# The Palgrave Handbook of African Colonial and Postcolonial History

T0387991

Martin S. Shanguhyia · Toyin Falola
Editors

# The Palgrave Handbook of African Colonial and Postcolonial History

Volume 2

palgrave
macmillan

*Editors*
Martin S. Shanguhyia
History Department, Maxwell School of
   Citizenship and Public Affairs
Syracuse University
Syracuse, NY, USA

Toyin Falola
University of Texas at Austin
Austin, TX, USA

ISBN 978-1-137-59425-9      ISBN 978-1-137-59426-6   (eBook)
https://doi.org/10.1057/978-1-137-59426-6

Library of Congress Control Number: 2017950403

Cover credit: ilbusca/Getty Images

Printed on acid-free paper

This Palgrave Macmillan imprint is published by Springer Nature
The registered company is Nature America, Inc.
The registered company address is: 1 New York Plaza, New York, NY 10004, U.S.A.

# ACKNOWLEDGEMENTS

This book is the result of unlimited effort from various individuals and institutions. The topics and themes came from an enriching brainstorming and back-and-forth communication and conversation between Toyin Falola and Martin Shanguhyia. Most important, we are grateful to the contributors to this volume who were willing to share some perspectives on how certain topics have been essential to the development of modern African history. They spent their invaluable time making endless revisions to their chapters under time constraints. Our constant communications and conversations were more rewarding than an inconvenience to all involved. We would also like to thank Amy Katherine Burnette, then a Dissertation Fellow at the Humanities Center at Syracuse University, and Thomas Jefferson West III, a doctoral candidate in the Department of Languages, Literatures, and Linguistics, Syracuse University, for the endless hours they spend editing the chapters. Special thanks also to the History Department at Syracuse University for subsidizing funds for editorial services. We also wish to acknowledge Jamie DeAngelo for her expertise in producing the maps.

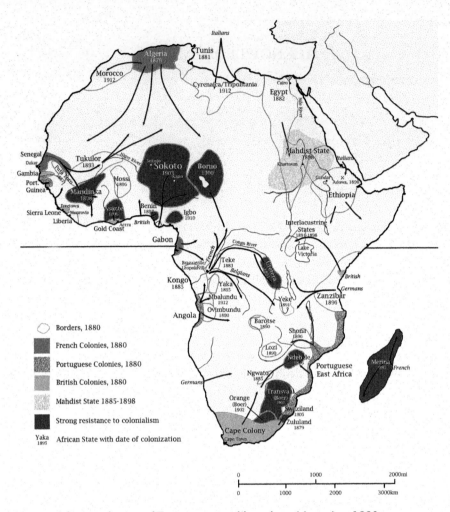

**Map 1**  Africa on the eve of European scramble and partition, circa 1880

**Map 2**   Colonial Africa, circa 1914

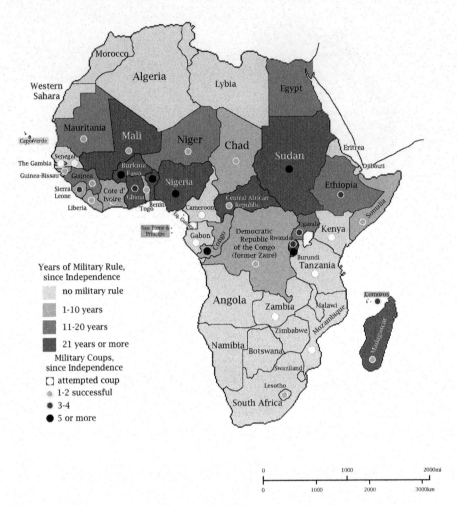

**Map 3** Modern Africa: Countries that have experienced military rule

**Map 4**  Modern Africa: Countries that have experienced political conflict

# Contents

# EDITORS AND CONTRIBUTORS

## About the Editors

**Martin S. Shanguhyia, Ph.D.** is an Associate Professor of African History at the Maxwell School of Citizenship and Public Affairs at Syracuse University, New York. He received his Ph.D. in African history at West Virginia University, Morgantown. He is the author of *Population, Tradition and Environmental Control in Colonial Kenya, 1920–1963* (Rochester, NY: University of Rochester Press, December 2015). His work has also been published in the *International Journal of African Historical Studies* as well as the *Journal of Colonialism and Colonial History* and in several chapters in edited books on themes reflecting the intersection between colonialism, environment, agrarian change, conservation, land, and conflict. His current research focuses on the political economy of state–community and intercommunity relations across Kenya's borderlands with Uganda, South Sudan, and Ethiopia during the colonial period.

**Toyin Falola, Ph.D.** is the Frances and Sanger Mossiker Chair in the Humanities and University Distinguished Teaching Professor, University of Texas at Austin. He has received various awards and honors, including seven honorary doctorates. He is the author and editor of over 150 books.

## Contributors

**Jamaine M. Abidogun,** is Professor in history, Missouri State University, holds a Ph.D. in curriculum and instruction in secondary education, minor in African and African-American studies, from the University of Kansas. She is a two-time Fulbright Scholar recipient for her work 'Gender Perspectives in Nigeria Secondary Education: A Case Study in Nsukka' (2004–2005) and 'Strengthening Gender Research to Improve Girls' and

Women's Education in Nigeria' (2013–2014). Her co-edited works with Toyin Falola include *Education, Creativity and Economic Empowerment in Africa* (2014) and *Issues in African Political Economies* (2016). Her publications include several chapters and articles in *African and Education Studies*. She is the editor-in-chief of the *African Journal of Teacher Education* (AJOTE), University of Guelph, Ontario and a member of the Fulbright Academy and the Mid-America Alliance for African Studies (MAAAS).

**Augustine Agwuele,** is an Associate Professor of linguistics in the Department of Anthropology, Texas State University. As an interdisciplinary scholar, he combines the conceptual rigors of theoretical linguistics with ethnographically grounded scholarship in socio-cultural anthropology. With this he studies language, culture, and society, addressing common and habitual practices involved in encoding, transmitting, and decoding messages. He studies closely Yoruba people of Nigeria.

**Chukwuemeka Agbo** is currently a Ph.D. student in the Department of History, University of Texas at Austin. He is also affiliated to the Department of History and Strategic Studies at the Federal University, Ndufu-Alike, Ikwo (FUNAI), Nigeria. His research focuses on the labor history of Southeastern Nigeria in the nineteenth and twentieth centuries.

**Kwabena O. Akurang-Parry,** is a Full Sabbatical Professor of Africana studies and world history at the University of Cape Coast, Cape Coast, Ghana. He received his Ph.D. in African history and comparative slavery as well as a Post-Graduate diploma in refugee and migration Studies at York University, Toronto, Canada. Professor Akurang-Parry has authored over 50 peer-reviewed articles in major journals, including *Slavery and Abolition, History in Africa, African Economic History, The International Journal of African Historical Studies, The International Journal of Regional and Local Studies, Left History, Transactions of the Historical Society of Ghana, African Identities,* and *International Working-Class and Labor History.* He is the co-editor of *African Agency and European Colonialism: Latitudes of Negotiation and Containment* (2007). He has held teaching and research positions at: Tulane University, New Orleans, USA; York University, Toronto, Canada; Shippensburg University, Pennsylvania, USA; and the University of Cape Coast, Ghana.

**Temilola Alanamu,** is a Leverhulme Early Career Fellow at the University of Kent. Her current research focuses on the intersection of gender and the life cycle in Southern Nigeria and encompasses the social experiences of the sexes from birth until death. She has published articles and book reviews in *Africa, Gender and History* and *Church History and Religious Culture* amongst others. She also has other forthcoming projects in *Oxford Bibliographies, Journal of World History* and *The Journal of Colonialism and Colonial History.* She is currently co-editing the *Encyclopaedia of African Religions Beliefs and Practices through History* with Douglas Thomas.

**Ademola Araoye,** has practiced political analysis, with particular focus on conflict, mediation, and post-conflict reconstruction for over three decades. A former Nigerian diplomat, he was head of the Political, Policy Planning Section of the United Nations Mission in Liberia (UNMIL), and later head of the Peace Consolidation Service of the mission. He is author of *Cote d'Ivoire: The Conundrum of a Still Wretched of the Earth* and *Sources of Conflict in the Post-Colonial Africa State.* He taught part time at the Ibrahim Babaginda Graduate School of the University of Liberia.

**Andrew E. Barnes,** teaches history at Arizona State University in Tempe, Arizona. He studies the history of Christianity in Africa and Europe. The primary focus of his present research is Christian missions and their interactions with African Christians during the era of European colonialism. He is the author of *Making Headway: The Introduction of Western Civilization in Colonial Northern Nigeria* (2009). His new book, *Industrial Education and the Christian Black Atlantic,* is forthcoming from Baylor University Press.

**Davies Banda,** is an active researcher in the field of sport and international development and is Deputy Director of the Unit for Child and Youth Studies at York St. John University, UK. His research covers sport-for-development, corporate social responsibility, national sports policies, and social inclusion interventions. He has been engaged as a consultant for the Commonwealth Secretariat, Euroleague Basketball, UK Sport, Laureus Sports for Good Foundation and some charities in Zambia and the United Kingdom.

**Judith A. Byfield,** is an Associate Professor in the History Department, Cornell University. She is the co-editor of *Africa and World War II* (Cambridge University Press, 2015) and author of *The Bluest Hands: A Social and Economic History of Women Indigo Dyers in Western Nigeria, 1890–1940* (Heinemann, 2002). A former President of the African Studies Association (2010–2011), Byfield has received numerous fellowships including the NEH and Fulbright.

**Kelly Duke Bryant,** is an Associate Professor of History at Rowan University (New Jersey), where she teaches African history. Her research focuses on colonial education, children and youth, and political change in Senegal. This research has generated several articles and a book, *Education as Politics: Colonial Schooling and Political Debate in Senegal, 1850s–1914* (2015).

**Elias Kifon Bongmba,** holds the Harry and Hazle Chavanne Chair in Christian theology and is Professor of religion at Rice University, Houston, Texas. His areas of specialization include African religions, theology, and philosophy. His book *The Dialectics of Transformation in Africa* won the Franz Fanon Prize. He has published widely on religion, theology, and is completing a monograph on same-sex relations in Africa.

**Nancy L. Clark,** is an historian with over 25 years' experience of teaching and research in South African history. She serves as the Jane DeGrummond Professor of history at Louisiana State University where she also served as Dean of the Honors College for over 10 years. Her areas of research have focused on twentieth-century South African history, with special emphasis on the apartheid era. She has published extensively on the impact of segregation and apartheid on the labor force, and most recently published the third edition of *The Rise and Fall of Apartheid,* co-authored with William Worger.

**Horace G. Campbell,** holds a joint Professorship in the Department of African American Studies and Department of Political Science, Maxwell School-Syracuse University. He has recently published *Global NATO and the Catastrophic Failure in Libya: Lessons for Africa in the Forging of African Unity* (2013) and *Barack Obama and twenty-first Century Politics: A Revolutionary Moment in the USA* (2010). He is also the author of *Reclaiming Zimbabwe: The Exhaustion of the Patriarchal Model of Liberation* (2003), and *Pan Africanism, Pan Africanists and African Liberation in the twenty-first Century* (2006). His most famous book, *Rasta and Resistance: from Marcus Garvey to Walter Rodney* (first published in 1985) is going through its eighth printing. He co-edited (Howard Stein) *Tanzania and the IMF: The Dynamics of* Liberalization (1992). He has published more than 60 journal articles and a dozen monographs as well as chapters in edited books. He was the Kwame Nkrumah Chair of African Studies at the Institute of African Studies, University of Legon, Ghana during 2016–2017.

**Benedict Carton,** is Robert T. Hawkes Professor of History and Africa Coordinator of African and African American Studies at George Mason University, Fairfax, Virginia. He is the author of *Blood from Your Children: The Colonial Origins of Generational Conflict in South Africa* (University of Virginia Press, 2000) and co-editor of *Zulu Identities: Being Zulu Past and Present* (2008).

**Tony Chafer,** is a historian specializing in Francophone Africa and French relations with Africa in the late colonial and postcolonial era. He is Director of the Centre for European and International Studies Research at the University of Portsmouth (UK). Recently he has published widely on French military policy in Africa and is currently working on a new edition of his book *The End of Empire in French West Africa: France's Successful Decolonization?*

**Eric Charry,** is a Professor of Music at Wesleyan University. He has published extensively on music in Africa, including dictionary and encyclopedia entries as well as the books *Mande Music* (2000) and *Hip Hop Africa* (2012).

**Hikabwa D. Chipande,** is a social historian of twentieth-century Africa. His research work focuses on the relationship between popular culture and politics, particularly football (soccer) and sport. He earned his Ph.D. in African history from Michigan State University in 2015 and is currently teaching at the University of Zambia in Lusaka.

**Gloria Chuku,** is a historian with over 25 years of teaching and research experience. She is Professor and Chair of Africana Studies, and Affiliate Professor of Gender and Women's Studies, and the Language, Literacy and Culture Ph.D. Program at the University of Maryland, Baltimore County, USA. Her work centers on Nigerian history with particular focus on gender, entrepreneurship, nationalism, ethnonationalisms and conflicts, and Igbo intellectual history. She has published extensively in these areas, including: a monograph, *Igbo Women and Economic Transformation in Southeastern Nigeria, 1900–1960* (2005); two edited volumes, *The Igbo Intellectual Tradition: Creative Conflict in African and African Diasporic Thought* (2013) and *Ethnicities, Nationalities, and Cross-Cultural Representations in Africa and the Diaspora* (2015). She has also publsihed over 50 scholarly articles.

**Alicia C. Decker** is an Associate Professor of women's, gender, and sexuality studies and African studies at the Pennsylvania State University, where she also co-directs the African Feminist Initiative. Her research and teaching interests include gender and militarism, African women's history, and global feminisms. She is the author of *In Idi Amin's Shadow: Women, Gender, and Militarism in Uganda* (Ohio University Press, 2014), and co-author with Andrea Arrington of *Africanizing Democracies: 1980 to Present* (Oxford University Press, 2014).

**Mamadou Diouf,** is an historian, and has taught at the Université Cheikh Anata Diop in Dakar (Senegal), and directed the Research and Documentation Department of the Council for the Development of Social Sciences Research. He was the Charles Moody Jr. Professor of History and African and African American Studies at the University of Michigan, Ann Arbor. He is currently the Leitner Family Professor of African studies and history at Columbia University in the City of New York, and a Visiting Professor at Sciences PIO, Paris (France). His research interests have focused on African intellectual and urban histories and youth cultures. His more recent publications include the co-edited book *Tolerance, Democracy and the Sufis in Senegal,* (2014), and co-edited volumes *The Arts of Citizenship in Africa. Spaces of Belonging* (with R. Fredericks), 2015); *Les arts de la citoyenneté au Sénégal. Espaces Contestés et Civilités Urbaines* (with F. Fredericks, 2013); *Rhythms of the Afro-Atlantic: Rituals and Remembrances,* (with I. Nwankwo, 2010) and *New Perspectives on Islam in Senegal: Conversion, Migration, Wealth, Power and Femininity* (with Mara Leichtman, 2009).

**Joshua Eisenman,** is Assistant Professor at the University of Texas at Austin's LBJ School of Public Affairs and senior fellow for China studies at the American Foreign Policy Council in Washington, DC. His second book, *China and Africa: A Century of Engagement,* co-authored with former US Ambassador to Ethiopia David H. Shinn, was named one of the top three books on Africa in 2012 by *Foreign Affairs* magazine. In 2007, he co-edited *China and the Developing World: Beijing's Strategy for the twenty-first Century,* and wrote the book's chapter on China–Africa relations.

**Ibrahim J. Gassama,** is the Frank Nash Professor of law at the University of Oregon. His research interests include international humanitarian, human rights, and economic law. His recent international law articles have appeared in the international law journals of Brooklyn (2012), Fordham (2013), Washington (2013), and Wisconsin (2014) Universities. Prior to becoming a law professor, he worked for TransAfrica, the African-American lobby for Africa.

**Fikru Negash Gebrekidan,** is an Associate Professor of History at St Thomas University in Fredericton, Canada. He regularly teaches courses on African history, world history, and the history of genocide. His major publications have appeared in *Northeast African Studies,* the *International Journal of Ethiopian Studies,* the *Journal of Ethiopian Studies, Callaloo,* and the *African Studies Review.* He is the author of *Bond without Blood: A History of Ethiopian and New World Black Relations, 1896–1991* (2005).

**Philip J. Havik,** is senior researcher at the Instituto de Higiene e Medicina Tropical of the Universidade Nova in Lisbon (IHMT/UNL) where he also teaches the history of medicine. His multidisciplinary research centers upon the study of public health and tropical medicine, state formation and governance, cultural brokerage and entrepreneurship in West Africa, with special emphasis on Lusophone countries, including Guinea Bissau. His most recent publications include (with co-authors Alexander Keese and Maciel Santos) *Administration and Taxation in the former Portuguese Empire, 1900–1945* (2015).

**Matthew M. Heaton,** is an Associate Professor in the Department of History at Virginia Tech. His research interests are in the history of health and illness, migration, and globalization in Africa with particular emphasis on Nigeria. He is the author of *Black Skin, White Coats: Nigerian Psychiatrists, Decolonization, and the Globalization of Psychiatry* and co-author of *A History of Nigeria.*

**Isaac Indome** is an M.Phil. History student at the Department of History, University of Cape Coast, Cape Coast, Ghana. He obtained his B.A. (Hons) degree in history from the University of Cape Coast in June 2015 and taught in the same department during the 2015/2016 academic year. His research interests are in migration in colonial Africa, specifically focusing on health and migration in colonial Ghana.

**Marloes Janson,** is Reader in West African anthropology at SOAS, University of London. Her areas of ethnographic interest include religious reform (both Muslim and Christian), oral history, gender, and youth in the Gambia and Nigeria. She has published extensively in these areas, most recently *Islam, Youth, and Modernity in the Gambia: The Tablighi Jama'at* (Cambridge University Press/International African Institute, 2014). She is the book reviews editor of the *Journal of Religion in Africa*.

**Kenneth Kalu,** received his Ph.D. from the School of Public Policy and Administration, Carleton University, Ottawa, Canada. He is currently an Assistant Professor at Ted Rogers School of Management, Ryerson University, Toronto, Canada. His research interests revolve around Africa's political economy; with special focus on the nature, evolution, and interactions of economic and political institutions; the political economy of foreign development assistance; and the history of foreign direct investment in Africa. His essays have appeared in several edited volumes, and his article on state–society relations in Africa is forthcoming in *Development Policy Review*. His forthcoming book is on development assistance and the future of Africa. He has held several senior positions in the public and private sectors in Nigeria and Canada.

**Edward Kissi,** is Associate Professor in the Department of Africana Studies at the University of South Florida. He studies the economic and diplomatic history of Ethiopia and the Horn of Africa, and the comparative history of genocide and human rights, and has published extensively on these subjects. He is the author of 'Obligation to Prevent (02P): Proposal for a Community Approach to Genocide-prevention in Africa' to be published in *African Security Review*, in September 2016.

**Kwasi Konadu,** is Professor of history at The City University of New York. Among other books, he is the author of *The Akan Diaspora in the Americas* (2010), *Transatlantic Africa, 1440–1880* (2014), and co-editor of *The Ghana Reader: History, Culture, Politics* (2016). He is also the founding director of the non-profit educational publisher Diasporic Africa Press, Inc.

**Benjamin N. Lawrance,** is Professor of African History at the University of Arizona, and also the Editor-in-Chief of African Studies Review. His research interests include comparative and contemporary slavery, human trafficking, cuisine and globalization, human rights, refugee issues and asylum policies. Among his books are *Amistad's Orphans: An Atlantic Story of Children, Slavery, and Smuggling* (2014), and *Adjudicating Refugee and Asylum Status: The Role of Witness, Expertise, and Testimony* (2015), with Galya Ruffer; and, *Trafficking in Slavery's Wake: Law and the Experience of Women and Children in Africa* (2012), with Richard L. Roberts.

**Xavier Livermon,** is an Assistant Professor of African and African diaspora studies at the University of Texas at Austin. He has published widely in the fields of African popular culture and African queer studies. His forth-coming book *Kwaito Futurity* discusses the rise of post-apartheid South African popular culture and its articulation with contemporary politics of race, gender, and sexuality.

**Paul E. Lovejoy,** is Distinguished Research Professor in the Department of History, York University, Toronto, and holds the Canada Research Chair in African Diaspora History. He is a Fellow of the Royal Society of Canada and was the founding director of the Harriet Tubman Institute for Research on the Global Migrations of African Peoples. His recent publications include *The Transatlantic Slave Trade and Slavery: New Directions in Teaching and Learning* (2013), co-edited with Benjamin Bowser, and *Jihád in West Africa During the Age of Revolutions* (Athens, OH: Ohio University Press, 2016). He has been awarded the Honorary degree of Doctor of the University, by the University of Stirling in 2007, the Distinguished Africanist Award by the University of Texas at Austin in 2010, a Life Time Achievement Award from the Canadian Association of African Studies in 2011, and Faculty of Graduate Studies Teaching Award at York University in 2011. He is General Editor of the Harriet Tubman Series on the African Diaspora, Africa World Press.

**Robert M. Maxon,** is an historian with more than 45 years of teach-ing, research and supervision of students at West Virginia University and Moi University. His research interests include East African history, Kenyan political and economic history, the economic history of western Kenya, and Kenya's constitutional history. He has published in these areas, most recently *Kenya's Independence Constitution: Constitution-Making and End of Empire* (2011), *Britain and Kenya's Constitutions 1950–1960* (2011), and *Historical Dictionary of Kenya* (3rd edn, 2014).

**John Mukum Mbaku,** is an economist, lawyer, and legal scholar with more than 30 years of teaching and research experience. He is currently Brady Presidential Distinguished Professor of economics and John S. Hinckley Fellow at Weber State University (Utah, USA), a Nonresident Senior Fellow at The Brookings Institution (Washington, DC), and an Attorney and Counselor at law (licensed in Utah). His research interests are in constitu-tional political economy and governance in Africa. He has published exten-sively in these areas, most recently, *Governing the Nile River Basin: The Search for a New Legal Regime* (2015), with Mwangi S. Kimenyi.

**Enocent Msindo,** is Associate Professor of History at Rhodes University, South Africa. He has published widely on Africa's social and political history. He is the author of *Ethnicity in Zimbabwe: Transformations in Kalanga and Ndebele Societies* (2012) and is currently completing a monograph on the state, information policy and propaganda in Zimbabwe from 1890 to the pre-sent.

**Mukoma Wa Ngugi,** is an Assistant Professor of English at Cornell University and the author of the novels *Mrs. Shaw* (2015), *Black Star Nairobi* (2013), *Nairobi Heat* (2011), and a book of poetry, *Hurling Words at Consciousness* (2006). *Logotherapy* (poetry) is forthcoming. He is the co-founder of the Mabati–Cornell Kiswahili Prize for African Literature and co-director of the Global South Project—Cornell. The goal of GSP is to facilitate public conversations among writers and scholars from Africa, Latin America, and Asia as well as minority groups in the West. In 2013, *New African* magazine named him one of the 100 most Influential Africans. In 2015 he was a juror for the Writivism Short Story Prize and the Neustadt International Prize for Literature.

**Oluwatoyin B. Oduntan,** is an Assistant Professor of History at Towson University in Maryland where he teaches courses in world, African and intellectual histories, and historical methods. He focuses his research on elite formation, cultural identity, and modernity in Africa.

**Moses E. Ochonu,** is Professor of African History at Vanderbilt University. He holds a Ph.D. in African history from the University of Michigan, Ann Arbor, and Graduate Certificate in conflict management from Lipscomb University, Nashville. He is the author of three books: *Africa in Fragments: Essays on Nigeria, Africa, and Global Africanity* (New York: Diasporic Africa Press, 2014); *Colonialism by Proxy: Hausa Imperial Agents and Middle Belt Consciousness in Nigeria* (Indiana University Press, 2014), which was named finalist for the Herskovits Prize; and *Colonial Meltdown: Northern Nigeria in the Great Depression* (Ohio University Press, 2009). Ochonu's articles have been published as book chapters and in several scholarly journals. He is currently working on a book project dealing with a unique form of colonial patronage which saw British colonial authorities sponsor Northern Nigerian emirs and other Muslim aristocrats to London and other metropolitan destinations for sightseeing adventures. Ochonu is two-time recipient of the research fellowship of the American Council of Learned Societies (ACLS). He has also received research grants and fellowships from the Harry Frank Guggenheim Foundation, the Social Science Research Council (SSRC), Rockefeller Foundation, Ford Foundation, National Endowment for the Humanities (NEH), and the British Library.

**Sharon Adetutu Omotoso,** is a Philosopher  (Applied Ethicist) with years of teaching,  research and supervision of students, formerly at Lead City University and currently at the Institute of African Studies, University of Ibadan. Her areas of research interest include Applied Ethics, Political Communications, Media & Gender studies, Philosophy of Education, Socio-Political Philosophy, and African Philosophy. She has published significantly in these areas, most recently, a co-edited book: *Political Communication in Africa* (Cham: Springer Publishers, 2017).

**Tanure Ojaide,** is a writer and scholar, currently The Frank Porter Graham Professor of Africana studies at the University of North Carolina at Charlotte. He has won major awards for his poetry and scholarly works.

**Peter Otiato Ojiambo,** is an Associate Professor in the Department of African and African-American Studies at the University of Kansas with several years of teaching, research and student supervision experience. His areas of research include: African-centered educational biographies, comparative and international education, educational leadership and non-western educational thoughts. He has written and published extensively on these areas. His recent publication is entitled "Perspectives on Empowering Education", 2014.

**Meshack Owino,** is an Associate Professor of History at Cleveland State University, Cleveland, Ohio. He earned his B.Ed and M.A at Kenyatta University, Kenya, and an M.A. and Ph.D.. at Rice University, Houston, Texas. Owino's areas of academic interests include the social experience of African soldiers in pre-colonial and colonial wars; and the nature and permutation of the modern African state. Owino has taught African History at several universities, including Egerton University, Kenya and Bloomsburg University, Bloomsburg, Pennsylvania. He has served as a Visiting Professor of African history at Stanford University, Palo Alto, California, and as an Adjunct Professor at Texas Southern University, Houston, Texas.

**Adebayo Oyebade,** is Professor of history and Chair of the History Department at Tennessee State University at Nashville. He has authored numerous journal articles and book chapters on African and African diasporan history. He is the author, editor, and co-editor of nine books including *United States' Foreign Policy in Africa in the twenty-first Century: Issues and Perspectives* (2014).

**Sylvester Okwunodu Ogbechie,** is Professor of art history and visual cultures of global Africa at the University of California Santa Barbara. He received his Ph.D. at Northwestern University and is the author of *Ben Enwonwu: The Making of an African Modernist* (2008) which was awarded the 2009 Herskovits Prize of the African Studies Association for best scholarly publication in African studies. He has also authored *Making History: The Femi Akinsanya African Art Collection* (2011), and is editor of *Artists of Nigeria* (2012). Ogbechie is also the founder and editor of *Critical Interventions: Journal of African Art History and Visual Culture*. He is currently a Smithsonian Institution Senior Fellow at the National Museum of African Art.

**Ruth Rempel,** is a historian in the international development studies program at Canadian Mennonite University. Her research and teaching interests include global and African development history, structural adjustment in Africa, narratives of African development since 1990, and development theory. She has written on these and other topics, and has a forthcoming book on African development history from 1970 to 2010.

**David H. Shinn,** has been teaching as an Adjunct Professor in the Elliott School of International Affairs at George Washington University since 2001. He previously served for 37 years in the US Foreign Service with assignments at embassies in Lebanon, Kenya, Tanzania, Mauritania, Cameroon, Sudan, and as ambassador to Ethiopia and Burkina Faso. Shinn, who has a Ph.D. from George Washington University, is the co-author of *China and Africa: A Century of Engagement* and the *Historical Dictionary of Ethiopia*, and the author of *Hizmet in Africa: The Activities and Significance of the Gülen Movement.* Shinn has authored numerous journal articles and book chapters on China–Africa issues. He blogs at http://davidshinn.blogspot.com.

**Charles G. Thomas,** is an Associate Professor of comparative military studies at the Air Command and Staff College. He is the co-editor of *Securing Africa: Local Crises and Foreign Interventions* (2013) and the *Managing Editor of the Journal of African Military History* (Brill Academic Press).

**Uyilawa Usuanlele,** studied in Nigeria, Sweden, and Canada and majored in African History, Peace, and Conflict Studies. He worked as a researcher with the National Council for Arts and Culture, Nigeria. He was a founding member/Coordinator of Institute for Benin Studies, Benin City, Nigeria. He has contributed articles and chapters to journals and books. He currently teaches African history, as well as peace and conflict Studies at State University of New York (SUNY) Oswego, New York, USA.

**Sarah Van Beurden,** is an Associate Professor of African studies at the Ohio State University. She received her Ph.D. from University of Pennsylvania, and is the author of *Authentically African: Arts and the Transnational Politics of Congolese Culture* (2015). She has also written several articles and chapters on the colonial and postcolonial history of Congo/Zaire, and cultural heritage and museum politics.

**Natalya Vince,** is a Lecturer in North African and French Studies at the University of Portsmouth. Her subject area is modern Algerian and French history, and her research interests include oral history, gender studies, and state and nation building in Algeria and France, and more broadly in Europe and Africa. Her monograph *Our Fighting Sisters: Nation, Memory and Gender in Algeria, 1954–2012* was published in 2015.

**Michael O. West,** is Professor of Sociology, Africana Studies and History at Binghamton University. He has published broadly in the fields of African studies, African diaspora studies, African-American studies, Pan-Africanism, history, and historical sociology. His current research centers on the Black Power movement in global perspectives.

# LIST OF FIGURES

# LIST OF TABLES

# PART II

# Postcolonial Africa

# CHAPTER 27

# Africa and the Cold War

## Kenneth Kalu

'When elephants fight, it is the grass that suffers.'—*An African proverb.*

The Atlantic slave trade and colonialism have been the two major historical events often seen as the principal forces that shaped and continue to shape Africa's political economy and its relationship with the rest of the world. For sure, the Atlantic slave trade and colonialism were unique in their crass exploitation and harsh cruelty towards Africa's peoples and natural resources. The literature on the Atlantic slave trade is unambiguous on the devastating impacts of slave trade on Africa's culture, sociology, and political economy.[1] Slavery thrived on the use of extreme force, raids, kidnapping, and acts of inhumanity to Africans. Likewise, the European colonial experiment in Africa has been described as the foundation of Africa's inefficient and extractive institutions that have contributed to keeping Africa in its present state of underdevelopment.[2] These historical epochs had devastating impacts on the continent. European colonial administration set up institutions primarily designed to facilitate the extraction and transfer of Africa's natural resources to Europe. These extractive institutions and predatory state structures, which have persisted, have been the major cause of Africa's poor economic performance.[3]

Having suffered under colonial domination for decades, African countries began to gain political independence during the late 1950s. This period also coincided with the time of the Cold War. The Cold War can be seen as the

K. Kalu (✉)
Ted Rogers School of Management,
Ryerson University, Toronto, ON, Canada

© The Author(s) 2018
M.S. Shanguhyia and T. Falola (eds.),
*The Palgrave Handbook of African Colonial and Postcolonial History*,
https://doi.org/10.1057/978-1-137-59426-6_27

period, from 1945 to 1991, of intense struggle for ideological supremacy between capitalist forces led by the USA and the forces of communism spearheaded by the USSR.[4] The Cold War shaped Africa's decolonization process and transition to nationhood in very significant ways. According to Jeremi Suri,[5] there are two distinguishable genres of literature on the place of the Cold War in shaping international relations and the global political economy after the Second World War. The first school of thought posits that the Cold War had a tremendous impact on the global political economy. Along this line, US foreign policy during the Cold War, however nuanced, is seen as some form of continuation of imperialism in all material respects.[6] According to this view, the major Cold War actors (the free market ideologues led by the USA, and the Soviet Union with its allies who were inspired by communism) played the most important roles in defining the direction of international relations and the global political economy at the end of the Second World War. The second school of thought argues that the whole narrative about the Cold War and its significance in the world system gives undue primacy to the USA and Europe and undermines the critical contributions of local actors in the peripheries, including Africa, Asia, and Latin America.[7] This school of thought argues, for example, that instead of framing decolonization around the actions and inactions of the USA, Europe, or the USSR, analysis should focus on the nationalist movements, on local struggles, and on domestic forces of change and liberation whose actions and sometimes ultimate sacrifices had significant impacts on the changes that took place, especially in developing countries. These actors may or may not have had any connections whatsoever with either the West or the East but were wrongly labeled to be sympathetic to either the Right or the Left. The latter argument seeks to bring to the fore the often neglected actors whose contributions shaped the socio-political trajectories of the time. This second strand of literature questions the seeming conventional wisdom that the principal Cold War rivalries shaped the nature of international relations after the Second World War.

The two distinct analytical frames summarized above have their arguments anchored on some premises: while one gives primacy to the activities of the superpowers in the postwar period, the other privileges local actors and domestic struggles as the most appropriate narrative for global dynamics, especially relating to the changes in Africa and the rest of the Third World. In aligning with one strand or the other, it is important to emphasize the economic strength and political clout of the actors and the role these variables play in shaping international relations. For sure, local nationalist movements are about the only legitimate vehicles to push for independence and self-government for their respective countries, but local actors needed the right resources to be able to organize a formidable pressure group to push forward their demands. Domestic pressure groups needed the international media, financial resources, and sometimes materials to stage a credible opposition.

Across the developing world, domestic actors received support from external forces, but such support or interventions were never without strings attached. Take the case of Guinea, which voted to exit the French Union in 1957. It is reported that French President de Gaulle was so irked by Guinea's decision that he chose to make an example of the West African country by withdrawing all forms of assistance, including taking away hospital beds, school tables, and French personnel in order to make life unbearable for its citizens.[8] For sure, domestic actors voted for Guinea to leave the French Union, but the country would have been crippled without the timely intervention of the USSR. The intervention of the USSR set Guinea on the path to communism, which may not have been the original idea or intention of the domestic actors who voted for Guinea to severe ties with France. The case of Guinea and other such countries show that a more nuanced narrative that recognizes the critical roles of each actor (domestic and foreign) is perhaps a more appropriate frame. This chapter argues that the Cold War had important implications for Africa's decolonization process. In addition, the Cold War shaped the form of institutions and political culture that evolved in Africa in the post-independence period. This by no means undermines the important contributions of domestic actors whose struggles also shaped the independence movement in significant ways and whose actions have continued to define Africa's development trajectory up to the present.

## The Cold War and Africa's Decolonization

The Second World War and its aftermath heralded a new vista in the global system. Besides its huge cost in human and material resources, the War led to the formation of new global alliances, altered existing relationships, created new superpowers, and demystified empires that had hitherto commanded respect, especially in the colonies. It was during the War that Africans finally realized that the European military wasn't invincible. Africans who were drafted to fight in the war alongside their imperial masters saw, perhaps for the first time, that the European military which had conquered and colonized Africa could be vulnerable. Having participated in the War alongside the Europeans, Africans came back more emboldened to confront their European colonizers. As Crawford Young noted, the War created a 'rupture in expectations', as colonial subjects pressed for enhanced political and economic stature for Africans.[9] During the War, European colonists had been concerned that the US military forces that fought were a multiracial contingent which included African Americans, Asian Americans, Hispanics, Native Americans, and other 'non-European Americans'. The concern of the European colonists was that dealing with the 'black Americans would explode some of the racial stereotypes they had consciously cultivated in their colonies'.[10] In effect, because the colonial policy directly denigrated Africans as being inferior to the white man, the colonists were concerned about how to relate with African Americans without contradicting the stereotype they had institutionalized in the African colonies. As Westad noted, this apparent contradiction came to a head when an adviser to the Belgian Government in the Congo, Felix de Muelenaere, tried to explain this contradiction to the African American diplomat Ralph Bunche in 1942. Felix de Muelenaere noted that black American soldiers 'would have a bad effect on the Congo natives, especially on the detribalized native clerks ... The Congo native would begin to think that he should have the same privileges as the highly developed American blacks who are college graduates, doctors, and professors'.[11]

After first-hand experience of the devastation which Europe suffered, Africans began to question the toga of invincibility which was associated with the European military. The new realization that the colonial army was not infallible helped to strengthen the resolve of African freedom fighters to intensify the struggles for independence. In addition, the exposure of Africans from the colonies to black Americans during the War helped colonial subjects to begin to question some of the racial prejudices that the European colonists had consciously laid in the minds of Africans. Although the black Americans were still facing a series of racial challenges in the USA, at least the native African believed that the black American prospects were much better than those of Africans in the hands of the colonial masters. The first decade of the postwar period therefore witnessed intensified pressures for changes to colonial policies. However, the initial response of the French and the British imperial powers to Africa's demands was violent resistance and suppression as witnessed in Algeria, Cameroon, Ivory Coast, Madagascar and Tunisia, where local uprisings were brutally crushed by the French military. The British colonial government equally used violent forces to suppress the Mau Mau insurgency in Kenya, and this led to the death of many civilians in the area where the Mau Mau group held sway.[12]

Nationalist movements and the struggle for independence in the African colonies had been in process to varying degrees for as long as colonialism had lasted, and the struggle had understandably focused on internal issues relevant to the local population. However, following the end of the War, external interests began to alter the dynamics of independence struggles in significant ways. In a bid to promote their economic interests or to push forward one ideology or the other, external forces besides Africa's colonial masters began to take a more than passive interest in the geopolitical dynamics in the continent. Consequently, local independence struggles in the African colonies began to take on new forms. The two Cold War rivalries (the USA-led Western forces and the Soviet Union with its allies) began to play active roles in the political economy of African colonies. These foreign interventions meant that some conflicts that should otherwise have been on a small scale and prosecuted by contending domestic forces escalated and took on larger dimensions. The external interventions usually resulted in more destruction, exacerbated instability, and produced more permanent devastation in the region.[13] In effect, one of the legacies of the Cold War on the continent is a higher degree of violence in the region during independence struggles and up to the period immediately following political independence. Take the case of Angola, where the struggle took on a different dimension, so much so that about 30,000 Cuban troops had to be deployed to the fight alongside revolutionaries. The Cuban troops were deployed because Cuba felt that Angola was towing the communist line and thus qualified as an ally. Although the USSR had no direct interest in Angola, Moscow had to lend its support to the revolutionaries there because of their communist leanings. As expected, the USA also intervened in the Angolan crisis, using the South African army to quell opposition from forces that were believed to be pro-communist.[14] One can only imagine the consequence of such multilateral interventions in Angola, as in other equally struggling African countries at that time.

The USA and its allies were always willing to show sympathy to movements that supported (or were seen to lean towards) capitalism as opposed to communism. Interestingly, all the major colonial powers in Africa (Belgium, Britain, France, and Portugal) were US allies. An easy option for the USA would have been to offer unconditional support for the continuation of these allies' empires, but this option was not a feasible one for the USA for several reasons. First, the USA had no colonies in Africa but was desirous of promoting both its influence and economic interests in the region. Therefore, allowing Western European colonists to continue with their empires would not have given the USA the opportunity to enter the lucrative African market for raw materials. Second, at the end of the War, the notion of self-determination was creeping into global political ideology. With the emergence of the United Nations, that had been set up to promote world peace and to emphasize the human rights of all peoples irrespective of race or creed, colonialism had become a sort of contradiction to the dictates of self-determination. Colonial subjects had their human rights largely denied by the colonial masters, and colonial subjects had no say on how they were governed. Colonialism thus became an anachronism in the emerging world order. Third, there was the palpable fear in the minds of US policymakers that the Soviet Union would find ready and available converts to communism among the oppressed peoples of the colonies. These factors put the USA in a rather difficult position with respect to its appropriate role in Africa's decolonization struggles. The USA therefore supported decolonization, in part to dilute the influence of Europe over African countries. However, the US government was careful not to allow the independence struggles to be hijacked by socialist elements or for the independent states to move towards communism.[15]

By the late 1940s, the economic challenges faced by Europe following the War had become clearer, and the cost of maintaining the colonies was becoming a major issue for the colonial governments. In Europe, questions were being raised about the reasonableness of maintaining the African colonies. It would be recalled that the colonies were mainly a source of raw materials for European industries, but the War had devastated the European economy, destroyed infrastructure, and led to general decline in industrial production and capacity. This meant that the demand for African raw materials had also declined since the industries that needed them were not functioning at the scale of the prewar period. The effects of the War on Europe thus gave rise to questions about the appropriate place of the African colonies. However, because the colonies were still largely considered assets for the metropolitan governments, the resolve of Europe was to maintain them and suppress the rising agitations.

After the initial violent suppression of internal agitations by the colonial governments in the immediate postwar period, especially in the French colonies, it became clear to imperial Europe that changes were inevitable. By the 1950s, the British colonial government had given more representations to Africans, and more responsibilities were accorded to domestic political actors. However, Britain adopted a strategy to mentor a crop of new African elites that would protect British interests when power was eventually handed over to them. It was only in Kenya that the Mau Mau uprising posed a difficult challenge to the British colonial administration, leading to the use of British military to crush the uprising. The rather brutal reaction to the Mau Mau insurgency had severe consequences for the civilian population, where an estimated 200,000 Africans became victims.[16] The British hoped that setting up the Commonwealth of former colonies would help safeguard British interests whenever the countries eventually gained independence. This strategy meant that the British colonial governments were not deeply bothered by the increasing wave of independence struggles. However, for the African population, it meant that politically independent status would actually mean little in substance as the imperial power would remain largely in control of the economy and continue to have significant influence on political developments in the independent states. This strategy of planning for the protection of European interests, as against preparing the colonies for balanced and sustainable growth and development after colonial rule, set the stage for neo-colonialism in the postcolonial period.

In the French colonies the situation differed considerably from the fairly straightforward post-empire strategy of Britain. France felt that it would lose its place in the global political and economic equation if it lost its African colonies. Consequently, the French government fought devastating wars to suppress nationalist agitations, leading to the vicious conflict in Algeria and the use of military forces against independent struggles in the West African colonies. However, the global environment in the postwar period was generally not conducive to the maintenance of empires. The US government was concerned that revolutionaries in the colonies could be easy prey for communist infiltration, and France could not get the support from the US government to maintain the status quo in the French African colonies. As nationalist struggles continued, the French government had no option but to concede more grounds to African nationalists. The French first created more seats in the French Parliament for French Africans. With less than 3% of the seats reserved for Africans, the gesture was aimed at appeasing the natives and creating a more conducive environment for the continuation of French colonial rule. However, by 1960, most of the French African colonies had gained independence, although France negotiated a range of military, political, and economic partnership agreements that would protect the country's interests in the post-independence period.[17]

France was reluctant to grant independence to its African colonies, but Belgium and Portugal were even less willing to do so. The violent dictatorship of King Leopold II in Congo and the subsequent transfer of the colony's administration to Belgium had done little to prepare Africans for self-government. In the Congo, education was not readily available to Africans, as the colonial government was reluctant to bring Western education for fear that it would enhance the exposure of the natives and lead to more potent agitations, thereby creating problems for the colonial government. In 1960, when Congo gained political independence, there were only 20 Congolese who had obtained a university degree.[18] As such there were not many Western-educated Africans to assume positions of leadership in the new country. This meant that Belgium maintained a significant presence in independent Congo, controlling the large mining corporations and running the country's military. Like Belgium, Portugal was unwilling to embrace self-government for its African colonies. Not being as powerful as Britain or France, Portugal felt that it would lose whatever strength it had if it lost its African colonies. In Angola and Mozambique, the Portuguese fought a protracted war against African independence movements, but again the balance of global power was tilted against colonialism, and Portugal had to reluctantly grant self-government to its African colonies.

During the decolonization process, the two major Cold War actors had begun to take on major roles in the African colonies beyond those they had played before the War. The USA generally supported decolonization but wanted independent African states to embrace free-market principles instead of falling into the hands of the communist USSR. The USA wanted access to raw materials from African colonies. The European imperialists had hitherto maintained exclusive control over African trade. While the USA supported self-government and independence for the colonies, it frowned at violent revolutionaries who were often accused of receiving support from the communist USSR. The USA therefore encouraged the colonial governments to embrace changes that would leave no room for violent agitations. On the other hand, the USSR, China, and Cuba provided assistance to nationalist movements that were seen to be sympathetic to socialist principles, or, at least, that were not aligned with US capitalism. Along these lines, the USSR at one time or another extended assistance to nationalist movements in Algeria, Angola, Congo, Ghana, Guinea, Kenya, Mali, and Mozambique, among others.[19]

In general, while one may not conclude that the Cold War led to decolonization in Africa, the Cold War significantly altered the dynamics of independence struggles. The pursuit of economic and ideological domination by the superpowers turned Africa into a center for a proxy war. African nationalists took advantage of the interest shown by the USA, the USSR, Cuba, and China in the political and economic development of the region. Financial and material support became more readily available to independence movements and revolutionaries that were seen to be sympathetic to the ideology of the donor nation. Although this increased support helped the independence movements in different countries, it also led to the influx and proliferation of arms in African countries, leading to more violent struggles and a spike in the number of crises, wars, and associated fatalities. As Schmidt observed, 'from Kennedy through the Nixon administrations, American weapons, tanks, planes, ships, helicopters, napalm, and chemical defoliants were used against Africans in the Portuguese colonies ...'.[20] This was the case across the continent wherever the US government and its European allies felt that domestic revolutionaries were receiving support from the USSR or any other country on the communist side. The unfortunate end product of the military interventions by the USA and the USSR and their allies was the increased militarization of African societies, because once arms are in the hands of agitators or revolutionaries, it is difficult to retrieve them even after the object of the initial struggle has been won or lost. The infiltration of external powers through the provision of financial and military support during the Cold War contributed significantly to the proliferation of arms in the region. The consequence was continued conflict, unnecessary militarization, and civil wars in the post-independence period.

While the Cold War may have helped to quicken the decolonization process, it had deeper negative consequences in fueling violent conflicts, arming state and non-state actors, and heightening social and political instability in the region. The result of arms proliferation was more wars, increased guerilla warfare, armed robbery, and general crisis in the region even after independence. Within the first decade of independence (1960–1970), Africa had experienced 27 military coups d'état that led to change of government, and 12 failed coup attempts, making a total of 37 military coups in the continent.[21] Although one may not conclude that external interventions during the Cold War were the only causes of the crises, the activities of the main Cold War actors had significant impacts on all the major political and economic events in the region. The ease with which the Cold War superpowers supplied arms and other forms of military assistance to African countries helped to militarize the region and turned many countries into a keg of gunpowder waiting to explode. As Europeans departed at the dawn of independence, the seed of instability that was being sown from the period of colonial rule to the Cold War era germinated and produced military coups, communal conflicts, and civil wars. The Cold War superpowers were adept at identifying local champions, who were then supported to promote the ideology of the particular superpower. In many African countries, one would see the USA providing resources to one group and the USSR supporting a different factional leader. The propping-up of puppets (a major foreign policy strategy of the USA during the Cold War era) was a precursor to political crises, wars, and the destruction that characterized the African continent up to the 1970s and 1990s.

## THE COLD WAR AND POLITICAL INSTITUTIONS
## IN INDEPENDENT AFRICA

It is well established that colonialism left a legacy of extractive institutions and predatory states that was not conducive to real economic growth and development.[22] As African countries began to gain political independence in the 1960s, there was growing optimism that with the United Nations in place, the world would make an effort to ameliorate some of the problems that had hindered Africa's social, political, and economic development. However, as Christopher O'Sullivan noted, the world missed that opportunity to address the myriad of challenges facing Africa largely due to the bitter rivalry between the two factions of the Cold War era.[23] The USA and the USSR failed to forge the global cooperation and partnerships necessary for Africa and the international community to work together towards correcting the evils that European colonial exploitation had unleashed on Africa and its people. As the superpowers struggled for supremacy, the developing nations, including some of the newly independent African countries, formed the Non-Aligned Movement (NAM), which was a coalition of nations that were not aligned to the Right as dictated by the USA nor to the Left under the leadership of the USSR at that time. For sure, members of the NAM had neither the economic capacity nor the political clout to effect the kind of changes that would fundamentally alter the trajectories of failure and despondency laid for Africa by European imperialists.

The world superpowers in the immediate postwar period were interested in spreading their influence and parallel ideologies across the globe. Engrossed in ideological warfare, the superpowers and the rest of the world paid no attention to the deficient foundations laid in Africa by European imperialists: the arbitrary borders created by colonial Europe, the destructive exploitation of Africa's natural resources, the conscious establishment of extractive institutions that were not amenable to development, the creation of a perverse economic structure dependent only on the export of a few cash crops to European firms, and the colonial masters' strategy to retain a firm grip over the region even after the end of formal colonialism. The period of independence would have been a great time for the world to review the conditions and prospects of the emerging African states. But instead of setting Africa on a developmental trajectory, the politics of the Cold War turned the continent into a site for proxy wars between the two superpowers and their allies. As the African saying quoted at the beginning of this chapter aptly states, Africa again suffered as the two big elephants (the USA and the USSR) fought for ideological supremacy.

As colonialism was fading away, the USA became increasingly concerned about the direction that independent African states could take. The fear expressed within the US government was that the USSR might infiltrate the newly independent states, and entice African leaders to embrace communism. The thinking was that the exit of European colonists could exacerbate this problem. It was against this background that President J.F. Kennedy made the following statements in 1961:

> We live in a world which has changed tremendously in our lifetime—history only will secure a full perspective on that change. But there is Africa, which was held by Western European powers for several centuries, now independent—which holds within its countries masses of people, many of them illiterate, who live on average incomes of 50 or 60 or 75 dollars a year, who want a change, who now are the masters of their own house but who lack the means of building a viable economy, who are impressed by the example of the Soviet Union and the Chinese, who—not knowing the meaning of freedom in their lives—wonder whether the Communist system holds the secrets of organizing the resources of the state in order to bring them a better life.[24]

The US government therefore focused on counter-strategies. African leaders who appeared to have sympathy for socialist ideas were rebuffed and isolated by the USA, regardless of whether they were loved by their people. For example, Ghana's President, Kwame Nkrumah, although very popular amongst the people of Ghana, was seen by the USA as being too radical and almost pandering towards communist ideas. Consequently, the US government thought he was becoming a threat that must be isolated in order to ensure he did not drag his country to communism. In a memo to President Kennedy, Chester Bowles (the President's special envoy), stated as follows, after a visit to Africa in 1962:

> Nkrumah is continuing to lose ground as a political force and is likely to become increasingly isolated from the mainstream of African politics ... Our policy in Ghana should therefore be one of restraint. By denying Nkrumah a demagogic issue ... we will help to assure his increasing isolation.[25]

The Cold War era somehow made it impossible for the USA to consider other factors (such as domestic preferences or the long-term interest of African countries) in its policies towards Africa. African leaders increasingly realized that US foreign policy during the Cold War was not necessarily premised on promoting Africa's long-term interest despite the grants and aid provided by the US government. Consequently, the atmosphere of distrust which defined the relationships between the West and African countries after the period of colonialism persisted despite the independent status of most African countries. Besides protecting capitalist ideas and ensuring that the USSR did not infiltrate African countries with communism, the USA sought to expand its economic interests into the African region. In the same vein, the major imperial powers of Britain and France were not in a hurry to relinquish their hold on the colonies.

Even as many African countries gained independence in the 1960s, the colonists were not willing to give up control of the region's economy. At the time of independence, the colonial forces took proactive steps to safeguard their economic interests and investments in the colonies. The determination to maintain control over African countries and to avoid the intrusion of communism into Africa led Europe, with its US ally, to play principal roles in deciding who would succeed the colonial government. The result was selective support for political leaders who were expected to safeguard the economic interests of the departing colonists and embrace capitalism over communism. In supporting one African politician over another, the external interventionist paid little or no attention to what would advance the interests of the African population but focused only on protecting the selfish interests of the external forces. Beginning in the late 1950s, external interventions in Africa's politics were widespread, and the primary mission of such interventionists was to raise and foist on African countries new sets of leaders who would entrench the ideology of the benefactor. Perhaps the situation in the former Belgium colony of Congo best illustrates the callousness of foreign actors who cared less about the welfare of Africans. Even by colonial standards, Congo (now the Democratic Republic of Congo) suffered terrible exploitation under King Leopold II, who ruled the Central African country with an iron hand and perpetrated some of the worst forms of abuses in colonial Africa. For Congo, independence should have marked a breath of fresh air and the discontinuation of the exploitation and expropriation that occurred on a grand scale during colonial rule. Instead, the intrigues of the Cold War brought devastation to the region, such that Congo has never seen stability since gaining independence in 1960. At independence, the people of Congo elected Patrice Lumumba as the country's first prime minister. Lumumba was a Pan-Africanist who believed in the emancipation and unification of Africa. He opposed the brutal exploitation of colonialism in all its ramifications and he was not afraid to show his disdain for the colonial forces. His tough stance on reclaiming Congo and its resources from Belgian imperialists did not go down well with Belgium and the USA. Lumumba faced strong opposition from external forces who feared that this new leader would embark on reforms that would dilute Belgium's control over the country.

Prime Minister Patrice Lumumba was not afraid to tell the truth to the colonists. It was reported that in his speech on the day of Congo's independence, he reminded the audience, including the departing colonial officials, as follows: 'We are proud of this struggle, of tears, of fire, and of blood, to the depths of our being, for it was a noble and just struggle, and indispensable to put an end to the humiliating slavery which was imposed upon us by force'.[26] These words, spoken by the new Prime Minister in the presence of Belgian officials, foreign press and King Baudouin of Belgium at Congo's independence celebration in 1960, irked the latter, who had earlier counselled the new Prime Minister to retain the 'structures' that Belgium was handing over to him at independence. From the beginning of Patrice Lumumba's administration, he did not have the support of Belgium and the USA. He was seen as a radical nationalist, concerned about Africa's liberation and unity, and who would not protect European interests in Congo. Within the first days of his government, a factional force declared independence for the province of Katanga from Congo on July 11, 1960. The secessionist forces were supported wholly by Belgium, thus plunging the nascent nation into avoidable crisis.

Lumumba sought the support of the United Nations to quell the secessionist forces and restore peace to the new nation,[27] but help was not forthcoming as the USA supported Belgium. Lumumba then sought the support of the USSR to maintain peace in the Congo. This action was the straw that broke the camel's back, as it was viewed as a declaration for communism by Lumumba. The crisis took on an international dimension and the battle was fought not just in Congo but also on the floor of the United Nations. The USSR demanded that the United Nations secure the immediate release of Lumumba who had, at that time, been arrested by the military forces led by General Mobutu. The USSR also asked the then UN Secretary-General Dag Hammarskjold to order Belgian officials to leave Congo for the Congolese.[28] These demands were not met because the USA had thought that Congo, which had uranium deposits, would fall into the hands of the Soviets if Belgium left. The US's interest was not about the welfare of Africans in Congo; neither was it concerned about restoring stability in the country according to the wishes of Congolese. Rather, the USA's preoccupation was on how to ensure that Congo did not enter into any relationship with the USSR or allow the latter access to its uranium deposits. The crisis escalated, culminating in the assassination of Patrice Lumumba and the eventual emergence of the Western-backed Joseph Mobutu.

The assassination of Prime Minister Lumumba was greeted with protests across the world, and not a few believed there was Western complicity in his death. Patrice Lumumba had been very determined to turn the fortunes of Congo around for the good of the Congolese. In his often celebrated independence speech, he had reminded the world that the wounds inflicted on Africa and Africans were:

> too fresh and too smarting for us to be able to have known ironies, insults, and blows which we had to undergo morning, noon and night because we were Negroes. We have seen our lands spoiled in the name of laws which only recognized the right of the strongest. We have known laws which differed according to whether it dealt with a black man or a white.[29]

The USA thought he was too radical and as such susceptible to communist ideas. Congo represents a classic example of the devastating impacts of the Cold War on Africa. From the time of independence, Congo has not known peace and the exploitative structures that began under King Leopold II have largely persisted. Prime Minister Patrice Lumumba might not have achieved complete transformation of the Congo if he had been allowed to lead his people, but he was clear about his detestation for colonialism and the slavery that was the hallmark of Congo's colonial experience. The Congo crisis in the 1960s devastated not only Congo, but also affected other countries in the region.

Sometimes, events like the Congo crisis are analyzed on the surface, perhaps in terms of the destruction of lives and properties only. While the loss of life and property are indeed some of the negatives of the crisis, a major effect of such development is the institutional legacy it created in the country and the region at large. The Cold War and the crisis it generated created institutions that reinforce exploitation and are continuously prone to crisis. It also liberalized the culture of violence with the influx of arms from external forces to support one group or another. Despite Congo's enormous resources, poverty has persisted and the country has rarely enjoyed peace and stability since its independence. The form of institutions that promote a culture of violence and inhibit inclusive productive engagements by all are not conducive to growth and development, irrespective of the policy adopted, and irrespective of the volume of foreign aid extended to the country.

As his Western supporters expected, Mobutu did not dismantle the exploitative structures that had been set up by the colonial government. Rather, Mobutu continued with the crass exploitation of Congo's resources even to a scale that was as much as, or even more devastating, than had been the case during the rule of King Leopold II.[30] The USA and Belgium supported the rise of Mobutu in Congo and provided him cover, just as he protected the interest of Belgium, shunned the overtures of the USSR, and pursued the free market ideas of the West. For his loyalty to the West, President Mobutu at first received the foreign support he needed to continue to exploit his people. Congo's experience shows that international interventions in the continent during the Cold War period were not always for the overall long-term interest of Africans.

While decolonization and the principles of self-determination are good ideas on their own, the process of decolonization and the emergence of independent African countries could have taken a different form. The colonial government was predatory, and all political and economic institutions during colonial rule were extractive, designed to exploit and expropriate Africa's resources. In effect, the colonial state and its structures were not anchored on any social contract between the state and its citizens. The government belonged to the colonial masters and their respective home governments. Africans were alienated from the government and state–society relations were defined by exploitation in all material respects. Given the structure of colonial rule, one would have expected that at the end of colonialism, Africa's development partners would work with the incoming African leaders to dismantle those colonial institutions that fostered exploitation and expropriation. An African-centered process of decolonization should have included the restructuring of all institutions of the state from the civil service to the military, and from the electoral process to the judiciary, and property rights should have been properly defined to reduce the risk of expropriation. Independent African states needed to launch into statehood with inclusive institutions that would redefine the essence of the state and create mutually beneficial relationships between the state and its citizens.

The Cold War focused the attention of the world on the distinction between capitalism and communism and on the superiority of one over the other. International politics revolved around these two models, and the search for recruits for either of these ideas became the major concern of the world superpowers of that era. Africa and other developing countries across the world became the center of contestation, as the USA sought to enmesh the newly independent nations within the free market, while the USSR and China were busy seeking new converts to communism. As Schmidt noted, many African leaders took advantage of the rush for new converts. These countries courted different parties to the ideological divide, and often simultaneously received support from opposing forces.[31] While this contestation lasted, the superpowers that should have invested in recreating the new nations just emerging from many decades of exploitation and devastation abandoned this role and concentrated on hawking ideas. Africa needed a fundamental restructuring in the 1960s to have a real chance of achieving meaningful development after decades of colonial exploitation.

The arbitrary division of the continent into incoherent and unworkable units for the convenience of the colonial masters, the brutal exploitation of the region's resources, and the establishment of political and economic structures that were by all accounts exploitative are good reasons for believing that African countries needed restructuring at the end of colonial rule. Instead, the Cold War diverted the attention of the world from the precarious state of the continent to vain pursuit of ideological supremacy between the West and the East. While new dictators emerged following the withdrawal of old ones, the world looked the other way for as long as the dictator conformed to the 'free market ideas' and allowed the West access to natural resources in the region. It is not likely that the devastation suffered by Europe during the Second World War was anything close to the institutionalized looting and massive destruction that took place in Africa during several decades of colonial rule. Yet while the USA was quick to put in place the Marshall Plan designed to rebuild Europe after the War, no such plan was designed to rebuild Africa after the devastation of colonialism and its aftermath. The Cold War diverted the world's attention to the propagation of ideologies that served the interest of the First World, and restricted the choices available to the periphery. Even the setting up of the Non-Aligned Movement by some countries in Africa and parts of Asia could not help these countries to fend off the powerful influence of the USA and Western Europe.

One must note that Africans are also culpable for their complicity in carrying on with the exploitative structures set up by colonial Europe even after colonialism had ended. Regional bodies like the then Organization of African Unity, now the African Union (AU), could have taken a hard look at the continent immediately after political independence. But the AU failed to initiate the critical restructuring that was needed to change the independent states. This failure on the part of the regional body should be expected because of the global dynamics of that time. Radical movements were promptly crushed by the US government and its allies, as such movements were dubbed communist insurgencies that must be curbed in order to give the world the free market that the USA and its allies believed would enhance society's welfare. One can excuse African leaders in the first decade of independence for following the European colonial exploiters and prioritizing America's free market over restructuring of their countries. Perhaps many of the African leaders were rather too naïve to embark on such a fundamental project. The support of the superpowers was what Africa needed to restructure its societies out of the perverse anti-development structures that colonialism bequeathed on the continent.

Although the Cold War is over, Africa continues to bear the real cost of the ideological battle that occurred at a time when the continent was just emerging from colonialism. Africa's political space of today remains dominated by a few 'big men'. Just like in the era of colonialism, most African governments are detached from the people and state–society relations are largely defined by exploitation and predation on citizens. In most of Africa, economic institutions are not inclusive and do not support productive engagements by every citizen. The restructuring of institutions and state-society relations that needed to happen at the end of colonialism did not take place because the key actors that should have championed this critical restructuring were engaged in a needless Cold War. Consequently, the colonial institutions that served mainly the interests of the colonial government persisted, and African governments now only seem to exist to serve a privileged few. Instead of restructuring the governance arrangements, the emerging African leaders, supported by the West, maintained the colonial structures that paid little attention to serving the general population. Continuation of the colonial institutions helped to safeguard the interests of the former colonists at the expense of the African population. Real development has therefore been difficult to achieve because the extant political and economic institutions were never designed to produce broad-based growth and development. One should note that it is actually disingenuous to expect the colonial institutions that once treated Africans as objects of exploitation to turn and serve the same population as citizens. The overall effects of these perverse institutions is scandalous levels of inequality between a privileged few and the masses, with abject poverty and misery being the norm for the general population. There is no attempt here to suggest that the Cold War is to blame for all of Africa's developmental challenges. The argument is that the Cold War helped to shift the attention of the world from appraising the devastation of colonialism in Africa and coming up with an Africa-type Marshall Plan to restructure the continent.

The Cold War also facilitated the emergence of a new set of dictators who took over the reins of leadership at the twilight of colonialism. Once these dictators appeared to protect the interest of the departing colonial masters or were in tune with the free-market ideology that was spearheaded by the USA at that time, the world overlooked the atrocities of the dictator and actively supported his reign over Africans. In many respects, the Cold War facilitated the transfer of African countries from European colonial masters to African dictators. The implication is that no real change took place following the end of colonialism. What happened was the transfer of the colonies from European taskmasters to African dictators and emperors, while the fate of the ordinary citizen remained largely the same. The departing colonial powers consciously transferred power to Africans who would maintain the status quo and not implement fundamental restructuring to alter the colonial order and produce real benefits for Africans. Cold War actors were more interested in the pursuit of parochial interests than the interests of African countries.

## CONCLUSION

At the end of the Second World War, the USA was determined to spread free-market ideas to Africa and the rest of world. It was also an opportunity for America to gain access to Africa's markets, which had hitherto been dominated exclusively by European imperialists. On the other hand, the USSR and its allies were hawking communist ideas and found the emerging African nations a fertile ground for the spread of communism. The USSR believed that the struggles of Africans and other Third World populations against colonialism and other forms of domination and exploitation were natural tenets of communism. Therefore, the communist countries could identify with Africans in the struggle for freedom. The two superpowers (the USA and USSR) were both interested in the fate of the Third World. However, this interest was not necessarily out of love for the oppressed people of the developing world but was based on the self-interest of the superpowers and the pursuit of ideological supremacy. Perhaps the USSR genuinely supported the liberation movement in Africa out of principle, but such cannot be said of the USA. The USA supported decolonization, in part to dilute the economic influence of Europe over African countries and to make an inroad into the African market. While the USA supported decolonization, it was conscious not to allow the independence struggles by African nationalists to be hijacked by communist elements. It was based on this paradigm that President Eisenhower wrote to Prime Minister Winston Churchill on the need for an end to colonialism as follows:

> [T]here is abroad in the world a fierce and growing spirit of nationalism. Should we try to dam it up completely, it would, like a mighty river, burst through the barriers and could create havoc. But again, like a river, if we are intelligent enough to make constructive use of this force, then the result, far from being disastrous, could rebound greatly to our advantage, particularly in our struggle against the Kremlin's power.[32]

In effect, the US government felt the appropriate strategy was to 'moderate' Africa's independence so as to avoid the 'infiltration' of communist elements in the struggle for independence.

International relations during the Cold War were dominated by the self-ish interests of the superpowers. Although the Cold War afforded African countries access to finance and the military support of one or other Cold War superpower, it created a permanent stain on the political culture and development trajectory of these countries. Because financial and military support were readily available to domestic forces (from either side of the divide), these forms of support helped to escalate and broaden conflicts that would otherwise have had far less disastrous effects on the people. The protracted wars in Algeria between 1954 and 1962, and the conflict in Congo in the 1960s that ousted Prime Minister Patrice Lumumba and installed one of Africa's worst dictators, are major examples of the negative influence of the Cold War in African countries. Instead of serving to liberate African countries, Cold War rivalries fostered the continuation of imperialism in a different form. Africans were not allowed to pursue development and statehood in ways that worked for African societies. Rather, the USA had its own definition of modernism which had to be followed by the nascent countries, otherwise they were accused of following the communist agenda. Instead of enjoying true independence, African countries did not have the freedom to pursue their own ideas of modernity. Their near pathological attachment to opposing ideologies developed into feelings of insecurity in the minds of the two superpowers, such that US foreign policy became one based on the belief that 'my enemy's enemy is my friend' and vice versa.[33] In effect, if a country was not following communist ideas, such a country or its leader was considered a US ally.

While political independence should have been a great opportunity for African countries to evolve institutions and a development paradigm that worked for African communities, the Cold War politics blocked such opportunities for the nascent nations and led to the confusion that has characterized Africa's political economy ever since. Again, the intrigues in Congo at the time of independence readily come to mind. The people of Congo overwhelmingly voted for Patrice Lumumba to direct the affairs of independent Congo, but the US government was not comfortable with Lumumba's ideas and rhetoric. In pursuit of its Cold War objectives, the USA and its Belgian ally helped to thwart the wishes of the people of Congo. Patrice Lumumba was removed from office and the more US-friendly General Mobutu was helped onto the throne. The fate of Congo under Mobutu is well known. While we may not know whether Congo would have fared better under Prime Minister Patrice Lumumba, the brazen manner in which the wishes of the Congolese were truncated left a permanent scar in the minds of Africans and helped to entrench a political culture defined by violence and brute force.

The process of decolonization presented an opportunity for the world to assist Africa in dismantling the extractive political and economic institutions established in the continent by European colonial powers. However, the intrigues of the Cold War deviated the attention of the world to the real problems facing Africa and the rest of the Third World. Instead of targeting the utterly destructive legacies of colonialism, US foreign policy towards

Africa focused on dictating the type of modernity that independent African states must pursue. The battle for supremacy between the US-led forces of capitalism and the apostles of communism anchored by the USSR and China often resulted in violent conflicts. The destructive forces of political brigandage, frequent military overthrow of popular government, and civil wars in African countries after political independence are direct consequences of the Cold War.

## NOTES

1. See Paul E. Lovejoy, *Transformation in Slavery: A History in Slavery in Africa*, 2nd ed. (New York: Cambridge University Press, 2000); and Patrick Manning, *Slavery and African Life: Occidental, Oriental and African Slave Trades* (Cambridge: Cambridge University Press, 1990).
2. Daron Acemoglu, Simeon Johnson, and James Robinson, "The Colonial Origins of Comparative Development: An Empirical Investigation," *The American Economic Review* 91, no. 5 (2001): 1369–401.
3. Daron Acemoglu and James A. Robinson, "Why is Africa Poor?" *Economic History of Developing Regions* 25, no. 1 (2010): 21–50.
4. Odd Arne Westad, *The Global Cold War* (Cambridge: Cambridge University Press, 2007), 3.
5. Jeremi Suri, "The Cold War, Decolonization, and Global Social Awakenings: Historical Intersections," *Cold War History* 6, no. 3 (2006): 353–63.
6. See for example the important contributions by: Thomas McCormick, *America's Half Century: United States Foreign Policy in the Cold War and After* (Baltimore, MD: John Hopkins University Press, 1995); Greg Grandin, *The Last Colonial Massacre: Latin America in the Cold War* (Chicago, IL: University of Chicago Press, 2004); among others.
7. See for example the work of: Dipesh Chakrabarty, *Provincialising Europe: Postcolonial Thought and Historical Difference* (Princeton, NJ: Princeton University Press, 2000); Matthew Connelly, "Taking Off the Cold War Lens: Visions of North-South Conflict During the Algerian War for Independence," *The American Historical Review* 105, no. 3 (2000), 739–69; among others.
8. Richard J. Reid, *A History of Modern Africa: 1800 to the Present* (West Sussex: John Wiley & Sons Ltd, 2012), 278.
9. Crawford Young, *The African Colonial State in Comparative Perspective* (New Haven, CT: Yale University Press, 1994): 184–85.
10. Westad, *The Global Cold War*, 132.
11. Conversation between Bauche and de Muelenaere, November 16, 1942, quoted in Westad, *The Global Cold War*, 132.
12. Elizabeth Schmidt, *Foreign Interventions in Africa: from the Cold War to the War on Terror* (Cambridge: Cambridge University Press, 2013).
13. Schmidt, *Foreign Interventions in Africa*, 23.
14. Jeremi Suri, "The Cold War, Decolonization, and Global Social Awakenings: Historical Intersections."
15. Schmidt, *Foreign Interventions in Africa*, 23.
16. Frantz Fanon (English translation by Richard Philcox), *The Wretched of the Earth* (New York, NY: Grove Press, 2004), 38.

17. Richard Reid, *A History of Modern Africa*, 277–78.
18. David Wallechinsky, *Tyrants, the World's 20 Worst Living Dictators* (New York, NY: Harper Collins Publishers, 2006).
19. Schmidt, *Foreign Interventions in Africa*, 25.
20. Ibid., 82.
21. Habiba Ben Barka and Mthuli Ncube, "Political Fragility in Africa: Are Military Coups d'état a Never Ending Phenomena?," *AfDB Chief Economist Complex*, September 2012.
22. See the seminal work by Acemoglu et al., *The Colonial Origins of Comparative Development*; and Daron Acemoglu and James Robinson, "Why is Africa Poor," *Economic History of Developing Regions*, 25, no. 1 (2010), 21–50; among others.
23. Christopher O'Sullivan, "The United Nations, Decolonization, and Self-Determination in Cold War Sub-Saharan Africa, 1960–1994," *Journal of Third World Studies* 12, no. 2 (2005): 103–20.
24. "Special Message to Congress on Foreign Aid," March 22, 1961, *Public Papers of the Presidents of the United States, John F. Kennedy*, Vol. 1, 340–43 (quoted in Wested, 134–35).
25. Chester Bowles to President J.F. Kennedy, "Report on a Mission to Africa," October 17–November 9, 1962, DDRS (Quoted in Westad, 135).
26. Godfrey Mwakikagile, *Africa 1960–1970: Chronicle and Analysis* (Dar es Salaam: New Africa Press, 2009), 20.
27. Christopher O'Sullivan, "The United Nations, Decolonization, and Self-Determination in Cold War Sub-Saharan Africa, 1960–1994."
28. United Nation, *Yearbook of the United Nations, 1960* (New York: United Nations, 1961), 52–129.
29. "Marred: M. Lumumba's Offensive Speech in King's presence." London: *The Guardian*, July 1, 1960. https://www.theguardian.com/world/1960/jul/01/congo.
30. Reid, *Modern Africa*, 288.
31. Schmidt, *Foreign Interventions*, 27–28.
32. Quoted in Gregory A. Olson, "Eisenhower and the Indochina Problem," in *Eisenhower's War of Words: Rhetoric and Leadership*, ed. Martin J. Medhurst (East Lansing, MI: Michigan State University Press, 1994), 98.
33. Westad, *Global Cold War*, 399.

## BIBLIOGRAPHY

Acemoglu, Daron, and James A. Robinson. "Why is Africa Poor?" *Economic History of Developing Regions* 25, no. 1 (2010): 21–50.
Acemoglu, Daron, Simeon Johnson, and James Robinson. "The Colonial Origins of Comparative Development: An Empirical Investigation." *The American Economic Review* 91, no. 5 (2001): 1369–401.
Barka, Habiba, and Mthuli Ncube. "Political Fragility in Africa: Are Military Coup d'états a Never Ending Phenomena?" *AfDB Chief Economist Complex*, September 2012.
Chakrabarty, Dipesh. *Provincialising Europe: Postcolonial Thought and Historical Difference*. Princeton, NJ: Princeton University Press, 2000.

Connelly, Matthew. "Taking Off the Cold War Lens: Visions of North–South Conflict During the Algerian War for Independence." *The American Historical Review* 105, no. 3 (2000): 739–69.

Fanon, Frantz. *The Wretched of the Earth*. New York, NY: Grove Press, 2004.

Grandin, Greg. *The Last Colonial Massacre: Latin America in the Cold War*. Chicago, IL: University of Chicago Press, 2004.

Lovejoy, P.E. *Transformation in Slavery: A History in Slavery in Africa*. 2nd ed. New York, NY: Cambridge University Press, 2000.

Manning, P. *Slavery and African Life: Occidental, Oriental and African Slave Trades*. Cambridge: Cambridge University Press, 1990.

McCormick, Thomas. *America's Half Century: United States Foreign Policy in the Cold War and After*. Baltimore, MD: John Hopkins University Press, 1995.

Mwakikagile, Godfrey. *Africa 1960–1970: Chronicle and Analysis*. Dar es Salaam: New Africa Press, 2009.

Olson, Gregory. "Eisenhower and the Indochina Problem." In *Eisenhower's War of Words: Rhetoric and Leadership*, edited by Martin J. Medhurst. East Lansing, MI: Michigan State University Press, 1994.

O'Sullivan, Christopher. "The United Nations, Decolonization, and Self-Determination in Cold War Sub-Saharan Africa, 1960–1994." *Journal of Third World Studies* 12, no. 2 (2005): 103–20.

Reid, Richard. *A History of Modern Africa: 1800 to the Present*. West Sussex: John Wiley & Sons Ltd, 2012.

Schmidt, Elizabeth. *Foreign Interventions in Africa: From the Cold War to the War on Terror*. Cambridge: Cambridge University Press, 2013.

Suri, Jeremi. "The Cold War, Decolonization, and Global Social Awakenings: Historical Intersections." *Cold War History* 6, no. 3 (2006): 353–63.

United Nation. *Yearbook of the United Nations, 1960*. New York: United Nations, 1961.

Wallechinsky, David. *Tyrants, the World's 20 Worst Living Dictators*. New York, NY: Harper Collins Publishers, 2006.

Westad, Odd Arne. *The Global Cold War*. Cambridge: Cambridge University Press, 2007.

Young, Crawford. *The African Colonial State in Comparative Perspective*. New Haven, CT: Yale University Press, 1994.

CHAPTER 28

# African Politics Since Independence

*Ademola Araoye*

Engaging the complexities of politics in Africa since independence poses the challenge of distilling commonalities across a wide universe of 56 African postcolonial political entities and their equally vast panoply of governance paradigms. African states and political entities are diverse, significantly differentiated in their antecedents, including in the different trajectories to their emergence as states in the global system, their colonial experiences and traditions bequeathed to them, the varying strength and salience of impositions of neo-colonial affinities, and their heterogeneous internal constructions that together impact the variegated internal processes and dynamics of each state. Patrick Chabal, for instance, notes that although the five Lusophone countries in Africa (which gained independence in 1974/1975 mainly through military defeats of the Portuguese colonial administrations) share a common colonial heritage, a heritage that is quite distinct from that of the other two main colonial powers, Britain and France. However, they are also diverse and complex in many other ways. This diversity and complexity consists of their sociological constructions, size, and geo-physical structure that impact their politics. For example, Cape Verde is an archipelago of ten islands and constituted by a creole society more akin to the Caribbean than the African; whereas Mozambique, also multiracial in its composition and based on a community of established Indian Portuguese 'Goans' and a more recent Indian trading population, is much less multiracial in its outlook. Mozambique was also far less successfully integrated than Angola.[1]

A. Araoye (✉)
Independent Researcher, Johannesburg, South Africa

© The Author(s) 2018
M.S. Shanguhyia and T. Falola (eds.),
*The Palgrave Handbook of African Colonial and Postcolonial History*,
https://doi.org/10.1057/978-1-137-59426-6_28

African states have different internal constructions. Nigeria, with a land area of 910,770 square kilometers and an estimated population of 184,932,822 as of Thursday, January 28, 2016[2] and composed of over 250 ethnic groups is divided into 36 states in a quasi-federal arrangement that is broadly demarcated along ethnic boundaries. The Nigerian society and state have managed, in recent times, to render more complex their ethno-regional mosaic and tensions by exacerbating a major line of cleavage in the thinly veiled struggle for ascendancy between Christianity and Islam in national life. Liberia's internal cleavages are along the lines of a hegemonic Americo-Liberian elite society constituted by descendants of returnee free slaves on the one hand and an indigenous population of 15 major ethnic groups that, on the other hand, challenge the legitimacy of the Liberianess of the identities of some of the indigenous groups. Superimposed on these divisions in post-conflict Liberia is a clamor for the declaration of Liberia as founded on Christian foundations, even while some want the state to be directed by Only Indigenous Liberians (OIL). In the same vein, the central theme of the politics of Guinea Bissau has traditionally been how to manage the vaunted political aspirations of the Ballanta, the single largest ethnic group and, paradoxically, the widely perceived ambivalence of the status of the Mettise community that produced Amilcar Cabral, the founding father of the nation. In Ivory Coast, long dominated by Houphouët-Boigny working in close collaboration with the French establishment, the Ivorianness of the Mossi and Foula are often questioned. The Republic of South Sudan, the world's latest independent country, gained independence from Sudan on 9 July 2011 as the outcome of a 2005 agreement that ended Africa's longest-running civil war. Its population of ten million people is made up of the 10 southernmost states of Sudan. South Sudan is one of the most diverse countries in Africa. It is home to over 60 different major ethnic groups, and the majority of its people follow traditional religions.[3] The diversity of South Sudan, as in most of Africa, has proven to be a challenge for national cohesion.

Senegal's estimated population of 15,684,159 is comprised of over ten main ethnic groups, though five account for the majority of the country's people. The largest group is the Wolof in the northwest and central regions, who make up nearly half of the population. The Wolof language has become a national lingua franca of sorts. In the North are the Fula/Peul/Fulbe/Fulani, one of West Africa's largest and most diverse ethnic groups, speaking two distinct languages and accounting for around a quarter of the population. Religion plays a significant role in Senegal, where 92% of the population is Muslim, mainly Sunni of Maliki school of jurisprudence intermingled with Sufi influences. Christians, mostly found in the Casamance region, represent 7% of the population. Traditional beliefs are officially practiced by 1% of the population, but a significant proportion of the population partake in traditional practices. The Diola, who straddle the Gambia and Guinea-Bissau, predominate in the region of Casamance. The Casamance was ceded by Portugal to French control following negotiations between the two in 1888, in which Portugal lost possession of Casamance, then the commercial hub of its colony Portuguese Guinea, which later became Guinea Bissau. A local variant of Kriol known as Ziguinchor Creole has been retained in the region, and the members of the deep-rooted Creole community carry Portuguese surnames like Da Silva, Carvalho and Fonseca. Interest in Portuguese colonial heritage has been revived in order to exert a distinct identity, particularly in Baixa (Lower) Casamançe.

The Islamic Republic of Mauretania further sharpens the cultural complexity, the contrasts, and the tensions in the historicity and sociological constructions of African states and societies. In bridging the Arab Maghreb and western Sub-Saharan Africa, Mauretania has retained the tensions in Afro-Arab relations in officially sustaining the slavery of its black population until 1981. This largely desert country presents a cultural contrast, with an Arab-Berber population to the North and black Africans to the South. Many of its people are nomads. For a while controlling the Islamic part of Spain, Mauritania in the Middle ages was the cradle of the Almoravid movement, which spread Islam throughout the region. Slavery is deeply rooted in the structure of Mauritanian society and closely tied to the ethnic composition of the country.[4] Mauritania was the last country in the world to formally abolish slavery; the continued vibrancy of the centuries-old practice is a fossilized residue of the trans-Sahara slave trade when Arabic-speaking Moors raided African villages. Society is organized around a rigid caste system that favors mainly Moorish noble-borns, who are uncompromising about their country as an Arab republic. Power and wealth is concentrated among majority lighter-skinned Moors. The descendants of slaves and darker-skinned Moors, as well as black Africans, live on the margins of society. It is estimated that up to 800,000 people in a nation of 3.5 million remain chattels.[5]

The implications of the internal constructions of postcolonial African states acquire greater salience for the nature of the governance that emerged in the post-liberation era in states that emerged through armed liberation struggles. This is pronounced in cases where white settler minorities had made Africa their homes and had entrenched minority rule. Nationalist liberation movements, confronted by a refusal of the incumbent, internal, minority colonial regimes to relinquish power, had been forced to take up arms to dislodge settler colonialism. Roger Southall advances that the ensuing armed struggle required the transformation of nationalist movements into what have become known as National Liberation Movements (NLMs).[6] In dealing with what he terms the ambiguous heritage of settler colonialism in the post-liberation state (exemplified in South Africa, Mozambique, Namibia, and Zimbabwe), the centralized and hierarchical protocols as well as the organizing principles of the NLMs gave birth to vastly different organizational forms, strategies, and tactics of struggle. These attributes significantly impacted the governance practices of the post-liberation state as the armed movements became the ruling parties. The structure of society and the history of minority rule threw up profound multiple challenges regarding identity legitimation and the skewed political economy in the new states. These multidimensional challenges included the fundamental characteristic that the pivots of the economy remained white-dominated; the hitherto subordinated racial populations lacked the necessary skills required to be meaningfully integrated into the political economy. These challenges also reflected the ambiguity around the concepts of race and citizenship in the post liberated state. Southall observes of this connection that:

> It was easy enough to depict 'white settlers' as the principal beneficiaries of 'white domination'. Yet what constituted a 'settler'? Was it someone who themselves had just recently settled upon Africa as their home? If so, what about those whites whose forebears had settled in their countries of residence two, three, or even more generations ago, and who had known no other home but Africa? ... Suffice it to say that NLM found themselves awkwardly situated with regard to the status of whites who viewed themselves as living at 'home' while at the same time they identified white settlers whose power was embodied in racially exclusionary regimes, as manifestly 'the enemy' of political liberation. ... Even so, questions around whether the 'white citizen' could also claim to be authentically 'African' were to linger on well into post liberation era and were to retain political volatility.[7]

Navigating these complexities of the continental landscape, some have concluded that there is not one, but many Africas.[8] In this diversified universe, the specific contexts and make-up of each African state drive its politics.

Meanwhile, the extant construction of Africa is an important context and a crucial pointer to the evolution of politics in and of African states since independence. This problematic construction reflects the inability of the leaders of Africa in the immediate post-independence era to surmount the fundamental historic challenge. This challenge was expressed in fractious structures and institutions of a fragile states system that was bequeathed as a legacy of colonialism. The main existential dilemma before the continent in 1963, as new states emerged (often variously directed and controlled by the colonial powers), was clearly defined. The question was whether in forging ahead in the post-independence era, Africa would maintain the fractious and divisive structure of the evolving continental states system that was based on the outcome of the Berlin Conference of 1884, at which the colonial powers partitioned the continent according to their national interests, or whether it would mobilize the will to transcend these contrived divisions and build a strong and viable continental state. The failure of an ideo-philosophically divided leadership of the continent to consolidate the colonially designed states system into a single strong and viable continental federation (thereby radically realigning the continental political geography) has haunted the evolution of Africa since independence. Two camps emerged in the struggle: the Casablanca group, whose integrationist vision was encapsulated in the struggles of Kwame Nkrumah of Ghana, and a conservative Monrovia group led by the likes of Houphouët-Boigny of Ivory Coast (officially the Republic of Côte d'Ivoire), Leopold Sedar Senghor of Senegal, and William Tubman in Liberia, whose insistence on a gradualist approach to substantive African unity merely reflected the interests of their neo-colonial controllers and their personal predilections, which were informed by personal political interests to maintain the status quo. Before then, the French idea of a united Francophone West African colonial state, for example, crumbled over the personal rivalry of Boigny and Senghor, who both sought to maintain a postcolonial fiefdom under their respective control. On the other side, Kwame Nkrumah, the preeminent articulator of the integrationist perspective, canvassed total political integration in the form of a continental union. The Union was to have three main objectives: overall continental planning on a continental scale; a unified land, sea, air, military, and defense strategy; and a common foreign policy. Nkrumah emphasized that the interests of neo-colonialism and the objectives of African governments are directly opposed, for whereas the strength of African countries lies in their unity, the strength of neo-colonialism lies in their disunity.[9] The subversion of the integrationist project of the visionaries also reflected the lack of will of most of the leaders of early post-independence Africa to rise above parochial and personal interests in resolving the first and defining political challenge that faced the continent. This failure presaged the transformation of independent African states into mere personal fiefdoms of these early leaders through their complete appropriation of the socio-political and economic spaces of post-independence African states. The personal appropriations of state spaces by early political leaders were convenient for the sustenance of external and neo-colonial control and fed well into the calculus of the Cold War that prevailed as African states emerged as proxy entities into the global system of states.

Meanwhile, Adebayo Olukoshi observes that the last decade-and-a-half in Africa's recent history has been marked by some dramatic and significant developments on the continent's political terrain. These developments have been as varied as they have been contradictory. This evolution, he concludes, has also constituted a major source of challenge to political theory as different schools of thought have grappled with them in terms of their weight and meaning.[10] Despite the continuing evolution, complexity, and diversity across the African continent, it is safe to hazard that the politics of postcolonial Africa has been shaped by the interplay of a myriad of factors and especially by the expansive activities and interactions of an unholy trinity of associated forces. Among these may be cited the ideological bifurcation of the global system at the emergence of African statehoods in that system that impacted the internal dynamics and governance arrangements in the new states. Western powers viewed African independence through the lens of the Cold War,[11] and the determination to coopt them as instruments or proxies of their ideological camps directed their interaction with the new states. Ultimately, culturally and politically, and in the face of the rejection by African leaders of constructive realignment and consolidation of the political geography of the continent to enhance the capacity of a united Africa to resist foreign domination in the 1960s, the legacy of European dominance remained evident in the national borders, political infrastructures, education systems, national languages, economies, and trade networks of each of the newly emerged nations.[12] The location of the new states as weak postcolonial entities that largely served as proxies of the major protagonists in the Cold War ensured the projection of strategic interests of neo-colonial powers during the Cold War at the expense of the continent. In relation to these factors, with the outbreak of the Cold War after the Second World War, the USA and its Western allies were prepared to let emerging new states in Africa enjoy neither political autonomy nor effective control over strategic raw materials in their territories. That was in order to avoid these strategic minerals falling under the control of their enemies in the USSR.

In the post-Cold War period, the resurgence of the Berlin 1884 syndrome has been notable, even as the liberating consequences of the end of the Cold War instigated social forces, however feeble, for the liberation of Africa's political spaces from entrenched maximum rulers in a raft of sovereign national conferences. The sovereign national conferences sought to renegotiate the normative political settlements and impositions that had evolved and seemingly been validated in the context and by the externally derived logic of the Cold War. The post-Cold War redemocratization impulse fizzled out as democratic practice was again instrumentalized to revalidate neo-patrimonialism as the normative governance paradigm. In state after state in the post-Cold War era, constitutionalism was assaulted with varying results and consequences. It has eventually paved the way for a post-Cold War club of sit-tight presidents and national leaders with varying legitimacy depending on the specific national contexts. Many of these leaders have their antecedence in military interventions in the political process in the Cold War era. The challenging situations in Pierre Nkurunziza's Burundi are as different from the situation of Paul Kagame as those in Rwanda are from Yoweri Museveni in Uganda, which in turn is very different from Dos Santos in Angola. The consolidated, permanent, personal appropriation of the state spaces in scenarios (such as in Paul Biya's Cameroon, Sassou Nguesso's Congo Brazzaville, the now dethroned Yahya Jammeh in the Gambia, Joseph Kabilla in the Democratic Republic of Congo or Robert Mugabe in Zimbabwe) reflects problematic continuities that have defied the feeble redemocratization wave of the post-Cold War. In some of these instances, the residual logics of neo-colonial control have been at play despite the political rhetoric of neo-colonial forces, such as France, to the contrary. Even then, some consolidated personal appropriations of the totality of the public spaces (by leaders such Yoweri Museveni and Robert Mugabe) are paradoxically validated by perceived threats of neo-colonial interventions to reverse the radical gains made. Yet the strength of political institutions that have prevailed in a country like Nigeria, where the spirited efforts of a claimed born-again democrat in Olusegun Obasanjo, a former military dictator, to change the constitution to facilitate his term elongation; the smooth transitions of power and substantive democratic consolidation in Ghana; and the dramatic turnaround and democratic consolidation in the former quasi Marxist-Republic of Benin offer some hope for the future.

Finally, the third of the unholy trinity is the internal security dilemmas associated with the structural heterogeneity of the postcolonial African state and the pathologies of postcoloniality. In newly independent states cobbled together by external forces and structured to advance the interests of their creators, social and constituent groups who perceive themselves as trapped in the newly demarcated political spaces and entities have to determine whether their new compatriots pose a threat to them. This is especially so as the colonial creators of the postcolonial state manipulated the various groups to attain their strategic objective of continued and long term control. Consequently, Ademola Araoye notes that in the postcolonial environment each group must look out on its own for its own to protect its integrity and autonomy. Thus, the state, once appropriated by one dominant group through the political settlement that emerges or through control of the coercive machinery of the state, potentially poses a mortal threat to the continued integrity and autonomy of the other constituent communities or groups. Each group must ensure that it has enough coercive instruments to protect itself.[13] Invariably, perceptions of security dilemmas have been in the affirmative, as the Rwandan genocide, the case of Nigeria and Biafra or in Guinea Bissau, or even challenges to the legitimacy of certain identities in countries such as Liberia have shown. The pervasive contest for ascendancy between Christianity and Islam has added a new dimension to perceptions of threat to deeply held values by religious minorities as in the Gambia, Angola, Liberia, Nigeria, among others. The security dilemma has been exacerbated by the manipulations of the colonial powers, expressed in the role of France in the conflict in Ivory Coast and in the Central African Republic (CAR). Also, the existence of transnational and extraterritorial stakeholders who perceive legitimate interests to protect in the outcomes of the strategic interactions in the environment of the postcolonial African state has critical implications. The internal construction and processes of the postcolonial state impact the nature of relationships generated with the immediate 'external' environment of the postcolonial state. The immediate environment of the postcolonial state has an intermestic attribute.[14]

Africa is geophysically the center of the universe. It is also acknowledged as the cradle of humankind. Africa is the second-largest and second-most populous continent on earth. It is the most endowed of all continents. It has the largest deposition of natural wealth on the surface of planet Earth. Africa has 25% of the world's arable land. About 65% of the uncultivated arable land needed to feed 9 billion people globally by 2050 is in Africa. Africa has an abundance of human resources. The UN Population Fund stated in 2009 that the population of Africa had hit the one billion mark and had therefore doubled in size over the course of 27 years. As of 2015, the population estimates are around 1.166 billion.[15] With these endowments, Africa is of immense strategic interest to humanity. These factors have impacted the fortunes of the continent, from the social through the economic to the political evolution of the continent. Developments in Africa, including political, social, and economic, since its contact with the world (mainly the Arab world and Islam as well with Europe and Christianity) have significantly been impacted or even directed by powerful external forces mobilized around the control of the immense strategic values, material, spiritual, and the commodified black humanity, of the continent. External forces have also influenced the character of the political landscape, the structure of political, social, and economic entities, as well as the overall dynamics that have shaped the evolution of the African colonized spaces that began to be transformed into sovereign states in the 1950s.

Postcolonial African states[16] began to emerge from the 1950s when six African nations, notably Ghana in 1957, gained independence from colonial Britain. In the 1960s, 11 other independent African states emerged. In 2016, Africa is home to 54 recognized sovereign states and countries, 9 territories, and 2 de facto independent states with very little recognition. Africa thus groups together 56 of over 193 entities that constitute a complex universe of hierarchically arranged state actors in the global order. These factors constitute a context that has crucially defined Africa's locus in the global system and its relationship with the world that have all affected, and in instances directed, the internal dynamics of its diverse states. The multiplicity of Africa's relationships with the world have been skewed, reflecting Africa's subordinate status in a highly hierarchical global system. These relationships have impacted the socio-cultural and political development and evolution of the continent, spanning formal debilitating enslavement of Africans to the neo-colonial status of Africa in contemporary times. Still directed and pummeled by the same global forces that created the African state in their own images and interests, the neo-colonial state that emerged and its internal dynamics were a continuity of sorts of the historic complexities and travails of Africa and of black humanity given its locus in global affairs.

Against this general background, African politics (the ways in which political protocols, rules, norms, methods, and modes of interaction are established, maintained and change) in the postcolonial era has been marred by authoritarianism, corruption, military intervention, and leadership failures amidst a broader socio-economic crisis characterized by poverty.[17] In the pervading climate of poverty, African politics in the first five decades of independence witnessed an era of exuberant expressions, on the part of both civil and military interventionists in the political sphere. The exuberance exhibited in the ideo-philosophical engagements of the dominant and often hegemonic political forces that emerged in early decades of post-independence entailed deleterious consequences for state and nation building as well as for peace, stability and development; political and socio-economic development in the postcolonial state. The situation was the same whether the main actors were nationalists and revolutionaries as in most of Lusophone Africa or in post-liberated states in Southern Africa; nationalists as in most of Anglophone Africa; or plain conservatives as in most of Francophone Sub-Saharan Africa. This was a natural consequence of the mass mobilization required to overthrow the *ancien* colonial administration in most of Africa, including internal minority colonial regimes that instigated revolutionary responses in Southern Africa. African politics since independence has generally been turbulent and characterized by violence. The culture of political violence associated with African statecraft carried forward an experience that was integral to colonial control of subordinated territories by the creators of the neo-colonial African state. Specifically, colonial administrative systems were not based on democratic foundations. Governance followed the top-down approach that was largely arbitrary and not geared toward the well-being of the governed.[18] Since the purpose of colonial government was to control the population and ensure the continuous exploitation of natural resources for the benefit of the European colonizing powers, the objective was met through authoritarian rule that was bolstered by strong police and military forces. In this context, political legitimacy was attached to the unequivocal control of force. Colonialism thus implanted the notion that authoritarianism is an appropriate mode of political rule and that force is an acceptable instrument of that rule.[19] Democratic practice in the post-independence era, often alternating with military regimes and revolutions of various hues, competed with and or often complemented political violence in postcolonial Africa. The military emerged in post-independent Africa as the most critical segment of all in the struggle for power.[20]

However, both political violence (Including civil wars and armed liberation struggles) and Africa's myriad versions of democracy have been instruments in the service of exclusive parochial objectives, in contradistinction to national consensus and the overall public good. Democratic practice, thus also instrumentalized, acquired a unique flavor that subverted substantive democratic values and ethics as well as procedures. It was used to advance the parochially exclusive acquisition of loot instead of instilling the intrinsic value of democracy to attain the publicly inclusive good in the post-independence era. Given the structural heterogeneity and the internal polarities of society in postcolonial political entities struggling to be nations, the search for parochial loot by powerful constituents, often seeking hegemonic status in the political space, is a pivotal motive driving the political process. In the postcolonial state, the search for loot by agencies associated with and loyal to identifiable and specific competing constituents undermines the policy of advancing the inclusive and positively non-exclusive public good. Accordingly, in the post-colonial state setting, the search for parochial loot by the dominant political force, in contradistinction to the non-exclusive national public good, is facilitated through the struggle for the absolute appropriation of the public space by the dominant parochial force. This national process, driven by parochial objectives of the dominant competing forces, sets apart the internal political process of the postcolonial state from the internal politics and policy processes of modern and postmodern states. The latter operates on the basis of the constant search for compromises among competing forces. Public policy formulation equates the search for the non-exclusive public good. Southall observes the same tendency for exclusive public policy in post-liberated states. He highlights that in the post-liberation era, the capturing of the state and its transformation are major policy objectives of the different liberation movements. This is illustrated in the commitment to transformation agendas that is a feature common to all post-liberated states that emerged from settler colonial regimes. In the transformation was implied the need for a revolutionary state capable of overcoming all obstacles.[21] Given their backgrounds and the challenges emanating from the struggle and the ambiguity of their heritage, it is scarcely surprising that liberation movements in their transformed role as ruling parties regarded the state as requiring not merely Africanization (as in Zimbabwe) or affirmative action to ensure 'representivity' (as in Namibia and South Africa), but its becoming the key instrument of transformation.[22] The policy to deploy party personnel to all key institutions of the state, which is a central tenet of the process of state transformation, is to enable the liberation movement to control the levers of power. In the final analysis, though, the implementation of the transformation policy, especially its deployment strategy, became an instrument of patronage, material accumulation, and upward mobility. It acquired the character of a neo-patrimonial system associated with the classic postcolonial African state.

The struggle for the partisan absolute appropriation of the totality of the state space has been the driving motif of politics in Africa since independence. The search for the parochial good as against the public or national good threw up creative structures such as the one-party states that effectively were one-man states, as well as political parties or military formations structured largely as the vessels for the articulation of the parochial and partisan interests of local dominant forces and their external allies and sponsors. The outcome of the struggle has been a pervasive deployment of violence and manipulation of democratic practice by powerful forces to retain absolute control of the state space against all other contestants. It is in this context that some have argued that multiparty politics have made things worse, not because of the theoretically admirable principles of political competition but because of the dirty and messy business which such competition can mean in practice.[23]

At the domestic level, partisan absolute appropriation of the socio-economic and political spaces by contesting stake holders and constituent units of the postcolonial state has been the central motif of African politics since independence. At a second level, external forces are heavily implicated in the internal politics to consolidate control over what they perceive as their neo-colonial possessions. Indeed, the process of independence often laid the foundations for neo-colonial control of the emerging state. These are exemplified in manipulating key internal facts such as demography (as in Anglophone Nigeria and Kenya), or in the institution of mechanisms to effect direct placement of stooges as leaders of new states (as throughout Francophone Sub-Saharan Africa, including Ivory Coast, Gabon, Democratic Republic of Congo, or Congo [Brazzaville] and lately in Guinea). In Lusophone Africa, where revolutionary forces forced out the Portuguese, the decay of these revolutions compromised the integrity of the movement towards nationhood as they over time slid into big-power manipulations, as in Guinea Bissau and ultimately in Angola. In this climate, the dominant political settlements were largely impositions of the interests of the most powerfully placed interest group, mainly ethno-regional or ethno-religious groups, or a coalition of interest groups against all other stakeholders. The prevailing political settlements were thus fragile and they unraveled as the internal configuration of domestic forces changed or when the external guarantor of the prevailing settlements switched loyalty. In these situations, armed conflict became the currency to resolve the stalemate that often led to the implosion of the state. Nigeria, Guinea Bissau, Rwanda, Liberia, Angola, Chad, Ivory Coast, CAR, Somalia, Burundi, and Mobutu's Zaire present classic examples of this.

The pervasive search for partisan absolute control of the state space by contesting political forces within the postcolonial African state ensures instability in the political process. Political conflict is perennially generated over control of the state, where conflict is about who governs and does not envisage the creation of a new state. The unity of the state is tacitly accepted by competing elites, and conflict centers on control of the state and state resources.[24] However, this is conditioned on the expectation that the competing constituent units will be able to outsmart the extant dominant power over time. The political process is an attempt to capture the state through the use of political or military power by one group at the expense of another, but ultimately it is a process of the search for absolute partisan appropriation of the state space by anyone of the competing constituent groups by outmaneuvering the others. The process elicits conflict. As expressed in Nigeria, Liberia, and Angola, the most difficult conflict is that around the control of the state and its resources. This control is often attained by one of the groups of contesting forces institutionalized in the dominant neo-patrimonial system of governance. The political process in Africa since independence has thus been characterized by crisis and ultimately war to attain absolute partisan appropriation of the state space. In the unending struggle for absolute control of the political space, succession struggles in the postcolonial African state focus upon the presidency and the institutions in which competition for national leadership takes place.[25] Also, dynastic succession has posed a challenge to democratic transitions in the post-Cold War era. Accordingly, although power transfers and transitions are effected by four means in the politics of Africa,[26] irregular power transfers remain the norm.

In the second half-century of post-independence that has been character-ized by strong international sentiments for the entrenchment of democracy, the vogue has been for African leaders to abridge democratic practice through the unconstitutional renewal of executive tenure and controversial adjust-ments of executive mandates that also represent avenues of open subversion of the Constitution. Mwaura identifies the four means of power transfers in Africa as:

1. 'Regular executive transfer', which occurs according to the relevance of the established rules, constitution, laws, customs, etc. which regulate succession and facilitate a peaceful and orderly transition. Power transi-tion from one ruling party or elite to another competing party or group of power aspirants remains an aberration.
2. 'Renewal of executive tenure' or 'self-succession', which involves the search for regime legitimacy in elections, 'constitutional' amendments, and centralized control of political-party and state-administrative structures.
3. 'Executive adjustments' involving succession of political and economic elites, through cabinet shuffles, party (re)alignments and alliance shifts, and the ethnic equation of governmental positions.
4. 'Irregular power transfer', according to the key event which leads to succession, such as assassinations and political murder, deposition, res-ignation and coups d'état as the instruments for succession.

The implications of executive adjustments are aptly demonstrated in the case of Kenya by Lakidi and Mazrui. Affirming the 'the East African Experi-ence' as a 'third model' of power transfer, they note that initially the Ken-yan constitution was based on the Westminster experience. In that model, the prime minister derived his legitimacy from parliament. When the East African countries went 'presidential', it was not in the direction of the US system. The relationship between the president and parliament changed; it was no longer a system in which the president derived legitimacy from parliament, nor one in which the president was constitutionally separate from the legis-lature, but one in which the parliament in reality came to derive its legiti-macy from the president (Lakidi and Mazrui 1973: 3). As Lakidi and Mazrui further elaborate, the presidency in East Africa became the primary source of legitimization for proposed political policies and social values. While in Brit-ain the prime minister cannot afford to lose the confidence of parliament, in East Africa, parliament cannot afford to lose the confidence of the president. Constitutional amendments and changes in Kenya have over the years consol-idated presidential power against parliamentary initiatives. Political expediency and prudence determine political survival or the ability of a political leader to retain political office or political efficacy. Political recruitment is the other side of the coin of political survival; those who fail to survive are by definition out of the center of politics; those who are recruited come either to replace the losers or to supplement the survivors. Political survival therefore dictates that political recruitment be regulated and controlled so as to limit leadership succession at all levels of the political ladder. Kenyatta attempted to reduce competition for political recruitment through, firstly, an internal purge in KANU, and, secondly, control of the electoral process. The roots of conflict in independent Kenya revolved around ideology and policies of the new state.[27]

With the scant prospect of a constitutional transfer of power, the outcome of the political processes since independence has been the entrenchment of violence to achieve political goals. This is often expressed in coups d'états, revolutions, conflict, wars, and associated humanitarian disasters that are prominent features of African politics. The challenge therefore has been how to reinvent political processes to address the multidimensional deficits of democratic practice. It is against this background that John W. Harbeson[28] advances that postcolonial politics in Africa since independence has been, and continues to be, very much work in progress. It is surmised that the originally prevailing designs for building prosperous, viable, stable states have changed markedly over Sub-Saharan Africa's first half-century of independence through reliance upon various hypothesized keys to overcoming fundamental and endemic manifestations of political and economic underdevelopment. Harbeson concludes that the assumed first vision of nationalist leaders of the mass-based parties who brought their countries to independence, centering upon rapid, egalitarian, state-led political development, dissolved amid political disarray with their objectives largely unrealized.[29] Many of the nationalist leaders became victims of the strategic interferences of elite states determined to keep Africa within their spheres of influence during the Cold War. Many of the leaders in Africa were and are still directly imposed or manipulated into office by elite states to consolidate their control over what many analysts still refer to as neo-colonial states, rather than postcolonial states. The controversial emergence of Alhassan Ouattara as president in Ivory Coast following the removal of nationalist Laurent Gbagbo, the entrenchment of Sassou Nguesso as quasi-permanent president of Congo (Brazzaville), Ali Bongo, son of Omar Bongo, as successor to his father, or the continuing rule of Paul Biya, among many others, all reflect the continued leverage of France to determine who rules and on what terms in Francophone Africa.

A good appreciation of the antecedence and structure of the state are critical elements in understanding the internal dynamics (whether political, social, and/or economic) of African states since independence. Some analysts advance that because of its antecedence as a mechanical creation and it being an unintended derivative of early globalization driven by elite state actors, the postcolonial African state has been unable to keep pace with the evolutionary advance of the cluster of modern states that emerged from the impulses of the mid-seventeenth century to a postmodern phase. Because of its sluggish adaptive capacity, the African postcolonial state is characterized by institutional lags that have militated against its evolution. Consequently, it has remained a marginalized member of the global interstates system. The postcolonial African state also grapples with the tensions and struggles that characterized if not the formative stages of Westphalia then at least its phase of state consolidation that gave birth to the nation by 1781. Nation building has remained a formidable challenge to the consolidation of the postcolonial state. Its fragmented and unpacified society is the biggest threat to its continued existence as a member of the global states system. Conventional wisdom perceives the interstate system as one of anarchy in which those states which fail to help themselves, or which do so less effectively than others, will fail to prosper. In this self-help system, units worry about their survival due to the danger posed by the external environment. The weak postcolonial African state paradoxically deviates from the general principles that govern the states system. The double paradox is that the threat to the perpetuation of the postcolonial state is largely internal, as the state is permanently in danger of imploding or disintegrating in the context of the pervasive struggle for absolute partisan appropriation of the state space by its constituent units. The evidence illustrates that many postcolonial African states have lived with powerful proto states[30] within their territory as rival claimants to the sovereignty of that state. A second paradox is that the postcolonial state owes its continued existence to the protocols and myths of the global interstate system and often to direct patronage of elite state actors in this system. These caveats reflect the complexities of the underpinnings of politics in the postcolonial African state.[31] Independence would seem to have complicated the conditions of Africa's engagement with its self and the world around it.

The intermestic character of the immediate environment in which the postcolonial African state is located is therefore conceptually distinct from the conventional environment of the interstate system. Although the immediate intermestic environment is integral to the structure of the overall external environment, the character of the immediate environment is principally defined by the potential presence of proto-states whose existence are facilitated by the cross-border flow of transnational interest groups perceiving legitimate stakes in the affairs of the postcolonial state. These distinctions have radical implications for the political process and have been manifest in politics since independence. The formal postcolonial state may seek the perpetuation of the structure of the state as presently constituted, while the goal of the proto-state or disaffected communities is either to transform the structure of the state to its partisan advantage or to carve out a new autonomous political space from the formal state. In instances, the proto-state (exemplified by Greater Liberia with its capital in Gbarnga under Charles Taylor, greater Ivory Coast with its capital in Bouake of the Forces Nouvelle, the SPLA in South Sudan with its Juba capital) have sometimes demonstrated more coercive capabilities than the opposing postcolonial state. In other instances (such as the wide enclave in Angola of the Jonas Savimbi-led UNITA, which lasted for over three decades), they fizzle out as anachronistic elements in an evolved global strategic landscape that is inimical to their survival. Their objectives are mostly achieved through war that has become a feature of political bargaining since independence. The constraints posed by the intermestic immediate environment of the postcolonial state are therefore different from those posed to the modern state by the structure of the interstate system.

A configuration of power may emerge that advances the vested partisan interests of the key actors in the international community in controlling the internal political forces in the postcolonial state and dominating the immediate and larger environment. The nature of relationships elicited by the structure of the external environment, including the state system, also impacts the internal characteristic of the postcolonial state. The politics of the postcolonial state may thus be impacted or exacerbated by the confrontation between strategic interests between blocs of transnational forces supporting or challenging the civil order of the postcolonial state. Harbeson observes that the outcome of the intertwining of the rapidly and profoundly changing contours of late twentieth and early twenty-first century world politics and the global economy with predominant weakness and political decay in African politics, as well as endemic economic underdevelopment, have had deleterious consequences for the continent. These pathologies are intrinsic to the incongruous internal structure of the African state. In terms of their attributes, especially their domestic and Westphalian sovereignties, as well as the multiple loci of power, many of the political entities in Africa barely qualify as states, except in the convenient recognition afforded them as such by other states expressed in pragmatic respect for their international legal sovereignties. The interactions of external forces and associated factors and domestic forces and factors have shaped the dominant governance patrimonial paradigm in Africa since independence.

The distinctive institutional hallmark of African regimes is neo-patrimonialism.[32] This dominant governance paradigm is variously expressed in a statism that paradoxically consolidates power outside the public realm in the private hands of a patriarchal figure operating in the context of patrimonial, neo-patrimonial, civilian and military autocratic structures and institutions of governance of African states since independence. In its classic expression, patrimonialism is a social system in which a royal elite rules through personal and arbitrary control over a bureaucracy and over slaves, mercenaries, and conscripts who have no power themselves and serve only to enforce the monarch's rule. It was most often associated with Asia, and China in particular. Patrimonial systems, representing tenuous political settlements, are known to be far less stable (and have attracted coups d'état and revolutions) than other types of systems. Proponents of the concept of neo-patrimonialism assert that distinct features distinguish governance in the African state from its counterparts in other world regions. It is highlighted that this particular attribute of the African state is characterized by the lack of separation between the public and the private spheres.[33] This is consistent with the experience in Africa where patrimonial systems with respectable economic successes have resulted in social and political instability and ultimately violent transitions as exemplified in Ivory Coast since Houphouët-Boigny, the revolution against Moussa Traore in Mali, and the overthrow of Siad Barre in Somalia. Bratton and Van de Walle highlight that although neo-patrimonial rule may outwardly resemble a democratic society, the underlying system has more in common with a patrimonial system, in which society is governed by a powerful leader for whom personal ties are central. In this system, an individual rules by dint of personal prestige and power. Authority is entirely personalized, shaped by a ruler's preference rather than any codified system of laws. The neo-patrimonial system modifies this structure while maintaining the basic relationships; while laws and bureaucracies do exist, the underlying system is little different from patrimonialism. Neo-patrimonialism merely incorporates patrimonial logic into bureaucratic institutions.[34] Finally, neo-patrimonial systems, with their emphasis on the individual prestige of the leader, are inherently undemocratic, despite the fact that democratic elections take place. Though ostensibly governed by rules and bureaucracy, they in fact employ these means in order to be instilled in society. Democratic institutions are subverted in order to fit within this power structure.[35]

In its workings, patrimonialism is based on a patron–client relationship where a president first occupies the political space by entrenching substantial centralized control over social and economic affairs in the state. With the power of patronage concentrated in one hand, as a patron the president deploys state resources to court the loyalty of cronies who serve as clients within his primary constituency, as well as others coopted from opposing constituencies or interest groups. Bratton and van de Walle delineate the three features of neo-patrimonialism as: a systematic concentration of power: a penchant of the patron for awarding personal favors to cronies; and the use of state resources for political legitimation. Patrimonialism connotes that a patron in a certain social and political order bestows gifts from their own resources upon followers in order to secure loyalty and support (Weber 1980 [1922]: 133–134, 136). Clients, in turn, obtain material benefits and protection.[36] To achieve this end, constitutionalism is abrogated to create what some have described as authoritarian statism that entails the management of the concept of life presidency intrinsic to patrimonialism. Patrimonialism is thus the principle or policy of concentrating extensive economic, political, and related controls in the hands of an individual. With the immense power of the state to intrude into society, the real cost of patrimonial regimes is the loss of individual liberty. It is intended to concentrate power in the hands of one man, thus making it easier for the consolidation of political power as well as accentuating the consolidation security and of all levels of influence in the state mechanism. Power is concentrated in one man or one party in what may be referred to as a 'one-man state' or (OMS) or 'one-party state' or (OPS). Neo-patrimonialism undermines the constitutional process through the destruction of the constitution. Patrimonial arrangements survive by oiling political clientelism that is operated as an extant political settlement among the elite. This political arrangement involves 'give-and-take' relationships between actors controlling political, economic, and social resources. Meanwhile, a fourth attribute of neo-patrimonialism is that opposition figures are assassinated or hunted out of the state. It is thus observed that in conflicts emerging from 'new independent consolidation' or attempts by postcolonial regimes to achieve consolidation and control of national political space ('an attempt to subdue regional, ethnic, ideological and personal ambitions which resisted state authority') the loser often has to flee into exile as a survival option.[37]

The character and operations of neo-patrimonial systems have been well codified in the case of Zambia by Christian von Soest.[38] Soest observes that the first President Kaunda served for 27 years in office and entrenched his power with a corps of personal advisors which in turn reduced the influence of the cabinet and other units of the ruling United National Independence Party (UNIP). He not only gained from particular legitimacy as Zambia's founding President who had led the struggle for independence but also augmented his control of the political process by promulgating the one-party state in December 1972.

The neo-patrimonial centralization of power in Zambia also finds expression in the frequent change of ministers. The average tenure of key ministers from independence until today stands at only 2.4 years. Consequently, the most important cabinet members have exercised their functions for only half of a legislative period, on average. Christian von Soest cites Burnell as noting that this pattern of 'elite circulation' has shown a high degree of consistency and has endured during Zambia's one-party Second Republic (from the end of 1972 to 1991) and during the multiparty Third Republic (since November 1991).

It is also noted Kaunda's successor, President Frederick Chiluba, adopted the same technique. According to Erdmann and Simutanyi,[39] in a major cabinet reshuffle in April 1993 for instance, President Chiluba removed from office those reform-minded ministers he perceived to be a threat to his rule. Others were frustrated to the extent that they resigned from government. With an average tenure of less than two years, the 'ministerial game of musical chairs' in the key departments did not slow down under President Mwanawasa, who was reelected on 28 September 2006 (Electoral Commission of Zambia, 2006). In sum, the neo-patrimonial concentration of political power has been a feature consistently applied in Zambian politics.[40]

Politics since independence has been within the context of a febrile democratic environment across the continent, characterized by the subversion of constitutions and the erosion of constitutionalism. Attempts at entrenching the practice of democracy in Africa since independence, including in the post-Cold War era, have thus been largely only convenient as an instrument in advancing the parochial interests of internal forces and advancing strategic objectives of elite external forces. These forces and factors now include the emerging struggle of powerful main systemic hegemonic faiths, fundamentalist Christian sects, and radical and militant Islamic institutions for ascendance in Africa's polluted spiritual spaces. This accounts for the continued assault on the legitimacy of the secularity of African political spaces by faith-mobilized civil society. Its impact has been the increasing lack of salience of the ideational and the degradation of the role of conventional civil society in giving direction to the evolution of political processes in Africa.

Accordingly, the undercurrents of politics since independence in Africa include the fact that black Africa has also presented a particularly inviting arena to be conveniently coopted to serve extra-African interests by willing African proxies. The interests represented are not just political in the conventional understanding. In more recent times, the polarization of society mobilized on fundamentalist religious credos that seem to assault the integrity of all other faiths and belief systems (including demonization of traditional systems of worship, explicit in particular in the growing rift and deep antagonism between fundamentalist Islam and Pentecostal Christian evangelicalism) has evolved as a major line of cleavage across the continent. This cleavage is discernible in Nigeria, where the fierce contest for ascendance between Islam and Christianity has incrementally intruded into public life and politics and has now has been institutionalized, reflecting the increasing danger in the long term de-secularization of the public sphere in Africa. In Nigeria, balancing religious faiths in presidential and gubernatorial tickets is the conventional wisdom. There is also a palpable contest in Nigeria between Christianity and Islam in all spheres off human endeavor, from education to careers in government,. In Liberia, the intense clamor to declare the state as founded on Christian foundations is the biggest political challenge facing the country. This division reverberated during the country's long civil war. Angola has informally banned Islam, and in the Gambia, President Yahya Jammeh has declared the state an Islamic Republic. East Africa is caught in the throes of Al Shabab's agenda to Islamize the region. Boko Haram has acquired the same ideology to turn West Africa into a caliphate. In January 2016, in Central Africa, the Seleka, a largely Muslim militia, has been fighting to stave off a counter-coup by forces of the Christian majority in this 'state' in the capital Bangui and the northern city of Bossangoa.[41] Mozambique is also caught in the throes of the expansion of hegemonic faiths. Religious animosities continue to surface from time to time. Although the Mozambican government has historically been secular and has refused to recognize the traditional Christian holidays as religious, the declaration of two Muslim festivals as public holidays has created some furor among Catholics. Renamo promptly seized the opportunity to condemn the move, in the process alienating Muslims who had supported its campaign in 1994. The situation reignited the controversy surrounding Mozambique's joining the Organization of Islamic Conference a few years ago. The growing influence of Iran and the ease with which Islam is taking hold in the traditional African milieu has irked Catholics.[42]

The deployment of religion to serve political ends and vice versa has led to the exacerbation of religious elements and symbols. This has been glaring in Nigeria, where it is fast becoming a political convention to balance presidential and gubernatorial tickets on religious lines. The volatility of ethnoreligious passions has become one of the most combustible factors of African politics. These developments are consistent with Alain Rouvez's[43] assertion that sub-Saharan Africa has proven to be particularly vulnerable to external influence. Independence made little difference to the exploitation of Africa's wealth by European colonial powers. Indeed, this remains at the core of France's agenda in its neo-colonial relations with black Africa. Power and politics in Africa remain servants to the economic strength of the West, and now possibly of Arab oil-producing countries such as Iran, which is fanning the embers of Shiite expansionism in Nigeria and in the Gambia. China too is expanding its economic zone of influence throughout Africa. As poor countries, independence created a power vacuum to be exploited by those who care enough to graft Africa into their orbits of influence. Rouvez attests that the ex-colonizers learned to convert remnants of their imperial liabilities into postcolonial assets. In the same manner, hegemonic faiths have sought to appropriate the totality of spiritual spaces on the continent. Religion has become a core political factor in Africa, especially in the twenty-first century. The virulence of Boko Haram in Nigeria, Al Shabab in Somalia, and the Séléka movement in the CAR are sharp pointers to this challenge.

The situation in the CAR manifests the complexities of African politics since independence, as all the deleterious factors converge. Observers believe that at Séléka's core is a very diverse cast of characters. The Séléka rebel movement has no concept or structure of a political program, no clear or coherent ideology, and no precise demands.[44] Government officials from Bangui accused Séléka of harboring 'foreign provocateurs' greedy for the country's vast mineral wealth. Suspicions are cast that mainly Muslim elements from Chad, Nigeria, and Sudan make up Séléka's ranks. Others have noted that rather than being a simple revolt by the CAR's civil society, money to pay Séléka's soldiers may originate from the same sources that funded the Malian, Libyan, and Tunisian revolts: amongst others, this would imply Chad and possibly al Qaeda.[45] According to other reliable sources, the numbers of the Seleka coalition rebels were swollen by soldiers coming from Darfur (or even mercenaries from other countries such as Mali or even Northern Nigeria) where Boko Haram Islamists are based, while noting that the Seleka coalition is made up of rebel groups from the North of the CAR (who are all Muslims), or even from the Darfur region. Darfur is where Rwanda and Uganda have deployed hundreds of troops, paid for by the USA, to stop what they call mass killing by the Sudanese government against the Darfurians.[46]

Other observers, however, interpret the Séléka phenomenon as a northern resistance to the continuing struggle of the central government in the CAR to fully appropriate the totality of the economic space, in particular those formerly under the control of northern (mostly Muslim) merchants. It is highlighted that it is impossible to say which of the numerous grievances and motivations were dominant in the uprising of the Séléka against the central government of Francois Bozizé. The North is seen as economically poor and politically marginalized, a zone mostly out of the control of the state, where its people make their living in a variety of ways, including artisanal diamond mining and trading, forestry, wildlife conservation and poaching, and smuggling along ancient Sahelian trade routes. From 2003 to 2013, President Bozizé attempted to centralize control of diamond extraction and trade by cutting out of the market many northern diamond traders. Bozizé also attempted to gain greater control over the smuggling and trade routes throughout the country, threatening the little access to trade and revenue many in the North had remaining to them. Accordingly, reports indicate that many of the original commanders of the Séléka coalition were 'Big Men' of the northern economy who fought to grow their control of the country's resources and to keep Bangui out of their existing networks. Some of François Bozizé's ministers even claimed that the Séléka takeover of the country was 'a "coup" by the diamond merchants'.[47] The perceived coup was led by the Séléka from the northeastern CAR, a predominantly Muslim region. It bears highlighting that President Bozizé is Christian, as is 71% of the Central African population.[48]

In the varying appreciations of the Séléka phenomenon emerge the following expressions of African politics: an ethno-religiously and ethno-regionally mobilized struggle for control of the economic space, contention around the attempt of the state to penetrate its society fully, and the intermestic role of communities across the national frontiers of the CAR with defined stakes in the internal processes of the country. Yet other analysts have advanced crucial geo-strategic imperatives that link both the USA and France to the situation in the CAR. According to these analysts, controversies around the non-intervention posture of France and the USA in the overthrow of Francois Bozizé abound. They highlight that Bozizé had urged the USA and France to intervene against the rebel forces, but his call fell on deaf ears. Demonstrators reportedly accused Paris of supporting the rebels. In response to the claims of French President François Hollande to neutrality in the internal affairs of the country, the question was raised of why France intervened in the internal affairs of Ivory Coast then, literally kidnapping Laurent Gbagbo, who had really won the elections and putting Alassane Ouattara into power? Also, in its report of January 2, 2013, GlobalResearch.ca concluded that behind this bogus 'non-intervention' posture, the French government was undoubtedly working hand in hand with the Obama Administration to determine the outcome of the crisis in the CAR because France has been intimately involved in every change of government in its former colony since 1960. It was observed that after declaring himself president, Djotodia, who briefly was in power, through the Séléka said that he would invite France, the CAR's former colonial power, along with the European Union and the USA, to retrain the country's army.[49]

The response to the encroachment of these destructive external forces in post-independence Africa has also been the emergence of strong nationalist leaders determined to ward off all manner of extraneous forces, from the neo-colonial political and economic to the extra-African religious forces seeking the appropriation or consolidation of their hold on local and even the continental social, economic, and political spaces. This has bred new forms of nationalist insurgencies which have radically repudiated the extant political dispensations. The drawback is that these nationalist leaders have also demonstrated a penchant for validating their endless tenures through controversial constitutional amendments that abrogate term limits. Accordingly, this has perpetuated the OPS/OMS state syndrome in a new strain of neo-patrimonial dispensation dominated by the singular vision of the progressive nationalist leader on the way forward for state and society. Yoweri Museveni in Uganda and Paul Kagame in Rwanda or even Robert Mugabe in Zimbabwe are classic examples of this form of governance arrangement. Patrimonial arrangements have thus become a challenge to the deepening of democratic culture in Africa.

Museveni is a product of a revolutionary rejection of a dangerous national circumstance as the Idi Amin regime exploited ethno-religious sentiment to entrench a brutal dictatorship. Idi Amin's coup in the 1970s launched Yoweri Museveni's political career. By October 1978, when Amin ordered the invasion of Tanzania in order to claim the Kagera province for Uganda, Museveni had already trained a significant number of fighters in his Front for National Salvation (FRONASA). This fed into a people's protracted war that he had waged for many years, because Museveni perceived that it was the only way to cement the involvement of the population.[50] The FRONASA collaborated with the Tanzanian forces deployed by President Julius Nyerere, who was irritated and tired of the embarrassment Ugandan dictator Amin had become and sought to oust him from power. Yoweri Museveni relaunched a guerrilla war on February 6, 1981 against the Ugandan government in which he had served as a minister, arguing that that the 1980 elections were rigged. His National Resistance Army eventually took power in January 1986 and introduced the Movement system of politics; described as a broad-based, alternate system of democracy in which people compete for political office on individual merit. Mr. Museveni argued that political-party activity split underdeveloped countries like Uganda along ethnic and religious lines.[51] Promising not a mere change of guard, but a fundamental change, Museveni was sworn in as president of Uganda on January 29, 1986. On inauguration, he affirmed that the people of Africa and the people of Uganda were entitled to a democratic government and that he did not consider a favor from any regime. He declared that the sovereign people must be the public, not the government. 'The main problem in Africa is of leaders who do not want to leave power', he asserted. By 2015, when he sought constitutional change to remain president, Yoweri Kaguta Museveni had been in power for 29 years. Meanwhile, Mr. Museveni's government accuses Dr. Besigye, a former comrade and now a prominent opposition figure who has stood against the President, of trying to organize an Egypt-style uprising.[52]

Paul Kagame is in this same genre of neo-patrimonial OMS mode. In the 1980s, Paul Kagame came into the limelight fighting in Yoweri Museveni's army (FRONASA) that had launched him to power as Ugandan president. He later joined the Rwandan Patriotic Front (RPF), which invaded Rwanda in 1990 and assumed control of it following the death of leader Fred Rwigyema. He played a prominent role in the civil war that was reignited as a result of the assassination of Rwanda's President Juvénal Habyarimana and ended the genocide in that country with a military victory. He became vice president and was in charge of operations to neutralize Hutu insurgents who were destabilizing the country from hideouts in neighboring Zaire. As part of the counter-insurgency operations, Kagame sponsored two controversial rebel wars in Zaire. The Rwandan and Ugandan-backed rebels' Armed Forces for the Liberation of Congo/Zaire (AFLCZ) won the first war (1996–1997) that removed French-backed dictator Sese Sesko Mobutu from office and installed Laurent-Désiré Kabila as president in his place. Kagame later turned against his ally.

Paul Kagame became president in 2000. His tenure has been marked by stability and relative prosperity. As president, he has focused on a national development plan to transform Rwanda into a middle-income country by 2020. By 2013, Rwanda had demonstrated strong performances on key indicators, such as health care and education. Annual growth between 2004 and 2010 averaged 8% per year. With impressive indicators of progress in Rwanda, Kagame has strong support among the population, although human-rights groups note political repression. He won an election in 2003 under a new constitution adopted that year, and was elected for a second term in 2010. In a referendum to amend the constitution to end term limits on December 18, 2015, more than 90% of Rwandan voters said yes to the proposed changes. That cleared the way for Kagame to run for office again—and again and again. With the outcome of the referendum, Kagame, in theory, could remain in power for another 17 years.[53]

The dominant governance paradigm on the African continent, arising from the interplay of the unholy trinity of factors and associated forces, has been expressed in normative statist autocracies, civilian and military dictatorships alike, and orchestrated through strategic patron–client relationships. This patrimonial and, more contemporaneously, neo-patrimonial paradigm of governance and a snapshot of the conundrum of African governance are illustrated in the trajectory of the Democratic Republic of the Congo (DRC), which since independence in 1960 has not recovered from the assassination of Patrice Lumumba, its first nationalist national leader. Between 1961 and 1973, it is reckoned that six African independence leaders have been assassinated by their ex-colonial rulers, including Patrice Lumumba of Congo.[54] Accordingly, the problem of governance since independence in Africa is epitomized by the career of Mobutu Sese Seko Kuku Ngbendu Wa Za Banga and the travails of the Congo that are still raging to this day. Joseph Desire Mobutu was implicated in what Ludo De Witte has qualified as 'the most important assassination of the 20th century'.[55] Patrice Lumumba, the democratically elected prime minister of the DRC, was assassinated on January 17, 1961, barely a year into the country's independence. His assassination by a Belgian execution squad working in collaboration with Congolese accomplices was a culmination of two interrelated assassination plots by US and Belgian governments.[56] Also, according to remarks attributed to Baroness Park of Monmouth, who was head of the MI6 station in the central African country at the time, the Congo's first democratically elected prime minister was abducted and killed in a Cold War operation run by British intelligence. The contention was that it was the fear of the Western allies that Lumumba would have handed over the high-value Katangese uranium deposits as well as the diamonds and other important minerals largely located in the secessionist eastern state of Katanga to the Soviets.[57] Colonel Mobutu was thus propelled into office in 1965 as a direct beneficiary of an international conspiracy involving the USA, Belgium and Britain. With the support of the USA and its Western allies, he was through dubious democratic maneuvers transformed into a life president of the DRC.

Mobutu Sese Seko ruled the Republic of Zaire with an iron hand from 1965 to 1997, when he was overthrown by a coalition of forces organized under the umbrella of the Armed Forces for the Liberation of the Democratic Republic of Congo/Zaire (AFLDC/Z). These anti-Mobutu forces comprised both state and non-state actors, including the national armies of Tanzania, Uganda, Rwanda, and Angola fighting alongside the Laurent Kabila-led AFLDC/Z. In the changing calculus of elite forces in the post-Cold War period, the regional coalition of forces, the AFLDC/Z and its regional allies that were paradoxically supported by the USA, were arrayed against an opposing alliance of regional, mainly Francophone, countries including Morocco, status quo forces and non-state actors such as the UNITA from Angola, mobilized by France. In 1967–1968, Mobutu Sese Seko served as chairperson of the Organization of African Unity.

Lumumba's assassination had significant historical import because of a multitude of factors. It starkly demonstrated the deleterious pertinence of the global context, its impact, specifically in this instance on Congolese politics and, generally, on the evolution of African politics since independence. It was also a reflection of Lumumba's overall fate and the legacy of Africa's nationalist leaders at independence. The powerful forces arrayed against African states at their emergence as states onto the world stage have remained. The continued salience of elite forces of the global states system, although modified in the transformed geo-strategic landscape of Africa characterized in the post-Cold War era by behavioral transformations of African states, is again illustrated in the fate of Laurent Kabila, also of the Congo. Laurent Kabila, the hero of the liberation from the rule of Mobutu Sese Seko, was assassinated in what remain mysterious circumstances in 2001. Kagame sent Rwandan troops into Zaire in late 1996 to battle the Hutu forces. While there, the troops also intervened in the rebellion taking place, supporting Laurent Kabila in his successful quest to depose Zairean president Mobutu Sese Seko. Kagame was one of several African leaders operating military forces in Congo during that country's civil war, dubbed Africa's 'first world war'.[58]

In 1998, after Laurent Kabila had been in power for a little more than a year, his former allies, Museveni and Kagame, shifted support to rebels who sought to oust Kabila. They mounted a campaign that reached the suburbs of the capital, Kinshasa. Kabila was only saved by the intervention of other neighbors (Angola, Namibia, and Zimbabwe) to protect their strategic interests in the region. Notwithstanding a peace agreement, Uganda and Rwanda, with the support of several Congolese rebel groups, controlled half of the territory of the country for a long time.[59] Incursions from these Congolese rebels are rampant and uncontrolled despite the deployment of the largest United Nations peacekeeping force in the country. Under its Chap. 7 mandate, the United Nations Peacekeeping Forces have engaged in direct combat to address catastrophic humanitarian consequences of rebel forces suspected of being proxies of neighboring states. Given the humanitarian challenges in the Congo, UN forces continue to provide support to a Congolese army that is reputed for its indiscipline.

The assassination of Patrice Lumumba was the second in the killing of five leaders of independence movements in African in the 1960s orchestrated by Africa's former colonial masters, or their agents. Amilcar Cabral, leader of the West African liberation movement against Portugal of the African Party for the Independence of Guinea and Cape Verde, (Partido Africano da Independência da Guiné e Cabo Verde or PAIGC) in Guinea Bissau and Cape Verde, was assassinated in Conakry in 1973 by Portuguese agents. Before Lumumba's death in 1961, Felix Moumie, the Cameroonian opposition leader, had been poisoned in 1960. Meanwhile, Sylvanus Olympio, leader of Togo, was killed in 1963. Mehdi Ben Barka, leader of the Moroccan opposition movement, disappeared in France in 1965. Finally, Eduardo Mondlane, leader of Mozambique's Frelimo, fighting for independence from the Portuguese, died from a parcel bomb in 1969.[60] Also, Kwame Nkrumah of Ghana was ousted in a Western-backed coup in 1966. He died in exile in Guinea.

A second archetype of patrimonial governance, with the strong connivance of metropolitan controllers of puppet African leaders and neo-colonial forces, is the life presidency of civilian and civilianized military dictatorships. These regimes, mainly expressed in the OPS/OMS, are often rationalized in many (frequently contradictory) terms, as there are autocratic patriarchal figures heading patrimonial arrangements. The political evolution of Ivory Coast, under its OPS the Democratic Party of Ivory Coast (PDCI), and doubling as an OMS under the life presidency of Felix Houphouët-Boigny, a trained medical assistant, who has led the country since 1945 or even in Sassou Nguesso's

Republic of Congo (Brazzaville) or Mobutu's Sese Seko in Zaire or now Democratic Republic of Congo, are classic exemplars. Other more contemporaneous variants of the OMS with some controversial historic validation are in Paul Kagame's Rwanda or Museveni's Uganda or even Zimbabwe's 92-year-old President Robert Mugabe.

In all these cases, constitutional term limits are abrogated through constitutional referenda almost always to the benefit of the incumbents. In Burundi, Pierre Nkurunziza forced his way, through a muscled Supreme Court ruling, to rig to enthrone an unconstitutional third term. In a few cases, with strongly entrenched institutions such as Nigeria, the institutions have proven to be resilient enough to thwart attempts at undermining the integrity of the constitutional process. The strenuous effort of Olusegun Obasanjo to manipulate the constitution for an elongated tenure was robustly defeated. In Sierra Leone, the ambition of President Kabbah to secure a third term has led to serious schisms within the ruling party. As for Zimbabwe's Robert Mugabe, his unending validation is the leadership of the 1970s guerrilla war where he made his name. At the time, he was seen as a revolutionary hero, fighting white minority rule for the freedom of his people; this is why many African leaders remain reluctant to criticize him.[61]

As with most African states, the trajectory of Houphouët-Boigny's politics in Ivory Coast essentially reflected the political history of the country. With antecedence as a local tax collector for the French colonial administration, he appreciated the prejudices against indigenous farmers, leading him in 1933 to organize the first African planters' association Syndicate Agricole Africain (SAA) in Ivory Coast. With over 20,000 members, the SAA became one of the first anti-colonial movements in the country. Houphouet-Boigny entered the *Assemblée Constituante* (French National Assembly) in 1945, occupying the seat reserved for the indigenous constituency. In 1946, he collaborated with the French Communist Party to found the Democratic Party of Ivory Coast (PDCI) that allied itself with the African Democratic Rally, a transterritorial movement across French West Africa. Given that the climate in the Cold War presented risks to associations with communism in Africa, including French West Africa, and specifically in Ivory Coast, the RDA and its Ivorian expression in the PDCI abandoned their ideological leaning and association with the French communists.

These developments paved the way to his recognition as a moderate in the French Assembly. It earned him the acquaintanceship of General Charles de Gaulle. Houphouët-Boigny effectively became an ally of the French establishment. His whole political career thereafter was dedicated to the protection of French interests in Ivory Coast and Africa. Félix Houphouët-Boigny is associated with the drafting and ultimate adoption of the *loi-cadre*, passed by the French National Assembly in 1956, authorizing the right to vote for all African subjects in French colonies. The law also presaged the autonomy of French colonies in Africa.[62] His life and times as a benign civilian dictator represented one polar end of the OPS/OMS syndrome, while Mobutu Sese Seko represented the military end of the continuum. Invariably, all Africa's major political actors fall within this continuum.

Military interventions in the political processes of African states that were initially perceived as political aberrations became instrumental to the consolidation of the extant political settlements under threat or to institute new settlements that were driven by the partisan agenda of the triumphant interventionists or a coalition of partisan stakeholders determined to overthrow the old regime. Political settlements describe the types of informal as well as formal political bargains that can end conflict and bring sustainable peace, promote reform, development, and reduce poverty; or fail to achieve any such progress.[63] It is argued that political settlement is central to all development and one that does not exclude powerful players is more likely to prevent conflict.[64] The reality, however, is that political settlements in post-independence Africa have not been achieved through consensual engagement. They have been a product of impositions through various means, including Africa's distorted brand of democracy, or purely forceful interventions in the political process.

Forceful changes of political settlements through military interventions such as coups d'état, rebellions, and revolutions of various hues have been a prominent part of the politics of post-independence Africa. The period between 1960 and 1970 and slightly beyond has generally been called the decades of coups.[65] Military intervention entails the conscious act of displacing and supplanting an existing political order, a government, by soldiers with the objective of either governing or influencing the political affairs of the country in a particular direction determined largely by the interventionists themselves.[66] Military interventions in the form of a coup or military regimes are the most extreme forms of the military impacting the policy process. These interventions effect an irregular transfer of the state's executive power by the regular armed forces or internal security forces through the threat or actual use of force. They usurp the legislative or executive power or in some cases the judicial powers.[67]

During the decade of coups the scoreboard read something like this:

1. Congo-Kinshasa, 1960. Colonel Mobutu seizes power temporarily.
2. Togo, January 1963. Coup deposes President Olympio who gets killed in the process.
3. Congo-Brazzaville, August 1963. Government of Abbe Youlou overthrown by Marien Ngouabi.
4. Dahomey, December 1963. Colonel Sogho overthrows President Albert Magai.
5. Gabon, February 1964. Coup d'état occurs but is reversed by French forces.
6. Algeria, June 1965. Colonel Boumedienne overthrows President Ben Bella.

7. Dahomey, December 1965. A second coup is staged.
8. Burundi, October 1965. The monarchy is overthrown by Army officers.
9. Central African Republic, January 1966. President David Dacko is ousted by Colonel Jean Bokassa.
10. Upper Volta, January 1966. Colonel Lamizana deposes President Yameogo.
11. Nigeria, January 1966. General Ironsi is installed after a coup led by young majors.
12. Ghana, February 1966. President Kwame Nkrumah is overthrown by the military led by General Ankrah.
13. Nigeria, July 1966. General Gowon overthrows General Ironsi.
14. Burundi, November 1966. Captain Micombero takes over in another coup.
15. Sierra Leone, March 1967. President Margai deposed by Lieutenant Colonel Juxon-Smith.
16. Algeria, December 1967. A second coup attempt is made.
17. Sierra Leone, April 1968. A coup from the ranks overthrows Lieutenant Colonel Juxon-Smith. Civilian government reinstalled under President Siaka Stevens.
18. Mali, November 1968. Young officers led by Lieutenant Moussa Traore depose the government of President Modibo Keita.
19. Sudan, May 1969. Free Officers' Movement seizes power.
20. Libya, September 1969. The monarchy is deposed.
21. Somalia, October 1969. A revolutionary Council led by the military overthrows the government.

Among the prominent military takeovers in the 1960s were those in: Congo (Kinshasa) in November 1965 by Colonial Joseph Desire Mobutu, and in the same year in Algeria by Colonel Houari Boummedienne; Nigeria in January 1966, by Major Nzeogwu followed later by a counter-coup by Major-General Johnson Aguiyi-Ironsi; a month later in Ghana, by Colonel Akwasi Amankwaah Afrifa; Togo in January 1967, by Lieutenant Colonel Etienne Gnassingbe Eyadema; Mali in 1968, by Lieutenant Moussa Traore; and Libya in September 1969, by Colonel Muammar Gaddafi. Prominent among the military coups in the 1970s were those in: Uganda in 1971 by Idi Amin Dada; Ethiopia in 1974 by Colonial Mengistu Haile Mariam; Nigeria in July 1975 by General Muhammad Murtala; and Ghana in 1979 by Flight-Lieutenant Jerry Rawlings.

After 1970, numerous other governments were overturned. The progressive government of Dr. Milton Obote in Uganda was deposed by General Idi Amin in January 1971. Uganda, under General Amin, went through one of the most tragic experiences in recent African history. The feudal monarchy of Emperor Haile Selassie in Ethiopia was deposed by the military in

September 1974. By 1975, approximately half of the continent's states were led by military or civil-military governments. Other states also had records of predatory attacks by their military forces. In the 1980s, changes of government through the coup d'état have occurred in Ghana, Burkina Faso, Congo (Brazzaville) and Nigeria, among others. No doubt, the coup d'état and the military regime had become the most prevalent political phenomena in Africa.

The era of military interventions in post-independence Africa seriously impacted the overall direction of the politics here up to contemporary times. For one reason, many of the usurpers of power validated themselves through patrimonial arrangement or legitimized their order through external recognition and validation by powerful external forces that exploited them to advance their strategic ideological or material interests. In this class are the interventions that brought the likes of Congo's (later Zaire's) Sese Seko Mobutu to power through the removal of Patrice Lumumba or, more lately, the overthrow of Muammar Gaddafi in Libya or even the assassination of Africa's 'Che' Thomas Sankara by Blaise Compaore in Ouagadougou, Burkina Faso. These interventions were often underwritten by external forces advancing their global strategic objectives. This was mostly the case in Francophone Africa, from Zaire/Democratic Republic of Congo, Republic of Congo (Brazzaville), Gabon, the CAR etc. Military intervention has not always been conducted to 'rescue' the nation from political ills. Coups have been linked directly or indirectly with personal ambitions and the craving for power by some specific key players. This was in fact the case in Dahomey in 1965. In other instances, officers have led coups to regain lost prestige or to preempt an impending purge. Coupled with this, interpersonal clashes have occurred between the civilian and military elites and thereby provoked takeovers. Cases in point have been Uganda in 1971, Togo in 1963, Congo in 1968, Dahomey in 1967, and several others.

In that connection, Murat Önder notes that:

> For the centrality of the military approach, the greater the resources and the cohesion of the military, the greater the likelihood of interventions are (Mayer and Burnett, 1977). One view emphasize the sectoral interests of the military, treating the military as a potentially parasitic institution which, given its centrality to the state's claim on legitimate violence, is prone to use this to dominate politically, and especially if civilian institutions are weak (Jenkins and Kposowa, 1992). The stronger the military's resources, either as a percent of state resource or relative to the national economy, the weaker the institution of civil society and thereby the greater the probability of military interventions. Several studies have found that larger armies and those with greater claims to the government revenues have been more coups prone. A second view argues that a centralized chain of command, military discipline, and extensive communication make military officers a cohesive group, capable of organizing effective seizure.[68]

The distinctive characteristic of military bureaucracy from civilian bureaucracy is that they are more hierarchical, authoritative, and their attribute as a legitimate source of coercion make it easy for them to influence political institutions.[69] The deployment of coercive instruments of the state and, at the same time, the use of force by competing unpacified domestic forces to advance partisan political objectives, partly accounts for many coups and generally the turbulence of the internal processes of postcolonial states in Africa. The outcomes of the interactions of these factors, feeding into the pervasive struggle of all forces, both domestic and external, to appropriate the totality of the social, political, and economic space, were expressed in the prevalence of classical patrimonial structures of governance in the first decades of independence. With political development processes of African states based largely on coercion, the nodal state has in the long term been weak and susceptible to unraveling. In this environment, African politics in the postcolonial era has been marred by authoritarianism, corruption, military interventions, and leadership failures amidst a broader socio-economic crisis characterized by poverty.[70]

Benjamin Talton observes that although by 1990 formal European political control had given way to African self-rule (except in South Africa), the legacy of European dominance remained evident in the national borders, political institutions and infrastructures, education systems, national languages, economies, and trade networks of each nation. Accordingly, in the post-Cold War period coinciding with the post-Mandela world order, the accent on democratic practice as the validating principle of governance imposed by Western European masters turned out to be subverted by the continued unrestrained interest articulation of the same neo-colonial forces (especially France) as the leading force for the sustenance of the status quo on the continent. Decolonization failed to transform the political structures to bring about true autonomy.[71] Democracy in Africa in the post-Cold War period has therefore been doubly instrumentalized. First, it is to project the strategic interests of neo-colonial forces, which connive in institutionalizing neo-patrimonial structures and institutions that advance their strategic interests. African leaders, often in collusion with neo-colonial handlers, have also instrumentalized democracy to consolidate illegitimate political settlements negotiated often after protracted electoral controversies. The consolidation of the status quo that absolutely appropriates the state space for a particular ethnic constituency is attained through one-man life rule as reflected in Houphouët-Boigny in Ivory Coast, Omar Bongo in Gabon (who became the longest ruling head of state before he passed away), Gnasingbe Eyadema in Togo, and Paul Biya in Cameroon, among others.

A second route to the consolidation of the neo-patrimonial status quo is via dynastic succession, as in the Eyadema clan in Togo, the Omar Bongo dynasty in Gabon, the Kabila family in Democratic Republic of Congo, and an attempt by President Wade in Senegal to invest control of Senegal in his son Karim Wade. The idea of father-to-son inheritance of state power in Senegal began to emerge after President Abdoulaye Wade's first presidential victory as Karim Wade, who was in his 40s, like Ali Bongo in Gabon before him, was placed in a post in the presidential office. He was soon appointed to the strategic position of president of the Agence Nationale de l'Organization de la Conference Islamic in charge of preparing a summit of the Islamic Conference Organization.[72] President Abdoulaye Wade's father-to-son power-transfer plan was foiled through mass protests. Houphouët-Boigny manipulated the political process to ensure the seeming constitutional takeover of the state by his Baoule ethnic heir and godson Bedie. He ensured the rise of Bedie as the president of the legislature in line for the presidency in the event of the incapacitation of the president. The project failed. As earlier noted, abrogation of constitutionally sanctioned term limits has become the norm to subvert the will of the people. This has been the case with Pierre Nkuruzuza in Burundi, Sassou Nguesso in Congo (Brazzaville), Bai Koroma in Sierra Leone, Paul Kagame in Rwanda, Kabila in Democratic Republic of Congo (Kinshasa), Dos Santos in Angola, and Yoweri Museveni in Uganda. Olusegun Obasanjo's attempt to elongate his rule in Nigeria was robustly confronted and defeated. All such cases of confrontations with assaults on constitutional term limits have been costly in term of human lives and financial losses.

The consequence is that politics in the African state environment involves a struggle for the appropriation of the totality of the social-economic and political spaces by all against all others. Force is more likely to be deployed from within, in collaboration with transnational interests groups in the immediate intermestic environment, to unravel perceived illegitimate political institutions, processes, and imposed settlements of the OMS/OPS structure across the continent. This significantly explains the rise of many proto-states with the support of such neo-colonial forces as France's instigation and support for the rebellion of the Forces Nouvelles in Ivory Coast against a nationalist Laurent Gbagbo administration and the support of the USA, France, Belgium, Morocco, and apartheid South Africa for Joseph Mobutu Sese Seko, who came to power in 1965 in the Congo (later Democratic Republic of Congo) and was overthrown in May 1997 by the Laurent Desire Kabila led coalition of African forces including Rwanda, Uganda, Tanzania, and Angola, supported by post-apartheid South Africa in what is popular dubbed as Africa's first world war. In Liberia, Charles Taylor was ousted by a coalition of rebellious forces mobilized in Sierra Leone and Guinea with the active support of Houphouët-Boigny in Ivory Coast, acting to execute the interests of France in derailing the attempt to transcend colonial divisions of the subregion through the Economic Community of West African States. This coincided with the withdrawal of US support for Liberian President and warlord Charles Taylor due to arguments around concessions in respect of oil finds in commercial quantities in the country.

Overall, military interventions have been instituted for three and a quasi-fourth reasons. These interventions may be inspired by revolutionary objectives, to advance nationalist goals, or to consolidate a failing partisan status quo and, finally, merely to advance the personal ambitions of military officers. Revolutionary interventions are exemplified by Muammar Gaddafi's overthrow of King Idris in September 1969. Idris's government was increasingly unpopular by the later 1960s; it had exacerbated Libya's traditional regional and tribal divisions by centralizing the country's federal system in order to take advantage of the Libya's oil wealth. Corruption was entrenched by widespread patronage throughout the oil industry. Muammar Gaddafi effectively overcame these challenges while binding all Libya's fractious elements into a nation or at least a working state. Thomas Sankara's coup in Burkina Faso in 1983 was founded on Marxist revolutionary, pan-Africanist theories. He was a charismatic and iconic figure of revolution, commonly referred to as 'Africa's Che Guevara'. His coup was undertaken with the goal of eliminating corruption and the dominance of the former French colonial power. He mobilized the population at the grassroots level across the country and launched one of the most ambitious programs for social and economic change ever attempted on the African continent. He was assassinated by forces loyal to his deputy Blaise Compaore, who was supported by France and the regional overseer of French interests in the region, Ivorian president Houphouët-Boigny. General Murtala Mohammed in Nigeria attempted to radically alter the moral foundations of the Nigerian state and society and institute transformative policies. He was assassinated by status quo forces determined to halt programs of change. In general, conservative military regimes have greater longevity in Africa: Nigeria, Congo Brazzaville, Zaire, and Mali are some of the examples. Whether in the case of Muammar Gaddafi, Thomas Sankara, or Murtala Mohammed, external forces with strategic interests to protect were implicated in the ultimate neutralization of revolutionary regimes in Africa.

The decisive involvement of neo-colonial external forces in the internal affairs of the African state locates the African state within the workings of a world system. Accordingly, in the manner predicted by Immanuel Wallenstein,[73] the life of the African state, a unit of the larger world system, and its internal processes are made up of tensions of rival conflicting forces, contending for supremacy in the polity. The state is held together by tension and torn apart as each contending constituent unit seeking to transform the system to its absolute advantage in conjunction with its conniving external metropoles. The transition of power from one dominant group to another emergent force, either through demographic transitions or the introduction of new factors that change the internal balance of power, or even the reversal of sympathy or loyalty of the metropolitan force, is marked by extreme violence. In this climate, the military institution plays a prominent and decisive role, and control of the military is a prime political objectives of major contending forces in the African state. Some analysts emphasize the centrality of the military institution in the politics of Africans states.

Postcolonial and post-independence Africa has witnessed a few revolutions. A revolution is a process that seeks to violently overthrow an established socio-political order with a view to creating a new and better one founded on radically different visions of society and fresh new principles and ideas. Ademola Araoye advances that revolutions are motivated by the uncompromising rejection of the foundational values and fundamental principles that underpin the subsisting social order and system. Frantz Fanon argues that the end of a revolution is to bring into being an entirely new world that must be absolutely free of the past. A revolutionary process would aim to achieve 'a total, complete, and absolute substitution' of certain specie of men by another specie without any period of transition. It is an abrupt transformation of society. Given the 'willed' abruptness and the absolute substitution it seeks to attain, the desired transformation requires the application of absolute violence.[74] It may be surmised that revolutions seek seismic systemic transformations that are based on a total rejection of the foundational premises and value systems on which the rejected system is constructed. These thoughts were shared by Amilcar Cabral. Seen from this light, only in a few cases in post-independence Africa have military interventions attained revolutionary proportions.

Military interventions in African politics may be broadly delineated into four classes. These are the interventions of revolutionary 'madmen' and nonconformists to fundamentally reorder the national value system and realign relations with dominant external forces and neo-colonial forces intruding or outrightly directing the internal affairs of the state. In the vision of Thomas Sankara, one of those revolutionary madmen, he

> would like to leave behind me the conviction that if we maintain a certain amount of caution and organization we deserve victory ... You cannot carry out fundamental change without a certain amount of madness. In this case, it comes from nonconformity, the courage to turn your back on the old formulas, the courage to invent the future. It took the madmen of yesterday for us to be able to act with extreme clarity today. I want to be one of those madmen. We must dare to invent the future. https://answersafrica.com/by-these-quotes-you-know-thomas-sankara.html.

This genre of intervention would include Thomas Isidore Noel Sankara's revolution in Upper Volta and its transformation to Burkina Faso (meaning land of people of integrity) or Colonel Muammar Gaddafi's revolutionary Great Socialist People's Libyan Arab Jamahiriya or the ill-fated Derg-led Ethiopian revolution that in September 1974 brought the rule of Emperor Haile Selassie to an end.

A second genre of military interventions is the nationalist coup d'état that may be motivated by grand or limited objectives to sanitize the internal processes and introduce some order to national affairs. The case of Flight Lieutenant Jerry Rawlings in Ghana comes to mind. Often the perpetrators of this kind of intervention begin with revolutionary rhetoric reflecting a reading of the national mood for drastic action to contain a slide to national trauma. In Ghana, Jerry Rawlings executed key members of the ousted regime for economic sabotage. At the same time, his revolution coincided with mysterious assassination of many prominent members of the judiciary.

The two classes of military intervention often begin with the proclamation of a revolution but become more clearly delineated with the passage of time and the articulation of policy. The modalities of engagement, in particular the acceptance of revolutionary means (political executions) as state policy to advance radical political ideology, often separate revolutions from nationalist military interventions in the political process. A third kind of military intervention, often in the form of counter-coups, is driven by the need to reverse the movement or a gathering momentum toward radical transformations of the system. Such counter-coups may be reactionary and may be motivated by the perceived need to consolidate the status quo, whatever the character of that status quo. In Ghana, the 1966 coup of the National Liberation Council appears to have been a reactionary response to Kwame Nkrumah's radical political visions. Also, with the imminent threat to partisan interest represented by a particular regime, civilian or military, to its partisan constituency, a coup may be staged to forestall another coup that could effect a power transition from one partisan constituent unit to another contesting constituent of the state. Most of the military interventions in Nigeria's public life have been staged by Northern officers fearful of a forced change of Northern-dominated governments that are often in power. When the Northern-dominated Nigerian military struck in 1983, it was to preempt a coup from outside their military circuit to remove the widely condemned Northern-aligned and performance-challenged Shehu Shagari regime from office. The reactionary military regime of General Ibrahim Babaginda that overthrew the draconian regime of General Muhammadu Buhari and his right-hand man, the Northern Yoruba Muslim General Tune Idiagbon instituted a hegemonic regime. General Ibrahim Babaginda's self-styled military presidency was not only anti-South, but is reputed to have systematically begun the destruction of the country's morality and value system. It formally entrenched corruption as quasi-state policy and institutionalized the physical elimination of political opponents by the administration. Strategic neutralization of opponents became a part of the political culture of the country that spilled over into the democratic era. Also, at the height of General Ibrahim Babaginda's administration, all members of the Supreme Military Council, with the exception of two, were Northerners. When a Yoruba politician finally won what is generally acclaimed as the freest and most democratic presidential election ever held in the country after a tortuous transition program, Moshood Abiola's mandate was annulled because the top brass of the Northern-dominated military would not hand over power to a non-Hausa-Fulani. The Nigerian military acquired the reputation of being the most potent political instrument of the Hausa-Fulani North.

Also, many coups are undertaken by partisan forces seeking to reverse radical changes to the status quo by a revolutionary regime. This would include the September 2002 attempted coup staged by the France and Burkina Faso-backed Forces Nouvelles to remove the nationalist and Pan-Africanist government of Laurent Gbagbo from office in Ivory Coast. The coup was manipulated by French authorities to become a full-blown war in order to consolidate its continued hold over the country. That objective was finally secured in the controversial kidnapping of the Ivorian president Laurent Gbagbo, who was handed over to the Hague-based International Criminal Court which is perceived in most of Africa to be a political hatchet institution to advance the strategic interests of neo-colonial powers. The quasi-fourth motivation is the coup for personal aggrandizement of military officers. Moussa Traoré's coup in Mali on 19 November 1968 exemplifies this. Lieutenant Moussa Traoré led a coup d'état against Mali's one-party government, personally arresting the president, Modibo Keïta, a Pan-Africanist. In March 1971, Traoré arrested his co-conspirators and main rivals, including his deputy Captain Yoro Diakité, for plotting to overthrow his government. In 1972, they were convicted to life imprisonment in the Taoudem Salt Mines, where Diakité died a year later. On May 18, 1977, ex-president Modibo Keïta died in prison.

The driving motif of African politics in post-independence Africa, including military engagement in the political domain, may be the search for absolute appropriation of the totality of the socio-political and economic space of the African state by internal forces, in connivance with external vested interests. This situation has engendered the challenge of resolving a pervasive security dilemma that has afflicted the African state process since independence. Gerard Hagg (2008) highlights that in postcolonial African countries, political power struggles generally take two forms: the state is in conflict with identity groups (state-identity conflict), and identity groups compete for 'ownership' or dominance of the state (inter-identity conflict).[75] The two levels of conflict seldom occur or remain in isolation but are interactive and can develop in two directions: from the state to society and from society to the state. The state may actively support one identity in inter-identity conflict if this identity occupies powerful positions within the state. In reality, such states often encourage dominant identities to use state resources and institutions to suppress other identities. Therefore, strategic interaction among groups is characterized by competition for control of the state as the dominant group in the state sets the terms of competition between its rivals. Accordingly, Lake and Rothchild (1996) assert that the pursuit of particularistic objectives often becomes embodied in competing visions of just, legitimate, and appropriate political orders.[76] Interpreting interaction between political forces, the dominant patrimonial and neo-patrimonial governance paradigm may be better understood as part of a mechanism to consolidate the absolute partisan appropriation of the African state space.

Perhaps these have influenced the failures of sovereign national conferences (SNCs), mainly in Francophone Africa, to change the dominant governance paradigm in the post-Cold War era. Participants in SNCs have often comprised prominent intellectuals, including a few from the diaspora, representatives of political parties and of civil-society groups, notably labour unions, media and youths. In practice, participation has been manipulated and skewed to ensure that the outcome of the conference is consistent with views and interests of the administration. This has been a major drawback of SNCs organized by the various administrations in Nigeria. The phenomenon of the SNC was employed by the Republic of Benin as the long-entrenched degenerate Marxist OMS of Mathew Kerekou was forced to acknowledge the bankruptcy of his regime and apologise to the population. The two-week frank and critical deliberation led to a broad national consensus on the adoption of principles of liberal democracy, respect of fundamental human liberties, rule of law, separation of power with checks and balances, multiparty system, competitive choice of political leaders through free and fair elections, good governance, etc. It was this broad national consensus that was later enshrined in the constitution that was adopted through a referendum on December 11, 1990.[77] The crucial and unusual success factor in Benin Republic was a collapsed state and economy and a leader who admitted failure. The experience in the Republic of Benin is seen as the only success of the wave of SNCs that took place in several Francophone African countries in the early 1990s. Without exception, incumbent leaders in the other countries who considered themselves in effective control engineered the failure of the conferences in their respective countries. Two notable examples were Bongo of Gabon and Eyadema of Togo. SNCs failed in the other countries. In Zaire, where the longest conference lasted over seven years, the dinosaur state of Mubutu ensured that the proceedings were consistently interrupted, even while Étienne Tshisekedi wa Mulumba, a convenient on-and-off ally of Mobutu, led opposition Sacred Union and its coalition partners battled the state to no avail. It is paradoxical that it was the decision of the conference to formally denaturalize all Zairean Tutsis of Zairean nationality that provided the rationale for Rwanda and others to raise Laurent Kabilla's rebellion that finally overthrew Mobutu from office. The rebellion succeeded largely because of the liberating implications of the end of the Cold War for Africa as the USA teamed up with Nelson Mandela's South Africa to negotiate an end to the Mobutu regime against the stout opposition of France that had mobilized neighboring Francophone proxy states to put up a last battle in Kinshasa.

In Congo Brazzaville, the elected sovereign post-conference president Pascal Lissouba was removed from office by the old dictator Sassou Nguesso, who with the financial support of ELF Acquitaine, launched a war to remove President Lissouba, who had opened up the hitherto French-controlled oil sector in that country to US interests. In December 2015, President Denis Sassou Nguesso, 71, after a new constitution removed age and term limits obstructing his bid to extend his rule, announced that a presidential election would be held several months early. Under the controversial new charter adopted after a referendum in the preceding October, an election was due to be held in the Republic of Congo in July 2016, but he said he wanted to bring it forward to the first quarter of 2016 to usher in a 'new dynamic' following the referendum.

Meanwhile, the relationship between France and its African proxies can often take on the character of a roadshow or circus, especially when the occasional simmering disagreements between them blow into the open or when domestic pressure forces the government to distance itself momentarily from its protégés. It is in this context that, in September 2015, French judges ordered the seizure of properties tied to Sassou Nguesso's family in an investigation over suspected ill-gotten wealth.[78] He is among a number of African leaders targeted by a long-running French investigation into suspected ill-gotten wealth in France.[79] About the same time, French authorities began investigating Gabon president Ali Bongo's chief of staff on suspicion of having taken a bribe to help secure a contract for a French company. Under Omar Bongo, put in office by the French, Gabon had excellent relations with France for decades under a system known as 'la Françafrique'. The Paris establishment granted political and military support to long-serving presidents in its former African colonies in exchange for commercial favors. But the skewed and exploitative relationship has cooled since Ali Bongo, who was supported by France to succeed his father as president in a disputed election in 2009, sought to distance himself from France's exploitative relations sustained by his father. His chief of staff, Maixent Accrombessi, under investigation by the French authorities, had asserted that Gabon had been like a drinking trough for the biggest French companies, which, under Omar Bongo, had been behind unprecedented crimes, illicit agreements, abuse of public goods, and abuse of their dominant position. While the scandal unfolded, past presidents, including Jacques Chirac and Nicolas Sarkozy, denied allegations of having benefited from millions of dollars in illegal campaign funds from figures like Omar and Ali Bongo. Also, France's top multinationals are overrepresented in the former colonial nations. Home to one of four French military bases in Africa, Gabon remains the 'epicenter of Françafrique' and the sphere of influence *par excellence*, where French businesses control more than 30% of some market sectors.[80] Observers note that the revelations are an indictment of a corrupt regime that reflects shamefully on both the former colonial master France and the unabashedly high-living governing family that has treated the national treasury like its own private bank account.[81] Before relations with France went awry, Francois Stifani, the grand master of the National Grand Lodge of France (GLNF), one of the largest Masonic orders with 38,000 members, was in Libreville in May of 2010 to ordain Ali Bongo as the grand master of Gabonese Freemasons. Until then, Ali Bongo had occupied the rank of Assistant Grand Master, i.e., at least three levels below the peak of the hierarchy. At age 53, Ali Bongo was catapulted to be the grand master of the Grand Lodge of Gabon (GLB) and the Grand Equatorial Rite, the two predominant Freemason orders in Gabon.

These problematic relationships have fed into the internal dynamics of governance in post-independence Africa and have been sustained in the post-Cold War era. Gary K. Busch explains that Freemason lodges maintain a formidable, covert influence within the French judicial and police structures. Their tentacles spread all over Francophone Africa and are a potent instrument to keep control over political developments across the African continent, in particular in Francophone Sub-Saharan Africa. All three Free-mason lodges in France have gained reputations in recent years for being caught out peddling political influence and pursuing false invoicing on state contracts, particularly in companies controlled by the state. It is the responsi-bility of the Freemasons in the judiciary to hamper any investigations through bureaucratic measures designed to torpedo any serious attempt at reform. One of the topmost grievances raised by the muzzled press is the National Grand Lodge of France (GLNF) open-armed embrace of brutal or corrupt African dictators who are Masons. The other two Grand Lodges are no differ-ent. Just as in France, Freemasonry is ubiquitous at the very top in many Afri-can states. Denis Sassou Nguesso, the Congolese president, is Grand Master of the Grand Lodge of Congo (Brazzaville), which was linked to the GLNF; President Mamadou Tanja of Niger, and Chad's Idriss Deby and Francoisois Bozize of the Central African Republic are among at least 12 African presi-dents linked to the Masons. In November 2009, Ali Bongo, the new Gab-onese president, was ordained as the Grand Master of the Grand Lodge of Gabon (GLB) and the Grand Equatorial Rite, the two predominant Freema-son orders in Gabon.

In Congo-Brazzaville, both the current president, Denis Sassou Nguesso, and the former president, Pascal Lissouba, are freemasons, although they belong to different chapters of the order. Lissouba is an initiate of the Grand Orient of France, while Sassou Nguesso belongs to a Senegalese lodge affili-ated to the GLNF. Most of these African presidents, but not exclusively, are Francophone: Paul Biya, president of Cameroon; Blaise Campaore, president of Burkina Faso; Robert Guei, former head of Ivory Coast; John Kuffuor, former president of Ghana, to name but a few. There are scores more at cabi-net level and among those staffing African regional organizations and banks.[82]

In effect, governance and governmental institutions in Francophone Africa are caught in formidable unofficial strictures and neo-colonial institu-tions that constitute the real informal platforms that in fact govern the Fran-cophone African state. Significantly, this critical factor has remained constant since the independence of the Francophone Sub-Saharan African state. The end of the Cold War paradoxically merely liberated neo-colonial forces to pursue their national interests with extra vigor at the expense of the peoples of those states. Gary Busch, citing the work of Francois Xavier Verschave, extensively codified the depth and reach of these affairs.

Francois Xavier Verschave in 1994 coined the concept of 'Françafrique' to describe a conspiracy between African proxies and stooges and the French establishment as the tip of the iceberg that is Franco-African relations. He said the term refers to the secret criminality in the upper echelons of French politics and economy, where a kind of underground Republic is hidden from view. Putting it in historical context, he observes that in 1960, events forced De Gaulle to grant independence to the French colonies of black Africa. He described the newly proclaimed international legality as the unsullied tip of the iceberg as France insinuated the idea of being the best friend of Africa, development, and democracy. Meanwhile, Jacques Foccart, 'the man in the shadows', was given the task of enforcing African states' dependence, using inevitably illegal, secret, and shameful methods. Focart, also known as Monsieur Afrique, selected African heads of state who were 'friends of France'. Verschave documents that through war more than 100,000 civilians have been massacred in Cameroon since 1956; the Madagascan resistance was broken in 1947 by carnage of a similar magnitude, assassination, or electoral fraud. Verschave highlights that to these African guardians of the neo-colonial order, Paris offered a share of the income from raw materials and development aid. Military bases, the CFA franc which could be exchanged in Switzerland, the secret services and the outwardly-innocent businesses acting on their behalf (Elf and numerous supply or 'security' companies) completed the system.[83]

Verschave observes that a lot of this ability to hide what it happening from the public derives from two interlinked processes. The first is the absence of any democratic procedures in the French political system for debating African policy, and the second is the role of French Masons (and their African presidential lodge brothers) in enforcing the narrow interests of French business throughout Africa by using the institutions of the French state. In return, the African presidents pay a tithe to the French politicians which funds French political parties and enriches others on a personal basis.

He exemplifies the workings of the system with Gabon's late president Omar Bongo, who allegedly pocketed millions in embezzled funds from the Central African state, channeling some of it to French political parties in support of Nicolas Sarkozy. Verschave alludes to a US embassy cable referencing a senior official at the Bank of Central African States (BEAC) who gave information to a US diplomat in Cameroon. This information comprised Bongo's 'brazen' defrauding of the BEAC, which holds the pooled reserves of six Central African countries, including Gabon, Cameroon, and the Democratic Republic of Congo. Shortly after Bongo's death in 2009, the US embassy in Yaounde said the bank source told them: 'Gabonese officials used the proceeds for their own enrichment and, at Bongo's direction, funneled funds to French political parties, including in support of French President Nicolas Sarkozy'. The cable, released by WikiLeaks, continued: 'Asked what the officials did with the stolen funds, the BEAC official responded, 'sometimes they kept it for themselves, sometimes they funneled it to French political parties'. Asked who received the funds, the official responded, 'both sides, but mostly the right; especially Chirac and including Sarkozy'. The BEAC official said 'Bongo was France's favourite president in Africa', and 'this is classic FrancAfrique'.[84] Gary Busch cites Francois Xavier Verschave's revelations that the Ivorian crisis was the war of the French against Ivory Coast instigated by Jacques Chirac. It was his fit of pique which ordered the French peacekeepers to attack and destroy the Ivorian air force. It was his order to send over a hundred tanks to surround the Hotel Ivoire and President Gbagbo's house. It was his decision to allow his soldiers to open fire on a crowd of singing youths, totally unarmed and non-threatening, seeking only to stop the French from carrying out a coup or killing President Gbagbo. It was his African advisor Michel Bonnecorse, Defense Minister Aliot-Marie, and Pierre Brochand, chief of the General Directorate for External Security (DGSE) who made and controlled French policy and programs in Africa under Chirac. They were aided by a web of French agents assigned to work undercover in French companies like Bouygues, Delmas, Total, and other multinationals; pretending to be expatriate employees.[85]

In this climate, the SNCs that took place in the wake of the end of the Cold War, with the singular exception of the Republic of Benin, failed in Chad, Comoros, Gabon, Mali, Niger, and Togo. They made no dent on the prevailing governance paradigm. In post-conference Togo, under the reign of Gnasingbe Eyadema, who was president from 1967 until his death, aged 69, in 2005, family dynastic rule has been entrenched for 38 years. He took power definitively in January 1967, but was already notorious for having, as a 28-year-old sergeant in 1963, assassinated the first president of Togo, Sylvanus Olympio, in West Africa's first post-independence coup.[86] With Benin under him, such was his inexperience and incompetence that President Charles de Gaulle's African adviser, Jacques Foccart, was said to rule Togo by telephone.[87] Significantly, the country is now ruled by his son Faure Essozimna Gnassingbé. In like manner, Omar Bongo in Gabon, who ruled from December 1967 to June 2009, became the world's longest-serving non-monarch ruler. He was one of the longest serving rulers in history. Bongo was criticized for in effect having worked for himself, his family, and local elites and not for Gabon and its people. For instance, French Green politician Eva Joly noted that during Bongo's long reign, despite an oil-led GDP per capita growth to one of the highest levels in Africa, Gabon built only 5 kilometers of freeway a year and still had one of the world's highest infant mortality rates by the time of his death in June 2009. After Bongo's death, his son Ali Bongo (who, as part of preparations to assume office after his father, had been assigned key ministerial responsibilities by the latter) was elected to succeed him in a controversial election that was marred by violence in August 2009.[88] In Lusophone Africa, violence continues to play a significant role in the resolution of political contentions. Guinea Bissau, where virtually a whole generation of mainly old cadres of the African Party of Independence of Guinea and Cape Verde (PAIGC) militocrats has been wiped out in political violence (from President Bernandino Viera through General Ansumane Mane, the former head of the military junta, to his chief of staff General Verissimo Seabra) in internecine quasi-ideological struggles, it may be said that violence is the principal mode of political engagement. Mozambique remains mired in intermittent political flashes while Angola would seem to have overcome the challenge of violence in its national life. Hopefully, for good.

In Anglophone Africa in the post-Cold War era, constitutional conferences, convened in particular in Kenya and Nigeria, often became mere talking shops as their recommendations were never implemented. Nigeria's tortuous experience of formulating a balanced constitution presents a unique case of the problem of constitution making in Africa. In Nigeria, one channel through which the NGN 550 billion appropriated to fund the National Assembly has been drained in the last 17 years is the Constitution Review project. Though only one of the three attempts at amending the constitution has succeeded, at least NGN 9 Billion has gone into what has become a very expensive ritual.[89] Since the end of the civil war, several constitutional conferences have been held, from the Murtala/Obasanjo Constitutional Drafting Committee headed by Chief F.R.A. Williams, through the era of states creation by General Ibrahim Babaginda, the General Sani Abacha Constituent Assembly, the General Abdul Salami Abubakar 1999 Constitution, the President Olusegun Obasanjo National Political Reform Conference of 2005, to President Jonathan's Constitutional Conference on 2014. In all these attempts at constitution making, the trend has always been for Nigerians to demand the creation of more federating units.[90] The constitutional and political reform initiatives embarked upon by the various executive and legislative arms of the government since 1999 (at least two by each arm) have had no impact on the constitution that the Sani Abacha military regime foisted on the country. The Ibrahim Mantu-led attempt to amend the constitution in 2006 was entangled in the manipulation of the process by President Olusegun Obasanjo to advance his project of unconstitutionally extending his tenure in office.[91] The review was thus thrown out with Olusegun Obasanjo's third-term project by the Legislature. The successor Goodluck Jonathan administration also hosted what observers thought was a jamboree designed to woo mostly old political horses who were offered seats by the administration in the conference and who dominated its proceedings to support the controversial second-term bid of President Goodluck Jonathan. Accordingly, the clamor for authentic and politically unencumbered constitutional reform has remained a permanent issue that all administrations, including the Mohammadu Buhari administration, have had to confront. The Eighth National Assembly has decided to resume the attempt to review and amend the country's extant constitution as there is universal recognition that Nigeria's existing constitution is neither one that derived legitimacy from 'we the people of Nigeria' nor one that provides an adequate basis for tackling the country's two major challenges: socio-economic development and enduring political stability. In Kenya, constitutional review efforts undertaken over two decades prior to the governance crisis of 2008 were only partially implemented by successive governments that conveniently picked from the reforms proposed by the review. The main objective of the administrations was to avoid any threats to their continued power and interests. Not even the catastrophic events of 2008 around its elections led to any comprehensive changes in the constitution. The subsequent constitutional reform exercise was a root-and-branch affair: all political, economic, and social issues that were dodged or skirted in the past were addressed and the national consensus that emerged was incorporated into a new constitution.[92]

Post-conflict Liberia has not been immune to the rigmaroles of constitution making. The more attempts that have been made to overcome institutional prejudices in its founding 1847 constitution, the more newer challenges have emerged on the nationality clause that proscribes people of non-negro descent from acquiring citizenship. There have even been attempts to bar the poor from electoral competition by demands for unaffordable registration fees to contest elections. Attempts to review the 1986 constitution since 2014 have run up against the reluctance of establishment Liberia to accept changes that would completely equilibrate the rights of all citizens by eliminating the special privileges of Americo-Liberians. Also, a new reactionary movement to declare Liberia as founded on Christian foundations has gained a degree of momentum that may ultimately drive the country back to sectarian hostilities. Across the continent, as earlier noted, in Uganda, Rwanda, Burundi, Congo Brazzaville, and Senegal among others, constitution making and review have been manipulated to consolidate or entrench personal and partisan interests, including absolute appropriation of the totality of the state space by these sectarian interests.

The outcome is that today only a handful of African countries (including Kenya, Benin, Senegal, Ghana, Cape Verde, and South Africa) have constitutions that may be said to reflect the wishes of the population and are owned by the citizens. The Republic of Benin, Ghana, Cape Verde, and South Africa would arguably remain the reference for democratic consolidation in Africa given their strings of successive regime transitions through the ballot box devoid of violence. Besides the experience of the transition from apartheid to black majority rule in South Africa, the Republic of Benin probably signposts one potential future trajectory of democracy in Africa. Against the backdrop of overcoming coups d'état, overthrowing an OPS/OMS through a popular SNC, the removal in 1990 of General Mathieu Kerekou, whose OPS/OMS was anchored in a convenient Marxism/Leninism and his acceptance of the first democratic presidential elections in 1991 that he lost to Nicephore Soglo, the Republic of Benin has survived all the pathologies of post-independence Africa.

## CONCLUSION

These morbid pathologies have remained a common challenge of most African states since independence. Paradoxically, in the evolved new syndrome of sit-tight presidencies and dynastic succession among African leaders of all hues in the post-Cold War era (ranging from the failed attempt by Nigeria's Olusegun Obasanjo, through Sassou Nguesso in Congo Brazzaville, Pierre Nkunrunziza in Burundi, or the Eyademas in Togo among many others), some cite the demonstrably reformed dictator Mathieu Kerekou as the preeminent change driver in Africa in his role in building a stable democracy by calling and accepting the resolutions of the SNC which put an end to his quasi-Marxist Leninist regime.[93] His return to a constitutional two-term tenure in office as president in the post-SNC period and voluntary transfer of power thereafter revalidated his general vision of a constitutional order and specifically a democratic Republic of Benin as the exemplar of the assured future of Africa in the post-Cold War era. The future of Africa two decades into its second half-century of independence would probably lie in repudiating the pervasive normative struggles for the appropriation of the totality of the political spaces through the realignment of the vision of its diverse leaderships to advance the distilled corporate will and collective interests of its peoples. Hopefully the dysfunctional and hazardous exuberance of politicians and the military that characterized the first half-century of independence of African states will give way to more rational, reasoned, structured, institutional, transparent, and ordered paradigms of inclusive governance based on the imperative to project the common will and collective interests of the peoples of the continent as the very raison d'être of the African state.

## NOTES

1. Patrick Chabal, "The Transition to Multi-Party Politics in Lusophone Africa, Problems and Prospects," *Lusophone* (1996): 57–69.
2. Source: http://www.worldometers.info/world-population/nigeria-population/.
3. South Sudan Country Profile. Source: http://www.bbc.com/news/world-africa-14069082.
4. Slavery in Mauritania: https://en.wikipedia.org/wiki/Slavery_in_Mauritania.
5. Slavery Still Shackles Mauritania, 31 Years after its Abolition. Source: http://www.theguardian.com/world/2012/aug/14/slavery-still-shackles-mauritania.
6. Roger Southall, *Liberation Movements in Power, Party and State in Southern Africa* (Pietermaritzburg: James Curry, University of KwaZulu Natal, 2013), 2.
7. Roger Southall, ibid., 136.
8. Naomi Chazan, Peter Lewis et al., *The Diversity of African Politics in Politics and Society in Contemporary Africa*, 3rd ed. (Boulder: Lynne Rienner Publishers), 14.
9. Kanu, Ikechukwu Anthony (OSA), "Nkrumah and the Quest for African Unity," *American International Journal of Contemporary Research* 3, no. 6 (June 2013).
10. Adebayo Olukoshi, Changing Patterns of Politics in Africa. Source: http://cea.revues.org/1045.
11. Benjamin Talton, The Challenge of Decolonization in Africa. Source: http://exhibitions.nypl.org/africanaage/essay-challenge-of-decolonization-africa.html.
12. Ibid.
13. Ademola Araoye, *Sources of Conflict in the Postcolonial State* (Trenton, NJ: Africa World Press, 2014), 66.
14. Ademola Araoye and Hegemonic Agendas, "Intermesticity and Conflicts in the Post-colonial State," *African Journal on Conflict Resolution* 12, no. 1 (2012).
15. Source: http://worldpopulationreview.com/continents/africa-population/.

16. The reference to African states in the context of postcoloniality raises issues around the perpetuation of externally and colonially derived structures and institutions that are founded around the logic of the continued subordination and appropriation of African spaces by neo-colonial forces that remain actively engaged in the internal processes of the Africa state. Postcoloniality may then be defined as the complete and absolute retrenchment in actuality of all structures and protocols that perpetuate the subordinate status of Africa in its interaction with the global system of states. The term neo-colonial state would seem to convey the true character of the African state as it currently is.

17. Donald L. Gordon, "Overview of Politics in the Postcolonial Era 'African Politics'," in *Understanding Contemporary Africa*, ed. April A. Gordon, and Donald L. Gordon (Boulder, CO: Lynne Rienner, 2007).

18. Ibid., 62–63.

19. Ibid.

20. Chris A. Agoha, "Elites, Leadership and Governance: The Triple Dilemma of Democratic Development in Nigeria," in *The African Power Elite*.

21. Roger Southall, ibid., 137.

22. Ibid.

23. Chabal, "The Transition to Multi-Party Politics."

24. Charles N. Mwaura, *Political Succession and Related Conflicts in Kenya*, http://erepository.uonbi.ac.ke/bitstream/handle/11295/38631/Political%20Succession%20and%20Related%20Conflicts%20in%20Kenya.pdf?sequence=1.

25. Ibid.

26. Ibid.

27. Lakidi and Mazrui, cited Mwaura in *Political Succession and Related Conflicts in Kenya*.

28. John W. Harbeson, "Postcolonial Sub-Saharan African Politics," http://www.oxfordbibliographies.com/view/document/obo-9780199846733/obo-9780199846733-0057.xml.

29. Ibid.

30. The idea of quasi-sovereign entities with putative powers of the state existing within the postcolonial African state and side-by-side in the same state environment while conducting various forms of informal or formal relations with the states was captured as proto states by Ed Haley, Professor of International Relations at the Claremont McKenna College, Claremont, CA.

31. Ademola Araoye, *Sources of Conflict in the Post Colonial African State* (Trenton, NJ: Africa World Press, 2014).

32. Bratton and van de Walle, Cited in Christian von Soest, *How Does neo-Patrimonialism Affect the African State? The Case of Tax Collection in Zambia*. Source: http://papers.ssrn.com/sol3/papers.cfm?abstract_id=946092.

33. von Soest, *How Does neo-Patrimonialism Affect the African State?*

34. Discussions: Bratton, and Van de Walle, http://www.jennyweatherup.com/artwork/writing/bratton.html.

35. Ibid.

36. Christian von Soest, *How Does neo-Patrimonialism Affect the African State?*

37. C.N. Mwaura, *Political Succession and Related Conflicts in Kenya*.

38. von Soest, *How Does neo-Patrimonialism Affect the African State?*

39. Ibid.
40. Ibid.
41. Seleka: The Militia Terrorising Central African Republic's Christian Population. Source: http://www.telegraph.co.uk/news/worldnews/africaandindianocean/centralafricanrepublic/10502752/Seleka-the-militia-terrorising-Central-African-Republics-Christian-population.html.
42. Mozambique: History and Politic. Source: https://www.issafrica.org/af/profiles/Mozambique/Politics.html.
43. Alain Rouvez, *Disconsolate Empires* (New York: University Press of America, 1994).
44. Jason Warner, Who Are Seleka? Source: http://globalpublicsquare.blogs.cnn.com/2013/01/17/who-are-seleka/.
45. Ibid.
46. Antoine Roger Lokongo, Central African Republic: The Hidden Hands Behind 'Yet Another Good Coup', http://www.pambazuka.net/en/category.php/features/87025/print.
47. Emilly Mellgard, What Is the Seleka? 29 January, 2015. Source: http://tony-blairfaithfoundation.org/religion-geopolitics/commentaries/backgrounder/what-seleka.
48. Ibid.
49. See note 46 above.
50. President of Uganda, H.E. Yoweri K. Museveni, http://www.statehouse.go.ug/people/h-e-yoweri-k-museveni.
51. Uganda's Yoweri Museveni in Profile, accessed: December 21, 2015, http://www.bbc.com/news/world-africa-12421747.
52. Ibid.
53. Gregory Warner, Rwanda's President Dangles the Possibility of a Third Term. Source: http://www.npr.org/sections/parallels/2015/12/21/460595912/rwandas-president-dangles-the-possibility-of-a-third-term.
54. Africa: A Continent Drenched in the Blood of Revolutionary Heroes, accessed on December 16, 2015. Source: http://www.theguardian.com/global-development/poverty-matters/2011/jan/17/lumumba-50th-anniversary-african-leaders-assassinations.
55. Georges Nzongola-Ntalaja, Patrice Lumumba: The Most Important Assassination of the 20th Century, accessed December 16, 2015. Source: http://www.theguardian.com/global-development/poverty-matters/2011/jan/17/patrice-lumumba-50th-anniversary-assassination.
56. Ibid.
57. MI6 'Arranged Cold War Killing' of Congo Prime Minister, accessed on December 16, 2015. Source: http://www.theguardian.com/world/2013/apr/02/mi6-patrice-lumumba-assassination.
58. Paul Kagame, President of Rwanda, Encyclopaedea Britannica, accessed December 21, 2015. Source: http://www.britannica.com/biography/Paul-Kagame.
59. Profile: Laurent Kabila, accessed December 16, 2015. Source: http://news.bbc.co.uk/2/hi/africa/1121068.stm.
60. See note 54 above.

61. Joseph Winter, Zimbabwe's Robert Mugabe. Source: http://www.bbc.com/news/world-africa-23431534.
62. Félix Houphouët-Boigny of Côte d'Ivoire, accessed December 16, 2015. Source: http://africanhistory.about.com/od/ctedivoir1/a/Bio-Houphouët-Boigny.htm.
63. The Politics of Poverty: Elites, Citizens and States, Center for the Future State, Development Research Contre et al. (Department for International Development DFID) 2010.
64. Ibid.
65. Major Jimmi Wangome, Military Coups in Africa-The African Neo-Colonialism That Is Self-Inflicted, CSC 1985.
66. Which of the Military Intervention Theory that Best Explain Military Intervention in Nigeria and Reasons, Wednesday, March 5, 2014. Source: http://chrisdonasco.blogspot.com.ng/2014/03/which-of-military-intervention-theory.html.
67. Murat ÖNDER, What Accounts for Military Interventions in Politics: A Cross-National Comparison, http://www.eakademi.org/incele.asp?konu=WHat.%20ACCOUNTS%20FOR%20MILITARY%20INTERVENTIONS%20IN%20POLITICS:%20A%20CROSSNATIONAL%20COMPARISON&kimlik=1285708304&url=makaleler/monder-1.htm.
68. Ibid.
69. Ibid.
70. Gordon, "African Politics," 62–63.
71. Benjamin Talton, The Challenge of Decolonization in Africa. Source: http://exhibitions.nypl.org/africanaage/essay-challenge-of-decolonization-africa.html.
72. Wading In, Africa Confidential, Vol. 48, no. 23. November 16, 2007, 8.
73. Immanuel Wallenstein, *The Modern World System: Capitalist Agriculture and the Origin of the European World-Economy in the Sixteenth Century* (New York: Academic Press, 1976), 229–33.
74. Frantz Fanon, *The Wretched of the Earth* (New York: Grove Press, 1963).
75. Gerard Hagg, and Peter Kagwanja, Identity and Peace: Reconfiguring Conflict Resolution in Africa, African Journal on Conflict Resolution, Vol. 7, no. 2, 2007. https://www.files.ethz.ch/isn/98398/ajcr_volume-7_2007_no2.pdf.
76. David A. Lake, and Donald Rothchild, "Containing Fear: The Origins and Management of Ethnic Conflict," *International Security* 21, no. 2 (1996), 41–75.
77. Ladipo Adamolekun, SNC Notes: The Present Nigerian Constitution Is Neither Owned by the People nor Is It Really Federal. October 19, 2013. Source: http://emotanafricana.com/2013/10/19/snc-notes-the-present-nigerian-constitution-is-neither-owned-by-the-people-nor-is-it-really-federal-ladipo-adamolekun/.
78. French Court Orders Seizures of Properties Tied to Congo's President's Family, September 29, 2015. Source: http://www.reuters.com/article/us-france-congo-corruption-idUSKCN0RT2HL20150929.
79. Laudes Martial Mbon, Armed with New Constitution, Congo Leader in a Hurry for New Elections. December 22, 2015. Source: http://news.yahoo.com/congo-leader-plans-bring-forward-presidential-vote-132308818.html.

80. A Fight Inside Gabon's Kleptocratic Dynasty Exposes the Complicity of French Business. Source: http://qz.com/395572/a-fight-inside-gabons-kleptocratic-dynasty-reveals-the-complicity-of-french-business/.
81. Ibid.
82. Gary K. Busch, West African Leaders on the Square against Gbagbo. Source: http://www.ocnus.net/artman2/publish/Editorial_10/West-African-Leaders-On-The-Square-Against-Gbagbo_printer.shtml.
83. Defining Françafrique by François Xavier Verschave. Internet Source: https://www.scribd.com/document/65598907/Defining-Francafrique-by-Francois-Xavier-Verschave.
84. Gary K. Busch, West African Leaders on the Square against Gbagbo. Source: http://www.ocnus.net/artman2/publish/Editorial_10/West-African-Leaders-On-The-Square-Against-Gbagbo_printer.shtml.
85. Busch, West African Leaders on the Square against Gbagbo, accessed: November, 2015. Source: http://www.villagesquare.org/xenforo/index.php?threads/west-african-leaders-on-the-square-against-gbagbo.60059/page-2.
86. Kaye Whiteman, Gnassingbe Eyadema, Dinosaur Dictator Who Ruled Togo for 38 Brutal and Bearful Years. Source: http://www.theguardian.com/news/2005/feb/07/guardianobituaries.
87. Ibid.
88. Omar Bongo. Source: https://en.wikipedia.org/wiki/Omar_Bongo.
89. Azimazi Momoh Jimoh, "The Burgeoning Economy of Constitution Review," *The Guardian* (Nigeria) Sunday, January 24, 2016, 19.
90. Emeka Anyaoku, Nigeria: In Urgent Need of a True Federalism, Address at the Ibadan School of Government and Public Policy at the International Conference Center, University of Ibadan, Ibadan, February 1, 2016.
91. Jimoh, The Burgeoning Economy, 19.
92. See note 77 above.
93. Nigeria-Benin Siamese Relations Will Reach New Heights When I Become President, Says Edah, Interview with Daniel Edah," *The Guardian* (Nigeria), February 3, 2016, 48–49.

## BIBLIOGRAPHY

Adamolekun, Ladipo. SNC Notes: The Present Nigerian Constitution Is Neither Owned by the People nor Is It Really Federal. October 19, 2013. Source: http://emotanafricana.com/2013/10/19/snc-notes-the-present-nigerian-constitution-is-neither-owned-by-the-people-nor-is-it-really-federal-ladipo-adamolekun/.
Agoha, Chris A. Elites, Leadership and Governance: The Triple Dilemma of Democratic Development in Nigeria. In *The African Power Elite*.
Anyaoku, Emeka. Nigeria: In Urgent Need of a True Federalism, Address at the Lbadan School of Government and Public Policy at the International Conference Center. Ibadan: University of Ibadan, 1 February 2016.
Araoye, Ademola. "Hegemonic Agendas, Intermesticity and Conflicts in the Post-colonial State." *African Journal on Conflict Resolution* 12, no. 1 (2012): 9–32.
———. *Sources of Conflict in the Postcolonial State*. Trenton, NJ: Africa World Press, 2014, 66.
Bratton, and Van de Walle. Discussions, accessed December, 2015, http://www.jennyweatherup.com/artwork/writing/bratton.html.

Busch, Gary K. West African Leaders on the Square Against Gbagbo, accessed November, 2015. Source: http://www.ocnus.net/artman2/publish/Editorial_10/West-African-Leaders-On-The-Square-Against-Gbagbo_printer.shtml.

Chabal, Patrick. "The Transition to Multi-Party Politics in Lusophone Africa, Problems and Prospects." *Lusotopie* (1996): 57–69.

Chazan, Naomi, Peter Lewis, et al. *The Diversity of African Politics in Politics and Society in Contemporary Africa*. 3rd ed. Boulder: Lynne Rienner Publishers, 14.

Edah, Daniel. "Nigeria-Benin Siamese Relations Will Reach New Heights When I Become President." *The Guardian* (Nigeria), February 3, 2016, 48–49.

Fanon, Frantz. *The Wretched of the Earth*. New York: Grove Press, 1963.

Gordon, Donald L. "Overview of Politics in the Postcolonial Era, 'African Politics.'" In *Understanding Contemporary Africa*, edited by April A Gordon, and Donald L. Gordon. Boulder, CO: Lynne Rienner, 2007.

Hagg, Gerald. "Identity and Violent Conflict in Africa." *HSRC (Human Science Research Council) Review* 6 (2008): 14.

Harbeson, John W. Postcolonial Sub-Saharan African Politics. http://www.oxfordbibliographies.com/view/document/obo-9780199846733/obo-9780199846733-0057.xml.

Jimoh, Azimazi Momoh. "The Burgeoning Economy of Constitution Review." *The Guardian* (Nigeria) Sunday, January 24, 2016, 19.

Kanu, Ikechukwu Anthony (OSA). "Nkrumah and the Quest for African Unity." *American International Journal of Contemporary Research* 3, no. 6 (June 2013).

Lake, David A., and Donald Rothchild. "Containing Fear: The Origins and Management of Ethnic Conflict." *International Security* 21, no. 2 (1996): 41–75.

Lakidi and Mazrui, cited Mwaura, C.N. in *Political Succession and Related Conflicts in Kenya*. Source: http://erepository.uonbi.ac.ke/bitstream/handle/11295/38631/Political%20Succession%20and%20Related%20Conflicts%20in%20Kenya.pdf?sequence=1.

Lokongo, Antoine Roger. Central African Republic: The Hidden Hands Behind 'Yet Another Good Coup'. http://www.pambazuka.net/en/category.php/features/87025/print.

Mbon, Laudes Martial. Armed with New Constitution, Congo Leader in a Hurry for new elections. December 22, 2015, accessed November, 2015. Source: http://news.yahoo.com/congo-leader-plans-bring-forward-presidential-vote-132308818.html.

Mellgard, Emilly. What Is the Seleka? 29 January, 2015. Source: http://tonyblairfaithfoundation.org/religion-geopolitics/commentaries/backgrounder/what-seleka.

Mwaura, C.N. *Political Succession and Related Conflicts in Kenya*. Source: http://erepository.uonbi.ac.ke/bitstream/handle/11295/38631/Political%20Succession%20and%20Related%20Conflicts%20in%20Kenya.pdf?sequence=1.

Nzongola-Ntalaja, Georges. Patrice Lumumba: The Most Important Assassination of the 20th Century, accessed December 16, 2015. Source: http://www.theguardian.com/global-development/poverty-matters/2011/jan/17/patrice-lumumba-50th-anniversary-assassination.

Olukoshi, Adebayo. *Changing Patterns of Politics in Africa*. Source: http://cea.revues.org/1045.

Önder, Murat. What Accounts for Military Interventions in Politics: A Cross-National Comparison. http://www.eakademi.org/incele.asp?konu=WHAT%20 ACCOUNTS%20FOR%20MILITARY%20INTERVENTIONS%20IN%20POLI-TICS:%20A%20CROSSNATIONAL%20COMPARISON&kimlik=1285708304& url=makaleler/monder-1.htm.

Rouvez, Alain. *Disconsolate Empires.* New York: University Press of America, 1994.

Southall, Roger. *Liberation Movements in Power, Party and State in Southern Africa.* Pietermaritzburg: James Curry, University of KwaZulu Natal, 2013, 2.

Talton, Benjamin. *The Challenge of Decolonization in Africa.* Source: http://exhibitions.nypl.org/africanaage/essay-challenge-of-decolonization-africa.html.

Verschave, François Xavier. Defining Françafrique. Internet Source: https://www.scribd.com/document/65598907/Defining-Francafrique-by-Francois-Xavier-Verschave.

von Soest, Christian. How Does neo-Patrimonialism Affect the African State? *GIGA German Institute of Global and Area Studies,* Working Paper 22, accessed November, 2015. Source: https://papers.ssrn.com/sol3/papers.cfm?abstract_id=946092.

Wallenstein, Immanuel. *The Modern World System: Capitalist Agriculture and the Origin of the European World-Economy in the Sixteenth Century.* New York: Academic Press, 1976, 229–33.

Wangome, Major Jimmi. Military Coups in Africa-The African Neo-Colonialism That Is Self-Inflicted, CSC 1985, accessed November, 2015. Source: http://www.globalsecurity.org/military/library/report/1985/WJ.htm.

Warner, Gregory. Rwanda's President Dangles the Possibility of a Third Term. Source: http://www.npr.org/sections/parallels/2015/12/21/460595912/rwandas-president-dangles-the-possibility-of-a-third-term.

Warner, Jason. Who Are Seleka? accessed October, 2015. Source: http://globalpublicsquare.blogs.cnn.com/2013/01/17/who-are-seleka/.

Which of the Military Intervention Theory That Best Explain Military Intervention in Nigeria and Reasons, Wednesday, 5 March, 2014. Source: http://chrisdonasco.blogspot.com.ng/2014/03/which-of-military-intervention-theory.html.

Whiteman, Kaye. Gnassingbe Eyadema, Dinosaur Dictator Who Ruled Togo for 38 Brutal and Fearful Years. Source: http://www.theguardian.com/news/2005/feb/07/guardianobituaries.

Winter, Joseph. Zimbabwe's Robert Mugabe. Source: http://www.bbc.com/news/world-africa-23431534.

# CHAPTER 29

# Secession and Separatism in Modern Africa

## Charles G. Thomas

The states of Africa have been objects of contention among their citizens since the emergence of the modern independent polities of the continent. The boundaries of Africa's modern countries were delineated along the lines of the European colonies that had been established following the 1885 Berlin Conference. However, there were no African powers present at this conference, only the representatives of the European states interested in the continent. The borders the representatives drew were based upon the negotiations of these powers as they expressed their political and economic desires in their newly claimed continent. These negotiations were not informed by the populations living upon the land they were discussing, but instead upon the balance of power in Europe, the treaties powers could already claim, and the rights of conquest and occupation. As such, these boundaries cut across social, cultural, political, and even economic linkages as they already existed on the continent.

This social fracturing was carried forward following independence, with each new state lacking historical or cultural connections to bind the state together. Even worse, each of these states also lacked the capacity to forge such connections within its newly independent populace.[1] With unrelated groups now sharing political and economic boundaries, often with their traditional connections severed by the new political order, significant discontent developed amongst those populations who felt marginalized within these new borders. This discontent found an outlet in non-violent and eventually violent attempts to revise the local political order. Especially as strong ethnic

C.G. Thomas (✉)
The Air Command and Staff College, Maxwell AFB, Montgomery, AL, USA

© The Author(s) 2018
M.S. Shanguhyia and T. Falola (eds.),
*The Palgrave Handbook of African Colonial and Postcolonial History*,
https://doi.org/10.1057/978-1-137-59426-6_29

or linguistic groups attempted to revise their local order, the ideas of local national identity groups governing them instead of a distant and unrepresentative state carried a strong appeal. As these groups fought for governance and in some cases direct sovereignty, postcolonial Africa grappled for the first time with secession and separatist conflicts. These conflicts have become ubiquitous since the first shots were fired in Sudan's 1956 civil war, and there has not been a single year without a secessionist or separatist conflict since then. This chapter will discuss the political aims of secessionism and separatism, what drives them, the evolution of secessionist and separatist conflicts in Africa, and why these have evolved as they have during the past 60 years.

## WHAT ARE SECESSION AND SEPARATISM?

In the modern postcolonial era, the Westphalian nation-state is considered the most desirable and representative political unit across the globe. This state carries with it many specific characteristics, including the maintenance of a bureaucracy to administer its functions, the policing of criminal behavior, the existence of an armed force to defend its borders, the provision of services to its citizens, the raising of revenue to pay for its servants and services, and the acquisition of political legitimacy to ease the creation of the foregoing.[2] While most states of the developed world are able to affirmatively pursue all of these characteristics, in many African states there are significant challenges to achieving these solely through the state. These developing states maintain their legitimacy through the recognition of the international community, but will often afford fewer services, less political representation, and fewer legal protections to marginalized groups within their borders. These groups might be an ethno-linguistic group, a political party, or even a local geographic socio-political subdivision, but the marginalization in the services and protection by the state leaves the targeted group with second-class citizenship in the state and most often drives a desire to revise the political order. However, given that the state itself has little incentive to voluntarily let this revision occur, these groups will often have to turn to violent means to compel this revision. If the desired revision is to devolve the political governance of the marginalized group to the group itself, essentially granting autonomy, then the conflict is a separatist conflict. In these cases, the local political actors will take over the internal aspects of their own governance, creating and enforcing their own laws, often collecting their own taxes, and providing their own services to their populations. However, in such cases these local autonomous groups are still understood to be part of the same larger state structure by the international community and any formal international exchange will pass through the formal state structures.

For some marginalized African groups, local autonomy isn't enough. Due to the weakness of the state in Africa and the centrality of international connections for political legitimacy and economic aid, separatism is sometimes not enough to fully address the grievances of marginalized groups. Since the sovereign state is the only authority recognized by the international community, the state retains extraordinary control over social, economic, and even political development within its borders.[3] This means that if an autonomous region wishes to access these networks of international capital and development aid, it needs to negotiate access to them with the existing state. These negotiations can sometimes be accomplished, but far more often the marginalized group either cannot reach an acceptable agreement with their host state or more often refuses to negotiate such access. In this case, the marginalized groups will enter into an armed struggle for not only their local autonomy but their internationally recognized sovereignty in the form of their own state. These struggles for an independent state are secessionist struggles, and what marks their difference is exactly this fight to attain and maintain independent, internationally recognized sovereignty over the territory the group governs.

Given this, all of these struggles are ultimately ones for control over the functions of the state (that is, the application and enforcement of laws, the taxing of the populace, and the provision of services), but secession also involves the creation of an entirely separate and recognized political body. As such, all secessions are ultimately part of separatism, but not all separatist conflicts necessarily involve secession. These lines will often become even more blurred over the course of a conflict, when a secessionist movement may instead settle for local autonomy, such as has been seen in the Malian conflicts in the 1990s. Conversely, the struggles of separatists and their subsequent relations with their host state might convince them that a settlement cannot be reached and instead secession must be adopted as a conflict goal. This pattern was seen through the long wars in South Sudan, where initial struggles for local autonomy eventually led to such a fractious relationship with the North that secession was seen as the only remedy. As such, it must always be understood that these related but distinct concepts are rarely cleanly declared or pursued, and it is only in the wake of conflicts that the final determination of separatism and secession is understood.

## Separatism and Secession in Colonial Africa

Separatism and secession in Africa is a difficult subject to effectively approach. The concepts of secession and separatism rely strongly on the concepts of the Westphalian nation-state, the creation of which was a liminal moment in the emergence of European modernity. Given that the processes of European modernity only began being impressed on Africa during the decades of colonial rule, and even then only piecemeal, it is hard to say whether secession or separatism is an idea that can be applied to any study of Africa prior to independence. This isn't to say that there weren't efforts by marginalized groups to exercise their own local control, but often this was a local control that was not as developed in terms of participation, function, or capacity as those of the later nation-state. However, it is useful to look at some occurrences of political fracturing and local autonomy in these periods to understand how and why these historical attempts both resembled and were foreign to the modern African secessionist and separatist conflicts.

Following the 'Scramble for Africa' in the nineteenth century, the vast majority of the continent was colonized by European powers. Aside from Liberia and Ethiopia, the continent was divided into colonial administrations where the political, economic, and military control was exercised by the colonial power. The colonial systems that these powers put in place were state-like, but not states. Whereas states exist explicitly to protect and provide for their citizens, these colonies had the provision of services and the protections of their subjects as generally a secondary objective. Instead, control was exercised in such a way as to maintain order for the economic exploitation of the regions. The local laws, taxes, and administrative structures were rarely designed by the locals, instead being alien systems put in place to compel the obedience of the ruled. While there were regions where the original indigenous political systems continued to exist, such as the Sokoto caliphate, they did so as sub-imperial agents of the colonizing power. As such, these local political organizations, while maintaining their own state-like attributes, could only exercise their own sovereign power under the auspices and direction of their colonial masters.

Within the colonial context there certainly were violent conflicts waged by Africans to throw off the control of the colonial powers. There are literally hundreds of histories of local resistance to the European empires in Africa. The Germans fought against the Maji-Maji revolt in East Africa[4] while the British faced a Zulu revolt in 1906,[5] to name but two of the indigenous uprisings against the established colonial control of their colonial conquerors. However, in these cases they were not done with the explicit intent to split from an existent local state authority and then join Ethiopia and Liberia in independence. Instead, these were violent rebellions against local authorities without a greater goal of state creation. As such, they are commonly viewed as either resistance or liberation struggles, conflicts that are similar to the later secessionist and separatist wars, but ones which, instead of overthrowing the authority of a local state or state structures, were instead throwing off the colonial structures of distant European states.[6] It would not be until local independent state structures existed that secession and separatism could be exercised on the continent.

## THE INDEPENDENCE ERA

Following the Second World War the colonial powers that ruled the majority of the continent found themselves either severely weakened in victory or crushed in defeat. This weakness, combined with local unrest and international opposition, saw the first major cracks in the colonial system. By the late 1940s it had become apparent that colonial Africa was firmly on the track to independence, and by the late 1950s it was plain this independence would be happening sooner rather than later. While Sudan, Tunisia, and Morocco each gained their independence in 1956, the full torrent in Sub-Saharan Africa began with Ghana in 1957 and over the next decade the vast majority of African countries gained their own self-rule. However, independence had come quickly and even those colonial powers which felt some responsibility for the development of governing institutions were caught flat-footed. As such, very little progress had been made in creating robust, local, and modern governing institutions; effective bureaucracies; African leaders for the military and police services; or even general educated civil societies. The states that emerged had in many cases not completed the transition from sites of colonial extraction and thus had incomplete capacities to effectively provide the services and protections that state legitimacy is founded upon.

These weak states in turn often found that in the absence of the unifying nationalist cause of independence there was little holding the various political and cultural groups together within their borders. Those groups which were poor and marginalized called upon the state to provide for their uplift, a task often well beyond the capacity of the state. Those groups which had resources within their purview such as copper, gold, iron, diamonds, or oil often found the state wished to redistribute this wealth to a greater degree than those groups hoped. Those groups which were a minority found themselves without much political power and felt unrepresented within their new government, while their ethnic group might have considerably more representation on the other side of a state border. These subnational groups, whether political or social, proved to be potent rivals to the state, especially as they often had far more cohesion than the state itself. These groups then often found themselves even more aggrieved as the states of Africa began to take the initiative in nation building, frequently asking for labor and funds from the peoples who felt little loyalty or care towards their independent regimes.

It is within this context of independent states that the initial conflicts demanding autonomy or secession began in Africa. These secessionist and separatist groups had several arguments in their favor. The first was that the new wave of decolonization had been supported by the United Nations (UN), which enshrined a people's right to self-determination.[7] While this had often been deferred in the past, such as with the League of Nations and later UN Trustee territories,[8] the cornerstone of the dismantling of the European empires was the concept that the postwar moment was when the promises would be made good for all of the colonized peoples of the world. However, while self-determination was a right, there had been no pronouncement on the limitations of self-determination. To those aggrieved, marginalized populations in Africa, this offered the legal possibility of their own state under the current international order. The second argument in their favor was that these groups often had an arguable precedent for independence. While the colonial boundaries had been set as the initial new state borders, the colonies themselves had been subdivided within their own borders many times over; different administrative areas might be ruled under completely different legal codes, marking an existent and arguably legitimate boundary. For example, South Sudan had been administered under an entirely different Anglo-Egyptian administration than the North since 1930,[9] with each having its own legal code and philosophical basis. With these two ideas taken hand-in-hand, secessionist groups felt they had a strong and legitimate argument for their secession from the sovereign states that the former colonies had become. It would not take long for some of these aggrieved groups to test these arguments in the wider world.

## THE CIVIL SECESSIONS

The first and most notable secessionist attempts are what might be termed the 'civil secessions'. In both cases, the secessionist territories (in the Republic of the Congo and Nigeria) had been administered separately to the rest of the colony into which they had been amalgamated. Due to the resources at hand and their relations with the colonial powers, both had managed to become well-developed colonial territories. They featured developed infrastructure, good public services, a strong bureaucracy, and a firm identity as a people. As such, when both found themselves at odds with their new state, they found themselves in much stronger positions than might be expected; both might be able to form its own state directly from the regional structures it had already developed. Given this, when secession came, it came as a whole, multi-ethnic civil political unit; thus a civil secession.[10]

The strategy of both of these secessions would prove to be the same. Given their political and economic development and precedent for independence, the secessionist powers simply declared their secession and went about administering their territories as a state. Taxes were collected, services procured, legal codes revised and enforced, and defense forces organized to defend the borders of their new states. These efforts were intended to underscore the true independence of these territories, building their internal legitimacy while at the same time hopefully gaining them the international recognition that would see them join the great community of nations.

However, in both cases, this declaration of independence was seen as a crisis of sovereignty by their host nations. In both instances, attempted negotiations failed, leading inevitably to military confrontations. Given that the secessionist states were just subdivisions of their host nations, they invariably lacked the military strength to effectively fight a decisive war against them. Instead these secessionist states attempted to fight a defensive conflict while waiting for international actors to recognize their independence and step in to negotiate an end to the conflict. However, in both cases their assumptions about the strength of their home states, the reaction of the international community, and the viability of civil secession as a whole would prove to be wrong. The precedents thus set within the family of African states and the global communities would shape all future secessionist and separatist conflicts on the continent.

The first of these civil secessions was Katanga in the newly independent Republic of the Congo. The former Belgian colony had had a precipitous dive into independence, with the Belgians doing little to develop their massive colony aside from its mineral-rich southeastern province. When elections were held in May of 1960, the populist leader Patrice Lumumba led his Mouvement National Congolais party to victory but managed to do little to bring together the fractious political factions within his nation. One of those members left out in the cold was the Katangan political leader Moise Tshombe, who saw little reason to compromise with the new government. His province of Katanga had always been administered separately from the rest of the Congo under the auspices of the Comité Spéciale du Katanga.[11] This separate administration had been due to the mineral riches of Katanga itself, with the province holding deposits of copper, cobalt, silver, platinum, uranium, and zinc. Given Tshombe's antipathy to the new Congolese government, the precedent of separate administration, and the tacit support of the Belgian government (which wished for continued access to the riches of Katanga), it was hardly surprising that Katanga would look for any opportunity for secession.

Such an opportunity presented itself less than a week after independence, when the Congolese army mutinied on July 4, 1960.[12] In the confusion of the mutiny and Lumumba's attempts to reimpose order, Tshombe declared Katanga an independent state on July 11. Tshombe assumed the presidency of the new state with the support of the Union Minière du Haute Katanga, the largest of the mining companies in the region. Tshombe quickly established a small state with vast mineral wealth and excellent relations with their former colonial power. With the aid of Belgian expatriates and technical advisors, Katanga quickly established a central bureaucracy and resumed its extractive industries. Just as importantly, with the aid of Belgian troops and the recruitment of mercenaries, the new state quickly established a potent defensive force to guard its borders until such time as Katanga might be recognized by the international community.

In the meantime, Lumumba's situation had become critical, with much of his political base fracturing and Katanga's secession creating an internal crisis that sparked other possible secessionist fronts. The Prime Minister appealed for support to the United Nations. Under the direction of Secretary General Dag Hjammarskold, the UN deployed a strong contingent of international peacekeepers with the intent of ending the bloodshed in the Congo and stabilizing its increasingly threatened government.[13] However, while the UN was willing to keep the peace, it initially was unwilling to take any action against Katanga despite Lumumba entreating it to do so. The increasing instability of the central government and the UN's unwillingness to do anything more than demand the removal of Belgians from Katanga eventually doomed Lumumba, whose appeal for additional aid to the Soviet Union led to his arrest by the commander of his army, Joseph Mobutu. Following an escape attempt, Lumumba was again captured, but this time flown to Katanga where he was tortured and murdered on Tshombe's orders.

However, it was this act that likely doomed Katanga. While there had been some attempts to bring Katanga back under the auspices of the Congolese government in a loose federal structure, this killing turned international opinion decisively against the Katangans. The United Nations' forces began a series of offensive actions against Katanga on the premise that the foreign mercenaries within its borders were in violation of international law and must be ejected. Katanga saw these actions as inimical to its sovereignty and resisted, leading to several sharp clashes between mercenaries and the UN.[14] In the midst of these confrontations, Dag Hammarskjöld's plane was shot down near the Katangan border and his death forced the UN's hand. The peacekeepers finally undertook decisive offensive operations and despite their involvement with Katanga the Belgians could no longer offer aid following such a heinous act. The final Katangan stronghold of Kolwezi was occupied on January 21, 1963 and Moise Tshombe fled the country. Following this action, Katangan secession was finally finished and the province was returned to the central control of the Congolese government.

The second and final civil secessionist attempt would occur a mere four years later. The Federal Republic of Nigeria had entered into independence better equipped than most of the former colonial possessions when it gained independence on October 1, 1960. Britain had established a well-staffed professional civil service and a military with a well-deserved reputation for professionalism. The country itself had a strong economy with oil reserves in the southeast and a historically flourishing coastal trade. The Federal Republic had even seen all three of its major ethnic groups join together to push for national independence despite the historic cleavages between the Northern Hausa, the Western Yoruba, and the Eastern Igbo.[15] However, within the first few years of independence, splits had begun opening within the nationalist coalition. The Hausa of the North were more populous but hewed towards traditional Islamic values whereas the Igbo were the smaller part but had far more modern Western ideas. The Yoruba and Igbo quickly became concerned that the Hausa would electorally dominate the new Federation, locking them out of the governance of the state. Conversely, these Hausa were concerned that the bureaucracy of the country, where much of the power lay, was dominated by their coalition partners. Their fears were particularly focused on the Igbo, who not only made up a large amount of the state administration but also made up a significant amount of the mercantile sector within the country.

Electoral dysfunction plagued the country during its first few years of independence, with each of the three major ethnic groups attempting to game the federal system to retain power. Violence finally erupted in 1966 when back-to-back coups rocked the young republic in January and July. The first was primarily driven by young officers in the Army, the majority of whom were Igbo.[16] The second was a counter-coup by Northern officers that brought Lieutenant Colonel Yakubu Gowon to power.[17] Both coups saw targeted violence, with the plotters of the first murdering prominent Northern and Western politicians and the plotters of the second killing many of the Igbo officers involved in the first.[18] In addition, the second coup triggered a series of pogroms in the North against the Igbo communities that had settled there, leading many to flee back to the East.

Following the second coup there was a brief period of uncertainty. The new Northern military ruler, General Yakubu Gowon, placed officers in charge of each of Nigeria's four major regions and made gestures towards unifying the reeling country. However, these gestures would not be enough and in May of 1967 the military ruler of the Eastern Region, Lieutenant Colonel Emeka Ojukwu, declared the Eastern Region the independent state of Biafra. Ojukwu and the other Biafrans' argument was simple: the Federal Republic of Nigeria was now under illegitimate governance and the Eastern Province had a historical precedent to independent administration. The first half of the argument was premised on the idea that Gowon's government was not an elected government as provided for within the Federal Constitution but had instead come to power in a coup. In addition, it had offered scant representation or protection to the Eastern region and thus had lost any legitimacy it might claim. The latter half originated in the British colonial governance of Nigeria, which had seen the North and South governed separately until 1914, when the two had been unified under an umbrella administration. However, the South and particularly the East had been developed and administered very differently to the North even following this union and as such there was a legal argument for this separation.

The new state of Biafra then continued down the path of statehood, providing services to its people, promulgating its new codes of law, developing its own military to defend its borders, and reaching out the rest of the international community for recognition and aid. Much like Katanga before it, Biafra placed its hopes in declaring itself a state and then defending that state long enough for the international community to force Nigeria to recognize it. This plan started out well when Biafra repelled the initial Nigerian invasion in July 1967. However, in a perhaps misguided strategy to force a reckoning with the Federal system, the Biafrans launched a strike westward in the hopes of driving the Yoruba-dominated Western Region into rebellion against the North as well. This strategy backfired when the lightning offensive failed and the Western Region then reaffirmed its allegiance to the Federal structure.[19] Now isolated, Biafra settled into the military defensive while the North and West mobilized their own armed forces to bring the secessionist state to heel.

Even before the failure of Biafra's westward offensive in September, the Nigerians had begun to drive inroads into Biafran territory. Beginning in July, the Federal forces captured Enugu and by October were threatening Onitsha and Calabar. The Biafrans mobilized what manpower they could and created massive workshops to produce the materials of war that they could not import. However, with the Federal capture of Port Harcourt in May 1968, Biafra was entirely surrounded and could only be resupplied by airlift.[20] At this point, the war was militarily unwinnable and the only remaining hope that the Biafrans had was for the intervention of the international community.

Unfortunately for Biafra, the international community did not respond as they had hoped. Britain and the United States wished to stay out of the conflict and quietly backed the Federal Government, strengthening their support once the oil-producing regions of the Niger Delta were captured.[21] France saw an opportunity to intervene in an oil-rich region and supplied arms, medical supplies, and food, but did not recognize Biafra.[22] Russia immediately backed the Federal Government. Within Africa, the only countries that recognized Biafra were Tanzania, Zambia, Gabon, and Ivory Coast. The latter two largely did so in support of French policies and the former two for humanitarian reasons.[23] However, with this meager international support it quickly became evident that external enforcement of independence would not be forthcoming.

Despite this denial of recognition, Biafra struggled on. International humanitarian aid was still delivered via airlift, and arms and war materials were smuggled into the embattled enclave. However, food was quickly depleted for the population left inside and the remaining Biafrans adopted a siege mentality. Their print media declared now that Biafra was an Igbo nation and that the Federal Army was intending to commit genocide. The struggle became desperate throughout 1969, but the Biafrans simply did not have the power to push the Nigerians away with the limited foreign aid they were receiving. Finally, in December 1969, the reorganized and rearmed Nigerians pressed through the thin Biafran perimeter and split the tiny enclave in two. The next month Ojukwu fled his declared country and the remaining Biafrans surrendered. The second and final civil secession in Africa came to an end in 1970.

However, while the civil secessions had been finally brought to a close, they set several precedents that would continue to resonate through the coming decades. The central concept behind both had been secession, an end goal that could only be accomplished politically and militarily with the support and recognition of the international community. However, whether from individual actors, regional organizations, or even the UN, this support and recognition were denied as a matter of policy. Both secessionist actors had largely assumed that the United Nations' guarantees of self-determination would support their claims. However, as the Congo crisis unfolded, the UN eventually set the precedent that secession was not a recognized political end goal. Instead, the UN enforced the practice that in such situations the recognized government must remain unitary. The UN would enshrine the right of territorial and political integrity for the existing, recognized government versus secession attempts within its Resolution 161.[24]

This same resolution also reinforced the UN's earlier call for the removal of all external military forces that were present without the consent of the recognized nation, which had begun with Resolutions 143 and 145. This combination of resolutions led to the removal of Belgian technical and military personnel from the Congo, effectively creating the precedent that foreign personnel supporting an unrecognized secessionist conflict, whether at the behest of another state or not, was not accepted. This precedent then broadly became part of the international consensus with the general understanding that states that were part of the UN would not create relations with these unrecognized armed political actors.

Finally, in terms of the continent of Africa, the Organization of African Unity (OAU) was formed in the very year that Katanga was toppled. The OAU was intended to bring together all the states of Africa and establish the aspirations, rules, and norms involved in the Pan-African community. While the charter called for African unity, the push for the liberation of the remaining colonial states, and beneficial trade relations, Article III spoke directly to the issues that the Congo was facing. Article III promised both 'non-interference in the internal affairs of states' and 'Respect for sovereignty and territorial integrity of each State'.[25] With this signing of the charter by every independent African state, there was now a continent-wide consensus against the recognition of secession or the support of secessionist actors.

While each of these precedents was set during or in the aftermath of the Congo Crisis, and thus might be attributed to Katanga's attempted secession, it was the Biafra conflict that saw them put into effect. When Biafra declared independence there was not a single country that rushed to recognize its sovereignty. The UN did not intervene as they had in Katanga because the recognized government of the Federal Republic of Nigeria did not request their aid, but without United Nations recognition Biafra could not even begin to ask for their help. In terms of independent states, as noted, only the French intervened to aid Biafra, but this was at the margins and without official recognition. All the other world powers, no matter their alignment in the Cold War, refused to recognize or offer aid to the state of Biafra outside of providing humanitarian assistance to its starving populace. Finally, in terms of African states, only four offered recognition and all largely bore the enmity of their fellow OAU member states for their recognition.[26]

In the end, these precedents set in the wake of the two civil secessions would essentially end the possibility of civil secessions in Africa. For this model of secession to succeed it required the intervention of the international community which would open the possibility either of military aid or diplomatic negotiations. However, this necessity for foreign intervention proved to be disastrous for the would-be secessionist states, as the international community not only refused to intervene in such conflicts but actively shaped international norms to prevent any future intervention. This closed the most obvious path towards secession, but as the next few decades would come to show, those dedicated to secession and separatism would prove resourceful in the pursuit of their goals.

## THE LONG WARS

At the same time that Katanga was busy fighting pitched battles to defend what it claimed were its independent borders, there were other conflicts ongoing that would bloom into secessionism and separatism. These conflicts tended not to draw the attention that the civil secessionists had done due to their method of pursuing their political separation. Where the civil secessionists had proclaimed their independence and fought to maintain the territorial integrity of the state they had declared, these parallel efforts were more flexible. Over the next several decades these wars would be waged not for territory but for social and political legitimacy, and took the approach not of declaring a state and fighting to maintain it, but of fighting a war to gain a state. These would be what might be characterized as the long wars, as they took decades of slow-burning conflict to build parallel capacity and eventually force the recognition of their host.

These long wars took the longer struggles of global liberation as their model for the structure and pursuit of independence. Prior to the 1960s, the decolonization struggles of Vietnam and Algeria and the political struggle of the Chinese Civil War had offered a pathway forward with minimal formal state organization and even less outside support. What these models instead showed was the path of using a protracted struggle to raise political awareness and legitimacy, which would help form a mass movement for the political purpose of liberation or secession.[27] In turn, these mass movements would translate not only into military capacity, but also allow the creation of an administrative organization and a political framework. In the end, these political, military, and administrative structures would allow for the creation of what would essentially be a ready-made state if victory were achieved.

It was of course through this process of creating a state that the mass movements would also pursue their ultimate goal of secession. While the civil secessionists had looked beyond their borders for international recognition of their independence, those behind the long wars instead took the view that the only possibility of recognition was through their host state. This daunting task was undertaken with the understanding that no African state would willingly allow a subnational group to separate from its sovereign territory. This meant that the host state would need to be compelled to do so. However, the host state had direct advantages that the secessionist and separatist movements could never hope to match. The host state had access to the vast resources of a formal state, could trade on the international markets for arms and war material, and could negotiate with its neighbors to cut off any succor for its secessionist foe. To nullify these, the secessionist movements took on a long-term strategy, one that could weather the strengths of the host state while building their own capacity to resist.

The model of these long wars was also the first of them to be successful: Eritrea. While initially an Italian colony dating to the 1889 Treaty of Uccialli, in the wake of the Second World War the UN was uncertain what to do with the small territory on the shore of the Red Sea. While it was adjacent to the Empire of Ethiopia, its citizens argued that they had never been formally part of that state. Conversely, Emperor Haile Selassie of Ethiopia argued that historically Eritrea had been claimed by his state and that in the postwar settlement that territory should properly revert to the Crown. The UN eventually split the difference, declaring Eritrea a separate republic under the federal control of the Ethiopian Crown in 1950.[28] However, federation under an absolute monarchy proved to be an unstable system, and over the next decade Ethiopia dismantled most of the governmental structures of Eritrea and placed it under the direct control of the Ethiopian government.[29]

Ethiopian rule was not necessarily pleasant for much of the Eritrean population and by 1961 the first shots had been fired in what would be the long war for Eritrean secession from Ethiopia.[30] Initially disjointed, much of the resistance to Ethiopian rule found its way under the flag of the Eritrean Liberation Front (ELF) by 1965, and the new politico-military group was waging an effective guerrilla campaign against the Ethiopian forces. The ELF formed five regional commands to coordinate its struggle against the Ethiopians over the next five years, but found itself largely at a stalemate due to factional infighting and political divisions between the regional commands.[31] Already at the brink of suppression, the ELF splintered in 1970 into the ELF and the Eritrean People's Liberation Front (EPLF). While the ELF retained its identity as a nationalist guerrilla force, the EPLF took on a more revolutionary cast, looking to transform the economic, social, and political underpinnings of Eritrea. While the two Fronts remained largely hostile to one another, both carried on their struggle against Haile Selassie's forces. With the war now entering its second decade, the Ethiopian forces had weakened and turned to harsher measures, drawing more support to the two guerrillas.

The weakness of the Ethiopian state finally caused a crisis and in 1974 Selassie was overthrown by Marxist revolutionaries calling themselves the Derg.[32] During the confusion of this overthrow, the two liberation Fronts declared a ceasefire and began to recruit and implement their plans within the regions of Eritrean they controlled. The ELF proposed modest reforms, drawing mild support, while the EPLF offered land redistribution, education, health care, and even an expansion of women's rights.[33] Over the next four years both fronts made advances, with the Ethiopians being largely pushed out of Eritrean territory aside from scattered garrisons in Asmara, Massawa, and Barentu. However, during this period, the transformative programs of the EPLF gained them significantly more legitimacy and popular support than their rivals the ELF. This would stand them in good stead during the hard years beginning in 1978.

Starting in 1977 the shifting Cold War dynamics in the Horn saw Ethiopia become the recipient of massive Soviet military aid. This infusion of weaponry and expertise allowed Ethiopia to rebuild massive forces to both drive away their Somali adversaries in the Ogaden and direct powerful operations against the Eritreans in 1978. The offensives that followed, involving over 100,000 Ethiopian troops equipped with armor and artillery, swept the ELF forces away while forcing the more flexible EPLF to retreat to more defensible positions.[34] While the veteran EPLF guerrillas bloodied the Ethiopians, over the next two years they were driven back to their mountainous bastion of Nacfa, where they continued fighting an irregular struggle against the Derg's forces. However, despite being bowed, the EPLF was unbroken and it continued to carry out and support the social and political programs within Eritrea despite the Ethiopian occupation. Over the next several years the EPLF forces in Nacfa fought off several powerful offensives while guerrillas in the countryside bled the Ethiopians dry, even through the terrible famines that struck the Horn in 1984–1985.[35]

By 1987 the EPLF had regained enough strength to launch several counter-offensives against the weakened Derg forces, eventually inflicting a crushing defeat on the Ethiopians at the 1988 Battle of Afabet.[36] As the Eritrean soldiers advanced, they were welcomed by the social and political organizations that EPLF had continued to foster within their state. In addition, these structures had allowed for the fostering of other domestic liberation fronts within Ethiopian, such as the Tigrayan People's Liberation Front (TPLF). In the late 1980s, the TPLF and other domestic armed groups formed an alliance called the Ethiopian Peoples Revolutionary Democratic Front (EPDRF). Although the EPLF had a fractious relationship with the TPLF and other members of the EPDRF, they joined forces in a final offensive against the Derg forces. By 1991, the EPLF had liberated Asmara and Massawa and aided in the capture of Addis Ababa, which placed the EPDRF in control of Ethiopia.[37] In return for the aid of the EPLF, the EPDRF offered a plebiscite to the Eritrean populace, a UN-overseen popular referendum that in 1993 decisively chose secession and independence. The now independent country of Eritrea was governed by the very social structures that had sustained the EPLF's long war; the political structures, the provision of health care, the land-tenure regime, and the educational administration. The Eritreans had built their state in the process of winning its freedom.

The other major example of the long wars comes from Sudan, which saw similar dynamics to those in Eritrea. The South had been administered separately under the Anglo-Egyptian government since the late nineteenth century, eventually having its own legal regime, military forces, and bureaucracy.[38] With the beginning of decolonization in 1955, the North of the country quickly set about politically dominating the South, replacing the British officials with heavy-handed Northern administrators. The South had little representation in the government of Sudan and all senior ranks of the now-unified military went to Northern officers.[39] This state of affairs proved untenable for the South, and within months the Southern military had mutinied against Northern control. While the mutiny was put down, many of the soldiers fled into the bush to continue the struggle. By 1963, these soldiers had named themselves the Land and Freedom Army, although they would more commonly be called the Anya-nya.[40] The Anya-nya carried out guerrilla raids against the Northerners garrisoning the South and quickly the conflict turned into a pattern of raid and reprisal within the fractious South.

This military resistance was paralleled by political resistance, as a series of Southern political groups rose to challenge Northern rule. First the Sudan African Closed Districts National Union (SACDNU) and later the Sudan African National Union (SANU) rose to try and create a unified political front, but dealt with constant splintering. The North fared little better as the initial independence government of Premier Abdullah Khalil was swept away in a military coup led by Brigadier Abboud in 1958, and then Abboud himself was toppled in 1964 and replaced by Premier al-Khatim al-Khalifa who in turn lost his base and was replace in 1965 by Mohammed Ahmed Maghoub. With both sides dealing with political turmoil, there was little chance for the advancement of the conflict on either side. The South continued its decentralized raids while the North attempted to tamp down the political and military chaos in the South. It was not until 1969–1970 that the civil war would enter a new phase.

In 1969, the Northern government of Maghoub was overthrown in a bloodless coup by Colonel Gaafar Mohammed al-Numeiry, who wished to compel the South to come to the bargaining table. The following year, the splintered Southern opposition was finally welded together by a fighter named Joseph Lagu, who had gained a monopoly on the flow of Israeli arms and ammunition into the South.[41] Using this monopoly, he managed to coerce many of the armed fronts to join his faction, which eventually unified the South under the banner of the Southern Sudan Liberation Movement (SSLM). With this unified command and a steady flow of war material, Lagu carried the struggle forward and inflicted significant damage on the Northern forces in a series of raids throughout 1971. This unitary control also allowed Lagu to finally form a central administration for the resistance movements, allowing for a degree of political, social, and economic cohesion amongst the armed groups of the South.[42] This project was just coming to fruition in 1972 when al-Numeiry's offer of a ceasefire reached his headquarters.

The ceasefire led to negotiations in Addis Ababa between the still fragile SSLM and a Northern government tired of war. While the Anya-nya and members of the SSLM had wanted secession from the North, the Northern government was categorically against the splitting of the nation. The SSLM would settle for the next best thing, separatism under the control of the local administration which had been being developed. The South would have regional autonomy but in return remained limited in the central government in Khartoum. In addition, the armed forces would be steadily integrated, with the unified army, absorbing elements of the South's armed forces but with the central government largely retaining control of these forces. However, despite the obvious flaws of this agreement, at this point both sides were willing to sign to end the conflict and in 1972 the First Sudan Civil War ended.

The Addis Ababa agreement would buy 11 years of peace, but in that time the weakness of the agreement would become manifest. The South, already feeling marginalized, found its lack of control in Khartoum left it out of the country's major decisions. While the North increasingly expanded its irrigation capacity and mechanized its agriculture, the South remained moribund and economically backward. Beyond this, the integration of the military had still left many of the Southern soldiers marginalized and the Southern officers who had been accepted into the new armed forces found themselves distrusted.[43] Fights often broke out between the Northern and Southern units, leading to armed tension throughout the country. While autonomy and accommodation had brought the South peace, it had brought them little else that they had wanted when they initially went to war.

Beginning in 1983, Southern military units began deserting, beginning renewed resistance to the Sudanese government. The Commandant of the Sudanese military academy, a Southerner named John Garang, travelled to one of the troubled military units, claiming he would calm the difficult soldiers. Instead he led the unit and its sister unit into a mutiny, beginning the larger conflict that would engulf the South for the next three decades.[44] Garang, using the troops under his control and connections with the Derg's Ethiopia, managed to weld together the disparate armed groups in the South. While these forces had been fighting under the general sobriquet of Anya-nya II, Garang's new unified command was now called the Sudanese People's Liberation Movement (SPLM) with its armed wing called the Sudanese People's Liberation Army (SPLA). Having been part of the original Anya-nya, Garang was determined to avoid the loose structure and constant divisions that had marked that organization. Instead, the SPLM was quickly structured as a disciplined and harsh centralized organization, with Garang using his access to military materials as the carrot to his armed forces' stick.[45] This unity of command allowed Garang to quickly establish results far in excess of those of his predecessors.

Under the SPLM, numerous administrative centers were created in the South, restarting the social and political transformation that had only partially occurred over the previous decade. In addition, the SPLA reached out to the West and East of Sudan, attempting to spark more regional resistance to the Northern government. While Numeiry's government increased its counter-insurgency operations to try and tamp down this resistance, the brutality of his soldiers and their related militias just caused a more general conflagration. By 1986, the harsh measures of the central government saw Numeiry overthrown and replaced by Sadiq al-Mahdi, the leader of the Islamist Umma Party. Unfortunately, even this did not halt the spread of resistance to the Khartoum government and by 1989 the central government was willing to negotiate with the increasingly powerful SPLM government and its various regional allies. However, while victory appeared in their grasp, two separate occurrences would again shift the strategic balance.

The first was that in 1989 Sadiq al-Mahdi was overthrown in a coup led by Omar al-Bashir. This coup halted the peace process and caused general chaos within the North. Without a partner to offer terms, the SPLM and its increasingly independent allies found themselves at a halt. Additional offensive military action seemed counter-productive, but the unity of purpose of the allies was unraveling during this period of inaction. The second was the ongoing collapse of the Derg regime in Ethiopia. The Derg had been the central supplier of arms and war materiel to Garang, and in turn these arms and materiel had been what allowed him to keep control of the more far-flung or fractious factions under his direction. However, by 1990, the pipeline of Derg weapons was closing off as that government faced several decisive defeats at the hands of the EPLF and the EPRDF. Without these arms at his command, Garang lost unified control of his forces. Beginning in 1991, several splinter factions emerged, many of them taking more effort to try and overthrown Garang than fight the North.[46] These internecine conflicts would continue throughout the early 1990s, and the North often found itself supporting several of these splinter factions as spoilers towards Garang's forces.

Despite these setbacks, Garang's faction, called SPLM-Torit and later SPLM-Mainstream, managed to weather the storm largely thanks to its established administrative zones in the South. While the SPLM-Nasir (later SPLM-United) eventually began running out of steam and relying more on Northern support, Garang's forces rallied within their home territories, where the social and economic transformation had made several safe zones. By 1996 the SPLM-United had failed in a rebranding and then splintered further, with most of the splinters finding their way back to the SPLM-Mainstream camp. By 2000, the Southern forces had largely reconstituted themselves under the stable banner of Garang's SPLM.

This would prove to be excellent timing, as al-Bashir's government had found itself increasing isolated since 1991. With the collapse of the Soviet

Union and the subsequent end of the Cold War, the USA had seen little gain in continuing to support the Islamic government in Sudan.[47] Instead, the USA had seen it as far more preferable to see peace in the Sudan and they began to exert firm pressure on al-Bashir to draw this long-running conflict to an end. Although the conflict continued for some time, usually through the North supporting Southern splinter groups, by 1994 the Khartoum government had largely accepted the principles of Southern self-determination and by 2000 it had begun drafting the documents necessary for the plebiscite in the South. Finally, on January 9, 2005 an agreement was signed, one that demarcated the spheres of the North and South and set the date for a plebiscite on secession in 2011. Six years later, that plebiscite was carried out under the auspices of the UN, and the South formally seceded from the North.

Both of these examples of long wars are exceptional for a singular reason—they succeeded. Both Eritrea and South Sudan managed to achieve their political goal of a separate, recognized sovereignty from their host country. This stands out in stark contrast to the cases of the civil secessions, both of which not only failed but seemed to close the doors of secession behind them. As such, it is important to discuss how these succeeded despite the barriers put in place following the failures of the civil secessions.

In terms of the lack of recognition or support from individual states, the precedent essentially held. Neither South Sudan nor Eritrea was recognized by an outside power. While the Eritrean Liberation Front would receive some help attaining arms and supplies from Islamic countries early on, and arms from Israel and Ethiopia would be decisive for the South Sudanese groups, this was not that different to what had been seen before. Katanga had received arms and aid from Belgium during its secessionist attempt and Biafra was sustained in large part due to smuggled French arms.

Furthermore, the precedents binding the OAU saw less disruption than during the Biafran conflict. While Tanzania, Zambia, Gabon, and Ivory Coast had recognized the breakaway Eastern Region of Nigeria, no African state recognized or offered open aid to these participants in the long wars. In fact, aside from the illicit arms that Ethiopia was providing to the South Sudanese, there was remarkably little relation between any African states and the long-wars secessionist movements.

This leaves the United Nations, which played a unique role in both of these conflicts. In both cases it was the UN that oversaw the plebiscites that conferred secession and then welcomed these new sovereign states into the international community. As such, the UN was the key player in the formal attainment of the secessionist goal. It is, however, the nature of this intervention that is the crux of the different outcomes between the long wars and the civil secessions. In both long-wars cases, the UN intervened decisively for the secession because the host state invited them to do so; in turn, this invitation was the result of the military victory of the secessionist groups.

Ultimately, then, the question concerns how the long-wars secessionist states achieved victory where the civil secessions did not. The answer is rather simple: the strategy adopted by Eritrea and South Sudan could prevail despite the crippling lack of international recognition or large-scale foreign aid, whereas that of Katanga and Biafra could not. Given the advantages in manpower, materiel, organization, and resources, the host state invariably could marshal almost overwhelming strength against a secessionist enclave. As such, once recognition and therefore aid was denied to Katanga and Biafra, their conventional approach to guarding territory was doomed to failure. However, the EPLF and SPLM both took an approach reminiscent of liberation fronts. Instead of facing the forces of their host state directly, they fought a guerrilla campaign to weaken them while building their own administrative and logistics hubs to sustain the fight, even in the absence of outside aid. This allowed them to carry on the fight until such time as the balance of power tipped in their favor and they could carry our more decisive actions. Even when the balance tipped back in favor of the host, as seen in Eritrea in 1978, the EPLF could retreat back to its safe, organized strongholds to continue the struggle. Given the weakness of the postcolonial African state and the potent organizing done by the secessionist Fronts, eventually both forced a tipping point and seized victory from their state-based opponents.

## THE NEW WAVE

With the end of the Cold War following the 1989 revolutions and the 1991 break-up of the USSR, there was a dramatic revision of the global order that would have wide-ranging implications for phenomena of secession in Africa. Before the end of the Cold War, secession in Africa had largely been seen as an impossibility. The UN and the OAU had both set their firm precedents against such activity, and while at the time the Eritreans, South Sudanese, and many others were in the midst of their struggles, there was no perceivable positive ending for these combatants. However, the fall of the Soviet Union and the reordering of the global community triggered a series of alterations that would change the strategic calculus for would-be separatists in Africa and set off a new wave of conflict.

The first of these alterations was the fracturing of many of the Eastern Bloc states in the wake of the Cold War and the welcoming of their successors into the global community. While several of the post-communist states such as Poland and Bulgaria were brought into the new capitalist world order without territorial alteration, other states underwent massive transformations. Czechoslovakia was split into the Czech Republic and Slovakia in 1992, and Yugoslavia broke into seven successor states in 1990. With the maps being redrawn in Europe following the dissolution of the USSR and the broader communist bloc, this offered marginalized groups in Africa the hope that their borders might prove mutable as well.

The second major alteration involved the fracturing of the USSR proper, which began during the same period. The USSR had encompassed the territories of the former Russian Empire, which had expanded to include a multitude of ethnicities during the nineteenth century. During the break-up of the USSR, these populations were encouraged to reclaim their states from Russian control. This was an explicit call to reform what were termed nation-states, those states that were built to specifically offer services and protection to a particular nation or ethnicity. In the USSR this process achieved the creation of an Uzbekistan for the Uzbeks, Kazakhstan for the Kazakhs, and several other nation-states for the former Soviet minority groups. However, this fostering of nation-states was a departure from the Cold War era, where the excesses of nationalism before and during the Second World War had been perceived as the driver of the worst of the atrocities committed and perhaps even as the main cause of the war. As such, in the decades following that conflict there had been a conscious decision within the international community to deny the formation of specifically ethnically derived states and instead foster ethnically diverse ones.

However, within the African context, the 'nation', that is informal associations of ethno-linguistic groups, had generally always existed in competition with the state. These groups had often been able to form their own legitimate authority within the state, providing a degree of services or protection, but had never been able to take on the functional recognition as a state. The fear of ethnically based states had essentially allowed for the suppression of any state ambitions that these groups might have held. However, with the acceptance of ethnically based states in the wake of the collapse of the USSR, these groups now felt there was a precedent being set. Ethno-nation states were now no longer a taboo within the global context and as such the nationalist ambitions of several sub-national groups were reignited.

Finally, and perhaps most critically, the end of the Cold War directly disrupted the governing capacity of the majority of states in Africa. As noted earlier, most states in Africa had not emerged from colonialism fully developed, with many lacking effective administrative apparatuses or large and professional security services. This administrative underdevelopment was exacerbated due to economic underdevelopment, with the extractive economies of these states being both relatively poor and subject to severe global shocks. However, due to the fierce rivalries of the Cold War, many African states gained significant support from either the First or Second World, thus allowing a degree of technical assistance, material support, and economic buttressing to be applied to their weak state structures. This meant that while the states themselves remained relatively weak, they were able to maintain their core functions with the assistance of their international patrons.

With the end of the Cold War, the support from either pole effectively ended. For those powers that had largely aligned themselves with the communist bloc, there simply were no patrons left to offer assistance. Countries like Ethiopia that had relied heavily on Soviet aid found their state functions failing and their governments crumbling. Even those states like Angola that were Marxist in alignment but had significant resources found themselves diminished in their capacity. For those countries that were aligned with the USA and other capitalist powers, the aid did not necessarily end but it did change form. While the capitalist powers were willing to support illegitimate regimes like Mobutu's in Zaire during their proxy struggle with the USSR, now they wished to see democratic reform and a more free market system. These states, so long dependent on more direct aid, found themselves caught in the lurch, with diminished capacity right at the moment when questions about the future of sovereignty were being opened.

These factors combined to help drive a wave of new insurgencies against the states of Africa. The weak states of Africa combined with strong sub-national groups and the possibility of revising the political order of Africa created a new dynamic context that saw the rise of new armed groups devoted to taking over the government of their state, seizing local power, or even forming their own new state. Especially with the states being weakened in the wake of the Cold War, smaller and less organized groups could still manage to sustain a longer and more effective conflict than they might previously have been able to.

Admittedly, with the questions of the new political order and the diminished capacity of many states, there was one alteration in the end goals of many conflicts. While during the previous decades it was far more common for armed groups to push for a secessionist outcome, with the new armed groups it was just as common to see armed force as a negotiation for local autonomy, which might have been unthinkable previously. Simply put, the post-Cold War African states did not necessarily have the capacity to effectively put down their local aggressors and so found themselves negotiating local solutions more than previously. While many of these conflicts are still underway in places such as the Casamance in Senegal and Cabinda in Angola,[48] there are several other regions that have seen secessionist conflicts begin and end—notably Mali and Somaliland.

The conflict in Mali was waged between the nomadic Kel Tamasheq of northern Mali and the state government, which was largely based in the South near the Niger bend. The Kel Tamasheq, commonly called the Tuareg, had always had difficulties with the central government.[49] They had been administered by the French separately from the African populations and felt culturally superior to the Bambara and Mande populations whom they had enslaved for centuries.[50] With the end of colonialism the Kel Tamasheq had suddenly found themselves suborned to the Malian government despite assurances by the French that there would be a separate Saharan zone for them and the Bidan populations.[51] The central government tried to conscript their young men into development projects and to tax their trade across the Sahara. A brief nationalist guerrilla struggle broke out in 1962, but there were never many fighters and by 1964 the resistance had generally been suppressed.[52] While many of the Kel Tamasheq population fled across the desert to Algeria and Libya, there remained a considerable number of them in Mali and over the next two decades many drifted back as conditions allowed. However, the Malian government never managed to effectively integrate members of the Kel Tamasheq and they suffered terribly in several droughts and famines that occurred in 1972–1974 and 1984–1985.

This marginalization was not forgotten and in 1990 a civil war began with the Kel Tamasheq in the North attacking the city of Gao.[53] This began a series of hit-and-run attacks where the Kel Tamasheq would raid the cities bordering the North and the Malian army would attempt to send columns to pacify them. Reprisals were taken on both sides and despite initial efforts at a ceasefire in 1992, the conflict carried on. Interestingly, the 1992 ceasefire included the creation of the Kidal Region in Mali, which would be self-governing and largely inhabited by the Kel Tamasheq. Despite another devastating raid on the city of Gao in 1994, the Kel Tamasheq were unable to decisively defeat the Malian armed forces nor were the Malians able to effectively stop the Kel Tamasheq. Finally, in 1995, moderates on both sides negotiated a peace and the Kel Tamasheq was largely given autonomy in the North and offered additional connections to the resources of the state. While some groups still wished for their own Kel Tamasheq state in relation to a parallel revolt that was occurring in Niger, the peace deal was signed in 1996 and this separatism was largely accepted for the moment.[54]

As for Somaliland, it retains a very unusual pedigree. While born in conflict, its secession occurred almost by default and, even more strangely, its secession was from Africa's first nation-state. The territory now known as Somaliland was a strip of the Red Sea coast that was inhabited predominantly by the Isaaq clan family of the Somalis. During the Scramble for Africa it was conquered by the British, who let the Isaaq traditional leaders administer most of the interior while they retained the coast for control of the Red Sea traffic. With the end of the Second World War, the UN combined this British Somaliland with the larger Italian Somaliland to create Somalia, the first nation-state of Africa in 1960. General Mohamed Siad Barre seized control of this unified state in 1969 in a coup, quickly establishing fervent pan-Somalism as his central binding ideology.[55] While historically the seven major clan families of Somalia had had a fractious and sometimes violent relationship, Barre's regime attempted to keep these groups together by focusing on their unified Somali identity and the Somali territories that still lay outside their state. The prime example of these territories was the Ogaden in Ethiopia, which had been conquered by the Ethiopian empire in the nineteenth century. To maintain his control in the state, Siad Barre launched a war to retake the Ogaden from Ethiopia in 1977.[56]

Due to the currents of the Cold War, the Ogaden War would prove to be a disaster for Barre's Somalia. Although the major military operations were completed in 1978 following the USSR's abandonment of its client state

Somalia in favor of the Derg regime in Ethiopia, Barre kept up desultory operations until 1988.[57] At this point, his army largely depleted, his overseas support gone, and with increasing opposition by the clans within Somalia, Siad Barre attempted to end the war and maintain control of his country. However, at this point the clan-driven opposition to his rule had become too organized and too coordinated and in 1991 he was overthrown by a coalition of clan-affiliated armed fronts. For those clans of the southern regions, such as the Hawiye and the Darod, the power vacuum led to an armed struggle that eventually caused the southern region to collapse into a vicious civil war and humanitarian disaster.

For the Isaaq the results were quite different. At the outset of the armed struggle against Siad Barre, their armed forces from the Somali National Movement swept into their territories in former British Somaliland and quickly took control of the major city of Hargeisa and the port at Berbera.[58] Although the late 1980s had seen fierce struggles against the forces of Siad Barre, this new offensive met little organized resistance. By May, the country was mostly under the control of the SNM and the Isaaq clan. With the rest of the state of Somalia falling rapidly into a civil war, the Isaaq declared their territory the new state of Somaliland during a grand conference of the clan leaders in mid-May of 1991.[59] While Somaliland would continue to face internal challenges from some of the marginal clan group militias, by the middle of 1993 there had already been a transition in their government from President Abdirahman Ahmed Ali Tuur to Muhammed Haji Ibrahim Egal, and the security of the state had been improved through negotiations between various militias.

Interestingly, while the rest of Somalia has still struggled to create a unified government, Somaliland has remained generally pacific and stable and remains autonomous to this day. In 2003 they held their first full election for president and continue to use a bicameral parliament to decide most legislative questions.[60] In addition, they have used their access to the strategic port of Berbera to forge economic ties with the other Red Sea nations and also serve as an exit port for Ethiopian goods. However, despite all of this, Somaliland remains an unrecognized state and to the present day much of the global community insists on maintaining the federal government in Mogadishu as the only legitimate government for all of Somalia.

In both these cases, the dynamics of the post-Cold War wave of secessions can be examined. For both cases it was the weakness of the host state that allowed the secessionist/separatist struggles to gain a foothold and even succeed despite small numbers of combatants and relatively short conflicts. In Somaliland's case it was not just the weakness of Somalia, but that state's collapse following the overthrow of the Siad Barre regime. In addition, in the case of Mali, it can be seen that a secessionist group can find it far more useful to negotiate separatism with its weak host state. For this, the armed groups can gain autonomy and oftentimes additional concessions, such as additional government employment or aid like that the Kel Tamasheq were offered.

However, there is also one more as yet undiscussed characteristic of these conflicts: their uncertain ends. While Somaliland currently has its unrecognized secession, without that recognition it has only a small amount of international legitimacy. Indeed, as Somalia's Federal Government continues to gain capacity, there will likely be calls for Somaliland to rejoin the nation of Somalia. Under such circumstances they might maintain significant autonomy, but there would still be less local control than they currently have. Even more uncertain is Mali. While the moderates in the Kel Tamasheq community accepted autonomy and aid in 1996, many in the Kel Tamasheq community did not. Newer splinter groups emerged such as the May 23, 2006 Democratic Alliance for Change, which was formed of former combatants of the 1990 war who were unsatisfied with its outcome. Beginning in 2007, a new conflict erupted in Mali and Niger as Kel Tamasheq in both states fought for more representation within their states and more recognition of their traditional rights. While these conflicts both continued at best sporadically, beginning in 2012 a new wave of combatants, armed with weapons drawn from Libyan stockpiles, reignited the general conflict in northern Mali, this time calling for the direct creation of a Kel Tamasheq state in the Sahara called Azawad.[61] Like these conflicts, many of the other ethnically based secessions of the new wave have uncertain ends, as the states of Africa are still attempting to build capacity and the political order on the continent is by no means concrete.

## CONCLUSION

Secession and separatism in postcolonial Africa have not been especially common occurrences. Although the first decade of independence saw several secession attempts begin, these were seemingly suppressed very quickly and international precedent apparently made them impossible. For most African states, the idea of a Katanga or Biafra was a nightmare, yet one that passed quickly as the international community refused to recognize these attempts and the OAU enshrined territorial integrity within its charter. However, despite the concept of secession seeming to be dead, after thirty years of conflict combatants in Eritrea managed to seize their own sovereignty and those in South Sudan soon followed. What had seemed an impossibility had now been achieved and with the post-Cold War world being reordered, new struggles for secession, autonomy, and irredentism are again in progress on the continent. While no other new state has yet been recognized, in this brave new world it seems only a matter of time before one is.

# NOTES

1. Much of this discussion is covered in Basil Davidson's excellent *The Black Man's Burden: Africa and the Curse of the Nation State*. See Basil Davidson, *The Black Man's Burden: Africa and the Curse of the Nation State* (New York: Three Rivers Press, 1997).

2. These attributes are discussed at length in Ricardo Rene Laremont, "Borders, States, and Nationalism," in *Borders, Nationalism, and the African State*, ed. Ricardo Rene Laremont (London: Lynne Rienner Publishers, 2005), 5.

3. This is most often discussed as the Gatekeeper State, as noted in Frederick Cooper's *Africa Since 1940: The Past of the Present*. See Frederick Cooper, *Africa Since 1940: The Past of the Present* (New York: Cambridge University Press, 2002), 141.

4. For a broader perspective on the Maji Maji Revolt, see James Giblin, and Jamie Monson, eds., *Maji Maji: Lifting the Fog of War* (Leiden: Brill Academic Press, 2010).

5. For a broader perspective on the 1906 Zulu Revolt, see Thompson Paul S., "The Zulu Rebellion of 1906: The Collusion of Bambatha and Dinuzulu," *The International Journal of African Historical Studies* 36, no. 3 (2003): 533–57.

6. This also tracks with the analytic framework used on African insurgencies by Christopher Clapham. See Christopher Clapham, "Introduction: Analyzing African Insurgencies," in *African Guerrillas*, ed. Christopher Clapham (Bloomington: Indiana University Press, 1998), 6.

7. The right of self-determination is specifically noted in Article I, Chapter I of the United Nations Charter. See "Chapter I, Charter of the United Nations," accessed March 9, 2017, http://www.un.org/en/sections/un-charter/chapter-i/.

8. For example Tanganyika, a League of Nations Trustee Territory was denied self-determination until the era of decolonization.

9. Douglas H. Johnson, *The Root Causes of Sudan's Civil Wars* (Bloomington: Indiana University Press, 2003), 10–11.

10. The idea of a civil state is expounded on at length in Philip White, "Globalization and the Mythology of the 'Nation State'," in *Global History: Interactions Between the Universal and the Local*, ed. A.G. Hopkins (New York: Palgrave Macmillan, 2006), 257–84.

11. Jules Gérard-Libois, *Katanga Secession*, trans. Rebecca Young (Madison: University of Wisconsin Press, 1966), 316

12. Ernest Lefever and Wynfred Joshua, *United Nations Peacekeeping in the Congo, 1960–1964, Volume 2: Full Text* (Washington, DC: Brookings Institution, 1966), 14.

13. Georges Abi-Saab, *The United Nations Operation in the Congo, 1960–1964* (New York: Oxford University Press, 1978), 14. The particular resolution deploying UN forces was Resolution 143.

14. Conor Cruise O'Brien, *To Katanga and Back: A UN Case History* (London: Hutchinson, 1962), 252–88.

15. For an accessible source on the formation of colonial and postcolonial Nigeria, see Sir Rex Niven, *The War of Nigerian Unity, 1967–1970* (Ibadan: Evans Brothers, 1971).

16. John de St. Jorre, *The Nigerian Civil War* (London: Hodder and Stoughton, 1972), 31.
17. Ibid., 69.
18. Ibid., 60 and 69.
19. Zdenek Cervenka, *The Nigerian Civil War, 1967–1970* (Frankfurt am Main: Bernard and Grafe, 1971), 57.
20. Ibid., 63.
21. de St. Jorre, *The Nigerian Civil War*, 181–84.
22. Ibid., 210.
23. Ibid., 193–96.
24. Resolution 161 effectively outlawed secession and also authorized extremely aggressive action on the part of the UN to enforce integrity.
25. "OAU Charter, article III, Sects. 2 and 3," accessed March 9, 2017, https://www.au.int/web/sites/default/files/treaties/7759-file-oau_charter_1963.pdf.
26. For example, Tanzania's later appeals for OAU support against Idi Amin's Uganda were generally rejected by the Nigerians, who still held the recognition against Biafra against Julius Nyerere's government.
27. This was most effectively discussed in Mao Tse-Tung's classic "On Protracted War." See Mao Tse-Tung, "On Protracted War" in *Mao Tse-Tung on Revolution and War*, ed. M. Rejai (Garden City, NY: Anchor Books, 1970), 271–79.
28. Richard Sherman, *Eritrea: The Unfinished Revolution* (New York, NY: Praeger Publishing, 1980), 23.
29. Ibid., 29.
30. Dan Connell, *Against All Odds: A Chronicle of the Eritrean Revolution* (Trenton, NJ: Red Sea Press, 1993), 58.
31. Sherman, *Eritrea*, 74.
32. *Derg* is the Amharic word for "Committee," reflecting the initial character of the regime, although it was swiftly dominated by Colonel Mengistu Haile Miriam who purged most dissent.
33. Connell, *Against All Odds*, 38–39 and 109–26.
34. Ibid., 160–61.
35. The best discussion of the famines and their effects are in Alex DeWaal, *Evil Days: 30 Years of War and Famine in Ethiopia.* (New York: Human Rights Watch, 1991).
36. Connell, *Against All Odds: A Chronicle of the Eritrean Revolution*, 228.
37. DeWaal, *Evil Days*, 272–73.
38. Douglas H Johnson, *The Root Causes of Sudan's Civil Wars* (Bloomington; Kampala: Indiana University Press; Fountain Publishers, 2003), 10–11.
39. Scopas Sekwat Poggo, *The First Sudanese Civil War Africans, Arabs, and Israelis in the Southern Sudan, 1955–1972* (Basingstoke: Palgrave Macmillan, 2011), 37; and Dunstan M. Wai, *The African-Arab Conflict in the Sudan* (New York: Africana Pub. Co., 1981), 74.
40. Ibid., 92.
41. Robert O Collins, *A History of Modern Sudan* (New York: Cambridge Univ. Press, 2008), 103.
42. Ibid., 106.
43. Johnson, *The Root Causes of Sudan's Civil Wars*, 41.

44. Philippa Scott, "The Sudan Peoples' Liberation Movement (SPLM) and Liberation Army (SPLA)," *Review of African Political Economy* no. 33 (August 1, 1985): 70.
45. Douglas H. Johnson, "The Sudan People's Liberation Army and the Problem of Factionalism," in *African Guerrillas*, ed. Christopher Clapham (Oxford: James Currey, 1998), 61.
46. Ibid., 63.
47. Johnson, *The Root Causes of Sudan's Civil Wars*, 102.
48. However, both of these conflicts have been intermittently fought by their populations since independence.
49. The name Kel Tamasheq means "The people who speak Tamasheq" and is generally accepted as the most inclusive and accurate name for this group. See Jean Sebastian Lecocq, *Disputed Desert: Decolonisation, Competing Nationalisms and Tuareg Rebellions in Northern Mali* (Leiden; Boston: Brill, 2010), 2.
50. See Priscilla Ellen Starratt, "Tuareg Slavery and Slave Trade," *Slavery & Abolition* 2, no. 2 (1981): 88; and Baz Lecocq, "The Bellah Question: Slave Emancipation, Race, and Social Categories in Late Twentieth-Century Northern Mali," *Canadian Journal of African Studies / Revue Canadienne Des Études Africaines* 39, no. 1 (January 1, 2005): 52.
51. This was called the Organisation Commune des Regions Sahariennes (OCRS), a French project that would have seen a communal organization of the Saharan territories, which held much more promise for them. However, this was abandoned in the face of decolonization. LeCocq, *Disputed Desert*, 41.
52. This conflict was called the Alfellagha. Ibid., 186.
53. Baz Lecocq and Georg Klute, "Tuareg Separatism in Mali," *International Journal: Canada's Journal of Global Policy Analysis* 68, no. 3 (September 1, 2013), 426.
54. LoCocq, *Disputed Desert*, 307.
55. I.M. Lewis, *Making and Breaking States in Africa: The Somali Experience* (Trenton, NJ: Red Sea Press, 2010), 65.
56. Lewis, *Making and Breaking States in Africa*, 119; Gebru Tareke, *The Ethiopian Revolution: War in the Horn of Africa* (New Haven: Yale University Press, 2009), 187.
57. Compagnon Daniel, "Somali Armed Movements," in *African Guerrillas*, ed. Christopher Clapham (Oxford: James Currey, 1998), 80.
58. Mark Bradbury, *Becoming Somaliland* (Oxford: James Currey, 2008), 62.
59. Ibid., 82.
60. This legislature features a lower house of elected representatives and an upper house of clan elders, making the structure somewhat analogous to the House of Commons and the House of Lords.
61. The state of Azawad had been part of the initial goals of the Alfellagha and the 1990–1996 insurgency, but the specific demands for an irredentist Kel Tamasheq state have been more strident in the 2007 and 2012 insurgencies.

## BIBLIOGRAPHY

Abi-Saab, Georges. *The United Nations Operation in the Congo, 1960–1964.* New York: Oxford University Press, 1978.
Bradbury, Mark. *Becoming Somaliland.* Oxford: James Currey, 2008.

Cervenka, Zdenek. *The Nigerian Civil War, 1967–1970.* Frankfurt am Main: Bernard and Grafe, 1971.

Clapham, Christopher. "Introduction: Analyzing African Insurgencies." In *African Guerrillas*, edited by Christopher Clapham, 1–18. Bloomington: Indiana University Press, 1998.

Collins, Robert O. *A History of Modern Sudan.* New York: Cambridge Univ. Press, 2008.

Compagnon, Daniel. "Somali Armed Movements." In *African Guerrillas*, edited by Christopher Clapham, 73–90. Bloomington: Indiana University Press, 1998.

Connell, Dan. *Against All Odds: A Chronicle of the Eritrean Revolution.* Trenton, NJ: Red Sea Press, 1993.

Cooper, Frederick. *Africa Since 1940: The Past of the Present.* New York: Cambridge University Press, 2002.

Davidson, Basil. *The Black Man's Burden: Africa and the Curse of the Nation State.* New York: Three Rivers Press, 1997.

de St. Jorre, John. *The Nigerian Civil War.* London: Hodder and Stoughton, 1972.

DeWaal, Alex. *Evil Days: 30 Years of War and Famine in Ethiopia.* New York: Human Rights Watch, 1991.

Gérard-Libois, Jules. *Katanga Secession.* Translated by Rebecca Young. Madison: University of Wisconsin Press, 1966.

Giblin, James, and Jamie Monson, eds. *Maji Maji: Lifting the Fog of War.* Leiden: Brill Academic Press, 2010.

Johnson, Douglas H. "The Sudan People's Liberation Army and the Problem of Factionalism." In *African Guerrillas*, edited by Christopher Clapham, 53–72. Bloomington: Indiana University Press, 1998.

———. *The Root Causes of Sudan's Civil Wars.* Bloomington: Indiana University Press, 2003.

Laremont, Ricardo Rene, ed. *Borders, Nationalism, and the African State.* London: Lynne Rienner Publishers, 2005.

Lecocq, Jean Sebastian. "The Bellah Question: Slave Emancipation, Race, and Social Categories in Late Twentieth-Century Northern Mali." *Canadian Journal of African Studies / Revue Canadienne Des Études Africaines* 39, no. 1 (January 1, 2005): 42–68.

———. *Disputed Desert: Decolonisation, Competing Nationalisms and Tuareg Rebellions in Northern Mali.* Leiden; Boston: Brill, 2010.

Lefever, Ernest, and Wynfred Joshua. *United Nations Peacekeeping in the Congo, 1960–1964, Volume 2: Full Text.* Washington, DC: Brookings Institution, 1966.

Lewis, IM. *Making and Breaking States in Africa: The Somali Experience.* Trenton, NJ: Red Sea Press, 2010.

Niven, Sir Rex. *The War of Nigerian Unity, 1967–1970.* Ibadan: Evans Brothers, 1971.

O'Brien, Conor Cruise. *To Katanga and Back: A UN Case History.* London: Hutchinson, 1962.

Poggo, Scopas Sekwat. *The First Sudanese Civil War Africans, Arabs, and Israelis in the Southern Sudan, 1955–1972.* Basingstoke: Palgrave Macmillan, 2011.

Scott, Philippa. "The Sudan Peoples' Liberation Movement (SPLM) and Liberation Army (SPLA)." *Review of African Political Economy* no. 33 (August 1, 1985): 69–82.

Sherman, Richard. *Eritrea: The Unfinished Revolution.* New York, NY: Praeger Publishing, 1980.

Starratt, Priscilla Ellen. "Tuareg Slavery and Slave Trade." *Slavery & Abolition* 2, no. 2 (1981): 83–113.

Tareke, Gebru. *The Ethiopian Revolution: War in the Horn of Africa.* New Haven: Yale University Press, 2009.

Thompson, Paul S. "The Zulu Rebellion of 1906: The Collusion of Bambatha and Dinuzulu." *The International Journal of African Historical Studies* 36, no. 3 (2003): 533–57.

Tse-Tung, Mao. "On Protracted War." In *Mao Tse-Tung on Revolution and War,* edited by M. Rejai, 271–79. Garden City, NY: Anchor Books, 1970.

Wai, Dunstan M. *The African-Arab Conflict in the Sudan.* New York: Africana Pub. Co., 1981.

White, Philip. "Globalization and the Mythology of the 'Nation State.'" In *Global History: Interactions between the Universal and the Local,* edited by A.G Hopkins, 257–84. New York: Palgrave Macmillan, 2006.

# CHAPTER 30

# Postcolonial Africa and the West

*Enocent Msindo*

When he pronounced his famous saying, 'Seek Ye First The Political Kingdom ...', Kwame Nkrumah, the first president of independent Ghana, a leading African philosopher and proponent of Pan-Africanism, unwittingly set the tone for what became the preoccupation of African political leaders after independence—the pursuit of political power. In the last 60 years, Africa has experienced genocides, rebel movements, coups, xenophobia, economic crises and much else. Associated with these has been the slowness of economic, political, and institutional change as venal leaders have cloven to power. This was not in line with Nkrumah's vision for Africa. For Nkrumah, political power was not an end in itself, but a prerequisite if Africans were to jettison global capitalism and establish a just society in which national goods and endowments would be fairly distributed under a socialist dispensation. African socialism was envisaged as a complete package to drive Africa's political, economic, and social agendas.

However, the African socialist experiment failed for a number of reasons, including: the structural conditions of the inherited states; the nature of African politics since independence; and, chiefly, the nature of Africa's relationship with the West after independence. As in the years of Western colonial control, post-independence Africa remained tied to Western capitalist systems that dictated Africa's pace and nature of economic (under)development. In many parts of Africa, Western corporations did not withdraw following the demise of formal empires, but continued to extract resources for their mother countries. Coupled with this was the rise of US economic imperialism, whose

E. Msindo (✉)
Department of History, Rhodes University, Grahamstown, South Africa

© The Author(s) 2018
M.S. Shanguhyia and T. Falola (eds.),
*The Palgrave Handbook of African Colonial and Postcolonial History*,
https://doi.org/10.1057/978-1-137-59426-6_30

multinational corporations (MNCs) also prowled in Africa looking for primary goods. This situation meant that Africa's efforts to transform its economy were doomed to fail. Neither capitalist-oriented African leaders, like Félix Houphouët Boigny of Ivory Coast (aka Côte d'Ivoire) and Mobutu of Zaire (Congo), who increased their economic ties to the West, nor the avowed socialists like Nkrumah, Nyerere of Tanzania and Machel of Mozambique who had radical, Pan-Africanist ideas ultimately transformed the African economy. Afro-pessimists and some scholars tend to blame Africa's poor economic performance on Africa's bad policy choices and bad African leadership. There is some truth in this critique, but these scholars do not sufficiently examine Africa's economic and political relationship with the West and how this perpetuates Africa's problems. The West's parasitic economic agenda, we argue, has been and still is the major contributory factor not only to the failure of Africa's economic performance, but also to the rise of toxic forms of political expression such as coups, military rule, and other forms of instability in post-independence Africa. To demonstrate this point, we will take a number of examples from Sub-Saharan Africa since independence.

## AFRICA (1956–1973)

Between 1956 and 1973, about three-quarters of African countries attained political independence, with Ghana leading the way in Sub-Saharan Africa. In North Africa, Egypt had already become independent in 1922, followed by Sudan in 1956. The exceptions were Southern Africa colonies which were under repressive white-settler regimes. Whereas decolonization was relatively peaceful in British West Africa, where the British had exercised indirect rule, this was not the case in settler colonies of East and Central Africa. In Kenya, the struggle for independence was as violent as it was in French controlled Algeria. In this section, we examine how Africa's attempt to negotiate its transition was affected not only by its bad political leadership and the colonial legacy on African institutions, but also by the overall international political environment, especially the politics of the Cold War. We also examine Western responses to certain African challenges and the efficacy of such responses. Additionally, we examine the challenges faced by African countries that tried to replace capitalism with socialism as an ideology and economic principle, and how this brought those states onto a collision course with Western powers. Finally, we will briefly analyze Africa's economic performance and dealings with Western MNCs.

Independent Africa inherited weak and anachronistic social, political, and economic institutions, yet at the same time they weren't easy to change as changing them would lead to instability. In the Great Lakes region, for instance, colonial politics of divide and rule created tensions between ethnic groups. Here, the Belgians and British practiced forms of indirect rule that solidified ethnic animosity between the ruling classes (usually the *nilotes* and mainly Tutsi), who served in administrative and political positions, and the majority (usually *bantu*) who endured various abuses from the colonial agents. Following the rapid withdrawal of the British and Belgians there was chaos in Rwanda, Burundi, and Uganda after 1959 as majority governments replaced colonial regimes.

In Rwanda, a predominantly Hutu government came to power, resulting in many Tutsi, who feared retribution, leaving for exile mainly to eastern Congo and Uganda. In Uganda, Tutsi refugees became involved in local politics, ultimately forming in exile a Tutsi militia called the Rwanda Patriotic Front, which helped Yoweri Museveni to ascend to power after he ousted Milton Obote. With the support of Museveni, the Rwanda Patriotic Front invaded Rwanda in 1990, eventually leading to the 1994 genocide in which close to a million Tutsi and moderate Hutu were killed. In Burundi, a Tutsi monarchy was retained under Michel Micombero, resulting in the formation of all-Hutu political organizations in 1972 that attacked Tutsi people. This gave the Tutsi military regime the excuse to attack Hutu people in revenge. The result was a loss of more than 100,000 Hutu lives and massive numbers of refugees outside the country, mainly in Tanzania and Rwanda, where the new governments were pro-Hutu. The crisis in Burundi eventually led to further coups in 1987 and later. Contemporary Burundi is still struggling to move beyond this identity-based politics which have their origins in the colonial era. Attempts to resolve conflicts by way of unity governments, power-sharing arrangements, and peace accords reaped short-term benefits between the years 1960 and 2000.

In Kenya, the new government of Jomo Kenyatta inherited in 1964 a weak constitution that limited the powers of the central government by promoting an ethnic based quasi-federal system. However, as a Unitarian nationalist and Pan-Africanist, Kenyatta used his ingenuity (a mixture of paternalism and good statesmanship) to create a unitary government and to run the economy by combining strong capitalist ideas and very mild socialist ideas. Although Kenyatta's interventions ensured peace and economic development in Kenya during his rule, the unity between powerful ethnic groups (especially Kikuyu and Luo) was fragile. This became evident even in Kenyatta's own political party where members of his own party aligned themselves to ethnic-based factions which made it difficult for them to agree on national priorities.[1] His successor, Daniel Arap Moi, failed to reconcile these factions, resulting in him having to use violence against opponents and cronyism to stay in power.[2] Many aspiring Luo politicians went into exile for fear of Arap Moi.

The challenges of regionalism, political tribalism, and even xenophobia are common problems in Africa. However, these emerged primarily within the colonial politics of divide and rule. Africa's fundamental challenge was its failure to reform the social and political architecture of the states they inherited. In this regard, Crawford Young is correct when he says, 'New political superstructure directed by the triumphant nationalist leaders was bolted onto the sturdy frame of colonial autocracy ... In many silent ways, the mentalities and routines of the colonial state were absorbed into the quotidian action of its postcolonial successor'.[3]

By the mid-1970s, many African countries had experienced political instability of one form or another. More than thirty military coups had occurred in Africa, with at least nine countries experiencing coups two or more times. Benin alone (formerly Dahomey) experienced six coups between 1963 and 1972.[4] Although bad African leadership is often blamed for instability in Africa (and some of the African leaders are indeed culpable), the role of Western powers in political processes in Africa also requires closer scrutiny. In some African states, political instability happened as a result of either direct or indirect Western political interference. Africa gained independence amidst the international political divide created by the Cold War rivalries between the Eastern and Western blocs. African countries that took the socialist path were subjected to various forms of political and economic sabotage, with some Western countries sponsoring rebel movements, secessions, and coups, especially in the first two decades of independence. Instability became the order of the day because of a combination of the internal weakness of African social and political institutions and the political and economic agenda of the intervening Western powers. Pro-Western independent African countries were not spared as, because of economic and political dependency, they too were turned into quasi-states that relied on Western patronage.[5] During the Cold War, the USA sought strategic international allies to form a bulwark against the spread of Soviet communism. A number of African countries were seen as strategically important in their regions. Zaire (Congo), Morocco, Ethiopia, Somalia, and Kenya were identified as allies, and had diplomatic support and foreign aid provided to them for their support of the USA and other Western countries.[6]

In some cases, Western governments intervened directly in the internal affairs of African countries, such as the USA's involvement in the Angolan civil war in support of UNITA, a Cold War ally. In the Central African Republic, the French government helped Jean-Bedel Bokassa, a military ruler, into power through a 1966 coup, only to depose him through another army coup that they sponsored in 1979 when Bokassa no longer served their economic and political interests.[7] In Chad, the French supported Christian southerners in seizing power from Muslim northerners in exchange for continued French economic control over Chad. French troops were stationed in most parts of Chad. This cemented regional animosities in Chad which eventually led to a civil war in 1968 as rebel movements from the North tried to seize power in 1968. The incumbent, Tombalbaye, who was supported by the French, failed to control this civil war and was eventually ousted from power in 1975. In a typical Cold War scenario, the northerners were supported by Libya's Muammar Gaddafi in their fight against the French-supported southerners.[8] This chaos continued into the 1980s and beyond.

It is because of the traditional rivalry between the French and Libya that French troops directly intervened in Libya in 2011, leading to the killing of Muammar Gaddafi.

In Congo, Belgian and US governments interfered in the country by supporting Moise Tshombe, a secessionist who wanted to control Katanga, a rich copper-mining region, and use proceeds from corporate taxes to advance his agenda. Lumumba was murdered within a year of assuming office because he was an avowed communist ally. Since Lumumba's death, Congo has never known peace, beginning with the thirty-two year dictatorship of Mobutu.[9] For this reason, his human rights abuses on the Banyamulenge of eastern Zaire, his killing of opposition politicians, his kleptocracy, his patronage system, and other forms of misrule were never questioned, but rather abetted by the US and Belgian authorities who had close corporate and political interests in Zaire. During this time, Congo, renamed Zaire, received massive financial aid from Western multilateral institutions, which Mobutu diverted to sustain his dictatorship by paying his patronage networks.[10] It only became prudent for the West to criticize Mobutu's excesses in the 1990s after the end of the Cold War.

Western governments dumped Mobutu and began supporting his rivals. His successor Laurent Kabila was also a dictator, so is the incumbent Joseph Kabila, who, like his predecessors, has failed to deal with the multiple crises facing the country. Perpetual instability in the Democratic Republic of Congo has created an ideal environment for MNCs to loot the Congolese economy as they have done since the colonial era. So, overwhelming evidence demonstrates the relationship between political instability in Africa and bad Western interference. Another challenge for some African countries was their adoption of socialism, which strained their relationship with the predominantly capitalist West. We will briefly examine that below.

Liberation movements came into power by winning the hearts and minds of the poor African populace who had been victims of capitalism in many ways. They did so by promising to replace the capitalist state with a new socialist one that would curtail inequality and capitalist accumulation. Socialism was seen as an alternative model for Africa due to the frustrations with failure to develop Africa using Western economic models. The third reason for preferring socialism was the mistaken belief that it would stem rampant corruption and misappropriation of funds by political leaders. It was believed that capitalism was inherently corrupt. The fourth reason for wanting to adopt socialism was the assumption that African societies had traditionally been collectivist, and were therefore closer to socialism than capitalism.[11]

But socialism, as espoused by the new African governments, was not along the lines of 'primitive' communalism where societies operated on the basis of consensus, with multiple centers of power in the form of ethnic groups, clans, and kingdoms. The socialism of the post-1960s was based on centralized political control, with one-party governments dictating the socialist agenda, as was the case in Asia and Russia. This undermined participatory development in Africa, eventually leading to popular discontent. Moreover, broadly based collectivist understandings of socialism were imposed on African societies which had been fragmented into rival ethnic groups and economic classes, which made state development projects difficult to implement on a one-size-fits-all basis. Additionally, African political elites never fully agreed on how to implement socialism in their countries, often clashing on state policy matters.

Finally, socialism on the continent was doomed to fail because it was being adopted without adaptation to economies here which had long been tightly linked to global capitalism but had no control over it. As Ali Mazrui correctly said:

> If the genius of capitalism is production, the genius of socialism is distribution. And yet one cannot distribute poverty or socialize the means of *non*-production. Africa will need to develop a productive capacity before it can meaningfully implement a programme of distribution. At least to some extent Africa has to become capitalist before it can genuinely become socialist.[12]

Africa's socialist countries were well meaning in their attempt to champion an alternative to capitalism. However, such efforts were not successful because of certain systemic flaws in the inherited economy and also because any move towards socialism was a total affront to the Western powers, whose corporations chose to withdraw their capital from such socialist countries. We will take a few examples below to illustrate the fate of African countries that took the socialist route.

In Ghana, Kwame Nkrumah believed that socialism should be the central political philosophy, the unifying social ideology, and the driving force behind Africa's economic development. He was too radical and did not understand how intricately linked to the West and how small and fragile the Ghanaian economy was. Nkrumah's immediate goal of industrializing Ghana through state-controlled enterprises was very noble when he came to power in 1957. He was attempting to move Ghana beyond the limited, colonial, cocoa cash-crop economy. A key project was the Upper Volta hydro-electric project, from which Ghana would tap electricity required for major industrial projects. However, this project was too expensive and drained most of the loans that Ghana had borrowed from the Americans, deepening Ghana's debt crisis. Ghana tried to service this loan by overtaxing the already underpaid cocoa-farming peasants.[13] The Upper Volta dam was completed in 1966, the very year Nkrumah was ousted through a coup. Nkrumah also had great difficulties convincing his opponents in government about economic strategy as they were divided between those who wanted private enterprise against his faction, which preferred public enterprise. A key limitation was that Nkrumah's Ghana did not have sufficient capital to develop import substitution industries. The mechanized farms and other state-run businesses and those which had been developed realized massive losses because of mismanagement and possibly corruption.[14]

To deal with Ghana's financial crisis, Nkrumah tried to nationalize some gold mines, but for fear of immediate Western criticism, he targeted smaller ones instead of the Ashanti mines which were the largest and most profitable. As the urban population grew, Ghana faced an urban food crisis, which further alienated Nkrumah from the very young people who had voted him into power. Soon he requested food aid from the USA, which was not approved because of his radical ideas against neo-colonialism.[15] In rural areas, the plight of the peasants did not improve from what it had been during colonialism because the state's parasitic relationship with them continued. The indigenous business sector was unhappy with the tight controls on exchange rates, business permits, and other impediments. The army, whose older leaders were quickly removed and sometimes overlooked in promotion in favor of younger and inexperienced ones, became divided and disloyal. Nkrumah no longer had guaranteed military support. Some of his ministers felt sidelined as Nkrumah arrogantly pursued his socialism. Neighboring countries did not help Nkrumah's fate as capitalist-oriented ones such as Ivory Coast were thriving economically in the first decade up to the early 1970s. As internal opposition grew, Nkrumah became dictatorial, regularly using the colonial preventive detention law to detain critics without trial. He was eventually ousted in absentia through a bloodless coup and exiled.[16]

Although Nkrumah's socialism was driven by the noble aim to indigenize the economy, it failed because the Ghanaian economy remained in the hands of Western corporations. Nkrumah's governance was a kind of charismatic leadership that depended on inspiring awe and fear and had almost built a personality cult around his figure. He did not do enough to ensure that his ideas were well understood at grassroots level and in his party leadership. He also failed because of the influence of the West. Since his disagreement with the USA in the 1960 Congo crisis, when he advocated for non-Western intervention, his relations with the USA and other Western countries had been severely tainted. Western governments used pro-capitalist African states such as Ivory Coast, Malawi, Zaire, Kenya, and Nigeria to thwart Nkrumah's Pan-Africanist ideas. These African countries had no option as they risked losing financial aid and loans should they not be acquiescent. In Ghana itself, Nkrumah came under increasing US pressure, with CIA spies secretly meeting some of his unhappy government ministers and inciting them to rebel against Nkrumah for his alleged Soviet leanings and alleged authoritarianism.[17] Evidence from CIA files and other sources suggests that the CIA actively aided the coup plotters.[18]

Nkrumah was replaced by a military regime which ruled and handed over power to a civilian government following the 1969 elections; but in 1981, Flight Lieutenant Gerry Rawlings took over power in a military coup once again. He engaged in pro-International Monetary Fund (IMF) and World Bank structural adjustment policies in an attempt to gain access to Western loans. He is credited with the good use of IMF money, but he did not deal with the fundamental problems of creating economic self-sufficiency and alleviating poverty.[19] Rawlings also failed to democratize Ghana and entrenched repression, yet he continued to receive financial support from Western multilateral institutions.[20]

In Tanzania between 1967 and 1980, socialism as epitomized in the Ujamaa village system did not take into account various preexisting community economies, such as those of people who had survived on cattle ranching since the pre-colonial era. When they were forced into villages, the evictees had to start to learn a new farming-based economy, which drove them into abject poverty. Traditional local authorities, mainly chiefs, were undermined and slowly became redundant because of the ruling party's inordinate political interference in directing rural agricultural production. The Tanganyika African National Union (TANU) organized people into cells, with cell leaders systematically replacing those who had previously been called headmen during the colonial era. TANU leaders became the new elites in rural areas, perpetuating inequality.[21] The limited successes of the Ujamaa villages program was undermined in the mid-1970s by the drought of 1974 and the oil price hikes of the same decade, which made Tanzania a net food importer.[22] The economy slowed down, the Tanzanian currency devalued significantly, debts continued to mount, and inflation rose sharply. This led to the decline in public support for Ujamaa.[23]

The Tanzanian story is not so different from that of the socialist government of Haile Mengistu in Ethiopia, which moved huge populations into resettlements after the 1973 droughts. These movements are largely blamed for the devastating famine of 1983 to 1985. Western attempts to pour in aid and loans did not help the country to emerge from its economic and social crisis. Instead, this increased Ethiopia's dependence on the West for its survival.[24] In Mozambique, in the late 1970s and 1980s, Samora Machel's socialist government compelled peasants to work on village cooperatives, in almost the same way they had been exploited under the Portuguese regime.[25] Like Nkrumah, Machel did not live to see the end of his vision as he was killed by agents of the South African apartheid state. Elsewhere in Africa, many grand projects failed not merely because of corruption, bloated expenditures, mismanagement, and the general inefficiency of the African state in conducting business, but also because of declining terms of trade with the West. Having said this, we will briefly examine below other facets of Africa's economic condition since independence.

Many African states attained independence partly because of the ideological and military support of the socialist countries. At the time of independence, their diplomatic and military ties with these socialist countries remained. However, Africa's economic and cultural ties with the Western capitalist bloc remained in place after independence, even in those states that were supposedly socialist. African education continued to be offered in the languages of the former colonizers, with very little effort to intellectualize African languages for broader adaptation to the curricula. This had implications for indigenous knowledge systems, as this was also not intellectualized, sufficiently embraced, and legitimized for economic development.

In general, the African economy continued to be run on Western models that privileged foreign capitalist extraction and accumulation with no critical thinking about alternatives to empower the locality. Even socialist countries were not free from the trappings of accumulation as the state itself became a capitalist entity of sorts by controlling and directing production using state-controlled businesses, by nationalizing some businesses, and also by forcing peasants to work for the state agricultural projects, supposedly to attain the goals of socialism. These failed dismally. African countries like Ivory Coast that took the capitalist route endured for just over a decade after independence before their economies collapsed in the late 1970s, consequently relapsing into dependency on Western patronage. At the time Ivory Coast was being hailed as the African miracle, its leader Houphouët Boigny, a conservative French *assimilado*, was busy using the profits of the land to extend his personal rule, thwarting opposition and trade unions, and also to engage in the grand project of turning his village home of Yamoussoukro into the state capital of Ivory Coast.[26]

But how is it that neither the capitalist nor socialist model worked for Africa? The answer lies in the fact that neither socialism nor capitalism were fundamentally African ideologies, but were convenient models borrowed from elsewhere. Moreover, Africa's ties to the West and the role of Western MNCs in African politics and economy were also limiting factors. Moreover, during the struggle for independence, there had been no careful thinking about how the African economies would be sustained after independence. The assumption had been that by attaining political independence, the new leaders would use state power to control and dictate economic policy. African nationalists were wrong in underestimating the power of international corporations and their links to global politics and multilateral institutions. They also did not realize that Western governments were planning carefully on how to dictate terms of engagement with Africa after the 1960s.

Relations between the European Economic Community (EEC) and the African, Caribbean and the Pacific (ACP) countries were dictated by the 1957 Treaty of Rome, which set in place the broader neo-colonial frameworks for multilateral relations that would saddle Africa in the long run. This led to further conventions, generally known as the Lome Conventions, which built upon this Treaty and further refined the original thoughts in the Rome Treaty.[27] The 1957 Rome Treaty hinged on three critical points, which were:

- the gradual opening of markets of associated African countries to the exports of the EEC member states without discrimination
- the opening of EEC markets to the produce of associated African countries under preferential arrangements
- the inauguration of social and economic investment programs in these overseas countries, financed by the European Development Fund.[28]

Africa played no part in determining terms of trade with the West under this Treaty or even in deciding on the nature of development finance that would be loaned to her. The first two points of the Treaty illustrate the West's intention to continue with the colonial system of extracting raw material from Africa and trading of finished goods to Africa. There was no intention by the Western powers to encourage Africa to fully industrialize. The 'bail-out' strategy in the Rome Treaty was a bait to pull Africa into the vortex of economic dependency. Former colonial powers knew exactly the fragility of the economies they left in African states, and how Africans would soon come for various forms of aid and loans.

With the economic crisis of the 1970s that was mainly caused by the oil price hikes of 1973 and 1979, Africa's fragile economies were severely affected as governments had no financial reserves and the necessary foreign currency to buy capital goods and food to feed the starving population. Africa consequently turned to Western loans and aid. This paved the way for them to come under the neo-liberal regime of controls, with the IMF and World Bank imposing new, restrictive conditions under its structural adjustments programs. Since then, Africa has never recovered from the huge debts incurred from these loans, which kept being rescheduled as African governments failed to service them.

The ballooning debts and the associated badly performing economies had serious political ramifications for ruling regimes, as they had to deal with widespread political opposition including Western-sponsored rebel movements at a time when Africa's (economically effective) population was being decimated by the HIV-AIDS virus. African dictatorships went a step further to contain this rising discontent. In Malawi, the Banda regime became more repressive; so did the Kaunda regime in Zambia, which had also been struggling since the 1970s because of falling copper prices. In Zimbabwe, the economy struggled to weather the challenge of restructuring, leading to the radicalization of the trade union movement, which eventually became a political party in the late 1990s. In Somalia, Siad Barre's regime became more repressive, leading to clans revolting, and to the eventual collapse of his regime in 1991. This marked the beginning of the Somalian crisis. In the same year, Haile Mengistu's regime collapsed in Ethiopia. Barre and Mengistu were 'collateral damage' of the end of the Cold War, they having been strong socialists. But a salient issue that also requires some analysis is the role of MNCs that we alluded to above.

In postcolonial Africa, MNCs continued to maintain the old exploitative relationship with Africa, with the continued support of their mother countries, which were supposedly democratic yet financially propping up dictatorial African regimes. In nine Francophone West African states (Benin, Ivory Coast, Mauritania, Mali, Burkina Faso, Senegal, Gambia, Guinea, and Niger), French MNCs invested considerably more money between 1960 and 1970 than they had invested during the colonial era. Their investment by far exceeded that which the African governments themselves invested in those states for industrial development during the same period. Consequently, any assumed economic growth in these states was basically capital growth of the MNCs themselves, not real sustainable growth of the African countries' economies.[29] As Samir Amin argues, the distribution of this foreign investment to the different sectors has continued to follow the colonial pattern of investing in agriculture, mining, energy, and fishing. However, the total investment in these sectors was only a third of the total investment, with the rest going into infrastructure, housing, social services, and transport that were not directly linked to the productive sector. For this reason, only two countries (Ivory Coast and Mauritania) out of all the former French West African states realized reasonable economic growth between 1960 and 1970.[30]

The US corporations also invested in Africa, especially in apartheid South Africa in the 1970s. Ironically this was the time South Africa was under economic sanctions for its gross human rights violations against the black populace, as evident in the Sharpeville massacres and other cases of violence. We do not know exactly how much was invested by the USA into Africa between the 1960s and 1970. Suggested figures range from about $500 million to $755 million, with US exports to settler-ruled South Africa and Namibia alone totaling $563 million and their imports totaling only $208 million, epitomizing a negative balance of trade scenario for Africa.[31] The story of negative balance of trade is pervasive all over Africa because of low industrialization levels and declining terms of trade.

Multinational companies continued to siphon investable surpluses from Africa in almost the same way other corporations did during the colonial era. Seidman and Makgetla argue that between 1965 and 1975, US firms alone directly sent home more than $601 million, which was twenty five percent more than their original investments.[32] This figure does not include other unreported capital leakages and income from their shady business deals in war-torn countries. Having recouped their investments, MNCs are under no pressure to stay in some African countries, especially when there is a drastic change in the investment climate in that country. They can leave at will or siphon money from one part of Africa to invest in another continent. Moreover, the fact that some of these companies are in a stronger position financially than the state in Africa encourages them to defy government orders and threaten to disinvest should African governments pass laws that seek to demand them to invest a larger portion of the profits locally or to sell shares to indigenous populations. Facing demands to sell some of its shares to Nigerian indigenous businesspeople in the mid-1970s, US-owned Citibank chose to leave Nigeria instead.

In many cases, Western countries directly intervened to contain the threats of nationalization of some MNCs by signing investor protection agreements to protect their companies in Africa.[33] This protection is always necessary because MNCs are the chief agents of Western neo-colonialism. As Markovitz argued, the power of the MNCs lies in the fact that they 'represent the forces that have created the world market system', the Western countries. In this regard, one may note the address of US Secretary of State, Henry Kissinger to the United Nations General Assembly in 1975. In this he declared that transnational enterprises were the 'engine of development', warning that the host governments must treat these enterprises 'equitably without discrimination ... [and] not as objects of economic warfare'.[34] Kissinger had to defend the MNCs because they are the mainstay of the US economy. In the mid-1970s, US MNCs accounted for 62% of US exports, 35% of US imports of manufactured goods, and about a third of the USA's domestic economic activity. In the early 1970s, their largest MNC, General Motors, was bigger than the Gross National Product of most of the countries internationally, including some European countries, having a turnover of more than $36 billion.[35]

MNCs also thrived in Africa, as they did elsewhere, because of their patronage networks with corruptible African politicians and rebel movements. In the Congo, Belgian and US MNCs supported and even paid 'taxes' to Moise Tshombe so as to thwart communist supporter Lumumba whom they feared would nationalize the economy. During the reign of Mobutu, MNCs promoted his kleptocracy and dictatorship in exchange for favorable business deals and limited scrutiny. During Kabila's era, they helped foment political chaos that helped them to continue extracting mineral resources during the conflict. In Nigeria, soon after the discovery of oil and the beginning of oil-drilling operations, a coup took place resulting in military rule. This was followed by a second crisis, the Biafra civil war (1967–1970), with the Igbo-dominated Biafra region, the source of most of the oil, turning to French support to secede from the Nigerian state even as the British and the Soviet Union supported the unitary Nigerian government. Whereas the French hoped to enter the Nigerian oil market by supporting a secessionist movement, the British government supported the central government under which its oil corporations Shell-BP were already operating, having long secured oil prospecting licenses during the colonial era.

Concluding his analysis of the role of MNCs in Africa, Markovitz had no kind words:

The MNCs pour asbestos into drinking water, Sulphur dioxide into the air, hormones into cattle, mercury into fish. The MNCs pollute, they corrupt. They buy prime ministers and pay the 10 percent to administrative officials. The willingness of indigenous nationalists to accept bribes should not divert attention from the bribers. If the MNCs can, as alleged, bribe the Dutch royal family and arrange payoffs to Japanese prime ministers, they can do it to anybody … the multinational corporation represents the latest chapter in the long history of the continued expansion of national capitalism.[36]

Markovitz's criticism was not off the mark. By the mid-1970s, Africa had been driven by the same corporations into bankruptcy, with negative balance of trade and very limited foreign currency reserves. Africa had become more indebted and her economy was in dire straits.

## 'The Lost Years' (1973–1990)

Between 1973 and 1990, Africa's economic performance was generally disappointing, especially due to the fall in oil prices and declining terms of trade. In this misery, Africa turned to the World Bank and the IMF for help. However, assessing the economic environment, the IMF and the World Bank took on more interventionist approaches guided by the new neo-colonial world order supported by strong neo-liberalist thinking. Politically, Africa witnessed a rise in the number of military dictatorships which stifled political change. Because of a combination of lack of political change and the economic crisis, this period is characterized as Africa's lost years.

Earlier, we examined how post-colonial Africa inherited narrow, unindustrialized economies. In the 1960s and 1970s, African governments tried different economic development initiatives, most of which failed because of inordinate political interference, lack of sufficient skills, and Africa's weak finance capital base. In Ivory Coast, the government continued profiteering from cocoa monoculture, but did not diversify the economy early enough to hedge against falling cocoa prices. In Nigeria, the discovery of oil resulted in a switch from a predominantly agrarian economy that produced cocoa, palm oil, palm kernel, and groundnuts to a spigot economy. With her farmers driven out of business because of the rising costs of farming, Nigeria became one of Africa's biggest net food importers.[37] In Ghana, Nkrumah tried to industrialize by first investing in hydro-electricity generation, but this noble investment drained most of the country's financial reserves. We have also noted how governments of Mozambique, Tanzania, Ethiopia, and elsewhere engaged in ambitious state-controlled agricultural ventures, which led to opposition from below and to serious food shortages.

Many African governments tried to deal with the problem of dependency, especially the skewed balance of trade by establishing small manufacturing industries which produced certain goods locally so as to substitute the huge import costs. Import substitution would have been a noble strategy had there been sufficient capital, managerial, and political capacity to deal with the growing international economic competition of the 1970s and 1980s. Under the import substitution strategy, governments incentivized industry through access to cheap credit, protected markets, favorable exchange rates, and state subsidies. The assumption was that such industries would eventually grow and generate surpluses to make them self-sustaining and competitive in the international markets.[38]

Unfortunately, these industries failed to compete with bigger international corporations which had better technology and had already established themselves in Africa at independence. Consequently, these industries experienced retarded growth, became moribund, and those that survived continued to require financial bailout from the state.[39] The urban development bias and the inefficiency of state controls were also partly to blame for the failure of these industries. Whereas state-controlled economies worked during the colonial era because the colonies were themselves controlled by the Western governments that in turn controlled international economic processes, state control of the local African economies after independence did not work because Africa was not a key global economic player. Increased *statism* led to disinvestment and capital flight, which made Africa more vulnerable economically. To stem capital flight, desperate African governments had to acquiesce to the demands of belligerent Western corporations even where these corporations competed with new African industries.

There were other efforts to grow the African economies which also failed. Attempts to modernize agriculture and encourage peasant production failed because they were premised on the colonial parasitic model of exploiting peasants. Other efforts, such as encouraging economic growth via regional integration initiatives, also failed because of lack of political will to unite and also because of the lack of agreement between regional states on the overall economic strategy.[40] Today, some parts of African countries are still not linked to other countries as the existing road networks have not yet been developed beyond the old colonial trade routes.[41]

Although Africa's economic challenges predate the 1970s, African economies became more precarious in that decade than they had been in the 1960s. This was mainly due to the global recession hitting Sub-Saharan Africa, whose economies were based on exporting raw materials. Between 1970 and 1975, Africa's growth rates were lower than other least-developed countries. This was mainly due to the global hike in oil prices of 1973, which affected agricultural and industrial development, and the drought of 1974 which increased Africa's food import costs. As African economies tried to recover, they were further constrained by the oil-price shocks of 1979. Concurrently, international financial institutions drastically hiked their lending rates, supposedly to curtail reckless spending, at a time when African governments expected to borrow more to revive their economies.

In addition, Africa also experienced serious droughts between 1983 and 1984. Consequently, Africa's economic growth rate was as low as one and half to two percent in the mid-1980s, the lowest since 1960.[42] Economies that had thrived in the 1960s began to collapse, and Ivory Coast, which had been hailed as the African miracle, suffered severe economic decline as all its financial reserves dried up. Zambia's once a successful copper industry also collapsed due to declining terms of trade. In Zaire (Congo), Mobutu's patronage was tested as he no longer had enough wealth to distribute to his loyalists due to the falling copper prices. In the 1980s, pictures of famished Ethiopian people began to appear on British televisions, all heralding the sorry state of Africa. The widespread economic crisis made it difficult for Africa to service her earlier debts to international, multilateral financial institutions.

By 1987, Sub-Saharan Africa's external debt stood at US$129 billion, which was roughly about 47% of the continent's Gross Domestic Product.[43] This indebtedness was worsened by the fact that in the 1960s and 1970s, dictatorial regimes had accessed cheap credit from Western funders because of their Cold War loyalty. They used most of the monies to defend themselves from coups and rebel movements instead of developing their countries. The economic crisis made it difficult for African countries to import capital goods to revive the collapsing import substitution industries. To recover the monies owed by African governments to them, the IMF and World Bank, starting in the late 1970s, began to tighten their funding criteria in a manner that fundamentally deepened Africa's economic crisis. They forced Africa into what was called structural adjustment programs (SAPs).

The basic assumption of the World Bank, as evident in their ideologue Berg in his 1981 report, was that Africa's economic crisis was a product of it local economic distortions that he blamed on inappropriate government policy interventions and lack of institutional reform. Berg cited, among other factors: overprotection of industry hampering external competition; exchange-rate controls that made African currencies stay overvalued and discouraged international trade; a raft of state subsidies which were increasing public debt; the bloated civil service; and the agriculture development bias. Except for Ghana, where food production temporarily increased in the mid-1980s, SAPs severely affected African cash crop and food-based agriculture. The removal of state subsidies led to high input costs which increased producer prices, yet without a corresponding increase of the price of the final product on the international market. This worsened rural poverty levels and further slowed down Africa's economic growth.[44] Education and health-care services became more expensive, and job losses increased as companies downsized by retrenching workers.[45]

SAPs did not deal with the problem they proposed to address, but drove Africa into acute economic and political crisis. This increased Africa's dependency on the West. As Loxley and Campbell argued:

Never before have the international financial institutions wielded such pervasive influence on policy formulation in Africa: not since the days of colonialism have external forces been so powerfully focused to shape Africa's economic structure and nature of its participation in the world system.[46]

SAPs reduced African governments' capacity to industrialize as their emerging industries came under severe competition from international suppliers from more industrialized countries under the market deregulation regime. The export bias of the SAPs also meant continued focus on cash crops, which compromised Africa's food security. Additionally, the SAPs did not lay out any clear strategy to take Africa out of debt.

What was clear was the intention to increase lending to Africa, even to highly indebted countries. This increased Africa's economic dependency on the West, with more money transferred to the West than was initially loaned. Between 1984 and 1990, there was a net transfer of $156 billion from Sub-Saharan Africa to Western countries, with $4.7 billion being repaid to the IMF and the World Bank alone between 1986 and 1990; this, incidentally, at a time when Africa was struggling economically.[47] This compromised Africa's ability to develop alternative economic models beyond IMF and World Bank patronage. However, what are not usually mentioned are the political repercussions of the SAPs on Africa.

Evidence suggests a corresponding relationship between SAPs-oriented economic change and the entrenchment of one-party dictatorships in Africa as governments tried to contain popular discontent from every direction. As Legum correctly observed, 'By the beginning of the 1990s, forty-two [African] states were under either military or single party rule, and only five still maintained multiparty systems'.[48] Legum, however, did not see the SAPs and politics nexus. In Morocco, the mere announcement by government in 1984 that subsidies would be cut led to countrywide street protests which prompted extreme police and military brutality as government sought to contain its restless population, arresting over 9000 protesters and killing about 400 people in the process.[49] In Zimbabwe, the implementation of SAPs radicalized the trade union movement and the student organizations, with the result that government also used police force to control protests in 1989 and in the early 1990s. In Ivory Coast, economic hardships brought about increasing xenophobia as the politics of citizenship were evoked in claims to land. Boigny's pro-IMF regime used brute force to suppress protesting students, teachers, and workers in 1990, arresting more than 100 people. His regime eventually collapsed in 1993. In Zambia in 1985, rioting against the state happened following almost a decade of government implementation of the SAPs. This forced Kaunda to temporarily break from the IMF and World Bank reforms, before reintroducing them in 1986. The Zambian riots led to the death of 15 people as government sought to contain discontent. Citizens soon started mass gatherings demanding political change.[50] In Zaire, the state collapsed as civil servants could no longer financially afford to travel to work. Soldiers abandoned Mobutu as he could no longer financially sustain his patronage networks in the country. The list is endless. However, all this points to the fact that in the 1980s, dictatorial tendencies had their origins deeply rooted in economic crises facing neo-liberal Africa. Therefore, we rightly argue that dictatorship was not *causa sui* and that it was not always to be blamed on the characteristics of individual African politicians.

When it became evident that Africa's economies were not improving and that there was a rise in African political turmoil, the West changed its political game in the late 1980s. For the first time, Africa's poor economic performance was blamed on her bad politics and fragile institutions. Democracy and economic development began to be seen as Siamese twins. This became an important facet of Africa's engagement with the West in the post-Cold War era, following the weakening and collapse of communist regimes.

## From the 1990s Onward

The collapse of international communist regimes in the late 1980s had serious repercussions for Africa. African countries that had benefitted militarily, diplomatically, and financially from communist countries were in a crisis. Revolts in communist-controlled Ethiopia, Somalia, and Liberia, for instance, resulted in chaotic second transitions in these countries, the first transitions being the transition from colonialism. Countries that had sided with neither the capitalist nor the communist blocs, in what was called the Non-aligned Movement (NAM), did not perform better as they were also beset by increasing poverty. African leaders who had benefited from Western support during the Cold War were also uncertain about the future. Some of their governments collapsed as a result of declining Western financial support in the 1990s.

Although most African countries crafted investor-friendly laws in the late 1980s and 1990s with a view to attracting foreign capital, Sub-Saharan Africa in the 1990s experienced low levels of foreign direct investment (FDI) when compared to Latin America and Asia. Ghana, which had a sound economic development package in 1985, had secured a total FDI of only one billion (US$) by 1991, which was insufficient to meet its development needs. Uganda, Nigeria, Zimbabwe, Malawi, and many other countries had similar experiences. Although this poor FDI situation is easily blamed on the grounds that many African governments were still under coups and military rule, therefore not investor friendly, it is also true that the West has generally been unwilling to promote industrialization projects in Africa that would have resulted in Africa becoming economically self-sufficient. In this section, we examine the changes in the West's terms of engagement with Africa, especially the rise of the language of democracy and human rights which had not been important to them before 1989.

Backed by their governments, that drew up country 'fact files', Western financiers came up with one alibi: that African dictatorships were the major cause of their countries' poor economic performances. With this, Africa had entered a new phase in which economic men (the IMF and World Bank) ruled African politics with the political backing of the West in a neo-liberal era. There were increased calls by Western countries for Africa to twin good governance and democratization to the broader issues of economic reform and public accountability.[51] Consequently, Western-sponsored civil society organizations emerged as whistleblowers and watchdogs to safeguard human rights and the rule of law. But whose whistleblowers were they? When the IMF and World Bank started their SAPs in Africa, they never concerned themselves with Africa's political questions. This concern started in 1989 with the World Bank mentioning the term 'governance' in its discussion of Africa's developmental issues, blaming Africa's internal political conditions and weak commitment to policy and political reform for the failures of their SAPs.[52]

Given its global reach, especially in the West, the World Bank set the pace for other international investors and donors to Africa, who immediately joined the governance bandwagon. The World Bank led attacks on Africa, arguing that the continent had severely declining quality of governance, creeping bureaucracies, weak judiciary, inadequate rule of law, corruption and rent-seeking tendencies, and a 'deep political malaise' which were making it impossible for the continent to cope with 'rapid modernization'.[53] Following this negative slant, many Afro-pessimists rose in the academy pandering to the same World Bank whim. Thus, Africa began to be described by scholars of the post-1990s as having parasitic or vampire states, rogue regimes, failed states, and so on. Such depictions usually sought to diminish the interface between Africa's bad governance and bad Western economic interventions that we have explained above.

In its attempts to operationalize reforms in Africa, the World Bank had, by 1994 initiated civil-service reforms in 29 countries to contain bloated costs and to privatize state enterprises. The bank also enforced legal reforms in Uganda, Angola, Ivory Coast, Cape Verde, Ghana, Mali, and Guinea to promote human rights and enforce contracts relating to private-sector loans and credits. It also sponsored projects that focused on legal training and legal awareness such as the ones offered by the Legal Resources Foundation in Zimbabwe and many others in Tanzania, Mozambique, Burkina Faso, and Zambia. The Bank also sponsored female-gender activist movements in Africa, assuming that this would ultimately empower them economically. Considerable efforts were made to support grass-roots non-governmental organizations (NGOs) to empower people to counter the neo-patrimonial state. Some of the NGOs were given much money to undertake development work and were trained on capacity building. In schools, curricula were subjected to scrutiny for their overall economic value, so were funds made available to laboratories and libraries within the overall rationalization schema.[54] All this was not helpful for many reasons.

First, the World Bank systematically distorted Africa's postcolonial developmental experience and did not appreciate a myriad of reasons why certain development initiatives had failed. The World Bank did not appreciate Africa's global constraints and its very own role in deepening Africa's debt crisis. Moreover, there was no proven link between economic development and democracy, and as the Asian economies demonstrated, their economies grew the most under dictatorial regimes that enforced and directed economic programs in almost the same way pre-1970s Ivory Coast had developed under the dictatorship of Boigny.

African countries accepted the World Bank's political demands so as to meet the lending criteria. According to Crawford Young, by 1991, more than forty states had either undertaken political liberalization or had promised to implement such reforms. By the same year, a number of old African regimes had been voted out of office, in addition to those who that were ousted through military coups. Curiously, even as the IMF and World Bank spoke strongly about democracy and good governance, these institutions were still keen to work with amenable dictatorial regimes such as those of Senegal, Gambia, and Zimbabwe in the 1990s. The dictatorial Yoweri Museveni of Uganda received much foreign aid in the 1990s, being well liked by the West, especially after the demise of Mobutu. In Rwanda, Paul Kagame continued to gain Western support by playing the victim card after the 1994 Rwandan genocide, even when evidence of extra-judicial killings of political and ethnic enemies in the country continued to surface.[55] The West itself watched the genocidal horror of Rwanda that claimed almost 1 million lives.

Another point is that where communist regimes collapsed lase in Somalia, the West watched the country degenerate into chaos, perhaps because there was relatively little wealth for its corporations to tap from the country. In Ethiopia, the fall of Mengistu's socialist regime did not lead to democratization, but to protracted ethnic fights particularly over state resource allocation. In the 1990s, both countries continued to rely heavily on donor aid as they had been doing since the late 1970s. In the Democratic Republic of Congo, Western donors have persistently supplied food and military aid for decades, without corresponding action on how to deal with the civil conflict in the country. Throughout the Congo crisis, some Western companies were involved in mining and mineral smuggling.

An important development in the post-1990 era was the proliferation of NGOs in Africa such as Oxfam, Care International, World Vision, Action Aid, Catholic Relief Services, and many others promoting peace, security, and development. By the mid-1990s, many locally based NGOs had also emerged, usually with links to international NGOs and funding agents. This rise of NGOs happened against the backdrop of Africa's economic decline, which weakened governments' capacity to provide basic services.[56] It also coincided with increasing cases of HIV and AIDS-related illnesses in Africa and also with efforts by some African countries to reconstruct, following protracted civil wars, military rule, and other forms of instability from the 1970s to the 1980s. In Tanzania, NGOs grew from numbering seventeen in the early 1980s to about 1000 in the late 1990s. Tanzania's neighbor Uganda had 2,655 registered NGOs in 2000 and 5200 in 2004.[57]

Most importantly, the growth in the number and prominence of NGOs was also triggered by the rise of Western liberal internationalism that sought to re-educate former communist countries and the so-called 'Third World' countries supposedly to curtail human rights abuses as a precondition for economic development. In this regard, NGOs were meant to drive the agenda of international capital that financed them and the politics of their sending countries.[58] Unlike the earlier period when funds had been recklessly advanced to some unaccountable, usually authoritarian, political regimes in Africa, substantial amounts of funds were now being channeled to Africa through NGOs. In eastern Zaire, NGOs became the major employers after 1994. They offered better salaries when compared to those in the public service. This NGO factor contributed to the collapse of the country's public service and by extension, poor service delivery, leading to protests. International NGOs and the local ones took over the conventional functions of the state, setting themselves on a collision course with African leaders who perceived NGO activities to be an affront to state sovereignty. In Somalia, where most of the people survived on food aid from NGOs, this food aid was a disincentive to Somalian peasant production as food became freely available.

Although international NGOs are often mistaken for disinterested altruistic organizations, evidence of their operations in Africa suggests that they are not completely divorced from the covert agenda of their sending countries. As we alluded to above, some NGOs played a critical part in enforcing compliance to the World Bank's problematic 'good governance' and 'democratization' program.[59] By their aid programs and activities, some became complicit in sustaining dictatorships.[60] In the eastern provinces of Zaire, NGOs continued to support Hutu refugees even when these refugees formed a militia that raided and attacked the local Banyamulenge who were Mobutu's enemies. Their food aid distribution was biased against the Banyamulenge who were not in the refugee camps, yet the same Banyamulenge could not produce food because of persistent attacks from the Hutu militia and Mobutu's army.

Furthermore, in areas where NGOs have been involved in community development, their interventions have usually been one-offs and have not offered long-lasting solutions. As soon as the NGOs leave, villagers relapse into their old circumstances. For this reason, we believe that Africa's future will depend on collective efforts by Africans to develop the necessary skills to expropriate and properly use Africa's own resources, not her reliance on NGOs. Although civil societies and NGOs have helped to raise important questions about democratization, Africa must still strengthen its institutions and develop political and economic models that are best suited to its own contexts.

## CONCLUSION: WHITHER AFRICA?

In concluding this chapter, we must emphasize a few key observations that are important to our understanding of post-colonial African economies, politics, and relationship with the West. First, colonial economic structures were replicated in the postcolonial era, and where there were attempts to modify them, there were more often than not uprisings in African states. In Congo, this happened with Belgian and US companies and intelligence forces supporting the secessionist Moise Tshombe against the nationalist Patrice Lumumba. Second, African leaders who took over power had no political model to learn from. Colonialism had not showcased good governance, but had thrived on divide-and-rule, racist, capitalist dictatorship, and forms of patronage. Thus, the politics of patronage in Africa were mainly an extension of bad leadership that was inherited from the colonial era, and of course perfected after independence as the new leaders tried to sustain the ungovernable states marred by rebellions, banditry, political tribalism, calls for secession, and other forms of political expression. Third, Kwame Nkrumah's vision of seeking first the political kingdom as a pathway to gaining economic freedom was noble, but it was not fulfilled. The trap of state sovereignty deprived the African leaders of the opportunity to work closely with their neighbors to rethink better models of economic integration and development, and to smoothe over the challenges of regional economic communities such as the Economic Community of West African States (ECOWAS), the East African Communities (EAC), the Southern African Development Community (SADC), and others. Thus, African countries continued to sustain their traditional parasitic links with Western African countries in ways that consolidated the Western economic stranglehold over Africa. Very little was done to invest in processing industries, and where this happened, ambitious projects met the challenges of narrow revenue bases, which made it difficult to complete such projects. The debt crisis which encumbered Africa as a result of the IMF and World Bank's neo-liberal regime intensified the economic crisis.

Except for a few African countries where political leaders had clear plans of action (such as Ghana, Senegal, Tanzania, Ivory Coast, Mozambique, and others), some new African leaders had not necessarily prepared themselves for leadership over the new states, with many lingering questions about the future having never been considered. In contrast, the West had planned more carefully about it engagement with post-independence Africa. Where their planning was not so good, Western countries took advantage of opportunities that presented themselves in Africa (particularly political and economic instability, ideological confusion, and the lack of unity between African states) to reassert their new forms of control in the different African countries. Following the collapse of communism, Africa became a site for both political and economic control as the financiers imposed conditions that had political repercussions across the continent. Monitoring Africa's good governance and democratization levels were important for the World Bank after 1990. But as we have argued, this has not made Africa a better place economically and politically.

## NOTES

1. S.A. Akintoye, *Emergent African States* (London: Longman, 1976), 198–203.
2. C. Young, *The Postcolonial State in Africa: Fifty Years of Independence, 1960–2010* (Madison: University of Wisconsin Press), 165.
3. Young, *The Postcolonial State in Africa*, 337.
4. I.L. Markovitz, *Power and Class in Africa: An Introduction to Change and Conflict in African Politics* (Upper Saddle River, NJ: Prentice-Hall, 1977), 286.
5. Robert Jackson quoted in W. Reno, *Warlord Politics and African States* (London: Lynne Reinner Publishers, 1998), 2.
6. A. Thomson, *An Introduction to African Politics*, 2nd ed. (London: Routledge, 2005), 154, 155.
7. N. Chazan, P. Lewis et al., *Politics and Society in Contemporary Africa*, Boulder, 3rd ed. (Lynne Reinner, 1999), 424–25.
8. B. Davidson, *Modern Africa*, 211, 212; and K. Somerville, *Foreign Military Intervention in Africa* (London: Pinter Publishers, 1990), 61–82.
9. Z. Laidi, *The Super-powers and Africa: The Constraints of a Rivalry, 1860–1990* (Chicago: University of Chicago Press, 1990), 14–17; A.A. Mazrui, *Africa's International Relations: The Diplomacy of Dependency and Change* (London, Heinemann, 1984), 162, 163; and Chazan et al., *Politics and Society in Contemporary Africa*, 441.
10. Reno, *Warlord Politics*, 148–62.
11. A.A. Mazrui, *The Africans: A Triple Heritage* (London: BBC Publications, 1986), 188–89.
12. Mazrui, *The Africans*, 223.
13. T. Falola, *Key Events in African History: A Reference Guide* (Westport: Greenwood Press, 2002), 258.
14. D. Rooney, *Kwame Nkrumah: The Political Kingdom in the Third World* (London: I.B. Tauris, 1988), 183–94.
15. W.S. Thompson, *Ghana's Foreign Policy, 1956–1966: Diplomacy, Ideology, and the New State* (Princeton: Princeton University Press, 1969), 397.
16. D. Birmingham, *Kwame Nkrumah: The Father of African Nationalism* (Athens: Ohio University Press, 1998), 63–92; and Markovitz, *Power and Class in Africa*, 256–57.
17. D. Rooney, *Kwame Nkrumah*, 226–28.
18. Ibid., 252–54.
19. K. Donkor, *Structural Adjustment and Mass Poverty in Ghana* (Aldershot: Ashgate, 1997), 190–240.
20. J. Haynes, "Inching Towards Democracy: The Ghanaian "Revolution," the International Monetary Fund, and the Politics of the Possible," in *Democracy and Socialism in Africa*, ed. R. Cohen, and H. Goulbourne (Boulder: Westview Press, 1991), 142–64; and J. Ibrahim, *Democratic Transition in Anglophone West Africa* (Dakar: CODESRIA), 8–22.

21. Markovitz, *Power and Class in Africa*, 167–68; and John Saul, "Socialism in one Country: Tanzania," in *Essays on the Political Economy of Africa*, Saul and Arrighi, 237–335.
22. P. Nugent, *Africa Since Independence* (Basingstoke: Palgrave Macmillan, 2004), 150.
23. Falola, *Key Events in African History*, 258.
24. D. Rahmato, "The Political Economy of Development in Ethiopia," in *Afro-Marxist Regimes: Ideology and Public Policy*, ed. E. Keller, and D. Rothchild (Boulder: Lynne Reinner, 1987), 155–79.
25. A. Isaacman, and B. Isaacman, *Mozambique: From Colonialism to Revolution* (Harare, Zimbabwe Publishing House, 1985), 145–70; and J. Hanlon, *Mozambique: The Revolution Under Fire* (London: ZED Books, 1984), 93–114. See also E. Keller, and D. Rothchild, *Afro-Marxist Regimes: Ideology and Public Policy* (Boulder: Lynne Reinner, 1987).
26. A. Thomson, *An Introduction to African Politics*, 117, 123–26.
27. R.I. Onwuka, "Beyond Lome III: Prospects for Symmetrical EurAfrican Relations," in *Africa in World Politics: Into the 1990s*, ed. R.I. Onwuka and T.M. Shaw (Basingstoke: Macmillan, 1989), 64–86.
28. C. Coquery-Vidrovitch, "Economic Changes in Africa in the World Context," in *UNESCO General History of Africa, Vol. 8: Africa Since 1985*, ed. Ali Mazrui (California: Heinemann, 1993), 285–316.
29. S. Amin, *Neocolonialism in West Africa* (New York: Monthly Review Press, 1973), 270–71.
30. S. Amin, *Neocolonialism in West Africa*, 268–69.
31. Mazrui, *Africa's International Relations*, 165.
32. Seidman and Makgetla, *Outposts of Monopoly Capitalism*, 49.
33. Chinweizu, "Africa and the Capitalist countries," in *Africa Since 1935*, Mazrui and Wondji, 769–97.
34. Markovitz, *Power and Class in Africa*, 92, 95.
35. Ibid., 92–93.
36. Markovitz, ibid., 96–97.
37. M. Watts and R. Shenton, "State and Agrarian Transformation in Nigeria," in *The Politics of Agriculture in Tropical Africa*, ed. J. Barker (London: Sage, 1984), 173–203.
38. T. Mkandawire, "30 Years of African Independence: The Economic Experience," in *30 Years of Independence in Africa: The Loss Decades?* ed. P.A. Nyongó (Nairobi: Academy Science Publishers, 1992), 86–102.
39. R. Tangri, *The Politics of Patronage in Africa: Parastatals, Privatization and Private Enterprise* (Oxford: James Currey, 1999), 18–33.
40. I. Wallerstein, *Africa: The Politics of Independence and Unity* (Lincoln: University of Nebraska Press, 2005), 111–28, first published in 1967.
41. I.E. Griffiths, *The African Inheritance* (London: Routledge, 1995), 184–90.
42. J.H. Wagao, "Economic Aspects of the Crisis in Africa," in *30 Years of Independence in Africa*, ed. P.A. Nyongó, 103–30.
43. Wagao, "Economic Aspects of the Crisis," 107.
44. P. Gibbon, K.J. Havnevik, and K. Hermele, *A Blighted Harvest: The World Bank and African Agriculture in the 1980s* (London: James Currey, 1993), 8–10, 128–30.

45. A. Adepoju, ed., *The Impact of Structural Adjustment on the Population of Africa*, 5–6.

46. J. Loxley and B.K. Campbell, "Introduction," in *Structural Adjustment in Africa*, ed. Loxley, and Campbell (New York: St Martins Press, 1989), 1–11, see page 1 for quoted text.

47. B. Turok, "Towards a Democratic Coalition against SAP," in *30 Years of Independence in Africa*, ed. P.A. Nyongó, 131–44.

48. C. Legum, *Africa Since Independence*, 49.

49. D. Seddon, "The Politics of 'Adjustment' in Morocco," in *Structural Adjustment in Africa*, ed. Campbell, and Loxley, 234–65.

50. B. Turok, "Towards a Democratic Coalition against SAP," 131–44.

51. C. Young, "Democratization in Africa: The Contradictions of a Political Imperative," in *Economic Change and Political Liberalization in Sub-Saharan Africa*, ed. J.A. Widner (Baltimore: John Hopkins University Press, 1994), 230–50.

52. A.O. Olukoshi, "The Elusive Prince of Denmark: Structural Adjustment and the Crisis of Governance in Africa," in *African Voices on Structural Adjustment*, ed. T. Mkandawire and C.C. Soludo (Trenton: Africa World Press, 2003), 229–73.

53. Olukoshi, "The Elusive Prince of Denmark," 246.

54. Ibid., 249–54.

55. R. Lemarchand, *The Dynamics of Violence in Central Africa* (Philadelphia: Pennsylvania University Press, 2009), see chap. 7 generally.

56. R. Pinkney, *NGOs, Africa and the Global Order* (Basingstoke: Palgrave Macmillan, 2009), 47.

57. R. Pinkney, *NGOs, Africa and the Global Order*, 18.

58. A. Choudry and D. Kapoor, "Introduction: NGOisation: Complicity, Contradictions and Prospects," in *NGOisation: Complicity, Contradictions and Prospects*, ed. A. Choudry, and D. Kapoor (London: ZED Books, 2013), 1–23.

59. Nugent, *Africa Since Independence*, 348, 350.

60. C. Lancaster, *Aid to Africa: So Much to Do, So Little Done* (Chicago University of Chicago Press, 1999), 94.

# BIBLIOGRAPHY

Adepoju, A., ed. *The Impact of Structural Adjustment on the Population of Africa: The Implications for Education, Health, & Employment*. London: James Currey, 1993.

Akintoye, S.A. *Emergent African States*. London: Longman, 1976.

Amin, S. *Neocolonialism in West Africa*. New York: Monthly Review Press, 1973.

Arrighi, G., and J.S. Saul. *Essays on the Political Economy of Africa*. New York: Monthly Review Press, 1973.

Birmingham, D. *Kwame Nkrumah: The Father of African Nationalism*. Athens: Ohio University Press, 1998.

Chazan, N., P. Lewis, et al. *Politics and Society in Contemporary Africa*. 3rd ed. Boulder: Lynne Reinner, 1999.

Chinweizu. "Africa and the Capitalist countries." In *UNESCO General History of Africa, Vol. 8: Africa Since 1985*, Mazrui, and Wondji, California: Heinemann, 1993, 769–97.

Choudry, A., and D. Kapoor, eds. *NGOisation: Complicity, Contradictions and Prospects.* London: ZED Books, 2013.

Coquery-Vidrovitch, C. "Economic changes in Africa in the world context." In *UNESCO General History of Africa, Vol. 8: Africa Since 1985,* edited by Ali Mazrui. California: Heinemann, 1993, 285–316.

Davidson, B. *Modern Africa: A Social and Political History.* 2nd ed. London: Longman, 1989.

Donkor, K. *Structural Adjustment and Mass Poverty in Ghana.* Aldershot: Ashgate, 1997.

Falola, T. *Key Events in African History: A Reference Guide.* Westport: Greenwood Press, 2002.

Gibbon, P., Havnevik, K.J., and Hermele, K. *A Blighted Harvest: The World Bank and African Agriculture in the 1980s.* London: James Currey, 1993.

Griffiths, I.E. *The African Inheritance.* London: Routledge, 1995.

Hanlon, J. *Mozambique: The Revolution Under Fire.* London: ZED Books, 1984.

Haynes, J. "Inching Towards Democracy: The Ghanaian "Revolution," the International Monetary Fund, and the Politics of the Possible." In *Democracy and Socialism in Africa,* edited by R. Cohen, and H. Goulbourne Boulder: Westview Press, 1991, 142–64.

Isaacman A., and B. Isaacman. *Mozambique: From Colonialism to Revolution.* Harare: Zimbabwe Publishing House, 1985.

Laidi, Z. *The Super-powers and Africa: The Constraints of a Rivalry, 1860–1990.* Chicago: University of Chicago Press, 1990.

Lancaster, C. *Aid to Africa: So Much to Do, So Little Done.* Chicago: University of Chicago Press, 1999.

Legum, C. *Africa Since Independence.* Bloomington: Indiana University Press, 1999.

Lemarchand, R. *The Dynamics of Violence in Central Africa.* Philadelphia: Pennsylvania University Press, 2009.

Loxley, J., and B.K. Campbell. Structural Adjustment in Africa. New York: St Martins Press, 1989.

Markovitz, I.L. *Power and Class in Africa: An Introduction to Change and Conflict in African Politics.* New Jersey: Prentice-Hall, 1977.

Mazrui, A.A. *Africa's International Relations: The Diplomacy of Dependency and Change.* London: Heinemann, 1984.

Mazrui, A.A. *The Africans: A Triple Heritage.* London: BBC Publications, 1986.

Mkandawire, T. "30 Years of African Independence: The Economic Experience." In *30 Years of Independence in Africa: The Loss Decades?* edited by P.A. Nyongó. Nairobi: Academy Science Publishers, 1992, 86–102.

Nugent, P. *Africa Since Independence.* Basingstoke: Palgrave Macmillan, 2004.

Olukoshi, A.O. "The Elusive Prince of Denmark: Structural Adjustment and the Crisis of Governance in Africa." In *African Voices on Structural Adjustment,* edited by T. Mkandawire, and C.C. Soludo. Trenton: Africa World Press, 2003, 229–73.

Onwuka, R.I., and T.M. Shaw, eds. *Africa in World Politics: Into the 1990s.* Basingstoke: Macmillan, 1989.

Pinkney, R. *NGOs, Africa and the Global Order.* Basingstoke: Palgrave Macmillan, 2009.

Rahmato, D. "The Political Economy of Development in Ethiopia." In *Afro-Marxist Regimes: Ideology and Public Policy,* edited by E. Keller, and D. Rothchild, Boulder: Lynne Reinner, 1987, 155–79.

Reno, W. *Warlord Politics and African States*. London: Lynne Reinner Publishers, 1998.

Rooney, D. *Kwame Nkrumah: The Political Kingdom in the Third World*. London: I. B. Tauris, 1988.

Seidman, A., and N.S. Makgetla *Outposts of Monopoly Capitalism: Southern Africa in the Changing Global Economy*. London: ZED Press, 1980.

Somerville, K. *Foreign Military Intervention in Africa*. London: Pinter Publishers, 1990.

Tangri, R. *The Politics of Patronage in Africa: Parastatals, Privatization and Private Enterprise*. Oxford: James Currey, 1999.

Thompson, W.S. *Ghana's Foreign Policy, 1956–1966: Diplomacy, Ideology, and the New State*. Princeton: Princeton University Press, 1969.

Thomson, A. *An Introduction to African Politics*, 2nd ed. London: Routledge, 2005.

Wagao, J.H. "Economic Aspects of the Crisis in Africa." In *30 Years of Independence in Africa: The Loss Decades?* edited by P.A. Nyongó. Nairobi: Academy Science Publishers, 1992, 103–30.

Wallerstein, I. *Africa: The Politics of Independence and Unity*. Lincoln: University of Nebraska Press, 2005, first published in 1967.

Watts, M., and R. Shenton. "State and Agrarian Transformation in Nigeria." In *The Politics of Agriculture in Tropical Africa*, edited by J. Barker. London: Sage, 1984, 173–203.

Young, C. "Democratization in Africa: The Contradictions of a Political Imperative." In *Economic Change and Political Liberalization in Sub-Saharan Africa*, edited by J.A. Widner. Baltimore: John Hopkins University Press, 1994.

———. *The Postcolonial State in Africa: Fifty Years of Independence, 1960–2010*. Madison: University of Wisconsin Press, 2012.

# CHAPTER 31

# The USA and Africa

*Adebayo Oyebade*

For much of the history of US foreign relations, Africa has been a somewhat overlooked entity and sometimes entirely ignored. The primary interests of the postcolonial USA, for 150 years, resided chiefly in the Americas, Europe, and Asia. In Europe, for example, during the Second World War, bilateral cooperation with Britain elevated Anglo-US ties to a pedestal described by wartime British prime minister Winston Churchill as a 'special relationship'. In Latin America, the Monroe Doctrine of 1823 declared the region out of bounds to European colonization and, by the early twentieth century, American hegemony in the region was fully at play. In Asia, the threat to the USA's economic interests compelled a demand for free trade in China in 1899 through the Open Door policy. The promotion of free trade would become the centerpiece of the USA's foreign policy in Southeast Asia for much of the twentieth century.

In sharp contrast, before the Second World War Africa was virtually invisible in the USA's external relations and dealings. The USA had no foreign-policy doctrine that defined distinctive interest in Africa, nor did it establish significant treaties and alliances with the continent. Indeed, for the most part, the USA considered colonial Africa as the purview of European imperialist states, not a part of its own sphere of influence.

Yet deep-rooted connections between the USA and Africa had always existed. Interactions between North America and West Africa could possibly have begun in pre-Columbian America, as expressed in some Afrocentric

A. Oyebade (✉)
History Department, Tennessee State University,
Nashville, TN, USA

© The Author(s) 2018
M.S. Shanguhyia and T. Falola (eds.),
*The Palgrave Handbook of African Colonial and Postcolonial History*,
https://doi.org/10.1057/978-1-137-59426-6_31

literature. Taking this hypothesis as a point of departure, this chapter will discuss the major historical and contemporary themes that have defined relationships between the USA and Africa.

## 'A DARK CONTINENT:' THE US PERCEPTION OF AFRICA

The lack of US interest in Africa, particularly before the Second World War, was a reflection of many Americans' historical perception of the continent as 'dark'. This Eurocentric perception of Africa as a 'dark continent' was, in one sense, an expression of the inherent ignorance of the land and its people by the Euro-American public. In another sense, 'dark Africa' was essentially a perception of the continent as lacking in human advancement, cultural sophistication, and a history worthy of note. This idea was rooted in the Eurocentric historical tradition vividly represented in the early nineteenth-century Hegelian theorization of ahistorical and inconsequential Africa.[1] This Eurocentric conceptualization of Africa found further expression in racist Euro-American scholarship and popular culture and literature from the late nineteenth and early twentieth centuries. The British-born US journalist-turned-explorer Henry Morton Stanley, perhaps more than any other single individual, propagated the idea of Africa as a 'dark continent'.[2]

## AFRICA AND PRE-COLUMBIAN AMERICA

The earliest period of interaction between North America and Africa could possibility have been in the pre-Columbian era. This idea has been expressed in some Afrocentric literature, although without wide scholarly acceptance. Afrocentricity (or Afrocentrism) itself is an intellectual movement which gained some prominence, particularly in the 1990s, among black scholars in the USA. Its fundamental principle is its insistence on a paradigm shift in which the elements of African culture (religion, philosophy, history, and sociology) form the core of any scholarly discourse about Africa.

One of the basic claims of Afrocentric scholarship is Pre-Columbian contacts between North America and West Africa. The pioneering proponent of this hypothesis was the one-time Rutgers University scholar Ivan Van Sertima, whose controversial book *They Came Before Columbus* postulated the presence of Africans in the New World, particularly South America, before the arrival of Christopher Columbus.[3] Since the publication of Van Sertima's book, Molefi Kete Asante, often credited with propounding Afrocentric theory, and a number of African American scholars, have argued that there were transatlantic crossings that brought voyagers from West Africa to the Americas before Columbus's arrival in the New World in 1492.

Yet the notion of a pre-Columbian black presence in the Americas has not been embraced by mainstream US scholarship. In particular, there is strong reservation about the Afrocentric claim of significant African contribution to Mesoamerican culture.[4] In essence, as the idea of a pre-Columbian black presence in America has not met with definitive validity, it remains at best a hypothesis, despite the work of a handful of Afrocentric apologists.

## THE EARLY US REPUBLIC AND AFRICA

With the Declaration of Independence in 1776 and the conclusion of the American Revolution in 1783, the American Republic was effectively established, and the new nation entered the fray of foreign relations. Even though Africa had no place in the external relations of the early American Republic, one of the first countries to formally recognize its independence was the North African state of Morocco. This occurred on June 23, 1786, when it signed a treaty of peace and friendship with the USA. What followed was a period of American consular presence in Morocco, with the establishment of a consulate in Tangiers in March 1791, which was elevated to a legation in March 1905. Following the first consulate in Tangiers, in the next hundred years the USA opened other ones in Moroccan cities, including Casablanca and Rabat.[5] The USA also had official representation in another North African state, Tunisia, dating to 1795 when the state recognized the American republic. A treaty of friendship and trade was concluded with Tunisia in 1799, and an American consulate was established in Tunis in 1800.[6]

Although US foreign policy in its first century was not globally focused, the North African region was certainly of considerable importance to it. In the early nineteenth century, a number of states in the region known as the Barbary States were involved in international piracy that impacted US shipping on the Mediterranean. The states, namely present-day Morocco, Algeria, Tunisia, and Libya, were sponsors of pirates who seized Western and US sailors and extorted ransom from their countries. The US attempt to stamp out the activities of the pirates prompted the Barbary Wars of 1801–1805 and 1815–1816 against Tripoli and Algiers respectively.[7]

## INTERACTIONS IN THE ERA OF THE ATLANTIC SLAVE TRADE

An epochal period in the early history of US interaction with Africa was the era of the Atlantic slave trade. The rise of the USA's plantation system in the South needed a massive infusion of labor for success. However, poor and indentured whites and Native Americans were unable to meet the requirement. Beginning in the early sixteenth century, Africans had begun to be transported by Euro-American slave merchants to the New World, many of them enslaved on southern plantations.

Enslaved Africans were brought from the entire stretch of the west coast of Africa and the West-Central region as far as Angola. Most came from the region known in the parlance of slave merchants as the 'slave coast'; that is, the Bight of Benin, an area coterminous with the coastline of present-day

Republic of Benin and Nigeria up to the Niger Delta. However, there were other major slave-exporting regions, namely Senegambia in the upper Guinea coast, the 'Gold Coast', and the Bight of Biafra. Dotting this coastal landscape were trading posts such as Goree, Cape Coast, Elmina, Porto Novo, Whydah, Badagry, Lagos, Bonny, and Luanda, where European slave merchants and their African collaborators conducted the business of buying and selling slaves.

In the USA, the agrarian southern economy became exclusively dependent on slave labor. Enslaved Africans, put to work on the plantations to cultivate cotton, tobacco, sugar cane, corn, rice, indigo, and other crops, constituted an instrument of wealth creation and accumulation for the southern, white, slave-owning class that dominated the society. With time, the black population began to exceed that of whites in some southern counties. In South Carolina, for example, by the 1790s the black population had surpassed that of whites, and, indeed, more than doubled it by 1860. The growing population of enslaved Africans through the Atlantic trade became a major problem to the privileged white society. The belief that this increased number of blacks accentuated the possibility of slave revolts led some states, by the end of the American Revolution, to pass legislation restricting the importation of slaves. Between 1776 and 1787, ten states banned the importation of slaves. In any case, the slavery system was now self-perpetuating and the need hardly existed to import more Africans. Congress itself outlawed the Atlantic trade in 1808. By this time, according to estimates, between 10 and 12 million transplanted Africans had been enslaved in the Americas, mostly in the cotton states of the US South.[8]

The transatlantic slave trade lasted for almost 400 years. Its most profound legacy was the establishment of the African diaspora in the Americas, a community of the descendants of enslaved Africans. As of 2015, people of African descent, now known as African Americans, numbered 46.3 million, representing 14.4% of the entire population of the USA, but contemporary United States has also seen the emergence of a new black diaspora that is fast expanding. While the old black diaspora was shaped by the Atlantic slave trade that, from the fifteenth to the nineteenth century, brought enslaved Africans to the New World, the new black diaspora is being created by the massive influx of African-born immigrants into the USA, particularly since the closing decades of the twentieth century. Consequently, the US black community has expanded to include new social, cultural, and religious identities.[9]

## LIBERIA: THE USA's STEPCHILD

The African diaspora in the USA notwithstanding, the antebellum USA had no dynamic relationship with Africa beyond Liberia. An independent republic located on the West Coast of Africa, Liberia was a US creation which existed in its early decades as a virtual colony of the latter.

As a colony, Liberia was founded in 1821 by the American Society for Colonizing the Free People of Color in the United States (otherwise known as the American Colonization Society, ACS) as a haven for emancipated American slaves. Its foundation was a direct product of a combination of factors in the USA: the abolitionist movement, the South's race dilemma occasioned by an increased free black population, and the emancipation and colonization project that had become very prominent by the early nineteenth century.

As far back as the 1790s, there had been a number of groups, mostly in the North, dedicated to the emancipation of the slaves and the ending of chattel slavery in the USA. This campaign was driven not only by white Christian liberals, but also by other groups not necessarily motivated by altruism. In the South, some in the slave-holding class had grudgingly accepted the inevitability of the end of slavery and were troubled by the prospect of the significant expansion of blacks that emancipation would bring about. Thus, while subscribing to abolitionism, they tied it to the colonization of free blacks outside the USA. In essence, the early nineteenth-century politics of abolitionism was interwoven with the twin concept of emancipation and colonization.

Many blacks in the South were convinced that they would never be truly free citizens in the racist US society and thus welcomed relocation outside the South, though not necessarily outside North America. Colonization in Africa never appealed to the vast majority of free blacks, who saw the Liberian project as a ploy by whites to rid the USA of blacks. In any case, by the early nineteenth century, many of the free blacks were US-born with no connection to Africa whatsoever. Indeed, one the most prominent black abolitionists, Fredrick Douglass, opposed the colonization scheme.

The ACS, under whose auspices Liberia was founded, only managed to ship a small number of freed slaves to the colony. Some other colonization societies also established colonies in the same locality and sent free blacks there. By 1824, the different colonies had consolidated to be officially known as 'Liberia', and Monrovia became its capital, named after James Monroe, the fifth US president who had supported the colonization enterprise. However, the Liberian colonization scheme was never a huge phenomenon as a mass exodus of US blacks to the colony did not materialize.[10]

In its early years under the governing authority of the ACS, Liberia struggled to survive amidst numerous arduous challenges, including financial difficulties, hostility from indigenous communities, and encroachment on its territory by European colonizing powers, notably Britain and France. The ACS eventually went bankrupt, which largely led to the colonists' demand for independence, granted in 1847.

Post-independence Liberia maintained close ties with the USA, especially after the establishment of diplomatic relations in 1862. However, prior to the Second World War, US interest in Liberia was largely economic, primarily an investment in rubber production. This venture was largely the work of

Harvey Firestone, owner of the US-based Firestone Rubber Company, who established extensive rubber plantations at Harbel on the Farmington River in 1926. The rubber company came to exert a great deal of influence over the Liberian economy. A year after its establishment, the company secured a concession agreement with the Liberian government which granted it one million acres of land for a period of ninety nine years. Also, Liberia was required to accept a $5 million loan from the company, an arrangement that put the African nation in a long-term debt.

## The Second World War: Changing Dynamics of US-African Relations

The advent of the Second World War significantly altered USA's interest in Africa. The continent formally entered the US war effort on November 8, 1942, when Anglo-US forces invaded North Africa in a military operation called Torch. This operation was a campaign directed at wresting French North Africa from the control of the Germans, which would deliver to the Allies a platform from which to halt the Axis gains in Europe.

US wartime interest in Africa manifested in two major arenas: economic and strategic. The war demand on the US economy, even before the nation's entry into the war in December 1941, required stepping up its external trade. The dramatic increase in the volume of US import/exports trade reflected on Africa, catapulting the continent into an important portion of the USA's economic warfare. The fall of Southeast Asia to Japanese forces by early 1942 had significant repercussions for the US economic war effort. This region had been an important source of raw materials for the USA. The consequent loss of the traditional markets of British Malaya, French Indochina, and Burma spelled the denial of vital strategic raw materials to the USA. In this precarious situation, the USA turned to other regions, including Africa, for the supply of vital commodities to meet domestic industrial need and the war effort. West Africa, for example, became an important supplier of strategic mineral raw materials including Liberian iron ore, Nigerian tin ore, Gold Coast's manganese ore, Sierra Leone's diamonds. The USA also obtained vital minerals from other parts of the continent such as South Africa and the Belgian Congo. Besides strategic mineral resources, the USA also obtained critical agricultural products such as palm oil and cocoa from Nigeria, Gold Coast, and Sierra Leone and rubber from Liberia.[11]

The Second World War also brought Africa into the USA's strategic plan in the Mediterranean where the Germans and the Italians had established control over the coastal stretch from Egypt to Tunisia. In May 1943, the USA provided much needed military assistance to the Allied powers in order to defeat the Axis in North Africa and end the campaign in that sector that had begun in 1940. Although North Africa was a major theatre of war in Africa, West Africa was also brought into the US war strategy in the Southern

Atlantic. The region not only played an important role in Allied victory in the Mediterranean; US war planners saw it as vital to the defense of the Western Hemisphere. Consequently, the USA established military bases in strategic locations, from the western tip of Africa through Central Africa to North Africa and onward to the Middle East. Points on this line included: Dakar, Bathurst, Freetown, Monrovia, Takoradi, Lagos, Kano, Maiduguri in West Africa; Fort Lamy in Central Africa; Khartoum in the Anglo-Egyptian Sudan; and Cairo in North Africa. These bases served as terminal points on a trans-Africa air-ferry service across West and Central Africa to the Middle East. This was a pre-war route which the USA took over in 1941, expanded, and operated through Pan American Airways (Pan Am), a leading aviation company that had been operational in South America since the 1930s. Through this ferry service, British desert forces received critical military supplies and hardware including US-manufactured combat aircraft.

The USA greatly expanded its strategic interest in Liberia during the Second World War, as was evident by its conclusion of a defense pact with Monrovia in 1942. A major airbase, Roberts Field, was constructed by Pan Am and financed by the USA. The USA maintained a military presence in Liberia by stationing military units there made up of predominantly African Americans troops and other servicemen. Liberia eventually formally joined the Allied powers in 1944 when it declared war on Germany and Japan. The strategic importance of wartime Liberia was underscored by President Franklin D. Roosevelt's visit to the country in January 1943, where he held war-related talks with the Liberian president, Edwin James Barclay, and met the 2000-plus American troops stationed in the country.

## THE USA AND COLD WAR DYNAMICS IN AFRICA

After the Second World War, Africa witnessed the advent of the era of decolonization, as European colonies in Africa began to attain political independence. This period coincided with the shaping of the Cold War, the ideological tension between the two global powers, the USA and the USSR. US foreign policy in Africa during this period was necessarily affected by the prevailing Cold War dynamics. The USA began to view Africa almost exclusively from the logic of the Cold War. The overriding US foreign policy goal in Africa was to prevent newly independent states from joining the Eastern bloc and to see them adopt Western-oriented economic principles and democratic governments.

The independence of Ghana (formerly Gold Coast) in 1957, the first state to be free of colonial rule in sub-Saharan Africa, posed a challenge to the US vision of a democratic Africa secured within the Western capitalist bloc. Kwame Nkrumah, Ghana's foremost nationalist leader, who led his country to independence from Britain and became its prime minister, was known for promoting a radical form of Pan-Africanism which called for the political union of African states. Although not overtly anti-West and espousing non-alignment, he vehemently opposed European imperialism, subscribed to Leninist-Marxist principles, and flirted with communism. Ghana under Nkrumah's dictatorship and one-party rule was hardly a model for Western democratic tradition.

The late 1950s and early 1960s saw the intensification of the Cold War and consequent US anti-communist covert interventions overseas. In Africa, an important example of the USA's Cold War meddling was the Congo Crisis of the early 1960s. Western and US interest in the former Belgian colony rested on its vast mineral resources, the access to which could be jeopardized by the budding Soviet influence in the state. The new Congolese prime minister, Patrice Lumumba, had sought Soviet assistance as the newly independent nation's crisis deepened. President Dwight Eisenhower's administration regarded Lumumba as a stooge of the Kremlin who must not be allowed to aid the expansion of Soviet influence in Africa. The Congo Crisis culminated in the unceremonious murder of Lumumba in January 1961, in which the Central Intelligence Agency (CIA) was implicated. The USA also facilitated the enthronement of Mobutu Sese Sekou, a staunch ally of the West, as the new Congolese leader. Indeed, the West, particularly the USA, helped to sustain Mobutu's corrupt and autocratic rule till the end of the Cold War. As elsewhere during the Cold War, the USA had subordinated its much touted principles of human rights and democracy to an anti-communism foreign policy that tolerated contrary authoritarian ideals.

Following the Congo Crisis that ushered in the Cold War to Africa, other parts of the continent emerged as proxies in the Soviet-US ideological confrontation. In Southern Africa, the USA sought to undermine the increasing Soviet presence in the region. In the 1970s, the Portuguese colonies of Angola and Mozambique had turned to Warsaw Pact states and the USSR for military and economic assistance in their anti-colonial struggle. The post-independence civil wars in both countries threatened a continued Soviet presence which the USA wished to end. At independence in 1975, Angola declared itself a Marxist state as the People's Republic of Angola, under its pro-Soviet leader Agostinho Neto. In the immediate post-independence Angola civil war, the USA supported the pro-Western rebel organization the National Union for the Total Liberation of Angola (União Nacional para a Independência Total de Angola, UNITA), which was fighting the ruling Marxist, Cuban and Soviet-supported Popular Movement for the Liberation of Angola (Movimento Popular de Libertação de Angola, MPLA).[12]

The same Cold War pattern of overt and covert superpower intervention occurred elsewhere in Southern Africa. During Mozambique's post-independence civil war, the ruling Mozambique Liberation Front (Frente de Libertação de Moçambique, FRELIMO), professedly Marxist, enjoyed extensive military aid from the Soviet Union and some East European states in its war against the rebel forces of the Mozambican National Resistance

(Resistência Nacional Moçambicana, RENAMO), which was covertly supported by the USA through its proxy, apartheid South Africa. In Zimbabwe (formerly Rhodesia) and Namibia (formerly South West Africa), their respective liberation organizations, the Zimbabwe African People's Union (ZAPU) and the South West Africa People's Organization (SWAPO), received Soviet military and technical aid and other forms of support from East European communist states in their guerrilla wars against racist white minority rule. The African National Congress (ANC), in a similar struggle in South Africa against apartheid, was viewed with distrust by Washington, which erroneously assumed it was a communist organization with direct Soviet influence.

The US reluctance to support the anti-apartheid movement in South Africa amounted to a tacit approval of apartheid. But this was primarily dictated by Cold War dynamics, although it also had to do with the USA's extensive economic investment in the country. In the early 1980s, international condemnation of the apartheid regime was rife, but Cold War considerations continued to prevent the USA from making a meaningful change in its policy toward South Africa. President Reagan's administration opposed demands, especially from the black congressional leadership, for sanctions against South Africa. Instead, the administration pursued a reactionary policy called 'constructive engagement', by which Washington expected to encourage the apartheid regime to gradually end its racist policies. Not unexpectedly, this policy failed to bring about change in South Africa; rather, it sanctioned the apartheid state's repression of the black struggle.[13]

## US Post-Cold War Interest in Africa

The end of the Cold War in the late 1980s freed the USA from the anti-communist foreign-policy straitjacket it had been constrained by for almost half a century. In Africa, Cold War concerns that had restricted US opposition to apartheid were removed, and US engagement with Africa was now defined by a new interests-based partnership. One key area of partnership on which the USA placed a premium was African democratization. The US policy was to promote in Africa the building of viable democratic institutions, respect for human rights, elimination of corruption, and the fostering of transparency in governance. Sustainable economic growth and development was another component of partnership. To assist in achieving this, in 2000 the US Congress passed into law the African Growth and Opportunity Act (AGOA), which offered eligible sub-Saharan African states tangible trade incentives and preference to tap into the US market. This initiative was intended to promote economic expansion and free markets in Africa.[14]

Strengthening African democratic institutions and promoting US-African trade has continued to be a critical element of contemporary US policy. The administration of President Barak Obama repeatedly underscored these core values in US foreign policy in Africa. However, there are other arenas of US partnership with Africa. One important dimension has been promoting health care on the continent. The administration of President George W. Bush, in particular, pursed an active agenda in this area. As part of the US Global Health Initiative (GHI), the US government expended significant material and financial resources on combating the HIV/AIDS pandemic in Africa. This effort was largely pursued through the President's Emergency Plan for AIDS Relief (PEPFAR) which was launched in 2003. The US health-care initiative in Africa also included the fight against other debilitating diseases such as malaria and tuberculosis.[15]

## ALTERNATIVE APPROACH TO CONFLICT PREVENTION IN AFRICA

Post-Cold War Africa continued to witness intractable conflicts, some of which attracted international attention because of their destructive intensity and extended duration.[16] One of the legacies of the Cold War was a massive infusion of arms into African conflicts by both superpowers, which undoubtedly exacerbated the conflicts. The US arms transfers to many African states continued even after the Cold War had ended. For example, the conflicts in the Great Lakes region in Central Africa, that began in the mid-1990s, were fueled by the US supply of arms to the warring parties, worth $125 million by the end of the decade.[17]

However, in the post-Cold War period, the USA exercised restraint in direct humanitarian intervention in Africa. This was evident in Rwanda, where the Clinton Administration refused to intervene in the country's brewing crisis in a way that some observers believed could have prevented the 1994 genocide in the country. The US reluctance to intervene in African conflicts where its vital interests were not at stake had a direct relation to the lesson of the failed US-led humanitarian intervention in Somalia in December 1992, codenamed Operation Restore Hope. During the course of this, some 18 US soldiers were killed in a most dastardly manner by Somali militiamen at the so-called Battle of Mogadishu in October 1993. Eschewing interventionist policy, US strategy toward African conflicts was to help African states build up viable mechanisms to address continental crises. This peace-building strategy involved US assistance in creating an all-Africa rapid response force that could be deployed to hotspots on the continent.

The immediate result of this strategy was the launching of the African Crisis Response Initiative (ACRI) in October 1996 by the State Department, supported by the Department of Defense. This was an initiative that aimed at enhancing the capability of the militaries of designated African states to respond efficiently in a peacekeeping capacity to crisis situations on the continent.[18] ACRI immediately began training programs for the military in these states. However, some African countries, including Nigeria, were unreceptive, at least initially, to the idea of US military training for their militaries, which they considered condescending. Nevertheless, in 2004, ACRI was restructured as the African Contingency Operations Training and Assistance Program (ACOTA) and continued to provide military training and technical and logistical support to more African militaries.[19]

## COMBATING TERRORISM AND THE MILITARIZATION OF AFRICA

With the emergence of Africa as a front in the US-led global anti-terrorist project in the late 1980s, the level of US military partnership with the continent increased dramatically. The perceived terrorist threat to Western and US interests from Africa dates to at least 1986, when President Reagan accused Muammar Gaddafi's Libya of fomenting terrorism worldwide, supporting terrorist organizations that killed US diplomats and tourists, and allegedly setting up camps in the country to train terrorists. Viewing the Libyan regime as hostile to the USA, Reagan ordered US strategic bombing of alleged terrorist installations in Libya.[20] However, it was the coordinated bombing of the US embassies in Dar es Salaam (Tanzania), and Nairobi (Kenya), on August 7, 1998, with heavy casualties, that crystallized the reality of terrorist threat to American interests in Africa. Henceforth, Africa became a part of the broader war on terrorism which would necessitate a US military presence on the continent.

Islamist terrorism has been rife, principally in the Horn of Africa, North Africa, East Africa, and West Africa. The USA's counterterrorism campaign on the continent has thus been focused on key terrorist organizations based in these regions, such as al-Qaida in the Islamic Maghreb (AQIM); al-Shabaab, active in Somalia; Ansar Dine, operational in Mali; and the Nigerian-based Boko Haram. These groups not only pose a threat to American and Western interests in Africa; they also have a history of destabilizing their regions of operation.

The US approach to countering terrorism in Africa has been to forge counter-terrorism partnerships with some African states with the aim of equipping them with the necessary tools to enhance their capacity to effectively combat terrorism. In order to degrade terrorist cells and deny them a platform from which to operate, the US partnership has focused on providing support to its African partners in a number of areas. One critical area is bolstering the capacity of state militaries and law-enforcement agencies to conduct counter-terrorism operations. Another important area is working with partners to eliminate sources of funding for terrorist groups and at the same time helping governments to institute poverty-alleviating strategies that would benefit impoverished youths and discourage them from gravitating towards extremist groups.

To manage the US counter-terrorism collaboration with North and West African states, the Trans-Sahara Counterterrorism Partnership (TSCTP), an initiative of the Bureau of Counterterrorism (BCT), was established by the State Department in 2005. An equivalent agency, the Partnership for

Regional East Africa Counterterrorism (PREACT), was created in 2009 for the East African partner states. These initiatives have provided support for partner states as well as regional organizations at the forefront of the war against terrorism. For example, PREACT has provided military and financial support for the governments of Somalia and Kenya and for the African Union (AU) Mission in Somalia (AMISOM) against al-Shabaab.[21] A repercussion of the broader war on terrorism is a major US military presence in Africa. An indication of the prevailing militarization of the continent was the establishment of the United States Africa Command (AFRICOM) in 2007, as one of the six Department of Defense's regional combatant commands. AFRICOM uses the major US military base, Camp Lemonnier, in Djibouti, as operational ground for its military activities and counter-terrorism crusade in Africa. The military command has been roundly criticized for the alleged militarization of the continent. This opinion was aptly expressed by political scientist Olayiwola Abegunrin, when he stated:

> AFRICOM is an example of U.S. expansion in the name of the war on terrorism. ... It represents a policy of U.S. military-driven expansionism that will only enhance political instability, conflict, and the deterioration of state security in Africa.[22]

## CONCLUSION

The history of interactions and relations between the USA and Africa is a long one, although too often episodic. Nevertheless, it has been an enduring one that promises to continue to expand. This chapter has attempted to interrogate the major themes that have defined this history, from pre-Colombian America to the contemporary age of Islamist terrorism and its destabilization of states and entire regions. The latter period has given birth to significant US military presence on the continent. Perhaps justifiably, US strategic and security concerns will be the yardstick for delineating contemporary relations with Africa for some time to come. This has overshadowed other forms of US engagement with the continent such as partnership with African states and development assistance to promote trade and investment, political transparency and democratic institutions, health-care needs, and educational development.

## NOTES

1. For critique of Hegel's African thesis, see the following: Teshale Tibebu, *Hegel and the Third World: The Making of Eurocentrism in World History* (New York: Syracuse University Press, 2011); Babacar Camara, "The Falsity of Hegel's Theses on Africa," *Journal of Black Studies* 36, no. 1 (2005): 82–96; and Ronald Kuykendall, "Hegel and Africa: An Evaluation of the Treatment of Africa

in The Philosophy of History," *Journal of Black Studies* 23, no. 4 (1993): 571–81.

2. Among Stanley's works are, *Through the Dark Continent, Vol. 1 and II*, (1878); *In Darkest Africa: Or the Quest, Rescue, and Retreat of Emin Governor of Equatoria* (1890); and *My Dark Companions and Their Strange Stories* (1893). Note the reference to "dark" and "darkness" in the titles of the works.

3. Ivan Van Sertima, *They Came Before Columbus: The African Presence in Ancient America* (New York: Random House Publishing Group, 1976).

4. An example of a critique of this notion is provided in Gabriel Haslip-Viera, Bernard Ortiz de Montellano, and Warren Barbour, "Robbing Native Cultures: Van Sertima's Afrocentricity and the Olmecs," *Current Anthropology* 38, no. 3 (1997): 419–41.

5. US Department of State, Office of the Historian, "A Guide to the United States' History of Recognition, Diplomatic, and Consular Relations, by Country, Since 1776: Morocco." Retrieved Feb. 28, 2016 at https://history.state.gov/countries/morocco.

6. See The White House, Office of the Press Secretary, "FACT SHEET: Enduring U.S.-Tunisian Relations," May 21, 2015. Retrieved Sept. 13, 2016 at [https://www.whitehouse.gov/the-press-office/2015/05/21/fact-sheet-enduring-us-tunisian-relations]; and U.S. Department of State, Office of the Historian, "A Guide to the United States' History of Recognition, Diplomatic, and Consular Relations, by Country, since 1776: Tunisia." Retrieved Feb. 26, 2016 at https://history.state.gov/countries/tunisia.

7. On this subject, see Frank Lambert, *The Barbary Wars: American Independence in the Atlantic World* (New York: Hill and Wang, 2005); and Ray W. Irwin, *The Diplomatic Relations of the United States with the Barbary Powers 1776–1816* (Chapel Hill, NC: University of North Carolina Press, 1931).

8. The Trans-Atlantic Slave Trade Database provides a figure of 12.5 million. See the website at http://slavevoyages.org/.

9. For more on this subject, see Toyin Falola, and Adebayo Oyebade, eds., *The New African Diaspora in the United States* (New York: Routledge, 2017).

10. For more on this subject, see the following: John David Smith, ed., *The American Colonization Society and Emigration: Solutions to "The Negro Problem"* (New York: Garland Publishers, 1993); James Wesley Smith, *Sojourners in Search of Freedom: The Settlement of Liberia of Black Americans* (Lanham, MD: University Press of America, 1987); and Tom Shick, *Behold the Promised land: A History of Afro American Settler Society in Nineteenth-century Liberia* (Baltimore, MD: Johns Hopkins University press, 1984).

11. This subject is further discussed in Adebayo Oyebade, "Feeding America's War Machine: The United States and Economic Expansion in West Africa during World War II," *African Economic History*, no. 26 (1998): 119–40.

12. For more analysis on this subject, see Toyin Falola, and Adebayo Oyebade, *Hot Spot Sub-Saharan Africa* (Santa Barbara, CA: Greenwood, 2010), 99–125.

13. On this subject, see the following, Sanford J. Ungar, and Peter Vale, "South Africa: Why Constructive Engagement Failed," *Foreign Affairs* 64, no. 2 (1985): 234–58; Christopher Coker, *The United States and South Africa, 1968–1985: Constructive Engagement and its Critics* (Durham, NC: Duke University Press 1986); Robert I. Rotberg, "Reagan Era in Africa," in *Reagan and*

*the World*, ed. David E. Kyvig (New York: Greenwood Press, 1990), 119–38; and J.E. Davies, *Constructive Engagement?: Chester Crocker and American Policy in South Africa, Namibia & Angola* (Athens, OH: Ohio University Press, 2007).

14. See, One Hundred Sixth Congress of the United States of America, H.R. 434. Retrieved Oct. 11, 2016, at [http://trade.gov/agoa/legislation/agoa_main_002118.pdf] For an assessment of AGOA, see Kenneth E. Kalu, "Anchoring Development on Trade: Another Look at AGOA as an Instrument of Growth and Development," in *The United States' Foreign Policy in Africa in the 21st Century: Issues and Perspectives*, ed. Adebayo Oyebade (Durham, NC: Carolina Academic Press, 2014), 41–53.

15. This subject is further discussed in Victor Eno, "International Health Intervention as Foreign Policy: Case Study of United States' Global Health Initiative's (GHI) HIV/AIDS Program in Sub-Saharan Africa," in *The United States' Foreign Policy in Africa*, ed. Oyebade., 27–39.

16. For an overview of major conflicts, see Falola, and Oyebade, *Hot Spot: Sub-Saharan Africa*.

17. William D. Hartung, and Bridget Moix, "Deadly Legacy: U.S. Arms to Africa and the Congo War," World Policy Institute—Research Project, Feb. 2000. Retrieved Oct. 12, 2016 at http://www.worldpolicy.org/projects/arms/reports/congo.htm#table1.

18. See "Africa Crisis Response Initiative (ACRI)." Retrieved Oct. 13, 2016 at http://www.globalsecurity.org/military/ops/acri.htm.

19. For a scholarly evaluation of ACRI, see Emmanuel K. Aning, "African Crisis Response Initiative and the New African Security (Dis)order," *African Journal of Political Science* 6, no. 1 (2001): 43–67.

20. For more on this subject, see Nicholas Laham, *The American Bombing of Libya: A Study of the Force of Miscalculation in Reagan Foreign Policy* (Jefferson, NC: McFarland & Co., 2008).

21. The American counter-terrorism project in Africa is further discussed in Frederic Wehrey, "The Islamic State in Libya: U.S. Policy Options," in *Diplomacy and Extremism: Iran, ISIS and U.S. Interests in an Unraveling Middle*, ed. Dan Glickman (Washington, DC: The Aspen Institute, 2015), 47–51; U.S. Department of State, "Bureau of Counterterrorism and Countering Violent Extremism, Country Reports on Terrorism 2015: Africa." Retrieved Oct. 14, 2016, at [https://www.state.gov/j/ct/rls/crt/2015/257514.htm]; Hussein Solomon, *Terrorism and Counter-Terrorism in Africa: Fighting Insurgency from Al Shabaab, Ansar Dine, and Boko Haram* (New York: Palgrave Macmillan, 2015), 117–27; and George H. Rasmussen, ed., *U.S. Counter Terrorism Efforts in Africa* (Hauppauge, NY: Nova Science, 2009); and Jessica R. Piombo, "Terrorism and U.S. Counter-Terrorism Programs in Africa: An Overview," *Strategic Insights*, Volume VI, Issue 1 (January 2007). Retrieved Oct. 14, 2016 at https://calhoun.nps.edu/bitstream/handle/10945/11360/piomboJan07.pdf?sequence=1&isAllowed=y.

22. Olayiwola Abegunrin, "Africa Command Center (AFRICOM) and U.S. Foreign Policy of Militarization of Africa under the Obama Administration," in *The United States' Foreign Policy in Africa*, ed. Oyebade, 77–97.

# BIBLIOGRAPHY

Coker, Christopher. *The United States and South Africa, 1968–1985: Constructive Engagement and Its Critics.* Durham, NC: Duke University Press, 1986.

Davies, J.E. *Constructive Engagement?: Chester Crocker & American Policy in South Africa, Namibia & Angola.* Athens, OH: Ohio University Press, 2007.

Falola, Toyin, and Adebayo Oyebade. *Hot Spot Sub-Saharan Africa.* Santa Barbara, CA: Greenwood, 2010.

Falola, Toyin, and Adebayo Oyebade, eds. *The New African Diaspora in the United States.* New York: Routledge, 2017.

Irwin, Ray W. *The Diplomatic Relations of the United States with the Barbary Powers 1776–1816.* Chapel Hill, NC: University of North Carolina Press, 1931.

Lambert, Frank. *The Barbary Wars: American Independence in the Atlantic World.* New York: Hill and Wang, 2005.

Oyebade, Adebayo, ed. *The United States' Foreign Policy in Africa in the 21st Century: Issues and Perspectives.* Durham, NC: Carolina Academic Press, 2014.

Rasmussen, George H., ed. *U.S. Counter Terrorism Efforts in Africa.* Hauppauge, NY: Nova Science, 2009.

Smith, John David, ed. *The American Colonization Society and Emigration: Solutions to "The Negro Problem".* New York: Garland Publishers, 1993.

Solomon, Hussein. *Terrorism and Counter-Terrorism in Africa: Fighting Insurgency from Al Shabaab, Ansar Dine and Boko Haram.* New York: Palgrave Macmillan, 2015.

Van Sertima, Ivan. *They Came Before Columbus: The African Presence in Ancient America.* New York: Random House Publishing Group, 1976.

# CHAPTER 32

# Franco-African Relations: Still Exceptional?

*Tony Chafer*

The notion of exceptionalism in Franco-African relations has a long pedigree.[1] It can be traced back to the colonial period and the idea that French colonial policy was fundamentally different from, and indeed superior to, British policy. In contrast to the British approach of indirect rule, which did not seek to 'remake' the colonized in the image of the colonizer and which allowed the indigenous population to retain certain administrative, legal, and other powers, the French republican colonial project, rooted in direct rule and assimilation, was presented as progressive and modernizing. Many commentators have pointed to the 'myth of the contrast'[2]: yet the 'thin white line' of colonial administrators was just as much of a reality in French as it was in British Africa, with the result that colonial rule in practice, on the ground, was 'the art of the possible', involving improvisation and 'making do'. Many other factors (lack of resources, both financial and human, the underlying racism and assumption of superiority, and the overriding concern among colonial administrators to maintain stability) militated in favor of such convergence of practice between the colonial powers. However, French claims to exceptionalism were not entirely without substance. France was different from the other European colonizing powers, which were essentially conservative monarchies. To be sure, there was never any systematic attempt to transpose French republican traditions south of the Sahara but, unlike under British colonial rule, there was an underlying assumption that colonial administrators, through the system of direct rule, would seek to rid the

T. Chafer (✉)
Professor of French and African Studies, Centre for European and International Studies Research, University of Portsmouth, Portsmouth, UK

© The Author(s) 2018
M.S. Shanguhyia and T. Falola (eds.),
*The Palgrave Handbook of African Colonial and Postcolonial History*,
https://doi.org/10.1057/978-1-137-59426-6_32

colonies of their 'feudal' aristocracies by undermining hereditary chiefs and promoting Francophile, French-speaking elites to positions of limited power.[3] The influence of this conception of French colonial rule was far from uniform across the period: during the interwar years the policy of association cut in the opposite direction, with its stress on rural society and 'traditional' authority rather than urban educated elites. Nonetheless, the Republican modernising instinct continued to underpin French policy and this difference in approach came to the fore after the Second World War.

Both France and Britain emerged from the war much weakened. Not only were they confronted by the emergence of two new global superpowers (the USA and the USSR) but their relation to their colonial empires fundamentally changed as a result of the war. The notion of white superiority was undermined in the eyes of many Africans by the sight of whites, for the second time in less than thirty years, fighting each other in a global conflict. Moreover, the war was fought in the name of freedom and the Atlantic Charter of 1941 asserted the right of all peoples to choose the form of government under which they are governed. Although the colonial powers were quick to assert that this did not apply to their colonized territories as they were not yet ready to exercise such freedoms themselves, this was not a view that the majority of the colonized could be expected to share. Other factors, specific to France, undermined the notion of French superiority. The colonial empire in Africa divided in 1940, with French North and West Africa declaring for Vichy and French Equatorial Africa declaring for de Gaulle and Free France. Further underlining French weakness, liberation from Vichy rule came with the Allied landings in North Africa in November 1941 and was the result of Allied, not French, action. African troops subsequently played a significant role in the liberation of metropolitan France[4] and in some cases even found themselves, in Syria for example, fighting each other for two 'different Frances': Vichy France and Free France.

Thus, the maintenance of empire became even more important to France's continuing claim to world power status than it was before the war. However, de Gaulle's Free French government was acutely aware that for this to be possible, profound reforms would be needed in the colonial relationship. He therefore decided to convene a conference (to be held in the capital of French Equatorial Africa in January–February 1944 and called the Brazzaville African Conference) with the dual aim of making clear France's intention to hold onto its colonial empire after the war and promising wide-reaching reform to the colonized peoples of Africa who had remained loyal to France during the war. Although the conference had no legislative power and could only make recommendations, a significant number of its recommendations were subsequently enacted, including the abolition of forced labor and the *indigénat*,[5] the establishment of a fund for economic and social development in the colonies, and the plan for African deputies to be elected to the future National Assembly in Paris.

This laid the basis for a distinctive French approach to decolonization in Sub-Saharan Africa. Whereas British Colonial Secretary Malcolm MacDonald had expressed the view before the war that Britain's ultimate aim was to bring its colonies to self-government,[6] any form of self-government for France's colonial empire was explicitly ruled out at the Brazzaville Conference.[7] In keeping with this, France's Fourth Republic (1946–1958) embarked on a project to bring about decolonization through closer integration with the Republic and the full application of its core values of liberty, equality, and fraternity, rather than through secession from it.[8] This was enshrined in the constitution of the Fourth Republic by the declaration that France forms with the peoples of overseas France (as the colonized were now called) 'a Union based on the equality of rights and duties, without distinction of race or religion'. Indeed, each of the major colonial reform projects after 1944 (reconfiguring the empire and renaming it the French Union [Union Française] in 1945; the *loi-cadre* [framework law] of 1956, which devolved certain powers over internal affairs to the government councils that were established in the individual colonial territories; the creation of the Community [La Communauté] in 1958) was seen at the time not as a series of stages on the road to self-government and eventual independence but rather as a means of reconfiguring the French presence in order to maintain influence. To be sure, France was not alone among the colonial powers in seeking to ensure that decolonization did not mean complete withdrawal and in searching for ways to continue to exercise influence, albeit more cheaply; what was distinctive in the French case was that decolonization was taken to mean closer integration with metropolitan France. Decolonization was equated with the modernizing of Africa through economic and social development, while political independence was ruled out. In Indochina and Algeria, this policy would lead France into two highly destructive wars of decolonization[9]; in Sub-Saharan Africa it laid the basis for the Franco-African special relationship that would subsequently come to be characterized as the 'Franco-African state'[10] or *Françafrique*.[11]

The foundations for this special relationship were, first, the decision to provide for direct political representation of France's Sub-Saharan African colonies in the National Assembly in Paris. In some cases this even led to African politicians being appointed government ministers, such as, for example, Félix Houphouët-Boigny, who was a minister in the Mollet Government from 1956 to 1957. The consequence of this was to establish Paris as a key focus for the political activity of African political leaders under the Fourth Republic. Many of them affiliated to metropolitan political parties (Houphouët-Boigny, for example, having initially affiliated to the Communist Party in 1946, subsequently joined François Mitterrand's center-left Union Démocratique et Socialiste de la Résistance in 1950). They became thoroughly socialized into the French political system and culture[12] and formed close alliances (and often friendships) with leading French politicians. These political associations, which endured in many cases for up to thirty years beyond political independence in 1960, formed the bedrock of the post-colonial Franco-African special relationship.

Second, the creation of the Economic and Social Development Fund (FIDES) for overseas territories in 1946 played an important role. For the first time it channeled significant sums of money from the metropole to France's colonial territories in Sub-Saharan Africa. Yet FIDES could never hope to provide sufficient funds to meet the vast development needs of France's Sub-Saharan African empire. African political leaders thus inevitably competed with each other, lobbying the government for investment in major infrastructural projects such as roads, ports, hospitals, and schools since their legitimacy as political leaders depended, to a significant degree, on their success in obtaining these funds for their territories. This had two consequences. It reinforced the relationship of economic dependency between France and its African colonies, and laid the basis for a patron–client relationship in which the patron (France) and its African clients (its colonial territories, soon to become independent states) were locked into a relationship of mutual obligation, from which both parties expected to derive benefits. Finally, and just as importantly, it gave a number of large French companies, which benefited from these large infrastructure projects within what was a de facto protected market, a stake in the Franco-African special relationship.

## BELATED MOVES TOWARDS GRANTING POLITICAL INDEPENDENCE

This vision of an African future as part of a Franco-African, or 'Eurafrican', bloc with France at its head, came under growing challenge from within Africa, notably after the Bandung Conference of 1955.[13] The twenty-nine countries, most of them newly independent, that participated in the conference aimed to promote 'South–South' economic and cultural cooperation and to oppose all forms of colonialism and neo-colonialism. Following Bandung, African intellectuals and social movements increasingly saw themselves as part of a wider 'Third World' grouping, embracing North and Sub-Saharan Africa. At the same time as their political horizons were shifting, the military situation in Algeria was deteriorating and the Fourth Republic fell in 1958. The new French government under de Gaulle, who had left power in 1946 but was now recalled to restore order in Algeria and save France from a possible military coup d'état, was forced rapidly to improvise an 'exit strategy' that would both avert the danger of another colonial crisis developing in Sub-Saharan Africa and enable France to maintain its position and influence in the region. Initially, in the 1958 referendum on the new constitution that established the Fifth Republic, he offered the colonial territories in Sub-Saharan Africa the option of joining a renovated French Union, to be renamed the Community, or immediate independence. Only Sékou Touré's Guinea chose the latter course, while all the other territories voted 'yes' to de Gaulle's offer. However, the Community was to prove short-lived and, in the presence of General de Gaulle, on December 13, 1959, the president of the Mali Federation[14] and future president of Senegal Léopold Sédar Senghor announced that he was requesting the right to independence. Expressing his gratitude to, and confidence in, 'the man of the 18th of June' ('l'homme du 18 juin'), who had launched the struggle for the liberation of France in 1940, he declared:

> You are, Mr President, the inheritor of the French Revolution, which for the first time in the world dared to proclaim the rights of man and of the citizen ... We trust in you to 'do the rest' with us ... You have understood us: you have understood the History of this Century.

Significantly, he concluded:

> [W]e aim to achieve our national independence, not against France, but with France, in a great Franco-African grouping, by friendly and constitutional means ... Beyond constitutional independence, we aim to achieve 'real independence and guaranteed cooperation,' which is what you are offering.

De Gaulle's response was similarly gracious and eloquent. He pointed to France and Africa's shared language and ideas and acknowledged the legitimacy of their claim to 'international sovereignty', recognizing that without a state, you 'do not exist in the international order'. He stated his preference for the term 'international sovereignty' rather than 'independence', as it accorded better with the spirit of the age, and he went on:

> No one in truth enjoys total independence ... But international sovereignty means ... a lot. It means that a people takes responsibility for managing its affairs itself ... There is no international existence that is not first of all a national reality.

He finished by saying that the Mali Federation and its member states would achieve this objective 'with the agreement, the support, the help of France'.[15] Thus, only in 1959 did the French government finally abandon its efforts to hold back the rising tide of anti-colonialism and announce that it would grant independence to any colonial territories that requested it. Within little more than twelve months, the process was complete, and all the territories of former French West and French Equatorial Africa had achieved political independence.

The strategy for granting independence was called the 'transfer of competences'.[16] It involved transferring power to African political leaders who were for the most part friendly towards France, while at the same time putting in place an array of official agreements and other links which ensured that the future of France and its newly independent former colonies remained closely tied.

## THE ESTABLISHMENT OF THE FRENCH *PRÉ CARRÉ* IN AFRICA

Having accepted the inevitability of political independence, the priority was to ensure that decolonization did not mark an end, but rather a restructuring, of the imperial relationship in Sub-Saharan Africa. This was to be achieved in a number of different ways. Crucially, under the Fifth Republic, decision making on Africa policy largely bypassed the Ministry of Foreign Affairs; key decisions were instead made by the president in close consultation with his 'Africa cell' of special advisors at the presidential palace, and were not subject to parliamentary scrutiny. Indeed, Africa policy was for many years the 'reserved domain' of the president. This personalization of policy making was an important vehicle for the cultivation of regional friends among Africa's political leaders, a practice that was facilitated by the fact that many of the leaders of the newly independent states of Francophone Africa had, as we have seen, been *députés* in the National Assembly in Paris under the Fourth Republic. France's privileged sphere of influence in Africa was known as the *pré carré*.

Crucially, also, France signed cultural, technical and military cooperation accords with most of its ex-colonies at independence. The sending of large numbers of *coopérants*, often as teachers or government advisors to former French Africa served to maintain, and indeed reinforce, the French presence. In some cases the latter were sent to Africa to assist the newly independent governments, while in others former colonial officials simply exchanged their previous post as employee of the colonial government for a new one as advisor to the president or to an African minister in the government of the newly independent state.[17] A Ministry of Cooperation, successor to the colonial Ministry for Overseas France, was created. Its role was to oversee the cooperation agreements and it became in effect a ministry for Sub-Saharan Francophone Africa.

The policy of cooperation, which was at the heart of the Franco-African special relationship, rested on three pillars: the economic, the cultural, and the military.

### *The Economic Pillar*

Central to the economic pillar was the Franc zone. Maintained by most of the former French colonies at independence, it tied their currency, the CFA franc, to the French franc at a fixed rate and obliged the countries using the CFA franc to deposit 65% of their foreign currency reserves with the Trésor in Paris. No decision concerning the Franc zone could be taken without the approval of the Bank of France.

We have seen that, thanks to FIDES, a number of large French companies were already involved in Africa in the late colonial period. Thanks to the retention of the Franc zone, these economic links intensified after political independence. FIDES was abolished in 1959 and replaced by the Fonds d'Aide à la Coopération (FAC) with a brief to oversee the *coopération* agreements (economic, cultural, technical, military, and defense) with the newly independent Francophone African states. Two-thirds of French development aid went to France's former colonies in Sub-Saharan Africa, and a government agency, the Caisse Centrale de Coopération Economique, was created to provide development loans.[18] The contracts to carry out projects funded by these bodies went to French companies, some of them state-controlled or with strong links to the state, such as the Compagnie Générale des Eaux, Bouygues, Bolloré, Eiffage, and France Télécom.

The French oil company Elf-Aquitaine, which was established in 1966 under de Gaulle as a state-run company with a brief to secure French access to oil, also played a key part in Franco-African relations during the post-independence years. A key area of operation for the company was West and Central Africa, where it operated effectively as a state within a state.[19] It had its own security and intelligence services and was headed for many years by a former Gaullist intelligence officer, Pierre Guillaumat. Its role was in effect to act as the 'oil arm' of the French state, to ensure its energy independence and challenge the dominance of the big Anglo-American companies in this crucially important sector.[20] Before its merger with Total-Fina, it was accused of interference in African politics, contributing to military conflicts and corruption, which culminated in legal proceedings and a crisis in relations with the ruling regime in Congo-Brazzaville in 2003.

Economic relations between France and Francophone Africa have benefited from several special conditions. In particular, economic and financial ties were reinforced through the maintenance of the Franc zone and the policy of coopération which, while making a contribution to the development of the newly independent countries, maintained the relationship of dependency between France and Francophone Africa.

### *The Cultural Pillar and* Francophonie

The projection of French power overseas (the so-called *besoin de rayonnement*) is integral to France's image of itself on the international stage and often seen as independent from its material power.[21] In keeping with this, the second pillar of the Franco-African special relationship was the maintenance of the French language and promotion of French culture. This meant that central importance was attached to sustaining the position of French within the education systems of the newly independent states. This is reflected in the large sums disbursed through the *coopération* budget to secondary and higher education, which were seen as the most strategically important. Thus, from 1959 to 1967, the FAC devoted more than 38% of its budget to higher education and 27% to secondary education, with just 13% going to primary education and only 7.4% to the technical and vocational sector.[22] The sending of large numbers of *coopérants* as teachers, university lecturers, and educational advisors to former French Africa thus served to maintain, and indeed reinforce, the French cultural presence.[23]

This 'soft power' dimension of French power in Africa should not be underestimated and derives from the prestige attached to France as a beacon of humanist republicanism, promoting liberty, equality, fraternity, and universal human rights. Its role as perceived champion of the 'Third World' and its position at the forefront of promoting universal values not designed solely for the French people of France but for enlightened citizens throughout the world remains an important vector of French influence in Africa. This is despite the uses and abuses of these ideas during the colonial period, when supporters of empire sought to justify France's imperial enterprise through various forms of the civilizing mission (*mission civilisatrice*), which aimed to bring progressive enlightenment to the backward populations of Africa through exposure to the values, traditions, and culture of France.[24]

The Francophonie movement has also played a key role in maintaining the position of the French language in Africa. Its origins date back to a special issue of the review *Esprit* (1962), to which a group of intellectuals and politicians, including Senghor, contributed. The movement was supported through the Agence de Coopération Culturelle et Technique (ACCT), which was created in 1970 at the instigation of, among others, Senghor of Senegal and Diori of Niger. The movement only became formalized, however, when François Mitterrand hosted the first Francophonie Summit in Versailles in 1986. Since then, the summits have taken place biannually, usually outside France. The movement also underwent various changes, including the election of a secretary-general from 1998, before becoming the Organisation Internationale de la Francophonie (OIF) with a permanent secretariat in 2005. Despite these changes, the idealistic discourse portraying France and French culture to the world as a beacon of progressive values remains largely intact and Africa continues to play a key role within Francophonie; nearly half the organization's member states are in Africa, which is also the continent with the largest number of countries whose official language is French. With over 96 million French-speakers, the future of French as a global language is inescapably bound up with its development in Africa.

### The Military Pillar

Arguably the most important pillar of the Franco-African special relationship is the military one. At one level, the significance of the military dimension actually predates the colonial period, since African soldiers (the so-called *tirailleurs sénégalais*[25]) played a key role in the French conquest of Africa. In the twentieth century, hundreds of thousands of Africans served under the French flag in metropolitan France and other theaters in both world wars and in the two major wars against French colonial rule in Indochina and in

Algeria. Indeed, alongside African students who went to France in increasing numbers from 1945 onwards, they represent the largest social group that traveled to the metropole.[26] At independence these veterans also expected their role to continue to be recognized and took their demands directly to de Gaulle and Jacques Foccart. However, in 1960, in what appears to have been a unique legislative act, the French Parliament froze the military pensions of all veterans who were not French citizens, thus leading to discriminatory treatment of these veterans compared to their army colleagues who held a French passport.[27] Moreover, at independence, a parallel 'transfer of competences' played out in the military sphere, notably in former colonial territories such as Mauritania and Cameroon, where the French army remained on the ground after 1960 to assist the new governments of these countries in the fight against 'insurgents'. It is also worth noting that many of the coups d'état staged against post-colonial governments from the early 1960s were carried out by African military officers who had been educated in the French service. When deciding for or against intervention in a putsch situation, France's African affairs specialists often had to take account of the fact that these leaders had an older, military-related connection with France.[28]

At another level, the Ministry of Defense has been a key actor in French Africa policy since 1960. France maintained military bases in several countries, including the Central African Republic (CAR), Ivory Coast, Gabon, Senegal, and Djibouti and a large presence of permanently stationed troops, which numbered 58,500 in 1962, dropping to 21,300 in 1964 and 6700 in 1981,[29] before rising again thereafter. In line with the bilateral defense agreements signed at or shortly after independence, France intervened militarily in Africa more than thirty times between 1960 and the early 1990s, an average of one intervention a year and a record that led France to be dubbed the 'gendarme of Africa'.[30] It also had large numbers of military advisors working in the defense ministries of African governments and military officers embedded within African armies. In addition, France remains a major supplier of military equipment, including aircraft and armaments, to African countries. Moreover, in geopolitical terms, the Cold War afforded France a 'space' on the international stage in which it was able to present itself as the guarantor of Western interests in Sub-Saharan Africa, in a part of the world that the USA did not know well and which it did not see as central to its own security. The USA was therefore happy to delegate to France the task of ensuring that the region did not fall into the clutches of Moscow. These factors taken together have combined to ensure that the Ministry of Defense, together with the 'Africa cell' at the presidential palace, have played a pivotal role in determining and implementing Africa policy in the post-independence period, not least because the former has direct access to the Africa cell through the president's military chief of staff stationed within the palace.

*France's African Networks*

Alongside these official policy instruments there existed a complex range of unofficial, family-like, and often covert relationships.[31] For much of the thirty years after political independence these networks (*réseaux*), as they were called, were associated with Jacques Foccart, de Gaulle's 'man in the shadows' and special advisor on African affairs, to whom he had entrusted the task of maintaining France's position in Africa after independence.[32] Foccart subsequently also acted as advisor to President Pompidou and to Jacques Chirac, both when he was prime minister and president. There were also the Franco-African summits, instituted at the instigation of President Hamani Diori of Niger in 1973, which brought the French president and key ministers together with African political leaders in an annual celebration of their special relationship. These meetings were traditionally more like a family gathering than an official summit meeting, as there was no published agenda and no final communiqué afterwards. Finally, regular French presidential visits to Africa and visits by African presidents to Paris further helped to maintain the special relationship. The close interlinking of these official, semi-official, and unofficial dimensions of the relationship, together with support for them at the summit of the French state, were the key to France's success in establishing its African *pré carré* that was at the heart of its special relationship with Africa after political independence. Thus was the post-colonial Franco-African special relationship born, giving credence to, and further perpetuating, the notion of French exceptionalism.

## THE WATERSHED OF THE EARLY 1990s

With the end of the Cold War in 1990, the Cold War rationale for France maintaining its African *pré carré* disappeared. Acknowledging this new context, President Mitterrand's announcement to African leaders at the 1990 La Baule Franco-African summit that France intended in future to reward those regimes which undertook political reform signaled a significant break with past French practice, as political conditionality in this form had never been part of French African policy. His speech was clearly intended to send a message to African political leaders that they needed to initiate a process of political reform if they wished to continue to receive French support.[33] Although the new policy was actually implemented very unevenly across Francophone Africa, it nonetheless set in motion a profound process of political change, which started with the holding in Benin in 1990 of the first of a series of national conferences to reform the political systems of Francophone African countries.[34]

In the economic sphere, the introduction of economic conditionality, the so-called 'Balladur doctrine', or 'Abidjan doctrine' (because the new policy was unveiled in the Ivoirian capital) was a further sign of profound change. Concerned about the rising cost to France of its African relationship, Prime Minister Balladur announced in September 1993 that the granting of French public development aid would henceforth be conditional upon the prior signature of an accord with the International Monetary Fund (IMF) and World Bank. This was followed in January 1994 by the devaluation of the CFA franc by 50%.[35] Taken together, these two measures aimed to promote economic reform in France's former colonies, thereby reducing the cost to France of its African policy and making it more financially sustainable. A major reconfiguration of the Franco-African special relationship was underway.

The pressure for change increased further as a result of the 1994 genocide in Rwanda. Following the shooting down of President Habyarimana's plane in April 1994, his supporters were responsible for the killing of some 800,000 Rwandan Tutsis and moderate Hutus in the space of two months.[36] Having been the main external backer from 1990 to 1994 of the Habyarimana regime that prepared the genocide,[37] France was widely criticized for its failure both to see what was happening in the country and take measures to prevent it. France's response, in the aftermath of the genocide in June, was to seek United Nations support for a humanitarian mission to the country to protect refugees and establish, where possible, safe humanitarian areas. Operation Turquoise, as it was called, drew further criticism for two reasons. First, it was seen as an attempt to prop up the genocidal Hutu regime by providing many of the perpetrators of the genocide with a safe escape route into neighboring Zaire (now called the Democratic Republic of the Congo: DRC). Secondly, by deploying a second UN mission, Operation Turquoise, the French government was accused of undermining the mandate of the existing UN mission (UNAMIR) in the country.[38]

The Rwanda genocide and its aftermath marked a major turning point in French military policy in Africa. Since then, successive French governments have been careful to seek United Nations Security Council (UNSC) approval for military operations on the continent. It was also following the Rwanda debacle that the idea of creating an African peacekeeping force emerged, driven on the one hand by the need to gain increased international acceptance and consolidate domestic support for France's military effort on the continent, and on the other by the desire to share the burden, both militarily and politically, of this effort. Moreover, after the much criticized Operation Turquoise, France initially showed far less willingness to intervene militarily on the continent and substantial reductions were made in the number of French troops stationed in Africa, with two bases in the CAR being closed in 1999. Thus, under pressure from external forces which it could not control, France was forced to undertake major changes in its Africa policy.

## FROM BILATERALISM TO MULTILATERALISM

In the immediate aftermath of decolonization, bilateral ties with the newly independent African countries of France's African *pré carré* were preferred. From the late 1990s, a multilateral approach was increasingly adopted and

France sought to engage with African countries outside the *pré carré*. Various initiatives were launched with this in mind. The so-called 'P3' initiative began in 1997. This was an informal grouping that brought the USA, Britain, and France together at the level of the UNSC to coordinate their positions and harmonize their peacekeeping capacity-building programs in Africa. In the following year, at the Anglo-French summit in Saint-Malo, the British and French governments announced their intention to set aside a century of rivalry and cooperate more closely on African issues.[39] Also in 1998, in an effort to reduce its deployment of troops in Africa, France introduced its Renforcement des Capacités Africaines de Maintien de la Paix (RECAMP) program to build African peacekeeping capacity. This represented a watershed in French policy, as it marked a move away from its traditional approach of direct, unilateral military intervention towards a policy of training and supporting Africans to peacekeep themselves. At the same time, there was a recognition that France needed to engage beyond its traditional *pré carré* if it were to address security concerns effectively on the continent: Liberia, where ongoing instability threatened to affect neighboring countries that were part of France's *pré carré*, was an important object lesson in this respect. The attacks on the World Trade Center and the Pentagon in September 2001 further reinforced the converging focus on security issues between France, Britain, and the USA, as Africa now emerged as a key arena of the 'war on terror'.

Two key principles underpinned France's Africa policy from the late 1990s: 'Africanization' and 'Europeanization'. Africanization was supposed to mean ensuring that any military intervention has been requested by the government of the country, that it had the prior approval of the relevant African regional body, and involved African forces taking the lead role. The Europeanization of Africa policy was defined in various ways. It could mean, for example, European Union (EU) member states, through the European External Action Service, sharing responsibility for the protection (and eventual evacuation) of EU citizens in Africa; it could mean Europeanizing the French military presence on the continent, thereby freeing up more French troops and resources for operations in Africa led by NATO or the UN[40]; or, less ambitiously, Europeanization was a means of avoiding the charge of neo-colonialism, insofar as an EU military operation would not have the same direct association with France and would thus be seen as more politically 'neutral'. Above all, from a French point of view, 'Europeanization', like 'Africanization', is about burden sharing: sharing the risks and costs, of military operations in Africa with other actors.

In addition to the factors already mentioned, another key driver of this change was pressure on public finances. Lacking the resources to continue to do everything it wanted to do in Africa, French governments sought to make alliances, to be integrated into UN or EU actions and to build coalitions in which France would play a lead role, so as to benefit from the 'multiplier of influence' effect.[41] Under Presidents Chirac (2002–2007) and

Sarkozy (2007–2012) there was an effort to Europeanize French military interventions in Africa. There were three French-inspired European Security and Defense Policy (ESDP) military missions on African soil between 2003 and 2009: Operation Artemis in the DRC from June to September 2003; EUFOR, also in the DRC, from July to November 2006; and EUFOR Chad/CAR from January 2008 to March 2009. Also, President Sarkozy oversaw the Europeanization of the RECAMP program, which was renamed EURORECAMP in 2008.[42]

Within Africa, the move towards multilateralism has meant working increasingly with African regional organizations such as the Economic Community of West African States (ECOWAS) and the African Union (AU). Thus, after the 2003 Marcoussis agreement was signed between the political forces involved in the Ivoirian conflict, a largely Francophone force was deployed under the auspices of ECOWAS in 2003–2004.[43] Meanwhile, the French intervention force (Licorne) remained under French command, with ECOWAS's blessing but without its formal approval, and played a key role in supporting the ECOWAS (subsequently UN) peacekeeping force in Ivory Coast.[44] This trend towards increased engagement with multilateral organizations continued under President Sarkozy. Thus, French intervention to support Ivoirian troops in arresting President Gbagbo, after he refused to step down following his defeat in the 2010 presidential election, was carried out with the blessing of ECOWAS and the AU.[45] There were, however, limits to this cooperation, as was seen when, under the auspices of NATO, the French and UK governments launched air strikes on Libya in 2011 despite the opposition of the AU to any form of military intervention.[46]

## A New Partnership with Africa?

A recurring theme in French policy discourse on Africa in recent years has been the idea of partnership. Before his election as president, in a speech in Benin in 2006, Nicolas Sarkozy called for a new partnership with Africa, saying that Franco-African ties should 'not merely depend on the quality of the personal relations between heads of state' but should engage Africans 'as equal, responsible partners', supporting their efforts to build democracy and respect individual freedoms.[47] Similarly, prior to the 2012 presidential election, the Socialist Party's Africa specialist, Thomas Mélonio, published a pamphlet promising a 'modern' partnership with Africa, based on transparency and greater involvement of civil society and with a renewed emphasis on human rights and democracy.[48] The theme of partnership was taken up by Hollande after his election and placed at the center of his Africa policy. In a speech before the Senegalese National Assembly in Dakar in October 2012 he said: 'The time of *Françafrique* has passed. There is France and there is Africa. There is the partnership with relations based on respect, clarity and solidarity'.[49]

France has sought to portray itself, in particular, as a partner for peace and security in Africa. President Hollande announced in January 2013 that he was launching Operation Serval at the request of the Malian president to assist the country in fighting 'terrorist elements coming from the north,' to protect Malian sovereignty and 'the right of a population ... to live in freedom and democracy'.[50] Serval finished in July 2014 and was followed by a new operation, Barkhane, launched in August 2014, whose theater of operations stretches across the whole of the Francophone Sahel/Sahara region, spanning five countries (Mauritania, Mali, Burkina Faso, Niger, and Chad; referred to on the French Ministry of Defense website as the 'G5 Sahel'). It comprised, in 2015, 3000 men, 200 supply vehicles, 200 armored carriers, 6 fighter planes, 20 helicopters, 7 transport planes, and 4 drones. The operation is similarly justified by reference to the need to support the armed forces of the participating countries in their interventions against armed terrorist groups and to help prevent the reestablishment of terrorist sanctuaries in the region.[51] However, while the policy discourse regarding Barkhane is very much one of partnership with, and support for, African forces, the reality is that the capacity of the armed forces of these countries (with the exception of Chad) to intervene outside their national territory is limited and the operation is very much dependent on French troops, materiel, logistics, and intelligence.

It should be noted that this discourse of partnership is not motivated only by security concerns. France has seen its share of the African market reduced by 50% in the last ten years. A priority for the Hollande Government was to reverse this downward trend and double French trade with Africa, creating over 200,000 jobs in France.[52] President Macron has also placed emphasis on improving economic links with Africa. However, if this is to be achieved, France will have to continue the major reorientation of its trade links away from its Francophone *pré carré* towards the big economic powers in Africa, such as Nigeria, South Africa, and Angola.

## CONCLUSION

France's special relationship with Africa needs to be understood, first and foremost, in the context of the continuing importance attached to Africa in French foreign policy. Since the colonial period, Africa has been, and remains to this day, the foundation stone of France's ambition to remain a global power; outside Europe, it is *the* privileged arena for the projection of French power overseas. The various changes in French Africa policy, and the efforts to reconfigure Franco-African relations since the Second World War, need to be seen in this light.

The move away from exclusive, bilateral relations with (mainly Francophone) African states towards a multilateral approach was important, both in terms of reducing the cost of the French presence in Africa and addressing the accusation that France was behaving as a neo-colonial actor on the continent. The 'Europeanization' and 'Africanization' of policy were the twin pillars of a new African policy that was supposed to provide the means to avoid such criticisms in future. They were also seen as a way of relegitimizing France's military role in Africa. Following widespread domestic and international criticism of its role in Rwanda, in the late 1990s French governments initially abandoned unilateral military actions that had earned France the reputation of being the 'gendarme' of Africa. However, in recent years, the fight against terrorism has provided a new legitimacy for French military actions on the continent. The French military's traditional focus on territorial defense has been redirected to meet new global challenges, in particular the 'war on terror'[53] and the promotion of peace and security in Africa. Under the Hollande Presidency, France apparently became less afraid of criticism of its role as a 'neo-colonial' actor in Africa, which in turn facilitated the move back to more unilateral interventions, as we saw in 2013 with the interventions in Mali and CAR. The discourse of partnership with Africa remains, but the reality is that the EU and African actors were reduced to essentially supporting roles under President Hollande. France's relations with Africa thus remain in many respects 'exceptional'.

## NOTES

1. "Africa" in this article refers to Sub-Saharan Africa. French relations with Algeria are the subject of a separate chapter in this volume by Natalya Vince.
2. M. Semakula Kiwanuka, "Colonial Policies and Administrations in Africa: The Myths of the Contrasts," *African Historical Studies* 3, no. 2 (1970): 295–315.
3. Gordon D. Cumming, "Transposing the 'Republican' Model? A Critical Appraisal of France's Historic Mission in Africa," *Journal of Contemporary African Studies* 23, no. 2 (2005): 233–52.
4. African troops subsequently played a significant role in the liberation of metropolitan France; see Tony Chafer, "Forgotten Soldiers," *History Today* 58, no. 11 (2008): 35–37.
5. The *indigénat* was the native civil code that, according to Gregory Mann, defined "the very status of 'native' on which colonial rule relied" and listed offenses that "by definition only 'natives' could commit." Gregory Mann, *From Empires to NGOs in the West African Sahel: The Road to Nongovernmentality* (Cambridge: Cambridge University Press, 2015), 44.
6. John D. Hargreaves, *Decolonization in Africa*, 2nd ed. (London: Longman, 1996), 50.
7. Jacques Dalloz, *Textes sur la Décolonisation* (Paris: Presses Universitaires de France, 1989), 21.
8. Tony Chafer, *The End of Empire in French West Africa: France's Successful Decolonization?* (Oxford: Berg, 2002).
9. Anthony Clayton, *The Wars of French Decolonization* (London: Longman, 1994).
10. Jean-Pierre Dozon, *Frères et Sujets: la France et l'Afrique en Perspective* (Paris: Flammarion, 2003).

11. François-Xavier Verschave, *La Françafrique: le Plus Long Scandale de la République* (Paris: Stock, 1998).
12. Tony Chafer, "Education and Political Socialisation of a National-colonial Political Elite in French West Africa, 1936–47," *Journal of Imperial and Commonwealth History* 35, no. 3 (2007): 437–58.
13. Chafer, *The End of Empire*, 145–46.
14. The Mali Federation comprised Senegal, and French Soudan. It was dissolved in August 1960.
15. Charles de Gaulle, "Senghor Speech," Federal Assembly of Mali, December 13, 1959, Archives de l'Afrique Occidentale Française, Dakar, Series Fédération du Mali, File No. FM00018.
16. Article 78, Constitution of the Fifth Republic, in Dalloz, *Textes*, 77–78. See also Tony Chafer, "Senegal," in *Exit Strategies and State Building*, ed. Richard Caplan (New York: Oxford University Press, 2012), 48–51.
17. There were many examples of this throughout former French West and Equatorial Africa. One of the best known was former French colonial administrator Jean Collin, who became a government advisor in Senegal after independence and occupied the posts of finance and later interior minister. Yves Gounin, *La France en Afrique* (Brussels: Editions De Boeck, 2009), 24.
18. Gordon D. Cumming, *Aid to Africa* (Aldershot: Ashgate, 2001), 60.
19. Jean-Pierre Bat, *Le Syndrome Foccart* (Paris: Gallimard, 2012), 425–42.
20. Jacques Amalric, "Une création de De Gaulle pour contrer l'Amérique," *Libération* (2003, 13 January), 3.
21. John Keiger, *France and the World since 1870* (London: Arnold, 2001), 18.
22. Samy Mesli, "French *Coopération* in the Field of Education (1960–1980): A Story of Disillusionment," in *Francophone Africa at Fifty*, ed. Tony Chafer, and Alexander Keese (Manchester: Manchester University Press, 2013), 124.
23. Gérard Bossuat, "French Development Aid, and Co-operation under De Gaulle," *Contemporary European History* 12, no. 4 (2003): 447.
24. Margaret A. Majumdar, "France in the World," in *The Routledge Handbook of French Politics and Culture*, ed. Aurélien Mondon, Marion Demossier, Nina Parish, and David Lees.
25. Despite their name, the *tirailleurs sénégalais* actually came from across French Sub-Saharan Africa, not just from Senegal.
26. Myron Echenberg, *Colonial Conscripts. The Tirailleurs Sénégalais in French West Africa, 1857–1960* (Portsmouth, NH: Heinemann, 1991); and Marc Michel, *Les Africains et la Grande Guerre: l'appel à l'Afrique (1914–1918)* (Paris: Karthala, 2003).
27. "Une dette de sang", *Le Monde*, January 5, 2002.
28. Alain Rouvez, *Disconsolate Empires: French, British, and Belgian Military Involvement in Post-Colonial Sub-Saharan Africa* (Lanham, MD: University Press of America, 1994), 18; and Camille Evrard, "Transfer of Military Power in Mauritania: from Ecouvillon to Lamantin (1958–1978)," in *Francophone Africa at Fifty*, ed. Tony Chafer, and Alexander Keese (Manchester: Manchester University Press, 2013), 100.
29. Robin Luckham, "French Militarism in Africa," *Review of African Political Economy* 9, no. 24 (1982): 55–84.

30. Tony Chafer, "Hollande and Africa Policy," *Modern and Contemporary France* 22, no. 4 (2014): 517; and Victor-Manuel Vallin, "France as the Gendarme of Africa, 1960–2014," *Political Science Quarterly* 130, no. 1 (2015): 79–101.

31. Jean-François Médard, "France-Africa: Within the Family," in *Democracy and Corruption in Europe*, ed. Donatella Della Porta, and Yves Mény (London: Pinter, 1997), 22–24.

32. Bat, *Le Syndrome Foccart*.

33. Tony Chafer, "Chirac and '*la Françafrique*': No Longer a Family Affair," *Modern and Contemporary France* 13, no. 1 (2005): 14–15; and Gounin, *La France en Afrique*, 41.

34. Fabien Eboussi Boulaga, *Les Conférences Nationales en Afrique Noire - une Affaire à Suivre* (Paris: Karthala, 2009).

35. Chafer, "Chirac and '*la Françafrique*,'" 14–15; Gounin, *La France en Afrique*, 44.

36. Linda Melvern, *Conspiracy to Murder: The Rwandan Genocide* (London: Verso, 2006).

37. Daniela Kroslak, *The Role of France in the Rwandan Genocide* (London: Hurst, 2007).

38. Bruno Charbonneau, *France and the New Imperialism: Security Policy in Sub-Saharan Africa* (Aldershot: Ashgate, 2008), 140–41.

39. Tony Chafer, "Beyond Fashoda: Anglo-French Security Cooperation in Africa since St-Malo," *International Affairs* 86, no. 5 (2010): 1129–47.

40. Thomas Mélonio, *Quelle Politique Africaine pour la France en 2012?* (Paris: Fondation Jean Jaurès), 33–34.

41. Daniel Bourmaud, "From Unilateralism to Multilateralism: The Decline of French Power in Africa," in *From Rivalry to Partnership?: New Approaches to the Challenges of Africa*, ed. Tony Chafer, and Gordon Cumming (Farnham: Ashgate, 2011), 52.

42. Tony Chafer, "The AU: A New Arena for Anglo-French Cooperation in Africa?" *Journal of Modern African Studies* 49, no. 1 (2010): 64.

43. Douglas A. Yates, "France, the EU, and Africa," in *The EU and Africa: from Eurafrique to Afro-Europa*, ed. Adekeye Adebajo, and Kaye Whiteman (London: Hurst, 2012), 336–37.

44. Charbonneau, *France and the New Imperialism*, 165–66.

45. Tony Chafer, "The UK and France in West Africa: Towards Convergence?" *African Security* 6, no. 3–4 (2013): 246.

46. Thomas Alberts, "The African Union and Libya, on the Horns of a Dilemma," *African Arguments* (blog), November 2, 2011, http://africanarguments.org/2011/11/02/the-african-union-and-libya-on-the-horns-of-a-dilemma-by-thomas-alberts/.

47. Gounin, *La France en Afrique*, 70–72.

48. Mélonio, *Quelle Politique Africaine pour la France?*

49. Christophe Chatelot, "M. Hollande veut un 'partenariat' avec l'Afrique," *Le Monde*, October 14, 2012.

50. Stephen W. Smith, "In Search of Monsters," *London Review of Books* 35, no. 3 (2013): 3.

51. Ministry of Defense, *Opération Barkhane* (French Government, 2015) http://www.defense.gouv.fr/operations/sahel/dossier-de-presentation-de-l-operation-barkhane/operation-barkhane.

52. Marie Bezou, "La France appelle l'Afrique à prendre en charge sa sécurité," *Bulletin Quotidien*, December 8, 2013: 6; and Pierre Moscovici, "Mon objectif: doubler les flux commerciaux entre la France et l'Afrique," *Jeune Afrique*, no. 2760, 1–7 (2013): 82.

53. Yates, "France, the EU and Africa," 329–30.

## BIBLIOGRAPHY

Bat, Jean-Pierre. *Le Syndrome Foccart*. Paris: Gallimard, 2012.

Bossuat, Gérard. "French Development Aid and Co-operation under De Gaulle." *Contemporary European History* 12, no. 4 (2003): 431–56.

Bourmaud, Daniel. "From Unilateralism to Multilateralism: The Decline of French Power in Africa." In *From Rivalry to Partnership?: New Approaches to the Challenges of Africa*, edited by Tony Chafer, and Gordon Cumming, 41–54. Farnham: Ashgate, 2011.

Chafer, Tony. *The End of Empire in French West Africa: France's Successful Decolonization?* Oxford: Berg, 2002.

———. "Chirac and 'la Françafrique': No Longer a Family Affair." *Modern and Contemporary France* 13, no. 1 (2005): 7–23.

———. "Education and Political Socialisation of a National-colonial Political Elite in French West Africa, 1936–47." *Journal of Imperial and Commonwealth History* 35, no. 3 (2008): 437–58.

———. "Forgotten Soldiers." *History Today* 58, no. 11 (2008): 35–37.

———. "The UK and France in West Africa: Towards Convergence?" *African Security* 6, no. 3–4 (2013): 234–56.

Chafer, Tony, and Alexander Keese, eds. *Francophone Africa at Fifty*. Manchester: Manchester University Press, 2013.

Charbonneau, Bruno. *France and the New Imperialism: Security Policy in Sub-Saharan Africa*. Aldershot: Ashgate, 2008.

Clayton, Anthony. *The Wars of French Decolonization*. London: Longman, 1994.

Cumming, Gordon D. *Aid to Africa*. Aldershot: Ashgate, 2001.

———. "Transposing the 'Republican' Model? A Critical Appraisal of France's Historic Mission in Africa." *Journal of Contemporary African Studies* 23, no. 2 (2005): 233–52.

Dozon, Jean-Pierre. *Frères et Sujets: la France et l'Afrique en Perspective*. Paris: Flammarion, 2003.

Echenberg, Myron. *Colonial Conscripts. The Tirailleurs Sénégalais in French West Africa, 1857–1960*. Portsmouth, NH: Heinemann, 1991.

Gounin, Yves. *La France en Afrique*. Brussels: Editions De Boeck, 2009.

Hargreaves, John D. *Decolonization in Africa*. 2nd ed. London: Longman, 1996.

Keiger, John. *France and the World since 1870*. London: Arnold, 2001.

Kroslak, Daniela. *The Role of France in the Rwandan Genocide*. London: Hurst, 2007.

Majumdar, Margaret A. "France in the World." In *The Routledge Handbook of French Politics and Culture*, edited by Aurélien Mondon, Marion Demossier, Nina Parish, and David Lees. London: Routledge, 2017.

Mann, Gregory. *From Empires to NGOs in the West African Sahel: The Road to Nongovernmentality*. Cambridge: Cambridge University Press, 2015.

Médard, Jean-François. "France-Africa: Within the Family." In *Democracy and Corruption in Europe*, edited by Donatella Della Porta, and Yves Mény, 22–34. London: Pinter, 1997.

Michel, Marc. *Les Africains et la Grande Guerre: l'appel à l'Afrique (1914–1918)*. Paris: Karthala, 2003.

Rouvez, Alain. *Disconsolate Empires: French, British, and Belgian Military Involvement in Post-colonial Sub-Saharan Africa*. Lanham, MD: University Press of America, 1994.

Verschave, François-Xavier. *La Françafrique: le Plus Long Scandale de la République*. Paris: Stock, 1998.

Yates, Douglas A. "France, the EU and Africa." In *The EU and Africa: From Eurafrique to Afro-Europa*, edited by Adekeye Adebajo, and Kaye Whiteman, 317–42. London: Hurst, 2012.

# CHAPTER 33

# Algeria and France: Beyond the Franco-Algerian Lens

## Natalya Vince

The dominant metaphor used to describe relations between Algeria and France is that of a forced marriage which ended in a bitter separation, fraught with recrimination on both sides. Writing in 1991, Benjamin Stora, one of the leading historians of France and Algeria, argued:

> Franco-Algerian relations were forged in violence, by the imposition of the colonial system and by a seven-year war which enabled Algeria to acquire independence. This is why, thirty years later, time has not appeased passions ... From 1962 onwards, the Mediterranean, whose name in Arabic, *al-bahr al-abyad al-mutawassat* means 'the white sea in the middle,' became a fracture line, an imaginary blue 'wall.' The violent divorce has unceasingly fed tensions, obsessions and fantasies from one shore to the other.[1]

This language of intimate enemies captures what is often depicted as the exceptionality of the Franco-Algerian relationship. In the context of France's African empire and subsequent Franco-African relations, this relationship is characterized on both sides of the Mediterranean and in much academic literature as both exceptionally close and exceptionally bad.

Yet while there were many distinctive features to the French colonial presence in Algeria (the form which decolonization took and post-independence relations), the case for exceptionalism has been overstated. This has resulted from the tendency to study Algeria solely through a French lens.

N. Vince (✉)
University of Portsmouth, Portsmouth, UK

M.S. Shanguhyia and T. Falola (eds.),
*The Palgrave Handbook of African Colonial and Postcolonial History*,
https://doi.org/10.1057/978-1-137-59426-6_33

For the colonial period, relatively little attention has been paid to Algeria's connections to other parts of the French empire in terms of people, policy, and intertwined chains of events. For the post-independence period, Algeria has continued to be predominantly viewed through the perspective of its relationship to France, and rarely located in broader African, Middle Eastern, or Third Worldist contexts.

## COLONIAL ALGERIA: THREE DEPARTMENTS OF FRANCE, A LARGE SETTLER POPULATION, MULTIPLE FORMS OF FRENCH CITIZENSHIP

The 1830 invasion of Algiers, at the time under Ottoman rule, marked the beginning of three decades of military conquest. Algeria was thus neither part of France's 'first wave' of empire in the Americas from the sixteenth to the eighteenth century, nor was it part of the 'second wave' of empire acquired by the French Third Republic (1870–1940) in West and Equatorial Africa, and in Tunisia and Morocco, during the late nineteenth-century 'Scramble'. Moreover, Algeria was neither a colony (as French possessions were in Sub-Saharan Africa) nor a protectorate (like Tunisia and Morocco). Instead, from 1848 onwards, Algeria was three departments of France: Oran, Algiers, and Constantine. The Sahara would remain under direct military control until it was turned into departments in 1957.

Algeria was also distinctive in the French empire because it had a large settler population. These settlers came not only from France, but also from Spain, Italy, Malta, Germany, and Switzerland. They were a heterogeneous group of political exiles, landless farmers, urban laborers, and large farming and business interests. In 1889, in a bid to shore up the Frenchness of 'French Algeria', all children of European settlers were automatically given French citizenship. This contrasted sharply with the citizenship status of the autochthonous population. A decree passed in 1865 declared that all 'Muslim natives' were French nationals, but barred them from benefiting from full French citizenship unless they renounced their Muslim personal status; that is to say, those aspects of Muslim family law which were considered at odds with the French civil code, such as polygamy, repudiation, and the right of parents to choose their child's spouse. Renouncing their personal status was considered an act of apostasy by most Muslims, and for the few thousand who did seek naturalization the colonial legal system put significant obstacles in their way. Thus, under the cloak of 'respect for tradition' and the supposed lack of Muslims' cultural readiness to embrace full French citizenship, the French state had found the means for a numerical minority to politically dominate the majority of the population. The 1865 law also applied to Algeria's autochthonous Jewish minority for five years (with their personal status being Jewish Mosaic Law). In 1870, the Crémieux Decree collectively accorded full citizenship to around 30,000 Jews in the three departments of Algeria. The

1891 census counted 530,924 'Europeans' (a category which now included the Jews of Algeria) for 3,577,000 'Muslims', a ratio of 1: 6.7. By 1954, however, the European presence of 984,000 could not keep pace with the Muslim population of 8,675,000 and this ratio was 1: 8.8.[2]

## CONNECTIONS AND PARALLELS ACROSS EMPIRES: SETTLER MYTHS, UNDER-ADMINISTRATION, THE *INDIGÉNAT*, COLONIAL TROOPS, AND ANTI-COLONIAL CAMPAIGNS

Settlers in Algeria sustained many of the same myths to justify their presence that white settlers did in other parts of Africa. Europeans credited themselves with having 'made the desert bloom' after centuries of supposed environmental mismanagement by the 'natives'.[3] The Tamazight-speaking (Berber) peoples of the region of Kabylia were depicted as a lost European Christian tribe, 'noble savages' more susceptible to being assimilated into French culture and becoming loyal colonial administrators than the Arabic-speaking majority.[4] Many settlers appropriated the label 'Algerian' (*Algérien*) for themselves, seeing their identity and culture as distinct from both that of metropolitan France and the autochthonous majority who were attributed a variety of labels, including 'natives' (*indigènes*), 'Muslims', and later 'French Muslims'.

For the colonized population of Algeria, the experience of colonialism had many similarities to that of peoples living under French rule south of the Sahara. Although the European presence in Algeria was far greater than in other parts of the empire, this presence was largely concentrated in Algeria's coastal cities. Vast swathes of Algerian territory had very little contact with the colonial administration or indeed anyone of European origin. In 1948, less than one in ten Muslim children aged between six and fourteen were in primary school (this increased to just under 17% by 1954) while all European children had access to education.[5] In 1954, there were only 1900 doctors in Algeria, equating to 5300 patients per doctor, most of whom were based in the major cities where the settlers lived.[6] As French nationals, not full citizens, Muslims were also subject to the *indigénat*: a series of laws and rules which applied only to the 'native' population. Codified in 1881, it proscribed a whole range of activities, such as organizing a meeting without a permit, leaving the territory without permission, and disrespecting figures of authority. First trialed in Algeria, versions of the *indigénat* were subsequently applied all over the French empire, before being repealed after the Second World War.

As ideas about how to 'run' empire circulated, so did the men used to conquer territory and enforce colonial rule. Louis Faidherbe is best known as the general and colonial administrator who vastly increased France's West African empire, but he had received his military training in Algeria, under the ruthless Marshall Thomas Robert Bugeaud. Regiments of colonized men also moved across the empire. *Tirailleurs sénégalais* (literally, Senegalese riflemen, but including troops from across France's Sub-Saharan empire) participated in brutal massacres of local populations in Sétif, Guelma, and Kherrata (eastern Algeria) in the wake of anti-colonial demonstrations on May 8, 1945. Algerian 'French Muslims' went to fight in the French army in Indochina between 1946 and 1954. Tirailleurs sénégalais fought against the Front de Libération Nationale (National Liberation Front, FLN) during the War of Independence, as did some Algerian men, today commonly referred to as *harkis*.

In the first political movements to emerge in the interwar period to challenge colonial domination and discrimination, there were also connections across different parts of the French empire. When the French army conscripted colonized men during the First World War, politicians in Algeria and in Senegal's Four Communes seized on the occasion to demand, in return for the 'blood tax', citizenship rights for a much wider segment of the population. In 1916, Deputy Blaise Diagne successfully secured full citizenship for the black residents of Saint-Louis, Dakar, Gorée, and Rufisque, in return for his participation in the French army's recruitment campaigns. In Algeria, the Emir Khaled, a captain in the French army as well as being the grandson of the Emir Abdelkader who had led resistance against the French invasion in the 1830s and 1840s, also sought to link citizenship to conscription and lobby for an extension of full citizenship to more 'Muslims', but with less success.[7]

Migration to the metropole from across North Africa, Indochina, and Sub-Saharan Africa, of both intellectual elites and factory workers, meant that mainland France, and particularly Paris, became a hub for the emergence of critiques of colonial rule in the interwar years.[8] There was a greater degree of political freedom compared to the colonies, and the first nationalist movements found an early, although not sustained, source of support from the French Communist Party. In 1926, Messali Hadj created the first overtly nationalist organization, the Etoile Nord-Africaine (North African Star, ENA) in Paris. In 1927, Messali and other ENA members attended the conference of the League Against Imperialism in Brussels, alongside representatives from Senegal, Tunisia, Indonesia, the African National Congress (ANC), and the Syria-Palestinian Congress. Although the massacres of Sétif are described by some historians as the beginning of the War of Independence,[9] in post-Second World War Algeria, Algerian politicians such as Messali and Ferhat Abbas sought to participate in the political process like their counterparts in Sub-Saharan Africa. Abbas was a deputy in the First Constituent Assembly, which played a major role in shaping the French Union of the 1946 constitution, alongside Lamine Guèye, Léopold Sédar Senghor, and Félix Houphouët-Boigny. Members of both Messali and Abbas's post-Second World War political parties (respectively, the Mouvement pour le Triomphe des Libertés Démocratiques [Movement for the Triumph of Democratic Liberties, MTLD] and the Union Démocratique du Manifeste Algérien

[Demoratic Union of the Algerian Manifesto, UDMA]) stood as candidates in local elections, although the blatant ballot rigging by colonial authorities left a bitter taste.

## THE VIOLENT ALGERIAN WAR VS PEACEFUL DECOLONIZATION IN SUB-SAHARAN AFRICA?

The main claim to difference between Algeria and France's Sub-Saharan African colonies (and indeed the protectorates of Tunisia and Morocco) is based on contrasting Algeria's anti-colonial war, in which independence was wrenched from a recalcitrant France, with the peaceful 'transfer of power' in the rest of France's African empire; although as Tony Chafer has highlighted, this 'successful decolonization' was less the result of careful planning on the part of the French and much more accidental and ad hoc.[10] Just months after the French government had extricated itself from Indochina after the army's humiliating defeat at Dien Bien Phu, on November 1, 1954, a newly formed organization called the FLN, frustrated with what it saw as the failings of previous anti-colonial movements to make progress, carried out a series of explosions, assassinations, and acts of sabotage across Algeria. The attacks were accompanied by a statement calling for 'The restoration of the sovereign, democratic, and social Algerian state, within the framework of Islamic Principles'.[11] The response of the French government was unequivocal; Algeria, senior politicians repeated, was France.

The conflict would drag on for another seven-and-a-half years. Some 1,400,000 French soldiers, the vast majority conscripts, were sent to Algeria. Around 25,000 of these men were killed, as were 4000–5000 European settlers and an estimated 15,000–30,000 *harkis*. Hundreds of thousands of Algerian combatants and civilians were killed; the official figure in Algeria is one and a half million martyrs; historians are more cautious in their estimations of between 350,000 and 400,000 Algerians killed.[12] The conflict wreaked economic devastation and brought about major social upheaval. Vast areas of the Algerian countryside were declared no-go zones and populations forcibly displaced. Bombing campaigns by the French army destroyed land and livelihoods. The 'Battle of Algiers' between autumn 1956 and autumn 1957 pitched the FLN's clandestine urban networks, which carried out bomb attacks and assassinations against military and civilian targets in the capital, against the might of the French army. Within a year, the army had largely dismantled the FLN's Algiers network. However, the methods which they had used to do so (systematic use of torture, assassination, forced 'disappearances') both reinforced divisions between 'Europeans' and 'Muslims' and undermined the Republic's claim to its 'civilizing mission'.

The ongoing conflict would bring down the Fourth Republic, as settlers and army generals in Algiers, unconvinced of the center-left government's resolve to hold on to Algeria, staged the beginnings of a coup in May 1958.

The Algerian crisis provided the conditions for the political comeback of General Charles de Gaulle, posited as the savior (once again) of France, and the creation of the Fifth Republic.

This was a war very much fought on the world stage with both sides producing extensive propaganda for global consumption and seeking to win supporters and international legitimacy through formal and informal diplomacy. The FLN sent delegates to the Afro-Asian conference in Bandung in April 1955, which in turn issued a declaration of support for the rights of the peoples of North Africa to self-determination and independence. The FLN scored a major political victory in December 1960, when the United Nations General Assembly recognized the right of the Algerian people to self-determination and independence.

The war was not a straightforward confrontation between the 'French' and the 'Algerians'. While the majority of the Algerian population had rallied to the FLN by 1956–1957, internecine conflict continued between supporters of the FLN and supporters of the rival Mouvement National Algérien (Algerian National Movement, MNA), created by Messali at the end of 1954. In addition, 200,000–400,000 Algerians (through ideological conviction, coercion, or economic necessity) served in the French army.[13] They would come to be known as *harkis*. In early 1961, the Organisation de l'Armée Secrète (Secret Armed Organisation, OAS) was created, composed of hardline settlers and disillusioned members of the French army, to wage war against the French army, the FLN, and the wider Algerian civilian population.

A peace treaty, the Evian Accords, was finally signed between France and the FLN in March 1962. An immediate ceasefire was announced, political prisoners released, and a referendum planned on self-determination. The violence however, did not end. The OAS accelerated its assassinations and participated in a 'scorched earth' campaign to leave no functioning infrastructure behind. The European population of Algeria, fearing that their only choice in independent Algeria was 'the coffin or the suitcase' fled between spring and summer 1962, becoming 'repatriates' in a country most had never seen. Many *harkis* and their families also sought to escape, but the French state was much more reluctant to accommodate their arrival. Thousands were parked in camps in France; many others were left behind and became victims of reprisals, although others integrated back into their local communities. In summer 1962, the FLN imploded into its competing factions, with the army generals who had spent much of the war based in Tunisia and Morocco gaining the upper hand over both the combatants fighting on Algerian territory and the politicians who had participated in much of the FLN's peace negotiations and international diplomacy. By the start of autumn 1962, a single party state (under the banner of the party of the FLN) had taken shape.

The distinctiveness of Algeria in the context of the decolonization of France's African empire seems clear in a number of ways. First, the scale of the violence and the tortuous length of the conflict compared to other colonies are undeniable. Second, the way in which FLN politicians appealed to and used the international context to press home their demands for total independence was, for Matthew Connelly, a 'diplomatic revolution', an example which would go on to inspire the African National Congress and the Palestinian Liberation Organization.[14] In this perspective, Algeria broke with the pattern of French decolonization in the rest of Africa and established a new road map. Less attention, however, has been paid to how decolonization in Algeria was, in other ways, similar in pattern and also intertwined in process to decolonization in the rest of the French empire.

The French response to nationalist demands and anti-colonial critiques across its African empire held a number of similarities. In Algeria, there was military repression on a massive scale, but this always went hand in hand with major reform programs. The logic driving this reform was much the same as in Sub-Saharan Africa ('decolonization through integration' [Chafer, this volume]), that is to say, applying the oft-proclaimed but rarely practiced Republican values of liberty, equality, and fraternity through according equal political rights and investing in economic and social development.[15] Between 1955 and 1958, Jacques Soustelle, as Governor General of Algeria, pushed forward with his idea of 'integration' and the creation of what he saw as a modern, inclusive Franco-Algerian nation. (Bitterly disappointed at the failure of this to come to fruition, he went on to join the OAS.) Extensive efforts were made to win over Muslim women, notably between 1957 and 1959, through a program of increasing access to schooling and health care, implementing voting rights and replacing the 'Muslim personal status' with the French civil code in matters of family law.[16] The Constantine Plan, launched by de Gaulle in October 1958, was an ambitious series of economic and social reforms, with the indisputably political aim of reducing the stark inequalities between the 'European' and 'Muslim' populations.

As in Sub-Saharan Africa, voters in Algeria were called to the polls in September 1958 to vote on the new Fifth Republic constitution and the creation of the 'French Community', with greater devolved powers passed over to the colonies. The population of Algeria voted for the constitution and for the Community by a large majority and with a fairly high turnout. Indeed, de Gaulle's ideal solution to the Algerian crisis at this point in the war would have been for Algeria to remain within the Community, alongside Senegal, Ivory Coast, Chad, and so forth. In a televised speech in September 1959, de Gaulle laid out three options for Algeria: total integration (which, unlike Soustelle, he viewed as neither feasible nor desirable), total independence (as Guinea had chosen in 1958, which in de Gaulle's view presented a grave danger for Algeria politically and economically), or (his preferred option) a federal relationship between a French-backed Algerian government, with interdependency in key areas such as the economy, education, defense, and foreign policy. The FLN was not prepared to accept interdependency, but this should not distract us from the fact that this was de Gaulle's preferred option, which would have made France's 'decolonized' relations with Algeria closely resemble those which France established with its former Sub-Saharan African colonies. By 1960, as a 'Community' solution in Algeria came to be understood as politically impossible by senior French politicians, the all-consuming nature of the Algerian crisis sped up decolonization elsewhere, and all of France's Sub-Saharan African colonies became formally independent.

## THE BASIS OF POST-INDEPENDENCE FRANCO-ALGERIAN RELATIONS: CONFRONTATION IN RHETORIC, COOPERATION IN PRACTICE, AND A WORLD OF CONNECTIONS

If the way in which decolonization took place shaped the basis of post-independence French-Sub-Saharan African relations (see Chafer, this volume), this was also true in the Algerian case. In the Sub-Saharan African case, French politicians and civil servants in the post-independence period engaged with interlocutors with whom they had long relationships and mutual understanding of their shared interests. In Algeria in the 1960s and 1970s, key politicians and foreign policy actors were not career diplomats or civil servants but war veterans with 'revolutionary experience'.[17] Algerian statesmen unequivocally positioned their newly independent country as part of the Arab and Muslim world, while at the same time building relations with the Eastern Bloc. Algeria also saw itself as a leader of the wider Third Worldist movement, pioneering a 'third way' between capitalist exploitation and the more oppressive aspects of communism. Algeria proudly hosted the 1969 Pan-African Festival in Algiers, as well as providing a haven and training ground for anti-colonial activists and revolutionaries from around the world.[18] While nourishing these transnational connections, Algeria maintained a principle of neither allowing other countries to meddle in its affairs, nor meddling in the affairs of other countries, and a marked preference for bilateral, as opposed to multilateral, relations.

France, meanwhile, its colonies gone, threw itself into achieving that Gaullist buzzword 'greatness' through other means. The commonly held idea that France 'replaced' empire with a leading role in European construction requires nuance, however; the two were not mutually exclusive. As an integral part of French territory, Algeria was part of France's European Economic Community (EEC) negotiations, and indeed part of the EEC between 1957 and 1962. After independences, de Gaulle sought to reinvent himself as a decolonizer and France as a friend (and leader) of the 'Third World', not least to counteract the negative impact of the Algerian War on France's international standing, notably in the eyes of newly independent countries. This meant that *coopération* (technical and educational cooperation) was not only more necessary than ever, it also needed to be exemplary.[19] In short, how France and Algeria positioned themselves in relation to each other was important in constructing their future away from each other.

The Evian Accords of March 1962 put in place a road map for future relations in key areas such as nationality and citizenship, property ownership, *coopération*, financial investment, shared control of petrol exploitation, nuclear testing, and military bases. Apart from nuclear testing (which continued in the Sahara until 1967, with devastating results for the health and livelihoods of local populations) and the French military bases (which remained until the end of their rental periods), many of the agreements contained in the Evian Accords were rapidly rendered a dead letter by both events and subsequent political decisions. The guarantee of property rights for Europeans became obsolete in spring and summer 1962 as the majority of Europeans left and their vacant homes and properties were spontaneously occupied by Algerian families, many of whom were rural to urban migrants who had been made homeless by the war. In the following years, land and industry would be nationalized. The Evian Accords had allowed for European settlers to choose Algerian nationality within three years, as long as they fulfilled certain residence clauses. However, in March 1963, the Nationality Code stated that only those whose father and grandfather had been born in Algeria under the (colonial) 'Muslim personal status' were automatically Algerian.

While the French state and French economic interests were desperate to maintain a major stake in petrol exploitation in the Sahara (and saw this as their 'right' as a result of their initial financial outlay in discovering petrol), the Algerian political discourse was one of economic, as well as political, independence. The Algerian state rapidly sought to bring the technical knowledge associated with petrol discovery and extraction and the wealth it generated under greater Algerian control. In 1971, President Houari Boumediène (who had seized power in a coup in June 1965) unilaterally nationalized Algerian petrol. 'If we were to analyze Algerian petrol', he declared in one speech, 'We would discover that the blood of our martyrs makes up one of its components because the possession of this wealth was paid for in our blood'.[20] This emotive political discourse (and sincere desire to bring Algerian resources under Algerian control) found an echo in popular culture. While the French singer Michel Sardou penned 'Ils ont le pétrole, mais c'est tout' (They've got petrol, but that's it), vaunting France's 'Latin paradise' in retaliation against Algerian nationalization, Algerian singer Rabah Driassa sang his own hit 'Petrol' in which nationalization was depicted as the continuation of the liberation struggle. Nevertheless, economic relations were maintained. Thousands of *coopérants* traveled to Algeria, including as government advisors whose technical expertise shaped Algeria's nominally socialist economy. Until 2014, when it was overtaken by China, France was Algeria's main trading partner.

Much of the political rhetoric of independent Algeria was about cultural decolonization. Algeria, successive presidents of Algeria repeated, was Arab, Muslim, and Arabic-speaking. Unlike in Sub-Saharan Africa, where French was maintained as the official language, Arabic was immediately made Algeria's sole official language. In the course of the next decades, Arabicization laws were steadily introduced across education, the judiciary, and other state institutions. While Léopold Sedar Senghor, first president of Senegal, and Habib Bourguiba, first president of Tunisia, among others, embraced ideas about 'Francophonie' (a community of French speakers with shared humanist values), Algeria kept its distance. Algeria refused to become a member of the Agence de Coopération Culturelle et Technique (Agency for Cultural and Technical Cooperation, ACCT) established in 1970, and its successor, the Organisation Internationale de la Francophonie (International Organisation of Francophonie, OIF), despite having one of the largest French-speaking populations in the world. Indeed, Algerian authors writing in French have made a major contribution to Francophone literature, with writer Kateb Yacine famously describing the French language as a 'war booty' ('*butin de guerre*').

Up until the 1980s, the Algerian government was considered by the French government to be the main actor in the organization and control of the large numbers of Algerians who migrated to France after 1962, seeking to escape economic misery which was not quickly resolved by independence. Both states viewed migration as a temporary phenomenon. The Friendly Society for Algerians in Europe (Amicale des Algériens en Europe, AAE) took the form of 'a true ministry for emigration' ('*un veritable ministère de l'émigration*'),[21] collecting subscriptions from Algerians for repatriation insurance in case of death on French soil, bringing imams to France, organizing Arabic lessons and concerts, and training youth workers. The Amicale represented the interests of the FLN and sought to extend their control over Algerian immigrants, conscious that France, both during and after the war, was a space for Algerian political movements challenging the hegemony of the FLN. Indeed, in 1965, the French authorities connived in suppressing Amicale dissent in France in the wake of Boumediène's coup.[22]

By the early 1980s, the Algerian state was in a far weaker position to negotiate its place in the world. In the context of falling oil prices, and in need of financial assistance, under President Chadli Benjedid (1979–1992), Algeria moved away from its state-led socialist economy towards economic liberalization, and Algerian debt was rescheduled within the International Monetary Fund's (IMF) structural readjustment program. The crisis of the 1980s in Algeria was political as well as economic. As elsewhere in North Africa and the Middle East, Islamism was rapidly gaining ground in the wake of the 1979 Iranian Revolution. Large sections of a new, post-independence generation had a burning sense of injustice at being excluded from the political system and the employment market. In October 1988, youth riots took place across Algeria. In February 1989, the introduction of political pluralism brought to an end twenty-seven years of single-party rule. The political party which gained the most from this was the Front Islamique du Salut (Islamic Salvation Front, FIS). In December 1991, the FIS scored a landslide victory in the first round of legislative elections. In January 1992, the Algerian army stepped into prevent a second-round victory for the FIS. Chadli resigned, the National Assembly was dissolved and a state of emergency declared. A decade of violence pitching the forces of the Algerian state against armed Islamists ensued, during which many civilians found themselves caught in the crossfire. An estimated 200,000 Algerians were killed.[23] The conflict also 'spilled over' into France, for example, in the Saint Michel metro bombing in 1995.

During this period, Franco-Algerian relations underwent a significant shift. No longer primarily state-to-state and predicated on competing claims to be leaders on the world stage, the fight to crush what was perceived to be a shared threat (Islamist terrorism) led to an opaque imbrication of Algerian and French secret services and senior politicians, with France becoming the privileged interpreter of what was going on in Algeria for the rest of the world. For Hugh Roberts, 'Paris's relations with Algiers degenerated into the French government's involvement with the *personnel* of the Algerian regime', which in turn generated a 'complex and unsavory system of patronage, reciprocal back-scratching and corruption'.[24] The system of elite imbrication and dodgy deals across the Mediterranean at the expense of the 'ordinary' people is sometimes referred to using the pejorative term Françalgérie, an adaptation of Françafrique.[25]

## THE IMPACT OF THE 1990S: A FRANCO-ALGERIAN LENS LOCKED IN PLACE BY TRANSNATIONAL MEMORY FRAMES AND POLITICAL EXPEDIENCY

In the 1990s, the way in which Franco-Algerian relations came to be understood was shaped by the coalescence of the civil violence raging in Algeria, developments in the academic field of memory studies, and the turn to legalistic strategies to seek historical redress by memory activists. The language used to talk about how states, societies, and individuals have addressed (or not) the Holocaust (terms and concepts such as amnesia, repressed memory, trauma, unhealed wounds, recognition, and repentance) began to be applied to colonial contexts. Stora's evocatively titled *La Gangrène et l'oubli: la mémoire de la guerre d'Algérie* (Paris: La Découverte, 1991) established the framework for much future work on France and Algeria. In 1997–1998, Maurice Papon was found guilty of crimes against humanity for his role in the deportation of Jews between 1942 and 1944. The Papon trial also flagged up to the French public his role as Paris chief of police in the deadly repression of Algerians participating in a peaceful demonstration in the French capital on October 17, 1961, protesting against the wartime curfew imposed on them.

In part because of the wide-ranging amnesties put in place at the end of the War of Independence to protect civilian and military personnel from being prosecuted for illegal acts committed during the conflict, memory activists on both sides of the Mediterranean and from a wide range of political positions during the war (from OAS to FLN) have sought to bring court cases for crimes which are not covered by the amnesties, albeit with little success. Associations of former settlers have demanded that the French state recognize its responsibility for having 'abandoned' French civilians to their fate in the months between the Evian Accords and formal independence in July 1962, while harki memory activists use the language of 'crimes against humanity' to frame their experiences. In 2002, General Paul Aussaresses and the publishers of his 2001 memoirs were found guilty of 'apology for war crimes', for stating that he had used torture during the war, and would do so again. In 2003, Louisette Ighilahriz, a former member of the FLN bomb network who was brutally tortured and raped during the war, took French army General Maurice Schmitt to court for libel when he accused her of fabricating her account.

The law of February 23, 2005, whose Article four declared that the French school curriculum should recognize 'the positive role of the French overseas presence, notably in North Africa', prompted a sustained campaign by French and Algerian historians against state interference in the writing of history. It also led to a brief attempt in 2010 by a group of Algerian deputies to pass a law declaring colonialism a crime against humanity; the Algerian government had little appetite for this and the idea was quietly dropped. Indeed, senior politicians in Algeria and France studiously shied away from taking a position on the February 23, 2005 law, although it is widely seen as having dashed a planned 'Friendship Treaty' between Algeria and France. Article four was revoked by President Jacques Chirac (1995–2007) in January 2006, when he described it as a text that 'divides the French'.

Indeed, these debates (often referred to as 'Franco-Algerian memory wars') are in many cases less Franco-Algerian than they initially seem. First, both in the political language used and the legal strategies employed, they are part of transnational debates which go far beyond the Franco-Algerian relationship. The February 23, 2005 law, for example, is part of a wider pattern of memorial laws in France, including the Taubira Law, which recognized slavery as a crime against humanity, and the law criminalizing Armenian genocide denial, both passed in 2001.

Second, these 'memory wars' are often closely tied to Algero-Algerian or Franco-French national, local, and regional politics, and the ensuing debates do not always find an echo on the other side of the Mediterranean. The February 23, 2005 law initially attracted very little media attention. Few deputies and senators participated in its various readings as it made its way through the French legislature, and those who supported it were, broadly speaking, a cross-party group from the South of France, where the former settler or *harki* voters are based. At the same time, at the national level, taking a particular view on France's colonial legacies has become a means for French politicians to position themselves. On the far right, nostalgia for the colonial period is a common theme, flying in the face of the far right's simultaneous insistence on the 'inassimilable' nature of immigrants and its hatred of multi-ethnic, multicultural contemporary France. On the right, President Nicolas Sarkozy (2007–2012) has been a loud supporter of the 'refusal of repentance' (*'refus de la repentance'*), that is to say, the claim that reexamining the colonial past equates to national self-hatred and the decline of Frenchness. On the left (despite the fact that the Republican center-left historically constituted the most enthusiastic supporters of the 'civilizing mission' and that it was a center-left government that escalated the war in Algeria in 1956), confronting the colonial past and making carefully worded apologies is a way of demonstrating a vision of France as open, diverse, and united. François Hollande's first official engagement as the Socialist Party's (PS) presidential candidate on October 17, 2011 was to throw a rose (the symbol of the PS) into the Seine, in memory of the Algerians who died there on October 17, 1961.

In Algeria, meanwhile, borrowing from the language of the anti-colonial struggle has become a means to contest the political system in place. Since 1962, the war has been both the foundational block of Algerian national identity and the key source of legitimacy for the political establishment ('the system'). In his 1999 election campaign and subsequently, Abdelaziz Bouteflika (president 1999–present) played on his veteran status. Critics of 'the system' also use the language of the war to claim that those who took power in 1962 were not 'true' veterans. Some liberal, secular critics argue that the post-1962 insistence by the state and the party of the FLN on Islam and Arabic effaced a much longer nationalist tradition of political and cultural plurality. Other critics, more sympathetic to Islamist ideas, argue that the process of cultural decolonization begun during the war has not yet been completed, and that Algerian identity needs to become more Muslim and Arabophone. In both the French and Algerian cases, 'memory wars' are moving farther and farther away from the colonial past. Instead, this past has been boiled down to a series of key words, increasingly emptied of the historical substance linking back to a shared Franco-Algerian past, which provide instantly accessible political languages to debate the French *or* Algerian presents.

## CONCLUSION: CHANGING THE LENS

Franco-Algerian state-to-state relations today may best be characterized as noisy, sometimes confrontational rhetoric accompanied by quiet, pragmatic collaboration. The idea that Franco-Algerian relations are 'exceptional' is a mythologized, if not entirely mythological, claim. The mythologizing contrast between, on the one hand, Franco-Algerian relations, and on the other hand, relations between other former colonial powers and their former colonies, is sustained by two states both with very strong national myths. In France, the idea that Algeria was the exception which proved the rule of France's 'successful' decolonization, chosen and driven by France, with France always the center and the principal actor, persists. In Algeria, the idea that the Algerian people led a unique struggle to overthrow colonial oppression, at the cost of the lives of 1.5 million martyrs is sacrosanct. Both countries see themselves as bearers of a distinct model with a special place in the world. The frame of national exceptionalism, and its corollary, exceptional Franco-Algerian relations, provides a potent political language which has permeated wider culture. Yet rather than being locked in a suffocating embrace, Franco-Algerian relations have always existed and functioned in wider contexts. For the colonial period, a number of academics have now produced work which steps beyond the Franco-Algerian binary. The work on post-independence Algerian history which goes beyond Algeria's relationship with France is only just beginning to be done.[26] This work is nevertheless essential in order to avoid what Frederick Cooper has termed the fallacy of 'leap-frogging legacies',[27] whereby postcolonial states and societies are reduced to being permanently viewed through the lens of the former colonial power.

## NOTES

1. Benjamin Stora, *La Gangrène et l'oubli: la mémoire de la guerre d'Algérie* (Paris: La Découverte, 1991), 317. "Les rapports franco-algériens se sont noués dans la violence, par l'imposition du système colonial, et par une guerre de sept ans qui a permis l'accession de l'Algérie à l'indépendance. Voilà pourquoi, trente ans après, le temps n'a pas pu apaiser les passions … Dès 1962, la Méditerranée, dont le nom arabe, *[A]l [b]ahr [al-abyad] al moutawassat*, signifie 'la mer blanche du milieu,' est devenue ligne de fracture, 'mur' bleu imaginaire. Le divorce, violent, n'a cessé de nourrir tensions, obsessions, fantasmes d'une rive à l'autre."

2. Dominique Maison, "La Population de l'Algérie," *Population* 28, no. 6 (1973): 1080–82.

3. Diana Davis, "Desert 'Wastes' of the Maghreb: Desertification Narratives in French Colonial Environmental History of North Africa," *Cultural Geographies* 11, no. 4 (2004): 359–87.

4. Patricia Lorcin, *Imperial Identities: Stereotyping, Prejudice and Race in Colonial Algeria* (London: I.B. Tauris, 1995).

5. Kamel Kateb, *Ecole, population et société en Algérie* (Paris: L'Harmattan, 2005), 27–28.

6. Jennifer Johnson, *The Battle for Algeria: Sovereignty, Healthcare, and Humanitarianism* (Philadelphia: University of Pennsylvania Press, 2016), 66.

7. Saliha Belmessous, *Assimilation and Empire: Uniformity in French and British Colonies, 1541–1954* (Oxford: Oxford University Press, 2013), 161–64.

8. Michael Goebel, *Anti-Imperial Metropolis: Interwar Paris and the Seeds of Third World Nationalism* (Cambridge: Cambridge University Press, 2015).

9. For example, the former member of the FLN and leading Algerian historian Mohamed Harbi, "La guerre d'Algérie a commencé à Sétif," *Le Monde diplomatique*, May 2005.

10. Tony Chafer, *The End of Empire in French West Africa: France's Successful Decolonization?* (Oxford: Berg, 2002).

11. Todd Shepard, *Voices of Decolonization: A Brief History with Documents* (Boston: Bedford/St Martin's, 2015), 96–100.

12. Benjamin Stora, *Les mots de la guerre d'Algérie* (Toulouse: Presses Universitaires du Mirail, 2005), 23–25.
13. François-Xavier Hautreux, "Quelques pistes pour une meilleure compréhension de l'engagement des harkis (1954–1962)," *Les Temps Modernes* 666 (2011): 44–52.
14. Matthew Connelly, *A Diplomatic Revolution: Algeria's Fight for Independence and the Origins of the Post-Cold War Era* (Oxford: Oxford University Press, 2003), 5.
15. Todd Shepard, *The Invention of Decolonization: The Algerian War and the Remaking of France* (Ithaca, NY: Cornell University Press, 2006).
16. Neil Macmaster, *Burning the Veil: The Algerian War and the "Emancipation" Of Muslim Women, 1954–62* (Manchester: Manchester University Press, 2009).
17. Amine Ait Chaalal, "La politique étrangère de l'Algérie: entre héritage et originalité," in *La politique étrangère: le modèle classique à l'épreuve*, ed. Claude Roosens, and Valérie Rosoux (Belgium: PIE-Peter Lang, 2004), 206.
18. Jeffrey James Byrne, *Mecca of Revolution: Algeria, Decolonization and the Third World Order* (Oxford: Oxford University Press, 2016).
19. Jean-François Daguzan, "Les Relations franco-algériennes ou la poursuite des amicales incompréhensions," *Annuaire français des relations internationales* 2 (2000): 438–50.
20. Nicole Grimaud, "Le Conflit pétrolier franco-algérien," *Revue française de science politique* 22, no. 6 (1972): 1276–307. "S'il nous était donné d'analyser le pétrole algérien, nous découvririons que le sang de nos martyrs constitue l'une de ses composantes car la possession de cette richesse a été payée du prix de notre sang." Boumediène speaking in Skikda on July 16, 1970.
21. Jean-Charles Scagnetti, "Pays d'origine et encadrement des pratiques religieuses: l'Algérie et ses émigrés (1962–1988)," *Cahiers de la Méditerranée* 78 (2009): 177–202.
22. Ed Naylor, "The Politics of a Presence: Algerians in Marseille from Independence to 'immigration sauvage' (1962–1974)" (PhD diss., University of London, 2011), 190–93.
23. Martin Evans, and John Phillips, *Algeria: The Anger of the Dispossessed* (New Haven: Yale University Press, 2007), xiv. Like the statistic of "one and a half million martyrs" killed during the War of Independence, the figure of 200,000 killed during the "black decade" is increasingly challenged by academics and civil society activists. Nazim Mekbel, founder of the association Ajouad Algérie Mémoires, which campaigns for the recognition of victims of terrorism, and author of an MA dissertation on the subject, puts forward the figure of 40,000–70,000 killed, drawing on a wide variety of sources and a decade-long study. Ameyar Hafida, "La Société ne peut pas se contenter de lois d'amnésie et d'amnistie," *Liberté*, October 18, 2016.
24. Hugh Roberts, *The Battlefield Algeria 1988–2002: Studies in a Broken Polity* (London: Verso, 2003), 307.
25. Lounis Aggoun, and Jean-Baptiste Rivoire, *Françalgérie: Crimes et mensonges d'Etat* (Paris: La Découverte, 2004).
26. As Malika Rahal underlines, "in contemporary Algeria, it seems no history is possible after the War of Independence." Malika Rahal, "Comment faire l'histoire de l'Algérie indépendante?," *La vie des idées*, March 13, 2012. See

her trilingual blog http://texturesdutemps.hypotheses.org as a starting point for collaboratively writing the post-1962 history of Algeria.

27. Frederick Cooper, *Colonialism in Question: Theory, Knowledge, History* (Berkeley: University of California Press), 17–18.

## BIBLIOGRAPHY

Aggoun, Lounis, and Jean-Baptiste Rivoire. *Françalgérie: Crimes et mensonges d'Etat.* Paris: La Découverte, 2004.

Ait Chaalal, Amine. "La politique étrangère de l'Algérie: entre héritage et originalité." In *La politique étrangère: le modèle classique à l'épreuve*, edited by Claude Roosens and Valérie Rosoux, 203–15. Belgium: PIE-Peter Lang, 2004.

Belmessous, Saliha. *Assimilation and Empire: Uniformity in French and British Colonies, 1541–1954.* Oxford: Oxford University Press, 2013.

Byrne, Jeffrey James. *Mecca of Revolution: Algeria, Decolonization and the Third World Order.* Oxford: Oxford University Press, 2016.

Chafer, Tony. *The End of Empire in French West Africa: France's Successful Decolonization?* Oxford: Berg, 2002.

Connelly, Matthew. *A Diplomatic Revolution: Algeria's Fight for Independence and the Origins of the Post-Cold War Era.* Oxford: Oxford University Press, 2003.

Cooper, Frederick. *Colonialism in Question: Theory, Knowledge, History.* Berkeley: University of California Press.

Daguzan, Jean-François. "Les Relations franco-algériennes ou la poursuite des amicales incompréhensions." *Annuaire français des relations internationales* 2 (2000): 438–50.

Davis, Diana. "Desert 'wastes' of the Maghreb: Desertification Narratives in French Colonial Environmental History of North Africa." *Cultural Geographies* 11, no. 4 (2004): 359–87.

Evans, Martin, and John Phillips, *Algeria: The Anger of the Dispossessed.* New Haven: Yale University Press, 2007.

Goebel, Michael. *Anti-Imperial Metropolis: Interwar Paris and the Seeds of Third World Nationalism.* Cambridge: Cambridge University Press, 2015.

Grimaud, Nicole. "Le Conflit pétrolier franco-algérien." *Revue française de science politique* 22, no. 6 (1972): 1276–307.

Harbi, Mohamed. "La guerre d'Algérie a commencé à Sétif." *Le Monde diplomatique*, May 2005. https://www.monde-diplomatique.fr/2005/05/HARBI/12191.

Hautreux, François-Xavier. "Quelques pistes pour une meilleure compréhension de l'engagement des harkis (1954–1962)." *Les Temps Modernes* 666 (2011): 44–52.

Johnson, Jennifer. *The Battle for Algeria: Sovereignty, Healthcare, and Humanitarianism.* Philadelphia: University of Pennsylvania Press, 2016.

Kateb, Kamel. *Ecole, population et société en Algérie.* Paris: L'Harmattan, 2005.

Lorcin, Patricia. *Imperial Identities: Stereotyping, Prejudice and Race in Colonial Algeria.* London: I.B. Tauris, 1995.

Macmaster, Neil. *Burning the Veil: The Algerian War and the 'Emancipation' Of Muslim Women, 1954–62.* Manchester: Manchester University Press, 2009.

Maison, Dominique. "La Population de l'Algérie." *Population* 28, no. 6 (1973): 1080–82.

Naylor, Ed. "The Politics of a Presence: Algerians in Marseille from Independence to 'immigration sauvage' (1962–1974)." Ph.D. diss., University of London, 2011.

Rahal, Malika. "Comment faire l'histoire de l'Algérie indépendante?" *La vie des idées*, March 13, 2012. http://www.laviedesidees.fr/Comment-faire-l-histoire-de-l-Algerie-independante.html.

Roberts, Hugh. *The Battlefield Algeria 1988–2002: Studies in a Broken Polity*. London: Verso, 2003.

Scagnetti, Jean-Charles. "Pays d'origine et encadrement des pratiques religieuses: l'Algérie et ses émigrés (1962–1988)." *Cahiers de la Méditerranée* 78 (2009): 177–202.

Shepard, Todd. *Voices of Decolonization: A Brief History with Documents*. Boston: Bedford/St Martin's, 2015.

Shepard, Todd. *The Invention of Decolonization: The Algerian War and the Remaking of France*. Ithaca, NY: Cornell University Press, 2006.

Stora, Benjamin. *La Gangrène et l'oubli: la mémoire de la guerre d'Algérie*. Paris: La Découverte, 1991.

———. *Les mots de la guerre d'Algérie*. Toulouse: Presses Universitaires du Mirail, 2005.

# CHAPTER 34

# China and Africa

## Joshua Eisenman and David H. Shinn

### Historical Overview

In the 1950s and 1960s, Beijing's primary motivation in Africa was the affirmation of its own brand of communism and support for revolutionary movements. In the 1970s, following the most tumultuous period of Mao Zedong's Cultural Revolution and the deepening of the Sino-Soviet split, an increasingly pragmatic leadership sought to secure China's borders by keeping Soviet resources bogged down in distant conflicts. In the 1980s and 1990s, China's attention to Africa receded as the country turned inward and devoted more attention to relations with the West. Since the turn of the millennium, however, to support China's growing economy, China has developed extensive commercial, diplomatic, and political ties with Africa.

The 1955 Asian–African conference at Bandung, Indonesia, marked an important watershed in China's relations with Africa.[1] Premier Zhou Enlai, who led the Chinese delegation, interacted for the first time with delegations from six African countries: Egypt, Ethiopia, Liberia, Libya, and soon-to-be independent Sudan and Ghana.[2] The Bandung Conference marked a change in China's relations with Africa. The Chinese developed a good relationship with the Egyptians and met with representatives of several African liberation movements. Bandung provided a forum for China to condemn colonialism

J. Eisenman (✉)
The University of Texas, Austin, TX, USA

D.H. Shinn
George Washington University, Washington, DC, USA

© The Author(s) 2018
M.S. Shanguhyia and T. Falola (eds.),
*The Palgrave Handbook of African Colonial and Postcolonial History*,
https://doi.org/10.1057/978-1-137-59426-6_34

839

and imperialism in Africa, and to support independence movements in Algeria, Morocco, and Tunisia, and Egypt's claim to the Suez Canal.[3]

Building on its success at Bandung, China expanded its engagement with the Afro-Asian world in an effort to mold its thinking and actions in accordance with Chinese ideology. The USSR, which had not been invited to the conference, and its supporters resisted this effort. China sent a delegation to the first Afro-Asian People's Solidarity Organization Conference in Cairo, which began in late 1957, and took note of Africans' growing role in the movement. Before the conference opened, Beijing held a rally to support several African national liberation movements and afterward acknowledged the growing importance of Africa in world politics.[4]

During this period China portrayed itself as shepherding a flock of African nations moving toward a 'new democratic revolution'. At the Moscow Summit of Communist Parties in November 1960, China's state-run press reported that African revolutionaries were 'studying Mao's works and using Chinese guerilla methods'.[5] Premier Zhou Enlai nurtured the idea that Africa was engulfed in revolutionary zeal and that Soviet revisionists had betrayed the ideals of revolutionary communism. Some African leaders had indeed become steeped in Maoist revolutionary thought and liberation ideology.[6]

Zhou's historic ten-country visit to Africa at the end of 1963 and beginning of 1964 began China's emphasis on the importance of regular, senior, face-to-face contact with African leaders—a practice that continues today.[7] In Africa, Zhou unveiled five principles to guide China–Africa relations: opposition to imperialism and colonialism, non-alignment, African-Arab unity, peaceful resolution of disputes, and national sovereignty. These principles are sufficiently general that they have withstood the test of time, yet China has not always adhered to them. Chinese support in the 1960s for several African revolutionary movements committed to the overthrow of independent governments violated them.[8] Nevertheless, the principles continue to be quoted by Chinese officials and scholars, and were updated and expanded in China's 2006 African policy statement.[9]

During the Cultural Revolution (1966–1969), the Communist Party of China (CPC) brought African policy to the Chinese people via the state-run press. To reinforce domestic support and publicize its conviction, CPC propaganda promoted what Mao called 'righteous struggle' in Africa. This meant supporting Mao-style revolutionary mass movements as an extension of China's own unfinished revolution.[10] By citing Africa as proof of the widespread appeal of Mao Zedong's thinking, China aimed to highlight Maoist ideology's broad appeal and establish its position as the vanguard of global proletarian revolutionary orthodoxy.

Beijing aided many African revolutionary forces fighting a guerrilla war by hastening 'the development of [African] political opposition groups and guiding them towards conceptions of action closely akin to her own'.[11] Speeches, editorials, and publications condemned vestiges of Western colonialism and stressed the role of Maoist ideology and the scope of armed struggles.[12] By asserting that conflicts in Algeria, Cameroon, the Congo, Uganda, and elsewhere were proletarian revolutions, China showcased its influence. Calls for armed struggle and the export of small arms cost little, so Beijing supported revolutionary groups with zealous rhetoric and modest materiel support.[13]

China's willingness to place geopolitical objectives before ideological consistency grew apace with the Soviet threat. In 1969, roughly 400,000 Soviet troops equipped with battlefield nuclear weapons appeared on China's border. While the Soviets never attacked, the threat prompted Beijing to devise a strategy to cope with the threat. Although Beijing advocated a dual-adversary approach directed against both the USA and USSR, in practice the latter was prioritized.[14] China sought to preoccupy Soviet forces in far-off conflicts, particularly in Africa.[15] The CPC supported revolutionary movements that fought against 'imperialist forces', a term synonymous with groups supported by Moscow. This shift from dogmatism to pragmatism was catalyzed by widespread cynicism as the Cultural Revolution's worst days subsided. This less radical approach succeeded in 1971 when twenty six African countries supported Beijing's successful effort to replace Taipei on the UN Security Council. In the 1970s, China initiated a strategy that prioritized national-security interests and was predicated on state-to-state relations, themes that continue today.[16]

Throughout the 1970s, the CPC's pragmatists gradually gained power. Although Mao had already been enshrined as 'the great leader of the international proletariat and the oppressed nations and the oppressed people', his followers had suffered a crisis of conscience.[17] Maoism had failed to fulfill its promise as a panacea for society's ills. Free from the need to insist all rebel movements were Maoist, and desperately poor, China began promoting African self-reliance. Beijing became willing 'to grant ideological autonomy, and when African countries seemed to embark on a policy closely akin to Chinese thinking, Peking refrained from claiming that the Africans were following a Maoist path'.[18] China increased state-to-state relations and put most leftist radicals on notice that they could not expect much support.

In the late 1970s and early 1980s, changes in China's domestic landscape diverted attention from Africa. By the time the pragmatists had wrested power from the residual Maoists, widespread rural poverty and urban disenchantment required a reorientation of priorities. Led by Deng Xiaoping, China's leadership focused on expanding market forces in the economy. Chinese people were told to get rich, leading many to turn to trade with the West to make their fortunes. Economic reforms, a receding Soviet threat, and the waning role of revolutionary ideology diverted Chinese attention from Africa. It was not until the nation's need for raw materials and support on diplomatic issues (e.g. repeated Western attempts to condemn China's human-rights abuses in the UN in the 1990s) that Beijing turned back to Africa via the Forum on China–Africa Cooperation (FOCAC) framework initiated by President Jiang Zemin in 2000.[19] Throughout the twenty-first century, China has emphasized its economic ties with Africa but never lost sight of its political and security interests.

## CHINA'S INTERESTS IN AFRICA

China has become, in the words of Zimbabwe's strongman Robert Mugabe, 'an alternative global power point' in Africa.[20] Beijing has designed a strategy in Africa to ensure access to energy and other natural resources, open new export markets, safeguard its interests in international institutions, and gain external validation for its socialist political ideology. In pursuit of these objectives, Beijing has shown little regard for the financial or humanitarian constraints that give pause to leaders in liberal democratic societies.

China has five primary interests on the continent, the first of which is access to raw materials. In 2009, China became Africa's largest trading partner, surpassing the USA. About 85% of China's imports from Africa are raw materials, mainly oil, minerals, and hardwood timber. Five oil/mineral exporting nations (South Africa, Angola, DRC, South Sudan, and Zambia) account for most of Africa's exports to China. While China's imported oil from Africa as a percentage of global oil imports fell from 28% in 2008 to 22% in 2014, the total volume imported from Africa has remained about the same. China also imports large quantities of minerals such as cobalt, copper, manganese, and tantalum to supply China's robust manufacturing and construction sectors. Beginning in mid-2014, the fall in oil and commodity prices resulted in a sharp reduction by dollar value of China's imports from Africa, declining from $115 billion in 2014 to $55 billion in 2015. Previous dollar values are likely to return if the global economy improves and prices recover.

Second, China wants to increase its exports to Africa, which has more than 1 billion people and a growing middle class with increasing expendable income. Most Chinese exports to Africa are consumer products or high-value manufactured goods such as transport equipment, machinery, and electronic products. From 2014 to 2015, even as the value of China's imports from Africa dropped sharply, the value of China's exports to Africa increased slightly. China's most important African markets are South Africa, Nigeria, Egypt, Algeria, and Angola. Still, Africa accounts for only about 5% of China's global exports; China, by contrast, supplies about 19% of all African imports.[21]

Third, China seeks African support in international forums on various global issues ranging from climate change to trade disputes in the World Trade Organization. African countries constitute more than one quarter of the members of the UN General Assembly and hold thirteen of the forty-seven seats on the UN Human Rights Council.[22] Beijing uses its seat on the

Security Council to support the positions of African countries, and they, in return, support China when it faces Western criticisms for its human-rights practices. China seeks African support on three additional internal issues: first, backing for China's position on Tibet, which has attracted little interest in Africa, except when the South African government turned down the Dalai Lama's visa request; second, rhetorical opposition to the East Turkestan Islamic Movement, a Muslim separatist group of militant Uighurs in Xinjiang Province; third, and most recent, China has solicited African leaders' support for its territorial claims in the East and South China Seas. Although this issue is geographically far from Africa, African leaders have provided substantial support for China's position.[23]

Fourth, China is committed to ending Taiwan's diplomatic presence in Africa. From the late 1950s until 2008 there was intense competition between Beijing and Taipei for recognition by African countries. In the early years, Taipei maintained diplomatic relations with numerous African countries but over time Beijing has successfully pushed Taipei's diplomats out of all but Burkina Faso and Swaziland. Following the election in 2008 of the more Beijing-friendly Ma Ying-jeou as Taiwan's president, the two sides agreed upon an unofficial diplomatic truce that temporarily stopped their rivalry for recognition. Taiwan's election of the more independence-minded Tsai Ing-wen in 2016 ended the truce and China quickly established diplomatic relations with The Gambia, which had broken ties with Taiwan in 2013.[24] São Tomé and Principe switched from Taipei to Beijing late in 2016. Although the competition for diplomatic recognition is largely over in Africa, Taiwan's status remains among China's core interests.

Fifth, China wants to minimize illicit activities including terrorism, international crime, narcotics trafficking, and piracy so they do not harm Chinese in Africa or the homeland. Chinese nationals, who number between one and two million in Africa, are increasingly subject to attacks. More than twenty Chinese nationals have been kidnapped in Nigeria by the Movement for the Emancipation of the Niger Delta. Rebel groups in Sudan have attacked Chinese oilfields and kidnapped Chinese personnel near Darfur, resulting in several deaths. Nine Chinese employees of a Sinopec subsidiary died in Ethiopia's Ogaden region when they were caught in the crossfire between Ethiopian security personnel and a rebel group. Al-Qaeda in the Islamic Maghreb, citing China's crackdown on Muslim Uighurs in Xinjiang, attacked Chinese highway construction workers in Algeria. Boko Haram kidnapped ten Chinese construction workers in northern Cameroon and three Chinese nationals were among eighteen killed when Muslim militants stormed a hotel in Bamako, Mali. During the height of Somali piracy in the Gulf of Aden, Chinese crews and vessels came under attack, prompting China to join the international anti-piracy operation. The overthrow in 2011 of Muammar Qaddafi in Libya resulted in the evacuation of almost 36,000 Chinese working on contracts valued at $20 billion. Dozens of Chinese were injured when Libyans looted their work sites. China has also arrested a number of Africans in China for engaging in narcotics trafficking, and had Chinese deported for engaging in fraudulent online activities.

## CHINA'S ENGAGEMENT WITH AFRICA

China prioritizes its engagement with African states, and its high-level leaders make frequent visits. Beijing has diplomatic relations with fifty-two African countries and maintains an embassy in all of them; all but The Gambia and São Tomé and Principe have an embassy in Beijing. Former President Hu Jintao visited Africa four times, and President Xi Jinping made his first overseas visit to Russia followed immediately by a trip to Africa. Xi returned in 2015 to attend the Sixth FOCAC summit in Johannesburg. Every year since 1991, China's foreign minister has made his first overseas visit to Africa, usually in January. Senior CPC and People's Liberation Army (PLA) personnel also make regular visits to Africa. The CPC has developed strong ties with African ruling political parties in countries such as Ethiopia, Angola, Sudan, Zimbabwe, and South Africa. China annually hosts hundreds of senior African government, party, and military officials.

China created FOCAC in 2000 to coordinate its interaction with individual African countries. FOCAC was designed to help Beijing regularize its diplomatic initiatives, technical training, infrastructure financing and construction, and aid and trade policies. FOCAC institutionalizes China's outreach to African governments and advances Sino-African solidarity. It meets at the ministerial or summit level every three years, alternating between Beijing and an African capital. At its last meeting in 2015, Xi announced $60 billion in new financing for ten major initiatives, including: $10 billion for an industrial cooperation fund to invest in manufacturing, hi-tech, agriculture, energy, and infrastructure; $5 billion for aid and interest-free loans; $35 billion for preferential loans and export credits; and $10 billion for the expansion of the China Africa Development Fund.[25]

Since the Mao era, China has trained cadres from African political parties and organizations. The primary vehicle for foreign political party outreach and training is the Central Committee of the CPC International Department (ID). CPC training is based on sharing its own experiences with African counterparts. In recent years, the CPC's cadre training efforts in Africa have expanded their focus to include younger political leaders. African political delegations visiting China as guests of the ID receive lectures at China's educational and training institutions, attend cultural programs, visit state-owned and private businesses, and meet a variety of officials.[26] The countries with the largest number of exchanges since 2006 are Sudan, Ethiopia, Zimbabwe, Morocco, Algeria, South Africa, Tanzania, and Mauritius. Since 2012, more African party delegations have visited China each year than CPC delegations have visited Africa.

Chinese foreign direct investment (FDI) in Africa began growing rapidly after 2000 and reached $32 billion at the end of 2014. Although fast growing, Chinese investment represents less than 5% of the global FDI stock in Africa.[27] As of 2011, 31% of Chinese FDI in Africa was in oil and mining, 20% in banking and finance, 16% in construction, 15% in manufacturing, and the remainder in services, technology, wholesale and retail, agriculture, and real estate.[28] At the end of 2012, South Africa, Zambia, Nigeria, Algeria, Angola, and Sudan accounted for 58% of China's FDI in Africa.[29]

From 2010 through 2012, almost 52% of China's $14.41 billion in overseas development assistance (ODA) (about $2.5 billion per year) went to African countries. The aid was in the form of grants, both cash and in-kind, interest-free loans, and concessional loans. Most of China's aid consists of concessional loans managed by the Export-Import Bank.[30] Between 2000 and 2014, the Chinese government, banks, and contractors extended $86.3 billion worth of loans to African governments and state-owned enterprises primarily in Angola, Ethiopia, Sudan, Kenya, and the Democratic Republic of the Congo (DRC). Most of these loans financed infrastructure projects and did not qualify as ODA.[31] China has a good record of providing debt relief to heavily indebted poor countries. Beijing prides itself on attaching no political strings to its ODA other than the 'One China' principle, but requires nearly all recipients to hire Chinese companies and use a determined amount of Chinese materials and labor.

To improve its image, China has an extensive public-relations operation in Africa. The official news services Xinhua, China Central Television, and China Radio International have branches in Africa and reach millions of Africans. China promotes a positive image of itself and works to counter the negative coverage in the Western media. One of China's oldest programs in Africa is the sending of some 18,000 medical personnel to forty-six countries since 1963. China offers 5500 university scholarships annually, although many of them are not being utilized. It has provided technical training for 30,000 Africans. In 2016, there were forty-five Confucius Institutes in African universities and twenty-three Confucius Classrooms in secondary schools in thirty-five African countries.[32] In 2009, FOCAC announced the twenty plus twenty program whereby twenty Chinese universities established formal ties with African counterparts.[33]

China has long been a major supplier of military equipment to African countries. From 2011 to 2014, China provided about 24% of the conventional arms entering Sub-Saharan Africa.[34] China also transfers the single largest quantity of small arms and light weapons to Africa.[35] Countries, especially those facing Western sanctions such as Sudan and Zimbabwe, welcome low-cost and good-quality Chinese weapons, which are increasingly appearing in conflict zones. On the positive side, China is active in UN peacekeeping operations. In 2016, some 2200 Chinese peacekeepers were serving in seven of the nine UN peacekeeping operations in Africa, including combat units in

South Sudan and Mali.[36] Since its engagement in the anti-piracy operation in the Gulf of Aden, China has expanded its bilateral security relationships with African countries and the size and role of the PLA Navy (PLAN). Since 2010, there have been more than thirty PLAN port calls in about a dozen African countries.[37] China is also constructing a permanent military facility in Djibouti to support its growing naval presence in the region and secure its interests in Africa.[38]

Over the last decade, China has expanded its security presence in Africa and along African coasts. The CPC and Xinhua are extending their outreach to African political parties and press outlets, hosting more visitors than ever before and training the next generation of African party cadres and media, respectfully. Chinese investment and trade have helped many African countries develop their industries and unearth their resources. Yet Chinese economic, diplomatic, and security policies have faced criticism for facilitating corruption and poor governance. These approaches have also had unintended consequences for China: its state-run firms lost billions in Libya after Gaddafi fell, and despite its contribution to UN peacekeeping in South Sudan, Chinese oil investments have been undermined by civil war. In Zimbabwe, a looming political transition threatens to bring similar economic losses.

## AFRICAN PERCEPTIONS OF CHINA'S AFRICA STRATEGY

Perceptions of China are generally positive in Africa. A 2014 Pew survey conducted through interviews with 7062 individuals in Tanzania, Kenya, Senegal, Nigeria, Uganda, Ghana, and South Africa found that in all countries (except South Africa) over half of those surveyed hold favorable views of China, perceive China's economic growth as beneficial for their country's economy, and believe that the Chinese government respects personal freedoms.[39] In a subsequent 2015 Pew survey, which looked at favorable/ unfavorable views of China in nine countries in Sub-Saharan Africa, China's favorable rating was about 70%.[40]

Many Africans appear to welcome the benefits of newly constructed roads, schools, communication facilities, and factories, as well as rising energy and commodity prices driven by China's growing demand. It remains to be seen, however, whether a fall in oil and other commodity prices in 2014 and China's diversification of petroleum imports towards non-African suppliers will alter these positive perceptions.[41] Summarizing China's economic engagement in Africa, the governor of the Bank of Botswana, Linah Mohohlo, generally praised China's efforts in promoting development throughout the Continent. At the same time, he expressed concern that there may be a second Scramble for Africa that results in the plundering of Africa's resources. Mohohlo concluded that 'Africa should be careful not to rely too much on China and its development model as the panacea for its economic ills'.[42]

China has cordial, and in some cases warm, relationships with all fifty-two African governments that recognize Beijing. Autocratic African governments, like Zimbabwe, Ethiopia, and Sudan, have been particularly attracted to China's political and economic systems. These close relations also extend to the North African countries of Algeria and Morocco. Like many countries, China was forced to adjust its policies in North Africa in the aftermath of the Arab spring. Relations with Tunisia have returned to normal and ties with Egypt are particularly strong, although Libya remains a challenge. Beijing has cordial relations with the Sahel countries except for Burkina Faso, which recognizes Taipei. China's economic ties are strong throughout the region, including trade with Burkina Faso.

China has good relations with leading countries in West Africa: Nigeria, Ghana, Senegal, Ivory Coast, and Liberia. The autocratic governments of Central Africa have warm relations with China, largely because Beijing does not hector their leaders over their poor human rights practices and reluctance to democratize. China has good relations with central Africa's most important country, the DRC. China is a major trade partner for the DRC, which has received billions in Chinese loans.

The six countries in the Horn of Africa present challenges for China because of internal conflict and problems with neighbors. China has strong economic and political ties with most of them, particularly Ethiopia and Sudan. At the same time, it has struggled to preserve its oil interests in South Sudan, where it contributes more than 1000 troops to the UN peacekeeping operation. China has developed close ties in East Africa with Kenya, Tanzania, and Uganda, and has good relations with the four Indian Ocean Island governments. Beijing's economic and political relations with the governments of Southern African countries are uniformly strong except for Swaziland, which recognizes Taipei. Angola and South Africa are China's major African trade partners, and a high percentage of China's FDI has gone to Southern Africa.

While China generally has close relations with African governments, elite African perceptions of China are not uniformly positive. The bluntest criticisms of Chinese business practices liken them to European colonialism. 'The potential danger, in terms of the relationship that could be constructed between China and the African continent, would indeed be a replication of that colonial relationship', former South African president Thabo Mbeki said in 2006. 'It is possible to build an unequal relationship, the kind of relationship that has developed between African countries as colonies. The African continent exports raw material and imports manufactured goods, condemning [it] to underdevelopment'.[43] In 2013, Nigeria's Central Bank governor, Lamido Sanusi, observed that:

> China takes our primary goods and sells us manufactured ones. This was also the essence of colonialism. The British went to Africa and India to secure raw

materials and markets. Africa is now willingly opening itself up to a new form of imperialism.[44]

In 2016, despite winning numerous government contracts, several Chinese multinationals, including the massive telecoms giant ZTE, were placed under investigation by the Kenya Revenue Authority for using accounts in Hong Kong to facilitate tens of millions dollars in tax evasion.[45] Some members of African elites, like John Mangudya, the governor of the Reserve Bank of Zimbabwe (RBZ), have refused to publicly criticize the Chinese even as they are transporting hundreds of millions in hard currency out of the country in 'suitcases and depositing cash with a Chinese bank in Johannesburg'. In 2015, Mangudya acknowledged that $684 million was illicitly externalized by individuals 'under the auspices of free funds for various dubious and unwarranted purposes'. That year, in a case bankers called 'just the tip of an iceberg', the Chinese diamond mining firm, Jinan Mining, was investigated for externalizing $546 million. 'It's not just the currency; it's also ivory and precious stones. A few of them have been arrested but the fines have not been deterrent', an anonymous RBZ official said. An anonymous source within the ruling ZANU-PF party said the capital flight had 'disturbed the political system'.[46]

Other elements of African societies that have responded less favorably to China's increasing presence on the continent include civil-society organizations, opposition political parties, independent labor unions, and the non-government media sector. They periodically express concerns about existing China–Africa trade patterns and the treatment of African workers. Mixed perceptions of China among Africans have had some negative social and political externalities. One young Chinese woman in Kenya explained how 'traditional' Chinese attitudes damaged African perceptions:

> Traditional Chinese businessmen came to Africa simply to pursue fortune. They usually ignore labor complaints, environmental pollution, wildlife conservation and relationship with local residents. Besides, when meeting problems, especially facing government officials, they tend to solve problems by corrupting them. All of these leave a bad impression of Chinese to African people.[47]

Tensions have precipitated urban protests in a number of African countries. Zambia and Zimbabwe, for instance, have seen riots against Chinese merchants and products, and the exclusion of Chinese from business and other communities.[48] In 2015, in Kinshasa, DRC, local protesters attacked and looted about fifty Chinese-owned shops in working-class neighborhoods. Demonstrators shattered windows, broke down doors, and picked shelves clean. 'Nothing was touched besides the Chinese stores', said one Congolese who owns dozens of businesses in the area. Thousands of Chinese laborers in the DRC work on Chinese-financed infrastructure projects or run businesses that serve their compatriots. 'They sell everything, [and] we're no longer doing any business because of them', complained one local vendor, who said he hoped the looting would be a 'lesson' to his Chinese rivals.[49]

If China-Africa trade continues in accordance with existing patterns, China's interests will be increasingly pitted against emerging African resistance narratives at both the grass-roots and elite levels. Generally, positive perceptions of China as an African development partner seem to turn negative when large numbers of Chinese enter African communities, usually as traders and entrepreneurs in the local market. In Kampala, Uganda, for instance, local merchants held a two-day strike in 2011 against the 'influx of Chinese traders associated with Chinese investments'. Issa Sekito of the Kampala City Traders Association explained: 'Over the years, we have been complaining to government over the aliens doing petty trade, especially the Chinese—who come in as investors'.[50] In a move aimed at Chinese, the Ugandan Parliament in 2016 gave foreigners engaged in retail business three months to either make larger investments or leave the country.[51] Similarly, in 2014, Tanzania's labor unions publicly criticized the government for letting in small Chinese traders.[52]

'China inadvertently follows the same pattern of other preceding great powers, spreading the seeds of discontent in a continent with diversified ethnicities and cultures', Eric Kiss and Kate Zhou observe.[53] China's indifference to, or active aid of, autocratic regimes in countries like Zimbabwe, Equatorial Guinea, Guinea, Sudan, and Ethiopia risks partnering with repressive political elites against local people. By selling African governments weapons, censorship technology, and monitoring equipment to maintain social order, Chinese firms are unwittingly tapping into a reservoir of historic anti-foreign resistance narratives that remain widespread among some communities. Grass-roots anti-Chinese critiques frequently veer into charges against African governments; many Africans are aware that their political leaders sanction or turn a blind eye toward adverse Chinese business practices.

At the heart of such criticism is a perception that has become increasingly widespread within African civil society: China's predilection for autocratic regimes determines its choice of African trade partners and is thus exploitative.[54] To examine how widely held this perception is, in 2014 the Ethics Institute of South Africa conducted an online survey of 1056 African civil society representatives from fifteen countries.[55] The study found that African perceptions of Chinese businesses are indeed overwhelmingly negative. Africans are skeptical about the quality of Chinese goods, Chinese enterprises' environmental and economic practices, and Chinese businesses' employment policies toward their African workers. 'There is a perception that Chinese companies do not treat their African staff with respect, do not provide decent working conditions, have little regard for health and safety conditions of their employees and have little regard for basic workers' rights', the study noted.[56] It seems likely that the study's small sample size, focus on urban civil-society representatives, and reliance on an online questionnaire (rather than face-to-face interviews like the Pew survey) led to a selection bias.

African resistance to Chinese firms takes many forms, but is often organized via social media and led by an emergent African civil society that demands more opportunities for locals, ethical business practices, and worker-friendly policies. Mark Kaigwa and Yu-Shan Wu argue that as the number of social-media communication platforms expands in Africa, so too do outlets for anti-Chinese sentiment.[57] In Zimbabwe, there has been a government crackdown on Chinese business activity and a wave of popular anti-Chinese journalism. In Kenya and Uganda, there is resistance among some communities to Chinese railway construction practices. Soon after construction on the East Africa railway began, protestors blocked highway traffic, burned tires and accused the project contractor, China Road and Bridge Construction Company, of denying them jobs in favor of Chinese workers. 'Contracts for the projects are shrouded in secrecy, this cannot be good for us as well as future generations', said Ugandan parliamentarian Geoffrey Ekanya. 'The Chinese are giving us cheap loans, but this should also translate into good jobs for our people'.[58]

## NOTES

1. For a detailed description of this period see David H. Shinn, and Joshua Eisenman, *China and Africa: A Century of Engagement* (Philadelphia: University of Pennsylvania Press, 2012), 31–38.
2. Shinn, and Eisenman, China, and Africa, 33.
3. Mon'im Nasser-Eddine, 60–104, has a detailed account of Chinese–Egyptian contacts leading up to diplomatic recognition in 1956 in *Arab-Chinese Relations 1950–1971* (Beirut: The Arab Institute for Research and Publishing, 1972); see also Bruce D. Larkin, *China in Africa 1949–1970: The Foreign Policy of the People's Republic of China* (Berkeley, CA: University of California Press, 1971), 16–20. For an account of the Bandung Conference, see Richard Wright, *The Color Curtain: A Report on the Bandung Conference* (Jackson, MS: Banner Books, 1956).
4. Larkin, China, and Africa 1949–1970, 20, 32–36.
5. W.A.C. Adie, "Chinese Policy Towards Africa," in *The Soviet Bloc, China and Africa*, ed. Sven Hamrell and Carl Gosta Widstrand (Uppsala: The Scandinavian Institute of African Studies, 1964), 53.
6. Patrick Tyler, *A Great Wall* (New York: Public Affairs, 1999), 204.
7. Julia C. Strauss, "The Past in the Present: Historical and Rhetorical Lineages in China's Relations with Africa," *China Quarterly* 199 (2009): 781–82.
8. CIA, "What the Chinese Communists are Up to in Black Africa," declassified secret report, March 23, 1971, 7.
9. For a discussion of the principles, see Alaba Ogunsanwo, *China's Policy in Africa 1958–71* (London: Cambridge University Press, 1974), 120.
10. Adie, "Chinese Policy Towards Africa," 44.
11. Larkin, China, and Africa 1949–1970, 157.
12. Adie, "Chinese Policy Towards Africa," 53.
13. Larkin, China, and Africa 1949–1970, 156.

14. S.S. Kim, "China and the Third World: In Search of a Neorealist World Policy," in *China and the World: Chinese Foreign Policy in the Post-Mao Era*, ed. S. S. Kim (Boulder: Westview Press, 1984), 184; and Harold C. Hinton, *The People's Republic of China, 1949–1979: A Documentary Survey* (Wilmington, DE: Scholarly Resources, 1980), 2414–23.

15. Richard Lowenthal, "The Sino-Soviet Split and Its Repercussions in Africa," in *The Soviet Bloc, China and Africa*, ed. Hamrell, and Widstrand, 132.

16. James Lilley, and Jeffrey Lilley, *China Hands: Nine Decades of Adventure, Espionage, and Diplomacy in Asia* (New York: Public Affairs, 2004), 155.

17. "Text of the Announcement Issued by Peking Reporting Death of Chairman Mao," *The New York Times*, September 10, 1976, http://www.nytimes.com/learning/general/onthisday/bday/1226a.html.

18. Eugene K. Lawson, "China's Policy in Ethiopia, and Angola," in *Soviet and Chinese Aid to African Nations*, ed. Warren Weinstein and Thomas H. Henriksen (New York: Praeger, 1980), 172.

19. For a more extensive analysis of China–Africa relations in the 1980s and 1990s see Shinn, and Eisenman, 43–48, 66–69, 111–14.

20. "Mugabe Moots Alliance with China," *Mail and Guardian*, December 2, 2003, http://mg.co.za/article/2003-12-02-mugabe-moots-alliance-with-china.

21. Louis Marc Ducharme, *Direction of Trade Statistics Yearbook 2015* (Washington, DC: IMF, 2015), 37, 160–61.

22. "Current Membership of the Human Rights Council, 1 January–31 December 2016," United Nations Human Rights, http://www.ohchr.org/EN/HRBodies/HRC/Pages/CurrentMembers.aspx.

23. Michael Green, and Gregory Poling, "Arbitration Support Tracker," June 16, 2016, *Asia Maritime Transparency Initiative*, https://amti.csis.org/arbitration-support-tracker/.

24. Austin Ramzy, "China Resumes Diplomatic Relations with Gambia, Shutting Out Taiwan," *The New York Times*, March 18, 2016, http://www.nytimes.com/2016/03/19/world/asia/china-gambia-taiwan-diplomatic-relations.html.

25. "Home Page," *Forum on China-Africa Cooperation*, http://www.focac.org/eng/.

26. Hui Ma (International Department, Central Committee of CPC), interview by Joshua Eisenman, June 20, 2016.

27. David Dollar, "Setting the Record Straight on China's Engagement in Africa," *Brookings*, July 11, 2016, https://www.brookings.edu/blog/order-from-chaos/2016/07/11/setting-the-record-straight-on-chinas-engagement-in-africa/.

28. China Information Office of the State Council, "China-Africa Economic and Trade Cooperation," August 2013, https://dilemmaxdotnet.files.wordpress.com/2013/08/china-africa-economic-and-trade-cooperation-2013.pdf.

29. Denise Leung and Lihuan Zhou, "Where Are Chinese Investments in Africa Headed?" World Resources Institute, May 15, 2014, http://www.wri.org/blog/2014/05/where-are-chinese-investments-africa-headed.

30. China Information Office of the State Council, "China's Foreign Aid," *Xinhua*, July 2014, http://news.xinhuanet.com/english/china/2014-07/10/c_133474011.htm.
31. China Africa Research Initiative, "Chinese Loans and Aid to Africa," http://www.sais-cari.org/data-chinese-loans-and-aid-to-africa/.
32. "Hanban," Confucius Institute, http://english.hanban.org/node_10971.htm.
33. Kenneth King, *China's Aid & Soft Power in Africa: The Case of Education and Training* (Suffolk: James Currey, 2013), 75.
34. Catherine Theohary, *Conventional Arms Transfers to Developing Nations, 2007–2014* (Washington, DC: Congressional Research Service, 2015), 44.
35. Mark Bromley, Mathieu Duchâtel, and Paul Holtom, *China's Exports of Small Arms and Light Weapons* (Stockholm: SIPRI, 2013), 43.
36. "UN Mission's Summary Detailed by Country," UN Peacekeeping, June 30, 2016, http://www.un.org/en/peacekeeping/contributors/2016/jun16_3.pdf.
37. Andrew S. Erickson, and Austin M. Strange, "China's Blue Soft Power: Antipiracy, Engagement, and Image Enhancement," *Naval War College Review* 68 (2015): 81–82.
38. Jeffrey Payne, "China Sets Up Shop in Africa," *Fair Observer*, September 14, 2016, http://www.fairobserver.com/region/asia_pacific/chinese-military-base-in-djibouti-23320/.
39. "Global Opposition to U.S. Surveillance, and Drones, but Limited Harm to America's Image—Chapter 2: China's Image," Pew Research Center, July 14, 2014, http://www.pewglobal.org/2014/07/14/chapter-2-chinas-image/.
40. Richard Wike, "5 Charts on America's (Very Positive) Image in Africa," Pew Research Center, July 23, 2015, www.pewresearch.org/fact-tank/2015/07/23/5-charts-on-americas-very-positive-image-in-africa/.
41. Yenling Song, and Wendy Wells, "China's October Pipeline Gas Imports Rise 9% on Year to 2.75 Bcm," *Platts*, November 24, 2014, http://www.platts.com/latest-news/natural-gas/singapore/chinas-october-pipeline-gas-imports-rise-9-on-27862135.
42. Mark Leonard, et al., "Geo-Economics with Chinese Characteristics: How China's Economic Might is Reshaping World Politics," *World Economic Forum*, January 2016, http://www3.weforum.org/docs/WEF_Geoeconomics_with_Chinese_Characteristics.pdf.
43. Victor Mallet, "The Chinese in Africa: Beijing Offers a New Deal," *The Financial Times*, January 23, 2007, https://business-humanrights.org/en/the-chinese-in-africa-beijing-offers-a-new-deal.
44. Lamido Sanusi, "Africa Must Get Real About Chinese Ties," *The Financial Times*, March 11, 2013, https://www.ft.com/content/562692b0-898c-11e2-ad3f-00144feabdc0.
45. Edwin Okoth, "China Firms Caught Up in Billion-Shilling Tax Probe," *Daily Nation* (Kenya) September 25, 2016, http://www.nation.co.ke/news/KRA-accuses-Chinese-firms-of-tax-evasion/1056-3393812-1313bve/.
46. Dumisani Ndlela, "Zimbabwe: Panic in Government as Chinese Loot Economy," *All Africa*, April 21, 2016, http://allafrica.com/stories/201604210612.html.

47. Yao Zongfu, "Chinese Youth in Kenya: A New Generation of Sino-African Relations," *The China Africa Project*, August 26, 2015, http://www.chinaafricaproject.com/chinese-youth-kenya-sino-africa-new-generation/.
48. Barry Sautman, "Racialization as Agency in Zambia–China Relations," in *Africa and China: How Africans and Their Governments Are Shaping Relations with China*, ed. Aleksandra Gadzala (Lanham, MD: Rowman and Littlefield, 2015), 127–48.
49. Marthe Bosuandole, "Chinese Become Targets in DR Congo Riots," *Agence France Presse* January 26, 2015, http://www.dailymail.co.uk/wires/afp/article-2925241/Chinese-targets-DR-Congo-anti-government-riots.html.
50. "Uganda Traders Close Shops in Protest," *BBC News*, July 6, 2011, http://www.bbc.com/news/world-africa-14053516.
51. Amos Ngwonmoya, "MPs Give Foreigners in Retail Business Three Months to Quit," *The Monitor*, September 6, 2016, http://www.monitor.co.ug/News/National/MPs-give-foreigners-in-retail-business-three-months-to-quit/688334-3370554-12yenfaz/index.html.
52. "China in Africa: One Among Many," *The Economist*, January 17, 2015, http://www.economist.com/news/middle-east-and-africa/21639554-china-has-become-big-africa-now-backlash-one-among-many.
53. Eric Kiss, and Kate Zhou, "China's New Burden in Africa," in *Dancing with the Dragon: China's Emergence in the Developing World*, ed. Dennis Hickey, and Baogang Guo (Lanham, MD: Rowman & Littlefield, 2010), 156.
54. For African commentaries that reflect this emerging anti-Chinese narrative see: Catherine Sasman, "Chinese in Gobabis," *The Namibian*, January 12, 2012, http://www.namibian.com.na/index.php?id=90247&page=archive-read. Also see: Bisong Etabohen, "Cameroon Looks to Fix Chinese Employment Blues," *Africa Review*, January 15, 2012, http://www.africareview.com/Special+Reports/Cameroon+looks+to+fix+Chinese+employment+blues/-/979182/1305980/-/view/printVersion/-/69xk9i/-/index.html; and Ephrem Madebo, "Autocracy: The Unsolicited Export of China," *Ethiopian News & Opinions*, August 12, 2010, http://ecadforum.com/blog/autocracy-the-unsolicited-export-of-china/.
55. Angola, Benin, Cameroon, Democratic Republic of Congo, Ethiopia, Ghana, Kenya, Mozambique, Nigeria, South Africa, South Sudan, Sudan, Tanzania, Zambia, and Zimbabwe.
56. Sofie Geerts, Namhla Xinwa, and Deon Rossouw, *Africans' Perceptions of Chinese Business in Africa: A Survey* (Geneva: Globethics, 2014), 34.
57. Calestous Juma, "Afro-Chinese Cooperation: The Evolution of Diplomatic Agency," in *Africa and China: How Africans and Their Governments Are Shaping Relations with China*, ed. Gadzala, 171–90.
58. Nicholas Bariyo, "East African Rail Expansion Meets Growing Opposition," *The Wall Street Journal*, November 14, 2014, http://blogs.wsj.com/frontiers/2014/11/14/east-african-rail-expansion-meets-growing-opposition/.

## SELECT BIBLIOGRAPHY

Bromley, Mark, Mathieu Duchâtel, and Paul Holtom. *China's Exports of Small Arms and Light Weapons*. Stockholm: SIPRI, 2013.

Erickson, Andrew S., and Austin M. Strange. "China's Blue Soft Power: Antipiracy, Engagement, and Image Enhancement." *Naval War College Review* 68 (Winter 2015): 71–91.

Gadzala, Aleksandra, ed. *Africa and China: How Africans and Their Governments Are Shaping Relations with China*. London: Rowman & Littlefield, 2015.

Geerts, Sofie, Namhla Xinwa, and Deon Rossouw. *Africans' Perceptions of Chinese Business in Africa: A Survey*. Geneva: Globethics, 2014.

Hamrell, Sven, and Carl Gösta Widstrand, eds. *The Soviet Bloc China and Africa*. Uppsala: The Scandinavian Institute of African Studies, 1964.

Hickey, Dennis, and Baogang Guo, eds. *Dancing with the Dragon: China's Emergence in the Developing World*. Lanham, MD: Rowman & Littlefield, 2010.

Hinton, Harold C. *The People's Republic of China, 1949–1979. A Documentary Survey*. Wilmington, DE: Scholarly Resources, 1980.

Kim, Samuel S., ed. *China and the World: Chinese Foreign Policy in the Post-Mao Era*. Boulder: Westview Press, 1984.

King, Kenneth. *China's Aid & Soft Power in Africa: The Case of Education and Training*. Suffolk: James Currey, 2013.

Larkin, Bruce D. *China and Africa 1949–1970: The Foreign Policy of the People's Republic of China*. Berkeley, University of California Press, 1971.

Lilley, James R., and Jeffrey Lilley. *China Hands: Nine Decades of Adventure, Espionage, and Diplomacy in Asia*. New York: Public Affairs, 2004.

Nasser-Eddine, Mon'im. *Arab-Chinese Relations 1950–1971*. Beirut: The Arab Institute for Research and Publishing, 1972.

Ogunsanwo, Alaba. *China's Policy in Africa 1958–1971*. London: Cambridge University Press, 1974.

Shinn, David H., and Joshua Eisenman. *China and Africa: A Century of Engagement*. Philadelphia: University of Pennsylvania Press, 2012.

Strauss, Julia C. "The Past in the Present: Historical and Rhetorical Lineages in China's Relations with Africa." *China Quarterly* 199 (September 2009): 777–95.

Theohary, Catherine. *Conventional Arms Transfers to Developing Nations, 2007–2014*. Washington: Congressional Research Service, 2015.

Tyler, Patrick. *A Great Wall*. New York: Public Affairs, 1999.

Weinstein, Warren, and Thomas H. Henriksen, eds. *Soviet and Chinese Aid to African Nations*. New York: Praeger, 1980.

Wright, Richard. *The Color Curtain: A Report on the Bandung Conference*. Jackson, MS: Banner Books, 1956.

# CHAPTER 35

# Africa and Global Financial Institutions

## *John Mukum Mbaku*

Since independence, African countries have had an uneasy and somewhat ambivalent relationship with international financial institutions (IFIs). On the one hand, African countries have looked to IFIs, such as the World Bank (International Bank for Reconstruction and Development [IBRD] and the International Development Association [ADA]) and the International Monetary Fund (IMF) for access to international capital markets so that they can secure the resources that they need to finance national development projects. Specifically, many African countries have looked to the World Bank for access to credit to finance important capital projects and to the IMF for help with balance-of-payments problems. On the other hand, they have resented these international institutions' interference in the domestic policy process in the continent. Many African countries give as an example of the interference of IFIs in political economy in the continent the IMF and World Bank-mandated structural adjustment programs (SAPs), which were imposed on many African economies as a condition for, inter alia, further access to international financial markets.[1]

Developing countries, including those in Africa, have looked to the World Bank and the IMF (the so-called 'Bretton Woods institutions') to help them improve their ability to participate fully and gainfully in the global economy and, at the same time, deal more effectively with domestic economic problems, including especially the eradication of poverty. The Bretton Woods institutions, which form the heart of the international financial architecture, were founded after the Second World War and were expected to serve as a conduit or mechanism through which the rich industrial countries of the

J.M. Mbaku (✉)
Weber State University, Ogden, UT, USA

© The Author(s) 2018
M.S. Shanguhyia and T. Falola (eds.),
*The Palgrave Handbook of African Colonial and Postcolonial History*,
https://doi.org/10.1057/978-1-137-59426-6_35

855

economic North could participate fully and effectively in the elimination of global poverty and material deprivation and help the poor countries of the economic South significantly improve their national standards of living.

Critics of the World Bank and the IMF have argued that despite the fact that, at their founding, these global financial institutions were given clear mandates, they have proceeded to pursue other goals, including an effort to 'integrate countries into the capitalist world economy'.[2] Although the Bretton Woods institutions came to view themselves as agents of social and economic transformation in the developing countries of the economic South, and of the eradication of mass poverty and deprivation, their critics claim that these institutions have, during the last six or so decades, been interested primarily in integrating the elites and governments of the poor and relatively weak states of Africa, Asia, and Latin America into a global economy that is dominated and controlled by large and highly powerful transnational companies head-quartered in the industrial market economies of the economic North.[3]

During the last six decades, both the World Bank and the IMF have gained significant political and economic power, as well as influence. Today, these global financial institutions have emerged as very important (and, to a certain extent, dominant) players in the global lending and donor communities. In fact, the World Bank and the IMF have become so powerful economically and politically that they now control much of the lending to developing countries, including those in Africa. First, these institutions are themselves major lenders to African countries, a significant number of which are not able or lack the capacity to source funds directly from private lenders in international financial markets.[4] Second, many international lenders (both private and public) now require IMF/World Bank clearance before credit is extended to the governments of developing countries, including those in Africa.

Thus, while many African countries see the Bretton Woods institutions as effective conduits to the international financial market, they also resent the power that these institutions can exercise over them. The African countries resent the gatekeeper role played by the World Bank and the IMF and consider programs such as the SAPs as interference with national sovereignty and the ability of each African country to carry out macroeconomic policy. In fact, some African countries have argued that World Bank and IMF involvement in domestic policy has been extremely harmful and has retarded inclusive growth and development. The World Bank and IMF conditionalities in Mozambique are usually offered as an example of these institutions' overreach. With reference to its activities in Mozambique, the World Bank is said to have stated that, 'partly by design, partly by default, the Bank [i.e., World Bank] today has a near-monopoly on development strategy dialogue with the [Mozambican] Government'.[5] In the process, African governments have been forced to the sidelines (i.e. the periphery of the international economy), with the multilateral agencies having a significant impact on the policy agenda in these countries.

This chapter will rigorously examine the relationship between Africa and the international financial system with specific emphasis on the impact of the activities of the IFIs on public-policy design and implementation in the continent, as well as on the continent's ability to source funds from the international market.

## INTERNATIONAL FINANCIAL INSTITUTIONS: WHAT ARE THEY?

IFIs, together with the United Nations system, are responsible for most of today's global governance. The IFIs function specifically to enhance economic and financial cooperation among countries, including especially the transfer of financial resources.[6] Thus, mobilization of financial resources at the global level is a key function of the IFIs. Specifically, IFIs provide: (a) financial assistance to countries; and (b) technical and professional advice, primarily for the purpose of advancing economic growth and human development. In the process, the IFIs also promote international economic cooperation, including trade.

The expression 'international financial institutions' is usually used in the literature to refer to the IMF and the five multilateral development banks. The latter consist of: (a) the World Bank Group; (b) the African Development Bank; (c) the Asian Development Bank; (d) the Inter-American Development Bank; and (e) the European Bank for Reconstruction and Development. The last four financial institutions are regional banks and focus their activities on specific regions of the world. The activities of the World Bank Group and the IMF are global in perspective and scope.

Membership of the IFIs is limited to sovereign countries only, which are referred to as 'owner-members'; both developed and developing countries are eligible for membership in the IFIs. Historically, the developed countries have been *donors* to the IFIs, while the developing countries have been *borrowers*. Membership in the regional development banks is open to all countries, including those which do not belong to the region in question. For example, membership of the African Development Bank includes not only African countries but also many countries from outside the region, including Britain, the USA, Canada, Brazil, Saudi Arabia, The Netherlands, the People's Republic of China (PRC), South Korea, Germany, and Argentina, to name just a few. Although each IFI has its own 'independent legal and operational status',[7] there is a significant level of cooperation among all these IFIs because of the structure of their memberships.

While the IMF offers temporary financial assistance to member countries to help them deal with balance-of-payments problems, the regional development banks provide resources for member countries to invest in national development projects. Three types of financial instruments dominate the relationship between the regional development banks and their members: (a) long-term loans (with maturities of up to twenty years); (b) very long-term loans (with maturities of thirty to forty years); and (c) grants, specifically for 'technical assistance, advisory services, or project preparation'.[8]

Within the global financial system, there are other 'publicly owned international banks and funds', which also extend credit to developing countries. However, these institutions are usually classified as 'other multilateral financial institutions' (OMFIs) as opposed to IFIs.[9] These OMFIs (such as the European Investment Bank, the International Fund for Agricultural Development, the Islamic Development Bank, and the Organization of the Petroleum Exporting Countries Fund for International Development) usually focus on specific and much narrower economic sectors or have extremely narrow membership structures.[10]

The IMF was established in 1945 as the primary regulator of the international monetary system. In performing its functions, the IMF was expected to 'prevent crises in the [international monetary] system by encouraging countries to adopt sound economic policies'.[11] In addition to monitoring countries to make sure that they were adhering to the principle of sound economic policy making, the IMF also stood ready to provide these countries with financial assistance to meet balance-of-payments problems.

The IMF, since its founding, has engaged in three important types of activities: (a) it monitors financial and economic developments, globally and at the country level, and offers advice to countries; (b) it provides loans to member countries, which are having balance-of-payments problems; and (c) it provides technical assistance and training to the governments (usually finance ministries) and central banks of member countries.

The IMF is headquartered in Washington, DC and is accountable to its 188 member governments. In recent years, the IMF has emerged as a global forum for examining issues of importance to the stability of the international economy; for example, the design and implementation of standards and codes of conduct in such areas as data management, fiscal transparency, and financial and monetary policy transparency.

The World Bank was founded in 1945 and was initially geared toward financing the reconstruction of countries that had been destroyed by the Second World War. Nevertheless, as war-torn European economies slowly and steadily recovered, the Bank began to turn its attention to the other task that had been envisioned for it at its founding; that is, to assist in and, to a certain extent, oversee the economic development of what came to be referred to as developing and non-industrialized countries.

The World Bank Group's shareholders are the same countries which make up the membership of the IMF. The Bank is governed by a Board of Governors, which is made up of the representatives of ministers of finance/development of the member countries. However, since the Board of Governors meets only annually, the power to make decisions for the Bank on a daily basis is delegated to twenty four executive directors who are located and work at the Bank's location in Washington, DC.

The World Bank Group consists of five institutions, namely: (a) the International Bank for Reconstruction and Development (IBRD, usually referred to as the World Bank); (b) the International Development Association (IDA); (c) the International Finance Corporation (IFC); (d) the Multilateral Investment Guarantee Agency (MIGA); and (e) the International Center for Settlement of Investment Disputes (ICSID). All five institutions have different roles to play in fulfilling the World Bank Group's corporate mission, which is to fight poverty and improve the living conditions of people throughout the world. As a group, they 'provide low-interest loans, interest-free credits, and grants to governments and the private sector in developing countries for investments in education, health, infrastructure, communications, and many other purposes, as well as services in support of those investments'.[12]

The African Development Bank (AfDB), whose headquarters are located in Abidjan, Ivory Coast, is engaged principally in the development of its African member countries. The AfDB is owned by fifty three African countries and twenty four others from the Americas, Europe, Asia, and the Middle East. According to the Agreement Establishing the African Development Bank,[13] the latter's main purpose is to 'contribute to the sustainable economic development and social progress of its regional members individually and jointly' (Article 1).[14] The AfDB's functions include:

- To use the resources at its disposal for the financing of investment projects and programs relating to the economic and social development of its regional members
- To undertake, or participate in, the selection, study and preparation of projects, enterprises and activities contributing to such development
- To mobilize and increase in Africa, and outside Africa, resources for the financing of such investment projects and programs
- Generally, to promote investment in Africa of public and private capital in projects or programs designed to contribute to the economic development or social progress of its regional members
- To provide such technical assistance as may be needed in Africa for the study, preparation, financing and execution of development projects or programs; and
- To undertake such other activities and provide such other services as may advance its purpose (Article 2 (1) (a–f)).[15]

In carrying out its functions, the AfDB is instructed by its enabling law to 'seek to co-operate with national, regional and sub-regional development institutions in Africa' (Article 2[2]).[16] Additionally, the AfDB is instructed to cooperate with 'other international organizations [which are] pursuing a similar purpose and with other institutions concerned with the development of Africa' (Article 2[3]).[17]

The AfDB's financial base is made up of subscribed capital, reserves, and funds that the Bank sources through loans, and its accumulated net income.

In terms of the AfDB's subscribed capital, two-thirds is held by its regional member countries and one-third by member countries outside the continent. In terms of governance, the AfDB's highest policy-making body is the Board of Governors, each member country being assigned one governor. In terms of actual governance, however, the Board of Governors delegates some of its powers to the Board of Directors, which consists of 18 executive directors, 12 of whom represent the regional members, and 6 of whom represent the outside or non-regional members. Its founding law, however, mandates that the president of the AfDB must be a national of one of the regional member countries.[18]

## AFRICA AND THE INTERNATIONAL FINANCIAL SYSTEM

Before we take a look at Africa's post-independence experience with the international financial system, it is instructive to see how the IFIs view their role in Africa and other developing regions of the world. Regardless of the dictates of their mandates, many IFIs purport to provide certain specific services to countries in Africa and other poor regions of the world in an effort to enhance economic growth and human development.[19]

First, IFIs provide *financing*, usually loans and grants, to African countries to undertake various development projects. Although such financing may support projects in infrastructure and other areas critical to the development of each country's productive capacity, all projects financed are based on national priorities designed in consultation with the IFIs. In certain cases, the financial assistance offered the African country is directed at projects associated with structural adjustment programs (SAPs).[20]

Second, staff members from the IFIs enhance the capacity of African countries to design and implement public policies, especially those dealing with economic growth and development. In addition to providing dedicated staff who consult extensively with elites from both the public and private sectors of the African countries, the IFIs (e.g. World Bank and IMF) may actually send staff members to work with central banks and finance ministries in the African countries. The two parties (technocrats from the IFIs and Africa's private and public sectors) ideally are expected to produce policy packages which are informed by recommendations of the IFIs and the African countries. These policies, of course, are expected to reflect the poverty and development needs of the respective African countries.

Third, IFIs help African countries develop and adopt internationally accepted codes of good practices; for example, the IMF's *Code of Good Practices on Fiscal Transparency* and *Code of Good Practices on Transparency in Monetary and Financial Policies*.[21] The development and adoption of these internationally recognized or accepted codes of conduct for use in both the public and private sectors is supposed to generally improve both economic and political governance and enhance economic growth and development.

In addition to promoting improvements in domestic economic performance, adoption of codes of good practices is expected to enhance the ability of the African economies to integrate into and participate gainfully in the global economy.

Fourth, the IFIs provide various sectors of the African economies with opportunities for human capital development. Training can be undertaken within the framework of specific development projects undertaken by the African countries with the support and guidance of the IFIs or as stand-alone training programs designed to build capacity in the African countries. For example, the training arm of the World Bank or IMF may bring staff from both private and public sectors in the African countries to Washington, DC to attend short courses or workshops that help these individuals acquire new competences and return home to improve the capacities of their work units.

Finally, IFIs offer financial and other assistance to capacity-building institutions (e.g., the African Capacity Building Foundation and the African Economic Research Consortium) to train researchers, improve and enhance knowledge transfer, support economic and financial research, provide continuing education courses for staff in both private and public sectors, and generally assist the continent in capacity-building projects.

While, in theory, the IFIs can provide many services to the African economies (e.g. help them build capacity and develop and implement monetary policies that enhance financial and economic stability), it is important to point out that these external institutions, including even the African Development Bank, must play only an advisory and subordinate role. Each African country must not allow these institutions to dominate and control domestic public policy. Economic policy in each country must be the purview and responsibility of the country's policymakers.

## Africa's Post-Independence Experience with the International Financial Community

In the mid-1970s, many countries in Africa suffered from significantly high levels of external debts and, by the mid-1980s, the failure of these countries to effectively manage their debts had evolved into a major constraint on economic growth and development.[22] In order to deal effectively and fully with these debts and provide the wherewithal for economic growth and development, many of these African countries appealed to the international financial community for assistance. Most of the effort was directed at two of the most important IFIs—the World Bank and the IMF. Eventually these so-called Bretton Woods institutions became involved in what came to be referred to as 'conditional lending'. Under the latter regime, African countries which sought loans or loan-extensions from the international financial system (primarily from the Bretton Woods institutions and/or the developed market economies) were required to implement a basket of institutional reforms, which included, inter alia: (a) reductions in the public sector; (b) devaluation of the national currency; (c) deregulation of the foreign trade sector; and (d) greater reliance on markets for the allocation of resources.[23]

As a result of the fact that the World Bank and the IMF had essentially become gatekeepers for certain types of financial flows (primarily debt and development assistance) to the African countries, these institutions played a significant role in the transition to democratic governance that started in the continent in the mid-1980s.[24]

But how did the Bretton Woods institutions become so intimately linked to structural or institutional adjustments in the African countries? As argued by Baylies, the involvement of these multilateral financial organizations in Africa's reform efforts can be traced to 'a broader discourse promoted by the World Bank from the mid-eighties which expressed the need for an ena-bling environment to facilitate prescribed economic reforms'.[25] At the time, the World Bank felt that many of its development projects in Africa were not functioning efficiently because recipient countries were pervaded by extremely inefficient and dysfunctional bureaucratic structures and govern-ance systems that were actually constraints on entrepreneurial activities and the creation of wealth.[26] In other words, the World Bank argued that the governance architectures of many African countries were actually a hindrance to wealth creation, economic growth, and development. The World Bank subsequently engaged in a concerted effort to coerce African countries into undertaking institutional reforms, which were expected to improve economic performance and significantly increase the efficiency and performance of the multilateral organization's projects in these countries. Thus, since the mid-1980s, the World Bank and the IMF have become very critical participants in the transition to more effective governance systems in the African countries.

The involvement of both the World Bank and the IMF in the African economies beginning in the mid-1980s was supposed to assist these coun-tries resolve an economic crisis that was threatening to wipe out most of the improvements in human development that had been achieved in the conti-nent since the 1950s and 1960s. By the early 1980s, many countries in Africa suffered from significant balance-of-payments deficits and their development efforts were threatened by rising external debts. The Bretton Woods institu-tions' structural adjustment programs (SAPs) were supposedly designed to help the African countries improve macroeconomic performance and create the environment for rapid economic growth. The latter would then provide each African government with the resources that it needed to fight poverty and material deprivation and improve the quality of life for all citizens. By 1994, the World Bank[27] was still quite optimistic regarding the positive role that the SAPs could play in economic transformation in the African coun-tries. However, many scholars criticized the World Bank's assessment of the SAPs and argued that although African countries were in need of institutional reforms and structural adjustment, the top-down and elite-driven approach adopted by the World Bank and other IFIs would not produce outcomes that were beneficial to the African countries. In order for institutional reforms to significantly improve governance, and hence, entrepreneurship and economic growth in the African countries, the reforms had to be undertaken through a bottom-up, inclusive, and people-driven process; that is, the African people had to initiate and own the reforms, and implement them without the active involvement of the IFIs.[28]

The IMF and the World Bank are the cornerstone of the international financial system. The IMF, for example, is expected to help minimize interruptions in global trade and assist countries in meeting any temporary shortfalls in their balance-of-payments. The financial assistance to be provided by the IMF was supposed to ensure that 'these countries continued to participate in the international economy without any interruptions'.[29]

The World Bank's raison d'être was to promote and enhance rapid economic growth and development in the post-Second World War period, not just in war-torn Europe but also in the developing countries, most of which were former colonies of the European countries. As part of the duty to assist developing countries fight poverty, the Bank was expected to lend these countries money so that they could invest in social overhead capital, which included 'roads, railways and other communication infrastructures, utilities, dams, irrigation facilities, schools, health care centers, including hospitals, and other structures that were expected to enhance the rapid creation of the wealth that these countries needed to deal with poverty'.[30] An important argument at the time was that in the newly independent countries in Africa, Asia, and the Americas, the private sector was either unwilling or incapable of providing the necessary economic infrastructures. It was, therefore, critical that the government intervene and provide the necessary social overhead capital, which was a *sine qua non* for postwar economic transformation in the continent. In addition, the World Bank was also expected to encourage and facilitate the flow of foreign private investment into the African countries through loan guarantees or the direct participation of the Bank with private entrepreneurs in development projects.

Policymakers in the African countries came to view the Bretton Woods institutions as financial organizations that could help them secure the necessary resources they needed to invest in poverty eradication programs. Specifically, these multilateral organizations were expected to function as a conduit through which the rich industrial countries of the economic North could contribute to job creation and poverty eradication in the economic South. Critics of the World Bank and the IMF, however, have argued that although these IFIs were granted clear mandates, they nevertheless have pursued other objectives, the most important of which is to 'integrate countries into the capitalist world economy'.[31]

Although the Bretton Woods institutions came to view themselves as 'agents of social and economic transformation in the Third World, and of the elimination of global poverty, their critics claim that the primary function of these institutions during the last fifty years has been the integration of the elites and governments of the poor and relatively weak states of Africa, Asia, and Latin America into an international economy that is dominated and controlled by large transnational firms located in the industrial market economies'.[32]

During more than fifty years of operations, both the World Bank and the IMF have gained a lot of political and economic influence; in fact, today, they are considered the global economy's most important financial institutions. The IMF has expanded its duties from ensuring an effective international payments system to performing other functions associated with general global financial health, international trade, job creation and economic growth, and poverty alleviation. In fact, during the financial crisis of 2008, the IMF restructured its policies toward poor countries and introduced a more flexible regime of conditionality, making it easier for these countries to access resources for poverty alleviation. In addition, the IMF reformed its lending framework and adopted a system that allowed it to tailor 'loan terms to countries' varying strengths and circumstances'.[33]

The control of lending to the African countries by the World Bank and the IMF has been undertaken in the following ways. First, both organizations have emerged as the most important lenders to developing countries, including those in Africa. Most of these countries are not in a position to independently access resources directly from international private lenders.[34] Second, since the early 1990s, so-called 'conditional lending' has become an important part of the flow of resources from the developed countries to the African economies. It was at this time that many donor countries implemented policies that linked 'official development aid to political and economic liberalization as recommended under the IMF/World Bank structural adjustment programs'.[35]

Of course, the developed countries that extend financial assistance to the African countries do not actively engage in monitoring the recipient countries to make certain that they engage in the necessary institutional reforms. That job is left to the IMF and the World Bank. As a consequence, the recommendations of the IMF and the World Bank now constitute an important aspect of the approval of development aid to developing countries, including those in Africa.[36] In the African countries, many policymakers believe that the IMF and the World Bank are now important gatekeepers in the flow of financial resources from the developed countries to the continent.

The enormous economic power that the Bretton Woods institutions have amassed since their founding in the 1940s has allowed them to exercise significant influence on macroeconomic policies in the developing countries, including those in Africa. One can use the involvement of these IFIs in the economy of Mozambique to illustrate the extent to which these organizations have usurped public policy in many countries in Africa. After Mozambique's civil war ended, the World Bank and the IMF became de facto governors of Mozambique's political and economic systems. As stated by Dunn, '[a]s the World Bank and IMF have enlarged the scope of conditionalities beyond economic policies, the Mozambican state now exists to the extent that the Western lending agencies allow it to exist'.[37] According to David Plank, 'public officials [in Mozambique] now have little choice but to do whatever the aid agencies demand of them'.[38]

As argued by Young, 'despite equipping Mozambique with all the trappings of a democratic state, the sheer leverage of outside powers, and in particular the coordinating role of the IMF/World Bank, have subjected Mozambique to an extraordinary degree of foreign tutelage. Indeed, Mozambique has been made into a virtual laboratory for new forms of Western domination'.[39] In fact, the World Bank eventually admitted its culpability in Mozambique's disastrous macroeconomic performance when it stated that, 'partly by design, partly by default, the Bank today has a near-monopoly on development strategy dialogue with the [Mozambican] Government'.[40]

As a consequence of these developments, many scholars came to view the Mozambican state as merely an extension of international donor and aid agencies instead of a servant of the citizens (i.e., the domestic electorate). As accurately summed up by Dunn,[41] the Mozambican state has become 'largely an interlocutor for international agents and domestic interests, and distinguishing between the two has become increasingly difficult'.[42]

Beginning in the mid-1980s in Africa, many countries were literally forced to 'adopt and implement programs designed in Washington, DC by the World Bank and the IMF in order to qualify for additional loans from the international lending community'.[43] During the negotiations that produced these programs, individual African countries were usually represented by 'urban-based elites who lack both time-and-place information about economic and social conditions in the rural areas of their respective countries'.[44] In addition, these elites were not likely to bear a significant portion of the costs of implementing these programs. For example, in a study of SAPs in Nigeria, Julius O. Ihonvbere[45] determined that most of the costs of these programs were borne primarily by rural peasants, the urban poor, and historically marginalized individuals and groups (e.g. women and minority ethnic and religious groups).[46]

One important aspect of the SAPs was for each African government to get rid of price controls on the marketing of foodstuffs in urban markets in an effort to improve the prices received by rural farmers for their produce. Unfortunately, the implementation of price deregulation in the African countries was undertaken capriciously by governments that were eager to maintain the 'goodwill of the politically volatile urban sectors' and, as a consequence, many rural farmers rarely benefited from the implementation of the SAPs.[47]

In fact, the decision by the IMF and policymakers in the African countries to emphasize the production of cash crops (e.g. coffee, cocoa, rubber, palm kernels, and bananas) at the expense of foodstuffs was made without widespread consultation; it was a top-down, elite-driven and non-participatory policy that came to be an important cause of food shortages in many of these countries. While the policy significantly improved the capacity of many African countries to secure the foreign exchange (through the export of cash crops) to service their external debts, it crippled economic activities in many rural areas and 'dealt a severe blow to foodstuff production and consequently, food security'.[48]

In Cameroon, for example, the government designed an incentive system that encouraged and enhanced the production of coffee, a policy which, in the country's grasslands, 'worked directly against the production of food staples such as cocoyams, several varieties of yams, plantains, and other crops essential for the maintenance of a healthy and productive population'.[49] The outcome was major food shortages that forced many people to depend on imported foods. Unfortunately, dependence on imported foods created many nutritional and health problems, particularly in children. Many families were forced to change their diets, including those of infants and young children, creating such dietary problems as tooth decay and diabetes that the country's health-care system was not equipped to fully and effectively handle.

Although the World Bank and the IMF intended their adjustment programs to enhance the ability of African countries to promote and enhance human development through strengthening markets and greatly enhancing rapid economic growth and the creation of wealth, many researchers now argue that, with respect to the African countries, the Bretton Woods institutions have evolved into 'vehicles through which the income and wealth of the poor countries is redistributed in favor of the rich developed countries'.[50] For example, in its 1992 annual report, the World Bank[51] reported that it and the International Development Agency had remitted $16.441 billion to its borrowers in developing countries. In terms of net disbursements (gross disbursements minus payments on outstanding loans and credits), the amount was $6.258 billion. In the same year, developing countries, which were debtors to the World Bank, collectively sent $6.547 billion to private business enterprises in the Organization for Economic Cooperation and Development (OECD) countries as payments for goods and services on the Bank's outstanding loans. From the point of view of net transfers, the poor countries paid $198 million more to the developed industrial countries for World Bank-associated purchases than the developing countries had received from the Bank.[52]

During the last several decades, the World Bank and the IMF have made great efforts to help the African countries service their debts. Many critics, however, have argued that the reality is that the programs promoted by these institutions have resulted in the continuous bleeding of the African economies; there has been a net transfer of resources from the continent to the industrial market economies. It is argued, however, that the more important issue is that at the same time as the multilateral financial institutions have been helping the African countries to remain viable borrowers, levels of poverty and material deprivation have continued to rise in these countries. Improved access to international financial markets has allowed many of these countries to increase their debt levels but most of the resources secured through this process have not been invested in productive capacity or in providing welfare-enhancing services to the populations. Instead, a lot of the borrowed resources have been used by unscrupulous civil servants and political elites to minimize the impact on themselves of the austerity measures that are part of the IMF and World Bank imposed conditionalities.[53] In addition, spending on health care, education (especially at the primary and secondary levels) housing, HIV/AIDS education, and other areas that are critical to human development, have been neglected in favor of debt service. As a consequence, many researchers have come to see both the IMF and the World Bank programs (e.g. the SAPs) as mechanisms designed to exploit and plunder the African economies for the benefit of national elites (civil servants and politicians) and their foreign-based benefactors. The bulk of the citizens in these countries, especially those who historically have been marginalized and pushed to the political and economic periphery (e.g. women, rural inhabitants, the urban poor, and ethnic and religious minorities) have received virtually no benefits from these adjustment programs. Instead, they have been forced to bear most of the costs of the SAPs and other austerity programs.[54]

The origins of IMF and World Bank involvement in African political economy, argue some economists,[55] can be traced to the desire by the World Bank to improve the institutional environment in economies in which it had development projects. The World Bank is said to have indicated that many of its development projects in several countries, including those in Africa, were not performing effectively and efficiently because of the presence of several institutional impediments; specifically, severely weak, inefficient, and parasitic bureaucracies, and governments that were either not willing or did not have the capacity to design and implement policies that support markets and enhance entrepreneurial activities. The Bank sought to have recipients of its financial assistance programs implement a basket of policy reforms designed to significantly improve their governance architectures.[56]

Specifically, the World Bank desired that countries participating in its development programs should undertake specific adjustments to the structure of their governance institutions—here, 'adjustment' refers to 'changes made in the economy (as well as in the institutional environment) to enhance the latter's (i.e., the economy's) ability to cope with external shocks'.[57] The Bank argued that if the reforms were fully and effectively implemented, the domestic economy would be more able to properly respond to both negative and positive external shocks such as, for example, trade deficits, changes in global commodity prices, and inflows of foreign resources (e.g. official development aid, private investment, and loans).

The structural adjustment programs, as promoted by the World Bank and the IMF in Africa, can be seen as consisting of two separate but connected elements: (a) changes in public policy whose main objective is to enhance the ability of the domestic economy to achieve both internal and external balances and which are considered to be within the purview of the IMF and policymakers in the adjusting African country; and (b) institutional reforms that force each African economy to rely more on markets and prices for the allocation of resources. The latter reforms, those designed to enhance and improve the functioning of markets, are considered the purview of the World Bank.[58] As implemented in the African countries during the last several decades, SAPs have essentially involved efforts to, inter alia[59]:

- significantly reduce state ownership and management of productive resources through the privatization of state-owned enterprises
- abolish the regime of price controls, including especially price ceilings on agricultural produce in an effort to improve incentives for farmers and enhance productivity in this critical sector
- devalue the domestic currency in order to improve the country's ability to compete globally
- remove most government subsidies on goods sold and consumed domestically
- reduce state regulation of private exchange and rely more on markets for the allocation of goods and services
- upgrade the national investment code and create an enabling environment for the inflow of foreign investment
- significantly enhance free trade by eliminating protectionist laws and statutes.

Africa's post-independence experience with the international financial community has been dominated by its involvement with the IMF and the World Bank. In addition, the relationship between Africa and the Bretton Woods institutions has been overshadowed by the latter's preoccupation with the SAPs. The argument given by economists at the World Bank and the IMF at the time was that full and effective implementation of the SAPs would: (a) significantly decrease national debt levels and free up revenues for investment in critical sectors, such as education and training, health, and agriculture; (b) improve macroeconomic performance and enhance the creation of wealth; and (c) generally strengthen economic and political governance. Although many of the African countries that implemented the SAPs continued to suffer deterioration in their economies, the World Bank and the IMF continued to argue that the SAPs would eventually improve political economy in many of these countries and bring about inclusive and sustainable economic growth and development.[60]

By the 1990s, many Sub-Saharan African countries were no longer able to service their national debts, and this was partly responsible for their decision to seek assistance from the IMF and the World Bank. Despite the assistance provided by the Bretton Woods institutions, many of these countries continued to struggle with a debt burden that threatened to destroy prospects for economic growth and effective elimination of poverty. While several reasons were offered by researchers to explain why the implementation of the SAPs had not had a major positive impact on macroeconomic performance, the most important of them was the fact that the SAPs were seen by most Africans as external impositions; these reform programs were 'designed abroad without effective participation by [each country's] relevant stakeholders'[61] and were implemented arbitrarily and capriciously.

Of course, African countries were duly represented at the negotiations that produced these structural adjustment schemes. Nevertheless, the truth of the matter is that representation was limited to urban-based elites, who worked closely with economists at the IMF and the World Bank. Important stakeholders (notably inhabitants of the rural sectors, the urban poor, and women) who ultimately were forced to bear most of the costs of the adjustments were not provided the facilities to participate fully and effectively in the design and implementation of the adjustment programs. The urban-based elites lacked the time-and-place information, especially information about social and economic conditions in the rural areas of many of the African countries that were subjected to the SAPs and, without such information, they could not design programs that were capable of dealing effectively with the problems these communities suffered from. Additionally, the fact that many of these countries had governing processes that were not truly representative meant that the elites at the center (i.e. the individuals who were in charge of public-policy design and implementation) were not in a position to maximize *national* objectives.

Even after the many institutional transformations that have taken place in the continent since the pro-democracy movements of the early 1990s (including the recent Arab Spring events), many African countries still have institutional arrangements or governance systems that: (a) do not adequately constrain the state, allowing civil servants and political elites to act with impunity and engage in growth-inhibiting behaviors such as corruption and rent seeking; (b) constrain entrepreneurial activities and the creation of wealth; (c) fail to enhance the effective management of diversity (especially ethnic and religious diversity); and (d) do not provide effective participation of all relevant stakeholders in policy design and implementation.

Although many African governments still optimistically believe that the involvement of the Bretton Woods institutions in their economies will significantly improve their capacity to manage their debts fully and effectively, the citizens of these countries continue to see the SAPs and other impositions of the international financial system as new forms of colonialism and exploitation. There is a belief in the African countries that both the World Bank and the IMF are part of an effort by external actors, based primarily in the developed Western economies, to recolonize the continent and exploit the latter's resources for the benefit of the metropolitan economies and collaborating urban-based elites in the African countries. Nevertheless, the implementation of the programs demanded by the IFIs as conditions for African countries to continue to participate in and access global financial markets has imposed significant costs on the poor and historically marginalized and deprived groups and communities such as ethnic and religious minorities, women, rural inhabitants, and the urban poor.[62]

Virtually all the research carried out on the effects of SAPs on African economies has contradicted the excessive optimism expressed by the World Bank and the IMF.[63] As argued by Lall, for example, SAPs have provided virtually no benefits to industry in Africa and have, in addition, not helped in the diversification of industry in the continent.[64] While many countries continue to adhere to the demands of the international financial system, including those of the IMF and the World Bank, the benefits to these economies are, at best, dubious, and at worst, injurious. Throughout the continent, the SAPs and other foreign-imposed institutional reforms have been politicized and have emerged as instruments for the enrichment of domestic political elites.[65] As a consequence, many citizens do not consider these structural adjustment programs as genuine tools for effective transformation of their economic and political governance systems. The view among many Africans is not just that the SAPs should be abandoned, but that all foreign or externally imposed reforms should be avoided in favor of bottom-up, locally focused, inclusive, and people-driven institutional reform programs, which are most likely to reflect local values, interests, and problems, and hence allow the Africans to own their transformation processes.

While some policymakers argue that the Bretton Woods institutions still have a role to play in Africa's struggle to develop, others argue that both institutions are actually obstacles to the continent's effective economic transformation. Those policymakers who oppose the intervention of the Bretton Woods institutions in African political economy argue that these organizations' obsession with institutional reforms (that many African countries do not consider as priorities) is interfering with the ability of policymakers in the continent to engage in the promotion of policies that are relevant to and informed by the multifarious problems that plague their economies.

The World Bank and the IMF offer the African countries a basket of 'services' including:

- granting a 'seal of approval' for commercial lending
- providing coordination of donors in-country
- participating in the Paris Club consultations, which determine aid and credit to developing countries, including those in Africa (but some

critics argued that both the IMF and the World Bank attend these consultations to bully participants into adopting these institutions' views on the transfer of resources to developing countries)[66]

- conditionalities on structural adjustment loans and debt relief (most of which conditionalities have remained the same despite changes in the political economy of many of these countries)
- significant power to interfere in domestic monetary policy, including sending individuals to oversee activities at central banks and finance ministries
- balance-of-payments support in cases of emergency
- loans for countries to undertake major infrastructure projects such as dams, roads and transport, mineral extraction, energy projects, and other economic infrastructures.

While these services may appear as benefits to the African economy, critics argue that the financial reforms (e.g. exchange rate liberalization) imposed on these economies by the World Bank and the IMF usually induce capital flight, with the latter wiping out any gains from any inflow of financial resources into the continent induced by the Bretton Woods institutions. Research by James Boyce and Léonce Ndikumana has shown that Africa is a net exporter of financial resources and that, by 2004, more than 30% of African citizens' investments (cash and assets) were held offshore.[67] As argued by other researchers, Africans do not benefit from the loans accumulated by their governments; most of these resources are siphoned off by corrupt civil servants and politicians and then 'invested' in offshore accounts in the same banks that extended the credit to the African governments, with benefits accruing to the corrupt elites and their benefactors and not to the people.

Over the years, researchers have uncovered evidence to support the position that World Bank projects in Africa have been mired in corruption and have produced virtually no benefits for the people. Africans argue that there is a total disconnect between their aspirations and the values promoted by their leaders, the latter being the ones who deal with the IFIs; these individuals are primarily interested in maximizing their personal interests and usually engage in activities and behaviors that enrich them but do not promote national development. For example, in the World Bank-funded Chad–Cameroon oil pipeline, while the multinational companies exploiting Chad's oilfields were making record profits, communities around the oilfields and along the pipeline were left to swelter in poverty and high levels of material deprivation, thanks to corruption at the highest levels of the Bank and in the African capitals.[68]

The AfDB began effective operations on July 1, 1966, and until 1973 it struggled to meet its many functions, including especially the promotion of economic growth and development in African countries. The main issue for the Bank at this time in its existence was an inadequate capital stock.

The latter was supposed to come from subscriptions by its member countries. Unfortunately, most of these countries were poor and highly underdeveloped, and hence were not able to pay the money that they had pledged as part of their membership in the AfDB. During the period 1967–1974, the Bank financed its investments in the African economies primarily through funds received as paid-in capital by member countries.[69]

Beginning in 1974, the AfDB began to support its work through the borrowing of resources from the central banks of member countries. Nevertheless, it still continued to operate with a very limited resource base, investing only US $119,500,000 during its first six years of operations in projects in the African countries.[70] At this time, however, the AfDB did not have the necessary creditworthiness to access resources from international markets. The main source of the AfDB's financial problems can be traced to the fact that its membership was essentially made up of severely underdeveloped and extremely poor economies, each of which individually had very poor credit. However, that creditworthiness did not improve after they consolidated their resources and formed the AfDB. Of course, there were a few economies within the continent (Algeria, Nigeria, and Libya) that were relatively large and provided the Bank with significant capital. Nevertheless, the Bank was still unable to secure enough resources to provide the type of capital base that would have significantly enhanced its ability to access international financial markets. In addition to the fact that this state of affairs limited the Bank's investment portfolio, it also discouraged external lenders from extending credit to the Bank. A further exacerbating factor was the failure of many member countries to make good on their financial commitments to the Bank.[71]

In 1975, the AfDB was able to secure funds worth US $65,000,000 from a syndicate of commercial banks in the USA.[72] Finally, with access to funds in the international financial markets, the AfDB was able to safeguard its paid-in capital, as well as expand its investment programs in the African economies. Slowly, the AfDB began to gain the confidence of external lenders, specifically those in the Western industrial economies, such as the USA and other OECD countries.

Over the years, the AfDB's ability to access funds from external sources (i.e. sources outside Africa) continued to increase. This was due partly to the fact that the Bank significantly improved its internal efficiency, especially in the management of its loan portfolio. With an increased ability to source loans from international financial markets, the AfDB was now in a position to engage in multinational projects throughout the continent.[73]

The AfDB's main objective is to promote sustainable economic growth and development in Africa. A fundamental issue that the Bank has tackled in recent years is poverty alleviation, and in doing so, it has spearheaded the African Union's New Partnership for Africa's Development (NEPAD). Within the framework of the NEPAD, the Bank has had to deal with additional issues besides poverty alleviation, including, especially, climate change and the environment, health (especially in view of the HIV/AIDS pandemic), gender equality, and the reconstruction of post-conflict societies. Over the years, the AfDB has taken an active role in infrastructure development throughout the continent, including the building of roads and highways, railway and port facilities, and other structures designed to significantly increase the productive capacity of many countries. In keeping with changes in technology, the Bank has gradually increased its investment in clean energy projects. In fact, the Bank now manages a Sustainable Energy Fund for Africa, the latter supported by donations from the governments of the USA and Denmark and designed to support the development of clean, affordable, and renewable energy for commercial and household use in the African countries, as well as the creation of jobs in this fast-emerging economic sector.

## CONCLUSION

During the last several decades, African countries have had a rather ambivalent relationship with the IFIs. The ruling elites of many countries on the continent have looked to the IFIs (notably the IMF and the World Bank) to provide funds for and facilitate the implementation of major industrial projects (e.g. the Chad–Cameroon pipeline project). However, many civil-society organizations in Africa (e.g. community, human-rights, and environmental activists and their organizations) have argued that a lot of projects funded by the IFIs have generated benefits almost exclusively for national elites and their foreign benefactors. At the same time, these projects have imposed significant social, economic, political, and environmental costs on the general population. For example, civil-society groups in Chad have argued that the US $4.8 billion Chad–Cameroon pipeline, cofunded by the World Bank, provided many benefits for the multinational companies (including especially Exxon-Mobil, the consortium leader) involved in the project, as well as for Chadian political elites. But, as argued by many of the country's civil society groups, the additional revenues flowing to the government were used to fund the military and significantly increase the state's capacity to oppress and exploit citizens. In addition, the project created many environmental problems for the villages located along the pipeline's route but provided them with virtually no benefits.

Critics have also argued that flows of financial resources to the continent facilitated by IFIs have usually been accompanied by pressure from multilateral agencies such as the World Bank and the IMF for the African countries to undertake certain prescribed institutional reforms, most of which are not designed with the full participation of each country's relevant stakeholders. As a consequence, many of these reforms, such as the SAPs, do not reflect the values and priorities that are most important to the mass of the African peoples. For example, emphasis of the SAPs on debt service skewed agricultural production in many African countries in favor of cash or export crops (e.g. coffee, palm kernel, cocoa, and bananas) and neglected foodstuff production, a process that led to severe food shortages and threatened food security in many communities throughout the continent.

The way forward, as argued by a host of civil-society organizations and community activists across Africa, is a total reconstruction of global finance so that the IFIs do not remain, as they have been in the last several decades, instruments for the economic, political, and social exploitation of the African peoples. While the reform of international finance is a desirable goal, it is important that Africans provide themselves with governance systems that cannot be easily turned into instruments of plunder by national elites for their own benefit and that of their foreign benefactors. For one thing, the IFIs cannot fund exploitative projects in the continent without the cooperation and acquiescence of each African country's civil servants and political elites. Hence, it is important that each country provide itself with institutional arrangements that adequately constrain the state and hence prevent its custodians (i.e. civil servants and political elites) from acting with impunity. Perhaps, more important, is the fact that significantly improved and more democratic governance systems would greatly enhance the ability of civil society to serve as an effective check on the exercise of government power and hence prevent the engagement of ruling elites in IFI-funded projects that undermine the protection of human rights, gender equality, environmental and ecosystem preservation, peaceful coexistence, poverty eradication, and national development.

## NOTES

1. See e.g. Carolyn Baylies, "'Political Conditionality' and Democratization," in *The Review of African Political Economy* 22, no. 65 (1995): 321–37; and World Bank, *Accelerated Development in Sub-Saharan Africa: An Agenda for Action* (Washington, DC: The World Bank, 1981).
2. Kevin Danaher, "Introduction," in *50 Years Is Enough: The Case against the World Bank and the International Monetary Fund*, ed. Kevin Danaher (Boston, MA: South End Press, 1994), 2.
3. For more on this subject, see the following: Kevin Danaher ed., *50 Years Is Enough: The Case against the World Bank and the International Monetary Fund* (Boston, MA: South End Press, 1994); and Boris Bernstein and James M. Boughton, "Adjusting to Development: The IMF and the Poor," Finance and *Development* 31 (1995): 42–45.
4. See e.g. World Bank, *African Development Indicators, 1998/1999* (Washington, DC: The World Bank, 1998), 177.
5. Quoted in Tom Young, "'A Project to Be Realized': Global Liberalism and Contemporary Africa," *Millennium* 24, no. 3 (Winter 1995): 538–39.
6. Vinay K. Bhargava, "The Role of the International Financial Institutions in Addressing Global Issues," in *Global Issues for Global Citizens: An Introduction*

*to Key Development Challenges*, ed. Vinay K. Bhargava (Washington, DC: The World Bank, 2006), 393.

7. Ibid., 394.
8. Ibid.
9. Ibid.
10. Vinay K. Bhargava, "The Role of the International Financial Institutions in Addressing Global Issues," 394–95.
11. Ibid., 395.
12. Ibid., 396.
13. African Development Bank, "Agreement Establishing the African Development Bank," last visited on December 31, 2016. Available at http://www.afdb. org/fileadmin/uploads/afdb/Documents/Legal-Documents/Agreement%20 Establishing%20the%20ADB%20final%202011.pdf.
14. Ibid., Article 1.
15. Ibid., Article 2.
16. Ibid.
17. Ibid.
18. Ibid., "Agreement Establishing the African Development Bank."
19. See e.g. Saleh M. Nsouli, "Capacity Building in Africa: The Role of International Financial Institutions," *Finance and Development* 37, no. 4 (2000): 34–37; and Michael A. Dessart, and Roland E. Ubogu eds., *Capacity Building, Governance, and Economic Reform in Africa* (Washington, DC: The World Bank, 2001).
20. See "Capacity Building in Africa."
21. See John Mukum Mbaku, *Institutions and Development in Africa* (Trenton, NJ: Africa World Press, 2004), 247, 261.
22. See e.g. Simeon Ibidayo Ajayi, and Mohsin S. Khan eds., *External Debt and Capital Flight in Sub-Saharan Africa* (Washington, DC: IMF, 2000); and Richard E. Mshomba, *Africa in the Global Economy* (Boulder, CO: Lynne Rienner Publishers, Inc., 2000).
23. See e.g. Mbaku, *Institutions and Development in Africa*, 141.
24. See e.g. Fantu Cheru, *The Silent Revolution in Africa: Debt, Development and Democracy* (London, UK: Zed Books, 1989); Timothy M. Shaw, "Reformism, Revisionism, and Radicalism in African Political Economy during the 1990s," *The Journal of Modern African Studies* 29, no. 2 (1991): 191–212; Stephen R. Weissman, "Structural Adjustment in Africa: Insights from the Experiences of Ghana and Senegal," *World Development* 18, no. 12 (1990): 1621–34; Julius O. Ihonvbere, *Nigeria: The Politics of Adjustment & Democracy* (New Brunswick, NJ: Transaction Publishers, 1994); and George W. Shepherd, "The African Right to Development: World Policy and the Debt Crisis," *Africa Today* 37, no. 4 (1990): 5–14.
25. Baylies, "Political Conditionality," 322.
26. Mbaku, *Institutions and Development*, 142.
27. See e.g. World Bank, *Adjustment in Africa: Reforms, Results, and the Road Ahead* (New York: Oxford University Press, 1994).
28. See generally Sanjaya Lall, "Structural Adjustment and African Industry," *World Development* 23, no. 12 (1995): 2019–31; Ihonvbere, *Nigeria: The Politics of Adjustment*; Kempe R. Hope Sr., ed., *Structural Adjustment, Reconstruction and Development* (Aldershot, UK: Ashgate, 1997); and Fantu Cheru,

*The Silent Revolution in Africa: Debt, Development and Democracy* (London, UK: Zed Books, 1989).

29. Mbaku, *Institutions and Development in Africa*, 145.
30. Ibid.
31. Danaher, "Introduction," 2.
32. Mbaku, *Institutions and Development in Africa*, 146; see also Danaher, "Introduction," op. cit., 2; and Bernstein and Boughton, "Adjusting to Development."
33. IMF, "Factsheet: The IMF's Response to the Global Economic Crisis," last visited on December 31, 2016. Available at http://www.imf.org/About/Factsheets/Sheets/2016/07/27/15/19/Response-to-the-Global-Economic-Crisis?pdf=1.
34. See e.g. World Bank, *African Development Indicators, 1998/1999* (Washington, DC: The World Bank, 1998).
35. Mbaku, *Institutions and Development in Africa*, 146.
36. John Mukum Mbaku, "A Balance Sheet of Structural Adjustment in Africa: Towards a Sustainable Development Agenda," in *Preparing Africa for the Twenty-First Century: Strategies for Peaceful Coexistence and Sustainable Development*, ed. John Mukum Mbaku (Aldershot, UK: Ashgate, 1999), 119–49; Baylies, "Political Conditionality"; and Peter Gibbon, "The World Bank and the New Politics of Aid," *European Journal of Development Research* 5, no. 1 (1993): 35–62.
37. Kevin Dunn, "Tales from the Dark Side: Africa's Challenges to International Relations Theory," *Journal of Third World Studies* XVII, no. 1 (2000): 69. See also Kevin Dunn, and Timothy M. Shaw, eds., *Africa's Challenge to International Relations Theory* (New York: Palgrave, 2001).
38. David N. Plank, "Aid, Debt, and the End of Sovereignty: Mozambique and Its Donors," *The Journal of Modern African Studies* 31, no. 3 (1993): 417.
39. Tom Young, "'A Project to Be Realized': Global Liberalism and Contemporary Africa," *Millennium* 24, no. 3 (Winter, 1995): 542.
40. Quoted in Young, "A Project to Be Realized," 538–39.
41. Dunn, "Tales from the Dark Side," 69.
42. Ibid.
43. Mbaku, *Institutions and Development in Africa*, 147.
44. Ibid.
45. Ihonvbere, *Nigeria: The Politics of Adjustment & Democracy*.
46. For the effects of SAPs on poor African economies, see also the following: Fantu Cheru, *The Silent Revolution in Africa: Debt, Development and Democracy* (London, UK: Zed Books, 1989) and the series of essays in Kempe R. Hope Sr., ed., *Structural Adjustment, Reconstruction and Development in Africa* (Aldershot, UK: Ashgate, 1997).
47. See e.g. Ihonvbere, *Nigeria: The Politics of Adjustment & Democracy*, op. cit.
48. Mbaku, *Institutions and Development in Africa*, 148.
49. Ibid.
50. Ibid.
51. World Bank, *The World Bank Annual Report 1992* (Washington, DC: The World Bank, 1992).

52. Bruce Rich, "World Bank/IMF: 50 Years Is Enough," in *50 Years Is Enough: The Case against the World Bank and the International Monetary Fund*, ed. Kevin Danaher (Boston, MA: South End Press, 1994), 6–13.
53. Ihonvbere, *Nigeria: The Politics of Adjustment & Democracy*; and Cheru, *The Silent Revolution in Africa*, op. cit.
54. Ihonvbere, *Nigeria: The Politics of Adjustment & Democracy*; Rich, "World Bank/IMF," op. cit.; and Cheru, *The Silent Revolution in Africa*, op. cit.
55. See e.g. Baylies, "Political Conditionalities"; and World Bank, *Accelerated Development in Sub-Saharan Africa*.
56. Mbaku, *Institutions and Development in Africa*, 149–50.
57. Ibid., 15.
58. Sanjaya Lall, "Structural Adjustment and African Industry," *World Development* 23, no. 12 (1995): 2020.
59. See e.g. World Bank, *Accelerated Development in sub-Saharan Africa*; and Danaher, "Introduction."
60. See e.g. the overtly optimistic assessment in World Bank, *Adjustment in Africa, Reforms, Results, and the Road Ahead* (New York: Oxford University Press, 1994); and F.L. Osunsade, IMF *Support for African Adjustment Programs: Questions and Answers* (Washington, DC: IMF, 1993).
61. Mbaku, *Institutions and Development in Africa*, 151.
62. See e.g. Danaher, "Introduction"; Ihonvbere, *Nigeria: The Politics of Adjustment & Democracy*; and Cheru, *The Silent Revolution in Africa*.
63. See e.g. Mbaku, *Institutions and Development in Africa*, 154.
64. Lall, "Structural Adjustment and African Industry," 2019–31.
65. See e.g. Mbaku, *Institutions and Development in Africa*, op. cit.; and John Mukum Mbaku, "Providing a Foundation for Wealth Creation and Development in Africa: The Role of the Rule of Law," *Brooklyn Journal of International Law* 38, no. 3 (2013): 959–1051.
66. P. Bond, and A. Patel, "International Financial Institutions in Africa: Is Reform on the Agenda?," Open Society Initiative for South Africa, Rosebank, South Africa (n.d.), last visited on December 31, 2016. Available at http://ccs.ukzn.ac.za/files/Bond%20Patel%20intl%20finance.pdf.
67. Léonce Ndikumana, and James K. Boyce, *Africa's Odious Debts: How Foreign Loans and Capital Flight Bled a Continent* (London, UK: Zed Books, 2011).
68. See e.g. Joyce B. Endeley, and F. Sikod, *The Social Impact of the Chad-Cameroon Oil Pipeline: How Industrial Development Affects Gender Relations, Land Tenure, and Local Culture* (Lewiston, NY: The Edwin Mellen Press, 2007).
69. Craig S. Barnes, "The African Development Bank's Role in Promoting Regional Integration in the Economic Community of West African States," in *Boston College Third World Law Journal* 4, no. 2 (1984): 156.
70. AfDB, *Annual Report, 1974* (Abidjan, Côte d'Ivoire: African Development Bank, 1974), 10; see also Barnes, "The African Development Bank's Role," 157.
71. See e.g. Barnes, "The African Development Bank's Role," 157.
72. AfDB, *Annual Report, 1975* (Abidjan, Côte d'Ivoire: African Development Bank, 1975), 30.
73. See e.g. Barnes, "The African Development Bank's Role," 173–74.

## References

Ajayi, Simeon Ibidayo, and Mohsin S. Khan, eds. *External Debt and Capital Flight in Sub-Saharan Africa*. Washington, DC: IMF, 2000.

Barnes, Craig S. "The African Development Bank's Role in Promoting Regional Integration in the Economic Community of West African States." *Boston College Third World Law Journal* 4, no. 2 (1984): 151–82.

Baylies, Carolyn. "'Political Conditionality' and Democratization." *The Review of African Political Economy* 22, no. 65 (1995): 321–37.

Bernstein, Boris, and James M. Boughton. "Adjusting to Development: The IMF and the Poor." *Finance and Development* 31 (1995): 42–45.

Bhargava, Vinay K. "The Role of the International Financial Institutions in Addressing Global Issues." In *Global Issues for Global Citizens: An Introduction to Key Development Challenges*, edited by Vinay K. Bhargava, 393–410. Washington, DC: The World Bank, 2006.

Bond, P., and A. Patel. "International Financial Institutions in Africa: Is Reform on the Agenda?," Open Society Initiative for South Africa, Rosebank, South Africa n.d., last visited on January 2, 2017. Available at http://ccs.ukzn.ac.za/files/Bond%20Patel%20intl%20finance.pdf.

Cheru, Fantu. *The Silent Revolution in Africa: Debt, Development and Democracy*. London: Zed Books, 1989.

Danaher, Kevin. "Introduction." In *50 Years Is Enough: The Case against the World Bank and the International Monetary Fund*, edited by Kevin Danaher, 1–5. Boston, MA: South End Press, 1994.

———, ed. *50 Years Is Enough: The Case against the World Bank and the International Monetary Fund*. Boston, MA: South End Press, 1994.

Dessart, Michael A., and Roland E. Ubogu, eds. *Capacity Building, Governance, and Economic Reform in Africa*. Washington, DC: The Word Bank, 2001.

Dunn, Kevin. "Tales from the Dark Side: Africa's Challenges to International Relations Theory." *Journal of Third World Studies* XVII, no. 1 (2000): 61–90.

Dunn, Kevin, and Timothy M. Shaw, eds. *Africa's Challenge to International Relations Theory*. New York: Palgrave, 2001.

Endeley, Joyce B., and F. Sikod. *The Social Impact of the Chad-Cameroon Oil Pipeline: How Industrial Development Affects Gender Relations, Land Tenure, and Local Cuture*. Lewiston, NY: The Edward Mellen Press, 2007.

Gibbon, Peter. "The World Bank and the New Politics of Aid." *European Journal of Development Research* 5, no. 1 (1993): 35–62.

Hope, Kempe R. Sr., ed. *Structural Adjustment, Reconstruction and Development*. Aldershot, UK: Ashgate, 1997.

Ihonvbere, Julius O. *The Politics of Adjustment & Democracy*. New Brunswick, NJ: Transaction Publishers, 1994.

Lall, Sanjaya. "Structural Adjustment and African Industry." *World Development* 23, no. 12 (1993): 2019–31.

Mbaku, John Mukum. "A Balance Sheet of Structural Adjustment in Africa: Towards a Sustainable Development Agenda." In *Preparing Africa for the Twenty-First Century: Strategies for Peaceful Coexistence and Sustainable Development*, edited by John Mukum Mbaku, 119–49. Aldershot, UK: Ashgate, 1999.

———. *Institutions and Development in Africa*. Trenton, NJ: Africa World Press, 2004.

———. "Providing a Foundation for Wealth Creation and Development in Africa: The Role of the Rule of Law." *Brooklyn Journal of International Law* 38, no. 3 (2013): 959–1051.

Mshomba, Richard E. *Africa in the Global Economy*. Boulder, CO: Lynne Rienner Publishers, Inc., 2000.

Ndikumana, Léonce, and James K. Boyce. *Africa's Odious Debts: How Foreign Loans and Capital Flight Bled a Continent*. London: Zed Books, 2011.

Nsouli, Saleh M. "Capacity Building in Africa: The Role of International Financial Institutions." *Finance and Development* 37, no. 4 (2000): 34–37.

Osunsade, F.L. *IMF Support for African Adjustment Programs: Questions and Answers*. Washington, DC: IMF, 1993.

Plank, David N. "Aid, Debt, and the End of Sovereignty: Mozambique and Its Donors." *The Journal of Modern African Studies* 31, no. 3 (1993): 407–30.

Rich, Bruce. "World Bank/IMF: 50 Years Is Enough." In *50 Years Is Enough: The Case against the World Bank and the International Monetary Fund*, edited by Kevin Danaher, 6–13. Boston, MA: South End Press, 1994.

Shaw, Timothy M. "Reformism, Revisionism, and Radicalism in African Political Economy during the 1990s." *The Journal of Modern African Studies* 29, no. 2 (1991): 191–212.

Shepherd, George W. "The African Right to Development: World Policy and the Debt Crisis." *Africa Today* 37, no. 4 (1990): 5–14.

Weissman, Stephen R. "Structural Adjustment in Africa: Insights from the Experiences of Ghana and Senegal." *World Development* 18, no. 12 (1990): 1621–34.

World Bank. *Accelerated Development in Sub-Saharan Africa: An Agenda for Action*. Washington, DC: The World Bank, 1981.

———. *Adjustment in Africa: Reforms, Results, and the Road Ahead*. New York: Oxford University Press, 1994.

———. *African Development Indicators, 1998/1999*. Washington, DC: The World Bank, 1998.

Young, Tom. "'A Project to Be Realized': Global Liberalism and Contemporary Africa." *Millennium* 24, no. 3 (Winter 1995): 327–548.

# CHAPTER 36

# Development History and Postcolonial African Experience

*Ruth Rempel*

Poet Okot p'Bitek asked his readers: 'Do you remember/The night of *uhuru*' (freedom, independence), when 'men and women wept with joy/As they danced,/Hands raised in salute/To the national flag?' He continued, giving voice to the hopes of Uganda's rural majority, by asking:

> Did someone tell you
> That on the morning of *uhuru*
> The dew on the grass
> Along the village pathways
> Would turn into gold?[1]

Nationalist historians, like p'Bitek's villagers, saw political independence as a historical watershed. However, if we use development as a lens, political independence appears as the redirection of a watercourse, rather than a watershed. p'Bitek was one of many who went on to identify painful continuities between development in the colonial and postcolonial eras.

R. Rempel (✉)
International Development Studies, Menno Simons College,
Canadian Mennonite University, Winnipeg, MB, Canada

© The Author(s) 2018
M.S. Shanguhyia and T. Falola (eds.),
*The Palgrave Handbook of African Colonial and Postcolonial History*,
https://doi.org/10.1057/978-1-137-59426-6_36

881

## DEVELOPMENT IN NEW AFRICAN STATES

Nationalists promised that if they held the levers of power they would provide good jobs and markets, as well as modern education, health care and other services Africans were coming to expect, like roads and mail.[2] The word 'development' carried all these and other desired changes. But how was it to be accomplished?

Governments of newly independent African countries generally maintained the development approach established under imperial rule. In part, this was because imperial officials continued to occupy senior positions due to the scarcity of educated nationals.[3] Another factor was the attractiveness of some inherited policies, exemplified by the 1951 UN report's influence in African countries.[4] Even where a reversal of approach might be expected, there were continuities. For example, the 1962 Evian Accords that ended Algeria's bitter war for independence used the 1958 Constantine Plan to structure postwar development and French aid for it.[5]

Development continuity was also the product of the constrained choices African countries faced.[6] Most were small. The median population size in 1960 was three million, and 15 countries were under one million. Despite this, imperial boundaries made for diverse populations, so national unity was a challenge.[7] On average, 15% of African countries' land was arable, giving reasonable agricultural prospects. A handful of countries had known mineral deposits, but few were thought to have oil.[8] Most lacked the capacity to extract sub-surface resources, or to compete with established processors and manufacturers. They depended heavily on trade, but were disadvantaged by small market share, distance from global markets, and ties to a single trade partner. Their influence with investors, lenders, or donors outside their imperial metropole was limited. This was a hindsight view, however. At the time of independence, development experts believed African countries' prospects for economic growth were fairly good; African leaders believed they were excellent.[9]

'Political independence, in itself, does not satisfy anything', Senegalese politician Mamadou Dia remarked. 'But it is necessary, and without it, nothing is possible'.[10] What independence chiefly made possible was a new pace of development, often through intensification of existing approaches.[11] Uganda's economy, for example, remained overwhelmingly agricultural after independence in 1962, its subsistence sector largely outside the purview of government policy and its main export crops subject to policies established around the Second World War. Coffee and cotton marketing boards continued to accumulate surpluses through indirect taxation. Trade-based taxes generated much of government revenue, as had been the case since 1920.[12] Cash-crop growers continued to exercise economic and political agency in cooperatives, legalized in 1946.[13] Public investment followed patterns established in the early 1950s. Experts noted that the years of high investment and growth before independence were also years of booming exports and high world prices. Spending restraint would be needed in non-essential areas to meet the robust, but status quo economic growth targets of the 1961–1966 Five-Year Plan—four to five percent per year—or the more ambitious seven to eight percent target of the subsequent plan. Alternatively, higher taxes, 'semivoluntary' savings schemes, and stronger incentives for private investment would be required.[14] The new government preferred to rely on external aid and borrowing, though it attracted less of these than neighboring Kenya.[15] Likewise, community development and women's development followed already established patterns, with existing volunteer organizations complemented by formal structures set up in the early 1950s.[16] Staples of nationalist policy like diversification of agricultural exports, promotion of light industry focused on the domestic market, and participating in an International Coffee Agreement to manage the market for the country's main export all predated Uganda's independence, and were continued afterwards.[17] Regional integration, a signature policy of the Organization of African Unity (OAU), was built on East African institutions created between 1917 and 1961. The pace of practical integration did not increase after independence, despite the creation of the East African Community in 1967.[18] It is worth remembering, though, that Uganda's early five-year plans differed from those of its regional partners, with whom it shared history and geography as well as institutional ties. That diversification accelerated after independence, within both East Africa and the continent.

## EMERGING AFRICAN APPROACHES

Despite the constraints and challenges they faced, African governments viewed the creation of national development plans as an exercise of sovereignty.[19] However, a study of plans from 22 Sub-Saharan countries found that it was the second post-independence plan—generally drafted in the mid- to late 1960s—in which a national development model of some sort was advanced.[20] This effort was tempered, though, by the political structures emerging in a number of African countries. As Claude Ake observed, once in power, nationalist leaders tended to use their position for accumulation since they had been unable to build up economic strength under imperial rule. These leaders sought to contain social and economic divisions, both to build national unity and to protect their own positions. They deliberately narrowed the political system, creating effective, if not formal, one-party states, and enhanced the power of the executive within the state. They also limited the space in which non-state actors—whether private businesses, unions, non-profit organizations or popular movements—could operate. 'Besieged by a multitude of hostile forces that their authoritarianism and exploitative practices had engendered', Ake went on, 'those in power were so involved in the struggle for survival that they could not address the problem of development'. They also could not abandon it, since development was an important rationale for their rule. Leaders 'responded to this dilemma by making token gestures to development while trying to pass the responsibility for [it] to foreign patrons'.[21] Poet p'Bitek was blunter. He railed against the leaders who rejected the works of Europeans, 'the famine relief granaries/And the forced-labour system', even as they invited 'Foreign "experts" and peace corps [to] swarm the country like white ants'. They proclaimed the need for 'all the tribes' to 'become one people' while sowing fierce new political divisions. They talked endlessly about how 'They fight with diseases/Poverty and ignorance', while they ate 'thick honey/and ghee and butter'. They opened a gulf between the rural poor and urban '"big car" tribesmen'.[22] These leaders, p'Bitek charged:

> Throw themselves into soft beds,
> But the hip bones of the voters
> Grow painful
> Sleeping on the same earth
> They slept
> Before Uhuru![23]

Whether token or not, national development models and their underlying ideologies can be categorized by their emphases: African socialism and African pragmatism were initially popular; Afro-Marxism and populism made an appearance toward the end of the 1960s.[24] Despite their diversity of name and focus, these models shared the idea of state-led development, then a globally accepted element of development.[25] It was particularly powerful in Africa because recent independence had made the state a collective and an individual prize. The desirability of modernity was a second shared assumption. It was not understood as openness to ongoing change, which could be destabilizing; a fear nationalist leaders shared with their imperial predecessors. The appeal of modernization was increased productivity and capacity through adoption of new technology and techniques.[26] Nationalists believed these could be blended with valued elements of tradition. The third assumption was the need for indigenization, protectionism, nationalization, and often also nativism. The territorial nation and the continent were the units to which this assumption was generally applied, but at both these levels, the indigenous had to be adapted or (re)constructed. An example of this was consensus seeking—what Ali Mazrui and others called the palaver tradition—which became a rationale for 'one-party democracies' in a number of countries after independence.[27] The development goal that flowed from all these assumptions was an internationally respected, unified country governed by a state with agency. It should have a revitalized, harmonious social order linked to a national identity, and a self-reliant economy that financed modernization.[28]

Nationalist models proved difficult to translate into specific development policies, even where governments were genuinely interested in doing so. The Tanzania African National Union (TANU) government under Julius Nyerere was one that made the effort.[29] Tanzania's new development principles were set out in the 1967 Arusha Declaration.[30] The country's second five-year plan (1969–1974) called for full mobilization behind the core principle of *ujamaa* (familyhood). *Ujamaa* bundled together values abstracted from familial relations, which Nyerere and TANU saw as the heart of traditional African societies, and extended them to the nation. *Ujamaa* was also linked to villagization. It would create rural communities that farmed more productively through collective work and improved methods. The villages would also be vehicles for more effective service delivery, for national planning and defense, plus incubators for appropriate norms and roles. Women as mothers should improve food security and familial well-being, for example, while young men were to guard the nation, though both groups' energies were channeled rather than genuinely mobilized.[31] After 1973, the creation of *ujamaa* villages was enforced, since voluntary participation was not achieving official targets. Industrial workers and students were also subordinated to the government. As this suggests, the direction and pace of change did not please all Tanzanians, and the government's increasingly authoritarian posture grieved and angered many. The impacts of villagization and other initiatives linked to *ujamaa* varied.[32] Improved access to health and education services helped increase average life expectancy from 42 to 52 years between 1960 and 1980, while literacy increased from 10 to 66%.[33] Production of food crops also grew over these two decades, but at a slower rate between 1967 and 1973 than in the immediately preceding or following years.[34] After leaving office, Nyerere said the Arusha Declaration had not banished poverty, but claimed that it had not promised to do so; rather, its purpose had been to offer hope for a future of justice and peace.[35]

Rural development received more attention in Tanzania than was common in African countries at that time, but structural change based on industrialization was still TANU's long-term goal.[36] Neglect of the rural, especially smallholders (or peasant farmers), was an emerging concern about the 1951 development model. It was an acute omission in African countries, which had overwhelmingly rural populations. African women played important agricultural roles, but women were another of the model's blind spots. By the late 1960s, both critics and supporters of development were also questioning the assumed connection between international aid, state-led economic growth, and bettered lives. Addressing these problems created opportunities for non-profit actors, ranging from foundations and non-governmental organizations (NGOs) operating at a global scale, to associations and organizations that worked at very local ones. More of these were active in African countries by the 1970s, though the non-profit sector varied considerably by country.[37]

Fears of a global food crisis intensified development experts' interest in agriculture toward the end of the 1960s. To the extent that African governments delegated national development to external actors, they followed this trend, though their most acute concern was usually to keep food affordable and prevent unrest. Mali's government, for example, retooled the *Office du Niger* after independence, with the goal of ensuring national food security. The area under irrigation increased, and the government endorsed the preindependence switch from cotton to rice production; the project's top-down approach was also retained.[38] As the *Office* had never been profitable, foreign aid was needed to support it and thus subsidize the rice it produced, mostly for urban consumers.[39] Food imports were another tactic some African governments used, though in doing so they sacrificed national self-reliance and rural prosperity for stability.

## FROM CHALLENGE TO CRISIS

The mid-1970s was a watershed for African development because global economic changes that significantly affected the resources available for development interacted with changes underway within African countries. The most visible global change was the oil price increase of 1973, which occurred after members of the Organization of Petroleum Exporting Countries (OPEC) cut production to enforce their demand for better prices. A simultaneous embargo by Arab oil exporters against Israel's allies in the Yom Kippur war magnified the cut's impact. Real international oil prices doubled. Observers believed that 'the energy crisis has deprived the less developed countries of any chance of further development'. A second large price increase occurred in 1979, triggered by fears of shortages after an oil-worker strike in revolutionary Iran and the Iran-Iraq war.[40]

Another change whose effects were becoming clearer by the mid-1970s was the American government's 1971 decision to end the convertibility of its dollar to gold. Rapid fluctuations in the value of major currencies followed, and by early 1973 the International Monetary Fund (IMF)-supervised system of exchange rates negotiated after the Second World War was effectively dead.[41] Banks seeking to protect themselves from these fluctuations and from rising inflation switched from lending with fixed interest rates to variable ones. Added to this, monetary policy changes in countries that housed international banks, especially the USA and Britain, provoked substantial increases in real interest rates at the start of the 1980s. As Susan Strange observed, the decade-and-a-half following 1973 was characterized by significant economic instability as the prices of commodities, of currencies, and of credit all became more volatile.[42] This severe turbulence was even more striking by contrast with the stability of the preceding decade. In retrospect, the 1960s and the 1950s before them looked like a golden age for development.

Commodity-price fluctuations interacted with exchange-rate volatility to increase the risk and cost of trading. Businesses and governments both faced greater challenges in planning economic activity and managing their finances. Powerful economic actors, whether industrialized countries or multinational corporations, were able to cope with or deflect these problems. Their negative effects fell most heavily on weaker actors, including low-income, trade-dependent countries.[43] Where these countries had only been independent for a short time and had relatively inexperienced governments—as was the case in Africa—the harm was amplified. In addition, international economic volatility had a more damaging effect on countries experiencing internal conflicts.[44] Between 1970 and 1985, armed conflict affected roughly half of Africa's countries.[45]

As this suggests, global changes interacted negatively with socio-political processes in African countries. When commodity prices fell, national income contracted as did state revenue, since African governments still relied heavily on taxation of trade. Reduced revenue affected the state's ability to provide public services and jobs, to subsidize essential goods, to invest, or to provide the counterpart funds required for many aid projects. Windfalls, like the dramatic coffee-price spike of the mid-1970s, could be equally destabilizing.[46] African governments, both those committed to development and those not, interpreted dramatic price increases as signs of an upward trend. The pressure to spend rather than save the increased income was powerful, and once spending commitments were made it was hard to counter the expectation they would continue. In Uganda, Ethiopia, and Rwanda—all heavily dependent on coffee exports—management of the price spike was fumbled by military governments.[47] Even where either government or the private sector invested the windfall, limited capacity to absorb a sudden burst of spending undermined the investments' effectiveness and caused inflation. All these problems were compounded by poor advice from external development experts whose commodity-price forecasts tended to be optimistic, and whose understanding of the causes of price volatility was limited.[48]

The national development models advanced in the late 1960s could not reach healthy maturity in such an environment, no matter what their content. International turbulence strained the compact nationalists made with citizens at independence: loyalty to the state and contributions to its development agenda in exchange for prosperity and social harmony. It also exacerbated tensions between ethnic groups and classes. Not surprisingly, 30 African countries experienced coups between 1973 and 1985, and 13 of them multiple coups, a greater concentration than during any other period between 1950 and the present.[49] About half of these coups were successful, and the names of the regimes they engendered implied renewed promises: Democracy, Progress, Unity, and Redemption.[50] But a reported exchange between Liberia's military ruler and future president Ellen Johnson Sirleaf summed up what most offered in practice: "'General Doe, you promised the people so many things, and you are not keeping those promises." Doe just looked straight at me and said, "I didn't promise them shit"'.[51]

Different, but equally difficult conflicts consumed Southern Africa as the struggle for liberation from white minority rule intensified, together with destabilization of frontline states by embattled settler regimes.

The Portuguese colonies' independence struggles ended abruptly after a 1974 coup in Portugal, but were followed by destructive civil wars in Angola and Mozambique.

Post-independence crises like the Suez (1956) and Congo (1960) ones had drawn an international response from governments and the UN. The Nigeria-Biafra war (1967–1970) was different. The official response was limited, but non-profit actors like the Red Cross, together with European and North American church organizations, played a significant role. They provided both relief aid and Track Two (or citizen) diplomacy. Their public appeals, together with international media coverage, prompted an outpouring of donations.[52] The war was another turning point in development history. Biafra shaped a new generation of humanitarian workers and NGOs, successors to those who assisted postwar Europe. By 1970, a recognizable international humanitarian system that paralleled and overlapped with that of development assistance was emerging.[53]

Meanwhile, another crisis was unfolding close by. Drought started in the Sahel in 1968, and the hunger it caused intensified into famine over the next few years. Several million people in six countries required food aid and an estimated 100,000 died.[54] Sahelian governments did not declare a state of emergency until early 1973, though, the point when the disaster also started to receive international media coverage.[55] In its aftermath, many questions were raised about the humanitarian response. Nonetheless, aid to the continent increased substantially, both for relief and for development. Drought-stricken Sahelian countries almost doubled their per capita aid receipts between 1975 and 1980.[56] Unfortunately, this caused them to suffer aid indigestion, as they had a limited ability to absorb the sudden influx of resources or deal effectively with a mass of donors.[57]

A decade later, famine in the Horn of Africa drew unprecedented international attention. In development circles it was clear that the mid-1980s drought and food shortages were not confined to the Horn; they affected 22 countries spanning West, East, and Southern Africa.[58] This humanitarian emergency fed a sense that the continent was suffering a development crisis. The appeals for extraordinary aid by African governments and intergovernmental organizations helped to distinguish the continent's needs from those of other regions.

The number of aid-dependent African countries almost tripled between 1975 and 1979. Two types of countries were added to the existing list: drought-affected Sahelian countries and small countries like Gambia, Lesotho, and the Seychelles that were particularly vulnerable to economic turmoil. By the end of the 1980s, almost half of the continent's countries were aid-dependent.[59] This reflected both the success of pleas for aid made with increasing intensity in the 1980s, and the dramatic reduction in incoming foreign investment that distinguished Africa from other developing continents during the 1980s.[60]

## The UN Development Decades
## in Africa—Were They a Disaster?

Crises, which entrenched the image of the entire continent as a disaster zone, suggest the need for a review of Africa's development performance during the UN Development Decades, roughly also the first two decades after independence. The most common metric for development during this period was economic growth, and by this standard African countries' performance was, on average, respectable. Tanzania's economy, for example, grew by an annual average rate of six percent in the 1960s and five percent in the following decade.[61] Most countries, though, did not reach the very ambitious growth targets prescribed in their national plans. These echoed or exceeded the targets of the UN Development Decades, on which African governments had been an important influence.[62] Economic growth was not only jeopardized by global turmoil after 1973, it was undercut by rapid population growth. The average per capita income growth in the continent was a limited, though still positive, 0.9% over the two UN Development Decades.[63]

With respect to structural change, commodities continued to make up the vast majority of African exports, though some countries were able to diversify into non-traditional commodities whose prices were better. However, outside of export enclaves, production techniques and productivity did not improve much.[64] The share of manufactures in African exports rose, indicating that the goal of industrial development was being met, albeit modestly. Although trade with former imperial powers remained important, most African countries were able to diversify their trade relationships.[65] More importantly, as Table 36.1 shows, life expectancy and literacy both improved, though slowly, and levels of social development in many Sub-Saharan countries remained very low. As with income, these averages concealed significant variation between countries, and growing inequality within them.

Developing countries were responsible for the proclamation of a second UN Development Decade in 1970. Its agenda was more substantial than that of the first, though mostly still through intensification of the 1951 model.[66] An important difference, though, was the collective action taken

**Table 36.1**  Trends in social development

|                                    | Life expectancy (years) | | | | Literacy rate (percent) | | | |
| --- | --- | --- | --- | --- | --- | --- | --- | --- |
|                                    | 1950 | 1960 | 1970 | 1979 | 1950 | 1960 | 1970 | 1979 |
| Low-income Sub-Saharan countries    | 35  | 39 | 43 | 46 | –    | 17 | 17 | 29 |
| Middle-income Sub-Saharan countries | 37  | 41 | 46 | 50 | 16   | 22 | 37 | –  |
| North African countries             | 42[a] | 47 | 52 | 57 | 19[a] | 19 | 24 | 40 |
| All developing countries            | 43  | 48 | 54 | 58 | 33   | 38 | 46 | 56 |

*Source* World Bank, *World Development Report 1982* (New York: Oxford University Press for the World Bank, 1982), 24
[a]The 1950 data for North Africa include the Middle East

by governments in the Non-Aligned Movement and the Group of 77. They sought to change the global context in which their national development occurred, and the New International Economic Order they desired became a defining development initiative of the 1970s.[67] The UN Conference on Trade and Development (UNCTAD), created in 1964, was a vehicle for it. African countries, working in concert, provided crucial support for this in the UN and ensured that the problems of commodity-exporting countries were prominent on UNCTAD's agenda.[68] African governments hedged their trade-and-development bets, though, by negotiating special market access to the European Economic Community (EEC) on terms similar to those they had from their former imperial rulers.[69]

## TEMPLATES FOR AFRICAN DEVELOPMENT

At the national level, African states were also adjusting their development agendas. As Claude Ake noted, external actors played an increasing role in this. The space ceded by African leaders, whose governing capacity did not keep pace with the growth of their populations or with the challenges of the 1970s, was one reason for this. The engagement of a larger and more diverse group of external actors, who had more encompassing ideas about development, was another. The Integrated Rural Development Project (IRDP) was emblematic of both trends, as John Cohen's work on the Chilalo Agricultural Development Unit in Ethiopia illustrates.[70] Donor pressure had given agriculture a new prominence in Ethiopia's third five-year plan (1968–1973). Both donors and the government agreed that a few well-resourced interventions would be the most effective way to spark change, given the depth of Ethiopia's rural poverty and the government's limited capacity. Chilalo, started in 1967 by the Swedish International Development Authority (SIDA), was the first of three IRDPs. It demonstrated that an integrated set of measures—improved rural markets, infrastructure and services, together with the Green Revolution inputs of high-yielding seed and fertilizer—could increase agricultural production in Ethiopia. However, the benefits were unevenly distributed, and they were not accompanied by either popular participation or progressive social change.

The Chilalo project represented a negotiation of interests among the participants. SIDA chose to believe Emperor Haile Selassie's promise that land-reform legislation, something the Swedes thought essential to rural transformation, was imminent. In turn, the emperor approved the Chilalo project—and its inflow of resources—as proposed, and allowed it to be administered autonomously by SIDA. At the project level, tenants who increased production faced demands for higher rent from feudal landowners. Some even evicted their tenants and used the project's inputs and subsidized farm machinery for themselves.

The Swedish evaluation of Chilalo concluded that a few inputs had been crucial to the productivity gain, so SIDA said it would help provide these in more locations via a less complex and much less expensive Minimum Package Program starting in 1971. This program continued after the military coup in 1974, as did the Chilalo project though it was renamed and extended throughout the Arsi region.[71] Ethiopia's new revolutionary government initiated one of the more substantial applications of the Soviet agricultural model to an African country. It nationalized land and distributed user-rights to small farmers. It required the formation of peasant associations and cooperatives, started resettlement and villagization programs, and created some state farms, though subsistence farming was for the first time a national priority. Nonetheless, the new government continued to receive rural development aid from SIDA and other prerevolutionary donors. This enabled a sharp increase in government spending on agriculture. Though it insisted on greater national control over planning and implementation, the government still needed aid and multilateral loans to finance development. Another important continuity with the prerevolutionary era was use of national marketing bodies to tax farmers.[72]

The sense of development crisis was far from universal in the continent after 1973. The oil-price increases gave Africa's oil exporters an unprecedented opportunity to fund national development. Though Algeria's model of oil-financed development had its problems, the price windfall of the 1970s was invested to a greater extent than in other African countries.[73] Nigeria's experience, by contrast, gave development analysts grounds for talking about a resource curse.[74] Botswana and Mauritius offered national models for prospering, and not just surviving the economic turmoil. Mauritius used income from sugar exports to the EEC, earned with a large Lomé agreement quota, to diversify its economy and industrialize. However, its distinctive socio-political and geographic conditions led observers to question whether other African countries could repeat its experience.[75] Botswana parlayed its diamond wealth into economic growth, improved social development and political stability, though diamond processing was as far as its economic transformation proceeded.[76] Both have been tagged as African developmental states, though the debate about the character and desirability of such states continues.[77]

The UN Economic Commission for Africa (ECA) was the scene of another kind of positive work: drafting a continental blueprint for development. It started in 1975, the year in which a driven new executive secretary, Adebayo Adedeji, was appointed. The ECA undertook an audit of development trends in the continent from 1960 to 1975 and found that, despite an average economic growth rate of 4.8%, there was an increasing gap between nationalist promises and African performance, as well as between Africa and other developing regions.[78] Adedeji was convinced that blind acceptance of Western development models was behind this, and set the ECA to create an African one. The result was a set of connected documents, including the

Monrovia Strategy (1979) and the Lagos Plan of Action (1980), that were adopted by the OAU. These documents showed that the 1950s development consensus continued to exercise a strong hold on African intellectuals and leaders, though they adapted it to the continent's particular needs.[79] The Lagos Plan assumed the modernization of society as a goal, to be achieved through import-substituting industrialization, with the state playing a central role in development. African unity was a means of accomplishing development objectives through collective self-reliance via an African Economic Community.[80] The Plan's drafters were conscious of the changing global context, though. Rising international food prices and falling African production moved neglected agriculture into the Plan's first chapter, with the goal of food self-sufficiency via an agricultural revolution.[81] Urgent action was also prescribed in the Plan's energy section, since shortages were identified as an existential threat to non-oil-exporting African countries.[82] Despite evident worry over worsening development prospects, the Lagos Plan displayed a mid-1970s optimism that collective Third World action could change an unjust international system. Adedeji, the Plan's sponsor, argued though that global change must flow from national and continental transformation; only then would commodity-dependent African countries experience economic decolonization.[83]

The Lagos Plan's existence was more distinctively African than its content. No other region of the world felt the need for a continental model of development, let alone put significant effort into creating one. The Plan embodied a confidence that elements of disparate development approaches could be successfully harmonized, a trait evident in other individual and national African development prescriptions. Unfortunately, the Lagos Plan fell into an established pattern for continental pronouncements: leaders assented, but did not follow through with national public engagement or sufficient resources. The Lagos Plan quickly became the first in a series of what Adedeji called 'Battles for the African Mind'.[84] Its opponent was the World Bank's *Accelerated Development in Sub-Saharan Africa* (1981), which set out a very different agenda for change. As African governments had few resources they were able, or willing, to devote to the Lagos Plan, and external donors and creditors preferred to support its opponent, the battle was short.[85] The African Development Bank was the one organization that did adopt the Lagos Plan, as a response to critics who said it lacked a clear development strategy for its lending.[86]

Despite successes in a few countries, the decade after 1974 was one of uncertainty and confusion about the direction of development in Africa. By the time the Lagos Plan was formally adopted the conditions in which and for which it had been created were gone. The OAU's next major statement about continental development, Africa's Priority Programme for Economic Recovery (APPER, 1985), referenced the Lagos Plan but was effectively an elegy for it. Though stating that the Lagos principles were 'more valid today than ever', APPER concerned itself with crisis recovery and called for a new relationship with aid donors.[87]

## ECONOMIC SHOCKS AND NATIONAL SURVIVAL PROGRAMS

Between 1980 and 1986, the global context for African development changed further. International commodity prices, including that of oil, fell sharply. In 1986, real commodity prices stood at levels below those of the 1920s and 1930s. Price volatility, though less severe than during the 1970s, continued.[88] The resulting terms of trade losses were worse in Africa than the average for developing countries. While Africa's oil exporters suffered the most dramatic losses, between 1981 and 1986 the non-oil-exporting countries of Sub-Saharan Africa collectively earned an estimated US$1.6 billion a year less than they would have done if commodity prices had stayed at 1980 levels. This was in spite of generally increasing export volumes.[89] Indeed, the greater export effort made the problem worse, as oversupply further lowered prices.

Ghana's situation illustrates the ongoing interaction between external and internal pressures. A series of venal military regimes gave way to a weak civilian government at the end of the 1970s, but none of them offered policies that engaged much public support or responded effectively to the turmoil Ghana experienced. When Flight Lieutenant Rawlings seized power for a second time in 1981, his military government inherited an economy close to collapse. Unlike some other African governments, it did not have an immediate debt problem because of rescheduling carried out in the early 1970s.[90] However, cocoa production, which accounted for more than 70% of the country's exports, had been falling steadily for a decade. Worse, cocoa's international price dropped in 1980.[91] Ghana was also experiencing a severe drought, which caused food shortages, destructive fires, and a drastic cut in hydroelectric generation that limited national economic activity and power exports. Nigeria caused additional problems when it expelled foreigners, including between 500,000 and 1,000,000 Ghanaians, who had to be reabsorbed.[92]

Import strangulation was the first and most visible symptom of crisis in Ghana and elsewhere. By the mid-1980s, African countries had a sharply reduced capacity to pay for crucial imports of productive goods, consumer items and, in some cases, even food.[93] Many African governments borrowed to cover the resulting trade deficits, but rising real interest rates and a scarcity of credit after the international debt crisis broke in mid-1982 made this a problematic strategy.

The governments of several countries—Algeria, Burkina Faso, Ghana, Mozambique, and Tanzania among them—responded by creating national survival programs in the early 1980s. These were country-specific programs used to solicit support from bilateral creditors and aid donors. They generally included measures to bridge the gap between imports and exports, and to deal with food deficits; some also dealt with budget deficits and allowed private businesses more of a role in the economy.[94] Burkina Faso's program, for example, responded to a worsening deficit and debt situation that, while modest in comparison with other African countries, were significant given the country's small income and cautious financial policies. The revolutionary military government installed in 1983 quickly introduced a self-designed policy package to address the economic shocks and, more unusually, to promote social equity and structural change in the economy. This included cuts to civil-service wages and perks, new taxes and fees, an end to the fertilizer subsidy, as well as measures to increase agricultural production and mining. There were also primary-education, health, and housing initiatives. This echoed parts of the Lagos Plan, but the Burkinabe program was formulated independently of it. Although the program had positive effects, the country's debt-service burden worsened.[95] The program was also not successful in attracting international aid: while the USA increased its assistance to Burkina Faso, this was outweighed by French aid cuts.

Other countries with national survival programs were similarly unable to attract funding from either socialist donors or Organization for Economic Co-operation and Development (OECD) ones. They were consequently forced to turn to the IMF and World Bank.[96] The survival programs were also swamped by the severity of the crisis, especially where new shocks were piled onto serious existing problems, as was the case in Mozambique.[97] While these programs had mixed policy effects, one thing they consistently failed to do was reduce the debt of the countries concerned. Indeed, in most cases the debt increased. Over the next several years, these survival programs evolved into narrower economic stabilization packages, usually financed by the IMF. Initially, this was short-term credit from the IMF's Stand-By Facility, whose conditions were not quite as onerous as those of the Fund's Extended Facility. When drawing on the latter, countries were forced to adopt stabilization policies that were controversial both because their effect on the least developed countries was debated, and because their sharp impact on the public made them politically unpopular.[98]

## ADJUSTMENT VS DEVELOPMENT

Jacques de Larosière, the IMF's managing director, could report in 1984 that adjustment was 'now virtually universal' and the debt crisis was being successfully managed.[99] However, in 1986, the Fund had to create a Structural Adjustment Facility (SAF), followed a year later by an Enhanced Structural Adjustment Facility (ESAF) as it became increasingly clear that standard stabilization packages were not addressing the economic problems of African countries.[100] In hindsight, the early 1980s were the high-water mark of direct IMF involvement with indebted countries, as new forms of World Bank lending allowed it to play an increasing role.[101] The World Bank's Structural Adjustment Loans (SALs) and smaller-scale Sectoral Adjustment Loans (SECALs), created in 1980 and 1982 respectively, had two conflicting purposes: to promote policy dialogue with borrowing countries and to provide money to countries in economic crisis, money that was available quickly and was not tied to a particular project.[102] The policy dialogue occurred when the loans were negotiated, but given the financial desperation and limited capacity of African governments, together with the superficial deference many paid to donors and creditors, lenders dominated the dialogue. Adjustment loans consequently had a consistent core of policy conditions.[103] This included a substantial dose of stabilization, followed by policy changes to reorient the economy and promote economic growth. A switch from state-led to market-led development, involving liberalization and privatization, was central to the reorientation. While adjusting countries were encouraged to diversify their exports, in practice, adjustment programs emphasized producing more of what was already being exported. Indeed some of the policy tools needed for diversification, especially a shift toward commodity processing and manufacturing, were put out of bounds by adjustment conditionality.[104] All this was an axe to the root of the nationalists' program of development, which neoliberal advocates dismissed as a set of growth-killing policies that primarily benefited corrupt African politicians and bureaucrats.[105]

Behind stabilization and adjustment was an increasingly powerful monetarist view of the economic problems of industrialized countries. It made the leap to development policy in the late 1970s with the assertion that the problems of poor people and poor countries were not distinctively different from those of others.[106] The weakness of existing development models, under attack from both the right and the left, facilitated this leap. Supporters proclaimed the end of development and a new era of reform with the conviction of military spokespersons announcing a redemptive new regime. Simultaneously, a New Political Economy that used neo-classical economic tools to generate a radically negative view of the state was gaining influence, fueling a preference for small, authoritarian, and technocratic states.[107]

The reform process, which IMF and World Bank experts initially expected to last two to three years, would need more time, maybe a decade or more.[108] As the period for neo-liberal policy intervention lengthened, its scope also broadened, giving structural adjustment the characteristics of a development model despite the neo-liberal rejection of development. By the end of the 1990s, the rationale for adjustment had become retroactively and openly developmental: 'to prevent or reverse unsustainable economic conditions that hurt the poor and to establish or restore the conditions for sustainable development'.[109]

The election of governments espousing these ideas in influential creditor and aid donor countries meant they were communicated to bilateral aid agencies and to institutions like the IMF and World Bank. In turn, these were the channels through which these ideas were transmitted to African countries and became powerful there.[110] Structural adjustment lending played a key role in this process, but it is worth noting that these World Bank loans were not created as an evangelical tool for neo-liberal views.[111] However, in giving policy space and influence to monetarism and the New Political Economy, adjustment lending helped to establish these views in the development mainstream and to keep them there during the 1980s and much of the 1990s.[112]

While structural adjustment lending was generally no more than a quarter of the World Bank's and IMF's total lending, it became a crucial means of engagement with African countries for both organizations.[113] Having an IMF agreement is a good indicator of the intensity of a country's adjustment experience, since the World Bank together with other lenders and aid donors required the IMF's 'seal of approval' before they would provide funds.[114] Between 1980 and 1999, indebted non-African countries with IMF stabilization programs spent an average of nine of those years under the discipline of these programs, while indebted African countries spent an average of eleven years, and among the ten most adjusted African countries, it was almost 18 years. The ten most adjusted non-African countries spent an average of only ten years under IMF discipline. Nine out of ten African countries had an IMF program at some point during the 1980s and 1990s. In Latin America and the Caribbean, the next most adjusted region of the world, this was true for just over three-quarters of the countries.[115]

African governments responded to neo-liberal reform ideas and to conditionality on much needed funding in a variety of ways. Some rejected specific conditions, as when Ghana's government refused to privatize its cocoa marketing board, Cocobod, choosing to reform it instead.[116] Rejection of an entire adjustment program was relatively rare, though Zambia was one country that did so. Its 1985 Economic Recovery Program (ERP), supported with World Bank and IMF loans, was a program whose conditions frustrated even those members of the government who favored reform. When riots provoked by removal of the maize subsidy spread from Copperbelt towns to the capital in 1987, the government changed course. President Kaunda announced the ERP's replacement with a nationally designed reform program that was to be financed by diverting foreign exchange from unproductive uses like luxury imports and foreign debt payments. Debt service was unilaterally limited to ten percent of net export earnings. Like the national salvation plans, this reform program had mixed results. The least ambiguous one was the withholding of funds by donors and lenders who disapproved of Zambia's action. Under growing financial pressure, the government returned to an orthodox adjustment program one year later, and maintained it despite renewed rioting and a coup attempt.[117]

A much more common response to structural adjustment programs was to agree to what external funders proposed and then delay, or fail to implement reforms, or undermine them with countervailing measures. Independent studies suggest that about half of the conditions were implemented, but only a quarter of them on the timetable set by the Fund or the Bank.[118] Since multilateral lenders were under pressure to keep loans flowing, and bilateral donors wanted to support client countries, non-cooperation was an effective way for some African governments to avoid unwanted change. It did not, however, amount to an alternate strategy for addressing national crises. Regimes and leaders often embraced those reforms that fitted with their interests, rather than national ones. In Tunisia, for example, the 1986 *infitah* (opening) of the economy intensified a process of liberalization already underway, adding in resources and policy advice from the IMF and World Bank. The government of Zine al-Abidine Ben Ali, installed in a bloodless 1987 coup, maintained a close relationship with the Bretton Woods institutions, especially the IMF. Ben Ali's government was quite willing to remove currency controls and restrictions on foreign investment and profit repatriation to liberalize the crucial tourism sector, among others. Nonetheless, it insisted on a more gradual pace of reform than its Bretton Woods advisors wanted. Significantly, the government also did not remove itself from the tourist industry. A number of the state-owned hotels that were privatized were in fact purchased by state-owned banks and refurbished; the banks then sold off some shares in the hotels. This was part of a pattern of liberalization in which new channels of patronage were created for a small number of well-connected and wealthy Tunisians.[119]

The human costs of stabilization and adjustment were also significant. In Ivory Coast, one of the continent's ten most adjusted countries, poverty was a long-standing problem. It worsened significantly, though, after the government started to draw extensively on the IMF in 1989. An IMF-supported study found that between 1988 and 1995 the incidence and the intensity of poverty in the country doubled, and poverty affected a wider range of social groups.[120] The share of the population earning less than US$1 per day rose from 18 to 37%, and the incidence of stunting (low height-for-age among young children) rose from 20 to 35% over the same period. Despite efforts to protect social expenditure, stabilization measures resulted in small per capita decreases in real health spending and dramatic cuts in real education spending. As primary school enrollment was increasing, the quality of education deteriorated as student–teacher ratios increased and teacher salaries fell. In the health sector, user fees introduced in 1991 did not reduce visits by the poorest Ivorians. However, their health suffered because they were no longer able to supplement low-quality public health services with formal private-sector care, and instead had to fall back on traditional medicine. A program to mitigate the short-term effects of adjustment on the urban poor—the rural poor were expected to benefit from adjustment—was only partly implemented and it failed to prevent a worsening of urban poverty. Ivory Coast's reforms were initiated by the autocratic regime of Félix Houphouët-Boigny. With no prior opportunity for public input, it was no surprise that the public expressed opposition to the reforms when political liberalization started in the early 1990s.

As in Zambia, public protest was one, though not a universal part of the popular response to structural adjustment. Campaigning by African NGOs, national church bodies and trade unions was another, some of it directed at national decisionmakers and some at external targets, like the World Bank. Involvement in international campaigns in turn helped create space for African NGOs in some countries to participate in national dialogue on adjustment issues through the Structural Adjustment Participatory Review Initiative (SAPRIN) and subsequent Poverty Reduction Strategy Paper (PRSP) consultations. This advocacy and policy work was only one part of the response of non-profit organizations, though. NGOs, both national and international ones, were also under pressure to return to the fields of health, education, and income generation as government budget cuts left substantial gaps in their provision of basic services and community development.

Circumvention of stabilization and adjustment's effects was a common response at the level of households and individuals. Migration was an option for some, as was movement, not always voluntary, into the informal sector. In many African countries, the informal sector grew substantially. It and subsistence agriculture were the means by which many Africans, especially women and the poor, supported themselves during the years of crisis. The informal sector helped insulate its participants from economic contraction, but it also meant they were excluded from new economic opportunities in the reformed formal sector.[121]

## AN AFRICAN SYNTHESIS?

In the 1980s, most African intellectuals were, if not completely opposed to structural adjustment, then critical pragmatists, though there were also some African enthusiasts for structural adjustment. The critics denounced adjustment as a set of policies that opened African economies to external exploiters, impoverishing both citizens and states, as well as stereotyping Africans as corrupt and incompetent. In other words, it was a thinly disguised recolonization of the continent. The critical pragmatists acknowledged that some adjustments were necessary to deal with external shocks and poor policy choices, but they were adamant that many parts of the standard structural adjustment package were unsuited to African conditions and inconsistent with any idea of long-term development.

Under Adebayo Adedeji's leadership, the ECA became a center of high-level African opposition to structural adjustment. Adedeji was also conscious of the need for 'an alternate paradigm' that donors and the Bretton Woods institutions would fund.[122] In 1988 and 1989, the ECA sponsored assessments of existing adjustment programs and consultation on alternatives. The outcome was the African Alternative Framework to Structural Adjustment

Programmes for Socio-Economic Recovery and Transformation (AAF-SAP), a document without counterparts in Latin America or Asia, though there was no shortage of opposition to adjustment in those continents. This document echoed the views of the critical pragmatists in several respects: adjustments were needed, but should be done in a way that addressed long-standing development problems and were appropriate to the circumstances of the adjusting country. While it looked back to the Lagos Plan for its development content, in some areas the AAF-SAP went further than the reforms envisioned by the Bretton Woods institutions. For example, it added unsustainable, import-dependent Western lifestyles to the list of economic imbalances where transformation was needed.[123]

However, the 'war of visions' that had developed between the UNECA and the World Bank ensured that the AAF-SAP was seen as a riposte, not a basis for negotiating change in the practice of adjustment.[124] It was also not well received by bilateral aid donors, and lacked champions among Africa's national leaders.[125] Although adopted by the OAU in 1989, member support was perfunctory. Some NGOs and trade unions picked up the Framework as a campaigning and popular education tool, but no African government implemented it.[126] Although a few of the earlier national survival programs, particularly that of Burkina Faso, bore some resemblance to the AAF-SAP, these programs were, like Zambia's self-designed adjustment program, generated through national processes and had no explicit links to the AAF-SAP.

By the mid-1990s, views had shifted. While radical critiques were still being penned, blanket opposition to adjustment had diminished in many circles. This was the result of tiredness, a shift in focus to the impact of post-Cold War conflicts, and new development possibilities emerging in the last half of the 1990s. Neo-liberal ideas were also evolving: becoming more nuanced and pragmatic in the eyes of some; in the eyes of others, becoming so well entrenched that harsh dogmatism and external enforcement were no longer necessary. On the part of donor countries and a range of multilateral lenders, politicians, and economic officials across various African governments, there was agreement that it was time to move beyond structural adjustment.[127]

The resulting, rough Africa policy consensus recognized the need to maintain financial and trade balances, but in a way that incorporated a long-term plan for development and investment in key sectors.[128] It agreed on the need to reduce the debt overhang, and that generating government revenue through a better tax system would reduce dependence on external funds. It accepted the need for policies to reduce poverty, recognizing that economic growth alone would not do so. It also recognized that agriculture, especially smallholder agriculture, needed more attention. It saw that trade liberalization had benefits, but acknowledged that African countries had been required to liberalize heavily and unilaterally. Likewise, continuing commodity dependence was not desirable, though there was less agreement on how to change that. A series of financial crises starting in 1994 undermined arguments for full financial liberalization, but debate about the appropriate degree of liberalization continued. Overall, both states and markets were seen to have important roles to play, and to be in need of improvement in African countries. The rough consensus also recognized that, in Africa, regional cooperation and the institutions to foster it were important, though admitting that there were lessons to be learned from past failures. The New Partnership for Africa's Development (NEPAD, 2001) was a later expression of this synthesis.

## A Long Lost 'Decade'—the Impacts of Adjustment

Within the continent, the years of stabilization and adjustment are widely seen as lost ones for African development. Conventionally, the lost years are the decade of the 1980s, but as intensive reform did not start until the end of the decade in many countries and was preceded by years of turmoil that also hindered development, the 'decade' was a long one, lasting from the mid-1970s to the late 1990s. It is not a stretch to argue, as some have done, that this long decade's impacts on African countries have been as great as the decades of direct imperial rule.[129]

While post-independence governments had their faults, African countries together with other debtor countries running financial and trade deficits were made to do most of the adjusting to the changes engineered in the global economy in the 1970s. Countries that accumulated trade and financial surpluses at their expense did little adjusting. The costs of that adjustment were high: a worsened international trade position and, more seriously, substantial foregone investment in education, health, and infrastructure. As with the promises of the nationalists, the rapid economic growth that was supposed to follow structural adjustment was in short supply. Wealthy and well-connected Africans were able to insulate themselves to some degree from the shortages and problems that stabilization and adjustment caused, but most citizens were not. Improvement in mortality, literacy, and other indicators of well-being slowed dramatically, and were reversed in some cases. Girls and women were usually the most affected. Gaps of income and opportunity widened within countries. Alterations to adjustment packages that were supposed to address poverty provided some belated relief, but critics argued that in the poorest and least developed countries, adjustment needed a human body, not just a human face.

Another significant impact of the lost 'decade' was the changes it wrought in the balance of development actors. The dramatic decrease in the size of the state, together with a change in its character, was foremost among them. If the face of the state in the 1970s was a mass of clerks, industrial workers, teachers, doctors, nurses, and soldiers with status jobs but falling real wages, the face of the state in the 1990s was a few powerful, but overworked senior officials in the Ministry of Finance and Central Bank. This shrinking and distracted state became the focus of popular movements for political renewal in many African countries, as well as external donors newly interested in good governance and democratization. These changes created openings for a wide range of non-state actors: businesses, as well as non-profit actors like NGOs and community-based organizations. Growth of the informal sector removed large swathes of the economy from state purview, while new decentralization initiatives called out, but did not resource other levels of government and 'traditional' authorities. This posed new challenges for leaders who subsequently tried to muster the resources and support for a revival of development linked to the nation-state.

Reformed African states required a rewrite of their post-independence public narratives as well. The technocratic elite who occupied, or sought powerful positions within them understood themselves to be fulfilling the promise of independence. The source of the continent's development problems, they believed, had been its postcolonial states and their policies. By dismantling and reversing these, they would end poverty, create both opportunity and stability, and restore the international credibility of African countries. Neo-nationalist reformers—and the external experts they worked with—paid less attention to the regional and ethnic balances that postcolonial states had achieved, however rough and unsatisfactory, even as new disparities grew under stabilization and adjustment. Subsequent identity- and resource-based conflicts were intensified by the liberal distribution of weapons from national armories and transnational smuggling networks.

The power conferred by holding debt triggered another change in the balance of development actors in the continent: it gave external donors and international financial institutions, particularly the World Bank, a new prominence in most African countries. There were more foreign advisors in the continent than at the height of imperial rule, with fewer lines of accountability and less public acknowledgement.[130] Expatriates were also maneuvered into senior government positions, as with the Canadian who was appointed governor of Zambia's central bank in 1990.[131] Related to this, another legacy of the lost decade has been a narrowed range of national economic-development policies. For some this represented a hard-won, though still partial, consensus; for others, the hegemonic power of approaches introduced in the 1980s. These policies featured many points raised by the critical pragmatists in response to adjustment and stabilization, but also contained more neo-classicism than would have been the case in a consensus built prior to the mid-1980s. Elements of the New Political Economy also continued to shape the intellectual landscape, with the concept of the neo-patrimonial African state a widely assumed backdrop to discussions of both economic policy and democratization.[132] Neo-liberal ideas also trickled down to influence the practice of development by NGOs, contributing to the emergence of new tools like micro-loans, fair-trade certification, and cash transfers.

Conditionality was the final legacy of the lost decade. It would be inaccurate to say that every policy condition was forced on an unwilling African government, but even where support for economic reform existed, the intensity, scope, and speed of the changes external actors demanded far exceeded it. Many Africans felt their countries had become laboratories for a massive policy experiment, one that their poverty left them no option to refuse.[133] Unfortunately, poverty also meant that the conditions needed to support positive results from the experimental economic 'medicine' were scarce. Worse yet, international lenders and donors rarely provided enough funding to help their 'patients' implement multiple reforms in a harsh global economic environment.[134] Poor results did not cause the experimenters to doubt their assumptions or question their prescriptions; it caused them to look for new variables to control with more conditionality, or to chide their 'patients' for their failure to follow instructions. Some World Bank and IMF officials were openly patronizing; others occasionally gave incomplete or misleading information to adjusting-country governments, apparently believing they had the right to decide what it was proper for debtor country officials to know.[135] All this left a bitter taste.

## RELAUNCHING DEVELOPMENT

The new millennium is associated with new energy for international development, embodied in such things as the Jubilee 2000 and Make Poverty History campaigns, and the Millennium Development Goals (MDGs).[136] These international initiatives garnered attention, but more complex things were happening within the continent under many names. 'Restoration' was one of them, a term that started to appear with regularity in the literature on African development in the late 1990s. It was applied to post-conflict settings and to situations that followed the removal of authoritarian governments, among others. Restoration had parallels in the call that people like Abiola Irele made for a return to the 'modernity project'.[137] The 'African Renaissance', floated by Thabo Mbeki, was another term for change in the new millennium. It meant different things to different people, but often included the revival—in modified form—of Pan-Africanism and of development-minded nation-states. There were many sources of inspiration for this relaunch on the part of African leaders, intellectuals, and activists. Some looked to the South, as mutual development cooperation with other Southern countries grew in importance again; some looked East to the developmental states of East Asia, while others sought in reinvigorated tradition—whether ethnic, national, or African—a model for change. The idea of a new, more effective partnership with OECD donors also returned to prominence with NEPAD. It did not explicitly reference the 1969 new aid partnership of the Commission on International Development, but it included development ideas from that era, like investment in infrastructure and regional economic cooperation. It also included novel tools, like the African Peer Review Mechanism. Gender was briefly mentioned in NEPAD, and in other relaunching development discussions, but did not play a clear or significant role in them.[138]

These initiatives paralleled and intersected with the rediscovery of poverty by external actors at the end of the 1980s, followed by their discovery that the character of institutions, whether public or private, mattered. At the World Bank, the bellwether for a flock of donors and the IMF, programs to mitigate the social costs of adjustment were an early step in this process. The understanding of poverty and the tools needed to deal with it harked back in several ways to *Redistribution with Growth*, which had expressed the World Bank's general position on poverty in the early 1970s.[139] A more substantial and innovative step was the joint introduction of Poverty Reduction Strategy Papers (PRSPs) by the World Bank and IMF in 1999. These were comprehensive blueprints for medium-term poverty-focused development and they were supposed to be created through participatory national processes. Preparing a satisfactory PRSP became a requirement for countries needing either policy-based loans or debt relief, as did conditionality that mandated certain political and legal reforms. The Bank's engagement with African countries was the driver of this 'governance' conditionality, and African countries were disproportionately subject to these kinds of conditions. Africa was the continent with the highest concentration of programs to reduce the social costs of adjustment, also known as social funds; in addition, it was the continent in which the PRSP approach was the most thoroughgoing.[140]

The pattern was similar in global initiatives like the MDGs, where Africa was consistently singled out as a region of focus because special effort would be needed to achieve the goals there. Bilateral donors, most explicitly in the British Labour Government's Commission for Africa (2004), echoed this focus on Africa.[141] However, Africans played a relatively small role in formulating these initiatives. With the MDGs, for instance, African governments and African NGOs participated in the UN conferences and meetings that provided input for the goals. However, the role of African actors, other than UN Secretary General Kofi Annan, in drafting the goals and targets was much more limited.[142] Situations like this were the basis for the belief that non-African actors were responsible for the revival of development, even as the continent became the focus of the international development and humanitarian systems. However, below the surface things were less clear-cut. African governments were involved in multiple processes for setting development goals. For most, the national goals set out in their PRSP were more compelling than the universal MDGs, since aid and debt relief depended directly on them.

A closer look at PRSPs reveals examples of more African agency, in a context where the meaning and funding of development remained a negotiation between internal and external actors. PRSPs were explicitly modeled on the Poverty Eradication Action Plan (PEAP) Uganda's government had put forward in 1997.[143] The PEAP built on Ugandan initiatives from earlier in the 1990s, including a national seminar on poverty, as well as a standard program to mitigate adjustment's social costs. However, it received new energy and direction from the interaction between voters, President Museveni, and opposition candidates during the 1996 national elections. Subsequent consultation created a new consensus on poverty within government, and between government, civil-society organizations, and external donors. Economic growth was seen as the foundation for poverty eradication, but the PEAP also offered both a comprehensive strategy and plans for poverty-focused policy and spending in each sector. It required that government spending be evaluated in terms of its effect on poverty, and protected spending in priority areas from cuts.[144] The Ugandan government proposed its revised second PEAP (2000) as its PRSP for purposes of the Enhanced Highly Indebted Poor Country debt relief initiative. However, the World Bank and IMF were surprisingly reluctant. In the end, they agreed that a summary of the lengthy document would qualify, but the summary underwent translation into language acceptable to the Bank and Fund. Ugandan civil-society organizations were excluded from this translation process, though they had been substantially involved in revisions to the full PEAP.[145]

The first two PEAPs resulted in increased funding for designated Ugandan poverty initiatives. Some of this was money no longer needed for debt payment, which was channeled through a Poverty Action Fund. However, bilateral aid was crucial to implementation of PEAP, though use of budget support by donors reduced their control over the money somewhat. There was a similar mixture of internal and external resources in the Uganda Debt Network (1996), which became an institutionalized channel for civil-society participation in and monitoring of subsequent PEAPs, among other things. It received funding from INGOs and some bilateral aid agencies, but also relied on volunteer input at the community level and membership contributions from individuals and national NGOs.[146]

Uganda's PRSP experience was distinctive. In other African countries, bilateral donors and the World Bank played a substantial role in the PRSP process and the PRSPs, despite their supposed national character, had many common elements.[147] Nevertheless, Uganda displayed other trends with broader relevance. In its ongoing political restructuring, elements of a one-party state mingled with an array of private-sector actors and the military; elements of a 'developmental state' and a neo-patrimonial one were also comingled. Some, though not all of the conflicts that had catastrophically undermined Uganda's national and East African regional development were ended. External actors—bilateral donors, multilateral lenders, INGOs, and foreign firms—were more involved than ever before, but the Ugandan state and, to a lesser degree, other internal actors showed an ability to manipulate and manage them. Development continued to be important to the legitimacy of the ruling party, and of the state, and ideas from the era of state-led development and African Socialism continued to echo. Development tools such as national plans and budget support from the 1950s were revived and used side-by-side with new ones, like the Poverty Action Fund.

Underlying this were important development finance trends. Bilateral aid, which had dried up and narrowed to a core of OECD donors during the 1990s, was more readily available and from a competing array of donors in the new millennium. There was more investment money as well, though much of it was concentrated in resource extraction. Remittances to African countries quadrupled in the twenty years after 1990; reported amounts stood at almost US$40 billion in 2010, slightly exceeding the official aid coming into the continent.[148] Most importantly, commodity prices, still central to African economies and to government revenue, rose again in the late 1990s. African actors who had access to these unevenly distributed resources had options that had not been available for decades. What use they made of them and what impact it is having on the well-being of Africans are not yet easy to judge, especially since these financial flows have shrunk again in recent years.

Assumpta Acam-Oturu, another poet from Uganda, lamented what post-independence generations like hers experienced: 'this land has waited/Under the perennial sun in those twenty years/The dawns of those years were a prayer, a rise in hope' even as 'her ravaged arteries bled to waste'. Writing as a 'gory sunset' ended the century and the millennium, she voiced a widespread, though cautious optimism, looking for 'A transition that may one day draw/ From its unknown source, a resurrection, a new spirit?'[149]

## NOTES

1. Okot p'Bitek, "The Song of Ocol," in *Song of Lawino, Song of Ocol* (1966, 1967; reprint, Long Grove, IL: Waveland Press, 2013), 142.
2. Immanuel Wallerstein, "Elites in French-Speaking West Africa: The Social Basis of Ideas," *Journal of Modern African Studies* 3, no. 1 (1965): 5; and Toyin Falola, *Development Planning and Decolonization in Nigeria* (Gainsville: University Press of Florida, 1996), 31, 68, 70, 88, 91.
3. Uma Kothari, "From Colonialism to Development: Continuities and Divergences," *Journal of Commonwealth and Comparative Politics* 44, no. 1 (2006): 118–36. See also Joseph M. Hodge, *Triumph of the Expert: Agrarian Doctrines of Development and the Legacies of British Colonialism* (Athens, OH: Ohio University Press, 2007).
4. For example, S. Herbert Frankel, "United Nations Primer for Development," *Quarterly Journal of Economics* 66, no. 3 (1952): 301–26; and Kenneth Dadzie, "The UN and the Problem of Economic Development," in *United Nations, Divided World: The UN's Roles in International Relations*, ed. Adam Roberts and Benedict Kingsbury (Oxford: Clarendon Press, 1993), 299.
5. Phillip Naylor, *France and Algeria: A History of Decolonization and Transformation* (Gainesville: University Press of Florida, 2000), 19–21, 36–37, 60.
6. Dudley Seers, *The Political Economy of Nationalism* (Oxford: Oxford University Press, 1983), 91.

7. Social scientists point to the high levels of ethnic diversity in Sub-Saharan countries compared to those in other continents. For instance, William Easterly and Ross Levine note that "fourteen out of the fifteen most ethnically heterogeneous societies in the world are in Africa," in "Africa's Growth Tragedy: Policies and Ethnic Divisions," *Quarterly Journal of Economics* 112 (1997): 1207, 1219. See also Ted Robert Gurr (ed.), *Minorities at Risk: A Global View of Ethnopolitical Conflicts* (Washington, DC: United States Institute for Peace Press, 1993).

8. IFAD Rural Poverty Portal (accessed 9 March 2016), http://www.ruralpovertyportal.org; and Jonathan Baker, "Oil and African Development," *Journal of Modern African Studies* 15, no. 2 (1977): 175–76.

9. For example, Paul Rosenstein-Rodan, "International Aid for Underdeveloped Countries," *Review of Economics and Statistics* 43, no. 2 (1961): 111–12; and Colin Leys, "African Economic Development in Theory and Practice," *Daedalus* 111, no. 2 (1982): 99.

10. Mamadou Dia in Leopold Senghor et al., "Dakar Colloquium: Search for a Definition," *Africa Report* 8, no. 5 (1963): 17.

11. David Fieldhouse, *Black Africa, 1945–1980: Economic Decolonization and Arrested Development* (London: Allen & Unwin, 1986), 42.

12. Thomas Taylor, "The Struggle for Economic Control of Uganda, 1919–1922: Formulation of an Economic Policy," *International Journal of African Historical Studies* 11, no. 1 (1978): 7; Paul Clark, "Development Strategy in an Early-Stage Economy: Uganda," *Journal of Modern African Studies* 4, no. 1 (1966): 48–49; and Michael Schultheis, "The Ugandan Economy and General Amin, 1971–1974," *Studies in Comparative International Development* 10, no. 3 (1975): 6, 8. See also J.J. Oloya, "Marketing Boards and Post-War Economic Development Policy in Uganda, 1945–1962," *Indian Journal of Agricultural Economics* 23 (1968): 50–58.

13. Crawford Young, Neal Sherman, and Tim Rose, *Cooperatives and Development: Agricultural Politics in Ghana and Uganda* (Madison: University of Wisconsin Press, 1981), 42–44, 61.

14. A. B. Adimola, "Uganda: The Newest 'Independent'," *African Affairs* 62, no. 249 (1963): 326–32; Clark, "Development Strategy in an Early-Stage Economy," 49–51, 56; and Reginald Green, "Uganda's Plan for Growth and Development: An Analysis of and Preliminary Reflections on Work for Progress," ERRP No. 103 (Institute for Development Studies, University of Sussex, 1966), 3, http://opendocs.ids.ac.uk/opendocs/bitstream/handle/123456789/1511/EDRP103-329701.pdf?sequence=1. See also C.C. Wrigley, *Crops and Wealth in Uganda*, East African Studies No. 12 (Kampala: East African Institute of Social Research, 1959).

15. Paul Clark, "Co-Ordination of Development Plans in East Africa" (Institute for Development Studies, University of Sussex, 1963), 6, http://dev.opendocs.ids.ac.uk/opendocs/bitstream/handle/123456789/1571/EDRP14-327419.pdf?sequence=1; and Paul Clark, *Development Planning in East Africa* (Nairobi: East African Publishing House for the Makerere Institute of Social Research, 1965), 50–55.

16. See Edward Manson et al., *The Economic Development of Uganda* (Baltimore: Johns Hopkins Press for the IBRD, 1962), 401–3; Kathleen Heasman,

"Women and Community Development in Kenya and Uganda," *Community Development Journal* 1, no. 4 (1966): 16–22; Hilda Mary Tadria, "Uganda Women's Organizations: Their Contribution Towards Raising Uganda's Standard of Living," *Africa Spectrum* 8, no. 2 (1973): 217–26; and Jeff Grischow and Glenn McKnight, "Rhyming Development: Practising Post-Development in Colonial Ghana and Uganda," *Journal of Historical Sociology* 16, no. 4 (2003): 517–49.

17. See Christopher Youé, "Peasants, Planters and Cotton Capitalists: The 'Dual Economy' in Colonial Uganda," *Canadian Journal of African Studies* 12, no. 2 (1978): 163–84; Keith Ede, "An Analysis of Regional Inequality in Uganda," *Tijdschrift voor economische en sociale geografie* 72, no. 5 (1981): 296–303; and Bart Fisher, *The International Coffee Agreement: A Study in Coffee Diplomacy* (New York: Praeger Publishers, 1972). For commodity market management in the early twentieth century see Fiona Gordon-Ashworth, *International Commodity Control: A Contemporary History and Appraisal* (London: Croon Helm, 1984).

18. See Reginald Green, "The Treaty for East African Co-Operation: A Summary and Interpretation," *Journal of Modern African Studies* 5, no. 3 (1967): 414–19; and "History of the EAC," East African Community, 2016, http://www.eac.int/about/EAC-history.

19. Tekalign Gedamu, "Economic Planning in Africa," *Africa Today* 10, no. 9 (1963): 30, 32; and Reginald Green, "Four African Development Plans: Ghana, Kenya, Nigeria and Tanzania," *Journal of Modern African Studies* 3, no. 2 (1965): 249.

20. T.Y. Shen, "Macro Development Planning in Tropical Africa: Technocratic and Non-Technocratic Causes of Failure," *Journal of Development Studies* 13, no. 4 (1977): 417.

21. Claude Ake, *Democracy and Development in Africa* (Washington, DC: The Brookings Institution, 1996), 5, 7.

22. p'Bitek, *The Song of Lawino*, 104, 110; Okot p'Bitek, "Indigenous Ills" (1967), reprint in *Transition* 75/76 (1997): 40–42.

23. p'Bitek, *The Song of Lawino*, 110.

24. See Naomi Chazan et al., *Politics and Society in Contemporary Africa*, 3rd ed. (Boulder: Lynne Rienner, 1999), 160–67 for a concise overview; and Crawford Young, *Ideology and Development in Africa* (New Haven: Yale University Press, 1982) for a longer one. Guy Martin, *African Political Thought* (New York: Palgrave Macmillan, 2012) offers a detailed discussion of socialist, Marxist and populist ideas.

25. John Rapley, *Understanding Development: Theory and Practice in the Third World*, 3rd ed. (Boulder: Lynne Rienner, 2007), 28–33.

26. Bahru Zewde, *Pioneers of Change in Ethiopia: The Reformist Intellectuals of the Early Twentieth Century* (Oxford: James Currey, Ohio University Press, and Addis Ababa University, 2002), 1–3.

27. J.F. Ade Ajayi, "Expectations of Independence," *Daedalus* 111, no. 2 (1982): 3; and Ali A. Mazrui, "Elements of the New Africa," *Index on Censorship* 21, no. 4 (1992): 9.

28. Ajayi, "Expectations of Independence," 2; Saleh Omar, "Arab Nationalism: A Retrospective Evaluation," *Arab Studies Quarterly* 14, no. 4 (1992): 25–26; and Ake, *Democracy and Development in Africa*, 8, 11.

29. The literature on Tanzania's post-independence development model is vast. For recent overviews see Paul Bjerk, "Sovereignty and Socialism in Tanzania: The Historiography of an African State," *History in Africa* 37 (2010): 275–319; plus the "Tanzania at 50" section in *Review of African Political Economy* 39, no. 131 (2012): 101–31.

30. Copies of this and related documents can be found in Julius Nyerere, *Freedom and Development/Uhuru na Maendeleo: A Selection from Writings and Speeches, 1968–1973* (London: Oxford University Press, 1973).

31. Priya Lal, "Militants, Mothers, and the National Family: *Ujamaa*, Gender, and Rural Development in Postcolonial Tanzania," *Journal of African History* 51, no. 1 (2010): 6–7.

32. See *Tanzania Human Development Report 2014: Economic Transformation for Human Development* (Dar-es-Salaam: Economic and Social Research Foundation, United Nations Development Programme Tanzania Office, and the Ministry of Finance, 2015), xvi. A widely cited contemporary view is offered by Goran Hyden, *Beyond Ujamaa in Tanzania: Underdevelopment and an Uncaptured Peasantry* (Berkeley and Los Angeles: University of California Press, 1980).

33. *World Development Report 1982* (New York: Oxford University Press for the World Bank, 1982), 150, 154.

34. FAOSTAT (accessed 7 May 2016), http://faostat.fao.org/DesktopDefault. aspx?PageID=339&lang=en&country=215.

35. Issa Shivji, "Nationalism and Pan-Africanism: Decisive Moments in Nyerere's Intellectual and Political Thought," *Review of African Political Economy* 39, no. 131 (2012): 113.

36. Gedamu, "Economic Planning in Africa," 32; and Mathew Costello, "Market and State: Evaluating Tanzania's Program of State-Led Industrialization," *World Development* 22, no. 10 (1994): 1513.

37. Helmut Anheier, "Private Voluntary Organizations and the Third World: The Case of Africa," in *The Third Sector: Comparative Studies in Nonprofit Organizations*, ed. Helmut Anheier and Wolfgang Seibel (Berlin: de Gruyter, 1990), 371. Surveys of the non-profit sectors in six African countries are presented in Lester Salamon et al., *Global Civil Society: Dimensions of the Nonprofit Sector*, Vol. 2 (Bloomfield: Kumarian Press, 2004).

38. John de Wilde, *Experiences with Agricultural Development in Tropical Africa*, Vol. 2, *The Case Studies*, trans. A. Guinard et al. (Baltimore: Johns Hopkins University Press for the IBRD, 1967), 249–51; Djibril Aw and Geert Diemer, *Making a Large Irrigation Scheme Work: A Case Study from Mali*, Directions in Development No. 31672 (Washington, DC: World Bank, 2005), 6, http://elibrary.worldbank.org/doi/abs/10.1596/0-8213-5942-8; and Sander Zwart and Lucie Leclert, "A Remote Sensing-Based Irrigation Performance Assessment: A Case Study of the *Office Du Niger* in Mali," *Irrigation Science* 28, no. 5 (2010): 373.

39. de Wilde, *Experiences with Agricultural Development*, Vol. 2, 246–47, 286–87.

40. Jacqueline Braveboy-Wagner, *Institutions of the Global South* (London: Routledge, 2009), 56–57; and Joshua Goldstein, Xiaoming Huang and Burcu Akan, "Energy in the World Economy, 1950–1992," *International Studies Quarterly* 41, no. 2 (1997): 250. The quote is from Wolfgang Bartke, *China's Economic Aid* (Delhi: Vikas Publishing for the Hamburg Institute of Asian Affairs, 1975), 9.

41. J. Ernesto López-Córdova and Christopher Meissner, "Exchange-Rate Regimes and International Trade: Evidence from the Classical Gold Standard Era," *American Economic Review* 93, no. 1 (2003): 344–53; and Owen Humpage, "Smithsonian Agreement," Federal Reserve History, 22 November 2013, http://www.federalreservehistory.org/Events/DetailView/34.

42. Susan Strange, *Mad Money: When Markets Outgrow Governments* (Ann Arbor: University of Michigan Press, 1998), 4.

43. Gerald Helleiner, "The Impact of the Exchange Rate System on the Developing Countries," in *The New Global Economy and the Developing Countries: Essays in International Economics and Development* (Aldershot: Edward Elgar, 1990), 75–101; see also Alfred Maizels, "Commodities in Crisis: An Overview of the Main Issues," *World Development* 15, no. 5 (1987): 537–49.

44. Dani Rodrik, "Where Did All the Growth Go? External Shocks, Social Conflict, and Growth Collapses," *Journal of Economic Growth* 4, no. 4 (1999): 385–412.

45. UCDP/PRIO Armed Conflict Dataset v.4-2015 (accessed 29 March 2016), http://www.pcr.uu.se/research/ucdp/datasets/ucdp_prio_armed_conflict_dataset/.

46. Jean-Louis Combes and Tahsin Saadi-Sedik, "How Does Trade Openness Influence Budget Deficits in Developing Countries?" *Journal of Development Studies* 42, no. 8 (2006): 1404.

47. See Aidan Southall, "Social Disorganisation in Uganda: Before, During, and After Amin," *Journal of Modern African Studies* 18, no. 4 (1980): 627–56; Godfrey Asiimwe, *The Impact of Post-Colonial Policy Shifts in Coffee Marketing at the Local Level in Uganda: A Case Study of Mukono District, 1962–1998* (Maastricht: Shaker Publishing, 2002); Philip Verwimp, "The Political Economy of Coffee, Dictatorship, and Genocide," *European Journal of Political Economy* 19, no. 2 (2003): 161–81; Zerihun Gudeta Alemu, Lukas Oosthuizen and H. D. van Schalwyk, "Agricultural Development Policies of Ethiopia since 1957," *South African Journal of Economic History* 17, nos. 1–2 (2002): 1–24; and Berhanu Abegaz, "The Economics of Surplus Squeeze under Peripheral Socialism: An Ethiopian Illustration," *Studies in Comparative International Development* 23, no. 3 (1988): 51–77.

48. David Sapsford and Hans Singer, "The IMF, the World Bank and Commodity Prices: A Case of Shifting Sands?," *World Development* 26, no. 9 (1998): 1653–60; and Angus Deaton, "Commodity Prices and Growth in Africa," *Journal of Economic Perspectives* 13, no. 3 (1999): 31–32.

49. Jonathan Powell and Clayton Thyne, "Coups in the World, 1950-Present" (dataset v2015.09.30; accessed 30 March 2016), http://www.jonathanmpowell.com/coup-detat-dataset.html; and Patrick McGowan, "African military coups d'état, 1956–2001: frequency, trends and distribution," *Journal of Modern African Studies* 41, no. 3 (2003): 339–70.

50. Naomi Chazan et al., "Appendix 3: Basic Political Data," in *Politics and Society in Contemporary Africa*, 3rd ed., 505–25.

51. Ellen Johnson Sirleaf, *This Child Will Be Great: Memoir of a Remarkable Life by Africa's First Woman President* (New York: HarperCollins, 2009), 117.

52. John Stremlau, *The International Politics of the Nigerian Civil War, 1967–1970* (Princeton: Princeton University Press, 1977), 238–52; Alex de Waal, *Famine Crimes: Politics and the Disaster Relief Industry in Africa* (Oxford: African Rights, The International African Institute, James Currey, and Indiana University Press, 1997), 73–77; and Eno Blankson Ikpe, "Migration, Starvation and Humanitarian Intervention During the Nigerian Civil War," *Lagos Historical Review* 1 (2001): 91. On citizen diplomacy see Tom Princen, *Intermediaries in International Conflict* (Princeton: Princeton University Press, 1992), 186–213.

53. de Waal, *Famine Crimes*, 72–73; and Peter Walker and Daniel Maxwell, *Shaping the Humanitarian World* (London: Routledge, 2009), 46–48.

54. Hal Sheets and Roger Morris, *Disaster in the Desert: Failures of International Relief in the West African Drought* (Washington, DC: Carnegie Endowment for International Peace, 1974), 10–11; and William Torry, "Social Science Research on Famine: A Critical Evaluation," *Human Ecology* 12, no. 3 (1984): 228.

55. John Esseks, "Review: Humanitarian Assistance in Africa: Some Case Studies," *Africa Today* 24, no. 3 (1977): 77; and Nicole Ball, "Drought and Dependence in the Sahel," *International Journal of Health Services* 8, no. 2 (1978): 271.

56. Edward Bunting, "The Sahel: Still Causing Concern Despite the Aid," in *Africa Contemporary Record: Annual Survey and Documents 1982–1983*, ed. Colin Legum (New York: Africana Publishing, 1984), A194–95; and OECD QWIDS (accessed 25 March 2016), https://stats.oecd.org/qwids/.

57. For example, John Esseks, "The Food Outlook for the Sahel: Regaining Self-Sufficiency or Continuing Dependence on International Aid?," *Africa Today* 22, no. 2 (1975): 46–47.

58. de Waal, *Famine Crimes*, 121–22; and John Borton and Edward Clay, "The African Food Crisis of 1982–1986," *Disasters* 10, no. 4 (1986): 261.

59. Arthur Goldsmith, "Foreign Aid and Statehood in Africa," *International Organization* 55, no. 1 (2001): 126. It is worth noting that aid dependence, often measured as net ODA greater than 10% of GNP, does not go hand in hand with the largest flows of aid. As Cold War developments directed more rather than less attention to the continent after the mid-1970s, the largest aid recipients were strategically important countries like Egypt, and they were not aid-dependent by this measure.

60. Roger Riddell and Lawrence Cockcroft, "Foreign Direct Investment," in *African External Finance in the 1990s*, ed. Ishrat Husain and John Underwood (Washington, DC: The World Bank, 1991), 139.

61. Leys, "African Economic Development in Theory and Practice," 100; and World Bank, *World Development Report 1980* (Washington, DC: World Bank, 1980), 112.

62. Gedamu, "Economic Planning in Africa," 32; Shen, "Macro Development Planning in Tropical Africa," 415; Leys, "African Economic Development in Theory and Practice," 99–100.

63. Leys, "African Economic Development in Theory and Practice," 100.
64. Adebayo Adedeji, "Transforming Africa's Economies," *Africa Report* 31, no. 3 (1986): 5.
65. See Richard Grant and John Agnew, "Representing Africa: The Geography of Africa in World Trade, 1960–92," *Annals of the Association of American Geographers* 86, no. 4 (1996): 729–44.
66. Olav Stokke, *The UN and Development: From Aid to Cooperation* (Bloomington: Indiana University Press, 2009), 139, 141, 157, 170.
67. The most lucid guide to this initiative remains Craig Murphy, *The Emergence of the NIEO Ideology* (Boulder: Westview Press, 1984).
68. Nassau Adams, *Worlds Apart: The North–South Divide and the International System* (London: Zed Books, 1993), 75–76; and Jock Finlayson and Mark Zacher, "International Trade Institutions and the North/South Dialogue," *International Journal* 36, no. 4 (1981): 732–65.
69. Trevor Parfitt, "The Lomé Convention and the New International Order," *Review of African Political Economy* no. 22 (1981): 85–95; and Louis Sicking, "A Colonial Echo: France and the Colonial Dimension of the European Economic Community," *French Colonial History* 5 (2004): 207–28.
70. John Cohen, "Rural Change in Ethiopia: The Chilalo Agricultural Development Unit," *Economic Development and Cultural Change* 22, no. 4 (1974): 580–614; and John Cohen, *Integrated Rural Development: The Ethiopian Experience and the Debate* (Uppsala: The Scandinavian Institute of African Studies, 1987). See also Seleshi Sisaye and Eileen Stommes, "Agricultural Development in Ethiopia: Government Budgeting and Development Assistance in the Pre and Post 1975 Periods," *Journal of Development Studies* 16, no. 2 (1980): 156–85.
71. John Cohen and Nils-Ivar Isaksson, "Villagisation in Ethiopia's Arsi Region," *Journal of Modern African Studies* 25, no. 3 (1987): 439–40.
72. Abegaz, "The Economics of Surplus Squeeze under Peripheral Socialism;" Alemu et al., "Agricultural Development Policies of Ethiopia since 1957".
73. See Miriam Lowi, "Oil Rents and Political Breakdown in Patrimonial States: Algeria in Comparative Perspective," *Journal of North African Studies* 9, no. 3 (2004): 83–102; and Clement Henry, "Algeria's Agonies: Oil Rent Effects in a Bunker State," *Journal of North African Studies* 9, no. 2 (2004): 68–81.
74. For example, Xavier Sala-i-Martin and Arvind Subramanian, "Addressing the Natural Resource Curse: An Illustration from Nigeria," *Journal of African Economies* 22, no. 4 (2012): 570–615.
75. For example, Richard Sandbrook, "Origins of the Democratic Developmental State: Interrogating Mauritius," *Canadian Journal of African Studies* 39, no. 3 (2005): 549–81; and Kalle Laaksonen, Petri Mäki-Fränti, and Meri Virolainen, "Mauritius and Jamaica as Case Studies of the Lomé Sugar Protocol" (TradeAg Working Paper 06/21, Pellervo Economic Research Institute, 2006), http://purl.umn.edu/18855.
76. Ralph Hazelton, "Diamonds: Forever or for Good? The Economic Impact of Diamonds in Southern Africa" (Diamonds and Human Security Project occasional paper #3, Ottawa: Partnership Africa Canada, 2002); Ian Taylor, "The Developmental State in Africa: The Case of Botswana," in *The Potentiality of "Developmental States" in Africa: Botswana and Uganda Compared,*

ed. Pamela Mbabazi and Ian Taylor (Dakar: CODESRIA, 2005), 44–56; and Ellen Hillbom, "Diamonds or Development? A Structural Assessment of Botswana's Forty Years of Success," *Journal of Modern African Studies* 46, no. 2 (2008): 191–214.

77. See Chalmers Johnson, "The Developmental State: Odyssey of a Concept," in *The Developmental State*, ed. Meredith Woo-Cumings (Ithaca, NY: Cornell University Press, 1999), 32–60; and Thandika Mkandawire, "Thinking About Developmental States in Africa," *Cambridge Journal of Economics* 25, no. 3 (2001): 289–314.

78. Kwame Akonor, *African Economic Institutions* (London: Routledge, 2009), 21; and Organization of African Unity, "Lagos Plan of Action for the Economic Development of Africa, 1980–2000," 1980, 5–6, http://www.merit. unu.edu/wp-content/uploads/2015/01/Lagos-Plan-of-Action.pdf.

79. Tony Killick, "Trends in Development Economics and Their Relevance to Africa," *Journal of Modern African Studies* 18, no. 3 (1980): 368.

80. Adebayo Adedeji, "The ECA: Forging a Future for Africa," in *Unity and Diversity in Development Ideas: Perspectives from the UN Regional Commissions*, ed. Yves Berthelot (Bloomington: Indiana University Press, 2004), 253–59; and Adekeye Adebajo, "Two Prophets of Regional Integration: Prebisch and Adedeji," in *International Development: Ideas, Experience, and Prospects*, ed. Bruce Currie-Alder et al. (Oxford: Oxford University Press, 2014), 330–33.

81. "Lagos Plan of Action," 8; and Uma Lele, "The MADIA Countries: Aid Inflows, Endowments, Policies, and Performance," in *Aid to African Agriculture: Lessons from Two Decades of Donors' Experiences*, ed. Uma Lele (Washington, DC: Johns Hopkins University Press for the World Bank, 1991), 14.

82. "Lagos Plan of Action," 79.

83. Adebayo Adedeji, "The Evolution of the Monrovia Strategy and the Lagos Plan of Action: A Regional Approach to Economic Decolonization" (lecture, Nigerian Institute for Social and Economic Research, Ibadan, 24 March 1983; UN Economic Commission for Africa Knowledge Repository, Bib-45065), 8–9, http://repository.uneca.org/handle/10855/5726.

84. Adedeji, "The ECA: Forging a Future for Africa," 266.

85. For example, Richard Jolly, "The Economic Commission for Africa: Fighting to Be Heard," Briefing Note No. 21 (Ralph Bunche Institute for International Studies, City University of New York, 2009), http://www.unhistory. org/briefing/21ECA.pdf; Yash Tandon, "Reflections on African Renaissance and the Lagos Plan of Action" (Oxford, 8 February 2016), http:// yashtandon.com/wp-content/uploads/2016/02/08-Reflections-on-African-Renaissance-and-the-Lagos-Plan-of-Action.pdf.

86. Karen Mingst, "Inter-Organizational Politics: The World Bank and the African Development Bank," *Review of International Studies* 13, no. 4 (1987): 284.

87. Sadig Rasheed and Eshetu Chole, "Human Development: An African Perspective" (occasional paper no. 17, Human Development Report Office, UNDP, 1994), 3, http://hdr.undp.org/en/content/human-development-african-perspective. APPER was submitted to the UN a year later and

adopted by the General Assembly as the Programme of Action for Africa's Economic Recovery and Development (UNPAAERD).

88. Alfred Maizels, "The Continuing Commodity Crisis of Developing Countries," *World Development* 22, no. 11 (1994): 1685–86; and Roy Culpeper, *Forced Adjustment: The Export Collapse of Sub-Saharan Africa* (Ottawa: North-South Institute, 1987), 2–3.

89. Culpeper, *Forced Adjustment*, 8–9, 17–19.

90. John Loxley, "Structural Adjustment in Africa: Reflections on Ghana and Zambia," *Review of African Political Economy* 47 (1990): 19; and John Loxley, *Ghana: The Long Road to Recovery, 1983–1990* (Ottawa: North-South Institute, 1991), 46.

91. World Bank, *Commodity Trade and Price Trends* (Baltimore: Johns Hopkins University Press for the IBRD, 1985), 45; and Commodity price long-term trends in UNCTADSTAT (accessed 15 May 2016), http://unctadstat.unctad.org/wds/ReportFolders/reportFolders.aspx?IF_ActivePath=P,8.

92. Loxley, *Ghana: The Long Road to Recovery*, 7, 9.

93. Raúl Prebish, "Two Decades After," in *UNCTAD and the South-North Dialogue: The First Twenty Years*, ed. Michael Zammit Cutajar (Oxford: Pergamon Press, 1985), 8; and Culpeper, *Forced Adjustment*, 8–9.

94. Benedict Mongula, "Development Theory & Changing Trends in Sub-Saharan African Economies 1960–89," in *African Perspectives on Development*, ed. Ulf Himmelstrand et al. (London: James Currey, 1994), 92; and Charles Chukwuma Soludo, "In Search of Alternative Analytical and Methodological Frameworks for an African Economic Development Model," in *African Voices on Structural Adjustment*, ed. Thandika Mkandawire and Charles Soludo (Trenton, NJ: Africa World Press for CODESRIA and IDRC, 2003), 24.

95. See Kimseyinga Savadogo and Claude Wetta, "The Impact of Self-Imposed Adjustment: The Case of Burkina Faso, 1983–1989" (Innocenti occasional papers no. 15, UNICEF International Child Development Centre, Florence, 1991), https://www.unicef-irc.org/publications/pdf/eps15.pdf.

96. For example, Kwabena Donkor, *Structural Adjustment and Mass Poverty in Ghana* (Aldershot: Ashgate, 1997), 118–20; and Haidari Amani et al., "Understanding Economic and Political Reform in Tanzania," in *Understanding Economic Reforms in Africa: A Tale of Seven Nations*, ed. Joseph Mensah (Houndmills: Palgrave Macmillan, 2006), 214–15.

97. Channing Arndt, Henning Tarp Jensen and Finn Tarp, "Stabilization and Structural Adjustment in Mozambique: An appraisal," *Journal of International Development* 12, no. 3 (2000): 301–2.

98. Justin Zulu and Saleh Nsouli, "Adjustment Programs in Africa: The Recent Experience" (occasional paper no. 34, International Monetary Fund, Washington, DC, 1985), 11, http://dx.doi.org/10.5089/9781557750563.084; John Loxley, "The IMF, the World Bank, and Sub-Saharan Africa: Policies and Politics," in *The IMF and the World Bank in Africa*, ed. Kjell Havnevik (Uppsala: Scandinavian Institute of African Studies, 1987), 52; and Mongula, "Development Theory & Changing Trends in Sub-Saharan African Economies," 92–93.

99. Jacques de Larosière, "Adjustment Policy Rationale … Fund Managing Director Describes Case Studies," *IMF Survey* (6 February 1984), 46; and

Margaret Garritsen de Vries, *The IMF in a Changing World 1945–85* (Washington, DC: International Monetary Fund, 1986), 191.

100. Devesh Kapur, "Conditionality and Its Alternatives," in *The IMF and the World Bank at Sixty*, ed. Ariel Buria (London: Anthem Press, 2005), 49.

101. Robert Wood, *From Marshall Plan to Debt Crisis: Foreign Aid and Development Choices in the World Economy* (Berkeley and Los Angeles: University of California Press, 1986), 300.

102. Devesh Kapur, John Lewis, and Richard Webb, *The World Bank: Its First Half Century*, Vol. 1, *History* (Washington, DC: Brookings Institution Press, 1997), 507, 510.

103. Kapur et al., *The World Bank*, Vol. 1, 537; and Reginald Green, "A Cloth Untrue: The Evolution of Structural Adjustment in Sub-Saharan Africa," *Journal of International Affairs* 52, no. 1 (1998): 218.

104. Thandika Mkandawire, "Maladjusted African Economies and Globalisation," *Africa Development* 30, nos. 1–2 (2005): 20.

105. For example, Gustav Ranis, "Debt, Adjustment and Development," in *Economic Development and World Debt*, ed. Hans Singer and Soumitra Sharma (New York: St. Martin's Press, 1989), 227–38; and Anne Krueger, "The Need for Policy Reform," in *Economic Policy Reform in Developing Countries* (Oxford: Blackwell, 1992), 1–58.

106. Paul Mosley, Jane Harrigan, and John Toye, *Aid and Power: The World Bank and Policy-Based Lending*, 2nd ed., Vol. 1: *Analysis and Policy Proposals* (New York: Routledge, 1995), 9–10; Jan Nederveen Pieterse, *Development Theory: Deconstructions/Reconstructions* (Los Angeles: Sage Publications, 2001), 41; and John Williamson, "A Short History of the Washington Consensus," in *The Washington Consensus Reconsidered: Towards a New Global Governance*, ed. Narcis Serra and Joseph Stiglitz (Oxford: Oxford University Press, 2008), 16.

107. Mosley et al., *Aid and Power*, 2nd ed., Vol. 1, 13–16; and Rapley, *Understanding Development*, 3rd ed., 59–62.

108. Adebayo Adedeji, "Structural Adjustment Policies in Africa," *International Social Science Journal* 51, no. 4 (1999): 522.

109. "Adjustment Lending Retrospective: Final Report" (World Bank Operations Policy and Country Services, World Bank, Washington, DC, 2001), 2, http://siteresources.worldbank.org/PROJECTS/Resources/ALR06_20_01.pdf.

110. Thandika Mkandawire and Charles Soludo, *Our Continent, Our Future: African Perspectives on Structural Adjustment* (Trenton, NJ: Africa World Press for CODESRIA and IDRC, 1999), 41.

111. Kapur et al., *The World Bank*, Vol. 1, 513–15; and Green, "A Cloth Untrue: The Evolution of Structural Adjustment," 210.

112. Kapur et al., *The World Bank*, Vol. 1, 588.

113. Kapur et al., *The World Bank*, Vol. 1, 518, 541; and Tony Killick, *IMF Programmes in Developing Countries: Design and Impact* (London: Routledge, 1995), 14–16.

114. Gerald Helleiner, "The IMF and Africa in the 1980s," Essays in International Finance No. 152 (Department of Economics, Princeton University, July 1983), 9, https://www.princeton.edu/~ies/IES_Essays/E152.pdf; and William Easterly, "What Did Structural Adjustment Adjust? The Association

of Policies and Growth with Repeated IMF and World Bank Adjustment Loans," *Journal of Development Economics* 76, no. 1 (2005): 7.

115. IMF *Annual Reports*, 1980–2000, https://www.imf.org/external/pubs/ft/ar/; "Agreements Concluded with Paris Club," Paris Club (accessed 22 February 2016), http://www.clubdeparis.org/en/traitements?tid_1=All&tid_2=All&tid=All&field_treatment_date_value%5Bvalue%5D%5Byear%5D=; and Easterly, "What Did Structural Adjustment Adjust?," 5. By this measure, the ten most adjusted African countries were: Senegal, Togo, Malawi, Ivory Coast, Uganda, Madagascar, Mali, Mauritania, Central African Republic, and Kenya with Guinea tied for tenth place.

116. John Toye, "Ghana," in *Aid and Power: The World Bank and Policy-Based Lending*, ed. Paul Mosley et al. (London: Routledge, 1991), 174–75; and Tracy Williams, "An African Success Story: Ghana's Cocoa Marketing System" (working paper Vol. 2009, no. 318, Institute for Development Studies, University of Sussex, January 2009), http://www.ids.ac.uk/idspublication/an-african-success-story-ghana-s-cocoa-marketing-system.

117. See Roger Young and John Loxley, *Zambia: An Assessment of Zambia's Structural Adjustment Experience*, rev. ed. (Ottawa: The North-South Institute, 1990); Venkatesh Seshamani, "Zambia," in *The Human Dimensions of Africa's Persistent Economic Crisis*, ed. Adebayo Adedeji et al. (London: Hans Zell for the UNECA, 1990), 104–23; and Gladstone Bonnick, "Zambia Country Assistance Review: Turning an Economy Around," World Bank Operations Evaluation Study (World Bank, Washington, DC, 1997), http://documents.worldbank.org/curated/en/1997/03/440761/zambia-country-assistance-review-turning-economy-around.

118. Tony Killick, *Aid and the Political Economy of Policy Change* (New York: Routledge, 1998), 29–31.

119. Robert Poirier, "Tourism and Development in Tunisia," *Annals of Tourism Research* 22, no. 1 (1995): 157–71; Waleed Hazbun, "Images of Openness, Spaces of Control: The Politics of Tourism Development in Tunisia," *Arab Studies Journal* 15/16, no. 2/1 (2007): 10–35; and Myriam Blin, "The Political Economy of IMF and World Bank Interventions: Is Tunisia Really a Model Student?" in *Aid and Power in the Arab World: IMF and World Bank Policy-Based Lending in the Middle East and North Africa*, ed. Jane Harrigan and Hamed El-Said (London: Palgrave Macmillan, 2009), 105–47.

120. Kwesi Botchwey et al., "Report of the Group of Independent Persons Appointed to Conduct an Evaluation of Certain Aspects of the Enhanced Structural Adjustment Facility" (International Monetary Fund, Washington, DC, June 1998), Part 2, 44, 64–73, http://www.imf.org/external/np/esaf/evaluat.htm. The information on people living below US$1 per day is taken from Robert Naiman and Neil Watkins, "A Survey of the Impacts of IMF Structural Adjustment in Africa: Growth, Social Spending, and Debt Relief" (Center for Economic and Policy Research, Washington, DC, 1999), http://cepr.net/documents/publications/debt_1999_04.htm.

121. William Easterly, "The Effect of International Monetary Fund and World Bank Programs on Poverty" (Policy Research working paper 2517, Development Research Group, World Bank, Washington, DC, January 2001), http://elibrary.worldbank.org/doi/abs/10.1596/1813-9450-2517.

122. Adebayo Adedeji, "The UN Economic Commission for Africa," in *From Global Apartheid to Global Village: Africa and the United Nations*, ed. Adekeye Adebajo (Scotsville: University of KwaZuluNatal Press, 2009), 389.

123. UN Economic Commission for Africa, "African Alternative Framework to Structural Adjustment Programmes for Socio-Economic Recovery and Transformation," 1989, http://repository.uneca.org/handle/10855/5670; Reginald Green and Mike Faber, "Editorial: The Structural Adjustment of Structural Adjustment: Sub-Saharan Africa 1980–1993," *IDS Bulletin* 25, no. 3 (1994): 4.

124. Soludo, "In Search of Alternative Analytical and Methodological Frameworks," 32.

125. For example, Pádraig Carmody, "Constructing Alternatives to Structural Adjustment in Africa," *Review of African Political Economy*, no. 75 (1998): 39; and Mbaya Kankwenda, "The UN Development Programme," in *From Global Apartheid to Global Village*, 404.

126. Abdalla Bujra, "Africa: From the OAU to the African Union," *Cooperation South* (2002): 115; and Soludo, "In Search of Alternative Analytical and Methodological Frameworks," 31.

127. Soludo, "In Search of Alternative Analytical and Methodological Frameworks," 33.

128. Discussion of the rough consensus can be found in Gerald Helleiner, "From Adjustment to Development in Sub-Saharan Africa: Consensus and Continuing Conflict," in *From Adjustment to Development in Africa: Conflict, Controversy, Convergence, Consensus?* ed. Giovanni Andrea Cornia and Gerald Helleiner (Houndmills: Macmillan, 1994), 3–24; K. Mengisteab and B. Ikubolajeh Logan, eds., *Beyond Economic Liberalization in Africa: Structural Adjustment and the Alternatives* (London: Zed Books, 1995); and Thandika Mkandawire and Charles Soludo, *Our Continent, Our Future*.

129. Soludo, "In Search of Alternative Analytical and Methodological Frameworks," 28.

130. Mkandawire and Soludo, *Our Continent, Our Future*, 35–37.

131. Young and Loxley, *Zambia*, rev. ed., 76.

132. Thandika Mkandawire, "Adjustment, Political Conditionality and Democratisation in Africa," in *From Adjustment to Development in Africa*, 166.

133. Ali Abdel Gadir Ali, "The Rediscovery of the African Alternative Framework to Structural Adjustment Programmes," in *African Development in the 21st Century: Adebayo Adedeji's Theories and Contributions*, ed. Amos Sawyer et al. (Trenton, NJ: Africa World Press, 2015), 38.

134. Gerald Helleiner, "External Resource Flows, Debt Relief and Economic Development in Sub-Saharan Africa," in *From Adjustment to Development in Africa*, 317.

135. For example, see Robert Klitgaard, *Tropical Gangsters: One Man's Experience with Development and Decadence in Deepest Africa* (New York: Basic Books, 1990), 264–70; and Lance Taylor, *Varieties of Stabilization Experience* (Oxford: Clarendon Press, 1988), 165.

136. See Joshua W. Busby, "Bono Made Jesse Helms Cry: Jubilee 2000, Debt Relief, and Moral Action in International Politics," *International Studies Quarterly* 51, no. 2 (2007): 247–75; Nicolas Sireau, *Make Poverty History:*

*Political Communication in Action* (Houndmills: Palgrave Macmillan, 2009); and David Hulme, "The Millennium Development Goals (MDGs): A Short History of the World's Biggest Promise" (Brooks World Poverty Institute working paper no. 100, University of Manchester, September 2009), http://papers.ssrn.com/sol3/papers.cfm?abstract_id=1544271.

137. Abiola Irele, "The Political Kingdom: Toward Reconstruction in Africa," *Socialism and Democracy* 21, no. 3 (2007): 5–35. This article was first published online in 1999.

138. See Zo Randriamaro, "NEPAD, Gender and the Poverty Trap: The Challenges of Financing for Development in Africa from a Gender Perspective," in *Africa and Development Challenges in the New Millennium: The NEPAD Debate*, ed. 'Jìmí O. Adésínà, Yao Graham, and A. Olukoshi (Dakar: CODESRIA, Zed Books & UNISA Press, 2006), 207–34.

139. Hollis Chenery, Montek Ahluwalia et al., *Redistribution with Growth* (London: Oxford University Press for the World Bank and the Institute of Development Studies (Sussex), 1974); and Robert Ayers, *Banking on the Poor: The World Bank and World Poverty* (Cambridge, MA: MIT Press, 1983).

140. Kapur, "Conditionality and Its Alternatives", 35–37; and Anthony Bigio, "Social Funds and Reaching the Poor: Experiences and Future Directions" (Washington, DC: World Bank, 1988), 12. See also John Factora, "Poverty Reduction Support Credits (PRSC): A Stocktaking," in *Budget Support as More Effective Aid? Recent Experiences and Emerging Lessons* (Washington, DC: World Bank, 2006), 47–80.

141. For example, Anthony Payne, "Blair, Brown and the Gleneagles Agenda: Making Poverty History, or Confronting the Global Politics of Unequal Development?," *International Affairs* 82, no. 5 (2006): 917–35.

142. David Hulme, *Global Poverty: How Global Governance Is Failing the Poor* (New York: Routledge, 2010), 85.

143. Alan Whitworth and Tim Williamson, "Overview of Ugandan Economic Reform since 1986," in *Uganda's Economic Reforms: Insider Accounts*, ed. Florence Kuteesa et al. (Oxford: Oxford University Press, 2010), 15.

144. Anne Mette Kjaer and Fred Muhumuza, "The New Poverty Agenda in Uganda" (DIIS working paper 2009: 14, Danish Institute for International Studies, 2009), 11–12, https://www.ciaonet.org/attachments/15041/uploads; and Kenneth Mugambe, "The Poverty Eradication Action Plan," in *Uganda's Economic Reforms: Insider Accounts*, 158–60.

145. African Network on Debt and Development (AFRODAD), "Africa: Retracing the Path to Sustainability," in *The Reality of Aid 2002*, ed. Judith Randel et al. (Manila: IBON Books, 2002), 40–41; and Mugambe, "The Poverty Eradication Action Plan," 165.

146. Paolo de Renzio, Vitus Azeem, and Vivek Ramkumar, "Budget Monitoring as an Advocacy Tool: Uganda Debt Network," Case study for the research project "Lessons from Civil Society Budget Analysis and Advocacy Inititatives" [Namati (Legal Empowerment Network), Washington, DC, 2006], https://namati.org/resources/budget-monitoring-as-an-advocacy-tool-uganda-debt-network/.

147. Whitworth and Williamson, "Overview of Ugandan Economic Reform since 1986," 15.

148. Dilip Ratha et al., *Leveraging Migration for Africa: Remittances, Skills, and Investments* (Washington, DC: World Bank and the African Development Bank, 2011), 47, 51.

149. Assumpta Acam-Oturu, From "An Agony … A Resurrection," in *The New African Poetry: An Anthology*, ed. Tanure Ojaide and Tijan Sallah (Boulder: Lynne Rienner, 1999), 44.

## BIBLIOGRAPHY

Abegaz, Berhanu. "The Economics of Surplus Squeeze under Peripheral Socialism: An Ethiopian Illustration." *Studies in Comparative International Development* 23, no. 3 (1998): 51–77.

Adams, Nassau. *Worlds Apart: The North-South Divide and the International System.* London: Zed Books, 1993.

Adebajo, Adekeye, ed. *From Global Apartheid to Global Village: Africa and the United Nations.* Scottsville: University of KwaZuluNatal Press, 2009.

———. "Two Prophets of Regional Integration: Prebisch and Adedeji." In *International Development: Ideas, Experience, and Prospects*, edited by Bruce Currie-Alder, Ravi Kanbur, David Malone, and Rohinton Medhora, 323–38. Oxford: Oxford University Press, 2014.

Adedeji, Adebayo. "Transforming Africa's Economies." *Africa Report* 31, no. 3 (1986): 4–8.

———. "Structural Adjustment Policies in Africa." *International Social Science Journal* 51, no. 4 (1999): 218–521.

———. "The ECA: Forging a Future for Africa." In *Unity and Diversity in Development Ideas: Perspectives from the UN Regional Commissions*, edited by Yves Berthelot, 233–306. Bloomington: Indiana University Press, 2004.

Adésínà, 'Jìmí. "Development and the Challenge of Poverty: NEPAD, post-Washington Consensus and Beyond." In *Africa and Development Challenges in the New Millennium: The NEPAD Debate*, edited by 'Jìmí Adésínà, Yao Graham, and A. Olukoshi, 33–62. Dakar: CODESRIA, Zed Books and UNISA Press, 2006.

Ajayi, J.F. Ade. "Expectations of Independence." *Daedalus* 111, no. 2 (1982): 1–9.

Ake, Claude. *Democracy and Development in Africa.* Washington, DC: The Brookings Institution, 1996.

Akonor, Kwame. *African Economic Institutions.* London: Routledge, 2009.

Alemu, Zerihun Gudeta, Lukas Oosthuizen, and H. D. van Schalwyk. "Agricultural Development Policies of Ethiopia Since 1957." *South African Journal of Economic History* 17, no. 1–2 (2002): 1–24.

Ali, Ali Abdel Gadir. "The Rediscovery of the African Alternative Framework to Structural Adjustment Programmes." In *African Development in the 21st Century: Adebayo Adedeji's Theories and Contributions*, edited by Amos Sawyer, Afeikhena Jerome, and Ejeviome Eloho Otobo, 29–52. Trenton, NJ: Africa World Press, 2015.

Amani, Haidari, Samuel Wangwe, Dennis Rweyemamu, Rose Aiko, and Godwill Wanga. "Understanding Economic and Political Reform in Tanzania." In *Understanding Economic Reforms in Africa: A Tale of Seven Nations*, edited by Joseph Mensah, 205–36. Houndmills: Palgrave Macmillan, 2006.

Anheier, Helmut. "Private Voluntary Organizations and the Third World: The Case of Africa." In *The Third Sector: Comparative Studies in Nonprofit Organizations*, edited by Helmut Anheier and Wolfgang Seibel, 361–76. Berlin: de Gruyter, 1990.

Arndt, Channing, Henning Tarp Jensen, and Finn Tarp. "Stabilization and Structural Adjustment in Mozambique: An Appraisal." *Journal of International Development* 12, no. 3 (2000): 299–323.

Aw, Djibril, and Geert Diemer. *"Making a Large Irrigation Scheme Work: A Case Study from Mali."* Directions in Development No. 31672, IBRD, Washington, DC, 2005.

Ayers, Robert. *Banking on the Poor: The World Bank and World Poverty.* Cambridge, MA: MIT Press, 1983.

Baker, Jonathan. "Oil and African Development." *Journal of Modern African Studies* 15, no. 2 (1977): 175–212.

Ball, Nicole. "Drought and Dependence in the Sahel." *International Journal of Health Services* 8, no. 2 (1978): 271–98.

Bartke, Wolfgang. *China's Economic Aid.* Delhi: Vikas Publishing for the Institute of Asian Affairs (Hamburg), 1975.

Bjerk, Paul. "Sovereignty and Socialism in Tanzania: The Historiography of an African State." *History in Africa* 37 (2010): 275–319.

Bonnick, Gladstone. *Zambia Country Assistance Review: Turning an Economy Around.* Washington, DC: World Bank, 1997.

Borton, John, and Edward Clay. "The African Food Crisis of 1982–1986." *Disasters* 10, no. 4 (1986): 258–72.

Braveboy-Wagner, Jacqueline Anne. *Institutions of the Global South.* London: Routledge, 2009.

Busby, Joshua William. "Bono Made Jesse Helms Cry: Jubilee 2000, Debt Relief, and Moral Action in International Politics." *International Studies Quarterly* 51, no. 2 (2007): 247–75.

Carmody, Pádraig. "Constructing Alternatives to Structural Adjustment in Africa." *Review of African Political Economy* 25, no. 75 (1998): 25–46.

Chazan, Naomi, Peter Lewis, Robert Mortimer, Donald Rothchild, and Stephen John Stedman. *Politics and Society in Contemporary Africa*, 3rd ed. Boulder: Lynne Rienner, 1999.

Clark, Paul. *Development Planning in East Africa.* Nairobi: East African Publishing House for the Makerere Institute of Social Research, 1965.

Cohen, John. "Rural Change in Ethiopia: The Chilalo Agricultural Development Unit." *Economic Development and Cultural Change* 22, no. 4 (1974): 580–614.

———. *Integrated Rural Development: The Ethiopian Experience and the Debate.* Uppsala: The Scandinavian Institute of African Studies, 1987.

Cohen, John, and Nils-Ivar Isaksson. "Villagisation in Ethiopia's Arsi Region." *Journal of Modern African Studies* 25, no. 3 (1987): 435–64.

Combes, Jean-Louis, and Tahsin Saadi-Sedik. "How Does Trade Openness Influence Budget Deficits in Developing Countries?" *Journal of Development Studies* 42, no. 8 (2006): 1401–16.

Costello, Matthew. "Market and State: Evaluating Tanzania's Program of State-Led Industrialization." *World Development* 22, no. 10 (1994): 1511–20.

Culpeper, Roy. *Forced Adjustment: The Export Collapse of Sub-Saharan Africa.* Ottawa: North-South Institute, 1987.

Dadzie, Kenneth. "The UN and the Problem of Economic Development." In *United Nations, Divided World: The UN's Roles in International Relations*, edited by Adam Roberts and Benedict Kingsbury, 297–326. Oxford: Clarendon Press, 1993.

de Vries, Margaret Garritsen. *The IMF in a Changing World 1945–85*. Washington, DC: International Monetary Fund, 1986.

de Waal, Alex. *Famine Crimes: Politics and the Disaster Relief Industry in Africa*. Oxford: African Rights, The International African Institute, James Currey and Indiana University Press, 1997.

de Wilde, John. *Experiences with Agricultural Development in Tropical Africa*. Translated by A. Guinard et al. Vol. 2: *The Case Studies*. Baltimore: Johns Hopkins University Press for the IBRD, 1967.

Deaton, Angus. "Commodity Prices and Growth in Africa." *Journal of Economic Perspectives* 13, no. 3 (1999): 23–40.

Donkor, Kwabena. *Structural Adjustment and Mass Poverty in Ghana*. Aldershot: Ashgate, 1997.

Easterly, William. "*The Effect of International Monetary Fund and World Bank Programs on Poverty*." Policy Research Working Paper No. 2517, World Bank, Washington, DC, January 2001.

———. "What Did Structural Adjustment Adjust? The Association of Policies and Growth with Repeated IMF and World Bank Adjustment Loans." *Journal of Development Economics* 76, no. 1 (2005): 1–22.

Easterly, William, and Ross Levine. "Africa's Growth Tragedy: Policies and Ethnic Divisions." *Quarterly Journal of Economics* 112, no. 4 (1997): 1203–50.

Esseks, John. "The Food Outlook for the Sahel: Regaining Self-Sufficiency or Continuing Dependence on International Aid?" *Africa Today* 22, no. 2 (1975): 45–56.

Factora, John. "Poverty Reduction Support Credits (PRSC): A Stocktaking." In *Budget Support as More Effective Aid? Recent Experiences and Emerging Lessons*, 47–80. Washington DC: World Bank, 2006.

Falola, Toyin. *Development Planning and Decolonization in Nigeria*. Gainsville: University Press of Florida, 1996.

Fieldhouse, David K. *Black Africa, 1945–1980: Economic Decolonization and Arrested Development*. London: Allen & Unwin, 1986.

Finlayson, Jock, and Mark Zacher. "International Trade Institutions and the North/South Dialogue." *International Journal* 36, no. 4 (1981): 732–65.

Fisher, Bart. *The International Coffee Agreement: A Study in Coffee Diplomacy*. New York: Praeger Publishers, 1972.

Frankel, S. Herbert. "United Nations Primer for Development." *Quarterly Journal of Economics* 66, no. 3 (1952): 301–26.

Gedamu, Tekalign. "Economic Planning in Africa." *Africa Today* 10, no. 9 (1963): 30–34.

Godfrey, Asiimwe. *The Impact of Post-Colonial Policy Shifts in Coffee Marketing at the Local Level in Uganda: A Case Study of Mukono District, 1962–1998*. Maastricht: Shaker Publishing, 2002.

Goldsmith, Arthur. "Foreign Aid and Statehood in Africa." *International Organization* 55, no. 1 (2001): 123–48.

Goldstein, Joshua, Xiaoming Huang, and Burcu Akan. "Energy in the World Economy, 1950–1992." *International Studies Quarterly* 41, no. 2 (1997): 241–66.

Gordon-Ashworth, Fiona. *International Commodity Control: A Contemporary History and Appraisal*. London: Croon Helm, 1984.

Grant, Richard, and John Agnew. "Representing Africa: The Geography of Africa in World Trade, 1960–92." *Annals of the Association of American Geographers* 86, no. 4 (1996): 729–44.

Green, Reginald. "Four African Development Plans: Ghana, Kenya, Nigeria and Tanzania." *Journal of Modern African Studies* 3, no. 2 (1965): 249–79.

———. "Uganda's Plan for Growth and Development: An Analysis of and Preliminary Reflections on Work for Progress." EDRP No. 103, Institute for Development Studies, University of Sussex, Brighton, 1966.

———. "The Treaty for East African Co-operation: A Summary and Interpretation." *Journal of Modern African Studies* 5, no. 3 (1967): 414–19.

———. "A Cloth Untrue: The Evolution of Structural Adjustment in Sub-Saharan Africa." *Journal of International Affairs* 52, no. 1 (1998): 207–32.

Grischow, Jeff, and Glenn McKnight. "Rhyming Development: Practising Post-development in Colonial Ghana and Uganda." *Journal of Historical Sociology* 16, no. 4 (2003): 517–49.

Gurr, Ted Robert, ed. *Minorities at Risk: A Global View of Ethnopolitical Conflicts*. Washington, DC: United States Institute for Peace Press, 1993.

Harrigan, Jane, and Hamed El-Said. *Aid and Power in the Arab World: IMF and World Bank Policy-Based Lending in the Middle East and North Africa*. Houndmills: Palgrave Macmillan, 2009.

Hazbun, Waleed. "Images of Openness, Spaces of Control: The Politics of Tourism Development in Tunisia." *Arab Studies Journal* 15/16, no. 2/1 (2007): 10–35.

Hazelton, Ralph. *"Diamonds: Forever or for Good? The Economic Impact of Diamonds in Southern Africa."* Diamonds and Human Security Project Occasional Paper #3, Partnership Africa Canada, Ottawa, 2002.

Heasman, Kathleen. "Women and Community Development in Kenya and Uganda." *Community Development Journal* 1, no. 4 (1966): 16–22.

Helleiner, Gerald. "The IMF and Africa in the 1980s." Essays in International Finance No. 152. Princeton, NJ: Princeton University, 1983.

———. "The Impact of the Exchange Rate System on the Developing Countries." In *The New Global Economy and the Developing Countries: Essays in International Economics and Development*, edited by Gerald Helleiner, 75–101. Aldershot: Edward Elgar, 1990.

———. "From Adjustment to Development in Sub-Saharan Africa: Consensus and Continuing Conflict." In *From Adjustment to Development in Africa: Conflict, Controversy, Convergence, Consensus?* edited by Giovanni Andrea Cornia and Gerald Helleiner, 3–24. Houndmills: Macmillan, 1994.

Henry, Clement. "Algeria's Agonies: Oil Rent Effects in a Bunker State." *Journal of North African Studies* 9, no. 2 (2004): 68–81.

Hillbom, Ellen. "Diamonds or Development? A Structural Assessment of Botswana's Forty Years of Success." *Journal of Modern African Studies* 46, no. 2 (2008): 191–214.

Hodge, Joseph M. *Triumph of the Expert: Agrarian Doctrines of Development and the Legacies of British Colonialism*. Athens, OH: Ohio University Press, 2007.

Hulme, David. *Global Poverty: How Global Governance Is Failing the Poor*. New York: Routledge, 2010.

Hydén, Göran. *Beyond Ujamaa in Tanzania: Underdevelopment and an Uncaptured Peasantry.* Berkeley: University of California Press, 1980.

Ikpe, Eno Blankson. "Migration, Starvation and Humanitarian Intervention during the Nigerian Civil War." *Lagos Historical Review* 1 (2001): 84–96.

Irele, Abiola. "The Political Kingdom: Toward Reconstruction in Africa." *Socialism and Democracy* 21, no. 3 (2007): 5–35.

Johnson, Chalmers. "The Developmental State: Odyssey of a Concept." In *The Developmental State*, edited by Meredith Woo-Cumings, 32–60. Ithaca, NY: Cornell University Press, 1999.

Johnson Sirleaf, Ellen. *This Child Will Be Great: Memoir of a Remarkable Life by Africa's First Woman President.* New York: HarperCollins, 2009.

Kapur, Devesh. "Conditionality and Its Alternatives." In *The IMF and the World Bank at Sixty*, edited by Ariel Buria. London: Anthem Press, 2005.

Kapur, Devesh, John Lewis, and Richard Webb. *The World Bank: Its First Half Century.* Vol. 1 *History.* Washington, DC: Brookings Institution Press, 1997.

Killick, Tony. "Trends in Development Economics and Their Relevance to Africa." *Journal of Modern African Studies* 18, no. 3 (1980): 367–86.

———. *IMF Programmes in Developing Countries: Design and Impact.* London: Routledge, 1995.

Killick, Tony, Ramani Gunatilaka, and Ana Marr. *Aid and the Political Economy of Policy Change.* London: Routledge, 1998.

Kjaer, Anne Mette, and Fred Muhumuza. *"The New Poverty Agenda in Uganda."* DIIS Working Paper 2009: 14, Danish Institute for International Studies, Copenhagen, 2009.

Klitgaard, Robert. *Tropical Gangsters: One Man's Experience with Development and Decadence in Deepest Africa.* New York: Basic Books, 1990.

Kothari, Uma. "From Colonialism to Development: Reflections of Former Colonial Officers." *Commonwealth and Comparative Politics* 44, no. 1 (2006): 118–36.

Krueger, Anne. "The Need for Policy Reform." In *Economic Policy Reform in Developing Countries*, 1–58. Oxford: Blackwell, 1992.

Kuteesa, Florence, Emmanuel Tumusiime-Mutebile, Alan Whitworth, and Tim Williamson, eds. *Uganda's Economic Reforms: Insider Accounts.* Oxford: Oxford University Press, 2010.

Lal, Priya. "Militants, Mothers, and the National Family: *Ujamaa*, Gender, and Rural Development in Postcolonial Tanzania." *Journal of African History* 51, no. 1 (2010): 1–20.

Lele, Uma. "The MADIA Countries: Aid Inflows, Endowments, Policies, and Performance." In *Aid to African Agriculture: Lessons from Two Decades of Donors' Experiences*, edited by Uma Lele, 14–106. Washington, DC: Johns Hopkins University Press for the World Bank, 1991.

Leys, Colin. "African Economic Development in Theory and Practice." *Daedalus* 111, no. 2 (1982): 99–124.

Lowi, Miriam. "Oil Rents and Political Breakdown in Patrimonial States: Algeria in Comparative Perspective." *Journal of North African Studies* 9, no. 3 (2004): 83–102.

Loxley, John. "The IMF, the World Bank, and Sub-Saharan Africa: Policies and Politics." In *The IMF and the World Bank in Africa*, edited by Kjell Havnevik, 47–63. Uppsala: Scandinavian Institute of African Studies, 1987.

———. "Structural Adjustment in Africa: Reflections on Ghana and Zambia." *Review of African Political Economy*, no. 47 (1990): 8–27.

———. *Ghana: The Long Road to Recovery, 1983–1990*. Ottawa: North-South Institute, 1991.

Maizels, Alfred. "Commodities in Crisis: An Overview of the Main Issues." *World Development* 15, no. 5 (1987): 537–49.

———. "The Continuing Commodity Crisis of Developing Countries." *World Development* 22, no. 11 (1994): 1685–95.

Martin, Guy. *African Political Thought*. New York: Palgrave Macmillan, 2012.

Mazrui, Ali A. "Elements of the New Africa." *Index on Censorship* 21, no. 4 (1992): 9, 22.

McGowan, Patrick. "African military coups d'état, 1956–2001: frequency, trends and distribution." *Journal of Modern African Studies* 41, no. 3 (2003): 339–70.

Mengisteab, K., and B. Ikubolajeh Logan, eds. *Beyond Economic Liberalization in Africa: Structural Adjustment and the Alternatives*. London: Zed Books, 1995.

Mingst, Karen. "Inter-organizational Politics: The World Bank and the African Development Bank." *Review of International Studies* 13, no. 4 (1987): 281–93.

Mkandawire, Thandika. "Adjustment, Political Conditionality and Democratisation in Africa." In *From Adjustment to Development in Africa: Conflict, Controversy, Convergence, Consensus?* edited by Giovanni Andrea Cornia and Gerald Helleiner, 155–73. Houndmills: Macmillan Press, 1994.

———. "Thinking About Developmental States in Africa." *Cambridge Journal of Economics* 25, no. 3 (2001): 289–314.

———. "Maladjusted African Economies and Globalisation." *Africa Development* 30, no. 1–2 (2005): 1–33.

Mkandawire, Thandika, and Charles Soludo. *Our Continent, Our Future: African Perspectives on Structural Adjustment*. Trenton, NJ: Africa World Press for CODESRIA and IDRC, 1999.

Mongula, Benedict. "Development Theory and Changing Trends in Sub-Saharan African Economies 1960–89." In *African Perspectives on Development*, edited by Ulf Himmelstrand, Kabiru Kinyanjui, and Edward Mburugu, 84–96. London: James Currey, 1994.

Mosley, Paul, Jane Harrigan, and John Toye. *Aid and Power: The World Bank and Policy-based Lending*. 2nd ed. Vol. 1: *Analysis and Policy Proposals*. New York: Routledge, 1995.

Murphy, Craig. *The Emergence of the NIEO Ideology*. Boulder: Westview Press, 1984.

Naylor, Phillip. *France and Algeria: A History of Decolonization and Transformation*. Gainesville: University Press of Florida, 2000.

Nyerere, Julius K. *Freedom and Development/Uhuru na Maendeleo: A Selection from Writings and Speeches, 1968–1973*. London: Oxford University Press, 1973.

Oloya, J.J. "Marketing Boards and Post-War Economic Development Policy in Uganda, 1945–1962." *Indian Journal of Agricultural Economics* 23 (1968): 50–58.

Omar, Saleh. "Arab Nationalism: A Retrospective Evaluation." *Arab Studies Quarterly* 14, no. 4 (1992): 23–37.

p'Bitek, Okot. "Indigenous Ills." *Transition* No. 75/76 (1997/1967 reprint): 40–42.

Parfitt, Trevor. "The Lomé Convention and the New International Order." *Review of African Political Economy* no. 22 (1981): 85–95.

Payne, Anthony. "Blair, Brown and the Gleneagles Agenda: Making Poverty History, or Confronting the Global Politics of Unequal Development?" *International Affairs* 82, no. 5 (2006): 917–35.

Poirier, Robert. "Tourism and Development in Tunisia." *Annals of Tourism Research* 22, no. 1 (1995): 157–71.

Prebish, Raúl. "Two Decades After." In *UNCTAD and The South-North Dialogue: The First Twenty Years*, edited by Michael Zammit Cutajar, 3–9. Oxford: Pergamon Press, 1985.

Ranis, Gustav. "Debt, Adjustment and Development." In *Economic Development and World Debt*, edited by Hans Singer and Soumitra Sharma, 227–38. New York: St. Martin's Press, 1989.

Rapley, John. *Understanding Development: Theory and Practice in the Third World*, 3rd ed. Boulder: Lynne Rienner, 2007.

Rasheed, Sadig, and Eshetu Chole. "Human Development: An African Perspective." Occasional Paper No. 17, Human Development Report Office, United Nations Development Programme, New York, 1994.

Ratha, Dilip, Sanket Mohapatra, Çaglar Özden, Sonia Plaza, William Shaw, and Abebe Shimeles. *Leveraging Migration for Africa: Remittances, Skills, and Investments*. Washington, DC: World Bank and the African Development Bank, 2011.

Riddell, Roger, and Lawrence Cockcroft. "Foreign Direct Investment." In *African External Finance in the 1990s*, edited by Ishrat Husain and John Underwood, 139–50. Washington, DC: The World Bank, 1991.

Rodrik, Dani. "Where Did All the Growth Go? External Shocks, Social Conflict, and Growth Collapses." *Journal of Economic Growth* 4, no. 4 (1999): 385–412.

Rosenstein-Rodan, Paul. "International Aid for Underdeveloped Countries." *Review of Economics and Statistics* 43, no. 2 (1961): 107–38.

Sala-i-Martin, Xavier, and Arvind Subramanian. "Addressing the Natural Resource Curse: An Illustration from Nigeria." *Journal of African Economies* 22, no. 4 (2012): 570–615.

Sandbrook, Richard. "Origins of the Democratic Developmental State: Interrogating Mauritius." *Canadian Journal of African Studies* 39, no. 3 (2005): 549–81.

Sapsford, David, and Hans Singer. "The IMF, the World Bank and Commodity Prices: A Case of Shifting Sands?" *World Development* 26, no. 9 (1998): 1653–60.

Savadogo, Kimseyinga, and Claude Wetta. "The Impact of Self-Imposed Adjustment: The Case of Burkina Faso, 1983–1989." Special Series: Structural Adjustment in Sub-Saharan Africa, UNICEF International Child Development Centre, Florence, 1991.

Schultheis, Michael. "The Ugandan Economy and General Amin, 1971–1974." *Studies in Comparative International Development* 10, no. 3 (1975): 3–34.

Seers, Dudley. *The Political Economy of Nationalism*. Oxford: Oxford University Press, 1983.

Seshamani, Venkatesh. "Zambia." In *The Human Dimensions of Africa's Persistent Economic Crisis*, edited by Adebayo Adedeji, Sadig Rasheed, and Melody Morrison, 104–23. London: Hans Zell for the UNECA, 1990.

Sheets, Hal, and Roger Morris. *Disaster in the Desert: Failures of International Relief in the West African Drought, Humanitarian Policy Studies*. Washington, DC: Carnegie Endowment for International Peace, 1974.

Shen, T. Y. "Macro Development Planning in Tropical Africa: Technocratic and non-Technocratic Causes of Failure." *Journal of Development Studies* 13, no. 4 (1977): 413–27.

Shivji, Issa. "Nationalism and pan-Africanism: Decisive Moments in Nyerere's Intellectual and Political Thought." *Review of African Political Economy* 39, no. 131 (2012): 103–16.

Sicking, Louis. "A Colonial Echo: France and the Colonial Dimension of the European Economic Community." *French Colonial History* 5 (2004): 207–28.

Sireau, Nicolas. *Make Poverty History: Political Communication in Action.* Houndmills: Palgrave Macmillan, 2009.

Sisaye, Seleshi, and Eileen Stommes. "Agricultural Development in Ethiopia: Government Budgeting and Development Assistance in the pre and post 1975 Periods." *Journal of Development Studies* 16, no. 2 (1980): 156–85.

Soludo, Charles Chukwuma. "In Search of Alternative Analytical and Methodological Frameworks for an African Economic Development Model." In *African Voices on Structural Adjustment*, edited by Thandika Mkandawire and Charles Soludo, 17–72. Trenton, NJ: Africa World Press for CODESRIA and IDRC, 2003.

Southall, Aidan. "Social Disorganisation in Uganda: Before, during, and after Amin." *Journal of Modern African Studies* 18, no. 4 (1980): 627–56.

Stokke, Olav. *The UN and Development: From Aid to Cooperation.* Bloomington: Indiana University Press, 2009.

Strange, Susan. *Mad Money: When Markets Outgrow Governments.* Ann Arbor: University of Michigan Press, 1998.

Stremlau, John. *The International Politics of the Nigerian Civil War, 1967–1970.* Princeton: Princeton University Press, 1977.

Tadria, Hilda Mary. "Uganda Women's Organizations: Their Contribution towards Raising Uganda's Standard of Living." *Africa Spectrum* 8, no. 2 (1973): 217–26.

Taylor, Ian. "The Developmental State in Africa: The Case of Botswana." In *The Potentiality of 'Developmental States' in Africa: Botswana and Uganda Compared*, edited by Pamela Mbabazi and Ian Taylor, 44–56. Dakar: CODESRIA, 2005.

Taylor, Lance. *Varieties of Stabilization Experience.* Oxford: Clarendon Press, 1988.

Torry, William. "Social Science Research on Famine: A Critical Evaluation." *Human Ecology* 12, no. 3 (1984): 227–52.

Verwimp, Philip. "The Political Economy of Coffee, Dictatorship, and Genocide." *European Journal of Political Economy* 19, no. 2 (2003): 161–81.

Walker, Peter, and Daniel Maxwell. *Shaping the Humanitarian World.* London: Routledge, 2009.

Williams, Tracy. "*An African Success Story: Ghana's Cocoa Marketing System.*" Working Paper 318, Institute for Development Studies, University of Sussex, Brighton, 2009.

Williamson, John. "A Short History of the Washington Consensus." In *The Washington Consensus Reconsidered: Towards a New Global Governance*, edited by Narcis Serra and Joseph Stiglitz, 14–30. Oxford: Oxford University Press, 2008.

Wood, Robert. *From Marshall Plan to Debt Crisis: Foreign Aid and Development Choices in the World Economy.* Berkeley: University of California Press, 1986.

Young, Crawford. *Ideology and Development in Africa.* New Haven: Yale University Press, 1982.

Young, Crawford, Neal Sherman, and Tim Rose. *Cooperatives and Development: Agricultural Politics in Ghana and Uganda.* Madison: University of Wisconsin Press, 1981.

Young, Roger, and John Loxley. *Zambia: An Assessment of Zambia's Structural Adjustment Experience*, rev. ed. Ottawa: The North-South Institute, 1990.

Zewde, Bahru. *Pioneers of Change in Ethiopia: The Reformist Intellectuals of the Early Twentieth Century.* Oxford: James Currey, Ohio University Press, Addis Ababa University, 2002.

Zulu, Justin, and Saleh Nsouli. *"Adjustment Programs in Africa: The Recent Experience."* Occasional Paper No. 34, International Monetary Fund, Washington, DC, 1985.

# CHAPTER 37

# African Diasporas and Postcolonial Africa

## Kwasi Konadu

In recent decades, research on a narrowly constituted 'African diaspora' has given way to an increasingly expanded focus on multifarious diasporic communities in Africa, Eurasia, and the Americas.[1] State and economic crises, military rule, civil war, natural disasters, violence and oppression, desires for belonging and home(land), and potential economic opportunities (for both incoming and outgoing migrants) have all shaped African diasporas spawned in the 'postcolonial' moment. In light of the circuits of movement and reconstitution, the forms of violence (economic, political, and 'ethnic') that animated the colonial state and that underpin ongoing diasporas have stubbornly endured in the present, making the 'postcolonial' moment a meaningless marker indexing how Africans moved through historical time. Those circuits, instead, belong to an elongated historical process rather than a 'postcolonial'

---

[1] On the definition of the "African diaspora," see: Brent H. Edwards, "The Uses of Diaspora," *Social Text* 19, no. 1 (2001), 45–73; Colin A. Palmer, "Defining and Studying the Modern African Diaspora," *Journal of African American History* 85, no. 1–2 (2000), 27–32; Joseph E. Harris, ed., *Global Dimensions of the African Diaspora* (Washington, DC: Howard University Press, 1993); Kim Butler, "Defining Diaspora, Refining a Discourse," *Diaspora* 10, no. 2 (2002): 189–219. For a standard, narrative account (in all its bewildering details), see Patrick Manning, *The African Diaspora: A History through Culture* (New York: Columbia University Press, 2009). On the African diaspora contextualized as a "migration," see Tiffany R. Patterson and Robin D. G. Kelley, "Unfinished Migrations: Reflections on the African Diaspora and the Making of the Modern World," *African Studies Review* 43, no. 1 (2000): 11–45.

---

K. Konadu (✉)
The City University of New York, New York, NY, USA

© The Author(s) 2018
M.S. Shanguhyia and T. Falola (eds.),
*The Palgrave Handbook of African Colonial and Postcolonial History*,
https://doi.org/10.1057/978-1-137-59426-6_37

moment, where intra-African movement remains just as dynamic as that of those who move and resettle beyond the borders of continental Africa and its offshore island-states. To be sure, the influx and outflow of individuals to, from, and within Africa have multiple geneses, but these movements must be understood within the historiography of African diasporas and within the specific contexts that help explain departures and arrivals, sources and destinations. This chapter discusses two of the more recent and significant trends in diasporic approaches to African history, and makes a case for addressing methodological and other shortcomings inherent in those trends, in terms of approaches in the field of African history that might engender an African world perspective and practice.

Conventional accounts of the 'African diaspora' in African historiography view Africa as bounded unto itself and as an imaginary source for its diasporic folk to draw upon in their (re)imagined selves and communities.[2] According to this view, there is only Africa *and* the diaspora. The conjunction 'and' envisages diasporic movement and community formation as something that has (and continues) to occur *outside* of continental Africa. Rarely do such accounts consider diasporic movement and community making *within* Africa writ large. It is precisely out of this framework that we have been held captive to binary debates about the continuity or creolization of African cultures, about imagined communities and invented identities, about diaspora as principally a return or reconnection to Africa, and about the relationship between Africa and African America, docked in their impervious hemispheres. Within this framework, a fashionable lexicon populates its universe: hybridity, creolization, cosmopolitanism, (re)invention, imagination, and (Black) Atlantic. Unsurprisingly, there exists a clear asymmetry in knowledge production (where Atlantic diasporas have received far more scholarly attention than Indian Ocean or Mediterranean or Eurasian varieties) in addition to the global and chronological breadth of African diasporas reduced to a singularly constituted 'African diaspora', itself a shorthand for the fashionable but defective 'Atlantic creole' and 'black' Atlantic conceptualizations of diaspora.

---

[2]Giles Mohan and A. B. Zack-Williams have rightfully lamented, "African Studies has retained its generalist colonial (and neo-imperial) features and resolutely sees Africa as a self-contained continent." See Giles Mohan and A. B. Zack-Williams, "Globalisation from below: Conceptualising the Role of the African Diasporas in Africa's Development," *Review of African Political Economy* 29, no. 92 (2002): 213. For the most recent statement of the conventional view, see: John Parker, "The African Diaspora," in *The Oxford Handbook of Modern African History*, ed., John Parker and Richard Reid (New York: Oxford University Press, 2013), 132–48; John Parker and Richard Rathbone, *African History: A Very Short Introduction* (New York: Oxford University Press, 2007), 32–37, 82–86. For more on so-called "imagined" identities, see Sidney J. Lemelle and Robin D. G. Kelley, *Imagining Home: Class, Culture and Nationalism in the African Diaspora* (New York: Verso, 1994), and, on the African side of the Atlantic equation, see V.Y. Mudimbe's *The Invention of Africa* (Bloomington: Indiana University Press, 1988) and *The Idea of Africa* (Bloomington: Indiana University Press, 1994).

## Atlantic Creoles: Creolization
## in the Atlantic Diaspora and Africa

Though the concept of 'Atlantic creoles' came out of linguistics in the late 1960s and 1970s, especially Ian Hancock's work around 'Negro English' of West Africa and the Americas, the current iteration of the concept was adopted by North American scholars who fell in love with the postmodernist ideas of 'hybridity', 'fluidity', or 'plasticity' as applied to cultures and identities.[3] Chief among the targets of these postmodernists are the ideas of race and 'blackness', both squarely rooted in the politics of knowledge and in the cauldron of US racial politics and violence. To many scholars, 'blackness' is a commodity that is fluid and permeable, though without the distinct burden of 'living-while-black'. A survey of the literature reveals an increased use of the terms 'creole' and 'creolization' during the very height of the Black Power movement and the use of 'Africa' in the 1960s and 1970s, but a sharp downward trend in the use of 'Africa' in the late 1970s and the equally steep over-the-cliff descent in 'Black Power' by 1980. What does this mean? Scholars peddling the 'creolization' idea (as a framing device) were pushing back ideologically against what they perceived as Black Power interpretations of and claims to African cultural history and identity. The year 1980, not surprisingly, witnessed a parallel but sharp rise in the use of 'creole' and 'creolization', peaking in the late 1990s and into the early 2000s.[4] The normative skill set and lives of most Africans, with or without contact with Europeans, constituted a history for which scholars deeply shaped by the politics of knowledge and race in twentieth-century North America were not writing about. Instead, their preoccupations with the present moment framed narratives of a past in which the key categories and logic at play had little to do with the African lives at stake.

In the early twentieth century, the idea of 'acculturation' occupied the intellectual space that 'creole' and 'creolization' would assume. Both the category of creole and the process of creolization took off during the socio-political context of the 1960s, and both were shaped by white anthropologists working on 'black people' at the nexus of Africa and the Americas. Between the publications of *The American Negro: A Study in Racial Crossing* (1928), *Acculturation: The Study of Culture Contact* (1938), and the

---

[3] See e.g. Ian F Hancock, "A Provisional List of English-based Atlantic Creoles," *African Language Review* 8 (1969): 7–72; idem, *The Relationship of Black Vernacular English to the Atlantic Creoles* (Austin: African and Afro-American Studies and Research Center, University of Texas at Austin, 1978).

[4] I have used Google's Ngram Viewer (https://books.google.com/ngrams), an online graphing tool, that shows the usage or trend of a word or phrase by searching over 5 million books, or some 500 billion words, published in North American English (and other languages) between the years 1500 and 2010. My Ngram search settled on the years between 1900 and 2010, using the terms "creole," "creolization," "Black Power," and "Africa."

*Myth of the Negro Past* (1941), anthropologist Melville J. Herskovits became the 'authority' on African and African diasporic affairs and on race in North America. Though W.E.B. Du Bois's trilogy (*The Negro* [1915], *Black Folk: Then and Now* [1939], and *The World and Africa* [1946]) and Carter G. Woodson's *The Negro in our History* (1922) covered much of the ground on which Herskovits's 'authority' rested, it was Herskovits's ideas about race and culture that came to shape the study of Africa and its diasporas. It is no surprise Herskovits had an adversarial relationship with leading intellectuals such as Du Bois and Woodson. Herskovits feuded with Woodson and, through his influence amongst corporate funders and politicians, he sabotaged Du Bois's *Encyclopedia Africana* project. (Herskovits considered Du Bois's project an instrument of 'racial uplift' propaganda.[5]) Armed with the financial and political means to control the study of Africa and its Atlantic diasporas, Herskovits institutionalized his ideas of race and culture (framed around African studies) through the African Studies program established at Northwestern University in 1948 and the African Studies Association (ASA) founded in 1957.[6] To be sure, Herskovits built his ideas of race and culture around interracial ideals shaped by the racial politics of US society. In spite of Herskovits's later attention to African cultural 'retentions', his linear and teleological conception of acculturation was to be understood as 'Negro acculturation to European patterns'.[7] Other anthropologists working in the turbulent decades of the 1960s and 1970s, notably Sidney Mintz and Richard Price, assumed much of the content and context of Herskovits's work on acculturation, replacing it with a linguistic brand of 'creolization' that served to 'underemphasize the African past' in the study of African cultures in the Americas.[8]

In *Anthropological Approach to the Afro-American Past: A Caribbean Perspective* (1972–1973), Mintz and Price stipulated their essay was written 'in the immediate aftermath of the Civil Rights [and Black Power] struggle and the swift establishment of Afro-American and Black Studies programs in U.S. universities'. The provocation, then, for the essay was 'certain polarizations emerging

---

[5] Jerry Gershenhorn, *Melville J. Herskovits and the Racial Politics of Knowledge* (Lincoln: University of Nebraska Press, 2004), 106–7, 147–56.

[6] Readers need to be reminded or made aware that the first African Studies Program in the USA was founded at Fisk University in Tennessee in 1943 with the help of linguist Lorenzo Turner, and the first such program to grant a Bachelor's and Master's degree was the one at Howard University in 1954. See Margaret Wade-Lewis, *Lorenzo Dow Turner: Father of Gullah Studies* (Columbia: University of South Carolina Press, 2007), 140.

[7] Melville J. Herskovits, *The Myth of the Negro Past* (New York: Harper & Brothers, 1941), 114; Gershenhorn, *Herskovits*, 65.

[8] Sidney W. Mintz and Richard Price, *Anthropological Approach to the Afro-American Past: A Caribbean Perspective* (Philadelphia: Institute for the Study of Human Issues, 1976), reprinted (with a new preface) as *The Birth of African-American Culture: An Anthropological Perspective* (Boston: Beacon, 1992), 95 n. 16.

in Afro-American Studies' such as 'ideological preoccupations might deflect the scholarly quest'.[9] In the 1960s, African and African diasporic scholars fought to interrogate the reigning paradigms and personnel exercising hegemony over the study of Africa(ns) and its worldwide diasporas. This intellectual fight erupted in the very organization Herskovits helped establish (the ASA) at Montreal in 1969 and in elite (historically white) universities such as Northwestern, Cornell, and Columbia.[10] When the aforementioned hegemony and the subjugation of (diasporic) African claims to African studies were challenged in 1969, entrenched stakeholders in ASA framed the issue as one of 'untrammeled scholarly inquiry' with respect to whites studying Africa against 'black interests' driven by 'strong emotion' and 'progressive politics'.[11] Nothing short of invoking Herskovits's spirit, ASA stakeholders had no ambiguity about what was at stake; 'the future of African studies in the United States'.[12] The intellectual ownership of a discipline and a continent were also at stake, and so those principally white stakeholders in elite US universities and in the US State Department acted as Herskovits did against Du Bois and Woodson, ceding little control in the study of the African world. In response, some African and diasporic African scholars created their own professional organizations (e.g. the African Studies Heritage Association and the National Council of Black Studies) and established several African/a studies programs, departments, and centers at principally white universities and colleges. These individuals were the targets of Mintz and Price. Both anthropologists assumed their posture against such 'black interests' with abiding 'ideological preoccupations' would not expose their own 'ideological preoccupations', namely propagating a 'miracle of creolization' theology in a society where Americanization was the end game and where Africans were destined to acculturate to 'European patterns'.[13] Insofar as Mintz and Price's essay 'built on and extended

[9] Mintz and Price, *Birth of African-American Culture*, iv.

[10] Among others, see Iris Berger, "Contested Boundaries: African Studies Approaching the Millennium," *African Studies Review* 40, no. 2 (1997): 1–14. On the Black Studies/Power protest movement on historically white colleges and universities, see: Joy Ann Williamson, *Black Power on Campus: The University of Illinois, 1965–75* (Urbana: University of Illinois Press, 2003); Noliwe M. Rooks, *White Money/Black Power: The Surprising History of African American Studies and the Crisis of Race in Higher Education* (Boston: Beacon Press, 2006); Fabio Rojas, *From Black Power to Black Studies: How a Radical Social Movement Became an Academic Discipline* (Baltimore: Johns Hopkins University Press, 2007); Stefan M. Bradley, *Harlem vs. Columbia University: Black Student Power in the Late 1960s* (Urbana: University of Illinois Press, 2009); Ibram X. Kendi, *The Black Campus Movement: Black Students and the Racial Reconstitution of Higher Education, 1965–1972* (New York: Palgrave Macmillan, 2012); Martha Biondi, *The Black Revolution on Campus* (Berkeley: University of California Press, 2012); and Delores Aldridge and Carlene Young, eds., *Out of the Revolution: the Development of Africana Studies* (New York: Lexington Books, 2000).

[11] Benjamin Nimer, "Politics and Scholarship in African Studies in the United States," *African Studies Review* 13, no. 3 (1970): 353, 355–56.

[12] Nimber, "Politics and Scholarship," 353.

[13] See Richard Price, "The Miracle of Creolization: A Retrospective," *New West Indian Guide-Nieuwe West-Indische Gids* 75, no. 1–2 (2001): 35–64; idem, "African Diaspora and

the ideas of Melville J. Herskovits', so too did it fail to consider the profound cultural and socio-linguistic mutual intelligibility amongst African societies or the systemic racialization and colonial regimes that forced diasporic Africans to fight against 'social death' through life-sustaining institutions that affirmed their humanity and shaped their lives.[14]

In 1992, Mintz and Price 'republished [their] original essay largely unchanged'.[15] The essay contained a new title (*The Birth of African-American Culture: An Anthropological Perspective*) with no reference to an under-emphasized 'African past' or the 'Caribbean' (the locus of their research). The essay was strategically reprinted in a socio-political climate where ideas of 'biracial', 'mixed race' and 'creolization' were on the rise with a steep decline in the 'Afrocentric' idea. It is in this climate that historian Ira Berlin published an essay and then a monograph outlining his version of the 'Atlantic creole' idea; an idea appropriated, once more, from the study of languages. Following Mintz and Price, Berlin eschewed the 'African past' and the African continent, claiming, 'Black life on mainland North America originated *not* in Africa or in America but in the *nether world* between the two continents'.[16] Berlin's teleological thinking is yet another installation of the inexorable procession toward Europeanization and Americanization in arguing the first generation of Africans in British North America were 'Atlantic creoles' because of their acculturation to European cultural norms.[17] Berlin uses particles of evidence about a minute cast of 'creoles' granted legal emancipation as representation of a people and their predicament; in his parallel universe, these outliers become the norm. Berlin eschews African cultures and histories, statistics for these 'Atlantic creoles', and focuses almost exclusively on a distinct minority rather than the bulk of Africans because it is impossible for him to specify how prevalent 'Atlantic creoles' were in seventeenth-century North America. To be sure, there was little that was 'creole' about the 20

Anthropology," in *The African Diaspora and the Disciplines*, ed. Tejumola Olaniyan and James H. Sweet (Bloomington: Indiana University Press, 2010), 67.

[14] Price, "African Diaspora and Anthropology," 57.

[15] Mintz and Price, *Birth of African-American Culture*, xi. Price, as recently as 2007, amended his perspective on the "creolized" nature of African diasporic cultures: rather than "continuous creolization," he has opted for the unfolding of "creolization-like process." See Richard Price, *Travels with Tooy: History, Memory, and the African American Imagination* (Chicago: University of Chicago Press, 2007), 299.

[16] Berlin, *Many Thousands Gone*, 17 (emphasis added); idem, *Generations of Captivity: A History of African-American Slaves* (Cambridge, MA: Belknap Press, 2003), 23; and Alison Games, "Atlantic History: Definitions, Challenges, and Opportunities," *American Historical Review* 111, no. 3 (2006): 752.

[17] Berlin, *Many Thousands Gone*, 18. The same argument (that is, "Atlantic creoles" only become so upon contact with Europeans) formed the foundation of Berlin's *Generations of Captivity*, which can be read as an abridged version of *Many Thousands Gone*.

or so captive Africans from West-Central Africa brought to the Jamestown colony in 1619.[18] Those Africans brought to the colony were too atomized to constitute a community or self-identify as 'Atlantic creoles'. Unlike so-called 'Luso-Africans' who traded in captives but whose numbers were also very small, the mass of captive Africans from West and West-Central Africa had trivial exposure to European culture and were involuntary parties, for instance, to the bureaucratic mass baptisms (e.g. naming, salt on the tongue, water on the head) that some scholars parade as 'creolization'. Most Africans, however, interpreted this baptismal ritual as witchcraft and as preparation for consumption by European witches![19]

In 2007, Linda M. Heywood and John K. Thornton published their *Central Africans, Atlantic Creoles, and the Foundation of the Americas*, adopting Berlin's 'Atlantic creole' idea but in a historical moment punctuated by the profusion of 'creolization' and 'black Atlantic' verbiage and by Barack Obama's presidential candidacy and its 'post-racial' outgrowth. If Berlin sought to make a handful of 'quasi-black people' originating from an imaginary 'nether world' the founders of African-American culture, Heywood and Thornton simply shifted the locus of Berlin's personnel from West to West-Central Africa. Using the updated Trans-Atlantic Slave Trade Database, Heywood and Thornton argue large parts of West-Central Africa had developed an 'Atlantic creole' culture by the early seventeenth century and it was an 'Angola wave', and not those from Berlin's West Africa, that were the 'charter generation' of Africans in the early Americas.[20] Their ambitious project, however, is less insightful than it is a symptomatic chorus where 'creolization' translates into Europeanization and where 'Atlantic creoles' corresponds to 'Europeanized Africans'. Claims of pervasive Catholic influence saturate their work. Whatever the innermost content of some expressions

---

[18] James H. Sweet, "African Identity and Slave Resistance in the Portuguese Atlantic," in Peter C. Mancall, ed., *The Atlantic World and Virginia, 1550–1624* (Chapel Hill: University of North Carolina Press, 2007), 225–47.

[19] Joan Cameron Bristol, *Christians, Blasphemers, and Witches: Afro-Mexican Ritual Practice in the Seventeenth Century* (Albuquerque: University of New Mexico Press, 2007), 73; and James H. Sweet, *Recreating Africa: Culture, Kinship, and Religion in the African-Portuguese World, 1441–770* (Chapel-Hill: University of North Carolina Press, 2003), 197.

[20] Linda M. Heywood and John K. Thornton, *Central Africans, Atlantic Creoles, and the Foundation of the Americas, 1585–1660* (New York: Cambridge University Press, 2007), 2, 236. This work builds upon an earlier volume: Linda Heywood, ed., *Central Africans and Cultural Transformations in the American Diaspora* (New York: Cambridge University Press, 2002). For doubts about the 'creolized' nature of those from Angola, see Roquinaldo Ferreira, *Cross-Cultural Exchange in the Atlantic World: Angola and Brazil during the Era of the Slave Trade* (New York: Cambridge University Press, 2012), 247–48. For non-creolized views of the culture and identities of West-Central Africans, see Christina F. Mobley, "The Kongolese Atlantic: Central African Slavery & Culture from Mayombe to Haiti" (PhD dissertation, Duke University, 2015); Barbaro Martinez-Ruiz, *Kongo Graphic Writing and Other Narratives of the Sign* (Philadelphia: Temple University Press, 2013); and Maureen Warner Lewis, *Central Africa in the Caribbean: Transcending Time, Transforming Cultures* (Mona: University of West Indies Press, 2003).

of faith, the records make it clear those expressions were linked to political expediency, operating through the machinations of ruling elites, persistent warfare, acute slaving, and exile. Viewed from this perspective, it is no wonder the authors *cannot* show how most West-Central Africans, especially those (to be) enslaved, became seduced by Portuguese and Catholic ideals and how 'creolized' their daily lives became. Efforts to elucidate African ideas and intra-African histories are aborted in favor of fervently seeking to prove the existence of 'Atlantic creoles' and to minimize the extent of fraudulent baptisms received by captives prior to embarkation. Rather than lay bare the processes by which Africans incorporated or rejected Portuguese cultural or religious ideas, the authors quantify 'creolization' through a set of maps scaled from 'no creolization' to 'most creolization'.[21]

If, as they argue, 'Atlantic creoles' from West-Central Africa were the 'most homogeneous group of Africans to enter the Americas in the whole history of the slave trade' and they were 'culturally much closer to the Europeans', then how do we explain their short-lived social compatibility and how quickly their 'race' mattered in the inchoate European overseas colonies?[22] They tell us it was only in the late seventeenth century that English and Dutch colonists came to view Africans as 'slaves' in the strictest sense, but this explanation fails to integrate earlier Anglo-Dutch understandings of race and caste appropriated from their Iberian slaving partners and competitors. The English learned much of the racial and economic contours of Atlantic slaving from the Iberians and then the Dutch. Early English merchants in Iberia and English privateers regularly plundered Iberian ships in the Atlantic and Mediterranean, and readily adopted the racial category 'negro' and expelled undesirable 'negars and blackamoors' through a series of edicts.[23] Indeed, there is little evidence for their interpretation of Anglo-Dutch racial thinking, 'Atlantic creole' influences on Anglo-Dutch colonies, or for the culture of Africans of the late seventeenth century being 'different and more alien to Euro American expectations' than 'creolized' Africans.[24] The absence of significant evidence, especially for the bulk of common folks among a 'most homogenous group', severely undermines the 'Atlantic creole' argument.

It is difficult, therefore, to figure out how scholars can measure the sincerity of one's conversion or the adoption of European culture among sociopolitical elites much less the commoners cast as political subjects, social undesirables, and converted souls. Matthew Restall has lamented the same

---

[21] Heywood and Thornton, *Atlantic Creoles*, 227–35.

[22] Ibid., 238, 293.

[23] Peter Fryer, *Staying Power: The History of Black People in Britain* (London: Pluto Press, 1984), 10–2; Steven A. Epstein, *Speaking of Slavery: Color, Ethnicity, and Human Bondage in Italy* (Ithaca: Cornell University Press, 2001), 108; and April L. Hatfield, "A 'Very Wary People in the Bargaining' or 'Very Good Merchandise': English Traders' Views of Free and Enslaved Africans, 1550–1650," *Slavery and Abolition* 25, no. 3 (2004): 1–2.

[24] Heywood and Thornton, *Atlantic Creoles*, 331.

in his study of Africans and their descendants in the Yucatan under Spanish colonial rule: 'It is thus hard to determine whether professions of faith were sincere or whether Africans slaves paid lip service to the religion of their [Spanish] masters'.[25] We can apply these same misgivings to the claim of 'significant acculturation' to European values, especially Catholicism, and the claim that what mattered 'was the assertion of a Christian identity rather than a sectarian Catholic one'.[26] The repetition of an argument does not make it more convincing. We are told many times that 'Atlantic creole' culture was 'best represented by the profession of Christianity', among other features, but *how* an Africanized form of Catholicism found expression in the lives of those who allegedly had a substantial impact on African-American culture formation, or in the embryonic Anglo-Dutch colonies, is left unattended.[27] To their credit, Heywood and Thornton skillfully lay out the context of warfare and disintegration that produced West-Central African captives in stunning detail, but their sources say comparatively little about the 'creole culture' these captives supposedly transferred to the Americas. Ultimately, they are unable to demonstrate the 'ways in which this generation of Africans helped lay the foundation for the subsequent development of African American culture'.[28]

Rather than assume, at face value, the categories and content of the European-supplied sources, teasing out the broader historical patterns central to the formation of African diasporas requires a pan-European approach instead of a 'national' one for those sources. The very networks of merchants, clerics, capital, and commodities that would seriously contest Iberian quasi-monopolies in the constant but shifting relations between European partners and competitors sustained the Iberian presence in Africa and the Americas. Thus, for instance, the English colony in Virginia or in Barbados would have been established earlier and with enslaved labor if the Iberian slaving monopoly had been broken sooner. Once the Virginia colony was established and tobacco became a profitable staple crop, its colonial elites, planters, and the gentry 'began purchasing slaves as soon as they could get them and continued to buy more as fast as the limited supply and their individual resources would allow'.[29] As early as 1637, officials of the Company of Adventurers of London Trading to the Ports of Africa, 'to whom the King has granted a patent for the sole to trade to Guinea, Binney [Benin], and Angola', began 'to trade upon

---

[25] Matthew Restall, *The Black Middle: Africans, Mayas, and Spaniards in Colonial Yucatan* (Stanford: Stanford University Press, 2009), 235.

[26] Heywood and Thornton, *Atlantic Creoles*, 272.

[27] Ibid., 67.

[28] Ibid., i.

[29] John C. Coombs, "The Phases of Conversion: A New Chronology for the Rise of Slavery in Early Virginia," *The William and Mary Quarterly* 68, no. 3 (2011): 347; Douglas M. Bradburn and John C. Coombs, "Smoke and Mirrors: Reinterpreting the Society and Economy of the Seventeenth-Century Chesapeake," *Atlantic Studies* 3 (2006): 131–57. See also Edmund Morgan, *American Slavery, American Freedom: The Ordeal of Colonial Virginia* (New York: W. W. Norton, 1975), whose ideas about the rise of slavery Coombs challenges.

the coasts of Guinea, to take "nigers," and carry them to foreign parts'.[30] The number of enslaved individuals soon surpassed indentured servants by end of 1650s, but this would have been quicker had greater supply reached the colony through Dutch and other foreign traders. In 1664, the English capture of New Netherland ended the Holland–Virginia–Barbados trade link and the capture of Carolusborg (Cape Coast) in Gold Coast established direct supply lines between West Africa and the English plantation colonies, especially Barbados.[31] Settled in 1627, Barbados became a fully fledged slave society within a generation, punctuated by laws enslaving Africans for life (1636) and a slave code (1661).[32] By the late seventeenth century, Barbados was 'a laboratory of labor [and racialized slavery]', diffusing its racialized ideas and plantation practices through planters who left the island with their captives and settled in the Carolinas, the Chesapeake region, Jamaica, and other islands.[33]

These developments in the Anglo-Dutch Americas, however, came after a century of Iberian plantation slavery and where an 'Angola wave' allegedly responsible for the foundation of African-American culture was preceded by dominant patterns of Senegambia importation into Spanish America. The Spaniards had virtually no presence in West-Central Africa. But under a united Iberian crown (c.1580–1640), Portuguese merchants had access to Spanish America, while other Europeans attacked Iberian ships and settlements (from 1581), (re)sold captives to Spanish settlers in the Caribbean, and adopted sugar production techniques (from São Tomé to Brazil to Barbados) and ideas about racialized slavery. By 1640, the Spanish Caribbean was flooded with other Europeans through *asientos* granted by the Spanish Crown. Between the 1660s and 1670s, Genoese merchants procured enslaved Africans in the Caribbean from Anglo-Dutch traders, and resold them to major Spanish American ports. Late seventeenth and eighteenth-century Dutch and French merchants supplied Veracruz, Havana, Cartagena, and Panama with captives from their West African enclaves, while English merchants and loggers remained active in the Yucatan and Belize between 1655 and 1722.[34] Until the mid-seventeenth century, the idea that an almost

[30]W. Noël Sainsbury, ed., *Calendar of State Papers Colonial, America and West Indies, Volume 1, 1574–1660* (London: Her Majesty's Stationery Office, 1860), 1: 260.

[31]For some contemporary accounts of Anglo-Dutch wars and English activity in Gold Coast, see UK National Archives at Kew (TNA): Public Records Office (PRO), Colonial Office (CO) 1/19, no. 5 (1665), "A Breife Narrative of the Trade and Present Condition of the Company of Royall Adventurers of England Trading into Africa;" CO 1/17, no. 60 (1663), "An Extract of Letters from Cormantine and Other Places in Affrica;" CO 1/17, nos. 110–1 (1663), "The Company of Royal Adventurers Trading into Africa to [the King]."

[32]Simon P. Newman, *A New World of Labor: The Development of Plantation Slavery in the British Atlantic* (Philadelphia: University of Pennsylvania Press, 2013), 250.

[33]Newman, *A New World*, 251. For accounts of early English sugar plantations, see TNA: PRO, CO 1/22, no. 20.

[34]Restall, *The Black Middle*, 19–20.

exclusive West-Central African cast was trafficked to the early Americas is deeply at odds with the statistics for the sixteenth and seventeenth centuries, especially for the major Spanish American slaving hubs in Cartagena, Veracruz, and Buenos Aires.[35] Between 1525 and 1640, the vast majority of slaving voyages and the number of captive Africans went to Spanish America, with peaks between 1586 and 1640.[36] Between 1595 and 1640, half of all recorded captive Africans to Spanish America came from Senegambia with some 4000 per annum to Cartagena alone.[37] The year 1640, of course, corresponds to the end of the united Iberian crown and the lost of an Atlantic monopoly, illustrated by some two-thirds of all recorded captives flowing from Angola to the region between 1626 and 1640.[38] From 1641 to 1650, the largest number of slaving voyages went to Brazil and Barbados.[39]

Until the early or mid-seventeenth century, transatlantic slaving was largely an Iberian affair when we look at the numbers, though we should be very much aware of the multitude of hands that stirred this transatlantic pot. In Linda A. Newson and Susie Minchin's *From Capture to Sale*, the authors show the value of kin networks for Portuguese slavers who used kin and compatriots in Senegambia and Angola and in negotiating the imperial South American bureaucracy to further their commerce in 'pieces of slaves' (Span. *pieza de esclavo*). To this, we must add what the available databases do not account for concerning any 'wave' of captive Africans: contraband trafficking, bribes to royal and other officials, and intentional concealments of arrivals and departures to bolster self-interest in Atlantic Africa and in the Americas. Lastly, we must reckon with the perception of slavers in their procurement of captive Africans. In 1622, royal officials in Bogota wrote:

> The black slaves that are brought to Cartagena and sold are of three types – the first and most esteemed are those of the Rivers of Guinea [i.e. Senegambia], who are also called *de ley* ['authentic' or 'top-quality']. They have different names, and their common price is 200 pesos of assayed silver. The second type is that of the Ardas or Ararás [i.e. Allada]. These are brought with least frequency, and are sold at 160 *ducados* of 11 *reales*. The third and worst is that of the Angolas and Congos, who are infinitely numerous in their lands, and who commonly sell for 150 *ducados* each.[40]

[35] Linda A. Newson and Susie Minchin, *From Capture to Sale: The Portuguese Slave Trade to Spanish South America in the Early Seventeenth Century* (Leiden: Brill, 2007), 153.

[36] Data from the Trans-Atlantic Slave Trade database, accessed December 3, 2014, www.slavevoyages.org/tast/database/search.faces.

[37] Newson and Minchin, *From Capture to Sale*, 62, 66.

[38] David Wheat, "The First Great Waves: African Provenance Zones for the Transatlantic Slave Trade to Cartagena De Indias, 1570–1640," *The Journal of African History* 52 (2011): 4, 12, 14–15.

[39] Data from the Trans-Atlantic Slave Trade database, accessed December 3, 2014 www.slavevoyages.org/tast/database/search.faces.

[40] Cited in Wheat, "The First Great Waves," 19.

Captive Africans from Senegambia also reached a price double the value of Angolan counterparts in Africa.[41] Taken together, these factors and their numerical support point to a composite African (rather than an 'Angolan' wave that reached the shores of the Americas) with an equally composite culture that looked inside to their foundational understandings of life to deal with external forces they could not fully control. The countervailing fight for life against such forces was neither a 'miracle' nor a function of 'creolization'. It is what humans held captive on land or at sea do.

## 'BLACK' ATLANTIC HISTORIES

For millions of captive Africans dispatched to what became worldwide African diasporas, the Atlantic Ocean was experienced as a medium of alienation from natal kin and community. Between 1400 and 1900, this was true for the vast majority of Africans evicted from their homeland and from humanity en route to the Americas or Eurasia. Framing devises such 'Atlantic creoles' and 'creolization' remain out of sync with their lived experiences, languages, and ideas. As Pier Larson has shown for Madagascar and the western Indian Ocean, in *Ocean of Letters*, 'creole' ideas and cultures have been overvalued at the expense of indigenous cultures among captive Africans in the region.[42] Wherever supposed creolization occurred, it grew out of conquest, rupture, displacement, and in moments of asymmetrical power relations. Proponents of 'Atlantic' or whatever creoles have a difficult time substantiating the latter's existence in specific human details and cannot show beyond reasonable doubt how a 'creolized culture' operated in their daily lives because of weak evidence and a view of the Atlantic as a transformative portal that hollowed out Africans' ancestral inheritances. Rather than view the Atlantic as some magical threshold that miraculously created new peoples and cultures, an integrated space where power relations among the participants was symmetrical, or a transfer point for 'creolized' cultures, we need abstinence from grandiose claims framed by contemporary politics. What did imprisonment in one dungeon, stepping aboard yet another (floating) dungeon, estrangement from kin and community, and faced with perpetual incarnation in a foreign land and religion mean to those who followed the characteristically one-way Atlantic route? Diasporic scholarship might be served better by focusing on the lives, experiences, and ideas of Africans. In so doing, we would elucidate contemporary socio-political contexts borne out of transatlantic slaving and against their deep histories, rather than be guided by fashionable trends.

---

[41] Newson and Minchin, *From Capture to Sale*, 300.

[42] Pier M. Larson, *Ocean of Letters: Language and Creolization in an Indian Ocean Diaspora* (New York: Cambridge University Press, 2009).

Scholars are, in fact, 'creatures of fashion and this ... affects the fate of ideas. The ebb and flow of fashion is, at least, exhausting and, at worst, quite pernicious'.[43] Most fashionable ideas have a shared storyline. Take, for instance, the 'invention of the tradition' idea popularized in an edited volume by historians Eric Hobsbawm and Terence Ranger in 1983. Though a volume largely unconcerned with Africa (except one chapter by Ranger), the 'invented tradition' idea became contagious, reaching epidemic proportions with new articles and books donning titles such as 'the invention of Africa' and hundreds of books whose titles contained 'The Invention of'.[44] In the end, Hobsbawm and Ranger's argument about culture change, packaged in the distinction between 'invented' and 'genuine' tradition, was pointless because all human traditions are innovations with specific durability. and culture change is not the only outcome of encounters. The fashion of 'creolization' (Atlantic or otherwise) followed an identical trajectory: a linguistic concept applied to historical processes by anthropologists unconcerned with the 'African past' became a popular explanation for African cultures in various diasporas. One of the latest kindred fashions, in this genealogy of vogue ideas, is the concept of Atlantic history.

Like 'creolization', Atlantic history is a multicolored world unto itself (with red, black, green, and white Atlantics) that stubbornly eschews Africa and African histories. To be sure, 'Atlantic Africa is largely ignored in all [current] schemas [of Atlantic history]', but Atlantic history falters as a 'discrete unit' of inquiry by its wholesale obsession with Western Europe and North America and in circumnavigating most of the global systems of exchanges that flowed through Africa, Eurasia, and the Americas, especially 'non-Atlantic' parts.[45] For many, Atlantic history had its origins in the 'sudden and harsh encounter between two old worlds [i.e. indigenous America and Western Europe] that transformed both and integrated them into a single New World'.[46] Although some have disputed this framework by pleading the 'most urgent and immediate challenge is to restore Africa to the Atlantic', such well-intentioned appeals concede to, rather than seriously confront, a white/European constructed 'Atlantic world' in which Africa(ns) might be

---

[43] Quoted in Paul J. Cloke, Chris Philo, and David Sadler, *Approaching Human Geography: An Introduction to Contemporary Theoretical Debates* (New York: Guilford Press, 1991), 93.

[44] Eric Hobsbawm and Terence Ranger, eds., *The Invention of Tradition* (New York: Cambridge University Press, 1983), 211–62; Derek R. Peterson, *Ethnic Patriotism and the East African Revival: A History of Dissent, c. 1935–1972* (New York: Cambridge University Press, 2012), 3. See also Terence Ranger, "The Invention of Tradition Revisited: The Case of Colonial Africa," in Terence Ranger and Olufemi Vaughan, eds., *Legitimacy and the State in Twentieth-Century Africa: Essays in Honour of A. H. M. Kirk-Greene* (New York: Palgrave, 1993); Valentin Y. Mudimbe, *The Invention of Africa: Gnosis, Philosophy, and the Order of Knowledge* (Bloomington: Indiana University Press, 1988).

[45] Jack P. Greene and Philip Morgan, eds., *Atlantic History: A Critical Appraisal* (New York: Oxford University Press, 2009), 18, 21 (quotation), 339, 345 (quotation).

[46] Bernard Bailyn, *Atlantic History: Concept and Contours* (Cambridge, MA: Harvard University Press, 2005), 55–56; Donald W. Meinig, *The Shaping of America: A Geographical Perspective on 500 Years of History*, Vol. 1 (New Haven: Yale University Press, 1986), 4.

integrated.[47] The challenge for scholars of the 'Atlantic world', in whatever hue, is to comprehend that significant parts of 'Atlantic history' are sub-plots of larger (intra)African historical processes for which the Atlantic was a marginal frontier. For many Africans, the Atlantic was peripheral and remained so even with increased European contact.

Atlantic history can only be 'Atlantic' and a human history when we engage Africans in the full profile of *their* own world(s) and lived experiences. Ironically, most of the sixteenth to eighteenth-century travel accounts, however exoticized and problematic, did place Africa(ns) at the center of their 'Atlantic' narratives. But since the eighteenth-century era of racial science and slavery, there has been an explicit if not coordinated 'straw man' argument made (Africans are 'black-unchristian-slaves' and slavery was justified by this racial profile) as if Africans ever opted out of their humanity for any slaving nation, merchant company, or planter. Too many scholars have taken quite literally the enslaved or the emancipated Africans' appropriated use of non-African categories of being and belonging to affirm their humanity as evidence of the Africans' self-understanding.[48] In what seems like an out-of-body experience, scholars seek distance rather than the discovery of African understandings of self, kin, and society, embedded in the violence and trauma that birthed the 'modern' world. African experiences of the Atlantic were ones of permanent alienation from place of birth and socialization and from those who mattered in their life (kin and community). To them, this Atlantic world was neither a stable concept, theoretical frame, nor a 'master text' made intelligible through literary criticism and racialized hermeneutics. Regardless of whether we 'whiten' or 'blacken' the Atlantic, we would still miss the opportunity to take our cues from their lived experiences.

The 'Black' Atlantic idea is therefore woven from threads of a falsely perceived shared geography that did not exist in either the minds or the archived experiences of most Africans who traveled as prisoners on the Atlantic. The root problem is that the conjoined histories of Africa *and* the Atlantic region has been hijacked, first, by a cast of anthropologists and, more recently, literary critics who collectively have little desire to seriously engage the 'African past', the Africans' foundational self-understandings accessed through *their* languages and cultures, and *their* categories of family and community rooted in bio-genetics and ancestry. It is not that historians are the only ones capable of producing such histories; their record is at best mixed and at worst makes

---

[47] Games, "Atlantic History," 754.

[48] Ironically, the "face value" approach rarely occurs or is taken seriously when Africans and their progeny self-identity themselves using one or several toponyms/ethnonyms, such as "Congo," "Angola," "Mina," etc. In a recent and otherwise exceptional book on revolutionary Haiti and Cuba, the author describes one Juan Bautista Lisundia as a practitioner of "Afro-Cuban religion," a drummer, and one who identified himself as "Congo." The author, however, categorized him as a "creole." See Ada Ferrer, *Freedom's Mirror: Cuba and Haiti in the Age of Revolution* (New York: Cambridge University Press, 2015), 298.

them accessories to a protracted crime against African historicity by reducing them to supporting cast or invisibility in their own histories. Regardless of who researches and writes, we need context, not simply the interpretation of text! This is even truer for Africans who dictated or created some archived remembrance calibrated to specific economic and socio-political contexts: they cannot engage in nor protest our interpretations of their lives!

In the current 'Black Atlantic' fashion, the multiplicity of these lives, especially for the vast majority who were either illiterate in European languages or lacked the opportunity for documentary representation, matters little. Instead, what seems to matter is the autobiographical anxiety or 'the special stress' these literary critics-cum-intellectuals feel about *their* own 'African' ancestry and *their* own 'striving to be both European and black'.[49] Not unlike the travel accounts of earlier centuries, travelogues of the tourist kind produced by 'black' scholars, especially those inclined to literary criticism, have come to stand in place of deep contextualization and an engagement with historical processes in Atlantic and non-Atlantic Africa over time.[50] Rather than sober us by charting how race was ideologically determined in fifteenth and sixteenth-century Iberia and grafted onto human bodies (especially African ones) by so-called Enlightenment thinkers, these literary critics and their theorizing peers have reified the very thing that triggers their anxiety and which they persistently argue against: the idea of 'blackness'.[51] This ironic and intoxicating trend has led to the branding of a 'black Mediterranean', a 'black Pacific,' and a 'black Indian Ocean'.[52] Perhaps there is some meaning in following today's or tomorrow's fashion. In either case, this much is clear: neither 'blackenizing' an ocean nor intellectual voyeurism (where there

---

[49] Paul Gilroy, *The Black Atlantic: Modernity and Double Consciousness* (Cambridge, MA: Harvard University Press), 1, 3. For a thorough and largely accurate critique of Gilroy, see chapter three ("Gilroy: Neither Black nor Atlantic") of Don Robotham's *Culture, Society, Economy: Globalization and Its Alternatives* (London: Sage, 2005), 43–61.

[50] Specimens of this anxiety can be found, for instance, in Henry Louis Gates's *Wonders of the African World* video series and the book of the same title; idem, *Tradition and the Black Atlantic: Critical Theory in the African Diaspora* (New York: Basic Civitas Books, 2010); Saidiya V. Hartman, *Lose Your Mother: A Journey Along the Atlantic Slave Route* (New York: Farrah, Straus and Giroux, 2007).

[51] On locating "race" in early Iberia, see Francisco Bethencourt, *Racisms: From the Crusades to the Twentieth Century* (Princeton: Princeton University Press, 2013). On science and race-making related to African bodies, see Andrew Curran, *The Anatomy of Blackness: Science and Slavery in an Age of Enlightenment* (Baltimore: The John Hopkins University Press, 2011), 6, 168.

[52] Jay B. Haviser and Kevin C. MacDonald, eds., *African Re-Genesis: Confronting Social Issues in the Diaspora* (Walnut Creek, CA: Left Coast Press, 2006), 251; John Parker and Richard Reid, eds., *The Oxford Handbook of Modern African History* (New York: Oxford University Press, 2013), 144; Seifudein Adem and Ali A. Mazrui, *Afrasia: A Tale of Two Continents* (Lanham, MD: University Press of America, 2013), 261; Heather Smyth, "The Black Atlantic Meets the Black Pacific: Multimodality in Kamau Brathwaite and Wayde Compton," *Callaloo* 37, no. 2 (2014); 389–403; Yasuhiro Okada, "Gendering the 'Black Pacific': Race Consciousness, National Identity, and the Masculine/Feminine Empowerment Among African Americans in Japan Under

is only the 'idea of Africa') will allow us to see the stories that need telling, especially the ones creolization and Atlantic perspectives obfuscate.

## MOVEMENT PEOPLE

Since antiquity, there has been a series of human movements in and outside of Africa and at various scales, but in the past five centuries we have witnessed unprecedented forms of forced migration and dispersal of peoples outside of Africa. This outflow of diverse yet overlapping cultures and histories was coalesced into servile and racialized categories, settling in (slave) societies bordering the Mediterranean Sea and the Indian and Atlantic Oceans. For scholars who have focused on parcels of the past half millennium, the locus of inquiry has been the Americas. Understandably, most scholars of a singularly constituted 'African diaspora' are based in the Americas (the region most transformed by captive African labor, ideas, and cultures) and so African diasporic research and writing have been stubbornly centered on the Atlantic basin. A few scholars who are proficient in African and Asian languages and cultures bordering the Mediterranean and Indian Ocean have begun to address this imbalance in the study of African diasporas in Asia. In the case of either the Americas or Eurasia, however, even fewer scholars have sought to bring these diasporic strands into a cohesive and broader history of the ways in which African cultures and histories took shape in and outside of Africa. Though a modest attempt, my *Transatlantic Africa, 1440–1888* provides a number of methodological tools and substantial storylines that push us toward that cohesive and broader history. The sources and narrative in the book spanned the past 500 years, geographically integrated the Atlantic, Indian Ocean, Trans-Saharan, and Mediterranean worlds, and told a composite story that foregrounded global African voices and perspectives.[53] This kind of history offers a crucial turning point in how we can think and write about global African history and African diasporas as integral perspectives on world history.

U.S. Military Occupation, 1945–1952" (PhD dissertation, Michigan State University, 2008); Wanni Wibulswasdi Anderson and Robert G. Lee, eds., *Displacements and Diasporas: Asians in the Americas* (New Brunswick: Rutgers University Press, 2005), Chap. 7; Robbie Shilliam, *The Black Pacific: Anti-Colonial Struggles and Oceanic Connections* (New York: Bloomsbury Publishing, 2015). On the different "colored" Atlantics, see, more generally, Jack P. Greene and Philip D. Morgan, eds., *Atlantic History: A Critical Appraisal* (Oxford University Press, 2008), and more specifically works such Jace Weaver's *The Red Atlantic: American Indigenes and the Making of the Modern World, 1000–1927* (Chapel Hill: University of North Carolina Press, 2014).

[53] Kwasi Konadu, *Transatlantic Africa, 1440–1888* (New York: Oxford University Press, 2015).

In the past twenty years, the study of African diasporas has provided a wealth of new information and interpretations. However, very little research and analysis have been devoted to studying the interconnections between worldwide African diasporas. We need to know more than just the statistical evidence for Africans transported to the Americas, the personal story of exceptional yet less than representative enslaved Africans who attained notoriety in Asia or Islamic empires, or the silence that surrounds the lives of enslaved Africans brought to Czarist Russia or imperial China. We need to understand the relationship between these various facets of a composite African diaspora as strands that constitute a quilt rather than discrete and isolated phenomena unto themselves. Consequently, emergent scholarship on African diasporas may need to adopt a global framework (as a prerequisite methodology) for specific and broader diasporic strands studied in isolation or in comparative perspectives.[54] This way, we firstly lay bare the processes by which the types and formation of African diasporas relate or diverge and what, for instance, the endurance and transformation of African cultural forms (in response to mechanisms of socio-political inclusion and exclusion) reveal about the substance and inner corridors of diasporic lives. Secondly, we need a critical assessment of how the global forces at play and local conditions, such as the population density and range of Africans within specific regions of the world, influenced the content and course of memory, culture, and identities. Finally, we need, on the one hand, to account for the presence or absence of so-called 'back-to-Africa' and 'black consciousness' movements in specific times and regions of the world, socio-political movements that invariably engaged in and promoted the very idea of African diasporic scholarship and networks across boundaries that human movement created. On the other hand, we also need to account for intra-African dispersal as well as transborder circulations within Africa, especially after the decade of African political independence from formal colonial rule, and the inflow of peoples of African ancestry in West, East, and Southern Africa during the same historical moments.[55]

---

[54]Though focused on the Atlantic, a number of methodological questions raised by James Sweet may have broader salience. See James H. Sweet, "Mistaken Identities? Olaudah Equiano, Domingos Álvares, and the Methodological Challenges of Studying the African Diaspora," *The American Historical Review* 114 (2009): 279–306.

[55]On internal circulation of peoples in continental Africa in the contemporary moment, see, for instance, Aderanti Adepoju, ed., *International Migration within, to and from Africa in a Globalised World* (Accra: Sub-Saharan Publishers, 2009); Victor Agadjanian, "Research on International Migration within Sub-Saharan Africa: Foci, Approaches, and Challenges," *Sociological Quarterly* 49, no. 3 (2008): 407–21; Giles Mohan and A.B. Zack-Williams, "Globalisation from Below: Conceptualising the Role of the African Diasporas in Africa's Development," *Review of African Political Economy* 29, no. 92 (2002): 211–36. On the historic inflow of diasporic Africans to various parts of Africa, see Kwame Essien, *Brazilian-African Diaspora in Ghana: The Tabom, Slavery, Dissonance of Memory, Identity and Locating* (East Lansing: Michigan State

Pioneering scholarship on African diasporas in Asia offers a striking contrast to trends that privilege an Atlantic or North American ownership of the 'African diaspora'. During the past three decades, several important monographs and edited volumes have appeared. These include the likes of: Joseph Harris's *The African Diaspora in Asia*; Shihan de Silva Jaysuriya's *African Identity in Asia*; Edward Alper's *East Africa and the Indian Ocean*; Shaun Marmon's *Slavery in the Islamic Middle East*; Paul E. Lovejoy's *Slavery on the Frontiers of Islam*; and John Hunwick and Eve Troutt Powell's *The African Diaspora in the Mediterranean Lands of Islam*. Taken together, these studies focus on excavating silenced African and African-descended histories and adding other integral strands to our worldwide diasporic knowledge base. These works and others have made concerted efforts to create new ground for research, but underlying both this and the Atlantic history/creole development is the tendency to concentrate on specific historical topics, peoples, and places without pushing us toward a cohesive and broader history of African diasporas. Whether the loci have been the Americas or Eurasia, these studies have illuminated some of the key socio-political and cultural underpinnings of studying African diasporas, and so have provided a nascent framework for interpreting diasporic histories in specific nation-states and regions. However, historians have not traced the historic and cultural links between African diasporas or their relation to broader patterns at the level of world history. By taking a holistic and global view of historic Africa and its diasporas we can perceive, for example, how the memory and culture of a 'homeland' affected the outcomes of diasporic (trans)formation in 'foreign' lands. This perspective might prove fruitful in framing the ways in which cultural identity, memory, and production proved crucial in how dispersed and forced migrants within and outside of Africa dealt with mechanisms of socio-political inclusion and exclusion in host societies. Thus, by analyzing the connection between African diasporas, a more developed interpretation of how African peoples, ideas and cultures moved (in all their various forms) through their global histories. In 1946, W.E.B. Du Bois published *The World and Africa*, and, in it, he argued for the contributions made by Africa to world history, but for reasons of funding and what was known said little about diasporic African histories throughout the world. With our current tools and state of knowledge, our understanding of 'Africa' and 'the world' should coalesce around a field of knowledge and perspective we might call 'African world histories'. African world histories attuned to the specifics of local communities, their self-understandings and optics, and the flow of global exchanges (where Africa is porous and an integral part of those exchanges) seem to be where diasporic approaches to African history should take us.

University Press, 2016); Kwasi Konadu, *The Akan Diaspora in the Americas* (New York: Oxford University Press, 2010); and Nemata A. Blyden, *West Indians in West Africa, 1808–1880: The African Diaspora in Reverse* (Rochester: University of Rochester Press, 2000).

# BIBLIOGRAPHY

## ARCHIVAL SOURCES

"A Breife Narrative of the Trade and Present Condition of the Company of Roy-all Adventurers of England Trading into Africa." UK National Archives at Kew (TNA): Public Records Office (PRO), Colonial Office (CO) 1/19, no. 5 (1665).

Account of early English plantations in Barbados. TNA: PRO, CO 1/22, no. 20.

"An Extract of Letters from Cormantine and Other Places in Affrica." TNA: PRO, CO 1/17, no. 60 (1663).

"The Company of Royal Adventurers Trading into Africa to [the King]." TNA: PRO, CO 1/17, no. 110–1 (1663).

## SECONDARY LITERATURE

Adem, Seifudein, and Ali A. Mazrui. *Afrasia: A Tale of Two Continents*. Lanham, MD: University Press of America, 2013.

Adepoju, Aderanti, ed. *International Migration within, to and from Africa in a Globalised World*. Accra: Sub-Saharan Publishers, 2009.

Agadjanian, Victor. "Research on International Migration within Sub-Saharan Africa: Foci, Approaches, and Challenges." *Sociological Quarterly* 49, no. 3 (2008): 407–21.

Aldridge, Delores, and Carlene Young, eds. *Out of the Revolution: The Development of Africana Studies*. New York: Lexington Books, 2000.

Anderson, Wanni Wibulswasdi, and Robert G. Lee, eds. *Displacements and Diasporas: Asians in the Americas*. New Brunswick: Rutgers University Press, 2005.

Bailyn, Bernard. *Atlantic History: Concept and Contours*. Cambridge, MA: Harvard University Press, 2005.

Berger, Iris. "Contested Boundaries: African Studies Approaching the Millennium." *African Studies Review* 40, no. 2 (1997): 1–14.

Berlin, Ira. *Generations of Captivity: A History of African-American Slaves*. Cambridge, MA: Belknap Press of Harvard University Press, 2003.

———. *The First Two Centuries of Slavery in North America*. Cambridge, MA: The Belknap Press of Harvard University Press, 1998.

Bethencourt, Francisco. *Racisms: From the Crusades to the Twentieth Century*. Princeton: Princeton University Press, 2013.

Biondi, Martha. *The Black Revolution on Campus*. Berkeley: University of California Press, 2012.

Blyden, Nemata A. *West Indians in West Africa, 1808–1880: The African Diaspora in Reverse*. Rochester: University of Rochester Press, 2000.

Bradburn, Douglas M., and John C. Coombs, "Smoke and Mirrors: Reinterpreting the Society and Economy of the Seventeenth-Century Chesapeake." *Atlantic Studies* 3 (2006): 131–57.

Bradley, Stefan M. *Harlem vs. Columbia University: Black Student Power in the Late 1960s*. Urbana: University of Illinois Press, 2009.

Bristol, Joan Cameron. *Christians, Blasphemers, and Witches: Afro-Mexican Ritual Practice in the Seventeenth Century*. Albuquerque: University of New Mexico Press, 2007.

Butler, Kim. "Defining Diaspora, Refining a Discourse." *Diaspora* 10, no. 2 (2002), 189–219.

Cloke, Paul J., Chris Philo, and David Sadler. *Approaching Human Geography: An Introduction to Contemporary Theoretical Debates.* New York: Guilford Press, 1991.

Coombs, John C. "The Phases of Conversion: A New Chronology for the Rise of Slavery in Early Virginia." *The William and Mary Quarterly* 68, no. 3 (2011): 332–60.

Curran, Andrew. *The Anatomy of Blackness: Science and Slavery in an Age of Enlightenment.* Baltimore: The John Hopkins University Press, 2011.

Edwards, Brent H. "The Uses of Diaspora." *Social Text* 19, no. 1 (2001): 45–73.

Epstein, Steven A. *Speaking of Slavery: Color, Ethnicity, and Human Bondage in Italy.* Ithaca: Cornell University Press, 2001.

Essien, Kwame. *Brazilian-African Diaspora in Ghana: The Tabom, Slavery, Dissonance of Memory, Identity and Locating.* East Lansing: Michigan State University Press, 2016.

Ferreira, Roquinaldo. *Cross-Cultural Exchange in the Atlantic World: Angola and Brazil during the Era of the Slave Trade.* New York: Cambridge University Press, 2012.

Ferrer, Ada. *Freedom's Mirror: Cuba and Haiti in the Age of Revolution.* New York: Cambridge University Press, 2015.

Fryer, Peter. *Staying Power: The History of Black People in Britain.* London: Pluto Press, 1984.

Games, Alison. "Atlantic History: Definitions, Challenges, and Opportunities." *American Historical Review* 111, no. 3 (2006): 741–57.

Gates, Henry Louis. *Tradition and the Black Atlantic: Critical Theory in the African Diaspora.* New York: Basic Civitas Books, 2010.

Gershenhorn, Jerry. *Melville J. Herskovits and the Racial Politics of Knowledge.* Lincoln: University of Nebraska Press, 2004.

Gilroy, Paul. *The Black Atlantic: Modernity and Double Consciousness.* Cambridge, MA: Harvard University Press.

Greene, Jack P., and Philip Morgan, eds. *Atlantic History: A Critical Appraisal.* New York: Oxford University Press, 2009.

Hancock, Ian F. *The Relationship of Black Vernacular English to the Atlantic Creoles.* Austin: African and Afro-American Studies and Research Center, University of Texas at Austin, 1978.

———. "A Provisional List of English-based Atlantic Creoles." *African Language Review* 8 (1969): 7–72.

Harris, Joseph E., ed. *Global Dimensions of the African Diaspora.* Washington, DC: Howard University Press, 1993.

Hartman, Saidiya V. *Lose Your Mother: A Journey Along the Atlantic Slave Route.* New York: Farrah, Straus and Giroux, 2007.

Hatfield, April L. "A 'Very Wary People in the Bargaining' or 'Very Good Merchandise': English Traders' Views of Free and Enslaved Africans, 1550–1650." *Slavery and Abolition* 25, no. 3 (2004): 1–17.

Haviser, Jay B., and Kevin C. MacDonald, eds. *African Re-Genesis: Confronting Social Issues in the* Diaspora. Walnut Creek, CA: Left Coast Press, 2006.

Heywood, Linda M., and John K. Thornton. *Central Africans, Atlantic Creoles, and the Foundation of the Americas, 1585–1660.* New York: Cambridge University Press, 2007.

Heywood, Linda, ed. *Central Africans and Cultural Transformations in the American Diaspora*. New York: Cambridge University Press, 2002.

Hobsbawm, Eric, and Terence Ranger, eds. *The Invention of Tradition*. New York: Cambridge University Press, 1983.

Kendi, Ibram X. *The Black Campus Movement: Black Students and the Racial Reconstitution of Higher Education, 1965–1972*. New York: Palgrave Macmillan, 2012.

Konadu, Kwasi. *The Akan Diaspora in the Americas*. New York: Oxford University Press, 2010.

———. *Transatlantic Africa, 1440–1888*. New York: Oxford University Press, 2015.

Larson, Pier M. *Ocean of Letters: Language and Creolization in an Indian Ocean Diaspora*. New York: Cambridge University Press, 2009.

Lemelle, Sidney J., and Robin D.G. Kelley. *Imagining Home: Class, Culture and Nationalism in the African Diaspora*. New York: Verso, 1994.

Manning, Patrick. *The African Diaspora: A History through Culture*. New York: Columbia University Press, 2009.

Martinez-Ruiz, Barbaro. *Kongo Graphic Writing and Other Narratives of the Sign*. Philadelphia: Temple University Press, 2013.

Meinig, Donald W. *The Shaping of America: A Geographical Perspective on 500 Years of History*, Vol. 1. New Haven: Yale University Press, 1986.

Melville J. Herskovits. *The Myth of the Negro Past*. New York: Harper & Brothers, 1941.

Mintz, Sidney W., and Richard Price. *The Birth of African-American Culture: An Anthropological Perspective*. Boston: Beacon, 1992.

———. *Anthropological Approach to the Afro-American Past: A Caribbean Perspective*. Philadelphia: Institute for the Study of Human Issues, 1976.

Mobley, Christina F. "The Kongolese Atlantic: Central African Slavery & Culture from Mayombe to Haiti." PhD diss., Duke University, 2015.

Mohan, Giles, and A.B. Zack-Williams. "Globalisation from below: Conceptualising the Role of the African Diasporas in Africa's Development." *Review of African Political Economy* 29, no. 92 (2002): 211–36.

Morgan, Edmund. *American Slavery, American Freedom: The Ordeal of Colonial Virginia*. New York: W. W. Norton, 1975.

Mudimbe, V. Y. *The Idea of Africa*. Bloomington: Indiana University Press, 1994.

———. *The Invention of Africa*. Bloomington: Indiana University Press, 1988.

Newman, Simon P. *A New World of Labor: The Development of Plantation Slavery in the British Atlantic*. Philadelphia: University of Pennsylvania Press, 2013.

Newson, Linda A., and Susie Minchin. *From Capture to Sale: The Portuguese Slave Trade to Spanish South America in the Early Seventeenth Century*. Leiden: Brill, 2007.

Nimer, Benjamin. "Politics and Scholarship in African Studies in the United States." *African Studies Review* 13, no. 3 (1970): 353–61.

Okada, Yasuhiro. "Gendering the 'Black Pacific': Race Consciousness, National Identity, and the Masculine/Feminine Empowerment Among African Americans in Japan Under U.S. Military Occupation, 1945–1952." PhD diss., Michigan State University, 2008.

Palmer, Colin A. "Defining and Studying the Modern African Diaspora." *Journal of African American History* 85, no. 1–2 (2000): 27–32.

Parker, John, and Richard Rathbone. *African History: A Very Short Introduction.* New York: Oxford University Press, 2007.

Parker, John. "The African Diaspora." In *The Oxford Handbook of Modern African History,* edited by John Parker and Richard Reid, 132–48. New York: Oxford University Press, 2013.

Patterson, Tiffany R., and Robin D.G. Kelley. "Unfinished Migrations: Reflections on the African Diaspora and the Making of the Modern World." *African Studies Review* 43, no. 1 (2000): 11–45.

Peterson, Derek R. *Ethnic Patriotism and the East African Revival: A History of Dissent, c. 1935–1972.* New York: Cambridge University Press, 2012.

Price, Richard. "African Diaspora and Anthropology." In *The African Diaspora and the Disciplines,* edited by Tejumola Olaniyan and James H. Sweet, 53–74. Bloomington: Indiana University Press, 2010.

———. *Travels with Tooy: History, Memory, and the African American Imagination.* Chicago: University of Chicago Press, 2007.

———. "The Miracle of Creolization: A Retrospective." *New West Indian Guide-Nieuwe West-Indische Gids* 75, no. 1–2 (2001): 35–64.

Ranger, Terence. "The Invention of Tradition Revisited: The Case of Colonial Africa." In *Legitimacy and the State in Twentieth-Century Africa: Essays in Honour of A. H. M. Kirk-Greene,* edited by Terence Ranger and Olufemi Vaughan, 62–111. New York: Palgrave, 1993.

Restall, Matthew. *The Black Middle: Africans, Mayas, and Spaniards in Colonial Yucatan.* Stanford: Stanford University Press, 2009.

Robotham, Don. *Culture, Society, Economy: Globalization and Its Alternatives.* London: Sage, 2005.

Rojas, Fabio. *From Black Power to Black Studies: How a Radical Social Movement Became an Academic Discipline.* Baltimore: Johns Hopkins University Press, 2007.

Rooks, Noliwe M. *White Money/Black Power: The Surprising History of African American Studies and the Crisis of Race in Higher Education.* Boston: Beacon Press, 2006.

Sainsbury, W. Noël, ed. *Calendar of State Papers Colonial, America and West Indies, Volume 1, 1574–1660.* London: Her Majesty's Stationery Office, 1860.

Shilliam, Robbie. *The Black Pacific: Anti-Colonial Struggles and Oceanic Connections.* New York: Bloomsbury Publishing, 2015.

Smyth, Heather. "The Black Atlantic Meets the Black Pacific: Multimodality in Kamau Brathwaite and Wayde Compton." *Callaloo* 37, no. 2 (2014); 389–403.

Sweet, James H. *Recreating Africa: Culture, Kinship, and Religion in the African-Portuguese World, 1441–1770.* Chapel-Hill: University of North Carolina Press, 2003.

———. "African Identity and Slave Resistance in the Portuguese Atlantic." In *The Atlantic World and Virginia, 1550–1624,* edited by Peter C. Mancall, 225–47. Chapel Hill: University of North Carolina Press, 2007.

———. "Mistaken Identities? Olaudah Equiano, Domingos Álvares, and the Methodological Challenges of Studying the African Diaspora." *The American Historical Review* 114 (2009): 279–306.

Trans-Atlantic Slave Trade database. www.slavevoyages.org/tast/database/search.faces.

Wade-Lewis, Margaret. *Lorenzo Dow Turner: Father of Gullah Studies.* Columbia: University of South Carolina Press, 2007.

Warner-Lewis, Maureen. *Central Africa in the Caribbean: Transcending Time, Transforming Cultures.* Mona: University of West Indies Press, 2003.

Weaver, Jace. *The Red Atlantic: American Indigenes and the Making of the Modern World, 1000–1927.* Chapel Hill: University of North Carolina Press, 2014.

Wheat, David. "The First Great Waves: African Provenance Zones for the Transatlantic Slave Trade to Cartagena De Indias, 1570–1640." *The Journal of African History* 52 (2011): 1–22.

Williamson, Joy Ann. *Black Power on Campus: The University of Illinois, 1965–75.* Urbana: University of Illinois Press, 2003.

# CHAPTER 38

# Islam in Sub-Saharan Africa

## Marloes Janson

Sub-Saharan Africa is frequently, but unjustly, seen as the periphery of the Muslim world, in terms of both geography and religious influence. By contrast, North Africa is considered to be directly linked to the alleged center of the Muslim world; that is, the Arab Middle East. In fact, Islam has had a presence in Sub-Saharan Africa since the earliest days of its history. This chapter tries to redress the periphery bias in the analysis of African Muslim societies; a correction that, as Loimeier points out,[1] is long overdue. After all, Africa is home to one of the largest agglomerations of Muslims in the world today.[2]

Stretching south across the Sahara, the vast savannah zone (known as the Sahel) is Muslim until it reaches the forest belt of West and Central Africa. Moving south, the Horn of Africa represents a second major zone of Muslim influence. Via contact with seafaring traders in the Indian Ocean, Islam came to dominate in what is now known as the Swahili coast, stretching as far south as Mozambique and the island of Madagascar. From these areas, the religion spread gradually over the centuries, moving south and west into more tropical zones, and the expansion continues today.[3] At present, Muslims constitute a majority in North Africa and in most of the countries in the Sahel. In Sudan, Chad, and Tanzania, Muslims are the largest group. The population is almost equally divided between Muslims and Christians in Africa's most populous country, Nigeria. Even where Muslims are a minority, they constitute large majorities in certain regions, as for example on the Cape

M. Janson (✉)
Department of Anthropology and Sociology,
SOAS University of London, London, UK

© The Author(s) 2018
M.S. Shanguhyia and T. Falola (eds.),
*The Palgrave Handbook of African Colonial and Postcolonial History*,
https://doi.org/10.1057/978-1-137-59426-6_38

in South Africa,[4] northern Benin, northern Cameroon, northern Ghana, and in highland Ethiopia and coastal Kenya.[5] Although being a minority, Muslims are nevertheless important in politics in Uganda,[6] and are a force to be reckoned with at the national level in Malawi and Mozambique.[7] This chapter begins by mapping historical processes in the expansion of Islam in pre-colonial Sub-Saharan Africa, before moving on to the colonial and post-colonial periods. The focus is on West and East Africa; regions that have been well documented in the literature.[8] Compared with the study of Muslim societies in West and East Africa, the topic of Islam in Southern Africa is still in its infancy.[9]

Scholars studying Islam in Sub-Saharan Africa have long written about an 'African Islam', reflecting the Sufi bias typical of scholarship on Islam in Africa.[10] This chapter aims at demonstrating that the recurrent idea of an 'African Islam' hampers a better understanding of the emergence of Islamic reformist-oriented movements.[11] I conclude by pointing out new approaches to the study of Islam in Sub-Saharan Africa that capture the complexity and fluidity of the different ways of 'being Muslim' in everyday living, thereby challenging ingrained analytical binaries such as an 'African Islam' versus 'Arab Islam', and an accommodating Sufi Islam versus an orthodox reformist Islam.

## HISTORY OF ISLAM IN SUB-SAHARAN AFRICA

The Muslim penetration of Sub-Saharan Africa has traditionally been associated with conquest, trade, migration, and missionary activities, occurring in four main phases.[12] The first phase dates to the seventh and eight centuries, with the military conquest of much of North Africa, where political submission and conversion to Islam were considered one and the same act.[13] Converted Berber-speaking nomads were well positioned to mediate Islamic influences between the Maghreb and the Western Sudan. The Almoravid movement, translated as 'the movement of those who engaged in holy war', originated in the desert space between North and West Africa in the eleventh century.[14] It initiated the implantation of the Maliki law school (*madhab*),[15] thus giving the region a shared intellectual-legal frame of reference.[16] The Almoravid movement is also held responsible for conquering the Ghana Empire in the eleventh century, resulting in its Islamization.[17]

During the second phase, Islam spread across the Sahara into West Africa along the trans-Saharan trade routes. From the tenth century onward, North African Muslim merchants settled in the main towns along the trade routes.[18] In addition to goods like salt, merchants brought Islamic ideas and practices to West Africa. Due to its central location on the rim of the Indian Ocean, trade was also the avenue through which Islam spread in East Africa. Whereas in West Africa Islam expanded gradually from the Sahel toward the tropical forest belt of the Guinea coast, Islam in East Africa remained confined to a chain of settlements on the shore of the Indian Ocean and the islands off the coast until the nineteenth century.[19] A second difference was that whereas the spread of Islam in East Africa went hand-in-hand with linguistic and cultural 'Arabization',[20] in West Africa Arabic failed to achieve the status of a vernacular language and became the lingua franca only in scholarly circles; the 'Latin of Africa'.[21]

During the third phase, the influence of Muslim traders along with Muslim scholars was instrumental in the formation of states ruled by Muslims. 'It is not always easy', writes Lewis, 'to distinguish between the Islamizing role of Muslim traders, on the one hand, and of teachers and holy men, on the other, since these two activities are often associated in Muslim communities and regularly combined in the same person'.[22] Traders and Muslim clerics propagated Islam under the patronage of local rulers. In the thirteenth century, Islam became the religion of state in the Mali Empire, by then the dominant political and commercial power in the Western Sudan.[23]

Here it should be noted that throughout the third phase of the Islamic expansion, Islam remained a court religion. Because only the king and his immediate entourage came under the influence of Islam, the ruling aristocracy adopted a middle position between Islam and the traditional religion, patronizing both Muslim clerics and traditional priests.[24] Both categories provided services to local rulers, in the form of amulets, prayers, blessings, healing, and other supernatural means at their disposal to guarantee the prosperity of the polity as well as of its king. The symbiotic relation of Islam with traditional religion was attested by the Moroccan traveler Ibn Battuta when he visited the Malian court in the middle of the fourteenth century. He attended two Islamic festivals, and in his book *Travels* he condemned the 'vile practices' of the Malian participants, who mixed Islamic practices with traditional ones.[25]

Despite its expansion, Islam remained marginal in Sub-Saharan Africa until the time of the jihadist movements in the eighteenth and nineteenth centuries, which were motivated by the desire to eliminate *shirk* (idolatry) at chiefly courts in order to establish systems of government based on Islamic principles. The most prominent was Usman dan Fodio's jihad in Hausaland (modern Northern Nigeria), which resulted in the creation of the Sokoto caliphate in 1809; the largest state in West Africa until it was conquered by the British in 1903.[26] While the Sokoto caliphate determined Islamic practice in West Africa, the Zanzibar sultanate became the focal point of the religious and cultural life of the East African coast in the nineteenth century. The bombardment of Zanzibar by British naval forces in 1896 sealed its transformation into a British protectorate.[27]

Loimeier concludes that the Muslim caliphates and sultanates resulting from jihadist movements in the eighteenth and nineteenth centuries constituted an important political experience, because for the first time in Sub-Saharan history Islam became the only source of political legitimacy.[28] Jihadist movements were, however, crucial not only in the expansion of Islam as a political force, but also in anti-colonial resistance. For example, the man whom the British characterized as the 'mad Mullah' (Sayyid Muhammad Abdallah Hassan) of Somalia conducted a jihad between 1898 and 1920 to resist the territorial ambitions of the British, Italians, and Ethiopians. The Sayyid (an honorific title for the alleged descendants of the Prophet Muhammad) belonged to the Shadhiliyya Sufi order and confronted the Qadiriyya, who collaborated with the European rulers with the aim of establishing an independent Islamic state for Somalis.[29]

The final phase of the Islamic expansion in Sub-Saharan Africa began in the nineteenth century under the influence of the Sufi orders (turuq). Starting in the mid-nineteenth century, the Tijaniyya, under the leadership of al-Hajj 'Umar Tall (d. 1864), gradually superseded the Qadiriyya (which had originated in Baghdad in the thirteenth century) as the largest Sufi order in West Africa. Al-Hajj 'Umar Tall led a large-scale jihadist movement in the area of present-day Mali, resulting in mass conversion.[30] Popularly based Sufi orders reached the East African coast much later; only near the end of the nineteenth century did the Qadiriyya, Alawiyya, and Shadhiliyya become active and trigger a movement of conversion to Islam.[31] But although they had a much shorter history than the Sufi orders in West Africa, the East African Sufi orders played an important role in bringing newcomers to Islam. Their egalitarian attitude attracted migrants, marginalized upcountry converts, and (ex-)slaves who had been routinely excluded from power.[32]

Remarkably, although none of the European colonial powers developed a coherent Muslim policy, the colonial period (i.e. the late nineteenth and early twentieth centuries) saw the large-scale conversion of Africans to Islam.

## THE COLONIAL PERIOD

The relationship between colonialism and Islam was a complex one. Although colonial rule put an end to the jihadist movements and colonial governments attempted to prevent Islam from expanding, the process of Islamization accelerated during the colonial period and the number of converts increased due to colonial policies and activities. According to Launay and Soares,[33] the rise in the number of Muslims during the colonial period can be explained in terms of developments within the 'Islamic sphere'; a Muslim public arena that existed separately, though not detached from, the colonial public sphere. Muslims throughout Sub-Saharan Africa took advantage of the new possibilities created by colonialism, thereby expanding the Islamic sphere.

In order to be better able to control their Muslim subjects perhaps, colonial officials maintained close contacts with local Muslim rulers and religious scholars. Only a minority of Muslim leaders resisted colonialism or tried to avoid conquest by making the hijra (migrating beyond the reach of colonial authorities)[34]; the majority chose accommodation or collaboration.[35] For instance, Senegalese marabouts (Muslim clerics) collaborated closely with the French colonial rulers, for whom they mobilized support and collected taxes, in return for some level of influence on the shaping of Senegalese society and polity.[36,37] In neighboring Gambia, the British colonial rulers acknowledged the centrality of Islam by making room for some elements of the Sharia law in the legal system.[38] Likewise, the *ulama* (Islamic scholars) of the East African protectorates were coopted into the regime's service as salaried *qadis* (Islamic judges) and other 'native' officials.[39]

Second, new means of communication and transport facilitated travel and the flow of ideas among African Muslims and between African Muslims and their counterparts elsewhere. The explicit aim of the improved infrastructure was to stimulate the flow of raw materials (peanuts, palm oil, cotton, wild rubber, coffee, and cocoa) and labor to support the colonial enterprise. By building roads to previously inaccessible areas of the country and opening the hinterland, colonial rulers unwittingly enabled Muslim clerics and traders to communicate with one another and expand their spheres of influence.[40] Moreover, by putting an end to jihads and local warfare, colonial governments were able to guarantee safe travel over long distances.[41] Africans from the countryside migrated to the growing urban centers, where they came under Muslim influence. Mobility thus facilitated the expansion of Islam. As a result, more standardized ways of being Muslim emerged during the colonial period. In this context Eickelman speaks of a 'generic Islam' that centered around the assumed universals of Islam.[42] This new trend was reflected in the increasing number of African Muslims who were able to set out on the *hajj*, the pilgrimage to Mecca. It is here that Muslims were brought face-to-face with a diversity of their fellow Muslims. As such, the hajj is a tool to integrate the worldwide community of Muslims, the *umma*.[43]

The advent of Islam in South Africa also occurred in conjunction with colonialism. The first Muslims in South Africa, the 'Malay', were taken from Southeast Asia by the Dutch colonists in 1658. A second group (1860–1911) came from India as indentured laborers to work on Natal's sugar plantations. The 'Malay' and Indian Muslims make up the two largest groups among the Muslim population of South Africa today.[44] Under British rule, the Cape Muslim population gained religious freedom and the number of mosques increased. However, the growing size of the Cape Muslim community triggered a number of communal disputes over the leadership of mosques, as a result of which it was never able to achieve the kind of political unity that would have been necessary to influence Cape Town's political development in decisive ways in the late nineteenth century.[45]

While colonial attitudes towards Muslim subjects remained ambivalent, Islam turned into a majority religion in large parts of Sub-Saharan Africa in the twentieth century. At the transition to independence, a new wave of Islamic reform erupted.

# THE NEW WAVE OF ISLAMIC REFORM
## IN POSTCOLONIAL AFRICA

Despite the colonial impetus to the expansion of Islam, Christian missions spread throughout Sub-Saharan Africa in the twentieth century. While many Africans acquired literacy and formal Western education and became Christian, Muslims (who continued to follow their traditional Islamic system of education) had less access to formal education and less opportunity for development. Consequently, Christians came to have a 'privileged position' in society.[46] With the rise of a class of literate African Christians, Muslims became less important to the colonial administration, and Muslim communities tended to become marginalized from the modern economic sector. The imbalances created by these unequal circumstances make up much of the legacy being experienced by Muslims in postcolonial Africa.[47] Thus began a wave of Muslim emancipation with Muslim parties and pressure groups calling for a Muslim equivalent to the Christian mission schools established in the colonial period. Money coming from oil-producing Muslim countries since the 1970s has facilitated the implementation of these demands.[48]

From the 1970s onwards, an increasing number of African students also received scholarships to universities and colleges in Egypt, Sudan, Libya, Saudi Arabia, and Kuwait. Upon their return to Sub-Saharan Africa, they attempted to reform Islam by purifying it from local traditions. Their attempts resulted in local disputes about the 'correct' practice of Islam. An example is the *qabd-sadl* dispute; that is, the dispute over the position of the arms in prayer in parts of West Africa. Whereas the Maliki school of law recommended *sadl* (arms outstretched), new Muslim movements of reform affiliated with the Saudi-oriented Wahhabiyya and the Indo-Pakistani Tablighi Jama'at insisted on *qabd* (arms folded over the chest).[49] Other forms of ritual practice over which conflict broke out in East African Muslim communities were the celebration of Muslim holidays and in particular the birthday of the Prophet Muhammad, the *maulidi* (*mawlid* in Arabic [Ar]). Although maulidi is celebrated by significant parts of the Muslim population of the Kenyan coast (and elsewhere in Africa), the form of the celebrations (the use of musical instruments, textual recitation in either Arabic or Kiswhahili, etc.) is highly contested from within. The strong influence of Islamic reformism over the last few decades has largely rejected *maulidi* as undue religious innovation in Kenya.[50]

Due to the importance of proper ritual, ritual practices have often been at the center of local disputes in African Muslim communities.[51] These disputes touch on questions of education, authority, and religious identity. On the grounds that they were educated in formal institutions in the Arab world, reformist Muslims claimed to have more insight into the proper interpretation of Islam than scholars who were trained in the traditional Muslim education system. Owing to the new Afro-Arab cooperation in the

1970s, a number of international Muslim organizations involved in both *da'wa* (mission) and development-oriented activities capitalized on this new interpretation of Islam.[52]

Under the influence of the Iranian Revolution, with the increased presence and resources of the Arab Gulf States and Saudi Arabia, the exposure to a more reformist type of Islam stirred up an Islamic revival in Sub-Saharan Africa.[53] This resulted in an increased visibility and assertiveness of Islam in society, as manifested in the mushrooming of mosques, Islamic schools, and clinics, which identify much of the public (and especially urban) space as Islamic. Since the 1990s, media-savvy Muslim intellectuals have captured the media. They publicly called into question the religious authority of the established Muslim scholars, the *ulama*, leading to a fragmentation of religious authority.[54] The spread of new media technologies thus set in motion the process of the democratization of religious knowledge. No longer are the ulama regarded as the sole guardians of Islam; religious authority is now in many hands. Islamic radio and television broadcasts, as well as audiotapes of preaching and religious pamphlets, have brought about a public debate on what 'true Islam' involves.[55]

Transnational movements such as the Jama'at Izalat al-Bid'a wa-Iqamat as-Sunna (the Society for the Removal of Innovation and Reinstatement of the Sunna, or Izala for short) in West Africa,[56] and the Tablighi Jama'at (a missionary movement that originated in India and that has made inroads in West Africa,[57] East Africa,[58] and South Africa[59]) fed on and contributed to increasing internal debates about Islam and Muslim subjectivity in Sub-Saharan Africa. The efforts of (trans)national Muslim movements of reform to popularize religious knowledge by offering Muslims autonomous access to the sources of faith have created the basis for a new interpretation of Islam and a novel understanding of 'being Muslim'.[60]

(Trans)national reformist Muslim movements shed light not only on the divergent opinions of what being Muslim means, but also on the interconnections between Muslims in Africa and elsewhere. They offer African Muslims the means through which to surpass local identities and local modes of belonging and to identify instead with the umma. As such, these movements connect the local with the national and the global, and open up an avenue for mapping the complex articulations between religion and politics.[61] The emergence of a 'transnational Islam'[62] thus helps us to think beyond binaries such as an allegedly tolerant and 'traditional' local Islam versus an orthodox and 'modern' global Islam, which for a long time have dominated the study of Islam and African Muslim communities.[63]

Since the 1990s, increased global interconnections, along with economic and political reform, liberalization, and the weakening of the postcolonial state, have played major roles in the transformation of the religious landscape in Sub-Saharan Africa.[64] In virtually every Muslim community on the continent, the decades since the 1990s have been marked by heated debates about who is authorized to speak in the name of Islam and for whom. In many cases these debates have taken the form of increased tensions between reformist Muslims and Sufi practitioners. In countries as diverse as Niger and Ethiopia, religious disputes resulted in reformists accusing Sufi Muslims of not being 'true Muslims'.[65] *Bid'a*, 'innovation' or deviation from the Prophet Muhammad's path, is in the opinion of reformist Muslims largely related to the Sufi practice of Islam. By attacking 'superstitions' such as the veneration of Sufi saints and the trade in amulets and other manifestations of Sufi Islam, reformist movements thus represent a 'de-mystifying trend in religion'.[66]

But Islamic reform not only resulted in religious disputes; the new possibilities for claiming religious authority also had the effect of empowering marginalized groups in society, including women and youth. Most significantly, political liberalization in African Muslim societies has given voice to Muslim women's organizations, which have played an active role in redefining notions of family life, sexuality, and moral self-fashioning.[67] Furthermore, Muslim women nowadays take an active part in movements of popular learning and piety in many parts of Africa.[68] Not only women, but also young people have gained a greater and more visible role in religious life in present-day Africa. Inverting intergenerational relationships, young people are now assuming positions of religious authority for themselves, leaving the established Muslim elders in a state of powerlessness; a position normally associated with youth.[69] For example, the Durban-based Muslim Youth Movement of South Africa (MYMSA) played a pivotal role in disseminating reformist ideas, thereby carving a niche for Muslim youth in politics.[70] Many Muslim youths have made use of South Africa's new political freedoms and its liberal constitution to pursue their distinctive rights. For many, this is part of a broader reformist program of introducing stricter Islamic codes in public and private spheres.[71]

It can be concluded that although most Sub-Saharan independent nation-states (with the exception of Mauritania, set up as an 'Islamic Republic' at independence[72]; Ethiopia, which historically has been identified with the Coptic Church or Orthodox Christianity; and the special case of South Africa under apartheid rule) started off with secular constitutions, the efforts of postcolonial governments served to foster the spread of Islam. With religion becoming politically salient, a heated debate erupted between different religious communities about who 'owns' the state. Indeed, much of post-independence history has been a conflict over the control of the state. A case in point is Tanzania, where religion constitutes a platform of political mobilization for both Muslims and Christians, and where historical legacy and postcolonial policy have led to the emergence of religious disputes over development and national political leadership. The number of Muslims in Tanzania has grown considerably since the late nineteenth century. Yet this growth has not been translated into a corresponding increase in the number of Muslims holding positions in the political, educational, and economic arenas. In the eyes of many Muslims, Tanzania has become a Christian country. The Baraza

Kuu la Waislamu Tanzania (BAKWATA), that is, the National Muslim Council of Tanzania, was established in 1968 to serve Muslim interests. Nevertheless, Muslims increasingly became dissatisfied with the Council, seeing its role as representing the government instead of representing Muslim aspirations for political development. To redress the structural imbalance between Muslims and Christians, several new Muslim organizations proliferated in Tanzania in the 1980s, with the aim of opposing state-informed concepts of 'true Islam' as presented by BAKWATA and developing modern Islamic education. Since then, Muslim-Christian disputes have dominated public debates in Tanzania, with Muslims and Christians attacking each other's faiths in their public preaching, resulting in religious violence.[73]

Contradicting the typical image promulgated in the Western media of the radicalization of African political Islam and deteriorating Christian-Muslim relations (a tendency that has gained more currency since 9/11 and the recent upsurge of Boko Haram in northeastern Nigeria),[74] many African Muslims emphasize the significance of individual reform rather than political struggle in bringing about social transformation. Moreover, a striking feature of interreligious relations in several African countries is their peaceful nature and their relative lack of political cleavages.[75] Although conflict and violence are closely associated with the image that people (both outsiders and Nigerians themselves) have of Nigeria, religious clashes are just one aspect of manifold Christian-Muslim relations in the country. Christians and Muslims have long lived side-by-side in southwestern Nigeria, often in harmony with 'traditional' practitioners; the boundaries between the three are not always sharply demarcated.[76] In a similar vein, the East African upcountry regions are informed today by a multitude of interfaces between Islam, Christianity, and African religions.[77] These interfaces have inspired Africanists to adopt a comparative approach that focuses on how Christians and Muslims align with and copy each other, sometimes in interaction with so-called traditionalists.[78] Where Christian-Muslim conflicts prevail,[79] it would be better to describe the causes of these conflicts as a mixture of different factors, with religion being only one of them, and many of them rooted in postcolonial development.[80]

## 'African Islam' Versus 'Islam in Africa'

Despite the long history of Islam in Sub-Saharan Africa, the study of Islam has long been neglected by Africanists. They considered Islam not 'authentically' African and therefore not a legitimate subject of study. Conversely, Sub-Saharan Africa is often perceived as peripheral to the field of Islamic studies. Somewhat ironically, whereas Islam has not been 'African' enough for some, Africans have not been 'Islamic' enough for others.[81]

As Triaud points out,[82] the scientific partition between African Studies and Islamic Studies (or its predecessor Orientalism) superimposed itself over an epistemological divide between an 'African Islam' (referred to as *Islam noir*, literally 'black Islam', by French colonial authorities),[83] which is inherently syncretic, and an 'orthodox' or 'Arab Islam.' The idea that there is a specifically 'African Islam' formed the basis of colonial policy with regard to Islam from the second decade of the twentieth century onwards. Although the concept of Islam noir has been severely criticized,[84] there is still a tendency to depict Islam as practiced in Sub-Saharan Africa as less orthodox than that which is practiced in the Arab Middle East. For example, in their edited volume *African Islam and Islam in Africa*, Westerlund and Rosander describe 'African Islam' as more flexible and adaptable than what they portray as 'Islam in Africa', thereby reviving the colonial tradition of Islam noir.[85] Another example of the endurance of Islam noir is Robinson's *Muslim Societies in African History*, in which one chapter is devoted to 'The Islamization of Africa' and the subsequent one to 'The Africanization of Islam.'[86]

Following Geertz's lead, who in his pioneering book *Islam Observed* compared Moroccan and Indonesian cultures through the lens of Islam,[87] social scientists finally started dealing seriously with Islam as an object of study. But once again African Muslim societies were analyzed along contrasting paradigms as either 'Sufi' or 'reformist.' A major concern in the Africanist study of Islam has been how to document the diversity within Muslim communities without violating the religion's universal features.[88] Or, in the words of Launay, 'how can the very diverse (if not diverging) religious beliefs and practices of Muslims be comprehended within a single idea of "Islam"?'[89] The contrasting and competing Islamic discourses and practices in Muslim Africa are often studied in terms of a distinction between a Sufi and a reformist tradition; a distinction that is redolent of the earlier 'African Islam' versus 'Arab Islam' contrast.

In the so-called Sufi understanding of Islam, Muslims treat certain charismatic persons (living or deceased religious leaders, saints, or marabouts) as intermediaries between ordinary believers and Allah. Such charismatic religious leaders, their descendants, and their followers are organized into Sufi orders (Ar. *turuq*, singular *tariqa*), which have become one of the main organizational forms for the practice of Islam in Sub-Saharan Africa.[90] Adherence to a Sufi order is expressed through a special litany of prayers as well as by engagement in Sufi practices, including the consultation of religious specialists for divination, healing, and the request of amulets, pilgrimages to Sufi shrines, and the performance of religious festivals commemorating the birth of the Prophet or a Sufi saint. Largely because of the prominent position that Sufi orders occupy in the religio-political landscape (mainly in Senegal), they have attracted a great deal of scholarly tradition.[91]

The Sufi tradition is often studied in opposition to a reformist tradition, which is believed to call much of the former into question. As we have seen above, reformists condemn Sufis' 'incorrect' practice of Islam and seek to reform the way Islam is practiced locally by modeling themselves on the Arab Middle East. Through trade networks and education, reformist ideas reached

Muslim communities in Sub-Saharan Africa.[92] Starting in the 1970s, with money coming from the oil countries, an increasing number of Africans have received scholarships to study at universities and colleges in the Arab world. Upon their return to their home countries, they spread a reformist interpretation of Islam.

Although the binary between a Sufi and reformist Islam is challenging, it oversimplifies the fragmented and fluid nature of religious practice in Muslim Africa. Most Muslims in Sub-Saharan Africa today are neither members of Sufi orders nor self-proclaimed reformists.[93] During my ethnographic field research in the Gambia, it struck me that the majority of my interlocutors identified themselves as 'ordinary Muslims'; they did not affiliate themselves officially with any of the Sufi orders, and since the term 'reformist' is associated with religious 'radicalism' they did not call themselves reformists either.[94] A second flaw, as outlined above, is that the analytical model that opposes Sufism and reformism implies a hierarchical structuring of Islam in that Sufism is often believed to be less 'orthodox' than reformism, which is termed a 'purer' form of Islam. A related shortcoming is that the Sufi-reformist dichotomy frequently involves a teleological perspective in which Sufi Islam eventually gives away to a version of 'true', reformist Islam. For instance, Umar claims that Islam in Nigeria today has to be understood as a historical transformation from Sufism into anti-Sufism or reformism.[95]

In practice, however, Islamization does not proceed along a unilinear path from an accommodating, syncretic religion to a pure, orthodox one. Recent scholarship has illustrated that the moral and spiritual transformation Muslims go through in ongoing Islamization processes is often filled with temptations and struggles.[96] Finding ways to cope with these challenges, they move in and out of religious movements, often shifting their religious allegiances. Muslims' shifting allegiances explain why the study of new formations of Muslim identity in Africa (and beyond) should take into account not only the cultivation of piety, but also the imperfection and failure of everyday living. According to Marsden, studies of Muslim societies that focus narrowly on moral self-fashioning are 'unable to confront the ways in which Muslims are called upon to face, explain and contend with inconsistencies and complexities in their attempts to live virtuous lives'.[97] I would therefore like to conclude with a plea for a study of Islam that takes lived religiosity as its starting point and that warrants against the essentialism encapsulated in many of our analytical concepts, including an 'African Islam' versus 'Arab Islam' or a 'Sufi Islam' versus 'reformist Islam.'

## LIVING ISLAM

The commonplace approach to Islam in social-science scholarship is as a 'discursive tradition.' According to Asad,[98] Islam needs to be interpreted as a tradition consisting of discourses that seek to instruct Muslims in the correct form and purpose of a given practice. In this view, a practice is Islamic because it is authorized by the discursive traditions of Islam as represented by the Quran and *hadith*; the accounts of what the Prophet Muhammad said and did. Although the interpretation of Islam as a discursive tradition sheds light on the interplay of its singular terms and its universal, global import, it also has certain shortcomings because it passes over the fact that for many Muslims Islamic tradition is not merely discursively shaped.[99] In fact, many Muslims put more emphasis on religious orthopraxy (emphasis on correct religious practice) than on orthodoxy (emphasis on correct belief and doctrinal conformity). This prompts us to search for an approach to Islam that is more perceptive about everyday religious practice.

The current focus on 'living Islam'[100] resulted from a shift in scholarship whereby Islam was no longer studied as another aspect of social structure in the same way as, for example, kinship,[101] but as a part of the actual world in which Muslims live. As Seesemann points out, a focus on the quotidian may facilitate a deeper understanding of how Islam operates in a particular social setting.[102] Taking such a course shifts the emphasis from the narrowly political, macro-oriented analysis in studies of Muslim societies towards a perspective that focuses on how ideas, doctrines, and practices related to Islam undergo a process of contextualization in specific localities.

Drawing upon Haenni and Holtrop, Otayek and Soares capture Muslims' everyday experience of religion in the notion of *islam mondain*, that is, 'Islam in the present world'.[103] Islam mondain helps us to apprehend the variety of Muslim identities and the porosity of boundaries between these identities in the contemporary world in which Muslims find themselves, making efforts to produce themselves as modern religious subjects within contexts of considerable political and economic uncertainty, as well as increased global interconnections.

One can see this way of 'being Muslim' especially among mainstream African Muslims,[104] like the Nigerian Muslim youths cited by Masquelier, who ask themselves, in media outside the control of established religious authorities and the state, 'what it means to be Muslim, a citizen, or simply a youth with moral convictions'.[105] The Islamic revival in African Muslim societies needs to be interpreted in terms of these questions rather than in normative categories or unhelpful binaries, including 'African Islam' versus 'Arab Islam' or 'Sufi Islam' versus 'reformist Islam.' Indeed, questions about what it means to be Muslim challenge us to shift the attention from a narrow analysis of Islam in Africa as a coherent belief system towards a perspective that focuses on how Muslims actually live religion in their daily lives, and the ambiguities, contradictions, and aspirations as the constitutive moments in their lived religiosity.

## NOTES

1. Roman Loimeier, *Muslim Societies in Africa: A Historical Anthropology* (Bloomington: Indiana University Press, 2013), ix–x.
2. According to the CIA World Factbook, about half of Africa's population professes Islam, https://www.cia.gov/library/publications/the-world-factbook.
3. Nehemia Levtzion and Randall L. Pouwels, "Introduction: Patterns of Islamization and Varieties of Religious Experience among Muslims of Africa," in *The History of Islam in Africa*, ed. Nehemia Levtzion and Randall L. Pouwels (Athens: Ohio University Press, 2000), 1–18; and Roman Loimeier, *Muslim Societies in Africa: A Historical Anthropology* (Bloomington: Indiana University Press, 2013).
4. As Abdulkader Tayob, "Counting Muslims in South Africa," *Annual Review of Islam in South Africa* 5 (Cape Town: Centre for Contemporary Islam, University of Cape Town, 1998) observes, although Muslims form less than 2% of the South African population, statistics do not reflect their religious experience. Residential concentration of Muslims in racially segregated areas in Cape Town means that many of them live in proximity to mosques and Islamic schools and have a strong sense of being Muslim. See Goolam Vahed and Shamil Jeppie, *Multiple Communities: Muslims in Post-Apartheid South Africa* (2005), 252–53, www.hsrcpress.ac.za.
5. René Otayek and Benjamin F. Soares, "Introduction: Islam and Muslim Politics in Africa," in *Islam and Muslim Politics in Africa*, ed. Benjamin F. Soares and René Otayek (New York: Palgrave, 2007), 1–24, 2.
6. Abdin N. Chande, "Radicalism and Reform in East Africa," in *The History of Islam in Africa*, ed. Nehemia Levtzion and Randall L. Pouwels (Athens: Ohio University Press, 2000).
7. Edward A. Alpers, "East Central Africa," in *The History of Islam in Africa*, ed. Nehemia Levtzion and Randall L. Pouwels (Athens: Ohio University Press, 2000), 315–19.
8. Given the sheer number of countries and their diversity in these regions, individual cases cannot be described but I will point out broad patterns with reference to some key examples.
9. But see Abdulkader Tayob, *Islam in South Africa: Mosques, Imams, and Sermons* (Gainesville: University Press of Florida, 1999).
10. Sufism (Ar. *tasawwuf*) refers to the mystical tradition in Islam characterized by esoteric practices, special litanies of prayer, and techniques of invoking Allah's names as ways of approaching Him.
11. These movements are variously known as Wahhabi, Salafi, Islamist, or simply Sunnite Islam in Sub-Saharan Africa. For example, see: Lansiné Kaba, *The Wahhabiyya. Islamic Reform and Politics in French West Africa* (Evanston: Northwestern University Press, 1974); Elizabeth Hodgkin, "Islamism and Islamic Research in Africa," *Islam et Sociétés au sud du Sahara* 4 (1990): 73–130; Roman Loimeier, "Patterns and Peculiarities of Islamic Reform in Africa," *Journal of Religion in Africa* 33, no. 3 (2003): 237–62; William F. S. Miles, "West African Islam: Emerging Political Dynamics," in *Political Islam in West Africa: State-Society Relations Transformed*, ed. William F.S.

Miles (Boulder: Lynne Rienner Publishers, 2007), 1–18. What these move-ments have in common is what Roy calls "a quest to define a pure religion beyond time and space;" and Olivier Roy, *Globalised Islam* (London: Hurst, 2004), 11. They aim at purging Islam of unlawful innovations (*bid'a*) by returning to the purported origins of Islam.

12. For example, see: John S. Trimingham, *Islam in West Africa* (Oxford: Clar-endon Press, 1959); John S. Trimingham, *Islam in East Africa* (Oxford: Clarendon Press, 1964); Peter B. Clarke, *West Africa and Islam: A Study of Religious Development from the 8th to the 20th Century* (London: Edward Arnold, 1982); Mervyn Hiskett, *The Development of Islam in West Africa* (London: Longman, 1984); Randall L. Pouwels, *Horn and Crescent: Cul-tural Change and Traditional Islam on the East African Coast, 800–1900* (Cambridge: Cambridge University Press, 1987); Nehemia Levtzion, *Islam in West Africa: Religion, Society and Politics to 1800* (Aldershot: Variorum, 1994); David Robinson, *Muslim Histories, African Societies: The Venture of Islamic Studies in Africa* (Cambridge: Cambridge University Press, 2004); and Roman Loimeier, *Muslim Societies in Africa: A Historical Anthropology* (Bloomington: Indiana University Press, 2013).

13. Nehemia Levtzion and Randall L. Pouwels, "Introduction: Patterns of Islami-zation and Varieties of Religious Experience among Muslims of Africa," in *The History of Islam in Africa*, ed. Nehemia Levtzion and Randall L. Pouwels (Athens: Ohio University Press, 2000), 1–18, 2.

14. Peter B. Clarke, *West Africa and Islam: A Study of Religious Development from the 8th to the 20th Century* (London: Edward Arnold, 1982), 13.

15. The majority of Muslims in Africa are Sunnis belonging to the Maliki (domi-nant in North and West Africa) and Shafi'i (predominant on the East African coast) legal schools of thought. Exceptions are Shi'i Muslims in parts of West Africa, Ahmadis (a Muslim movement with a strong missionary component going back to Mirza Ghulam Ahmad (d. 1908) from Punjab in India) and Isma'ilis in East Africa and in areas of Asian Muslim immigration in South Africa. For Shi'i Muslims, see Mara A. Leichtman, *Shi'i Cosmopolitanisms in Africa: Lebanese Migration and Religious Conversion in Senegal* (Blooming-ton: Indiana University Press, 2015). For Ahmadis, see Humphrey J. Fisher, *Ahmadiyyah: A Study in Contemporary Islam on the West African Coast* (Lon-don: Oxford University Press, 1963).

16. Peter Von Sivers, "Egypt and North Africa," in *The History of Islam in Africa*, ed. Nehemia Levtzion and Randall L. Pouwels (Athens: Ohio University Press, 2000), 21–36, 25–26.

17. Nehemia Levtzion, "Islam in the Bilad al-Sudan to 1800," in *The History of Islam in Africa*, ed. Nehemia Levtzion and Randall L. Pouwels (Athens: Ohio University Press, 2000), 63–91, 64.

18. Peter B. Clarke, *West Africa and Islam: A Study of Religious Development from the 8th to the 20th Century* (London: Edward Arnold, 1982), 10–12.

19. Roman Loimeier, *Muslim Societies in Africa: A Historical Anthropology* (Bloomington: Indiana University Press, 2013), 239–40.

20. Randall L. Pouwels, *Horn and Crescent: Cultural Change and Traditional Islam on the East African Coast, 800–1900* (Cambridge: Cambridge Univer-sity Press, 1987), 129–31.

21. John O. Hunwick, "West Africa and the Arabic Language," *Sudanic Africa* 15 (2004): 133.
22. Ioan M. Lewis, ed. *Islam in Tropical Africa* (London: International African Institute, Oxford University Press, 1966). See also: Lamin Sanneh, *The Jakhanke Muslim Clerics: A Religious and Historical Study of Islam in Senegambia* (Lanham: University Press of America, 1989); and Nehemia Levtzion, *Islam in West Africa: Religion, Society and Politics to 1800* (Aldershot: Variorum, 1994).
23. Nehemia Levtzion, "Islam in the Bilad al-Sudan to 1800," in *The History of Islam in Africa*, ed. Nehemia Levtzion and Randall L. Pouwels (Athens: Ohio University Press, 2000), 63–91, 66–68.
24. Nehemia Levtzion and Randall L. Pouwels, "Introduction: Patterns of Islamization and Varieties of Religious Experience among Muslims of Africa," in *The History of Islam in Africa*, ed. Nehemia Levtzion and Randall L. Pouwels (Athens: Ohio University Press, 2000), 1–18, 3.
25. Nehemia Levtzion, "Islam in the Bilad al-Sudan to 1800," in *The History of Islam in Africa*, ed. Nehemia Levtzion and Randall L. Pouwels (Athens: Ohio University Press, 2000), 63–91, 67–68.
26. Murray Last, *The Sokoto Caliphate* (London: Longman, 1967).
27. Randall L. Pouwels, "The East African Coast, c. 780–1900 C.E.," in *The History of Islam in Africa*, ed. Nehemia Levtzion and Randall L. Pouwels (Athens: Ohio University Press, 2000), 251–71, 265; and Roman Loimeier, *Muslim Societies in Africa: A Historical Anthropology* (Bloomington: Indiana University Press, 2013), 229–34.
28. Roman Loimeier, *Muslim Societies in Africa: A Historical Anthropology* (Bloomington: Indiana University Press, 2013), 291.
29. Lidwien Kapteijns, "Ethiopia and the Horn of Africa," in *The History of Islam in Africa*, ed. Nehemia Levtzion and Randall L. Pouwels (Athens: Ohio University Press, 2000), 227–50, 235–37; and Roman Loimeier, *Muslim Societies in Africa: A Historical Anthropology* (Bloomington: Indiana University Press, 2013), 202–9.
30. David Robinson, *The Holy War of Umar Tal* (Oxford: Clarendon Press, 1985).
31. Anne K. Bang, *Sufis and Scholars of the Sea: Family Networks in East Africa, 1960–1925* (London: Routledge, 2003).
32. Roman Loimeier, *Muslim Societies in Africa: A Historical Anthropology* (Bloomington: Indiana University Press, 2013), 237.
33. Robert Launay and Benjamin F. Soares, "The Formation of an 'Islamic Sphere' in French Colonial West Africa," *Economy and Society* 28, no. 4 (1999): 497–519.
34. A prominent example is Shaykh Amadu Bamba M'Backe, the founder of the Senegalese Muridiyya Sufi order, who was sent by the French rulers into exile twice: to Gabon from 1895 to 1902, and to Mauritania from 1903 to 1907. Bamba's vexed relationship with the French has prompted later followers of the Muridiyya to praise him as a hero of the anti-colonial struggle. See Cheikh Babou, *Le Jihad de l'âme: Ahmadou Bamba et la fondation de la Mouridiyya au Sénégal, 1853–1913* (Paris: Karthala, 2011).

35. Nehemia Levtzion and Randall L. Pouwels, "Introduction: Patterns of Islamization and Varieties of Religious Experience among Muslims of Africa," in *The History of Islam in Africa*, ed. Nehemia Levtzion and Randall L. Pouwels (Athens: Ohio University Press, 2000), 1–18, 13.

36. Although borrowed from the French colonial lexicon, the term *marabout* is widespread in local discourse in West Africa and has grown into a self-designation. It refers to a wide range of religious specialists, from head of a Sufi order to Islamic healer and Quranic teacher. See Benjamin F. Soares, *Islam and the Prayer Economy: History and Authority in a Malian Town* (Edinburgh: Edinburgh University Press, 2005), 30–32.

37. Leonardo A. Villalón, *Islamic Society and State Power in Senegal: Disciples and Citizens in Fatick* (Cambridge: Cambridge University Press, 1995).

38. Marloes Janson, *Islam, Youth, and Modernity in the Gambia: The Tablighi Jama'at*, International African Library (New York: Cambridge University Press, 2014), 41.

39. Lidwien Kapteijns, "Ethiopia and the Horn of Africa," in *The History of Islam in Africa*, ed. Nehemia Levtzion and Randall L. Pouwels (Athens: Ohio University Press, 2000), 227–50, 238–39.

40. Sulayman S. Nyang and Marloes Janson, "Gambia," in *The Oxford Encyclopedia of the Modern Islamic World*, ed. John Esposito (New York: Oxford University Press, 2009), 283–86, 284.

41. Robert Launay and Benjamin F. Soares, "The Formation of an 'Islamic Sphere' in French Colonial West Africa," *Economy and Society* 28, no. 4 (1999): 505.

42. Dale F. Eickelman, "National Identity and Religious Discourse in Contemporary Oman," *International Journal of Islamic and Arabic Studies* 6, no. 1 (1989): 1–20; see also Robert Launay and Benjamin F. Soares, "The Formation of an 'Islamic Sphere' in French Colonial West Africa," *Economy and Society* 28, no. 4 (1999): 506.

43. Dale F. Eickelman and James Piscatori, eds. *Muslim Travellers. Pilgrimage, Migration, and the Religious Imagination* (Berkeley: University of California Press, 1990).

44. Goolam Vahed, "Changing Islamic Traditions and Emerging Identities in South Africa," *Journal of Muslim Minority Affairs* 20, no. 1 (2000): 44–45.

45. Roman Loimeier, *Muslim Societies in Africa: A Historical Anthropology* (Bloomington: Indiana University Press, 2013), 16, 261.

46. Abdin N. Chande, *Islam, Ulamaa, and Community Development in Tanzania: A Study of Islamic Trends in Tanzania, East Africa* (San Francisco: Austin & Lawrier, 1998), 6–8; see also Jean Comaroff and John Comaroff, *Of Revelation and Revolution. Vol. 1, Christianity, Colonialism, and Consciousness in South Africa* (Chicago: The University of Chicago Press, 1991).

47. David C. Sperling, "The Coastal Hinterland and Interior of East Africa," in *The History of Islam in Africa*, ed. Nehemia Levtzion and Randall L. Pouwels (Athens: Ohio University Press, 2000), 273–302, 297.

48. David E. Skinner, *Islam, Education and Politics in West Africa*. Proceedings of the Fifth Birmingham Sierra Leone Studies Symposium, 15–17 July 1988 (Birmingham: University of Birmingham, 1990), 133–38, 133–35.

49. Roman Loimeier, *Muslim Societies in Africa: A Historical Anthropology* (Bloomington: Indiana University Press, 2013), 23–24.

50. Kai Kresse, "Debating Maulidi: Ambiguities and Transformations of Muslim Identity Along the Kenyan Swahili Coast," in *The Global Worlds of the Swahili. Interfaces of Islam, Identity and Space in 19th and 20th-Century East Africa*, ed. Roman Loimeier and Rüdiger Seesemann, 209–28 (Berlin: Lit Verlag, 2006).

51. Robert Launay, *Beyond the Stream: Islam and Society in a West African Town* (Long Grove: Waveland Press, 2004), 27, 105.

52. Examples are the Africa Muslims Agency (Kuwait), International Islamic Relief Organization (Saudi Arabia), *Al-Haramain* (Saudi Arabia), World Islamic Call Society (Libya), *Munazamat al-Da'wa al-Islamiyya* (Sudan), and the International African Relief Agency (Sudan). Ahmed interprets the widening of the concept of *da'wa* linking moral reform with social welfare as the "Red Cross complex." See Chanfi Ahmed, "Networks of Islamic NGOs in Sub-Saharan Africa: Bilal Muslim Mission, African Muslim Agency (Direct Aid), and al-Haramayn," *Journal of Eastern African Studies* 3, no. 3 (2009): 426–27. In competition with the Christian Red Cross and non-governmental organizations, contemporary Muslim associations feel obliged to provide all kinds of educational services and charity. See Mohamed A. Salih, "Islamic NGOs in Africa: The Promise and Peril of Islamic Voluntarism," in *Islamism and Its Enemies in the Horn of Africa*, ed. Alex de Waal (London: Hurst, 2004), 141–81.

53. Justo Lacunza-Balda, "Translations of the Quran into Swahili, and Contemporary Islamic Revival in East Africa," in *African Islam and Islam in Africa. Encounters between Sufis and Islamists*, ed. David Westerlund and Eva Evers Rosander (London: Hurst, 1997), 95–126; Roman Loimeier, *Muslim Societies in Africa: A Historical Anthropology* (Bloomington: Indiana University Press, 2013); Adeline Masquelier, *Women and Islamic Revival in a West African Town* (Bloomington: Indiana University Press, 2009); and Dorothea E. Schulz, *Muslims and New Media in West Africa: Pathways to God* (Bloomington: Indiana University Press, 2012).

54. Dale F. Eickelman and James Piscatori, eds. *Muslim Politics* (Princeton: Princeton University Press, 1996).

55. Rosalind I.J. Hackett and Benjamin F. Soares, "Introduction: New Media and Religious Transformations in Africa," in *New Media and Religious Transformations in Africa*, ed. Rosalind I.J. Hackett and Benjamin F. Soares (Bloomington: Indiana University Press, 2015), 1–16.

56. Roman Loimeier, *Islamic Reform and Political Change in Northern Nigeria* (Evanston: Northwestern University Press, 1997); and Ousmane Kane, *Muslim Modernity in Postcolonial Nigeria: A Study of the Society for the Renewal of Innovation and Reinstatement of Tradition* (Leiden: Brill, 2003).

57. Marloes Janson, *Islam, Youth, and Modernity in the Gambia: The Tablighi Jama'at*, International African Library (New York: Cambridge University Press, 2014).

58. Abdin N. Chande, "Radicalism and Reform in East Africa," in *The History of Islam in Africa*, ed. Nehemia Levtzion and Randall L. Pouwels (Athens: Ohio University Press, 2000), 349–69; and Halkano Abdi Wario and Ramzi

Ben Amara, "Door to Door Da'wa in Africa: Dynamics of Proselytization in Yan Izala and Tablīghī Jamā'at," in *Religion on the Move: New Dynamics of Religious Expansion in a Globalizing World*, ed. Afe Adogame and Shobana Shankar (Leiden: Brill, 2013), 159–77.

59. Ebrahim Moosa, "Worlds 'Apart:' Tablīghī Jamā'at in South Africa under Apartheid, 1963–1993," in *Travellers in Faith: Studies of the Tablīghī Jamā'at as a Transnational Islamic Movement for Faith Renewal*, ed. Muhammad Khalid Masud (Leiden: Brill, 2000), 206–21; and Golam Vahed, "Contesting 'Orthodoxy': The Tablighi-Sunni Conflict among South African Muslims in the 1970s and 1980s," *Journal of Muslim Minority Affairs* 23, no. 2 (2003): 313–34.

60. Roman Loimeier, "Patterns and Peculiarities of Islamic Reform in Africa," *Journal of Religion in Africa* 33, no. 3 (2003): 256.

61. Benjamin Soares and Filippo Osella, "Islam, Politics, Anthropology," *Journal of the Royal Anthropological Institute* 15, no. 1 (2009): 8–9.

62. See Olivier Roy, *Globalised Islam: The Search for a New Ummah* (London: Hurst, 2004).

63. Roman Loimeier and Rüdiger Seesemann, "Introduction: Interfaces of Islam, Identity and Space in 19th and 20th Century East Africa," in *The Global Worlds of the Swahili. Interfaces of Islam, Identity and Space in 19th and 20th-Century East Africa*, ed. Roman Loimeier and Rüdiger Seesemann (Berlin: Lit Verlag, 2006), 1–14.

64. René Otayek and Benjamin F. Soares, "Introduction: Islam and Muslim Politics in Africa," in *Islam and Muslim Politics in Africa*, ed. Benjamin F. Soares and René Otayek (New York: Palgrave, 2007), 1–24.

65. Adeline Masquelier, "Debating Muslims, Disputed Practices: Struggles for the Realization of an Alternative Moral Order in Niger," in *Civil Society and the Political Imagination in Africa: Critical Perspectives*, ed. John L. Comaroff and Jean Comaroff (Chicago: The University of Chicago Press, 1999), 219–50; and Terje Østebø, *Localising Salafism: Religious Change among Oromo Muslims in Bale, Ethiopia* (Leiden: Brill, 2012).

66. Roman Loimeier, "Patterns and Peculiarities of Islamic Reform in Africa," *Journal of Religion in Africa* 33, no. 3 (2003): 260.

67. Ousseina D. Alidou, *Engaging Modernity: Muslim Women and the Politics of Agency in Postcolonial Niger* (Madison: University of Wisconsin Press, 2005); Rosa de Jorio, "Between Dialogue and Contestation: Gender, Islam, and the Challenges of a Malian Public Sphere," *Journal of the Royal Anthropological Institute* 15 (2009): 95–111; and Erin J. Augis, "Jambaar or Jumbax-Out? How Sunnite Women Negotiate Power and Belief in Orthodox Islamic Femininity," in *New Perspectives on Islam in Senegal: Conversion, Migration, Wealth, Power, and Femininity*, ed. Mamadou Diouf and Mara Leichtman (New York: Palgrave, 2009), 211–33.

68. Saba Mahmood, *Politics of Piety: The Islamic Revival and the Feminist Subject* (Princeton: Princeton University Press, 2005); Adeline Masquelier, *Women and Islamic Revival in a West African Town* (Bloomington: Indiana University Press, 2009); Dorothea E. Schulz, *Muslims and New Media in West Africa: Pathways to God* (Bloomington: Indiana University Press, 2012); and Marloes Janson, *Islam, Youth, and Modernity in the Gambia: The Tablighi*

*Jama'at*, International African Library (New York: Cambridge University Press, 2014).

69. Murray Last, "The Power of Youth, Youth of Power: Notes on the Religions of the Young in Northern Nigeria," in *Les jeunes en afrique. La politique et la ville*, Vol. 2, ed. Hélène d'Almeida-Topor (Paris: L'Harmattan, 1992), 375–99; Fabienne Samson, *Les marabouts de l'islam politique: Le Dahiratoul Moustarchidina Wal Moustarchidaty, un mouvement néo-confrérique sénégalais* (Paris: Karthala, 2005); Adeline Masquelier, "Negotiating Futures: Islam, Youth, and the State in Niger," in *Islam and Muslim Politics in Africa*, ed. Benjamin F. Soares and René Otayek (New York: Palgrave, 2007), 243–62; and Marloes Janson, *Islam, Youth, and Modernity in the Gambia: The Tablighi Jama'at*, International African Library (New York: Cambridge University Press, 2014).

70. Abdulkader Tayob, *Islamic Resurgence in South Africa: The Muslim Youth Movement* (Cape Town: University of Cape Town Press, 1995).

71. Goolam Vahed and Shamil Jeppie, *Multiple Communities: Muslims in Post-Apartheid South Africa* (2005), 267, www.hsrcpress.ac.za.

72. On 11 December 2015, President Jammeh declared the Gambia an Islamic Republic. The Gambia follows Mauritania as Africa's second Islamic republic, although the country's secular constitution remains unaltered, http://www.africaresearchinstitute.org/the-gambia-expert-briefing/.

73. Roman Loimeier, "Perceptions of Marginalization: Muslims in Contemporary Tanzania," in *Islam and Muslim Politics in Africa*, ed. Benjamin F. Soares and René Otayek (New York: Palgrave, 2007), 137–56.

74. Since 9/11, the Western world's line-drawing of Islam has resulted in a binary view of what Mamdani calls "Good Muslim" versus "Bad Muslim." See Mahmood Mamdani, *Good Muslim, Bad Muslim: A Political Perspective on Culture and Terrorism. America, the Cold War, and the Roots of Terror* (New York: Pantheon Books, 2004). This way of understanding Islam has resulted in various US "counterterrorism" initiatives in Sub-Saharan Africa, such as the Pan Sahel Initiative and the follow-up program, the Trans-Sahara Counterterrorism Initiative. See Peter J. Schraeder, "La guerre contre le terrorisme et la politique Américaine en Afrique," *Politique africaine* 98 (2005): 42–62; and Baz Lecocq and Paul Schrijver, "The War on Terror in a Haze of Dust: Potholes and Pitfalls on the Saharan Front," *Journal of Contemporary African Studies* 25, no. 1 (2007): 141–66.

75. Benjamin F. Soares, *Muslim-Christian Encounters in Africa* (Leiden: Brill, 2006).

76. J. D. Y. Peel, *Religious Encounter and the Making of the Yoruba* (Bloomington: Indiana University Press, 2000).

77. Janet McIntosh, *The Edge of Islam: Power, Personhood, and Ethnoreligious Boundaries on the Kenya Coast* (Durham: Duke University Press, 2009).

78. Brian Larkin and Birgit Meyer, "Pentecostalism, Islam and Culture: New Religious Movements in West Africa," in *Themes in West African History*, ed. Emmanuel K. Akyeampong (Oxford: James Currey, 2006), 286–312; J. D. Y. Peel, *Christianity, Islam, and Orisa-Religion: Three Traditions in Comparison and Interaction* (Berkeley: University of California Press, 2015); and Marloes Janson and Birgit Meyer, "Introduction: Towards a Framework for the Study

of Christian–Muslim Encounters in Africa," *Africa: The Journal of the International African Institute* 86, no. 4 (2016): 615–19.

79. It should be noted here that disputes among Muslims are as virulent today as are polemics between Muslims and Christians. See Adeline Masquelier, "Debating Muslims, Disputed Practices: Struggles for the Realization of an Alternative Moral Order in Niger," in *Civil Society and the Political Imagination in Africa: Critical Perspectives*, ed. John L. Comaroff and Jean Comaroff (Chicago: The University of Chicago Press, 1999), 219–50.

80. Toyin Falola, *Violence in Nigeria: The Crisis of Religious Politics and Secular Ideologies* (Rochester: University of Rochester Press, 1998); and Roman Loimeier, *Muslim Societies in Africa: A Historical Anthropology* (Bloomington: Indiana University Press, 2013), 292.

81. Robert Launay, "An Invisible Religion? Anthropology's Avoidance of Islam in Africa," in *African Anthropologies: History, Critique and Practice*, ed. Mwenda Ntarangwi, David Mills, and Mustafa Babiker (London: Zed Books, 2006), 188–203; and Roman Loimeier, *Muslim Societies in Africa: A Historical Anthropology* (Bloomington: Indiana University Press, 2013), ix.

82. Jean-Louis Triaud, "Giving a Name to Islam South of the Sahara: An Adventure in Taxonomy," *The Journal of African History* 55, no. 1 (2014): 3–15.

83. See Vincent Monteil, *L'Islam noir* (Paris: Éditions du Seuil, 1980).

84. Robert Launay and Benjamin F. Soares, "The Formation of an 'Islamic Sphere' in French Colonial West Africa," *Economy and Society* 28, no. 4 (1999): 497–519; Louis Brenner, *Controlling Knowledge: Religion, Power, and Schooling in a West African Muslim Society* (London: Hurst, 2000); Rüdiger Seesemann, "African Islam or Islam in Africa? Evidence from Kenya," in *The Global Worlds of the Swahili. Interfaces of Islam, Identity and Space in 19th and 20th-Century East Africa*, ed. Roman Loimeier and Rüdiger Seesemann (Berlin: Lit Verlag, 2006), 229–50; and Jean-Louis Triaud, "Giving a Name to Islam South of the Sahara: An Adventure in Taxonomy," *The Journal of African History* 55, 1 (2014): 3–15.

85. David Westerlund and Eva Evers Rosander, eds. *African Islam and Islam in Africa: Encounters Between Sufis and Islamists* (London: Hurst, 1997).

86. David Robinson, *Muslim Histories, African Societies: The Venture of Islamic Studies in Africa* (Cambridge: Cambridge University Press, 2004).

87. Clifford Geertz, *Islam Observed: Religious Development in Morocco and Indonesia* (New Haven: Yale University Press, 1968).

88. Ladislav Holy, *Religion and Custom in a Muslim Society: The Berti of Sudan* (Cambridge: Cambridge University Press, 1991); and Louis Brenner, "Introduction: Muslim Representations of Unity and Difference in the African Discourse," in *Muslim Identity and Social Change in Sub-Saharan Africa*, ed. Louis Brenner (Bloomington: Indiana University Press, 1993), 1–20.

89. Robert Launay, *Beyond the Stream: Islam and Society in a West African Town* (Long Grove: Waveland Press, 2004), 5.

90. Benjamin F. Soares, *Islam and the Prayer Economy: History and Authority in a Malian Town* (Edinburgh: Edinburgh University Press, 2005), 9–10.

91. For example, see Donal B. Cruise O'Brien and Christian Coulon, eds. *Charisma and Brotherhood in African Islam* (Oxford: Clarendon Press, 1988); Leonardo A. Villalón, *Islamic Society and State Power in Senegal: Disciples*

*and Citizens in Fatick* (Cambridge: Cambridge University Press, 1995); and Khadim Mbacké, *Sufism and Religious Brotherhoods in Senegal*, trans. Eric Ross (Princeton: Markus Wiener Publishers, 2005).

92. Louis Brenner, *Controlling Knowledge: Religion, Power, and Schooling in a West African Muslim Society* (London: Hurst, 2000); Roman Loimeier, "Patterns and Peculiarities of Islamic Reform in Africa," *Journal of Religion in Africa* 33, no. 3 (2003); and Marie Miran, *Islam, histoire et modernité en Côte d'Ivoire* (Paris: Karthala, 2006).

93. René Otayek and Benjamin F. Soares, "Introduction: Islam and Muslim Politics in Africa," in *Islam and Muslim Politics in Africa*, ed. Benjamin F. Soares and René Otayek (New York: Palgrave, 2007), 1–24, 7.

94. Marloes Janson, *Islam, Youth, and Modernity in the Gambia: The Tablighi Jama'at*, International African Library (New York: Cambridge University Press, 2014), 10.

95. M. Sanni Umar, "Changing Islamic Identity in Nigeria from the 1960s to the 1980s: From Sufism to Anti-Sufism," in *Muslim Identity and Social Change in Sub-Saharan Africa*, ed. Louis Brenner (Bloomington: Indiana University Press, 1993), 154–78.

96. Samuli Schielke, "Ambivalent Commitments: Troubles of Morality, Religiosity and Aspiration among Young Egyptians," *Journal of Religion in Africa* 39, no. 2 (2009): 158–85; and Marloes Janson, "'How, for God's Sake, Can I Be a Good Muslim?' Gambian Youth in Search of a Moral Lifestyle," *Ethnography* 17 (2016): 22–46.

97. Magnus Marsden, *Living Islam: Muslim Religious Experience in Pakistan's North-West Frontier* (Cambridge: Cambridge University Press, 2005), 260–61.

98. Talal Asad, *The Idea of an Anthropology of Islam*. Occasional Paper Series (Washington, DC: Center for Contemporary Arab Studies, Georgetown University, 1986), 14.

99. Samuli Schielke and Liza Debevec, "Introduction," in *Ordinary Lives and Grand Schemes. An Anthropology of Everyday Religion*, ed. Samuli Schielke and Liza Debevec (New York: Berghahn Books, 2012), 1–16.

100. Ayşe Saktanber, *Living Islam: Women, Religion and the Politicization of Culture in Turkey* (London: I. B. Tauris, 2002); Magnus Marsden, *Living Islam: Muslim Religious Experience in Pakistan's North-West Frontier* (Cambridge: Cambridge University Press, 2005); and Samuli Schielke and Liza Debevec, eds., *Ordinary Lives and Grand Schemes. An Anthropology of Everyday Religion* (New York: Berghahn Books, 2012).

101. Ernest Gellner, *Muslim Society* (Cambridge: Cambridge University Press, 1981).

102. Rüdiger Seesemann, "The Quotidian Dimension of Islamic Reformism in Wadai (Chad)," in *L'islam politique au sud du Sahara. Identités, discours et enjeux*, ed. Muriel Gomez-Perez (Paris: Karthala, 2005), 327–46, 327.

103. Patrick Haenni and Tjitske Holtrop, "Mondaines spiritualités: 'Amr Khalid, 'shaykh' branché de la jeunesse dorée du Caire," *Politique africaine* 87 (2002): 45–68; and René Otayek and Benjamin F. Soares, "Introduction: Islam and Muslim Politics in Africa," in *Islam and Muslim Politics in Africa*, ed. Benjamin F. Soares and René Otayek (New York: Palgrave, 2007), 1–24, 17–19.

104. By way of a better term, "mainstream Muslims" stands here for those Muslims who combine piety with pragmatism in their struggle to participate in the definition of Islamic modernity. See also Adeline Masquelier, "Negotiating Futures: Islam, Youth, and the State in Niger," in *Islam and Muslim Politics in Africa*, ed. Benjamin F. Soares and René Otayek (New York: Palgrave, 2007), 243–62; and Marloes Janson, "'How, for God's Sake, Can I Be a Good Muslim?' Gambian Youth in Search of a Moral Lifestyle," *Ethnography* 17 (2016): 22–46.

105. Adeline Masquelier, "Negotiating Futures: Islam, Youth, and the State in Niger," in *Islam and Muslim Politics in Africa*, ed. Benjamin F. Soares and René Otayek (New York: Palgrave, 2007), 243–62, 257–58.

## BIBLIOGRAPHY

Ahmed, Chanfi. "Networks of Islamic NGOs in Sub-Saharan Africa: Bilal Muslim Mission, African Muslim Agency (Direct Aid), and al-Haramayn." *Journal of Eastern African Studies* 3, no. 3 (2009): 426–37.

Alidou, Ousseina D. *Engaging Modernity: Muslim Women and the Politics of Agency in Postcolonial Niger*. Madison: University of Wisconsin Press, 2005.

Alpers, Edward A. "East Central Africa." In *The History of Islam in Africa*, edited by Nehemia Levtzion and Randall L. Pouwels, 251–71. Athens, OH: Ohio University Press, 2000.

Asad, Talal. *The Idea of an Anthropology of Islam*. Occasional Paper Series. Washington, DC: Center for Contemporary Arab Studies, Georgetown University, 1986.

Augis, Erin J. "Jambaar or Jumbax-Out? How Sunnite Women Negotiate Power and Belief in Orthodox Islamic Femininity." In *New Perspectives on Islam in Senegal: Conversion, Migration, Wealth, Power, and Femininity*, edited by Mamadou Diouf and Mara Leichtman, 211–33. New York: Palgrave, 2009.

Babou, Cheikh. *Le Jihad de l'âme: Ahmadou Bamba et la fondation de la Mouridiyya au Sénégal, 1853–1913*. Paris: Karthala, 2011.

Bang, Anne K. *Sufis and Scholars of the Sea: Family Networks in East Africa, 1960–1925*. London: Routledge, 2003.

Brenner, Louis. "Introduction: Muslim Representations of Unity and Difference in the African Discourse." In *Muslim Identity and Social Change in Sub-Saharan Africa*, edited by Louis Brenner, 1–20. Bloomington, IN: Indiana University Press, 1993.

———. *Controlling Knowledge: Religion, Power, and Schooling in a West African Muslim Society*. London: Hurst, 2000.

Chande, Abdin N. *Islam, Ulamaa, and Community Development in Tanzania: A Study of Islamic Trends in Tanzania, East Africa*. San Francisco: Austin & Lawrier, 1998.

———. "Radicalism and Reform in East Africa." In *The History of Islam in Africa*, edited by Nehemia Levtzion and Randall L. Pouwels, 349–69. Athens, OH: Ohio University Press, 2000.

Clarke, Peter B. *West Africa and Islam: A Study of Religious Development from the 8th to the 20th Century*. London: Edward Arnold, 1982.

Comaroff, Jean, and John Comaroff. *Of Revelation and Revolution: Christianity, Colonialism, and Consciousness in South Africa,* Vol. 1. Chicago: The University of Chicago Press, 1991.

Cruise O'Brien, Donal B., and Christian Coulon, eds. *Charisma and Brotherhood in African Islam.* Oxford: Clarendon Press, 1988.

De Jorio, Rosa. "Between Dialogue and Contestation: Gender, Islam, and the Challenges of a Malian Public Sphere." *Journal of the Royal Anthropological Institute* 15 (2009): 95–111.

Eickelman, Dale F. "National Identity and Religious Discourse in Contemporary Oman." *International Journal of Islamic and Arabic Studies* 6, no. 1 (1989): 1–20.

———. *Muslim Travellers. Pilgrimage, Migration, and the Religious Imagination.* Berkeley: University of California Press, 1990.

Eickelman, Dale F., and James Piscatori, eds. *Muslim Politics.* Princeton, NJ: Princeton University Press, 1996.

Falola, Toyin. *Violence in Nigeria: The Crisis of Religious Politics and Secular Ideologies.* Rochester, NY: University of Rochester Press, 1998.

Fisher, Humphrey J. *Ahmadiyyah: A Study in Contemporary Islam on the West African Coast.* London: Oxford University Press, 1963.

Geertz, Clifford. *Islam Observed: Religious Development in Morocco and Indonesia.* New Haven, CT: Yale University Press, 1968.

Gellner, Ernest. *Muslim Society.* Cambridge: Cambridge University Press, 1981.

Hackett, Rosalind I.J., and Benjamin F. Soares. "Introduction: New Media and Religious Transformations in Africa." In *New Media and Religious Transformations in Africa,* edited by Rosalind I.J. Hackett and Benjamin F. Soares, 1–16. Bloomington, IN: Indiana University Press, 2015.

Haenni, Patrick, and Tjitske Holtrop. "Mondaines spiritualités: 'Amr Khalid, 'shaykh' branché de la jeunesse dorée du Caire." *Politique africaine* 87 (2002): 45–68.

Hiskett, Mervyn. *The Development of Islam in West Africa.* London: Longman, 1984.

Hodgkin, Elizabeth. "Islamism and Islamic Research in Africa." *Islam et Sociétés au sud du Sahara* 4 (1990): 73–130.

Holy, Ladislav. *Religion and Custom in a Muslim Society: The Berti of Sudan.* Cambridge: Cambridge University Press, 1991.

Hunwick, John O. "West Africa and the Arabic Language." *Sudanic Africa* 15 (2004): 133–44.

Janson, Marloes. *Islam, Youth, and Modernity in the Gambia: The Tablighi Jama'at.* International African Library. New York: Cambridge University Press, 2014.

———. "'How, for God's Sake, Can I Be a Good Muslim?' Gambian Youth in Search of a Moral Lifestyle." *Ethnography* 17 (2016): 22–46.

Janson, Marloes, and Birgit Meyer. "Introduction: Towards a Framework for the Study of Christian–Muslim Encounters in Africa." *Africa: The Journal of the International African Institute* 86, no. 4 (2016): 615–19.

Kaba, Lansiné. *The Wahhabiyya: Islamic Reform and Politics in French West Africa.* Evanston, IL: Northwestern University Press, 1974.

Kane, Ousmane. *Muslim Modernity in Postcolonial Nigeria: A Study of the Society for the Renewal of Innovation and Reinstatement of Tradition.* Leiden, NL: Brill, 2003.

Kapteijns, Lidwien. "Ethiopia and the Horn of Africa." In *The History of Islam in Africa,* edited by Nehemia Levtzion and Randall L. Pouwels, 227–50. Athens, OH: Ohio University Press, 2000.

Kresse, Kai. "Debating Maulidi: Ambiguities and Transformations of Muslim Identity along the Kenyan Swahili Coast." In *The Global Worlds of the Swahili. Interfaces of Islam, Identity and Space in 19th and 20th-Century East Africa*, edited by Roman Loimeier and Rüdiger Seesemann, 209–28. Berlin: Lit Verlag, 2006.

Lacunza-Balda, Justo. "Translations of the Quran into Swahili, and Contemporary Islamic Revival in East Africa." In *African Islam and Islam in Africa. Encounters Between Sufis and Islamists*, edited by David Westerlund and Eva Evers Rosander, 95–126. London: Hurst, 1997.

Larkin, Brian, and Birgit Meyer. "Pentecostalism, Islam and Culture: New Religious Movements in West Africa." In *Themes in West African History*, edited by Emmanuel K. Akyeampong, 286–312. Oxford: James Currey, 2006.

Last, Murray. *The Sokoto Caliphate*. London: Longman, 1967.

——. "The Power of Youth, Youth of Power: Notes on the Religions of the Young in Northern Nigeria." In *Les jeunes en afrique. La politique et la ville*, Vol. 2, edited by Hélène d'Almeida-Topor, 375–99. Paris: L'Harmattan, 1992.

Launay, Robert. *Beyond the Stream: Islam and Society in a West African Town*. Long Grove, IL: Waveland Press, 2004.

——. "An Invisible Religion? Anthropology's Avoidance of Islam in Africa." In *African Anthropologies: History, Critique and Practice*, edited by Mwenda Ntarangwi, David Mills, and Mustafa Babiker, 188–203. London: Zed Books, 2006.

Launay, Robert, and Benjamin F. Soares. "The Formation of an 'Islamic Sphere' in French Colonial West Africa." *Economy and Society* 28, no. 4 (1999): 497–519.

Lecocq, Baz, and Paul Schrijver. "The War on Terror in a Haze of Dust: Potholes and Pitfalls on the Saharan Front." *Journal of Contemporary African Studies* 25, no. 1 (2007): 141–66.

Leichtman, Mara A. *Shi'i Cosmopolitanisms in Africa: Lebanese Migration and Religious Conversion in Senegal*. Bloomington, IN: Indiana University Press, 2015.

Levtzion, Nehemia. *Islam in West Africa: Religion, Society and Politics to 1800*. Aldershot: Variorum, 1994.

——. "Islam in the Bilad al-Sudan to 1800." In *The History of Islam in Africa*, edited by Nehemia Levtzion and Randall L. Pouwels, 63–91. Athens, OH: Ohio University Press, 2000.

Levtzion, Nehemia, and Randall L. Pouwels. "Introduction: Patterns of Islamization and Varieties of Religious Experience among Muslims of Africa." In *The History of Islam in Africa*, edited by Nehemia Levtzion and Randall L. Pouwels, 1–18. Athens, OH: Ohio University Press, 2000.

Lewis, Ioan M., ed. *Islam in Tropical Africa*. London: International African Institute, Oxford University Press, 1966.

Loimeier, Roman. *Islamic Reform and Political Change in Northern Nigeria*. Evanston, IL: Northwestern University Press, 1997.

——. "Patterns and Peculiarities of Islamic Reform in Africa." *Journal of Religion in Africa* 33, no. 3 (2003): 237–62.

——. "Perceptions of Marginalization: Muslims in Contemporary Tanzania." In *Islam and Muslim Politics in Africa*, edited by Benjamin F. Soares and René Otayek, 137–56. New York: Palgrave, 2007.

——. *Muslim Societies in Africa: A Historical Anthropology*. Bloomington, IN: Indiana University Press, 2013.

Loimeier, Roman, and Rüdiger Seesemann. "Introduction: Interfaces of Islam, Identity and Space in 19th- and 20th-Century East Africa." In *The Global Worlds of the Swahili. Interfaces of Islam, Identity and Space in 19th and 20th-Century East Africa*, edited by Roman Loimeier and Rüdiger Seesemann, 1–14. Berlin: Lit Verlag, 2006.

Mahmood, Saba. *Politics of Piety: The Islamic Revival and the Feminist Subject*. Princeton, NJ: Princeton University Press, 2005.

Mamdani, Mahmood. *"Good Muslim, Bad Muslim: America, the Cold War, and the Roots of Terror*. New York: Pantheon Books, 2004.

Marsden, Magnus. *Living Islam: Muslim Religious Experience in Pakistan's North-West Frontier*. Cambridge: Cambridge University Press, 2005.

Masquelier, Adeline. "Debating Muslims, Disputed Practices: Struggles for the Realization of an Alternative Moral Order in Niger." In *Civil Society and the Political Imagination in Africa: Critical Perspectives*, edited by John L. Comaroff and Jean Comaroff, 219–50. Chicago: The University of Chicago Press, 1999.

———. "Negotiating Futures: Islam, Youth, and the State in Niger." In *Islam and Muslim Politics in Africa*, edited by Benjamin F. Soares and René Otayek, 243–62. New York: Palgrave, 2007.

———. *Women and Islamic Revival in a West African Town*. Bloomington, IN: Indiana University Press, 2009.

Mbacké, Khadim. *Sufism and Religious Brotherhoods in Senegal*. Translated by Eric Ross. Princeton, NJ: Markus Wiener Publishers, 2005.

McIntosh, Janet. *The Edge of Islam: Power, Personhood, and Ethnoreligious Boundaries on the Kenya Coast*. Durham, NC: Duke University Press, 2009.

Miles, William F.S. "West African Islam: Emerging Political Dynamics." In *Political Islam in West Africa: State-Society Relations Transformed*, edited by William F.S. Miles, 1–18. Boulder, CO: Lynne Rienner Publishers, 2007.

Miran, Marie. *Islam, histoire et modernité en Côte d'Ivoire*. Paris: Karthala, 2006.

Monteil, Vincent. *L'Islam noir*. Paris: Éditions du Seuil, 1980.

Moosa, Ebrahim. "Worlds 'Apart': Tablīghī Jamā'at in South Africa under Apartheid, 1963–1993." In *Travellers in Faith: Studies of the Tablīghī Jamā'at as a Transnational Islamic Movement for Faith Renewal*, edited by Muhammad Khalid Masud, 206–21. Leiden, NL: Brill, 2000.

Nyang, Sulayman S., and Marloes Janson. "Gambia." In *The Oxford Encyclopedia of the Modern Islamic World*, edited by John Esposito, 283–86. New York: Oxford University Press, 2009.

Østebø, Terje. *Localising Salafism: Religious Change among Oromo Muslims in Bale, Ethiopia*. Leiden, NL: Brill, 2012.

Otayek, René, and Benjamin F. Soares. "Introduction: Islam and Muslim Politics in Africa." In *Islam and Muslim Politics in Africa*, edited by Benjamin F. Soares and René Otayek, 1–24. New York: Palgrave, 2007.

Peel, J.D.Y. *Religious Encounter and the Making of the Yoruba*. Bloomington, IN: Indiana University Press, 2000.

———. *Christianity, Islam, and Orisa-Religion: Three Traditions in Comparison and Interaction*. Berkeley: University of California Press, 2015.

Pouwels, Randall L. *Horn and Crescent: Cultural Change and Traditional Islam on the East African Coast, 800–1900*. Cambridge: Cambridge University Press, 1987.

————. "The East African Coast, c. 780 to 1900 C.E." In *The History of Islam in Africa*, edited by Nehemia Levtzion and Randall L. Pouwels, 251–71. Athens, OH: Ohio University Press, 2000.

Robinson, David. *The Holy War of Umar Tal*. Oxford: Clarendon Press, 1985.

————. *Muslim Histories, African Societies: The Venture of Islamic Studies in Africa*. Cambridge: Cambridge University Press, 2004.

Roy, Olivier. *Globalised Islam: The Search for a New Ummah*. London: Hurst, 2004.

Saktanber, Ayşe. *Living Islam: Women, Religion and the Politicization of Culture in Turkey*. London: I. B. Tauris, 2002.

Salih, Mohamed A. "Islamic NGOs in Africa: The Promise and Peril of Islamic Voluntarism." In *Islamism and Its Enemies in the Horn of Africa*, edited by Alex de Waal, 141–81. London: Hurst, 2004.

Samson, Fabienne. *Les marabouts de l'islam politique: Le Dahiratoul Moustarchidina Wal Moustarchidaty, un mouvement néo-confrérique sénégalais*. Paris: Karthala, 2005.

Sanneh, Lamin. *The Jakhanke Muslim Clerics: A Religious and Historical Study of Islam in Senegambia*. Lanham, MD: University Press of America, 1989.

Schielke, Samuli. "Ambivalent Commitments: Troubles of Morality, Religiosity and Aspiration among Young Egyptians." *Journal of Religion in Africa* 39, no. 2 (2009): 158–85.

Schielke, Samuli, and Liza Debevec. "Introduction." In *Ordinary Lives and Grand Schemes. An Anthropology of Everyday Religion*, edited by Samuli Schielke and Liza Debevec, 1–16. New York: Berghahn Books, 2012.

Schraeder, Peter J. "La guerre contre le terrorisme et la politique Américaine en Afrique." *Politique africaine* 98 (2005): 42–62.

Schulz, Dorothea E. *Muslims and New Media in West Africa: Pathways to God*. Bloomington, IN: Indiana University Press, 2012.

Seesemann, Rüdiger. "The Quotidian Dimension of Islamic Reformism in Wadai (Chad)." In *L'islam politique au sud du Sahara. Identités, discours et enjeux*, edited by Muriel Gomez-Perez, 327–46. Paris: Karthala, 2005.

————. "African Islam or Islam in Africa? Evidence from Kenya." In *The Global Worlds of the Swahili. Interfaces of Islam, Identity and Space in 19th and 20th-Century East Africa*, edited by Roman Loimeier and Rüdiger Seesemann, 229–50. Berlin: Lit Verlag, 2006.

Skinner, David E. "Islam, Education and Politics in West Africa." Proceedings of the Fifth Birmingham Sierra Leone Studies Symposium, 15–17 July 1988, 133–38. Birmingham: University of Birmingham, 1990.

Soares, Benjamin F. *Islam and the Prayer Economy: History and Authority in a Malian Town*. Edinburgh: Edinburgh University Press, 2005.

————. *Muslim–Christian Encounters in Africa*. Leiden, NL: Brill, 2006.

Soares, Benjamin, and Filippo Osella. "Islam, Politics, Anthropology." *Journal of the Royal Anthropological Institute* 15, no. 1 (2009): 1–23.

Sperling, David C. "The Coastal Hinterland and Interior of East Africa." In *The History of Islam in Africa*, edited by Nehemia Levtzion and Randall L. Pouwels, 273–302. Athens, OH: Ohio University Press, 2000.

Tayob, Abdulkader. *Islamic Resurgence in South Africa: The Muslim Youth Movement*. Cape Town: University of Cape Town Press, 1995.

————. "Counting Muslims in South Africa." *Annual Review of Islam in South Africa* 1. Cape Town: Centre for Contemporary Islam, University of Cape Town, http://www.cci.uct.ac.za/usr/cci/publications/aria/download_issues/1998/1998_9.pdf, 1998.

————. *Islam in South Africa: Mosques, Imams, and Sermons.* Gainesville: University Press of Florida, 1999.

Triaud, Jean-Louis. "Giving a Name to Islam South of the Sahara: An Adventure in Taxonomy." *The Journal of African History* 55, no. 1 (2014): 3–15.

Trimingham, John S. *Islam in West Africa.* Oxford: Clarendon Press, 1959.

————. *Islam in East Africa.* Oxford: Clarendon Press, 1964.

Umar, M. Sanni. "Changing Islamic Identity in Nigeria from the 1960s to the 1908s: From Sufism to Anti-Sufism." In *Muslim Identity and Social Change in Sub-Saharan Africa,* edited by Louis Brenner, 154–78. Bloomington, IN: Indiana University Press, 1993.

Vahed, Goolam. "Changing Islamic Traditions and Emerging Identities in South Africa." *Journal of Muslim Minority Affairs* 20, no. 1 (2000): 43–73.

————. "Contesting 'Orthodoxy': The Tablighi-Sunni Conflict Among South African Muslims in the 1970s and 1980s." *Journal of Muslim Minority Affairs* 23, no. 2 (2003): 313–34.

Vahed, Goolam, and Shamil Jeppie. *Multiple Communities: Muslims in Post-Apartheid South Africa,* 2005, www.hsrcpress.ac.za.

Villalón, Leonardo A. *Islamic Society and State Power in Senegal: Disciples and Citizens in Fatick.* Cambridge: Cambridge University Press, 1995.

Von Sivers, Peter. "Egypt and North Africa." In *The History of Islam in Africa,* edited by Nehemia Levtzion and Randall L. Pouwels, 21–36. Athens, OH: Ohio University Press, 2000.

Wario, Halkano Abdi, and Ramzi Ben Amara. "Door to Door Daʻwa in Africa: Dynamics of Proselytization in Yan Izala and Tablīghī Jamāʻat." In *Religion on the Move: New Dynamics of Religious Expansion in a Globalizing World,* edited by Afe Adogame and Shobana Shankar, 159–77. Leiden, NL: Brill, 2013.

Westerlund, David, and Eva Evers Rosander, eds. *African Islam and Islam in Africa: Encounters Between Sufis and Islamists.* London: Hurst, 1997.

# CHAPTER 39

# The Unfinished Business of Postcolonialism: Theological Perspectives

*Elias Kifon Bongmba*

In this chapter, I argue that postcolonialism argument is a discourse and practice that has two aims. Firstly, it denounces and rejects imperial domination. Secondly, it turns a critical gaze on the new configurations of power in former colonies that are now independent, and thus postcolonies. I work with a loose definition of postcolonial to refer to the shadow and effects of the imperial colonial order on nations around the world, and to the lingering effects of colonialism that continue to shape global relations. This short working framework derives from Pramod K. Nayar who states: 'Postcolonialism is the academic, intellectual, ideological and ideational scaffolding of the condition of decolonization (the period following political independence for nations and cultures in Africa, Asia and South America)'.[1] Postcolonialism is a multidisciplinary inquiry and practice that debunks the views that colonial societies did not have any histories before the birth of the imperial age and that rejects colonial domination.[2] In this chapter, I focus briefly on the religious dimensions and within that field of study I will reflect specifically on the theological perspectives of Fabien Eboussi Boulaga, referring only in a tangential manner to philosophical arguments. This is a simple division of labor that allows me to focus on one line of argument and should not be seen as neglect of the rich literature on postcolonialism in the social sciences and the humanities, or more broadly, African studies. For example, I do not specifically address postcoloniality in literature, where African writers like Ngugi wa Thiogo, Chinua Achebe, Mongo Beti, Mariama Bâ, Cheikh Hamidou Kane

E.K. Bongmba (✉)
Rice University, Houston, TX, USA

© The Author(s) 2018
M.S. Shanguhyia and T. Falola (eds.),
*The Palgrave Handbook of African Colonial and Postcolonial History*,
https://doi.org/10.1057/978-1-137-59426-6_39

Calixthe Beyala, and more recently Chimamanda Adichie, have been some of the most creative interpreters of the postcolonial condition and the postcolony.[3] Therefore, my goal is to highlight and reflect on theological perspectives on the African postcolony.

## THE POLITICAL PHILOSOPHY OF DECOLONIZATION

To begin with, postcolonial discourses and criticism reject the imperial order because what masqueraded for many decades as cultural diffusion, religious benevolence, or an intellectual and educational project was a practice of domination. Ali Mazrui described the colonial aptly:

> God, gold and glory! Captured in a slogan, these are in in fact the three basic imperatives in the history of cultural diffusion. Why do men burst forth from their boundaries in search of new horizons? They are inspired either by a search for religious fulfillment (the God standard) or by a yearning for economic realization (the gold standard) or by the passion for renown (the quest for glory).[4]

Mazrui captured the essence of the imperial project, but the task was to name and overcome it. Here the postcolonial project was articulated from many perspectives, but one of the predominant modes of discourse was what Toyin Falola has called cultural nationalism.[5] Falola covers a wide timeline and includes intellectuals like Edward Wilmot Blyden, but he maps out the ideas African intellectuals deployed to counter imperialism. However, many of them focused on identity politics in writings and pronouncements that reclaimed and affirmed the African personality that had suffered ignominy under colonialism. The Négritude movement promoted black thought that was grounded in African cultural and social realities.[6] Writers like Aimé Césaire and Léopold Séda Senghor carried their epistemological project from a solid grounding in black identity and African thought systems. This approach did not ignore rationality, but instead asserted the African *will* to think and theorize, hence the term Négritude. Both Césaire and Senghor used their poetry to reaffirm Africanness and blackness.

Such a project was not without its critics. For example, Emmanuel Chukwudi Eze has argued that postcolonial critique must 'adopt an explicitly philosophical standpoint' to analyze and articulate morality and politics. He laments the fact that ideas like *ubuntu* dominate contemporary philosophical discourses and scholars have ignored other rational approaches in postcolonial critique. He argues that ubuntu as a philosophical category is not helpful and does not serve a useful function because it is grounded on luck, miracles, and is largely 'an aestheticized, quasi-religious political thought for a particular place and time'.[7] Cultural nationalism and a short essay like this cannot do justice to the amount of literature that discusses and assesses the postcolonial project in the African context.

In politics, one of the clearest statements on postcolonialism came from Dr. Kwame Nkrumah, arguably one of the most distinguished intellectual and active politicians in Africa.[8] Nkrumah, whose statue stands outside the African Union buildings, in many ways remains the 'Patron Saint' of African Unity and one of its most eloquent critics of colonialism. In his book, *Consciencism*, Nkrumah provided a philosophical and ideological perspective with the goals of effecting the decolonization and reconfiguration of sociopolitical practice in the postcolony.[9] Other African politicians articulated positions on their own thought and direction in which they would go such as Ahmadou Ahidjo of Cameroon in *The Political Philosophy of Ahmadou Ahidjo*, and Julius Nyerere's widely studied *Ujamaa*.[10] Nkrumah constructed his text carefully, beginning with a long section in which he interpreted the history of philosophy, making his case that philosophy is a contextual activity which offers critical perspectives on understanding and responding to reality and the social world in which people live.[11] Nkumah argued that early philosophical thinking focused on society, politics, sociality, and the natural world. Philosophical positions that serve the society always have an ideology that unites people and provides the justification for the kinds of institutions and structures that would work for a revolution to change things. For Nkrumah, ideology unites the actions of people, orders the life of the society, and manifests itself in political theory as well as in moral theory. Nkrumah described ideology as 'a network of principles and rules for the guidance and appraisal of conduct'.[12] Ideology embraces all aspects of life and 'manifests itself in their class-structure, history, literature, art, religion'.[13] Nkrumah argued that ideology should also aim for social control in a context that should allow for unity and diversity without foregoing the need for coercion. Establishing coercion, as envisaged by Nkrumah, did not mean brute force, but included the use of different instruments such as legislative action because a society 'must count among its instruments of coercion and cohesion, prohibitions and permissions which are made explicit in a statutory way'.[14] To articulate an ideology that would serve Africa, Africans ought to appreciate African history but also consider the impact of Western and Islamic thought.[15] Nkrumah argued that philosophical studies did not help Africans very much because the universalist perspective of philosophy lacks the kind of specificity needed to address the concrete realities of Africans.

Nkrumah grounded his revolutionary project on the presupposition that Africa faced competing ideologies: traditional beliefs and way of life, Islamic thought, and Christian thought.[16] Africans needed a philosophical idea that would galvanize the fight against the imperial order and he named that idea philosophical consciencism. Nkrumah grounded consciencism on materialism because matter has power to move. Additionally, he argued that this would enable Africans to change their perspectives on ethics and morals. The weapons of the philosophy lay in the 'living conditions of the African people'.[17] Its project would restore egalitarianism and mobilize African resources to attain the objectives laid down by African leaders emerging from colonialism. Consciencism had to combine action with promoting egalitarianism at the social level and was therefore ethical, requiring human conduct that conformed to this philosophy. Nkrumah argued: 'The cardinal ethical principle of philosophical consciencism is to treat each man as an end in himself and not merely as a means'.[18] Nkrumah distinguished his perspective from Kant's categorical imperative by arguing that his perspective was grounded on materialism and African perspectives on personhood, life, and reality.

Nkrumah condemned the exploitation of people. He argued:

> By reason of its egalitarian tenet, philosophical consciencism seeks to promote individual development, but in such a way that the conditions for the development of all become the conditions for the development of each; that is, in such a way that the individual development does not introduce such diversities as to destroy the egalitarian basis.[19]

Nkrumah tied the notion of individuality to the idea of African personality, which is a broad term that is difficult to determine because various scholars and politicians have used it, but there are two possibilities. The idea of African personality referred to the personality of individual Africans or referred to a collective African personality.[20] Olúfémi Táíwó has argued that scholars like Blyden, and politicians like Nkrumah and Nnamdi Azikiwe of Nigeria, adopted the latter view of African personality, thus promoting a view of personality that assumes a common Africanness. Táíwó argues for an African personality that promotes individuality to refer to difference and 'individuality that gives full scope to agency and its occasional display of caprice'.[21]

The imperative task for Africans was to end colonialism and the economic exploitation of Africa. Therefore, acting to emancipate Africa was the first step to securing economic independence. It was important for people to choose between positive and negative actions.

> Positive action will represent the sum of those forces seeking social justice in terms of the destruction of oligarchic exploitation and oppression. Negative action will correspondingly represent the sum of those forces tending to prolong colonial subjugation and exploitation. Positive action is revolutionary and negative action is reactionary.[22]

He argued that the implications for politics are that there is always tension in plurality. He called for institutions that would monitor the behavior of individuals in the community and recognize that each individual has worth.

Nkrumah argued that consciencism faced colonial and imperialist forces of disunity, as well as lack of development. In order to get rid of these problems, it was necessary to end the colonialism that existed to extort Africans' raw materials. He contended that both social forces and matter must be changed through positive action. However, the problem with Nkrumah's thesis was that all along he privileged socialism. In addition, he called for the establishment of a one-party state, claiming it would enable people to express themselves and follow their common aspirations more effectively than would a multi-party democracy. Since colonials were not happy to be booted out, Nkrumah argued that they would do all they could to stay in charge through the project of neo-colonialism. Africans struggling for liberation ought not to take advice from them. Instead, Africans needed to carry out an objective analysis of the situation as they prepared for positive action that would lead to liberation.

One wonders if Nkrumah thought about the political dimension of his project carefully, especially since he was also appealing for an African individuality. Proposing a one-party state indicates that Nkrumah actually conceived of African personality as a collective at the expense of individual thought. The one-party structure in most countries actually eliminated free thought. Nkrumah argued that the colonialists would fight back through the more dangerous practice and tool of neo-colonialism, which divides the people and causes leaders to ignore the those who elected them, preferring the neo-colonialist. It was necessary then to use positive action to bring people together to promote development and unite forces to prevent it from collapsing.

Positive action needed an ideology that would unite the masses, offer a regenerative view of their life-world, and help them to perceive the past, present, and future. Ideology was important because it set criteria to evaluate positive action and make sure that it was rooted in the life of the people. Nkrumah called for Africans to practice socialism.

> When socialism is true to its purpose, it seeks a connection with the egalitarian and humanist past of the people before their social evolution was ravaged by colonialism; it seeks from the results of colonialism those elements (like new methods of industrial production and economic organization) which can be adapted to serve the interest of the people; it seeks to contain and prevent the spread of those anomalies and domineering interests created by the capitalist habit of colonialism; it reclaims the psychology of the people, erasing the 'colonial mentality' from it; and it resolutely defends the independence and security of the people.[23]

Nkrumah understood this to involve a dialectical process that would let the forces and tensions play out and introduce change through materialism. Nkrumah had thought through his ideas carefully, defending what some would have called totalitarian rule by arguing that even in ancient Greece the well-articulated ideals of democracy were left to the sophist to execute and society was never as democratic as one thinks because there were class factions and even slavery. However, I should emphasize that the African thought and ideals to which Nkrumah appealed were not as conclusive on one side as Nkrumah assumed. Kwasi Wiredu has argued that although the Akan chiefship was hereditary, decision making was representative and included the building of consensus through persuasion.[24]

Nkrumah was also criticized by one of Africa's leading postcolonial scholars, Ali Mazrui, who himself rejected the colonial project and focused his intellectual and scholarly output to articulate Africanness and the African will to be different. The temptation of the one-party system and its practice in Africa was detrimental, and Mazrui argued that most African countries that gained independence failed to sustain democratic rule by the end of the first decade of independence. 'Within the first decade either the military captured power or the elected president became a dictator, or a civil war broke out, or the ruling party outlawed any rival political party and turned the country into a single-party state'.[25] Mazrui also bemoaned the strivings and conflicts in Africa and argued that Africans should work for solutions that required looking inward (drawing from Africa's own ancestral resources) and looking outward to other parts of the world.[26]

According to Mazrui, Africans continued to live through a set of paradoxes, which included the paradox of habitation in which Africa is seen as the ancestral home of humanity, but many see it today as the least hospitable place. There is the paradox of humiliation that Africans have suffered through the ages; slavery, colonialism, and racial discrimination. Ali pointed to the paradox of acculturation because foreign cultures, political, economic, and social models have been imposed on Africa, creating conflicts with identities. Africa also suffered from the paradox of fragmentation because capitalist exploitation disrupted Africa. Africa had the paradox of retardation, seen in the fact that it could not seem to act as single continent due to national, ethnic, ideological, and religious differences make it challenging for Africans to do so. The final paradox was that of location, because Africa was on the margins of global politics, even though it seemed to be located at the center of the map.[27] Therefore, the task of postcolonial scholars and actors emerged in different forms and there was never unanimity. Even Mazrui himself at some point argued that using non-Africans to commit atrocities could be a way of achieving peace in Africa.[28]

## THE MALAISE OF THE POSTCOLONY

If the second goal of postcolonial theory is to focus on the postcolony, then its task involves not only the ability to redefine Africa and Africans on their own terms, but to provide a diagnosis of the Africa that was invented through Western discourse and colonial practice. V. Y. Mudimbe has clearly demonstrated this in *The Invention of Africa*.[29] The act of invention was an obsession which Achille Mbembe argues marked out Africa as a space of 'absence, lack, non being, of identity and difference, of negatives—in short of nothingness'.[30] Postcolonial discourse, then, would address what Lewis R. Gordon has argued, is the way Africa has been 'invented by systems of knowledge constituted by the processes of conquest and colonization … always erupted … [through] the processes of resistance borne out of those events'.[31] In exposing colonial invention, postcolonial critique and practice intended to create new spaces, redefining identities with an enabling and ennobling discourse. This would assert the African will to be and act in political communities that were always global, but were being dragged into a globalized world not merely by neo-colonial forces which continued to serve as bastions of domination, but by postcolonial regimes that were a disappointment to many Africans. That is why the discourse of postcoloniality was as concerned with the postcolony as it was with imperial forces.

What is significant about postcolonial studies is that while the authors in different fields held the searchlight and deployed their critical tools to examine colonialism beyond the struggles of the postwar era and the influence of Marxist critiques, it was also clear that postcolonial studies, while not establishing a deceptive time line, has also turned its critical gaze on the postcolony. From a theoretical perspective, one could argue that postcolonial theories and the scholars who articulated them had become self-reflexive to the extent that much of the discourse focused on the postcolony itself.[32]

While there are numerous examples here, in the social sciences it was Achille Mbembe's 1992 essay 'Provisional Notes on the Postcolony' that set the gold standard for this type of critique.[33] For Mbembe, the postcolony referred to the countries that had just emerged from the barbarism of colonialism and demonstrated what he called a chaotic pluralism but also ironically demonstrated 'an internal coherence'.[34] Describing the postcolony as a system of signs for mirroring and imagining power, as he said at the beginning of the essay 'The Banality of Power', Mbembe provided an apt description of the postcolony that remains hauntingly true today. He argued: 'the postcolony is characterized by a distinctive style of political improvisation, by a tendency to excess and a lack of proportion as well as by distinctive ways in which identities are multiplied, transformed, and put into circulation'.[35] Mbembe's analysis of the banality of power, which he would further flesh out in his book *On the Postcolony*, gave robust postmodern 'position' to his analysis of power which other scholars had discussed, especially if one thinks of the critique of power by Robert Jackson, Carl Rosberg, and Jean-François Bayart.[36]

Some critics suggested that Mbembe's characterization ought to be matched with ethnographic realities from Africa. Yet what is clear to many readers is that Mbembe had landscaped nearly all the features of personal and presidential governance in Africa to present a purposefulness to it when he conceptualized the postcolonial exercise of power not merely as a continuation of colonial abuse but as a groomed aesthetics and stylistic approach to power which he would also call the 'vulgarity of power'.[37] In his *On the Postcolony*, Mbembe broadened his analysis of the brutality of power as he painted the portrait of 'big man' politics in Cameroon, which he laid out in 'provisional notes' which raised many concerns because critics thought he had painted such a bleak portrait of Africa and left no room for optimism. In a response to Mbembe's essay on the banality of power, V. Y. Mudimbe argued that Mbembe had an excellent grasp of 'the economy of life and its exploitation by demagogic politicians', adding that Mbembe had left readers with a depressing portrait of the continent: 'either to confirm Africa in an absolute status of incompetence ... or to claim that the whole scandal going on right now might be a regrettable accident of the extension of capitalism'.[38] However, in what clearly was a call for Africans to go beyond pessimism, Mudimbe asked:

> Could not we go further? Should we not add to what Achille has provided (and most of us have done rather poorly) a paragraph, a chapter, a book or (why not?) a political engagement that might indicate how to save the African Continent? I believe the masochist period has lasted long enough. Let us remain critical and, at the same time, try to balance our critiques with concrete and programmatic projects.[39]

In effect Mudimbe agreed with the portrait of the postcolony painted by Mbembe. Africa is at the crossroads, and those who control the traffic lights are its leaders, who must give their citizens the green light to action that will lead them out of despair. In the next section, I will discuss how Fabien-Eboussi Boulaga's postcolonial discourse frames a way out.

## CONDITIONS FOR VIBRANT POSTCOLONIAL PRAXIS: THEOLOGICAL PERSPECTIVES

Postcolonial discourses on religion and theology developed multiple themes that centered on colonial abuse and neglect of African cultures and religions, the imperative of liberation, and a critical political theology that addressed the human condition in Africa. Beginning with the significant text *Des Prêtres Noirs s'Interrogent*, African theologians criticized missionary practice for ignoring African cultures and passing on Western culture to Africans as authentic Christianity.[40] One of the major responses to the crisis of religion and culture came from John Mbiti of Kenya and E. Bolaji Idowu, who as Christian theologians popularized the teaching of African religions in schools and universities through their publications, bringing to the scholarly world a systematic organization of the themes that constitute the idea of religion in Africa which at that time had become part of the standard social-scientific studies of Africa.[41] These studies concretized the study of African religions in the postcolony and were in themselves a potent critique of colonial and Christian attempts to wipe African indigenous religions off the map. Idowu also argued: 'There are in Africa men of faith who are finding the prefabricated theology imported into Africa inadequate for her spiritual and academic needs ... [They are] advocators and promoters of theology which bears the stamp of original thinking and mediation of Africans'.[42] The scholarly output of African theologians focused on articulating liberation on the continent, but more especially in Southern Africa, where colonial domination remained in Angola, Namibia, Zimbabwe, and Mozambique.[43] In calling for a complete liberation, theologians like Jean Mar Ela focused on poverty and hunger as part of their greater concern for liberation in Africa. From his ecclesial assignment in North Cameroon, Ela, using African metaphors, argued that for many in Africa, 'the granary is empty'.[44] Discussing the food situation in Africa in light of the Christian experience, Ela stated: 'our churches today expose us to the dangers of atheism each time we celebrate the Eucharist in areas where no one is working to create conditions that would allow hungry people to feed themselves'.[45] It is important to note that by 1988, Ela was highlighting the seriousness of the situation because Africa was experiencing phenomenal Church growth, even when its masses were going without food. Ela argued that the poor must be part of the process of change. In order for Africans to bring about the plan of God in their context they must start a 'ministry of the granary' to address the food situation. 'Today the question of food must again become the center of daily life—starting from an African culture that is based on granaries and dynamics of the revelation as it is read in Genesis through Mathew.'[46] In the African postcolony, Ela asked the haunting question: '[H]ow can we speak of the Lord of life, knowing full well that famine is the messenger of death?'[47] Food security remains a huge problem in the African postcolony, and it has been compromised by land and boundary disputes, farmer–grazier problems, and a growing *latifundia* which has arisen in the wake of the expansion of large agro-pastoral projects which have initiated a new land grab on the continent.[48]

One of the most devastating critiques of colonial practice came from philosopher and theologian Fabien Eboussi-Boulaga, who prosecuted that criticism in what is one of the most creative theological treatises in Africa, *Christianity without Fetishes: An African Critique and Recapture of Christianity* (CWF).[49] Eboussi-Boulaga's agenda involved four critical questions:

1. Can Western dogmas of Christianity and its civilization remain the same when transmitted to other places?
2. Can the identity of Christianity remain the Western experience?
3. Can other societies whose cultures have been criticized and rejected and lived the death of their own myths 'seriously accept Christianity's pretensions to be the foreordained truth and norm of all authentic existence ...?'[50]
4. Does God's identity as proclaimed by Christians not suffer because he is presented as a partisan who privileges others and excludes others?

Eboussi-Boulaga asked '[H]ow is it possible to take the metaphors of revelation and word of God literally when they authorize a like human conception, too human a conception, and make of monotheism a political problem?'[51] These questions frame what was intended to discard fetishes of Christianity, but it was also an itinerary that provided one of the strongest criticisms of the colonial Christian project. He discussed the worldwide spread of dogmatic Christianity as an untouchable tradition, carrying with it a 'form of certitude' grounded on the claims that Christianity was revealed by an almighty God, although each Church presents its own interpretation of that revelation:

> Revelation rests on the premise that there are empirically observable realities that are substantially sacred and afford direct access to God—that symbols exist expressing God's nature, symbols of God. From these one can ascend toward him, know what he is, know what he wills and what he does. They can occur in the form of persons, words, formulas, books, defined behavior, on inward sentiments or certitudes.[52]

This view of revelation is grounded in a belief that would be transported to all parts of the Earth, and those people who accepted it were supposed to give up their own myths. In Africa it perpetuated an alienating practice which classified Africans as pagans who lived in evil, were not part of God, and suffered intellectual and moral regression. This justified the exercise of authority over them by colonials and missionaries. Even when individuals changed, they were not equal to Western colonials.[53] These proclamations extirpated Africans, stripped them of their space, rendered them naked and despoiled. In terms of time, conversion was supposed to wipe away the past of the pagan and lead to a situation where 'faith finds its phenomenological locus in the manifold renunciation of the presence of inculturation'.[54] In other words, the doctrine of revelation presented the absoluteness of Christianity and removed (or at least so the missionaries thought) Africans from their worldviews and their cultures.

To effect that kind of domination, missionary discourse involved the language of derision, which mocked to death the gods of the locals. It employed the language of refutation, and rejected pagan beliefs because they emerged from 'unbridled silliness'. Missionaries also employed the language of demonstration, through which they explained 'the Christian faith in all its order, coherence, and transforming power'. They considered what they taught truths Africans had to believe, commands they were to obey, and the sacraments they were to receive. Missionaries also employed the language of orthodoxy, which emphasized the difference of the Christian faith which ought to be received as truth. Finally, they employed the language of conformity through which African lives, social time, and spaces were remodeled through rites and works they were to perform. The missionary promoted might, which sometimes permitted violence if it would lead to conversion, and its theological pronouncements about a strong and vengeful God dissuaded other spirits from intervening. It promoted a rationalism which militated against indigenous beliefs and thought systems, since it was assumed the missionary message was grounded on natural reason. In running away from other myths, Christianity created its own myths and called them history. They promoted miracles, prophecy, and stressed the historicity of Christian myths and, in what appears as a commentary on Rudolf Bultmann, Eboussi-Boulaga argues that the search for something that distinguishes Christianity as the supernatural and exceptional constituted fetishes.[55]

The messengers of the Christian tradition imposed Western ways of perceiving divinity and divine beings. Their presentation not only privileged but also imposed a Western rationalist perspective which ignored the symbolic world to which they had taken their message. The personalist ethos of the new religion was troubling to Africans because it championed individualisms and disassociations. Eboussi-Boulaga then proposed a recapture of Christianity through what he described as the Christic model. A clear understanding of the Christic model called for rethinking the Christian message in the postcolonial context in a way that would entail going back to the beginning of the Christian mythos in order to reinvent Christianity, transform it, and give it a local name and habitation. Eboussi-Boulaga then reviewed the different movements and schools of thought that offered alternative teachings at the time of Jesus, who for the most part had some version of the reign of God. The vision of Jesus was distinct because its eschatological component stressed (and required) actions through which one would integrate 'historical conditions into one's own lot, for receiving one's self from others ... a realistic horizon of collective and individual self'.[56] The eschatological activity thus relativized ideologies, institutions, and privileged actions in the tradition of Jesus who in his lifetime associated frequently with the outcasts and those who lived on the underside of society. The eschatological vision of Jesus made explicit that those in need are my neighbors. The eschatological engagement takes care of the people and the things that have been ignored or neglected by the system. In this view of eschatology, God is initiated by the actions of other human beings for others. 'The God who begets is the God who arrives, who supervenes. He is the Ancestor'.[57] Therefore the Christic model requires a theology of God who should be seen as a parent of all who live in relationship with one another and guardian of the institutions that preside over human relations.

The Christic model is not grounded primarily in the imposition of Western myths over African myths and worldview but is the habituation of love which makes the faith community one of love, a communion of brothers, sisters, and friends. It is a self-limiting community which underscores its radical openness to others. In such a community, miracles are a product of faith and are analogous to what we see in the African context, and the stress that there are verifiable practices is beside the point of miracles themselves. The only difference is the cultural conditioning of the message about miracles. Most of them were used in liturgy, hence they were stories meant to encourage and serve the believing community. These activities reflect Christ, whose life was filled with mythic symbols and had a destiny that was concerned not with one's self but with the community. Eboussi Boulaga's probe lays bare the historical record on Christianity in Africa to highlight not only a methodological blunder but also a serious flaw in its anthropological vision, since they articulated an ethic that ignored the Christic model and mission.

Prior to *Christianity without Fetishes*, Eboussi Boulaga defined the African condition as *La Crise fu Muntu*, which he called a moral imperative that must be addressed by Africans by drawing from Africa's cultural and intellectual system which had been undermined by the global system of domination. Such an intellectual and moral vision called for perspectives that would effect a critical reconstruction of the self in light of African traditions, and respond to the distortion caused by international imperial forces.[58] Such a self is one who thinks broadly about the past, the present, and the future of Africa but does not dwell in the past.[59] That subjectivity would deliver Africans from captivity within European thought. Eboussi Boulaga rejects domination and invites Africans to assume responsibility, take charge of their affairs, and face the future in the grand task of reconstituting the self, whose success depends on Africans. Therefore, an appropriate postcolonial posture placed African traditions at the center of the process that required a critical rethinking and reorientation of all notions of self. Rethinking the idea of Muntu was a critical engagement that required that each individual reorganize his or her mentality and make critical choices to sift through and recover African traditions and the self-awareness compromised by colonial domination. For Eboussi Boulaga, this called for a self that would think and act like a subject on his or her own terms, whose self-determination would give a clear message that he or she is not an object but an individual who can act decisively in search of self-fulfillment. Eugène Didier A. Goussikindey is correct to argue that in posing the question of identity in relation to the idea of a subject, Eboussi-Boulaga prioritizes responsibility of the subject to determine the self.[60]

Taking such a posture required a deconstructive process that would place everything Africans had received from the imperial and its religious traditions on the table for scrutiny, appropriation, or rejection. Eboussi-Boulaga offered a more thoroughgoing deconstruction in light of the fact that what appeared to be African tradition (modern, Christian, or even African) was actually constructed by forces of domination both in and outside Africa. In light of this, Eboussi-Boulaga argued that from the colonial perspective, there was no African tradition because the colonials did not believe in those things or there were no Africans (only people to be dominated).[61] This was not a denial of the view that there was something in Africa which colonial forces destroyed, nor is this a claim that Muntu culture lacked ideals, but a recognition of the falsehood that had been perpetrated about Muntu which now required revolutionary thinking for Africans to overcome falsehood. The task for Muntu called not only for a restart, or reform, but for what he described in different places as a fresh start, or new beginning.[62]

The goal of such revolutionary thinking in the postcolony was to offer a critique of practices that did not work to the benefit of Muntu and their communities. This critique would focus on imperial domination, thoughts, and ideas that have distorted Muntu, but the critique would reaffirm Muntu. This required a new perspective on tradition from Africans which would reject all notions that their traditions were static or locked somewhere in the past. The traditions of Muntu and their communities were active and alive and what we see is an appeal to employ those to create viable communities.[63] This theme of transformation and change has remained a constant in the thought of Eboussi Boulaga. During the movement toward democracy in Africa, when the Catholic Church helped establish National Sovereign Conferences all over the continent, Eboussi Boulaga argued that what was needed was the emergence of a superior engagement that would overturn completely the previous economic (and we might add, political and social) system.[64]

Seeing local traditions as creative forces would turn away negativity and replace it with a bold assertion of the self. Postcolonial discourse ought to be liberating discourses which would reject the negativity of the imperial world which constrains the creativity of Muntu.

A liberating discourse should unleash Muntu to become engaged in the creative process that not only interprets the individual's being but asserts it as a subject on his or her own terms. This requires a love experience whose phenomenology involves *being* and *doing* as practices which rethink and redefine the historical process and articulate a vision not concerned primarily with survival, but with self-creation in an authentic dialectical engagement of being and doing. One may be tempted at this point to think that Mobuto Sese Seko, the disgraced dictator of Zaire, might have read Eboussi Boulaga, but Mobitu's *authenticité* was self-serving and meant to promote his vision of the Congo, then Zaire.

This search for authenticity is a complex process, which according to Eboussi Boulaga should also be seen as a communal project because it involves all black people. Like some of the early thinkers such as Aimé Césaire who previewed postcoloniality, he viewed blacks as sharing a common and varied experience of marginalization, and believed fighting it would require the contribution of all black people. Such a communal project could not be used to eviscerate individual subjectivity, which was and should remain a cardinal virtue of the process to reclaim the black self and restore African communities from the doldrums of imperial domination. Self-affirmation called for a critical evaluation of what had been taught to Africans by the forces of destabilization. Muntu had an obligation to search and affirm what liberated Muntu from the clutches of destabilization, even when those clutches masqueraded in the guise of modernity. In order to succeed, Muntu had to reject negative priorities used by colonials and postcolonial forces who had acted as if they owned other people and as if the postcolony was a private estate to be managed or destroyed at will. Eboussi Boulaga's call for a strong self of individuality was not a descent into solipsism, but a recognition that change only happens when all recognize who they are and work to reject imputed identities that have been a hindrance to the realization of the *sommum bonum*. The activities of the self in this regard should complement the activities of the other. Rebuilding the authenticity of Muntu called for the marshaling of mutual interest that drew from local resources to mount critical perspectives on reconstruction and development.

Eboussi Boulaga offers solutions that emphasize Muntu's self-assertion because Muntu faces crisis in all areas of life. It is a political crisis because of the abuse of colonial and postcolonial domination. It is a social crisis because Africa's march from colonial times to the postcolonial era has been marred by inequality and inequity. It is an intellectual crisis because colonial thought denigrated African thought as irrational. Georg W. F. Hegel, talking about the development of philosophical thinking, argued: 'Africa is no historical part of the world: it has not movement or development to exhibit'. He also argued that Egypt did not belong to the African spirit.[65] Muntu's crisis is also a cultural crisis because Muntu has been told his or her culture is backward and primitive and needs to be transcended by a cultural outlook brought to Muntu by the forces of domination. Finally, and for our purpose, it is a theological crisis because Muntu, who like the Western missionary is a bearer of the *imago dei*, has been told that he has to ignore all of that cultural baggage and become a Christian, especially a Western version which contributed to the loss of African subjectivity.[66] The significant theological move here is that the recovery of African subjectivity is grounded on the self and the culture in which the self is located. The recovery of lost or shattered subjectivity, especially in the postcolony, must prioritize the self in community.[67] One would think this is something that could be taken for granted, but that is not the case because there is always a debate about the place of individuality and community in African life and worldview. A recovery of subjectivity does not doom community; if anything, it enhances it because the self exists in dialogue with other selves in community.

## RESPONSIBILITY IN THE POSTCOLONY

Responding to the crisis of Muntu and recapturing Christianity for Africans was more than a philosophical and theological project. Eboussi Boulaga departed from dominating discourse, and engaged in rigorous thought analysis and critique to invite Africans to think and act ethically against the most devastating projects of the colonial and postcolonial abuse of power. Africans must assert the will to be now in the postcolony. Postcolonial discourse must be about the postcolony and must be about liberation and reconstruction.[68] The postcolonial project today implies several things. First, in religious language, it is an ongoing revelation which opens the mind and the eye of the African on a daily basis to practices that incapacitate people from reaching their full potential. Such a revelation calls on Africans to speak the truth to those who currently dominate Africans and the global forces which colluded with African leaders to hijack market forces to deprive Africans of resources to sustain life and participate meaningfully in the global economy.

In this respect, postcolonial discourse proclaims the rejection of the world constructed by the political and economic practice of the postcolony described by Achille Mbembe as 'necropolitics', a term he coins to explore 'the ultimate expression of sovereignty [which] resides to a large degree, in the power and the capacity to dictate who may live and who must die'.[69] Notice that Mbembe's terminology refers to necropolitcs as those practices in which some 'must die' and some 'may live', suggesting the inevitability of a culture of death as a calculation of the modality of power in the postcolony. Thinking and speaking in that context is an act of resistance that for the African postcolony has so far proved futile for many, but such thinking and acting are perhaps an indication that dictators will not have the last word.[70]

In religious language, one could argue that what is revelatory here is the reaffirmation that Muntu is a thinking and acting subject. Africans have been misrepresented in all ways, and Eboussi-Boulaga argues that Christianity and the missionaries who were its messengers did everything for the blacks (negroes) but they did not do anything for the Africans who started to question their paternalism, context of ignorance, and the violence with which this was carried out.[71] Africans should take up the responsibility to reclaim themselves in their own space and context and resist the culture of death that surrounds them. Africans must decry and reject the crises of today which include political prisoners, torture chambers, the mixing of the state of Africans today with that of the victims jailed by colonials.[72] In other words, the urgent task of today is to speak up for the freedom of all people, especially members of the lesbian, gay, bisexual, and transgender community (LGBT), defined as undesirables in many African communities.[73]

Second, the postcolony requires responsible actions to overcome the despoliation that has been meted out and create a new society. Those responsibilities are varied and contextual, but share one common feature: the rejection of political anachronism and the building of a vibrant political community that is open to all persons and not just the ruling class. Africans today face issues of domination and abuses of power that have exploited them for many generations. All concerned, like Eboussi Boulaga and Frantz Fanon, must raise critical questions about what it means to be human and part of the human family in the African context, making the major postcolonial task today a recovery of humanity in Africa.[74] In the 'post-neo-colonial' state, that idea of restating the subjectivity of the African is urgent because the political elite have taken over. If we remain in the field of theology, a new responsibility must rethink the imperatives of living in a political community. In addition to the political theologies of Africa, two developments of the last four decades remain crucial to the kind of ecclesial community.

The Circle of Concerned African Women Theologians (Circle) launched, by Mercy Amba Oduyoye of Ghana, has carried out research, published, and carried out activism for gender equality and justice in Africa. Their first publication, *The Will to Arise*, articulated the quest for justice in three areas: African culture, sexuality, and women in the Church. They raised their voices as women in 'a call to action ... to wholeness that challenges the will and the intellect'.[75] The Circle has published many studies on the status of women and the ongoing quest for justice in Africa, including insightful analysis of the HIV and AIDS pandemic.

Another development in Africa is critical perspectives on postcolonial biblical interpretation designed to critique the past and transform the present.

Musa Dube has championed this theoretical orientation in biblical studies in Africa, and has argued that African readers of the Bible must engage in several key areas in the postcolony such as land, race, power, readers, internationalism, the history of liberation, and gender. Since Africans claim the Bible, Dube calls for new scrutiny of it from a postcolonial perspective. According to Dube:

> The postcolonial landscape is drawn with colors of western imperialism, depicting inclusive histories of unequal geographies, unequal races, unequal distribution of power, denial of difference, and silencing of women. Simultaneously, the postcolonial landscape is flashed with the riotous colors of resisting African voices and others of the Two-Thirds World, who assert the dignity of the lands, cultures, races, and differences, and challenge Westerners to ethical distribution of power over the globe.[76]

Because patriarchy remains a hindrance in the struggle for emancipation in the postcolony, the African community has a lot to learn from a feminist reading of the sacred texts that continue to hold sway over it. Outside religious communities, women have risen to leadership positions in several African countries and even at the African Union. Yet African women do not yet enjoy full rights human rights, and until that happens the postcolony will not experience total liberation and engage in long-standing reconstruction.

In addition, one cannot stress enough the responsibility of deconstructing the Bible in light of postcolonial projects. The Bible remains one of the most authoritative texts in Africa, and has been widely received and explored by both experts and members of the ecclesial community.[77] It has had a complex history and been used to justify colonial practice and compel obedience to coloniality, abused by postcolonial leaders who claim they should be obeyed because the Bible commands that all should be subject to the powers that be, and has also been used to subjugate women and justify inequality. It has received a new sense and purpose in the rise and growth of Pentecostal/ Charismatic Churches whose members have returned to the Bible in ways one would not have anticipated, with mixed reviews. While others may condemn the uncritical use of texts, and application of the Bible in magical terms, there is no doubt that it is central to the worldview that defines contemporary Pentecostal/Charismatic Churches in Africa.[78] Ogbu Kalu has argued that their turn to the Bible is generating a new public persona that is attuned to the individual's world and needs, and generates a sense of *Tembisa*, hope.[79] Pentecostals ignore criticism that the claims they make about miracles reflect a world that we do not inhabit anymore. Nimi Wariboko points out that when you confront them with such a worldview, they respond, quoting the biblical text that Jesus promised that later disciples would perform more miracles than he did.[80] One cannot deny that the Bible has been used by many Pentecostal Christians to find support, healing, engage in ethical practices that range from works of charity to entrepreneurial activities such as the broad ministries of Mensa Otabil in Ghana. However, one must not forget that in terms of the impact on the postcolony, people influenced by commitment to the Bible in the Pentecostal tradition still leave a lot to be desired in terms of public-policy actions that transform Africa and ensure that all experience full rights and equality. While one cannot dismiss the strength of the Pentecostal/Charismatic movement which is exporting its 'brand' overseas, I still think that Mbembe was correct when he argued in *Afrique indociles: Christianisme, pouvoir et état en société postcoloniale*, that Africans were turning to Christianity (and here one should add Pentecostalism) as a recourse to meaning in the wake of the disappointing project of the postcolony.[81] If anything, one worries that the Bible has just become a drug for the people and is less effective in curbing political excesses and ushering in justice. A postcolonial responsible reading of the Bible must continue to work for justice for all.

Finally, a postcolonial reading of the Bible is needed to articulate an appropriate political theology and social praxis. Churches have played a significant role in social transformation in Africa. The transformation in Southern Africa enjoyed wide support from the denominations whose members fought racial injustice and illegal regimes. Religious communities have contributed significantly to conflict resolution on the continent.[82] A political theology using biblical insights must recognize the realm of the secular, with citizens as democratic subjects who are members of religious communities and are committed to public discourse and practices intended to facilitate social change. Democratic values incorporated into a political theology would give members of the political community the basis to work for freedom and economic justice for all. Unfortunately, the literal reading of the Bible on many issues allows Churches in Africa to appropriate many biblical texts that do not speak for the times. But such use of biblical texts allows some politicians to claim they are the ones who have been appointed by God to lead the 'chosen nation', as Laurent Gbagbo has done in Ivory Coast.[83]

In closing, I want to return to the idea of a Muntu who thinks and acts. Such a person is what is needed today in the postcolony. In addition to economic and political challenges, Africa has lived for more than 30 years under the scourge of HIV and AIDS, which continue to devastate many communities, and the Ebola Virus Disease has wreaked havoc in several West African communities, exposing the vulnerabilities which are still prevalent in the postcolony. This calls for a sustained postcolonial critique which removes vestiges of postcolonial ineptitude and engages in a critical reconstruction and transformation of the postcolony. Muntu must find ways of achieving autonomy, knowing that governing forces at home and international market forces that continue to abuse the prospects of globalization may stifle such a search. The excessive, bloated bureaucratic nightmare of the postcolony, as exemplified by the Cameroon state with over 40 ministers, is a telling sign that autonomy still eludes the postcolony and it is of our own doing.

In a previous argument in *The Dialectics of Transformation in Africa*, I have called for an intersubjective approach to postcolonial politics. The crisis of the postcolony is largely a crisis of intersubjectivity, and members of African political communities could begin to treat politics as an intersubjective practice. At the end of *The Dialectics* I discussed what I called 'beyond pessimism to optimism: in love with Africa', in which I argued that transcending the postcolonial nightmare which I had portrayed as the privatization of power, the pauperization of the state, the prodigalization of the state, and the proliferation of violence, which were rooted in the manifestation of personal political will, required not only transformative programs like democracy and an African renaissance, but the cultivation of an intersubjective political community animated by love which, among other things, prioritizes others and 'translate[s] into specific political behavior that is consistent with the ideals of a democratic and free society'.[84] This would be one example of how individuals' and groups' discussion of the postcolony could lay out paths and actions that could lead to the transformation of the postcolonial condition and the postcolony.

## NOTES

1. Pramod K. Nayea, *Postcolonialism: A Guide for the Perplexed* (New York: Continuum, 2010), 1.
2. Eric Wolf, *Europe and the People without History* (Berkeley: University of California Press, 1982); Johannes Fabian, *Time and the Other: How Anthropology makes Its Object* (New York: Columbia University, 1983); and McGrane Bernard, *Beyond Anthropology: Society and the Other* (New York: Columbia University Press, 1989).
3. See Bill Ngugi wa Thiongo, *Decolonising the Mind: Moving the Centre* (London: James Currey); Ngugi wa Thiongo, *Moving the Center: The Struggle for Cultural Freedoms* (London: James Curry, 1993); Ranjini Mendis Aschroft, Julie McGonegal, and Arun Mukherjee, eds., *Literature for Our Times: Postcolonial Studies in the Twenty-First Century* (Amsterdam: Rodopi, 2012); and Bill Ashcroft, Gareth Griffiths, and Helen Tiffin, *Postcolonial Studies: The Key Concepts*, 3rd ed. (New York: Routledge, 2013).
4. Ali A. Mazrui, *Cultural Forces in World Politics* (London: James Curry, 1990), 1.
5. Toyin Falola, *Nationalism and African Intellectuals* (Rochester, NY: Rochester University Press, 2001).
6. See C.V. Michael, *Negritude: An Annotated Bibliography* (West Cornwall: Locust Hill Press, 1988).
7. Emmanuel C. Eze, "Hume, Race, and Human Nature," *Journal of the History of Ideas* 61, no. 4 (2000): 234.
8. Kwame Nkrumah's publications are numerous. He published at least 10 books and wrote numerous essays and gave many speeches, all proclaiming political freedom and revolution in Africa.
9. Kwame Nkrumah, *Consciencism: Philosophy and the Ideology of Declonization* (New York: St. Martin's Press, 1964).
10. Julius Nyerere, "Ujamaa: The Basis of African Socialism," in *Readings in African Political Thought*, ed. G.M. Mutiso and S.W. Rohio (London: Heinemann Educational Books, 1975), 512–15.

11. Nkrumah, *Consciencism: Philosophy and Ideology* 1, 30.
12. Ibid., 1966, 58.
13. Kwame Nkrumah, 1966, 59.
14. Ibid., 61.
15. Ibid., 68.
16. Ibid., 70.
17. Ibid., 78.
18. Kwame Nkrumah, 1966, 95 use ibid.
19. Ibid., 98.
20. Nkrumah's critics, raised questions and doubts about what seemed to be a broad sweep of individualism in the project of consciencism.
21. Olúfémi Táíwó, *How Colonialism Preempted Modernity in Africa* (Bloomington: Indiana University Press, 2010), 86.
22. Kwame Nkrumah, 1966, 99.
23. Ibid., 1966, 106.
24. Kwasi Wiredu, *Cultural Universals and Particulars: An African Perspective* (Bloomington: Indiana University Press, 1996), 174.
25. A.P. Ali Mazrui "Pro-democracy Uprisings in Africa's Experience: From Sharpeville to Benghazi" (paper presented at the African Studies Centre, University of the Free State, Bloemfontein, 2011), 1.
26. A. Ali Mazrui, *The Africans: A Triple Heritage* (London: BBC Publications, 1986).
27. A. Ali Mazrui, *The African Condition: A Diagnosis* (Cambridge: Cambridge University Press, 1980).
28. A. Ali Mazrui, *Towards a Pax Africana: A Study of Ideology and Ambition* (Chicago: University of Chicago Press, 1967).
29. V.Y. Mudimbe, *The Invention of Africa: Gnosis, Philosophy, and the Order of Knowledge* (Bloomington: Indiana University Press, 1988).
30. Achille Mbembe, *On the Postcolony* (Berkeley: University of California Press, 2001), 4.
31. Lewis R. Gordon, *An Introduction to Africana Philosophy* (New York: Cambridge University Press, 2008), 204.
32. Leela Ghandi, *Postcolonial Theory: A Critical Introduction* (New York: Columbia University Press, 1998).
33. Achille Mbembe, "Provisional Notes on the Postcolony," *Africa* 62, no. 1 (1992).
34. Achille Mbembe, 1992, 1.
35. Ibid.
36. Achille Mbembe, *On the Postcolony* (Berkeley: University of California Press, 2001); Robert H. Jackson and Carl G. Roseberg, *Personal Rule in Africa: Prince, Autocrat, Prophet, Tyrant* (Berkeley: University of California Press, 1982); and Jean-François Bayart, *The State in Africa: The Politics of the Belly* (London: Longman, 1993). See also Elias K. Bongmba, *The Dialectics of Transformation in Africa* (New York: Palgrave Macmillan, 2006).
37. Achille Mbembe, "The Banality of Power and the Aesthetics of Vulgarity in the Postcolony," *Public Culture* 4, no. 2 (1992): 1–30.
38. V.Y. Mudimbe, "Save the African Continent," *Public Culture* 5, no. 1 (Fall 1992): 61.

39. V.Y. Mudimbe, 1992, 62.
40. Albert Abble, *Des Prêtres noirs s'interrogent,* Reconntres 47 (Paris: Editions du Cerf, 1956); See other texts such as Kwesi Dickson, *Uncompleted Mission: Christianity and Exclusivism* (Maryknoll, NY: Orbis Books, 1993).
41. John Mbiti, *African Religions and Philosophy* (London: Heinemann; 2nd Revised & enlarged edition, 1990); See also his classic *Concepts of God in Africa* (London: SPCK, 1970); John Mbiti, *New Testament Eschatology in an African Background* (London: Oxford 1971); E. Bolaji Idowu, *African Traditional Religions: A Definition* (Maryknoll, NY: Orbis Books, 1973); See also his *Olódùmarè: God in Yoruba Belief* (New York: Wazobia, 1994). See other studies of African religions in the tradition established by Mbiti and Idowu; Laurenti Magesa, *African Religions: The Moral Traditions of the Abundant Life* (Maryknoll, NY: Orbis Books, 1997); and Laurenti Magesa, *African Religion in the Dialogue Debate: From Intolerance to Coexistence* (Münster: LIT Verlag, 2010).
42. E. Bolaji Idowu, 1973, xi.
43. For a recent discussion of the work of these theologians see: Bénézét Buho and Juvénal Ilungu Muya, eds., *African Theology: The Contributions of the Pioneers,* Vol. 1 (Nairobi: Paulines Publication, 2003); Bénézét Buho and Juvénal Ilungu Muya, eds., *African Theology: The Contributions of the Pioneers,* Vol. 2 (Nairobi: Paulines Publications, 2006). See also Canaaan Banana, "The Case for a New Bible," in *Rewriting the Bible: The Real Issues,* ed. I. Mokunyora, J.L. Cox, and V.J. Verstraelen (Gweru, Zimbabwe: Mambo Press, 1993).
44. Jean Marc Ela, *My Faith as an African,* trans. from the French by John Pairman Brown and Susan Perry (Maryknoll, NY: Orbis Books, 1988), 87. Part of this discussion is taken from a keynote address I presented at a conference at the University of Zambia and Justo Mwale University, April 7, 2016.
45. Jean Marc Ela, 1988, 87–88.
46. Ibid., 92.
47. Ibid., 93.
48. Elias Kifon Bongmba, "Land and Authority in Postcolonial Cameroon" Inaugural lecture at "Africa at Crossroads Trans-Institutional Program" Vanderbilt University, September 28, 2016.
49. Fabien Eboussi-Boulaga, *Christianity without Fetishes: An African Critique and Recapture of Christianity,* trans. Robert Barr (Maryknoll, NY: Orbis Books, 1981).
50. Fabien Eboussi-Boulaga, 1981, 2.
51. Ibid.
52. Fabien Eboussi-Boulaga, 1981, 11.
53. Ibid., 21.
54. Ibid., 26.
55. Ibid., 53.
56. Ibid., 104.
57. Ibid., 110.
58. Fabien Eboussi Boulaga, *La Cris du Muntu, Authenticité africaine et philosophie* (Paris Présence Africaine, 1997).
59. Fabien Eboussi Boulaga, *Notes de Synthése: Doctorat d'Eta ten Philosophie* (Dakar: Université de Dakar, Janv. 1994), 4. I am indebted to Eugéne Didier A. Goussikindey for this reference and some of the discussion in this section of

this chapter. See his "The Christic Model of Eboussi Boulaga: A Critical Exposition and Evaluation of an African 'Recapture' of Christianity" (PhD diss., University of Saint Michael's College, 1997), 7.

60. Eugéne Didier A. Goussikindey, "The Christic Model of Eboussi Boulaga," 1997, 12, 14 ff.
61. *La Crise du Muntu*, 145.
62. The term he uses is "*un autre commencement.*"
63. *La Crise du Muntu*, 156.
64. Fabien Eboussi Boulaga, *Les Conférences Nationales en afrique noir. Une affaire à suivre* (Paris: Karthala, 1993), 89.
65. G.W.F. Hegel, *The Philosophy of History* (New York: Dover, 1956), 99.
66. Fabien Eboussi Boulaga, "L'Adventure ambigüge de Cheik Hamidou Kane," *Abbia* 6 (1964): 207–13.
67. Dismas Masolo, *Self and Community in a Changing World* (Bloomington: Indiana University Press, 2010).
68. Charles Villa-Vicencio, *A Theology of Reconstruction* (New York: Cambridge University Press, 1992); and Jesse N.K. Mugambi, *From Liberation to Reconstruction: African Christian Theology after the Cold War* (Nairobi: East African Educational Publishers, 1995).
69. Achille Mbembe, "Necropolitics," trans. Libby Meintjes, *Public Culture* 15, no. 1 (2003): 11–40.
70. Fabien Eboussi-Boulaga, "L'Honneur de Penser," *Terriors* 001 (1992): 4–5.
71. Fabien Eboussi-Boulaga, "L'Africain Chrétien à la Recherche de son Identité," *Concilium* 126 (1977): 39–48.
72. Fabien Eboussi-Boulaga, *Les Conférences Nationales en Afrique Noire, Une affaire à suivre* (Paris: Karthala, 1993), 24–25.
73. Elias Kifon Bongmba, "Homosexuality, Ubuntu, and Otherness in the African Church," *Journal of Religion and Violence* 4, no. 1 (2016): 15–37.
74. Jacob Agossou, *Christianisme africain. Une fraterité au-delà de l'ethnie* (Paris: Karthala, 1987).
75. Mercy Amba Oduyoye and Musimbi R.A. Kanyoro, *The Will to Arise: African Women, Tradition and the Church in Africa* (Maryknoll, NY: Orbis Books, 1992), 1.
76. Musa W. Dube, *Postcolonial Feminist Interpretation of the Bible* (St. Louis, MO: Chalice Press, 2000), 20.
77. Musa W. Dube and Gerald O. West, *The Bible in Africa* (Leiden: Brill, 2000).
78. J. Kwabena Assamouah-Gyadu, *Sighs and Signs of the Spirit: Ghanaian Perspectives on Pentecostalism and Renewal in Africa* (Oxford: Regnum Publishers, 2015), 16–17.
79. Ogbu Kalu, *African Pentecostalism* (New York: Oxford University Press, 2008), 212.
80. Nimi Wariboko, *Nigerian Pentecostalism* (Rochester, NY: Rochester University Press, 2014), 100.
81. Achille Mbembe, *Afrique indociles: Christianisme, pouvoir et état en sociéte postcoloniale* (Paris: Karthala, 1988).
82. James Howard Smith and Rosalind I.J. Hackett, *Displacing the State: Religion and Conflict in Neoliberal Africa* (South Bend, IN: University of Notre Dame Press, 2012).

83. Konstanze n'Guessan, "Pentecostalism, Politics, and Performances of the Past," *Nova Religio* 18, no. 3 (2015): 80–100, 82, 85. See also Karel Arnaut, "Performing Displacements and Reshaping Attachments: Ethnographic Explorations of Mobility in Art, Ritual, Media, and Politics" (PhD diss., Ghent University, Belgium, 2004).
84. Elias K. Bongmba, 2006, 210.

## BIBLIOGRAPHY

Abble, Albert, ed. *Des Prêtres noirs s'interrogent,* Reconntres 47. Paris: Editions du Cerf, 1956.

Agossou, Jacob. *Christianisme africain. Une fraterité au-delà de l'ethnie.* Paris: Karthala, 1987.

Ahidjo, Ahmadou. *The Political Philosophy of Ahmadou Ahidjo.* Monte Carlo: Paul Bory Publishers, 1968.

Arnaut, Karel. "Performing Displacements and Reshaping Attachments: Ethnographic Explorations of Mobility in Art, Ritual, Media, and Politics." PhD diss., Ghent University, Belgium, 2004.

Aschroft, Bill, Ranjini Mendis, Julie McGonegal, and Arun Mukherjee, eds. *Literature for Our Times: Postcolonial Studies in the Twenty-First Century.* Amsterdam: Rodopi, 2012.

Ashcroft, Bill, Gareth Griffiths, and Helen Tiffin, eds. *Postcolonial Studies: The Key Concepts,* 3rd ed. New York: Routledge, 2013.

Assamouah-Gyadu, J. Kwabena. *Sighs and Signs of the Spirit: Ghanaian Perspectives on Pentecostalism and Renewal in Africa.* Oxford: Regnum Publishers, 2015.

Banana, Canaan. "The Case for a New Bible." In *Rewriting the Bible: The Real Issues,* edited by I. Mokunyora, J.L. Cox, and V.J. Verstraelen. Gweru, Zimbabwe: Mambo Press, 1993.

Bayart, Jean-François. *The State in Africa: The Politics of the Belly.* London: Longman, 1993.

Bongmba, Elias K. *The Dialectics of Transformation in Africa.* New York: Palgrave Macmillan, 2006.

———. "Land and Authority in Postcolonial Cameroon" Inaugural lecture at "Africa at Crossroads Trans-Institutional Program." Vanderbilt University, September 28, 2016.

———. "Homosexuality, Ubuntu, and Otherness in the African Church." *Journal of Religion and Violence* 4, no. 1 (2016): 15–37.

Buho, Bénézét, and Juvénal Ilungu Muya, eds. *African Theology: The Contributions of the Pioneers,* Vol 1. Nairobi: Paulines Publication, 2003.

———. *African Theology: The Contributions of the Pioneers,* Vol 2. Nairobi: Paulines Publications, 2006.

Dickson, Kwesi. *Uncompleted Mission: Christianity and Exclusivism.* Maryknoll, NY: Orbis Books, 1993.

Dube, Musa W. *Postcolonial Feminist Interpretation of the Bible.* St. Louis, MO: Chalice Press, 2000.

Dube, Musa W., and Gerald O. West, eds. *The Bible in Africa.* Leiden: Brill, 2000.

Eboussi-Boulaga, Fabien. "L'Adventure ambigüge de Cheik Hamidou Kane." *Abbia* 6 (1964): 207–13.

———. *Christianity Without Fetishes: An African Critique and Recapture of Christianity.* Translated by Robert Barr. Maryknoll, NY: Orbis Books, 1981.

———. "L'Honneur de Penser." *Terrioirs* 001 (1992): 4–5.

———. *Les Conférences Nationales en Afrique Noire, Une affaire à suivre.* Paris: Karthala, 1993.

———. *Notes de Synthése: Doctorat d'Eta ten Philosophie.* Dakar: Université de Dakar, Janv. 1994.

———. *La Cris du Muntu, Authenticité africaine et philosophie.* Paris Présence Africaine, 1997.

———. "L'Africain Chrétien à la Recherche de son Identité," *Concilium* 126 (1977): 39–48.

Ela, Jean Marc. *Faith as an African.* Translated from the French by John Pairman Brown and Susan Perry. Maryknoll, NY: Orbis Books, 1988.

Eze, Emmanuel C. "Hume, Race, and Human Nature." *Journal of the History of Ideas* 61, no. 4 (2000): 691–98.

———. *On Reason, Rationality in a World of Cultural Conflict and Racism.* Durham: Duke University Press, 2008.

Fabian, Johannes. *Time and the Other: How Anthropology Makes Its Object.* New York: Columbia University, 1983.

Falola, Toyin. *Nationalism and African Intellectuals.* Rochester, NY: Rochester University Press, 2001.

Ghandi, Leela. *Postcolonial Theory: A Critical Introduction.* New York: Columbia University Press, 1998.

Gordon, Lewis R. *An Introduction to Africana Philosophy.* New York: Cambridge University Press, 2008.

Goussikindey, Eugéne Didier A. "The Christic Model of Eboussi Boulaga: A Critical Exposition and Evaluation of an African 'Recapture' of Christianity." PhD diss., University of Saint Michael's College, 1997.

Hegel, G.W.F. *The Philosophy of History.* New York: Dover, 1956.

Idowu, E. Bolaji. *African Traditional Religions: A Definition.* Maryknoll, NY: Orbis Books, 1973.

———. *Olódùmarè: God in Yoruba Belief.* New York: Wazobia, 1994.

Jackson, Robert H., and Carl G. Roseberg. *Personal Rule in Africa: Prince, Autocrat, Prophet, Tyrant.* Berkeley: University of California Press, 1982.

Kalu, Ogbu. *African Pentecostalism.* New York: Oxford University Press, 2008.

Magesa, Laurenti. *African Religions: The Moral Traditions of the Abundant Life.* Maryknoll, NY: Orbis Books, 1997.

———. *African Religion in the Dialogue Debate: From Intolerance to Coexistence.* Münster: LIT Verlag, 2010.

Masolo, Dismas. *Self and Community in a Changing World.* Bloomington: Indiana University Press, 2010.

Mazrui, Ali A. *Towards a Pax Africana: A Study of Ideology and Ambition.* Chicago: University of Chicago Press, 1967.

———. *The African Condition: A Diagnosis.* Cambridge: Cambridge University Press, 1980.

———. *The Africans: A Triple Heritage.* London: BBC Publications, 1986.

———. *Cultural Forces in World Politics.* London: James Curry, 1990.

———. "Pro-democracy Uprisings in Africa's Experience: From Sharpeville to Benghazi." Paper presented at the African Studies Centre, University of the Free State, Bloemfontein, 2011.

Mbembe, Achille. *Afrique indociles: Christianisme, pouvoir et état en sociéte postcoloniale*. Paris: Karthala, 1988.

———. "Provisional Notes on the Postcolony." *Africa* 62, no. 1 (1992).

———. "Necropolitics." Translated by Libby Meintjes. *Public Culture* 15, no. 1 (2003): 11–40.

———. *On the Postcolony*. Berkeley: University of California Press, 2001.

———. "The Banality of Power and the Aesthetics of Vulgarity in the Postcolony." *Public Culture* 4, no. 2 (1992): 1–30.

Mbiti, John. *Concepts of God in Africa*. London: SPCK, 1970.

———. *New Testament Eschatology in an African Background*. London: Oxford, 1971.

———. *African Religions and Philosophy*, 2nd Revised & Enlarged ed. London: Heinemann, 1990.

McGrane, Bernard. *Beyond Anthropology: Society and the Other*. New York: Columbia University Press, 1989.

Michael, C.V. *Negritude: An Annotated Bibliography*. West Cornwall: Locust Hill Press, 1988.

Mudimbe, V.Y. *The Invention of Africa: Gnosis, Philosophy, and the Order of Knowledge*. Bloomington: Indiana University Press, 1988.

———. "Save the African Continent." *Public Culture* 5, no. 1 (Fall 1992).

Mugambi, Jesse N.K. *From Liberation to Reconstruction: African Christian Theology after the Cold War*. Nairobi: East African Educational Publishers, 1995.

n'Guessan Konstanze. "Pentecostalism, Politics, and Performances of the Past." *Nova Religio* 18, no. 3 (2015): 80–100.

Nayea, Pramod K. *Postcolonialism: A Guide for the Perplexed*. New York: Continuum, 2010.

Nkrumah, Kwame. *Consciencism: Philosophy and the Ideology of Declonization*. New York: St. Martin's Press, 1964.

Nyerere, Julius. "Ujamaa: The Basis of African Socialism." *Readings in African Political Thought*, edited by G.M. Mutiso and S.W. Rohio, 512–15. London: Heinemann Educational Books, 1975.

Oduyoye, Mercy Amba, and Musimbi R.A. Kanyoro, eds. *The Will to Arise: African Women, Tradition and the Church in Africa*. Maryknoll, NY: Orbis Books, 1992.

Smith, James Howard, and Rosalind I.J. Hackett. *Displacing the State: Religion and Conflict in Neoliberal Africa*. South Bend, IN: University of Notre Dame Press, 2012.

Táíwó, Olúfémi. *How Colonialism Preempted Modernity in Africa*. Bloomington: Indiana University Press, 2010.

Villa-Vicencio, Charles. *A Theology of Reconstruction: Nation Building and Human Rights*. New York: Cambridge University Press, 1992.

Wa Thiongo, Ngugi. *Decolonising the Mind: The Politics of Language in African Literature*. London: Heinemann Education Books, 1986.

———. *Moving the Center: The Struggle for Cultural Freedoms*. London: James Curry, 1993.

Wariboko, Nimi. *Nigerian Pentecostalism*. Rochester, NY: Rochester University Press, 2014.

Wiredu, Kwasi. *Cultural Universals and Particulars: An African Perspective*. Bloomington: Indiana University Press, 1996.

Wolf, Eric. *Europe and the People without History*. Berkeley: University of California Press, 1982.

# CHAPTER 40

# South Africa: Apartheid and Post-Apartheid

*Nancy L. Clark*

The South African government enforced a policy formally known as 'apartheid' for 50 years, leaving the country scarred by this ordeal and still searching for ways in which to understand, remedy, and overcome the events of this period. The history of apartheid was not isolated; it was in fact preceded by nearly 300 years of imperial and colonial rule as was the rest of the continent, and it was initiated through a settler regime spawned by conquest. In 1994, this history ended with the country's first democratic elections and the inauguration of Nelson Mandela as president. And yet despite this historic shift in power from the white minority to the black majority, the political transition was an isolated event that left the overwhelming legacy of history (inequality, poverty, violence, and suspicion) to be solved by the new electorate. South Africa, like most of postcolonial Africa, gained political power but remained tied to its historical legacies.

## PRELUDE TO APARTHEID: ESTABLISHING A PATTERN

From the first landing of Europeans at the Cape of Good Hope in 1652, Africans had been coerced, bullied, and finally conquered and dispossessed of their land as the European settlers and their descendants spread eastward.[1] Even in the earliest settlements, Europeans had defined a hierarchical set of legal rights based on race, with those of Europeans at the top and Africans at the bottom.[2] When the most valuable mineral discoveries of the nineteenth century were made in Kimberley (diamonds, 1869) and Johannesburg (gold, 1886),

N.L. Clark (✉)
Department of History, Louisiana State University, Baton Rouge, LA, USA

© The Author(s) 2018
M.S. Shanguhyia and T. Falola (eds.),
*The Palgrave Handbook of African Colonial and Postcolonial History,*
https://doi.org/10.1057/978-1-137-59426-6_40

the serious conquest of remaining lands and peoples commenced under the British flag, culminating in the devastation of the South African War (1899–1903), leaving Dutch-speaking white settlers as well as Africans destitute and virtually landless.[3] The British left the country in the hands of the whites, including the descendants of the early Dutch settlers as well as more recent immigrants from England. Equipped with a racial franchise that made small concessions to property-owning 'non-whites' in the former Cape colony, South Africa entered the twentieth century with a firm framework of racial separation and discrimination.

Many of the most devastating restrictions on African freedoms and rights were legislated early in the twentieth century. Labeled as 'segregation', the new laws enacted under successive administrations robbed Africans, Coloreds, and Asians of most basic freedoms. Africans were barred from skilled jobs (Mines and Works Regulations Act, 1912), from purchasing land outside 7% of the land area of the country (Natives Land Act, 1913), from residing outside 'native' locations in the cities (Natives Urban Areas Act, 1923), from negotiating wages (Industrial Conciliation Act, 1923), from speaking freely (Native Administration Act, known colloquially as the 'hostility law', 1927), and from staying in urban areas for more than 14 days (Native Laws Amendment Act, 1937). With a firm framework for discriminatory racial separation established in both urban and rural areas well before the institution of apartheid policy, what more could be enforced and why?[4]

## The Apartheid Framework: From a Segregationist State to a Police State

When the National Party took control of the South African government in 1948 on a platform of 'apartheid', neither its leaders nor its critics knew precisely what to expect. The term 'apartheid' had served as a potent rallying cry for the party during the 1948 election but beyond its Afrikaans translation (apartness) there were few concrete plans attached to the concept.[5] Initially, apartheid policies that elaborated on the preceding period of segregationist legislation were enacted through laws and were enforced through the power of the courts. One of the first pieces of apartheid legislation, the Immorality Act of 1949, outlawed extramarital sexual intercourse between whites and Africans and was in fact an extension of a similar Act of 1927 which was itself an extension of previous laws from 1902 and 1903. Other legislation consolidated laws and policies that had previously been enacted and enforced through the provinces and municipalities including the classification of individuals by race (Population Registration Act, 1950), use of identity documents known as 'passes' (Natives Abolition of Passes and Co-ordination of Documents Act, 1952), restriction of access to public areas and services by race (Reservation of Separate Amenities Act, 1953), and provision of education for Africans (Bantu Education Act, 1953).[6] It should be noted that policies and enforcement varied widely throughout the provinces before the imposition of apartheid, and that the centralization of control over these practices allowed the Union government to override local concerns and in most cases to increase the severity of implementation.

The 1913 Natives Land Act began to elaborate on the system of 'Native Reserves', seeing them less as reserves for Africans than as their permanent dwelling place. Prior to Union, various laws in each of the provinces had already limited African ownership of land and designated areas for African 'communal' settlement.[7] In 1913, the Natives Land Act consolidated the situation, restricting African purchase of land to only 7% of the country, labeled Native Reserves. In 1927, the Native Administration Act took legal responsibility of the Reserves away from Parliament and instead stipulated that the Governor-General could rule in these areas by Proclamation. In 1951, the Bantu Authorities Act established 'tribal authorities' in each Reserve to implement the policies of the Governor-General. Finally, in 1959, the Promotion of Bantu Self-Government Act stipulated that these Reserves, now seen as 'homelands' for ethnically defined groups of Africans, would be developed as separate and independent nations providing citizenship rights in these areas for designated ethnicities. These 'homelands' would form the centerpiece of the Grand Apartheid scheme to fully disenfranchise Africans within South Africa.

But the most dramatic change under apartheid was the increasing power of the police. Beginning in 1950, the government began to institute laws which progressively took powers of arrest and conviction away from the courts and put them in the hands of the executive branch, especially the Governor-General, later to be State President, and the Minister of Justice. In 1950, amid concerns over popular agitation against the new government, the Suppression of Communism Act was passed, giving the Governor-General the power to declare any organization deemed to support political change unlawful and to seize its property as well as to 'ban' any individual pursuing similar aims. While earlier legislation (Native Administration Act, 1927) had outlawed the promotion of hostility between whites and Africans, the Suppression of Communism Act greatly expanded the scope of the law and added for the first time punishment for organizations as well as the new category of 'banishment' for the accused. In 1956, the Riotous Assemblies Act allowed the Governor-General to outlaw any public gathering; in 1962, the Terrorism Act allowed police to detain suspects without a warrant; and in1963, the General Laws Amendment gave police the power to detain anyone suspected of a political offense for 90 days without allowing contact with a lawyer. The power handed to the police progressively expanded over the years, and by 1965 they were allowed to hold anyone without charge for 180 days, to be renewed indefinitely.

The police were not the only ones responsible for security. In 1963, the Defense Amendment Act stipulated that the South African Defense Force

(SADF) was tasked not only with the defense of the country, but also with combating 'internal disorder'[8] at the direction of the Prime Minister. For the first time, the military would be asked to fight South African citizens, and they would be used relentlessly to quell protests throughout the 1970s and 1980s. Finally, leaving little doubt that the country had indeed lost all semblance of a legitimate state, the Bureau of State Security (BOSS) was established in 1969 under the Public Service Amendment Act as a body responsible only to the Prime Minister with a secret budget, legal protection, and freedom from accountability to the public or even Parliament.[9] Under a cloak of secrecy, the apartheid regime would commit unspeakable violence against its disenfranchised citizens.[10]

## No Political Solution

Although political organizations representing all races existed in 1948, many rising to challenge the ongoing decimation of freedom, only whites could vote. In most cases, political groups representing Africans, Coloreds, and Indians were punished and destroyed in the first two decades of apartheid rule, leaving the strictly political realm to those parties able to operate inside South Africa. Initially, the African National Congress (ANC), the Pan Africanist Congress (PAC), the South African Communist Party (SACP), and others challenged the apartheid spate of legislation before being successively outlawed, forcing them to work outside the country or underground and leaving the parliamentary debates to the National Party (NP) and its white opposition.

By 1948, the National Party had split with its founder, J.B.M. Hertzog, and had become, if possible, even more stridently pro-Afrikaner. Shocked by its victory in the election, especially since the party had polled fewer votes than the United Party but had prevailed through the apportionment of seats, the NP quickly set to work passing legislation under the belief that they would soon be voted out of office. In terms of parliamentary action, the Official Opposition Party, the United Party, and later its successors, the Liberal Party (1953–1968) and the Progressive Party (1959–1975) tried to block the litany of apartheid laws but increasingly lost both power and direction as the NP began to capture majorities of the white vote.[11]

The ANC was in the midst of transitioning from a delegation of petitioners asking for protection of their remaining rights to a popular mass protest movement in the 1940s. Not long after the NP took power, the ANC launched a 'Programme of Action' to challenge earlier apartheid restrictions, for the first time attempting to engage in widespread resistance. The ANC was quickly joined by the Communist Party of South Africa (CPSA), which had been actively representing workers' rights, since its founding in 1921, and by 1948 pledged a firm commitment to ending racial discrimination albeit through the establishment of a socialist state. The party worked closely with the ANC in the 1940s, but was one of the first political organizations 'banned' by the apartheid government in 1950. Thereafter, the party worked primarily through the ANC until that organization was also banned in 1960.[12]

In the first decade of apartheid rule, political opposition to apartheid became intense. As the imperative for mass action grew, political organizations representing all racial groups rose to challenge the government including the ANC, the South African Indian Congress (SAIC), the South African Congress of Trade Unions (SACTU), the African People's Organization (APO), the Congress of Democrats (COD), and the South African Coloured People's Congress (SACPO). Following a successful 'stay-away' protest in 1950, the anti-apartheid groups called on the government to repeal 'unjust laws', or face mass civil disobedience. With the government's refusal to do so, the constituent groups launched the Defiance Campaign in June of 1952. Over 6000 people were jailed for breaking the new apartheid laws. Despite the police crackdown, the opposition groups formed the Congress Alliance and planned for a 'Congress of the People', which in 1955 adopted the Freedom Charter calling for non-racial democracy. Over 150 activists were arrested and charged with treason, with most opposition political leaders banned or arrested. It was clear that the government would not yield to or even engage with the peaceful demonstration of opposition used by political groups in the 1950s.[13]

A decisive political turning point came in 1960 following the police massacre of over 69 Africans in Sharpeville. The Pan Africanist Congress (PAC) had recently split from the ANC over ideological issues and organized a demonstration against the laws that required Africans to carry a 'pass' to prove their right to work and reside in South Africa. Police fired on the crowd, resulting in the most shocking show of police force to date. The government declared a state of emergency, detained thousands of people, banned all public meetings, and outlawed both the ANC and PAC.[14] From this time until 1990, strictly political African organizations were banned, forcing them to operate from outside the country or, even more riskily, underground. Both the ANC and PAC established offices outside the country and also created military organizations (Umkonto we Sizwe and Poqo, respectively) to initiate sabotage inside the country and to prepare for an armed struggle.[15]

In the political vacuum created in the aftermath of Sharpeville, the political realm was reserved for whites and eventually the homeland leaders and other groups involved in the creation of separate representation for Coloreds and Indians. The NP garnered increasing percentages of the white vote while the liberal parliamentary opposition dwindled. The government pointed to the creation of Urban Bantu Councils in the cities and administrative offices in the homelands as providing some political power for Africans; however, these offices operated at the government's will and none was viewed as legitimate by its constituency or the rest of the world. It was in this environment that the Inkatha Freedom Party (IFP) first emerged in 1975 as a Zulu cultural organization headed by Gatsha Mangosuthu Buthelezi, a former ANC Youth League member and later Chief Executive Officer of the Zulu 'homeland', KwaZulu. Although Buthelezi never acceded to accepting 'independence' for the homeland from the South African government, he nevertheless cultivated an ethnic base of political support that was at odds with the goals of those African political organizations that had been banned and which he later attempted to use as leverage against the ANC after that organization was unbanned.[16]

Successive South African prime ministers pursued increasingly draconian policies, earning larger margins of victory with every election; the most serious political challenges came from even more conservative segments of the Afrikaner electorate while the English-speaking whites appeared increasingly irrelevant to the country's political life. Both D.F. Malan (1948–1954) and J.G. Strijdom (1954–1958) were responsible for laying most of the early framework for apartheid. H.F. Verwoerd (1958–1966), commonly referred to as the 'architect' of apartheid, indeed elaborated on the initial version, leading South Africa out of the British Commonwealth and introducing the plan for 'separate development' that the party would follow to the end of apartheid.[17] While these first three administrations had all but destroyed legal protest and freedom of speech, South Africa entered into a phase of security control that was unprecedented under B.J. Vorster (1966–1978) and P.W. Botha (1978–1984), both of whom had supported sabotage against the government during the Second World War in opposition to its support for the British war effort. Vorster had served as Minister of Justice responsible for sending Nelson Mandela to prison, and was Prime Minister during the national crackdown following the Soweto uprising. In addition, he created the Bureau of State Security. Botha had served as Minister of Defense for 14 years, and as Prime Minister he oversaw the expansion of 'counter insurgency' efforts including the creation of the infamous Vlakplaas unit responsible for the torturing and deaths of thousands of South Africans.[18] Whether through willful ignorance or misguided self-interest, white South Africans supported these administrations at the polls.

The turnaround in policies granting African political rights came finally under the presidency of F.W. de Klerk.[19] Taking office after Botha suffered a stroke, de Klerk followed up on overtures that Botha had already made to the ANC and to Mandela. Within six months of taking office, de Klerk announced the unbanning of the ANC, PAC, and other political organizations and the release of Mandela and other political prisoners. His decision opened the political scene wide, revealing serious splits within the white electorate as some die-hard conservatives threatened violence; more importantly, his decision restored a political voice to all South Africans. In unleashing these forces, he felt that he could control the situation and negotiate an end to the tension and international condemnation that was hurting the

South African economy. During the negotiations toward the 1994 election, Mandela accused de Klerk of duplicity and of attempting to destabilize the situation as violence spread throughout the country. Indeed, responsibility for arming opponents of the ANC was later traced to de Klerk and his government. Nevertheless, once the negotiations toward democracy began, South Africa was on the path to a political, not a military, solution.[20] But how could African organizations barred from the political structure for nearly 30 years finally force the end of this government?

## POPULAR PROTEST AND THE COLLAPSE OF APARTHEID

Apartheid finally collapsed, forcing a political change through massive popular protest and resistance to the country's discriminatory system. The constant challenge to apartheid that reverberated throughout the country eventually provided the pressure that would force the government to concede the impracticality, if not the immorality, of apartheid. It is difficult to find an area of South Africa that was not affected by resistance to apartheid as it became an all-encompassing system of repression. In the cities, women protested against the pass laws, Africans protested against bus fares, and homeowners and renters alike tried to challenge 'removals' to urban locations. Workers formed their own unions and went out on illegal strikes, and students questioned the entire system of oppression for even the most educated.

But in 1948, most Africans still lived in the rural countryside, trying to eke out a livelihood. Once the Native Reserves had been demarcated through the Natives Land Act in 1913, a process of restricting Africans to ever more crowded land began, which by the 1940s had reached crisis proportions. At that time, the government embarked on a policy of rehabilitating the soil, later known as 'betterment', forcing Africans onto smaller plots of land as well as culling their herds to limit animal grazing. The results of these policies were disastrous, leading to impoverishment and famine. In addition, under apartheid appointed 'chiefs' were designated to carry out government policies. leading to resentment over the usurpation of traditional leaders. And even worse, these rural policies were undertaken while the government was busy removing Africans from the cities to their official 'homelands', the overcrowded and impoverished reserves.[21]

Outbreaks of localized resistance took place throughout rural areas as the policies of land rehabilitation, administration of the reserves, and the extension of the pass system to women took hold in the 1940s and through the 1960s. The most famous and widespread rural revolt took place in 1960 in the Transkei among the Pondo, who formed their own political organization (Intaba, meaning Mountain) and organized store boycotts as well as attacks on government-appointed chiefs. This movement was so serious that the government declared a state of emergency as the power of the Bantu Authorities completely collapsed. In the end, over 5000 Pondo were arrested and the uprising was crushed. Grievances over restrictions on farming and grazing likewise led to the physical intimidation of officials in Witziehoek in 1950, leading to government retaliation that left at least 14 Africans dead. Women took center stage in Zeerust in 1957, boycotting local stores and schools in protest over new laws requiring them to carry passes and limiting their ability to move between the cities and the rural areas.[22] Similar movements continued throughout the countryside, driven and organized by local residents who refused to accede to apartheid.

While resistance in the countryside took place in obscure areas that garnered little attention, the activities of urban workers and their labor unions could not be ignored. Over 70,000 mineworkers staged a dramatic strike in 1946 demanding better wages and working conditions, only to be crushed by police action with 12 killed and 1200 injured. With the accession of the apartheid government, African unions united to form SACTU in 1954, joining with the Congress Alliance and adopting the Freedom Charter. Nevertheless, the labor movement was hamstrung during the 1960s as SACTU was decimated through arrests and the banning of its leaders under the Suppression of Communism Act.[23] When a spontaneous strike erupted at the Coronation Brick and Tile Company in Durban in 1973, it became clear that South African workers were still ready to risk imprisonment and even death to fight for better conditions. Within one month of the first strike, workers at 29 firms in Durban were on strike followed by similar strikes on the mines in Johannesburg.[24] The power of workers (and pressure from their employers) finally forced the government to allow Africans to form legal unions in 1979.

Throughout the 1980s, labor unions applied crucial pressure on the government to improve wages; significantly, unions also came to play a major role in political negotiations to end apartheid. During this period, the line between worker action and political goals unavoidably became blurred with labor unions increasingly taking on some of the responsibility for those political leaders in prison or exile. The considerable leverage held by the unions (representing a majority of African wage earners who drove the profits of South African industry) was not lost on various political actors who were themselves divided on the best strategies to end apartheid; and, more importantly, on which ideologies should guide post-apartheid South Africa. With the formation of the umbrella Congress of South African Trade Unions (COSATU) in 1985, many of these differences were subsumed under a generalized 'anti-apartheid' goal.[25]

Another group that would play an increasingly political role under the severe restrictions of the 1970s and 1980s was African students. Under Bantu Education, all facets of education had not only been segregated but also significantly downgraded for Africans. While expanding the number of state schools available for African students, the government had also effectively ended the type of private, mission education that had previously been available. African leaders including Nelson Mandela, Robert Sobukwe, and even Steve Biko had received at least primary education through the mission schools' mix of the classics imbued with the superiority of Western 'civilization'.[26] Bantu Education skipped the humanism of mission education and focused instead on minimal skills necessary for the limited careers available to blacks under apartheid. While more students attended schools, they were receiving a minimal education. By the late 1960s, black university students began to speak out, forming their own organization, the South African Students Organisation (SASO), in 1968. SASO's manifesto set out the doctrine of Black Consciousness, most famously articulated by Biko, stating 'We, the Black Students of South Africa, believing that the Black Man can no longer allow definitions that have been imposed upon him by an arrogant White world concerning his Being and his destiny and that the Black Student has a moral obligation to articulate the needs and aspirations of the Black Community …'[27] While certainly political by implication, the government initially believed Black Consciousness was in alignment with 'separate development' for the races.

But Black Consciousness energized students and communities alike to oppose rather than join apartheid institutions. Most famously, students in Soweto used Black Consciousness slogans while protesting against the circumstances of their education, leading to the historic student uprisings in 1976. Staging a well-organized protest against the use of Afrikaans in schools, Soweto students were quickly set upon by police and later the South African military with over 170 losing their lives in one day. Protests spread throughout the country, and within three months had affected over 50 additional municipalities. In effect, the country was experiencing over 50 Sharpevilles in this short time period.[28]

In the wake of Soweto, the government swept in once again and banned, imprisoned, or outlawed all leaders and organizations remotely opposed to its policies; but much of the work accomplished through the Black Consciousness Movement and its affiliates would spawn the next phase of opposition. Many young people fled the country, joining one or other of the exile political organizations; others turned to community work, choosing a grass-roots rather than structural approach to change. For those inside the country, P.W. Botha's announcement of a new constitution in 1983 (granting limited political rights to Coloreds and Indians and relegating African political rights to the homelands) galvanized their efforts within an umbrella organization, the United Democratic Front (UDF). The sprawling organization of over 600 'civics' formed a visible public focus for the widespread localized rebellions against apartheid restrictions. While UDF leaders admitted that they were 'trailing behind the masses' in the widespread efforts to resist apartheid, the UDF could articulate grievances and demands that would otherwise have been characterized by the government as local, random, and illegitimate.[29] Regardless, the country was wracked by revolt throughout the late 1980s, matched by the increasingly militarized response from the South African state. The country was at one more turning point: more violence, or more rights?

The groundswell of resistance and ever increasing levels of violent government repression throughout the 1980s drew the attention and alarm of the international community; by 1990, all factors combined to convince the government to begin negotiations with the opposition. Unrest continued unabated throughout the late 1980s, with the country under almost continuous States of Emergency with SADF troops stationed in the townships. The Anti-Apartheid Movement based in London had led consumer, academic, and sports boycotts against the country since the 1960s, and in the 1980s a serious divestment campaign began in the USA. By 1989, over 100 cities, counties and states in the USA had divested pension funds from companies doing business in South Africa. The 1986 Comprehensive Anti-Apartheid Act passed by the US Congress over President Ronald Reagan's veto banned new investment, bank loans, and certain imports. In 1987, the Act was extended to deny tax reimbursements for companies doing business in South Africa, cutting into their profits by 72%. International companies fled South Africa, resulting in an estimated R5.5 billion in capital flight from the country.[30] Combined with the tremendous costs (human as well as financial) involved in the continuous suppression of opposition, international pressure delivered the *coup de grace* to the continuation of apartheid.

## The Role of Ideology: Past, Present, and Future

The forces supporting and contesting apartheid were driven by a variety of concerns and interests that manifested themselves in differing ideologies and visions for the future. The ideology of the ruling government itself had evolved over time from an inchoate vision of 'apartheid' into the hypocritical policy of 'separate development', a fiction which argued that everyone in South Africa would exercise rights in their home areas and which, for Africans, meant the impoverished 13% of the land allocated for homelands.[31] The far right in the white electorate held on to that vision as protests intensified, while what was left of a parliamentary opposition vigorously but fruitlessly opposed it. Some white academics mooted the possibilities of a sort of consociational power-sharing which appealed to neither pro- nor anti-government forces; others worked tirelessly to support trade unions, the grass-roots movements, and the exile community at great risk to themselves.[32] In retrospect, most of the discussion that tried to justify or at least salvage the political status quo resembled the colloquial metaphor of rearranging deckchairs on the *Titanic*.

While much of white South Africa was looking toward continuing domination, the rest of the country had quite different plans for the future. All parties wanted to see the end of apartheid; but within the spectrum of opposition there were serious differences about the future. Over the course of the twentieth century, the ANC itself had divided between accommodation and outright change, but with the advent of apartheid, it was clear that the government had no interest in any accommodation for Africans.[33] The ideology of the SACP (founded in 1919, banned in 1950, and resurfacing again only in 1990) identified South Africa as 'colonialism of a special type', where oppression was exerted both along racial lines within the country and externally as part of the international capitalist system. Even with the end of racial domination through apartheid, the SACP saw capitalism as an enduring threat.[34] The workers themselves had formed their own unions (finally legal in 1979) and more firmly focused on issues of wages, benefits, and social services.[35]

The argument over how to achieve the end of apartheid had revolved around race, creating divisions within the liberation movement. As early as the 1930s, leaders who questioned whether a multiracial leadership could ever work to the advantage of Africans challenged the accommodationist forces within the ANC. Anton Lembede and Peter Mda, among others, began to advocate an African Nationalism not tied to ethnicity but rather to assert the rights of Africans to rule their own country.[36] This strain of nationalism would weave variously over the next five decades through the ANC Youth League, the PAC, and the Black Consciousness Movement and its affiliates.[37] Whether advocating Africa for Africans or questioning the role of whites in a movement that sought ultimately to destroy their privilege, ideologies of African nationalism raised crucial questions about the future nature of South African society. What would be the role of race in the future? And coupled with socialist ideologies, how would race and class intersect?

In the aftermath of the Soweto Uprising of 1976 and the severe repression that followed, ideology began to take a backseat to urgent calls for the end of apartheid. The local civic organizations had various interests, claims, and concerns, but shared few ideological positions other than to end their specific forms of oppression. As local activism gathered steam and the UDF began to advocate for these groups, a Charterist ideology took hold roughly based on the aims of the Freedom Charter drawn up in 1955 by a group of now banned and defunct organizations including the ANC, South African Indian Congress (SAIC), Congress of Democrats, and SACTU. The document had reflected the aims of all of the constituent organizations and therefore included a laundry list of demands. Notably, the Freedom Charter stated 'that South Africa belongs to all who live in it, black and white', reflecting the multiracial composition of the Congress of the People. It also declared that 'The mineral wealth beneath the soil, the Banks and monopoly industry shall be transferred to the ownership of the people as a whole', giving rise over successive decades to fears of a communist takeover of the economy. And workers' concerns were specifically addressed: 'There shall be a forty-hour working week, a national minimum wage, paid annual leave, and sick leave for all workers, and maternity leave on full pay for all working mothers'.[38]

Thus, the Charterists of the 1980s followed the Congress Alliance strategy of the 1950s by subsuming individual ideological differences between opposition forces within the imperative of doing away with apartheid.

Whereas Black Consciousness of the 1970s had energized and reinvigorated the opposition, the turn to Charterism was successful in organizing concrete demonstrations of opposition. Whether protesting against rents, low wages, poor education, or the tri-cameral parliament, Charterism as espoused through the UDF succeeded in providing a united opposition to the overriding ideology (and practice) of one basic enemy: apartheid. In that respect, Charterism provided a crucial organizing force against apartheid. At the same time, however, it provided only a vague and soon to be contested vision of the future.[39]

## THE END, AND THE BEGINNING

On February 2, 1990, South African President F.W. de Klerk announced the unbanning of anti-apartheid organizations and the release of political prisoners, naming Nelson Mandela in particular. He was clear: 'I wish to put it plainly that the Government has taken a firm decision to release Mr. Mandela unconditionally. I am serious about bringing this matter to finality without delay'.[40] Identifying Mandela as the leader with whom the government would negotiate, de Klerk acceded to the drumbeat of the international 'Free Mandela' campaign that had identified Mandela as the voice of the opposition and gave the ANC predominance as its representative. Thus began the process of negotiation that would last nearly four years until the country's first multiracial elections were held in April 1994.

But the negotiations did not halt the violence, which in fact increased over this period. It became clear that de Klerk and his party were playing for time, trying to divide the fragile coalition built up by the UDF, and hoping to turn international support back to the status quo ante. Almost immediately following Mandela's release, police attacked residents in the township of Sebokeng who were protesting against high rents, killing 14 and wounding more than 300. At the same time, 'war' broke out between Zulu followers of the UDF and those of the Inkatha Freedom Party (IFP) in KwaZulu-Natal and nearly 200 died. It was later revealed that the IFP forces were armed and aided by the police. The government, clandestinely supportive of if not instigating the violence, argued that the country would soon fall apart due to ethnic rivalries and unrest. The right wing, as represented by the Afrikanerweerstandbeweging (AWB), added to the chaos, staging its own 'Battle of Ventersdorp' when de Klerk came to the hometown of the movement's leader, Eugene Terreblanche, resulting in the deaths of three of its own members. Township violence escalated again in 1993 when the IFP attacked ANC supporters in Boipatong, allowing police to open fire on residents and resulting in a total of 45 deaths. The last straw for many came soon after with an attack by homeland troops killing 28 protestors at Bisho, capital of the Ciskei homeland. As the Goldstone Commission of Inquiry Regarding the Prevention of Public Violence and Intimidation later concluded, political violence between 1990 and 1994 was fueled by a 'third force'; that is, the South African military in an attempt to promote fighting between members of the black political parties (ANC/UDF vs IFP). Although government officials consistently denied the presence of a 'third force', weapons used by the IFP were traced to the South African Police and SADF. Between the time of Mandela's release and the elections in April 1994, over 14,000 people had been killed in political violence.[41]

What did the National Party hope to achieve, and what did they finally get? In short, NP proposals envisioned a country with guaranteed rights for minorities (in this case meaning whites) and a government run by consensus between the three parties earning the most votes. In effect, de Klerk sought a veto power for whites in any new government. But the ANC, the dominant party in negotiations that included a total of 19 political parties, turned the suggestion down flat.[42] The Record of Understanding that finally emerged in 1992 proposed elections to a Constitutional Assembly tasked with writing the new constitution, and a 'Government of National Unity' to last five years made up of the three top polling parties that would rule on the basis of that electoral strength rather than consensus. When elections took place in April 1994, the ANC won 62% of the vote, the National Party 20%, and the IFP 10%. In the end, the NP got a seat at the table, but not at the head of the table.

## THE NEW SOUTH AFRICA: POST-APARTHEID REALITIES

When Nelson Mandela was sworn in as the President of South Africa on May 10, 1994, he stated, 'Never, never and never again shall it be that this beautiful land will again experience the oppression of one by another'.[43] The country was now ruled as a democracy, all citizens were entitled to vote, and the rule of law was reinstated after nearly a decade of martial law. In 1996, the new constitution was implemented with a Bill of Rights detailing over 25 general rights protected for South African citizens including equality, human dignity, security, privacy, religion, speech, movement, access to courts, etc. No longer would South Africans face random arrest and imprisonment, state-sponsored discrimination, or the overall brutality of the apartheid state. The notorious prisons including Robben Island and the 'Fort' in Johannesburg were closed and turned into museums recalling the injustices of apartheid. South Africa's future was now in the hands of all citizens. What would that bring?

The transition to democracy embodied a purely political solution to dismantle a system (apartheid) which touched every aspect of South African life far beyond the political. Nelson Mandela and the ANC had emerged during the negotiations as the country's presumptive dominant political leadership and therefore inherited the responsibility for formulating policies that could address the overwhelming task of reshaping South Africa. The legal framework of apartheid had quickly been dismantled; most apartheid laws were repealed even before Mandela took office. But control over the government and the repeal of legislation could go only so far. What were the party's priorities? Following the unbanning of the political opposition, the UDF had disbanded and the ANC joined with the SACP and COSATU in a 'Tripartite Alliance' to put forward a unified slate of candidates for election. While the three groups represented a broad range of interests and shared a vision of economic transformation within a democratic South Africa, what would that mean and how could it be achieved within the economic and social frameworks left behind by apartheid?

Mandela and his government inherited a country rent by division with very few available resources to meet the need or expectations of its citizens. Four years of internecine violence preceding the elections, on top of decades of state repression, left a deeply divided electorate as evidenced by election results. While the ANC earned 62% of the vote (presumably representing a large segment of the African population as well as a significant percentage of whites) the NP got 20% of the vote from whites and some Coloreds who feared radical change, and the IFP got 10% primarily from Zulus. These parties had fought bitterly prior to the elections over the very issues they would now need to resolve. Within the ANC itself were a wide variety of organizations and ideologies united primarily by their opposition to apartheid. And the government had few resources to meet the demands of all of these groups, discovering that the NP had left the government accounts in the red by $25 billion, with government debt equaling 50% of gross domestic product (GDP). The country's credit rating had dropped to BB, or junk status.[44] Even if the government could find consensus on priorities among the differing parties, where were the resources to fund new goals?

Mandela began by preaching reconciliation, in line with the Charterist ideology that 'South Africa belongs to all who live in it', and also from a recognition that the country could little afford further violence and bloodshed.[45] Reconciliation was quickly addressed through the Promotion of National Unity and Reconciliation Act of 1995, which established the Truth and Reconciliation Commission (TRC). Following similar efforts to uncover human rights abuses in countries such as Argentina and Chile, the TRC held public hearings for victims and perpetrators alike beginning in 1995. Over 20,000 people gave testimony of over 35,000 human rights abuses. Although the commission had no judicial power, perpetrators could request amnesty for crimes, but out of 7112 applications for amnesty, only 849 were granted.[46] In the wake of the TRC's final report in 1998, criticism has arisen over perceptions that justice was denied or, alternatively, that the hearings did not reveal a complete truth.[47] Nevertheless, much of the information concerning the government's attacks on the opposition (the murders of Steve Biko, the Craddock Four, the Guguletu Seven, and many others) was revealed through the TRC hearings. The most shocking truths were now in the open.

South Africans also had a pressing need for basic services denied under apartheid. The new constitution guaranteed these rights, including access to basic education, food, water, health care, and housing. But the shortfall in services was overwhelming. Out of a population of 40 million in 1996, 17 million people lived below the poverty line, 12 million lacked clean drinking water, and 4.3 million were without housing. During the elections, the ANC put forward a broad plan, the Reconstruction and Development Plan (RDP) that proposed to address these issues. While less than 60% of South Africans had access to clean water in 1994, by 2010 the government claimed that figure had risen to over 90%. Likewise, in 1996, less than 50% of South Africans lived in a 'formal dwelling'. Since then, 3.7 million houses have been built, housing approximately 12.5 million people. The percentage of South Africans who are illiterate has dropped from 25 to 10%.[48] While the success of these measures is often criticized in terms of the remaining needs of the population, the situation has materially improved for many.

The problem that has proven most difficult to solve is the continuing level of poverty and the attendant inequality gap that is still largely defined by race. In 1994, approximately 92% of the African population was classified as 'poor'. The economy has grown since 1994 as investment came back into the country, national debt decreased, and GDP increased over 200% by 2014. At the same time, however, unemployment has remained at approximately 25%. The result is the continuation of staggering poverty among Africans, 85% of whom remain classified as 'poor', or 'below poverty datum line'. In comparison, 67% of whites are classified as 'middle-class' and 20% as 'upper class'.[49] Although poverty has been reduced slightly due to increased levels of government support through social grants, continuing unemployment, especially among the youth, suggests that poverty will remain a long-term problem.

When Nelson Mandela stepped down after one term as president in 1999, his administration had already pivoted away from the RDP, deferring many of its goals in favor of policies that were oriented toward market-based strategies. In particular, rather than promoting growth through the redistribution of wealth, new policies as embodied in the Growth, Employment, and Redistribution Program (GEAR) sought redistribution through growth. GEAR policies focused on a smaller role in the economy for the government and gave greater leeway to the private sector, pursuing the privatization of government assets and reining in wage increases. One reason for this change was pressure from the IMF and World Bank to reduce South Africa's debt burden with nearly 18% of the government budget spent on debt servicing. Under President Thabo Mbeki, who became president in 1999, market-oriented policies continued with mixed results: while foreign debt dropped from nearly 50% of GDP to less than 30% by 2007, both unemployment and South Africa's personal debt jumped. The redistribution of wealth had not only failed but inequality appeared to be worsening.[50]

Although Mbeki was re-elected to a second term of office in 2004, his popularity waned as a result of controversial statements and policies. Most famously, his lack of action on the HIV/AIDS epidemic was blamed for soaring infection rates that were one of the highest in the world.[51] But he was also perceived as seeking a role as statesman for all of Africa, ignoring his own country's problems. And his continuing adherence to market-friendly policies, including the perceived creation of a wealthy 'black middle class' through his policies of Black Economic Empowerment (BEE) smacked of favoritism and corruption to many. Increasingly seen as remote and unengaged in the many continuing problems of poverty and inequality, Mbeki was voted out as President of the ANC in 2007 and stepped down as President of South Africa shortly thereafter in 2008.[52]

Under Mbeki's administration, fissures also began to appear in the political landscape. The ANC's formidable ally COSATU had locked horns with Mbeki over what the unions saw as an increasingly market-oriented approach to the economy at the expense of workers. In particular, the unions worried over the new government's willingness to continue the apartheid government's privatization of government assets which COSATU, as well as the SACP, saw as dangerous. During Mbeki's presidency he also came in for heavy criticism from the unions over his policies towards the HIV/AIDS crisis and his initial refusal to fund the antiretroviral drug treatments that could have prevented so many deaths. When Mbeki attempted to run for a third term as president of the ANC, being constitutionally barred from a third term as president of South Africa, the COSATU president Zwelinzima Vavi formally opposed him, easing the path for Jacob Zuma. Vavi has since expressed regret for the move, but he was also expelled from COSATU in the 2015 purge of the National Union of Metalworkers of South Africa (NUMSA). The disagreement within COSATU over police violence during the Marikana platinum mineworkers strike fractured the trade union federation and strained relations between the ANC and its labor allies.[53]

Mbeki had been forced from office by his successor, Jacob Zuma, who became President of South Africa in 2009. Unlike Mbeki, Zuma was outgoing and personable; but he carried considerable baggage including multiple accusations of corruption and an indictment on a charge of rape. Zuma had no formal education, but he was seen as a party loyalist, having served time on Robben Island and with the ANC's armed wing (MK) in Mozambique. He was also instrumental in defusing some tensions between the ANC and IFP in the run-up to the 1994 elections, and in winning over many Zulu (his own ethnic affiliation) to the party. Following his election, he pledged to address many of the problems facing the general populace including the HIV/AIDS crisis, job creation, health care, and land redistribution. Although the government succeeded in halting the rise in HIV/AIDS infection, most other areas of concern remained problematic.[54]

By 2016, the ANC faced serious but still not threatening opposition at the polls.[55] From the left, the former president of the ANC Youth League, Julius Malema, formed the Economic Freedom Fighters (EFF) in 2013 to challenge the government's economic policies, calling for nationalization of the mines and radical land reform. Although he (like Vavi) had been one of Zuma's active supporters in the rivalry with Mbeki, Malema was expelled from the ANC in 2012 over a host of incidents that embarrassed the party. The EFF has garnered notoriety but more importantly votes, holding 25 seats in Parliament. Also making inroads on ANC hegemony is the Democratic Alliance (DA), an heir to the white liberal parties of the apartheid period including the United Party and the Progressive Party. Attacking from the right of the ANC, the DA proposes smaller government and charges the ANC with gross corruption and incompetence. The DA has operated as the Official Opposition party in Parliament and polled approximately 22% of the vote in the 2014 election. In 2016, the EFF successfully petitioned the Constitutional Court to hear a case against President Zuma for misappropriation of state funds to refurbish his private residence and won the case in 2016 initiating a political crisis. An increasingly divisive figure, Zuma refused to step down from office as the ANC faced growing electoral challenges.

## CONCLUSION: THE LONG WALK

While the country was briefly united in a spirit of hope under Nelson Mandela in 1994, the many divisions and injustices sown over the centuries proved difficult to overcome in the first 20 years of the 'new' South Africa. The traces of the ideological differences which emerged under the stress of apartheid remain between and within racial and ethnic groups. More than 80% of the population, overwhelmingly black, remains mired in poverty. And the government is now accused of personal corruption, rather than the moral corruption of apartheid. Yet all South Africans exercise their freedom of speech, are not imprisoned or detained as a result of the color of their skin or their political beliefs, and do not disappear to be tortured or killed by the state. The country has earned many freedoms, including the freedom to determine its own fate.

## NOTES

1. For example, see: Eric A. Walker, *The Great Trek* (London: A & C Black, 1960); J.B. Peires, *House of Phalo: A History of the Xhosa People in the Days of Their Independence* (Berkeley: University of California Press, 1982) and *The Dead will Arise: Nongqawuse and the Great Xhosa Cattle-Killing Movement of 1856–7* (Johannesburg: Ravan Press, 1989); Martin Legassick, *The Politics of a South African Frontier: The Griqua, the Sotho-Tswana and the Missionaries,*

*1780–1840* (Basel: Basler Afrika Bibliographien, 2010); and Richard Elphick, *Kraal and Castle: Khoikhoi and the Founding of White South Africa* (New Haven: Yale University Press, 1977).

2. Richard Elphick and Hermann Giliomee, eds., *The Shaping of South African Society, 1652–1820* (Cape Town: Longman, 1979).

3. William Worger, *South Africa's City of Diamonds: Mine Workers and Monopoly Capitalism in Kimberley, 1867–1895* (New Haven: Yale University Press, 1987); Charles van Onselen, *Studies in the Social and Economic History of the Witwatersrand, 1886–1914, Volume 1: New Babylon, Volume 2: New Nineveh* (London: Longman, 1982); S.B. Spies, *Methods of Barbarism? Roberts and Kitchener and Civilians in the Boer Republics: January 1900–May 1902* (Cape Town: Human and Rousseau, 1977); and Thomas Pakenham, *The Boer War* (New York: Random House, 1979).

4. For the formation of segregationist polices, see Saul Dubow, *Racial Segregation and the Origins of Apartheid in South Africa, 1919–1936* (New York: St. Martin's Press, 1989). For policies in rural areas, see Nancy Jacobs, *Environment, Power and Injustice: A South African History* (Cambridge: Cambridge University Press, 2003); Timothy J. Keegan, *Rural Transformations in Industrializing South Africa: The Southern Highveld to 1914* (Braamfontein: Ravan Press, 1986) and *Facing the Storm: Portraits of Black Lives in Rural South Africa* (London: Zed Books, 1988).

5. Saul Dubow, *Apartheid 1948–1994* (Oxford: Oxford University Press, 2014); Deborah Posel, *The Making of Apartheid, 1948–1961: Conflict and Compromise* (Oxford: Oxford University Press, 1992).

6. Immorality Act of 1927. See Muriel Horrell, *Laws Affecting Race Relations in South Africa to the End of 1976* (Johannesburg: South African Institute of Race Relations, 1978).

7. In the South African Republic, Resolution 159 of 1855, Occupation Act of 1886, Squatters Act of 1887; in the Cape Colony, the Glen Grey Act of 1894.

8. Defence Amendment Act, No. 77 of 1963.

9. For a complete compilation and explanation of the evolution of apartheid legislation, see Muriel Horrell, *Laws Affecting Race Relations in South Africa to the End of 1976* (Johannesburg: South African Institute of Race Relations, 1978).

10. These crimes came to light during the investigations of the Truth and Reconciliation Commission (TRC) following the transition to democracy. See: De Wet Potgieter, *Total Onslaught: Apartheid's Dirty Tricks Exposed* (Cape Town: Zebra Press, 2007); Bill Minter, *Apartheid's Contras: An Inquiry into the Roots of War in Angola and Mozambique* (London: Zed Books, 1994); Eugene de Kock, *A Long Night's Damage: Working for the Apartheid State* (Saxonwold: Contra Press, 1998); Jacob Dlamini, *Askari: A Story of Collaboration and Betrayal in the Anti-Apartheid Struggle* (Oxford: Oxford University Press, 2015); and Antjie Krog, *Country of My Skull: Guilt, Sorrow, and the Limits of Forgiveness in the New South Africa* (New York: Crown Books, 1999).

11. For a critical history of the National Party see Dan O'Meara, *Forty Lost Years: The Apartheid State and the Politics of the National Party, 1948–1994* (Ravan Press, 1997). For differing explanations of the rise of Afrikaner nationalism see Dunbar Moodie, *The Rise of Afrikanerdom: Power, Apartheid and the Afrikaner Civil Religion* (Berkeley: University of California Press, 1975);

Dan O'Meara, *Volkskapitalisme: Class, Capital and Ideology in the Development of Afrikaner Nationalism, 1934–1948* (Cambridge: Cambridge University Press, 1983). For a critical discussion of the white parliamentary opposition, see Eddy Maloka, *Friends of the Natives: The Inconvenient Past of South African Liberalism* (Durban: 3rd Millenium Publishing, 2014).

12. On the history of the ANC, see: Andre Odendaal, *The Founders: The Origins of the ANC and the Struggle for Democracy in South Africa* (Lexington: University Press of Kentucky, 2013); Francis Meli, *A History of the ANC: South Africa Belongs to Us* (Harare: Zimbabwe Publishing House, 1988); and Tom Lodge, *Black Politics in South Africa Since 1945* (Johannesburg: Ravan Press, 1983). On the South African Communist Party see: A. Lerumo, *Fifty Fighting Years: The Communist Party of South Africa, 1921–1971* (London: Inkululeko Publications, 1980); Eddy Maloka, *The South African Communist Party, 1963–1990* (Pretoria: Africa Institute of South Africa, 2002); and Thomas Stanley Kolasa, *The South African Communist Party: Adapting to Thrive in a Post-Communist Age* (Jefferson, NC: McFarland and Co., 2016). For a discussion of ANC-SACP collaboration see Stephen Ellis, *Comrades Against Apartheid: The ANC and the South African Communist Party in Exile* (London: Currey, 1992).

13. For a personal account of these events, see Albert Luthuli, *Let My People Go* (New York: McGraw-Hill, 1962).

14. Tom Lodge, *Sharpeville: An Apartheid Massacre and Its Consequences* (Oxford: Oxford University Press, 2011); Philip Frankel, *An Ordinary Atrocity: Sharpeville and Its Massacre* (New Haven: Yale University Press, 2001); and Ambrose Reeves, *Shooting at Sharpeville: The Agony of South Africa* (New York: Houghton Mifflin, 1961).

15. Janet Cherry, *Spear of the Nation: Umkhonto We Sizwe: South Africa's Liberation Army, 1960s–1990s* (Athens: Ohio University Press, 2012); Stephen Davis, *Apartheid's Rebels: Inside South Africa's Hidden War* (New Haven: Yale University Press, 1987). See also biographies by many of the ANC and PAC members forced into exile or prison such as: Nelson Mandela, *Long Walk to Freedom: The Autobiography of Nelson Mandela* (New York: Back Bay Books, 1994); Padraig O'Malley, *Shades of Difference: Mac Maharaj and the Struggle for South Africa* (New York: Penguin Books, 2007); Ronnie Kasrils, *Armed and Dangerous: From Undercover Struggle to Freedom* (Oxford: Heinemann, 1993); Govan Mbeki, *Learning from Robben Island: The Prison Writings of Govan Mbeki* (London: J. Currey, 1991); Winnie Madikizela-Mandela, *491 Days: Prisoner 1323/69* (Athens, OH: Ohio University Press, 2014); Elinor Sisulu, *Walter and Albertina Sisulu: In Our Lifetime* (Claremont: David Philip, 2002); and Luli Callinicos, *Oliver Tambo: Beyond the Engeli Mountains* (Cape Town: New Africa Books, 2012).

16. For a critical appraisal of Buthelezi see Gerhard Mare and Georgina Hamilton, *An Appetite for Power: Buthelezi's Inkatha and South Africa* (Bloomington: Indiana University Press, 1988).

17. Lindie Koorts, *D. F. Malan and the Rise of Afrikaner Nationalism* (Cape Town: Tafelberg, 2014); J.L. Basson, *J. G. Strijdom: Sy Politieke Loopbaan van 1929 tot 1948* (Pretoria: Wonderboom, 1980); Alexander Hepple, *Verwoerd*

(Harmondsworth: Penguin, 1967); and Henry Kenney, *Architect of Apartheid: H.F. Verwoerd, an Appraisal* (Johannesburg: J. Ball, 1980).

18. Hermann Giliomee, *The Last Afrikaner Leaders: A Supreme Test of Power* (Cape Town: Tafelberg, 2012).

19. F.W. de Klerk, *The Last Trek – A New Beginning: The Autobiography* (London: Macmillan, 1998).

20. Jan Heunis, *The Inner Circle: Reflections on the Last Days of White Rule* (J. Ball: Johannesburg, 2007).

21. Nancy Jacobs, *Environment, Power and Injustice.*

22. Tom Lodge, *Black Politics in South Africa Since 1945.*

23. Edward Feit, *Workers Without Weapons: The South African Congress of Trade Unions and the Organization of the African Workers* (Hamden: Archon Books, 1975).

24. David Hemson, "Dock Workers, Labour Circulation, and Class Struggles in Durban, 1940–59," *Journal of Southern African Studies* 4, no. 1 (1977): 88–124.

25. Glenn Adler and Eddie Webster, eds., *Trade Unions and Democratization in South Africa, 1985–97* (New York: Palgrave Macmillan, 2000).

26. Ian Macqueen, "Students, Apartheid and the Ecumenical Movementin South Africa, 1960–1975," *Journal of Southern African Studies* 39, no. 2 (2013): 447–63.

27. Steve Biko, *I Write What I Like: Selected Writings* (University of Chicago Press, 1978).

28. Sifiso Ndlovu, *The Soweto Uprisings: Counter-Memories of June 1976* (Ravan Press, 1999); Gail Gerhart, *Black Power in South Africa: The Evolution of an Ideology* (Berkeley: University of California Press, 1979); Baruch Hirson, *Year of Fire, Year of Ash: The Soweto Revolt: Roots of a Revolution?* (London: Zed Press, 1979); and Daniel Magaziner, *The Law and the Prophets: Black Consciousness in South Africa, 1968–1977* (Athens: Ohio University Press, 2010).

29. Popo Molefe quoted in Jeremy Seekings, *The UDF: A History of the United Democratic Front in South Africa: 1983–1991* (Athens: Ohio University Press, 2000), 121. See also Ineke Van Kessel, *Beyond Our Wildest Dreams: The United Democratic Front and the Transformation of South Africa* (Charlottesville: University of Virginia Press, 2000).

30. Roger Fieldhouse, *Anti-Apartheid: A History of the Movement in Britain: A Study in Pressure Group Politics* (London: Merlin Press, 2005); and Hakan Thorn, *Anti-Apartheid and the Emergence of a Global Civil Society* (New York: Palgrave Macmillan, 2006).

31. H.F. Verwoerd, *Separate Development: The Positive Side* (Pretoria: Information Service of the Department of Native Affairs, 1958).

32. Arend Lijphart, *Power-Sharing in South Africa, Policy Papers in International Affairs Number 24* (Berkeley: Institute of International Studies, 1985); Frederick van zyl Slabbert and David Welsh, *South Africa's Options: Strategies for Sharing Power* (New York: St. Martin's Press, 1979). For examples of some white South Africans who risked their lives fighting against apartheid see: Beverley Naidoo, *Death of An Idealist: In Search of Neil Aggett* (Johannesburg: J. Ball, 2012); Billy Keniston, *Choosing to be Free: The Life Story of Rick Turner* (Auckland Park: Jacana, 2013); Albie Sachs, *The Soft Vengeance of a Freedom*

*Fighter* (Berkeley: University of California Press, 2000); and Julie Frederikse, *They Fought for Freedom: David Webster* (Cape Town: Maskew Miller Longman, 1998).

33. Xolela Mangcu, "Retracing Nelson Mandela Through the Lineage of Black Political Thoughts," *Transition* 112, (2013): 101–16.

34. Thomas Stanley Kolasa, *The South African Communist Party: Adapting to Thrive in a Post-Communist Age* (Jefferson, NC: McFarland and Co., 2016); and Eddy Maloka, *The South African Communist Party: Exile and After Apartheid* (Auckland Park: Jacana, 2013).

35. Jeremy Baskin, *Striking Back: A History of Cosatu* (London: Verso, 1990).

36. Robert Edgar and Luyanda Ka Msumza, eds., *Freedom in Our Lifetime: The Collected Writings of Anton Muziwakhe Lembede* (Athens: Ohio University Press, 1996). See also Gail Gerhart, *Black Power in South Africa*.

37. Benjamin Pogrund, *Robert Sobukwe: How Can Man Die Better* (London: P. Halban, 1990); and Jabulani Christian Mbatha, Sibusiso Andreas Mncwabe, and Zibukele Richard Mqadi, eds., *Bestowing a Human Face: A Black Consciousness Perspective* (Wandsbeck: Reach Publishers, 2016).

38. For the Freedom Charter, see http://www.anc.org.za/show.php?id=72.

39. For a full discussion of the ideological dimensions of opposition politics, see Anthony Marx, *Lessons of Struggle: South African Internal Opposition, 1960–1990* (New York: Oxford University Press, 1992).

40. "F.W. de Klerk's speech at the opening of Parliament 2 February 1990," https://www.nelsonmandela.org/omalley/index.php/site/q/03lv02039/04l v02103/05lv02104/06lv02105.htm.

41. See TRC Report, Volume 3 "Final Report," for Regional Profiles of conflict 1990–1994.

42. Jan Heunis, *The Inner Circle: Reflections on the Last Days of White Rule* (Johannesburg: J. Ball, 2007); and Allister Sparks, *Tomorrow is Another Country: The Inside Story of South Africa's Road to Change* (Chicago: University of Chicago Press, 1996).

43. See "Inaugural Speech, Pretoria [Mandela] – 5/10/94" at http://www.africa.upenn.edu/Articles_Gen/Inaugural_Speech_17984.html.

44. Goldman Sachs, 9.

45. Sabelo J. Ndlovu-Gatsheni, *The Decolonial Mandela: Peace, Justice and the Politics of Life* (Oxford: Berghahn Books, 2016).

46. "Amnesty Hearings and Decisions," at http://www.justice.gov.za/trc/amntrans/.

47. Deborah Posel and Graeme Simpson, eds., *Commissioning the Past: Understanding South Africa's Truth and Reconciliation Commission* (Johannesburg: Witwatersrand University Press, 2003).

48. Goldman Sachs, *Two Decades of Freedom: A 20-Year Review of South Africa* (Johannesburg: Goldman Sachs, 2013), 2; http://www.goldmansachs.com/our-thinking/archive/colin-coleman-south-africa/20-yrs-of-freedom.pdf.

49. Goldman Sachs, *Two Decades of Freedom*, 23.

50. Hein Marais, *South Africa Pushed to the Limit: The Political Economy of Change* (London: Zed Books, 2011).

51. Mark Givisser, *Thabo Mbeki: The Dream Deferred* (Johannesburg: J. Ball, 2007).

52. Frank Chikane, *Eight Days in September: The Removal of Thabo Mbeki* (Johannesburg: Picador, 2012).
53. Sakhela Buhlungu and Malehoko Tshoaedi, eds., *COSATU's Contested Legacy: South African Trade Unions in the Second Decade of Democracy* (Pretoria: Human Sciences Research Council, 2013); and Vishwas Satgar and Roger Southall, eds., *Cosatu in Crisis: The Fragmentation of an African Trade Union Federation* (Sandton: KMM Review Publishing Co., 2015).
54. Jeremy Gordin, *Zuma: A Biography* (Johannesburg: J. Ball, 2011).
55. For explanations of mounting frustration with the ANC, see Malaika Wa Azania, *Memoirs of a Born-Free: Reflections on the Rainbow Nation* (Auckland Park: Jacana, 2016).

## BIBLIOGRAPHY

Adler, Glenn, and Eddie Webster, eds. *Trade Unions and Democratization in South Africa, 1985–97*. New York: Palgrave Macmillan, 2000.

Azania, Malaika Wa. *Memoirs of a Born-Free: Reflections on the Rainbow Nation*. Auckland Park: Jacana, 2016.

Baskin, Jeremy. *Striking Back: A History of Cosatu*. London: Verso, 1990.

Basson, J.L. *J. G. Strijdom: Sy Politieke Loopbaan van 1929 tot 1948*. Pretoria: Wonderboom, 1980.

Biko, Steve. *I Write What I Like: Selected Writings*. University of Chicago Press, 1978.

Buhlungu, Sakhela, and Malehoko Tshoaedi, eds. *COSATU's Contested Legacy: South African Trade Unions in the Second Decade of Democracy*. Pretoria: Human Sciences Research Council, 2013.

Callinicos, Luli. *Oliver Tambo: Beyond the Engeli Mountains*. Cape Town: New Africa Books, 2012.

Cherry, Janet. *Spear of the Nation: Umkhonto We Sizwe: South Africa's Liberation Army, 1960s–1990s*. Athens: Ohio University Press, 2012.

Chikane, Frank. *Eight Days in September: The Removal of Thabo Mbeki*. Johannesburg: Picador, 2012.

Couper, Scott. *Albert Luthuli: Bound by Faith*. Scottsville: University of KwaZulu-Natal Press, 2010.

Davis, Stephen. *Apartheid's Rebels: Inside South Africa's Hidden War*. New Haven: Yale University Press, 1987.

de Klerk, F.W. *The Last Trek—A New Beginning: The Autobiography*. London: Macmillan, 1998.

de Kock, Eugene. *A Long Night's Damage: Working for the Apartheid State*. Saxonwold: Contra Press, 1998.

Dlamini, Jacob. *Askari: A Story of Collaboration and Betrayal in the Anti-Apartheid Struggle*. Oxford: Oxford University Press, 2015.

Dubow, Saul. *Racial Segregation and the Origins of Apartheid in South Africa, 1919–1936*. New York: St. Martin's Press, 1989.

———. *Apartheid 1948–1994*. Oxford: Oxford University Press, 2014.

Edgar, Robert, and Luyanda Ka Msumza, eds. *Freedom in Our Lifetime: The Collected Writings of Anton Muziwakhe Lembede*. Athens: Ohio University Press, 1996.

Ellis, Stephen. *Comrades Against Apartheid: The ANC and the South African Communist Party in Exile*. London: Currey, 1992.

Feit, Edward. *Workers Without Weapons: The South African Congress of Trade Unions and the Organization of the African Workers.* Hamden: Archon Books, 1975.

Fieldhouse, Roger. *Anti-Apartheid: A History of the Movement in Britain: A Study in Pressure Group Politics.* London: Merlin Press, 2005.

Frankel, Philip. *An Ordinary Atrocity: Sharpeville and Its Massacre.* New Haven: Yale University Press, 2001.

Frederikse, Julie. *They Fought for Freedom: David Webster.* Cape Town: Maskew Miller Longman, 1998.

Gerhart, Gail. *Black Power in South Africa: The Evolution of an Ideology.* Berkeley: University of California Press, 1979.

Giliomee, Hermann. *The Last Afrikaner Leaders: A Supreme Test of Power.* Cape Town: Tafelberg, 2012.

Givisser, Mark. *Thabo Mbeki: The Dream Deferred.* Johannesburg: J. Ball, 2007.

Goldman Sachs. *Two Decades of Freedom: A 20-Year Review of South Africa.* Johannesburg: Goldman Sachs, 2013. See http://www.goldmansachs.com/our-thinking/archive/colin-coleman-south-africa/20-yrs-of-freedom.pdf.

Gordin, Jeremy. *Zuma: A Biography.* Johannesburg: J. Ball, 2011.

Hepple, Alexander. *Verwoerd.* Harmondsworth: Penguin, 1967.

Heunis, Jan. *The Inner Circle: Reflections on the Last Days of White Rule.* Johannesburg: J. Ball, 2007.

Hirson, Baruch. *Year of Fire, Year of Ash: The Soweto Revolt: Roots of a Revolution?* London: Zed Press, 1979.

Horrell, Muriel. *Laws Affecting Race Relations in South Africa to the End of 1976.* Johannesburg: South African Institute of Race Relations, 1978.

Jacobs, Nancy. *Environment, Power and Injustice: A South African History.* Cambridge: Cambridge University Press, 2003.

Kasrils, Ronnie. *Armed and Dangerous: From Undercover Struggle to Freedom.* Oxford: Heinemann, 1993.

Keegan, Timothy J. *Facing the Storm: Portraits of Black Lives in Rural South Africa.* London: Zed Books, 1988.

Keniston, Billy. *Choosing to Be Free: The Life Story of Rick Turner.* Auckland Park: Jacana, 2013.

Kenney, Henry. *Architect of Apartheid: H.F. Verwoerd, an Appraisal.* Johannesburg: J. Ball, 1980.

Khumalo, Fred. *Touch My Blood: The Early Years.* Houghton: Umuzi Press, 2006.

Kolasa, Thomas Stanley. *The South African Communist Party: Adapting to Thrive in a Post-Communist Age.* Jefferson, NC: McFarland and Co., 2016.

Koorts, Lindie. *D.F. Malan and the Rise of Afrikaner Nationalism.* Cape Town: Tafelberg, 2014.

Krog, Antjie. *Country of My Skull: Guilt, Sorrow, and the Limits of Forgiveness in the New South Africa.* New York: Crown Books, 1999.

Lerumo, A. *Fifty Fighting Years: The Communist Party of South Africa, 1921–1971.* London: Inkululeko Publications, 1980.

Lodge, Tom. *Black Politics in South Africa Since 1945.* Johannesburg: Ravan Press, 1983.

———. *Sharpeville: An Apartheid Massacre and Its Consequences.* Oxford: Oxford University Press, 2011.

Luthuli, Albert. *Let My People Go.* New York: McGraw-Hill, 1962.

Macqueen, Ian. "Students, Apartheid and the Ecumenical Movement in South Africa, 1960–1975." *Journal of Southern African Studies* 39, no. 2 (2013): 447–63.

Madikizela-Mandela, Winnie. *491 Days: Prisoner 1323/69*. Athens: Ohio University Press, 2014.

Magaziner, Daniel. *The Law and the Prophets: Black Consciousness in South Africa, 1968–1977*. Athens: Ohio University Press, 2010.

Maloka, Eddy. *The South African Communist Party, 1963–1990*. Pretoria: Africa Institute of South Africa, 2002.

———. *Friends of the Natives: The Inconvenient Past of South African Liberalism*. Durban: 3rd Millenium Publishing, 2014.

Mandela, Nelson. *Long Walk to Freedom: The Autobiography of Nelson Mandela*. New York: Back Bay Books, 1994.

Mangcu, Xolela. *Biko: A Biography*. Cape Town: Tafelberg Press, 2012.

———. "Retracing Nelson Mandela through the Lineage of Black Political Thoughts." *Transition* 112 (2013): 101–16.

Marais, Hein. *South Africa Pushed to the Limit: The Political Economy of Change*. London: Zed Books, 2011.

Mare, Gerhard, and Georgina Hamilton. *An Appetite for Power: Buthelezi's Inkatha and South Africa*. Bloomington: Indiana University Press, 1988.

Marx, Anthony. *Lessons of Struggle: South African Internal Opposition, 1960–1990*. New York: Oxford University Press, 1992.

Mbeki, Govan. *Learning from Robben Island: The Prison Writings of Govan Mbeki*. London: J. Currey, 1991.

Meli, Francis. *A History of the ANC: South Africa Belongs to Us*. Harare: Zimbabwe Publishing House, 1988.

Minter, Bill. *Apartheid's Contras: An Inquiry into the Roots of War in Angola and Mozambique*. London: Zed Books, 1994.

Moodie, Dunbar. *The Rise of Afrikanerdom: Power, Apartheid and the Afrikaner Civil Religion*. Berkeley: University of California Press, 1975.

Naidoo, Beverley. *Death of An Idealist: In Search of Neil Aggett*. Johannesburg: J. Ball, 2012.

Ndebele, Njabulo S. *Fine Lines from the Box: Further Thoughts About Our Country*. Houghton: Umuzi Press, 2007.

Ndlovu, Sifiso. *The Soweto Uprisings: Counter-memories of June 1976*. Ravan Press, 1999.

Ndlovu-Gatsheni, Sabelo J. *The Decolonial Mandela: Peace, Justice and the Politics of Life*. Oxford: Berghahn Books, 2016.

Odendaal, Andre. *The Founders: The Origins of the ANC and the Struggle for Democracy in South Africa*. Lexington: University Press of Kentucky, 2013.

O'Malley, Padraig. *Shades of Difference: Mac Maharaj and the Struggle for South Africa*. New York: Penguin Books, 2007.

O'Meara, Dan. *Volkskapitalisme: Class, Capital and Ideology in the Development of Afrikaner Nationalism, 1934–1948*. Cambridge: Cambridge University Press, 1983.

———. *Forty Lost Years: The Apartheid State and the Politics of the National Party, 1948–1994*. Ravan Press, 1997.

Pogrund, Benjamin. *Robert Sobukwe: How Can Man Die Better*. London: P. Halban, 1990.

Posel, Deborah. *The Making of Apartheid, 1948–1961: Conflict and Compromise.* Oxford: Oxford University Press, 1992.

Posel, Deborah, and Graeme Simpson, eds. *Commissioning the Past: Understanding South Africa's Truth and Reconciliation Commission.* Johannesburg: Witwatersrand University Press, 2003.

Potgieter, De Wet. *Total Onslaught: Apartheid's Dirty Tricks Exposed.* Cape Town: Zebra Press, 2007.

Reeves, Ambrose. *Shooting at Sharpeville: The Agony of South Africa.* New York: Houghton Mifflin, 1961.

Sachs, Albie. *The Soft Vengeance of a Freedom Fighter.* Berkeley: University of California Press, 2000.

Seekings, Jeremy. *The UDF: A History of the United Democratic Front in South Africa: 1983–1991.* Athens: Ohio University Press, 2000.

Simpson, Thula. *Umkhonto we Sizwe: The ANC's Armed Struggle.* Cape Town: Penguin Random House, 2016.

Sisulu, Elinor. *Walter and Albertina Sisulu: In Our Lifetime.* Claremont: David Philip, 2002.

South Africa. *Truth and Reconciliation Commission of South Africa Report. Volumes 1–5.* Cape Town: The Commission, 1999.

Sparks, Allister. *Tomorrow Is Another Country: The Inside Story of South Africa's Road to Change.* Chicago: University of Chicago Press, 1996.

Thorn, Hakan. *Anti-Apartheid and the Emergence of a Global Civil Society.* New York: Palgrave Macmillan, 2006.

van Kessel, Ineke. *Beyond Our Wildest Dreams: The United Democratic Front and the Transformation of South Africa.* Charlottesville: University of Virginia Press, 2000.

# CHAPTER 41

# The Pan-African Experience: From the Organization of African Unity to the African Union

## Horace G. Campbell

*The Pan-African World We Want: Building a People's movement for a just, accountable and inclusive structural transformation. A united and integrated Africa; an-Africa imbued with the ideals of justice and peace; an interdependent and virile Africa determined to map for itself an ambitious strategy; an-Africa underpinned by political, economic, social and cultural integration which would restore to Pan-Africanism its full meaning; an-Africa able to make the best of its human and material resources, and keen to ensure the progress and prosperity of its citizens by taking advantage of the opportunities offered by a globalised world; an-Africa engaged in promoting its values in a world rich in its disparities.*
*(Constitutive Act, African Union website)*

When the call was made in May 2013 for 'a united and integrated Africa' by the African Union (AU) in its roll-out of Agenda 2063, it was then a major restatement of the goals of the emancipation of the African people at home and abroad. In keeping with this emancipatory aspiration, one year after the launch of Agenda 2063, the AU signed a Memorandum of Understanding (MoU) with the global Pan-Africa Movement. This MoU was a major admission that if the AU were to achieve its goals, it would have to be grounded

H.G. Campbell (✉)
Syracuse University, Syracuse, NY, USA

© The Author(s) 2018
M.S. Shanguhyia and T. Falola (eds.),
*The Palgrave Handbook of African Colonial and Postcolonial History,*
https://doi.org/10.1057/978-1-137-59426-6_41

in the ideas of African freedom as articulated by progressive Pan-Africanists at the grass roots through the ages. In fact, when the AU Constitutive Act was ratified in 2000, its preamble stated explicitly that the AU had been 'INSPIRED by the noble ideals which guided the founding fathers of our Continental Organization and generations of Pan-Africanists in their determination to promote unity, solidarity, cohesion and cooperation among the peoples of Africa and African States'.[1]

It is from this consideration of the need for an AU grounded in the principles of the most progressive aspects of the Pan-African Movement that guides this intervention. In this sense, the chapter will seek a longer historical overview of the movement than the empiricism that does not draw from the founding principles of Pan-African struggles. It should be stated from the outset that there are as many definitions of Pan-Africanism as there are different factions of this movement. This writer, as a scholar and activist in the movement, has been partial to the definitions of Pan-Africanism by thinkers such as Kwame Nkrumah, Marcus Garvey, Eusi Kwayana, Wangaari Mathai, Tajudeen Abdul Raheem, Micere Githae Mugo, and Walter Rodney. Within this movement, however, there is unanimity about the origins of this Pan-African movement among the enslaved Africans after the fifteenth century. From the time of the 1829 David Walker appeal in the USA, the orientation of the movement has been internationalist. David Walker had defined the tasks of Pan-Africanism by declaring that 'it was an unshakeable fact and forever immovable fact that your full glory and happiness, as well as that of all other coloured people under heaven, shall never be consummated without the entire emancipation of your enslaved brethren all over the world'. The concept of emancipation of all had been a key aspect of Pan-Africanism. Independent Haiti had lent support for the anti-colonial struggles all over South America, and black soldiers had been prominent in the armies of Simon Bolivar.

This chapter is divided into seven parts. The first will deal with the background to Pan-Africanism and the short transition from the Organization of African Unity (OAU) to the AU. It is here that there will be an explicit explanation of what is meant by the Pan-African experience. The second section will interrogate the context of the epistemological questions that arise from an engagement with the AU in the present and the OAU in the past. The third section will draw from the traditions of vindicationism and the long historical background of the Pan-African movement, drawing from the traditions of Ethiopianism and Pan-Africanism at the grass roots. The fourth section will provide the immediate background to the link between Pan-Africanism and the OAU (drawing out the tensions that came out of the birth of the OAU at the height of the Cold War). The fifth section interrogates the strength and weakness of the Pan-African movement at the moment of the intensified drive for freedom in Southern Africa and the intervention by the World Bank to entrench structural adjustment and economic retrogression in Africa.

The sixth section examines the revitalization of the ideals of Pan-African solidarity and cooperation which emerged after the military defeat of the apartheid army and the independence of Namibia. The seventh section will draw out the lessons from the birth of the AU and the tensions generated by the struggles by Africans outside of Africa to be central to the planning of the AU. The establishment of a sixth region of the AU was an elementary concession, but the urgent questions that were thrown up in the international Black Lives Matter movement brought renewed attention to Pan-Africanism's core challenge of how to guarantee the dignity of the African at home and abroad.

With the dominance of neo-liberal thinking internationally, the bureaucratic sections of the AU Commission fiddled with ideas of a Peer Review Commission and a Standby Force while the USA organized to deploy a new military and ideological force under the US Africa Command. In this era of neo-liberalism, the European Commission established its own center for Pan-Africanism to tap into the intellectual energy of this historic movement. Constant meetings about the protocols of Peace and Security had substituted for a clear agenda for the all African army until 2011. African leaders who had equivocated about calls for the full unification were given a rude awakening by the NATO intervention and destruction in Libya. In the conclusion, this chapter will underline the tenacity of the cultural and grass-roots forces of Pan-Africanism and the Pan-African movement that placed questions of reparative justice at the forefront of the movement. In the process of the struggles for reparations, the progressive tendencies within the Pan-African movement (especially from the African descendants in South America) linked once again to the world revolutionary trend and connected the ideas of Pan-Africanism to the collective struggles of humanity.

## WHAT IS PAN-AFRICANISM? BACKGROUND FROM THE OAU TO THE AU

Pan-Africanism arose as a philosophy to restore the humanity and dignity of the African person and indeed all humans. The concept of dignity and humanity has gone through many iterations from the period of enslavement to the current period of biotechnology when corporations have given themselves the right to patent life forms. African–Americans, Caribbean persons, and African descendants in Europe and other parts of the world have always been at the heart of Pan-African thought and action. This point has been articulated by many of the leading scholars on Pan-Africanism. The violent separation and oppression of the transatlantic slave trade lent urgency to identification with Africa. The idea of Pan-Africanism emanated from the enslaved person who wanted to develop a larger conception of reality than the village and the clan from which he or she had been taken into captivity. The transtlantic slave trade had captured the bodies of the Africans but could not capture their minds. The concept of shipmate helped to foster a new kind of familyhood or kinship in a period when the forms of bondage denied Africans the right to organize in family structures. The Pan-African idea and movement grew out of black people's desire to rediscover their identity and dignity and to fight for their liberation from colonialism and racism. As the Pan-African thinker St Clair Drake observed, the ideology of Pan-Africanism began:

> with a political concept developed by men of action not scholars, by a group of American Negroes and West Indians between 1900 and 1945 – Pan-Africanism – the idea that Africans and peoples of African descent in the New World should develop racial solidarity for the purpose of abolishing discrimination, enforced segregation, and political and economic exploitation.[2]

Though this author would take issue with the dates mentioned by Drake and the idea of 'men of action', the important point was that Pan-Africanism did not emerge out of the brains of intellectuals, but out of oppressed people who were engaged in concrete struggles. Hence, in the literature on Pan-Africanism, the words 'community', 'struggle', 'survival,' 'solidarity', 'cooperation', and 'emancipation' keep reappearing. 'Pan' means all, so Pan-Africanism includes all people of African ancestry living in continental Africa and throughout the world. At the period of slavery when the ideas of inferiority of black humanity became one component of Enlightenment thinking, Pan-Africanism emerged as a complex set of ideas and ideologies containing social, cultural, political, and spiritual aspects of dignity and liberation.

It was in the struggles against slavery that the ideas and principles of Pan-Africanism were refined. C.L.R. James made this point eloquently in his book *A History of Pan-African Revolt*. Drawing from the rich traditions of self-organization and self-expression that arose in the varying black revolts such as the successful Haitian Revolution, James pointed out how the success of the Haitian Revolution dominated Pan-African thinking in the nineteenth century.[3] Toward the end of that century, especially after the partitioning of Africa, black intellectuals began to give clearer meaning to the body of ideas that was later to be called Pan-Africanism. The first Pan-African Conference was called in London by H. Sylvester Williams in 1900.

Kwame Nkrumah had been one of the foremost thinkers and activist in the Pan-African movement in the twentieth century and he worked very hard for the goal of the unification of the people of Africa at home and abroad. On May 25, 1963 in Addis Ababa, Ethiopia, the 32 African states that had achieved independence at that time agreed to establish the OAU. A further 21 members joined gradually, reaching a total of 53 by the time of the AU's creation in 2002. At the founding meeting of the OAU in Addis Ababa, Nkrumah stated clearly that:

> No single part of Africa can be safe or free to develop fully and independently while any part remains unliberated or while Africa's vast economic resources continue to be exploited by imperialist and neo-colonialist interests. Unless

Africa is politically united under an All-Africa Union Government, there can be no solution to our political and economic problems.[4]

At that moment, many of the leaders who were present had thought that the aspiration of an All-Africa Union government was unrealistic, but by the start of the twenty-first century, the massive push from below rose all around the Pan-African world and the leaders returned to the goal of uniting all of Africa. The goal was for an independent and free Africa that would offer support to dispersed Africans. Julius Nyerere, who was an earlier supporter of gradually working towards a Union government, later recanted and in 1997 declared in Ghana that, 'without unity there is no future for Africa ... My generation led Africa to political freedom. The current generation of leaders and peoples of Africa must pick up the flickering torch of African freedom, refuel it with their enthusiasm and determination, and carry it forward'.[5]

Nkrumah had been a major historical figure in this movement and the Agenda 2063 of the AU subscribes to many of the goals of economic independence that had been articulated by hundreds of meetings and conferences by Pan-African thinkers and activists. The Pan-African goal of freedom, independence, and unity had been compromised in the founding of the Organization of African Unity in 1963, and for thirty eight years the progressive wing of the Pan-African movement pushed for realizing the goals of freedom, independence, unity, and an end to racial discrimination.

It was on May 26, 2001 that the Constitutive Act of the AU entered into force. This dream of uniting Africans had taken legal form and the Constitutive Act of the AU had been drafted, circulated and completed for adoption at the thirty-sixth summit of the OAU on July 11, 2000. The first formal meeting of the AU took place in Durban, South Africa (July 2002) and at that moment the OAU ceased to exist. The speed with which the African states adopted and signed the Constitutive Act of the AU had emanated from the appearance of new social forces that had emerged in a revitalized Africa after the defeat of apartheid at Cuito Cuanavale in 1988.[6] The end of formal apartheid, the World Conference against Racism in South Africa in 2001, and the birth of the AU were episodes in the revitalization of Africa reflecting the emerging social forces that wanted a break with the old forms of politics. These forces were carrying forward the call of Frantz Fanon for the creation of a new Africa with new ideas. In a major sense, the conjuncture of the formation of the AU reflected the aspirations of Pan-Africanists over the centuries who had believed that the freedom of black people everywhere was linked to a free and united Africa.

In the process of calling for change, the voices of truth across the Global Africa had made an impact to the point that the energies behind the formation of the AU represented a contested turning from the state-centered concepts of unity. This contestation remains manifest in the efforts to give meaning to the representation within the AU of the millions of Africans dispersed outside of Africa. Temporarily, these Africans have been grouped in the sixth region of the AU. The idea of an African Parliament representing peoples is one new aspect of Africa that is slowly emerging from the exhaustion of the old patriarchal models of politics. The other idea that is most profound is the mandate of the AU to intervene in the internal affairs of member countries in the event of cases of gross violation of human rights, crimes against humanity, and genocide. The AU is a body that represents the interests of all Africans on the continent of Africa. This organization is to be the core of a number of institutions such as the Pan-African Parliament, the African Court on Human and People's Rights, and the Central Bank.[7] (See Appendix on the Objectives of the AU.)

While academics, social scientists, political careerists, and legal experts had been toiling to give juridical meaning to the Constitutive Act, new social forces had been active in the Economic, Social and Cultural Council (ECOSOC) as well as the Conference on Security, Stability, Development and Cooperation in Africa (CSSDCA), seeking to formulate a clear and consistent position on a new thrust for Pan-African unity. Starting from a position of validating the life and dignity of all humans, the dominant forces in the CSSDCA sought to make a break with the conception of the state as the key force for Pan-African Unity and reconstruction in Africa. This position on Pan-Africanism had been reinforced by the outpourings of popular artists who had participated in the major Pan-African cultural activities such as the World Negro Art Festival (Dakar, April, 1–24, 1966), the Algiers Pan-African Cultural Festival (July 21–August 1, 1969), FESTAC (Art and Culture Festival, Lagos, January, 15–February 12, 1977) and other festivals with more limited scope such as the Ouagadougou Pan-African Film Festival (FESPACO), the Pan-African Music Festival (FESPAM, Brazzaville, 1987), and the Julius Nyerere Cultural and Intellectual Festivals in Tanzania. These festivals increased the range of Pan-African activities that were deepening the Pan-African experiences across the planet.

In this contribution by Pan-African experience, we mean the process of getting knowledge or skill from doing, seeing, or feeling things associated with the emancipation of Africa. In this case, the getting of knowledge and skill came from the differing Pan-African activities that were undertaken to advance the cause of freedom. St Clair Drake had succinctly outlined what was meant by a Pan-African activity. 'What makes the activity Pan-African is the conceptualization on the part of the participants in their local struggle of their being a part of a larger world, involving black people everywhere with various segments having obligations and responsibilities to each other.'[8]

The centrality of cultural artists in the Pan-African activities and the experiences in the transition from the OAU to the AU were manifest in the cultural outpourings from all corners of Global Africa. After the explosive interventions of Bob Marley, Fela Ransome Kuti, Tupac and countless others who pushed the progressive consciousness in the era of corporate globalization, there were efforts to depoliticize the cultural front by commodifying and linking Pan-African culture to saleable commodities. Thus, a tug of ideas emerged between neo-liberal Pan-Africanism and that tradition that was working to build new social relations. Hundreds of Pan-African artists continued to surge, using new technical means to bypass corporate-controlled sources of information and communication. This tenacity was underlined by the legendary Hugh Masekala. Internationally acclaimed for decades, this trumpeter, bandleader, composer, and lyricist created a sound that was part of the global anti-apartheid culture. At the launch of the AU he was at the forefront of composing its theme song. The song that underlined the depth of the feeling of the mass of the people of Africa was the song entitled *Everything Must Change*. This involvement of cultural artists at the forefront of strengthening progressive consciousness was not new; Tony Martin has reported Trinidad's entertainment icon Lord Kitchener being commissioned to compose a calypso for Ghana's independence.

This intervention on the Pan-African Experience and the AU draws inspiration from the cultural artists and village dialecticians from across Global Africa who are searching for new standards of human dignity and the validation of human beings.[9] The Garveyites in the early twentieth century had been clear that the struggles were global when they adopted the chant, 'Africa for the Africans at home and abroad'. It was the genius of the Garveyites that they had recognized the strategic spaces occupied by African descendants in Brazil, Costa Rica, Jamaica, the USA, Haiti, and other parts of the world. Mobilizing around a Global Pan-African ideal had connected dispersed movements in the last century and signaled that strategically any struggle for liberation in Africa must be linked to the conditions of the lives of Africans everywhere. After the OAU abandoned this global outlook and sought to domesticate Pan-Africanism as a vehicle for solidifying the power of a small clique, mainstream social scientists had heralded the death of the Pan-African movement. However, the seeds of the ideals of Pan-African liberation had, as it were, hidden in the mountains and valleys awaiting the right conditions for germination. These conditions are sprouting in a reenergized youth and in every village and township. The lyrics of Bob Marley have been a constant reminder of the need for an emancipatory approach to the Pan-African movement. This chapter will seek to elaborate on the emancipatory traditions of Pan-Africanism in order to distinguish this movement from the intellectual traditions of oppression that dehumanizes Africans.[10]

## Epistemological Questions and Grasping the Emergence of the AU

A theory is a statement of how and why processes work or the world operates. Within the social sciences, theories attempt to explain why groups of people choose to perform certain actions and how societies function or change in a certain way. Western social sciences have sought to place a dominant theoretical stamp of positivism in the study of Pan-Africanism. This theoretical perspective promotes the view about the appropriate methodology of social science, emphasizing empirical observation. With claims of being scientific, positivism is associated with empiricism (the view that knowledge is primarily based on experience via the five senses), and it is opposed to metaphysics. Roughly, the philosophical study of what is real is on the grounds that metaphysical claims cannot be verified by sense experience. This theoretical outlook was developed at a time when social scientists had embraced eugenic thinking and believed that ideas about African emancipation were metaphysical dreams that had no relation to reality. So far, as for the Western social scientists, the logical step for Africa was to be guided out of backwardness and superstition by modern Western intellectuals.

Western social scientists in the main understood the world based on the belief that Europe had reached the highest pinnacle of human civilization and that Western norms were universal. This position was clearly articulated in the book by Walt Rostow, *Stages of Economic Growth*. It followed then that the expansion of European social, economic, and cultural domination was necessary to facilitate the spread of civilization. Many Marxists also internalized this linear understanding of human societies and the French communists held onto this to the point of opposing the anti-colonial movements in French colonies. Many of the educated Africans who had sought to place themselves at the head of the Pan-African movement had internalized varying aspects of Western intellectual culture. Michael West had designated the nineteenth-century aspiring Pan-African thinkers as 'redemptionist and vindicationist'. In his analysis:

[the] redemptionist project had as its principal objective the rehabilitation, regeneration, and development of Africa and its inhabitants – spiritually, materially, and culturally. The exponents of African redemption were motivated by deep Christian convictions, largely Protestant. They accepted the view, then dominant in the White Atlantic, that Africa was a benighted land, in dire need of the transformative powers of that alchemic nineteenth-century trinity: Christianity, Commerce, and Civilization; that is, Protestantism, capitalism, and North Atlantic bourgeois culture.[11]

He continued by explaining the vindicationist traditions within Pan-Africanism.

Redemption, in this vision, amounted to a civilizing mission in which Africans from the west bank of the Atlantic would become the vanguard. Vindication complemented redemption. Whereas redemption championed the modernization of the African continent, vindication constituted the intellectual armor of an emerging global Africa. The vindicationists sought to valorize the African past, if not the African present. Theirs was a search for a usable past, a quest for a historiography to disprove White supremacist notions that Africa and Africans had played no part in the development of world cultures and civilizations.[12]

## THE POSITIVIST APPROACHES TO PAN-AFRICANISM

Positivism and individualism dominated the writings on Pan-Africanism and coincided with the popularity of the ideas of realism in international-relations theory. Toward the end of the nineteenth century, especially after the partitioning of Africa, black intellectuals began to give clearer meaning to the body of ideas that was later to be called Pan-Africanism. As stated in our introduction, the first Pan-African Conference was called in London by H. Sylvester Williams in 1900 in the period when the European armies were plundering Africa after the European leaders had partitioned the continent at the Berlin Conference (1884–1885). Vincent B. Thompson has been among those intellectuals who have chronicled the evolution of the OAU and the Pan-African movement from the activities of vindicationists such as Edward Blyden and J.H. Casley Hayford down through the Garvey movement to the advocacy of Kwame Nkrumah and the birth pains of the OAU.[13] Peter O. Esedebe, in the book, *Pan-Africanism: The Idea and Movement 1776–1963*, also linked the formation of the OAU to the long history of rebellions in the era of revolutions through the contributions of Blyden, Garvey, and those who came together for the Fifth Pan-African Congress in 1945.[14] Michael West in his contribution to the study of the idea of Pan-Africanism had also grounded the evolution of the idea to the quadripartite revolution at the end of the eighteenth century as manifest in the abolitionist movement, and the American, French, and Haitian Revolutions. Michael West then divided the emergence of the Pan-African idea into four moments: (a) 1776–1900, (b) 1900–1945, (c) 1945–1963; and (d) 1963–present.[15] West elaborated on how the Pan-Africanist project in this era was both a racial and a gendered one insofar as the struggle to redeem Africa was associated with the struggle to redeem black manhood.

For West, the idea of redeemed black manhood was replaced by the push for 'sovereign African statehood' by the time of the partitioning of Africa in 1885. Implicit in the push for African statehood was an accommodation with global capital. Booker T. Washington of the USA was the figure associated with this accommodationist outlook, but the imperatives of imperialism, racism, war, and Jim Crow eroded the appeal of accommodationism and birthed the Garvey movement that took a more militant approach to Pan-African self-reliance and self-organization.

Negro intellectuals, then, and indeed up to the present were dismissive of Garveyism and thus confused the personality of Garvey with the mass movement that represented one of the highest points of Pan-African activity. Instead of grasping the conditions of Jim Crow, eugenics, and the Klan that produced a wave of white racist violence, Western scholars denigrated Garvey and focused on the differences between him and W.E.B. Du Bois.

In this positivist tradition, there has been a major emphasis on the seven congresses that were held between 1900 and 1994 prior to the formation of the AU. W.E.B. Du Bois had been associated with the five major congresses up to 1945 and has often been referred to as the Father of Pan-Africanism. In the literature, the work of Du Bois and the International African Service Bureau (IASB) are usually highlighted as one of the high points of Pan-African organization. This focus on individuals has dominated the scholarly and Western academic approach to Pan-Africanism with the study of the lives of major figures such as Kwame Nkrumah, George Padmore, Marcus Garvey, Jomo Kenyatta, Julius Nyerere, Nelson Mandela, Bob Marley, Malcolm X, and Walter Rodney. One significant text in this tradition was that of Immanuel Geiss, *The Pan-African Movement: A History of Pan-Africanism in America, Europe and Africa*. This book drew heavily from the study of great individuals and centralized the role of black males, especially educated black males. It is this body of scholarship that focuses on events, conferences, and great individuals that is emblematic of the positivist intellectual traditions of Pan-Africanism.

One of the major limitations of this positivist tradition is the fact that many African intellectuals had sought to challenge Europeans on their own terms, especially with respect to recreating nation-states in Africa. This was manifest in three areas. The first was from those Pan-African intellectuals who accepted the pseudo-science of social Darwinism and believed that the leadership of the Pan-African movement required a cadre of intellectuals who were as rational and learned as Europeans. This belief emanated from Africans who had been educated in missionary schools. These African leaders wanted to inherit the colonial state without a fundamental transformation of the social and economic relations.[16]

The second challenge for the Pan-African idea was how to navigate the ideas of nationalism and Pan-Africanism. Within the ideas of Western social science, the 'nation' had been the core intellectual concept within which the ideals of sovereignty and self-determination were embedded. Social formations that had existed with millions of people were dominated by external forces at the end of the nineteenth century when European nationalism had propelled capitalist societies in Europe to embrace national boundaries with national language, customs, currency, and national 'market.' In Africa, the great social formations of Ghana, Mali, Songhay, Egypt, the Hausa states, Abyssinia, and Zimbabwe were states with differing nationalities. The transatlantic slave trade disrupted the paths of evolution of these societies. The Pan-African movement was faced with a struggle for self-determination by Africans who lived in multinational and multiracial societies and in Africa where the colonial boundaries had lumped differing nationalities and ethnic groups into one polity. The question of how to organize politically within territories that were not 'nations' posed a daunting problem for the Pan-African thinkers. None of the African states after independence developed a class that could fashion a national project in the form of organizing an economy with backward and forward linkages between production and consumption. Up to the present, when the idea of the nation has been undermined by the powerful forces of global capital, sections of the intellectual cadre still hold on to this concept and in reality linked up with ethnic chauvinism in the struggles for political power, especially in the era of multiparty democracy. The challenges of managing linguistic and ethnic differences offered new possibilities for real democratic management of societies within Pan-Africanism. The goals of Agenda 2063 unleashed new possibilities to transcend the colonial borders with the economies of scale that could compete in the emerging multipolar world, but most of the leaders who are bent on power within nation-states conceive of the AU as a union of states, in part because they believe in nineteenth-century concepts of nation-state.

The third strand of this positivist tradition was represented by members of a variant of Pan-Africanism that was called Négritude. This Négritude movement was a powerful one among French educated individuals such as Aimé Césaire, Leopold Senghor, Jean Price-Mars, and Leon Damas. Inspired by the black intellectuals of the US-based Pan-Africanists, the writers of this movement dug deep into the African past to celebrate the richness of African cultures in order to oppose French colonial racism. In the words of West:

> Négritude – the fourth agency that helped to cohere pan-African consciousness during the second moment of the global Africa idea was a reaction to what may be called the French imperial quandary. That is the chasm between France's preachment in its colonies and the treatment accorded colonial subjects in the métropole. Brought up to believe they were French citizens who only incidentally happened to be Black, as Blaise Diagne liked to boast, elite Francophone colonial subjects from Africa and the Caribbean – the évolués – often experienced a different reality on arrival in France. Their brushes with racial exclusion were not consistent with previous assurances that color bar was an Anglo-American injustice, in contrast to France, with its meritocratic non racial culture.[17]

After the end of the Second World War, when there were young intellectuals searching for alternative platforms to the French Communist Party and the French socialists who supported colonialism, a number of African students in France formed study groups and organizations dedicated to understanding African history. Cheikh Anta Diop of Senegal and Samir Amin of Egypt were two outstanding Pan-African thinkers who were seeking to develop new methodologies at that time. It was in this environment that Alioune Diop's *Présence Africaine*, was born and published in Paris from 1947. This bilingual journal brought together writers, politicians, and thinkers across the language barrier and served as a platform for Pan-Africanists for over 50 years.

Some of these Négritude intellectuals, however, had been constrained by their emotive link to the French language. This movement was very significant in the period of colonialism and there were many intellectuals who were introduced to the black intellectual traditions of the Pan-African world through this movement but later moved beyond this brand of seeking to solve the identity crisis of individuals. Cheikh Anta Diop, Amilcar Cabral,

Mario Andrade, and Frantz Fanon were among the notable intellectuals who started out in this Négritude tradition but who broke with the romantic notions of the African.

Both Fanon and Cabral later made sterling contributions to a new materialist methodology for analyzing Pan-African questions. They both decried the theoretical deficiencies of the Western traditions of history and the accompanying conceptions of unity. Fanon was especially scathing in his critique of the intellectual and political orientation of the new political leadership after independence. Coming from the deformed racial ideas of Portuguese colonialism, Amilcar Cabral elaborated the need for re-Africanization of the assimilated for cultural liberation. This process was not simply an intellectual exercise since a reconversion of minds—of mental set—is thus, indispensable to the true integration of the people into the liberation movement. 'Such conversion re-Africanization, in our case may take place before the struggle, but it is completed only during the course of the struggle, through daily contact with the popular masses in the communion of sacrifice required by the struggle.'[18]

Here Cabral was putting forth a version of Pan-Africanism that was based on concrete struggles for liberation. The process of liberation was one that required political clarity, organized political activity, and theoretical rigor. Cabral warned about the necessity to move to the level of engagement to be able to give a clear political content to the responsibilities devolving to Pan-Africanists who move from the level of analysis of skin color to grasping the necessities of the struggle against imperialism. It was this struggle against imperialism that influenced the Marxist analysis of Pan-Africanism.

## Marxism and Pan-Africanism

This particular epistemological approach to Pan-Africanism had been refined in the period of behavioralism when the Western social scientists wanted to diminish the impact of the anti-imperialist ideas that had been embedded in concepts of self-determination. Pan-Africanism as a body of thought had been influenced during the period of the Great Depression by ideas of class struggles and struggles against imperialism. Thinkers and activists such as Samir Amin, Amilcar Cabral, W.E.B, Du Bois, C.L.R James, Claudia Jones, Kwame Nkrumah, Walter Rodney, Tomas Sankara, and Ngugu Wa Thiongo were Pan-Africanists who sought to use a class analysis to grasp the struggles of Africans and to consider paths forward. We have already referred to the importance of C.L.R. James as a Pan-African activist who was also a Marxist. James had been initiated into the socialist movement and was sensitive to the need to grasp the class and racial content of the Pan-African struggle. His understanding of the interplay between race and class remains one of the clearest formulations of the period of the Pan-African Marxist intellectuals. James had noted: 'The race question is subsidiary to the class question in politics, and to think of imperialism in terms of race is disastrous. But to neglect the racial factor as merely incidental is an error only less grave than to make it fundamental'.[19]

This formulation was written in the context of the class and racial struggles in revolutionary Haiti. Other Marxists who did not comprehend the centrality of race in the lives of African people dismissed nationalist and Pan-African formations and promoted a dichotomy between nationalism and Marxism. This dichotomy was particularly present in the period of the struggles in Southern Africa where many of the liberation movements identified themselves as Marxist. In the particular case of the liberation movement in South Africa, because one of the movements had explicitly labeled itself as the Pan-Africanist Congress, the ideological and intellectual struggles over the definitions of Marxism and Pan-Africanism were very protracted inside the debates on liberation in Southern Africa. It was only after the African National Congress acceded to political power in 1994 that the leadership embraced an explicit Pan-Africanist outlook and proposed ideas about the African Renaissance.[20] The dichotomy between race and class played itself out in political terms and was fought out practically in the struggles for independence in Angola and Mozambique.

This dialectical interplay between race and class had dogged the Pan-African movement and exploded when the African leaders turned their backs on the struggles of the peoples after independence. Walter Rodney summed up this position of the leaders of the OAU at the time of the Sixth Pan-African Congress in Dar es Salaam when he wrote:

> Pan-Africanism has been so flouted by the present African regimes that the concept of 'Africa' is dead for all practical purposes such as travel and employment. The 'Africanisation' that was aimed against the European colonial administrator soon gave way to restrictive employment and immigration practices by Ivory Coast, Ghana (under Busia), Zaire, Tanzania, Uganda, Zambia, and others, aimed against Dahomeans, Nigerians, Burundi nationals, Malawians, Kenyans and all Africans who were guilty of believing that Africa was for the Africans.[21]

It was only later after the intervention of African feminists that it was understood that Pan-Africanism had to address the intersections of race, class, gender oppression, religious alienation, and sexual identity. However, this is to anticipate. What is important is to grasp the limits of those who attempted to reproduce a brand of Marxism that linked the ideas of Karl Marx to the European Enlightenment and Western social science.

George Patmore's *Pan-Africanism or Communism*, written at the height of the Cold War struggles between Western capitalism and the Soviet conception of communism, sought to define a path for Africans which was independent of both sections of the Cold War.[22] However, because of the racism of many of those who called themselves Communist, George Padmore opposed parties allied to the USSR and became a staunch anti-communist. Ultimately, Padmore became prey to anti-communist sentiments to the point of supporting the government of Forbes Burnham in Guyana. This was especially significant because this regime assassinated one of the foremost Pan-African thinkers of the twentieth century, Walter Rodney. It was Walter Rodney who sought to bring back the emancipatory ideas of Marx as articulated in the idea of self-emancipation.

## FEMINISM AND PAN-AFRICANISM

The third analytical approach to the study of Pan-Africanism has been offered by African feminists who have critiqued the patriarchal basis of previous Pan-African writing and thinking. These African feminists come from a broad range, from liberal feminists and womanists to Marxist feminists and radical black feminists. By the end of the twentieth century, African women had emerged with a new definition of Pan-Africanism that emphasized the humanity of Africans and not simply the independence of states. At the seventh Pan-African Congress in Kampala, Uganda, the women who were present formed the Pan-African Women's Liberation Organization (PAWLO). The struggles against violence, warfare, destruction, and violation had taken the Pan-African discussion to a new level. Feminists or womanists such as Ifi Amadiume, Ulla Taylor, Micere Mugo, Ama Atta Aidoo, and Nawal El Saadawi were developing a radical brand of feminism that was different from liberal feminism. Pan-Africanists such as Ifi Amadiume and Micere Mugo sought to, as it were, reenvision Pan-Africanism. Micere Mugo in her essay on 'Re-Envisioning Pan Africanism: What is the role of gender, youth and the masses', noted that:

> ... though not cited in intellectual discourses that have so far come to be the literary canon on Pan-Africanism, in their activism, as well as participation, women were and have always been the heart of the Pan-Africanism's essence, or if you like, substance. My point is that Pan-Africanism may be seen as manifesting itself in two major ways, which are equally important: through the movement itself and through its lived aspects. As a movement, Pan-Africanism has been characterized by fluctuation, registering bouts of life and dormant lulls. On the other hand, its lived aspects, actual substance, or essence, have always remained alive and persistent over historical time. Ordinary people, or the masses, including the majority of African women, have been the key keepers or carriers of this essence.[23]

Mugo's grasp of the lived experiences of the masses within the Pan-African movement builds on the insights of radical black feminists who had theorized the idea of intersectionality; that is to say, the framework that can be used to understand how systemic injustice and social inequality occur on a multidimensional basis. Intersectionality holds that the classical conceptualizations of oppression within society (such as racism, sexism, classism, ableism, homophobia, transphobia, xenophobia and belief-based bigotry) do not act independently of each other. Instead, these forms of oppression interrelate, creating a system of oppression that reflects the 'intersection' of multiple forms of discrimination. Kimberle Crenshaw and Patricia Hill Collins were two radical feminists who had critiqued the invisibility of black women in classical feminism and brought to the fore the impact of multiple oppression of women of color.[24] Their scholarship critiqued the intersectionality of Pan-African scholars such as W.E.B. Du Bois who had linked class and racial oppression but had omitted gender oppression and oppression of persons of differing sexual orientation. Radical black feminists had critiqued both masculinism in the Pan-African movement and the liberal feminism that preached equality on the basis of the capitalist market. Through the NGO movement and Western foundations this liberal feminism was promoted within Africa and finds expression within the AU in the policy that decided on gender parity for all of the important posts within the Commissions of the AU.

## Constructivism

While African intellectuals had deployed the approaches of liberalism, Marxism, and feminism in the era of capitalist globalization, a new approach emerged that was labeled as constructivism. This approach, which starts from an examination of the new 'norms' in international relations after the Cold War, seeks to highlight questions of human rights, peace, good governance, and security without reference to the unequal economic relations of the international capitalist system. For example, Akokpari, Ndinga-Muvumb, and Murithi's book *The African Union and its Institutions* gives some of the background to the Lagos Plan of Action and the Abuja Treaty, but books on the institutional approach diminish the important struggles that had gone inside the movement of the people to reach the point of the Lagos Plan of Action in 1980. Makinda, Okumu, Wafula, and Mickler's *The African Union: Addressing the challenges of peace, security, and governance* deploys the constructivist and institutional approach, comparing the AU to a supranational organization such as the United Nations. The most explicit constructivist study is Edozie's *The African Union's Africa: New Pan-African Initiatives in Global Governance*. The author explicitly stated that she wanted to underscore 'the cultural elements of constructivist international politics.' Constructivists have also noted the role of international institutions as actors in their own right. Hence, there is an inordinate emphasis on non-governmental organizations (NGOs) and discourses on civil society.

After the end of the Cold War, US-backed foundations had expended over a billion dollars to shape the intellectual culture of the post-apartheid society in projects to 'aid democracy.'[25] Aiding democracy and 'good governance' were promoted within South Africa and from there to the NGO consultants across Africa. This conception of good governance was to take institutional form in the Peer Review Mechanisms of the AU. Good governance emerged from the postmodernist intellectual networks and found its way into the documents of the AU. Afro pessimists who wrote reams of books and articles on 'failed states' in Africa influenced a new school of what this chapter will call neo-liberal Pan-Africanism. Primitive accumulation and theft were not seen as aspects of global capital formation and the role of transnational capitalism but presented as aspects of 'politics of the belly'.[26] From this analysis it was concluded that good governance could only come from outside from 'credible' institutions such as the Bretton Woods Institutions. Constructivism as a methodological framework for understanding contemporary Pan-Africanism 'provided the moral and intellectual foundation for the development of a set of doctrines, policies and principles formulated and implemented by various international actors to manage specifically the Third World States and Third World people'.[27]

Other pillars of constructivism and its handmaiden neo-liberal Pan-Africanism were to be found in the articulation of the New African Partnership for Development (NEPAD). NEPAD was presented to Africa after the World Conference against racism in Durban as a product of the initiative taken by four African presidents: General Olusegun Obasanjo of Nigeria, Thabo Mbeki of the Republic of South Africa, Abdoulaye Wade of Senegal and Abdelaziz Bouteflika of Algeria. Pan-African scholars and activists critiqued the assumptions and content that informed the framing of NEPAD in so far as it reflected the mistaken view that the continent's leadership needs to take an accommodative approach to world politics, and to adjust to the realities of neo-liberal globalization. Just as constructivism had emerged as a post-Cold War construct, so neo-liberalism presented the view that Africa needed 'partnership' with 'donors' in order to tap into language of foreign direct investment and capital flows. African scholars, progressive NGOs, trade unionists, and cultural workers distanced themselves from this neo-liberal Pan-African platform that was linked to the Washington consensus.[28]

## Ubuntu and the Emancipatory Approach to Pan-Africanism and the AU

The final methodological approach worth considering is that of the emancipatory framework for analyzing society. Walter Rodney had been the foremost theoretician of this position in his work on the self-emancipation of the working peoples. As a scholar, Rodney had been focused on the dignity of labor and elevated the questions of liberation beyond the capture of state power by political parties. He was explicit in his critique of vanguardism; that is, the idea that had developed among Marxist parties that an advanced sector of the intelligentsia and workers should lead the revolutionary struggles. In uniting theory and practice in the Caribbean, Rodney called on the intelligentsia to use their knowledge and skills to advance the struggles of the working peoples. For this task there had to be an explicit history of the working peoples.[29]

In practice, Rodney had demonstrated that Pan-Africanists cannot be racialists and that in order to struggle against racism, one had to be an anti-racist in word and deed. They must become members of social-movement organizations and work with the people in building their capacity for self-organization or self-emancipation. It was the view of Rodney that working people, through the process of struggle, would take themselves from one level of consciousness to the next. This was the core of his conception of self-emancipation.

It is the oppressed who are responsible for liberating themselves. If liberation is conceived, directed, and executed by the usurpers-cum-vanguards of the people and their struggle, the people will end up with new masters on the morning after the 'successful' revolution. Tajudeen Abdul Raheem deepened this conception of self-emancipation when he continuously wrote of liberators who later became dictators. He had written of the leadership of Uganda, then the supposed headquarters of the Pan-African movement that:

> They have stayed so long in power that they have all forgotten their previous jobs, values and visions. From heralding 'fundamental change' they have become apostles of 'no change'. They have become reactionaries, tired revolutionaries exhausting the country they claim they have liberated. The challenge now facing Ugandans is similar to what is facing Zimbabweans, Ethiopians, Eritreans and other post-liberation societies: how to liberate themselves from their liberators. The liberators have become establishment reactionaries blocking future changes ... they are no longer changing the system because they are the system. The burden of change is now squarely on the shoulders of another generation. They are no longer part of the solution but very central to the problem.[30]

Here Tajudeen was signaling the need for a new emancipatory basis for Pan-Africanism. Wangari Maathai and Thomas Sankara took this emancipatory framework further by linking humans to nature and saving the planet.

This emancipatory framework has been most manifest in the freedom and creativity of cultural artists such as Fela Ransome Kuti, Paul Robeson, Hugh Masekala, John Coltrane, Aretha Franklin, Tupac Shakur, Tikhen Jah, Alpha Blondie, and Bob Marley. It was Bob Marley who, through both the medium and the message, called for a conception of African unity and human freedom which was linked to the emancipation from mental slavery. Bob Marley, the Rastafarian cultural leader, was another notable Pan-African spokesperson of the century, who wanted to transcend racial divisions with a universal message of African unity, love, peace, and human emancipation. Africans and non-Africans alike embraced his music and ideas and his message of Pan-African emancipation was an inspiration to all of humanity. The challenge for Pan-Africanism in the twenty-first century is to take the conception of emancipation beyond the material plane to grasp the limits of the human potential imposed by the eugenic civilization of the contemporary period.

It was within the anti-apartheid struggle that the articulation of the ideas of dignity along with the identity of personhood brought the philosophy of Ubuntu onto the international stage. There is no literal translation for Ubuntu, but it means 'I am a person whose personhood is achieved through others'. Ubuntu elevated the discourses above the individualism and competitiveness of Western liberalism and conveyed ideas of sharing, reconciliation, and forgiveness.[31] Under the leadership of Nelson Mandela and Desmond Tutu there had been an effort to take the concept of Ubuntu from the philosophical level to the practical level in the promulgation of the Truth and Reconciliation Commission.

These ideas of sharing, reconciliation, and forgiveness did not come out of an intellectual vacuum but were direct responses to the ideation system that celebrated apartheid, individualism, patriarchy, and domination over nature and the ability of science and technology to solve humans' problems. Liberalism with its handmaidens private property, competition, and survival of the fittest form the core of the philosophy that emanates from the dominant European knowledge system. The progressive Pan-African movement was seeking to inspire a body of ideas that is embedded in values of justice, spiritual health, sharing, truth, and healing. It is at the philosophical level that there are new breakthroughs in grasping the 'Politics of Memory' as a core element in making the break with huge historical atrocities. Wole Soyinka raised fundamental questions on the importance of memory in the pursuit of truth. He addressed the fundamental issue of memory in a collection of essays on the *Burden of Memory and the Muse of Forgiveness*. Here Soyinka was linking the concept of infinity to the concept of memory by arguing that memory is not governed by statutes. However, he pointed out that while memory is not governed by statutes, humans have the capability to lay down the prerequisites for breaking the simplistic narrowness of historical memory as represented in the written texts available at present. This theme of the politics of memory is reinforced in the essay on 'Facing Truth, Voicing Justice', edited by Ifi Amadiume and Abdullahi An-Na'im in the book on *The Politics of Memory: Truth, Healing and Social Justice*.

## BACKGROUND TO THE PAN-AFRICAN MOVEMENT

The Africans who came to the United States as slaves started their attempts to claim their African heritage soon after they arrived in this country. They were searching for the lost identity that the slave system had destroyed. Concurrent with this black man's search for an identity in America, has been the search for an identity in the world. Which means, in essence, his identity as a human being with a history, before and after slavery that can command respect.[32]

Thus wrote the historian John Henrik-Clarke in his summation of the importance of grasping African thought and the survival of the philosophies of Africa that maintained a balance between humans, the natural world, and the wider universe. This balance framed the ways in which Africans understood the universe as a unified spiritual totality. This unified spiritual totality was very different from the crude materialism that was reproduced in the so-called Cartesian rationality of Western European thought.

St Clair Drake had linked the question of history to economic exploitation in his definition, which noted that, 'the idea that Africans and peoples of African descent in the New World should develop racial solidarity for the purpose of abolishing discrimination, enforced segregation, and political and economic exploitation of Negroes throughout the world'.[33]

At the period of slavery when the ideas of inferiority of black humanity became one component of Enlightenment thinking, Pan-Africanism emerged as a force to oppose oppression. These ideas inspired the organized and spontaneous rebellions for liberation. Pan-Africanism was therefore associated with struggles for self-development, emancipation, and freedom from bondage. Thus, in all parts of the planet, Africans responded to the ideas of 'liberty, equality, and fraternity' with a larger vision of liberty and equality than the philosophers of the French and European revolutionary processes. Whether it was within the Maroon communities, in the Quilombos of Brazil or other liberated spaces, the concepts of freedom and liberty were written in the struggles. C.L.R James documented the spontaneous and organized resistance of the rebellions in *A History of Pan-African Revolts*.

The term 'Pan-Africanism' first entered the political lexicon in 1900 when the Trinidadian lawyer Henry Sylvestre Williams, then based in London, called a conference of black people to protest against stealing of lands in the colonies, and against racial discrimination, and to deal with all other issues of interest to blacks. This is the period that Michael West has designated as the second period of the Global Africa idea. However, long before, the intellectual understandings of Pan-Africanism and the spirit of freedom had been manifest in Pan-African movements such as the movement for freedom, anti-slavery, and independence in Haiti. The leaders of the Haitian revolution wanted to organize an expedition to Africa to end the slave trade. The leadership of the Haitian revolution was killed and there was an international conspiracy to crush Pan-Africanism in Haiti which continues to this day. Anti-slavery fighters such as Martin Delaney, Harriet Tubman, Frederick Douglas, Sojourner Truth, and Rev. Richard Allen of Philadelphia linked the future dignity of Africans under slavery to freedom in Africa. In fact, the dominant force that arise came in the form of religious Pan-Africanism in the formation of the African Methodist Episcopal Church (AME). The AME became a force although other nineteenth-century Pan-Africanists such as Edward Wilmot Blyden did not believe that Western Christianity could be a vehicle for Pan-Africanism and liberation. Blyden, who was from the Danish colony in the Caribbean that is now called the US Virgin Islands went back to Africa, embraced Islam, and was an organizer for African independence in West Africa. His writings and advocacy influenced many educated Africans who were mobilized to oppose colonial rule after the Berlin Conference of 1885 to partition Africa. During the nineteenth century, Ethiopianism was the dominant variant of Pan-Africanism. This was the view that the independence and liberation of Africans throughout the world was linked to the continuing freedom and independence of Ethiopia.

## ETHIOPIANISM AND VINDICATIONISM

Pan-African intellectuals at the turn of the nineteenth century had argued that Africa had its own history, its own past, and its own civilizations. Prior to the twentieth century, this vindicationist tradition was called Ethiopianism. After the defeat of Italy at Adowa (Abyssinia) in 1896, this brand of African vindicationism developed and inspired confidence among Africans at a moment when the eugenic ideas of white superiority represented a dominant stream of Western European thought.[34] Vindicationism, in brief, was a project to negate the whiting out of the African past by European intellectuals. Time and space do not allow an in-depth analysis of Ethiopianism and vindicationism here, but it is important to locate this movement as one of the precursors to the contemporary Pan-African movement. According to William G. Martin and Michael West, 'the vindicationist tradition had its origins in attempts by black intellectuals, writers, pamphleteers, and memorialists to vindicate Africa and Africans, to defend them against their traducers in Europe and the Americas who hurled calumnies about a dark Africa devoid of the African past'.[35] Those who were steeped in the Bible used the words of the Psalms, ('Ethiopia stretches forth her hands unto God') to mobilize a study and celebration of Ethiopia and the great kingdoms of Africa. The writings of St Clair Drake on the vindicationist traditions provide one consistent thread in linking the traditional Pan-African activities of leaders and the mass uprisings of the peoples. In my own text on the Rastafari movement, I have been able to distinguish between the vindicationism of great men and vindicationism at the grass roots.[36]

## GARVEYISM AND VINDICATIONISM
## IN THE BACKGROUND OF THE OAU

As Tajudeen Abdul Raheem observed, in the book that came out after the Seventh Pan-African Congress, that while the years 1900–1919 can confidently be cited as important reference points for the Pan-African movement, the movement stretches back further into the distant history of our people. Indeed, the roots of the Pan-African movement can be traced right back to the ravages of the first European slave ships to touch the African coast, some 500 years ago.

The first Pan-African Conference took place in London, from July 23 to July 25, 1900. Nevertheless, far more important that the meetings were the organized and spontaneous Pan-African revolts against European colonialism and occupation. Whether it was the resistance of the Ethiopian Emperor Menelik at the Battle of Adowa (1896), the Bambata Revolts in South Africa (1906), or the resistance of Simon Kimbangu (in the regions of Angola and the Congo), Pan-Africanism at the grass roots flourished all over Africa. In the Americas, the highest expression of the Pan-African movement emerged in the forms of Garveyism and the Universal Improvement Association (UNIA). In 1914, Marcus Garvey popularized the ideas of African liberation among the poor and oppressed workers from the banana plantations in Costa Rica to the elevator operators and domestic workers in New York. The Conventions of the UNIA were major milestones in the Pan-African movement. It was at the 1920 Conventions that the Garveyites issued the 'Declaration of the Rights of the Negro People of the World'.

It should be stated that the kind of vindicationism that emanated from intellectuals and religious leaders had been different from the yearnings among the poor share croppers and workers in the USA who yearned for a social power to challenge the oppression of eugenics and Jim Crow. Before travelling to the USA, Garvey had been in communication with Booker T. Washington and had journeyed from Kingston, Jamaica to Harlem, USA to seek support for the UNIA that had been formed in Kingston in 1914. In the USA, the black working population had the social weight, organizational capabilities and political autonomy to elevate any yearning for kings and kingdoms into a concrete social movement based in a specific class. Marcus Garvey, coming from a British colony where anti-colonialism had taken the form of rejecting British imperialism represented by the British monarch, had linked his organization to the need to create an alternative government for Africans.

Garvey had asked himself, he later recalled in his famous book *The Philosophy and Opinions of Marcus Garvey, or, Africa for the Africans*: 'Where is the Black man's government? Where is his king and his kingdom? Where is his president, his country, and his ambassador, his army, his navy, his men of big affairs?' 'I could not find them', Garvey lamented, 'and then I declared, 'I will help to make them'.[37] This call for a government to defend black people is very different from the present governments in Africa and the Caribbean that do not defend black lives. Garvey's call for the organization of the blacks was what distinguished the Garveyite movement and separated vindicationism at the grass roots from Vindicationism of the current leaders of Africa. This kind of organization was different from the organization of the black educated who had organized in Blue Vein Clubs and looked down on Marcus Garvey because he could not pass the brown paper bag test.

Not only was the UNIA the most efficient organization among Africans at home and abroad, but the *Negro World* newspaper was the most widely circulated African publication in the world. Within a few short years, the Garveyites had built a Pan-African organization with branches in the Americas,

Africa, Europe, and Australia. The Negro Factories Corporation employed over a thousand people in New York. The Black Star Line Steamship Corporation sailed the seas. It hoped to facilitate trade and travel within the African diaspora. 'Negro producers, Negro distributors, Negro consumers!' Garvey exulted, 'The world of Negroes can be self-contained. We desire earnestly to deal with the rest of the world, but if the rest of the world desire not, we seek not'.[38]

## INFLUENCE OF GARVEYISM ON KWAME NKRUMAH AND THE OAU

The Garvey movement was the most vibrant international movement among dispersed Africans in the twentieth century. This global African movement had more than four million members and 400 chartered divisions in over 40 countries. Each local organizing committee had the autonomy to deal with the principal issue in their area or locality. The UNIA was based on the principle of the self-organization of the working people, as an organization developed a militant brand of Pan-Africanism that stressed self-reliance, self-defense, and the liberation of the African continent. The most organized divisions were in New York, Philadelphia, Pittsburgh, Cleveland, Cincinnati, Detroit, and Chicago. These were sites of intense class and racial struggles, and the Garveyites were organizing at every level of the society. Through the newspaper, the *Negro World*, this organization was able to develop the ideas of African redemption (liberation) in a language that was accessible to the mass of the working people. Africans in Harlem had come from four corners of the African world in the period of the Great Migration (the era of great outpouring that is sometimes referred to as the Harlem Renaissance) and the energies of that political moment created a worldwide movement. The economic activities of the UNIA were based on the right of the poor black workers to control their economic livelihood. Only UNIA members could own stock in UNIA companies.

There are many who associate the Garvey movement with the individual Marcus Garvey and this is consistent with the individualism and nature of celebrity politics in the USA. Hence, in the literature, there are those who will refer to Marcus Garvey as the Black Moses, Redeemer and Uplifter of the Race. There are many who denigrated the Garvey movement as a simple back-to-Africa movement, but the dynamism of this organization transcended the simple proposition of setting up a place for Africans in Africa. The point was that a Garvey settlement in Africa represented a threat to the colonial authorities, especially the French and the British. These governments paid very close attention to the activities of Garveyites and the *Negro World* was banned in most colonial territories. The UNIA was an illegal organization in French-occupied territories and those caught with a copy of the *Negro World* faced life imprisonment. The UNIA searched diligently for a base in Africa to promote the ideas of African liberation and African unity. The foreign policies of the USA with respect to the UNIA plans for Liberia have been documented extensively. The UNIA called for decolonization in a militant fashion and this inspired anti-colonial forces all over Africa.

Kwame Nkrumah wrote of how the UNIA inspired him and spurred the Pan-Africanist activities in his lifetime. At the All-African Peoples' Conference in 1958, he said, 'Many of them have made no small contribution to the cause of African freedom. Names which spring immediately to mind in this connection are those of Marcus Garvey, and W.E.B. Dubois. Long before many of us were even conscious of our own degradation, these men fought for African national and racial equality'.[39] Nkrumah had spent ten years in the USA and had learnt practically from the organizational capabilities of the Garveyites. One of the important aspects of Nkrumah's contribution to Pan-Africanism was his independence at the intellectual level. Nkrumah was able to draw from the positive contributions of George Padmore, Du Bois, James, and the Garveyites without being dragged into the sectarian debates that were common among those who did not have to grapple with fundamental questions of social and economic transformation.

## Influence of Dubois on the Pan-African Traditions

W.E.B. Du Bois had not been shy to embrace Marxism and his epic study of *Black Reconstruction in America* had alerted him to the implications of racism in the USA and how this racism and eugenics held back the economic potential of the country. His tireless activism with the Pan-African movement and his massive intellectual output placed him in the ranks of those who grasped the need for world peace as one component of Pan-African liberation. Even before Lenin had written the pamphlet on imperialism, ('Imperialism, the Highest Stage of Capitalism') Du Bois had written on the African roots of the First World War, elaborating on how this war emanated from the unfinished questions of the imperialist rivalries in Africa. Du Bois had noted, 'We, then, who want peace, must remove the real causes of war... We must extend the democratic ideals to the yellow, brown and black people'.[40] Du Bois's contribution to Pan-Africanism and world peace is one aspect of the global Pan-African movement that has not received adequate attention.

Although the first Pan-African Conference had been held in London in 1900, in 1919 Dubois organized what he determined to be the First Pan-African Congress in Paris, February 17–21, 1919. The meeting was held on the sidelines of the Versailles Conference which repartitioned Africa at the end of the First World War. (The former German colonies of Cameroon, South West Africa, Tanzania, and Togo were given to Britain and France under a League of Nations Mandate.) Dubois and the first Congress demanded:

The Land [in the colonies] must be preserved with its natural resources for the natives, their working conditions must be regarded by the law, and slavery and corporal punishment abolished, as well as forced labour except for criminals. The natives of Africa must have the rights to participate in governments as rapidly as their development will permit with the goal that in due time Africa will be governed with the consent of Africans.[41]

This theme of independence and self-government for Africans dominated the meetings that Du Bois called the Second Pan African Congress of 1921 with sessions in London, Brussels, and Paris; the Third Pan-African Congress held in London and Lisbon, November and December 1923; and the Fourth Pan-African Congress was held in New York in August 1927.

### The Fifth Pan-African Congress and the Decolonization Process to the OAU

During the worst years of the capitalist depression, there were many organizational forms of Pan-Africanism; the Rastafari and Kimbangist movements were expressions of Pan-Africanism at the grass roots. Among intellectuals such as C.L.R James, George Padmore, Kwame Nkrumah, Paul Robeson, and W. Alphaeus Hunton, Jr., there were formations such as the International African Service Bureau (IASB) and the Council on African Affairs (CAA). The Italian invasion of Abyssinia in October 1935 elicited a wave of Pan-African response all over the world and the Fifth Pan-African Congress grew out of the galvanized and organized Pan-African forces. That Congress had taken place in Manchester, October 15–19, 1945. It took a decisive stand on colonialism and the racism of that period and set in motion the networks for the independence struggles all over Africa.

Amy Ashwood Garvey and Amy Jacques Garvey provided the crucial links between the forces of the UNIA conventions and the intellectuals who had been organized in the Council for African Affairs, the West African Students Union (WASU) and the International Africa Service Bureau (IASB). Shirley Graham Du Bois was another such force who went on to serve the movement with distinction for decades. At the 1945 Congress, the major forces of decolonization were represented. Along with the above named women were such IASB luminaries such as Kwame Nkrumah, George Padmore and Du Bois. There was Wallace Johnson (Sierra Leone), Awolowo and Nnamdi Azikiwe (Nigeria), Jomo Kenyatta (Kenya), Ken Hill and Dudley Thompson (Jamaica). Hasting Banda (Malawi), Peter Abrahams (South Africa), Ako Adjei (Ghana), Jaja Wachukwu (Nigeria), along with D.M. Harper and Ras T. Makonnen (Guyana). There was a very strong representation of trade unions at this meeting.

One of the limitations of the representation of the Congresses up to 1945 was the silencing of the frontline role played by progressive women. Two Africans who were children of one of the main organizers of this meeting have written a book about the male-centered narrative of the five Congresses. In their book, *In Search of Mr McKenzie: two sisters' quest for an unknown father*, these Pan-African women highlighted the limitations of the male-centered movement when the men were involved in Progressive Pan-African politics in public but in private neglected their families and children. The story of Ernest McKenzie Mavinga, who was a key organizer of the 5th Pan-African Congress, has been repeated by Pan-Africanist women since the publication of this book in order to highlight the fact that in the written narratives of the Pan-African Movement, women have been excluded. Books on the history of the Pan-African Movement by scholars such as Immanuel Geiss wrote black women out of the movement. Women, with the exception of Adelaide Casely-Hayford, Shirley Graham Du Bois, Amy Ashwood Garvey and Amy Jacques Garvey, were virtually invisible in this history, particularly for the first five Congresses. There were, however, several forthright women who participated in these. Some of the black women participants in the early Congresses included Annie J. Cooper, Jessie Faucet, Ida Gibbs Hunt and Mary McLeod Bethune. A group of 21 women of African descent were the main organizers of the Fourth Pan-African Congress held in New York, 1927. Many of them were members of a women's organization called The Circle of Peace and Foreign Relations. Dorothy Hunton, who was the president of this organization, was involved in the struggle for Pan-Africanism for many years.

## THE ROAD TO THE OAU

Vincent B. Thompson in the excellent book *Africa and Unity* outlined in great detail the organizational forms of Pan-Africanism that had emerged in the period of decolonization. In 1957, when Ghana became independent, Kwame Nkrumah sought to give Garveyism and Pan-Africanism a base and on independence night he proclaimed, 'the independence of Ghana is meaningless if it is not linked to the total liberation and continental union of the whole of Africa'. In order to pursue this goal, one year later in April 1958, Nkrumah along with George Padmore called the All-African Peoples' Conference in Accra, Ghana. Pan-Africanism had finally returned home to Africa. At this meeting, 62 nationalist and liberation movements were represented. Among the major Pan-African forces and individuals to be represented at that meeting were Frantz Fanon and Ahmed Ben Bella (representing the Algerian liberation struggles), Tom Mboya and A.M. Babu (representing East Africa and the Pan-African Freedom Movement of East and Central Africa, PAFMECA), T.B. Makonnen, Félix Moumie of the French Cameroons, Roberto Holden of Angola, Modibo Keita (Mali) Joshua Nkomo (Zimbabwe), Oliver Tambo (South Africa), Kenneth Kaunda (Zambia), and Sékou Touré (Guinea). It was at this meeting that Patrice Lumumba was introduced to the wider Pan-African world by A.M. Babu and the delegation from East Africa that had organized PAFMECA. These delegates from East Africa had stopped off in Leopoldville (now Kinshasa) and sought out the Pan-Africanists in the

Congo. When they were introduced to Patrice Lumumba, the delegates from East Africa paid the fare for him to travel to Accra.

Nkrumah had been supporting the idea of positive action in the decolonization process in Ghana but at the All-African Peoples' Conference in 1958 the representatives of Algeria (Fanon) and Kenya (Tom Mboya) argued that the Pan-African movement must support those waging armed struggles for independence. It was at this meeting that the Pan-African slogan emerged that independence would be achieved by any means necessary. Malcolm X popularized these ideas in the context of the Civil Rights struggles in the USA, where he argued that the principles of peaceful non-violence should be replaced with the posture of freedom 'by any means necessary'.[42] In the speech he had said,

> The purpose of our Organization of Afro-American Unity, which has the same aim and objective [as the OAU] to fight whoever gets in our way, to bring about the complete independence of people of African descent here in the Western Hemisphere and, first, in the United States. And bring about the freedom of these people by any means necessary. He called for freedom, justice, and equality "by any means necessary".

Many of the luminaries of the 5th Pan-African Congress went home to join the decolonization struggles being borne by market women, students, workers, poor peasants, traders, ex-soldiers, and intellectuals. Kwame Nkrumah (Ghana), Jomo Kenyatta (Kenya), Hastings Banda (Malawi), Obafemi Awolowo (Nigeria) were among the more famous of the activists of the Pan-African Movement. It was the expectation of W.E.B Du Bois that once Ghana was independent the Sixth Pan-African Congress would be called in Ghana. At that time Du Bois could not travel because of the harassment and impounding of his passport by the US government. Western imperial forces did not sit idly by as the Pan-African forces deliberated on the full decolonization of Africa.

In the face of the independence of Ghana and the liberation struggles in Algeria and Kenya, France worked hard to break up the Rassemblement Democratique Africaine (RDA) which addressed itself to the independence of French West Africa. After the defeat of France in Vietnam in 1954, the leaders of France decided to make a stand in Africa in order to maintain the prestige of France as a 'world' power. Areas of West and Central Africa which experienced French colonial rule as a unified bloc witnessed the shameless dismantling of those colonial politics which had a large territorial base. Whereas the French had maintained unity for exploitation, the African petty bourgeoisie lacked the capacity to demand both unity and freedom. In 1958, in the face of Ghana's independence, President Charles de Gaulle of France toured the French colonial territories with his famous oui-ou-non (yes-or-no) offer. The offer gave the African colonies a choice; become autonomous states in the French Union or become immediately and fully independent. De Gaulle actively campaigned for the colonies to join the Union, and only Guinea chose immediate independence. However, by 1960 the French Union had failed and the other French colonies soon gained their independence as well. This independence was granted on the condition that the societies would remain under French cultural, linguistic, military, commercial, and monetary domination. From that time to today these former territories have not been allowed monetary independence and their reserves have had to be kept in France. The Francophone leaders on the whole accepted French domination and they accepted the Balkanization which led to fragments called Ivory Coast, Upper Volta, Niger, Chad, the Central African Republic and so on. Since independence, little or no progress has been registered with respect to reversing this Balkanization. Leaders such as Félix Moumie and movements such as the Union of the Peoples of Cameroon were eliminated.

## IMPERIAL MACHINATIONS TO DIVIDE THE PAN-AFRICAN MOVEMENT

Ghana had become a magnet for Pan-Africanism and leaders such as Martin Luther King and Malcolm X made pilgrimages to Accra. Maya Angelou was another of the Pan-African forces that moved to live in Ghana. While the Nkrumah forces sought to build a coalition for the total independence of Africa, the experience of Britain and France after the Suez Canal nationalization and the subsequent Suez crisis led them to expand their military relations with former colonies. Conferences in Dakar and Nairobi had laid the framework for the constant deployment of imperial troops in Africa, a situation that continues to this day. Nkrumah had been calling for an African High Command and this call ensured that Britain, France, Belgium, Portugal, and the USA were committed to a political and diplomatic posture that opposed Kwame Nkrumah and the Pan-Africanists. There was thus realignment among Pan-Africanists in what was to be called the Monrovia Group.

The Monrovia Group had convened in Liberia after the radical call of the meeting of African leaders in Morocco in December 1960. The Casablanca Group had met in Morocco in December 1960, the year of African independence, and called for the immediate political union of Africa. This group included leaders such as Kwame Nkrumah of Ghana, Gama Abdel Nasser of Egypt, Sékou Touré of Guinea, Ben Bella of Algeria, King Mohamed V of Morocco, and Modibo Keita of Mali. They met in May 1961 in response to the December meeting of 1960 and their group included leaders from Nigeria, Liberia, Togo, and observers from the French-speaking areas. They argued for slow steps to be taken to lead to African unity. One of the primary aims of this group was to oppose the mobilization of an all-African army after the assassination of Patrice Lumumba in January 1961. Inside the USA, the anti-Communism of the Cold War had created a rupture among Pan-Africanists such as Paul Robeson and W.E.B. Du Bois on one side and others such as Alphaeus Hunton who became rabid anti-communist. Patrice Lumumba was also characterized as a communist and Britain, Belgium, and the USA conspired to eliminate him. The USA, France, Belgium, Portugal, Germany, Italy, and South Africa worked hard to break the cohesion of the Pan-African forces and unleashed intellectuals and operatives to undermine the Pan-African movement. It was in the wake of this imperial resistance that leaders such as Ben Bella, Nkrumah, and Keita were removed.

## THE OAU AFTER THE ELIMINATION OF PATRICE LUMUMBA

In the spirit of compromise between the groupings dedicated to Pan-Africanism, the OAU was officially launched in May 1963 in Ethiopia. The momentum and energy of the poor ensured that despite the compromises, the one fact that held the Global Pan-African movement together was the commitment to end colonial rule in Africa. This took practical form in the establishment of the OAU Liberation Committee with its headquarters in Dar es Salaam, Tanzania. The OAU, through the Liberation Committee, supported the process of decolonization in Southern Africa but for all intents and purposes, the OAU after 1963 acted against the interests of African Unity. This is obvious in the compromise of the different groups which could not agree on how to respond to the clear external manipulation of the Congo after those representing the interests of Western mining capital murdered Patrice Lumumba in 1961. Kwame Nkrumah in his book *Challenge of the Congo* exposed the work of imperialism to derail the efforts of the progressive forces in the embryonic OAU to come to the support of the people of the Congo, which was destabilized and later renamed Zaire.

When Patrice Lumumba was waging the heroic struggle against imperialism, it seemed as if those governments which supported real independence would form an alliance to remove the stooges of external control. It was in response to the imperial military activities in the Congo that Nkrumah called for an Africa High Command. The Western intelligence agencies stepped up their activities against Africa and Pan-Africanism to the point that they conspired to undermine the very efforts of the Pan-Africanists to support Patrice Lumumba. Major General Alexander, the British officer who commanded the Ghanaian troops in the Congo had been deployed by the government of Kwame Nkrumah to support the United Nations against the rebellion from Katanga and the Belgian military that had opposed independence. General Alexander has written for posterity the intrigues between the British and US diplomatic personnel in the Congo to ensure that Lumumba was not supported. His memoirs pointed out that he responded to the dictates of the British government rather the government of Ghana that he was supposed to serve.[43] Not only did the Ghanaian troops oppose the Pan-African ideas of the Nkrumah Government but the officers who served in the Congo were identified as future allies of the West and were recruited to be the lynchpin of the military coup that removed Kwame Nkrumah in February 1966.

At the time of the coup, many on the left had blamed Nkrumah for the deterioration of the internal political situation, but after US documents on the coup were declassified, it became clear that the US government had been determined to depose Nkrumah before he managed to achieve a united African government. As it turned out, the US government and some of its allies, including Britain, had financed, masterminded, and guided the coup from a distance.[44] Recent research work and the findings of three commissions of investigations have shown the depth of the West's hostility towards decolonization efforts. This hostility had resulted in the killing of the Secretary General of the United Nations, Dag Hammarskjold. The book by Susan Williams (*Who killed Hammarskjöld?*) provides a clear analysis of the range of powerful forces in the USA, France,

Portugal, Britain, Belgium, South Africa, and the Congo who were complicit in the conspiracy to eliminate the Secretary General of the UN. This same alliance was strengthened to oppose the OAU and this was manifest in the wave of coups d'état to extinguish leaders and organizations supporting genuine Pan-African freedom. Younger scholars can juxtapose the history of Patrice Lumumba and Kwame Nkrumah against the elevation of Mobutu, who was supported by Western powers to play an influential role in the OAU for over thirty years.

After the assassination of Patrice Lumumba, the poor of Africa were very willing to lend support to those who were fighting the white mercenaries backing Mobutism. Malcolm X, Mohamed Babu, and Che Guevara had met at the United Nations in November 1964 and agreed to mount an international campaign to reverse the imperial domination of the Congo, which was being stabilized and renamed Zaire. The landing of US, French and Belgian troops in the Congo in 1964 at Stanleyville (present Kisangani) was an affront to those seeking liberation everywhere. By the time assistance was forthcoming from as far away as Cuba to avenge the murder of Congolese independence, the OAU was crippled by the idea that no popular movement could receive support from other African countries. This was expressed in the idea of 'non-interference in the internal affairs of a member state'. In practical terms, this protected African dictators from criticism and ensured that the basic rights of the African people were trampled upon from Malawi to Chad and by the rule of the Emperor of Ethiopia.

Because the Congo in the heart of Africa was so strategic for the freedom and independence of Africa, imperialism used this territory as a base for destabilization in North, East, West, and Southern Africa. While the OAU spoke of non-interference, the Zairian army invaded Angola in 1975 along with the South Africans to prevent the full decolonization of that society. The legacies of Mobutism are still being felt by the people of Angola, who have not seen peace in their society for 500 years.

## Mainstream Efforts to Discredit Pan-Africanism

The speed of the decolonization exercise had caught the Atlantic planners by surprise and for a short while, these planners and intellectuals from the North sought to define Pan-Africanism and determine who could articulate clear Pan-African ideas. When Joseph Nye, Dennis Austin, Colin Legum, and David Apter turned to writing about Pan-Africanism and the Pan-African project at the height of the Cold War struggles, it was the view among mainstream scholars that Africans were too emotional to write 'rational' accounts of the Pan-African movement.[45] Immanuel Geiss went so far as to note that studying Pan-Africanism from authorities such as George Padmore and W.E.B. Du Bois would lead to confusion. Geiss, the German authority on Pan-Africanism, maintained, 'Any attempt at theorizing without a more detailed or objective knowledge of its history than offered by the subjective accounts and interpretations by Padmore and Du Bois is bound to increase the prevalent confusion or even malaise about Pan-Africanism'.[46]

## WESTERN INTELLECTUAL ONSLAUGHT
## AGAINST THE PAN-AFRICAN PROJECT

Although the formation of the OAU had demonstrated that Africans could work together and speak with one voice on questions such as the future of colonialism and apartheid, the voluminous literature that was produced in the 1960s was dominated by the recurring theme of the OAU as a failed institution.[47] The standard texts that had been produced by mainstream academics used the structural functional approach to provide detailed assessments of the OAU structures: the Assembly, Council, Commissions and Secretariat along with the legal implications of the Charter of the OAU. A 700-page bibliographical work on the OAU by Gordon Harris on *The Organization of African Unity*, in the International Organization Series, exposed the intense effort of Western societies seeking to understand the OAU. Foundations and think tanks in North America and Western Europe expended millions of dollars seeking to define the frameworks and standpoints for African and Pan-African studies. The recently published 9 volume study on Southern African liberation struggles has now provided new resources to grasp the depth of the work of the liberation forces from 1960 to 1994.[48] Pan-African scholars and activists who had taken an even-handed approach to the limitations of the OAU were always aware that the real demands and sacrifices of the freedom struggle were the glue that held the OAU together.

The Pan-African intellectual contribution complements the earlier struggle that had been undertaken by that generation of scholars who had been able to influence UNESCO to undertake the General History of Africa project. These fronts in the Pan-African struggles provide an antidote to the Afro pessimism that had been peddled by Western intellectuals and their financiers. As Michael West and William G. Martin observed, the growth of the Africanist establishment in the USA and the downgrading of the organic Pan-African intellectual culture in African communities in the Americas were not accidental. They drew attention to the role of the Federal government of the USA and intelligence agencies in seeking to delegitimize the study of Africa from the point of view of those dedicated to ending racism in education and the role of specialists who were to be later called, Africanists. West and Martin argued that:

> in the United States the prevailing school of Pan-Africanist scholars was denied access to the fruits of the growth of support for the study of Africa. This devolution of Africa into the hands of 'Africanists' was by design and not as many have recounted the result of the natural growth of a new school of thought. This hidden history is easily illustrated: take for example the actions of the renowned founding father of African Studies, Melville Herskovits. While his

early work could engage Pan-African scholarship, he was later to boast of his role in helping to deny funding to 'negrophile' W. E. B. Dubois's Encyclopedia Africana project, while offering the ASA's full assistance, in his capacity as its first president to the CIA's Allen Dulles.[49]

Embedded in the body of scholarship that examined legal questions concerning the efficacy of the OAU were issues of method and orientation. Western foundations supported methodological workshops and conferences to provide resources for intellectuals who could and would proclaim that Pan-Africanism was narrow and not objective. Mainstream academics differed with Pan-Africanists over whether the struggles of that period were over communism or the institutional and structural racism of international capitalism. These differences exploded at the annual meeting of the African Studies Association in Montreal in 1969.[50] Progressive Pan-African scholars were very aware of the *Kissinger Study of Southern Africa: National Security Study Memorandum 39 (Secret)* (NSSM 39), that had recommended that the, 'whites are here to stay and the only way that constructive change can come about is through them. There is no hope for the blacks to gain the political rights they seek through violence, which will only lead to chaos and increased opportunities for the communists'.[51]

This secret analysis, which served as the basis for the extended review of Southern African policy which went on in Washington between April 1969 and February 1970, had been a direct response to the black liberation struggles in the USA and the intensified anti-colonial struggles in Southern Africa. While scholars such as Anthony Lake had critiqued the racist assumptions of NSSM 39, they had failed to grasp the significance of Kissinger and his entourage on the academic work and methodological frameworks for engagement with Africa.[52] For US policymakers, the OAU was being misled by Pan-Africanist and communist sympathizers, thus the full range of US policy whether in areas of commerce, culture, education or finance was to isolate those supporting the liberation movements and stepping up engagement with the white regimes. This option was carried to its dismal failure under Chester Crocker, who had been one of the members of the staff of the National Security Council when NSSM 39 was being crafted.[53]

In this context of overt racism in the foreign policy of the European powers, the Pan-African forces aligned with the anti-racist and peace forces that had formed the rump of Afro-Asian solidarity following the Bandung spirit. Africans spoke with one voice at the United Nations on questions of racism and colonialism, and Pan-Africanist forces assumed moral and intellectual leadership within the OAU so that, despite impressive investments in the intellectual output of Western scholars on the OAU, comparatively small efforts such as those of practicing African diplomats like Salim Ahmed Salim, Mohamoud Sahoun, and C.O. Amate served to provide valuable information on the OAU and Pan-Africanism. *Inside the OAU, Pan Africanism in*

*Practice* was an early insider account and since the 1980s Salim, who had served as the Secretary General of the OAU, has written his memoirs.[54]

## Militarism and the OAU

Not only did the leadership of the OAU support dictators who were able to sit and drink at so-called summits with impunity, but also the ordinary African was punished for believing that Africa was for the Africans. By 1975, the OAU summit had been dominated by military men who had seized political power from the first independence leaders. After 1960, there had been about 21 military transfers of power with soldiers holding the reins of power in societies such as Nigeria, Ghana, Togo, Gabon, Congo, Congo Brazzaville, Central African Republic, Libya, Burundi, Somalia, and Uganda. The clause of non-interference allowed the militarists to consolidate the colonial frontiers while defending the interests of foreign monopolies. Virtually all of the leaders of the independence movement had paid lip service to regional freedom and unity of the whole continent. However, in the process of negotiating independence, these leaders reneged on a cardinal principle of Pan-Africanism, namely, 'that the people from one part of Africa are responsible for the freedom and liberation of their brothers and sisters in other parts of Africa, and indeed, black people everywhere were to accept the same responsibility.'[55]

The interests of French capitalism, which became important in the Congo, had prevailed in West Africa when France sought to create non-viable entities that required French military presence to maintain the ruling elements in power.[56] French military bases dot the African continent and continue to prevent the consolidation of the independence process. It was in East Africa that the legacy of the failure of the OAU was to be the most profound, with Kenya chosen as the beachhead for Western security interests in Africa. Ex-ambassadors of the USA have boasted in their memoirs about how they worked to undermine the OAU committee, which had been created to mobilize support for the Lumumbist forces.[57] Idi Amin of Uganda had emerged from the machinations of the British and US Americans to prevent the consolidation of the Lumumbist forces. As a military leader who had fought against the Land and Freedom Army in Kenya, Amin (like Jean Bedel Bokassa and Mobutu Sese Seko) extended the role of force in politics inside Africa. The election of Idi Amin to become the chairperson of the OAU in 1975 was one of the lowest periods in the history of that organization. When Ugandan forces under Amin invaded Tanzania in order to divert attention from the wars of liberation in Southern Africa, the other dictators were silent. However, when Tanzania acted to repel this incursion and to support the removal of Amin, the dictators invoked the clause of non-interference in other states to tie the hands of Tanzania. The struggles for liberation and independence had reached a decisive stage in 1974 when the struggles for independence in Mozambique, Angola, and Guinea Bissau had forced dynamic changes in Southern Africa and in Europe.

## Dar es Salaam 1974 and the Turning of the Tide for the Full Unification of Africa

Every major study on the OAU reiterates the mantra that it was formed in 1963 as a compromise between the Casablanca and Monrovia Groups. Whatever the differences, there were a number of issues that kept the global Pan-African movement together. Two of these issues were the outstanding struggles against racism, apartheid, and colonialism and the struggles against Jim Crow and apartheid in the USA. From the moment of the Brown vs Board of Education decision until the COINTELPRO efforts to crush the black liberation movement in the USA, the struggles for basic rights in the USA became a focal point of the international Pan-African Movement. By the year 1970, the forces of African Liberation in Africa and in the global African family coalesced to organize the 6th Pan-African Congress in Dar es Salaam in June 1974. The themes around which the 6th Pan-African Congress was called included total independence and self-determination, unity and self-reliance of Africans in all parts of the world. Central to the theme of self-reliance and self-determination was the question of advancing a command of science and technology. At that historical moment, Tanzania was the headquarters of the OAU Liberation Committee and Tanzania represented the principal example of self-reliance. The largest delegation of Africans outside of Africa at that Congress was the North American delegation and the forces of the black liberation movement in the USA that had been organized under the African Liberation Support Committee (ALSC).

The ideological leadership of the liberation movements from Angola, Mozambique, Guinea Bissau, and South Africa ensured that the outcomes of the Sixth Pan-African Congress were focused on material, military, financial, and moral support for the last struggles against colonialism and minority rule. Henry Kissinger, Chester Crocker, and France colluded with Portugal and the racist apartheid regime to break the solidarity of the Sixth Pan-African Congress. States such as Ivory Cost under Félix Houphouët-Boigny along with Zaire coordinated support for the apartheid regime in South Africa and promoted the diplomatic spin of 'dialogue' with South Africa.

From the proxy states allied to Washington and Paris came spokespersons who wanted to speak for the liberation movements. The declaration of the Sixth Pan-African Congress on the support for armed struggles exposed the ideological lead taken by the liberation movements. However, the anticommunist position promoted by France, the USA, and South Africa sought to create deep divisions and the depth of this division was manifest in the position of the Pan-African Movement over the question of the independence of Angola. Sections of the Pan-African Movement carried a racial line and argued after 1975 that the Angolans should not ally with the Cubans to fight against the invading South African Army. The battles for the independence of Angola had threatened to split the OAU. When an extraordinary meeting of the OAU was called to decide on the recognition of the Angolan government after November 11, 1975, the decisive intervention of Nigeria to rebuff Henry Kissinger and the USA moved the question of solidarity among Africans to a new level. At the emergency summit of the OAU on January 11, 1976, the Nigerian head of state delivered a moving speech arguing that Africa had come of Age. In his analysis of this decisive moment in Pan-African history, Patrick Wilmot noted that 'This was the most militant speech ever delivered by a Nigerian Head of State, and contributed significantly to the eventual recognition of the Angolan Government by the OAU later in the spring of 1976. It also situated apartheid not just as an emotional bogeyman but as part of western imperialist strategy on the rest of the continent'.[58] When Kissinger had undertaken a tour of Africa to persuade African societies to support the position of the apartheid state, Murtala Mohammed humiliated Kissinger by refusing to see him on his African tour or even to give his plane permission to land when it was already on its way. A few weeks later on February 13, 1976, Murtala Mohammed was assassinated in an attempted military coup.

In the period between 1976 and 1980, the foreign policy of Nigeria decisively supported the front-line states of the OAU to the point that the government of Nigeria nationalized the assets of British Petroleum to intensify pressures against Britain to end support for the Ian Smith regime in Rhodesia. After the independence of Zimbabwe in 1980, the African leaders convened in Nigeria to hammer out the Lagos Plan of Action (LPA) incorporating programs and strategies for self-reliance development and cooperation among African countries. In response, the World Bank issued the Berg Report in 1981 and went into overdrive to obstruct economic integration. Elliot Berg, the World Bank functionary, argued in this report that the reason why African economies were in difficulty was the role of the state in the economy. It was argued that there should be an emphasis on 'liberating the forces of the market' in order both to revive exports and to improve the incomes of the rural agricultural populace. Structural adjustment and IMF conditionalities strengthened foreign capital to the same extent that they weakened African governments.

## The Defeat of Apartheid and the Revitalization of Pan-Africanism

The defeat of the apartheid army at Cuito Cuanavale in 1988 laid the foundations for a new lease of life in the Global Pan-African Movement. The end of apartheid coincided with the fall of the Berlin Wall and a wave of struggles to end military dictatorship across Africa. In 1990, Namibia acceded to independence, and in 1990, the apartheid regime unbanned the liberation movements (the African National Congress and Pan Africanist Congress) and released Nelson Mandela. This was the context in which the 7th Pan-African Congress took place in Kampala, Uganda, April 3–8, 1994. It was originally scheduled to take place in December 1993 but had to be rescheduled due to lack of sufficient funds to host the meeting and the logistical problems that arose from that lack of funds. More important than the shortage of funds were the ideological differences over the future of the Pan-African movement.

There were questions as to whether it was possible to hold a Pan-African Congress in Uganda. Should African governments be invited? Who was an African? Could activists and opponents of governments take part in the Congress? In fact, there were two motions for the 7th Pan-African Congress. Apart from the Kampala Initiative that was driven by A.M. Babu and Karrim Esack, there was the Lagos Initiative for the 7th Pan-African Congress spearheaded by Naiwu Osahon of Nigeria. Tajudeen Abdul Raheem, who had been recruited by Babu to serve as the core organizer for the Congress, has written about the twists and turns between the varying factions that dogged the event. This Congress had been called under the broad theme of 'Facing the Future of Unity, Social Progress and Democracy'. Those who believed that governments should not be invited to the Congress stayed away. However, the very same governments, except for 17 of the 53, boycotted. Ghana, Libya, and Namibia provided important resources for the 7th Pan-African Congress. Most of the governments that had leaders such as Mobutu of Zaire feared that the Congress would be dominated by revolutionary groups opposed to dictatorial governments.

Once the Congress convened in April with over 2000 delegates, the ideological and political struggles in the wider Pan-African world exploded at the plenary sessions. The government of Sudan sent one of the largest delegations and sought to direct the proceedings by opposing the participation of the Sudanese Peoples Liberation Army/Movement (SPLA/M). Joseph Garang of the SPLM represented the ideas of self-determination that was coming out of that section of the Pan-African movement.

The other major question that was hotly debated was the question of who is an African. There was one tendency within the Congress that argued that Pan-Africanism should only include black Africans along with the African descendants in the wider African family outside of Africa. This tendency opposed what they called continentalism and the inclusion of Africans, for example, of Indian descent (such as Gora Ibrahim, who was the spokesperson for the Pan-African Congress of Azania). However, in the final declaration it was agreed that all those who accepted the goals of African freedom and were committed to this while living in Africa were Africans. In many ways this was a reaffirmation that the Pan-African movement could not oppose racism and replace the opposition to racism with anti-white ideas. In this sense the Congress reasserted positions taken earlier by Kwame Nkrumah and Nnamdi

Azikiwe. At the 2004 Pan-African intellectual festival, Professor Tony Martin reasserted this position by quoting Azikiwe.

A multiracial politically unified continent is an inescapable goal in the twenty-first century and one that Nnamdi Azikiwe endorsed. In a 1961 speech reprinted in *Présence Africaine*, Azikiwe asked, 'When we speak of Pan-Africanism, what do we exactly mean?' He answered, 'I would like to speak of the peoples of Africa in general terms to include all the races inhabiting that continent and embracing all the linguistic and cultural groups who are domiciled therein'. He continued, 'It is true that the roots of Pan-Africanism are, to a large extent, racial, but the evolution of the idea itself took different forms in the last four centuries so that today Africanism cannot be restricted to racial factors.'[59] Progressive women who had understood how women's bodies became markers of race and ethnicity were at the forefront of ensuring that the Progressive Pan-African position entailed an intersection of oppressions, race, class. gender, economic exploitation, and sexuality.

## THE PAN-AFRICAN WOMEN'S LIBERATION ORGANIZATION AND THE 7TH PAN-AFRICAN CONGRESS

Many of the discussions of the 7th Pan-African Congress were recorded in the book *Pan-Africanism: Politics, Economy and Social Change in the Twenty First Century*. Tajudeen Abdul Raheem, who was elected as Secretary General of the Secretariat established in Kampala exposed the differing ideological positions of the members who comprised the International Preparatory Committee of the Congress. He and A.M. Babu had worked diligently to ensure that despite wide differences, the Congress could accommodate those who supported the progressive traditions of Kwame Nkrumah, Malcolm X, Frantz Fanon, Walter Rodney, Amy Jacques Garvey, Bob Marley, and Patrice Lumumba. Betty Shabbazz, the widow of Malcolm X, was one of the many prominent leaders who articulated the need for women's leadership in the Pan-African movement. This Congress reaffirmed the question of the full unification of Africa and established a permanent secretariat of the Pan-African movement to advance the cause of African liberation and the total elimination of colonialism. The Congress took place in the same month that the historic elections took place in South Africa in 1994 to end formal colonial rule and elect Nelson Mandela as president.

In the meetings of the preparatory committee there had been intense debates about the history of the Pan-African Movement and the silencing of women within the movement. Progressive women reminded the participants of the history of women in the movement and the lessons that should be learnt from the continued exclusion of women from political spaces. Questions of citizenship, inheritance, bodily integrity, rape, child marriage, domestic violence, and the brutalization of women using ideas about tradition were mooted and many of the women present were involved in the preparatory meetings for Beijing 1995. The progressive forces of the IPC and the progressive women worked hard for the convening of the Women's Congress within the Pan-African Congress. This Women's Congress was held for one full day at Makerere University in Kampala, Uganda and out of this women's meeting emerged the Pan-African Women's Liberation Organization (PAWLO).

Organizing women in the context of Pan-Africanism was not new. On July 31, 1962, the Conference of African Women (CAF) was created at Dar es Salaam in Tanganyika, now known as Tanzania. Out of that meeting emerged the first Pan-African Women's Organization (PAWO). In July 1974, one month after the 6th Pan-African Congress, there was another Conference of African Women which was held in Dakar (Senegal). It was in Senegal that July 31 was designated African Women Day. This division between Senegal and Tanzania in 1974 represented some of the same divisions that had existed between the Casablanca and Monrovia Groups. In Senegal at the time, there were leaders who were unsupportive of armed struggles against apartheid.

The major limitation of PAWO, however, was that by the time of the growth of the international women's movement, it had become the forum for the wives of the very same repressive leaders who were oppressing African women. Miriam Babangida, wife of the dictator Ibrahim Babangida of Nigeria, was the poster child of the first wives club that sought to speak on behalf of oppressed women. Her organizational vehicle for manipulating the principles of women's liberation was Better Life for Rural Women. PAWLO emerged from the ranks of the progressive women and men at the 7th Pan-African Congress. Fatima Babiker Mahmoud from Sudan was elected PAWLO's first president, and in her address to the Congress she held that, 'As African Women, we share a common history. We have similar challenges to face and a better future to look forward to. On this basis, it is important to stress our similarities rather than differences if we are to achieve any meaningful change'.[60]

PAWLO was established to implement the women's action plans that had come out of the resolutions of the Congress. PAWLO brought together African women from the continent, from the oppressed societies in the USA, Europe, and Asia in a forum of their own for the first time in the history of Pan-African Congresses. The resolutions of the PAWLO Congress agreed to bring together women with the objective of liberation in a common program and sustained action of work for improving the situation of African women.

## OAU, PAN-AFRICANISM, AND GENOCIDE

If the OAU had been founded on the principles of Pan-Africanism, it soon forgot the history of the Black Holocaust which dispersed millions of Africans across the Americas, Europe, and Arabia. The OAU had neglected to fully represent the interests of the Africans overseas and this silence was to repeat itself with the holocaust that took place in Rwanda. It was significant that during the ninety-day period of genocide, not one African leader spoke out or condemned the mass killings.

Two issues are worth examining in this respect. In the first place, the OAU had allowed international non-African bodies to make millions of dollars out of a new humanitarian industry called 'looking after refugees'. Under the principles of Pan-Africanism, it is impossible for an African to be a refugee in the continent of Africa. One of the future tasks of the AU will be to ensure the free movement of people across Africa. The problem of refugees had simmered in Central Africa for more than thirty years and the dictatorship in Rwanda had kept power by violence and manipulating ethnic identity. When a guerilla force took up arms against this dictatorship in a just war, it was the very same Mobutu (of Congolese infamy) and France which moved to save the murderers. In April 1994, when organized genocide was going on and the bodies of over a million persons appeared on TV screens across the world, the OAU called upon those fighting to end genocide to enter into dialogue with the authors of the genocide. This would be similar to the forces fighting in the Second World War being told to make peace with Hitler and Hitlerism. No serious person would have made or heeded such a demand. What was required was the removal of the genocidists. However, at the moment when the murderers were facing defeat, France intervened in a so called humanitarian mission (amply supported by puppet states) to protect the murderers.

The second issue relates to how the new discourses on conflict management were used as a cover to embolden repressive regimes. There were scholars who became experts at conflict resolution in Africa and produced reams of papers on Africa as a conflict zone.[61] African scholars grouped around the Council for the Development of Social Science Research in Africa (CODESRIA) responded to alert policymakers that the conflicts had arisen from the very nature of Africa's Balkanization and the inherited social and economic structures. From the outset, the OAU had incorporated mechanisms for mediation, arbitration, and conciliation. During the anti-colonial struggles, the OAU liberation committee distinguished between conflicts in societies such as Burundi, Rwanda, and Chad and the wars of national liberation in Angola, Guinea Bissau, Mozambique, Namibia, South Africa, and Zimbabwe. It was in the closing days of apartheid when the OAU formally strengthened the Commission for the Mechanism for Conflict Prevention, Management and Resolution (1993). This apparatus was severely tested by wars in the Congo, Liberia, Sierra Leone, Chad, Sudan, and the Central African Republic.

On his attendance at the first meeting of the OAU, Mandela spoke firmly of the need for Africa to act more decisively:

> Even as we speak, Rwanda stands out as a stern and severe rebuke to all of us for having failed to address these interrelated matters. As a result of that, a terrible slaughter of the innocent is taking place in front of our very eyes. Thus

do we give reason to the peoples of the world to say of Africa that she will never know stability and peace, that she will never experience development and growth, that her children will forever be condemned to poverty and dehumanisation and that we shall forever be knocking on somebody's door pleading for a slice of bread. We know it is a matter of fact that we have it in ourselves as Africans to change all this. We must, in action, assert our will to do so. We must, in action, say that there is no obstacle big enough to stop us from bringing about a new African renaissance.[62]

## PAN-AFRICANISM AND THE REPARATIONS QUESTION

The release of Nelson Mandela from incarceration in 1990 had been a major milestone in the global anti-racist struggles and it was in this international context that the OAU took up the issue of reparations. The global African community had always linked reparative justice to African freedom, but the majority of leaders of the OAU were fearful of the repercussions of calling for reparations for the transatlantic slave trade. In 1991, for the first time, the issue of reparations was placed before the OAU with Resolution 1339, approved by the Council of Ministers of May 27–June 1, 1991. By this resolution, the OAU (under the chairpersonship of Salim Ahmed Salim) had decided to establish a group of eminent Africans and Africans of the diaspora in the relevant fields to set out clearly the extent of Africa's exploitation, the liability of the perpetrators, and the strategies for achieving reparation.

Between February 24–28 of the following year 1992, the Council of Ministers of the OAU adopted Resolution 1373 and mandated the Secretary General to form appropriate sructures to support the committee of eminent personalities. The same Resolution thanked Chief Bashorun M.K.O. Abiola of Nigeria for his commitment and its shares in favor of reparations. With Resolution 1391, adopted by the Council of Ministers of June 22–28, 1992, it calls on the committee of eminent personalities and the member states to give their full support to the measures undertaken by the OAU in reparations for the wrongs done to Africa with the exploitation and the slave trade. This was the genesis of the Eminent Persons Group (EPG) of 12 appointed by the OAU to mobilize and organize educating Africans at home and abroad about reparations and reparative justice. The original chair of the EPG was the Nigerian politician cum businessman Chief Bashorun M.K.O. Abiola, who was later elected president of Nigeria. Other members were the Nigerian historian J.F. Ade Ajayi; Professor Samir Amin of Egypt; US Congressman R. Dellums; Professor Josef Ki-Zerbo of Burkina Faso; Mme Gracha Machel, formerly first lady of Mozambique and later wife of Nelson Mandela. Others were: Miriam Makeba; Professor M. M'Bow, former director-general of UNESCO; former president A. Pereira of Cape Verde; Ambassador Alex Quaison-Sackey, former foreign minister of Ghana; and the Jamaican lawyer/diplomat Dudley S. Thompson. Of these twelve eminent persons, the three who were the most active and attended international meetings and conferences such as the World

Conference against racism were J.F. Ade Ajayi, Ali A. Mazrui, and Dudley Thompson.

The momentum for reparative justice had taken the form of a major Pan-African Conference on Reparations in Abuja (April 27–29, 1993) sponsored by the Committee of Eminent Personalities and by the Reparations Commission of the OAU. After deliberating, the Abuja Proclamation called 'upon the international community to recognise that there is a unique and unprecedented moral debt owed to the African people which has yet to be paid the debt of compensation to the Africans as the most humiliated and exploited people of the last four centuries of modern history'. It further urged:

> the Organization of African Unity to call for full monetary payment of repayments through capital transfer and debt cancellation ... Convinced that the claim for reparations is well grounded in International Law, it urges on the Organization of African Unity to establish a legal Committee on the issue of Reparations ... Serves notice on all states in Europe and the Americas which had participated in the enslavement and colonisation of the African peoples, and which may still be engaged in racism and neo-colonialism, to desist from any further damage and start building bridges of conciliation, co-operation, and through reparation ...',[63]

These demands for capital transfer, debt cancellation, skills transfer and direct power transfer formed an important component of the scholarly activism of Ali A. Mazrui in the 1990s.[64] This reparations campaign was so feared by the international powers that when the chairperson of this group, M.K.O. Abiola, was elected president of Nigeria in 1993, he was prevented from taking office. He was to die in custody in Nigeria five years later in 1998. The death of Abiola like that of Murtala Mohammed, derailed Nigeria and prevented it from playing its real role in the Pan-African movement.

Ali Mazrui, a member of the Committee of Eminent Personalities and a Pan-Africanist who had become embroiled in the debates about Afro-Arabs with Professor Wole Soyinka, was one who drew from the Rodneyite tradition and became a force in the Global Pan-African Movement. Mazrui had this to say of his involvement in the case for reparative justice: 'In 1993, I embraced the reparations cause seriously not only as an assignment of the OAU entrusted to us but also as an intellectual challenge. After all, issues like colonial damage-analysis or comparative slavery were of academic value independently of any activism'.[65] One of the limitations of the work of this period was the paucity of real scholarly work on reparative justice. Two main publications by Ali Mazrui about reparations did not reflect deep and committed research.[66] These texts however served to inspire wider research and scholarship that later appeared in books by Hilary Beckles (*Britain's Black Debt: Reparations for Slavery and Native Genocide*) and Edward E Baptist (*The Half Has Never Been Told: Slavery and the Making of American Capitalism*). What has emerged from these new studies is the major work that still has to be done to roll back the ideas about 'modernity' and the civilizing role of Western capitalism. It was this global pressure for reparative justice that pushed the South African leadership to host the World Conference against Racism (WCAR) in Durban in 2001.

Imperialism became alert to the progressive character of the Pan-African movement that was informed by reparative justice and Pan-Africanism of the people. Using pliant citizens of African descent within the imperial centers (especially Condoleezza Rice and Colin Powell),[67] the USA worked hard to oppose the World Conference Against Racism and to ensure that the program of action would not be supported among governments. It was in Latin America that the reparations forces among the Africa descendants' caucus inspired new forms of mobilization within the politics there. There were many efforts of the opponents of Pan-Africanism in Africa but by far the most far reaching was to co-opt the young and articulate in the NGO fad that became the weapon of neo-liberalism in Africa. Neo-liberalism opposed governments of all kinds and this anti-government position served those who wanted to end state expenditures on social services.

Within the Pan-African movement, the question of how to organize against oppressive governments gave way to the call for an end to big Congresses and instead to support the people's movements in the streets, the villages, and townships all over the Pan-African world. By the end of the twentieth century, the progressive wing of the Pan-African movement had merged with the reparations movement, progressive workers' movements, the anti-dictatorship movement, the peace movement, the anti-globalization movement, progressive women's forum and the environmental justice movements. The HIV/AIDS pandemic dictated that there would be a strong movement for health care in the Pan-African world and organizations such as the Treatment Action Campaign developed new techniques of mobilization and organization to oppose the Western pharmaceutical companies that wanted the HIV/AIDS virus to be a death sentence for Africans. Pan-Africanists such as Wangari Mathai of the Green Belt Movement embodied the maturation of such forces and one new Pan-African front that emerged in the twenty-first century was the Pan-African Climate Justice Movement. It was in Latin America in societies such as Bolivia, Colombia, and Brazil that the anti-racist and climate justice forces were making an impact on the progressive movements internationally.

In the period after the genocide in Rwanda in 1994, the necessity to intervene to stop genocide gained momentum and this was reflected in the speed of the formation of the AU after the leader of Libya took the initiative in September 1999 to call an extraordinary summit for its creation. After the Congress in 1994, Tajudeen Abdul Raheem had worked in the Secretariat at Kampala and organized initiatives for peace and unity. Mobilizing around the Nkrumah's principle of Don't Mourn, Organize, Tajudeen travelled up and down the continent calling for implementation of the Congress resolution that Africa should be united now.

## END OF APARTHEID AND THE PAN-AFRICAN MOVEMENT

The Libyan leader Muammar Gaddafi had been a direct beneficiary of the changed political circumstances in international politics after the end of apartheid. Nelson Mandela, then the president of South Africa, had intervened directly to end the diplomatic and political isolation of Libya in the aftermath of the controversy over the bombing of a Pan Am plane in 1988 (over Lockerbie, Scotland). It was at the extraordinary meeting of the OAU called on September 8, 1999 at Sirte, Libya that African leaders committed themselves to the formation of the AU. The Sirte Declaration had been the culmination of several efforts and actions undertaken by those forces in Africa which had been pressuring the OAU Council of Ministers, the Committee of Ambassadors and the General Secretariat of the OAU.

The formation of the AU has rekindled conceptions of reconstruction and renewal that had been derailed by the neo-liberal policies of structural adjustment after 1980. Strident efforts towards unity had been undertaken with the boldest articulated in the Lagos Plan of Action, adopted in April 1980. Elsewhere, African scholars have painstakingly outlined the reality that the structural adjustment programs of the international financial institutions emerged as a direct response to the elaborate plans for African economic recovery that had been premised on the establishment of an African Economic Community by the year 2000.[68] Working under the auspices of the Economic Commission for Africa, CODESRIA and other authentic bases of intellectual inquiry, African scholars outlined the destructive impact of the World Bank policies. These intellectuals sought to reflect their concern for the toiling masses and identified with their aspirations for a better life. It was within this context that economists worked hard to pose alternative conceptions of economic cooperation and reconstruction. This had culminated in the signing of the Treaty in Abuja, Nigeria, establishing the African Economic Community (June 3, 1991). This reality that the Abuja Declaration (African Economic Community Treaty) formed the background of the AU is restated in Article 1 of the Lome Treaty establishing the Constitutive Act of the AU.

The Abuja Treaty had spelt out the framework for the mobilization of African human and material resources to break the cycle of plunder and exploitation. The Abuja Treaty had come into force in May 1994 when the required number of instruments of ratification had been deposited. It was the convergence of the Abuja Treaty along with the African Charter on Human and People's Rights that emerged in the Constitutive Act of the AU. Even though there is no explicit reference to the Charter in the Constitutive Act, legal scholars and human-rights activists have been at the forefront of the call of the OAU to intervene to prevent the violation of humans in Africa.

The OAU Charter on Human and People's Rights and the Grand Bay Declaration and Plan of Action on Human Rights were among the instruments adopted by the Organization to promote human rights. Underlying these instruments was a determination to ensure that Africa responds to the challenge of observing, promoting, and protecting human rights and the rule of law.

Thus far, the dominant literature on the birth of the AU has used the laundry list and institutional approach that does not adequately chronicle the long historical struggles inside the Pan-African movement. Even with this institutional approach, there is clear effort to exclude the work of the struggles for reparations. The AU represented the culmination of decades of struggle and work after the formation of the OAU in 1963 that had gone into the following plans:

- Lagos Plan of Action (LPA) and the Final Act of Lagos (1980).
- The African Charter on Human and People's Rights (Nairobi 1981) and the Grand Bay Declaration and Plan of Action on Human Rights.
- Africa's Priority Program for Economic Recovery (APPER)—1985: an emergency program designed to address the development crisis of the 1980s, in the wake of protracted drought and famine that had engulfed the continent and the crippling effect of Africa's external indebtedness.
- OAU Declaration on the Political and Socio-Economic Situation in Africa and the Fundamental Changes.
- The Charter on Popular Participation, adopted in 1990.
- The Treaty establishing the African Economic Community (AEC)—1991: commonly known as the Abuja Treaty.
- The Mechanism for Conflict Prevention, Management and Resolution (1993).
- Cairo Agenda for Action (1995): a program for relaunching Africa's political, economic, and social development.
- African Common Position on Africa's External Debt Crisis (1997): a strategy for addressing the continent's external debt crisis.
- The Algiers decision on Unconstitutional Changes of Government (1999) and the Lome Declaration on the framework for an OAU Response to Unconstitutional Changes (2000).
- The 2000 Solemn Declaration on the Conference on Security, Stability, Development, and Cooperation: establishes the fundamental principles for the promotion of democracy and good governance in the continent.

## The Libyan Question, the Unification of Africa and the Pan-African Movement

Nelson Mandela worked hard after 1994 to oppose genocidal violence and genocidal politics in Africa. As a leader, who had been designated as a 'terrorist', Mandela mediated to end the sanctions against Libya. In appreciation, the President of Libya called the extraordinary meeting of the OAU at Sirte in 1999 and decided to set in motion the number-one resolution of the 7th Pan-African Congress that there should be an AU. Within two years, the Constitutive Act of the AU was written and ratified, and the AU came into being in 2002. The major difference between the AU and the OAU was the right of the AU to intervene in cases of genocide, gross violation of human rights, and crimes against humanity. By 2004, there was the establishment of the Pan-African Parliament but the main political leaders of Africa were afraid of this becoming a representative body.

One of the major advances of the AU over the OAU was the incorporation of the Global African Family (called the diaspora) as the 6th region of the AU. There were mechanisms set in motion to work out representation for the African descendants outside of Africa in the AU. The AU Commission's Citizens and Diaspora Directorate (CIDO) was the institutional body where the AU was supposed to manifest its diaspora initiatives. CIDO's goal is to hold regular dialogs with diaspora communities around the world.[69] This question of the African descendants outside of Africa became an avenue of intense struggle. The AU operatives in their preoccupation with the remittances sent back to Arica decided to make a distinction between the 'historic' diaspora and the 'contemporary Diaspora.' For the AU bureaucrats, there was a distinction between Africans who migrated as students and economic migrants and decided to settle in foreign lands. These 'diaspora' Africans were to be distinguished from those children of Africa who had been kidnapped from Africa and made chattel slaves and victims of other forms of servitude. Those who supported neo-liberal Pan-Africanism only viewed Africans overseas as the source of remittances and remained silent when Africans were killed on the streets of Brazil and the USA. It was in this new situation of global capital where the Pan-African voices inside Africa for free movement and for a full unification converged.

The Pan-African movement of the streets and villages did not wait on governments to give them the rights of freedom of movement. Traders and workers all across Africa claimed freedom of movement and opposed the maintenance of the borders erected at Berlin. Ngugi Wa Thiongo gave coherence to the ideas of Pan-Africanism calling for the unity of the people when he drew on the long traditions of the emancipatory framework and echoed the call that the united Africa must be a union of African peoples and not just of heads of states. The peoples and their respective languages and culture which are arbitrarily separated by colonial boundaries should be united internally. This idea of internally borderless continent becomes even more necessary when border communities are closely examined. The finds from such examination would show that a considerable number of border communities on either side of borders within Africa have a common spiritual leader, history, and culture. With this understanding, it is easier to observe, for instance, that the unification of Ethiopia, Djibouti, and Somalia is a union of cultural relatives. This idea of shared community can be extended 'from the Cape to Cairo' and 'from Kenya to Liberia'.[70]

## BEYOND THE GRAND DEBATE

Cultural workers and creative artists from Africa and in the global African family strengthened the bonds of the Pan-African Movement. The enemies of Pan-Africanism and reparative justice went overboard to demonize the leader of Libya and to represent the goals of African unification as if this came from the head of Gaddafi, discounting the long struggles for African redemption and unity since the period of Marcus Garvey and Kwame Nkrumah. The demonization and opposition to the unification of Africa was seen on full display in 2007 when there was the grand debate about forming the Union Government and the United States of Africa. Under the Constitutive Act of 2001 there had been timetables for the development of an African Monetary System, the African Central Bank and the Common Currency.

Just as in the division between the Casablanca and Monrovia Groups, there were some leaders who called for a gradual approach to establish the Regional Economic Communities (REC) as opposed to continental Communities of Africans. This faction of the African leadership argued for gradual unity. Whatever the differences, however, the political leaders of Africa were brought to an awareness of the plans of external forces when NATO invaded Libya in 2011 under the pretext of humanitarian intervention. The military destruction of Libya and the assassination and humiliation of President Gaddafi created a new sense of urgency for the rekindling of a strong Pan-African movement. From 2012, there were meetings and consultations about the strengthening of the AU. The AU Commissioner Jean Ping was replaced by Dr. Nkosasana Zuma of South Africa, and it was the energy from the new leadership that produced Agenda 2063, the bold plan for the full union government of Africa.

## PRESSURES FOR CLARITY OF THE GOALS
## OF THE PAN-AFRICAN MOVEMENT

Just as how, at the 7th Pan-African Congress in Kampala, there had been other initiatives such as the Lagos Initiative, so after 1994 there were parallel initiatives for the Pan-African Congress movement. The governments of South Africa, Brazil, Nigeria, Ghana, Jamaica, and Senegal held numerous meetings that brought together intellectuals, economists, and other branches of the Pan-African Movement. The government of Senegal hosted a major meeting of intellectuals and thus was followed up in Brazil in 2006. It was at that meeting that the African dignitaries came face to face with the militancy of the Brazilian youth. For over 50 years, Abdias Nascimiento had been toiling within Brazil to expose the fallacies of racial democracy there. By the time of the World Conference against Racism in 2001, the Brazilian delegation had matured to be one of the most militant fronts of the Pan-African movement. No government could ignore the potential of over 100 million African descendants in Brazil. The Workers Party under Lula da Silva attempted to make small concessions by establishing quotas and affirmative action policies, but not even these concessions were bold enough. In 2016, the hard right and racists in Brazil mounted a movement against any concessions to blacks and called for the affirmation of the most retrograde forms of white supremacy.

## THE AU AND THE CALL FOR AGENDA 2063

In 2009, Tajudeen Abdul Raheem, the General Secretary of the global Pan-African movement passed away. Even before his passing, the future of the Pan-African Secretariat was in limbo because of the nature of the politics of Uganda. This politics polluted the goals of the movement and diminished the global Pan-African movement in the eyes of many. Wars in the Congo and military clashes between the armies of Rwanda and Uganda in the Democratic Republic of the Congo exposed how far these leaders had departed from the goals of peace and reconstruction. At the 2012 meeting of Pan-Africanists to remember Tajudeen Abdul Raheem in Addis Ababa, Ethiopia, there was a committee established to work to build the 8th Pan-African Congress in Accra, Ghana and to link the movement back to the Nkrumah goals of full unification and emancipation. This goal was reaffirmed in 2013 when the AU celebrated its 50 years of unity and explicitly determined to bring back the Pan-African Movement and Pan-African agenda into the AU. These meetings in Addis Ababa brought out the reaffirmation of the vision of the AU as that of, 'An integrated, prosperous and peaceful Africa, driven by its own citizens and representing a dynamic force in the global arena'.[71] A series of meetings were held with the surviving members of the International Governing Council and it was agreed to request the government of Ghana to host the 8th Pan-African Congress and for a relocation of the Secretariat to Accra, Ghana. By June 2014, there was an agreement on the Call for the 8th Pan-African Congress emanating from the International Governing Council (IGC).

Stressing the mantra of the 7th Pan-African Congress that there should be mass-based organization, the call went out to all organizations and individuals to participate at the Congress scheduled to be held in Accra, Ghana. In the new push for remobilization, there was a definite effort to build on the most radical aspects of the Pan-African experiences, noting that in keeping with the broad character of all previous congresses, from 1900 to 1994, this one would be open to all shades of opinion, groups, and individuals in the whole Pan-African world. In addition, African governments on the continent and in the diaspora would participate on an equal footing with other delegates. The AU and its organs and institutions as well as regional economic blocs and platforms would also participate.

Recognizing the AU vision of 'Peace, Prosperity and Unity', the broad theme of the Congress was 'The Pan-African world we want: building a people's movement for just, accountable and inclusive structural transformation'. Although there were 19 different agenda items mentioned in the call, there was considerable overlap. Democracy, governance, popular democracy, African citizenship, justice, social justice, reparative justice, ecology, and environment are all mentioned in at least two separate agenda points. The Pan-African Agenda can be broadly clustered under four themes. At the top is the political unity of the African continent under a union government. The global rights for African peoples within and outside Africa is another consideration. These rights encompass: basic necessities of life, for instance, housing and education; freedom of religion and expression; freedom from racism; reparative justice; and gender equity of women vis-à-vis the humanization of the male gender. The agenda also seeks to end imperialism and all forms of colonialism in Africa and its diaspora such as the Caribbean. The agenda also seeks to demilitarize Africa and its peoples. Further, it strives to project progressive Pan-Africanism as opposed to neo-liberal Pan-Africanism which invariably strengthens the marginalization of the bold efforts of African peoples towards self-determination and self-governance. Additionally, the Agenda promotes sustainable infrastructure for the transformation of Africa and environmental repairs. The focus on infrastructure comprises canal systems, roads, bridges, ICT connectivity and energy. Environmental repair concerns the elimination of every form of environmental racism of the current social system and seeks to reverse the destruction of Planet Earth.[72]

This position of seeking to safeguard the progressive cultural heritage of the African peoples came up against the realities of leaders who were bent on suppressing that same progressive tradition. The signing of this MoU with the Pan-African Movement had come one year after the same AU embraced the European Union (EU) Pan-African Program because despite signing the MoU with the Pan-African movement, the AU Commission was dominated by operatives of states who paid lip service to the goals of Agenda 2063. After the global capitalist crash of 2008 and the downturn in African economies subsequent to sharp decreases in commodity prices, there were stirrings of the people all over Africa with the uprisings in Egypt, Tunisia, Ethiopia, the Democratic Republic of the Congo and the Sudan opposing neo-liberalism. The peoples of Africa were responding every day to the global capitalist crisis by stating that the goals of Agenda 2063 cannot be achieved with the crop of current leaders. Some youths sought to flee Africa by crossing the Sahara Desert and embarking on an even more dangerous journey across the Mediterranean Sea.

Genocidal economic relations in the South Sudan, presidents for life, idle threats to withdraw en masse from the International Criminal Court (ICC), war as a business in the so-called war against terror, and the illicit capital flight from Africa preserved the interests of a class in Africa that opposed real progressive Pan-Africanism. Non-payment of dues by member states of the AU represented a statement about their loyalties. Working together with the UN Economic Commission for Africa, the AU had established the High Level Panel on Illicit Financial Flows from Africa headed by former South African president Thabo Mbeki. This panel in its Report found out that in the previous thirty-year period, Africa had lost about $1 trillion in capital flight and that illicit financial flows were draining the continent of needed resources.[73] Instead of seeking to implement the recommendations of the High Level Panel on Illicit Financial Flows, the operatives of the African states signed a partnership agreement with the EU for the EU to promote its Pan-African program. The fact that over 70% of the AU Commission is funded by imperial states was one indication of the infrastructure of capital flight. These 'donors' actually have the intelligence on how much money is being shipped abroad by African leaders, hence they seek to keep up the fiction of providing 'aid' to Africa.

In 2014, the EU brought out their own program for Pan-Africanism and launched the EU-Pan-African partnership. This partnership is downplaying the aspirations of Agenda 2063 and in its place organizing meetings all over Africa on 'good governance' and 'security sector reform.' According to the EU Commission:

> The Pan-African Programme provides dedicated support to the Africa-EU Strategic Partnership and is the first ever EU programme in development and cooperation that covers Africa as a whole. It supports projects with a trans-regional, continental or global added-value in areas of shared interest, and offers new possibilities for the EU and Africa to work together.[74]

This EU Pan-African program constituted a major front for neo-liberal Pan-Africanism. African leaders who were afraid to establish a Specialized Technical Commission on Reparations were only too ready and willing to embrace programs for 'partnership.' In the process of coordinating plans for a joint EU–Africa partnership, the conservative forces within the AU pushed for the readmission of Morocco into the AU. Morocco had departed the OAU in 1984 over the question of the recognition of the Polisario movement by the OAU. However, after the Eurozone crisis, Morocco launched a diplomatic and political offensive to rejoin the AU, using its allies in France, Senegal, and Ivory Coast. In January 2017, Morocco was readmitted to the AU.

## CONCLUSION

After the 1935 invasion of Abyssinia by the Italians, there was urgency within the Pan-African Movement to build the independence movement. The 5th Pan-African Congress brought an alliance between the differing forces to inspire the decolonization process. Many of the leaders of the 5th Pan-African Congress went home to their societies and reneged on one of the cardinal principles of Pan-Africanism, the free movement of people and the goal of uniting Africans at home and abroad. In his document written on the eve of the Pan-African Congress, Walter Rodney wrote that the 'African petty bourgeois leadership since independence has been an obstacle to the further development of the African revolution'. Rodney himself was assassinated in Guyana by a political leadership which claimed to be at the forefront of Pan-African ideals. By 1980, Walter Rodney had made the clear point that Pan-Africanism could not be based on exclusion, because everywhere in the Pan-African world there were Africans living in multiethnic and multiracial societies.

In South Africa, a new philosophy of Ubuntu emerged to anchor the Pan-Africanism of the twentieth century to affirm the position that Pan-Africanism was linked to human emancipation. This concept of the liberation of humanity became even clearer with big companies claiming the right to patent life forms and the convergence of biotechnology and nanotechnology giving corporations power to invent life. The South African leadership had claimed moral and intellectual leadership of the Pan-African movement after 1994 but the euphoria about an African renaissance had been overtaken by xenophobia when the South African state demonized other Africans who moved to South Africa after 1994.

At the end of the Cold War there had been a resurgence of radical Pan-Africanism with the progressive African women at the forefront. The struggles against gender violence, warfare, destruction, sexual harassment and violation had taken the Pan-African discussion to a new level. With the emergence of fundamentalist forces which wanted to control the minds and bodies of women, there was also the clarity of the need for a secular Pan-African movement that was rooted in deep African spirituality. When a militarist group such as Boko Haram emerged in Nigeria and promised to sell young girls into slavery, the progressive women were reenergized and began to build new Pan-African networks against oppressive governments and the men and women who legitimized them. It is this emancipatory approach to Pan-Africanism that is informing one section of the forces that carry forward the Pan-African movement. The challenge for Pan-Africanism in the twenty-first century is to take the conception of emancipation beyond the material plane to grasp the limits of the human potential imposed by the eugenic civilization of the contemporary period.

In 2011, the people of Egypt and Tunisia launched a new phase of popular struggles for global rights. Since these interventions, external forces have doubled down to hijack the liberating processes in Africa. War situations, the arming of militias, and external forces plundering Africa dominated the news out of Africa, while among Africans overseas the rise of racism, xenophobia, and exclusion demanded new forms of solidarity in the struggles for peace and social justice. The call for the 8th Pan-African Congress offered new opportunities to rebuild the emancipatory traditions.

There were many new and creative forms of organizing and communicating that emerged in the period of the information revolution. After the destruction of NATO, the imperial forces doubled down to harness the tools of social media to create confusion, doubt, and insecurity among young people. Conservative and militaristic leaders employed tools of regionalism, ethnicity, religion, and sexual orientation to disorient the producing classes. Schools and places of learning became centers for intimidation and obscene competition while religious zealots tormented communities with divisive energies. It was from Latin America, with more than 150 million Africans, that there came a call for a new movement for emancipation and transformation. The social forces that are coalescing for the rebuilding of the Pan-African Movement and Pan-African Congress are seeking to learn the positive lessons of the movement in order to build a strong force for the full freedom of Africa in the twenty-first century.

## NOTES

1. Constitutive Act of the African Union; Adopted by the Thirty-Sixth Ordinary Session of the Assembly of Heads of States and Governments 11 July, 2000—Lomé, Togo (Excerpts). http://www.ohchr.org/EN/Issues/RuleOfLaw/CompilationDemocracy/Pages/AfricanUnion.aspx.
2. Quoted in Ronald W. Walters, *Pan Africanism in the African Diaspora: An Analysis of Modern Afrocentric Political Movements* (Michigan: Wayne State University Press, 1997), 43.
3. C.L.R. James, *The Black Jacobins: Toussaint L'Ouverture and the San Domingo Revolution* (1938; repr., New York: Vintage, 1963).
4. Kwame Nkrumah, *Africa Must Unite*, New Edition (London: Pan Africa Books, November 2006), Preface.
5. Julius Nyerere, Speech in Ghana in 1997, "Without Unity, There Is No Future for Africa," Reported in the New African Magazine, http://newafricanmagazine.com/nyerere-without-unity-there-is-no-future-for-africa/.
6. Horace G. Campbell, "The Military Defeat of South Africa in Angola," *Monthly Review*, April 1989.
7. There is already a respectable body of literature on the AU. See inter alia, John Akokpari, Angela Ndinga-Muvumba, and Tim Murithi, eds., *The African Union and Its Institutions* (South Africa: Fanele books, 2008); Rita Kiki Edozie, *The African Union's Africa: New Pan-African Initiatives in Global Governance* (Lansing, MI: Michigan University Press, 2014); Abdulqawi A. Yusuf and Fatsah Ouguergouz, *The African Union: Legal and Institutional Framework: A Manual on the Pan-African Organization* (London: Brill, 2012); and Samuel Makinda, F. Wafula Okumu, and David Mickler, *The African Union: Addressing the Challenges of Peace, Security, and Governance* (London: Routledge, 2016).
8. S.C. Drake, "Diasporan Studies and Pan-Africanism," in *Global Dimensions of the African Diaspora*," ed. J.E. Harris (Washington, DC: Howard University Press, 1993), 341–402.
9. Michael West had defined global Africa as "the continent of Africa plus, firstly, the diaspora of enslavement (descendants of survivors of the Middle passage)

and secondly, the diaspora of colonialism (the dispersal of Africans which continues to occur as a result of disruptions of colonization and its aftermath."

10. Claude Ake, *Social Science as Imperialism: The Theory of Political Development* (Ibadan University Press, 1982).

11. Michael O. West, "Global Africa: The Emergence and Evolution of an Idea," *Review* 28, no. 1 (2005): 85–108, The Black World and the World-System.

12. Michael West, "Global Africa," ibid., 90.

13. Vincent B. Thompson, *Africa and Unity: The Evolution of Pan Africanism* (New York: Humanities Press, 1969).

14. Peter Olisanwuche Esedebe, *Pan-Africanism: The Idea and Movement 1776–1963* (Howard University Press).

15. Michael O. West, "Global Africa: The Emergence and Evolution of an Idea," *Review* 28, no. 1 (2005): 85–108, The Black World and the World-System

16. For an elaboration see Alois S. Mlambo, "Western Social Sciences and Africa: The Exploitation and Marginalization of a Continent," *African Sociological Review* 10, no. 1 (2006).

17. Michael West, "Global Africa," op cit, 98.

18. Amilcar Cabral, National Liberation & Culture, in *Return to the Source: Selected Speeches of Amilcar Cabral*, ed. Africa Information Services (New York: Monthly Review Press), 5.

19. C.L.R. James, *The Black Jacobins, Toussaint L'Ouverture and the San Domingo Revolution* (1938; repr., New York: Vintage, 1963), 283.

20. When Thabo Mbeki became the President of South Africa he was one of the most ardent supporter of the ideas of Pan Africanism and African Renaissance. See two texts that analyzed this phenomenon: Washington A.J. Okumu, *The African Renaissance: History, Significance and Strategy* (Trenton, NJ and Asmara: Africa World Press, 2002); and Fantu Cheru, *African Renaissance: Roadmaps to the Challenge of Globalization* (London and New York: Zed Books, 2002).

21. Walter Rodney, "Towards the Sixth Pan African Congress: Aspects of the International Class Struggles in Africa, the Caribbean and the Americas," in *Pan-Africanism: Struggle Against Neo-colonialism and Imperialism – Documents of the Sixth Pan-African Congress*, ed. Horace Campbell (Toronto: Afro-Carib Publications, 1975), 18–41.

22. James Hooker, *Black Revolutionary: George Padmore's Path from Communism to Pan Africanism* (London: Pall Mall Press, 1967).

23. Micere Mugo, "Re-Envisioning Pan Africanism: What Is the Role of Gender, Youth and the Masses," in *Pan Africanism and Integration in Africa*, ed. Ibbo Mandaza and Dan Nabudere (Harare: Sapes Books, 2002).

24. Kimberle Crenshaw, "Demarginalizing the Intersection of Race and Sex: A Black Feminist Critique of Antidiscrimination Doctrine, Feminist Theory and Antiracist Politics," *The University of Chicago, Legal Forum* 140 (1989): 139–67; and Patricia Hill Collins, *Black Feminist Thought: Knowledge, Consciousness, and the Politics of Empowerment* (New York: Routledge, 1990).

25. Simon Stacey and Seth Aksartova, "The Foundations of Democracy: U.S. Foundation Support for Civil Society in South Africa. 1988–1996," *Voluntas, International Journal of Voluntary and Non-Profit Organizations* 12, no. 4 (2001).

26. Jean-François Bayart, *The State in Africa: The Politics of the Belly*, 2nd ed. (London: Longman, 1993).

27. *Decolonizing International Relations*, ed. Branwen Gruffydd Jones, 114.

28. *Declaration on Africa's Development Challenges.* Adopted at end of Joint CODESRIA-TWN-AFRICA Conference on Africa's Development Challenges in the Millennium, Accra, April 23–26, 2002.
29. Walter Rodney, *History of the Guyanese Working Peoples* (John Hopkins University Press, 1981).
30. Tajudeen Abdul Raheem, *Speaking Truth to Power: Selected Pan-African Postcards* (London: Pambazuka Books, 2010).
31. This concept of Ubuntu is very rich and can be located at the center of the cultural unity of Africa. Cheik Anta Diop had theorized on the cultural unity in the book, *The Cultural Unity of Black Africa: The Domains of Matriarchy and Patriarchy in Classical Antiquity* (London: Karnak House, 1989). See also Archie Mafeje, "Africanity: A Combative Ontology," *Codesria Bulletin,* no. 1 (2000).
32. John Henrik Clarke, "African–American Historians and the Reclaiming of African History," in *African Culture: The Rhythms of Unity,* ed. Molefi Asante and Kariamu Welsh Asante (Trenton, NJ: Africa World Press, 1992).
33. Quoted in the book by Jerry Gafio Watts, *Amiri Baraka: The Politics and Art of a Black Intellectual* (New York: New York University Press, 2001).
34. William R. Scott, *The Sons of Sheba: African Americans and the Italo-Ethiopian War* (Bloomington: Indiana University Press, 1993). For an excellent analysis of the vindicationist traditions, see St. Clair Drake, "Diaspora Studies and Pan Africanism," in *Global Dimensions of the African Diaspora,* ed. Joseph E. Harris (Howard University Press).
35. William G. Martin and Michael O. West, *Out of One, Many Africas: Reconstructing the Study and Meaning of Africa* (Urbana: University of Illinois Press, 1999), 87.
36. Horace G. Campbell, *Rasta and Resistance: From Marcus Garvey to Walter Rodney* (Africa World Press, 2006).
37. Amy Jacques Garvey, *The Philosophy and Opinions of Marcus Garvey: Africa for the Africans* (Frontline Books and Miguel Lorne Publishers, July 2016), 126.
38. Tony Martin, *Race First: The Ideological and Organizational Struggles of Marcus Garvey and the Universal Negro Improvement Association* (Dover, MA: The Majority Press, 1986, first published 1976), 35, quoting *Blackman* (Jamaica), April 10, 1929.
39. Quoted from Daryl Zizwe Poe, *Kwame Nkrumah's Contribution to Pan-African Agency: An Afrocentric Analysis* (New York: Routledge, 2003), 112.
40. W.E. Burghardt Du Bois, "The African Rots of War," *Atlantic Monthly* 115, no. 5 (May 1915): 707–14.
41. W.E. Burghardt Du Bois, "The Pan African Movement," in *History of the Pan-African Congress,* ed. George Padmore, 1947, https://www.marxists.org/archive/padmore/1947/pan-african-congress/ch05.htm.
42. Most reports on the use of this formulation by Malcolm X refer to the speech that he had given on June 28, 1964 at the founding rally of the Organization of Afro-American Unity Founding Rally. For an elaboration see the book, Walter Dean Myers, *Malcolm X: By Any Means Necessary,* New York: Scholasitic Books, 1993. "So we have formed an organization known as the Organization of Afro American Unity which has the same aim and objective—to fight whoever gets in our way, to bring about the complete independence of people of

African descent here in the Western Hemisphere, and first here in the United States, and bring about the freedom of these people by any means necessary."

43. Henry Alexander, *African Tightrope: My Two Years as Nkrumah's Chief of Staff* (Pall Mall Press, 1965), 67–71.

44. Stockwell John, *In Search of Enemies: A CIA Story* (New York: W.W. Norton & Company, 1978), 201. For the details of the long-term planning behind the coup, see Ama Biney, *Political and Social Thought of Kwame Nkrumah*.

45. Immanuel Geiss, "Notes on the Development of Pan-Africanism," *Journal of the Historical Society of Nigeria* 3, no. 4 (June 1967): 719–74.

46. Imanuel Geiss, "Notes on the Development of Pan Africanism," *Journal of the Historical Society of Nigeria* 3, no. 4 (June 1967): 719.

47. One can compare the writings of supporters of the OAU such as: Immanuel Wallenstein "The Early Years of OAU: The Search for Organizational Preeminence," *International Organization* 20, no. 4 (1966): 774–87 or Z. Cervenka (1977) *The Unfinished Quest for Unity. Africa and the OAU.* (New York with the books of Jon Woronoff, Organizing African Unity, Scarecrow Press, New Jersey, 1970); and Ian Brownlie, *Basic Documents on African Affairs* (Oxford University Press, 1971).

48. Arnold J. Temu and Joel das Neves Tembe, ed., *Southern Africa Liberation Struggles 1960–1994.*

49. Michael O. West and William G. Martin, "A Future with a Past: Resurrecting the Study of Africa in the Post-Africanist," *Africa Today* 44, no. 3 (July–September 1997): 313.

50. Pauline Guedj, "Pan-Africanism in the Academia: John Henrik Clarke and the African Heritage Studies Association," Nuevo Mundo 2015, https://nuevo-mundo.revues.org/69574. See also Edmond Keller, "Globalization, African Studies and the Academy," Paper presented at an International Conference, Africa, France and the United States, at the Institut d'Etudes Politiques, Bordeaux, France, May 22–24, 1997, http://www.lam.sciencespobordeaux.fr/old/pageperso/td57.pdf

51. Anthony Lake, *The 'Tar Baby' Option: American Policy Towards Southern Rhodesia* (Columbia University Press), 276.

52. Anthony Lake, *The 'Tar Baby 'Option: American Policy Towards Southern Rhodesia* (New York: Columbia University Press, 1976). See also: *The Kissinger Study of Southern Africa: National Security StudyMemorandum 39 (Secret)*, ed. Mohamed A. El-Khawas and Barry Cohen (Westport, CT: Lawrence Hill and Company, 1976).

53. Chester Crocker, "The Military Transfer of Power in Africa: A Comparative Study of Change in the British and French Systems of Order" (PhD thesis, John Hopkins University, 1969).

54. C.O. Amate, *Inside the OAU: Pan Africanism in Practice* (London: St. Martin's Press, 1986); see also Salim Ahmed Salim: Son of Africa, edited by Jakkie Cilliers, ISS, South Africa, 2016.

55. Walter Rodney, "Towards the Sixth Pan African Congress: Aspects of the International Class Struggle in Africa, the Caribbean and America," *Pan-Africanism: Struggle against Neo-colonialism and Imperialism – Documents of the Sixth Pan-African Congress*, ed. Horace Campbell (Toronto: Afro-Carib Publications, 1975), 18–41.

56. Jon Henley, "Gigantic Sleaze Scandal Winds Up as Former Elf Oil Chiefs are Jailed," https://www.theguardian.com/business/2003/nov/13/france.oilandpetrol

57. William Attwood, *The Reds and the Blacks.*

58. Patrick Wilmot, "Nigeria's Southern Africa Policy: 1960–1988," Current African Issues Series, Scandinavian Institute of African Studies, Uppsala, August 1989.

59. Quoted in the lecture of Professor Tony Martin at the African Union Conference of Intellectuals, Dakar, Senegal 2004. See also Nnamdi Azikiwe, "The Future of Pan Africanism," in *Ideologies of Liberation in Black Africa, 1856–1970,* ed. Ayo Langley (London: Rex Collings, 1979).

60. Fatima Babiker Mahmoud, "Building a Pan African Women's Movement," in *Pan Africanism, Politics, Economy and Social Change in the Twenty First Century,* ed. Tajudeen Abdul Raheem (New York: New York University Press, 1997), 237.

61. See in particular the scholarship of William Zartman, I. William Zartman, ed., *Traditional Cures for Modern Conflicts: African Conflict 'Medicine'* (Boulder: Lynne Rienner Publishers, 2000).

62. Speech of, http://www.sahistory.org.za/archive/statement-president-republic-south-africa-nelson-mandela-oau-meeting-heads-state-and-governm, Nelson Mandela to the meeting of the OAU in Tunis, June 13, 1994.

63. The Abuja Declaration, Outcomes of Conference on Reparations (Nigeria) from April 27 to 29, 1993, http://www.colonialismreparation.org/en/compensations/african-union-colonialism.html.

64. Ali A. Mazrui, "Global Africa: From Abolitionists to Reparationists," *African Studies Review* 37, no. 3 (December 1994): 1–18.

65. A.A.A. Mazrui, *Black Reparations in the Era of Globalization* (Binghamton, NY: Institute of Global Cultural Studies, 2002).

66. A.A. Mazrui, "From Slave Ship to Space Ship: Africa between Marginalization and Globalization," *African Studies Quarterly: The Online Journal for African Studies* 2, no. 4 (1999), http://www.africa.ufl.edu/asq/v2/v2i4a2.htm.2002; and A.A. Mazrui, *Black Reparations in the Era of Globalization* (Binghamton, NY: Institute of Global Cultural Studies).

67. Clarence Lusane, *Colin Powell and Condoleezza Rice: Foreign Policy, Race, and the New American Century* (New York: Praeger, 2006).

68. See the contribution of Adebayo Adeji on the "Lagos Plan of Action," in *New Partnership for African Development: NEPAD, A New Path?* ed. Peter Anyang Nyongo (Heinrich Boll Foundation: Nairobi, Kenya).

69. Rita Kiki Edozie, "The Sixth Zone: The African Diaspora and the African Union's Global Era Pan Africanism," *Journal of African American Studies* 16, no. 2 (June 2012): 268–99.

70. Ngugi Wa Thiongo, "African Identities: Pan-Africanism in the Era of Globalization and Capitalist Fundamentalism," *Macalester International* 14, Article 9 (2004).

71. African Union Commission, Agenda 2063: The Africa We Want, Addis Ababa 29015, http://www.un.org/en/africa/osaa/pdf/au/agenda2063.pdf.

72. Memorandum of Understanding between the AU Commission and the Global Pan African Movement, April 2015.

73. Report of the High Level Panel on Illicit Financial Flows from Africa, "Track It, Stop It, Get It," http://www.uneca.org/sites/default/files/PublicationFiles/iff_main_report_26feb_en.pdf.
74. See the Pan African Program of the European Union, http://ec.europa.eu/europeaid/regions/africa/continental-cooperation/pan-african-programme_en.

## Bibliography

Abdul Raheem, Tajudeen, ed. *Pan Africanism, Politics, Economy and Social Change in the Twenty First Century.* New York: New York University Press, 1997.

Adeji, Adebayo. On the "Lagos Plan of Action." In *New Partnership for African Development: NEPAD, A New Path?* edited by Peter Anyang Nyongo. Nairobi, Kenya: Heinrich Boll Foundation, 2002.

Ake, Claude. *Social Science as Imperialism: The Theory of Political Development.* Ibadan: University Press, 1982.

Akokpari, John, Angela Ndinga-Muvumba, and Murithi Timothy. *The African Union and Its Institutions.* South Africa: Fanele Books, 2008.

Alexander, Henry. *African Tightrope. My Two Years as Nkrumah's Chief of Staff.* London: Pall Mall Press, 1965.

Amate, C.O. *Inside the OAU: Pan Africanism in Practice.* London: St. Martin's Press, 1986.

Amilcar, Cabral. *Return to the Source: Selected Speeches of Amílcar Cabral.* New York: Monthly Review Press, 1974.

Attwood, William. *The Reds and the Blacks, a Personal Adventure.* New York: Harper & Row, 1966.

Bayart, Jean-François. *The State in Africa: The Politics of the Belly.* 2nd ed. London: Longman, 1993.

Biney, Ama. *Political and Social Thought of Kwame Nkrumah.* Palgrave Macmillan, January 2011.

Brownlie, Ian. *Basic Documents on African Affairs.* London: Oxford University Press, January 1971.

Campbell, Horace G. "The Military Defeat of South Africa in Angola." *Monthly Review*, April 1989.

———. *Rasta and Resistance: From Marcus Garvey to Walter Rodney.* Africa World Press, 2006.

Campbell, Horace. *Global NATO and the Catastrophic Failure in Libya: Lessons for Africa in the Forging of African Unity.* New York: Monthly Review Press, March 2013.

Cervenka, Z. *The Unfinished Quest for Unity. Africa and the OAU.* New York with the Books of Woronoff, Jon, Organizing African Unity, New Jersey: Scarecrow Press, 1970.

Cheru, Fantu. *African Renaissance: Roadmaps to the Challenge of Globalization.* London and New York: Zed Books, 2002.

Clarke, John Henrik. "African-American Historians and the Reclaiming of African History." In *African Culture: The Rhythms of Unity*, edited by Molefi Asante and Kariamu Welsh Asante. Trenton, NJ: Africa World Press, 1992.

Collins, Patricia Hill. *Black Feminist Thought: Knowledge, Consciousness, and the Politics of Empowerment.* New York: Routledge, 1990.

Constitutive Act of the African Union. Adopted by the Thirty-Sixth Ordinary Session of the Assembly of Heads of States and Governments 11 July, 2000—Lomé, Togo (Excerpts). http://www.ohchr.org/EN/Issues/RuleOfLaw/CompilationDemocracy/Pages/AfricanUnion.aspx.

Crenshaw, Kimberle. "Demarginalizing the Intersection of Race and Sex: A Black Feminist Critique of Antidiscrimination Doctrine, Feminist Theory and Antiracist Politics." *The University of Chicago, Legal Forum* 140 (1989): 139–67.

Crocker, Chester. "The Military Transfer of Power in Africa: A Comparative Study of Change in the British and French Systems of Order." PhD. thesis, John Hopkins University, 1969.

*Declaration on Africa's Development Challenges.* Adopted at end of Joint CODESRIA-TWN-AFRICA Conference on Africa's Development Challenges in the Millennium, Accra, April 23–26, 2002.

Diop, Cheik Anta. *The Cultural Unity of Black Africa: The Domains of Matriarchy and Patriarchy in Classical Antiquity.* London: Karnak House, 1989.

Drake, St. Clair. "Diasporan Studies and Pan-Africanism." In *Global Dimensions of the African Diaspora*, edited by J.E. Harris. Washington, DC: Howard University Press, 1993.

Edozie, Rita Kiki. "The Sixth Zone: The African Diaspora and the African Union's Global Era Pan Africanism." *Journal of African American Studies* 16, no. 2 (June 2012).

———. *The African Union's Africa: New Pan-African Initiatives in Global Governance.* Michigan University Press, 2014.

El-Khawas, Mohamed A., and Barry Cohen. *The Kissinger Study of Southern Africa: National Security Study Memorandum 39 (secret).* Westport, Conn: Lawrence Hill and Company, 1976.

Esedebe, Peter Olisanwuche. *Pan-Africanism: The Idea and Movement 1776–1963.* Howard University Press, 1980.

Geiss, Immanuel. "Notes on the Development of Pan Africanism." *Journal of the Historical Society of Nigeria* 3, no. 4 (June 1967).

Guedj, Pauline. "Pan-Africanism in the Academia: Clarke, John Henrik, and the African Heritage Studies Association," October 2016. https://nuevomundo.revues.org/69574.

Henley, Jon. "Gigantic Sleaze Scandal Winds Up as Former Elf Oil Chiefs are Jailed," November 2003. https://www.theguardian.com/business/2003/nov/13/france.oilandpetrol.

Hooker, James. *Black Revolutionary: George Padmore's Path from Communism to Pan Africanism.* London: Pall Mall Press, 1967.

James, C.L.R. *The Black Jacobins: Toussaint L'Ouverture and the San Domingo Revolution* (1938). Reprint, New York: Vintage, 1963.

Jones, Branwen Gruffydd. "Decolonizing International Relations," September 2006.

Keller, Edmond. "Globalization, African Studies and the Academy," by Centre D'Etude D'Afrique Noire Institut D'Et S de Bordeaux U, January 1998.

Lake, Anthony. *The 'Tar Baby' Option: American Policy Towards Southern Rhodesia.* New York: Columbia University Press, 1976.

Lusane, Clarence. *Colin Powell and Condoleezza Rice: Foreign Policy, Race, and the New American Century.* New York: Praeger, 2006.

Mafeje, Archie. Africanity: A Combative Ontology. *Codesria Bulletin*, no. 1 (2000).

Makinda, Samuel F., Wafula Okumu, and David Mickler. *"The African Union: Addressing the Challenges of Peace, Security, and Governance."* London: Routledge, 2016.

Mandaza, Ibbo, and Dan Nabudere. *Pan Africanism and Integration in Africa.* Harare: SAPES Books, 2002.

Martin, Tony. *Race First "the Ideological and Organizational Struggles of Marcus Garvey and the Universal Negro Improvement Association."* Dover, MA: The Majority Press, 1986, first published 1976. Quoting *Blackman* (Jamaica) (September 1986).

———. "At the African Union Conference of Intellectuals," Dakar, Senegal, 2004.

Martin, William G., and Michael O. West. *Out of One, Many Africas: Reconstructing the Study and Meaning of Africa.* Urbana: University of Illinois Press, 1999.

Mazrui, A.A. *Black Reparations in the Era of Globalization.* Binghamton, NY: Institute of Global Cultural Studies, 1999.

———. "From Slave Ship to Space Ship: Africa between Marginalization and Globalization." *African Studies Quarterly: The Online Journal for African Studies* 2, no. 4 (2002). http://www.africa.ufl.edu/asq/v2/v2i4a2.htm.2002.

Mazrui, Ali A. "Global Africa: From Abolitionists to Reparationists." *African Studies Review* 37, no. 3 (December 1994).

Memorandum of Understanding between the AU Commission and the Global Pan African Movement, April 2015.

Mlambo, Alois. S. "Western Social Sciences and Africa: The Exploitation and Marginalization of a Continent." *African Sociological Review* 10, no. 1 (2006).

Nelson Mandela to the Meeting of the OAU in Tunis. http://www.sahistory.org.za/archive/statement-president-republic-south-africa-nelson-mandela-oau-meeting-heads-state-and-governm. June 13, 1994.

Nkrumah, Kwame. *Africa Must Unite*, New Edition. London: Panaf Books, November 2006.

Nnamdi, Azikiwe. "The Future of Pan Africanism." In *Ideologies of Liberation in Black Africa, 1856–1970*, edited by Ayo Langley. London: Rex Collings, 1979.

Nyerere, Julius. Speech in Ghana in 1997. "Without Unity, There Is No Future for Africa." Reported in the New African Magazine. http://newafricanmagazine.com/nyerere-without-unity-there-is-no-future-for-africa/.

Okumu, Washington, A.J. *The African Renaissance: History, Significance and Strategy.* Trenton, NJ and Asmara: Africa World Press, 2002.

Pan African Program of the European Union. http://ec.europa.eu/europeaid/regions/africa/continental-cooperation/pan-african-programme_en.

Raheem, Tajudeen Abdul. *Speaking Truth to Power: Selected Pan-African Postcards.* London: Pambazuka Books, 2010.

Rodney, Walter. "Towards the Sixth Pan African Congress: Aspects of the International Class Struggles in Africa, the Caribbean and the Americas." In *Pan-Africanism: Struggle Against Neo-colonialism and Imperialism—Documents of the Sixth Pan-African Congress*, edited by Horace Campbell. Toronto: Afro-Carib Publications, 1975.

———. *History of the Guyanese Working Peoples.* John Hopkins University Press, 1981.

Salim Ahmed Salim: *Son of Africa*, ISS, South Africa edited by Jakkie Cilliers, 2016.

Scott, William R. *The Sons of Sheba: African Americans and the Italo-Ethiopian War.* Bloomington: Indiana University Press, 1993.

Stacey, Simon, and Seth Aksartova. "The Foundations of Democracy: U.S. Foundation Support for Civil Society in South Africa, 1988–1996." *Voluntas, International Journal of Voluntary and Non-Profit Organizations* 12, no. 4 (December 2001).

Stockwell, John. 1978. *In Search of Enemies: A CIA Story.* New York: W.W. Norton & Company, November 1997.

Tafirenyinka, Masimba. Report of the High Level Panel on "*Illicit Financial Flows from Africa, 'Track It, Stop It, Get It'.*" http://www.uneca.org/sites/default/files/PublicationFiles/iff_main_report_26feb_en.pdf. December 2013.

Temu, Arnold J., and Joel das Neves Tembe, eds. *Southern Africa Liberation Struggles 1960–1994,* 2015.

The Abuja Declaration, Outcomes of Conference on Reparations (Nigeria) from April 27 to 29 1993. http://www.colonialismreparation.org/en/compensations/african-union-colonialism.html.

Thompson, Vincent B. *Africa and Unity: The Evolution of Pan Africanism.* New York: Humanities Press, 1969.

Wallenstein, Immanuel. "The Early Years of OAU: The Search for Organizational Preeminence." *International Organization* (1966).

Walters, Ronald W. *Pan Africanism in the African Diaspora: An Analysis of Modern Afrocentric Political Movements.* Michigan: Wayne State University Press, 1997.

Watts, Jerry Gafio. *Amiri Baraka: The Politics and Art of a Black Intellectual.* New York: New York University Press, 2001.

West, Michael O. "Global Africa: The Emergence and Evolution of an Idea." *Review* 28, no. 1 (2005). The Black World and the World-System.

West, Michael O., and William G. Martin. "A Future with a Past: Resurrecting the Study of Africa in the Post-Africanist." *Africa Today,* 1997.

William, Zartman I., ed. *Traditional Cures for Modern Conflicts: African Conflict 'Medicine.'* Boulder: Lynne Rienner Publishers, 2000.

Wilmot, Patrick. "Nigeria's Southern Africa Policy: 1960–1988." Current African Issues Series. Uppsala: Scandinavian Institute of African Studies, August 1989.

Yusuf, Abdulqawi A., and Fatsah Ouguergouz. *The African Union: Legal and Institutional Framework: A Manual on the Pan-African Organization.* London: Brill, 2012.

# CHAPTER 42

# Africa and Human Rights

## Edward Kissi

The historiography of 'human rights' is a catalogue of debates over some contentious issues. They include the definition of human rights, the history of human rights thought, the historical experiences and cultural traditions from which our contemporary ideas of human rights come, the degree to which human rights are universally shared values or the extent to which they are specific to each human society, the circumstances under which human rights became the cornerstone of today's international laws, and how human rights laws are applied in global affairs.[1] While this chapter draws upon some of these debates, it takes a different approach to its study of human rights in African history. It focuses rather on how human rights ideas were used as the frameworks of protest against colonialism and the organizing principles to promote social justice and racial equality, in the early years of political independence in Africa. It also looks at how human rights were perverted for political and ideological purposes in the early postcolonial period, and how human rights are viewed and discussed in contemporary Africa.

This chapter argues that despite claims by some scholars that Africans have their own separate concepts of human rights, human rights are actually universal ethical values that exist in all human societies. The current global human rights narrative, often presumed as a Western liberal ideology, gained global prominence in the aftermath of the state-organized atrocities that characterized the Second World War. As this war, in which colonial subjects from Africa had participated, exposed 'national sovereignty' as the legal refuge of totalitarian states, 'human rights', codified in legal documents, became the

E. Kissi (✉)
Department of Africana Studies,
University of South Florida, Tampa, FL, USA

M.S. Shanguhyia and T. Falola (eds.),
*The Palgrave Handbook of African Colonial and Postcolonial History*,
https://doi.org/10.1057/978-1-137-59426-6_42

moral and juridical guardian of the vulnerable and powerless. The postwar internationalization of human rights had a catalytic effect on the transition from colonial statehood to postcolonial nationhood in Africa. African nationalists protesting against the inhumane character of colonialism drew upon global values of human dignity now validated in international human rights declarations to make their voices heard. However, no sooner had the euphoria of political independence subsided than the nationalist leaders who came to power on the crest of human rights advocacy began to violate the norms they had previously upheld. That is Africa's paradoxical embrace of human rights ideas.

## HUMAN RIGHTS AND THEIR DEFENDERS AND CRITICS

There is no consensus among scholars and activists about what human rights are by definition, although there is broad agreement about their significance in human societies. The Ghanaian philosopher Kwasi Wiredu has described 'human rights' as 'claims that people are entitled to make ... by virtue of their status as human beings'.[2] In his book *Human Rights*, the British political scientist Michael Freeman identifies human rights as a set of norms outlined in international documents for the protection of vulnerable groups against all forms of violence and 'unjust customs'.[3] The Canadian human rights activist Michael Ignatieff sees human rights as 'the language through which individuals have created a defense of their autonomy against the oppression of religion, state, family, and group'.[4] The debate over the definition of human rights tends also to devolve into ideological controversies over whether the idea of human rights as claims that people make or entitlements that their humanity grants them is shared across all cultures in the world (universal) or is peculiar to particular groups and their historical experiences (relative).[5]

At the heart of this ideological tussle is the claim by some scholars that today's global human rights norms enshrined in the Universal Declaration of Human Rights (UDHR) of December 1948, for instance, emerged from 'Western' (that is European and US) 'liberal values' and that these values emphasize the freedom or 'autonomy' of the 'individual' human being over the aspirations and prescriptions of the larger society or ethnic community upheld in 'African culture' as more important than the individual. In an influential paper written on this subject in 1982, the US political scientist Jack Donnelly argued, controversially, that 'the concept of human rights is an artifact of modern Western civilization'.[6] In Donnelly's view, respect for the 'dignity' of human beings (human dignity), an ethic that all societies share, is not the same as individual liberty, freedom, and autonomy (human rights), a fundamental norm that exists only in Western cultural and political traditions.

Those who have disagreed with Donnelly's arguments have often offered their own equally controversial claims that since every group has its own culture and values there could be no common or 'universal' ideas of human rights that all human societies share.[7] The Kenyan political scientist Makau Mutua has described human rights as a Western liberal canon masquerading as universal values. He sees human rights as 'a philosophy that seeks the diffusion of liberalism and its primacy around the globe ...'.[8] Mutua argues that in the historical experiences of Europe and the USA, 'the language of rights' developed in the context of 'claims against the state' for the purpose of seeking 'individual remedy for a wrong'. That, in his view, contrasts sharply with the 'African language of duty' of the individual to the community or larger society of which that individual is a part.[9] On this basis, Mutua concludes that the 'Western' notion of human rights as 'individual rights' is 'ill-suited' for Africa because it originated from 'a specific historical context in the Western world' that was different from the historical, political and social realities of Africa.[10] The Ghanaian philosopher Kwasi Wiredu and political scientist Josiah Cobbah agree with Makau Mutua on the issue of 'rights' accruing to a 'human' or 'person' by virtue of that person's membership in an ethnic community to which that human owes duties. Cobbah has argued that human rights should be discussed 'within a cultural context'.[11] On account of that, Cobbah shares Mutua's view of human rights as a set of values rooted in Western liberal cultural thought. Like Wiredu, the cultural context in which Cobbah discusses human rights is the Akan people of Ghana's subordination of the rights of individuals to 'the requirements of the [ethnic] group'.[12]

The Nigerian political scientist Oritsegbubemi Anthony Owoye has, however, expressed great skepticism about 'the claim' that a unique or distinctively 'African' concept of human rights exists. In his view, human rights are ideas about human nature and 'human nature is universal'.[13] While one cannot make sense of human nature without paying attention to the 'elements of culture' and the 'various contingencies of human life' that shape human dispositions, there is almost universal agreement 'among many human rights theorists' that 'human rights are basic entitlements owed to human beings simply because they are human beings'.[14] Owoye laments the tendency in the literature on 'African perspectives on human rights' to present 'a family of practices and ideas' held by one ethnic group in Africa, in one part of the continent, as the 'African' 'conception of human rights'.[15] What is odd about this approach to human rights thought, in Owoye's view, is that if one looks at notions of humanity and dignity solely in terms of one's existence in one's ethnic community, then what happens to the status of that person if he or she moves outside of the community of which he is a part to another place or different community? Owoye wonders whether under the so-called African conception of human rights 'human beings who have relocated to unfamiliar cultural terrain thereby lose their standing as human beings'.[16] It appears from this critique that the more important debate over human rights is not necessarily what they are and where they come from, but why they are important. As Owoye notes, we care about human rights because they protect us against policies and practices that infringe on our human dignity.[17] This author agrees with Owoye and adds that different people in different societies may place different emphases on what they need to maintain a functioning human community. Central to this universal desire for social order is the recognition of and respect for the humanity and dignity of all human beings irrespective of where they may live. Any act that tramples upon the dignity of any human being, individual or group, anywhere, is a violation of human rights.

Scholars may disagree over the centrality of the 'individual' or 'group' in human rights theory. However, even those who argue that there are different ways in which 'Africans' and 'non-Africans' perceive and promote these rights agree that human rights are values that confer dignity and respect on every human being and, therefore, should be guaranteed in every human society. In fact, while Mutua contests what he calls the 'singular obsession with the universalization' of Western cultural models in human rights thought, he concedes that at its core, human rights are about 'the reduction' or 'elimination of conditions that foster human indignity, violence, poverty and powerlessness'.[18] Michael Ignatieff is therefore correct in arguing that human rights have become a global phenomenon 'not because [they serve] the interest of the powerful', but 'because [they have] advanced the interests of the powerless'.[19] As a value system, human rights in all their manifestations (right to life, right to work, freedom of speech, respect for one's identity, etc.) offer a secular alternative to often discriminatory religious beliefs and social traditions in a culturally diverse world.[20]

## COLONIALISM AS PERVERSION OF HUMAN RIGHTS

An historical understanding of human rights in postcolonial Africa should not be rooted in a conceptual debate over what human rights are, and which cultural traditions produced them. Rather, it should start with analyses of the continent's collective experience of the most egregious violation of the human rights and dignity of people (colonialism) and how colonized peoples used human rights norms as instruments for their own liberation. Historian Dennis Laumann has offered one of the clearest definitions of colonialism and examined its abusive features in African history. Colonialism, Laumann argues, is 'the seizure and occupation of territory ... belonging to one group of people (the colonized) by another group of people (the colonizers)'.[21] As Laumann observes, this seizure and occupation of territory also led to the settlement of the colonizers on the captured territory. In many parts of Africa, from the mid-nineteenth century to the end of the twentieth, the colonizers were Europeans who not only seized and occupied African lands, but also administered them for the principal purpose of exploiting their natural resources. It was in that process of conquest and exploitation, and resistance to both in Africa, that European colonizers unleashed the gravest of human rights abuses on their colonial subjects.

Colonialism is a central theme in Raphael Lemkin's original idea of genocide as the gravest threat to human rights.[22] The architect of the concept of genocide saw colonialism as involving the deliberate destruction of the economic existence of a subjugated group, its political institutions, religious beliefs, languages and other ways of life and the replacement of these foundations of the subjugated group's dignity, identity, and survival with the colonizers' culture and social, political, and economic institutions. Lemkin, therefore, viewed colonialism as a form of cultural genocide; a permanent destruction of a group's culture or way of life even if the colonized group that embodied that culture was not physically annihilated.[23] He believed that genocide, fostered through colonialism, was the ultimate threat to human dignity, the essence of human rights.[24] Thus, notwithstanding what some scholars might celebrate as the benefits of colonial rule in Africa (the introduction of European languages as a means of unifying diverse ethnic groups around common languages, the introduction of roads, railways, telegraphy, and missionary schools as 'modern' infrastructure, among other things) European colonialism in Africa was marked by relentless assaults on the dignity of colonial subjects and their identity as human beings.[25]

Scholars of African history have long documented the violent wars and other forms of physical killing and oppression that characterized European colonial rule in Africa, as well as that of the white settler regime in South Africa. However, it is only in recent years that those who have studied colonial violence have started to draw instructive connections between these atrocities and human rights. Colonial atrocities that have received this kind of analytic attention include the genocide perpetrated by the German colonial administration against the Herero and Nama ethnic groups in the German colony of South-West Africa, the organized and deliberate killing and maiming of individual colonial subjects in the Congo Free State (administered as the personal property of Belgium's King Leopold II), and the brutal suppression of anti-colonial protests in the British colony of Kenya, among many abuses of the dignity and humanity of colonial subjects.[26]

Scholars who see genocide (the intentional destruction of a group) as the gravest assault on the right to life as a fundamental human right agree that the first genocide of the twentieth century took place in the German colony of South-West Africa in 1904. Since 1884, when Germany laid claim to South-West Africa as a colonial possession, German settlers had seized the land and cattle of the pastoralist Herero population and constructed railway lines through Herero pasturelands and arbitrarily captured and imprisoned Herero men. As these colonial policies undermined the foundations of Herero humanity and dignity, the Herero people rose in armed rebellion in January 1904. Historian Benjamin Madley has noted that the subjugated Herero rebelled 'in an attempt to end their dispossession, impoverishment, and political subordination'.[27] The German reaction, as Laumann has characterized it, was 'comprehensive and vicious'.[28] In the racial mindset of colonial administrators, in the age of empire building in Africa, the African was viewed as a savage bordering on subhuman. The German authorities in South-West Africa saw their response to the Herero rebellion in such racial terms. With about 10,000 European recruits, led by Lieutenant General Lothar von Trotha, this mercenary force hunted down and annihilated the Herero as a group. Von Trotha's army chased the Herero into the Omaheke desert, with deadly consequences of starvation and poisoned lakes and rivers that could give the fleeing Herero any chance of survival. The Herero suffered these outrages against their dignity with the Nama pastoralist community in the colony who had also rejected German colonialism and resisted 'European religious, cultural, and political influence'.[29] When the German response to both the Herero and Nama protests was over, 'up to 60,000 Herero and 10,000 Nama [had] lost their lives'.[30]

The German annihilatory response to colonial subjects protesting against inhumane conditions was no different from the British reaction to the Kikuyu protest against the seizure of their lands in the British colony of Kenya, in East Africa, in 1954. The British East Africa Protectorate, as Kenya was initially called, had become a British colonial possession in the late nineteenth century. British men and their families saw this East African colony, a prized colony of fertile lands, as their home. This idea required an appropriation of land, much of it belonging to the predominantly peasant Kikuyu ethnic group, for the benefit of British settlers. It was this colonial policy of land grab and forced labor that brought British settlers and the Kikuyu people into what Caroline Elkins has described as 'one of the bloodiest and most protracted wars of decolonization' in the twentieth century.[31]

British colonial policies in Kenya affected many individuals and groups but, as Elkins has observed, no group experienced so intense a 'transformation' of its dignity and identity that colonialism engendered as the Kikuyu of Kenya.[32] The dispossession of the Kikuyu of their land undermined the foundations of Kikuyu individual and group survival. In human rights terms, the Kikuyu notion of personhood and dignity that revolved around land possession took a severe hit. A Kikuyu needed land to cultivate and obtain the necessary wealth to marry, have a family and be able to perform his duty to his society and, thus, maintain a dignified status. A Kikuyu woman too needed land to grow food-crops and sustain her family without which no Kikuyu woman could be deemed 'an adult'. In short, 'A Kikuyu could not be a Kikuyu without land'.[33] It is worth emphasizing that the Kikuyu of colonial Kenya shared their conception of human rights and dignity in relationship to land ownership with many ethnic groups in other parts of colonial Africa, including the Akans of the British colony of Gold Coast.[34]

For the British, colonialism preserved the rights and dignity of British settlers in Kenya and Britain's status as a global power. For the Kikuyu, the preservation of British rights and Britain's status meant an assault on theirs. The advancement of the dignity of British settlers in East Africa at the expense of the Kikuyu on their own land provoked what has been called the Mau Mau rebellion. The Kikuyu rebels or their sympathizers had burned, mutilated and hacked some British settlers and their Kenyan allies to death in a manner that, by any understanding of human rights, constituted a grave infraction on human life and dignity.[35] Mau Mau killing methods with machetes and other tools had inflamed British settler anxieties and driven 'local Europeans into a frenzied state of terror'.[36] As Elkins has noted, Kukuyu resistance to British settler colonialism and the response of the settlers 'left blood on the hands of all involved'.[37] Historian David Anderson has also described the Mau Mau rebellion, and the British response to it, as a 'story of atrocity and excess on both sides'.[38] Nonetheless, in 'scope and scale', Kikuyu atrocities paled in comparison to the response the British colonial authorities unleashed.[39]

Colonial violence revealed the limited value that European colonial administrators placed on the dignity and humanity of their colonized subjects. In Africa, these kinds of violent assaults on the dignity of the colonized also took place in 'Southern Rhodesia, British Natal, the Belgian Congo and Italian Ethiopia'[40] Colonialism's 'wholesale condemnation of everything African', its inherent racial discrimination and 'constant humiliation and oppression' of Africans generated, as Adu Boahen has observed, 'a deep feeling of inferiority' and 'the loss of a sense of human dignity among Africans'.[41] Viewed against this 'psychological impact' of colonial atrocities, resistance to colonial rule, in all its forms, could be understood as political and social protests undertaken to restore the human rights of colonized subjects.

## ANTICOLONIALISM AS RESTORATION OF HUMAN RIGHTS

Opinions differ among scholars about the extent to which decolonization represented a continental social movement for human rights.[42] Nevertheless, because colonialism in practice represented an assault on the human rights of the colonized, resistance to colonial rule should be understood as a struggle of the colonized for human rights. Certainly, 'white racial supremacy' in colonial Kenya had expressed itself in a host of unjust treatment of Africans 'including public flogging, beating deaths, and summary executions'.[43] It was therefore not surprising that African nationalists, and their global sympathizers, spared no opportunity to invoke universal human rights ideals in their anti-colonial activities. They sought, as Meredith Terretta has noted, to define and also uphold rights for people who were not deemed 'citizens' on their own lands, but rather as 'subjects' by European settlers who had taken over ownership of land, monopolized economic privileges, and determined access to political and civil rights.[44]

The colonial 'trial' of the alleged masterminds of the Mau Mau rebellion that preceded the annihilatory phase of the rebellion itself revealed the disjuncture between British conceptions of justice and Kikuyu notions of human rights. Caroline Elkins has chronicled the British trial, in December

1952, of Jomo Kenyatta and five others as the leaders of a creeping Kikuyu revolt against the British colonial administration. In the post-Second World War atmosphere of rights talk and self-determination discourse, Kenyatta and his colleagues accused of instigating the Mau Mau rebellion appropriated the language of 'justice' and 'rights' in their defense. Although Kenyatta denied any involvement in the Mau Mau atrocities against British settlers and their families, the future leader of an independent Kenya attributed Kikuyu anger to colonial 'injustices' and the desire of the Kikuyu people to 'establish' and also 'demand the rights of the African people as human beings ...'.[45] Opposition to colonialism in Africa gave human rights values concrete and universal meaning. Kenyatta, and many African nationalists who were arrested, tried, flogged, or imprisoned for protesting against degrading colonial policies invoked prevailing universal ideas of human rights (self-determination, freedom, and racial equality) to expose the 'contradictions' between the inhumane nature of colonial rule and the European justification of it as a 'civilizing mission'.[46]

Kwame Nkrumah best summed up the frustrations of the colonized peoples of Africa when he chose the evocative statement 'We prefer self-government with danger to servitude in tranquility' as the motto for a newspaper (*Accra Evening News*) he founded in 1949 as the vehicle for anti-colonial resistance in Gold Coast.[47] Independence was achieved in Gold Coast (renamed Ghana) on 6 March 1957. The sigh of relief was prompt and noticeable in Nkrumah's proclamation, as leader of the new nation of Ghana, to a cheering crowd, at the dawn of independence, that finally 'the battle has ended' and Ghana, their 'beloved country is free forever'.[48] For Nkrumah, 'freedom' from colonialism also meant the rebirth of 'a new African ... ready to fight his own battles'.[49] That also required, as Nkrumah put it, a degree of self-reliance that permitted the 'new' and independent African nations to 'create [their] own African personality and identity'.[50] This anti-colonial and self-determinationist principle was reechoed, in 1958, by Patrice Lumumba, the future leader of an independent Congo, when he explained that the fight of his people for independence from Belgian colonialism was nothing more than a restoration of 'a right that the Congolese people have lost'.[51]

The meanings that African nationalists attached to human rights shifted throughout the decolonization process.[52] For Nkrumah, human rights meant self-determination and the creation by Africans of their own distinctive identity. Julius Nyerere, the future leader of an independent Tanganyika (Tanzania), saw human rights in the colonial context as a struggle for racial equality.[53] Nyerere's framing of the human rights discourse in racial terms (more than Nkrumah's cultural construction), in the early post-independence period, became the framework for the critiques of apartheid South Africa that led to the isolation of the white minority government in Africa and in much of the world.[54] Notwithstanding their various and shifting interpretations of human rights, by appropriating and applying prevailing global human rights ideas of self-determination, racial equality, and political and civil rights to advance their anti-colonial and anti-apartheid causes, African nationalists such as Kenyatta, Nkrumah, Lumumba, and Nyerere appear, initially at least, to have embraced the universality of human rights principle. That embrace was, however, short-lived. The cracks in the African nationalist subscription to a universalist human rights ethos were apparent in Nkrumah's advocacy of a new African personality and identity. That signified an emerging desire for a particular conception of human rights in postcolonial Africa with an African imprint.

## IRONIES OF HUMAN RIGHTS OBSERVANCE IN POSTCOLONIAL AFRICA

The transition from colonial statehood to postcolonial nationhood in Africa was initially marked by human rights-based political expressions and commitments. They included the emergence of constitutions as the new criteria of national identity with guarantees of human rights such as freedom to speak, assemble, and enjoy due process in courts of law denied to Africans in the colonial period. Added to these marks of postcolonial nationhood were ratifications of international and continental human rights instruments. The adoption, in June 1981, of an 'African Charter on Human and Peoples' Rights' (ACHPR) by member states of the then Organization of African Unity was a substantive affirmation of the universality of the rights and freedoms enshrined in the UDHR. The 68 human rights articles in the ACHPR may be larger in number than the 30 in the UDHR, but they are consistent with the rights to life and freedom from persecution that the UDHR grants to every individual human being. The African Charter affirms these as fundamental human rights to which '[e]very individual' in Africa is 'entitled' without discrimination on the bases of 'race, ethnic group, color, sex, language, religion, political or any other opinion, national and social origin, fortune, birth or other status'.[55]

The extent to which the postcolonial African states and their guardians promoted human rights or perverted them, and why, is one of the disturbing ironies of the history of postcolonial Africa. As Meredith Terretta, and Kwasi Wiredu, have accurately noted, in separate publications, human rights talk and guarantees had a short lifespan in independent Africa.[56] Politics in Ghana, under Kwame Nkrumah, Tanzania, under Julius Nyerere, and Cameroon under Amadou Ahidjo, highlighted the promise and contradictions of postcolonial Africa's perplexing embrace of human rights. What Nkrumah had advocated as a 'new African personality and identity' found disconcerting expression in arbitrary 'preventive detention' legislations that granted his own government in Ghana, and others in independent Africa, broad authority to clamp down on 'ambiguously defined' subversive acts.[57]

After political independence in December 1961, the new leaders of Tanzania did not hide their intention of defining and implementing their own conceptions of human rights. Ironically, Tanzania invoked, in July 1965, a colonial-era Preventive Detention Act to justify the detention of about 126 people on alleged espionage activities.[58] Cameroon's new leader Amadou Ahidjo used similar methods after independence in 1960 to destroy all political opposition to his government. Preventive detention, censorship of the press, shutting down of opposition newspapers and imprisonments of political opponents in the name of maintaining public order became the juridical tools Cameroon's new leader amassed to crush civil and political rights in the new nation.[59]

Certainly, the universalist ethos in which the first generation of African nationalists had understood human rights gave way to self-serving appeals to 'national sovereignty' and African cultural uniqueness. In many cases, this particularist notion of human rights served two key purposes, among others. First, it provided a perverted basis for holding on to political power. Second, it served as a means of deflecting international criticism of the creeping authoritarianism in the newly independent nations of Africa.[60] The era of 'Preventive Detention' (the incarceration of political opponents without trial) in early postcolonial Africa (late 1950s and the end of the 1960s), was soon followed by the period of military coups, extrajudicial killings, and more violations of human rights (post-1970). As Claude E. Welch, Jr, has noted, 'between 1965 and 1980' the continent of Africa experienced '75 successful seizures of power'.[61] Some of the most abhorrent human rights abuses, including summary executions of people in postcolonial Africa, took place in Uganda, Equatorial Guinea, Ethiopia, and Ghana, under military regimes, in the 1970s and 1980s.[62] Between 1977 and 1978, the new military government in Ethiopia arrested, tortured, and killed a wide range of civilians in the government's infamous Red Terror campaign of murder of alleged political subversives.[63] In Ghana, in 1979, Flight Lieutenant Jerry Rawlings's Armed Forces Revolutionary Council (AFRC), that had also seized power in a military coup, followed the Ethiopian example by summarily executing three former heads of state.[64] The AFRC's human rights abuses, and those of Rawlings's second coup-based Provisional National Defence Council (PNDC) military administration of the 1980s, featured the humiliating stripping and torture of imprisoned people, extra-judicial executions, and harrowing assaults on the dignity of Ghanaians reminiscent of the treatment of colonial subjects in the colonial era.[65] This catalogue of infringements on human dignity is by no means exhaustive on a continent that also witnessed harrowing atrocities, including genocide, committed in the context of wars in Liberia, Sierra Leone, Sudan, the Democratic Republic of Congo, Rwanda and the Central African Republic, to mention but a few, between the 1990s and the present.[66] Wiredu is therefore correct in observing that 'apart from the vexatious case of apartheid, the encroachment on human rights in postcolonial Africa has come from African governments'.[67] While the requirements of national liberation and rapid postcolonial economic emancipation could partially explain some of these authoritarian curtailments of human rights, they cannot adequately justify them. Postcolonial Africa's paradoxical embrace of human rights is, perhaps, best illustrated by the presence of 'few human rights NGOs [non-governmental organizations]', and, therefore, fewer human rights advocates, on a continent whose history has been forged in the furnace of human rights atrocities.[68]

## HUMAN RIGHTS AND THEIR DISCONTENTS IN AFRICA TODAY

The end of the 1990s, and the beginning of a new century further exposed postcolonial Africa's complicated dalliance with human rights. The self-serving appeals to African culture and identity as the refuge for human rights discussions coincided with the post-1970 drift towards dictatorial military and civilian regimes and their opposition to criticisms by Western governments and foreign NGOs of the human rights record of African governments.[69] Today, in contemporary Africa, human rights have become the means through which governments and the public debate with the industrialized West on moral values. Nowhere has this become much more evident than on discussions relating to sexuality.[70] Yet, it is one of contemporary Africa's distinguishing accomplishments in human rights values (democratization) that has created and also limited the political and social spaces for discussions of rights for sexual minorities.[71] Human rights discourse that came in the wake of democratization in Africa, after 1990, have reignited the debate over the autonomy of the individual in contemporary Africa. Amid this progress, there still exist, in some parts of Africa, the misconstrual of human rights as an ideological cover for a Western gay rights agenda. In Uganda, Malawi, Nigeria, and Ghana, interpretations of human rights that include respect for the way that individuals wish to live their lives have come up against a popular urban and pulpit discourse about the place of sexual diversity in Africa and the rights of sexual minorities in Africa's democracies. Central to that discourse is the idea that no social order (that is the stability of society through the absence of anarchy) can endure when individuals and groups are permitted to do what they wish; that unrestrained autonomy in all matters of human conduct is a form of moral license, deviance, or perversion that can threaten the very social fabric that nations exist to build.

Certainly, integration of human rights principles into national constitutions and affirmations of support for them became, initially, the criteria of postcolonial nationhood. Today, opposition to human rights and the misconstrual of them as Western neo-colonial millstones have cast a gloomy shadow on how human rights are discussed and pursued in some parts of Africa. Perhaps the fairest assessment of contemporary Africa's complicated history of human rights observance is to underscore not only the continent's rhetorical embrace of human rights, but also its symbolic observance of them. On a more hopeful note, the African Union's 'resolution' in 2004 (on the tenth anniversary of the genocide in Rwanda) to build a 'continental human rights memorial', close to the site of its new headquarters in Addis Ababa, Ethiopia, is the boldest recognition by African leaders of the checkered record of human rights observance in postcolonial Africa. The human rights memorial idea aims at addressing some disturbing ironies and some lingering memories in African history. The objectives of the envisioned memorial are 'to honor the memory and dignity of those Africans who perished in genocide and human rights violations ...' on African soil, and 'to educate young Africans' about these atrocities in the hope that they will 'denounce and confront human rights crimes' in the future.[72] A human rights memorial is also projected to memorialize those who resisted apartheid, genocide, and other human rights abuses on the continent.

The necessity for such a human rights memorial is also the result of an instructive irony. The 'new headquarters' of the African Union, in the Ethiopian capital, is located on the grounds of 'the notorious Alem Bekagn [Maximum Security] Prison'. It was here that, in 1937, the Italian fascist war criminal General Rodolfo Graziani tortured and killed thousands of Ethiopians during the Italian occupation of Ethiopia before the outbreak of the Second World War. It was also the place that, in 1977–1978, Ethiopia's authoritarian military government under Colonel Mengistu Haile Mariam tortured and killed tens of thousands of Ethiopians during the regime's infamous Red Terror campaign of murder of suspected political opponents. This irony was not lost on Ethiopia's late President Meles Zenawi, who led the liberation movement that helped to overthrow the Mengistu regime in 1993. President Meles reportedly noted the irony that the new Pan-African headquarters and conference center symbolizing 'hope for a brighter future' was also, for many years, 'the site of despair, doom, and death in his speech in January 2012 to inaugurate the new AU headquarters'.[73] Advocates for an African Union Human Rights Memorial (AUHRM) hope that it will 'inspire ... emergent generations of Africans ... to resist any infringement on the fundamental human rights of Africans, especially infringements through the agency or complicity of African states and leaders as well as through the misdeeds of militant, politicized faiths that have taken root in Africa'.[74]

## CONCLUSION

The post-Second World War global human rights revolution witnessed two similar revolutions in Africa. First, the ingenious appropriation of human rights ideas by African nationalists as a rhetorical critique of colonialism's human rights infractions. Second, textual affirmations of the need for human rights observance in the new nations of Africa as emblems of modern nationhood. However, the contradictions of postcolonial Africa's paradoxical embrace of human rights as an organizing principle too soon became evident. Awareness in Africa of Nazi and colonial atrocities had made the rights and dignity of oppressed groups the subject of human rights laws and discussions.

That reality had a catalytic effect on the transition from colonial statehood to postcolonial nationhood in Africa. Today, the unyielding chorus in urban and elite circles in many nations in Africa is that the continent's priority should be on 'economic development' rather than on 'human rights' while, at the highest levels of continental diplomacy, the idea of a human rights memorial has gained symbolic attention. It is, therefore, apt to end this chapter with the instructive thoughts of the Cameroonian opposition leader Bebey-Eyidi, victim of Amadou Ahidjo's political repression, on what political independence should mean for Africa:

> Wouldn't it be normal for the liberated African countries to prove to the world that their liberation engenders a complete restoration of the personhood and dignity of African mankind? It is right to work to accelerate economic development. But of what good would the greatest wealth be for us if it did not have as its foundation and its purpose the person worthy of being called human?[75]

Perhaps the envisioned African Union Human Rights Memorial might stand as an eternal monument to the admonition and also aspiration embodied in Bebey-Eyidi's thoughts.

## Notes

1. For detailed examination of these major debates in human rights literature, see: Abdullahi Ahmed An-Na'im and Francis M. Deng, eds., *Human Rights in Africa: Cross-Cultural Perspectives* (Washington, DC: The Brookings Institution, 1990); Makau Mutua, *Human Rights: A Political and Cultural Critique* (Philadelphia: University of Pennsylvania Press, 2002), especially Introduction and chap. 1; Peter N. Stearns, *Human Rights in World History* (New York: Routledge, 2012); Kwasi Wiredu, *Cultural Universals and Particulars: An African Perspective* (Bloomington, IN: Indiana University Press, 1996); Michael Ignatieff, *Human Rights as Politics and Idolatry*, ed. Amy Gutman (Princeton, NJ: Princeton University Press, 2001); and Michael Freeman, *Human Rights* (Malden, MA: Polity Press, 2002). This chapter also draws upon ideas and analyses in a position paper on Human Rights I wrote in 2015 on behalf of the International Institute for the Advanced Study of Cultures, Institutions, and Economic Enterprise (IIAS), a think-tank in Ghana. For that position paper, see "Human Rights as a Global Conversation on Human Dignity," http://www.interias.org.gh/sites/default/files/Position%20Paper/IIASPositionPaperHumanRights.pdf.
2. Kwasi Wiredu, *Cultural Universals and Particulars: An African Perspective* (Bloomington, IN: Indiana University Press, 1996), 157.
3. Michael Freeman, *Human Rights* (Malden, MA: Polity Press, 2002), 1–2.
4. Michael Ignatieff, *Human Rights as Politics and Idolatry*, ed. Amy Gutman (Princeton, NJ: Princeton University Press, 2001), 83.
5. For some analyses of this debate, see IIAS Position Paper on Human Rights, http://www.interias.org.gh/sites/default/files/Position%20Paper/IIASPositionPaperHumanRights.pdf.

6. Jack Donnelly, "Human Rights and Human Dignity: An Analytic Critique of Non-Western Conceptions of Human Rights," *The American Political Science Review* 76 (1982): 303. See also Jack Donnelly, "In Defense of the Universal Declaration Model," in Gene M. Lyons and James Mayall, ed., *International Human Rights in the 21st Century* (Lanham, MD: Rowman & Littlefield Publishers, Inc., 2003), 26. For further analyses of this approach to the discussion of the history of human rights, see Freeman, *Human Rights*, chap. 2.

7. Josiah A.M. Cobbah, "African Values and the Human Rights Debate: An African Perspective," *Human Rights Quarterly* 9 (1987): 309, 310, 320, 321, 322–23, 324–25. See also Amy Gutman's "Introduction" to Michael Ignatieff's book *Human Rights as Politics and Idolatry*, viii., and Peter N. Stearns, *Human Rights in World History*, xi, 5–8.

8. Makau Mutua, *Human Rights: A Political and Cultural Critique*, 3.

9. Ibid., 73, 77.

10. Ibid., 71.

11. Cobbah, "African Values and the Human Rights Debate," 310.

12. Ibid., 321. See also 322, 323, and Kwasi Wiredu, "An Akan Perspective on Human Rights," in *Human Rights in Africa: Cross-Cultural Perspectives*, ed. Abdullahi Ahmed An-Na'im and Francis M. Deng, 247.

13. Oritsegbubemi Anthony Owoye, "An African Conception of Human Rights?: Comments on the Challenges of Relativism," *Human Rights Review* 15 (2014): 329.

14. Ibid., 331.

15. Ibid., 330.

16. Ibid., 334–35.

17. Ibid., 338.

18. Mutua, *Human Rights*, 5.

19. Ignatieff, *Human Rights as Politics and Idolatry*, 7.

20. See IIAS Position Paper, "Human Rights as a Global Conversation on Human Dignity," http://www.interias.org.gh/sites/default/files/Position%20Paper/IIASPositionPaperHumanRights.pdf.

21. Dennis Laumann, *Colonial Africa, 1884–1994* (New York: Oxford University Press, 2013), xi.

22. See Michael A. McDonnell and A. Dirk Moses, "Raphael Lemkin as a Historian of Genocide in the Americas," in The Origins of *Genocide: Raphael Lemkin as a Historian of Mass Violence*, ed. Dominick J. Schaller and Jurgen Zimmerer (New York: Routledge, 2009), 57–58. For more information about Lemkin's association of genocide with colonialism, see Michelle Tusan, "Crimes Against Humanity: Human Rights, the British Empire and the Origins of the Response to the Armenian Genocide," *American Historical Review* (February 2014), 50.

23. Schaller and Zimmerer, eds., *The Origins of Genocide*, 5–6.

24. Tusan, "Crimes Against Humanity," 50.

25. Laumann, *Colonial Africa*, xi. See also Benjamin Madley, "From Africa to Auschwitz: How German South West Africa Incubated Ideas and Methods Adopted and Developed by the Nazis in Eastern Europe," *European History Quarterly* 35, no. 3 (2005): 429.

26. For a detailed study of colonial atrocities and infractions on the human rights of colonized peoples in Africa, see: Laumann, *Colonial Africa, 1884–1994*, chap. 3; Adam Hochschild, *King Leoplold's Ghost: A Story of Greed, Terror, and Heroism in Colonial Africa* (Boston: Houghton Mifflin Company, 1999); Caroline Elkins, *Imperial Reckoning: The Untold Story of Britain's Gulag in Kenya* (New York: Henry Holt and Company, 2005); David Anderson, *Histories of the Hanged: The Dirty War in Kenya and the End of Empire* (New York: W.W. Norton & Company, 2005): Madley, "From Africa to Auschwitz," 437, 441; and Dominik J. Schaller, "The Genocide of the Herero and Nama in German South-West Africa, 1904–1907," in *Centuries of Genocide: Essays and Eyewitness Accounts*, ed. Samuel Totten and William S. Parsons, 4th ed. (New York: Routledge 2013), 92.

27. Madley, "From Africa to Auschwitz," 430.

28. Laumann, *Colonial Africa*, 48.

29. Schaller, "The Genocide of the Herero and Nama," 92.

30. Ibid., 90.

31. Elkins, *Imperial Reckoning*, 28.

32. Ibid., 12.

33. Ibid., 14.

34. Wiredu, "An Akan Perspective on Human Rights," in *Human Rights in Africa*, ed. Ahmed An-Na'im and M. Deng, 245, 253–54. See also Cobbah, "African Values and the Human Rights Debate," 323.

35. Elkins, *Imperial Reckoning*, 32–43.

36. Ibid., 47.

37. Ibid., xv.

38. Anderson, *Histories of the Hanged*, 2.

39. Elkins, *Imperial Reckoning*, xv–xvi.

40. Madley, "From Africa to Auschwitz," 430. For a comprehensive study of human rights atrocities and genocide in King Leopold's Congo Free State, and later Belgian Congo, see Hochschild, *King Leoplold's Ghost*.

41. A. Adu Boahen, *African Perspectives on Colonialism* (Baltimore: The Johns Hopkins University Press, 1987), 108.

42. Meredith Terretta, "From Below and to the Left?: Human Rights and Liberation Politics in Africa's Postcolonial Age," *Journal of World History* 24, no. 2 (2013): 394–96. See also Jan Eckel, "Human Rights and Decolonization: New Perspectives and Open Questions," *Humanity: An International Journal of Human Rights, Humanitarianism, and Development* 1, no. 1 (Fall 2010): 113, for summaries of this difference of opinion.

43. Elkins, *Imperial Reckoning*, 47.

44. Terretta, "From Below and to the Left," 394–95.

45. Elkins, *Imperial Reckoning*, 45.

46. Terretta, "From Below and to the Left," 396. See also Tusan, "Crimes Against Humanity," 51.

47. Kwame Nkrumah, *Ghana: The Autobiography of Kwame Nkrumah* (New York: International Publishers, 1971), 184. This book was first published in London, UK, in 1957, by Thomas Nelson & Sons Ltd.

48. Quoted in Laumann, *Colonial Africa*, 62.

49. Ibid., 62.
50. Ibid.
51. Eckel, "Human Rights and Decolonization," 116.
52. Ibid., 120.
53. Ibid.
54. Ibid.
55. African (Banjul) Charter on Human and Peoples' Rights (Adopted 27 June 1981, OAU Doc. CAB/LEG/67/3 rev. 5, 21. L.L.M. 58 (1982), entered into force 21 October 1986, at http://www.achpr.org/files/instruments/achpr/banjul_charter.pdf. See also IIAS Position Paper on "Human Rights," http://www.interias.org.gh/sites/default/files/Position%20Paper/IIASPositionPaperHumanRights.pdf.
56. Wiredu, "An Akan Perspective on Human Rights," 256. See also Claude E. Welch, Jr., "Human Rights NGOs and the Rule of Law in Africa," *Journal of Human Rights* 2, no. 3 (2003): 318.
57. Terretta, "From Below and to the Left?," 398.
58. Ibid., 401.
59. Ibid., 413.
60. Ibid., 398.
61. Claude E. Welch, Jr., "Human Rights NGOs and the Rule of Law in Africa," *Journal of Human Rights* 2, no. 3 (2003): 318.
62. Eckel, "Human Rights and Decolonization," 121.
63. Ethiopian Red Terror Documentation & Research Center (edited by Anne Louise Mahoney), *Documenting the Red Terror: Bearing Witness to Ethiopia's Lost Generation* (Ottawa: ERTDRC North America, Inc., 2012), chaps. 1 and 3.
64. See Jeff Haynes, "Human Rights and Democracy in Ghana: The Record of the Rawlings Regime," *African Affairs* 90 (1991): 408.
65. See Mike Ocquaye, "Human Rights and the Transition to Democracy under the PNDC in Ghana," *Human Rights Quarterly* 17 (1995): 563–64.
66. For a detailed discussion of war and its effects on human dignity in Liberia, Sierra Leone, and the Democratic Republic of the Congo, see William Reno, *Warlord Politics and African States* (Boulder, CO: Lynne Rienner Publishers, 1998).
67. Wiredu, "An African Perspective on Human Rights," 260.
68. Welch, Jr., "Human Rights NGOs and the Rule of Law in Africa," 321.
69. Eckel, "Human Rights and Decolonization," 122.
70. For more analyses of this aspect of human rights discourse in contemporary Africa, see Edward Kissi, "Obligation to Prevent: (O2P): Proposal for enhanced community approach to genocide prevention in Africa," *African Security Review* 25, no. 3 (September 2016): 249–50; Alicia C. Decker and Andrea L. Arrington, *Africanizing Democracies, 1980–Present* (New York: Oxford University Press, 2015), 56, 70–71.
71. Decker and Arrington, *Africanizing Democracies*, 70. See also: Ronald Louw, "Advancing Human Rights Through Constitutional Protection for Gays and Lesbians in South Africa," http://www.haworthpress.com/web/JH; Kristen Cheney, "Locating Neocolonialism, "Tradition," and Human Rights in

Uganda's Gay Death Penalty," ASR Forum, *African Studies Review* 55, no. 2 (2012): 78–79.

72. The intent of the African Union Human Rights Memorial is outlined in the "Executive Summary" and "Foreword" of the *African Union Human Rights Memorial Project Report on In-Country Consultations 2013*, written by Professor Andreas Eshete, Chair of the Interim Board of the AUHRM, in July 2014. This is a primary document that is not widely distributed. For a published version of this report, see Justice Africa [a human rights NGO], "African Union Human Rights Memorial Project for Dignity, Rights and an End to Atrocities," 2014, www.justiceafrica.org. See especially 1–2, 9.

73. Justice Africa, "African Union Human Rights Memorial Project for Dignity, Rights and an End to Atrocities," 1. www.justiceafrica.org.

74. Ibid.

75. Terretta, "From Below and to the Left?" 414.

## BIBLIOGRAPHY

Anderson, David. *Histories of the Hanged: The Dirty War in Kenya and the End of Empire*. New York: W.W. Norton & Company, 2005.

An-Na'im, Abdullahi Ahmed, and Francis M. Deng, eds. *Human Rights in Africa: Cross-Cultural Perspectives*. Washington, DC: The Brookings Institution, 1990.

Boahen, Adu A. *African Perspectives on Colonialism*. Baltimore: The Johns Hopkins University Press, 1987.

Cheney, Kristen. "Locating Neocolonialism, "Tradition," and Human Rights in Uganda's Gay Death Penalty." ASR Forum, *African Studies Review* 55, no. 2 (2012): 77–95.

Cobbah, Josiah A.M. "African Values and the Human Rights Debate: An African Perspective." *Human Rights Quarterly* 9 (1987): 309–31.

Decker, Alicia C., and Andrea L. Arrington. *Africanizing Democracies, 1980-present*. New York: Oxford University Press, 2015.

Donnelly, Jack. "Human Rights and Human Dignity: An Analytic Critique of Non-Western Conceptions of Human Rights." *The American Political Science Review* 76 (1982): 303–16.

———. "In Defense of the Universal Declaration Model." In *International Human Rights in the 21st Century*, edited by Gene M. Lyons and James Mayall Lanham, MD: Rowman & Littlefield Publishers, Inc., 2003.

Eckel, Jan. "Human Rights and Decolonization: New Perspectives and Open Questions." *Humanity: An International Journal of Human Rights, Humanitarianism, and Development* 1, no. 1 (Fall 2010): 111–35.

Elkins, Caroline. *Imperial Reckoning: The Untold Story of Britain's Gulag in Kenya*. New York: Henry Holt and Company, 2005.

Ethiopian Red Terror Documentation & Research Center (edited by Anne Louise Mahoney). *Documenting the Red Terror: Bearing Witness to Ethiopia's Lost Generation*. Ottawa: ERTDRC North America, Inc., 2012.

Freeman, Michael. *Human Rights*. Malden, MA: Polity Press, 2002.

Haynes, Jeff. "Human Rights and Democracy in Ghana: The Record of the Rawlings Regime." *African Affairs* 90, no. 360 (1991): 407–25.

Hochschild, Adam. *King Leoplold's Ghost: A Story of Greed, Terror, and Heroism in Colonial Africa*. Boston: Houghton Mifflin Company, 1999.

Ignatieff, Michael. *Human Rights as Politics and Idolatry* edited by Amy Gutman. Princeton, NJ: Princeton University Press, 2001.

International Institute for the Advanced Study of Cultures, Institutions, and Economic Enterprise (IIAS). "Human Rights as a Global Conversation on Human Dignity," http://www.interias.org.gh/sites/default/files/Position%20Paper/IIASPosition PaperHumanRights.pdf.

Justice Africa [A Human Rights NGO]. "African Union Human Rights Memorial Project for Dignity, Rights and an End to Atrocities," at www.justiceafrica.org.

Kissi, Edward. "Obligation to Prevent: (O2P): Proposal for Enhanced Community Approach to Genocide Prevention in Africa," *African Security Review* 25, no. 3 (September 2016): 242–57.

Laumann, Dennis. *Colonial Africa, 1884–1994*. New York: Oxford University Press, 2013.

Luow, Ronald. "Advancing Human Rights Through Constitutional Protection for Gays and Lesbians in South Africa." In *Sexuality and Human Rights: A Global Overview*, 141–62. At http://www.haworthpress.com/web/JH.

Madley, Benjamin. "From Africa to Auschwitz: How German South West Africa Incubated Ideas and Methods Adopted and Developed by the Nazis in Eastern Europe." *European History Quarterly* 35, no. 3 (2005): 429–64.

McDonnell, Michael A., and A. Dirk Moses. "Raphael Lemkin as a Historian of Genocide in the Americas." In *The Origins of Genocide: Raphael Lemkin as a Historian of Mass Violence*, edited by Dominick J. Schaller and Jurgen Zimmerer. New York: Routledge, 2009.

Mutua, Makau. *Human Rights: A Political and Cultural Critique*. Philadelphia: University of Pennsylvania Press, 2002.

Nkrumah, Kwame. *Ghana: The Autobiography of Kwame Nkrumah*. New York: International Publishers, 1971.

Ocquaye, Mike. "Human Rights and the Transition to Democracy under the PNDC in Ghana." *Human Rights Quarterly* 17 (1995): 556–73.

Organization of African Unity. "African (Banjul) Charter on Human and Peoples' Rights" (Adopted 27 June 1981, OAU Doc. CAB/LEG/67/3 rev. 5, 21. L.L.M. 58 (1982), http://www.achpr.org/files/instruments/achpr/banjul_charter.pdf.

Owoye, Oritsegbubemi A. "An African Conception of Human Rights?: Comments on the Challenges of Relativism." *Human Rights Review* 15 (2014): 329–47.

Reno, William. *Warlord Politics and African States*. Boulder, CO: Lynne Rienner Publishers, 1998.

Schaller, Dominik J. "The Genocide of the Herero and Nama in German South-West Africa, 1904–1907." In *Centuries of Genocide: Essays and Eyewitness Accounts*, 4th ed., edited by Samuel Totten and William S. Parsons. New York: Routledge, 2013.

Stearns, Peter N. *Human Rights in World History*. New York: Routledge, 2012.

Terretta, Meredith. "From Below and to the Left?: Human Rights and Liberation Politics in Africa's Postcolonial Age." *Journal of World History* 24, no. 2 (2013): 389–416.

Tusan, Michelle. "Crimes Against Humanity: Human Rights, the British Empire and the Origins of the Response to the Armenian Genocide." *American Historical Review* (February 2014): 47–77.

Welch, Claude E. Jr. "Human Rights NGOs and the Rule of Law in Africa." *Journal of Human Rights* 2, no. 3 (2003): 315–27.

Wiredu, Kwasi. "An Akan Perspective on Human Rights." In *Human Rights in Africa: Cross-Cultural Perspectives*, edited by Abdullahi Ahmed An-Na'im, et al. Washington, DC: The Brookings Institution, 1990.

———. *Cultural Universals and Particulars: An African Perspective*. Bloomington, IN: Indiana University Press, 1996.

# CHAPTER 43

# Education in Postcolonial Africa

*Peter Otiato Ojiambo*

## INTRODUCTION

The development of education in postcolonial Africa has witnessed tremendous expansion at all levels despite mixed economic growth in various African countries and diminishing educational returns. The last six decades have seen various African countries undertake several educational reforms and experimentations with the aim of addressing their social, political, and economic needs. Some of these reforms and experiments have been internally led, and some have been externally steered. In order to understand the complex educational developments, reforms, and experiments that have taken place in Africa in the postcolonial period, their successes and challenges, it is vital to examine the historical happenings that have influenced and shaped the process. Drawing from my educational biographical research work in Kenya, where I have studied Kenya's educational development in the postcolonial period using historical frames, this chapter seeks to examine how the development of education in Africa has been influenced by its historical events, the progress that has been made, challenges that have been witnessed, and what the future holds.

Given the contextual educational differences that exist among the 55 African countries that are rooted in their colonial and postcolonial experiences, this chapter focuses mainly on Sub-Saharan African (SSA) countries. In this regard, the ideas advanced in this chapter must be regarded as broad generalizations and tentative hypotheses to be studied critically by the reader in the light of his/her personal knowledge as he/she seeks to relate them to

P.O. Ojiambo (✉)
University of Kansas, Lawrence, KS, USA

© The Author(s) 2018
M.S. Shanguhyia and T. Falola (eds.),
*The Palgrave Handbook of African Colonial and Postcolonial History*,
https://doi.org/10.1057/978-1-137-59426-6_43

particular SSA countries and the African continent in general. Having said this, however, it is vital to note that there are indeed several educational characteristics that are common to most SSA countries, sufficient to justify the approach this chapter takes and the conclusions it makes. Specifically, this chapter examines: educational trends in postcolonial Africa; education in postcolonial Kenya; African-centered educational biographies and their contributions to the understanding of Africa and its historical developments in the postcolonial period; and what the future holds for education in Africa.

## SURVEY OF EDUCATIONAL TRENDS IN POSTCOLONIAL AFRICA

### Educational Trends 1960s to 1980s, External Influences and Frameworks

Research on education in postcolonial Africa has received minimal scholarship. Peter Kallaway observes that research on the history of education is in a dire state. He posits that:

> Attempts to convene panels on postcolonial education in Africa at various educational conferences in recent years have demonstrated that only a few young scholars are committed to this important field of research. This has undermined the capacity to understand the roots of African educational problems and possible solutions to them.[1]

Most of the written works on education on the African continent in the postcolonial period illustrate that much of the African educational historiography is dominated by the seminal studies of the formal history of colonial education systems for particular colonies or regions up to the independence period. There is very little in-depth work on the history of education in the post-independence era, and even less in the way of comparative studies between African national educational systems and other Third World regions. Even within the British, French, Portuguese, Spanish colonial, and postcolonial contexts, comparisons between educational policies in Africa and other parts of the world (for instance, India in the case of the British) are lacking. Therefore, this presents a challenge for educational researchers that is of utmost importance for a deeper understanding of the roots of African educational reforms and policies and their correlation to societal reconstruction and change process, something that would make a vital contribution to the solution of the numerous intractable problems currently facing modern African education.[2] It is against this backdrop of the dearth of scholarship on education in postcolonial Africa that this chapter is framed.

In postcolonial Africa, no other field of national development has invited as much criticism, scrutiny, and experimentation, or needed such constant innovation and reinvigoration, as its educational systems. Affirming this, Simeon Ominde, one of the pioneer Kenyan educators, writes that 'indeed such frequent reforms and restructuring have raised the fear that African nations may be missing the more difficult challenge of understanding education as an essential dynamic area of human activity and its role in the societal reconstruction process'.[3] It is in this context and setting of thought that this chapter examines the framework of educational development and change in Africa in the postcolonial period, its milestones, challenges, and future prospects.

In the first decade after independence, many African countries placed considerable importance on the role of education in promoting social, political, and economic development. The education system was expected to fulfill two main objectives: the technical and the social objective.[4] The technical objective was concerned more with providing the future manpower with requisite skills and knowledge. The social objective on the other hand was more concerned with the inculcation of values that could enrich people's lives and maintain a cohesive society. Summing up the educational focus and reforms of most African nations in the first post-independence decade, Abdelhag Rharade states:

> The 1960s can be justly described as the decade of great expectations, and optimism about the developmental potential of education in Africa. It began with the historic 1960 Ashby Report on education in Nigeria and the equally widely quoted 1961 Addis Ababa conference of African Ministers of Education. Before the decade was over some 40 manpower education plans had been published, not to mention the reports of a host of commissions of inquiry and academic studies. In the first five years alone, school enrolment in Africa rose by almost a half; the average proportion of the government budget spent on education jumped from one-seventh to over one-sixth—the highest for any continent except North America—and the proportion of national income devoted to education increased from 3 percent to 4.3 per cent, exceeded only by Europe.[5]

Education in Africa during the first decade of independence was shaped by several external forces. First was the *Report of the Conference of African States on the Development of Education in Africa* that was held in Addis Ababa in May 1961, under the joint sponsorship of UNESCO and the United Nations Economic Commission for Africa (ECA). The central aim of this conference was to provide a forum for African states to prioritize educational needs that could promote their economic, political, and social needs. Emphasis was placed on educational reforms and training that could produce the required manpower essential for the new, independent African nations.[6] Much emphasis in educational development during this period was given to secondary and postsecondary education rather than universal primary education. Effecting the proposal required massive national budgetary allocations and external aid from UNESCO, several developed nations, and non-governmental bodies. In line with the resolution of the conference, African ministers of education met in Paris in March 1962 to discuss further the implementation of the Addis Ababa plan. The meeting underscored the need to set up firm structures in African countries.

The African educational framework for higher education during this period was also built on *The Tananarive Conference on the Development of Higher Education in Africa* deliberations that were held in September 1962 under the leadership of UNESCO and the ECA as a follow-up to the Paris meeting. The conference adopted the Addis Ababa Conference plan in estimating the qualitative and quantitative educational changes necessary to meet the manpower requirements of African nations. It established targets in higher education and made recommendations for the overall planning, financing, curriculum, and staffing of higher institutions in Africa. In addition, it also indicated the responsibility of higher educational institutions in the advancement of development of African nations in all spheres. The report recommended high enrolments of students in science, technology, and agricultural courses. Cooperation among African countries and aid from external agencies were seen as vital to the future development of the continent.[7]

The Tananarive Conference was followed by a Kinshasa meeting in February and March of 1963. The Kinshasa meeting reaffirmed the resolutions of the Paris and Tananarive meetings. It advocated for the provision of more funds from UNESCO and other agencies to help African nations meet their educational mandates and expenditures. Another conference held during this early period that spearheaded education in Africa was the *Abidjan Regional Conference on the Planning and Organization of Literacy Programs* of March 1964. It reviewed educational regional targets that were set up at the Addis Ababa, Tananarive and Kinshasa conferences. It accentuated the need for African countries to use targets of these conferences as a guide to their educational expansion and future development depending on their resources and human-resource capabilities. It put emphasis on the role of education in the economic and social progress of African rural communities. It encouraged the establishment of more institutions of higher learning. This conference was followed by two central conferences: *The Teheran Conference of September 1965*, that emphasized adult literacy; and *The Lagos Conference on the Organization of Research and Training in Africa in Relation to Study, Conservation and Utilization of Natural Resources*, that was held in July 1964. These two conferences addressed the organization and financing of scientific and technical training in African nations to enable them to utilize their natural resources and human personnel for industrialization purposes.

These conferences set the stage for educational development in Africa and influenced the educational frameworks and strategies of most African nations in their first and second decades. In line with the Addis Ababa Conference, the orientation of African education shifted towards training Africans to fill high-level positions in the public and private sectors. Although other aspects of education were considered, this was to a minimal extent. In order to achieve this, priority was put on secondary and higher education. To meet public demand pertaining to more manpower development, many African nations began to devote large portions of their national budgets to education.

For instance, in Ghana's Second Development Plan (1959–1964), projected investment in education was £27.8 million, 11.4% of the total expenditure; this later rose to £17.3 million, 13.4% of the budget in 1961–1962 recurrent expenditure. In Nigeria's six-year Educational Plan, £32.8 million, three-fifths of the federal expenditure on education, was earmarked for higher education. In Tanzania (mainland) the Three-Year Plan proposed that a high proportion of the central government budget available for education be devoted to secondary school expansion. Between 1961 and 1962, £30.5 million was spent on education, 16.5% of the national budget.[8] Similar plans were made in the French-speaking countries. Mark Bray, Peter Clarke, and David Stephens postulate that 'there were no marked differences between the Anglophone and the Francophone countries regarding the problem of manpower development during this period and large investments were put in the education sector'.[9] Due to these massive investments in education in the postcolonial period, primary-school enrolments rose from 12 million in 1965 to 50 million in 1983, and the number of students in higher education increased from 21,000 in 1960 to 430,000 in 1983.[10]

During the first two decades, the rate of education expansion within African schools outstripped the possibilities for employment that once existed for school-leavers. New job creation proved difficult, slow, and expensive. Nevertheless, the kind of employment which school-leavers and particularly their parents expected remained constant; the desire for wage-earning employment, especially pertaining to white-collar employment. The quest for modern employment of this nature led to considerable migration of young people from rural to urban areas. In the late 1960s, African governments began questioning the continued rapid expansion of formal educational systems that had minimal societal returns. It was clear during this period that the small, modern sector of the economy had been Africanized much more rapidly than most educational observers had forecasted, and jobs had already become scarce. The consequent frustration among the youth who had expected that more years of formal secondary education would provide automatic access to wage employment and a better life led to serious doubts among African leaders about the direction education in their various countries was expected to take in the second decade. It was clear to most of them that the postcolonial educational systems that were inherited from the colonial regimes were too academic and examination-centered, and not tailored to the needs of rural African societies.

It is important to note that Africa's educational developments in the 1960s conformed to United Nations strategies for development in Third World countries. The so-called First Development Decade of the 1960s accentuated the importance of education in the production of highly skilled manpower and the larger national development. By the end of the First Development Decade, educational results, though quantitatively impressive, were unsatisfactory. The unemployment problem was crucial in many African countries.

This prompted the United Nations resolution on the strategies of the Second Development Decade. The Second Development Decade placed greater emphasis on social factors in development, the reduction of social imbalances, and structural change in education and basic education. The *UNESCO General Conference of 1970*, that was held during this period, formulated a set of recommendations which placed emphasis on the need for long-term educational reforms and approaches that could mitigate unemployment challenges and critical societal needs of African nations. To achieve this, the *International Commission on Educational Development* was established. Its report, *Learning To Be*, became the seminal guide on the importance of universal education for African development.

Education policy evolution in various African national educational systems in the first two decades must be interpreted in the context of funding constraints and the relative economic frailties of most African states during this period, rather than their rhetoric of nation building, democratization, community development, or manpower development. In the heady atmosphere of independence there was a danger of overloading African schools with tasks of transformation beyond their capacity to deliver, and then blaming them for the failure. The ambiguity and quagmire of the situation lay in the pressing desire for change and for the expansion of the state education systems to offer mass education to all citizens while at the same time dealing with the demand for the best that the traditional colonial system of secondary education had offered in terms of a literary education. The new political leaders and educated elites, like the reforming missionaries or colonial officials before them, soon discovered that there were limits to the kinds of educational innovation possibilities that could be undertaken, given the high demand for formal education. Attempts to introduce a richer and innovative curriculum that could marry indigenous education with vocational and technical programs in the 1970s did not garner much support.[11]

It is in this vein that Daniel Sifuna asserts that it is important to examine the dramatic rhetoric of mass education for democracy that was prevalent in many African nations in the first decade-and-a-half of independence within the context of the perception by communities, parents, and students that a formal curriculum opened the door to the formal job market, especially in the new bureaucracy that was being established at the time.[12] This weighed the balance of education reform in favor of existing structures, which emphasized formal education and continuity with earlier perceptions of colonial schooling rather than contributing to the radical innovation that was required at the time and the national and global trends that demanded moving away from colonial educational postulations, theoretical frameworks, and approaches. There was an urgent need for more diversity and innovation in educational programs to enable them to address their critical societal needs. Many of the educational plans associated with the United Nations First Development Decade (1961–1971) can thus be interpreted as having been strong on rhetoric, hopes, and beliefs about the transformative power of education to African nations, but weak on a detailed historical educational analysis of the realities in most African nations in the postcolonial period that required a comprehensive and robust education system that could spearhead national development.[13]

### World Bank and International Monetary Fund Impact on African Education in the 1980s–2000s

From the end of the 1980s to the early 2000s an examination of national educational systems in several African nations showed that they were heavily influenced by the Structural Adjustment Programs (SAPs) of the World Bank (WB), International Monetary Fund (IMF), and UNESCO. Peter Kallaway states that:

> By the end of the 'eighties the milestone report of the WB on *Education in Sub-Saharan Africa* (1988) signaled a new phase in African education that was heavily influenced by neo-liberal policies of the West that flowed from major economic changes in the world system that attempted to steer away from the welfarism focus of education that had emanated from the post-War era towards an education that could meet the demands of the new emerging global economic order that was dominated and driven by the new market demands.[14]

This report, together with Philip Coombs's *The World Crisis in Education* (1985) and the 1990 report for the Jomtien conference on a sustained campaign for *Education for All* (EFA), signaled a 'deterioration of educational services' in various African countries within the 1960s, 1970s, and 1980s that was evidenced in enrolment stagnation, poor-quality schooling, non-completion, and gender bias among other educational challenges. These weaknesses were attributed to a combination of factors, principally unprecedented population growth, a context of weak political and administrative institutions, and mounting fiscal austerity. In this context, the WB's influence on Third World policy development, especially on the African continent, was pervasive in the 1980–2000s era. A key element of African educational policy during this period was 'a redefinition of the notion of equity in education that was marked with a dramatic shift from government responsibility for delivery of quality equal education for all, to increasing emphasis on the responsibility of parents, community, and private control in the education sector'.[15] This emphasized 'cost recovery', or the freedom to purchase quality education in the marketplace for those who could afford it. The overall effect was to make it increasingly difficult for minority groups such as the urban poor, rural youth, minority ethnic groups, or women to access quality education, especially at the secondary and tertiary levels. These policies, developed in an era of financial stringency and fragile African economies, gave rise to a range of responses to address the consequent fall in student enrolments, equity, physical facilities, and quality areas through new programs and approaches, and the increasing agency and NGO intervention.[16]

Through the SAPs, African governments were urged to seek to 'improve efficiency' through 'adjustment, revitalization and selective expansion' of their education sectors.[17] The WB recommended that, in order to lower the cost of mass education, African governments be required to introduce 'user charges' and cost-recovery or cost-sharing arrangements by passing a substantial amount of the responsibility for schooling to parents and communities and allowing more scope and room for the privatization of education. Several recommendations were made for selective expansion, particularly regarding Universal Primary Education that had been begun in the 1960s and later developed in the 1970s and 1980s. Vocational education in schools was seen as expensive and often ineffective in creating jobs and employment opportunities. While there was an emphasis on improving quality and academic standards, the climate of economic austerity along with poor and fragile economies in most African nations left little room for maneuver and innovation. The role of donors in effecting SAPs was identified as central to promoting equity and 'African nations catch-up' with other developing nations.[18] The research of the WB and IMF policy prescriptions was often controversial and the source of national resentment and suffering of many poor African parents who could not afford the new costs of education because the insights and opinions of the WB and IMF were not based on ordinary research findings and actual economic conditions within African nations but were one significant part of a series of conditions and negotiations about loans to education in the developing world that entailed complex and exorbitant repayment mechanisms. These recommendations were often a product of reports by foreign experts who had minimal knowledge of African conditions and realities.[19] The question of external aid to education in Africa remained controversial during this period and has remained so to date, as attempts to restructure African education systems more often have experienced ambiguous objectives, visions, implementation, and learning outcomes.

## ALTERNATIVE FORMS OF EDUCATION

Beyond the internal and external forces that have shaped education development in postcolonial Africa, there have been a variety of educational initiatives that have been undertaken by several African governments during this period to complement their formal education. These alternative forms of education have paralleled the global-education, radical reform movements of the 1960s, 1970s, 1980s, and 1990s, for instance: the Deschooling Movement associated with Illich, Goodman, and Kohl in the USA; Student Rebellions of the 1960s; the Chinese Cultural Revolution; the Cuban Revolution; and the challenges set by Paulo Freire in his *Pedagogy of the Oppressed* in Latin America, and by Mikhail Gorbachev's *glasnost* and *perestroika* tenets in the USSR of the 1990s, among others.[20] These alternative forms of education have also in part been influenced by the works of Frantz Fanon, Albert Memmi, Mwalimu Julius Nyerere and other scholars who have provided a trenchant critique of the African nationalists' endeavors on the role of education in shaping

Africa's social, political, and economic structures in the post-independence period.[21] Several terms have been used to describe some of these alternative forms of education, namely: 'basic/fundamental education', 'lifelong education', 'recurrent education', and 'continuing education', among others. Some of these alternative forms of education have fallen under the general umbrella of 'non-formal education' and 'mass education'. Alternative forms of education have a substantial history on the African continent in the postcolonial period. They were developed because of the growing recognition by most African governments that formal education was not adequate in serving the bulk of the population, particularly in rural areas; and because there was a need for greater equity of participation in education and national development.

Alternative forms of education in Africa have taken a variety of forms. Examples in the postcolonial period include: self-development programs; rural or village polytechnics; rural education development and cooperative programs; the brigades; mass literacy programs; the National Youth Service schemes; agricultural extensions and farmer training programs; pre-employment programs and multipurpose programs.[22] *Self-development programs* were common in Ethiopia, Benin, Tanzania, São Tomé and Príncipe, Ghana, Guinea, and Zambia. They sought to promote the capacity of local communities' self-development. *Rural or village polytechnics programs* were evidenced in Kenya, Tanzania, Nigeria, Guinea, and Gambia. They strived to offer cheaper programs that were closely related to the needs of the rural villages. *Rural education development and cooperative programs* were run in Ivory Coast, Ghana, Liberia, Kenya, and Zambia. They entailed artisan, craft vocational and pre-vocational preparation programs. *The Brigades programs* were conducted in Botswana, Ghana, Kenya, Zimbabwe, Zambia, Benin, Ivory Coast, and Mozambique. They were conceived as a means of providing more appropriate forms of postprimary education and training than what was offered in conventional secondary schools. They offered both general and skill-based training. They sought to promote rural development both indirectly through training activities needed in specific areas and directly through undertaking contracts for government, local people, and organizations. Some brigades also offered *in situ* programs that were closely related to job creation. *Mass literacy programs* were conducted in Algeria, Guinea, Tanzania, Malagasy, Ethiopia, Mali, São Tomé and Príncipe, and Sudan. They provided rudimentary general literacy that was essential for national development.

Examples of *The National Youth Service schemes* in Africa included Ghana Young Pioneers, National Youth Service Corps of Nigeria, Malawi Young Pioneers, Kenya National Youth Service, and Zambia Youth Service Corps. Their purpose was to mobilize unemployed youth to undertake projects that could promote national development. They sought to inculcate in the youth an ethos that could promote national unity, a strong work ethic, and a spirit of service. They emphasized rural development. They offered courses in masonry, carpentry, motor vehicle maintenance, electrical installation and repair among others. *Agricultural extensions and farmer training programs* included young farmers' clubs, youth land settlement schemes, and cooperatives' farm learning centers. They were common in Kenya, Tanzania, Zambia, Mauritius, Lesotho, and Botswana. Similar to these programs were *animation rurale* programs in Morocco, Tunisia, Algeria, Mali, Senegal, and several other French-speaking African countries that combined agricultural extension programs with training activities.[23] Their aim was to harness the energy and resources of local communities for societal development. The *pre-employment programs* sought to service urban industry. They were mainly vocational training or industrial centers. They offered courses in motor-vehicle mechanics, furniture making, building, carpentry, and electrical installation. They were common in Ghana, Nigeria, Ivory Coast, Liberia, Kenya, Uganda, Tanzania, and Zambia. Several of their programs sought to encourage the growth of small-scale industries and self-employment. Some of their programs offered skill-upgrading courses for industry. This was evidenced in the courses that were offered by the National Vocational Training Institute in Ghana, and the Industrial Development and Vocational Improvement Centers in Kenya, Nigeria, and Ethiopia.[24] *Multi-purpose programs* were common in Kenya, Tanzania, Ghana, Nigeria, and Cameroon. Several of them were single-purpose projects. They endeavored to utilize the meager resources of various African nations. Many of their programs were determined by local communities, had great flexibility, and drew their resources from various sectors. They included literacy and school equivalency progress, youth clubs, sports, cultural programs, and guidance activities.

It is important to note that, on the whole, alternative forms of education have been attempts at providing micro-solutions to macro-problems of development in various African nations.[25] They have challenged the formal education of various African nations and proposed various kinds of interventions aimed at rural-development strategies, skills, and vocational training. Most of them have been centered on immediate production and application. They have been viewed as 'tending to be part of life, integrated with life and inseparable from it. They are designed to change society and make it self-reliant, self-sustaining. They answer to the aspirations and needs of their clients and are relevant to national goals'.[26] In some ways these alternative forms of education have reflected a range of missionary and colonial endeavors of the colonial period, and in many instances they have repeated their failures, as the formal education set in place during the colonial era has proved to be an endurable legacy in the postcolonial period. Lacking an industrial base, the lessons of the Asian Tigers regarding vocational and technical education entailed in these programs failed to attract the imagination of African governments in the 1970s, 1980s, and early 1990s. The conservative model of education in most African nations remained the high road to jobs in the formal, government, and private sector.[27]

The general experience in various alternative forms of education that have been undertaken in Africa in the postcolonial period is that many of them have been viewed as being expensive compared to formal education and that they have seldom attracted large numbers of students. It is important to note that some of them were pushed by education scholars like Illich, Reimer, and Freire who felt that efforts to reform school systems were futile and there was a need for a fresh start. This is clearly seen in the influence of Freire's literacy work in Tanzania, São Tomé and Príncipe, and Guinea. In most African countries the alternative models of education discussed above remained a second choice for the majority of students and in many cases their results were disappointing. This was attributed to many factors such as: poor instruction, lack of adequate teachers and funds, lack of appropriate teaching materials, lack of motivation for taking the programs (as many of them were seen as inferior in comparison to formal education), and lack of immediate practical benefits.[28] These educational approaches and alternative models of education that were carried out in several African countries as noted in this section were also evident in Kenya, a country on which my larger research work on Africa-centered educational biographies has focused. It is to this that I turn in the next section to illustrate some of these educational trends.

## EDUCATION IN POSTCOLONIAL KENYA

### Kenya's Educational Developments 1960–1970

In the postcolonial period, Kenya's long and bloody struggle for political independence served as a major impetus for her educational development. During the struggle for independence, the nationalists' main educational aim was to provide Africans with an education that could serve the immediate needs of the country. In 1961, when independence was imminent in most African countries, a conference on the development of education in Africa was held in Addis Ababa (Ethiopia) and Antananarire (Madagascar) in 1962. At these two conferences, representatives from all over the continent set educational priorities that sought to foster economic and social development in Africa. It was on this framework that Kenya formulated its educational policies and programs. The expansion and reform of the education system in Kenya during this period was also motivated by political pressures. Almost every politician and election manifesto leading to the independence elections called for more educational opportunities of all types, cheaper or free education, universal primary education.[29]

There were also external forces which partly contributed to the expansion of Kenyan education especially at the higher level during this period. Among the important ones was the *Report of the Conference of African States on the Development of Education in Africa*, which met in Addis Ababa in May 1961. In addition to this conference, the Kenyan government and the United Kingdom requested the International Bank for Reconstruction and Development to undertake a survey of the economic development of the country in

1961. These reports had a significant bearing on the Kenyan government's formulation of its educational policies. Their implementation in the first decade of the postcolonial period saw rapid expansion and enrolments at all levels of the Kenyan education system.[30]

Based on its colonial historical education legacy and these reports, the Kenyan government embarked on various educational policies that could advance its socio-economic development. The first undertaking was the drafting of the *Sessional Paper Number 10* in 1965. It articulated the immediate needs and goals of the nation. It saw education as a key means of alleviating the shortage of skilled manpower and creating equal economic opportunities for all Kenyans.[31] During this period, the government established five major inquiries to look into the development of education: The Kenya Education Commission (The Ominde Commission, Republic of Kenya, 1964); The National Committee on Educational Objectives and Policy (Gacathi Report, Republic of Kenya, 1979); The Presidential Working Party on the Second University (Mackay Report, Republic of Kenya, 1981); The Presidential Working Party on Education and Manpower (Kamunge Report, Republic of Kenya, 1988); and The Commission of Inquiry into the Education System of Kenya (Koech Commission, Republic of Kenya, 1999).

The Ominde Commission was the blueprint of post-independence Kenyan education. It was mandated to survey the existing educational resources and to advise the government on the formation and implementation of the required national education policies. The Commission was strongly influenced by the then existing international opinion on education and the national economic and political factors, and available publications on the importance of education in accelerating national development. These included the reports on *High Level Manpower Requirements and Resources in Kenya 1964–1970*; the *Development Plan of 1964–1970*; and *1965 Sessional Paper No.10: African Socialism and its Application to Planning in Kenya*. These publications identified a direct relationship between education, economic growth, and national development. It was on this premise that the organization of education during this period was closely linked to manpower development and labor-market demands.[32] This link led to the growth of enrolment, especially in secondary schools, university, and tertiary education, a growth that continued to be experienced in the 1980s and 1990s.

Although formal education was expanding during this period, it was not directly accompanied by appropriate economic growth. Thus, most school dropouts were left with neither jobs nor adequate training. By 1970, many secondary-school dropouts began to experience a serious unemployment crisis. Due to increased demand for higher education and the need for highly qualified manpower, the government created more acts in the 1980s geared towards the improvement of education to enable it accelerate development. There was also investment in vocational and technical secondary education. By the end of 1970, there were ten vocational secondary schools offering programs intended to provide students with skills pertaining to specific occupations. By 1970, enrolment in these schools had risen to 2,426. The Kenya Polytechnic, the epicenter of vocational and technical education training, was greatly expanded, partly with a loan from USAID and UNESCO. Courses in this area also began to be offered at Kenya Science Teachers College and Kenyatta College.

The Kenyan government and other organizations responded further to the unemployment crisis by establishing non-formal institutions with a strong vocational emphasis. The first of these institutions was the National Youth Service (NYS). This was a two-year program that linked general education with productive labor-intensive vocational instruction. Voluntary agencies, such as the National Christian Churches of Kenya, began village youth polytechnics that were small, flexible, low-cost, and localized to community needs. Other establishments that operated along the same lines were Industrial training centers, YMCAs, YWCAs, vocational and craft training centers, government youth centers, and rural training centers. A number of these institutions had small enrolments. Although they were aimed at self-employment, there was great desire for wage employment among its trainees.[33]

## KENYA'S EDUCATIONAL DEVELOPMENTS, 1970s–2000s

In broad context, Kenya's educational developments in the 1960s, conformed to the United Nations strategies for development in Third World countries. The so-called First Development Decade of the 1960s underscored the importance of education in the production of highly skilled manpower and national development. By the end of the First Development Decade, the educational results were quantitatively impressive, but were generally unsatisfactory. The unemployment problem had greatly increased within the country.[34] This prompted the United Nations resolution on the strategies of the Second Development Decade. The latter placed greater emphasis on social factors in development, the reduction of social imbalances, and structural changes. They underscored the importance of basic education and universal education. Basic education was seen as an attempt to meet the needs of substantial portions of the population that had no access to education. It was intended 'to provide a functional, flexible and low-cost education for those whom the formal system could not reach or had passed by'.[35]

The employment problem during this period was also taken up by the International Labor Organization (ILO). The ILO World Employment Program was launched in 1969. It sought to understand the causes of unemployment in selected African countries and possible remedies. Kenya was one of the selected countries. The report emphasized the need for basic, free universal education. The school curriculum was expected to be integrated in community activities. There was to be a gradual increase in the proportion of the curriculum devoted to pre-vocational subjects to cater to the interests of terminal students.[36] The 1975 commission appointed to examine Kenya's educational objectives and policies (*The Gacathi Report*) endorsed the ILO report even though it had not been implemented because of financial reasons. However, there was adoption of some of its recommendations; for instance, in 1979, the Ministry of Basic Education was established, and there was a strong push by the government on pre-vocational subjects in the formal curriculum. *The Gacathi Report* reiterated further the objectives of the Ominde Commission and underscored the role of education in shaping Kenya's national character and development. It recommended the development of vocational, technical, and practical education. In 1975, the government realized that education was not doing much to achieve its stated development objectives. The existing curriculum was viewed as being too academic, narrow, and examination-centered.[37] The rate of unemployment was growing as increasing numbers of school-leavers headed to urban centers in search of non-existent white-collar jobs. These conditions led to the formulation of the Third Development Plan of 1974/78 to address some of these challenges. According to this plan, Kenyan education was required to provide high-level, industrial, vocational, and technical skills necessary for employment and development.[38]

It is important to note that education for manpower dominated Kenya's educational strategies and plans in the 1970s as well. As earlier noted, the Development Plan for 1970–1974 had envisaged massive educational expansion at all levels of the school system, and this was endorsed in subsequent Plan documents.[39] There was expansion in University education, and the government also embarked on an ambitious program of expanding technical secondary schools. The Swedish International Development Agency (SIDA) provided aid for new workshops, equipment, support services, laboratories, and dormitories in all the 15 technical schools. Earlier in its 1975/1976 plan, the International Development Agency (IDA) of the United Nations had provided a substantial amount of equipment to the technical schools. There was also further funding from the Canadian International Development Agency (CIDA). It provided grant-in-aid of Ksh. 265 million in 1977 to build the Kenya Technical Teachers College complex and to support technical education in general. During this period, there was also massive expansion of the Egerton College for Agriculture through US aid. Additionally, the Kenyan government established a second Polytechnic in Mombasa. Further, the Japanese government started the Jomo Kenyatta College of Agriculture and Technology. During this period, Kenya was also heavily involved in fund-raising campaigns to establish *harambee* (self-help) institutes of technology that could provide secondary school-leavers with vital technological skills that were required in the labor market and for national development.[40]

In the 1980s, the government changed its policy on education because of the difficulties which were being faced by graduates of its education system at both the primary and secondary levels. Most graduates who were matriculating from these levels could still not be absorbed into the shrinking labor market as it had been in the previous decade. This prompted the government to set up a Presidential Working Party in 1981. The new education system was expected to equip students with technical, scientific, and practical knowledge vital for self and salaried employment, lifelong skills, and nation building. The Commission was also mandated to investigate the feasibility of establishing a second university that could achieve these goals. The Commission advocated a practical curriculum that would offer a wide range of employment opportunities and equitable distribution of resources. It gave rise to the current Kenyan education system, the 8-4-4.[41] An in-depth examination of the rationale for introducing the 8-4-4 system shows that it owed more to political reasons than to educational needs at the time. The system has faced numerous challenges since its inception, including lack of adequate infrastructure, trained personnel, among others. It was based on these shortfalls that the Kenyan government appointed the Commission of Inquiry into the Education System of Kenya (The Koech Commission) in 1999.

The Koech Commission was expected to make recommendations on ways to provide quality education. It emphasized the need for Kenyan education to become a ticket to national development, equality, social justice, and a better life for the individual, the community, and the nation.[42] Its proposals encompassed important societal ideals that Kenyan education was expected to offer rather than the mere reliance on the number of students who had access to education. It called for cutting-edge educational reforms, including: totally integrated quality education and training, abolition of the 8-4-4 education system and its replacement with a 7-4-2-3 system. Despite its candid report, it was never implemented because of a lack of political will.

In the postcolonial period, one concrete area that the Kenyan government has made concerted efforts to address in its education policy has been Universal Free Primary Education (UPE). It has argued that providing equal educational opportunities to all its citizens is essential for national development. These sentiments have been underscored in all of Kenya's Five-Year Development Plans from 1964 to the present. There have also been attempts since 2013 to offer free Universal Secondary Education (USE). Despite the many challenges that have been experienced in these efforts, it can be argued that Kenya's efforts to offer UPE and USE as vehicles of strong social, economic, and political developments are commendable.[43] The policy has enabled many poor students to access schooling. Within this broad educational policy framework, the expansion of learning institutions and literacy to all its citizens has been one of Kenya's greatest achievements in the education sector in the postcolonial period. This has resulted in increased participation in various societal spheres by groups that previously had little or no access to schooling, such as women and other minorities.

Since independence, the emphasis on Kenya's educational expansion has been complimented by the increasing priority accorded to programs of quality improvement in education. The Kenyan education expansion has been closely linked to its national developmental agenda and process. Close scrutiny of the educational reforms that have been undertaken in Kenya in the postcolonial period indicate that they have operated under this framework. By any standards, Kenyan educational goals as formulated in numerous reports and commissions are of high quality. Nevertheless, one wonders why they have not brought as much development to Kenya in the last five decades as envisaged. There has been, I contend, a chasm between their theory and practice. A cursory glance at schooling in Kenya today shows that educational practice suffers chronically from what Richard Dore calls the 'diploma disease'.[44] The sole criterion of Kenya's educational quality, it appears, has been high performance in national examinations. This centering of the education process on examinations has tended to obliterate its holistic function. In addition, as earlier noted, there has also been a lot of political interference in the education-reform process.

Since the centerpiece of this handbook is to highlight major themes, research trends, and interpretations that have shaped African history in both colonial and postcolonial period, and how scholars in related disciplines have contributed to the process, in the following section I discuss my research on African-centered educational biographies and its contributions to the understanding of the development of education in Kenya and Africa in general since the 1960s. In my discussion, I weave in examples from my research that speak to how historical methods have shaped my work and what the contributions of my work have been to it as well.

## African Educational Biographies and Postcolonial African History

I am an educationist with a training in educational leadership. My larger research work focuses on African-centered educational biographies. This is an area that has received minimal scholarship in both the colonial and postcolonial periods. I recognized earlier on in my graduate studies that although I am an educationist, my area of focus is interdisciplinary and borrows heavily from history. It was in this regard that I was nudged by my graduate advisor to take courses in African history to enable me ground myself in its methodological processes. In this section, I will speak to how these historical methods have enriched my research work in the last decade and greatly clarified the contributions of my work to our understanding of Africa and its larger historical happenings in various spheres in both colonial and postcolonial periods.

The term 'educational biographies' denotes works of biographical subjects who are drawn from the field of education.[45] Broadly viewed, these are individuals who have worked or work in the field of education, or who have made significant marks on it. Educational biographies draw their structures from several disciplines. One of the disciplines they draw heavily from is history, and in my case (since I examine African educators), African history has been an important portal of my work. Many historians point out several benefits of educational biographies and general biographies that have inspired my research work. Examining carefully the benefits of educational biographies, Ezekiel Adeoti posits that they lead to an in-depth understanding of the complex and fluid historical, social, political, and economic contexts of various societies.[46] This implies that they serve as a focal device when individuals who might be of relatively little importance can be cited as a type or as a useful lead into issues of wider historical importance. The three Kenyan educators whom I have examined in the last decade (Geoffrey William Griffin, Joseph Kamiru Gikubu, and Edward Carey Francis) were men from relatively humble backgrounds who distinguished themselves in Kenyan education. My work has striven to examine their involvement and contributions to the development of Kenyan education as a gateway to understanding the journey of Kenya's educational history and various social, economic, political forces, both in the colonial and postcolonial periods that have shaped it, challenges that have been experienced, and what the future holds. My work has attempted to ascertain how some biographies can rise above the level of providing source material and become important essays in interpretation and analysis of complex historical-societal events.[47] Affirming this, Ngugi Wa Thiong'o, in his book *Moving the Centre*, writing on the historical significance of biographies using Nelson Mandela's role in South Africa's democratic struggle as an example, states:

> All these figures are heroic because they reflect more intensely in their individual souls the souls of their community. Their uniqueness is the uniqueness of the historical moment. They make history even as history makes them. They are torches that blaze out new paths. Such a torch has been set alight by the fire of the masses, and every time it seems to fade, the great ones turn to their people for more energy. Mandela has been such a torch for the South African people. The black people of South Africa are reflected in Mandela. In Mandela the people of the world have really been applauding the courage, the endurance, the resistance and spirit of the South African masses. The people of the world, particularly Africans and those of African descent outside Africa, have in turn seen themselves reflected in the struggling South African masses. Or put another way, Mandela is to black South Africa's struggles what black South Africa's struggles are to the democratic forces of the world in the twentieth century. Indeed, South Africa is a mirror of the modern world in its emergence over the last four hundred years.[48]

Edward Carr notes that educational biographies and general biographies affirm that individuals shape history and are also shaped by it.[49] He sees the historical individual as a product and agent of the historical process, at once the representative and the creator of social forces which change the shape of the world and its thought processes. According to Francis Coker, every biography is seen as representing a survey and scrutiny of the past, compromises, observations, and instructions for future societal changes.[50] They inform us about the specific and unique aspects of the subject and the context in which he/she functioned. It is in this regard that biographical studies lead to an in-depth understanding of the complex and fluid historical, social, political, and economic contexts of their communities. This historical recognition that individuals shape history and are also shaped by it, and examining educational development in Kenya through several spheres and their connections and impact on educational reforms have been beneficial to my research work. They have challenged me to provide in-depth historical analysis and interpretation of various African educators with regard to their involvement and contributions to Kenyan education. This approach has enabled me to collect in-depth data that I would have missed if I had only used educational research frames. In addition, the approach has also enabled me to more deeply understand the breadth of complexities, issues, and challenges of Kenyan education in both the colonial and postcolonial periods. The approach has also enabled me to bring to the fore significant details relevant to my work. It has given me a better understanding of how best to approach solving critical Kenyan and African educational challenges.

Further, my research work has benefited from the historical methods pertaining to the use of archival materials and written documents, as well as the appropriate analysis, interpretation, and triangulation approaches therein. As earlier noted, as an educationist this was a new area for me, and yet it has been a very significant data-gathering methodology for me. It has enriched my research and enabled me to create new pathways for data analysis and presentation in educational biographical works. The approach has enabled me to gather deep data that has benefited the African historical field on educational issues in both the colonial and postcolonial periods and our overall understanding of Africa and its educational history.

My educational biographical works have also benefited from the historical critiques of biographical studies. The critiques have pushed me to interrogate and triangulate several sources in order to authenticate and validate them. For instance, I have taken into consideration the general criticisms of biographical works by various historians who view them as having a tendency to promote the cult of the individual and to make heroes of relatively insignificant individuals in historical terms at the expense of a well-balanced understanding of varied, complex, societal influences. To navigate this, I have taken into consideration their advice that it is vital to apply in-depth critical standards in the analysis of biographical works.[51] This awareness has been seminal in my work and has enabled me to critically analyze much of the historical information on my biographical subjects with regard to their involvement and contributions to the development of Kenyan education, a strategy that has contributed to a deeper understanding of their engagements and the frequently overlooked historical details on their educational work. A good example that suffices here is my examination of Geoffrey William Griffin's contributions to Kenyan youth education: his work at the National Youth Service entailed a deeper historical engagement of why it was an urgent and first undertaking of the Kenyan government after independence and the enormous development work it did for the country in the first three decades of independence.

My research work overall has striven to contribute to the rapidly evolving field of African-centered educational biographies by elucidating why my earlier mentioned educators became involved in Kenyan education and the circumstances that necessitated their involvement. The studies illuminate the meaning of actions they undertook in addressing Kenyan educational challenges in both the colonial and postcolonial periods, and their insights into the vision and growth of Kenyan education in the past and what the future holds. It is this significance that has guided my work and the possibilities it provides to the understanding of Africa, and its educational history both in the colonial and postcolonial periods.

## Conclusion

An overview of education in Africa shows almost definite trends and concerns in Africa's education-reform process during varied periods of its postcolonial history. In the first decade of independence, the main concerns of most African nations were how to use education to create national consciousness, adequate personnel, and to address critical national needs. In the early 1970s, the central concerns were how to improve and enhance the quality of education to enable it to curb the increased levels of unemployment. Between 1975 and 1985, most African nations were preoccupied with revising the previous educational policies and creating new proposals that were relevant to their national needs. This was evidenced in numerous educational experiments in technical, vocational, and non-formal education that were undertaken to meet their sporadic, broad, and complex national and global needs. These efforts indicated a dynamic and rapidly changing African continent that constantly required a dialectical education system. These experiments were influenced by both internal and external forces. The late 1980s and the 1990s were marked by more educational challenges that necessitated more educational reforms, curriculum reviews, and further enhancement of educational quality. This was evidenced in the strong educational focus on commercial, industrial, and technological fields. From 2000 to the present, the main concerns of education have been how to improve the quality, equity, access, and global connectivity. This is clearly seen in enormous investments in tertiary-level education and the diversification and interdisciplinary focus of various educational programs at this level.

This chapter has accentuated the importance and contributions of African-centered educational biographies to the understanding of Africa and its history. It shows that they fill an important gap in the historiography of the evolution and growth of African education both in the colonial and post-colonial periods. The chapter recognizes that this is an underresearched area and there is a need for more research to examine the role and contributions of African educators to the growth of African education in the postcolonial period. The chapter demonstrates that the more we know about the role of these educators, the more we understand in depth the historical, social, political, and economic happenings of African nations and the specific contexts that have shaped them. The chapter argues that by exploring their lives and contributions, we explore the efforts of the African people in history to use their educational systems to shape their destiny.

## WHAT THE FUTURE HOLDS REGARDING EDUCATION IN AFRICA

Adriaan Verspoor's important report on *Education at the Crossroads: Choices in Secondary Education in Sub-Saharan Africa* provides a succinct picture of education's future in postcolonial Africa. He posits that the challenges of educational development in SSA at the beginning of the 21st century and beyond are 'urgent and unprecedented' and there is still a lack of a long-term view of national development in many African countries, as evidenced in the 'firefighting and politics' that have characterized their education sectors and most of their educational policies and frameworks.[52] Most of them are politically driven with minimal input from African educational experts and other relevant stakeholders, as earlier noted in this chapter. In addition, many of them are externally driven, funded, and are not sustainable. Though many lessons can be drawn from the many educational challenges that most African nations have faced in the postcolonial period, it is clear that no one educational policy approach and framework can apply to all African countries given their varied histories, contexts, and needs. As the De Lors Commission points out, educational reforms in Africa can only work if they fit a given country's context, development, objectives, vision, and mission.[53] Such strategies will need to: be parsimonious with resource use and sustainability; recognize the bottom-up sequential nature of educational development; be closely aligned with national development priorities and strengthen autonomy; ensure central direction and support; and build public-private partnerships.[54] All this implies that for education to yield transformative and developmental success in Africa, African government's will have to evolve towards an education-policy formulation that is clearly defined objectively, theoretically, philosophically, and in praxis. The education policy will also have to be legislatively protected from any political dictates, owned by relevant stakeholders, adequately financed, and periodically subjected to technical consultations and reviews to ensure that it is in harmony with both local, national, and global needs.

In addition, African nations are also expected to support a broadly based, equitable expansion of educational provision at all levels, thereby ensuring that the needs of disfranchised and vulnerable groups like the poor, people with special needs, children, women, and rural populations are adequately met. Such an educational approach will provide hope, empowerment, freedom, social justice, peace, equity, democratic and human liberation, wholeness, and transformation to these marginalized populations. Such improvements are essential for tackling challenges of national development and a new world order. It will be an approach according to Ngugi Wa Thiong'o that uses education as a societal reconstruction and transformative tool. It will be an education:

> That urges men and women to use their seriousness of study, cheerfulness of knowledge, and intellect creatively to fight against all social-cultural, political and economic struggles and various prejudices prevalent in most African nations. It will be a transformative education that is expected to turn various challenges of African nations into spheres of common knowledge and experience and above all justice and societal liberation and development into a passion. It will be an education that should make its recipients and most African nations part of those millions whom Martin Carter once saw sleeping not to dream but dreaming to change the world.[55]

This type of education will enable African nations' developmental agendas and frameworks to take off since it will be rooted in holistic societal reform frames. This approach will necessitate going beyond the current myth of traditional education pedagogy prevalent in most African nations that is examination and career-centered. It will require putting great emphasis on innovative and alternative models of education that permit African nations to utilize modern technological advances. To this end, future transformative African educational policies in the postcolonial period will be expected to transcend mere transmission of factual knowledge to also include knowledge, skills, and values that are liberating insofar as they create new horizons and opportunities that are essential for national development. This will require a paradigmatic shift in the conceptualization and management of the education process. For this to be effective, the education process will need to be multi-dimensional, broad, explicit, and systematic in its commitment to preparing students who can transform society. In addition, this type of education will be required to have a strong and secure base that links formal and informal education. Further, it will require decolonization that addresses Frantz Fanon's fears of having 'black skins in white skins' epistemological approaches that cannot address Africa's myriad societal challenges. It will have to be an education that is centered on transformative knowledge systems that can address Africa's unique challenges. It will have to be an education that, according to Maya Angelou and Ngugi Wa Thiong'o, can permit 'Africa's caged birds that are stuck in colonial education prisons that cannot solve their societal challenges to be free and sing in their own educational frames.'[56] It will be an education that is conscious of addressing Africa's historical dilemmas. Elaborating the latter point, Ngugi Wa Thiong'o writes:

The present predicaments of Africa often arise from a historical situation. Their solutions are not so much a matter of individual countries' own decisions as that of a fundamental social transformation of the structures of their societies starting with a real break with imperialism and its internal ruling allies. Imperialism and its comprador alliances in Africa can never develop the continent.[57]

From Ngugi's thoughts, which I strongly concur with, it can be argued that the question of the base is critical in addressing Africa's educational challenges. It points to the need for clarity with regard to the purpose and direction of African education, its relevance, philosophical stands, national objectives, and needs. It points to the path:

the teaching of African literature, as well as of history, politics, and all the other arts and social sciences, ought to take in Africa today. It is about the inherited colonial education system and the consciousness it necessarily inculcated in the African mind. What directions should an education system take in an African wishing to break with neo-colonialism? What should be the philosophy guiding it? How does it want the 'New Africans' to view themselves in the universe? From what base: Afrocentric or Eurocentric? What then are the materials they should be exposed to: and in what order and perspective? Who should be interpreting that material to them: an African or non-African? If African, what kind of African? One who has internalized the colonial world outlook or one attempting to break free from the inherited slave consciousness? And what were the implications of such an education system for the political and economic set up or status quo? In a neo-colonialist context, would such an education system be possible? Would it not in fact come into conflict with political and economic neo-colonialism? Whether recommendations in the quest for relevance are successful or not ultimately depends on the entire government policy towards culture, education and language, and on where and how it stands in the new anti-imperialist process in Africa today.[58]

The process will require African nations to lead and own their educational reform process. This will require African nations to be self-sufficient in their educational policy, management and implementation process and to ensure that their educational vision and planning are sustainable. Again, here I concur with Ngugi's reflections on this subject in his seminal work *Secure the Base*. He observes:

Were Africa to examine its history seriously, the continent could learn useful lessons for the present. The most successful struggles, including those of the Haitian Africans in 1789 and the Mau Mau in the Kenya of the 1950s, were based on self-reliance and a belief in their capacity to change the world. However weak it may now appear to itself, Africa has to take Nyerere's credo of self-reliance seriously. A belief in self is the beginning of strength.[59]

This type of education will entail shaking off the colonial groove. It is a type of education that will enable African nations to develop from within and be independent. This is because development can only come from within. It must be endogenous, thought out by people for themselves, springing from the soil on which they live and attuned to their aspirations, dreams, the conditions of their natural environment, the resources at their disposal and the particular genius of their culture. African education to all intents and purposes will be expected to contribute to its endogenous development. Supporting this view, Julius Nyerere argued:

> People cannot be developed. They can only develop themselves. For while it is possible for an outsider to build a man's house, an outsider cannot give a man pride and self-confidence in himself as a human being. Those things a man has to create in himself by his own actions. He develops himself by what he does; he develops himself by making his own decisions, by increasing his understanding of what he is doing and why; by increasing his own knowledge and ability, and by his own full participation – as an equal – in the life of the community he lives in. Thus for example, a man is developing himself when he grows or earns enough to provide decent conditions for himself and his family; he is not being developed if someone gives him these things.[60]

Education of most worth for postcolonial Africa in the twenty-first century and beyond will also require redefinition and reconceptualization in terms of its philosophy and purpose. It will be required to go beyond being a 'preparation for a career in the civil service or the bureaucracy, but a preparation for life'.[61] It will be an education that develops and nurtures talents in every person that can be utilized to create, invent, invest, and venture into the unknown. Its goal will be to:

> Produce citizens who will invest in the nation by creating wealth (both human and material), economic investment, entrepreneurial spirit, self-help, rather than plunder the people's treasury. Education thus will be a preparation for service to and for the upliftment of the community, not through handouts, but through investment in the economic, social and intellectual needs of the people. It is only then that Education will become a true investment in human capital in Africa.[62]

Additionally, it will have to be an education that lays emphasis on democracy and critical consciousness with a vision of creating wealth for African nations. It will entail preparing individuals for self-sufficiency, risk taking, awakening the moral, economic, political, and civic responsibilities, adventure, and 'creating opportunities and new ideas or something for others where none exists'.[63] Further, it will be an education that has ethical caring and respect at its core. It will be an education that enables people to identify with others' challenges, empathizes with their thoughts and feelings. It will have to be an education that raises people's consciousness and emancipation capacities against the dangers of totalitarianism, oppression, exploitation, kleptocracy, and sexism.

It will be an education that strives to inspire people to find ways to get involved in societal development and reconstruction with an intention of making a difference. It will be expected to provide, according to Paulo Freire, both reflection and action required in tackling critical societal challenges prevalent in African nations.[64] It will be required to be a transformative, citizenship and possibility-centered education that inspires dreaming dreams, exploring them and acting on them for the betterment of society and for all the citizens. Additionally, it will have to be an education that strives to produce informed, active, and critical citizens who are capable of making intelligent decisions about everyday problems. It will be an education that fosters critical consciousness which, according to Paulo Freire, has to be accompanied by active critical thinking and dialogical skills that are vital for inquiry into possible solutions to Africa's societal challenges.[65] These skills will enable African nations to explore, take risks, invent, invest, and create opportunities for others who are less fortunate.

In conclusion, I would like to note that the search for an effective education process in postcolonial Africa is not an easy undertaking, as evidenced in this chapter. It is an intricate, complex, and multilayered process. It requires bold, dynamic, and transformative leadership at the national, individual, and collective levels; and a vision and mission that are clear, holistic, flexible, purposeful, and historically attuned to educational policy development and implementation. African nations must get the process right and recognize the vitality of education to the future survival of their nations. As Dickson Mungazi reminds us, 'human history is a race between education and catastrophe and education is the main spring of all national action and survival. Unless it is right and purposeful the people either crawl or limp along'.[66] African nations must use education to transform their societies the same way other nations in history have used it to transform theirs. This is the challenge of history for African nations in the postcolonial period. This chapter by its eclectic approach does not provide a definitive answer. It merely extends an invitation to African educators, scholars, and relevant education stakeholders to ponder more deeply on this challenge with regard to the purpose and vision of education in postcolonial Africa.

## NOTES

1. Peter Kallaway, "The Rise of National Education Systems in Africa," in *Oxford Handbook of History of Education*, ed. John Rury and Eileen Tamura (Oxford: Oxford University Press, forthcoming).
2. Kallaway, "The Rise of National Education Systems in Africa" (forthcoming).
3. Daniel Sifuna, *Development of Education in Africa: The Kenyan Experience* (Nairobi: Initiative Publishers, 1990), ix.
4. Sifuna, *Development of Education in Africa: The Kenyan Experience*, 1.
5. Abdelhag Rharade, "Education Reform in Kenya," *Prospects* 27, no. 11 (1997): 29.

6. Sorobea Bogonko, *A History of Modern Education in Kenya, 1895–1992* (Nairobi: Evans Brothers, 1992).
7. Jeanne Moulton, *Education Reform in Sub-Saharan Africa: Paradigm Lost?* (Westport: Greenwood, 2002).
8. Daniel Sifuna and James Otiende, *An Introductory History of Education* (Nairobi: Nairobi University Press, 2006).
9. Mark Bray, Peter Clarke, and David Stephens, *Education and Society in Africa* (London: Edward Arnold, 1986), 81.
10. Daniel Sifuna and Nobuhide Sawamura, *Challenge of Quality Education in Sub-Saharan African Countries* (New York: Nova Science Publishers, 2010).
11. Kallaway, "The Rise of National Education Systems in Africa" (forthcoming).
12. Ibid.
13. Ibid.
14. Ibid.
15. Ibid.
16. Ibid.
17. World Bank, *Education in Sub-Saharan Africa: Policies for Adjustment, Revitalization and Expansion* (Washington, DC: World Bank, 1988).
18. Kallaway, "The Rise of National Education Systems in Africa" (forthcoming).
19. Ibid.
20. Ibid.
21. Ibid.
22. Richard Thompson, *Education and Development in Africa* (London: Macmillan Publishers, 1981).
23. Thompson, *Education and Development in Africa*.
24. Ibid., 255.
25. Ibid., 256.
26. Sifuna and Otiende, *An Introductory History of Education*, 251.
27. Kallaway, "The Rise of National Education Systems in Africa" (forthcoming).
28. Ibid.
29. Sifuna, *Development of Education in Africa: The Kenyan Experience*, 55.
30. Ibid.
31. Republic of Kenya, *Sessional Paper No: 10: African Socialism and Its Application to Planning in Kenya* (Nairobi: Government Printer, 1965).
32. Republic of Kenya, *Kenya Education Commission Report* (Nairobi: Government Printer, 1964).
33. Sifuna and Otiende, *An Introductory History of Education*, 244.
34. Ibid.
35. Ibid., 245.
36. International Labor Organization, *Employment, Incomes and Equality: A Strategy for Increasing Employment in Kenya* (Geneva: ILO, 1972).
37. Republic of Kenya, *Development Plan, 1979–1983* (Nairobi: Government Printer, 1979).
38. Ibid.
39. Republic of Kenya, *Development Plan, 1970–1974* (Nairobi: Government Printer, 1969).
40. Thompson, *Education and Development in Africa*, 260.

41. Republic of Kenya, *Second University in Kenya: Report of the Working Party* (Nairobi: Government Printer, 1981).

42. Republic of Kenya, *Kenya Commission of Inquiry into Education System of Kenya* (Nairobi: Government Printer, 1999).

43. Republic of Kenya, *Kenya Commission of Inquiry into Education System of Kenya*.

44. Ronald Dore, *The Diploma Disease* (London: Allen and Unwin, 1976).

45. Christopher Kridel, *Writing Educational Biography: Explorations in Qualitative Research* (New York: Garland Publishing, 1988).

46. Ezekiel Adeoti, *Alayande as Educationist 1948–1983: A Study of Alayande's Contribution to Education and Social Change* (Ibadan: Educational Books, 1997).

47. Jacob Ajayi, *History and the Nation and Other Addresses* (Ibadan: Spectrum Books, 1990).

48. Ngugi Wa Thiong'o, *Moving the Centre: The Struggles for Cultural Freedoms* (Oxford: James Currey Limited, 1993), 147–48.

49. Edward Carr, *What is History?* (London: Pelican, 1961).

50. Francis Coker, *The Rt. Revd. Seth Irunsewe Kale* (Lagos: C.S.S. Press, 1973).

51. Ibid.

52. Adriaan, Verspoor, *At the Crossroads: Choices in Secondary Education in Sub-Saharan Africa* (Washington, DC: World Bank, 2008).

53. Jacques, De Lors, *Learning: The Treasure Within: Report to UNESCO of the International Commission on Education for the Twenty-first Century* (Paris: UNESCO, 1998).

54. Kallaway, "The Rise of National Education Systems in Africa" (forthcoming).

55. Ngugi Wa Thiong'o, *Decolonizing the Mind: The Politics of Language in African Literature* (Oxford: James Currey Limited, 1986), 108.

56. Ngugi Wa Thiong'o, *Something Torn and New: An African Renaissance* (New York: Basic Civitas Books, 2009), 98.

57. Wa Thiong'o, *Decolonizing the Mind: The Politics of Language in African Literature*, xii.

58. Ibid., 101–2.

59. Ngugi Wa Thiong'o, *Secure the Base* (London: Seagull, 2016), 34.

60. Magnus, Bassey, *Western Education and Political Domination in Africa: A Study in Critical and Dialogical Pedagogy* (London: Bergin and Garvey, 1999), 111.

61. Bassey, *Western Education and Political Domination in Africa: A Study in Critical and Dialogical Pedagogy*, 108.

62. Ibid.

63. Ibid., 111.

64. Paulo, Freire, *Pedagogy of the Oppressed* (New York: Continuum, 2002).

65. Freire, *Pedagogy of the Oppressed*.

66. Dickson Mungazi, *Education Policy and National Character: Africa, Japan, the United States and the Soviet Union* (West Port, CT: Praeger, 1993), 43.

## BIBLIOGRAPHY

Adeoti, Ezekiel. *Alayande as Educationist 1948–1983: A Study of Alayande's Contribution to Education and Social Change.* Ibadan: Educational Books, 1997.

Ajayi, Jacob. *History and the Nation and Other Addresses.* Ibadan: Spectrum Books, 1990.

Bassey, Magnus. *Western Education and Political Domination in Africa: A Study in Critical and Dialogical Pedagogy.* London: Bergin and Garvey, 1999.

Bogonko, Sorobea, *A History of Modern Education in Kenya, 1895–1992.* Nairobi: Evans Brothers, 1992.

Bray, Mark, Clarke Peter, and Stephens David. *Education and Society in Africa.* London: Edward Arnold, 1986.

Carr, Edward. *What Is History?* London: Pelican, 1961.

Coker, Francis. *The Rt. Revd. Seth Irunsewe Kale.* Lagos: C.S.S. Press, 1973.

Coombs, Phillip. *The World Crisis in Education.* London: Oxford University Press, 1985.

De Lors, Jacque. *Learning: The Treasure Within: Report to UNESCO of the International Commission on Education for the Twenty-first Century.* Paris: UNESCO, 1998.

Dore, Ronald. *The Diploma Disease.* London: Allen and Unwin, 1976.

International Labor Organization. *Employment, Incomes and Equality: A Strategy for Increasing Employment in Kenya.* Geneva: ILO, 1972.

Kallaway, Peter. "The Rise of National Education Systems in Africa." In *Oxford Handbook of History of Education,* edited by John Rury and Eileen Tamura. Oxford: Oxford University Press, forthcoming.

Kridel, Christopher. *Writing Educational Biography: Explorations in Qualitative Research.* New York: Garland Publishing, 1988.

Moulton, Jeanne. *Education Reform in Sub-Saharan Africa: Paradigm Lost?* Westport: Greenwood, 2002.

Mungazi, Dickson. *Education Policy and National Character: Africa, Japan, the United States and the Soviet Union.* West Port, CT: Praeger, 1993.

Republic of Kenya. *Kenya Education Commission Report.* Nairobi: Government Printer, 1964.

———. *Sessional Paper No: 10: African Socialism and Its Application to Planning in Kenya.* Nairobi: Government Printer, 1965.

———. *Development Plan, 1970–1974.* Nairobi: Government Printer, 1969.

———. *Development Plan, 1979–1983.* Nairobi: Government Printer, 1979.

———. *Second University in Kenya: Report of the Working Party.* Nairobi: Government Printer, 1981.

———. *Commission of Inquiry on Kenyan Education System.* Nairobi: Government Printer, 1999.

———. *Kenya Commission of Inquiry into Education System of Kenya.* Nairobi: Government Printer, 1999.

Rharade, Abdelhag. "Education Reform in Kenya." *Prospects* 27 (1997): 165.

Sifuna, Daniel. *Development of Education in Africa: The Kenyan Experience.* Nairobi: Initiatives Publishers, 1990.

Sifuna, Daniel, and Nobuhide Sawamura. *Challenge of Quality Education in Sub-Saharan African Countries.* New York: Nova Science Publishers, 2010.

Sifuna, Daniel, and Otiende James. *An Introductory History of Education*. Nairobi: Nairobi University Press, 2006.

Thiong'o, Ngugi Wa. *Decolonizing the Mind: The Politics of Language in African Literature*. Oxford: James Currey Limited, 1986.

———. *Moving the Centre: The Struggles for Cultural Freedoms*. Oxford: James Currey Limited, 1993.

———. *Something Torn and New: An African Renaissance*. New York: Basic Civitas Books, 2009.

———. *Secure the Base*. London: Seagull, 2016.

Thompson, Richard. *Education and Development in Africa*. London: Macmillan Publishers, 1981.

Verspoor, Adriaan. *At the Crossroads: Choices in Secondary Education in Sub-Saharan Africa*. Washington, DC: World Bank, 2008.

World Bank. *Education in Sub-Saharan Africa: Policies for Adjustment, Revitalization and Expansion*. Washington, DC: World Bank, 1988.

# CHAPTER 44

# African Women and the Postcolonial State

*Alicia C. Decker*

'In our African societies, woman's awakening is not entirely well conceived, although society's progress requires it and a country cannot develop without women's participation in different parts of our rapidly developing age'. So wrote Celestine Ouezzin Coulibaly, a West African activist-turned-politician, in November 1961, in one of the first newspaper articles written by a woman in the newly independent Republic of Upper Volta.[1] Her article, simply titled 'We Women of the Upper Volta', was a revolutionary call to arms, a feminist manifesto that emboldened women to stake their claim on the front lines of national development. Coulibaly was no stranger to the political scene. She had helped to found, and then became secretary general, of the women's wing of the Rassemblement Démocratique Africain in Ivory Coast and Upper Volta. The following year, in December 1949, she had organized a large march of women from Abidjan to Grand Bassam Prison (an impressive distance of 30 miles) to protest against French colonial rule. Some historians suggest that this procession and subsequent demonstration at the prison comprised a 'pivotal event' that inspired France to begin negotiations for African independence.[2] Nearly a decade later, after the Republic obtained self-governing status in 1958, Coulibaly was appointed Minister of Social Affairs, Housing, and Employment. The following year, she was elected to represent Upper Volta in the French Community senate, a position she held for the next two years. Given her multiple professional accomplishments, Coulibaly served as a role model for many women, and was someone to whom they would listen. She therefore used her newspaper article to remind them of the

A.C. Decker (✉)
The Pennsylvania State University, State College, PA, USA

© The Author(s) 2018
M.S. Shanguhyia and T. Falola (eds.),
*The Palgrave Handbook of African Colonial and Postcolonial History*,
https://doi.org/10.1057/978-1-137-59426-6_44

not-so-distant past, a time when they were not taken seriously as social actors. She explained:

> In those days, not so long ago, women were totally disregarded. She was considered secondary, as an object or a tool in the hands of her husband, whose actions she had no right to control. We had no position in society and we had no political rights whatsoever. Legally, women were considered incapable and therefore unable to consent to their own marriage, so marriage, was rather, a bill of sale agreed upon by the future husband and her own family. The dowry consisted of inconsequential symbolic gifts, rather than gifts of serious meaning for a family one was joining. The dowry became, instead, a display of wealth and false power, no more than a purchase price for a woman. Thus, a woman's safety after marriage was in no way guaranteed, since a husband could send her back at will.

Coulibaly made a point of informing her readers that things had not always been this way, that in the pre-colonial past women had had value and power, and that they could have these things again if they took their role in nation building seriously. 'The truth is that, with independence', she predicted, 'women's real emancipation has begun. With independence, women can once again become full-fledged citizens in an African state'.[3] But could they actually do so? Was 'fully-fledged' citizenship even possible for most African women? Or was 'real emancipation' nothing but a sham?

This chapter takes up these important questions by examining African women's complex relationship to the postcolonial state. More specifically, it explores the ways in which African statecraft has created opportunities and challenges for African women on the continent. This is a complicated assignment because its very title rests on several problematic assumptions. First, it assumes that there is such a thing as 'African women' who will act, or be acted upon, by the postcolonial state. There are fifty-five African nations that are recognized by the United Nations or the African Union, or both. Morocco is a member of the former, but not the latter, while Western Sahara is a member of the latter, but not the former.[4] Morocco claims Western Sahara as a territory; Western Saharans claim they are independent. There are also contested territories, such as the Republic of Somaliland, which operates as an autonomous region of Somalia. Unlike Western Sahara, however, Somaliland is not recognized by the international community. Does an African woman from one of these places have anything in common with an African woman from an uncontested territory? How about women from North Africa, whose ties to the Middle East or Europe might be more salient? Are they just as African as women from south of the Sahara? We could also question the meaning of 'women'. Are we making an assumption that gender trumps other types of difference, such as sexuality, religion, or social class?[5] If we propose that women are women despite all other aspects of their identity, are we including those who identify as transgender? Or do we really only mean those who are cisgender, or 'normatively' gendered? The point is this: African women are very difficult to categorize and are never simply 'African women'.

The second assumption is that there is something called 'the' postcolonial state. This begs the question: What is postcolonial? South Africa gained its independence from Britain in 1910, but the vast majority of South Africans did not experience liberation until multiracial elections were held in 1994, so is independence really an accurate marker of postcolonial status? Or is postcoloniality contingent on some degree of majority rule? How do we reconcile the temporal aspects of postcolonial status? Is the postcolonial state of Ghana (independent in 1957) really similar to the postcolonial state of South Sudan (independent in 2011)? And what do we make of Ethiopia and Liberia? Can a country be postcolonial if it was never colonized? The state must also be called into question, as there have been a number of different types of states in postcolonial Africa (e.g. single-party 'democratic', multiparty 'democratic', military regimes, and various hybrid models). There have also been weak, parasitic, and collapsed states, so when we talk about African women and the postcolonial state, what do we really mean?

The final assumption rests on the 'and' in the title of this chapter. 'And' assumes that women are not part and parcel of the state, that both terms are not mutually constitutive (i.e. there are women *and* there are states). However, what if we were to work from the premise that women *are* the state or that states *are* women, at least in part? In other words, what would happen if we were to think of states as gendered institutions that shape and are shaped by women (and men), and ideas about women (and men), whosoever they may be? At the very least, we would have a more nuanced understanding of history, one that embraces difference and the complexities that such an analysis brings. This is one of the primary goals of this chapter.

I am certainly not the first to argue that African states are gendered. In 1989, Jane Parpart and Kathleen Staudt published *Women and the State in Africa*, an edited collection that theorized women's gendered relationship to 'the state'. In their introduction, they describe how masculine privilege has been inscribed within structures of the state:

> Whether in its indigenous, colonial, or modern forms, the state has been overwhelmingly controlled by men; this control has translated into laws, policies, and spending patterns which not coincidentally benefit men. Women's seemingly personal, everyday experiences are structured by policies, most of which are apparently 'gender neutral.' But these policies are in fact experienced very differently by men and women.[6]

Historically, African states have been made up of men who have enacted policies that have primarily benefited other men. So what happens to the gendering of African statecraft when more women enter into formal politics? Does the state become less patriarchal if more women take a place at the table? Or would women be better served by refusing to sit at the table in the first place, by agitating against the state from the outside? If 'the master's tools will never dismantle the master's house', as the late Audre Lorde so eloquently penned more than thirty years ago, then perhaps African women (and their allies) need to continue challenging the very system itself.[7] In the remainder of this chapter, I will consider several historical examples that help us think through these particular questions, as well as those raised above. I begin by looking at the status of women in a number of different countries in Sub-Saharan Africa to determine how state policies and practices have influenced their lives.[8] In the next section, I examine the political trajectories of several women who got involved in politics and thus became part of the state. And finally, in the last section, I consider the role of activism as a tool for engaging the state from the outside. I conclude by returning to the gendering of African statecraft, theorizing how and to what extent African women can make the postcolonial state less patriarchal.

## THE STATE OF AFRICAN WOMEN

Given that the vast majority of political leaders in postcolonial Africa have been men, it is not surprising that many state policies have promoted and protected male privilege. One way they have done this is by allocating greater resources to issues that are important to men and/or to the celebration of masculinity. Ministries of Defense, for example, have historically enjoyed larger budgets than Ministries of Education, Health, or Labor because security has been defined in militarized terms (i.e. a 'secure' state is a militarized state) and categorized as 'men's work' (e.g. most soldiers and Ministers of Defense are men).[9] Patricia McFadden suggests that 'a clear and unambiguous link has existed between the maintenance and expansion of state power and the growth and use of militarism as an expression of that state power'. Furthermore, male leaders in postcolonial Africa have used the militarized state 'as a site of accumulation' and 'as a vehicle of repression, surveillance, and exclusion of the majority of people, particularly women, the young, and the elderly in working communities'.[10] In other words, they have used militarism to enrich and protect a particular type of power structure, one that is gendered masculine. This does not mean that some women have not benefited from this patriarchal system (or that all men have), but instead, that the postcolonial state has privileged a select few at the expense of many.

Another way that African states have promoted male privilege is by enacting policies that do not take women's domestic and reproductive labor into account, assuming that such labor is 'free' or ancillary to 'real' work. In the late 1970s and early 1980s, for example, global economic crisis compelled many African governments to restructure their economies on the basis of various austerity measures recommended by the World Bank and the International Monetary Fund (IMF). In order to qualify for additional aid packages, governments needed to 'balance their budgets, cut social spending, eliminate subsidies, provide concessions to multinational corporations to encourage investment, privatize government agencies, promote cash-crop production, and retrench redundant public servants'.[11] Such measures, it was believed, would help African governments save money so that they could more readily service their external debts. The problem, however, was that the citizenry had to compensate for the retraction of the state. Much of this labor burden fell on the shoulders of women:

> Since women are frequently responsible for food provision, the elimination of subsidies and the move toward cash crop production made it difficult for many to provide food for their families. The privatization of social services also made health and education unaffordable for the poor. Women's reproductive labor burdens often increased as they attempted to compensate for these cutbacks. In Malawi, for instance, if a clinic was compelled to introduce user fees to offset the loss of government subsidies, a peasant farmer might be unable to bring her sick child to the doctor. She would have to provide care at home, which in turn, compromised her ability to care for the rest of her family and jeopardized her child's chance of recovery. If this same woman was unable to pay her children's school fees, she might decide to keep her daughters at home so that they could help with domestic and agricultural activities. This would significantly decrease their future earning potential and increase the likelihood that they would be married off at an earlier age, a harmful practice for a host of additional reasons.[12]

The World Bank and IMF eventually came to recognize these problems, and began moving away from structural adjustment in the late 1990s. In their place, they initiated poverty-reduction programs, which gave African governments more ownership over the restructuring process. Nonetheless, these programs still reproduced many of the same problems for African women and girls, not counting or compensating for unpaid labor within the household.[13]

African postcolonial states have also protected male privilege by targeting women for social reform. In the 1960s and 1970s, for instance, as newly independent states grappled with the meanings of national identity, morality campaigns became increasingly popular. African leaders used these campaigns to create (the appearance of) a particular type of nation, one that was 'decent' and 'virtuous'. Whether they enacted these reforms to 'establish their superiority over the west in at least one sphere', as Audrey Wipper has suggested, or to cultivate political legitimacy as I have argued elsewhere, one thing is clear: women's bodies were the ones that were policed.[14] In Uganda, for instance, young women were routinely chastised for wearing mini dresses. In one letter to the Editor, defiantly titled 'Minis Not for Us', Peace Nyenga articulated her position:

> To shame a woman is to shame a nation … any woman (and girl) who wears a mini-dress puts the whole nation—Uganda—to shame … The Government should realize that the 'mini' girls or daughters have failed their parents and the

state of Uganda ... Action must be taken to discipline and limit the freedom of mini dressers so that Uganda can unburden *herself* of the mini dress yoke.[15]

The author clearly believed that women (and girls) were important symbols of the nation, and that the nation (at least in its ideological form) was gendered feminine.[16] President Idi Amin also believed that women's fashion was linked to moral decay. On May 27, 1972, he enacted a decree 'to prohibit the wearing of certain dresses which outrage decency and are injurious to public morals'. The decree stipulated that:

> Every person of or above the apparent age of fourteen years who in any public place wears any dress, garment, skirts, or shorts the hem-line or bottom of which is 7.62 centimeter (3 inches) above the knee-line or wears any dress popularly known as a midi or a maxi having a slit on any part of the circumference of such dress the apex of which is above the knee-line [would be in violation].[17]

The decree also banned short, tight-fitting pants that were known popularly as 'hot pants'. Any person arrested for violating the dress code was labeled 'idle and disorderly' and subject to a fine and/or imprisonment. Although the law was supposed to be gender-neutral, the vast majority of those arrested or otherwise punished were women.[18] This pattern was not unique to Uganda as many African states read (and continue to read) morality as a feminine preserve.[19]

African states also codified male privilege within their national constitutions by refusing to outlaw gender discrimination and by exempting family and customary law from constitutional regulation.[20] This meant that women were not considered full citizens of the postcolonial state. Although a number of governments amended or drafted new constitutions in the 1990s, an important response to the international women's movement which gained greater traction in Africa after the Third World Conference on Women was held in Nairobi in 1985, there is still room for improvement. South Africa remains the only country in Africa that has constitutionally outlawed discrimination on the basis of sexual orientation and that recognizes the right of same-sex couples to marry.[21] If African women are to achieve the 'real emancipation' that Coulibaly predicted in 1961, then policymakers must work harder at dismantling male privilege within the postcolonial state.

## Women of the African State

If the postcolonial state is masculinist *because* most African leaders have been men, what happens when increasing numbers of women become involved in politics? Does the African state become less patriarchal? Since the mid-1980s, six women have served as unelected heads of state: Carmen Pereira (Guinea Bissau, May 14–16, 1984); Sylvie Kinigi (Burundi, October 27, 1993–February 5, 1994); Ruth Perry (Liberia, September 3, 1996–August 2, 1997);

Rose Francine Rogombe (Gabon, June 10–October 16, 2009); Monique Ohsan Bellepeau (Mauritius, March 31, 2012–July 21, 2012 and May 29, 2015–June 5, 2015); and Joyce Banda (Malawi (April 7, 2012–May 31, 2014). In the last ten years, three additional women have been elected president. These include Ellen Johnson Sirleaf (Liberia, January 16, 2006–present), Catherine Samba-Panza (Central African Republic, January 23, 2014–March 30, 2016), and Ameenah Gurib (Mauritius, June 5, 2015–present). A relatively small number of African women have also served as prime minister or acting prime minister.[22] Most of these women have garnered little international attention, save for Ellen Johnson Sirleaf because of her role as the first *elected* female president of an African nation and because of the enormous task that lay ahead of her; Liberia had just emerged from fourteen years of brutal civil war and had very little in the way of infrastructure. In her inaugural address to the nation, Sirleaf vowed to root out corruption, restore good governance, and promote national reconciliation. She also promised to promote the status of women:

> My Administration shall thus endeavor to give Liberian women prominence in all affairs of our country. My Administration shall empower Liberian women in all areas of our national life. We will support and increase the writ of laws that restore their dignities and deal drastically with crimes that dehumanize them. We will enforce without fear or favor the law against rape recently passed by the National Transitional Legislature. We shall encourage families to educate all children, particularly the girl child. We shall also try to provide economic programs that enable Liberian women to assume their proper place in our economic revitalization process.[23]

While opportunities for women and girls have increased significantly during Sirleaf's two terms in office, her administration has also been accused of nepotism, patronage politics, and corruption. Perhaps 'old habits' are simply 'intransigent' as Aili Tripp suggests in a blog post about African women and politics.[24] Or perhaps the assumption that women will 'do' politics differently, simply because they are women, is faulty. Until more women have the opportunity to serve as political leaders, we will not fully understand if their political paths are truly different from those of men.

In Rwanda, where women currently hold 63.8% of parliamentary seats (more than anywhere else in the world) we might expect to find a less patriarchal form of politics at play. In some respects this is true. Rwandan women legislators have introduced (and helped pass) legislation that enables women to inherit land, that combats gender-based violence, and that loosens restrictions on abortion. The problem, however, is that they are competing with a larger power structure that can easily undermine their authority. According to April Gordon, 'Real power is invested in the office of the president in most African countries and among a few loyalists at the upper levels of the executive branch of government. In other words, men still hold a monopoly of power regardless of how many women are in parliament'.[25] So, even in a country like Rwanda where the majority of legislators are women, 'real' power remains largely in the hands of men.[26]

This has not always been the case. In Tanzania, for instance, Bibi Titi Mohamed was known as the 'Mother of the Nation' because of her role mobilizing women during the liberation struggle. She led Umoja wa Wanawake wa Tanzania, the women's wing of the Tanganyika African National Union, and used community dance groups to recruit women to the nationalist cause.[27] After independence, she served as Minister of Women and Social Affairs and as a member of parliament. She resigned from government service in 1967 after the President enacted the Arusha Declaration, a wide-reaching program promoting African socialism and self-reliance. She resented 'the undemocratic manner in which it was being imposed upon us'.[28] Shortly thereafter, in 1969, she was implicated in a plot to overthrow the government, and sentenced to life imprisonment for treason. Although she was pardoned in 1972, she never returned to political life. Despite her lack of education, Mohamed did have 'real' political power and was known as the 'most important politician after [President] Nyerere'.[29]

Another important political figure was Constance Agatha Cummings-John, the first black African woman to run a city government. In 1966, she was elected mayor of Freetown, the capital of Sierra Leone. Prior to this historic achievement, she had been elected to the Freetown City Council (1938) and the House of Representatives (1957), although she never had a chance to serve in the latter because of factional conflicts. In *Memoirs of a Krio Leader*, Cummings-John described her first day in office as mayor:

> After the usual swearing-in ceremony, the Town Clerk, J.B. Jenkins Johnston, and the mayor's secretary, Mrs. Cecelia Parkinson, took me into the mayor's chambers where I was robed. Fully robed and wearing my chain of office, I returned to the council hall to conduct the remainder of that day's business. I briefly spoke about the importance of my election for the women of Sierra Leone. *They had been left behind in our politics for some time, but now we would show them that we could hold our own with men.* After the meeting, there was much celebrating.[30]

One of her first official tasks was to appoint a 'mayoress', a position traditionally held by the mayor's wife. Because the mayor's husband was stationed abroad as the ambassador to Liberia and Ivory Coast, he could not undertake the required duties. She therefore decided to appoint her sister-in-law to the position, later noting in her memoir that '[h]er support and assistance during this time was really invaluable'.[31] The mayor appointed a second woman, Lerina Bright-Taylor, to lead the city's women in various self-help activities. Although the women organized a number of successful projects, their efforts were ultimately curtailed by a military coup in 1967.

Cummings-John's decision to appoint another woman as first lady, or mayoress, speaks to the importance of this position within African politics. In addition to ceremonial functions, some African first ladies have attempted to organize and represent the nation's women: Nana Ageman Rawlings led the 31 December Women's Movement in Ghana; Maryam Babangida ran the Better Life for Rural Women Program in Nigeria; and Mariam Traoré headed the Union Nationale des Femmes du Mali.[32] Not surprisingly, each of these organizations have had a close relationship with the ruling party and their politics. Amina Mama describes this system as a femocracy, which is 'an anti-democratic female power structure which claims to exist for the advancement of ordinary women, but is unable to do so because it is dominated by a small clique of women whose authority derives from their being married to powerful men, rather than from any actions or ideas of their own'.[33] Instead of promoting a feminist agenda, elite wives undermine women's interests by supporting a patriarchal political system that enriches but a few.

Although a relatively small number of African women have been active in politics, African statecraft remains highly patriarchal. Until women make up a 'critical mass' within male-dominated institutions (this critical mass being at least 30% according to targets set by the United Nations Economic and Social Council and reaffirmed within the Beijing Platform for Action) they will not likely have a meaningful impact on the political system. At present, only fourteen nations in Sub-Saharan Africa have reached this critical mass within their legislatures.[34] But having a critical mass of women in leadership is not enough. Women in power must also be willing to support legislation that promotes gender equity. Some may not want to 'rock the boat' by going against the mainstream agenda and standing up for women's rights. However, feminist scholars maintain that it is only by 'making waves' that African women can craft a less patriarchal state.

## ACTIVISM AS A GENDERED STRATEGY OF POLITICAL ENGAGEMENT

Most African women have interacted with the postcolonial state as political outsiders. Their strategies of engagement have varied, depending on the extent to which they have been compelled, or felt willing and able, to support or confront the state. The state represents different things to different persons. For one woman, it may figure as a drunken soldier, 'manning' a makeshift roadblock along a deserted stretch of roadway. For another woman, it could take the form of a revenue officer who issues her yearly tax stub. And for yet another, it might look like the local magistrate who presided over her son's recent court case. All of these women 'know' the postcolonial state in different ways and have different types of relationships with it. For some women, particularly in rural areas, the state is an abstract entity that rarely enters into everyday life. For others, however, the state is everywhere at all times, and must be constantly negotiated. These negotiations are of particular interest because they help us to understand the ways in which African women have used activism as a gendered strategy of political engagement.

In the mid-1970s, a significant number of Ugandan women stood up to Idi Amin, one of the world's most notorious dictators. Their husbands, sons, and fathers had been 'disappeared' by the military state, and yet, they had the courage to speak out against the brutal regime. These women agreed to testify in front of a government commission of inquiry that was investigating the 'mysterious stealing and disappearance of people in Uganda' *while* the regime was still in power.[35] In gut-wrenching detail, more than 150 women from across the country described the pain of watching as their loved ones were beaten, bundled into the trunks of unmarked cars, and whisked away, never to be seen again. They recalled the trauma of trudging through the forests and swamps that had become unmarked graves, searching for clues or a body to bury. And they remembered the emotional and financial hardships that accompanied their losses. They framed their narratives in gendered terms, situating themselves as the wives, mothers, and daughters of the disappeared. Although we may not think of these women as activists in the traditional sense of the word, they spoke against tyranny. By testifying about the brutality of Amin's dictatorship, they used their voices 'to counter the deafening silence of disappearance, indelibly recording a crime that was supposed to leave no trace'.[36]

Women in Botswana also spoke out against injustice. In 1982, the government amended the Citizenship Act, denying citizenship to the children of married parents whose mother was from Botswana and whose father was not.[37] According to the new law, citizenship could only be passed down along the 'legitimate' male line. A number of different newspapers published letters to the Editor challenging this narrow definition of citizenship. One such letter, written by six Batswana women, chastised the Attorney General for telling women, 'Don't marry a stranger if you don't want his citizenship'.[38] They warned that 'because the Citizenship Act denies Batswana women the right to marry whoever they love and to live with them wherever they see fit, we are already thinking of how to circumvent its provisions. Your Honour, we shall "live in sin" with the men we love so that our children may retain Botswana citizenship'.[39] They asserted that 'children born to a Botswana parent (irrespective of sex and marital status) have sufficient descent links with this country to be given an option to acquire its citizenship'.[40] They concluded by requesting that the Attorney General and the Law Reform Committee reconsider the 'unjust abolition of dual citizenship', noting that they would be making further recommendations about 'other laws and practices that are unjust'. One year after this letter was published, a group of activists founded Emang Basadi, which means 'Stand Up Women' in Setswana, to fight for women's rights. They legally challenged the amendment and in 1992, the Botswana High Court ruled in their favor, determining that the citizenship law was indeed in conflict with women's rights as articulated by the constitution.[41] By confronting the state in the court of public opinion, as well as through the formal legal system, these women brought about important change.

The women in Uganda, just like the women in Botswana, used gendered rhetoric in their appeals to the state. They spoke out as wives, mothers, and daughters who had been harmed by patriarchal political systems that were discriminatory and/or violent. On July 12, 1990, a group of women in northwest Soweto removed their clothes to publicly protest the demolition of their homes by the South African police force. Two weeks earlier, the women had put up shacks in an expensive new residential area to raise awareness of the plight of the homeless. Despite the cold weather, and the fact that the women had nowhere else to go, the government moved in with teargas, dogs, an armored vehicle, and a bulldozer to raze their shacks to the ground. Sheila Meintjes, a South African feminist scholar and activist, described the scene: 'As the police moved to dismantle their shacks, the younger women shack dwellers stripped off their clothes, taunted the police, ululated, shouted in anger about their plight and their pain, sang and danced, and held up printed placards demanding homes and security of tenure'.[42] The women hoped that by taking off their clothes, they could stop the police from demolishing their shacks. Meintjes explains:

> The symbolism of their identity as women and as sexual beings was a central aspect of their action. The particularity of their actions drew attention to, was a signifier of and was, at the same time, a challenge to their status as social and sexual dependents. Their action challenged men and the state. The claims embedded in their action were specific—for the substantive right to housing. Access to housing provided the basis on which they would be able to nurture their families and provide a launching pad for them to create sustainable livelihoods. For the women, the right to housing also called for recognition of their specific responsibilities as women citizens.[43]

Although the government demolished their shacks and confiscated all of their personal property, the women were ultimately victorious. The government agreed to release an adjacent plot of land for a new settlement. And yet, stripping naked was not an easy decision for these women. As Meintjes found in her interviews with participants, it was simply a 'last resort', proof that 'their circumstances had driven them into "madness"'.[44]

Because most African women have not had the opportunity to sit at the political table, so to speak, they have been compelled to engage the state from the outside. They have spoken out against violence, injustice, and discrimination, utilizing gendered rhetoric and collective action to get their points across. Sometimes, as the examples presented here suggest, women have been successful in their efforts to confront or challenge the postcolonial state. Other times, however, victory has been more elusive. Indeed, many African women have been taunted, beaten, jailed, and even killed for daring to take on 'the state'. The risks of engagement are certainly high, but for those who are living within patriarchal political systems that do not work for them, the risks of not engaging are even higher.

## CONCLUSION

It has now been fifty-five years since Celestine Ouezzin Coulibaly predicted that political independence would result in women's emancipation, allowing them to become 'full-fledged citizens' of the postcolonial state. Sadly, for most African women, her prediction did not come to fruition. In fact, in Burkina Faso (the current name of the former Republic of Upper Volta) women and girls are still considered 'second-class citizens'. A recent investigation by Amnesty International UK found that 'women and girls in Burkina Faso are being discriminated against by a system that won't let them make decisions about their education, healthcare and contraception'.[45] As a result, they have one of the highest maternal mortality rates in the world, coupled with one of the lowest rates of contraceptive use. Here, and in many other countries in Sub-Saharan Africa, sexism remains embedded within the legal code. One of the major problems is that politics remains a male game. Only 9.4% of legislators in Burkina Faso are women; that is significantly lower than the average for Sub-Saharan Africa, which currently stands at 23.1%.[46] We know that having women in positions of power is not enough to create substantive change for gender equality. Such women must also be willing to promote a feminist agenda, and have enough colleagues who are willing to do the same. Women should also have the freedom to engage the state through various forms of activism without the risk of being harassed, jailed, or even killed. Until sexist policies and practices can be safely challenged by women (and men), both within the postcolonial state and beyond, African statecraft will remain highly patriarchal.

## NOTES

1. Celestine Ouezzin Coulibaly, "We Women of the Upper Volta" (1961), in *Women Writing Africa: West Africa and the Sahel*, ed. Esi Sutherland-Addy and Aminata Diaw (New York: The Feminist Press at the City University of New York, 2005), 225.
2. Kathleen Sheldon, *The A to Z of Women in Sub-Saharan Africa* (Lanham, MD: The Scarecrow Press, 2010), 93. See also Henriettte Diabate, *La Marche des Femmes sur Grand-Bassam* (Abidjan: Les Nouvelles Editions Africaines, 1975).
3. Coulibaly, "We Women of the Upper Volta," 226.
4. The African Union admitted Morocco as a member state on January 30, 2017.
5. For an important discussion on the fluidity of sex and gender in Africa, see Ifi Amadiume, *Male Daughters, Female Husbands: Gender and Sex in an African Society* (London: Zed Books, 1987). See also Oyeronke Oyewumi, *The Invention of Women: Making an African Sense of Western Gender Discourses* (Minneapolis: University of Minnesota Press, 1997).

6. Jane L. Parpart and Kathleen A. Staudt, "Women and the State in Africa," in *Women and the State in Africa*, ed. Jane L. Parpart and Kathleen A. Staudt (Boulder, CO: Lynne Rienner Publishers, 1989), 1.

7. Audre Lorde, "The Master's Tools Will Never Dismantle the Master's House," in *Sister Outsider: Essays and Speeches* (Trumansburg, NY: The Crossing Press, 1984), 112.

8. My focus on Sub-Saharan Africa is not meant to signify that the gender politics of contemporary North Africa are any less important or interesting. Instead, it reflects the primary geographical scope of this particular volume.

9. For a discussion of the links between militarism and masculinity in Africa, see: Nina Mba, "Kaba and Khaki: Women and the Militarized State in Nigeria," in *Women and the State in Africa*, ed. Jane L. Parpart and Kathleen Staudt (Boulder, CO: Lynne Rienner Publishers, 1989), 69–90; Jackyn Cock, "Keeping the Fires Burning: Militarization and the Politics of Gender in South Africa," *Review of African Political Economy* 45/46 (1989): 50–64; Amina Mama and Margo Okazawa-Rey, "Militarism, Conflict, and Women's Activism," *Feminist Africa* 10 (2008): 1–8; Amina Mama and Margo Okazawa-Rey, "Militarism, Conflict and Women's Activism in the Global Era: Challenges and Prospects for Women in Three West African Contexts," *Feminist Review* 101 (2012): 97–123; and Alicia C. Decker, *In Idi Amin's Shadow: Women, Gender, and Militarism in Uganda* (Athens, OH: Ohio University Press, 2014).

10. Patricia McFadden, "Plunder as Statecraft: Militarism and Resistance in Postcolonial Africa," in *Security Disarmed: Critical Perspectives on Gender, Race, and Militarization*, ed. Barbara Sutton, Sandra Morgen, and Julie Novkov (New Brunswick, NJ: Rutgers University Press, 2008), 152.

11. Alicia C. Decker and Andrea L. Arrington, *Africanizing Democracies: 1980-Present* (New York: Oxford University Press, 2015), 26.

12. Ibid., 26–27.

13. The implementation of Universal Primary Education, which was one of the Millennium Development Goals, had unintended gendered effects in many African countries as well. As girls and boys went off to school, African women often lost an important source of labor within the household and thus experienced a greater labor burden.

14. Audrey Wipper, "African Women, Fashion, and Scapegoating," *Canadian Journal of African Studies* 6, no. 2 (1972): 332; Decker, *In Idi Amin's Shadow*, chap. 3.

15. Peace Nyenga, letter to the Editor, *Uganda Argus*, November 12, 1971. [Italics mine].

16. For a discussion of women as symbols of the nation, see Floya Anthias and Nira Yuval-Davis, "Introduction," in *Women-Nation-State*, ed. Nira Yuval-Davis and Floya Anthias (London: MacMillan, 1989), 9–10.

17. Government of Uganda, Penal Code Act (Amendment) Decree, Decree 9 of 1972.

18. Decker, *In Idi Amin's Shadow*, 66–73.

19. For discussions of similar campaigns and debates, see: Ilsa Glazer Schuster, *New Women of Lusaka* (Palo Alto, CA: Mayfield Publishing, 1979); Thomas Burgess, "Cinema, Bell Bottoms, and Miniskirts: Struggles Over Youth and Citizenship in Revolutionary Zanzibar," *International Journal of African*

*Historical Studies* 35, nos. 2–3 (2002): 287–313; Cyprian Kambili, "Ethics of African Tradition: Prescription of a Dress Code in Malawi, 1965–1973," *Society of Malawi Journal* 55, no. 2 (2002): 80–100; Karen Tranberg Hansen, "Dressing Dangerously: Miniskirts, Gender Relations, and Sexuality in Zambia," in *Fashioning Africa: Power and the Politics of Dress*, ed. Jean Allman (Bloomington: Indiana University Press, 2004), 166–85; and Andrew M. Ivaska, "'Anti-Mini Militants Meet Modern Misses': Urban Style, Gender, and the Politics of 'National Culture' in 1960s Dar es Salaam, Tanzania," in *Fashioning Africa*, 104–21.

20. Iris Berger, *Women in Twentieth-Century Africa* (Cambridge: Cambridge University Press, 2016), 99.
21. Aili Tripp, Isabel Casimiro, Joy Kwesiga, and Alice Mungwa, *African Women's Movements: Changing Political Landscapes* (Cambridge: Cambridge University Press, 2009), 7.
22. This includes Elisabeth Domitien (Central African Republic, January 2, 1975–April 4, 1976), Agathe Uwilingiyimana (Rwanda, July 18, 1993–April 7, 1994), Mame Madior Boye (Senegal, March 3, 2001–November 4, 2002), Maria das Neves (São Tomé and Príncipe, October 7, 2002–July 16, 2003 and July 23, 2003–September 18, 2004), Luisa Diogo (Mozambique, February 17, 2004–January 16, 2010), Maria do Carmo Silveira (São Tomé and Príncipe, June 8, 2005–April 21, 2006), Cécile Manorohanta (Madagascar, December 18–20, 2009), Cissé Mariam Kaidama Sidibé (Mali, April 3, 2011–March 22, 2012), Adiato Djaló Nandigna (Guinea Bissau, February 10, 2012–April 12, 2012), Aminata Touré (Senegal, September 3, 2013–July 8, 2014), and Saara Kuugongelwa (Namibia, March 21, 2015–present).
23. Ellen Johnson Sirleaf, "Presidential Inaugural Address," Capitol Grounds, Monrovia, January 16, 2006.
24. Aili Mari Tripp, 'Women in Politics in Africa Today,' *Democracy in Africa*, December 9, 2013, http://democracyinafrica.org/women-politics-africa-today/.
25. April Gordon, "Women in Development," in *Understanding Contemporary Africa*, ed. April A. Gordon and Donald L. Gordon (Boulder, CO: Lynne Rienner, 2013), 319.
26. Timothy Longman, "Rwanda: Achieving Equality or Serving an Authoritarian State?" in *Women in African Parliaments*, ed. Gretchen Bauer and Hannah E. Britton (Boulder, CO: Lynne Rienner, 2006), 149.
27. Sheldon, *Women in Sub-Saharan Africa*, 155.
28. Bibi Titi Mohamed quoted in M.M. Mulokozi, "Introduction to 'Bibi Titi Mohamed: Sacrifices for Change,'" in *Women Writing Africa: The Eastern Region*, ed. Amandina Lihamba et al. (New York: The Feminist Press at the City University of New York, 2007), 229.
29. Ibid., 229.
30. Constance Agatha Cummings-John, "Mayor of Freetown" (1995) in *Women Writing Africa: West Africa and the Sahel*, ed. Esi Sutherland-Addy and Aminata Diaw (New York: The Feminist Press at the City University of New York, 2005), 234. [Italics mine].
31. Ibid., 235.
32. Tripp, et al., *African Women's Movements*, 47.

33. Amina Mama, "Feminism or Femocracy? State Feminism and Democratization in Nigeria," *Africa Development* 20, no. 1 (1995): 41. See also: Hussaina Abdullah, "Wifeism and Activism: The Nigerian Women's Movement," in *The Challenge of Local Feminisms: Women's Movements in Local Perspective*, ed. Amrita Basu (Boulder, CO: Westview Press, 1995), 209–25; Philomena Okeke, "First Lady Syndrome: The (En)Gendering of Bureaucratic Corruption in Nigeria," *CODESRIA Bulletin* 3–4 (1998): 16–19; and Jibrin Ibrahim, "The First Lady Syndrome and the Marginalization of Women From Power: Opportunities or Compromises for Gender Equality?" *Feminist Africa* 3 (2004): 1–14.

34. Inter-Parliamentary Union, "Women in National Parliaments: World Classification," June 1, 2016, http://www.ipu.org/wmn-e/classif.htm. In 2006, this figure stood at five nations, and in 1997 (the earliest year that data is available) no countries in Sub-Saharan Africa had reached this critical mass. See Inter-Parliamentary Union, "Women in National Parliaments: World Classification," January 1, 2006, http://www.ipu.org/wmn-e/arc/classif300606.htm and Inter-Parliamentary Union, "Women in National Parliaments: World Classification," January 1, 1997, http://www.ipu.org/wmn-e/arc/classif010197.htm.

35. "Disappearance of People Will Be Stamped Out," *Voice of Uganda*, December 5, 1973.

36. Decker, *In Idi Amin's Shadow*, 133.

37. Leloba Molema and Mary Lederer, "Introduction to 'Citizenship: An Open Letter to the Attorney General'" (1985) in *Women Writing Africa: The Southern Region*, ed. M.J. Daymond et al. (New York: The Feminist Press at the City University of New York, 2003), 386.

38. Athaliah Molokomme et al., "Citizenship: An Open Letter to the Attorney General" (1985) in *Women Writing Africa: The Southern Region*, 387.

39. Ibid., 388.

40. Ibid., 389.

41. Sheldon, *Women in Sub-Saharan Africa*, 66.

42. Sheila Meintjes, "Naked Women's Protest, July 1990: 'We Won't Fuck for Houses,'" in *Women in South African History: Basus'iimbokodo, bawel'imilambo/They Remove Boulders and Cross Rivers*, ed. Nomboniso Gasa (Cape Town: HSRC Press, 2007), 348. See also Jacqueline Maingard, Heather Thompson, and Sheila Meintjes, *Uku hamba 'ze: To Walk Naked*, DVD (New York: Third World Newsreel, 1995).

43. Ibid., 348.

44. Ibid., 360. African women have a long history of using nakedness to express anger and to curse perpetrators for unacceptable behavior. For a few examples from colonial and postcolonial Africa, see: Tabitha Kanogo, "Kikuyu Women and the Politics of Protest," in *Images of Women in Peace and War*, ed. Sharon MacDonald, Pat Holden, and Shirley Ardener (London: MacMillan, 1987), 78–99; Audrey Wipper, "Kikuyu Women and the Harry Thuku Disturbances: Some Uniformities of Female Militancy," *Africa* 59, no. 3 (1989): 300–37; Wangari Maathai, *Unbowed: A Memoir* (New York: Alfred A. Knopf, 2006), 220–21; and Leymah Gbowee and Carol Mithers, *Mighty Be Our Powers: How Sisterhood, Prayer and Sex Changed a Nation at War* (New York: Beast Books, 2011), 161–63.

45. Amnesty International UK, "Burkina Faso, Where Women and Girls are Second-Class Citizens," March 21, 2016, https://www.amnesty.org.uk/burkina-faso-women-girls-rights-early-forced-marriage. Ironically, Burkina Faso once had one of the continent's most progressive leaders. President Thomas Sankara saw women's rights as part of his revolutionary social vision. Sadly, he was assassinated in a military coup on October 15, 1987, just four years after seizing power in his own coup.

46. Inter-Parliamentary Union, "Women in National Parliaments: World Classification," June 1, 2016, http://www.ipu.org/wmn-e/classif.htm and Inter-Parliamentary Union, "Women in National Parliaments: Regional Averages," June 1, 2016, http://www.ipu.org/wmn-e/world.htm.

## BIBLIOGRAPHY

Abdullah, Hussaina. "Wifeism and Activism: The Nigerian Women's Movement." In *The Challenge of Local Feminisms: Women's Movements in Local Perspective*, edited by Amrita Basu, 209–25. Boulder, CO: Westview Press, 1995.

Amadiume, Ifi. *Male Daughters, Female Husbands: Gender and Sex in an African Society*. London: Zed Books, 1987.

Amnesty International UK. "Burkina Faso, Where Women and Girls Are Second-Class Citizens." March 21, 2016. https://www.amnesty.org.uk/burkina-faso-women-girls-rights-early-forced-marriage.

Anthias, Floya, and Nira Yuval-Davis. "Introduction." In *Women-Nation-State*, edited by Nira Yuval-Davis and Floya Anthias, 1–15. London: MacMillan, 1989.

Berger, Iris. *Women in Twentieth-Century Africa*. Cambridge: Cambridge University Press, 2016.

Burgess, Thomas. "Cinema, Bell Bottoms, and Miniskirts: Struggles over Youth and Citizenship in Revolutionary Zanzibar." *International Journal of African Historical Studies* 35, nos. 2–3 (2002): 287–313.

Cock, Jacklyn. "Keeping the Fires Burning: Militarization and the Politics of Gender in South Africa." *Review of African Political Economy*, nos. 45/46 (1989): 50–64.

Coulibaly, Ouezzin Celestine. "We Women of the Upper Volta" (1961). In *Women Writing Africa: West Africa and the Sahel*, edited by Esi Sutherland-Addy and Aminata Diaw, 225–27. New York: The Feminist Press at the City University of New York, 2005.

Cummings-John, Constance Agatha. "Mayor of Freetown" (1995). In *Women Writing Africa: West Africa and the Sahel*, edited by Esi Sutherland-Addy and Aminata Diaw, 233–38. New York: The Feminist Press at the City University of New York, 2005.

Decker, Alicia C. *In Idi Amin's Shadow: Women, Gender, and Militarism in Uganda*. Athens, OH: Ohio University Press, 2014.

Decker, Alicia C., and Andrea L. Arrington. *Africanizing Democracies: 1980-Present*. New York: Oxford University Press, 2015.

Diabate, Henriette. *La Marche des Femmes sur Grand-Bassam*. Abidjan: Les Nouvelles Editions Africaines, 1975.

Gbowee, Leymah, and Carol Mithers. *Mighty Be Our Powers: How Sisterhood, Prayer and Sex Changed a Nation at War*. New York: Beast Books, 2011.

Gordon, April. "Women in Development." In *Understanding Contemporary Africa*, edited by April A. Gordon and Donald L. Gordon, 293–316. Boulder: Lynne Rienner, 2013.

Hansen, Karen Tranberg. "Dressing Dangerously: Miniskirts, Gender Relations, and Sexuality in Zambia." In *Fashioning Africa: Power and the Politics of Dress*, edited by Jean Allman, 166–85. Bloomington: Indiana University Press, 2004.

Ibrahim, Jibrin. "The First Lady Syndrome and the Marginalization of Women from Power: Opportunities or Compromises for Gender Equality?" *Feminist Africa* 3 (2004): 1–14.

Inter-Parliamentary Union. "Women in National Parliaments: World Classification." January 1, 1997. http://www.ipu.org/wmn-e/arc/classif010197.htm.

———. "Women in National Parliaments: World Classification." January 1, 2006. http://www.ipu.org/wmn-e/arc/classif300606.htm.

———. "Women in National Parliaments: World Classification." June 1, 2016. http://www.ipu.org/wmn-e/classif.htm.

Ivaska, Andrew M. "'Anti-Mini Militants Meet Modern Misses': Urban Style, Gender, and the Politics of 'National Culture' in 1960s Dar es Salaam, Tanzania." In *Fashioning Africa: Power and the Politics of Dress*, edited by Jean Allman, 104–21. Bloomington: Indiana University Press, 2004.

Kambili, Cyprian. "Ethics of African Tradition: Prescription of a Dress Code in Malawi, 1965–1973." *Society of Malawi Journal* 55, no. 2 (2002): 80–100.

Kanogo, Tabitha. "Kikuyu Women and the Politics of Protest." In *Images of Women in Peace and War*, edited by Sharon MacDonald, Pat Holden, and Shirley Ardener, 78–99. London: MacMillan, 1987.

Longman, Timothy. "Rwanda: Achieving Equality or Serving an Authoritarian State?" In *Women in African Parliaments*, edited by Gretchen Bauer and Hannah E. Britton, 133–50. Boulder: Lynne Rienner, 2006.

Lorde, Audre. "The Master's Tools Will Never Dismantle the Master's House." In *Sister Outsider: Essays and Speeches*, 110–14. Trumansburg, NY: The Crossing Press, 1984.

Maathai, Wangari. *Unbowed: A Memoir*. New York: Alfred A. Knopf, 2006.

Maingard, Jacqueline, Heather Thompson, and Sheila Meintjes. *Uku hamba 'ze: To Walk Naked*, DVD. New York: Third World Newsreel, 1995.

Mama, Amina. "Feminism or Femocracy? State Feminism and Democratization in Nigeria." *Africa Development* 20, no. 1 (1995): 37–58.

Mama, Amina, and Margo Okazawa-Rey. "Militarism, Conflict, and Women's Activism." *Feminist Africa* 10 (2008): 1–8.

———. "Militarism, Conflict and Women's Activism in the Global Era: Challenges and Prospects for Women in Three West African Contexts." *Feminist Review* 101 (2012): 97–123.

Mba, Nina. "Kaba and Khaki: Women and the Militarized State in Nigeria." In *Women and the State in Africa*, edited by Jane L. Parpart and Kathleen Staudt, 69–90. Boulder: Lynne Rienner Publishers, 1989.

McFadden, Patricia. "Plunder as Statecraft: Militarism and Resistance in Postcolonial Africa." In *Security Disarmed: Critical Perspectives on Gender, Race, and Militarization*, edited by Barbara Sutton, Sandra Morgen, and Julie Novkov, 136–56. New Brunswick, NJ: Rutgers University Press, 2008.

Meintjes, Sheila. "Naked Women's Protest, July 1990: 'We Won't Fuck for Houses.'" In *Women in South African History: Basus'iimbokodo, bawel'imilambo / They Remove Boulders and Cross Rivers*, edited by Nomboniso Gasa, 347–67. Cape Town: HSRC Press, 2007.

Molema, Leloba, and Mary Lederer. "Introduction to 'Citizenship: An Open Letter to the Attorney General'" (1985). In *Women Writing Africa: The Southern Region*, edited by M.J. Daymond, Dorothy Driver, Shelia Meintjes, Leloba Molema, Chiedza Musengezi, Margie Orford, and Nobantu Rasebotsa, 386–87. New York: The Feminist Press at the City University of New York, 2003.

Molokomme, Athaliah, Leloba Molema, Opha Dube, Motsei Madisa, Ruth Motsete, and Onalenna Selolwane. "Citizenship: An Open Letter to the Attorney General" (1985). In *Women Writing Africa: The Southern Region*, edited by M.J. Daymond, Dorothy Driver, Shelia Meintjes, Leloba Molema, Chiedza Musengezi, Margie Orford, and Nobantu Rasebotsa, 386–89. New York: The Feminist Press at the City University of New York, 2003.

Mulokozi, M.M. "Introduction to 'Bibi Titi Mohamed: Sacrifices for Change'" (1965). In *Women Writing Africa: The Eastern Region*, edited by Amandina Lihamba, Fulata L. Moyo, M.M. Mulokozi, Naomi L. Shitemi, and Saida Yahya-Othman, 229–30. New York: The Feminist Press at the City University of New York, 2007.

Okeke, Philomena. "First Lady Syndrome: The (En)Gendering of Bureaucratic Corruption in Nigeria." *CODESRIA Bulletin*, nos. 3–4 (1998): 16–19.

Oyewumi, Oyeronke. *The Invention of Women: Making an African Sense of Western Gender Discourses*. Minneapolis: University of Minnesota Press, 1997.

Parpart, Jane L., and Kathleen A. Staudt. "Women and the State in Africa." In *Women and the State in Africa*, edited by Jane L. Parpart and Kathleen A. Staudt, 1–19. Boulder: Lynne Rienner Publishers, 1989.

Schuster, Ilsa Glazer. *New Women of Lusaka*. Palo Alto, CA: Mayfield Publishing, 1979.

Sheldon, Kathleen. *The A to Z of Women in Sub-Saharan Africa*. Lanham, MD: The Scarecrow Press, 2010.

Sirleaf, Ellen Johnson. "Presidential Inaugural Address." Capitol Grounds, Monrovia, January 16, 2006.

Tripp, Aili Mari. "Women in Politics in Africa Today." *Democracy in Africa*. December 9, 2013. http://democracyinafrica.org/women-politics-africa-today/.

Tripp, Aili Mari, Isabel Casimiro, Joy Kwesiga, and Alice Mungwa. *African Women's Movements: Changing Political Landscapes*. Cambridge: Cambridge University Press, 2009.

Wipper, Audrey. "African Women, Fashion, and Scapegoating." *Canadian Journal of African Studies* 6, no. 2 (1972): 329–49.

———. "Kikuyu Women and the Harry Thuku Disturbances: Some Uniformities of Female Militancy." *Africa* 59, no. 3 (1989): 300–7.

# CHAPTER 45

# Young People and Public Space in Africa: Past and Present

## Mamadou Diouf

In his review for the *New York Times*, 'Youth with Hopes and Bliss Intact' (May 28, 2011),[1] Ken Johnson writes about the video installation created by the Thai director Apichatpong Weerasethakul. 'Primitive', then at the New Museum of New York, focused upon the men of Thailand, yet the initial sentences of Johnson's review aptly describe the situation of young men in many places:

> All over the world, teenage boys and young men are a problem. With their irrepressible energies and strengths, they are always ripe for industrial, military and other kinds of services. But when they are uneducated, unemployed and unsupervised, many of them get into trouble. They join feral gangs and terrorist groups or become freelance criminals, dissipated addicts, deadbeat fathers, suicides. In stable, wealthy nations, schools and vocational programs provide guidance and protective incubation for many youths during the pre-adult years. But in areas afflicted by war and poverty, they can be exceptionally vulnerable to exploitation and bad luck.[2]

Along with Thailand, Africa is one of many regions of misfortune for youth. During the last decades of the twentieth century and at the beginning of the twenty-first century, the continent has been shaken by eruptions of violence, social and political movements, and cultural and democratic projects,

M. Diouf (✉)
Middle Eastern, South Asian and African Studies Department and
Department of History, Columbia University, New York, NY, USA

© The Author(s) 2018
M.S. Shanguhyia and T. Falola (eds.),
*The Palgrave Handbook of African Colonial and Postcolonial History*,
https://doi.org/10.1057/978-1-137-59426-6_45

of which young men and women have been both the principal perpetrators and the principal victims.

Formally and informally, African youth occupy a central place within public spaces: in the political realm, in music (as creators and producers), in media, in spiritual sites (churches, mosques, forests and other sacred places), in the street,[3] in the armed forces, and as public servants; whether serving the state, politicians, communities, or themselves.[4] In African contexts today, young people are triply positioned: in environments of crisis (of multiple causes, forms, and consequences), young people have come to constitute significant *actors* and *resources*, as well as the central *concern*, within the social movements that have convulsed African societies.

The course and the detours of youth actions, their formal and informal interventions within available social frameworks (both licit and illicit) concern not only their future, but also the future of society as a whole. African youth (in their expressions of violence, as in their artistic endeavors, musical and visual; in their economic ingenuity and community engagement; and in their religious affiliations and political allegiances) sketch out a multicolored, incomplete, and unpublished mapping of a particular social geography. It is a cartography intent upon conforming to '*le temps du monde*' ('the time of globalization') which, in its brutality, uproots the vernacular temporalities of indigenous modernities.

I define *le temps du monde* as the historical sequences that have brought various communities across the world closer to each other economically, politically, and culturally. This movement was initiated by the profound change in the international geopolitical order that began in the sixteenth century with the shift of the world's geopolitical axis towards the oceans, Atlantic and Indian, and concluded with the conquest of the Pacific in the second half of the nineteenth century. *Le temps du monde* is contained within a movement that begins in America in 1492 and finishes in America, now, in the beginning of the twenty-first century; that of the birth and consolidation of the nation-state, and the progressive turning away of politics from its foundation in religion and the rule of the aristocracy.[5] *Le temps du monde*, according to Tocqueville, captures vernacular temporalities, reenunciating them along lines of generational and gender inequality characteristic of traditional societies. One of the clearest expressions of Africa's intrusion into *le temps du monde* is the album *Positive Black Soul*; Paris and New York become, in effect, *banlieues* of Dakar.

The context of the emergence of youth into the public sphere is connected to the combined effects of economic crisis and structural adjustment policies upon employment, education, and health care in particular, and the crisis of legitimacy of the institutions and of the political class which has begun to irreversibly decline. The consequences of such a situation are numerous. I will mention here only two: the acceleration of a process of depoliticization caused by the desertion of formal institutions and the substitution of a moral critique for a political critique, driven by a profound disdain for political activities and for politics itself, characterized as 'dirty' and morally fraudulent. In addition, political space and political institutions became the exclusive playground of politicians; new spaces of bricolage emerged; and there was a quest for new codes of ethics and solidarity or a recycling and revival of old ones. Other consequences include: the increasingly central role occupied, or taken, by non-state actors, in particular youth and members of ethnic or community organizations; increasingly widespread police and military repression and abuse; the intensification of criminality, drug trafficking and use, and militia activity (whether the militias of neighborhoods, or of ethnic or religious groups); the strengthening of clientelist networks located outside of the spheres of administration and government, particularly in the domain of security (of people and possessions)[6]; the disintegration of the administrative structure; and, finally, the obliteration of public services. In short, the privatization of previously public functions and the constriction of the space in which the state operates. 'In response', writes Joseph Hellweg, 'ruling elites consolidated networks of support, bought off opponents, commandeered state resources, manipulated markets, broke laws, dismantled bureaucracies, held creditors at bay, and allied with national or international corporations to privatize public services'.[7]

These analyses, which foster a reflection upon the relations between young people and the project of the democratization of African societies, must pay close attention to the conditions of everyday life, to the internal dynamics of these societies, and to the stakes of, and cultural motivations of, their interventions. Furthermore, we must attend to the geographies, ecologies (of the city, the village, the forest, the European and US metropole), and social imaginaries that young people have set in motion in order to produce their own subjectivities. How do they interpret, and how do they act upon, the (dis)continuities and ruptures that emerge in their lives, keeping in mind that democratization is a moment in which public space is reorganized? In order to account for the participation, resistance, or indifference of African youth to the democratic project, one must recognize the border zones of the territories in transition that they have been ransacking, marked by signs of suffering and crisis, and in historical moments that require the reconfiguration of geographies of inclusion and exclusion, public and domestic, communal and private.

Such an analysis requires that we take into consideration the realities (factual and discursive) that recover, under varying circumstances and conditions, ideas about both young people and democratization and the interactions between the two.

While the literature on youth is abundant, much of it addresses employment and work, family, belonging and affiliation, gender, and religion. The dimensions of race, politics, and class, however, are neglected. It is, for example, important to identify the styles (of practice, artistic and rhetorical) through which young people experience both citizenship and daily forms of belonging (local, national, and global), in relation to democratic principles; in particular to pluralism, tolerance, civility, and gender equality. Such a course is indispensable if one is to understand the process through which young people formulate their responses and if one is to understand their extremely complex critiques of political and domestic spaces and of the forms of identification and belonging authorized by state power.

Youth presence in public space (whether in roles assigned or claimed) and participation in politics (within political parties, armed groups, unions, or associations) is constantly reconstituted through a tumultuous movement of inclusion and eviction which positions them, whether as the agents or the acted upon,[8] according to age and sex, ethnicity and religion.

If it appears simple to identify the expressions for which the population labeled 'youth' is responsible, the realities that are defined by this term are difficult to establish unambiguously. What is the usefulness of the notion for describing and analyzing a heterogeneous social category, one that lacks fixed borders whether in terms of class, interests, worldview, gender, or age? Is it a primary or secondary identity? Does it better account for the experience of men than of women? That indeed would be the case if one were to share the view of R. Waller, who maintains that 'youth' is largely, and implicitly, gendered, a category employed to refer to the conflicts between adolescent and adult men in generational terms, while conflicts between adolescent and adult women are imagined in specifically gendered terms.[9] This situation is reflected in the engagements, and the level of participation, of the two groups in the political and social space. In effect, one can frequently lose sight of the presence of women's associations (the political consequences of their social and economic interventions) that insert themselves outside of the political institutions, that terrain that political leaders have exclusively reserved for men.[10]

Setting aside semantic uncertainties and the absence of a precisely defined age group to which it refers, the dominance of 'youth' is a powerful variable in the demography of Africa. This situation makes generational conflict one of the most dynamic and persistent forces of African history to govern access to power, women, and spiritual authority.[11] Islam, Christianity, and the urbanization that followed colonial domination all intensified generational conflict by fueling it with new opportunities and new constraints, both ideological and material.[12] Religious and urban transformations led to a loss of the authority of the 'elders' upon 'youth', and upon women. Both groups could now migrate, convert, or resist (including through violence) in order to confront the 'generational obstacles' that the colonial and postcolonial transitions, identified respectively by John Iliffe[13] and Frederick Cooper,[14] had unleashed. How to understand youth actions, and the political implications of those actions (ranging from the recourse to violence to efforts to join or abandon ethnic, religious, or regional community institutions, the state, and *le temps du monde*) without taking into consideration not only the *longue durée* of history, but also local understandings and idioms, and changing, unstable circumstances?[15] The appreciation of youth contribution to, or hindering of, the democratic project depends upon a perspective that recognizes this historical and social context.

In turning our attention uniquely towards the age of the actors, does the analytical category 'youth' help us understand particular social expressions? Is 'youth' not a political category claimed, and a metaphor brandished, by actors seeking to legitimate their interventions into political and social terrain? Challenging the existing order or claiming positions of leadership within their communities, 'youth' are not necessarily defined by age but, instead, by expertise, experience within educational and administrative institutions. For example, the contestation of indirect rule that, within the British Empire gave the 'native elite' – the first generation to receive university diplomas – both the legitimacy and authority to participate in colonial governance and control early postcolonial African states.

It appears, then, that understanding the role of young people in democratic transitions demands a double movement. In the first place, it demands understanding democratic transition as a project located at the heart of social, cultural, and economic claims, tests of institutional and political strength that are inscribed in the *longue durée* and in accretions of experiences and discourses, constantly recycled and questioned within social circuits. These practices are shaped by sequences, the pre-colonial (including certain ideas of modernity and modernization), the colonial (including new national forms of an alternative modernity), and that of capitalist globalization, with its creole logics. This movement is necessary in order to decipher social movements, cultural and political processes that undergird assertions of democracy building or that, by contrast, contribute to resistance or indifference to it. The second movement consists of asking about the continuities and discontinuities between the three temporalities in the representations and roles that are (self-)assigned to youth in democracy building. Several factors, including the political, economic, social and cultural, interact within each of these temporalities and trace the political formation and the type of presence and participation of youth in each of them.

This analysis does not lose sight of a central fact: the terrain of its intervention is that of the last twenty years. It sets out to account for the trajectory of African youth within the context of the varied projects of democratic transition that began in African states during the 1990s, without losing sight of the global context of that trajectory and the historical itinerary that endows it with meaning. This analysis tracks the transformations of the construction of the social category of 'youth'; the roles that are assigned to young people, as well as their practices in the spaces of community, state, and globalization; and the languages, social logics, and resources (material and symbolic) that they mobilize in the three temporal sequences that I identify below.

The first sequence consists of the nationalist years, dominated by the mobilization of youth in order to achieve political autonomy, recover African culture, and reconcile tradition and modernity; the second sequence is that of the intensification of social movements and of a return to violence, a context characterized by an intensification of repression and of demands for democracy. It is a moment that brings together war, the ascent of a libidinal, criminal economy that combines violence, the desire to (merely) appear, and the obscene display of wealth. The third and final sequence initiates (that is, at least, the argument that I defend here) the emergence of the arts of citizenship outside of the political or, in new modes of doing politics. This time is one of moral economies (of mosques, churches, and religious groups) and of a recycling of the effects of globalization on the part of youth who are aware of participating in *le temps du monde*. We could even say that in the course of this final sequence we see the dissolution of the political and the reinvention of the everyday and of history. Are we not in the process of exiting the libraries, both colonial and national? It is a situation that demands that the democratic project, which could not take root, must be rethought in light of the experiences of the past 20 years.

## SITUATIONS

African demographic research emphasizes the 'bulge' of youth in the population: it is a significant trend that has considerably reshaped the African population and will continue to do so long into the future. Some 200 million Africans are between 15 and 24 years old.[16] Young people represent three-fifths of the unemployed, and 72% of them have an income of under two dollars per day.[17] The following solid demographic factors deserve mention: young people face xenophobia and exploitation, including sexual exploitation; they endure domestic and public violence; they work in the informal sector, one of generally poor productivity and revenue.[18] Relative to rural youth, urban youth have more educational opportunities, stay in school longer and enter the labor market later.[19] Girls are less educated, have significantly reduced access to school, and may experience early pregnancy and childbirth.[20]

The figures are chilling. As Michelle Garvin observes:

> More than 70 percent of all Zimbabweans, for example, are now under 30; the same is true in Kenya, Uganda, Ethiopia, Liberia, and Nigeria, among other countries. Over one-third of the entire population of Zimbabwe, and over 56 percent of the adult (over 15) population, is between 15 and 29 years old. In fact, young adults (aged 15 to 29) make up 40 percent or more of the total adult population in the vast majority of sub-Saharan countries; in roughly 30 African countries, they constitute more than half of the adult population.

In contrast, approximately 40 percent of the population in the United States is under 30, and young adults constitute less than 30 percent of the adult population as a whole.[21]

Meanwhile, these enormous and horrifying figures mask the heterogeneity of the social category that they purport to explain. The relevant age range varies according to country, language, and circumstances, while the common legal situation is that, at age 18 (the age of majority), citizens gain the right to vote and become equal before the law. In West Africa, for example, youth is defined variously: in Ghana, as aged between 18 and 35; in Sierra Leone, between 15 and 30; in Nigeria, between 18 and 35; and in Senegal, Gambia, Guinea-Bissau, Mali, and Ivory Coast, between 15 and 35. Certain international institutions attempt to establish a common understanding of the age range that 'youth' denotes: the United Nations and the World Bank propose ages 15–24; the Commonwealth, ages 15–29.

The impacts of youth presence on public space and youth participation in politics vary considerably, depending upon what ages 'youth' denotes. These impacts and consequences are forcefully shaped by the distinct historical sequences around which this reflection is organized.

## First Sequence: Education and Training

This first sequence, which begins with independence and continues into the middle of the 1970s, is marked by the logic that defined state-education policy: the training and bureaucratization of youth by the ruling party (which quickly became the sole party) and its affiliated organizations of women, youth, workers, and peasants.[22] It is a situation that Achille Mbembe describes well in his analysis of the familial, patriarchal dynamics of political subordination:

> [T]he head of state, titled owner of the wealth that the state constitutes, manages that patrimony in the interest of his children. Through the ideological force of seniority, the younger owes respect and submission to the elder. Obedience is, here, the sign of wisdom, and is rewarded as such through cooptation into the circles that draw on the national coffers. In this way, relations of subjection attempt to work through the channels of familial relationship: and thus, given the character of African family structure, along the lines of inequality likely to evoke the greatest level of consent. Old social categories are thus reinvigorated and endowed with new political ends.[23]

African young people constituted a critical social and political issue because they became the most significant measure of the success or failure of society, state, and nation. Young people were assigned the double function of achieving the emancipation of the continent and of launching African states into development, democracy, and social justice. 'Youth' thus became the agent of modernization through education. Harboring the double promise of national independence and social and economic development, youth was to be responsible for cultural renewal at the same time as it was to bow before the edicts of ancestral African culture. This doubled force, of both modern temptation and the implacable tyranny of the ancestors, is located at the heart of the paradox of postcolonial African societies from the 1960s until the end of the twentieth century. It finds form in the wave of single-party states and in the logics of command and bureaucratization, especially in the strict control over youth and youth movements. The recourse to force and violence was the dominant form of these modes of political organization.

The period is also characterized by some achievements, such as a steady decline in mortality, increased life expectancy, and verifiable progress in the area of education. In search of legitimacy and a monopoly over political and economic power, political leaders alternated between three strategies: development politics focused upon social services, patronage, and the systematic repression of dissidence. In response, certain segments of the population, youth in particular, called upon alternative, religious or ethnic, forms that offered security and resources, whether through violence or withdrawal.[24]

A triple balancing structured the rhythm of the period in a vacillation between the extension and contraction of the space of citizenship: on the one hand, a state power which provided social services and created networks of patronage and which also resorted to blind repression of dissent; and, on the other, a population that variously feigned adhesion to the state, withdrew into indifference, resisted, or revolted.[25]

A political resource existing on the margins of public space, restricted in the economic realm (young women in particular), African young people were the primary victims of public and private violence during the 1960s and 1970s. Examples include the terrible repression of student movements that reached its apex in the bloody accounting that followed the military (and revolutionary-movement) take-over of power in Ethiopia in 1974; the silent violence to which rural young people are subjected by both the state and traditional authority in most African countries; and the patriarchal authority that seeks to exercise rigid control over African girls and women from the moment that they became an active presence in the labor market and public space.

The absolute and categorical nature of authoritarian rule rested upon a systematic recourse to violence. The failure of the promises of independence, the dramatic vagaries of economic crisis, the massive presence of the 'forces of order', and the everyday harassment that they inflicted, testifies to the extraordinary human and psychological cost borne by youth, in service of every cause or conflict of which they were to be the heroes; whether in the image of the South African 'young lions' faced with the repressive apartheid machine, or as delinquents and vagabonds, as in Sierra Leone, Liberia, Congo, or Mozambique.[26] Emerging from these sometimes vain, always murderous, experiences of suffering are dreams of departure for a destination beyond an Africa that must permit the exit from a continent for which there is no hope.[27]

In the second sequence, the systematic recourse to force, combined with a fascination with the success of 'the West', will often prove lethal. Together, these two tendencies will transform the Straits of Gibraltar and the Sahara into vast cemeteries filled with navigators and wanderers who had sought hospitable shores.

## SECOND SEQUENCE: NATIONALIST CRISIS, VIOLENCE AND DEMOCRATIC TRANSITION

Democratic transitions in Africa are inscribed in a particular moment in the history of African societies, a moment marked by a triple transition: demographic, political, and economic. The end of the Cold War, the intensification of structural adjustment programs, and the relaxing of external political constraints and support, all informed a change in the character of conflicts in Africa; they gained a more indigenous dimension. The three transitions signaled a situation of crisis and adjustment that produced multiple options and configurations of power and resource allocations; constraints and opportunities that made African societies vacillate between negotiation and conflict, reform and violent rupture.[28] Civic, political, and public spaces fractured more pervasively along ethnic, religious, and regional fault lines. At the same time, the triple transition pervaded and amplified generational problems (the difficult transition to adulthood involving employment, access to resources, and marriage) as it had done at the end of the colonial period, thus reinvigorating youth contestation and nourishing its increasingly violent expression. More tragically, demographic, economic, and political transitions led young people to experience increasing material and spiritual insecurity.[29] Young people endeavored to open a breach in authoritarian apparatuses, whether through political mobilization and struggle or through violence; they exploited the idioms and networks of multiple ethnographies and geographies, ones through which arms, drugs, and traffickers of contraband of all kinds circulated.[30] Increasingly brutal and murderous conflicts thus multiplied during the course of the 1990s. Their effects, according to F. Cooper, 'have been devastating, undermining more sustainable forms of economic development, destroying hard-built social and economic infrastructure, turning a new generation of potential citizens and workers into youthful soldiers, spreading disease and malnutrition'.[31]

In losing the privileged place that the nationalist narrative had granted them (warriors of the present, crucial actors and resources in the construction of the future and in the restoration of devalued identities) young people lost a place within nationalist time and its missions. They thus also lost their central role as drivers of national projects, and found themselves instead on the margins, feared, disparaged, and held at bay. From these margins, or in the fallows that the state (now impelled to relinquish its totalitarian grip) had opened, youth set out to create their own geography and narrative. That narrative would give them the meaningful task of radically questioning the nationalist narrative, its imaginary and all of its texts, whether economic, political, or cultural. Confronted with the intention of their elders to dictate the law and ensure their own continued domination of all the registers of social life, youth created dissident and dissonant cultures and modes of civility within the fissures of the social fabric. Socially and ideologically the minority but demographically the majority, youth fractured public space or transformed it, creating alternative spaces that made African cities difficult to govern; whole areas were beyond the reach of the state.

While the interventions and practices of youth certainly play a part in the construction of an open and democratic society, they do so obliquely, a fact which considerably reduces their participation in the consolidation of a democratic space and its attributes: freedom of press and association, respect for the rights of the human person, tolerance, pluralism, and respect for the rights of minorities. Young people were the principal victims of colonial domination,[32] but they were also, at the end of that period, the principal intellectual and 'muscular'[33] participants within nationalist movements.[34] This trajectory, characterized by alternating periods of intensity and ebbing, lasted through the interwar period, the Second World War, and the decades of nationalist awakening, until the Ivorian electoral crisis of 2010–2011. Youth traveled along licit and illicit routes, on paths through the *maquis* and through obscure urban zones, on those of violence as well as those of negotiation.[35] Young people mobilized, as they did in Mali, where, with the decisive intervention of their mothers and sisters, they put an end to the dictatorship of President Moussa Traoré (1991).

A quasi-totality of West African countries has experienced an *année blanche*, a 'blank year'.[36] The recourse to violence, the idiom of purification by fire, and the destruction of sites and monuments of the postcolonial power (as if to de-territorialize its inscription in space) constitute the shared elements of youth-led social movements. The project of 'uprooting', in the literal sense of the word, the legitimacy of postcolonial powers is legible in several events: in the riots orchestrated by Malian students (April 5, 1993)[37]; in the withdrawal of parts of Lagos and whole Nigerian cities from the control of politicians and the administration, except through the mediation of *area boys*[38]; and the crucial role played by 'disaffected youth' in the armed struggles in Liberia and Sierra Leone.[39]

The breaches that African young people have opened in the seemingly impenetrable retaining walls of the state speak to a loosening of the authoritarian vice. This relaxation occurs through several processes: in the opening to democracy (*ouverture démocratique*), the recognition of opposition parties, the establishment of electoral administrations, and in the initiation of economic reform and media pluralism. The organization of national conferences

(Benin, Congo, Togo) and the establishment of commissions charged with constitutional reform (Ivory Coast, Kenya, Cameroon), and growth in the numbers of political parties, unions, and non-governmental organizations, have brought about a reconfiguration of the political landscape.

In a context of resource scarcity and the incapacity of state bureaucracy to respond to social demands for employment, education, and health care, new institutional mechanisms and policies (the principal function of which was to assert and maintain the legitimacy of the ruling power) did not meet their goals. As happened during the transitional period that led to independence, young people were either absent from national conferences or confined to their margins. Young people's abandonment of political space, or their entry into clientelist networks, formal and informal, licit and illicit (especially the militias of political parties, neighborhoods, and religious organizations) were major consequences of their retreat from the national institutions. Once again, Ivory Coast offers us multiple illustrations of this movement in, for example, the armed mobilization of 'young patriots'.

Although they may have succeeded in ensuring a degree of social stability and peace, democratic transitions failed in their primary mission: to consensually renegotiate the political, social, and economic pact. Corruption was not eliminated, nor even managed; governance remained poor; violence and massive fraud continued to characterize electoral processes; and authoritarianism took on new forms, principally that of generalized police repression, just as wealth became increasingly concentrated in the hands of a tiny ruling class.

This restricted citizenship did not prevent youth from beginning new projects and searching for new ways to make its presence felt in the public space. New geographies, charted by war, contraband, delinquency and militia activity, erased or reconfigured old forms of belonging and their public, private, and domestic expressions.[40] The infliction of death, sexual relations outside the bounds of social norms, rites of passage and initiation, all signaled the brutal entry of youth into adulthood: entry in the form of criminal activity and a social recognition gained through the force of muscles and of sex. The low value assigned to human life, the right to mutilate, kill, rape and steal, combined with the appearance of a tiny minority of 'golden boys' of the 'Dot Com Generation', signal a particular conclusion: of the classical anthropological figures of the elder and the youngest, of the orderly and strategic circulation of women in the interest of strengthening social institutions, of community civility, and of an expert mastery of witchcraft and of African, Western, and Eastern spiritualities. There is thus an explosive fusion of the visible and the invisible that signals the emergence of societies abandoned by God.[41]

The scenery and props of this culture of riot and violent protest seem to be influenced by globally circulating images (of rioting South African townships, of the Intifada in Israeli-occupied Palestinian territories) disseminated by news media and by the crude aestheticized violence of *Rambo* and *Terminator*-type films.

## THIRD SEQUENCE: DISSIDENT OR UNDISCIPLINED CITIZENSHIPS?

From the turmoil in which Africa is located, and the varied ways in which its youth inscribe themselves in the movement of globalization, with its gaps and disjunctures, new cultures and modes of civility emerge and reorganize social structures and experience: new social organizations, new ways of living and dying, and new forms of sociality propose a detachment from the continent that is not performed simply through physical departure but also through mental disconnections and erasures of African social imaginaries.

These movements come together and produce new rules, articulations of new desires, and the expression of new aspirations of which, for adults, the only legible moments are ones of violence. It is likely that the echo (always a deformation of youth speech and its guises in music, visual arts, sports, and fashion) seems to have favored the emergence of volatile vagabond figures who constantly elide the adult gaze, all the while constructing a shared language. Their discontent is at once a source of creativity and innovation, as well as of violent dissent and destructive currents (such as domestic violence, xenophobia, and homophobia).

Young Africans appear to have exited the logics and representations that define public space and institution-bound politics. Citizenship and national belonging are no longer perceived to hold the civic values of rights, obligations, and responsibilities. Marriage and access to formal employment both appear to have lost their social functions. The ([in]voluntary) confinement of youth to the space between the neighborhood and the world has nourished cosmopolitanism, xenophobia, and the invention of new forms of regional belonging that span state borders, opening the way to a contestation of the nation, its structure of governance and its claim to (national) representation.

In a sense, we are witnessing the end of adult representation of young people. The creations of adults have ceded place to the invention of young people, their own desires and aspirations. In becoming the writers and directors of their own dramas, they open the doors to the world and fill the vernacular national space with practices from elsewhere. In thus widening fissures in the social structure, they offer themselves doubly, as both threat and promise; they definitively place nationalist and Pan-Africanist narratives, and their traits, biographies, and temporalities, for which they substitute a close or far-away 'elsewhere', and the accompanying illusions of economic globalization and the hard reality of African economies subject to structural adjustment: life in a between-geography, between African reality and Euro-American dream. And it is at the precise heart of the tensions of 'off-balance' societies that new political practices and formulations of citizenship emerge, ones that I understand to be both dissident and insurrectional. One wonders if the majority of young Africans recognize themselves in the structures and discourses that democratic transitions promoted. Must not that absence of recognition be the reason for their desertion of public political space and their invention of new practices and expressions that those spaces do not account for? Might this not be the very reason for the uncertainties and hiccups of the democratic transitions?

The geography of urban violence in particular informs the shattered portrait of an African youth gripped in the double vice of patriarchal, gerontocratic, authoritarian social traditions, and the imperatives of globalization. Their simultaneous declension, in an environment ruled by institutional improvisation, of the disintegration of spaces of socialization and command on the one hand, and the disordered and unstable redefinition of life stages, from childhood to adulthood, on the other, created fresh opportunities to block social norms and prescriptions, and to erase rites of passage and the borders between childhood, adolescence, and adulthood. This situation asks that we investigate the imaginaries at work in the African continent, paying particular attention to their producers, to the images, representations, and desires that they reveal, but also to the shocks that force them to interact on an unstable set jammed with figures of the native and the cosmopolitan, the dissident and the conservative. Invented traditions are located in *le temps du monde*, in the multiplicity of its modernities, in the evident singularity of its sites and the power of its connections and networks. Young Africans today are located between the increasing fragmentation of an African world and the dreams, images, and histories that they themselves bring into being on the stages and screens of the world. There, where a dialogue with others is permanently taking place, the strictures of the continent's geography, history, and imaginary cede to the propulsion of other spaces, the territoriality and historicity of which transform center into periphery, and periphery into center.

Certainly, the African present, in particular that of youth, is marked by the rhythm of other possibilities and by the courses of other trajectories, ones that emphasize different forms of sociality, in sports, music, and dance. These different possibilities and their constraints emerge from a shared condition: the inadequacy of existing political discourses and institutions in the face of social, economic, and ideological realities. The institutional space of the citizen is not the terrain of social practices, particularly not that of youth social practices. Figures of citizenship do not echo their desires and dreams. The failure of contemporary political institutions to produce a civic culture of tolerance, democracy, and respect for pluralism demands a rigorous explanation of social processes and cultural transformations, but also a deep familiarity with the powerful tendencies that structure African societies and social groups. A primary question is this: How should one respond to the disengagement of youth from public space and political expression? Thinking otherwise, we might ask ourselves if it is possible to translate young people's political practices into the institutional space of politics. Youth political practices produce a dissident discourse that challenges the state, its police, its discipline and its pedagogy, its institutions and its nationalist mythology. Young people attempt clumsily to respond to questions of institutional representation and elections, social justice and human rights, and the role and responsibility of varied actors such as the state, local authorities, ethnic, regional, and religious communities, and family. Violently opposed to the state and its agents, some young people endeavor to replace it by providing their communities with security, hope, and stability.[42] Family, state, and nation, and what they offer (security, education, health care), as well as political parties, have lost their ability to enchant. The dream of the future 'good life' has dissolved. Repeated obstacles in the passage from one generation to the next have obliterated the meanings and value associated with marriage, employment, and a slightly longer lifespan. The attainment of adulthood has become an increasingly distant horizon for African adolescents. We must not, therefore, merely rethink political institutions (of representation in particular); we must also rethink the temporal horizon of politics. In response, as we have endeavored to articulate in this chapter, youth have placed themselves beyond these zones.

This chapter has been translated from the French by Cullen Golblatt, Mellon Postdoctoral Fellow, The Cogut Center for the Humanities, Brown University.

## NOTES

1. "The Arts Pages," *New York Times*, Saturday, May 2, C1, C5.
2. Ibid., 1.
3. In his novel, *Allah Is Not Obliged* (New York: Anchor Books, [2000], 2007). (Translated from the French by Frank Wynne), Ahmadou Kourouma offers a vivid portrait of the street child, in the context of an African war: «Before I got to Liberia, I was a fearless, blameless kid. I slept anywhere I wanted and stole all kinds of stuff to eat. My grandmother used to spend days and days looking for me: that is because I was what they call a street kid. Before I was a street kid, I went at school. Before that, I was a *bilakoro* back in the village of Togobala (according to the *Glossary*, *bilakoro* is an uncircumcised boy). I ran through the streams and down the fields and I hunted mice and birds in the scrubland. I was a proper Black Nigger African Savage.» p. 5.
4. A number of researchers, politicians, and activists refer to a "youth bulge" or "youth crisis" that threatens security and stability in Africa. The principal expressions of a youth crisis are chronic unemployment, delinquency, and criminality, the recourse to violence, HIV/AIDS infection, and the exit of family networks and of ethnic, religious, and state inheritances from social institutions. See: Robert Kaplan, *The Ends of the Earth: A Journey at the Frontiers of Anarchy* (New York: Vintage Book, 1996); Michelle Garvin, "Africa's Restless Youth," in *Beyond Humanitarianism*, ed. P. Lyman and P. Dorff (New York: Council of Foreign Relations, 2007); and Jon Abbink, "Being Young in Africa: The Politics of Despair and Removal," in *Vanguard or Vandals: Youth, Politics and Conflicts in Africa*, ed. Jon Abbink and Ineke Van Kesse (Leiden and Boston: Brill, 2005).
5. Here, I am referring to Sudipta Kaviraj's discussion of Tocqueville's "two types of democratic transition," from "non-democratic to democratic forms

of government takes place within the horizons of a more complex, comprehensive, and slow-moving change—from pre-modern to modern forms of politics," "The Empire of Democracy. Reading Indian Politics Through Tocqueville," in *Anxieties of Democracy. Tocquevillean Reflections on India and the United States*, ed. Partha Chatterjee and Ira Katznelson (Oxford: Oxford University Press, 2012), 21–22.

6. David Anderson, "Vigilantes, Violence, and the Politics of Public Order in Kenya," *African Affairs* 101 (2002): 531–55; Kate Maeger, "Hijacking Civil Society: The Inside Story of the Bakassi Boys Vigilante Group of South-eastern Nigeria," *Journal of Modern African Studies* 45, no. 1 (2007); *Identity Economics. Social Networks and the Informal Economy in Nigeria* (Woodbridge, Rochester and Ibadan: James Currey, 2010); Mamadou Diouf, "Afterword," in *Makers and Breakers: Children and Youth in Postcolonial Africa*, ed. Alcinda Honwana and F. de Boeck (Oxford: James Currey, 2005); and Tshikala Biaya, "Youth and Street Culture in Urban Africa," in *Makers and Breakers: Children and Youth in Postcolonial Africa*, ed. Alcinda Honwana and F. de Boeck (Oxford: James Currey, 2005).

7. Joseph Hellweg, *Hunting the Ethical State. The Benkadi Movement of Côte d'Ivoire* (Chicago: University of Chicago Press, 2011), 6.

8. See Jon Abbink and Ineke Van Kesse, eds., *Vanguard or Vandals: Youth, Politics and Conflicts in Africa* (Leiden and Boston: Brill, 2005); and Alcinda Honwana and F. de Boeck, eds., *Makers and Breakers: Children and Youth in Postcolonial Africa* (Oxford: James Currey, 2005).

9. Richard Waller, "Rebellious Youth in Colonial Africa," *Journal of African History* 47, no. 1 (2006): 82–83.

10. Tomothy Scarnecchi, *The Urban Root of Democracy and Political Violence in Zimbabwe* (Rochester: University of Rochester Press, 2008); and Elisabeth Schmidt, *Mobilizing the Masses: Gender, Ethnicity, and Class in the Nationalist Movement in Guinea, 1939–1958* (Portsmouth: Heinemann, 2005).

11. John Iliffe, *The Africans: The History of a Continent* (Cambridge: Cambridge University Press, 1995), 95.

12. On these questions, see Chinua Achebe, *Things Fall Apart* (Oxford: Heinemann Educational Publishers, 1958); and Chimamanda N. Adichie, *Purple Hibiscus* (London: Fourth Estate, 2004).

13. John Iliffe, *Honour in African History* (Cambridge: Cambridge University Press, 2005), 203.

14. Cooper observes that the generational blockages of the late twentieth century unleashed "the apocalyptic destructiveness" of young men. "Possibility and Constraint: African Independence in Historical Perspective," *Journal of African History* 49, no. 2 (2008): 189.

15. Jay Staker, "Youth, Globalization, and Millenial Reflection in a Guinean Forest Town," *Journal of Modern African Studies* 45, no. 2 (2007): 302, 314–15.

16. The World Bank, *Youth and Employment in Africa. The Potential, the Problem, the Promise. Africa Development Indicators 2008–2009* (Washington DC, 2008), 1.

17. Ibid.

18. The World Bank, *Youth and Employment in Africa*, 5–6.

19. Ibid., 7.

20. Ibid.

21. Michelle D. Gavin, "Africa's Restless Youth," in *Beyond Humanitarianism*, ed. Princeton Lyman and Patricia Dorff (New York: Council of Foreign Relations, 2007), 69–70. This article originally appeared in *Current History* 106, no. 700 (May 2007): 220–26.

22. See Achille Mbembe's discussion of the conflation of the state and the single party, *Les Jeunes et l'Ordre Politique en Afrique* (Paris: L'Harmattan, 1992), 14.

23. Ibid., 15.

24. F. Cooper, *"Possibility and Constraint,"* 170.

25. Ibid., 172.

26. K. Peters and P. Richards, «Jeunes combattants parlant de la guerre et de la paix en Sierra Leone», *Cahiers d'Etudes Africaines* XXXIX, nos. 150–52 (1998): 581–617; I. Abdullah and Y. Bangura, eds., "Lumpen Youth Culture and Political Violence: The Sierra Leone Civil War," special issue, *Africa Development* 23, nos. 3–4 (1997); and A. Honwana, "Negotiating Post-War Identities: Child Soldiers in Mozambique and Angola," *CODESRIA Bulletin* 1–2, 1999.

27. See "The Hopeless Continent," *The Economist*, May 13, 2000.

28. Nicolas van de Walle, *African Economies and the Politics of Permanent Crisis, 1979–1999* (Cambridge: Cambridge University Press, 2001).

29. Adam Ashforth, *Witchcraft, Violence, and Democracy in South Africa* (Chicago: Chicago University Press, 2005).

30. Alcinda Honwana and Filip de Boeck, eds., *Makers and Breakers: Children and Youth in Postcolonial Africa* (Trenton: Africa World Press, 2005); William Reno, *Warlord Politics and African States* (Boulder: Westview Press, 1998); Stephen Ellis, *The Mask of Anarchy. The Destruction of Liberia and the Religious Dimension of African Civil Wars*, 2nd revised and updated edition (New York: New York University Press, 2006); and Edna Bay and Donald Dunham, eds., *States of Violence: Politics, Youth, and Memory in Contemporary Africa* (Charlottesville: University of Virginia Press, 2006).

31. F. Cooper, *"Possibility and Constraint,"* 188.

32. John Lonsdale considers that colonial domination weakened self-mastery, sapped masculine energy, reduced ethical and political choice, and emphasized women's sexuality, within a context that questioned indigenous rights to their land, material economies, and knowledge. Confronted with the blocked passage between one generation and the next, the available solutions were migration, religious conversion, and revolt against "the elders." See especially some of Lonsdale's contributions to the volume that he co-authored with Bruce Berman, *Unhappy Valley: Conflict in Kenya and Africa* (Athens: Ohio University Press, 1992). See also John Ilife, *Honour in African History* (Cambridge: Cambridge University Press, 2005); and Jean and John Comaroff, "Reflections on Youth, from the Past to the Postcolony," in *Makers and Breakers*, ed. Honwana de Boeck.

33. F. Cooper, "Possibility and Constraint," 174.

34. See Jonathan Derrick, *Africa's 'Agitators.' Militant Anti-Colonialism in Africa and the West. 1918–1939* (New York: Columbia University Press, 2008).

35. K. Peters and P. Richards, «Jeunes combattants parlant de la guerre et de la paix en Sierra Leone», *Cahiers d'Etudes Africaines* XXXIX, nos. 150–52 (1998): 581–617; I Abdullah and Y. Bangura, eds., "Lumpen Youth Culture and Political Violence: The Sierra Leone Civil War," special issue, *Africa Development*

23, nos. 3–4 (1997); and A. Honwana, "Negotiating Post-War Identities: Child Soldiers in Mozambique and Angola," *CODESRIA Bulletin* 1–2, 1999.

36. An *année blanche* is a "lost" academic year, one that is not recognized because, due to strikes and an insufficient amount of instruction time, exams are not held. The consequence is that the year must be repeated; all students are "held back" one year.

37. On the Malian situation, consult C.O. Diarrah, «Les ambiguïtés et les difficultés de la concrétisation opérationnelle du projet démocratique du Mali», Unpublished paper presented at the workshop on West African cities, Présentée à l'Atelier sur les Villes ouest-africaines, WALTPS, Cinergie (BAD/OCDE, Dakar, 15–17 November 1993).

38. On "area boys," Abubakar Momoh writes: "The area boys as a social category became preponderant, popularised and organised from about 1986 when the Structural Adjustment Programme took its full course. Hence today, any form of crime or criminal in the entire South-Western Nigeria is identifiable or traceable to the area boys. The area boys are the equivalent of "Yanbada" in Hausaland, there are also called *allaayes, Omo oni ile* (son of the soil or landlords) sweet urchins, government pickin, untouchables, or alright sir." "The South-Western Nigeria Case Study," Paper presented at the West African Long Term Perspective Study, ADB-CINERGIE Conference, Lagos, 11–13 October 1993, 28.

39. P. Richards, *Fighting for the Rainforest: War, Youth and Resources in Sierra Leone* (Oxford: James Currey, 1996); Ibrahim Abdullah, "I Am a Rebel: Youth Culture and Violence in Sierra Leone," in *Makers and Breakers*, ed. Honwana, and de Boeck.

40. Mamadou Diouf, "Engaging Postcolonial Cultures: African Youth and the Public Space," *African Studies Review* 46, no. 1 (2003).

41. This is, at any rate, the ironic and tragic reading that Ahmadou Kourouma proposes, *Allah n'est pas oblige, Allah Is Not Obliged.*

42. Johannes Harbnischfeger, "The Bakassi Boys: Fighting Crime in Nigeria," *Journal of Modern African Studies* 41, no. 1 (2003): 61–89; Wale Adebanwi, "The Carpenter's Revolt: Youth, Violence and the Reinvention of Culture in Nigeria," *Journal of Modern African Studies* 43, no. 3 (2005): 339–65; Insa Nolte, "Identity and Violence: The Politics of Youth in in Ijebu-Remo, Nigeria," *Journal of Modern African Studies* 42, no. 1 (2004): 61–89; and Kate Maeger, "Hijacking Civil Society: The Inside Story of the Bakassi Boys Vigilante Group of South-eastern Nigeria," *Journal of Modern African Studies* 45, no. 1 (2007): (89–115); and J. Hellweg, *Hunting the Ethical State*, op. cit.

# BIBLIOGRAPHY

Abbink, Jon. "Being Young in Africa: The Politics of Despair and Removal." In *Vanguard or Vandals: Youth, Politics and Conflicts in Africa*, edited by Jon Abbink and Ineke Van Kesse. Leiden and Boston: Brill, 2005.

Abbink, Jon, and Ineke Van Kesse, eds. *Vanguard or Vandals: Youth, Politics and Conflicts in Africa*. Leiden and Boston: Brill, 2005.

Abdullah, Ibrahim. "I Am a Rebel: Youth Culture and Violence in Sierra Leone." In *Makers and Breakers: Children and Youth in Postcolonial Africa*, edited by Alcinda Honwana and F. de Boeck, 172–87. Oxford: James Currey, 2005.

Abdullah, I., and Y. Bangura, eds. Lumpen Youth Culture and Political Violence: The Sierra Leone Civil War. Special issue, *Africa Development* 22, nos. 3/4 (1997).

Achebe, Chinua. *Things Fall Apart*. Oxford: Heinemann Educational Publishers, 1958.

Adebanwi, Wale. "The Carpenter's Revolt: Youth, Violence and the Reinvention of Culture in Nigeria." *Journal of Modern African Studies* 43, no. 3 (2005): 339–65.

Adichie, N. Chimamanda. *Purple Hibiscus*. London: Fourth Estate, 2004.

Anderson, David. "Vigilantes, Violence, and the Politics of Public Order in Kenya." *African Affairs* 101 (2002): 531–55.

Ashforth, Adam. *Witchcraft, Violence, and Democracy in South Africa*. Chicago: Chicago University Press, 2005.

Bay, Edna, and Donald Dunham, eds. *States of Violence: Politics, Youth, and Memory in Contemporary Africa*. Charlottesville: University of Virginia Press, 2006.

Biaya, Tshikala. "Youth and Street Culture in Urban Africa." In *Makers and Breakers: Children and Youth in Postcolonial Africa*, edited by Alcinda Honwana and F. de Boeck. Oxford: James Currey, 2005.

Comaroff, Jean, and John Comaroff. "Reflections on Youth; From the Past to the Postcolony." In *Makers and Breakers: Children and Youth in Postcolonial Africa*, edited by Alcinda Honwana and F. de Boeck, 19–30. Oxford: James Currey, 2005.

Cooper, Frederick. "Possibility and Constraint: African Independence in Historical Perspective." *Journal of African History* 49, no. 2 (2008): 167–96.

Derrick, Jonathan. *Africa's 'Agitators.' Militant Anti-Colonialism in Africa and the West. 1918–1939*. New York: Columbia University Press, 2008.

Diarrah, C.O. Les ambiguïtés et les difficultés de la concrétisation opérationnelle du projet démocratique du Mali (Unpublished présentation) at the West African Cities workshop organized by the West African Long Term Perspective Study (WALTPS) and Cinergie (African Development Bank (ADB) and Organisation for Economic Co-operation and Development (OECD) Dakar, 15–17 November (1993).

Diouf, Mamadou. "Engaging Postcolonial Cultures: African Youth and the Public Space." *African Studies Review* 46, no. 1 (2003): 1–12.

———. "Afterword." In *Makers and Breakers: Children and Youth in Postcolonial Africa*, edited by Alcinda Honwana and F. de Boeck, 229–34. Oxford: James Currey, 2005.

Ellis, Stephen. *The Mask of Anarchy. The Destruction of Liberia and the Religious Dimension of African Civil Wars*. 2nd revised ed. New York: New York University Press, 2006.

Garvin, Michelle. "Africa's Restless Youth." In *Beyond Humanitarianism*, edited by P. Lyman and P. Dorff. New York: Council of Foreign Relations, 2007.

Gavin, D. Michelle. "Africa's Restless Youth." In *Beyond Humanitarianism*, edited by Princeton Lyman and Patricia Dorff. New York: Council of Foreign Relations, 2007.

Harbnischfeger, Johannes. "The Bakassi Boys: Fighting Crime in Nigeria." *Journal of Modern African Studies* 41, no. 1 (2003): 69–83.

Hellweg, Joseph. *Hunting the Ethical State. The Benkadi Movement of Côte d'Ivoire*. Chicago: University of Chicago Press, 2011.

Honwana, Alcinda. "Negotiating Post-War Identities: Child Soldiers in Mozambique and Angola." *CODESRIA Bulletin* (1999).

Honwana, Alcinda, and F. de Boeck, eds. *Makers and Breakers: Children and Youth in Postcolonial Africa*. Oxford: James Currey, 2005.

Illife, John. *The Africans: The History of a Continent*. Cambridge: Cambridge University Press, 1995.

———. *Honour in African History*. Cambridge: Cambridge University Press, 2005.

Kaplan, Robert. *The Ends of the Earth: A Journey at the Frontiers of Anarchy*. New York: Vintage Book, 1996.

Kaviraj, Sudipta. "The Empire of Democracy. Reading Indian Politics through Tocqueville." In *Anxieties of Democracy. Tocquevillean Reflections on India and the United States*, edited by Partha Chatterjee and Ira Katznelson. Oxford: Oxford University Press, 2012.

Kourouma, Ahmadou. *Allah Is Not Obliged*. New York: Anchor Books [2000], 2007.

Lonsdale, John, and Bruce Berman. *Unhappy Valley: Conflict in Kenya and Africa*. Athens: Ohio University Press, 1992.

Maeger, Kate. "Hijacking Civil Society: The Inside Story of the Bakassi Boys Vigilante Group of South-eastern Nigeria." *Journal of Modern African Studies* 45, no. 1 (2007).

———. "Hijacking Civil Society: The Inside Story of the Bakassi Boys Vigilante Group of South-eastern Nigeria." *Journal of Modern African Studies* 45, no. 1 (2007): 89–115.

———. *Identity Economics. Social Networks and the Informal Economy in Nigeria*. Woodbridge, Rochester and Ibadan: James Currey, 2010.

Mbembe, Achille. *Les Jeunes et l'Ordre Politique en Afrique*. Paris: L'Harmattan, 1992.

Momoh, Abubakar. "The South-Western Nigeria Case Study." Paper Presented at the West African Long Term Perspective Study, ADB-CINERGIE Conference, Lagos, 11–13 October 1993.

Nolte, Insa. "Identity and Violence: The Politics of Youth in Ijebu-Remo, Nigeria." *Journal of Modern African Studies* 42, no. 1 (2004): 61–89.

Peters, K., and P. Richards. Jeunes combattants parlant de la guerre et de la paix en Sierra Leone [1998]. *Cahiers d'Etudes Africaines* XXXIX, nos. 150–52 (1998): 581–617.

Reno, William. *Warlord Politics and African States*. Boulder: Westview Press, 1998.

Richards, Paul. *Fighting for the Rainforest: War, Youth and Resources in Sierra Leone*. Oxford: James Currey, 1996.

Scarnecchi, Tomothy. *The Urban Root of Democracy and Political Violence in Zimbabwe*. Rochester: University of Rochester Press, 2008.

Schmidt, Elisabeth. *Mobilizing the Masses: Gender, Ethnicity, and Class in the Nationalist Movement in Guinea, 1939–1958*. Portsmouth: Heinemann, 2005.

Staker, Jay. "Youth, Globalization, and Millenial Reflection in a Guinean Forest Town." *Journal of Modern African Studies* 45, no. 2 (2007): 299–319.

*The Economist*. "The Hopeless Continent." May 13, 2000.

*The New York Times*. May 28, 2011.

The World Bank. *Youth and Employment in Africa. The Potential, the Problem, the Promise. Africa Development Indicators 2008–2009*. Washington, DC: The World Bank, 2008.

van de Walle, Nicolas. *African Economies and the Politics of Permanent Crisis, 1979–1999*. Cambridge: Cambridge University Press, 2001.

Waller, Richard. "Rebellious Youth in Colonial Africa." *Journal of African History* 47, no. 1 (2006): 77–92.

CHAPTER 46

# Colonialism and African Sexualities

## Xavier Livermon

The field of 'African sexuality', broadly defined, subsumes a wide range of research foci, including studies directed toward public health, ethnographic studies of sexual communities, studies on the relationship between gender and sexuality, studies on shifting understandings of sexual behavior, and historical studies that situate the political and social production of sexual behaviors and discourses about sexuality within a diachronic and dynamic framework, among other areas. Its theoretical repertoire is no less diverse as it takes inspiration from feminist theory, queer theory, postcolonial theory, theories of gender, transnational theory, and theories of political economy, among others. Indeed, scholars exploring what may be referred to as 'African sexuality', inclusive of not only sexual behaviors but also the identities and communities constructed around these behaviors, are confronted with an analytical and theoretical labor similar to Africanists working on other issues. This includes a critical engagement with disciplinary and analytic terminology, an interrogation of the (often colonial) past in the production of both social and discursive realities, and the ways in which the political and social processes of postcolonial African nation-states have come to reconstitute African bodies in ways in which sexual practices and discourses of sexuality are in states of constant flux and discursive reinscription. But it can also be argued that Africanists working on sexuality may sense their analytic labor to be unique in the sense that the (sexualized) body of Africans was an initial and often central site for constituting discourses of alterity and deviance. In some respects, sexuality represented a key African cultural feature in which foreign

X. Livermon (✉)
The University of Texas at Austin, Austin, TX, USA

© The Author(s) 2018                                                                 1175
M.S. Shanguhyia and T. Falola (eds.),
*The Palgrave Handbook of African Colonial and Postcolonial History*,
https://doi.org/10.1057/978-1-137-59426-6_46

intervention in Africa (both scholarly and political) was legitimized, for it exemplified much about what needed to be moralized, tamed, and analytically unraveled. To be sure, several scholars note the pervasiveness of such notions even in the scholarship of today, suggesting that such ideas can never really be undone without radical paradigm shifts and sustained critical interrogating of the politics of engagement.[1] Several scholars, both African and non-African, have called for more African involvement in the process of research and theorization, but such inclusion is likely to advance the field rather than reflect any true sense of 'progress' without a program of critical interrogating and evaluation of the terminologies that are deployed in the production of knowledge about the sexual(ized) African body. This is not to suggest that what may be called 'Western theory' has no relevance in the area of African sexuality studies, or that the application of theoretical and analytical concepts from Western discourses lacks richness for illuminating African realities. As several scholars have noted, much of what is discussed as African sexual heritage has not only been filtered through Western notions of Christianity and respectability, but also through the ethnocentrism of academic disciplines, especially anthropology. Such insights reveal the intricate ways in which the colonial heritage is not only interlocked with the production of theoretical knowledge, but also with the production of supposed ethnographic fact. Thus, the programmatic picture becomes a messy one when attempting to understand African sexuality.

In the field of African sexuality, scholars are essentially working to fuse together three broad questions: (1) What is Africa? (2) What is sexuality? (3) How and why are the two brought together to delineate what might be referred to as African sexuality? The notion of a singular African sexuality, not dissimilar to other monolithic notions about African cultural practices, has been problematized in some of the recent literature in the field. Sylvia Tamale's edited collection aims to critique the deployment of African *sexuality* as a singular, generalizing and homogenizing concept for organizing empirical phenomena and theoretical reflection.[2] In considering the notion of African *sexualities* rather than *sexuality*, such studies do not necessarily proceed from the premise that the latter approach elides the variegated sexual subjectivities and expressions one sees on the African continent; but for whatever dismissals are made on the basis that such studies unnecessarily obfuscate unity or seem to be enamored with plurality for its own sake, these works must be appreciated for their attempt to critique long-standing analytic practices which homogenize African experience for the sake of analytical ease. Still, other studies reflect an even bolder approach in their critique of the recursive deployment of sexuality as a totalizing concept. Works in this vein aim to destabilize sexuality as a centralizing analytic in favor of privileging other analytics which sexuality works within, through, and around. For example, Serena Dankwa's study of 'same-sex intimacies' among women in Ghana examines erotic interaction among women and the use of erotic behavior in the constitution of an alternative community, but instead deploys intimacy rather than sexuality as an analytic tool.[3]

For whatever the rich literature on African sexuality has achieved, its results were not slow to come. Indeed, as both Signe Arnfred and Marc Epprecht discuss in their work, the discursive production of Africa and its socio-cultural dynamics shaped not only the slow growth of the field of African sexuality, but also what were considered legitimate areas of inquiry within the social-science disciplines.[4] As I previously noted, Arnfred argues that the construction of narratives of African 'tradition' have been fundamentally shaped by the Christian backgrounds of those who have structured these narratives. She also demonstrates how the Christian background has led to the pathologization of female sexuality, as well as to the lack of distinction between sex for pleasure and sex for procreation. Christian moralist ideas around sexuality, coupled with the notions of African sexuality as primitive and 'close-to-nature', worked together to establish a false framing of African sexual practice as directed toward procreative pursuits. In highlighting several examples from the southern part of the continent in which sexual practice was conceived outside of a non-reproductive framework, Arnfred challenges the monolithic construction of African sexual subjectivity, agency, and ontology. The theoretical breath of fresh air in Arnfred's continual dwelling on this issue is that it should challenge us to explore how certain forms of heterosexual formation have been historically constituted, rather than assuming such formations as the norm to which other forms represent a deviance; same-sex sexuality, of course, representing the ultimate deviation. Arnfred's argument that most, if not all, pre-colonial African societies made a distinction between sex intended for procreation and sex intended for pleasure not only seems to suggest that pre-colonial Africans had notions of sexual subjectivity (even if they were not articulated through Western-like identity constructs) but it also destabilizes heterosexuality as both an already given as well as an already understood construct.

As Basile Ndjio has pointed out in his study of sexuality in Cameroon, (hetero)sexuality has become standardized in the postcolonial state in a way that enables it to be deployed in various nationalist and nationalizing discourses.[5] In examining the hegemonic construction of African sexuality in a postcolonial and Pan-African context, Ndjio focuses on the normalization of heterosexual identity and how internalized heteronormativity has produced constructions of citizenship that link authenticity to the pursuit of specific heterosexual desires and the disparagement of any alternatives. Focusing on Cameroon, but extrapolating to other African countries, Ndjio's study looks at patriarchy, and the construction of what he refers to as the Muntu: the straight African with a high sex drive who upholds various dimensions of heterosexism. This construction works to normalize heterosexuality and construct non-heterosexualities as betrayals and linked to 'witchcraft'. Such work reveals much about how heterosexuality, patriarchy, and heterosexism have been implicated in postcolonial political regimes and discourses of identity. What is illuminated in such work is that the process of standardizing African sexuality has been for the benefit of a postcolonial labor of articulating sovereignty and constructing a proper national citizenry. Epprecht illuminates how African societies have been heterosexualized through both the unwillingness to explore non-heterosexual formations and the inability to accurately interpret erotic behavior not structured along gender-normative lines. While he points out that the field of anthropology has been central to the production of knowledge about African peoples and their sexual practices, he argues that this process of knowledge production has been negatively shaped by a number of discursive, methodological, and social practices which have misrepresented African sexuality. This is especially evident in the lack of attention to same-sex sexuality in African ethnography and dismissals of descriptions of some same-sex behavior as bisexual or incidental. For Epprecht, scant references to same-sexual practices without further in-depth investigation reflect not only ideas in the field about what was considered significant for ethnographic exploration, but also notions of respectability and heteronormativity. But, as Arnfred regularly explores, it was also the idea that African people, and thus their sexuality, were 'primitive' and thus only oriented to the baser and natural aims of reproduction that played a role in inquiries about non-heteronormative sexualities and analysis of behaviors which involved same-sex interaction. For Epprecht, it has only been since the 1960s that academic and social changes have helped shape a more accurate and useful production of knowledge around African sexual practices, though these discourses do linger, particularly in the construction of HIV/AIDS in Africa as a heterosexual disease.

Fortunately, the literature on African same-sex sexuality has come a long way. Stephen O. Murray and Will Roscoe's *Boy Wives/Female Husbands* represents the first significant and comprehensive theoretical and empirical look at African same-sex sexuality.[6] Their wide-ranging ethnological survey, divided into geographical regions, not only aimed to dispel the notion that same-sex sexual practice did not exist in African societies, but it also sought to illuminate both the unity and diversity of its social structuring. As a result, this monograph has become a foundational text in the research about the indigeneity of African same-sex sexual practices, though certainly it has not been without its criticism. A number of fruitful ethnographic studies have since entered the literature.[7] These studies have refined our understanding of specific same-sex communities, illuminated local understandings of queer identity and performance, and explored the ways in which local constitutions of same-sex sexuality engage or disengage with transnational and global process. Several historical studies on Southern Africa by Marc Epprecht have helped enrich our understanding of the historical production and trajectory of non-heternormative sexualities in Africa.[8]

Rudolf Gaudio's *Allah Made Us* enjoys the unique status of being the only monograph-length ethnographic study of same-sex sexuality in West Africa. In this work, Gaudio explores the multifaceted lives of the *yan dauda*: effeminate men who engage in socially constructed 'women's work' and also participate in same-sex sexual practices. His thesis is that the practices of the yan dauda' enable them to access a form of cultural citizenship and construct notions of subjectivity rooted in local cultural and social processes. Through an exploration of various social practices, Gaudio illuminates the interconnection between gender and sexuality, and also provides an example of how religious (in this case, Muslim) moral and sexual ideas structure sexual norms and delineate public discourses.

South Africa has been overrepresented in the literature on same-sex sexuality in Africa, most likely due to its comparative liberalism around such issues (same-sex marriage has been legal since 2006), but also due to the comparatively high visibility of political activities and activism in the country. Andrew Tucker's *Queer Visibilities: Space, Identity, and Interaction in Cape Town* was a critical monograph-length ethnographic work to foreground local South African queer subjectivities and explore how black South Africans deployed Western notions of identity constitution (here, visibility) as a central concept of political and social engagement. Tucker emphasizes the usefulness of the notion of queer visibility as an interrogative tool for understanding how varied practices destabilize heteronormativity. This approach also helps to challenge homogenous representations of queer experience and South African life more broadly. Tucker suggests that thinking about queer visibility should not be limited to queer engagements with public culture; visibility also figures prominently in how various groups construct their identities in relation to each other and in relation to broader structures in society. This work also draws attention to the importance of race and the legacy of apartheid as important factors that have shaped differing practices of visibility in Cape Town.

As a theoretical work, Neville Hoad's *African Intimacies* aims to delineate the central issues at stake in the research on queer African sexualities. This book considers the ways in which the social construction of homosexuality and the social construction of Africa intersect. Focusing on the interrogative concepts that are central to the analytic and theoretical labor of studying African same-sex sexualities, Hoad explores the ways in which 'Africa' and 'homosexuality' are put into a dialectical and confrontational dialogue with each other, and he provides an analysis of the salience of homosexuality in various discourses and public imagery, and how they work to delineate a contemporary African subjectivity. This work also seeks to critique the applicability of the terms 'sexuality' and 'homosexuality' in the African context. For Hoad, the discussions around same-sex sexuality must pay attention to the ways in which public discourse reflects particular aspirations and performances of sovereignty in postcolonial African states. Here, queer bodies become sites for the construction and manipulations of discourses about African-ness and its precarity in our postcolonial moment.

In addition to the body of works on African same-sex sexuality that dwell explicitly on interrogating the construction of its very categories (i.e. Africa, sexuality, and African sexuality), there are a number of sociological, ethnographic, public-health, and historical studies that look at the construction and semiotics of sexual subjecthood and the symbiotic relationship between these subjectivities and the larger political and social milieus. Several studies explore the ways in which sexuality is implicated in discourses and performances of nationalism. Here, violence provides a means through which certain sexualities become representative of an embodied national subjecthood through their appropriation, promotion, and sanction. For example, Amanda Swarr explores how butch lesbians are often victims of physical attacks and rapes.[9] Central to this discussion is an analysis of South African constructions of masculinity, which butch lesbians subvert through their gender performances and their same-sex relationships. This makes them both unavailable and threatening to men. Theoretically, the author argues that there is a 'tripartite' threat that causes butch lesbians to frequently be the victims of sexual violence: (1) they threaten heterosexuality through their same-sex relationships; (2) they challenge normative constructions of gender through their masculine performances, and (3) their sexual practices disrupt notions of how women should properly use their bodies. The practices of butch lesbians are paradoxical because they ascribe a certain social power to such lesbians while also rendering them vulnerable to sexual violence. Swarr hopes that her analysis can illuminate the ideological basis of 'corrective' rape and murder, and provide a useful theoretical basis for trying to stop its proliferation.

Astrid Reyes situates violence enacted on queer bodies in South Africa within ongoing practices of aggression stemming from the apartheid era.[10] But Reyes sees these historically constituted performances of violence as being intimately linked to social practice of patriarchal masculinity in which violence functions to both constitute and reinforce notions of gender idealism. Reyes argues that this is the reason that many citizens endorse various notions of patriarchal control and gender inequality despite the progressive legislation of the South African government. Thus, discussions about sexual violence and women's rights are tied up with discussions of Africa versus the West; that is, in which efforts to reclaim popular understanding of the 'traditional', especially in regard to notions of masculinity, help in establishing an authenticity and cultural sovereignty to African societies that distinguish Africa and the West, rather than blur the socio-cultural boundaries.

Roderick Brown seeks to disrupt understandings of the 'traditional' in the context of neo-liberal ideals of the postcolonial state.[11] Brown argues that the pervasiveness of corrective rape in South Africa violates international human-rights principles as well as national standards of non-discrimination and equality. South Africa's past may have planted the roots of gender inequality, homophobia, and violence, but the study argues that these must be transcended by directed legislative action. This may include revising hate crime legislation, educating state agents and schoolchildren, supporting a nationwide campaign for lesbian, gay, bisexual, transgender and intersex (LGBTI) rights, and providing support to civil society and attorneys to protect the rights of LGBTI people. The study argues that these and similar actions must be implemented in unambiguous terms if they are to be upheld.

For Thabo Msibi, homophobia thrives on the promotion of certain hegemonic forms of masculinity.[12] Based on research conducted at the University of KwaZulu-Natal in Durban, Msibi demonstrates how patriarchal notions of manhood which are deeply embedded in society produce fears about effeminate men as well as lesbians, thus leading to acts of violence to reestablish an order and exercise hegemonic male power. A national history of violence can produce a feeling of emasculation, which results in strategies of reassertion that employ violence, especially violence that is gender-based. Msibi argues that the problem of sexual violence will only improve when notions of hegemonic masculinity are appropriately addressed. For him, institutions of higher education can play a key role in ameliorating this problem by creating modules on gender awareness and challenging the teachers of these modules to interrogate their own social identities and the social dynamics that inform institutions of higher education.

A number of other studies have been more focused on the ways in which the politicization of sexual subjectivities and communities may be understood through the theoretical framing of 'activism', or on how strategies that are seen to constitute forms of resistance may intervene in the reconfiguration of local social landscapes. For example, in a seminal monograph, Ashley Currier explores practices of visibility (and invisibility) among Namibian and South African lesbian, gay, bisexual, and transgender organizations.[13] She frames her argument by illuminating an unsettling paradox: while these organizations appropriate Western sexual identity concepts they simultaneously seek to challenge the notion that queer sexuality is incompatible with African culture. The author compares the experiences of each country between 1995 and 2006, noting how Namibian activists worked to challenge political homophobia while South African activists worked to combat homophobia despite progressive legislation. In drawing comparisons with Pan-African LGBTI organizations, the author argues that visibility should be viewed as one strategy among many that queer groups may deploy in negotiating their local societies, rather than simply viewing visibility as the ultimate political aspiration and sexual rights achievement.

Msibi explores the dual potential of language to challenge homophobia and heterosexism but also to reinforce it through the objectification of queer subjects.[14] Based on life-histories of eight men, Msibi elucidates how language functions as a means to resist dominant discourses but also to circumscribe their lives by those very discourses. Focusing on black gay men who spoke an in-group language referred to as isiNgqumo, Msibi argues that this language may be understood as a tool of resistance, but since it was not spoken by all men and is only employed in certain social contexts, its resistance potential could not be fully realized.

Stephanie Rudwick explored how the isiNsqumo language, as well as other practices inscribed as 'traditional', worked to constitute particular forms of resistant and politicized identities.[15] Discursive and social practices were thus manipulated as strategic choices by a community of gay Zulu men in South Africa to both challenge and resist the argument that homosexuality is 'un-African'. Rudwick argues that her findings both challenge essentialist notions of Zulu identity and show how African ethnicities are malleable and transformable. Participants employed three main strategies in reconciling their queer identities against the discourse that Zulu identity and homosexuality are incompatible: the use of isiNgqumo, which uses ancient isiZulu vocabulary, engagement with the ancestors (*amadlozi*), and the appropriation of the traditional custom of showing respect (*ukulonipha*).

Epprecht is critical of the appropriation of Western constructions in understanding forms of African queer resistance, while also drawing attention to how greater involvement from African scholars may help to refresh some of the stale scholarly practices that informed research on queer African subjects.[16] Epprecht seeks to shift attention momentarily away from representations of homophobia on the continent to look at the grassroots efforts of queer Africans to create a sense of optimism and combat the myriad sexualized and gendered challenges that affect their lives. He also seeks to destabilize the dichotomies that have informed discussions of queer African lives; dichotomies such as modern versus traditional, African communitarian values versus Western individualism, African 'folk knowledge' versus Western academic theory, and so forth. He thus proposes using language centered on 'justice' to avoid the ethnocentric implications of 'rights' language. Such language, he feels, also decenters sex and instead includes the entire body. The study looks at spirituality (noting the contradictions inherent in discussions of traditional spirituality, Christianity, and Islam) and suggests the possibility of the values of Ubuntu in reshaping discussions. In focusing on the state, he looks at the impact of colonial rule in establishing a structure around homophobia that middle-class Africans in postcolonial contexts perpetuate. Finally, he suggests that advocating for health rights may be a more sensitive and welcome approach than advocating for sexual minority rights. Ultimately, the author calls for Africans to be at the forefront of these movements.

The literature on African same-sex sexuality has produced not only a wealth of ethnographic data about the diversity of sexual practices on the African continent, but also reveals an engagement with the discourses that have shaped the sociology of knowledge in the field of African sexuality studies, and the ways in which scholarship on African sexuality may be enacted against and through these discourses. Another important feature of this work has been how the various facets of the postcolonial state shape and are shaped by queer bodies and the types of discourses that are produced about them. Tamale's analyses of how discourses around non-normative sexualities in Africa are tied in with larger social and political anxieties and visions is especially helpful in this regard.[17] Tamale links the instability of democratic practices and ideals on the African continent to the recent hyper-focus on issues of same-sex sexuality. She critiques the notion that African homophobia is generated by foreigners, and instead argues that homophobic practices work to bolster both local and foreign interests. As mentioned earlier, colonial discourses and practices sought to represent African people as closer to 'nature', and thus their sexuality as oriented toward reproduction. This worked to create suspicions and hostility toward sexualities that did not conform to this model. Thus, it is the religious discourses, rather than same-sex practices themselves, that produce homophobia and represent a foreign influence on African sexualities. Tamale argues that homophobia is strategically deployed, rather ironically so, as a tool by political conservatives. She cautions against uncritically accepting a binarized view of sexuality on a global scale that romanticizes the freedom and equality of Western countries while portraying non-Western countries in a negative light.

Saheed Aderinto's work foregrounds the historical constitution of the intersectionality between sexuality and various political, cultural, and social processes.[18] Focusing on the ways in which British colonizers sought to moralize, police, and punish prostitution in colonial Nigeria, Aderinto highlights the nuanced confrontation between the relative liberalism of African sexual practices and ideation, and European ones. Such issues, however, figured prominently in notions of progress and civilization, and have continued to structure what Aderinto refers to as the 'sexualization of nationalism', in which deviant and marginalized sexual practices, such as prostitution, are constructed as antithetical to proper Nigerian nation building. Aderinto's analysis reveals how the linguistic distinctions and terminologies invoked in describing sexual practice are both historically constituted and embedded. He also demonstrates how competing discourses began to delineate between child and adult sexuality. Finally, as numerous scholars writing about same-sex sexuality in Africa have noted, Aderinto foregrounds how more recent debates in Nigeria about issues such as prostitution seem to index wider political, social, economic, and cultural concerns, anxieties, and visions, and thus, are less about prostitution or deviant sexuality in and of themselves than they at first may appear to be.

Long held notions of untamed African sexuality and excessive liberalism of African sexuality, along with notions of some African cultures as incorrigibly patriarchal and ridden by sexual deviance, helped buttress notions, in the realm of sexuality, that Africa must be a prime target for the *mission civilsatrice* and the lager 'civilizing' mission of the colonial project. In many ways, contemporary discussions around African bodies reflect this 'enlightened' and 'civilizing' position of the West to the 'untamed' and 'primitive' practices of Africa. This dichotomization is especially evident in discussions around female genital mutilation (FGM)/female genital cutting (FGC). Arnfred argues that discourses about FGM/FGC put into competition 'traditional' African culture, which is seen as repressive and patriarchal, with Western culture, which is seen as liberating and progressive.[19] In framing African women as victims of such 'traditional' cultures, the West legitimizes its intervention into African lives. However, Arnfred notes that one of the problems with this view is that this neat dichotomy can only be produced by glossing over the complex nuances of FGM/FGC practice. For example, she points out that in some instances the practice is deployed in performances of female agency and power, and she further notes that the term 'FGM' erroneously subsumes a range of practices, some of which are actually intended to increase women's pleasure. Postcolonial notions of sexual deviance and liberalism have thus been intimately shaped by the colonial encounter. As a few chapters in a volume edited by Felicitas Becker and Wenzel Geissler discuss, in some instances in Africa AIDS is framed as an outcome of sexual liberalism and deviance.[20]

Less historically based studies on African sexuality, and especially those concerned with aspects of public health, seemed marked by an attention to the role of gender and gender ideals in shaping sexual subjectivity and practice. This is especially evident in work that takes the nation-state as its boundary of analysis. This close relationship reveals the ways in which sexuality is centrally constituted through the political, economic, and cultural processes that shape gender subjectivity. For example, Nyokabi Kamau's study of the effect of HIV/AIDS on senior women in Kenyan universities seeks to push the boundaries on the representation of African women in social science research, as well as to illuminate some of the unique dynamics surrounding the experience of HIV/AIDS among senior women.[21] Her study challenges the notions that the experiences of HIV/AIDS among Kenyan women are shaped fundamentally by economic disadvantage; to the contrary, Kamau's study centralizes gender rather than class as a significant determinant of experience. Kamau also seeks to challenge the notion that institutions of higher education are necessarily progressive, for she elaborates on the ways in which these institutions still perpetuate practices of women's marginalization and silencing.

Anthony Simpson seeks to invigorate discussions surrounding HIV/AIDS and its relation to gender identity by focusing on the experiences of men.[22] Simpson critiques the hyper-focus on women in the research around HIV/AIDS in Africa; and while he argues that women are most significantly impacted by the epidemic, he notes that the sociology of HIV/AIDS cannot be understood apart from the vulnerabilities that shape men's lives and the gendered expectations which structure their sexual behavior. To redress this issue, Simpson collected a number of life-stories with a particular focus on how men engaged in the construction of gendered subjectivities, especially in the face of HIV/AIDS. A unique aspect of Simpson's study is its longitudinal focus: he first interviewed these men in 1983 and 1984 at the culmination of their secondary education, and conducted further interviews in 2002 among those who were still living.

Carolyn Baylies and Janet Bujra seek to revise intervention strategies by complicating narratives linking gender and HIV/AIDS, and by challenging monolithic understandings of vulnerability.[23] They explore how issues of consumption, capitalism, mobility, and the transformation of cultural ideas altered and reshaped gendered vulnerabilities as well as discourses about the symbolism of HIV/AIDS in Tanzanian and Zambian societies In illuminating the shifting discourses surrounding the vulnerability of women, especially as they relate to the pathologizing of women's sexuality, they also seek to challenge homogenous representation of women by looking at how women's experiences are differentiated along various social axes.

While much literature in African sexuality studies links sexuality with gender, Arnfred notes that much of the scholarship of African feminists surrounding gender gave little attention to discussions of sexuality.[24] Thus, she notes that she had to seek inspiration from elsewhere for her interpretation of female initiation rituals in Mozambique. Drawing on the notion of the 'coloniality of gender', Arnfred argues that certain notions of sexuality have led to misinterpretations of these rituals. Working to develop her own theoretical framework for understanding initiation rituals in Mozambique, she argues that these rituals are a key site in which ideas of sexuality are brought together with ideas of gender in an inextricable way.

Some scholars have focused on educational institutions, and on exploring the ways in which such institutions delineate cultural frameworks for young citizens and work to instill certain notions of gender and sexuality. For example, Deevia Bhana examines the regulation of sexuality as it is structured by secondary schools in South Africa.[25] Bhana highlights an incongruity between South Africa's progressive and protective policies around sexual diversity and gender and the lived experiences of its citizens. Focusing on schools as sites in which such incongruity takes on a special significance, Bhana explores how varied forms of violence emerge within a context in which conservative and moralist notions of sexuality and gender are reinforced in the socio-educational process.

Bolder still are studies that centralize pleasure, for they disrupt the idea that pre-colonial African sexuality was too liberal and thus required continuous control in the postcolonial state. Furthermore, they also centralize agency and corporeal meaning, which is sometimes missing from studies oriented toward public health. Rachel Spronk identifies this when she sets out to critique the hyper-focus on public health in the field of African sexuality.[26] She highlights this as a programmatic inadequacy by demonstrating how the semiotics of sexual practices and the ways in which people construct meanings around sexual experience are often lost in the analytic deployment and overarching agenda of public-health studies. Spronk's analysis focuses on how various sexual practices and forms of sexual interaction among middle-class Kenyans engage with postcolonial understandings of cultural, national, and global identity. She explores how some middle-class Kenyans frame their pursuit of temporary relationships as a pursuit of pleasure, and she analyzes how these notions of pleasure, which seem to centrally inform conceptions of temporary relationships, destabilize certain understandings of Kenyan identity which link stability to marriage. For Spronk, young Kenyan professionals are a unique site for examining the manipulation of postcolonial discourses and the anxieties and ambiguities surrounding notions of modernity, which seem especially significant in the narrative of middle-class Africans.

Shanti Parikh undertook a unique study of how heterosexual desire is constructed and negotiated through the writing of love letters.[27] Focusing on youths in Uganda, Parikh examines how notions of desire intersect with modernist notions of romance, gendered identity, anxieties surrounding HIV/AIDS, and the regulation and policing of young people's sexual behaviors. In looking at how desire is constituted through a literary practice, Parikh illuminates how both postcolonial sexual identity and its performance practices are situated within nuanced intersections between local and global processes.

## CONCLUSION

The body of work that transverses a field which may be referred to as African sexuality represents not only a diversity in topical foci and theoretical orientation, but also in how its objects of study (Africa, sexuality, and African sexuality) are constituted. Most of the historical literature, by nature of its diachronic focus, is confronted with these questions more boldly, since the colonial period marks a central historical period that not only shaped the subsequent and present postcolonial world, but also the discourse through which the postcolonial, colonial, and pre-colonial worlds are investigated. Perhaps this is why African languages' apparent lack of vocabulary for Western concepts of sexuality has seemed to bother or intrigue researchers. What was considered to constitute sexual practices was recorded and judged by Europeans, but they were taken for granted as constituting the very thing that they were said to constitute. In a similar manner, it seems that sexual identity and subjectivity, as categories of interrogation and analysis, only arise through Western framing and inscription. Thus, as I suggested earlier, the variegated practices of heterosexual sex which, as scholars such as Arnfred note, characterized pre-colonial societies, evade being theorized through the lens of subjectivity. Instead, only the more politicized identities, as we see especially in the sexual rights struggles in Southern Africa, enjoy theorization through those lenses.

Perhaps there is some value to this, however, for, as African scholars such as Ifi Amadiume have argued, age and lineage, rather than gender, were more important categories of social organization in pre-colonial African societies.[28] From this perspective, the inscription of sexualized subjectivities could be interpreted as a way to see African realities and practices through Western eyes or, at least, make them intelligible to Western theoretical programs. But this is more symptomatic of a problem rather than the problem itself, for in failing to interrogate the constitution of the categories of analysis, the scholarly project of African sexuality studies remains overwhelmingly indebted to Western notions, even for sexual ontology itself. This, of course, creates a strong emphasis on studies that are not historical, and are thus concerned with contemporary and postcolonial realities, since historical studies must perforce confront these ideas with deeper interrogation.

Studies that look at the ways in which sexual practice and identity are shaped by the political, economic, and social processes of the postcolonial state have done much to not only reveal how African subjectivities are in flux, but also how sexuality becomes a site through which even Africans themselves engage in debates about authenticity, sovereignty, and modernity. A unique value of these studies is that sexuality and its underpinnings are freed from the essentialist motivations embedded in the discursive constructions of Africa and are instead seen to be responsive to the shifting conditions of an ongoing historical trajectory. These studies, therefore, destabilize sexuality as an almost reified and fixed concept that can be interrogated and, instead, suggest that local and continental notions of sexuality are in an elusive state of constitution and reconstitution.

The literature on African sexuality thus must always engage in the constitution of its basic categories. Not only do the socio-political realities of Africa change, but so too do the discourses about Africa, past and present. Not only do notions of sexuality change, but also what does and could constitute sexuality in an African context changes. Moreover, studies of African sexuality regularly wrestle with whether African sexuality should be understood in a totalizing, homogenous manner, or whether it is more fruitful to talk about a multiplicity of sexualities on the continent. The focus on multiple and varied sexualities not only destabilizes ongoing Western discourses about Africa, but also the kind of discourse that, as some of the scholars previously mentioned demonstrate, postcolonial states seem interested in promoting by articulating their contemporary notions of national identity and proper citizenship. But delineating multiple sexualities does not totally free one from this scholarly conundrum if it does not take into account the ways in which African communities understood multiple sexualities, even if one type of sexuality was considered to be dominant or hegemonic. Sexuality, after all, is constituted as an analytic category through discursive practice, and this is why the call by scholars to have more African researchers and theorists is so important. Seemingly liberating models, such as the desire to see a plurality of sexualities rather than one sexuality, though superficially a 'progressive' analytic framework, is also not discursively divorced from a community of scholarly production. African researchers can help to not only clarify the politics of analytic engagement and production, but also to enrich local understandings which may instead see, for example, a singular sexuality with many manifestations, rather than a plurality of sexualities. Such a perspective could also enrich the literature with more class-based analyses and constitutions of sexuality, and suggest and introduce other categories of social distinction around which sexualities might be differentiated.

HIV/AIDS has occupied a major place in public-health literature because of its devastating impact on the continent, but studies still struggle to delineate to what extent the disease is seen as a sexuality-based illness with social manifestations, or a social illness shaped by sexual practice. This struggle has everything to do with how these analyses engage with shifting notions of African sexuality. A number of public-health studies which have investigated HIV/AIDS issues among African men who have sex with men have, to some extent, it could be argued, responded to the critique by Epprecht and others that public-health discourses have worked to construct HIV/AIDS in Africa as a heterosexual disease. In studies focusing on purportedly heterosexual Africans, investigating the impact of HIV/AIDS has revealed shifts in sexual practices and the reconstitution of sexual subjectivities, and remains a site in which local understandings confront Western notions of illness and propriety. Here, as in related literatures, the interconnection between gender and sexuality remains an inescapable analytic field.

## NOTES

1. For example see Adrian Flint and Vernon Hewitt, "Colonial Tropes and HIV/AIDS in Africa: Sex, Disease, and Race," *Commonwealth & Comparative Politics* 53, no. 3 (2015): 294–314.
2. Sylvia Tamale, ed., *African Sexualities: A Reader* (Oxford: Pambazuka Press, 2011).
3. Serena Owusua Dankwa, "'It's a Silent Trade': Female Same-Sex Intimacies in Post-ColonialGhana," *NORA- Nordic Journal of Feminist and Gender Research* 17, no. 3 (2009): 195–205.
4. Signe Arnfred, ed., *Rethinking Sexualities in Africa* (Upsala Sweden: The Nordic Africa Institute, 2004); Marc Epprecht, "Bisexuality and the Politics of Normal in African Ethnography," *Anthropologica* 48, no. 2 (2006): 187–201; Epprecht, *Heterosexual Africa? The History of an Idea from the Age of Exploration to the Age of AIDS* (Athens, OH: Ohio University Press, 2008); and Epprecht, *Unspoken Facts: A History of Homosexualities in Africa* (Harare: Gays and Lesbians of Zimbabwe, 2008).
5. Basile Ndijo, "Post-Colonial Histories of Sexuality: The Political Invention of a Libidinal African Straight," *Africa: The Journal of the International African Institute* 82, no. 4 (2012): 609–31.

6. Stephen O. Murray and Will Roscoe, *Boy Wives and Female Husbands: Studies in African Homosexualities* (New York: St. Martin's Press, 1998).

7. For example see William D. Banks, "Remembering Okomfo Kwabena: 'Motherhood,' Spirituality, and Queer Leadership in Ghana," *African Historical Review* 44, no. 2 (2012): 1–17; William D. Banks, "'This Thing is Sweet': Ntetɛɛ and the Reconfiguration of Sexual Subjectivity in Post-Colonial Ghana," *Ghana Studies* 14 (2011): 265–90; Dankwa, "'It's a Silent Trade';" Rudolf Pell Gaudio, *Allah Made Us: Sexual Outlaws in an Islamic African City* (Malden, MA: Wiley-Blackwell, 2009); and Sylvia Tamale, "The Complexities of Subversion: *Kuchu* Culture in Uganda," in *Africa After Gender?*, ed. Catherine M. Cole, Takyiwaa Manuh, and Stephan F. Miescher. (Bloomington: Indiana University Press, 2007).

8. Marc Epprecht, *Hungochani: The History of a Dissident Sexuality in Southern Africa* (Montreal: McGill-Queen's University Press, 2004); Epprecht, *Heterosexual Africa?*

9. Amanda Swarr, "Paradoxes of Butchness: Lesbian Masculinities and Sexual Violence in Contemporary South Africa," *Signs: Journal of Women in Culture & Society* 37, no. 4 (2012): 961–88.

10. Astrid Reyes, "Sexual Violence in South Africa: Negotiating Constitutional Rights and Cultural Discourses of Gender" (Thesis, Emory University, 2013).

11. Roderick Brown, "Corrective Rape in South Africa: A Continuing Plight Despite an International Human Rights Repsonse," *Annual Survey of International & Comparative Law* 18, no. 1 (2012): 45–66.

12. Thabo Msibi, "Homophobic Language and Linguistic Resistance in KwaZulu-Natal, South Africa," in *Gender and Language in Sub-Saharan Africa: Tradition, Struggle, and Change*, ed. Atanga, Lilian Lem, Sibonile Edith Ellece, Lia Litosseliti, and Jane Sunderland (Amsterdam: John Benjamins Publishing, 2013): 253–74.

13. Ashley Currier, *Out in Africa: LGBT Organizing in Namibia and South Africa* (Minneapolis: University of Minnesota, 2012).

14. Msibi, "*Homophobic language.*"

15. Stephanie Rudwick, "Defying a Myth: A Gay Subculture in Contemporary South Africa," *Nordic Journal of African Studies* 20, no. 2 (2011): 90–111.

16. Marc Epprecht, *Sexuality and Social Justice in Africa: Rethinking Homophobia and Forging Resistance* (London: Zed Books Ltd, 2013).

17. Sylvia Tamale, "Confronting the Politics of Nonconforming Sexualities in Africa," *African Studies Review* 56, no. 2 (2013): 31–45.

18. Saheed Aderinto, *When Sex Threatened the State: Illicit Sexuality, Nationalism, and Politics in Colonial Nigeria, 1900–1958* (Champaign: University of Illinois Press, 2014).

19. Arnfred, *Rethinking Sexualities.*

20. Felicitas Becker and Wenzel P. Geissler. *AIDS and Religious Practice in Africa* (Leiden: Brill, 2009).

21. Nyokabi Kamau. *Research AIDS, Sexuality, and Gender: Case Studies of Women in Kenyan Universities,* 2nd ed. (Limuru, Kenya: Zapf Chancery Publishers Africa Ltd, 2013).

22. Anthony Simpson, *Boys to Men in the Shadow of AIDS: Masculinities and HIV Risk in Zambia* (London: Palgrave Macmillan, 2009).

23. Carolyn Baylies and Janet Bujra. *AIDS, Sexuality and Gender in Africa: Collective Strategies and Struggles in Tanzania and Zambia* (New York: Routledge, 2000).
24. Arnfred, *Sexuality and Gender Politics in Mozambique.*
25. Deevia Bhana, *Under Pressure: The Regulation of Sexuality in South African Secondary Schools* (Johannesburg, South Africa: Mathoko's Books, 2014).
26. Rachel Spronk, *Ambiguous Pleasures: Sexuality and Middle Class Self-Perceptions in Nairobi* (New York: Berghahn Books, 2012).
27. Shanti Parikh, *Regulating Romance: Youth Love Letters, Moral Anxiety, and Intervention in Uganda's Time of AIDS* (Nashville: Vanderbilt University Press, 2016).
28. Ifi Amadiume, *Male Daughters, Female Husbands: Gender and Sex in an African Society* (London: Zed Book, Ltd, 1987).

## BIBLIOGRAPHY

Aderinto, Saheed. *When Sex Threatened the State: Illicit Sexuality, Nationalism, and Politics in Colonial Nigeria, 1900–1958.* Champaign: University of Illinois Press, 2014.

Amadiume, Ifi. *Male Daughters, Female Husbands: Gender and Sex in an African Society.* London: Zed Book, Ltd, 1987.

Arnfred, Signe, ed. *Rethinking Sexualities in Africa.* Sexuality, Gender and Society in Africa Research Programme. Upsala Sweden: The Nordic Africa Institute, 2004.

———. *Sexuality and Gender Politics in Mozambique: Rethinking Gender in Africa.* Suffolk, UK: James Currey, 2011.

Banks, William D. "'This Thing is Sweet': Ntetee and the Reconfiguration of Sexual Subjectivity in Post-Colonial Ghana." *Ghana Studies* 14 (2011): 265–90.

———. "Remembering Okomfo Kwabena: 'Motherhood,' Spirituality, and Queer Leadership in Ghana." *African Historical Review* 44, no. 2 (2012): 1–17.

Baylies, Carolyn, and Janet Bujra. *AIDS, Sexuality and Gender in Africa: Collective Strategies and Struggles in Tanzania and Zambia.* New York: Routledge, 2000.

Becker, Felicitas, and Wenzel P. Geissler. *AIDS and Religious Practice in Africa.* Leiden: Brill, 2009.

Bhana, Deevia. *Under Pressure: The Regulation of Sexuality in South African Secondary Schools.* Braamfontein, South Africa: Mathoko's Books, 2014.

Brown, Roderick. "Corrective Rape in South Africa: A Continuing Plight Despite an International Human Rights Repsonse." *Annual Survey of International & Comparative Law* 18, no. 1 (2012): 45–66.

Currier, Ashley. *Out in Africa: LGBT Organizing in Namibia and South Africa.* Minneapolis: University of Minnesota, 2012.

Dankwa, Serena Owusua. "'It's a Silent Trade': Female Same-sex Intimacies in Post-Colonial Ghana." *NORA-Nordic Journal of Feminist and Gender Research* 17, no. 3 (2009): 195–205.

Epprecht, Marc. *Hungochani: The History of a Dissident Sexuality in Southern Africa.* Montreal: McGill-Queen's University Press, 2004.

———. "Bisexuality and the Politics of Normal in African Ethnography." *Anthropologica* 48, no. 2 (2006): 187–201.

———. *Heterosexual Africa? The History of an Idea From the Age of Exploration to the Age of AIDS.* Athens, OH: Ohio University Press, 2008.

———. *Unspoken Facts: A History of Homosexualities in Africa.* Harare: Gays and Lesbians of Zimbabwe, 2008.

———. *Sexuality and Social Justice in Africa: Rethinking Homophobia and Forging Resistance.* African Arguments. London: Zed Books Ltd, 2013.

Flint, Adrian, and Vernon Hewitt. "Colonial Tropes and HIV/AIDS in Africa: Sex, Disease, and Race." *Commonwealth & Comparative Politics* 53, no. 3 (2015): 294–314.

Gaudio, Rudolf Pell. *Allah Made Us: Sexual Outlaws in an Islamic African City.* Malden, MA: Wiley-Blackwell, 2009.

Kamau, Nyokabi. *Research AIDS, Sexuality, and Gender: Case Studies of Women in Kenyan Universities,* 2nd ed. Limuru, Kenya: Zapf Chancery Publishers Africa Ltd, 2013.

Msibi, Thabo. "Not Crossing the Line: Masculinities and Homophobic Violence in South Africa." *Agenda: Empowering Women for Gender Equity* 23, no. 80 (2009): 50–54.

———. "Homophobic Language and Linguistic Resistance in KwaZulu-Natal, South Africa." In *Gender and Language in Sub-Saharan Africa: Tradition, Struggle, and Change,* edited by Atanga, Lilian Lem, Sibonile Edith Ellece, Lia Litosseliti, and Jane Sunderland. Amsterdam: John Benjamins Publishing, 2013; 253–74.

Murray, Stephen O., and Will Roscoe. *Boy Wives and Female Husbands: Studies in African Homosexualities.* New York: St. Martin's Press, 1998.

Ndjio, Basile. "Post-Colonial Histories of Sexuality: The Political Invention of a Libidinal African Straight." *Africa: The Journal of the International African Institute* 82, no. 4 (2012): 609–31.

Parikh, Shanti. *Regulating Romance: Youth Love Letters, Moral Anxiety, and Intervention in Uganda's Time of AIDS.* Nashville: Vanderbilt University Press, 2016.

Reyes, Astrid. "Sexual Violence in South Africa: Negotiating Constitutional Rights and Cultural Discourses of Gender." Thesis, Emory University, 2013.

Rudwick, Stephanie. "'Gay and Zulu, We Speak isiNgqumo': Ethnolinguistic Identity Constructions." *Transformation: Critical Perspectives on Southern Africa* 74 (2010): 112–34.

———. "Defying a Myth: A Gay Subculture in Contemporary South Africa." *Nordic Journal of African Studies* 20, no. 2 (2011): 90–111.

Simpson, Anthony. *Boys to Men in the Shadow of AIDS: Masculinities and HIV Risk in Zambia.* London: Palgrave Macmillan, 2009.

Spronk, Rachel. *Ambiguous Pleasures: Sexuality and Middle Class Self-Perceptions in Nairobi.* New York: Berghahn Books, 2012.

Swarr, Amanda. "Paradoxes of Butchness: Lesbian Masculinities and Sexual Violence in Contemporary South Africa." *Signs: Journal of Women in Culture & Society* 37, no. 4 (2012): 961–88.

Tamale, Sylvia. "The Complexities of Subversion: *Kuchu* Culture in Uganda." In *Africa After Gender?*, edited by Catherine M. Cole, Takyiwaa Manuh, and Stephan F. Miescher. Bloomington: Indiana University Press, 2007.

———, ed. *African Sexualities: A Reader.* Oxford: Pambazuka Press, 2011.

———. "Confronting the Politics of Nonconforming Sexualities in Africa." *African Studies Review* 56, no. 2 (2013): 31–45.

Tucker, Andrew. *Queer Visibilies: Space, Identity and Interaction in Cape Town.* Malden, MA: Wiley-Blackwell, 2009.

# CHAPTER 47

# Culture, Artifacts, and Independent Africa: The Cultural Politics of Museums and Heritage

*Sarah Van Beurden*

Upon visiting the museum of Niamey in Niger sometime in the early 1970s, Hugues de Varine-Bohan, Director of the International Council of Museums (ICOM), enthusiastically declared it was the museum of the future because of its wide range of artistic and educational activities, and its ability to represent a large and diverse country. Not only was it financed by the people of Niger, it drew up to 10% of the population in visitors every year. It was, he gushed, 'a real instrument of national unity and national conscience'.[1] De Varine-Bohan perfectly captures the role many African museums were widely expected to fulfill in the postcolonial era: they were seen as places where the objects of ethnographic and art collections, often colonial in origin, could be placed in service of the creation of postcolonial national identities, and serve as tools for a process of cultural decolonization. The history of museums in Africa, and the accompanying struggle over the possession and ownership of cultural heritage, however, demonstrate how fraught with tensions and contradictions these politics often were.

Much has been written about the lives of objects in European collections and museums, both during and after colonialism.[2] Less attention has been given to how the changed status of certain objects as art, heritage, and museum objects influenced the ways in which decolonization was imagined in postcolonial Africa.[3] In their reincarnation as museum objects, artifacts were

S. Van Beurden (✉)
Departments of History and African American and African Studies,
Ohio State University, Columbus, OH, USA

© The Author(s) 2018
M.S. Shanguhyia and T. Falola (eds.),
*The Palgrave Handbook of African Colonial and Postcolonial History*,
https://doi.org/10.1057/978-1-137-59426-6_47

inserted into institutions historically associated with progress and rationality, where the past is represented in order to carve out a present and project into an 'authentic' future.[4] Although marked as being about the past, discussions about art as heritage are in fact cultural processes that make meaning about the present.[5] Because they are so often approached as neutral categories, however, the cultural 'work' these categories do becomes obscured. This chapter demonstrates how the categories of art and heritage, shaped in late colonial contexts, impacted the way in which decolonization and postcolonial cultural sovereignty were imagined and expressed.[6] Specifically, the chapter will trace the ways in which postcolonial states viewed and used ethnographic and art museums to represent cultural sovereignty and how the possession of African art and ethnographic collections in the West became contested through claims for restitution.[7] Although the cultural histories of colonial and postcolonial African countries are incredibly varied, there are nonetheless certain historical developments that are shared across borders, sometimes, for example, because of the similarities across empires in the cultural technologies of European colonial rule, or because of the dominance of the European nation-state model for postcolonial African nations. African dispossession of cultural heritage often came to symbolize larger patterns of dispossession of land, rights, sovereignty, identity, etc. As De Jong and Rowlands have pointed out, museums, like archives, 'are seen to evolve as a privileged space in which the sense of loss and disruption can be contemplated and assessed and finally cured'.[8] As such, museums and the objects in their collections became one of the battlegrounds in the process of cultural decolonization.

This chapter uses my own primary research on museums in central Africa (Congo in particular) but branches out to include the histories of other African countries and institutions. It starts by laying out shifting colonial attitudes with regard to the protection and conservation of particular aspects of African cultures, both in situ and in the context of museum collections. This protection, linked to a particular understanding of colonialism as cultural guardianship, influenced postcolonial constructions of cultural sovereignty, at play in the demands for the restitution of objects and collections from the West, but also visible in the role accorded to museum institutions across the continent.

## African Art, Colonialism, and Cultural Guardianship

Colonial attitudes towards African cultures and their material production varied greatly over time and space, and ranged from destruction and neglect to admiration and conservation, but the collection of artifacts formed a part of European imperialism from the very beginning. The deceptive neutrality of the term 'collecting' obscured the reality of a wide range of practices, from plundering and confiscation to commercial exchange and gift-giving, in a variety of settings that ranged from the violent to the commercial, and for a variety of motivations, including religious, political, and artistic. Objects that initially were considered as trophies or curios gradually acquired different meanings and came to be regarded as objects of science and, eventually, art. Many of these objects ended up in museums and collections in the West. As such, the museum formed part of a larger set of institutions and disciplines that studied, appropriated, and classified African nature and culture.

Attitudes towards this material shifted over time, and objects became increasingly embedded in classificatory and art historical systems. The most important evolution for the purpose of this chapter was the growing acceptance of certain objects as 'art', which also impacted their value as heritage. From the beginning of European–African contacts, certain objects had a clear aesthetic appeal for Western audiences, but the twentieth century saw a significant broadening of the objects included in the category of African art, an evolution pushed in particular by the primitivist modernists' interest in African art. A market for these objects grew in tandem, and gradually the trend also had an impact on museum displays, which more systematically came to include African art displays.[9]

A reflection of changing ways of regarding African cultures, the interpretation of these artifacts as art and heritage, was in fact deeply embedded in colonial systems of thought and knowledge. Although superficially progressive, the reinterpretation of an increasing amount of objects as art in fact underwrote a renewed commitment to colonialism, justified as conservationism and protectionism. This was a characteristic of a shifting interpretation of colonialism that, from the 1930s on, moved away from the civilizing mission towards a 'colonial humanism' or 'welfare colonialism', imagined by colonizers as reformed and 'modern' systems that would prevent the collapse of empires under the pressures of anti-colonial sentiment.[10]

By lifting the objects away from their origin and into the pantheon of art, and consequently human and world heritage, it became the responsibility of the European states to protect the (now economically valuable) collections in the West. The impact of this change also extended into colonial policies directed at the preservation of arts and cultures in the colonies. Growing international attention to, for example, Ife bronzes, fueled a trade in objects from Nigeria, which raised the concern of colonials and led to the creation of the Department of Antiquities, along with museums in Jos (1952) and Esie (1954) and legislation to control art trafficking.[11] As Derek Peterson argues, systems of indirect rule in particular accelerated the interest in African culture as heritages, using cultural justifications in the selection of African intermediary leadership, which the latter exploited in contexts of 'strategic ornamentalism'.[12]

In the case of the Belgian empire, efforts to introduce the protection of African art and crafts as heritage into colonial law started in the 1930s, although these were met with significant resistance from colonial officials on the ground. A government Commission for the Protection of Indigenous

Arts and Crafts (La Commission pour la Protection des Arts et Métiers indigènes), founded in the 1930s, created policies for conservation efforts in the colonies by supporting small museums in the colony but also with initiatives to encourage local artisanal production and bring it under the control of the colonial state.[13] A similar concern animated some of the activities of the Institut Français d'Afrique Noire (IFAN) in French West Africa, created in 1936 and headquartered in Dakar. Several of the IFAN-associated research and museum institutions displayed a concern with the advancement and control of artisanal production. In the museums in Abidjan and Niamey, for example, objects were displayed to serve as models for artisans, who at times were also housed in workshops connected to the museums.[14]

The logic of decolonization translated to the field of cultural production, and conservation projected the recovery of a sovereign way of life onto the possession of culture, literally and metaphorically. Its literal sense will be explored in the next section, which examines the emergence and persistence of claims for the restitution of cultural property, particularly in the form of art and museum collections, to the African continent. Second, this chapter will explore the history of museums on the African continent. As the institution that housed objects, the museum became the metaphorical location of cultural sovereignty, which it exercised via the possession and display of collections and via the creation and representation of knowledge about African cultures.

## ARTIFACTS AND ART ON DISPLAY: MUSEUMS IN AFRICA

The museum landscape in Africa still consists overwhelmingly of museums that have their origin in the colonial era. Yet because of their perceived roles as key elements in landscapes of modernity, many of these museums became national institutions after independence, a transition that confirmed the transformation of their collections into national patrimony, and connected them to the cultural politics of the independent state.[15]

Museums in the colonies were, like their counterparts in the metropole, heavily embedded in the theory and practice of colonial sciences, both in terms of the systems of classification and the interpretation that guided their display and collecting practices, but also in literal terms; they often originated in the collections of colonial research institutions.[16] For example, the core collection of today's National Museum of Rwanda in Butare was gathered by the researchers of the Belgian colonial Institute for Scientific Research in Butare (then Astrida) in the course of their ethnographic research.[17] This is also the case for former French West Africa, where the IFAN founded research institutes and museums throughout the region.[18] Most of these have had long histories as postcolonial national museums.[19]

Schools were also common places for small museums to emerge, particularly in British West Africa, where the British colonizers felt a certain competition with the French creation of the IFAN. In Nigeria, the development of museums was championed by British art teacher Kenneth Murray, who was appointed to the new department of Antiquities in 1953 as Surveyor of Antiquities. Together with Bernard Fagg, his efforts led to the creation of museums in Jos (1952) and Esie (1954). While a formal, national, museum opened in Gold Coast in 1957, it was based on a collection started at Achimota College in Accra in the 1920s, which occupied a small museum on campus. The hope was that the college museum, led by a British archeologist and located on the campus of a school created to educate a local elite, would contribute to a feeling of pride and ownership of local culture.[20]

The creation of these museums and research institutes manifests shifting attitudes towards the value of African cultures in the late colonial period. A sense of custodianship over African cultures came to permeate colonial policies, replacing some of the earlier emphasis on the erasure or destruction of local cultures in the context of the 'civilizing' mission. This did not mean, however, that these institutions could all be considered blank technologies of power. Often being the initiatives or pet projects of small elites, these projects were contested,[21] as were interpretations of colonialism as cultural guardianship in general. Nonetheless, they were part of the infrastructural and institutional inheritance of newly independent African states.

Political independence did not automatically entail a process of cultural decolonization. Although museums (and the possession of cultural heritage more broadly) were imagined as avenues for the creation of cultural sovereignty, in practice, it turned out to be difficult to transform the structures of knowledge, practices of preservation, and patterns of possession that formed the cultural pillars of colonialism. Cultural politics were commonly seen as an avenue for the strengthening of the nation in the postcolonial period, taking the shape of cultural festivals, the creation of cultural infrastructure (in the form of libraries, archives, museums, etc.) and organizations (in the form of dance and music troupes, for example). Museums in Africa were seen both as the targets of processes of decolonization, and as tools for said processes in the postcolonial period, although the implementation of these desired changes was highly uneven and depended greatly on local and national political trends.[22] Making national museums out of colonial institutions without replicating colonial structures of knowledge and representation was (and continues to be) no easy feat. Colonial interpretations of museums as places of conservation in the face of the disorientation of modernity continued, although postcolonial modernity was also regularly imagined around a core of so-called traditional or 'pre-colonial' cultures. Displaying a variety of local cultures while promoting a national identity was also a delicate line to walk, particularly when Pan-Africanism was also added to the agenda. By and large, however, many museums continued to focus their collections on the cultures that fell within the territorial boundaries of the state.

The history of the National Museum of Ghana is instructive here. Although it opened after Ghanaian independence in 1957, like many African museums, it was in essence a colonial project that was adapted to postcolonial political purposes. While its collection dated back to the 1930s and had been located on the campus of Achimota College, its conception as an independent institution was the culmination of changing attitudes toward African cultures in the late colonial period. It was conceived of as an institution where a deeper, pre-historical past could provide the backdrop for a contemporary, aesthetic, appreciation of local cultures, and the education of an elite upper class and their role in a common future for the country. As such, the museum not only had a cultural purpose, but also a social and political one: it could help anchor a society facing the impact of colonial modernity and provide a backdrop for the projection of a colonial sponsored nationalism, while being a place where colonial administrators and an upper-class elite mingled. These views did not disappear with independence. On the contrary, they seeped into postcolonial ideas about the role of the museum for the state of Ghana, although attitudes toward the museum were often ambiguous.[23]

The issue of national coherence was a prime concern for the Nkrumah Government. Ghana's first post-independence government was faced with the prospect of uniting regions that encompassed different local cultures but had also been subject to different systems of colonial rule. This deeply marked the state ceremonialism of Ghana, which integrated 'traditional' artifacts (such as Kente cloth and Asante stools) while emphasizing their role in *national* politics. The same concern applied to the objects in the country's museum collections and displays: their identification with local cultures had to be in the service of a national culture and identity. The displays at the National Museum in 1957 however allowed for multiple readings. One curatorial strategy, influenced by Pan-Africanism, was to refer to cultures and histories from across the continent. Nonetheless, the main focus was on local cultures, which were generally represented as elements of the national. However, as Mark Crinson describes, the dominance of Asante material, which dated back to the creation of the collections during the colonial period, had an impact on the post-independence displays, making it loom large within the representation of the nation. Postcolonial collecting practices of the 1960s also replicated the collection's existing strengths, reinforcing certain cultural hegemonies.[24]

As opposed to the Ghanaian national museum, the Institute for National Museums in Zaire (Institut des Musées Nationaux du Zaïre, IMNZ) focused exclusively on local cultures. The Institute was created between 1969 and 1971 through a collaboration between the former museum of the Belgian Congo (now the Royal Museum for Central Africa) in Belgium and the presidential office of Mobutu (who had come to power in 1965 through a coup), in part because of restitution demands for the collections of the Belgian museum by Zaire. By the Zairian side, the IMNZ was envisioned as an element in the quest to reclaim cultural sovereignty, by creating a national collection and using the latter in national and international exhibitions, and by educating a young generation of Zairian museum professionals in order to reclaim the production of knowledge about Zairian cultures from Western academia.

Cultural politics came to the forefront of Mobutu's national politics in the 1970s under the state ideology of *authenticité* (authenticity), which envisioned a new, national, 'authentic', Zairian nation, born out of the values and traditions of pre-colonial Zairian cultures. Although this led to a 'Zairization' campaign to downgrade the influence of the Belgians at the IMNZ, the Museum Institute failed to develop much of an approach to the decolonization of representations and knowledge. Despite organizing a number of well-received international exhibitions in the 1970s (notably to France and the USA), it, like other African museums, relied heavily on modes of visual and knowledge representations developed during the colonial era (particularly the emphasis on objects as art). The IMNZ also never succeeded in developing much of an audience nationally. Although a lack of exhibition space certainly played a role here, so did the increased authoritarianism of the Mobutu regime, which resulted in a decline in state interest and support of cultural technologies of power like the museum. Despite this distancing, the population continued to see the IMNZ as a Mobutist institution.[25]

As colonial institutions, many of the museums discussed here had only limited local audiences, a problem that continued into the postcolonial period. Museums were considered to be spaces for tourists and privileged elites. Their location in major cities, often centers of state power, also served as an impediment to developing a broader local audience. This was compounded by the fact that many museums were located in the administrative quarters of town previously less accessible to Africans, which often continued to be spaces of exclusion.[26] The West African Museum Program (WAMP) attempted to counteract this in the early 1980s by promoting the establishment of smaller, local museums in towns far from the capitals, a program that met with modest success.[27]

With the continent-wide economic downturn of the 1970s came an era of structural adjustments programs and global financial and economic interference, the impact of which fully took hold of the African continent by the 1980s, with serious financial consequences for many of the continent's cultural institutions. As Claude Ardouin, long-time director of the museum in Mali, observed, culture continued to be a 'strategic issue for policymaking in Africa', but development institutions became key players.[28] With state support in decline, the help of non-governmental organizations and collaboration with Western institutions and international cultural organizations (such as UNESCO and ICOM), became a matter of survival for many. With this shift, the realm of culture became fully integrated into the development paradigm. Like postcolonial states, development and international agencies were interested in the educational potential of museums as political tools, this time as promotional institutions for democracy. The 1991 ICOM meeting of African museum professionals described the museum as 'a tool for cultural pluralism, national development democracy [as well as] public education'.[29] As in the post-independence period, the desire was to see museums become relevant to society, but the ambitions for a decolonization of representation and knowledge faded into the background. Some of the initiatives that started as development projects became quite successful. Notably the West African Museum Program (WAMP), which was started by the International Africa Institute in London in 1982, developed into an independent West African institution that, through its workshops, publications, and grants, worked to battle the institutional fragility of West African museums across former British and French imperial boundaries.[30]

The more recent revival of the museum and heritage scene in South Africa forms a hopeful note in the history of African cultural institutions. The developments in South Africa are part and parcel of a wider movement for the decolonization of public culture. The fall of the apartheid system, combined with the existence of an already extensive network of heritage sites and museums this political system had generated, created the conditions and the urgent need for a decolonization of the country's cultural infrastructure.[31] This led to the (at times contested) reimagining of existing sites, but also the creation of new institutions, such as the District Six Museum in Cape Town, with considerable grass-roots support.[32] The questioning of museological strategies was more successful in some cases than in others. Particularly older institutions, such as the MuseumAfrica in Johannesburg, had a more difficult time separating themselves from a colonial and apartheid apparatus, both in practice and in perception.[33]

## DECOLONIZATION: HERITAGE AND RESTITUTION CLAIMS

Heritage protection had been the provenance of international organizations for a number of decades by the time decolonization swept the African continent. The decolonization wave of the mid-twentieth century, however, had a profound impact on the role of heritage in global relations. As a consequence of the colonial thirst for collecting, large collections of cultural artifacts were now housed in museums in the West. With the advent of decolonization, these objects had acquired meaning as the national heritage of newly independent nations. In a context in which past colonial practices were now the subject of public and widespread criticism, questions arose about the ownership of these objects and collections. It soon became clear that the international protocols for the protection of cultural property and heritage were woefully inadequate to deal with discussions about objects moved during colonial rule.[34]

Although discussions about the return of cultural objects have been part of international relations for several centuries, the Second World War was a watershed moment for the emergence of international agreements about the role and protection of cultural property. Conceived of in the aftermath of Nazi art looting, the Hague Convention and protocol of 1954; the Convention for the Protection of Cultural Property in the Event of Armed Conflict, gave shape to the idea that cultural property ought to be protected from wartime destruction and maintained in its culture of origin.[35] Given the difficulties adapting such agreements to the context of mid-twentieth century decolonization, UNESCO organized the UNESCO Convention on the Means of Prohibiting and Preventing the Illicit Import, Export and Transfer of Ownership of Cultural Property in 1970. The convention demonstrated an evolution in the views on heritage policies by explicitly addressing the needs of former colonial states to prevent cultural heritage from leaving their territories. Its policies, however, focused largely on the prevention of illegal trafficking of heritage objects. So, while it addressed continuing loss, its regulations did not allow for a frank discussion of the material that left former colonies before 1970. In other words, the topics of colonial collecting or plundering were off limits. A preliminary draft of the convention did address the issues of restitution of property removed before 1970, but many former colonial powers objected, and the final text was explicitly non-retroactive.[36] Widespread dissatisfaction with the 1970 Convention among former colonies resulted in resolutions from several political bodies, among which was *The Conference of Heads of State or Government of Non-aligned Countries,* which affirmed 'the principles of the Universal Declaration on Human Rights and the African Cultural Convention on the rights of states to recover the art treasures and manuscripts looted from them'.[37] Zairian dictator Mobutu also raised the matter in front of the Assembly of the United Nations in 1973 by condemning 'colonial pillage' and emphasizing the need for postcolonial cultural restitution by arguing for the national importance of the possession of an 'authentic' heritage for the viability of the future of new nations. The proposed resolution was received enthusiastically by most African nations, but was strongly opposed by Western countries, which rejected the emphasis on colonialism as a cause for the absence of heritage objects in former African colonies, instead placing blame on art trafficking and African collaboration with the latter.[38] The resulting resolution had lost most of its teeth, although its existence does attest to the urge of newly independent countries to push back against the non-retroactive nature of the 1970 UNESCO convention.

UNESCO responded with the establishment of an Intergovernmental Committee, although the debate about the name of this committee (which had to be changed from the 'Intergovernmental Committee Concerning Restitution or Return of Cultural Property' to the clunky 'Intergovernmental Committee for Promoting the Return of Cultural Property to its Countries of Origin or its Restitution in Case of Illicit Appropriation', ICPRCP) continued to underscore the contentious nature of its subject.[39] Its first session took place in 1980, and it continues to meet. In essence, what the committee does is encourage and facilitate discussions about potential cases for restitution in situations where bilateral contacts have been unfruitful, usually in a context of preservation and development. Of the mere six cases which have been resolved before the ICPRCP, only one includes an African country. Tanzania filed a claim in 2006 for the return of a Makonde mask from the Barbier-Mueller Museum in Geneva, Switzerland. The mask, which was stolen from the Museum in Dar Es Salaam in 1984, was returned in 2010. Negotiations had in fact been going in since 1990, but had broken down several times.[40]

Clearly the cases the ICPRCP treats are the very top of the iceberg when it comes to objects that African cultural institutions and states would like to see returned, which begs the question: Why so few? The Tanzania–Switzerland case had several elements that help us understand why so few cases have been brought before the ICPRCP: it had clear indications of a relatively recent theft; it concerned only one object; Tanzania possessed a respected national museum to return the object to; the Tanzanian state made the claim; and Switzerland was willing to enter into talks. The very structure of the process for filing claims and its administrative requirements necessitate the involvement of the government, and these might have more pressing concerns than the recovery of an object in a process that could become tendentious and cause tension with the West. Nor is it always easy to clearly lay out how objects disappeared, which certainly applies to material that was moved during the colonial era. This brings us to an argument often made by museum curators in the West: not all removal of artifacts from Africa during the colonial era can be considered plundering: some instances were the result of regular commercial transactions or exchanges in the context of the establishment of a relationship, for example. Or sometimes locals colluded in the removal or sale of objects to their own benefit. Often, the scientific value of keeping collections together and in good conditions of conservation are also raised in the context of requests for return.

The focus on conservation and preservation is inevitably used to draw attention to the limited opportunities many African museums have to maintain the same standards, or the ability of African nations to enforce protective measures against illegal trade; an argument that conveniently neglects the colonial roots of much of this illegal trade.[41] Recently, the focus on the value of heritage for a nation is also questioned by depicting local communities and cultures (and not African states) as the rightful originators of claims for return. Or the concept of cultural belonging is undermined completely from a postmodern perspective that recognizes objects have multiple lives and meanings to multiple audiences. While on an academic level this questioning of identity politics and its ties to an essentialized idea of culture certainly has merit, its underestimation of the historical inequalities that led to particular patterns of movement and possession of these objects, and their continued impact today, can feel jarring.[42]

The emergence of the idea of a heritage of mankind, and an emphasis on the universal value of heritage, has also had mixed effects on the ability of African nations to claim a national heritage. On the one hand, a recognition of a heritage site as a UNESCO World Heritage Site can create access to financial resources for preservation and protection, and stimulates these locations as tourist destinations.[43] On the other hand, as heritage scholar David Lowenthal has written: 'universalism endows the haves at others' expense'.[44] Once objects are considered universal heritage, it becomes easier for museums in the West to argue against restitution because of the relevance the objects have for their audience, as well as their duty to help preserve the objects.[45]

The universalist approach has recently found expression in the cosmopolitanism argument, advanced by Kwame Anthony Appiah, who laments the equation of patrimony with *a* culture and with the nation, questioning, for example, the link between a Nok sculpture and the contemporary nation of Nigeria.[46] Instead, he reminds his readers of the positive effects a global audience being able to experience African art has on people's sense of cosmopolitanism, allowing them, as he puts it, to experience a connection 'not *through* identity, but despite difference'.[47] Appiah doesn't deny that there are cases in which repatriation makes sense (particularly in the context of theft from African museums), but argues we do not need the concept of cultural patrimony to make this happen.

Regardless of the limitations of approaching culture through the possession of cultural property, it is clear that desires for restitution were and are a part of the way in which African nations, people, and cultural institutions imagine a redressing of the relation with the Global North. It is also clear, however, that the regulative framework UNESCO offers, and the administrative path available through the ICPRCP, are not able to address the deeper motivation behind desires for restitution. The history of these demands, then, is not limited to the cases discussed before the ICPRCP; quite the contrary.

The majority of the cases in which some form of return or restitution occurred actually took place outside the international legislative framework provided by the UN and UNESCO. The example of Zaire is instructive here. Mobutu's intervention at the 1973 UN Assembly meeting was no coincidence. Demands for the restitution of the museum collections of the Museum of the Belgian Congo near Brussels had accompanied the negotiations about Congolese independence from the very start, since they were envisioned as part and parcel of the riches of the country, much like its mining resources. The debate over their rightful ownership continued through the 1960s and led to a Belgian–Congolese collaboration in the creation of a National Institute for Museums in the Congo. Part of the motivation for Belgium's participation was the desire to deflect attention away from the collections in Belgium by helping Congo (which was renamed Zaire in 1971) to create its own national collection of art and ethnographic artifacts. When

Mobutu settled into power after his second coup in 1965, he resurrected the debate over the collections in Belgium in the context of what was described as an unfinished process of decolonization. The conflict between both countries partially resided in a disagreement about the language in which a return of objects was to be discussed: while Zairian officials insisted on using the word 'restitution', which implied they saw it as a correction to a wrongdoing of Belgium during the colonial period, the Belgian side preferred to address the matter as 'development cooperation' or 'gift', concepts that carry very different implications about the nature and meaning of the initial collection and the possible return of the objects. When a return of objects (1042 in total, 896 of which were actually already the property of Zaire, and 114 from the Belgian museum's collection) did take place between 1977 and 1981, it was after Zaire had explicitly distanced itself from the language of restitution and a demand for the return of the full collection of the Belgian museum.[48]

The Belgian–Congolese example is not the only case of repatriation that took place outside the confines of the UN and UNESCO regulative conservation regimes. Other examples of object repatriation to Africa include the return of sculpture, originally from the Great Zimbabwe site, from Germany to Zimbabwe in 2003, and the repatriation of an Axum obelisk from Italy to Ethiopia after decades of negotiations.[49] Other highly contested objects and collections, notably the many Benin bronzes in the West, the result of looting during the Benin Punitive Expedition by the British in 1897, remain the subject of continued and frequent debate.[50]

## CONCLUSION

This chapter has considered the impact of the colonial transformation of objects from African cultures into art and heritage, on the role these objects came to play in processes of decolonization aimed at establishing or reclaiming cultural guardianship from former colonial powers. One avenue through which this could be achieved was the development of ethnographic and art museums as national and postcolonial institutions, although in practice decolonizing both the infrastructures and the epistemological structures that were central to those proved a difficult and at times contentious process. The other avenue through which these objects (and the sovereignty they stood for) were reclaimed was that of the politics of heritage possession.

As this short foray into heritage politics and restitution cases demonstrates, the multiplication of parties (be they individual, commercial, or government and state representatives) and interests (be they commercial, scientific, national, cultural, or global) make the issue of restitution a difficult one. The growing presence of UN and UNESCO in heritage debates means that, on the one hand, UNESCO has created global constituencies but, on the other hand, its regulative framework does not fully support conversations about restitution, while its policies encourage the use of heritage policies in state ceremonialism.[51] While the regulative framework has expanded tremendously in the postcolonial era, it has produced very few results from the perspective of the many African parties seeking redress for the large stream of objects that left the continent during the colonial era. It can be argued, in fact, that the heritage regime is premised upon certain principles of preservation (scientific value of collections, legal chains of custody, integrity of the objects, etc.) that reproduce late colonial interpretations of cultural custodianship. This means that although it allowed for international discussions to take place, it failed to provide a powerful enough framework to support the repatriation demands of former colonies and thus, perhaps inadvertently, served to reinforce existing structural inequalities.

Like museums elsewhere in the world, the decolonization process of museums on the African continent remains unfinished. The search for alternative models of representation and display for local audiences, and for financial stability, continues. More than 50 years after independence movements engulfed the continent, however, museums continue to be seen as relevant by a variety of communities, from the local to the international. In the Global North, the discussion about the future of ethnographic museums is gaining speed, with a growing choir of voices advocating in favor of a post-ethnographic age of museums.[52] The way in which these questions impact museum institutions on the African continent has been all but neglected, often in favor of (admittedly pressing) concerns about financing and audiences.[53] We are, however, seeing a resurgence of decolonization language in the context of educational and cultural institutions, both on and off the African continent, a trend that will perhaps reignite a debate around African museums.[54]

## NOTES

1. De Varine-Bohan, quoted in *Les musées dans le monde* (Lausanne–Paris: Grammont-Robert Laffont, 1975), 73.
2. For the relation between anthropology, colonialism, and museums, see e.g., George Stocking Jr., (1985 and 1991), Sally Price (1991), H. Glenn Penny (2007) on Germany, Annie Coombes (1994) on the UK, Nélia Diaz (1991) and Maureen Murphy (2009) on France and the USA.
3. Of course, a wide variety of African art and artifacts continued to be produced and consumed for a variety of reasons, including local use, during the period discussed here.
4. The word 'authentic' appears in quotation marks here in order to acknowledge its constructed nature and avoid essentialized references to the past. As Sidney Kasfir explains, ideas about the 'authenticity' of African art are based on flawed assumptions about pre-colonial African societies as homogeneous and isolated, and African artists as controlled by tradition. See: Sidney Littefield Kasfir, "African Art and Authenticity: A Text With a Shadow," *African Arts*, 25, no. 2 (1992): 41–53.
5. Laurajane Smith, *The Uses of Heritage* (London and New York: Routledge, 2006), 44–83.

6. This does not imply, however, that African cultures and societies did not appreciate these objects for their aesthetic appeal. It merely means that the particular category of art in which they became inserted was in origin a European one.

7. This chapter is not intended as an exhaustive overview of the history of museums in Africa. For a more comprehensive overview, see Anne Gaugue, *Les États Africains et Leurs Musées. La mise en scène de la Nation* (Paris-Montréal: Éditions l'Harmattan, Gaugue 1997). This chapter is focused on national museums with what were considered to be ethnographic and art collections, and relies mostly on examples from West, Central and Southern Africa.

8. Ferdinand De Jong and Michael Rowlands, eds., *Reclaiming Heritage. Alternative Imaginaries of Memory in West Africa* (Walnut Creek, CA: Left Coast Press, 2007), 17.

9. This trend occurred at various speeds in different places. In French museums, for example, African art displays were common by the 1930s, while in Belgium this trend was not institutionalized until the 1950s. See Sarah Van Beurden, "The Value of Culture: Congolese Art and the Promotion of Belgian Colonialism (1945–1959)," *History and Anthropology*, 24, no. 4 (2013): 472–92.

10. On colonial humanism, see Gary Wilder, *The French Imperial Nation-State: Négritude and Colonial Humanism between the Two World Wars* (Chicago: University of Chicago Press, 2005). On welfare colonialism see Sarah Van Beurden, *Authentically African. Arts and the Transnational Politics of Congolese Culture* (Athens: Ohio University Press, 2015), 28–29.

11. Okechukwu Nwafor, "Culture, Corruption, Politics," *Critical Interventions: Journal of African Art History and Visual Culture* 4, no. 2 (2010): 118–19.

12. Derek R. Peterson, Kodzo Gavua, and Ciraj Rassool, eds., *The Politics of Heritage in Africa. Economies, Histories and Infrastructures* (New York: Cambridge University Press, 2015), 7.

13. Van Beurden, *Authentically African*, 63–72.

14. Agbenyega Adedze, "Symbols of Triumph: IFAN and the Colonial Museum Complex in French West Africa (1938–1960)," *Museum Anthropology* 25, no. 2 (2000): 52; and Julien Bondaz, *L'exposition postcoloniale. Musées et zoos en Afrique de l'Ouest (Niger, Mali, Burkina Faso)* (Paris: L'Harmattan, 2014), 64–71.

15. David Lowenthal, *The Heritage Crusade and the Spoils of History* (Cambridge: Cambridge University Press, 1998).

16. The first museums on the African continent were founded at the start of the twentieth century in the British and Portuguese empires and were focused on the collection and display of geological and mineral specimens. The collection and display of ethnograhic material only appears in the 1930s. Gaugue, *Les États Africains et Leurs Musées*, 7.

17. Laura De Becker, "Imagining the Post-Colonial and Post-Genocidal Nation in the National Museum of Rwanda, Butare," *Critical Interventions: Journal of African Art History and Visual Culture* 10, no. 3 (2016): 293–308.

18. Philip L. Ravenhill, "The Passive Object and the Tribal Paradigm: Colonial Museography in French West Africa," in *African Material Cultures*, ed. Mary Jo Arnoldi, Christaud M. Geary, and Kris L. Hardin (Bloomington: Indiana University Press, 1996), 265–82; and Adedze, "Symbols of Triumph".

19. Bondaz, *L'exposition postcoloniale*.

20. Sophie Mew, "'Universal Museums' in West Africa," *Critical Interventions: Journal of African Art History and Visual Culture* 4, no. 2 (2010): 101–17; and Mark Crinson, "Nation-Building, Collecting and the Politics of Display—the National Museum, Ghana," *Journal of the History of Collections* 13, no. 2 (2001): 231–50.

21. Paul Basu, "A Museum for Sierra Leone? Amateur Enthusiasms and Colonial Museum Policy in British West Africa," in *Curating Empire. Museums and the British Imperial Experience*, ed. Sarah Longair and John McAleer (Manchester: Manchester University Press, 2012), 145–67.

22. Alexandre Adande, "L'impérieuse nécessité des musées africains," *L'Art nègre* (Paris: Présence Africaine, 1966), 163–66; Agbenyega Adedze, "Museums as a Tool for Nationalism in Africa," *Museum Anthropology* 19, no. 2 (1995): 58–64; A.E. Afigbo and S.I.O. Okita, eds., *Museums and Nation Building* (Imo, Nigeria: New African Publishing Co., 1985); and Flora Edouwaye S. Kaplan, "Nigerian Museums: Envisaging Culture as National Identity," in *Museums and the Making of 'Ourselves': The Role of Objects in National Identity*, ed. Flora Edouwaye S. Kaplan (London: Leicester University Press, 1994), 45–78.

23. Crinson, "Nation-Building, Collecting and the Politics of Display—the National Museum, Ghana," 236 and 239–47.

24. Ibid., 242–45; and Arianna Fogelman, "Colonial Legacy in African Museology: The Case of the Ghana National Museum," *Museum Anthropology* 31, no. 1 (2008): 19–27.

25. Van Beurden, *Authentically African*, 127–207.

26. Gaugue, *Les États Africains et Leurs Musées*, 139–43.

27. Claude Daniel Ardouin and Emmanuel Arinze, eds., *Museums and the Community in West Africa* (Washington and London: Smithsonian Institution Press—James Currey, 1995).

28. Claude Daniel Ardouin, "Culture, Museums, and Development in Africa," in *The Muse of Modernity: Essays on Culture as Development in Africa*, ed. Philip G. Altbach and Salah Hassan (Trenton, NJ, Asmara, Eritrea: Africa World Press, 1997a), 181.

29. International Council of Museums (ICOM). *What Museums for Africa? Heritage in the Future: Benin, Ghana, Togo, November 18–23, 1991* (Proceedings of the Encounters [Paris?]: International Council of Museums, 1992), 371.

30. For the results of some of the WAMP workshops and conferences, see e.g., Claude Daniel Ardouin, ed., *Museums and Archeology in West Africa* (Washington and London: Smithsonian Institution Press—James Currey, 1997b); Claude Daniel Ardouin and Emmanuel Arinze, eds. *Museums & the Community in West Africa* (Washington and London: Smithsonian Institution Press—James Currey, 1995) and ibid. *Museums and History in West Africa* (Washington and London: Smithsonian Institution Press—James Currey, 2000).

31. It has also resulted in a critical mass in terms of scholarship. See e.g., Ciraj Rassool, *Recalling Community in Cape Town: Creating and Curating the District Six Museum* (Cape Town: District Six Museum, 2001); Sara Byala, *A Place That Matters Yet: John Gubbins's Museum Africa in the Postcolonial World* (Chicago: University of Chicago Press, 2013); and Annie Coombes, *History After*

*Apartheid: Visual Culture and Public Memory in a Democratic South Africa* (Raleigh: Duke University Press, 2003).

32. Rassool, *Recalling Community in Cape Town.*
33. Byala, *A Place that Matters Yet.*
34. What this chapter does not address, given its focus on cultural artifacts, but which is nonetheless an important element in the discussions about restitution, are the debates over human remains in Western museum collections. See e.g. Legassick and Rassool on museums and the trade in human remains from South Africa. Ciraj Rassool, "Re-Storing the Skeletons of Empire: Return, Reburial and Rehumanisation in Southern Africa," *Journal of Southern African Studies* 41, no. 3 (2015): 653–70; and Martin Legassick and Ciraj Rassool, *Sketelons in the Cupboard: South African Museums and the Trade in Human Remains, 1907–1917* (Cape Town: South African Museum, 2000).
35. Ana Filipa Vrdoljak, *International Law, Museums and the Return of Cultural Objects* (Cambridge: Cambridge University Press, 2006).
36. Lyndel V. Prott, ed., *Witnesses to History. A Compendium of Documents and Writings on the Return of Cultural Objects* (Paris: Unesco Publishing, 2009) 12–13. It should be noted here that conventions are only effective if they are ratified by individual governments. In the case of the 1970 UNESCO convention, this occurred only slowly. To date, 131 countries have ratified or accepted the agreement (For a full list, see, consulted April 18, 2016, http://www.unesco.org/eri/la/convention.asp?KO=13039&language=E).
37. Prott, *Witnesses to History*, 13.
38. Van Beurden, *Authentically African*, 116–18.
39. Prott, *Witnesses to History*, 15; and Vrdoljak, *International Law, Museums and the Return of Cultural Objects*, 211–12.
40. ICOM, *Dossier de Presse: Masque Makonde. Signature d'un accord pour le don du Masque Makondé du Musée Barbier-Mueller de Genève au Musée National de Tanzanie* (Paris: ICOM, 2010). The international regulative framework on restitution continues to expand, for example by the reccomendations made by the 1982 World Conference on Cultural Policies, held in Mexico and the 1995 UNIDROIT Convention on Stolen or Illegally Exported Cultural Objects. The emphasis on bilateral negotiations and the reluctance to engage with potential claims about material removed in a colonial context also continue. For details see: Jeanette Greenfield, *The Return of Cultural Treasures* (Cambridge: Cambridge University Press, 1989), 222–37; and Lyndell V. Prott, "Saving Heritage: UNESCO's Action against Illicit Traffic in Africa," in *Plundering Africa's Past*, ed. Peter R. Schmidt and Roderick J. McIntosh (Bloomington: Indiana University Press, 1996), 29–44.
41. Van Beurden, *Authentically African*, 103.
42. For more on the perspectives of Western museums and curators on restitution, see John Henry Merryman, ed., *Imperialism, Art and Restitution* (New York: Cambridge University Press, 2006).
43. Being a UNESCO World Heritage Site does not necessarily provide protection against theft and art smuggling of course. On the contrary, it can even make a site more of a target, since it can have a positive effect on the value of objects from these sites, as is the case with the Kilwa Kisiwani site on the Tanzanian coast, for example. See: N.J. Karoma, "The Deterioration and Destruction of

Archeological and Historical Sites in Tanzania," in *Plundering Africa's Past.* 194–95.
44. Lowenthal, *The Heritage Crusade and the Spoils of History,* 242.
45. For an account of how the technical process of world heritage recognition and management is biased against non-Western locations, see chap. 3 in *The Uses of Heritage* by Laurajane Smith (Smith, *The Uses of History,* 87–113).
46. Kwame Anthony Appiah, *Cosmopolitanism. Ethics in a World of Strangers* (New York and London: W.W. Norton and Company, 2007), 199.
47. Ibid., 135.
48. For a complete history of the Congolese–Zairian restitution demands, see Sarah Van Beurden, "The Art of (Re)Possession: Heritage and the Cultural Politics of Congo's Decolonization," *Journal of African History* 56, no. 1 (2015): 143–64; *Authentically African,* chap. 3.
49. Dawson Munjeri, "The Reunification of a National Symbol," *Museum International* 61, nos. 1–2 (2009): 12–21; and Haile Mariam, "The Cultural Benefits of the Return of the Axum Obelisk," *Museum International* 61, nos. 1–2 (2009): 48–51.
50. Sylvester Ogbechie, "Give Me What Is Mine (Apologies Burning Spear)," consulted May 10, 2016, http://aachronym.blogspot.de/2010/12/give-me-what-is-mine-apologies-burning.html; and Okechukwu Nwafor, "Culture, Corruption, Politics," *Critical Interventions: Journal of African Art History and Visual Culture* 4, no. 2 (2010): 118–31.
51. Ferdinand De Jong and Michael Rowlands, eds., *Reclaiming Heritage. Alternative Imaginaries of Memory in West Africa* (Walnut Creek, CA: Left Coast Press, 2007), 13.
52. See e.g. Clare Harriss and Michael O'Hanlon, "The Future of the Ethnographic Museum," *Anthropology Today* 29, no. 1 (2013): 1–32; and Clémentine Deliss (2015) "Collecting Life's Unknowns," *L'Internationale,* consulted March 12, 2016, http://www.internationaleonline.org/research/decolonising_practices/27_collecting_lifes_unknowns.
53. This continues the trend of the ICOM and other conferenecs of the 1990s. See e.g. Anne Marie Bouttiaux, ed., *Afrique: Musées et patrimoines pour quels publics?* (Tervuren–Paris: RMCA-Karthala, 2007).
54. For example in the context of campus protests against the presence of colonial monuments in South Africa, a debate that is also taken up by the Black Lives Matter movement in the USA.

**Acknowledgement** The author is grateful to the Max Planck Institute for the History of Science in Berlin, Germany for providing her with the time, space and support to work on this chapter.

## BIBLIOGRAPHY

Adande, Alexandre. "L'impérieuse nécessité des musées africains." *L'Art nègre.* Paris: Présence Africaine, 1966: 163–66.
Adedze, Agbenyega. "Museums as a Tool for Nationalism in Africa." *Museum Anthropology* 19, no. 2 (1995): 58–64.

————. "Symbols of Triumph: IFAN and the Colonial Museum Complex in French West Africa (1938–1960)." *Museum Anthropology* 25, no. 2 (2000): 50–60.

Afigbo, A.E., and Okita S.I.O, eds. *Museums and Nation Building.* Imo, Nigeria: New African Publishing Co., 1985.

Appiah, Kwame Anthony. *Cosmopolitanism: Ethics in a World of Strangers.* New York and London: W.W. Norton and Company, 2007.

Ardouin, Claude Daniel. "Culture, Museums, and Development in Africa." In *The Muse of Modernity: Essays on Culture as Development in Africa*, edited by Philip G. Altbach and Salah Hassan. Trenton, NJ, Asmara: Africa World Press, 1996, 1997.

————, ed. *Museums and Archeology in West Africa.* Washington and London: Smithsonian Institution Press—James Currey, 1997.

Ardouin, Claude Daniel, and Emmanuel Arinze, eds. *Museums & the Community in West Africa.* Washington and London: Smithsonian Institution Press—James Currey, 1995.

————. *Museums & History in West Africa.* Washington and London: Smithsonian Institution Press—James Currey, 2000.

Basu, Paul. "A Museum for Sierra Leone? Amateur Enthusiasms and Colonial Museum Policy in British West Africa." In *Curating Empire. Museums and the British Imperial Experience*, edited by Sarah Longair and John McAleer. Manchester: Manchester University Press, 2012, 145–67.

Bondaz, Julien. *L'exposition postcoloniale. Musées et zoos en Afrique de l'Ouest (Niger, Mali, Burkina Faso).* Paris: L'Harmattan, 2014.

Bouttiaux, Anne Marie, ed. *Afrique: Musées et patrimoines pour quels publics?* Tervuren-Paris: RMCA-Karthala, 2007.

Byala, Sara. *A Place That Matters Yet: John Gubbins's Museum Africa in the Postcolonial World.* Chicago: University of Chicago Press, 2013.

Coombes, Annie E. *Reinventing Africa: Museums, Material Culture and Popular Imagination in Late Victorian and Edwardian England.* New Haven: Yale University Press, 1994.

————. *History After Apartheid: Visual Culture and Public Memory in a Democratic South Africa.* Raleigh: Duke University Press, 2003.

Crinson, Mark. "Nation-Building, Collecting and the Politics of Display—The National Museum, Ghana." *Journal of the History of Collections* 13, no. 2 (2001): 231–50.

De Becker, Laura. "Imagining the Post-Colonial and Post-Genocidal Nation in the National Museum of Rwanda, Butare." *Critical Interventions: Journal of African Art History and Visual Culture* 10, no. 3 (2016): 293–308.

De Jong, Ferdinand, and Michael Rowlands, eds. *Reclaiming Heritage. Alternative Imaginaries of Memory in West Africa.* Walnut Creek, CA: Left Coast Press, 2007.

Deliss, Clémentine. "Collecting Life's Unknowns." *L'Internationale.* http://www.internationaleonline.org/research/decolonising_practices/27_collecting_lifes_unknowns (2015, consulted March 12, 2016).

Dias, Nélia. *Le Musée d'Ethnographie du Trocadéro (1878–1908): Anthropologie et muséologie en France.* Paris: Editions CNRS, 1991.

Fogelman, Arianna. "Colonial Legacy in African Museology: The Case of the Ghana National Museum." *Museum Anthropology* 31, no. 1 (2008): 19–27.

Gaugue, Anne. *Les États Africains et Leurs Musées. La mise en scène de la Nation.* Paris-Montréal: Éditions l'Harmattan, 1997.

Greenfield, Jeanette. *The Return of Cultural Treasures.* Cambridge: Cambridge University Press, 1989.

Harriss, Clare, and Michael O'Hanlon. "The Future of the Ethnographic Museum." *Anthropology Today* 29, no. 1 (2013): 1–32.

International Council of Museums (ICOM). *What Museums for Africa? Heritage in the Future: Benin, Ghana, Togo, November 18–23, 1991. Proceedings of the Encounters.* Paris?: International Council of Museums, 1992.

———. *Dossier de Presse: Masque Makonde. Signature d'un accord pour le don du Masque Makondé du Musée Barbier-Mueller de Genève au Musée National de Tanzanie.* Paris: ICOM, 2010.

Kaplan, Flora Edouwaye S. "Nigerian Museums: Envisaging Culture as National Identity." In *Museums and the Making of 'Ourselves': The Role of Objects in National Identity,* edited by Flora Edouwaye S. Kaplan. London: Leicester University Press, 1994, 45–78.

Karoma, N.J. "The Deterioration and Destruction of Archeological and Historical Sites in Tanzania." In *Plundering Africa's Past,* edited by Peter R. Schmidt and Roderick J. McIntosh. Bloomington: Indiana University Press, 1996, 191–200.

Kasfir, Sidney Littefield. "African Art and Authenticity: A Text with a Shadow." *African Arts* 25, no. 2 (1992): 41–53.

Legassick, Martin, and Ciraj Rassool. *Sketelons in the Cupboard: South African Museums and the Trade in Human Remains, 1907–1917.* Cape Town: South African Museum, 2000.

———. "Community Museums, Memory Politics, and Social Transformations in South Africa: Histories, Possibilities, and Limits." In *Museum Frictions. Public Cultures/Global Transformations,* edited by Ivan Karp and Corinne A. Kratz et al. Raleigh: Duke University Press, 2007.

*Les musées dans le monde.* Lausanne-Paris: Grammont-Robert Laffont, 1975.

Lowenthal, David. *The Heritage Crusade and the Spoils of History.* Cambridge: Cambridge University Press, 1998.

Mariam, Haile. "The Cultural Benefits of the Return of the Axum Obelisk." *Museum International* 61, nos. 1–2 (2009): 48–51.

Merryman, John Henry, ed. *Imperialism, Art and Restitution.* New York: Cambridge University Press. 2006.

Mew, Sophie. "'Universal Museums' in West Africa." *Critical Interventions: Journal of African Art History and Visual Culture* 4, no. 2 (2010): 101–17.

Munjeri, Dawson. "The Reunification of a National Symbol." *Museum International* 61, nos. 1–2 (2009): 12–21.

Murphy, Maureen. *De l'imaginaire au musée: Les arts d'Afrique à Paris et à New York (1931–2006).* Dijon: Les presses du reel, 2009.

Nwafor, Okechukwu. "Culture, Corruption, Politics." *Critical Interventions: Journal of African Art History and Visual Culture* 4, no. 2 (2010): 118–31.

Ogbechie, Sylvester. "Give Me What Is Mine (Apologies Burning Spear)." Consulted 2010, May 10, 2016. http://aachronym.blogspot.de/2010/12/give-me-what-is-mine-apologies-burning.html.

Penny, H. Glenn. *Objects of Culture: Ethnology and Ethnographic Museums in Imperial Germany.* Chapel Hill: University of North Carolina Press, 2007.

Peterson, Derek R., Kodzo Gavua, and Ciraj Rassool, eds. *The Politics of Heritage in Africa. Economies, Histories and Infrastructures.* New York: Cambridge University Press, 2015.

Price, Sally. *Primitive Art in Civilized Places.* Chicago: University of Chicago Press, 1989.

Prott, Lyndell V. "Saving Heritage: UNESCO's Action against Illicit Traffic in Africa." In *Plundering Africa's Past*, edited by Peter R. Schmidt and Roderick J. McIntosh. Bloomington: Indiana University Press, 1996, 29–44.

———, ed. *Witnesses to History. A Compendium of Documents and Writings on the Return of Cultural Objects.* Paris: Unesco Publishing, 2009.

Rassool, Ciraj. *Recalling Community in Cape Town: Creating and Curating the District Six Museum.* Cape Town: District Six Museum, 2001.

———. "Re-storing the Skeletons of Empire: Return, Reburial and Rehumanisation in Southern Africa." *Journal of Southern African Studies* 41, no. 3 (2015): 653–70.

Ravenhill, Philip L. "The Passive Object and the Tribal Paradigm: Colonial Museography in French West Africa." In *African Material Cultures*, edited by Mary Jo Arnoldi, Christraud M. Geary, and Kris L. Hardin. Bloomington: Indiana University Press, 1996, 265–82.

Schmidt, Peter R., and Roderick J. McIntosh, eds. *Plundering Africa's Past.* Bloomington: Indiana University Press, 1996.

Smith, Laurajane. *The Uses of Heritage.* London and New York: Routledge, 2006.

Stocking, George, Jr., ed. *Objects and Others: Essays on Museums and Material Culture.* Madison: University of Wisconsin Press, 1985.

———. *Colonial Situations: Essays on the Contextualization of Ethnographic Knowledge.* Madison: University of Wisconsin Press, 1991.

Van Beurden, Sarah. "The Value of Culture: Congolese Art and the Promotion of Belgian Colonialism (1945–1959)." *History and Anthropology* 24, no. 4 (2013): 472–92.

———. "The Art of (Re)Possession: Heritage and the Cultural Politics of Congo's Decolonization." *Journal of African History* 56, no. 1 (2015): 143–64.

———. *Authentically African. Arts and the Transnational Politics of Congolese Culture.* Athens: Ohio University Press, 2015.

Vrdoljak, Ana Filipa. *International Law, Museums and the Return of Cultural Objects.* Cambridge: Cambridge University Press, 2006.

Wilder, Gary. *The French Imperial Nation-State: Négritude and Colonial Humanism Between the Two World Wars.* Chicago: University of Chicago Press, 2005.

# CHAPTER 48

# Building the African Novel on Quick sand: Politics of Language, Identity, and Ownership

*Mukoma Wa Ngugi*

Chinua Achebe's *Things Fall Apart* has been translated into over 50 languages, making it the most translated African novel. But almost 60 years after it was first published, there is no authoritative translation into Igbo, Achebe's mother tongue.[1] An equivalent would be if Conrad's *Heart of Darkness* had not been translated into Polish. But even then, the comparison would not work. As the late Obi Wali noted, 'Conrad's works, as we know, are considered part of English literature, not Polish literature, and the sole criterion for this is that his works are in English, not in Polish'.[2] Achebe, on the other hand, understood himself, and is read, as part of the African literary tradition. Indeed, *Things Fall Apart* has been translated into Polish at least two times while there are three competing translations in German.[3] To be sure, it has been translated into ten or so African languages, but considering there are over 2000 languages on the continent, that is still a tiny number. And, more generally, other novels considered seminal in the African literary tradition such as Ngugi Wa Thiong'o's *A Grain of Wheat*, Bessie Head's *A Question of Power*, and Soyinka's *The Interpreters* fare much worse in terms of translation into the author's mother tongue and the wider African languages index.

This chapter is based on my forthcoming book *The Rise of the African Novel: Politics of Language, Identity and Ownership* (University of Michigan Press, 2018).

M.W. Ngugi (✉)
Cornell University, Ithaca, NY, USA

© The Author(s) 2018
M.S. Shanguhyia and T. Falola (eds.),
*The Palgrave Handbook of African Colonial and Postcolonial History*,
https://doi.org/10.1057/978-1-137-59426-6_48

To answer the question of why there is no authoritative Igbo translation of what is understood as Africa's most famous novel, one has to go back to the 1962 'African Writers of English Expression' conference convened at Makerere University, Uganda. In 1962, Africa was in the throes of decolonization, and for the group of young writers attending the conference anything was possible. Their goal was to define, or at least agree upon, the parameters of an African literary aesthetic that would also be in the service of political and cultural decolonization. Reading their post-conference write-ups in the *Transition Journal,* the excitement with which they greeted their role as the instigators and vanguards of an emerging literary tradition is palpable.

The writers in attendance, Chinua Achebe (age 32), Christopher Okigbo (age 32), Wole Soyinka (age 28), James Ngugi (age 28),[4] Bloke Modisane (age 39), and Ezekiel Mphahlele (age 43)[5] set in motion, within a few years, a literary tradition that would engulf subsequent generations in debates around the definition and category of African literature, the languages of African literature, the role of writers in political change, the writer in continental Africa versus the diaspora, and the relationship of African aesthetics to European aesthetics. They would in just a few short years run against the repression and violence of post-independence African states. Disillusioned with the promises of decolonization, they would turn their pens against their neo-colonial governments and pay the price of death, detention, and exile. Achebe became a spokesperson for Biafran independence from Nigeria, doing ambassadorial work in both Africa and the West. Okigbo was shot dead fighting for Biafra's independence in 1967, five years after the conference. The Nigerian military government of General Yakubu Gowon detained Soyinka for his peace activism in 1966. In 1977, the Kenyan government of Jomo Kenyatta detained Ngugi for his political writing and theater work in Gikuyu, his mother tongue. Both Mphahlele and Modisane, coming from apartheid South Africa, were already living in exile at the time of the Makerere Conference, Mphahlele in France and Modisane in Britain. Achebe, Soyinka, and Ngugi each wound up in political exile, ultimately joined by writers like Micere Mugo from Kenya and Nawal El Saadawi from Egypt. The Makerere generation of African writers would suffer death, exile, and detention for not separating their literary aesthetics from the material work of politics, for not separating the author from the citizen.[6]

The young and optimistic Ngugi captured the excitement when he enthusiastically concluded in his post-conference write-up, 'With the death of colonialism, a new society is being born. And with it a new literature'.[7] Yet, even as they were heralding the new society,[8] the conference had declared boldly in its title that this was a gathering of 'African Writers of English Expression'. As Obi Wali asked in an essay published the same year as the Makerere conference, entitled 'The Dead End of African Literature', why was it so important to signal to the attendees that African writers using African languages were not welcome? One cannot conceive of English writers today writing English national literature in French, or the Chinese writing in Japanese, or the French in German. But for African writers, writing in an imperially enforced foreign language was taken as the starting point. The question for the Makerere writers was not how to write, translate, and market books written in African languages. Rather, it was how best to make English work for the African literary imagination.

## EARLY SOUTH AFRICAN WRITING: A MISSING LITERARY EPOCH

It was not for the lack of examples of literature written in African languages. In the early 1900s, South African writers were writing in Xhosa, Zulu, Sesotho, and other African languages, with translations into English: Thomas Mofolo's *Moeti oa Bochabela* (published in 1907, later translated into English as *Traveller to the East* in 1934); *Chaka,* written in 1909 but published in 1931[9]; R.R.R. Dhlomo's *An African Tragedy* (1928) and *UNomalanga kaNdengezi* (1934); Samuel Mqhayi's *Ityala Lamawele* (*The Lawsuit of the Twins*) (1912); and A.C. Jordan's *Ingqumbo Yeminyanya* (1940), translated as *The Wrath of the Ancestors* in 1964. Sol Plaatje's novel, *Mhudi* (1930), was the first full-length novel in English by a black South African writer.

James Currey, the editorial director for *Heinemann's* African Writers Series (AWS) from 1967 to 1984 was well aware of early writing.[10] In *Africa Writes Back* he noted: '[t]he historic contribution by the mission presses in the early part of the twentieth century was later to be reflected in two novels. Lovedale had published Thomas Mofolo's *Chaka* in Sotho in 1925 and the quaint translations published in English and French had an international impact, especially on the writers of negritude. Heinemann commissioned an unexpurgated translation from the academic and poet Dan Kunene'.[11] However, it was not the 'quaint' early writing that really interested Currey; it was more the political writing and contemporary literature produced by politically conscious Makerere writers. Currey. on commissioning books from apartheid South Africa. was very clear about this, saying he wanted books that 'reflected first and foremost the realities of life suffered by the people oppressed by the laws of colour'.[12]

But just like the Makerere generation, these South African writers and intellectuals belonged to their times, and as apartheid became entrenched so did their resistance. For example, the national anthem of the first African National Congress (formed in 1912) was a song of mourning to which Mqhayi added seven nationalist verses. Sol Plaatje, a nationalist and one of the founding members of the ANC, 'arranged for the recording of "Nkosi" in London'.[13] In his essay 'Retracing Nelson Mandela through the Lineage of Black Political Thought from Walter Rubusana to Steve Biko', Xolela Mangcu talks about how, as a young student, Nelson Mandela was influenced by Mqhayi's 'cultural nationalism'.[14] Ntongela Masilela, who has done major work on these early South African writers, sees them as a movement not only conscious of each other and immersed in their political and cultural contexts, but aware of and influenced by and influencing black Americans and the black diaspora in general.[15] In other words, they saw themselves in the larger context of a Pan-African network.

The point I want to make here, though, is that this early South African literary history provided an alternative path to the 1960s African literature in English consensus. Instead, the Makerere writers were like a literary tsunami that came and immersed early South African writing beneath a torrent of realist novels written in English. They derailed the African literary tradition from one of writing in African languages and subsequently getting translated into other languages, and started us on the path of the realist African novel in English. And they were so thorough that African literary criticism has failed to recover the missing literary epoch.

For example, in the authoritative and groundbreaking anthology of literary criticism, the 2009 *Cambridge Companion to the African Novel*, there is no sustained discussion of the early South African writing in African languages or English. In the *Cambridge Companion*, the chronology of literary events starts with the *Egyptian Book of the Dead* (*c.*1500) and ends with Achebe winning the Man Booker International Prize in 2007. In that chronology, the only mentions of the early South African writing are Mofolo's *Chaka* and Sol Plaatje's *Mhudi*. Mofolo's name is misspelled, rendered as Mfomo, and his earlier two titles are not featured. Instead of giving the 1925 original publication of *Chaka* in Sesotho, it gives the English translation publication date of 1930. Dhlomo and A.C. Jordan and others are nowhere to be found. The equally authoritative 2007 *African Literature: An Anthology of Criticism and Theory,* edited by Tejumola Olaniyan and Ato Quayson, has no essays on pre-Makerere writing, in African languages or in English. To put it another way, imagine an English-literature anthology missing a literary epoch like modernism, for example. W.B. Yeats, Ezra Pound, D.H. Lawrence, T.S. Eliot, or James Joyce would be absent; the English literary tradition would be unrecognizable.

## THE PUBLISHING INDUSTRY AND THE RISE OF AFRICAN AESTHETICS IN ENGLISH

Missionary presses in general were central to establishing early South African writing. Oyekan Owomoyela, in his essay 'The Literature of Empire: Africa', credits Lovedale Press with establishing isiXhosa literature, saying that it 'owes its birth to the Lovedale press; one of the earliest products of the Lovedale mission school, Tiyo Soga, translated John Bunyan's *The Pilgrim's Progress* into Xhosa as *U-hambo lom-hambi* (1868), and also played a central role in the translation of the bible into the same language'.[16] Lovedale Press first published A.C. Jordan's *Ingqumbo Yeminyanya*, and in fact two of the main fictional characters in Jordan's novel, Mphuthumi and Thembeka, attend Lovedale College.

Lovedale was founded by the Glasgow Missionary Society in 1823 with a mission to 'promote Christian knowledge in Southern Africa and to propagate 'civilised norms of conduct and moral behaviour'.[17] Even though it specialized in educational and Christian books, starting in 1932 it branched out to publishing general literature books under the directorship of R.H.W. Shepherd. Shepherd believed that a 'mission press needed to exercise a more creative responsibility and that it should provide more general reading matter for the African public'.[18] Shepherd himself did not believe that blacks and whites were equals; he saw himself as gently guiding Africans from heathenism to civilization.

With Lovedale largely having a monopoly there was pressure to write books sympathetic to the Christianizing mission, and sometimes outright censorship as Jeffrey Peires shows in his essay 'Lovedale Press: Literature for the Bantu Revisited'. And that pressure might explain why in *Traveller to the East*, Thomas Mofolo created an Africa straight out of the myth of the noble savage. And it very well could be that the writers at that time could not see the coming apartheid and just how far it would go in denying Africans their humanity. For the revolutionary Makerere writers writing in a time of decolonization, Fekisi, in *Traveller to the East* in his journey toward Christian enlightenment, would have appeared a caricature, a confirmation of internalized racism. It would have appeared antithetical to the struggle for political, economic, and cultural independence. It was not a literature one could take seriously enough to be studied as an integral part of the African literary tradition.

The Makerere consensus would not have survived and thrived without active participation by British publishers. They too were invested in propagating the myth of African literature beginning with their intervention. For example, James Currey in *Africa Writes Back* titled the opening chapter 'The Establishment of African Literature', with the subtitle 'The Starting Line'. And he begins the chapter by quoting a 1998 Achebe Harvard Lecture in which Achebe celebrates the AWS. In fact, it is Achebe who uses the phrase 'starting line' in a lecture that takes the myth of the beginning of African literature for a fact:

> [t]he launching of the Heinemann's African Writers Series was like the umpire's signal for which African writers had been waiting on the starting line. In one short generation an immense library of writing had sprung into being from all over the continent and, for the first time in history, Africa's future generations of readers and writers—youngsters in schools and colleges—began to read not only *David Copperfield* and other English classics that I and my generation had read, but also works by their own writers about their own people.[19]

So here is the publisher using the writer, and the writer using the publisher, to justify an African literary clock that starts with the AWS. In the same opening page, after using the Achebe speech to show the AWS as the start of African literature, he goes on to justify the use of English. Currey writes, 'English was the lubricant of the English-speaking world. It was not only how authority was imposed but it was also the way in which the subject peoples reacted to that imposition of power. Writers in India, the Caribbean and Africa came to take advantage of the language they shared, but they had to have publishing opportunities'.[20] It is the sentence 'English was the lubricant of the English world' that is the most arresting because it starts with the fact of an English-speaking world, not a world in which thousands of other languages, literatures, and writers in those languages existed. The British publisher of African fiction was so thoroughly educated in the myth of the English metaphysical empire that even those pronouncements that would otherwise be seen as presenting two opposed truths pass for a fact: English is the language of the English-speaking world.

The decision to publish the African novels through its Heinemann Educational Books (HEB) imprints was a practical one. The colonial cultural machinery had not been interested in cultivating African literary culture or reading for pleasure. Publishing was for educational books. It was easier for Hill to push books written by African writers through the educational publishing model. And this meant publishing African literary books with the idea that they would in turn become set books in Kenyan primary and high schools. As Hill explained, HEB was the only firm with 'the faith—the passion almost—and the will to do the job' and they had the 'necessary business set-up to sell the books' in a continent where the 'book trade ... was almost entirely educational'.[21] The idea was that the books that sold well would support newer and even experimental works.

But it did not work that way. The model for the hard fought for but lucrative educational books market took over. There was no market-driven incentive effort to develop a general readership because the goal was to have novels become exam-set books. In a 2015 interview aptly titled 'We'll stick to creative works, but textbooks bring in cash', Kiarie Kamau, the chief executive at East African Educational Publishers, said that:

> [t]he demand for a generous return on investment is there. The competition
> is stiff, and one must keep raising the bar in terms of strategy to perform bet-
> ter and better ... What I mean is that there is that book that reads so well, has
> a strong message, and has an almost eternal shelf life. But it just doesn't sell in
> huge quantities. What the shareholder wants to hear about is the percentage
> of dividend that has been declared, and that's only possible if you have a mass
> market product, bringing home a generous turnover. Often, that's a textbook.[22]

Like any other business, publishing has to be profitable in order to be viable. But when the managing director starts calling novels products, it is clear that the institutional orientation is towards the profitable; to stick with what has always been working with general readership, books being secondary.

Because the educational system is in English, books written in English get priority. Walter Bgoya, the publisher at the Tanzanian-based Mkuki na Nyota Press, said in a 2013 essay, 'Publishing in Africa from Independence to the Present Day', gave the example of a bilingual textbook that Mkuki na Nyota submitted to the Committee of the Ministry of Education. He narrated:

> ... Mkuki na Nyota Publishers submitted the first of four bilingual Swahili/English textbooks, covering the equivalent of the O-level chemistry syllabus, to the Educational Materials Approval Committee of the Ministry of Education for evaluation. Although the material in both languages adequately covered the chemistry syllabus for Form 1, it was rejected solely because it was bilingual. The publisher was informed that approval would be given if the Swahili pages were removed.[23]

Only colonial education and its vestiges can explain why the committee would reject such a painstaking and creative solution. The high premium is on English. African languages are not only unequal but also not worthy of being taught. An opportunity to grow Kiswahili chemistry vocabulary was lost. Novels follow the same model: they are more likely to be taught if in English.

## WHAT IS AFRICAN LITERATURE? THEN AND NOW

The Makerere Conference of 1962 is also important because it was there that the question of what constituted African literature was discussed.[24] As per Chinua Achebe's account in his 1965 essay, 'English and the African Writer', the participants spent considerable time debating and eventually failing to agree a definition of African literature. Was African Literature to be limited by being:

> ... produced in Africa or about Africa? Could African literature be on any subject, or must it have an African theme? Should it embrace the whole continent or South of the Sahara, or just Black Africa? And then the question of language. Should it be in indigenous African languages or should it include Arabic, English, French, Portuguese, Afrikaans, etc.?[25]

The conference failed to answer the question, but one year later a conference held at Faculté des Lettres of Dakar University in Senegal succeeded in 'tentatively' coming up with a definition. Ezekiel Mphahlele in a conference report for *Transition* recorded the definition:

> ... as creative writing in which an African setting is authentically handled or to which experiences originating in Africa are integral. This therefore includes among others, writing by white Africans like Nadine Gordimer, Dan Jacobson, Doris Lessing, Elspeth Huxley, Alan Paton and so on, and that by non-Africans

like William Plomer (a man of many fascinating worlds), Joyce Cary and Joseph Conrad (specifically, *The Heart of Darkness*). Graham Greene's *The Heart of the Matter* could have been given any setting outside Africa, and so it does not qualify.[26]

This definition raises many questions. Who defines what is an authentic African setting? And with regard to these experiences originating from Africa, what is the appropriate length of time for a character to experience them? Achebe pointed out the difficulty of limiting African literature. In the same 1965 essay, he wrote: 'I could not help being amused by the curious circumstances in which Conrad, a Pole, writing in English produced African literature! On the other hand if Peter Abrahams were to write a good novel based on his experiences in the West Indies it would not be accepted as African literature'.[27] Is the African novel an extension of the African writer so it qualifies no matter the setting and content? Or is it the setting alone that matters? This definition of African literature, that could allow for the inclusion of Conrad's *Heart of Darkness* as an African text, while a novel by an African writer set outside the continent could not, led Achebe to conclude that '... you cannot cram African literature into a small, neat definition. I do not see African literature as one unit but as a group of associated units—in fact the sum total of all the national and ethnic literatures of Africa'.[28] National literature for Achebe was 'literature written in English; and the ethnic literatures are in Hausa, Ibo, Yoruba, Effik, Edo, ijaw, etc'.[29] By raising writing in English to national and major literature, and relegating African languages to producing ethnic literature, Achebe contributed to a language hierarchy that still undergirds and informs African literature today. But language hierarchy notwithstanding, for Achebe, the term 'African literature' could carry within it an immediately assumed diversity[30] in the same way that when one says 'European literature' a diverse history and array of writers is assumed.[31]

More than 50 years after the Makerere Conference the debate continues. But whereas in 1965 the argument was for the recognition of African literature as diverse, the debate today is around whether the category of African literature has any meaning at all. Taiye Selasi, a contemporary African writer and the author of *Ghana Must Go*, delivered a keynote speech at the 2013 Berlin Book Fair titled, 'African Literature Doesn't Exist'.[32] Selasi was being deliberately provocative, stating, 'I'm sure I'll regret having given this talk once the scholars swoop in, but for now, I'm young and idealistic enough to relish the risk of defeat', and terming her own paper an act of 'blasphemy'.[33] Her main argument, that in the West, the category of African literature has come to mean one kind of writer and one kind of writing, has resonated with the younger generation of African writers. For her, ignoring Africa's diversity, where there are 'over two thousand languages spoken', or 'dismiss[ing] this linguistic complexity as a symptom of primitive clannishness, as if these two thousand languages were spoken by one hundred people apiece',[34] can only see a singular Africa. In addition, she argued, there is a tendency to see

African writers as 'sociologists in creative writers' clothing' which 'betrays a fundamental disrespect for those writers' artistry'.[35] She used Achebe's 1965 essay to make her point that the category of 'African literature' itself was the problem. For her the term is simply too opaque to allow for a diverse catalogue of literature and writers to shine through. But whereas for Achebe the point was to have the term 'African literature' carry the complexity that came with it, Selasi argued for the bankruptcy of the term itself; the category could not help but carry within it a simplified sociological/anthropological reading of African literature.

## THE AFRICAN POLITICAL NOVEL

When Taiye Selasi in her Berlin lecture called for the abolition of the term 'African Literature', she was eliding two central realities. First, the category of African Literature was a creation of Western critics that they then imposed on writers from Africa. Africans actively and consciously courted it as part and parcel of cultural and intellectual decolonization. Secondly, while African literature was not necessarily seen as a rejection of European literature, it was understood that while European literature was the center during colonialism, African literature would become the starting point for postcolonial African students embarking on literary journeys whether as writers or critics, all within a Pan-African literary identity that was decidedly political in nature; so political that Alan Hill could write:

> Our involvement in African writing introduced me to a new aspect of publishing—the author in prison. At one time or another our African authors have become political prisoners ... In fact at one time, our weekly in-house circular which lists forthcoming visits by authors carried a column headed 'Authors in Prison' which we updated each month.[36]

Thus, the novel, by being born of an imagination formed by colonialism and anti-colonial struggles, was simply political because it worked on Manichean ever-present contradictions. These African writers had a clear duty to expose those contradictions through their art. And this is what their publishers expected of them. James Currey, for example, in *Africa Writes Back,* explained, 'The South African books chosen for the African Writers Series reflected first and foremost the realities of life suffered by people oppressed by the laws of color.[37] The writers as a matter of principle were political. Wole Soyinka, in a 1967 essay titled *The Writer in the African State,* argued that African writers had undergone three stages: the first, during decolonization, required that the writers contribute to the nationalist cause toward independence, meaning that they had to 'postpone that unique reflection on experience and events which is what makes a writer and constitute himself into a part of that machinery that will actually shape events'.[38] In the second stage, the writers now became part of nation building and put 'energies to enshrining victory, to re-affirming his identification with the aspirations of nationalism and the stabilisation of society'.[39] And in the third stage the writers found themselves in a state of 'disillusionment' leading to Soyinka calling for 'an honest examination of what has been the failure of the African writer, as a writer'.[40] He concluded his essay by asking writers to reengage with the material reality of their societies:

> Where the writer in his own society can no longer function as conscience he must recognise that his choice lies between denying himself totally or withdrawing to the position of chronicler and post-mortem surgeon. But there can be no further distractions with universal concerns whose balm is spread on abstract wounds, not on the gaping jaws of black inhumanity. A concern with culture strengthens society, but not a concern with mythology.[41]

Soyinka was decrying Négritude and the concept of a return to a mythological past, 'the myth of irrational nobility' and 'racial essence', but it is clear that he recognized the existence of the African writer who, then, for better or worse had a duty to society. Indeed, while African writers in the 1960s debated what constitutes African literature, that they had a duty to society was never really in question.

Ngugi, a Makerere University alumnus, was still a student at the time of the 1962 conference. In 2013, 51 years later, he returned to give a keynote address in which he reminisced about the conference, the role it had played in African literature, and what Achebe (who had just died) and the other writers had come to mean:

> These writers would later give us what's the nearest thing to a genuine Pan African intellectual article: the book, African literature. When Achebe passed on recently he was mourned all over the continent. His novel, *Things Fall Apart*, the text most discussed at the conference alongside that of Dennis Brutus of South Africa, is read in all Africa. The work of others like Okot p'Bitek and Wole Soyinka, and that of the generations that have followed, Dangarembga, Ngozi Adichie and Doreen Baingana are equally well received as belonging to all Africa. Thus if Makerere was the site and symbol of an East African intellectual community, it also marked the birth of literary Pan-Africanism.[42]

Along the same lines, even though Simon Gikandi in his essay 'Chinua Achebe and the Invention of African Culture', first lamented 'the institutionalization of *Things Fall Apart* and the wisdom of using it as supplement for African culture or the authorized point of entry into Igbo, Nigerian, or African landscapes', he also recognized it for its Pan-African historical moment:

> It is not an exaggeration to say that my life was never to be the same again. For reading *Things Fall Apart* brought me to the sudden realization that fiction was not merely about a set of texts which one studied for the Cambridge Overseas exam which, for my generation, had been renamed the East African

Certificate of Education; on the contrary, literature was about real and familiar worlds, of culture and human experience, of politics and economics, now re-routed through a language and structure that seemed at odds with the history or geography books we were reading at the time.[43]

He added that, 'there is consensus that *Things Fall Apart* was important for the marking and making of that exciting first decade of decolonization'.[44] And with an emerging Pan-African literature, it was only a matter of time before the role of English literature (though not the English language) in African education was questioned.

In a 1968 essay titled 'On the Abolition of the English Department', three professors at the University of Nairobi (Ngugi Wa Thiong'o, Henry Owuor-Anyumba, and Taban Lo Liyong) argued that in the teaching of literature was a 'basic assumption that the English tradition and the emergence of the modern West is the central root of our consciousness and cultural heritage' in which 'Africa becomes an extension of the West'. 'Why can't African litera-ture be at the center so that we can view other cultures in relationship to it?' they asked. They called for the abolition of the English Department and in its place a Department of African Literature and Languages. They were clear that they were not 'rejecting other cultural streams, especially the Western stream'.[45] The ideal curriculum would constitute the oral tradition, Swahili literature (with Arabic and Asian literatures), a selected course in European literature, and modern African literature, and knowledge of Swahili, English, and French would be a must.[46] They concluded that:

> ... with Africa at the center of things, not existing as an appendix or a satellite of other countries and literatures, things must be seen from the African per-spective. The dominant object in that perspective is African literature, the major branch of African culture. Its roots go back to past African literatures, European literatures, and Asian literatures. These can be studied meaningfully in a Depart-ment of African Literature and Languages in an African University.[47]

Their goal was to change the curriculum from a British-based one to one that reflected world literature with African literature at the center. For Amoko Apollo Obonyo in *Postcolonialism in the Wake of the Nairobi Revo-lution: Ngugi Wa Thiong'o and the Idea of African Literature*, the docu-ment was contradictory. For him, 'To the extent that the movement sought to uncouple the study of literature in English from the nationalist history of England, it represented a radical contestation of the ideology of English lit-erature to date'. But he went on to argue, 'the movement embodied power-fully contradictory impulses, at once rejecting and reproducing the cultural nationalist fallacies of colonial discourse'.[48] But in my reading of the docu-ment, its authors were very careful to say their revolution was not reduction-ist and essentialist; European literature and languages were going to be part of the curriculum. The contradiction was that in calling for the Department of African Literature and Languages, they did not mean African literature written in African languages. Rather, they meant linguistics. That is, African languages should be taught within the Department. The only African language literature mentioned was Kiswahili.[49]

Early South African writing in African languages, in translation or written originally in English, was not mentioned at all. What it did call for was a study of orature to 'supplement (not replace) courses in Modern African Literature'. This document that was going to change literature departments throughout the postcolonial world also cemented the myth that before the Makerere writers there was only orature. And even though the call for orature meant there was a place for African languages, the caveat of supplementing showed that they would play a junior role. But still the document showed that the Makerere writers understood right from the beginning their written work as contributing to political and cultural decolonization. And when decolonization turned into a mess of neo-colonial authoritarian military and civilian regimes, they saw their work as contributing to egalitarian and democratic societies. And they saw themselves as African writers contributing to African literature.

Frantz Fanon in *The Wretched of the Earth* outlines several stages that the African intellectual would have to go through in order to become useful in the anti-colonial struggle. The first stage was complete identification with colonial culture.[50] The second stage found the intellectual trying 'to remember what he is'.[51] (222). In the second stage, the dissociation starts and the intellectual 'sets up high value on the customs, traditions, and the appearances of his people; but his inevitable painful experience only seems to be a banal search for exoticism. The sari becomes sacred, and shoes that come from Paris or Italy are left in favor of pampooties'.[52] In the last stage, 'which is called the fighting phase, the native after having tried to lose himself in the people and with the people, will on the contrary shake the people'.[53]

The novel, and novelists, in the fighting stage had to do the work of decolonization by contributing to national consciousness and by carrying dynamic African culture. No matter where one stood on the question of writer as a revolutionary versus writer offering a mirror to society, it was a given that literature as well as the writer had a duty to 'shake the people'. In his essay 'The Novelist as Teacher', Chinua Achebe argues that for him, his role as a writer is to 'help my society regain belief in itself and put away the complexes of the years of denigration and self-abasement'.[54] A little later, he argues that the 'writer cannot be excused from the task of re-education and regeneration that must be done', and then concludes that, 'I would be satisfied if my novels (especially the ones I have set in the past) did no more than teach my readers that their past—with all its imperfections—was not one long night of savagery from which the first Europeans acting on God's behalf delivered them'.[55] In other words, for Achebe, rolling back the myths used to justify colonialism was an integral part of the African writer's mission. The writer in short had a duty to speak out against the sort of internalized racism and belief in cultural inferiority that Africans had inherited from colonialism. In *Writing Against Neocolonialism*, Ngugi Wa Thiong'o argues that African writers had gone through 'the age of the anti-colonial struggle; the age of independence; and the age of neocolonialism'. The African writer:

> ... was born on the crest of this anti-colonial struggle and world-wide revolutionary ferment. The anti-imperialist energy and optimism of the masses found its way into the writing of the period ... It was Africa explaining itself, speaking for itself, and interpreting its past. It was Africa rejecting its past as drawn by the artists of imperialism. The writer even flaunted his right to use the language of the former colonial master anyway he liked. No apologies. No begging. The Caliban of the world had been given European languages and he was going to use them even to subvert the master.[56]

In this context, writers like Mofolo and his cannibals were not political writers. *Mhudi* and *Wrath of Ancestors* were not written with the ideologies of the third stage, the fighting stage. With their calls for synthesis, they would have been somewhere between the first and second stages, caught between identifying with African and European cultures. In short, for the Makerere writers, early South Africans would have seemed blind to the political contradictions sharpening around them.

## Conclusion

African writers and critics have suppressed early South African writing for a number of reasons. First, at a time of decolonization, early South African literature with its call for synthesis would have been seen as another way of collaborating with the colonizer. Second, the writers and their critics believed that they had a duty to contribute to decolonization. Third, publishers like Heinemann saw themselves as also contributing to decolonization but with English as the language of that decolonization. What ultimately united the publishers, writers, critics, and readers was the belief that the language of decolonization was English. We are dealing with a literature and literary criticism that has ignored time and space; time because of the ahistorical nature of the criticism, and space because the literary criticism has been confined to continental African writers of the decolonization era.

Part of my argument then is that the question about what constitutes African literature cannot be answered outside the question of how and why African writers and critics from former British colonies and their Western publishers created an African literary aesthetic that centered on the realist novel in English, and away from the example set by early South African writers. And why these same African writers and critics, after finding themselves in the peculiar position of producing national and Pan-African literatures and criticism in English, became the biggest defenders of English while condescending to African languages.

Literary scholars had a responsibility to take into account early African writing for no other reason than that it existed, instead of dismissing it as precursors to the modern African novel. But more than that, there were real questions to be asked. Can a failed synthesis in early South African writing lead to hybridity in the literature of decolonization? Under the guise of agreeing with the noble savage myth, yet writing for a people who know they were not, could Mofolo be subverting colonial racism as in mimicry with a wink to the audience? And what of the writing in Africa do these books reveal when analyzed within an African literary tradition that allows them to be in conversation with Makerere and Post-Makerere writers? But they did not ask these questions. That early writing in African languages or in English has no place in the African literary tradition points to the tragic state of an African literary criticism that begins the clock in the wrong literary era.

## NOTES

1. There are mentions of possible translations online, but as far as I can ascertain they have as yet to be published in any meaningful sense. In any case we should be talking about competing translations as opposed to whether a single translation might exist.
2. Obi Wali, "A Reply to Critics from Obi Wali," *Transition*, no. 50 (1975/1976): 46–47.
3. See D. Goluch, "Chinua Achebe Translating, *Things Fall Apart* in Polish and the Task of Postcolonial Translation," trans. Chinua Achebe, *Cross/Cultures*, no. 137 (2011): 197–219; and W. Kolb, "Re-Writing, *Things Fall Apart* in German," *Cross/Cultures*, no. 137 (2011): 177–96, 219.
4. Ngugi would later decolonize his name and drop the Christian name James to become Ngugi wa Thiong'o in 1977.
5. Mphahlele would later drop Ezekiel to become Es'kia Mphahlele to reflect his growing black consciousness in 1977, the same year as Ngugi's name change.
6. The Makerere Conference was not the first literary event to involve the African continent and diaspora. The First Congress of Black Writers and Artists was held in Paris in 1956, organized by *Presence Africaine*, a Paris-based literary journal, with a second in 1959, featuring writers such as Aimé Césaire, Léopold Sédar Senghor, Richard Wright, James Baldwin, George Lamming, Frantz Fanon, Édouard Glissant, Josephine Baker, and Jean-Paul Sartre (who had declared solidarity with Third World revolutionary causes).
7. James Ngugi, "A Kenyan at the Conference," *Transition*, no. 5 (1962): 7.
8. But as enthusiastic as he was, the young Ngugi also noted the apolitical nature of the conference. In the same write-up he observes that, "Although there were at times violent and deep differences of opinion on particular issues, for instance on the question of whether there was such a thing as African writing, yet the whole conference was almost quiet on such things as colonialism, imperialism and other isms. In this it differed from the 1956 and 1959

World Congresses of Negro writers where political discussions clouded the atmosphere" ("A Kenyan at the Conference," 7).

9. See Thomas Jeffrey, "A Hundred Years of Thomas Mofolo," *English in Africa* 37, no. 2 (2010): 37–55.

10. In a section subtitled, "A Long Tradition of Writing by Africans," Currey writes about publishing Lalage Brown's *Two Centuries of African English* that in passing also discusses the early South African literature.

11. James Currey, *Africa Writes Back: The African Writers Series and the Launch of African Literature* (Oxford: James Currey, 2008), 187.

12. Ibid., 189.

13. David Copland and Bennetta Jules-Rosette, "'Nkosi Sikelel' iAfrika': From Independent Spirit to Political Mobilization" *Cahiers d'Études Africaines* 44, nos. 1–2 (2004): 343–67.

14. Xolela Mangcu, "Retracing Nelson Mandela through the Lineage of Black Political Thought," in "The Django Issue," special issue, *Transition*, no. 112 (2013): 101–16.

15. Ntongela Masilela, *An Outline of the New African Movement in South Africa* (Trenton, NJ: Africa World, 2013).

16. Oyekan Owomoyela, 'The Literature of Empire: Africa'. *Empire Online* (Marlborough: Adam Matthew, 2004), 7.

17. Tim White, "The Lovedale Press during the Directorship of R. H. W. Shepherd, 1930–1955," *English in Africa* 19, no. 2 (October 1992): 69–84.

18. Ibid.

19. James Currey, *Africa Writes Back: The African Writers Series and the Launch of African Literature* (Oxford: James Currey, 2008), 1.

20. Ibid., 2.

21. Ibid., 6.

22. Sigei Julius, "We'll Stick to Creative Works, but Text Books Bring in Cash," *Nation*, August 22, 2015, http://www.nation.co.ke/lifestyle/weekend/Well-stick-to-creative-works-but-text-books-bring-in-cash/1220-2840110-format-xhtml-plhluez/index.html.

23. Bgoya, Walter, and Mary Jay. "Publishing in Africa from Independence to the Present Day." *Research in African Literatures* 44, no. 2 (Summer 2013): 17–34.

24. A question that for my generation of writers and scholars remains as central as it is divisive and that I discuss in greater length in chap. 6, "Toward a Rooted Transnational African Literature: Politics of Image and Naming."

25. Chinua Achebe, "English and the African Writer," *Transition*, nos. 75/76, The Anniversary Issue: Selections from Transition, 1961–1976 (1997), 342.

26. Ibid.

27. Chinua Achebe, "English and the African Writer," 343.

28. Ibid.

29. Ibid.

30. The poet John Pepper Clark, writing in 1965, had also called for African literature to be recognized as a body containing different identities and cultures. He argued that he places "high premium on difference of identity": "... because there is the need to do this so that we do not fall into the popular pastime of indiscriminately lumping together African peoples. The truth is that these differences do exist among the numerous peoples of Africa, forming for each that special cultural make-up and sensibility of which any artist anywhere must partake and be impregnated with before he can bring forth any work

of meaning to his people and mankind in general" (18). Clark, John Pepper. "Poetry in Africa Today." *Transition* No. 18, 1965.

31. There is the question of an established European literary canon and the "minor" writers who have been cast to the margins, but even then European literature is not immediately understood as a singular aesthetic, produced by the same kind of authors for a functional project such as nation building or to carry and showcase a singular European culture and history.

32. Taiye Selasi, *"Opening Speech", (GB /I): African Literature Doesn't Exist*, (September 4, 2013).

33. Ibid., 1.

34. Ibid., 6.

35. Ibid., 8.

36. Alan Hill, *In Pursuit of Publishing* (London: J. Murray in Association with Heinemann Educational, 1988), 127.

37. James Currey, *Africa Writes Back: The African Writers Series and the Launch of African Literature* (Oxford: James Currey, 2008), 189.

38. Wole Soyinka, "The Writer in the African State," *Transition*, no. 31 (1967): 11.

39. Ibid., 12.

40. Ibid.

41. Wole Soyinka, "The Writer in the African State," 13.

42. Ngugi Wa Thiong'o, "Makerere Dreams: Language and New Frontiers of Knowledge." University of East Africa 50th Anniversary Celebrations. Makerere University, Kampala. 29 June 2013. *Makerere University*. Web. 24 June 2014.

43. Simon Gikandi, "Chinua Achebe and the Invention of African Culture," *Research in African Literatures* 32, no. 3, Nationalism (Autumn, 2001): 4.

44. Ibid.

45. Ngugi Wa Thiong'o, "On the Abolition of the English Department," in *The Post-colonial Studies Reader*, ed. Bill Ashcroft, Gareth Griffiths, and Helen Tiffin (London: Routledge, 1995), 445.

46. Ibid., 440.

47. Ibid., 441.

48. See Amoko Apollo Obonyo's *Postcolonialism in the Wake of the Nairobi Revolution: Ngugi Wa Thiong'o and the Idea of African Literature*, 4–5.

49. Ngugi Wa Thiong'o, "On the Abolition of the English Department," in *The Post-colonial Studies Reader*, ed. Bill Ashcroft, Gareth Griffiths, and Helen Tiffin (London: Routledge, 1995), 440.

50. Frantz Fanon, *The Wretched of the Earth* (New York: Grove, 2004), 222.

51. Ibid.

52. Fanon Frantz, *The Wretched of the Earth*, 221.

53. Ibid.

54. ChinuaAchebe, "The Novelist as Teacher," in *African Literature: An Anthology of Criticism and Theory*, ed. Tejumola Olaniyan and Ato Quayson (Malden, MA: Blackwell Publishers, 2007), 105.

55. Ibid.

56. "Writing Against Neocolonialism," in *African Literature: An Anthology of Criticism and Theory*, ed. Tejumola Olaniyan and Ato Quayson (Malden, MA: Blackwell Publishers, 2007), 158.

## Bibliography

Achebe, Chinua. "An Image of Africa," in "Special Issue on Literary Criticism." Special issue, *Research in African Literatures* 9, no. 1 (1978): 1–15.

———. *Things Fall Apart*. New York: Anchor, 1994.

———. "English and the African Writer," in "The Anniversary Issue: Selections from *Transition*, 1961–1976." Special issue, *Transition*, nos. 75/76 (1997): 342–49.

———. "The Novelist as Teacher." In *African Literature: An Anthology of Criticism and Theory*, edited by Tejumola Olaniyan and Ato Quayson, 103–5. Malden, MA: Blackwell Publishing, 2007.

Appiah, Kwame Anthony. *In My Father's House: Africa in the Politics of Culture*. Methuen, 1991.

———. "Cosmopolitan Patriots." Front Lines/Border Posts, *Critical Inquiry* 23, no. 3, Front Lines/Border Posts (1997): 617–39.

Copland, David, and Bennetta Jules-Rosette. "'Nkosi Sikelel' iAfrika': From Independent Spirit to Political Mobilization ("'Nkosi Sikelel' iAfrika': De l'esprit indépendant à la mobilisation politique"). *Cahiers d'Études africaines* 44, nos. 1–2 (2004): 343–67.

Currey, James. *Africa Writes Back: The African Writers Series & the Launch of African Literature*. Oxford: James Currey, 2008.

Davis, Caroline. *Creating Postcolonial Literature: African Writers and British Publishers*. New York: Palgrave Macmillan, 2013.

Fanon, Frantz. *The Wretched of the Earth*. New York: Grove, 2004.

Gikandi, Simon. "Chinua Achebe and the Invention of African Culture," in "Nationalism." Special issue, *Research in African Literatures* 32, no. 3 (2001): 3–8.

Goluch, D. "Chinua Achebe Translating, *Things Fall Apart* in Polish and the Task of Postcolonial Translation." Translated by Chinua Achebe. *Cross/Cultures*, no. 137 (2011): 197–219.

Hill, Alan. *In Pursuit of Publishing*. London: John Murray in Association with Heinemann Educational, 1988.

Jordan, A.C. *The Wrath of the Ancestors: A Novel*. Cape Province: Lovedale, 1980.

Kolb, W. "Re-writing Things Fall Apart in German." *Cross/Cultures*, no. 137 (2011): 177–96, 219.

Mangcu, Xolela. "Retracing Nelson Mandela through the Lineage of Black Political Thought: From Walter Rubusana to Steve Biko," in "The Django Issue." Special issue, *Transition* no. 112 (2013): 101–16.

Modisane, Bloke. "African Writers' Summit." *Transition*, no. 5 (1962): 5–6.

Morapal, Koliswa. "Shehe! Don't Go There!: AC Jordan's Ingqumbo Yeminyanya (The Wrath of the Ancestors) in English." *Southern African Linguistics and Applied Language Studies* 26, no. 1 (2008): 69–85.

Mphahlele, Ezekiel. "African Literature and Universities: A Report on Two Conferences to Discuss African Literature and the University Curriculum." *Transition*, no. 10 (1963): 16–18.

Nagenda, John. "Conference Notebook." *Transition*, no. 5 (1962): 8–9.

Ngugi, J.T. "A Kenyan at the Conference." *Transition*, no. 5 (1962): 7.

Owomoyela, Oyekan. "The Literature of Empire: Africa." *Empire Online*. Marlborough: Adam Matthew, 2004. Web. Accessed March 16, 2016. http://www.empire.amdigital.co.uk/Essays/OyekanOwomoyela.

Plaatje, Sol T. *Mhudi*. Long Grove, IL: Waveland, 2015.

————. *Native Life in South Africa / Before and Since the European War and the Boer Rebellion*. Kindle Locations, 117–18.

Thiong'o, Ngũgĩ Wa. *Decolonising the Mind: The Politics of Language in African Literature*. London: James Currey, 1986.

Wali, Obiajunwa. "A Reply to Critics from Obi Wali." *Transition*, no. 50 (1976): 46–47.

————. The Dead End of African Literature. *Transition*, nos. 75/76 (1997): 330–35.

# CHAPTER 49

# Music and Postcolonial Africa

*Eric Charry*

A stunning newsreel showing Presidents Kwame Nkrumah, Sékou Touré, and Modibo Keita together in Conakry in December 1960 working on the Ghana-Guinea-Mali Union provides a vivid entry point into some of the issues covered in this chapter. It was a historic meeting, with what seems to be the whole nation mobilized for the occasion, including a motorcade passing by crowds lining the streets singing and dancing, processions of the military and the youth wing of the revolutionary party, speeches in a stadium, and a formal signing of documents. One scene in the silent newsreel shows the three leaders sitting together (along with Touré's wife Andrée) in a concert hall watching a drum and dance performance, probably a regional Guinean ballet. The recently nationalized Les Ballets Africains was abroad, on its second tour of North America performing in over a dozen cities, including a one-month run on Broadway in New York City. Touré was a pioneer in state patronage of the performing arts, and both Nkrumah and Keita would establish their own national dance company and ballet, respectively, within a few years.[1]

Within several months (in April 1961 in Accra), the three leaders agreed on a charter for a Union of African States, which was to form the nucleus of a United States of Africa. Article 4 of the charter laid out the fields of activity of the Union, with section 'E' devoted to culture: 'The rehabilitation and development of African culture, and frequent and diversified cultural exchange'.[2]

Their Union was short-lived, superseded by other larger factions (Casablanca, Brazzaville, and Monrovia Groups) and ultimately the Organization

E. Charry (✉)
Department of Music, Wesleyan University, Middletown, CT, USA

© The Author(s) 2018
M.S. Shanguhyia and T. Falola (eds.),
*The Palgrave Handbook of African Colonial and Postcolonial History*,
https://doi.org/10.1057/978-1-137-59426-6_49

1231

of African Unity (OAU) in 1963 with 32 member states.[3] State development of culture had more concrete results and promise, although with its ups and downs and uneven deployment throughout the continent. The notion that African culture needed to be rehabilitated, however, speaks to a gap between the political elite, many of whom were battling a pernicious legacy of European colonial education, and musicians working on the ground, many of whom either had not been indoctrinated into that system or took what they could from it and forged new forms of cultural expression. Understanding this gap, and how it was bridged, is crucial for contextualizing African music discourse and performance.

The generation of early ballet and theater troupe directors, including Mawere Opoku (b. 1915, Ghana), Fodeba Keita (b. 1921, Guinea), and Maurice Sonar Senghor (b. 1926, Senegal), each of whom had a colonial-style formal education, played a major role in bridging the divide, the first to choreograph African culture for the international stage. The generation born in the 1930s and early 1940s, who grew up under a colonial regime and matured in the first decade of postcolonial fervor, offered their own individual solutions in the 1960s and 1970s, independent of, and sometimes in opposition to, the state, including Miriam Makeba (b. 1932, South Africa), Manu Dibango (b. 1933, Cameroon), Fela Kuti (b. 1938, Nigeria), and Joseph Shabalala (b. 1941, South Africa). The generation born in the 15 years between the end of the Second World War and 1960 offered yet other solutions, thoroughly and comfortably reconciling some of the most deeply rooted traditions with the most modern global sonic currents, including Thomas Mapfumo (b. 1945, Zimbabwe) and Salif Keita (b. 1949, Mali) at the early end, and Youssou N'Dour (b. 1959, Senegal) and Angelique Kidjo (b. 1960, Benin) born right at the moment of political independence.[4]

## THREE LEGACIES

The musical legacies of Ghana, Guinea, and Mali show some of the varied results of postcolonial government intervention in the arts, drawing on them, especially music and dance, to help establish a national identity and cohesion. Touré, largely self-educated, invested heavily in state-supported regional and national music and dance groups.[5] Les Ballets Africains, founded by Guinean Fodeba Keita in Paris, toured the world as the premiere African drum and dance troupe before settling in Conakry after independence. A second Guinean national ballet (Ballet Djoliba) trained and supported Mamady Keita, now Africa's most globally known drummer and a primary force for helping to establish the *jembe* as the most visible African drum on the planet. Guinea's 1970s orchestras, in particular the nationalized Bembeya Jazz, are legendary for their electric guitar-based transformations of local traditions. Touré also established a national record label, Syliphone.

Nkrumah invested in the arts through the educational system, establishing the Institute of African Studies (IAS), which housed the new National Dance Company (later called the Ghana Dance Ensemble) and new School of Music and Drama, all in 1962 at the University of Ghana. As a result, music within the borders of Ghana is probably the most well researched and documented in print in all of Africa, due in large part to the academic leadership of musicologist J.H. Kwabena Nketia, who directed the School, co-directed the Dance Company, and would soon head the IAS. Drummers associated with the university-based company migrated early on to North American universities, establishing the canonical status of their traditions there beginning in the 1960s and continuing unabated to the present day. That early cohort of Ghanaian drummers is now seeing retirements after more than forty years of teaching at universities such as UCLA, UC Berkeley, CalArts, and Wesleyan.[6]

Landlocked Mali, with its northern border deep in the Sahara, had less European traffic to contend with and has a reputation for retaining its venerable musical traditions outside of government support, stemming from lavish noble patronage during the days of the gold-rich ancient Mali empire. That history proved fortuitous at the Pan-African cultural festival in Algiers in 1969 when the national instrumental ensemble won a gold medal, and when a commercial world music market opened up in the 1980s seeking its own brand of authenticity. In the largest music industry in the world (the USA), Malian artists have captured more Grammy Award nominations in the World Music category than any other country (23 in all since 1992), competing in a field with major contenders such as Brazil and India having ten, or even seventy times its population. The 21-stringed kora, played by Malian Toumani Diabate and others, is rivaling the Indian sitar as the most globally known non-Western string instrument. The government also sent a group of students to study at the conservatory in Havana in the mid-1960s. One of them, Boncana Maiga, would direct a national orchestra after he returned to Mali and in the 1990s found Africando, an extraordinary New York-based salsa band that featured guest African vocalists.

## COLONIAL EDUCATION

The growing body of literature on colonial education, especially its relationship to the arts, is a rich resource for music studies. Nkrumah, who attended Gold Coast's prestigious Achimota College, posed one kind of impact as follows:

> We were denied the knowledge of our African past ... We were taught to regard our culture and traditions as barbarous and primitive. Our text-books were English text-books, telling us about English history, English geography, English ways of living, English customs, English ideas, English weather.[7]

Newly elected President of the Republic of Tanganyika Julius Nyerere, who attended the select Tabora School, articulated some of the despair of Africa's elite in his inaugural address in 1962. Announcing the formation of the Ministry of National Culture and Youth, he took note of the worst crime of colonialism, which was:

> the attempt to make us believe we had no indigenous culture of our own; or that what we did have was worthless—something of which we should be ashamed ... Some of us, particularly those of us who acquired a European-type of education ... abandoned everything connected with our own past and learnt to imitate only European ways.[8]

On the other hand, Achimota, as well as its Francophone colonial equivalent, École William Ponty in Senegal, made room for students to connect with their cultures of origin, no matter the motivations, whether benign or to better control them. Achimota had a mission to produce a type of student who was: '"Western" in his intellectual attitudes towards life, with a respect for science and capacity for systematic thought, but who remains African in sympathy and desirous of preserving and developing what is deserving of respect in tribal life, custom, rule and law'.[9] Ghana Dance Ensemble artistic director Opoku recalled African nights at Achimota with 'tribal' drumming and dancing of four principal groups (Twi, Fante, Ewe, and Ga), which took place on two Saturdays each month.[10]

École Ponty required students to write up summer research projects on some aspect of their culture, which Conteh-Morgan suggests, was intended in part, to 'give them an intellectual rootedness into their traditional cultures at a time when they ran the risk of total alienation from them as a result of their new French education'.[11] Their theater program supported plays on African topics, which would have a decisive impact. Within a few years of leaving Ponty, Fodeba Keita, who attended from 1940 to 1943, would begin publishing his poems and dramatic presentations, which would form the nucleus of his Ballets Africains programs that would gain such world renown the following decade.[12]

## EUROPEAN TIME FRAMES, ETHNICITY

A singular focus on the European impact only tells partial stories about how music lives in Africa. The impact of Islam and the Arab culture that is carried with it, for example, has also been critical.[13] The historical markers 'precolonial', 'colonial', and 'postcolonial' can sometimes be counter-productive in musical contexts. Colonization as the overriding standard and narrative (before, during, after) for understanding how Africans create and respond to music can miss the mark in many cases. Specifically, it does a disservice to the historical depth and power of some traditions and it removes agency from artists; labeling these traditions 'pre-' anything denies their status as classic (and even classical) art forms and grafts them onto a European political time frame.

Furthermore, the unit of the single ethnic group (or people) and nation, while remaining viable and valuable, can occasionally obscure African creative life. As Chikowero recently noted, using the example of the 'composite identity' of vocalist Dorothy Masuku [Masuka]:

> to Zambians, Masuku is a Lozi; to South Africans, she is Zulu; and in Lesotho and Zimbabwe, she can answer to both Sotho and Ndebele, and compose Shona songs ... Her multilingual repertoire, transterritorial belonging, lived experiences, and standing as a heroine of regional liberation all underscore the need to rewrite the stories of African self-making and cultural consciousness beyond the alienating colonial boundaries, taxonomies of 'tribes,' bounded nation-states, and codified official languages.[14]

Nevertheless, state boundaries are very real, and ethnic boundaries can at times be just as real, with some foundations before colonial era reification, and can serve as helpful guides for how to hear (and not to hear) African sonic expression. I am just suggesting that the terms pre- and postcolonial, and the historiographic framework imposed by them be handled with care. It would be a cliché to warn about the historical reality of ethnicity, but also irresponsible to ignore its contemporary significance. Many excellent studies in the past two decades have done the exhaustive research necessary to carry out the requisite balancing act between the historical past and ethnographic present with regard to music and ethnic identity.[15]

## MUSICAL INSTRUMENTS AND THEIR STORIES

The vast majority of scholarship on African music is organized and bound within national contexts, but there are other important perspectives. The extraordinary number and diversity of music cultures, mirrored in a similar diversity of spoken languages, defines the African landscape, oftentimes spilling over national borders.[16] Uniquely marked musical instruments alone probably number in the thousands. No single musical system (or even tuning system) sets the standard as it does in Europe or large parts of South or East Asia, for example, although strong cases can be made for broad aesthetic affinities. The European system of tonal harmony has had a broad impact in colonial and postcolonial times, but it has by no means wiped out systems and traditions that predated contact, and it has opened up new avenues of musical expression.

Instrument tunings may be likened to language dialects ('tongues'), and so different tuning systems (or dialects) may coexist, and typically be embraced in a single ensemble. Similarly, many languages may be embraced within a national culture: Mali's Counsel of Ministers recently reaffirmed the promotion of its 13 national languages, for instance, 'as part of the protection and development of linguistic heritage and cultural diversity'.[17]

This diversity, as well as the embrace of difference, has been one of the main driving engines of nation building in postcolonial Africa. Faced with disparate musical traditions housed within arbitrary national borders, postcolonial national music and dance ensembles forged new multiethnic mixes for presentation on the domestic and world stage. Music here acts as both a unifying force and a differentiating one at the same time. Two key approaches can be discerned. Les Ballets Africains arranged the music and dance of diverse peoples for a set of predominantly Mande musical instruments, including jembe, *dundun* (double-headed cylinder-shaped drum), *bala* (xylophone), and *kora* (harp). The Ghana Dance Ensemble used different sets of instruments to represent the diverse dances and ethnicities within its borders (e.g. Akan, Dagbamba, Ewe, Ga).[18]

The esoteric work of studying musical instrument morphology, tuning systems, and playing styles can lead to insights that are among the most powerful in shredding outdated notions of jigsaw puzzle-like, bounded, immobile ethnic groups populating a pre-colonial African landscape. Such work includes mapping out the wide distribution of lamellophones (known locally as *mbira*, *kalimba*, *likembe*, among others), xylophones, fiddles, lutes, and harps. These studies, which have their roots in colonial-era research, all point to generations-old, rich, expansive, supraregional cultures which persist to the present day, transcending ethnicity and nation-state.[19]

Yet, they also point out unique identifiers that mark instruments as belonging to one or other group of people. These identifiers can be as subtle as several millimeters on the neck design on wooden pegs that fasten the skin head to a drum. As Anku has shown in Ghana, Akan and Anlo Ewe drum pegs differ primarily by an asymmetrical neck that protrudes on one side of the peg.[20] One of the oldest surviving Akan drums, an apentemma collected in the American colony of Virginia in the early eighteenth century, suggests that its peg construction has not changed in centuries.[21] Musical instrument morphologies contain hidden stories, known well by practitioners and overlooked by outsiders, that can point to deep histories without uttering a single word.

The frame xylophone band that stretches across the West African savanna is another fascinating case, demonstrating both the futility of ethnic categorization and also local recognition of difference. Atta Annan Mensah provided a detailed comparative analysis of the three principal xylophone traditions in northern Ghana, using the ethnonyms Dagaba, Lobi, and Sisala.[22] Since Mensah first began publishing about these traditions, well over a dozen others have followed.[23] Most recently, master xylophone (gyil) player Bernard Woma tried to come to terms with the diversity of ethnonyms within this compact region, providing an insider's perspective.[24] This is no mean feat.

Outsiders naming ethnic groupings where they previously did not exist only tells part of the story. 'Ethnic distinctions and commonalities' in this region, anthropologist Lentz notes, were 'created and continually re-defined' also by 'chiefs, migrant workers, catechists, peasants, and educated elites'.[25] I would add musicians and dancers to this list. The power of ethnicity, she continues, rests on an 'inherent contradiction':

> ethnic identifications claim to be primordial, dictated by birth, and are thus non-negotiable, creating permanent bonds, stability and security … At the same time the boundaries of the communities created and the specific traits and practices associated with them are malleable and can be adapted to serve specific interests and contexts.[26]

In short, ethnicity is not simply a product of colonization, but rather is rooted in a deeper past and remains a contested living concept. What a rich field music makes for understanding how such boundaries can be understood; communities of people in close contact with each other have defined, and continue to define themselves, through music (especially through funeral rituals in this case). And what goes for northern Ghana goes for much of rural Africa.

Urban Africa provides other kinds of cases of the contemporary life of ethnicity. When rural migrants flood African cities, they reconfigure not only their own cultures, but also the soundscapes of those cities. Polak has studied how urban professional jembe drummers in Bamako shape their repertories so they can successfully play for marriage celebrations for migrant communities coming from various regions of Mali. They refer to some pieces in their repertory simply by the name of the ethnic group: Fulafoli (Fula music) and Maraka don (Maraka/Soninke dance/rhythm). Given the pervasive soundscape blanketing the city on Sundays when those celebrations are held, urban jembe drumming could be considered a popular music, rendering the description 'traditional' inadequate.[27]

But this particular drum, like many other African instruments, lives in multiple worlds: in village life-cycle ceremonies, in urban manifestations of the same, as part of an electrified band that travels the world (e.g. in Salif Keita's regular line-up), in world tours of concert-hall ballet performances, and in master classes around the world and cultural study tours at home. The same might be said of the *sabar* drums that are so important in defining the Senegalese identity of Youssou N'dour's band, or the Yoruba dundun in the bands of Nigerians King Sunny Ade and Lagbaja, or the Shona mbira in Zimbabwean Thomas Mapfumo's band.

Those cultural study tours to Africa (the most prevalent being jembe camps in Mali, Guinea, and Senegal, and semester or other study-abroad programs in Ghana) may be stimulating interest at home.[28] This is to say that, rather than fading into irrelevance as Africa urbanizes and modernizes, some of its long-held traditions continue to revitalize as their practitioners transform their contexts.

## NATIONALIZATION

What happens when colonial boundaries are layered on top of these regional traditions? Colonial and subsequently national identities then become a polyglot project. Musical instruments and dance movements can stand in as metonyms for ethnicity and be used as tools for nation building. The efforts of state leaders to put music and dance into such service has received significant scholarly attention over the past few decades, and here I sample two of the more well-documented ones.[29]

Sékou Touré established the model for regional and national performing groups. Les Ballets Africains, formed by Guinean Fodeba Keita in the late 1940s while he was a student in Paris, went on world tours over the course of the 1950s.[30] When Guinea gained independence, the Ballet moved to Conakry, and was nationalized. Their first two tours of North America in 1959 and 1960 were major events, covered by the *New York Times*, *Time*, and *The Nation*.[31]

Touré established three kinds of state-supported performing groups within a sophisticated regional and national political network: ballets (drum and dance troupes); ensembles (traditional instruments playing local repertories); and orchestras (brass and electric guitar-based groups playing modern international dance music).[32] Guinea's national ballets put the nation and its drummers on the global map. Lead jembe drummer Ladji Camara moved to New York in the mid-1960s and became an initial catalyst for the later worldwide popularity of the jembe. Mamady Keita, lead drummer of Guinea's second national ballet, Ballet Djoliba, took the jembe to an unprecedented level of visibility. At the age of 12 (in the early 1960s) he was recruited into Touré's performing arts system, soon joining the national Ballet Djoliba where he remained for 22 years, eventually becoming the artistic director.

After Sékou Touré died in 1984, state patronage dried up. Keita moved to Abidjan and then Belgium, where he established a school for jembe drumming, began releasing CDs of his music, and gained a significant following of students. In 1991, a documentary about his life, *Djembefola*, proved to be an important stepping stone to becoming the most well-known African drummer in the world after Nigerian Babatunde Olatunji, who had gained a Columbia Records contract in the early 1960s.[33]

Touré's legacy, one part of which is the revolutionary hero of the decolonization era and a generous patron of the arts, is a painful one, given his ruthless turn not long after he ascended to the presidency. Les Ballets Africains founder Fodeba Keita and member Marof Achkar, who both took up major posts in Touré's government, were eventually imprisoned and executed.[34] In *Djembefola*, Mamady Keita seemed ambivalent about Touré's system of state patronage. The performing arts had become a revolutionary duty for those capable enough:

[Mamady Keita:] Around 1964–65 Sekou Toure built a stage in the president's palace for our rehearsals … [He] was our father; he considered us as his

children. We were like robots, like people drugged by the revolutionary mentality. We each considered ourselves to be true and honest revolutionaries. We
could not imagine quitting the Ballet to go somewhere else, because to flee the
Ballet would have been to betray the nation and the Revolution ... The training was hard, very very hard ... Balanka Sidiki [the director] was terrible. He
gave 50 lashes for the slightest reason. We formed a delegation to tell the governor that he was too tough. The delegation was immediately arrested and hand-
cuffed, and the rest of the troupe—both girls and boys—was thrown in jail!

[Balanka Sidiki:] Real performers aren't lazy. They were well trained ... But our
duty, was to develop the national spirit. Like the army. Yes, like the army.

[Mamady Keita:] It was terribly hard training. But if the revolution hadn't taken
me from the village, I would still be scratching the earth with my brothers.[35]

This dedication and rigorous training of Guinean state-sponsored ballet drummers and dancers seem remarkably similar to their counterparts in
Ghana, minus the revolutionary rhetoric: 'We are like soldiers. When they call
us into battle, we must go'.[36] Nkrumah invested in the arts too, but unlike
Touré, he was highly educated with two Bachelor's degrees (Lincoln University) and two Master's degrees (University of Pennsylvania). Nkrumah's
establishment of the Institute of African Studies at the University of Ghana
was key. As Chancellor of the University, Nkrumah appointed Kwabena
Nketia as Deputy Director. Nketia had a degree in music from Trinity College (London), had been a research fellow at the university since 1952 with
a significant body of publications on music in Ghana, and had travelled the
USA on a Rockefeller grant studying ethnomusicology and composition with
Henry Cowell at Columbia, Charles Seeger and Mantle Hood at UCLA, and
Melville Herskovits and Alan Merriam at Northwestern.[37]

## CHOREOGRAPHING NATIONAL UNITY

As director of the new National Dance Company, Nketia enlisted Mawere
Opoku as artistic director. Opoku had Asante chiefs on both sides of his family, had attended Achimota College (1931–1934), and had received a Rockefeller fellowship to study in the USA, working with Martha Graham and at
Julliard.[38] Opoku's approach was to aestheticize ethnicity, identifying and
working with ethnically marked body movements.

Ashanti ... often has the body tilting, swaying to a different time count, while
the arms and legs may be moving in counter rhythms ... the steps of the women
suggest gliding. The Anglo [Ewe] dances show the main action in the upper
torso in a series of contractions and releases, with a downward thrust of the
arms ...The Gas favor stamping and skipping with body sways and rotations
from side to side along with bent elbows. They love the staccato type of jump
and the occasional thrust of the fist into the air. The Fantis tend to run for short
spells, stagger, pause, and leap, or turn somersaults, or sway on the spot with
sliding and clapping arm movements.[39]

Opoku did not mix dance traditions, but rather presented them as sequences of ethnically distinct pieces in a program. One effect was to freeze in time, for what would turn out to be a canon, the products of culturally fluid practices.[40] Each member of the company performing all the dances in the repertoire, regardless of ethnic or regional origin, embodied the political ideal of unity in diversity.[41]

The process of choreographing outdoor dance events for the stage necessarily involved compromises, or, looking at it another way, innovations. Fodeba Keita understood this early on:

> On the stage new conditions have to be created by means of different devices in order, on the one hand, to retain the freshness and reality of the dance and, on the other, to destroy the monotony which is quick to arise due to the non-active participation of the audience.[42]

The official inauguration of the Ghana Dance Ensemble (GDE) included the following statement:

> Truly, if our traditional arts are to survive and be meaningful in present day Ghana ... they must be kept alive not just by mere repetition of the same age-old traditions or by a museum approach to the art, but by artistic imagination which clarifies their aesthetic values and renews their vitality.[43]

Francis Nii-Yartey, GDE's artistic director from 1976, called these forms *new traditional*.[44]

Ambassador Marof Achkar's spoken introduction for a United Nations General Assembly Hall performance claimed authenticity, using the term 'faithful' for these new traditions as national culture.

> Les Ballets Africains of the Republic of Guinea and the National Ensemble of Guinea, are one of the most faithful and perhaps the most eloquent expressions of Guinean culture, certainly, but also of African culture.[45]

Guinean historian Lansiné Kaba further clarifies the nature of Keita's authenticity with regard to his work in the 1950s:

> Fodéba Keita appeared to be a classic example of a 'popular' artist, this word suggesting a patient search for the best interpretation of the folklore and soul of the people, in a repertoire consistent both with old norms and modern play techniques and language. The songs and dances of the Ballets attempted to convey an authentic expression of the traditional musical heritage, as well as of the changing image of modern Africa.[46]

Nii-Yartey introduced changes and mixed ethnic styles together in the GDE, but that format would be called 'contemporary African dance' or 'creative dance'.[47] This seems similar to procedures in the early days of Senegal's national ballet.

> The day would start with a class taught by Sonar Senghor. Then every dancer, from Dakar or from elsewhere, would take turns to teach the others some of the steps they knew from home. Sonar Senghor would then select and re-arrange the moves into a choreographic sequence. Later in the day, we'd rehearse for the shows.[48]

President Nyerere may too have had a similar vision for his Tanganyikan Ministry of Culture: 'I want it to seek the best of the traditions and customs of all our tribes and make them part of our national culture'.[49] The government newspaper even suggested that ethnic origins should be attenuated in favor of a singular national culture:

> no ngoma should belong to one tribe. What are called tribal dances now should be transformed into national ngomas. They must be made to belong to the people as a whole. With a national language—Kiswahili—at the nation's disposal, this should not be difficult to do. The singing can be done in Kiswahili while the dancing can remain in original tribal style.[50]

Deciding which traditions should stay and which should be rejected can be a dangerous business, pointing to a clash between Pan-Africanist and socialist thought. Nkrumah posed it as follows: 'Within a society poising itself for the leap from pre-industrial retardation to modern development, there are traditional forces that can impede progress. Some of these must be firmly cut at their roots, others can be retained and adapted to the changing need'.[51] Nyerere echoed this in his 1967 Arusha Declaration: 'Only cultural practices considered progressive in an overtly socialist sense would be retained'.[52] Touré went so far as to carry out an eradication campaign aimed at some of the polytheistic religious and cultural practices of non-Muslim minority ethnic groups.[53] Ugandan Prime Minister and then President Obote sacked the King of Buganda's palace (and its musical instruments) in 1966 and abolished kingdoms the following year, including Buganda and Bunyoro. Centuries-old royal court music was silent until the kingdoms were restored, beginning in 1993.[54]

## PAN-AFRICAN ARTS FESTIVALS

Three Pan-African arts and culture festivals, which took place within a decade-and-a-half of the founding of the OAU in 1963 provide another focal point for understanding the role of music in postcolonial Africa. National ensembles figured prominently, as did extended conferences to hash out competing philosophies.[55]

Pan-Africanism can refer to a political movement and also a more general attitude toward cultural unity. In the latter sense, it is intertwined with the ideas of an African Personality, initially postulated by Edward Wilmot Blyden and later picked up by Nkrumah, and Négritude, which Léopold Senghor himself, one of its primary exponents, has noted 'is nothing more or less than what some English-speaking Africans have called the *African personality*'.[56] As a movement, Pan-Africanism can be dated to the First Pan-African Conference (London, 1900) and the subsequent series of five Pan-African Congresses held between 1919 and 1945.[57]

The founding of the journal *Présence Africaine* in 1947 in Paris by Senegalese Alioune Diop (with Senghor and Aimé Césaire among the patrons), their sponsoring of the First International Congress of Negro Writers and Artists in Paris (1956), at which Diop founded the Société Africaine de Culture (SAC), which sponsored a Second Congress in Rome (1959), ultimately led to the first festival in Dakar. The Commission on the Arts at that Second Congress issued a resolution:

> to institute as an essential part of its activities, a celebratory festival during the meeting of the next Congress ... The festival should include song, drums, and dance, and perhaps also readings of dramatic pieces and poetry.[58]

The First World Festival of Negro Arts (*Festival Mondiale des Arts Nègres*, FESMAN) was held in Dakar, Senegal in 1966 under the sponsorship of the SAC and Senegalese President Senghor.[59] Twenty African countries sent their national ensembles. Reiser has suggested that these national ensemble performances might be described as 'authentically modern' in that 'presenting a collective performance of multiple ethnicities on the same stage at such a pan-African arts festival was a distinctly modern phenomenon ... represent[ing] the current postcolonial environment'.[60] Senghor's vision of Négritude did not include North Africans, at least as full participants in the weeklong colloquium. Guinea boycotted the festival.

Three years later, Algeria hosted the First Pan-African Cultural Festival in its capital Algiers. The term 'Pan-African', rather than Negro or Black, highlighted the break with Senghor's Négritude, which was widely denounced at the daily Symposium on African Culture.[61] One speaker from Sudan rejected the negativism of racial philosophies which only 'serve the interests of the colonialists who have worked for two centuries to characterize people of different continents according to racial criteria'.[62] Stanislas Adotevi, Commissioner General for Culture and Youth from Dahomey (renamed Benin in 1975) delivered an especially well-received and harsh paper. Noting that 'Negritude today fixes and coagulates ... the most well-worn theories about African traditions', Adotevi, reflecting the time and place of the festival, proclaimed, 'There is no further place in Africa for literature other than that of the revolutionary combat. Negritude is dead'.[63]

Revolutionary politics ruled the day, with the host President Boumediène stressing 'the struggle against imperialism, rather than simply racial solidarity, to be what unified the continent', as Reiser suggests.[64] Medals were awarded for the best performances and Guinea, one of Africa's most potent symbols for revolution and for state support of the performing arts, won a gold medal for its national ballet, and four silver medals for drama, traditional instrumental music, modern instrumental music, and choral and solo singing. Mali received a gold medal for its National Instrumental Ensemble.[65]

In 1977, Nigeria hosted the Second World Black and African Festival of Arts and Culture (FESTAC) in Lagos. Nigeria was oil-rich at the time and spent lavishly. New venues were built and the official cost was estimated at $213 million–$225 million; other estimates had the cost much higher. With 15,000 participants from 70 countries, 100,000 people attending the opening ceremonies, and a new FESTAC Village built to accommodate 45,000 international visitors, it turned out to be Africa's biggest cultural event in the twentieth century.[66]

Lagos 1977 differed in part from Dakar 1966 in that an important theme was contemporary African life. In his opening address, Nigerian Head of State General Obasanjo (under whose watch Fela Kuti's Kalakuta Republic compound was burned to the ground just after FESTAC ended) noted:

> The occasion will surely lead to the abandonment of the 'museum approach' to our culture by which men of other cultures consider our culture only in terms of pre-historic objects to be occasionally dusted, displayed and studied instead as a living thing containing and portraying the ethos of our peoples.[67]

A Third World Black Arts Festival (FESMAN 3) took place in Dakar in 2010, with national ensembles playing a much smaller role, yielding to urban culture/hip hop (organized by Didier Awadi) and world music artists, including Salif Keita, Toumani Diabate, Habib Koite, Ladysmith Black Mambazo, Hugh Masekela, Seun Kuti, King Sunny Ade, Angelique Kidjo, Youssou N'Dour, and Manu Dibango.[68]

## COLONIAL IMPORTS: BRASS BANDS, CHRISTIAN AND ART MUSIC

Brass bands, including trumpets, trombones, and percussion, as well as drum and fife bands, were an important aspect of the British and German colonial and missionary presence in West and East Africa. Missionaries in the 1880s saw marching-band music as a tool for instilling discipline. They felt that the rhythms of hymns and band music could introduce African children to a European worldview, including industrial time that was measured by the clock. For the missionaries, European music represented a world of order in contrast to what they perceived to be frenzied drumming and dancing that they encountered. The military style of dress and marching were also an important symbol for projecting colonial authority.[69] By the early twentieth century, Africans were fully participating in brass and drum and fife bands, either via military, missionary, or school activities. These bands would not only continue, playing their own local styles of Christian hymns and military music, but would lay an important foundation for dance orchestras that emerged after the First World War, including Ghanaian highlife.[70]

One impact of missionary activity was the planting of the European system of tonality, with its 12-tone, equal-tempered tuning system and goal-directed chord structures, not to mention style of singing, onto African soil. These roots branched out in several directions. Through mission schools and church attendance an appreciation for European art music was instilled in some, giving birth to a small number of composers who wrote in European styles, but drew on African melodies, rhythms, and other techniques. African composers in this style typically came from Anglophone countries, especially those that offered post-secondary-school training in Western music: Ghana, Nigeria, and Uganda. Despite the hostile conditions for European wood and string instruments built for more temperate climates, several tropical African cities have symphony orchestras, including Accra, Kinshasa, and Luanda. At the more temperate northern and southern ends there are orchestras in Cairo, Morocco, and at least six in South Africa.[71]

A much larger part of the population took to heart Christian hymn singing and began to reshape Christian religious music in their own styles. Gospel music, with its world of solo singing stars, positive uplifting messages, and music that draws on local popular styles is probably Anglophone Africa's fastest growing musical genre, and it can be a lucrative profession. In Ghana and Kenya, gospel music has the largest share of the commercial market.[72] The fact that it can draw on a variety of local styles has only broadened its appeal.

## ARCHIVES

One result of government patronage of music is the production of a rich body of recordings preserving and stimulating the cultural heritage. Some of this material, initially made for radio or television broadcast or release on vinyl LPs, has been released on CDs or in more piecemeal fashion online. Some recent efforts have resulted in the extraordinary digitizing of archives, making them widely available.

Guinea's state-funded Syliphone label released 82 long-play albums and 75 singles from about 1967 to 1984, and Radio Télévision Guinée (RTG) made many recordings that were never released commercially. The whole Syliphone catalog as well as RTG's archives (over 1000 reels of tape) have been digitized with support from the British Library's Endangered Archives Program. Over 7700 of these recordings are available for streaming online on the British Library's website.[73]

British Library Sounds has made available online over a dozen more collections from Africa. They are not alone. The French Center for Research in Ethnomusicology (CREM), an outgrowth of the Ethnomusicology Department of the Musée de l'homme (1929–2008), has tens of thousands of recordings in their digitized collection available for online streaming, including commercial and field recordings. Furthermore, they have made available a variety of modes for viewing waveforms, spectrograms, and pitch while the recording is playing. They are also experimenting with various modes of multimedia analysis of the recordings.

The Ghana Broadcasting Corporation has digitized its collection of commercial and field recordings, although they are not yet available online. Cameroon Radio Television (CrTV) has done the same with its collection (over 10,000 items). The Digital Namibian Archive is making available recordings, photographs, and films from Namibia's national archives. Similar efforts are underway in South Africa and surely other places in Africa. Repatriation of recordings (that is, bringing them back to the communities in which they were recorded) has recently received significant scholarly attention.[74]

## Intellectual Property and the Internet

Virtually any musical tradition can be found on the Internet nowadays. Beyond simple access, two case studies demonstrate some powerful new developments. A YouTube clip of Tofo Tofo, a relatively unknown Mozambican dance trio, was seen by US pop superstar Beyoncé, who wanted to use their choreography for her video 'Run the World (Girls)'. Her autobiographical documentary *Beyoncé: Year of 4* shows scenes of Beyoncé and her dance crew unsuccessfully trying to replicate their moves. 'What country was it?', someone asks. No-one on camera could recall. The group was eventually found and flown to Los Angeles to teach their choreography, and they made a cameo appearance in the video. When they first meet in the dance studio, one of the members of Tofo Tofo asks, 'What's your name?' 'I'm Beyoncé', she responds, as they realize that this is the person who summoned them there, taking her celebrity in stride.

Here is a case of African dance moves (more specifically, a South African township style called *pantsula*), interpreted by neighboring Mozambicans, making their way into one of the more visible pop culture products on the planet, recontextualized and rendered generically diasporic.[75]

When Colombian pop superstar Shakira released 'Waka Waka (This Time for Africa)', which became the official 2010 FIFA World Cup song, some noted a similarity to 'Zangalewa', a 1986 song by the Cameroonian group Golden Sounds. The chorus is the same in both. Negative online publicity, including the easy online availability of the original version, forced FIFA to make the following acknowledgement: 'The chorus is similar to that of a popular Cameroon song made famous by Golden Voices [sic] in particular'. Her record label Sony negotiated an out-of-court settlement with the group.

Not only did the Internet facilitate the clear connection between the two songs, and provide a forum for protests, but it also provided a forum for identifying a probable path to Shakira, a Dominican merengue version ('El negro no puede' by Las Chicas del Can, released in 1988). A press conference (online as of 2016) in which she discussed the inspiration behind the song with no mention of any prior sources did not help her reputation.[76]

## INDEPENDENT ARTISTS

The most audible stream of music in postcolonial Africa, at least since the 1970s, comes from independent artists, outside of government intervention. Their sources of inspiration are global, although one can pinpoint the Caribbean (Cuba, Jamaica, Trinidad), the USA, and the former metropoles (France, Britain, Spain, and Portugal). The sheer size of Africa suggests that each country has its own story to tell. Two important keys to the stories are Cuba and the guitar.

Urban Senegalese and Congolese musicians embraced Cuban music in the 1950s and 1960s, as did those in many Francophone regions of Africa, and came up with their own unique transformations, based on their own local cultures. Some of those cultures, such as sabar and *tama* drumming and Islamic-tinged Wolof singing in the case of Senegal, which stretch back to pre-colonial times, continue to maintain relevance, both in their own musical worlds and as part of modern Senegalese bands. There are few such visible references in the *soukous*/Congolese rumba bands of Kinshasa. Perhaps this is because of the size and polyglot colonial legacy of Kinshasa, the largest Francophone city in the world (including Paris), and third largest city in Africa. Rather, it is in the guitar playing exemplified by Franco Luambo (1960s–1980s) and Diblo Dibala (who teamed up with Kanda Bongo Man in the 1980s), in which deeply rooted aesthetic sensibilities get repurposed to provide a soundtrack for the continent.[77]

The guitar took on this role throughout Africa. In Guinea, *bala* (xylophone) styles were grafted onto the guitar by Mande jelis. In Mali it was *ngoni* (lute) and kora (harp) styles. In Senegal, sabar drumming rhythms made their way to the guitar. In Kenya, it was the *nyatiti* (lyre) that informed *benga* guitar playing. In Zimbabwe, guitarists learned to play mbira music on their instruments.[78] The list can go on to include almost every African nation.

Senegalese assimilation of Cuban music allowed a group like Orchestre Baobab to present a kind of national identity that was an alternative to that of national ensembles. Baobab's three vocalists were each rooted in three major Senegalese cultures: the southern Casamance region; the predominant Wolof; and Tukolor in the north. 'Being grounded in the Afro-Cuban tradition', Shain proposes, 'allowed the band to sample Senegal's varied musical traditions without being too closely identified with any particular ethnicity or region'. This was an alternate, modern, and more global vision than the French-African model of exchange that was associated with President Senghor, and they opened up a different brand of authenticity and cosmopolitanism that bypassed Europe and the USA, reaching out to a distantly familiar diasporic current.[79] It is a similar strategy to that used by Breakdance Project

Uganda, but in a very different context: American breakdancing was used to heal youth in a war torn nation, in part because it was not associated with any particular Ugandan ethnicity; all could freely participate.[80]

'Independence Chachacha', the 1960 hit by the Congolese band African Jazz, highlights the importance of Cuban music at the time. The 1970s can be viewed as a decade when artists worked to shed those Cuban influences in favor of more local influences. This is one key to the emergence of Youssou N'Dour's mbalax style.

Digging deep into their own singular local cultures—rather than sampling the whole nation—marked the efforts of many. For example, in Zimbabwe, Shona mbira music informed Thomas Mapfumo in the 1970s to the point where he eventually added an mbira player to his band in the 1980s. Oliver Mtukudzi also drew directly from Shona culture, but rather from concepts of personhood and practices of social relationships in his lyrics, as well as ngoma drumming and dancing. Any concert of Youssou N'Dour, whether in Dakar, Paris, or New York, is marked by extended periods of Wolof sabar and tama drumming, accommodating audience members who jump the stage to engage in expressing their culture through dance.[81]

In Mali, Salif Keita publicly reconciled with his father Sina, addressing Maninka social codes including father–son competitive relationships, via his first album on a major international label, *Soro*. Keita records and travels with a jembe player, who similarly invokes Maninka identity in his rhythms and dance invitations. Oumou Sangare updated ancient hunter's harp music, using a modified new youth's harp, guitar, and violin, addressing issues of concern to women in the musical and sung language of the Wassoulou region in southern Mali. From Guinea, Mamady Keita turned Maninka village jembe drumming into a solo concert genre. In Ghana, Obrafour drew the admiration of his peers and elders alike for his use of Akan libation formulas in a tribute to Nkrumah using a hiplife format. Second and later generations of hip hop artists in Africa are increasingly coming to terms with their relationship to local music culture, just as previous generations of artists have done in relation to Cuban and other foreign imports.[82]

## SHARED AESTHETIC SENSIBILITIES

Finally, a search for shared aesthetic sensibilities, not only across the continent but also farther afield across the diaspora, marks one corner of African music scholarship.[83] Shared sensibilities are especially remarkable in light of the great geographic, topographic, and ethno-linguistic diversity, overlaid by differing colonial and religious proselytizing histories. Among them are the high value placed on participation (including hand clapping, dancing, or vocally responding), buzzing devices on musical instruments which give life to the sounds coming from them, forms based on steady rhythmic cycles requiring improvisation, the use of polyrhythms and offbeat phrasing, and the tight link between drumming and dancing. The ways in which these aesthetics play out, from the obligatory responders in Malian hunter's music (with jingling rings on their harps) to the horn section and vocal chorus engaging in a three-way dialogue with vocalist Fela Kuti (e.g. 'Zombie') to the built-in polyrhythms of Shona mbira music (with jangling bottle caps attached to the instruments) make for a wondrously multifaceted realm of experience.

Not all African music is open like this, however. Hunter's music from Mali, for example, is only for hunters who have proven themselves, and only hunters can dance to certain pieces. Secretive power societies, which often use drumming, may also restrict who can be present and participate. But these are exceptions to a more general rule.

## Conclusion

With such a vast and diverse African soundscape, it would seem to be impossible to find common ground. But that is part of the beauty and joy in listening to (and participating in) African music, which is finding that common ground, from the most micro to larger and larger levels. It may also seem just as impossible to find a center of discourse about African music. But it is just that breadth of African music discourse, only a small part of which has been reflected here, that speaks to the vitality of the field.

## Notes

1. 'President Nkrumah Visits Guinea, 1960–1961,' http://www.britishpathe.com/video/president-nkrumah-visits-guinea. The concert begins at 8'43". The North American tour of Les Ballets Africains, from at least September 1960 through February 1961, can be tracked via *Variety* magazine and local newspapers in online databases.
2. Nkrumah (1963, 142).
3. African Union, 'History of the OAU and UA,' http://www.au.int/en/history/oau-and-au.
4. See their autobiographies and biographies: Sonar Senghor (2004), Makeba (1987), Dibango (1994), Fela (Veal 2000), Shabalala (in Erlmann 1996), Mapfumo (Eyre 2015), Keita (C. Keita 2011), N'Dour (Cathcart 1989), and Kidjo (2014).
5. Touré did not complete his secondary-school education; he was expelled from professional technical training school for insubordination by leading a protest (Lewin 2009, Vol.1:37–38).
6. For information on these and other African drummers at US universities, see http://musc265.blogs.wesleyan.edu/drumming/. See Patterson (2007) for their history at UCLA. Dor (2014) provides an important study of West African drumming ensembles in North American universities.
7. Nkrumah (1963, 49).
8. Nyerere (1967, 186); also see Askew (2002, 171).
9. Achimota College, 1932, in Coe (2005, 59).

10. Coe (2005, 60).
11. Conteh-Morgan (1994, 51).
12. What may be Keita's (1944) first publication has the look of what his Ponty assignment may have been. For his early creative work, see Keita (1945, 1948a, 1948b, 1949, 1950, 1952). See Cohen (2012, 21–25) for further references about École Ponty, Sabatier (1980) for a tighter focus, and Conteh-Morgan (1994) for a broader window on Francophone theater. President Modibo Keita was a product of École Ponty (Cutter 1971, 253). See Askew (2002, 161–95) and Turino (2000, 34) for other examples.
13. Charry (2000b).
14. Chikowero (2015, 301).
15. For example, Kisliuk (1998) on BaAka, Askew (2002) on Swahili, Meintjes on Zulu (2003), Reed (2003) on Dan, Nannyonga-Tamusuza (2005) on Baganda, Ampene (2005, 2016) on Akan, C. Keita (2011) on Maninka, Omojola (2012) on Yoruba, Kidula (2013) on Logooli, and Kyker (2016) on Shona. Earlier examples are too numerous to list, but Berliner (1978), Euba (1990), and Waterman (1990) stand out.
16. Recent estimates put the number of distinct African languages at over 2000, notwithstanding the problems involved in distinguishing languages, dialects, and varieties (Heine and Nurse 2000; Lewis, Simons, and Fennig 2016). See Irvine (2008) for a critical review of colonial-era research in African languages and the delimitation of linguistic boundaries.
17. N'Diaye (2016).
18. For Les Ballets Africains, see their 1967 performance (Sarma 1967). For the GDE see Opoku (1968?) and Younge (2011).
19. See Kubik and Cooke (2016), Blench (1982, 2014), Charry (2000a), Djedje (2008, 2015), and Baroin (2011). Early examples are: the work of Boone (1936, 1951) and Laurenty (1960) mapping out xylophones, drums, and string instruments in Central Africa; Jones (1959) mapping out vocal harmonies; and Wachsmann (1964) mapping out harps. The five volumes covering Africa in the series *Musikgeschichte in Bildern* (1961–1989) continue this work. See Wegner (1984) for string instruments and Meyer (1997) for drums. Kubik (1998, 296–98) notes four means of musical instrument diffusion: human migration, contacts between neighboring groups, long-distance travel, and diffusion through media.
20. Anku (2009, 44–45).
21. http://www.britishmuseum.org/whats_on/all_current_exhibitions/akan_drum.aspx. See also the British Museum number: Am,SLMisc.1368.
22. Mensah (1982, 140).
23. Mensah (1965). An Internet search (adding 'Ghana xylophone') should provide full details for the following. PhD dissertations: Larry Godsey (1980), Mary Seavoy (1982), Francis Saighoe (1988), Michael Vercelli (2006), Brian Hogan (2011), Julie Beauregard (2012), John Dankwa (2017); Masters theses: Sidra Lawrence (2006), Corinna Campbell (2006), John Dankwa (2012), Bernard Woma (2013); articles and chapters: A.A. Mensah (1967), Mitchel Strumpf (1970), Saighoe (1984), Godsey (1984), Ben Aning (1989), Trevor Wiggins (1998, 1999, 2011), J.P. Kuutiero (2006), Peter Cooke (2013); and book: Trevor Wiggins and Joseph Kobom (1992). I thank John Dankwa,

whose 2017 Wesleyan University PhD dissertation (*When the Gyil Speaks*) attempts to clarify much of this material. Julie Strand (2009) has done a PhD dissertation on a neighboring Burkina Faso tradition, and Hugo Zemp (2001–2002, 2006, 2010) has published documentary videos and articles on neighboring Senufo traditions in Ivory Coast (http://www.der.org/films/masters-of-the-balafon.html).

24. Woma (2013).

25. Lentz (2006, 2–3).

26. Lentz (2006, 3).

27. Polak (2012).

28. For the worldwide dispersion of the jembe and African study tours, see Billmeier (1999), Polak (2000), Raout (2009), Flaig (2010), and Gaudette (2013). For a similar phenomenon with the mbira, see Muparutsa (2013).

29. Important recent studies on nation building and music and dance have been done on Angola (Moorman 2008), Ghana (Schramm 2000; Schauert 2015a), Guinea (Cohen 2012), Senegal (Castaldi 2006; Neveu Kringelbach 2015), Tanzania (Lange 1995; Askew 2002; Edmondson 2007), and Zimbabwe (Turino 2000). See Rubin (1997) for information about various national dance ensembles throughout Africa. For recent work on the contemporary musical life of two cities, see Perullo (2011) and Skinner (2015).

30. For further information, see Charry (2000a), Straker (2009), Cohen (2012), and Counsel (2009, 2015, 2016). The US entertainment industry magazine *Variety* reported on Ballets Africains performances in Paris (12/4/1957, p. 72), Buenos Aires (6/18/1958, p. 60), and Edinburgh (10/9/1957, p. 2). For sources on Keita's impact in the 1950s, see Gnaoulé-Oupoh (2000, 138–42). For a report on the abandoned state of Les Ballets in 2015 see Juompan-Yakam (2015).

31. *Time* (3/2/1959, p. 60), *The Nation* (3/7/1959, p. 215). The *New York Times* devoted four articles to their debut tour (February 8, 17, 22, and March 1, 1959). Touré was *Time* magazine's cover story while Ballets Africains was in New York (2/16/1959). A Broadway Database lists four runs there: February 16–March 28, 1959 (48 performances); September 26–October 22, 1960; November 16, 1966–January 28, 1967 (85 performances); and February 20–April 6, 1968 (https://www.ibdb.com/broadway-show/les-ballets-africains-9983).

32. See Ministry of Information, Guinea (1979). In the 1970s UNESCO published similar policy reports for Algeria, Ghana, Kenya, Nigeria, Senegal, Tanzania, Togo, and Zaire, which are all available online. Search: Cultural Policy in [country] UNESCO.

33. Chevalier (1991). See Keita's Wikipedia page for details about his extensive performance and instructional CDs and DVDs, and his films: https://en.wikipedia.org/wiki/Mamady_Keïta. See also Billmeier (1999).

34. David Achkar's film *Allah Tantou* (1991) tries to makes sense of his father Marof Achkar's life, imprisonment, and execution (in 1971). See Kaba (1976) for an analysis of Touré's reign and the arts, and Diawara's film *Conakry Kas* (2003), which explores the conflicted legacy of Sékou Touré among elder artists and intellectuals in Conakry in the early 2000s.

35. Chevalier (1991).

36. Ghanaian dancer Atsikpa quoted in Schauert (2015a, 122).
37. Trinity College has since been renamed Trinity Laban Conservatoire of Music and Dance. For biographical material on Nketia see Djedje and Carter (1989), Akrofi (2002), Nketia (2005), and Nketia Music Foundation (2016), which lists 218 of Nketia's publications.
38. Kwakwa (2015, 496), Schauert (2015a, 52–60). Writing about the National Dance Company, officially inaugurated as the Ghana Dance Ensemble in 1967, is especially rich. Primary sources by those in the ensemble include: Opoku and Bell (1965), Opoku (1968?, 1976), Adinku (1994), and Kwakwa (2015). Other sources include July (1987), Schramm (2000), Hirt-Manheimer (2004), Botwe-Asamoah (2005), and Schauert (2015a, 2015b), whose book has the most comprehensive listing of references.
39. Opoku (1964, 52–53).
40. Schauert (2015a, 64–69).
41. Schramm (2000, 343).
42. F. Keita (1957, 207). This quotation also appears in the translations and reprints listed under this entry (1958, 176; and 1959, 23).
43. Deku, 1967, in Schram (2000, 347).
44. Schauert (2015a, 108–9). Also see US dancer Drid Williams's specific objections to calling the early GDE dances traditional (the music is traditional, but the dance and costuming is not) and response by Nketia, 'our goal was not to present an anthropological specimen. It was to create art' (Schauert 2015a, 105–8).
45. Marof Achkar in Sarma (1967). My translation from the French.
46. Kaba (1976, 203–4).
47. Schauert (2015a, 66–67).
48. Ousmane Noël Cissé, interview, in Neveu Kringelbach (2014, 234).
49. Nyerere [1962] (1967, 187).
50. *The Nationalist*, November 10, 1967, in Lange (1995, 32, 100).
51. Nkrumah (1963, 83); Schramm (2000, 22).
52. Arusha Declaration, 1967, in Askew (2002, 178).
53. McGovern (2013).
54. Kahunde (2012), Kafumbe (forthcoming).
55. Documentaries of the festivals were made in Dakar in 1966 (Greaves, Borelli), Algiers in 1969 (Klein), and Lagos in 1977 (Gaunt, Penna). For online links, see http://musc265.blogs.wesleyan.edu/pan-african-festivals/.
56. L. Senghor (1970, 179).
57. See Diagne's (2014) analysis of Césaire's 1956 Paris Congress lecture ('Culture and Colonization'), in which Césaire postulated a horizontal (political) and vertical (cultural, through time) solidarity of people of African descent. The former was based on a common experience of colonialism and racism; the latter 'is the way people of African descent manifest different faces of an African *civilization* ... Césaire's distinction between cultures (characterized by difference) and civilization (defined by the existence of commonalities) would mean that the 'vertical' dimension of Pan-Africanism is what could be identified as Négritude'. For more on Négritude, see L. Senghor (1970), Irele (1981, 2010), Diagne (2011), and Jaji (2014). For Pan-Africanism see Ratcliff (2009), Haynes (2010), and Ki-Zerbo (2013).
58. Commission des Arts (1959, 417).

59. For more on FESMAN see Fuller (1966), L. Senghor (1966), documentaries by Borelli (1966), Greaves (1967), and Dagan (1987), Reiser (2014), and Murphy (2016).
60. Reiser (2014, 139).
61. Sources for the Algiers festival includes Klein's (1969) film, Hadouchi's (2011) analysis of the film, Lindfors (1970), and Ratcliff (2009).
62. Lindfors (1970, 6) quoting Osman.
63. Adotevi (1969, 28, 30). This echoes Lenin's 1905 essay 'Party Organization and Party Literature'. For a related discussion of Guinea's 1968 Cultural Revolution under Sékou Touré, see Kaba (1976). Part of Adotevi's lecture is shown in Klein's (1969) film.
64. Reiser (2014, 192).
65. For recordings celebrating the medals of Guinea and Mali, see Bembeya Jazz National, 1970, *Regard sur le passé, médaille d'argent, orchestre moderne, premier Festival Culturel Panafricain à Alger*, Syliphone, SLP 10; and L' Ensemble Instrumental du Mali, 1973, *Première anthologie de la musique malienne*, Vol. 4, *Médaille d'or au festival culturel panafricain d'Alger*, Bärenreiter Musicaphon, BM 30 L 2504. For links to film of Les Ballets Africains (or possibly Ballet Djoliba), a Senegalese troupe (probably its national ballet), the all-star Guinean Syli Orchestre National, and Miriam Makeba, see http://musc265.blogs.wesleyan.edu/postcolonial/pan-african-festivals/.
66. Apter (2005, 47–49, 202), Falola (2005, 281, 288).
67. International Festival Committee (1977, 7), quoted in Falola (2005, 283).
68. For information on the Third World Black Arts Festival in Dakar in 2010 see Reiser (2014) and the program of events: https://www.sangonet.com/eventc/Exposition/Fesman3/program_french-fesman-MAJ2dec2010.pdf.
69. Ranger (1975, 12–13), Rumbolz (2000, 44–45).
70. Plageman (2013). The Gangbe Brass Band from Benin has a unique mix drawing from African and New Orleans brass bands, jazz, funk, and traditional *vodun* drumming (Ojo 2007).
71. See Sadoh (2010) for a guide to art music in Nigeria. A sampling of other sources includes Mensah (1998), Omojola (2009, 2012), Agawu (2016), and Terpenning (2016). For links to African symphonic orchestras, see http://musc265.blogs.wesleyan.edu/postcolonial/orchestras/.
72. Kidula (2000), Collins (2012).
73. Counsel (2015), who carried out the RTG project, provides full details. Counsel's website *Radio Africa* contains a listing of the complete Syliphone discography: http://www.radioafrica.com.au/Discographies/Syliphone.html. Direct links to all of the following archives have been gathered here: http://musc265.blogs.wesleyan.edu/postcolonial/sound-archives/.
74. See Kahunde (2012), Lobley (2012), and Nannyonga-Tamusuza and Weintraub (2012).
75. The video has over 330 million views as of 2016, five years after it was released, https://youtu.be/VBmMU_iwe6U. For *Year of 4*, see http://www.vevo.com/watch/beyonce/year-of-4/USSM21101099; Tofo Tofo references begin at 7'05" and continue at 13'28". For more on pantsula, see http://www.okayafrica.com/tag/pantsula/, especially the article 'Five Reasons We Love the New Basement Jaxx Video' (8/12/2013) by Alyssa Klein.

76. Tande (2013), Mackey (2010). For more on music and copyright in Africa see Collins (2006) and Perullo and Eisenberg (2015). A well-known case of trying to recoup royalties (Malan 2000) concerns Solomon Linda's 1939 'Mbube' and its subsequent use by Pete Seeger ('Wimowe'), The Tokens ('The Lion Sleeps Tonight'), and Walt Disney Corporation (*The Lion King*).
77. See Stewart (2000) for a history of Congolese popular music; for the early history of Cuban records in Africa, see Fargion (2004).
78. Charry (2000a), Cathcart (1989), Durán (1989), Eagleson (2012), Turino (2000).
79. Shain (forthcoming, 110, 143).
80. See the documentary by Elderkin (2010).
81. Turino (2000), Eyre (2015), Kyker (2016, 13, 46). See Ba's (1994) documentary of N'Dour's African tour: 'I am much more sure of people's reaction at the end of a concert in Africa than in Europe or the United States ... In Africa, if you manage to move an audience, people get up, cheer, shout or come up on the stage to dance, and there you know you've got to them'.
82. C. Keita (2011, 43–57), Durán (2007), Odamtten (2013). Hip hop in Africa is the most recent genre to undergo large-scale scholarly analysis, with about a dozen books devoted to it already. See the edited collections by Saucier (2011), Charry (2012), and Clark and Koster (2014).
83. Two early surveys are Bebey (1969) and Nketia (1974). A sample of work on music theoretical aesthetics includes Arom (1991), Nzewi (1997), Locke (2009), Polak and London (2014), and Agawu (1995, 2016). See Nketia (1998) for an extended survey of African music scholarship by Africans. For recent general bibliographies, see Oxford Bibliographies Online.

## BIBLIOGRAPHY

Adinku, W. Ofotsu. 1994. *African Dance Education in Ghana*. Accra: Ghana Universities Press.
Adotevi, Stanislas. 1969. "The Strategy of Culture." *Black Scholar* 1 (1): 27–35.
Agawu, Kofi. 1995. *African Rhythm: A Northern Ewe Perspective*. New York: Cambridge University Press.
———. 2016. *The African Imagination in Music*. New York: Oxford University Press.
Akrofi, Eric A. 2002. *Sharing Knowledge and Experience: A Profile of Kwabena Nketia, Scholar and Music Educator*. Accra: Afram Publications.
Ampene, Kwasi. 2005. *Female Song Tradition and the Akan of Ghana: The Creative Process in Nnwonkoro*. Burlington, VT: Ashgate.
———. 2016. *Engaging Modernity: Asante in the Twenty-First Century*. 2nd ed. Ann Arbor, MI: Maize Books.
Ampene, Kwasi, Akosua Adomako Ampofo, Godwin K. Adjei, and Albert K. Awedoba, eds. 2015. *Discourses in African Musicology: J.H. Kwabena Nketia Festschrift*. Ann Arbor: University of Michigan; Legon: University of Ghana.
Anku, Willie. 2009. "Drumming Among the Akan and Anlo Ewe of Ghana: An Introduction." *African Music* 8 (3): 38–64.
Apter, Andrew. 2005. *The Pan-African Nation: Oil and the Spectacle of Culture in Nigeria*. Chicago: University of Chicago Press.

Arom, Simha. 1991. *African Polyphony and Polyrhythm: Musical Structure and Methodology*. Translated by Martin Thom, Barbara Tuckett, and Raymond Boyd. Cambridge: Cambridge University Press.

Askew, Kelly. 2002. *Performing the Nation: Swahili Music and Cultural Politics in Tanzania*. Chicago: University of Chicago Press.

Baroin, Catherine. 2011. "L'odyssée africaine d'un cordophone rudimentaire, le 'luth à pique intérieure'." *Afrique, Archéologie, Arts* 7: 55–72. https://aaa.revues.org/625.

Bebey, Francis. 1969. *Musique de l'Afrique*. English translation by Josephine Bennett, 1975, *African Music: A People's Art*. Brooklyn, NY: Lawrence Hill Books.

Berliner, Paul. 1978. *The Soul of Mbira*. Berkeley: University of California Press.

Billmeier, Uschi. 1999. *Mamady Keïta. Ein Leben für die Djembé, traditionelle Rhythmen der Malinke; A Life for the Djembé: Traditional Rhythms of the Malinke; Un vie pour le djembé: rythmes traditionels des Malinké*. Engerda, Germany: Arun.

Blench, Roger. 1982. "Evidence for the Indonesian Origins of Certain Elements of African Culture: A Review, with Special Reference to the Arguments of A.M. Jones." *African Music* 6 (2): 81–93.

———. 2014. "Using Diverse Sources of Evidence for Reconstructing the Past History of Musical Exchanges in the Indian Ocean." *African Archeological Review* 31: 675–703.

Boone, Olga. 1936. *Les xylophones du Congo Belge*. Tervuren: Musée du Congo Belge.

———. 1951. *Les tambours du Congo Belge et du Ruanda-Urundi*. Tervuren: Musée du Congo Belge.

Botwe-Asamoah, Kwame. 2005. *Kwame Nkrumah's Politico-Cultural Thought and Policies: An African-Centered Paradigm for the Second Phase of the African Revolution*. New York: Routledge.

Castaldi, Francsca. 2006. *Choreographies of Identities: Negritude, Dance, and the National Ballet of Senegal*. Bloomington: University of Illinois Press.

Cathcart, Jenny. 1989. *Hey You!: A Portrait of Youssou N'Dour*. Witney, UK: Fine Line Books.

Charry, Eric. 2000a. *Mande Music: Traditional and Modern Music of the Maninka and Mandinka of Western Africa*. Chicago: University of Chicago Press.

———. 2000b. "Music and Islam in Sub-Saharan Africa." In *The History of Islam in Africa*, edited by Randall Pouwels and Nehemia Levtzion, 545–73. Athens: Ohio University Press.

———, ed. 2012. *Hip Hop Africa: New African Music in a Globalizing World*. Bloomington: Indiana University Press.

Chikowero, Mhoze. 2015. *African Music, Power, and Being in Colonial Zimbabwe*. Bloomington: Indiana University Press.

Clark, Msia Kibona, and Mickie Mwanzia Koster, eds. 2014. *Hip Hop and Social Change in Africa: Ni Wakati*. Lanham, MD: Lexington Books.

Cohen, Joshua. 2012. "Stages in Transition: Les Ballets Africains and Independence, 1959–1960." *Journal of Black Studies* 43 (1): 11–48.

Coe, Cati. 2005. *Dilemmas of Culture in African Schools: Youth, Nationalism, and the Transformation of Knowledge*. Chicago: University of Chicago Press.

Collins, John. 2006. "Copyright, Folklore and Music Piracy in Ghana." *Critical Arts* 20 (1): 158–70.

———. 2012. "Contemporary Ghanaian Popular Music Since the 1980s." In Charry, 2012: 211–33.

Commission des Arts (Deuxième congrès des écrivains et artistes noirs). 1959. "Resolution de la commission des arts." *Présence Africaine* (nouvelle série) 24/25: 413–19.

Conteh-Morgan, John. 1994. *Theatre and Drama in Francophone Africa: A Critical Introduction*. Cambridge: Cambridge University Press.

Counsel, Graeme. 2009. *Mande Popular Music and Cultural Policies in West Africa: Griots and Government Policies Since Independence*. Saabrücken: VDM Verlag.

———. 2015. "Music for a Revolution: The Sound Archives of Radio Télévision Guinée." In *From Dust to Digital: Ten Years of the Endangered Archives Programme*, edited by Maja Kominko, 547–86. Cambridge: Open Book Publishers.

———. 2016. "Syliphone Discography." *Radio Africa*. http://www.radioafrica.com.au/Discographies/Syliphone.html.

Cutter, Charles. 1971. *Nation-Building in Mali: Art, Radio, and Leadership in a Pre-literate Society*. PhD dissertation, University of California, Los Angeles.

Diagne, Souleymane Bachir. 2011. *African Art as Philosophy: Senghor, Bergson, and the Idea of Negritude*. Translated by Chike Jeffers. London: Seagull Books.

———. 2014. "Négritude." In *The Stanford Encyclopedia of Philosophy*, edited by Edward N. Zalta (Spring 2016 Edition). http://plato.stanford.edu/archives/spr2016/entries/negritude/.

Dibango, Manu with Danille Rouard. 1994. *Three Kilos of Coffee: An Autobiography*. Translated by Beth G. Raps. Chicago: University of Chicago Press.

Djedje, Jacqueline Cogdell. 2008. *Fiddling in West Africa: Touching the Spirit in Fulbe, Hausa, and Dagbamba Cultures*. Bloomington: University of Indiana Press.

———. 2015. "Music and Diasporas Within West Africa: The Pre-colonial Era." In Ampene and Others, 2015: 256–75.

Djedje, Jacqueline Cogdell, and William Grandvill Carter. 1989. "J.H. Kwabena Nketia: A Biobibliographical Portrait; Bibliography; Compositions 1942–1965." In *African Musicology: Current Trends, A Festschrift Presented to J.H. Kwabena Nketia*, ed. Djedje and associate ed. Carter. Vol. 1, 3–29. Los Angeles: African Studies Center, University of California.

Dor, George Worlasi Kwasi. 2014. *West African Drumming and Dance in North American Universities: An Ethnomusicological Perspective*. Jackson, MS: University Press of Mississippi.

Durán, Lucy. 1989. "Key to N'Dour: Roots of the Senegalese Star." *Popular Music* 8 (3): 275–84.

———. 2007. "Transcript of Location Feature: Mali's Songbird, Oumou Sangaré." *BBC Radio 3, World Routes*. Broadcast 9/20/2003. http://eprints.soas.ac.uk/4297/.

Eagleson, Ian M. 2012. *From Thum to Benga International: Continuity and Change in the Music of the Luo of Kenya, 1950–2010*. PhD dissertation, Wesleyan University.

Edmondson, Laura. 2007. *Performance and Politics in Tanzania: The Nation on Stage*. Bloomington: Indiana University Press.

Erlmann, Veit. 1996. *Nightsong: Performance, Power, and Practice in South Africa*. Chicago: University of Chicago Press.

Euba, Akin. 1990. *Yoruba Drumming: The Dundun Tradition*. Bayreuth: E. Breitinger/Bayreuth University.

Eyre, Banning. 2015. *Lion Songs: Thomas Mapfumo and the Music That Made Zimbabwe*. Durham: Duke University Press.

Falola, Toyin. 2005. *Key Events in African History: A Reference Guide*. Westport, CT: Greenwood Press.

Fargion, Janet Topp (notes and compiler). 2004. *Out of Cuba: Latin American Music Takes Africa by Storm*. CD. Topic Records, CDTSCD927.

Flaig, Vera H. 2010. *The Politics of Representation and Transmission in the Globalization of Guinea's Djembé*. PhD dissertation, University of Michigan.

Fuller, Hoyt W. 1966. "World Festival of Negro Arts: Senegal Fete Illustrates Philosophy of 'Négritude'." *Ebony* (July): 96–102, 104, 106. https://books.google.com/books?id=-1rJTL1zGTwC.

Gaudette, Pascal. 2013. "*Jembe* Hero: West African Drummers, Global Mobility and Cosmopolitanism as Status." *Journal of Ethnic and Migration Studies* 39 (2): 295–310.

Gnaoulé-Oupoh. 2000. *La littérature ivoirienne*. Abidjan: CEDA; Paris: Karthala.

Hadouchi, Olivier. 2011. "'African Culture will be Revolutionary or will not be': William Klein's Film of the First Pan-African Festival of Algiers (1969)." *Third Text* 25 (1): 117–28.

Haynes, Jeffrey. 2010. "Pan-Africanism." In *Oxford Encyclopedia of African Thought*, edited by F. Abiola Irele and Biodun Jeyifo, 2: 207–11. Oxford University Press.

Heine, Bernd, and Derek Nurse. 2000. "Introduction." In *African Languages: An Introduction*, edited by Heine and Nurse, 1–10 Cambridge: Cambridge University Press.

Hirt-Manheimer, Isaac. 2004. *Understanding "Fast Agbekor:" A History of Ghana's National Dance Company and an Analysis of Its Repertory*. MA thesis, Wesleyan University.

International Festival Committee. 1977. *FESTAC 77*. London: Africa Journal Ltd.

Irele, Abiola. 1981. *The African Experience in Literature and Ideology*. London and Exeter, NH: Heinemann. Reprinted 1990, Indiana University Press.

Irele, F. Abiola. 2010. "Négritude." In *Oxford Encyclopedia of African Thought*, edited by Irele and Biodun Jeyifo, 2: 155–58. Oxford University Press.

Irvine, Judith T. 2008. "Subjected Words: African Linguistics and the Colonial Encounter." *Language and Communication* 28: 323–43.

Jaji, Tsitsi Ella. 2014. *Africa in Stereo: Modernism, Music, and Pan-African Solidarity*. New York: Oxford University Press.

Jones, A.M. 1959. *Studies in African Music*. 2 vols. London: Oxford University Press.

July, Robert W. 1987. *An African Voice: The Role of the Humanities in African Independence*. Durham: Duke University Press.

Juompan-Yakam, Clarisse. 2015. "Ballets africains: quand la Guinée abandonne ses danseurs." *Jeune Afrique* (April 14), http://www.jeuneafrique.com/229374/culture/ballets-africains-quand-la-guin-e-abandonne-ses-danseurs/.

Kaba, Lansiné. 1976. "The Cultural Revolution, Artistic Creativity, and Freedom of Expression in Guinea." *Journal of Modern African Studies* 14 (2): 201–18.

Kafumbe, Damascus. Forthcoming. *Kawuugulu: Oral History and Musical Politics in Buganda*. Unpublished manuscript.

Kahunde, Samuel. 2012. "Repatriating Archival Sound Recordings to Revive Traditions: The Role of the Klaus Wachsmann Recordings in the Revival of the Royal Music of Bunyoro-Kitara, Uganda." *Ethnomusicology Forum* 21 (2): 197–219.

Keita, Cheick M. Cherif. 2011. *Outcast to Ambassador: The Musical Odyssey of Salif Keita*. CreateSpace Independent Publishing Platform.

Keita, Fodeba. 1944. "Une ceremonie de mariage à Kankan (1943)." *Notes Africaines* 23: 10, 12.

———. 1945. "Le 'Douga' ou vautor du Mandingue (Sénégal)." *Notes Africaines* 26: 15–16.

———. 1948a. "Etrange destin: Minuit." *Présence Africaine* 3: 466–69.

———. 1948b. "Chansons du Dioliba." *Présence Africaine* 4: 595–98.

———. 1949. "La moisson." *Présence Africaine* 6: 79–82.

———. 1950. *Poèmes Africains*. Paris: Pierre Seghers.

———. 1952. *Le maître d'école, suivi de Minuit*. Paris: Pierre Seghers.

———. 1957. "La danse africaine et la scéne." *Présence Africaine* (nouvelle série) 14/15: 202–9. Reprinted with English translation, 1958, "African Dance and the Stage/La danse africaine et la scéne," *Le Theatre dans le Monde/ World Theatre* 7 (3): 164–78. English translation adapted, 1959, "The True Meaning of African Dances." *UNESCO Courier* 1: 18–23.

Ki-Zerbo, Lazare, ed. 2013. New edition. *Le mouvement panafricaniste au vingtième siècle*. Paris: Organisation internationale de la francophonie. http://www.franco-phonie.org/IMG/pdf/oif-le-mouvement-panafricaniste-au-xxe-s.pdf.

Kidjo, Angélique with Rachel Wenrick. 2014. *Spirit Rising: My Life, My Music*. New York: Harper Design.

Kidula, Jean. 2000. "Polishing the Luster of the Stars: Music Professionalism Made Workable in Kenya." *Ethnomusicology* 44 (3): 408–28.

Kidula, Jean Ngoya. 2013. *Music in Kenyan Christianity: Logooli Religious Song*. Bloomington: Indiana University Press.

Kisliuk, Michelle. 1998. *Seize the Dance!: BaAka Musical Life and the Ethnography of Performance*. New York: Oxford University Press.

Kubik, Gerhard. 1998. "Intra-African Streams of Influence." In *The Garland Encyclo-pedia of African Music*, edited by Ruth Stone, 293–326. New York: Garland.

———. 2015. "Africa." *Grove Music Online, Oxford Music Online*, Oxford University Press. http://www.oxfordmusiconline.com/subscriber/article/grove/music/00268.

Kubik, Gerhard, and Peter Cooke. 2016. "Lamellophone." *Grove Music Online, Oxford Music Online*, Oxford University Press. http://www.oxfordmusiconline.com/subscriber/article/grove/music/40069.

Kwakwa, Patience A. 2015. "Kwabena Nketia and the Creative Arts: The Genesis of the School of Music and Drama, and the Formation of the Ghana Dance Ensem-ble." In Ampene and Others, 2015: 480–506.

Kyker, Jennifer. 2016. *Oliver Mtukudzi: Living Tuku Music in Zimbabwe*. Blooming-ton: Indiana University Press.

Lange, Siri. 1995. *From Nation-Building to Popular Culture: The Modernization of Performance in Tanzania*. Bergen, Norway: Chr. Michelson Institute.

Laurenty, J.S. 1960. *Les cordophones du Congo Belge et du Ruanda-Urundi*. Tervuren: Musée Royal du Congo Belge.

Lentz, Carola. 2006. *Ethnicity and the Making of History in Northern Ghana*. Edin-burgh: Edinburgh University Press.

Lewin, André. 2009–2011. *Ahmed Sékou Touré (1922–1984): président de la Guinée de 1958 à 1984*. 8 vols. Paris: Harmattan.

Lewis, M. Paul, Gary F. Simons, and Charles D. Fennig, eds. 2016. "Africa." *Ethno-logue: Languages of the World*. 19th ed. Dallas, TX: SIL International. http://www.ethnologue.com/region/Africa.

Lindfors, Bernth. 1970. "Anti-Negritude in Algiers." *Africa Today* 17 (1): 5–7.

Lobley, Noel. 2012. "Taking Xhosa Music Out of the Fridge and into the Townships." *Ethnomusicology Forum* 21 (2): 181–95.

Locke, David. 1982. "Principles of Offbeat Timing and Cross-Rhythm in Southern Eve Dance Music." *Ethnomusicology* 26 (2): 217–46.

———. 2009. "Simultaneous Multidimensionality in African Music: Musical Cubism." *African Music* 8 (3): 8–37.

Mackey, Robert. 2010. "Shakira Remixes African Hit for World Cup." thelede. blogs.nytimes.com (May 24), http://thelede.blogs.nytimes.com/2010/05/24/shakira-remixes-african-hit-for-world-cup/?_r=0.

Makeba, Miriam with James Hall. 1987. *Makeba: My Story*. New York: New American Library.

Malan, Rian. 2000. "In the Jungle." *Rolling Stone* (May 25): 54–66, 84–85. http://reprints.longform.org/in-the-jungle.

McGovern, Mike. 2013. *Unmasking the State: Making Guinea Modern*. Chicago: University of Chicago Press.

Meintjes, Louise. 2003. *Sound of Africa! Making Music Zulu in a South African Studio*. Durham: Duke University Press.

Mensah, Atta Annan. 1965. "Musicality and Musicianship in Northwest Ghana." *Research Review* (Institute of African Studies, Legon) 4 (2): 42–45.

———. 1982. "Gyil: The Dagara-Lobi Xylophone." *Journal of African Studies* 9 (3): 139–54.

———. 1998. "Compositional Practices in African Music." In Stone, 1998: 224–47.

Meyer, Andreas. 1997. *Afrikanische Trommeln: West- und Zentralafrika*. Berlin: Museum für Völkerkunde.

Ministry of Education and Culture of Guinea, Guinean National Commission for UNESCO. 1979. *Cultural Policy in the Revolutionary People's Republic of Guinea*. Paris: UNESCO.

Moorman, Marissa J. 2008. *Intonations: A Social History of Music and Nation in Luanda, Angola, from 1945 to Recent Times*. Athens: Ohio University Press.

Muparutsa, Tendai. 2013. *Transformations in Zimbabwean Traditional Music of North America*. PhD dissertation, University of Alberta.

Murphy, David, ed. 2016. *The First World Festival of Negro Arts, Dakar 1966: Contexts and Legacies*. Liverpool: Liverpool University Press.

Musikgeschichte in Bildern. 1961–1989. *NordAfrika* (P. Collaer and J. Elsner, 1983, 1[8]); *Zentralafrika* (J. Gansemans and B. Schmidt-Wrenger, 1986, 1[9]); *Ostafrika* (G. Kubik, 1982, 1[10]); *Westafrika* (G. Kubik, 1989, 1[11]); *Ägypten* (H. Hickmann, 1961, 2[1]). Leipzig: VEB Deutscher Verlag für Musik Leipzig.

Nannyonga-Tamusuza, Sylvia A. 2005. *Baakisimba: Gender in the Music and Dance of the Baganda People of Uganda*. New York: Routledge.

Nannyonga-Tamusuza, Sylvia A., and Andrew Weintraub. 2012. "The Audible Future: Reimagining the Role of Sound Archives in Uganda." *Ethnomusicology* 56 (2): 206–33.

N'Diaye, Diakite Fatoumata. 2016. "Communiqué du Conseil des Ministres du mercredi 14 septembre 2016." maliweb.net (September 14), http://www.maliweb.net/politique/conseil-des-ministres/communique-conseil-ministres-mercredi-14-septembre-2016-1781232.html.

Neveu Kringelbach, Hélène. 2014. "Choreographic Revival, Elite Nationalism, and Postcolonial Appropriation in Senegal." In *Oxford Handbook of Music Revival*, edited by Caroline Bithell and Juniper Hill, 228–51. Oxford: Oxford University Press.

———. 2015. *Dance Circles: Movement, Morality and Self-fashioning in Urban Senegal*. New York: Berghahn Books.

Nketia, J. H. Kwabena. 1974. *Music of Africa*. New York: W.W. Norton.

———. 1998. "The Scholarly Study of African Music: A Historical Review." In Stone, 1998: 13–73.

———. 2005. *Ethnomusicology and African Music: Collected Papers. Vol. 1, Modes of Inquiry and Interpretation*. Accra: Afram Publications.

Nketia Music Foundation. 2016. http://www.nketiamusicfoundation.org/web/resources/publications/.

Nkrumah, Kwame. 1963. *Africa Must Unite*. New York: Frederick A. Praeger.

Nyerere, Julius. 1967. *Freedom and Unity/Uhuru na Umoja: A Selection from Writings and Speeches, 1952–65*. London: Oxford University Press.

Nzewi, Meki. 1997. *African Music: Theoretical Content and Creative Continuum. The Culture-Exponent's Definitions*. Oldershausen: Institut für Didaktik populärer Musik.

Odamtten, Harry Nii Koney. 2013. "Morality, the Sacred, and God in Ghanaian Hip Hop." In *Urban God Talk: Constructing a Hip Hop Spirituality*, edited by Andre E. Johnson, 189–205. Lanham, MD: Lexington Books.

Ojo, Philip A. 2007. "Gangbe Brass Band: Partager notre culture avec les autres peoples du monde." *West Africa Review* 10: 1–9.

Omojola, Bode. 2009. *The Music of Fela Sowande: Encounters, African Identity and Creative Ethnomusicology*. Point Richmond, CA: Music Research Institute Press.

———. 2012. *Yoruba Music in the Twentieth Century: Identity, Agency and Performance Practice*. Rochester: University of Rochester Press.

Opoku, A.M. 1964. "Thoughts from the School of Music and Drama." *Okyeame* 2 (1): 51–56.

———. 1968?. *The Ghana Dance Ensemble: Sponsored by The Arts Council of Ghana and the Institute of African Studies, University of Ghana, Legon*. Accra: Pierian Press.

———. 1976. "The Presentation of Traditional Music and Dance in the Theatre." *World of Music* 18 (4): 58–67.

Opoku, A.M., and Willis Bell. 1965. *African Dances: A Ghanaian Profile*. Legon: Institute of African Studies, University of Ghana.

Oxford Bibliographies Online. 2014–2016. "African Studies: Music, Dance and the Study of Africa" (Nate Plageman); "African Studies: Music, Traditional" (Andrew J. Eisenberg); "Music: East and West Africa" (Daniel Avorgbedor); "Music: North Africa" (Kristy Barbacane). http://www.oxfordbibliographies.com/.

Patterson, Karin Gaynell. 2007. *Expressions of Africa in Los Angeles Public Performance, 1781–1994*. PhD dissertation, University of California, Los Angeles.

Perullo, Alex. 2011. *Live from Dar es Salaam: Popular Music and Tanzania's Music Economy*. Bloomington: Indiana University Press.

Perullo, Alex, and Andrew J. Eisenberg. 2015. "Musical Property Rights in Tanzania and Kenya After TRIPS." In *The Sage Handbook of Intellectual Property*, edited by Matthew David and Debora Halbert, 148–64. Los Angeles: Sage.

Plageman, Nate. 2013. *Highlife Saturday Night: Popular Music and Social Change in Urban Ghana*. Bloomington: Indiana University Press.

Polak, Rainer. 2000. "A Musical Instrument Travels Around the World: Jenbe Playing in Bamako, in West Africa, and Beyond." *World of Music* 42 (3): 7–46. Reprint, 2006. In *Ethnomusicology: A Contemporary Reader*, edited by Jennifer Post, 161–85. New York: Routledge.

Polak, Rainer. 2012. "Urban Drumming: Traditional Celebration Music in a West African City (Bamako)." In Charry, 2012: 261–81.

Polak, Rainer, and Justin London. 2014. "Timing and Meter in Mande Drumming from Mali." *Music Theory Online* 20 (1). http://www.mtosmt.org/issues/mto.14.20.1/mto.14.20.1.polak-london.php.

Ranger, T.O. 1975. *Dance and Society in Eastern Africa 1890–1970: The Beni Ngoma*. Berkeley: University of California Press.

Raout, Julien. 2009. "Au rythme du tourisme: Le monde transnational de la percussion guinéenne." *Cahiers d'Études africaines* 49 (1–2): 175–201.

Ratcliff, Anthony. 2009. *Liberation at the End of a Pen: Writing Pan-African Politics of Cultural Struggle*. PhD dissertation, University of Massachusetts, Amherst.

Reed, Daniel. 2003. *Dan Ge Performance: Masks and Music in Contemporary Côte d'Ivoire*. Bloomington: Indiana University Press.

Reiser, Melissa D. 2014. *Music, Negritude, and the 'African Renaissance': Performing Blackness at the World Festivals of Black Arts in Dakar, 1966 and 2010*. PhD dissertation, University of Wisconsin, Madison.

Rubin, Don, ed. 1997. *World Encyclopedia of Contemporary Theatre, vol. 3: Africa*. London: Routledge.

Rumbolz, Robert. 2000. *"A Vessel for Many Things:" Brass Bands in Ghana*. PhD dissertation, Wesleyan University.

Sabatier, Peggy R. 1980. "African Culture and Colonial Education: The William Ponty School Cahiers and Theater." *Journal of African Studies* 7 (1): 2–10.

Sadoh, Godwin. 2010. "African Musicology: A Bibliographical Guide to Nigerian Art Music (1927–2009)." *Notes* 66 (3): 485–502.

Saucier, Paul Khalil, ed. 2011. *Native Tongues: An African Hip-hop Reader*. Trenton, NJ: Africa World Press.

Schauert, Paul. 2015a. *Staging Ghana: Artistry and Nationalism in State Dance Ensembles*. Bloomington: Indiana University Press.

———. 2015b. "Nketia, Nationalism, and the Ghana Dance Ensemble." In Ampene and Others, 2015: 552–73.

Schramm, Katharina. 2000. "The Politics of Dance: Changing Representations of the Nation in Ghana." *Africa Spectrum* 35 (3): 339–58.

Senghor, Léopold Sédar. 1966. "The Function and Meaning of the First World Festival of Negro Arts." *African Forum* 1 (4): 5–10.

———. 1970. "Négritude: A Humanism of the Twentieth Century." In *The Africa Reader, vol. 2: Independent Africa*, edited by Wilfrid Cartey and Martin Kilson, 179–92. New York: Random House.

Senghor, Maurice Sonar. 2004. *Souvenirs de théâtres d'Afrique et d'outre-Afrique: pour que lève la semence, contribution à l'édification d'un théâtre noir universel*. Paris: Harmattan.

Shain, Richard M. Forthcoming. *Roots in Reverse: Senegalese Afro-Cuban Music and Tropical Cosmopolitanism*. Unpublished manuscript.

Skinner, Ryan Thomas. 2015. *Bamako Sounds: The Afropolitan Ethics of Malian Music*. Minneapolis: University of Minnesota Press.

Stewart, Gary. 2000. *Rumba on the River: A History of the Popular Music of the Two Congos.* London: Verso.

Stone, Ruth M., ed. 1998. *The Garland Encyclopedia of World Music, Volume 1: Africa.* New York: Garland.

Straker, Jay. 2009. *Youth, Nationalism, and the Guinean Revolution.* Bloomington: Indiana University Press.

Tande, Dibussi. 2013. "Undermining African Intellectual and Artistic Rights: Shakira, Zangalewa and the 2010 World Cup Anthem." *Bakwa* (April 26), https://bakwamagazine.com/2013/04/26/commentary-undermining-african-intellectual-and-artistic-rights-shakira-zangalewa-the-2010-world-cup-anthem/.

Terpenning, Steven Spinner. 2016. "African Musical Hybridity in the Colonial Context: An Analysis of Ephraim Amu's 'Yen Ara Asase Ni'." *Ethnomusicology* 60 (3): 459–83.

Turino, Thomas. 2000. *Nationalists, Cosmopolitans, and Popular Music in Zimbabwe.* Chicago: University of Chicago Press.

Veal, Michael E. 2000. *Fela: The Life and Times of an African Musical Icon.* Philadelphia: Temple University Press.

Wachsmann, Klaus. 1964. "Human Migration and African Harps." *Journal of the International Folk Music Council* 16: 84–88.

Waterman, Christopher. 1990. *Jùjú: A Social History and Ethnography of an African Popular Music.* Chicago: University of Chicago Press.

Wegner, Ulrich. 1984. *Afrikanische Saiteninstrumente.* Berlin: Staatliche Museen Preussischer Kulturbesitz.

Woma, Bernard. 2013. *The Socio-Political Dimension of Dagara Funeral Ritual, Music and Dirge.* MA Thesis, Indiana University.

Younge, Pascal Yao. 2011. *Music and Dance Traditions of Ghana: History, Performance and Teaching.* Jefferson, NC: McFarland.

## VIDEOGRAPHY

(For online links, see: http://musc265.blogs.wesleyan.edu/postcolonial/).

Ba, Ndiouga Moctar (dir.). 1994. *You, Africa: Youssou N'Dour and Super Etoile, the African Tour.* California Newsreel.

Borelli, Sergio (writer). 1966. *Il Festival di Dakar.*

Chevalier, Laurent (dir.). 1991. *Djembefola.* Interama.

Dagan, Esther Amrad (dir.). 1966/1987. *Dance in Africa: The First World Festival of Negro Arts.* Gallery Amrad.

Diawara, Manthia (dir.). 2003. *Conakry Kas.* Third World Newsreel.

Elderkin, Nabil (dir.). 2010. *Bouncing Cats.* Red Bull Media House.

Gaunt, Philip (dir.). 1977. *Festac 77: Festival de Lagos.* Nigerian National Broadcasting Commision/UNESCO.

Greaves Williams (dir.). 1967. *First World Festival of Negro Arts.* Motion Picture and Television Service of the United States Information Agency.

Klein, William (dir.). 1969. *Festival Panafrican d'Alger/Panafrican Festival of Algiers.* Arte France.

Penna, Hermano (dir.). 1977. *África, mundo novo.*

Sarma, Ramakantha (dir.). 1967. *International Zone: Africa Dances. Les Ballets Africains at the United Nations.* Contemporary Films/McGraw-Hill.

# CHAPTER 50

# Sports and Politics in Postcolonial Africa

*Hikabwa D. Chipande and Davies Banda*

As many African states were gaining political independence in the 1960s, one major problem most states faced was how to unite local people of diverse ethnic backgrounds and political interests into nations, and how to maintain the colonial borders of their new nations. Scholars have argued that some postcolonial African political leaders adopted sport as a form of 'neutral culture' that they could use to create a sense of nationhood, recognition, and Pan-African solidarity.[1] New African states played soccer matches against other independent African states, providing African leaders with occasions to display their newly imagined nations in front of thousands of their people, showcasing independence, nationhood, and unity.[2]

This chapter explores the interplay of the complex relationships between sports and politics in postcolonial Africa. It examines how sport was used to assert political independence, project positive images of newly independent African states, foster Pan-Africanism, and fight racial segregation. The chapter further explores how postcolonial African leaders attempted to use sport as a tool for controlling their citizens to achieve their political goals, and how ordinary people and fans resisted such attempts. Conversely, the local populace also used sport politically to express their discontent against their new

H.D. Chipande (✉)
Department of Historical and Archaeological Studies, University of Zambia, Lusaka, Zambia

D. Banda
Moray House School of Education, Institute of Sport, PE and Health Science, University of Edinburgh, St Leonard's Land, Edinburgh, UK

© The Author(s) 2018
M.S. Shanguhyia and T. Falola (eds.),
*The Palgrave Handbook of African Colonial and Postcolonial History*,
https://doi.org/10.1057/978-1-137-59426-6_50

indigenous governments. Therefore, the chapter discusses the salient role played by sport in confronting colonial legacies, forms of imperialism, and domination of sports governance structures.

## SPORTS AND INDEPENDENCE CELEBRATIONS

While agents of imperialism introduced modern sports in Africa as a source of leisure, scholars argue that sport was also used in the pursuit of broader imperial motives, such as 'civilizing', disciplining, and controlling Africans to realize and maintain the colonial order.[3] John Bale and Joe Sang postulate that the '... Europeanisation of African movement culture has been viewed by many observers as a form of social control—that is, behavior of individuals regulated by groups in dominant positions'.[4] Regardless of the motives behind the introduction of modern sports in Africa, recipients of this new culture such as athletes and fans quickly adapted sport to suit the cultural and political interests of the localities in which they were introduced.[5] Towards the end of the colonial era, Africans in Algeria, Congo Brazzaville, Eritrea, Egypt, Zanzibar, South Africa, Nigeria, and Zambia used sport as a means to reinterpret their colonial relationships, to challenge colonial oppression, and as an avenue for expressing their desires for political independence.[6] Sport was part of a range of different groups, associations, and organizations that played a crucial role in fighting colonial domination in different parts of the continent.[7]

As African countries were gaining independence in the 1960s, sports such as soccer became a big part of independence festivities. For instance, in the British Central African Federation, Malawi was the first country to gain independence from Britain and invited neighboring Tanzania and Zambia for a three-nations independence football tournament that was held in Zomba and Blantyre.[8] The final of the independence tournament was played on July 6, 1964, the day that was chosen as Malawi's Independence Day. Zambia spoiled Malawi's political-freedom celebrations by beating the hosts 5–0 in a thrilling match played at the Central Stadium in Blantyre.[9]

Sports stadia on the continent were common places for political festivities that included sporting activities, particularly soccer. It became part of a larger trend which saw many newly independent African nations build soccer stadiums in their capital cities as 'symbols of modernity and pride'.[10] Similarly, upon gaining political independence, Zambia invited Kenya, Uganda, and Ghana for a four nations *ufulu* (independence) football tournament. Zambia's ufulu celebrations started with the lowering of the Union Jack (British flag) and raising of the new Zambian flag at midnight on October 23,1964 at the newly constructed Independence Stadium in Lusaka.[11] The climax of the celebration was an electrifying ufulu football tournament final between Zambia and Ghana on October 24, 1964 in the Independence Stadium. The hosts scored the first two goals, and the Ghanaians, who were then African Cup of

Nations football champions, responded by silencing the 8000 Zambians in the stadium that included their first president Kenneth Kaunda by thrashing Zambia 3–4.[12]

Political-freedom football tournaments were also common in West African independence celebrations in the 1960s. Tongo invited Nigeria for a football contest to celebrate her independence in 1960. The match, which was played before a full capacity crowd in the Municipal Stadium in the capital Lomé, ended in a 1–1 draw.[13] Later, Nigeria also hosted Ghana in the Nkrumah Gold Cup played in the National Stadium during similar independence celebrations, where the hosts lost 3–0 to Ghana in the final. Other countries, such as Uganda and Kenya, also organized football competitions to celebrate their political freedom from European colonizers, making football an important part of independence festivities and Africa's postcolonial, urban popular culture.[14] Following independence, many African athletes were now eligible to represent their new countries in international sports contests such as the Olympic Games. For example, Northern Rhodesia marched through the opening ceremony of the Tokyo Games as a colony of Britain but later marched as Zambia, an independent state, at the closing ceremony of the same Games. Using the platform of major events, the newly created state chose not to miss the opportunity to proudly assert its political freedom to the audience of a major sporting event.[15]

## SPORT AND A POSITIVE IMAGE OF AFRICA

The performance of African athletes on the international scene can be traced as far back as the 1920s, when boxers such as Senegalese Louis Phal (popularly known as 'Battling Siki') won the world light-heavyweight title.[16] Later, Ghanaian boxer Roy Ankrah won the British Empire featherweight title in 1951.[17] Footballers such as Senegalese Raoul Diane and Moroccan Larbi Ben Barek were superstars in the French national team in the 1930s.[18] However, the majority of these sportspersons of African descent did not represent their countries of birth until after the 1960s, when most countries gained independence from European colonizers. Sixteen African states gained independence in 1960, leading to the naming of 1960 as 'the year of Africa'.[19]

As already mentioned, the independence of many African states in the 1960s triggered a swift increase in the number of Africans who represented their countries in international sports competitions such as the Olympic Games. Before the 1960s, only 11 African nations had been members of the International Olympic movement; the following decade, the number increased to 28, which also increased the number of African athletes participating in the Games.[20] Remarkably, African athletes performed very well in these international events, which resulted in global familiarity with the names of both the athletes and their countries of origin, which had recently acquired their new political freedom. For instance, Abebe Bikila, an Ethiopian athlete who was a member of the last Ethiopian emperor Haile Selassie's Imperial Guard, was among the first to put Ethiopia and postcolonial Africa on the sporting map by winning the Rome Marathon, running barefoot in 1960. Second to Bikila was another African, Rhadi Ben Abdesselam Randi of Morocco.[21] Ghanaian boxer Ike Quartey also won a silver medal at the 1960 Rome Olympics.[22] Interestingly, Bikila won the gold medal in Rome, the capital city of Italy, which had invaded Ethiopia a few decades earlier. Belachew Gebrewold argues that athletic performance became an important function in the realization of Ethiopian nationalism. Bikila's 'victory became not only a sporting event but also a political event, implicitly indicating that Africans were ready for the big time'.[23] These victories announced the emergence of Africa on the international scene.

Following the successful performance of Africans at the 1960 Rome Games, further sporting successes by Africans in track events followed at the 1964 Tokyo Games. Bikila went on to claim another gold medal, Mohammed Gammoudi of Tunisia a silver medal in the 10,000 m, and Wilson Kiprugut of Kenya a silver medal in the 800 m race. In 1968, at the Mexico City Games, 13 African athletes performed even better, winning a total of fifteen medals, five of those being golds. These victories marked the beginning of Africans' dominance in middle and long-distance events with athletes such as Abebe Bikila, Haile Gabresellasie, Miruts Yifter, Wilson Kiprugut, Kipchoge Keino, Filbert Bayi, Frank Fredericks, Maria Matola, Genzele Dibaba, Asbel Kiprop, and many others dominating world sports.[24] Beyond Olympic track and field events, African national football teams were attaining positive results too. For example, Ghana reached the quarterfinals of the Tokyo Games football competition in 1964; Nigeria drew with South American football powerhouse Brazil at the 1968 Mexico City Games; and Zambia defeated European football giants Italy 4–0 at the 1988 Soul Korea Olympics.[25] Nigeria defeated Argentina in the 1996 Olympics, and Cameroon beat Spain in the 2000 Olympic Games.[26]

Other major sporting events such as the football World Cup finals attracted the attention of African sports administrators, particularly highlighting the absence of African independent nations at the finals. The formation of the Confédération Africaine de Football (CAF) in 1957 provided a lobbying body to exert pressure on the Fédération Internationale de Football Association (FIFA) world football governing body to give the African continent slots for participating in the football World Cup finals. When the CAF threatened to boycott the 1966 World Cup finals, Africa was finally assured a slot in the world football competition in 1970 and was first represented by Morocco. At the 1974 West Germany World Cup finals, Zaire represented the continent, losing all three group stage matches. However, doubts regarding the quality of African football were challenged during the 1978 World Cup finals, where Tunisia defeated Mexico 3–1, and went on to register a remarkable goalless draw with the world champions West Germany after narrowly losing to

Poland. At the 1982 football World Cup finals in Spain, Africa's lobbying for more teams had paid off with one more slot awarded to the continent. Algeria and Cameroon went on to prove that postcolonial African football was making progress both on the continent and during international major sporting events. The two countries' performances at the 1982 football World Cup proved that African national football teams could proudly compete and gain good results against other teams at major events. Such sporting trajectories were also evident during major youth-football events, where African countries such as Nigeria, Ghana, Mali, and Egypt[27] continued to perform exceedingly well.

The successes of individual African athletes and national teams on the international scene not only proclaimed the arrival of Africans on the international sports scene but also implicitly meant the realization of African nationalism. Similar to the role sport played in African-American society after emancipation, postcolonial African sportspersons used sport as a vehicle for 'social mobility, self-definition and cultural expression'.[28] Sport offered a 'place where ideas of [colonial] order [could openly] be contested', proving that Africans can hold their own after generations of colonial racism and domination.[29] As the international media shared these successes of African athletes and national teams worldwide, it painted positive images of newly independent African states and the continent as a whole.[30] William Baker argues that these sports victories 'provided instant recognition for new African nations, serving as an informal, unofficial, but highly visible corollary to the transnational activities of official diplomats and formal negotiations'.[31] Sports, therefore, contributed towards projecting positive images of the African continent.

In the newly independent African nations, successful performances in international sports not only created a sense of triumph, but also of nationhood among numerous ethnic groups that formed the new nations. The victories of athletes and teams, particularly against former European colonizers, served as national symbols displaying the power of African states. For instance, when Ethiopia emerged as the best African country at the World Athletics Championship in 2003, emerging third overall behind the USA and Russia, the victorious athletes in Addis Ababa were welcomed with 'a famous Ethiopian song against the Italians' evoking the victory of Emperor Menelik II against the Italians at the Battle of Adwa in 1896.[32] In line with Pan-Africanism, the victories of African athletes on the global sporting stage were also seen as victories of the African continent as a whole.

## EMERGENCE OF PAN-AFRICANIST SPORTS BODIES

The peak of Africa's decolonization in the 1950s and 1960s saw an emergence of a number of continental sports bodies whose aims were to develop sports on the continent and to foster Pan-Africanist ideals among newly independent African states. By the 1960s, it was clear that football had become the most popular sport on the continent, as it was even spilling out of the major cities and towns to the countryside where herd-boys adopted it as their pastime activity.[33] Despite this popularity, FIFA, which was dominated by European and South American administrators, did not recognize this development of the game. This compelled African football leaders to seek a united and well-coordinated African football confederation that would promote the development of the game on the continent and help in making their voices heard in the governance of world football.[34]

The aforementioned lobbying resulted in the formation of CAF in Khartoum, Sudan in 1957 by representatives from four independent African states: Sudan, Egypt, Ethiopia, and South Africa.[35] Abdelaziz Abdallah Salem from Egypt, who was a member of the FIFA executive committee, became CAF's first president. Committee members included Yidnecatchew Tessema of Ethiopia, Abdel Halim Mohamed of Sudan, and a white South African, Fred Fell. CAF became the supreme body of football and a pioneer Pan-African sports institution on the continent.[36] Paul Darby argues that CAF gave 'a considerable weight to the use of the game as a tool for asserting national and pan-African identity ... [making it a] highly visible podium for mediating that identity throughout Africa and on a global basis'.[37]

The establishment of CAF in 1957 also witnessed the first African Cup of Nations football competition held in Khartoum, where only three of the four founding members competed. South Africa was excluded from participation after failing to feature a racially integrated team inclusive of local blacks as well as white South Africans. Instead, the South African team comprised only white footballers, reflecting an apartheid South Africa. Their exclusion from the African Cup of Nations tournament was indicative of the CAF's strong position against the racial segregation of an 'independent' African state. Like the intentions for the formation of CAF, the main purpose of organizing the African Cup of Nations was to advance the interests of the game on the continent. CAF and the African Cup of Nations both offered avenues for achieving Pan-Africanist objectives and became models for many African sports bodies and contests that followed.

In 1963, an athletics competition called the Games of Friendship was held in Dakar, Senegal, involving France and 24 independent African states, bringing together 2400 track-and-field athletes. The Games of Friendship laid a foundation for the emergence of a Pan-African sports event that came to be known as the All-African Games. Following the planning that was started during the 1963 Games of Friendship; the first All-Africa Games competition was held in Congo Brazzaville in 1965, in which 3000 contestants from thirty independent African states participated in various track and field events.[38] The successful staging of the All-Africa Games led to the formation in December 1966 of a Pan-Africanist sports institution, the Supreme Council for Sports in Africa (SCSA). The SCSA, with its headquarters in Yaoundé, Cameroon, became an intergovernmental supreme body responsible for promoting, developing, and coordinating all sports on the continent.[39] However, its leadership was composed of representatives from countries above or near the equator, with no representation from politically independent Southern African countries. These were: Andre Hombassa from Congo Brazzaville as SCSA president; Abraham Ordia from Nigeria as vice-president; Badora Sow from Mali as second vice-president; and Jean-Claude Gaga from Congo Brazzaville as the secretary-general.

The continent's sporting confederations shared similar ideological perspectives to those of African states and their Pan-Africanist goals. With political freedom also came the desire to attain economic freedom and break the shackles of imperialism, which many Pan-African leaders acknowledged as still existing within Africa's economic systems.[40] Therefore, establishing governing structures managed by Africans was an expression of the many freedoms from colonial rule. For example, French-speaking African states saw their economic and political connections with Europe, particularly France, as key to their economic development. Conversely, many former British colonies favored a Pan-Africanist approach; a kind of African socialism that encouraged unity and common African markets while avoiding what they perceived as the cunning and exploitative economic relationships with the capitalist West.[41] Despite these ideological differences, the emergence of Pan-Africanist sports bodies on the continent, such as CAF and SCSA, provided a platform for the selection of sports leaders who represented the interests of Africa in global sports. This development also emphasized the use of sport as a medium for asserting the identity of newly independent African states and played an important role in unifying and proclaiming the presence of Africa in global sports. The introduction of continental sports competitions such the African Cup of Nations in football and the All-Africa Games in track-and-field not only fostered Pan-Africanist thoughts but also helped in the development of formalized sports on the continent.

## THE FIGHT AGAINST RACIAL DISCRIMINATION

The Organization of African Unity (OAU), an association of independent African states, was established on May 25, 1963 in Addis Ababa, Ethiopia. The OAU as defender of the sovereignty of African states and eliminator of any forms of imperialism recognized the SCSA in 1967 as the official organization responsible for organizing sports on the continent. By so doing, the SCSA and OAU worked hand-in-hand to confront racial discriminations in African sports, particularly that which was prevalent in apartheid South Africa and in Southern Rhodesia (now Zimbabwe), a country where the decolonization process would not be accomplished until 1980.[42]

While South Africa had been practicing segregationist policies as far back as 1948, in 1956 the Minister of Interior Affairs Theophilus Ebenhaezer Dönges announced that within South Africa sport had to be played in line with the custom of 'separate development'.[43] Furthermore, the policy prohibited any forms of interracial sports competitions within South Africa and failed to recognize any non-white sports-governing body which did not have the support of white sports-governing bodies.[44] This racial segregation policy contributed to the failure by the separatist South African Football Association (FASA) to send a racially integrated team to the first aforementioned African Cup of Nations in Khartoum, Sudan in 1957. Subsequently, the expulsion of South Africa from CAF occurred in what became 'the first use of sport as a political tool in the fight against apartheid'.[45] This was indicative of CAF's and the African Cup of Nations' political stance as symbols of nationalism and Pan-Africanism.

Thereafter, CAF, SCSA, and other organizations, such as the non-racial South African Sports Association (SASA), formed by Dennis Brutus in 1958, kept on mounting pressure on FIFA to take similar action. In 1961, the FIFA Executive Committee suspended South Africa.[46] However, in the same year, a new FIFA president, Sir Stanley Rous, who was sympathetic to the South African apartheid government, reversed the decision by the FIFA Executive Committee and reinstated South Africa. Despite that, global campaigns for the expulsion of South Africa continued, leading to the 1964 FIFA Congress suspending South Africa again.[47]

Another heated political debate was between supporters of apartheid sports in South Africa and opponents of racial discrimination in sports. Recognizing the importance of the Olympic Games and the potential the Games had to exert external pressure on the apartheid system in South Africa, SASA formed the South African Non-Racial Olympic Committee in 1963.[48] This organization worked together with black Africans through the OAU, SCSA, the Communist bloc (led by the Soviet Union), and Caribbean nations in putting pressure on the IOC, resulting in the suspension of South Africa from the 1964 Tokyo Games. As white South African sports also had a lot of sympathizers within the IOC Executive Committee and Western countries, South Africa was readmitted into the Olympic movement in February 1968. African countries were disappointed by this development, and the OAU through the SCSA called for an international Olympic boycott of the 1968 Mexico City Games.[49] Within a short time, all the 32 countries affiliated with the SCSA confirmed their commitment to boycotting the Mexico Games if South Africa was invited to participate. The feelings of most African countries can be summed up in the views of the ruling Tanganyika African National Union (TANU) in Tanzania:

> As long as South Africa adheres to its principle of apartheid in sport, it cannot be allowed to take part in international tournaments … Because South Africa insists on categorizing some sportsmen as human athletes and others as sub-human, she should not be allowed to pollute the Olympic atmosphere … It must be hoped that other members will be persuaded to this line of thinking so

that the pressure against South Africa's obnoxious policy of apartheid may gain further momentum.[50]

The USSR, the Communist bloc, Arabic, and Caribbean countries joined the protest, giving the Olympic movement the strongest opposition they have ever met, forcing them to withdraw their invitation of South Africa.[51]

The white South Africans organized what they called South African games using sponsorship from Shell Oil and invited white teams from Europe and North America to participate. This was in order to appease their disappointed athletes who were excluded from the 1968 Mexico City Games. This shows that South Africa's inability to participate in the 1968 Olympic Games in Mexico City was putting pressure on the apartheid government and their sports administrators. Some African countries responded by threatening to boycott the Commonwealth Games of 1970 that were to be held in Scotland if any of the members of the Commonwealth attended the South African games. The SCSA also threatened that its members would boycott the 1972 Olympic Games in Munich if West Germany participated in the South African games. In the end, most countries declined South Africa's invitation, making the South African games a failure. This international pressure made the IOC finally resolve to expel South Africa from the Olympic movement in May 1970.[52]

In the 1972 Munich Olympic Games, the thorny issue was not with South Africa, but Rhodesia, where Ian Smith had proclaimed a Unilateral Declaration of Independence (UDI) of white minority rule in 1965. Rhodesia participated in the 1964 Tokyo Olympic Games under the British flag, despite being condemned by most countries for proclaiming UDI; Rhodesia was also invited to the 1972 Munich Games.[53] African countries were outraged. Upon realizing this pressure, the IOC tried to ensure that Rhodesia athletes participated in the games using British passports, and President of Tanzania Julius Nyerere argued that the suggestion was 'nonsense': 'We are not quarreling about passports but about the things which are going on in Rhodesia'.[54] This shows the strong anger that these issues evoked among African political leaders. African countries threatened to boycott the Munich Games; it was only after the IOC cancelled Rhodesia's invitation to the Games that African countries agreed to participate. Rhodesia was finally expelled from the Olympic movement in 1975.[55]

In June 1976, when black schoolchildren were being brutality killed by whites in the Soweto Uprising, tension was also mounting in the Olympic movement because of the All Blacks (the New Zealand rugby team) tour of South Africa. The OAU through the SCSA called for a boycott of the 1976 Montreal Olympic Games if New Zealand were allowed to attend.[56] The IOC tried to downplay the threats; this led to 30 African countries boycotting the 1976 Montreal Games, the largest Olympic boycott.[57] This sent a clear warning message to all sports bodies that African political leaders and the continent's sports governing bodies were serious about breaking sporting ties with apartheid South Africa.

The boycotts discussed above demonstrate how sport became an important tool for fighting racial segregation in South Africa and Rhodesia. Since events such as the Olympic Games attracted a lot of attention, the media publicity that the boycotts attracted made the Games a powerful weapon to fight colonialism and European racism. As others have observed, economic sanctions were going to affect the young African economies, hence resorting to sport as a tool for political negotiations.[58] Meanwhile, some politicians even went as far as using sport as a tool for controlling their own citizens to achieve their selfish political goals.

## Sport as a Tool for Political Propaganda

By the 1960s, when most African states were gaining independence, modern sport had already been appropriated as part of their urban popular culture.[59] Sports such as netball, volleyball, boxing, basketball, cricket (with football as the most popular of all) were played across the continent. Hundreds and thousands of teams emerged with millions of enthusiasts.[60] The popularity of sports attracted the attention of some political leaders who saw it as an opportunity to bolster their political ideologies and power.[61] Many postcolonial African states mainstreamed sports by establishing ministries and enacting pieces of legislation to try and bring sport under government control.[62]

Some African leaders went as far as taking a page out of the British colonizers' playbook by quickly identifying football's value as a tool for nation building and ideological propaganda. For instance, following Ghana's independence from Britain in 1957, first president Kwame Nkrumah ardently believed that football had the 'capacity to transcend ethnic, linguistic, regional, religious and generational barriers'.[63] In line with the colonialists and missionaries who used sport as a tool for social control, Nkrumah felt that the game had potential to help him in the creation of national cohesion, identity, and international visibility of the nation, his ruling Convention People's Party (CPP), and strengthening his power.[64] To achieve this goal, he appointed Ohene Djan in 1958 to reorganize the Ghanaian football league.

Nkrumah and Djan even formed a new club they called Real Republic in 1961, modeled after the Real Madrid FC of Spain to challenge the Ghanaian traditional archrivals Hearts of Oak FC and Asante Kotoko FC.[65] Nkrumah also assigned Djan to improve the international image of the Ghanaian national football team and made sure that he regularly hosted a dinner for the national team before international competitions and encouraged them to 'die for their nation'.[66] Nkrumah identified himself with talented national team players and used the national team as his symbol of success and political power. This explains why the Ghanaian national team was invited to play matches during independence celebrations for countries such as Nigeria,

Kenya, Uganda, and Zambia; they were seen to 'symbolize African freedom and the Pan-African unity' that Nkrumah was preaching.[67] He was not the only African political leader who saw an opportunity in sport to strengthen his power and popularity.

Julius Nyerere's government in Tanzania also attempted to control football. Following Tanzania's independence from Britain in 1961, President Nyerere's ruling Tanganyika African National Union (TANU) passed the Arusha Declaration in 1967, which asserted the country's African Socialism ideology. The party and government formed many organizations to have greater control over different sections of the population. In 1967, they passed the National Sports Council Act that established the National Sports Council and gave it powers to oversee all sports activities in Tanzania.[68] The party and government were determined to control sport, particularly football, and to use it as a tool for implementing their socialistic polices. They tried to bring the Football Association of Tanzania (FAT) under control by ensuring that 'All those who wished to become club officers in the Dar es Salaam region were required to be 'screened' in order, in the words of the Regional Commissioner, 'to bring about Party superiority in sport'.[69] Despite these efforts, the party and government failed to bring football under their control, partly because the people were resistant 'to the political objectives which football was to be used to attain'.[70] Ordinary citizens and sports fans usually managed to find ways of outmaneuvering party and government policies and laws in order for them to remain in control and enjoying their sports. Similarly, first president of Zambia Kenneth Kaunda's United National Independence Party (UNIP) attempted to control football and use it as a tool for propagating their political agendas. Following Zambia's independence in 1964, the UNIP government's popularity started waning as a result of its failure to fulfill independence promises. President Kaunda's government resorted to suppressing opposition political party leaders, leading to the declaration of a one-party state in 1972.[71] However, the successful performance of the Zambia national football team, particularly during the 1974 African Cup of Nations in Cairo, Egypt, saw Zambia emerge as runner-ups to Zaire, the winners of the 1974 African Nations Cup, resulting in a lot of attention from citizens.[72] This popularity of the game attracted political attention and control by state apparatus to propagate Kaunda's ideology of Zambia Humanism.[73] To achieve this goal, UNIP's Central Committee, which was the party's supreme policy-making body, created a Sub-Committee for Youth and Sport that was tasked with governing sport in the country.[74] The political system in Zambia, particularly the declaration of a one-party participatory system by Kaunda, led to interference in sports governance by UNIP officials.[75] For instance, the Sub-Committee for Youth and Sport tasked the Minister of Sport with dissolving the National Football League and the Football Association of Zambia in 1975 and appointing an interim committee, accusing them of underdeveloping the game by constant disagreements and bickering. The minister formed one football governing body, which was renamed Football Association of Zambia. Interestingly, when it was time to elect new leaders for this football governing body on December 28, 1975, only candidates who were approved by the UNIP Central Committee were allowed to contest the elections.[76] This shows how far President Kaunda's UNIP Government was determined to bring football in Zambia under its political control.

On the other hand, Kaunda was a former football player himself; he even inspired his cabinet ministers to form a football team.[77] The Zambia national team was even nicknamed after him as KK11 (Kenneth Kaunda Eleven), partly because of his enthusiasm for the game. Like his Ghanaian counterpart, Kaunda attended most national team matches and dined with the national team before international competitions. Kaunda significantly invested in the game, despite Zambia's severe economic decline from the 1970s to the 1990s.[78] However, the massive investment in the game did not stop football fans from criticizing his UNIP Government whenever the national team performed poorly. Citizens were also vigilant of how the game was being managed and usually protested and threatened to riot whenever they felt that the game was being mismanaged. While Kaunda's Government controlled the game, it also made efforts to appease the citizens, as seen in how they were quick to dismiss the incumbent national coach whenever the national team underachieved in order to portray their concern for the state of the game.[79]

In Cameroon in 1990, President Paul Biya's ruling Cameroon People's Democratic Movement (CPDM) (that dominated politics from 1960, when Cameroon gained independence) was experiencing tension, as citizens were demanding democracy and multipartyism. Biya's ruling CPDM attempted to take advantage of the Indomitable Lions' (Cameroon national football team) good performance in the 1990 World Cup in Italy, where they were eliminated by England in the quarterfinals of the competition.[80] Biya tried to use the Lions' successful performance in 1990 not only to promote national unity but also to divert citizens' attention from a highly charged political atmosphere.[81]

In the 1992 elections, Biya faced serious opposition for the first time from the Social Democratic Front (SDF), led by Ni John Fru Ndi. Biya's campaign team tried to paint a picture of him as a lion to associate him with the successful Indomitable Lions. Paul Nkwi and Bea Vidacs argue that this attempt to 'Co-opt the Lions' victory, which was also seen as the Cameroonian people's victory, was immediately turned back against the government by the people to become a term of derision against the government in general and against Biya in particular'.[82] Although Biya won this tightly contested election, citizens believed that Fru Ndi only lost because of fraud and labeled the event as 'The stolen victory', once again proving that the people are capable of verbally getting their own back'.[83]

These examples of African political leaders and their involvement in sport demonstrate postcolonial African leaders' attempts to use sport to achieve their selfish political goals. Despite some politicians being determined to control and use sport to achieve their goals, ordinary citizens were vigilant and prevented politicians from having total control of sport. Citizens always found a way to circumvent government authority and sometimes used the same sport to challenge government authorities. However, Africans were not the only political leaders in the world who attempted to use sport to bolster their political beliefs, popularity, and power. Several leaders in the world have attempted to use sport as a tool for political propaganda; the most famous were dictatorial regimes in Germany and Italy in interwar Europe. Adolf Hitler's Nazi regime hosted the famous 1936 Olympic Games in Berlin and Benito Mussolini's fascist regime organized the 1934 FIFA World Cup in Italy.[84]

Towards the 1990s, the falling economies in most African countries made it difficult for governments to fully support sport. For example, governments like that in Zambia, which had reverted to private ownership of state-owned corporations, saw the demise of corporate social responsibility programs providing community sport.[85] Banda highlights that the shrinking of local-government provision resulted in the loss of parks and recreational budgets that funded the community welfare sports and facility maintenance. The loss of community welfare provision created gaps in community sports provision, which later contributed to the emergence of the sport-for-development (SfD) sector.

## New Wine Skins: Sport-for-Development and the Peace Sector

In the 1980s and 1990s, a number of non-governmental organizations (NGOs) emerged in Africa, some of which focused on sports. Iain Lindsey and Davies Banda argue that neo-liberal ideology among Western governments and multinational agencies such as the World Bank supported the concept of NGOs in the 1980s and 1990s because there was a perception that '[n]ational governments in African countries were both failing and corrupt'.[86] Therefore, international NGOs were encouraged, following the belief that they stimulated democratic principles and were an effective means of making sure that aid was delivered to poor African communities.[87]

This period coincided with a severe economic meltdown that hit most African countries in the 1980s and 1990s, compelling them to engage the World Bank and the International Monetary Fund (IMF) for support. These multinational agencies urged African nations to implement austerity measures such as the Structural Adjustment Program (SAP) in exchange for the desperately needed loans to revive their national economies and keep their governments operative.[88] As each affected country struggled to share its meager resources beyond the core sectors of education, health, and agriculture, the 'rollback of government assistance in sport in the 1990s paved the way for nongovernmental organizations … and community-based organizations' to provide basic social services such as sport and education.[89] The collapse of the economies and the HIV/AIDS pandemic that overwhelmed many African countries resulted in poverty and in many children failing to have access to formal education. NGOs and other development agencies came in and used sports as a means to an end in their implementation of health, education, and development programs, for example[90]: the Mathare Youth Sports Association (MYSA), established in Nairobi Kenya in 1987; Sports Coaches Outreach (SCORE), established in Cape Town, South Africa in 1991; Sports in Action and Education Through Sport (EDUSPORT) Foundation in Zambia in the early 1990s.[91] Intercontinentally, there are hundreds of such organizations, often referred to as Sport for Development and Peace (SDP).[92] We prefer the acronym SfD to refer to the same sector.

Most SfD organizations obtained their funding to implement programs from Western national government and multinational agencies.[93] Therefore, there is a fear that these agencies impose their programs and values that make little sense to the recipient communities.[94] Simon Darnell and Lyndsay Hayhurst argue that there is a need for scholars to explore decolonization of SfD programs because the funding agencies seem to have taken up a role of political and economic stewardship and not solidarity with communities struggling for self-determination.[95] While sport offers a means of achieving particular development goals, it can easily be used as a tool for a politics of social control. 'Sport can be mobilized (and is implicit) within the politics of intranational colonization in which marginalized groups struggle for full representation and access to success within the social political economy.'[96]

Darnell and Hayhurst argue that critical examinations of SfD programs show that they have 'colonizing tendencies and tensions'.[97] Others argue that there are complex local-level experiences and interactions between donor agencies and recipient organizations that should not be simplified.[98] However, contrary to the political struggles and aspirations of Pan-Africanists, these new organizations as providers of community sport have handed the power back to foreign agendas. The governance of such SfD organizations is heavily influenced in agenda setting, decision making, and program implementation by those who financially support them. The postcolonial dream of fighting imperialism has established new forms of shackles on the freedom of local communities to shape their own destinies in accordance with local needs. Instead, foreign agendas are at times pursued due to the heavy resource dependence on Western donors.

While SfD organizations have made huge contributions in terms of developing sports structures in underprivileged African communities and developing young athletes at the grass-roots level, one cannot completely disregard the political influence from Western governments and multinational development agencies that bankrolled the projects.[99] Although there is a need to be aware that SfD is a complex enterprise, it is also important, as Darnell and Hayhurst have argued, not to completely discount the colonizing tendencies of the movement. Brian Stoddart points out in reference to the British empire that sport's 'Capacity to masquerade as an apolitical agency enhanced its ability to influence; because it appeared as one area of the social arena in which otherwise differing people might meet'.[100] As discussed in the introduction of this chapter, British sports were diffused to Africa as tools for social control.[101] Therefore, sport has continued to play a role in postcolonial African politics.

## CONCLUSION

This chapter has explored some of the complex relationships between sport and postcolonial politics in Africa from the 1960s to the 1990s. When African countries were gaining independence in the 1960s, sports such as football were the main highlights in some countries' independence festivities. Independence made many Africans eligible to represent their countries in international competitions. Victory in these competitions, particularly over Europeans who had colonized them for a long time, became not only sports events, but also political events implicitly demonstrating that Africans were capable of beating Europeans. These sports successes were important because they projected positive images of newly independent African nations. The popularity of sport was also harnessed to pursue Pan-Africanist ideals and to fight racial segregation in South Africa and Rhodesia.

Some postcolonial African leaders also saw the popularity of sport, particularly football, as an important avenue for propagating their political ideologies and consolidating political power. This made them determined to control sports, but they did not find it easy as ordinary people and sports fans were continuously circumventing the laws and sometimes successfully used sport to make their political leaders accountable. The late 1980s and early 1990s saw the emergence of SfD projects in Africa that were also not free from Western financiers' stewardship and political agendas. Sports and politics continue to be two sides of one coin in postcolonial Africa.

## NOTES

1. William J. Baker, "Political Games: The Meaning of International Sport for Independent Africa," in *Sport in Africa: Essays in Social History*, ed. William J. Baker and James A. Mangan (New York: Africana, 1987), 272; Peter Alegi, *African Soccerscapes: How a Continent Changed the World's Game* (Athens: Ohio University Press, 2010), 54; Craig Waite, "Ghana's Black Stars: A Fifty-Year Journey to the World Cup Quarterfinals," in *Africa's World Cup: Critical Reflections on Play, Patriotism, Spectatorship, and Space*, ed. P. Alegi and C. Bolsmann (Ann Arbor: University of Michigan Press, 2013), 100; and Hikabwa Decius Chipande, "Chipolopolo: A Political and Social History of Football (Soccer) in Zambia, 1940s–1994" (PhD diss., Michigan State University, 2015), 107.

2. Baker, "Political Games: The Meaning of International Sport for Independent Africa," 283; Alegi, *African Soccerscapes*, 54–55.

3. J.A. Mangan, *The Games Ethic and Imperialism: Aspects of the Diffusion of an Ideal* (New York: Viking, 1986), 191; Anthony Kirk-Green, "Imperial Administration and the Athletic Imperative: The Case of the District Officer in Africa," in *Sport in Africa: Essays in Social History*, ed. William J. Baker and James A. Mangan (New York: Africana, 1987), 81–110; John Bale and Joe Sang, *Kenyan Running: Movement Culture, Geography and Global Change* (London: Frank Cass, 1996), 97; and Alegi, *African Soccerscapes*, 1.

4. John Bale and Joe Sang, *Kenyan Running: Movement Culture, Geography and Global Change*, 76. For more on how colonial administrators set the tone on sport as a tool for social control in the British empire see the role of sport and physical education in Kirk-Green, "Imperial Administration and the Athletic Imperative: The Case of the District Officer in Africa," 81–113.

5. Brian Stoddart and Keith A. P Sandiford, *The Imperial Game: Cricket, Culture, and Society* (Manchester: Manchester University Press, 1998), VI.

6. Phyllis Martin, *Leisure and Society in Colonial Brazzaville* (Cambridge: Cambridge University Press, 1995), 100–25; Laura Fair, *Pastimes and Politics: Culture, Community, and Identity in Post-abolition Urban Zanzibar, 1890–1945* (Athens: Ohio University Press, 2001), 226–66; Peter Alegi, *Laduma!: Soccer, Politics, and Society in South Africa, from Its Origins to 2010*, 2nd ed. (Scottsville: University of KwaZulu-Natal Press, 2010), 15–135; Gary Armstrong and Richard Giulianotti, *Football in Africa: Conflict, Conciliation, and Community* (New York: Palgrave Macmillan, 2004), 18; Alegi, *African Soccerscapes*, 14–35; and Chipande, "Chipolopolo: A Political and Social History of Football (Soccer) in Zambia, 1940s–1994," 40–113.

7. Paul Darby, *Africa, Football and FIFA: Politics, Colonialism and Resistance* (London: Frank Cass, 2002), 26.

8. *Ufulu* is a term that is used to denote independence among the ba Chewa people of both Malawi and Zambia.

9. Chipande, "Chipolopolo: A Political and Social History of Football (Soccer) in Zambia, 1940s–1994," 110.

10. Alegi, *African Soccerscapes*, 55.

11. David Gordon, *Invisible Agents: Spirits in a Central African History* (Athens: Ohio University Press, 2012), 157.

12. Chipande, "Chipolopolo: A Political and Social History of Football (Soccer) in Zambia, 1940s–1994," 112.

13. Alegi, *African Soccerscapes: How a Continent Changed the World's Game*, 55.

14. Alegi, *African Soccerscapes*, 55.

15. Davies Banda, "Zambia: Government's Role in Colonial and Modern Times," *International Journal of Sport Policy*, 2 (2010): 242.

16. Baker, "Political Games: The Meaning of International Sport for Independent Africa," 279.

17. Emmanuel Akyeampong, "Bukom and Social History of Boxing in Accra: Warfare and Citizenship in Postcolonial Ga Soceity," *The International Journal of African Historical Studies*, 35 (2002): 47.

18. Alegi, *African Soccerscapes*, 55; Raffaele Poli, "Migrations and Trade of African Football Players: Historic, Geographical and Cultural Aspects," *Afrika Spectrum* 41 (2006): 395.
19. Baker, "Political Games: The Meaning of International Sport for Independent Africa," 275.
20. Tenga, "Globalization and Olympic Sport in Tanzania: A Developmental Approach," 81.
21. Belachew Gebrewold, "Ethiopian Nationalism: An Ideology to Transcend All Odds," *Africa Spectrum* 44, 1 (2009): 79–97; Tenga, "Globalization and Olympic Sport in Tanzania: A Developmental Approach," 81; and Baker, "Political Games: The Meaning of International Sport for Independent Africa," 275.
22. Akyeampong, "Bukom and Social History of Boxing in Accra: Warfare and Citizenship in Postcolonial Ga Soceity," 47.
23. Gebrewold, "Ethiopian Nationalism: an Ideology to Transcend All Odds," *Africa Spectrum*, 83.
24. Baker, "Political Games: The Meaning of International Sport for Independent Africa," 275; Tenga, "Globalization and Olympic Sport in Tanzania: A Developmental Approach," 81.
25. Alegi, *African Soccerscapes*, 76; Chipande, "Chipolopolo: A Political and Social History of Football (Soccer) in Zambia, 1940s–1994," 180.
26. Alegi, *African Soccerscapes*, 76.
27. Ibid., 77.
28. Akyeampong, "Bukom and Social History of Boxing in Accra: Warfare and Citizenship in Postcolonial Ga Soceity," 47.
29. Ibid., 46.
30. Tenga, "Globalization and Olympic Sport in Tanzania: A Developmental Approach," 82.
31. Baker, "Political Games: The Meaning of International Sport for Independent Africa," 277.
32. Gebrewold, "Ethiopian Nationalism: An Ideology to Transcend All Odds," *Africa Spectrum*, 83. Ethiopia under Emperor Menelik II defeated the Italians in 1896 at the Battle of Adwa after killing 14,000 Europeans, sending shock waves "throughout the foundations of 19th-century European racism," Teshale Tibebu, "The 'Anomaly' and 'Paradox' of Africa," *Journal of Black Studies* 26 (1996): 414–30.
33. Alegi, *African Soccerscapes*, 34.
34. Darby, *Africa, Football and FIFA: Politics, Colonialism and Resistance*, 33.
35. Darby, *Africa, Football and FIFA: Politics, Colonialism and Resistance*, 35; Alegi, *African Soccerscapes*, 64.
36. Alegi, *African Soccerscapes*, 65.
37. Darby, *Africa, Football and FIFA: Politics, Colonialism and Resistance*, 35.
38. Baker, "Political Games: The Meaning of International Sport for Independent Africa," 283.
39. Sendau Titus Tenga, "Globalization and Olympic Sport in Tanzania: A Developmental Approach" (PhD diss., Norwegian University of Sport and Physical Education, 2000), 54.

40. Banda, "Sport and the Multisectoral Approach to HIV/AIDS in Zambia," 49.
41. Tenga, "Globalization and Olympic Sport in Tanzania: A Developmental Approach," 53.
42. Baker, "Political Games: The Meaning of International Sport for Independent Africa," 285.
43. Alegi, *Laduma!* 113; Alegi, *African soccerscapes,* 67; and Darby, *Africa, Football and FIFA: Politics, Colonialism and Resistance,* 71.
44. Alegi, *Laduma!* 113.
45. Darby, *Africa, Football and FIFA: Politics, Colonialism and Resistance,* 72.
46. Alegi, *African Soccerscapes,* 74.
47. Ibid.
48. Tenga, "Globalization and Olympic Sport in Tanzania: A Developmental Approach," 84.
49. Ibid., 87.
50. Dean E. McHenry, Jr., "The Use of Sports in Policy Implementation: The Case of Tanzania," 237–56.
51. Baker, "Political Games: The Meaning of International Sport for Independent Africa," 286.
52. Ibid., 287.
53. Tenga, "Globalization and Olympic Sport in Tanzania: A Developmental Approach," 89.
54. Dean E. McHenry, Jr., "The Use of Sports in Policy Implementation: The Case of Tanzania," 246.
55. Baker, "Political Games: The Meaning of International Sport for Independent Africa," 288.
56. Dean E. McHenry, Jr., "The Use of Sports in Policy Implementation: The Case of Tanzania," 246.
57. See note 55 above.
58. McHenry, Jr., "The Use of Sports in Policy Implementation: The Case of Tanzania," 237–56.
59. Allen Guttmann, *Games and Empires: Modern Sports and Cultural Imperialism* (New York: Columbia University Press, 1994), 63.
60. See note 58 above.
61. Alegi, *African Soccerscapes,* 58–59.
62. Alegi, *African Soccerscapes,* 58–59; Chipande, "Chipolopolo: A Political and Social History of Football (Soccer) in Zambia, 1940s–1994," 114–40.
63. Alegi, *African Soccerscapes,* 58.
64. Craig Waite, "Ghana's Black Stars: A Fifty-Year Journey to the World Cup Quarterfinals," in *Africa's World Cup: Critical Reflections on Play, Patriotism, Spectatorship, and Space,* ed. P. Alegi and C. Bolsmann (Ann Arbor: University of Michigan Press, 2013), 100.
65. See note 63 above.
66. Craig Waite, "Ghana's Black Stars: A Fifty-Year Journey to the World Cup Quarterfinals," 101.
67. Ibid.
68. McHenry, "The Use of Sports in Policy Implementation: The Case of Tanzania," 241.
69. Ibid.

70. McHenry, "The Use of Sports in Policy Implementation: The Case of Tanzania," *The Journal of Modern African Studies* 18 (1980): 241.
71. Giacomo Macola, "Harry Mwaanga Nkumbula, UNIP and the roots of authoritarianism in nationalist Zambia," in *One Zambia Many Histories: Toward a History of Post-colonial Zambia* (Leiden: Brill, 2008), 20.
72. Sam Sikazwe, "Government Honors Our Soccer Heroes," *Times of Zambia*, May 8, 1974.
73. Zambian humanism was an ideology that President Kenneth Kaunda adopted as Zambian national ideology and philosophy after independence in 1964. Similar to Julius Nyerere's *Ujamaa* in Tanzania, Zambian Humanism was a form of African socialism with a combination of African traditional values and Christian values. The ideology put God and the human person at the centre, creating a strong connection between God and humans.
74. Davies Banda, "Zambia: Government's Role in Colonial and Modern Times," *International Journal of Sport Policy*, 2 (2010): 242.
75. Davies Banda, Zambia: Government's role in colonial and modern times.
76. Chipande, "Chipolopolo: A Political and Social History of Football (Soccer) in Zambia, 1940s–1994," 137.
77. "MP's team off to Dar," *Times of Zambia*, July 5, 1974.
78. Chipande, "Chipolopolo: A Political and Social History of Football (Soccer) in Zambia, 1940s–1994," 119.
79. Ibid.
80. Paul Nchoji Nkwi and Bea Vidacs, "Football: Politics and Power in Cameroon," in *Entering the Filed: New Perspectives on World Football*, ed. Gary Armstrong and Richard Giulianotti (New Yourk: Berg, 1997), 127.
81. Bea Vidacs, "Through the Prism of Sport: Why Should Africanists Study Sports?" *Africa Spectrum* (2006): 331–49.
82. Nkwi and Vidacs, "Football: Politics and Power in Cameroon," 130.
83. Ibid.
84. Allen Guttmann, "Sport, Politics and the Engaged Historian," *Journal of Contemporary History* 38 (2003): 363–75.
85. Banda, Zambia: Government's role in colonial and modern times; Banda, "Sport and the multisectoral approach to HIV/AIDS in Zambia," 198.
86. Iain Lindsey and Davies Banda, "Sport, non-government organizations and the fight against HIV/AIDS," *International Review for the Sociology of Sport* (2010), 4.
87. Lindsey and Banda, "Sport, Nongovernment Organizations and the Fight Against HIV/AIDS," 4.
88. Alegi, *African Soccerscapes*, 114.
89. Ibid., 124.
90. Banda, "Sport and the Multisectoral Approach to HIV/AIDS in Zambia," 212.
91. Fred Coalter, "Sport-in-Development: Accountability or Development?" in *Sport and International Development*, ed. Roger Levermore and Aaron Beacon (Basingstoke: Palgrave Macmillan, 2009), 58; Ruth Jeans, Jonathan Magee, Tess Kay and Davies Banda, "Sport for Development in Zambia: The New or Not so New Colonialism?" in *Localizing Global Sport for Development* (London: Bloomsbury Academic, 2014), 132.

92. Bruce Kidd, "A New Social Movement: Sport for Development and peace," *Sport in Society: Culture, Commerce, Media, Politics,* 11 (2008): 370–80.
93. Jeans, Magee, Kay and Banda, "Sport for Development in Zambia: The New or Not so New Colonialism?" 128.
94. Kidd, "A New Social Movement: Sport for Development and Peace," 377.
95. Simon C. Darnell and Lydsay M. C. Hayhurst, "Sport for decolonization: exploring a new praxis of sport for development," *Progress in Development Studies* 11 (2011): 183–96.
96. Darnell and Hayhurst, "Sport for Decolonization: Exploring a New Praxis of Sport for Development," 189.
97. Ibid., 190.
98. Jeans, Magee, Kay and Banda, "Sport for Development in Zambia: The New or not so New Colonialism?" 129.
99. See note 90 above.
100. Brian Stoddart, "Sport, Cultural Imperialism, and Colonial Response in the British Empire," *Comparative Studies in Society and History* (1988): 673.
101. Bale and Sang, *Kenyan Running: Movement Culture, Geography and Global Change,* 76.

## BIBLIOGRAPHY

Akyeampong, Emmanuel. "Bukom and Social History of Boxing in Accra: Warfare and Citizenship in Postcolonial Ga Society." *The International Journal of African Historical Studies* 35, no. 1 (2002): 39–60.

Alegi, Peter. *African Soccerscapes: How a Continent Changed the World's Game.* Athens: Ohio University Press, 2010.

———. *Laduma!: Soccer, Politics, and Society in South Africa, from Its Origins to 2010.* Scottsville: University of KwaZulu-Natal Press, 2010.

Alegi, Peter, and Chris Bolsmann. *Africa's World Cup: Critical Reflections on Play, Patriotism, Spectatorship, and Space.* Ann Arbor: University of Michigan Press, 2013.

Armstrong, Gary, and Richard Giulianotti, eds. *Entering the Filed: New Perspectives on World Football.* New York: Berg, 1997.

Armstrong, Gary, and Richard Giulianotti. *Football in Africa: Conflict, Conciliation, and Community.* New York: Palgrave Macmillan, 2004.

Baker, William, and James Mangan. *Sport in Africa: Essays in Social History.* New York: Africana Pub. Co., 1987.

Bale, John, and Joe Sang. *Kenyan Running: Movement Culture, Geography, and Global Change.* London and Portland, OR: F. Cass, 1996.

Banda, Davies. "Zambia: Government's Role in Colonial and Modern Times." *International Journal of Sport Policy* 2, no. 2 (2010): 237–52.

———. *Partnerships Involving Sports-for-Development NGOs and the Fight Against HIV/AIDS: Research in Lusaka, Zambia, 2007.* York: York St. John University, Faculty of Health and Life Sciences, 2008.

Chipande, Hikabwa. "Chipolopolo: A Political and Social History of Football (Soccer) in Zambia, 1940s–1994." PhD diss., Michigan State University, 2015.

Darby, Paul. *Africa, Football, and FIFA: Politics, Colonialism, and Resistance.* London: Cass, 2002.

Darnell, Simon C., and Lydsay M.C. Hayhurst. "Sport for Decolonization: Exploring a New Praxis of Sport for Development." *Progress in Development Studies* 11, no. 3 (2011): 183–96.

Fair, Laura. *Pastimes and Politics: Culture, Community, and Identity in Post-Abolition Urban Zanzibar, 1890–1945.* Athens: Ohio University Press, 2001.

Gebrewold, Belachew. "Ethiopian Nationalism: An Ideology to Transcend All Odds." *Africa Spectrum* 44, no. 1 (2009): 79–97.

Gordon, David. *Invisible Agents Spirits in a Central African History.* Athens: Ohio University Press, 2012.

Guttmann, Allen. *From Ritual to Record: The Nature of Modern Sports.* New York: Columbia University Press, 1978.

———. "Sport, Politics and the Engaged Historian." *Journal of Contemporary History* 38, no. 3 (2003): 365–75.

Kidd, Bruce. "A New Social Movement: Sport for Development and Peace." *Sport in Society: Culture, Commerce, Media, Politics* 11 (2008): 370–80.

Levermore, Roger and Aaron Beacon, eds. *Sport and International Development.* Basingstoke: Palgrave Macmillan, 2009.

Lindsey, Iain and Davies Banda. "Sport, Non-government Organizations and the Fight Against HIV/AIDS." *International Review for the Sociology of Sport* (2010).

Macola, Giacomo. *Liberal Nationalism in Central Africa: A Biography of Harry Mwaanga Nkumbula.* New York: Palgrave Macmillan, 2010.

Martin, Phyllis. *Leisure and Society in Colonial Brazzaville.* Cambridge: Cambridge University Press, 1995.

McHenry, Dean E. Jr., "The Use of Sports in Policy Implementation: The Case of Tanzania." *The Journal of Modern African Studies* 18, no. 2 (1980): 237–56.

Poli, Raffaele. "Migrations and Trade of African Football Players: Historic, Geographical and Cultural Aspects." *Afrika Spectrum* 41, no. 3 (2006): 393–414.

Stoddart, Brian. "Sport, Cultural Imperialism and Colonial Response in the British Empire." *Comparative Studies in Society and History: An International Quarterly* 30, no. 4 (1988): 649–73.

Stoddart, Brian, and Keith A.P. Sandiford. *The Imperial Game: Cricket, Culture, and Society.* Manchester: Manchester University Press, 1998.

Tibebu, Teshale. "Ethiopia: The 'Anomaly' and 'Paradox' of Africa." *Journal of Black Studies* 26, no. 4 (1996): 414–39.

Tenga, Titus. *Globalisation and Olympic Sport in Tanzania: A Developmental Approach.* Oslo: Norwegian University of Sport and Physical Education, 2000.

Vidacs, Bea. "Through the Prism of Sports: Why Should Africanists Study Sports?" *Africa Spectrum* 41, no. 3 (2006): 331–49.

# CHAPTER 51

# Media, Society, and the Postcolonial State

## Sharon Adetutu Omotoso

### CONCEPTUAL PROLOGUE

Setting out on this project, it is important to briefly consider interconnections of postcolonialism (a key concept in this chapter), postmodernism, and post-independence. Postmodernism is a late twentieth-century movement characterized by broad skepticism, subjectivism, and relativism; a general suspicion of reason; and an acute sensitivity to the role of ideology in asserting and maintaining political and economic power.[1] Postmodernism is a basic feature of the modern mind, a deep-seated inquiry of what the real is made of; it is a reaction to the assumed certainty of scientific or objective efforts to explain reality and it emphasizes difference as against uniformity. For postmodern thinkers, reality only comes into being through our interpretations of what the world means to us individually. Huyssen Andreas[2] avers that postmodernism began to compete with modernism in the late 1950s and gained ascendancy over it in the 1960s. Postmodernism holds that an explanation cannot be held valid for all groups, cultures, or races; rather, it focuses on (personalized) relative truth. It means among other things, intense reflections over the foundations of knowledge, epistemological issues, and disciplinary boundaries.[3]

Post-independence can be literally interpreted as the period after which a state has obtained flag independence from colonial powers. It is best understood as a process, rather than a goal. It involves the amalgamation of the knowledge and practices needed in order to bring about the right to decide

S.A. Omotoso (✉)
University of Ibadan, Ibadan, Nigeria

© The Author(s) 2018
M.S. Shanguhyia and T. Falola (eds.),
*The Palgrave Handbook of African Colonial and Postcolonial History*,
https://doi.org/10.1057/978-1-137-59426-6_51

without previous determinism. The mid and late twentieth century is identified as the beginning of the post-independence period in Africa.[4]

Postcolonialism is an intellectual direction that has existed since around the middle of the twentieth century. This direction was created as colonial countries became independent; its major aim is to provide explanations and implications of colonial thinking after independence by deconstructing the prejudiced explanations of sporadic incidences involved in the struggles (socio-political, economic, psychological, gendered) between the colonizer and the colonized. Postcolonialism is a theoretical resistance to the 'mystifying amnesia' of the colonial era[5]; it is meant to succeed colonialism and neo-colonialism and to engender a new era in which African societies will finally rid themselves of the lingering political, economic, and ideological trappings that have been imposed by, and are in the interests of, Western imperialism.[6] 'Postcolonial state' is a term popularly used in modern-day intellectual and political spheres to represent varying views regarding societies that have undergone colonial incursions of different kinds. To study postcolonial states is to critically examine the underlying cultural legacies of colonialism, the politics of knowledge creation, control, and distribution and its implications for the colonized as they struggle toward decolonization. It challenges the negative portrayals of the developing world,[7] particularly Africa, on the basis of implied comparisons with the West and other parts of the world. In Africa, postcolonialism is an ideological crusade which condemns the dehumanization of races, distortion of worldviews and the *self-other* mentality; it seeks to establish the uniqueness of the continent and its capability to contribute meaningfully to all spheres of global development.

To summarize, postmodernism, post-independence, and postcolonialism are contemporary intellectual movements developed to question lingering Western influences on Africa in particular and other developing states in general.[8] Connections drawn from the three concepts are as follows. First, the postmodern era is periodized within the late twentieth century; postcolonial states in Africa emerged into statehood during the mid and late twentieth century. In addition, studies and ideologies that have emerged as a result of activities within the postmodern and post-independence eras have brought about postcolonial issues which have lingered into the present. Second, the idea of difference as embraced in postmodernism is an essential content in studies of postcolonial states and their post-independence experiences. Third, discussions surrounding postmodernism, post-independence and postcolonialism include a wide range of issues (social, economic, political, religious, gendered and so on) which are both interdisciplinary and multidisciplinary. This explains why, in the hands of postcolonial writers like Edward Said, Homi Bhabha, Abdul Jan Mohamed, Gayatri Spivak (mostly academics in European or North American universities), postmodernism becomes postcolonialism, a discourse which attempts to heal the 'epistemic violence' of imperialism.[9] Seeing that they share the rejection of Western culture as any sort of cross-cultural paradigm,[10] timelines, ideologies, and objectives, it is evident that there are undeniable senses in which the postmodern connects with post-independence in discussions of postcolonialism. This chapter will therefore approach the discourse on postcolonial states from the communication perspective by critically dissecting issues revolving around African media.

Media are apparatuses that 'come in-between' or mediate between two or more parties. Although 'medium' is a generic term used to describe vehicles of conveyance, 'media' (plural) generally describes means of communication and information; it becomes 'mass media' when it is designed to reach a large and heterogeneous audience via various means including radio, television, Internet, and social media, among others.[11] Certain scholars discuss media using the term 'press', as presented in the classic work of Sierbert, Peterson, and Schramm[12] where the term is more often identified with newspapers, journals, and magazines. Over time, the term 'press' became restrictive of what the print media entails and media was thereafter described as 'mass media', referring to outfits or organizations, modern or traditional, which take up the task of creating and disseminating ideas and information, aimed at influencing or controlling an audience or the institutions that constitute legalized power and authority. For convenience, this chapter will adopt the term 'media' to encapsulate other terms used to describe groups and apparatuses tasked with mass information and communication.

Recognizing the Reithian trinity of information, education, and entertainment, Oso[13] stresses that 'the mass media have become the most important social institution in the construction and circulation of meaning in any modern society', and scholars agree that the media provide essential services to society.[14] This is:

> Based especially on the notion that the media and journalism are key purveyors of information that helps people to make sense of events beyond their sensory experience, information that influences people's daily lives and operations, and information that helps people make sense of their world, and negotiate meaning of events and their society.[15]

McQuail[16] points out that the media are channels of communication which essentially serve to connect the sender and receiver of information while constituting perceptions and definitions of social reality as well as normality for the purpose of a public, shared life. The media provide the platform for discussion and dialogues on economic, political, religious, and social issues (among others) between members of the society. In essence, media can be seen as the fortifier of societies. We may approach media operations in Africa from two perspectives: media in traditional society and media in contemporary society; in other words, indigenous media usage which has been transited into conventional media usage. Wilson[17] describes traditional systems of communication as a continuous process of information dissemination, entertainment, and education used in societies which have not been seriously dislocated by Western culture or any other external influence. Madzingira notes that:

> Among the inter-personal forms of communication through which traditional societies used or rural people still use to receive and give information are the family and neighbourhood, friends and acquaintances, markets and washing areas, and festival gatherings for the village. Institutional networks involve the church or religious networks, the administrative structure, the political party, the school, police and army, and such government service agents as agricultural extension, health, and family planning among others that may operate in the village.[18]

Wilson[19] aptly asserts that under the traditional system, media ownership lies with the society. This reiterates the importance of the media even in traditional societies. The indigenous media of communication vary among societies, and include: idiophones, membranophones, objectifics, color schemes, music, and so on.

The conventional media could be viewed from two perspectives based on usage; that is, colonial media and postcolonial media. Conventional media include radio, television, newspapers, and magazines; these were introduced during and towards the end of colonialism and have pervaded the communication landscape for decades until the advent of new media in the past two centuries. Responding to the claim that conventional media are superior to the traditional media, Wilson describes it as more rewarding, 'to view this traditional/modern communication dichotomy from the point of view of a series of concentric circles with the folk (or traditional) communication occupying the innermost circle and mass communication the outermost circle' Wilson (1987: 89). This replaces the limiting sense of distance with a sense of convergence and sharing of characteristics. Thus, Wilson advises that it is useful to see the system as traditional from the standpoint of an ongoing, long-standing, and 'modernized' (modified) practice. While appreciating the fact that certain traditional media systems have stood the test of time by defying all efforts by Western media to cannibalize them and perhaps supplant them, the implication for society in the recent past is that the traditional, conventional, and new media have had to coexist in Africa. For instance, while traditional media was and is widely trusted by the majority, community radio (such as *radio trottoir*) can be seen as an improved version of the traditional, while the social media are also beginning to gain acceptance and make waves among the new media. On this, Madzingira[20] avers that the media reflect the continuation of long-standing cultural traditions by combining technology-based change with a long history of cultural tradition, and it is precisely this encounter between the very newest and the very oldest that makes the audio-visual mass media a unique meeting point in the emerging information society.

The term 'society' has been mainly conceived from political and social perspectives, among others. We may describe society as an organized group of persons associated together for religious, benevolent, cultural, scientific, political, patriotic, and other purposes, a politically structured group with shared historical, cultural, or geographical traditions. The society is expected to engage in meaningful participation in processes around them, confronting whatever poses threats to them, ensuring general welfare, and scrutinizing the rules and regulations by which they are guided. These duties are beginning to resemble those guiding civil societies, which are held distinct from society in general and saddled with the tasks of interacting and influencing states, acting as intermediaries between society and states in order to counteract states' excesses.[21] This is due largely to new and recent trends in communication and information landscapes, leaving a thin line between societies in general and civil societies. Having observed the shifting social, psychological, technological, and economic posture of societies, in an earlier work I pointed out how models and theories such as minimal effect, agenda setting, and knowledge gap which used to be popular in media studies are becoming questionable because new media are posing unequalled challenges to them.[22] As against the vertical communication structure of the colonial era via conventional media (which ensured that the media primarily disseminated information on government programs and expectations, and the masses recognized media as a one-way tool of communication, best captured by the Yoruba perception and description of media as '*Asoro ma gbesi*', meaning 'one who speaks without waiting for a response'), Chaffee and Metzger[23] predicted that 'the key problem for agenda-setting theory will change from what issues the media tell people to think about to what issues people tell the media they want to think about'. Corroborating this, Windeck[24] affirms that the introduction of the Internet and mobile telecommunications in Africa at the beginning of the millennium has significantly altered communication structures, shifting them from a 'top-down approach' to a polycentric system, thus promoting citizens' position as equal partners in the communication structure. Thus, 'the traditionally passive role of receiving information and contributing little or nothing that is conferred on citizens, have changed dramatically with the advent of the new media ... This passive role has been replaced by an informed and active audience due largely to the introduction of new technology'.[25] Although society is becoming more enlightened, challenging both media and governance, we must inquire if there is sufficient enlightenment, and in the right direction, to enable society to do so for holistic development.

Without ignoring the fact that a discourse on media and society could be approached from several and equally valid standpoints, I shall endeavor to strictly maintain a connection of my arguments in each section with their implications for postcolonial states.

## African Media and the Philosophy of Communication

Media in Africa and African media are two closely related but different concepts; I describe media in Africa as all media organizations both local and foreign operating within Africa, while African media are media organizations based in Africa, owned by Africans, and operated to serve Africa.[26] This distinction has tremendous effects on African philosophy of communication, although I shall focus on the latter (African media) in this chapter. With a strong recognition of the heterogeneous nature of the African continent, as exemplified in the works of William Rugh on Arab media, Elizabeth Dadi on media in Ethiopia, and Wasserman and De Beer[27] on media in South Africa, among others, this work will employ the term 'African' not in a strict sense of singularity but as a general term which addresses the struggles for oneness in the midst of diversities. By asserting through careful examination of the nature of the media in Africa that activities in the state gave birth to them,[28] inferences have been drawn that the press (media) has been closely linked with the state and, as such, its role in state organization is fundamental.[29]

Scholars have identified the dynamism which has transformed knowledge into information, that is coded messages within a system of transmission and communication[30] which, in a sense, is an acknowledgement of the media and their epistemic roles, among other roles in societies. The recognition of the media's ability to inform, educate, and entertain spans time and space, as media have been prominent in shaping ideological, political, economic, and religious landscapes. Following Afolayan's[31] assertion that philosophy is a means of interrogating human relationships with their surroundings, together with the various fundamental issues and problems they throw up for them, we may infer that communication raises fundamental issues, as well as problems, within societies. These attributes qualify communication to undergo philosophical scrutiny, which is described as philosophy of communication. Philosophy of communication straddles two important disciplines (philosophy and communication) and has been studied from the perspectives of linguistics and communication itself. Although claimed to be a rather difficult area of study in definition and clarification, it is popularly held that communication underlies all disciplines.

What then is an African philosophy of communication? To begin with, we must note that African philosophy of communication is a sub-set of both philosophy of communication and African philosophy. Given this fact, African philosophy of communication may be defined as critical and systematic reflections, focusing on philosophical issues of pre-colonial, colonial, and postcolonial communication landscapes in Africa. African philosophy of communication is premised on Africa's concept of a society. By placing a premium on the identities, images, and characters of actors, it is armed with critical and analytic skills to decipher what is being communicated and how such communications could and/or should be interpreted. It is rooted in cultural values such as truth, empathy, self-worth, and human dignity, commonly cherished by Africans and ensuring that communication promotes the good of the society.[32] The foregoing presupposes that philosophies of communication held by African media require scrutiny. Pre-colonial philosophy of communication in Africa can be described as a philosophy of symbiotic reciprocity, captured in a Yoruba proverb which says, '*bu fun mi, ki n bu fun e ni opolo nke l'odo*', meaning: 'what frogs at the river continually say is: water me and I will water you in return'. This philosophy was developed due to, on one hand, the communitarian and interdependent nature of pre-colonial African societies and, on the other hand, the influences of traders, explorers, and missionaries, whose business relationships raised issues of language and were tackled with traditional modes of communications such as objectifics, signs, signals, and music, among others.[33] Wilson maintains that media in traditional systems functioned as part of the larger sociopolitical organization, reporting on and criticizing organs within the system, issuing directives from the legitimate, or in some cases titular, head, and providing education in the areas of the norms and mores of the society, stimulating the emotions and generally providing the light to innovations and helping their diffusion.[34]

African media in the colonial era were largely designed to serve the colonialists, at the expense of the society (their colonies). Communication in that era was built on the self–other philosophy, which bred complexes in order to achieve conformity with colonists' standards. In his discussion of media in Tanzania during the colonial era, Matumaini notes that 'apart from the missionaries' papers, the government used newspapers to defend their interests. The contents of the papers included weather forecast news, news from their home country with their European neighbors and local news from Tanganyika and Zanzibar'.[35] In Nigeria, among other media, broadcasting began with a radio repeater station established in Lagos as an outlet of the British Broadcasting Corporation, with the primary objective of transmitting colonialists' native programs to their colony.[36] Here also, media failed to serve the purpose of the masses. Similar cases of colonial governments setting up media to communicate among themselves and mobilize for followership are recorded in Uganda, Kenya, Ghana, and South Africa, among other African states.[37] Also, since not many were literate enough to read newspapers, the colonial press basically served urban elites.

Responding to the postcolonial situation of the media, the Yaounde Declaration[38] affirms that 'the current communication structure still conforms to the old colonial patterns and not to the needs and aspirations of the African people'. In line with this, Momoh maintains that the three traditional functions of the press are, again, a one-way traffic flowing from the direction of rulers and elites towards the ruled and the people.[39] For him, the press in postcolonial times informs, educates, and entertains to shield and protect the governors and elites in a process that mesmerizes the people and hold them spellbound. He avers that: 'the people need bread as they are hungry, but the mass media are standing by to inform the people that there is no bread, educate them on why there is no bread and how they can cope with hunger, and finally, to entertain them so they'll forget about hunger and bread'. Although Momoh[40] wrote at a period when African leadership was largely characterized by military rule, the situation has not improved much in democratic regimes. However, it is being challenged by the new media, which provide a public sphere for the masses to vent their worries. Sadly, the Internet availability that is expected to aid this movement remains a challenge.

Ideally, globalization should stimulate African media to be guided by philosophies of difference, utility, and analysis, where difference would portray the uniqueness of African media in their obligations to societies both within and outside the continent. In this scenario, utility would present their ingenuity as they explore the gains of technological innovations within the global village, and analysis or scrutiny would come to bear as they carefully evaluate and domesticate information and communication in an atmosphere of freedom as the fourth estate of the realm. However, currently, African media are guided by philosophies of dependence and ego.

On dependence, I have argued that 'the relationship between Africa and the West, implies that (Africa as) the "Other", also variously described as the "world's poorest nations", "the debtors", "the recipients" and "former colonies" are forced to a life that strives to be like the West, replicating what their masters represent, thus promoting Western consciousness as global consciousness'.[41] No thanks to hegemonic influences on African media, this 'dogma of inferiority which pervades the Continent and makes her people revere Western-oriented ideas, products and services among others, above her own is a third culture which must be squarely dealt with'.[42]

The ego-based African philosophy of communication showcases an ethics-based standpoint which manifests in multiple dimensions. First, it defeats the utility principle which operated in the pre-colonial era, as African media organizations struggle to transmit on cable, identifying global audiences as their major target as against their primary objective of serving their local, national, and/or continental audiences. Second, it fails in the promotion of states' cohesion, a duty which African media owe societies. By implication, African media are largely compliant with Western-based principles in the name of civilization and globalization. Considering how 'mediascapes in Africa bring afore, the disjunctures, the separateness and the uniqueness of challenges facing media organizations in various parts of Africa, there is a high tendency that States may vary in their ethical dispositions'.[43]

In view of the necessary connections between language and society (with the characteristic nature of being a culturally conventional tool of power[44]), a major linguistic problem in the African philosophy of communication is that of defining the extent to which meanings can be communicated across cultures without distortion.[45] Observing the operation modes of African media in postcolonial states, based on their strong reliance on non-indigenous language, Hallen surmises that:

once one recognizes the weakness of the empirical constraints placed upon the communication of meanings between two languages that may historically have no cause to share a single cognate in common, what exactly is the *objective* basis upon which we assign virtually literal accuracy to theoretical translation?[46]

The philosophy of communication currently held by African media is based more on a neo-colonial mindset constituted by relics of colonialism where information, entertainment, and enlightenment standards are set by the 'civilized' and 'developed', rather than the postmodern stance, which criticizes the status quo with the objective of arriving at more pragmatic grounds for African media performance. This in turn calls for a need 'to turn the prison of language to a house of conceptual enrichment' via 'conceptual decolonization',[47] a role which African media must play. Thus, an African philosophy of communication is central to understanding communicative actions in postmodern culture and has a major task of intellectually strategizing to decolonize concepts, ideologies, and communication itself, seeking to uproot anti-nationalist and neo-colonialist intellectualism for the fulfillment of existential necessities.

## African Media Policies in Postcolonial Times

Policies are vital, particularly in terms of long-term goals and objectives, although they may have operational implications of short-term significance. Tony Momoh clarifies that a media policy is embedded in communication policy of states.[48] Communication policies are a set of principles and norms established to guide the behavior of communication systems.[49] While communication policy involves the total mobilization of all structures of human interaction, information exchanges, and sharing of life experiences in a society, media policy includes all kinds of proposals and strategies used by governments, media corporations, international policy institutions, as well as organizations and individuals in the media sector. Despite marked differences among states, all media policies possess a set of elements such as goals and objectives, values, or criteria by which they are recognized and defined, content and communication services to which the policy applies, the different distribution services, and policy measures or means of implementation. Thus, a media policy is a coherent set of principles and norms established to provide guidelines to relate the principles and values of the societies to existing and prospective opportunities of communication in those societies.

Focusing primarily on media policies of African states in postcolonial times, trends have shown that in most parts of Africa media-policy formulations have not followed patterns and definitions of the kind of society hoped to be built. Consequently, Mailafiya claims that 'for the mass media in developing countries to play their proper roles in preserving the cultural identity of their nations and to curtail the threat from foreign media, they must be guided by well-articulated principles'.[50]

Matumaini[51] notes three main phases in the evolution of media policy in Africa.

The first was an emerging communication policy from 1920 to 1945, which was characterized by a transition from a period of virtually no official guidelines where anyone could establish a press outlet and say whatever they wanted. The period had a general policy of media freedom interfered with by the emergence of electronic media which gave rise to the worrisome need to define media ownership, control, and benefits to society. Media policies of this period were characteristically technology-driven rather than public-oriented.

The second period, from 1945 to 1990, was guided by the public-service media paradigm, dominated by socio-political issues, questioning the roles of the media and how media were used as a catalyst for the Second World War. The third period, the 1990s, was characterized by convergence and the interlinking of different forms of media, concentration of ownership, and increased toleration of monopolies.

A fourth phase[52] which has emerged since the end of the 1990s is the globalized and hegemonized one in which African media policies were designed for global markets as against local markets and in the interest of hegemonies in international politics. While not ignoring the necessity for states to factor in globalization in their activities, the local has been widely trampled, thereby rendering the objectives of media policies in Africa useless.

Across Africa, there are similar records of media policies void of public interest; for instance, in Tanzania, lack of clear-cut media policies, press censorship, ownership issues, lack of philosophy (whether to prioritize profit or social responsibility), regulation issues, and legal prescriptions have been presented as banes behind society-oriented media policies.[53] Opubor, Akingbulu, and Ojebode present the Nigerian situation, stating that 'broadcast media policies and their impact have not played out precisely in line with theoretical expectations as the authoritarian dispensations have brought greater diversification than civilian dispensations'.[54] Chibita[55] reports on the Ugandan situation, where militarized media policies, unethical operations due to political vacuums caused by power struggles, strong government reliance on the media for political opinions, complications of media policies within constitution of states and, in the more recent past, a consciousness of the competitive nature of political space and technological development, have resulted in a shift toward firmer media freedom. The Kenyan situation reflects a failure to involve the masses in decision-making processes, problems of legislative melee, problems of window dressing (where policies included in constitutions have not been put into effect), and policy vacuum among others.[56] A strong attachment to colonial heritages, cultural impoverishment, a marginalization of local languages, technological incompetence, and a lack of public accountability are presented as obstacles to people-centered media policies in Ghana.[57]

Indeed, 'many African national leaders are quick to say they favor liberating communication policies, however, in practice, the broader environment does not match the rhetoric'.[58] Zambia is faced with a number of challenges, including a lack of policy clarity, lip-service to media freedom, public interest, and the downplaying of the welfare of women, among others. Recognizing that even silence is itself a form of communication,[59] Chibita notes that 'sometimes not articulating a policy is in itself policy'.[60] Contrary to the needs of society, African media have followed one or more of these principles on various occasions and leadership dispensations. Accordingly, Berger,[61] like other scholars, clearly identifies major trends in media policy across different political dispensations, namely: a lack of consistent, clearly articulated and documented policy; a level of ambiguity in the wording of legislation; a tendency to retain outmoded colonial legislation and to recycle aspects of repealed laws; deliberate efforts to curtail editorial independence in the laws; inadequate provisions for converting the state broadcaster into a public broadcaster; and so on. These are clear indications of how legacies of colonialism continually determine media policies from the Horn to the Cape of Africa. The foregoing completely neglects what previous centuries have taught, according to Dunn and Boafo,[62] who posit that communications policy making should not be primarily driven by the inexorable roll-out of technological innovations, but should be needs-based and should emanate from conscious critical analyses of the strategic needs of people within their policy environments.

## SUMMARY AND CONCLUSION

This chapter began by establishing the similar features of three terms: 'post-independence', 'postmodern', and 'postcolonial', arguing that they are periods of contemporary intellectual movements developed to question lingering Western influences on Africa's social, political, economic, and ideological spheres, in particular in developing states. By clarifying that media in Africa differ from African media, the chapter diagnoses a lack of well-grounded philosophy of communication and a media-policy vacuum as the fundamental problems hindering African media from serving the society as they ought to. It was also argued in this work that a philosophy should underlie policies and as such African philosophy of communication (made up of basic components and shared values cherished by Africans) should be the basis for media policies in the continent. Arguments raised in each section of this work show clearly that conventional media across African regions have succeeded only in limited ways to bridge the communication gaps between the elites and the grassroots. This is due to difficulties faced in mobilizing for social and political development. Conversely, as a public sphere that is powered by individuals in societies, new and social media are beginning to bridge such gaps left by conventional media and have been impactful as regards the economic, political, and moral life of societies in postcolonial states, despite marked shortcomings (of new and social media) which will be subject to scrutiny in future researches. While McQuail raises uncertainties in the future because of the new social phenomenon in communication policy derived from advancement in technology and the impact of globalization,[63] Matumaini argues that the current general goal of communication policy is still the same as has emerged since the 1930s; that is, to serve the public interest.[64] Matumaini nonetheless argues that the content of the public interest has changed as economic welfare has become more important than political and socio-cultural welfare. A careful observation of the content of the public interest in the twenty-first century shows that it has witnessed dramatic transformations which not only include economic welfare, but also a combination of political and socio-cultural welfare, among others. The argument here is that all forms of welfare are interlinked as politics, which have been seen as a great determinant of social, cultural, and economic welfare; in the same vein, societies and cultures have also largely influenced politics and the economy. More than in the past, societies in this century are faced with security challenges which ultimately define directions in other sectors of their lives. Thus, African media must take into account these challenges if they are to carry out their duties to society as expected.

## NOTES

1. For a comprehensive introduction to postmodernism, see Brian Duignan, https://www.britannica.com/topic/postmodernism-philosophy, 2014.
2. Andreas Huyssen, *After the Great Divide. Modernism, Mass Culture and Post-modernism* (Bloomington: Indiana University Press, 1986), 188.
3. Peter Dahlgren, Theory, Boundaries and Political Communication, *European Journal of Communication* 19, no. 1 (2004): 8.
4. African Timeline, Part V, accessed on November 20, 2015, http://web.cocc.edu/cagatucci/classes/hum211.
5. Leela Ghandi, *Postcolonial Theory: A Critical Introduction* (New York: Columbia University Press, 1998).
6. Barry Hallen, *African Philosophy: The Analytic Approach* (Trenton, NJ: Africa World Press, Inc., 2006), 303.
7. For details on this, see Edward Said, *Orientalism* (London: Penguin, 1985 [1978]).
8. The following publications explicitly address the issues: Gayatri Spivak, *In Other Worlds: Essays in Cultural Politics* (New York: Methuen, 1987); Vumbi Y. Mudimbe, *The Invention of Africa: Gnosis, Philosophy and Order of Knowledge* (Bloomington: Indiana University Press, 1988); Kwame Appiah, *In My Father's House: Africa in the Philosophy of Culture* (Oxford: Oxford University Press, 1992); and Homi Bhabba, *The Location of Culture* (London and New York: Routledge, 1994).
9. Julia Emberly, *Thresholds of Difference: Feminist Critique, Native Women Writings, Post Colonial Theory* (Toronto: University of Toronto Press, 1993), 5.

10. Barry Hallen, *African Philosophy: The Analytic Approach* (Trenton, NJ: Africa World Press, Inc., 2006), 303.
11. See William Rugh, "Do National Political Systems Still Influence Arab Media?" *Arab Media and Society* (2007).
12. Fred S. Siebert, Theodore Peterson, and Wilbur Schramm, *Four Theories of the Press* (Urbana, IL: University of Illinois Press, 1963).
13. Lai Oso, "A Political Economy of Indigenous Language Press in Nigeria," in *Indigenous Language Media in Africa*, ed. Abiodun Salawu (Lagos: Center for Black and African Arts and Civilization, 2006), 175.
14. For further details on media and society see David Swanson and Dan Nimmo, *New Directions in Political Communication: A Resource Book* (Thousand Oaks: Sage, 1990); Paul D' Angelo and Matthew Lombard, "Power of the Press: The Effect of Press Frames in Political Campaign News on Media Perceptions," *Atlantic Journal of Communication* 16 (2008): 1–32; and Vian Bakir, *Torture, Intelligence and Surveillance in the War on Terror: Agenda-Building Struggles* (Farnham: Ashgate, 2013).
15. George Nyabuga, *Mediatising Politics and Democracy: Making Sense of the Role of the Media in Kenya* (Nairobi: Media Focus Foundation in Africa, 2012), 8.
16. Dennis McQuail, *Mass Communication Theory*, 5th ed. (Los Angeles: Sage, 2005), 81–83.
17. Des Wilson, Traditional Systems of Communication in Modern African Development: An Analytical Viewpoint, *Africa Media Review* 1, no. 2 (1987): 89.
18. Nyasha Madzingira, "Culture, Communication and Development in Africa," A paper prepared for the African Itinerant College for Culture and Development (African Institute for Economic Development and Planning, 2001).
19. Des Wilson, Traditional Systems of Communication in Modern African Development: An Analytical Viewpoint, *Africa Media Review* 1, no. 2 (1987): 90.
20. Nyasha Madzingira, "Culture, Communication and Development in Africa," 10.
21. See Francis K. Drah, "Civil Society Organizations and Grass Roots Participation in Ghana," in *Local Government in Ghana: Grassroots Participation in the 2002 Local Government Elections*, ed. N. Amponsah and A.K. Boafo (Legon: Department of Political Science, University of Ghana, 2003), 117–35.
22. See Sharon A. Omotoso, "Political Communication in Africa: Towards a Peace Policy," in *Communication, Peace and Conflict*, ed. Isaac Albert, Olusola Isola, and Oyewo Olusola (Institute of African Studies: University of Ibadan, 2015), 329–30.
23. Steven Chaffee and Miriam Metzger, The End of Mass Communication, *Mass Communications and Society* 4 (2001): 375.
24. Frank Windeck, *Political Communication in Sub-Saharan Africa and the Role of New Media* (Berlin: International Reports, 2010), 19.
25. Sharon A. Omotoso, "Deploying African Philosophy of Political Communication for Functional Leadership in Africa," *Journal on African Philosophy* 8 (2013): 56.
26. My definition of African media here is postcolonially oriented and does not follow literal descriptions of African media as the traditional means of communication.
27. These cited works are samples in recognition of the existence of multiplicity of media experiences in Africa. William Rugh, "Do National Political Systems

Still Influence Arab Media?" *Arab Media and Society* (2007); Elizabeth Dadi, "Radio Trottoir," *Political Communication*, ed. Addis Ababa, Retrieved from www.nai.uu.se/ecas-4/panels/141-156/.../Elizabeth-Demissie-Dadi.pdf on April 28, 2013; and Herman Wasserman and Arnold S. De Beer, "Conflicts of Interest? Debating the Media's Role in Post-apartheid South Africa," in *Mass Media and Political Communication in New Democracies*, ed. K. Voltmer (London: Routledge, 2006), 59–75.

28. Fred Omu, *Evolution of the Media in Nigeria* (London: Longman Ltd, 1978); Lai Oso, "A Political Economy of Indigenous Language Press in Nigeria," in *Indigenous Language Media in Africa*, ed. Abiodun Salawu (Lagos: Center for Black and African Arts and Civilization, 2006); and Ayo Olukotun, *Repressive State and Resurgent Media Under Nigeria's Military Dictatorship 1988–1998* (Uppsala, Sweden: NURIDIC African Institute and College Press, 2004).

29. Sharon A. Omotoso, "Political Communication in Africa: Towards a Peace Policy," in *Communication, Peace and Conflict*, ed. Isaac Albert, Olusola Isola, and Oyewo Olusola (Institute of African Studies, University of Ibadan, 2015), 130.

30. See Jean F. Lyotard, *The Postmodern Condition: A Report on Knowledge*, trans. Geoff Bennington and Brian Massumi (Minneapolis: University of Minnesota Press, 1984 [1979]).

31. Adeshina Afolayan, "The Language Question in African Philosophy," in *Core Issues in African Philosophy*, ed. Olusegun Oladipo (Ibadan: Hope Publications, 2006), 21.

32. For details on African Philosophy of Communication, see Sharon A. Omotoso, "Deploying African Philosophy of Political Communication for Functional Leadership in Africa," *Journal on African Philosophy* 8 (2013): 52–67.

33. See Dennis L. Wilcox, *Mass Media in Black Africa: Philosophy and Control* (New York: Praeger Publishers, 1975); Frank Ugboajah, "Oramedia," in *Mass Communication, Culture and Society in West Africa*, ed. F.O. Ugboajah (Oxford: Hans Zell-Saur, 1985); Ernest Mrutu, *Media and Society in Tanzania* (Dar es Salaam: Ecoprint, 2003); and Joseph Faniran, *Foundations of African Communication* (Ibadan: Spectrum Books, 2008).

34. Des Wilson, Traditional Systems of Communication in Modern African Development: An Analytical Viewpoint, *Africa Media Review* 1, no. 2 (1987): 99.

35. Joseph Matumaini, "Research on National Communication Policy in Africa and Tanzania," *African Communication Research* 3, no. 1 (2010): 11.

36. Atilade Atoyebi, "The Origin of Radio Nigeria," in *Radio Nigeria: Yesterday, Today and Tomorrow*, ed. T. Amadi and A. Atoyebi (Abuja: Northwood Resources Ltd, 2001).

37. See Fred Omu, *Evolution of the Media in Nigeria*; Zie Gariyo, *The Press and Democratic Struggles in Uganda, 1900–1962* (working paper no. 24, Kampala: Centre for Basic Research, 1992); and Jakayo P. Ocitti, *Press Politics and Public Policy in Uganda: The Role of Journalism in Democratization* (Queenston Ont: Edwin Mellen Press, 2005).

38. Yaounde Declaration, *Final Report. Intergovernmental Congress on Communication Policies in Africa* (Paris: UNESCO, 1980), 1.

39. Campbell Momoh, "Philosophical Elements of National Communication Policy," in *Philosophy and Dimensions of National Communication Policy*, ed.

Tony Nnaemeka, Egerton Uvieghara, and Didi Uyo (Lagos: Center for Black Arts and Civilization, 1989), 49–66, 57.

40. Ibid.

41. See Sharon A. Omotoso, "Black Consciousness in the Global Public Sphere: Questioning the Order of Otherness," in *Taking Stock: Nigerian Media and National Challenges*, ed. Oluyinka Esan (Ontario, Canada: Canada University Press, 2016), 117.

42. Ibid., 120.

43. Sharon A. Omotoso, "Mediascapes and the Ethics of States' Cohesion in Africa" (Paper presented at the 2015 Toyin Falola Conference, Pretoria, South Africa, July 2–5, 2015), 18.

44. Bohdan Szuchewycz, Power in Language: Verbal Communication and Social Influence, *Canadian Journal of Communication* 20, no. 2 (1995): 3.

45. Insightful on this are: Willard V. Quine, *Word and Object* (Cambridge, MA: M.I.T. Press, 1960); and Ngugi wa Thiong'o, *Decolonising the Mind: The Politics of Language in African Literature* (London: James Currey; Nairobi: Heinemann Kenya; Portsmouth, NH: Heinemann; Harare: Zimbabwe Publishing House, 1986).

46. Barry Hallen, "Indeterminacy, Ethnophilosophy, Linguistic Philosophy, African Philosophy," *Philosophy: Journal of Royal Institute of Philosophy* 70, no. 273 (1995): 379.

47. Olusegun Oladipo, "Challenges of African Philosophy in the Twenty-first Century," in *Core Issues in African Philosophy*, ed. Olusegun Oladipo (Ibadan: Hope Publications, 2006), 147.

48. Tony Momoh, "A Framework for National Communication Policy," in *Philosophy and Dimensions of National Communication Policy*, ed. Tony Nnaemeka, Egerton Uvieghara, and Didi Uyo (Lagos: Center for Black Arts and Civilization, 1989), 11.

49. UNESCO Intergovernmental Conference on Communication Policies in Africa: Final Report, 1980.

50. Madu Mailafiya, "Media Policies in Nigeria and Selected Third World Countries," in *Philosophy and Dimensions of National Communication Policy*, ed. Tony Nnaemeka, Egerton Uvieghara, and Didi Uyo (Lagos: Center for Black Arts and Civilization, 1989), 131.

51. Joseph Matumaini, "Research on National Communication Policy in Africa and Tanzania," *African Communication Research* 3, no. 1 (2010): 7–8.

52. This phase was not captured by Joseph Matumaini; it is my intervention in the light of observed recent trends.

53. Joseph Matumaini, "Research on National Communication Policy in Africa and Tanzania," *African Communication Research* 3, no. 1 (2010): 1–36.

54. Opubor, Alfred, Akin Akigbulu, and Ojebode Ayobami, "Broadcast Media Policy in Nigeria: Across Many Dispensations," *African Communication Research* 3, no. 1 (2010): 81.

55. Monica Chibita, "The Evolution of Media Policy in Uganda," *African Communication Research* 3, no. 1 (2010): 85–120.

56. Absalom Mutere, "Media Policy Making in Kenya," *African Communication Research* 3, no. 1 (2010): 121–44.

57. Osei K. Adow, "The Politics of Communication Policy Making in Ghana," *African Communication Research* 3, no. 1 (2010): 45–184.
58. Isaac Phiri, "Groping for a New National Communication Policy in Zambia," *African Communication Research* 3, no. 1 (2010): 194.
59. Sharon A. Omotoso, "Political Communication in Africa: Towards a Peace Policy," in *Communication, Peace and Conflict*, ed. Isaac Albert, Olusola Isola, and Oyewo Olusola (Institute of African Studies, University of Ibadan, 2015), 330.
60. Monica Chibita, "The Evolution of Media Policy in Uganda," 86.
61. Guy Berger, *Media Legislation in Africa. A Comparative Legal Survey* (Rhodes University: Published for UNESCO by the School of Journalism and Media Studies, Rhodes University, 2007).
62. Hopeton Dunn and Kwame Boafo, "Digital Domains and New Development Strategies: Revisiting ICT Policy-Making in the Global South," *African Communication Research* 3, no. 1 (2010): 39.
63. Dennis McQuail, *Mass Communication Theory*, 5th ed. (Los Angeles: Sage, 2005), 32.
64. Joseph Matumaini, "Research on National Communication Policy in Africa and Tanzania," *African Communication Research* 3, no. 1 (2010): 1–36.

## BIBLIOGRAPHY

Adeshina, Afolayan. "The Language Question in African Philosophy." In *Core Issues in African Philosophy*, edited by Olusegun Oladipo. Ibadan: Hope Publications, 2006.

Adow, Osei K. "The Politics of Communication Policy Making in Ghana." *African Communication Research* 3, no. 1 (2010): 45–184.

African Timeline, Part V, accessed on November 20, 2015. http://web.cocc.edu/cagatucci/classes/hum211.

Appiah, Kwame. *In My Father's House: Africa in the Philosophy of Culture*. Oxford: Oxford University Press, 1992.

Atoyebi, Atilade. "The Origin of Radio Nigeria." In *Radio Nigeria: Yesterday, Today and Tomorrow*, edited by T. Amadi and A. Atoyebi. Abuja: Northwood Resources Ltd, 2001.

Bakir, Vian. *Torture, Intelligence and Surveillance in the War on Terror: Agenda-Building Struggles*. Famham: Ashgate, 2013.

Berger, Guy. *Media Legislation in Africa. A Comparative Legal Survey*. School of Journalism and Media Studies, Rhodes University, 2007.

Bhabba, Homi. *The Location of Culture*. London and New York: Routledge, 1994.

Chaffee, Steven, and Miriam Metzger. "The End of Mass Communication." *Mass Communications and Society* 4 (2001): 365–79.

Chibita, Monica. "The Evolution of Media Policy in Uganda." *African Communication Research* 3, no. 1 (2010): 85–120.

Dadi, Elizabeth. "Radio Trottoir." *Political Communication*, edited by Addis Ababa. Retrieved from www.nai.uu.se/ecas-4/panels/141-156/.../Elizabeth-Demissie-Dadi.pdf on 28th April 2013.

Dahlgren, Peter. Theory, Boundaries and Political Communication. *European Journal of Communication* 19, no. 1 (2004): 7–18.

D' Angelo, Paul, and Matthew Lombard. "Power of the Press: The Effect of Press Frames in Political Campaign News on Media Perceptions." *Atlantic Journal of Communication* 16 (2008): 1–32.

Drah, Francis K. "Civil Society Organizations and Grass Roots Participation in Ghana." In *Local Government in Ghana: Grassroots Participation in the 2002 Local Government Elections*, edited by N. Amponsah and A.K. Boito (Legon: Department of Political Science, University of Ghana, 2003), 117–35.

Duignan, Brian. https://www.britannica.com/topic/postmodernism-philosophy, 2014.

Dunn, Hopeton, and Kwame Boafo. Digital Domains and New Development Strategies: Revisiting ICT Policy-Making in the Global South. *African Communication Research* 3, no. 1 (2010): 37–60.

Emberley, Julia. *Thresholds of Difference: Feminist Critique, Native Women Writings, Post Colonial Theory*. Toronto: University of Toronto Press, 1993.

Faniran, Joseph. *Foundations of African Communication*. Ibadan: Spectrum Books, 2008.

Gariyo, Zie. *The Press and Democratic Struggles in Uganda, 1900–1962*. Working Paper No. 24, Centre for Basic Research, Kampala, 1992.

Ghandi, Leela. *Postcolonial Theory: A Critical Introduction*. New York: Columbia University Press, 1998.

Habermas, Jurgen. "*The Philosophical Discourse of Modernity.*" Translated by Fredrick Lawrence. Cambridge: Cambridge University Press, 1987.

Hallen, Barry. "Indeterminacy, Ethnophilosophy, Linguistic Philosophy, African Philosophy." *Philosophy: Journal of Royal Institute of Philosophy* 70, no. 273 (1995): 379–93.

———. *African Philosophy: The Analytic Approach*. Trenton, NJ: Africa World Press, Inc., 2006.

Huyssen, Andreas. *After the Great Divide. Modernism, Mass Culture and Postmodernism*. Bloomington: Indiana University Press, 1986.

Lyotard, Jean F. *The Postmodern Condition: A Report on Knowledge*. Translated by Geoff Bennington and Brian Massumi. Minneapolis: University of Minnesota Press, 1984.

Madzingira, Nyasha. "*Culture, Communication and Development in Africa.*" A paper prepared for the African Itinerant College for Culture and Development, African Institute for Economic Development and Planning, Senegal, October 2001.

Mailafiya, Madu. "Media Policies in Nigeria and Selected Third World Countries." In *Philosophy and Dimensions of National Communication Policy*, edited by Tony Nnaemeka, Egerton Uviehara, and Didi Uyo, 131–39. Lagos: Center for Black Arts and Civilization, 1989.

Matumaini, Joseph. "Research on National Communication Policy in Africa and Tanzania." *African Communication Research* 3, no. 1 (2010): 1–36.

McQuail, Dennis. *Mass Communication Theory*, 5th ed. Los Angeles: Sage, 2005.

Momoh, Campbell. "Philosophical Elements of National Communication Policy." In *Philosophy and Dimensions of National Communication Policy*, edited by Tony Nnaemeka, Egerton Uviehara, and Didi Uyo, 49–66. Lagos: Center for Black Arts and Civilization, 1989.

Momoh, Tony. "A Framework for National Communication Policy." In *Philosophy and Dimensions of National Communication Policy*, edited by Tony Nnaemeka, Egerton

Uvieghara, and Didi Uyo, 10–23. Lagos: Center for Black Arts and Civilization, 1989.

Mrutu, Ernest. *Media and Society in Tanzania*. Dar es Salaam: Ecoprint, 2003.

Mudimbe, Vumbi Y. *The Invention of Africa: Gnosis, Philosophy and Order of Knowledge*. Bloomington: Indiana University Press, 1988.

Mutere, Absalom. "Media Policy Making in Kenya." *African Communication Research* 3, no. 1 (2010): 121–44.

Nyabuga, G. *Mediatising Politics and Democracy: Making Sense of the Role of the Media in Kenya*. Nairobi: Media Focus Foundation in Africa, 2012.

Ocitti, Jakayo P. *Press Politics and Public Policy in Uganda: The Role of Journalism in Democratization*. Queenston, Ontario: Edwin Mellen Press, 2005.

Oladipo, Olusegun. "Challenges of African Philosophy in the Twenty-first Century." In *Core Issues in African Philosophy*, edited by Olusegun Oladipo, 135–51. Ibadan: Hope Publications, 2006.

Olukotun, Ayo. *Repressive State and Resurgent Media Under Nigeria's Military Dictatorship 1988–1998*. Uppsala, Sweden: NURIDIC African Institute and College Press, 2004.

Omotoso, Sharon A. "Deploying African Philosophy of Political Communication for Functional Leadership in Africa." *Journal on African Philosophy* 8 (2013): 52–67.

———. "Political Communication in Africa: Towards a Peace Policy." In *Communication, Peace and Conflict*, edited by Isaac Albert, Olusola Isola, and Olusola Oyewo, 325–46. Institute of African Studies, University of Ibadan, 2015.

———. "Media Ethics, Press Ownership and State Failure." *Journal of Communication, Lead City University* 1, no. 1 (2015a): 126–38.

———. "Mediascapes and the Ethics of States' Cohesion in Africa." Paper presented at the 2015 Toyin Falola Conference, Pretoria, South Africa, July 2–5 (2015b).

———. "Black Consciousness in the Global Public Sphere: Questioning the Order of Otherness." In *Taking Stock: Nigerian Media and National Challenges*, edited by Oluyinka Esan, 111–23. Ontario, Canada: Canada University Press, 2016.

Omu, Fred. *Evolution of the Media in Nigeria*. London: Longman Ltd, 1978.

Opubor, Alfred, Akin Akigbulu, and Ojebode Ayobami. "Broadcast Media Policy in Nigeria: Across Many Dispensations." *African Communication Research* 3, no. 1 (2010): 61–84.

Oso, Lai. "A Political Economy of Indigenous Language Press in Nigeria." In *Indigenous Language Media in Africa*, edited by Abiodun Salawu. Lagos: Center for Black and African Arts and Civilization, 2006.

Phiri, Isaac. Groping for a New National Communication Policy in Zambia. *African Communication Research* 3, no. 1 (2010): 185–206.

Quine, Willard V. *Word and Object*. Cambridge, MA: M.I.T. Press, 1960.

Rugh, William. "Do National Political Systems Still Influence Arab Media?" *Arab Media and Society* 2, (2007).

Said, Edward. *Orientalism*. London: Penguin, 1985 edition.

Siebert, Fred S., Theodore Peterson, and Wilbur Schramm. *Four Theories of the Press*. Urbana, IL: University of Illinois Press, 1963.

Spivak, Gayatri. *In Other Worlds: Essays in Cultural Politics*. New York: Methuen, 1987.

Swanson, David, and Dan Nimmo. *New Directions in Political Communication: A Resource Book*. Thousand Oaks: Sage, 1990.

Szuchewycz, Bohdan. Power in Language: Verbal Communication and Social Influence. *Canadian Journal of Communication* 20, no. 2 (1995).

Thiong'o, Ngugi wa. *Decolonising the Mind: The Politics of Language in African Literature.* London: James Currey, 1986.

Ugboajah, Frank. "Oramedia." In *Mass Communication, Culture and Society in West Africa,* edited by F.O. Ugboajah. Oxford: Hans Zell-Saur, 1985.

UNESCO. Intergovernmental Conference on Communication Policies in Africa: Final Report, 1980.

Van Cuilenburg, J., and D. McQuail. "Media Policy Paradigm Shifts Towards a New Communications Policy Paradigm." *European Journal of Communication* 1 (2003): 181–207.

Wasserman, Herman, and Arnold S. De Beer. "Conflicts of Interest? Debating the Media's Role in Post-apartheid South Africa." In *Mass Media and Political Communication in New Democracies,* edited by K. Voltmer, 59–75. London: Routledge, 2006.

Wilcox, Dennis L. *Mass Media in Black Africa: Philosophy and Control.* New York: Praeger Publishers, 1975.

Wilson, Des. Traditional Systems of Communication in Modern African Development: An Analytical Viewpoint. *Africa Media Review* 1, no. 2 (1987): 87–104.

Windeck, Frank. *"Political Communication in Sub-Saharan Africa and the Role of New Media."* Berlin: International Reports, 2010.

Yaounde Declaration. *Final Report. Intergovernmental Congress on Communication Policies in Africa.* Paris: UNESCO, 1980.

# CHAPTER 52

# Between Diaspora and Homeland: The Study of Africa and the African Diaspora in the USA

## Michael O. West

Diaspora studies is in vogue. Perusal of the literature on diasporas over the past quarter century reveals a pattern: diaspora studies is not an equal-opportunity investigator. Some diaspora communities have received more scholarly attention than others. The better studied ones include the Armenian, Chinese, Greek, South Asian (mainly Indian), and Jewish diasporas.[1] The African diaspora too has been a major beneficiary of the emerging intellectual trend.[2]

The renaissance in diaspora studies (and it is just that, a rebirth, not a birth) is not just a function of intellectual abstraction.[3] Diaspora studies, rather, has also been driven by events outside the academy, notably the affairs of state. The end of the Cold War, which is to say the defeat of the USSR by the United States, albeit without a military showdown, was an indispensable precondition for the diaspora studies renaissance. In this, as in other matters, the rising of the one was accompanied by, and indeed predicated on, the falling of another. To be precise, the rise of diaspora studies coincided with the decline of area studies. These two (area studies and diaspora studies) are veritable bookends of the Cold War,[4] which, one South Asian writer has astutely noted, was 'cold for only the rich in the privileged places of the planet'.[5]

Area studies emerged hard on the heels of the Second World War, in the context of both the Cold War and the decolonization of empires, notably in Asia and Africa.[6] It followed, willy-nilly, that area studies was based in the

M.O. West (✉)
Department of Sociolog, Binghamton University,
State University of New York, Binghamton, NY, USA

© The Author(s) 2018
M.S. Shanguhyia and T. Falola (eds.),
*The Palgrave Handbook of African Colonial and Postcolonial History*,
https://doi.org/10.1057/978-1-137-59426-6_52

USA, rather than in the old imperial centers of Europe.[7] In and out of the US state apparatus, the Cold War and decolonization highlighted the paucity of knowledge about the non-Western world. This intellectual deficit was further highlighted by the rise of the Third World, so conspicuously announced by the Asian-African Conference of 1955, better known as the Bandung Conference, which the USA opposed as an anti-Western conclave.[8] Two years later, in 1957, Ghana became independent.[9] The Ghanaian example proved to be politically contagious, and within a few years colonial rule had formally ended in the greater part (although not all) of the continent.[10] Against this backdrop, it is hardly accidental that the African Studies Association, the leading professional body of area-studies scholars specializing in African affairs in the USA, was also founded in 1957.[11] Indeed, 1957 was a red-banner year for area studies, which was a partnership between the state (the US state), foundations and the academy, politically, financially, and intellectually. Spectacularly, the year 1957 also marked the launching, by the USSR, of Sputnik, the world's first artificial satellite. The response to Sputnik, especially, was immediate in the USA, with equally immediate benefits for area studies.[12] Among other things, Congress passed the National Defense Education Act of 1958, which greatly increased state subsidies to area studies under the Title VI program.

Meanwhile, area studies specialists in the academy had decisions to make. Those decisions included, crucially, the relationship between area studies and the disciplines. Bluntly stated, it came down to a choice between autonomy and appendage. Would area studies become an autonomous academic unit in its own right, akin to a department? Or, would area studies become an appendage, more or less a fully owned subsidiary of the disciplines? The decision was not preordained. The tale of the post-Enlightenment Western academy is a tale of fragmentation in the organization of knowledge. It is a story of philosophy seceding from religion, of the natural sciences disaffiliating from philosophy, of the social sciences taking leave of the natural sciences, and of the emergence of the humanities. These divisions, in turn, begat the disciplines: biology, sociology, history, and so forth.[13] In fine, the academic past suggested the possibility of autonomy for area studies, if autonomy from the disciplines was what the founders of area studies desired. But it was not. In the end, the area studies founders opted for appendage over autonomy. In so doing, they reaffirmed the hegemony of the disciplines within the academy.[14]

Within area studies, the Africa section stood out on several counts.[15] One is that African area studies (or African studies, for short) did not exactly pioneer the study of Africa in the USA. Long before the advent of African studies, the study of Africa had gained some traction in the USA, but under Jim Crow or apartheid conditions. The US pioneers of the study of Africa were largely black, and they were based largely in the historically black universities, or else were independent scholars without academic affiliations. These predominantly black pioneers were also largely excluded from the new, Cold War-inspired field of African studies, which was centered largely in historically white universities.[16]

Significant, too, were the epistemic differences between the black pioneers and the African studies specialists, dubbed 'Africanists', a term the black pioneers never used. In effect, the pioneers practiced what is now called African diaspora studies. Theirs was a transcontinental undertaking that linked the study of peoples of African descent outside of Africa to the study of the African continent. By contrast, the Africanists took as their assignment the African continent, and more particularly Sub-Saharan Africa. Peoples of African descent outside of Africa figured only marginally, when they figured at all, in the new Africanist scholarship. The same was largely true of Africa north of the Sahara, which the black pioneers had claimed as African patrimony, especially ancient Egypt.[17] Conversely, the Africanist paradigm (if not all Africanist scholars) conceded North Africa to the Orientalists, members of an older academic guild that served as something of a model for the Africanists.[18]

The epistemic exclusion of the African diaspora from African studies was rather curious, given the intellectual genealogy of some of the Africanist founders. Consider, for example, Melville J. Herskovits. A white anthropologist, Herskovits became, in 1957, the founding president of the African Studies Association (ASA), which, for all its waxing and waning, is still the foremost professional body of Africanists in the USA. Formerly based at historically black Howard University, Herskovits was a leading scholar of the African diaspora.[19] His 1941 publication, *The Myth of the Negro Past*[20] (originally written as one of several monographs for *An American Dilemma*, Gunnar Myrdal's summative wartime work on the black condition in the USA[21]) remains an iconic text of African diaspora studies.[22]

Seen in this light, another scenario was possible. Indeed, the reality of Herskovits's own past was suggestive of such an alternative scenario. In this imaginary world of US African studies, the ASA would not have been formed. Similarly, the journals that emerged alongside the association (like the *African Studies Review* and the *International Journal of African Historical Studies*) would not have been created. In short, the postwar interest in Africa would not have resulted in something new. Rather, it would have resulted in a revitalization of something old. The outcome would have been a new lease on life for a black-created body, the Association for the Study of Negro Life and History, which had been formed back in 1915, more than four decades before the ASA.[23] Likewise, the *Journal of Negro History*, the house organ of the Association for the Study of Negro Life and History, would have become the outlet of choice for the postwar renaissance in the study of Africa. But this alternative scenario was not to be. Instead of continuity, there was discontinuity. The resulting rupture epistemically separated the study of continental Africa from the study of peoples of African descent outside of Africa, the study of the African homeland from the study of the African diaspora.

Into this broken household ethnic studies was born, a decade after the consolidation of African studies and area studies more broadly. Ethnic studies amounted to an indictment of the academy in general and area studies in particular. Ethnic studies moved in sync with the Revolution of 1968, that catch-all moniker for the global revolts, insurgencies, and antinomian tendencies so manifest in and around the year 1968. It was a year of momentous marches, 1968, including on campus. Figuratively, and literally too, black studies marched at the head of ethnic studies, helping to make straight the way for such academic coadjutors as Latino(a), women's, gender, and sexuality studies. Student-led, insurgent, irreverent, black studies embodied everything that African studies, still striving for academic respect under the yoke of disciplines, was not.[24] Invoking that dreaded epithet of the Revolution of 1968, the black studies militants announced that African studies was not relevant. (Everything, and everyone, was judged by their relevance; relevance to the anticipated revolution.) For the most part, the African studies specialists responded to the black studies challenge with scorn. The Africanists looked askance at the non-degreed autodidacts who, academic lore had it, were swarming into black studies with the avowed aim of ending the 'cultural genocide' against African peoples.[25] Overlooked amid the sophistry were the very accomplished scholars, most of them black, who were attracted to black studies.[26] The result was alienation between African studies and black studies. Rare though the occasions were, however, the African studies and black studies twain did meet.

Predictably, almost inevitably, in the fateful year of 1968 a black studies caucus emerged within the ASA. (Black caucuses were also formed in this period in most of the professional associations centered on the social sciences and humanities.) Throwing down the gauntlet to the ASA, the black studies caucus demanded (what else?) a relevant African studies. A relevant African studies meant two things, one intellectual and the other political. Intellectually, a relevant African studies meant putting the diaspora back into the study of Africa, which is to say repudiating a key pillar of the Africanist paradigm. Politically, the black caucus argued, the ASA could make itself relevant by supporting African liberation, most notably the armed struggles then being waged against white-settler colonialism in Southern Africa (in South Africa, Zimbabwe, and Namibia) and against Portuguese colonialism (in Guinea-Bissau, Angola, and Mozambique). To top it off, the black caucus also called for a racial redistribution of power and resources, which would have meant more positions and research funds for black scholars, within the ASA as well as in the individual African studies centers in the universities.[27]

The Africanists, most of whom were white, rejected the demands of the black caucus, taking refuge behind the veil of scholarly objectivity and dispassionate research. The rejection meant that the Africanist center, or the ASA, would barely hold. Indeed, it almost fell apart, to paraphrase Chinua Achebe, author of the novel *Things Fall Apart*, the title of which drew on a line by the poet W.B. Yeats.[28] (Achebe's subsequent career in the US academy was made possible by the black studies and African studies phenomena, hard on the heels of his participation in the failed attempt to carve out an independent nation-state, Biafra, from Nigeria.[29]) Incensed by the rebuff, a large part of the black caucus walked out of the ASA and formed a rival body, the African Heritage Studies Association.[30] It is noteworthy that, instead of joining forces with an established formation, namely the Association for the Study of Afro-American Life and History (as the Association for the Study of Negro Life and History was now called), the black caucus followed the ASA in staking out an autonomous existence. The black studies founders would similarly shun the Association for the Study of Afro-American Life and History, now thrice spurned, and form a separate professional body, the National Council of Black Studies. Thus were African studies and black studies solidified for a generation, separately, and indeed unequally too. Until, that is, the end of the Cold War, which had served as the glue to the area studies coalition of state, foundation, and academy.

In the new world order, it seemed that area studies, rather like the Soviet Union, was also coming to an end, its raison d'être now in question, its funding equally questionable. The US state, as befitting its increasing neo-liberal orientation, was retreating from area studies, with foundation and academic officials showing corresponding signs of weariness, epistemic and fiduciary.[31] Entered diaspora studies. The new world order, with its emphasis on globalization (which is to say the expansion of the capitalist mode of production and exchange into formerly restricted territories) was more receptive to diaspora studies than area studies had been. These, then, were among the conditions that gave rise to the renaissance in diaspora studies.

To a large extent, the renaissance is a function of the rediscovery of diasporas by area studies, in the new post-Cold War environment. That certainly seems to be the case with African diaspora studies. Not for nothing did so many in the forefront of African diaspora studies come out of African studies, as evidenced, for instance, in the founding of the Association for the Study of the Worldwide African Diaspora (ASWAD). In opting for an independent and separate existence, ASWAD too followed a well-trodden path, once again bypassing a potential amalgamation with the Association of the Study of African American Life and History, the latest nomenclature for the scholarly body founded in 1915.

Meanwhile, events outside the academy seemed to offer a flicker of hope to a declining area studies. The war on terror, launched in the wake of the 2001 attacks with hijacked planes on US civilian and military facilities, created new demands for specialized linguistic and cultural knowledge of selected world areas, with a focus on those with large Muslim populations. The resulting reopening of the monetary spigot was instrumental in helping area studies to regain some of its former balance. Even this unexpected bonus, however, was highly contested. Some area studies scholars decried the fact that much of the new money emanated from the military and intelligence branches of the government, instead of the Department of Education, previously a key disburser of government funding for area studies. Yet for all the florid rhetoric, including talk about a clash of civilizations,[32] Al Qaeda is no Soviet Union. The same is true of the Islamic State, or ISIS, which at the time of writing has overtaken Al Qaeda as a focus of US (and more broadly Western) political, military, and intellectual wrath. In sum, the windfall for area studies from the war on terror is unlikely to last. Projecting forward, the general trend likely will be one of diaspora studies gaining at the expense of area studies.

Ethnic studies, which necessarily is about the study of diasporas, even if only within a national framework, never shared area studies' epistemic aversion to diaspora studies. Left to be determined is the nature of the relationship between these three (area studies, ethnic studies, and diaspora studies) and whether, or in what form, each will survive.

So far as the African diaspora is concerned, the question inevitably arises: Which one? It is a very pertinent question because, in truth, there is not one but multiple African diasporas. Among spatially dispersed communities, the African diaspora is among the most disaggregated and diverse. Historically, there are two great branches of the African diaspora. One in the East and the other in the West; East and West, that is, of the African continent. The eastern branch is in Asia and the western one in the Americas and, to a lesser extent, Europe. The African diaspora in the East is much older than the one in the West. Both branches are further sub-divided along various national, regional, linguistic, cultural, and religious lines. The study of this very diverse African diaspora is also very uneven, with the western branch receiving far more scholarly attention than its eastern counterpart. To be sure, a number of scholars, over many years, have labored in the vineyard that is the study of the eastern African diaspora.[33] However, the ranks of such scholars are rather thin. The obstacles are numerous, among them a dearth of competence in various Asian languages.

In recent decades, the western African diaspora has become even more complex with significant migrations from Africa to Western Europe and North America. Today, for example, visitors to certain parts of Houston, Texas may be forgiven for mistaking it for a Nigerian city, say Lagos, or Enugu. Just in the last decade, or so, large numbers of Zimbabweans have migrated to Britain in the wake of the implosion of their country's economy.[34] In France, African migrants and their scions, from south and north of the Sahara, now pose what some (xenophobic observers) describe as an existential crisis for the French Republic.[35] There is also the question of relations between the new African migrants to the West and older and more long-standing African diaspora communities in the receiving societies. Often, those relations have been marked by social distance, and have even been known to be strained.[36] Relevant too is the connection, which again is often difficult, between the new migrants and their respective national homelands.[37] In fine, the African diaspora is diverse, very diverse. So diverse, in fact, that there is a real sense in which one can speak of the African diasporas, in the plural. Even so, the singular (African diaspora) has a certain heuristic value, historical continuity, and political imperative that I wish to maintain for the purposes of this chapter.

The African diaspora has never possessed the shared social artifacts around which many diaspora communities traditionally cohere; namely, a common language, religion, or culture, or an actual or imaginary national homeland, as distinct from an entire continent. The African diaspora has always lacked a spatial entity akin to, say, Armenia, Greece, Palestine, or China. It is, and has always been, a genuine Babel, the African diaspora. Yet amid all this multifariousness, a unifying theme, if not a unifying tongue, would emerge. In the form it has come down to us, the story of this unifying theme, this Pan-African concord of modernity, began with the first western African diaspora. It is the story, in other words, of the African diaspora that was called into being in the Americas, largely by plantation crops, which is to say the crops of modernity and some of the key drivers of the Industrial Revolution, chief among them sugar, rice, tobacco, cotton, coffee, and cocoa.[38]

Whatever it may have lacked (which was most things, beginning with freedom) the first western African diaspora possessed, and that in abundance, the crucial element in the making of diasporic consciousness: adversity. Above all else, adversity (oppression, exclusion) is the glue of diaspora. It is a sorrow song, the song of diaspora; at once a popular conveyor of oppression or exclusion and a call to action. It often doubles, the diaspora song, as a nostalgic tune of homeland lost and a concomitant yearning for return, physically or spiritually, or both. One encounters such a phenomenon in the biblical psalms, a trope originally associated with the Jewish diaspora but one that would later be adopted by other diasporas, including the first western African diaspora:

> By the rivers of Babylon, there we sat down, yea, we wept, when we remembered Zion. We hanged our harps on the willows in the midst thereof. For there they that carried us away captive required of us a song; and they that wasted us required of us mirth, saying, Sing us one of the songs of Zion. How shall we sing the Lord's song in a strange land?[39]

Set to music by reggae artists, spiritual descendants of Rastafari and iconic purveyors of the story of global black adversity, this particular psalm would gain great currency worldwide.[40] A key twist was that the reggae songsters replaced the biblical 'Lord's song' with 'King Alpha's song', a reference to the Rastafarian deity, the late Ethiopian emperor Haile Selassie.[41]

The Guyanese-born Walter Rodney, eminent scholar of the African world, offered that 'the West Indies has made a unique contribution to the history of suffering in the world'.[42] (He had in mind Caribbean people of both African and South Asian descent.) Of course, comparative suffering is not a recognized field of study, and probably ought not to be. Another Caribbean organic intellectual, Aimé Césaire, posited that 'no race has a monopoly on beauty, on intelligence, on strength'.[43] Césaire's list could have been expanded to include suffering. But while all may have suffered, they have not all suffered equally. It is probably not altogether unfair or inaccurate to say that, in the making of the modern world, the first western African diaspora (not just in the Caribbean but everywhere in the Americas) has suffered more than most. It is this shared suffering that provided the raw material for the making of modern African diasporic consciousness. Instead of linguistic, cultural, or religious concordance (which was largely absent, at the outset, anyway) the first western African diaspora was distinguished by common experiences of oppression, and the cultures of resistance fashioned from those experiences.

Ideologically, the defining contribution of the first western African diaspora was an African worldview. Postmodernist scholars now call it the 'invention' and 'imagination' of Africa.[44] It was a spatially unbounded project, the African worldview. It conceived of peoples of African descent not in ethnic, national, imperial, regional, or even continental terms, but in global ones. Thus was born the idea of Africans as a global people with a set of congruent interests. This was a novel conception of international black solidarity, one centered on common African ancestry and shared historical experiences of enslavement, colonialism, and racial oppression; that is, the degradation of blackness and Africanness. In a sharp riposte, the African worldview envisioned a world free of human bondage and racial oppression.

The African worldview emerged during the second half of the eighteenth century, amid the interstices of two other iconic intellectual and cultural movements of that era, notably the Evangelical Revival and the European Enlightenment.[45] For better or worse, in its foundations the African worldview betrayed deep Anglocentric Protestant biases.[46] From the Evangelical Revival, the African worldview derived an essential principle: monogenesis. That is to say, the oneness and equality of the human family, a principle for which its exponents found support in biblical scripture, most tellingly the passage declaring that God 'hath made of one blood all nations of men for to dwell on all the face of the earth'.[47] Declarations like these were a severe rebuke to polygenesis, the notion, born of the Enlightenment, that the various 'races' of mankind have different, and unequal, origins. Despite its association with such 'scientific racism', the Enlightenment also became a source of wisdom for the African worldview. Natural law, derived from the Enlightenment and deemed to be timeless and universally valid, emerged as a bulwark in support of human equality across the board, including racial equality.[48] It was the peculiar genius of the founders of the African worldview to fuse these two systems of thought (the Evangelical Revival and the Enlightenment, the sacred and the profane, the two at once contradictory and complementary) into a vision of universal black emancipation unbounded by space and time.

Such, then, are the origins of the political and intellectual projects that would later assume such appellations as Pan-Negroism, Pan-Africanism, and Black Internationalism.[49] The story of these projects is a saga of interlocution, much of it fraught and contested (as such encounters inevitably are) within and between the African diaspora and the African homeland. Over the past two centuries or so, since the emergence of the African worldview, these interlocutions have unfolded in and around various events, movements, and organizations. Some of the more iconic ones, to name a few, are the Haitian Revolution, the Universal Negro Improvement Association, the Pan-African Congresses, Négritude, the Communist International (which, although not a black or African-led movement, served as a important platform for Pan-African emancipatory thought and action in the years between the two world wars), the Organization of African Unity turned African Union, the global Black Power movement of the 1960s and 1970s, the South African-focused global anti-apartheid struggle in the 1970s and 1980s, and the Hip-Hop culture of the 1990s coming into the twenty-first century.

Historically, a distinguishing feature of the movements associated with the African worldview has been an insistence on a close correlation between political struggles and intellectual pursuits. This has never been, one should hasten to add, a demand that research should subserve the political agenda of any particular organization or individual, which would be a travesty, propaganda masquerading as scholarship. It is to say, rather, that over time exponents of the African worldview have, in their varied literary expressions, forcefully and consistently called attention to the oppression of African peoples, with an explicit or implied demand for their liberation. In other words, the African worldview seeks to give voice to revolutionary and prophetic traditions of freedom inherent in the struggles of African peoples across space and time. These are the traditions to which well-known Pan-Africanist intellectuals like Edward Blyden, W.E.B. Du Bois and Kwame Nkrumah belong. They are also the traditions of less well-known and less well-published, but no less astute, Pan-Africanist intellectuals like Amy Jacques Garvey, Adelaide Caseley-Hayford, and Funmilayo Ransome-Kuti. 'They fought, they suffered—they are still fighting.'[50] Such was C.L.R. James's pithy summation of the modern experiences of African and African-descended peoples globally. Such, too, has been the leitmotif of much of the scholarship produced by exponents of the African worldview.

Historically, some of the key literary exponents of the African worldview were based in the USA. In the nineteenth century, these individuals mostly labored alone. However, as that century (which was so momentous in the modern global African experience, witnessing as it did the end of the Atlantic slave trade, the end of African slavery in the Americas, and the colonization of the greater part the African continent) drew to a close, new institutional networks focused in part on the African worldview began to emerge. One of the first such organizations was the American Negro Academy, founded by Alexander Crummell, former missionary to Liberia, leading promoter of the African worldview, and mentor to the young W.E.B. Du Bois. Alas, the American Negro Academy did not long survive Crummell's death in 1898.[51] The most enduring institutional repository of the African worldview in the USA would turn out to be the Association for the Study of Negro Life and History, under its original nomenclature. But, as we have seen, from the 1950s on the founders of both African studies and black studies studiously avoided institutional amalgamation with the Association for the Study of Negro Life and History, and instead went their separate ways.

Times, however, have changed. The new academic order, with its emphasis on globalization, is less amenable to traditional area studies (including African studies), and perhaps ethnic studies, too (including black studies), and more accommodating to diaspora studies, including African diaspora studies.[52] For sure, the academic upheavals and contestations are far from over (they never are) and at this point there is no clear vision of what the future holds.[53] What is clear is that in the study of Africa, Africans and their far-flung descendants throughout the world, particularism, exceptionalism, and national historiography are no longer tenable. Equally untenable are elitist conceptions of black liberation struggles and androcentric narratives that elide the centrality of women in those struggles.[54] In all probability, the future study of Africa, homeland and diaspora alike, will be transnational, transcontinental, and transoceanic.[55] It will be, in the language of St. Clair Drake, one of its outstanding practitioners, the study of 'black folk here and there'.[56]

## NOTES

1. These trends can be followed in the journal *Diaspora*, which began publishing in 1991, but has since gone out of business. The generically titled *Diaspora Studies*, which is still being published, is largely (although not exclusively) concerned with the Indian diaspora.

2. In addition to an ever increasing number of monographs and edited collections, the renaissance in African diaspora studies has spawned a number of new journals, including *African Diaspora, Black Diaspora Review*, and *Contours: A Journal of the African Diaspora*. While most of these new journals focus on the humanities and social sciences, not all do. Thus, there is an *African Diaspora Journal of Mathematics*.

3. For a useful introduction to the new literature on diaspora, see Ato Quayson, and Girish Daswani, eds., *A Companion to Diaspora and Transnationalism* (Chichester, UK: Wiley Blackwell, 2013).

4. Masao Miyoshi, and Harry Harootunian, eds., *Learning Places: The Afterlives of Area Studies* (Durham: Duke University Press, 2002).

5. Cited in Pankaj Mishra, "Pakistan's Writers: Living in a Minefield," *New York Review of Books*, October 13, 2011, 39.

6. Rupert Emerson, *From Empire to Nation: The Rise of Self-Assertion of Asian and African Peoples* (Cambridge, MA: Harvard University Press, 1960).

7. Wendell Clark Bennett, *Area Studies in American Universities* (New York: Social Science Research Council, 1951).

8. Richard Wright, *The Color Curtain: A Report on the Bandung Conference* (Jackson: University of Mississippi Press, 1994, first published 1956); G.H. Jansen, *Afro-Asia and Non-Alignment* (London: Faber and Faber, 1966); and Christopher J. Lee, ed., *Making a World after Empire: The Bandung Moment and Its Political Afterlives* (Athens: Ohio University Press, 2010).

9. For a personal account of the Ghanaian nationalist struggle by its best-known leader, see Kwame Nkrumah, *Ghana: The Autobiography of Kwame Nkrumah* (New York: Nelson, 1957).

10. Frederick Cooper, *Africa since 1940: The Past of the Present* (New York: Cambridge University Press, 2002).

11. William G. Martin, and Michael O. West, eds., *Out of One, Many Africas: Reconstructing the Study and Meaning of Africa* (Urbana: University of Illinois Press, 1999).

12. Zuoyue Wang, *In Sputnik's Shadow: The Presidents Science Advisory Committee and Cold War America* (New Brunswick: Rutgers University Press, 2008).

13. Open the Social Sciences, *Report of the Gulbenkian Commission on the Restructuring of the Social Sciences* (Stanford: Stanford University Press, 1996).

14. David Szanton, ed., *The Politics of Knowledge: Area Studies and the Disciplines* (Berkeley: University of California Press, 2004); Robert H. Bates, V.Y. Mudimbe, and Jean F. O'Barr, eds., *Africa and the Disciplines: The Contributions of Research in Africa to the Social Sciences and Humanities* (Chicago: University of Chicago Press, 1993); Toyin Falola, and Christian Jennings, eds., *Africanizing Knowledge: African Studies across the Disciplines* (New Brunswick, NJ: Transaction Publishers, 2002); and Tejumola Olaniyan, and James H. Sweet, eds., *The African Diaspora and the Disciplines* (Bloomington: Indiana University Press, 2010).

15. On the emergence and evolution of African studies, see: Jane I. Guyer, *African Studies in the United States: A Perspective* (Atlanta: African Studies Association Press, 1996); Tiyambe Zeleza, *Manufacturing African Studies and Crises* (Dakar: CODESRIA, 1997); Martin, and West, eds., *Out of One, Many Africas*.

16. Martin, and West, eds., *Out of One, Many Africas*.

17. The Egyptology strain was always a key one in the insurgent black history movement. For a summation of this considerable and uneven literature, in time and space, see St. Clair Drake, *Black Folk Here and There: An Essay in History and Anthropology*, 2 Vols. (Los Angeles: Center for Afro-American Studies, University of California, 1987 and 1990). The black Egyptology demarche would ultimately find its highest expression in the work of the Senegalese historian and polymath Cheikh Anta Diop. The most readily available précis of Diop's work in English is Cheikh Anta Diop, *The African Origin of Civilization: Myth or Reality*, trans. Mercer Cook (Westport, CT: Lawrence Hill & Company, 1974).

18. The iconic critique of Western Orientalist thought is Edward W. Said, *Orientalism* (New York: Vintage Books, 1994).

19. Jerry Gershenhorn, *Melville J. Herskovits and the Racial Politics of Knowledge* (Lincoln: University of Nebraska Press, 2004).

20. Melville J. Herskovits, *The Myth of the Negro Past* (New York: Harper, 1941).

21. Gunnar Myrdal, *An American Dilemma: The Negro Problem and Modern Democracy*, 2 Vols. (New York: Harper & Brothers, 1944).

22. One of the first issues of the journal *Diaspora* carried an article about Herskovits. See Andrew Apter, "Herskovits's Heritage: Rethinking Syncretism in the African Diaspora," *Diaspora* 1, no. 3 (1991): 235–60.

23. August Meier, and Elliott Rudwick, *Black History and the Historical Profession, 1915–1980* (Urbana: University of Illinois Press, 1986); Jacqueline Goggin, *Carter G. Woodson: A Life in Black History* (Baton Rouge: Louisiana State University Press, 1993); and Pero Gaglo Dagbovie, *The Early Black History Movement, Carter G. Woodson, and Lorenzo Johnston Greene* (Urbana: University of Illinois Press, 2007).

24. Stefan M. Bradley, *Harlem vs. Columbia University: Black Student Power in the Late 1960s* (Urbana: University of Illinois Press, 2009); Martha Biondi, *The Black Revolution on Campus* (Berkeley: University of California Press, 2012); and Ibram H. Rogers, *The Black Campus Movement: Black Students and Racial Reconstruction in Higher Education, 1965–1972* (New York: Palgrave Macmillan, 2012).

25. Yosef Ben-Jochannan, *Cultural Genocide in the Black and African Studies Curriculum* (New York: The Author, 1972).

26. Armstead L. Robinson, Craig C. Foster, and Donald H. Ogilvie, eds., *Black Studies in the University: A Symposium* (New Haven: Yale University Press, 1969); John W. Blassingame, ed., *New Perspectives on Black Studies* (Urbana: University of Illinois Press, 1971); Rojas Fabio, *From Black Power to Black Studies: How a Radical Social Movement Became an Academic Discipline* (Baltimore: Johns Hopkins University Press, 2007); and Stanlie M. James, Frances Smith Foster, and Beverly Guy-Sheftall, eds., *Still Brave: The Evolution of Black Women's Studies* (New York: Feminist Press, 2009).

27. Martin, and West, eds., *Out of One, Many Africas*.

28. Chinua Achebe, *Things Fall Apart* (London: Heinemann, 1976, first published 1958).

29. On Achebe's account of his Biafran experience, written late in his life, see Chinua Achebe, *There was a Country: A Personal History of Biafra* (New York: Allen Lane, 2012).

30. On the intellectual and political journey of a leading architect of this breakaway, see James L. Conyers Jr., and Julius E. Thompson, eds., *Pan-African Nationalism in the Americas: The Life and Times of John Henrik Clarke* (Trenton, NJ: Africa World Press, 2004); and Ahati N.N. Toure, *John Henrik Clarke and the Power of Africana History: Africalogical Quest for Decolonization and Sovereignty* (Trenton, NJ: Africa World Press, 2009).

31. Miyoshi, and Harootunian, eds., *Learning Places*.

32. Samuel P. Huntington, *The Clash of Civilizations and the Making of World Order* (New York: Simon & Schuster, 1996).

33. See, for example: John Hunwick, and Eve Troutt Powell, *The African Diaspora in the Mediterranean Lands of Islam* (Princeton, NJ: Marcus Wiener Publishers, 2002); Shihan de Silva Jayasuriya, and Richard Pankhurst, eds., *The African Diaspora in the Indian Ocean* (Trenton, NJ: Africa World Press, 2003); and Edward A. Alpers, *East Africa and the Indian Ocean* (Princeton, NJ: Marcus Wiener Publishers, 2009). For a comparison of slave trading, the key factor

in the making of both the eastern and western diasporas, see Patrick Manning, *Slavery and African Life: Occidental, Oriental, and African Slave Trades* (New York: Cambridge University Press, 1991).

34. A recent issue of *African Diaspora*, 7, 1 (2014) was devoted to the Zimbabwean diaspora. Several other issues of this journal, which began publication in 2008, carry articles on the new Zimbabwean diaspora.

35. Trica Danielle Keaton, T. Denean Sharpley-Whiting, and Tyler Stovall, eds., *Black France/France Noire: The History and Politics of Blackness* (Durham: Duke University Press, 2012).

36. Alusine Jalloh, and Toyin Falola, eds., *The United States and West Africa: Interactions and Relations* (Rochester: University of Rochester Press, 2008).

37. Bahar Baser, *Diasporas and Homeland Conflicts: A Comparative Perspective* (Burlington, VT: Ashgate, 2015).

38. The classic statement on the relationship between the enslavement of Africans and the first industrial revolution in Britain is Eric Williams, *Capitalism and Slavery* (Chapel Hill: University of North Carolina Press, 1944). For a more recent statement on the relationship between slavery and capitalism in the USA, see Edward E. Baptist, *The Half Has Never Been Told: Slavery and the Making of American Capitalism* (New York: Basic Books, 2014).

39. Psalms 137:1–4 (King James Bible). Also called the Authorized Version, the King James Bible has always been the authorized version of pan-Africanist Bible thumpers, including the Rastafarians.

40. On the political roots of Rastafari, see Horace Campbell, *Rasta and Resistance: From Marcus Garvey to Walter Rodney* (Trenton, NJ: Africa World Press, 1987). For the biblical basis of Rastafari, see Ken Post, "The Bible as Ideology: Ethiopianism in Jamaica, 1930–38," in *African Perspectives: Papers in the History, Politics and Economics of Africa Presented to Thomas Hodgkin*, ed. Christopher Allen, and R.W. Johnson (Cambridge: At the University Press, 1970), 185–207.

41. The Rastafari quest for Zion, as seen in the experiences of those Rastafarians who have emigrated to Ethiopia, has fallen short of expectations, as such journeys almost always do. None of which, of course, makes them any less appealing or worth the going. See Erin MacLeod, *Visions of Zion: Ethiopians and Rastafari in the Search for the Promised Land* (New York: New York University Press, 2014).

42. Walter Rodney, *The Groundings with My Brothers* (London: Bogle-L'Ouverture Publications Ltd, 1969), 26.

43. Aimé Césaire, *Notebook of a Return to the Native Land*, trans. Clayton Eshleman Annette Smith (Middletown, CT: Wesleyan University Press, 2001), 44.

44. Zine Magubane, ed., *Postmodernism, Postcoloniality and African Studies* (Trenton, NJ: Africa World Press, 2003); and Kwaku Larbi Korang, *Writing Ghana, Imagining Africa* (Rochester: University of Rochester Press, 2009). In Africa, as elsewhere, the literature on communal "imagining" and "inventing" has been greatly influenced by Benedict Anderson, *Imagined Communities: Reflections on the Origin and Spread of Nationalism* (New York: Verso, 1991).

45. Adam Potkay, and Sandra Burr, eds., *Black Atlantic Writers of the Eighteenth Century: Living the New Exodus in England and the Americas* (New York: St. Martin's Press, 1995); Henry Louis Gates Jr., and William L. Andrews,

eds., *Pioneers of the Black Atlantic: Five Slave Narratives from the Enlight-enment, 1772–1815* (Washington, DC: Civitas Counterpoint, 1998); and Joanna Brooks, and John Saillant, eds., *"Face Zion Forward": First Writers of the Black Atlantic, 1785–1798* (Boston: Northeastern University Press, 2002).

46. Edward Blyden, Presbyterian minister and key nineteenth-century elaborator of the African worldview, was among the least chauvinistic in his Protestant-ism, writing sympathetically about Islam, especially on the question of race. Yet even he exhibited a certain Anglocentric Protestant bias. See Edward W. Blyden, *Christianity, Islam and the Negro Race* (Edinburgh: Edinburgh University Press, 1967, first published 1887).

47. Acts 17:26 (King James Bible).

48. Anthony Bogues, *Black Heretics, Black Prophets: Radical Political Intellec-tuals* (New York: Routledge, 2003). See also Emmanuel Chukwudi Eze, ed., *Race and the Enlightenment: A Reader* (Cambridge, MA: Blackwell, 1997); and Andrew S. Curran, *The Anatomy of Blackness: Science and Slav-ery in an Age of Enlightenment* (Baltimore: Johns Hopkins University Press, 2011).

49. The literature on this subject is vast, and increasing rapidly. One of the best summaries on its origins and development up to the middle of the twentieth century remains Imanuel Geiss, *The Pan-African Movement: A History of Pan-Africanism in America, Europe and Africa*, trans. Ann Keep (New York: Afri-cana Publishing Co., 1974).

50. C.L.R. James, *A History of Pan-African Revolt* (Chicago: Charles H. Kerr Pub-lishing Company, 1995, originally published in 1938), 118.

51. Alfred A. Moss Jr., *The American Negro Academy: Voice of the Talented Tenth* (Baton Rouge: Louisiana State University Press, 1981). On Crummel, see Wil-son Jeremiah Moses, *Alexander Crummell: A Study in Civilization and Dis-content* (New York: Oxford University Press, 1989).

52. A seminal work in African diaspora studies, in its post-Cold War incarnation, is Paul Gilroy, *The Black Atlantic: Modernity and Double Consciousness* (Cam-bridge, MA: Harvard University Press, 1993). Gilroy's book on the "Black Atlantic," like Benedict Anderson's on national "imagination," would spark many similarly titled works.

53. Neil L. Waters, ed., *Beyond the Area Studies Wars: Toward a New International Studies* (Middlebury, VT: Middlebury College Press, 2000).

54. Judith A. Byfield, LaRay Denzer, and Anthea Morrison, eds., *Gendering The African Diaspora: Women, Culture, and Historical Change in the Car-ibbean and Nigerian Hinterland* (Bloomington: Indiana University Press, 2010).

55. As could be expected, there has been pushback from defenders of nation-bound studies and national historiography. See, for example, Adolph Reed Jr., and Kenneth W. Warren, eds., *Renewing Black Intellectual History: The Ideo-logical and Material Foundations of African American Thought* (Boulder: Para-digm Publishers, 2010).

56. Drake, *Black Folk Here and There.*

## BIBLIOGRAPHY

Achebe, Chinua. *Things Fall Apart*. London: Heinemann, 1976. First published 1958.

———. *There Was a Country: A Personal History of Biafra*. New York: Allen Lane, 2012.

*African Diaspora*, 7, 1 (2014).

Alpers, Edward A. *East Africa and the Indian Ocean*. Princeton, NJ: Marcus Wiener Publishers, 2009.

Anderson, Benedict. *Imagined Communities: Reflections on the Origin and Spread of Nationalism*. New York: Verso, 1991.

Apter, Andrew. "Herskovits's Heritage: Rethinking Syncretism in the African Diaspora," *Diaspora* 1, no. 3 (1991): 235–60.

Baptist, Edward E. *The Half Has Never Been Told: Slavery and the Making of American Capitalism*. New York: Basic Books, 2014.

Baser, Bahar. *Diasporas and Homeland Conflicts: A Comparative Perspective*. Burlington, VT: Ashgate, 2015.

Bates, Robert H., V.Y. Mudimbe, and Jean F. O'Barr, eds. *Africa and the Disciplines: The Contributions of Research in Africa to the Social Sciences and Humanities*. Chicago: University of Chicago Press, 1993.

Ben-Jochannan, Yosef. *Cultural Genocide in the Black & African Studies Curriculum*. New York: The Author, 1972.

Biondi, Martha. *The Black Revolution on Campus*. Berkeley: University of California Press, 2012.

Blassingame, John W., ed. *New Perspectives on Black Studies*. Urbana: University of Illinois Press, 1971.

Blyden, Edward W. *Christianity, Islam and the Negro Race*. Edinburgh: At the University Press, 1967. First published 1887.

Bogues, Anthony. *Black Heretics, Black Prophets: Radical Political Intellectuals*. New York: Routledge, 2003.

Bradley, Stefan M. *Harlem vs. Columbia University: Black Student Power in the Late 1960s*. Urbana: University of Illinois Press, 2009.

Brooks, Joanna, and John Saillant, eds. *"Face Zion Forward": First Writers of the Black Atlantic, 1785–1798*. Boston: Northeastern University Press, 2002.

Byfield, Judith A., LaRay Denzer, and Anthea Morrison, eds. *Gendering the African Diaspora: Women, Culture, and Historical Change in the Caribbean and Nigerian Hinterland*. Bloomington: Indiana University Press, 2010.

Campbell, Horace. *Rasta and Resistance: From Marcus Garvey to Walter Rodney*. Trenton, NJ: Africa World Press, 1987.

Césaire, Aimé. *Notebook of a Return to the Native Land*. Translated by Clayton Eshleman Annette Smith. Middletown, CT: Wesleyan University Press, 2001.

Clark, Wendell Bennett. *Area Studies in American Universities*. New York: Social Science Research Council, 1951.

Conyers, Jr., James L., and Julius E. Thompson, eds. *Pan-African Nationalism in the Americas: The Life and Times of John Henrik Clarke*. Trenton, NJ: Africa World Press, 2004.

Cooper, Frederick. *Africa since 1940: The Past of the Present*. New York: Cambridge University Press, 2002.

Curran, Andrew S. *The Anatomy of Blackness: Science and Slavery in an Age of Enlightenment.* Baltimore: Johns Hopkins University Press, 2011.

Dagbovie, Pero Gaglo. *The Early Black History Movement, Carter G. Woodson, and Lorenzo Johnston Greene.* Urbana: University of Illinois Press, 2007.

Diop, Cheikh Anta. *The African Origin of Civilization: Myth or Reality,* Translated by Mercer Cook. Westport, CT: Lawrence Hill & Company, 1974.

Drake, St. Claire. *Black Folk Here and There: An Essay in History and Anthropology.* 2 vols. Los Angeles: Center for Afro-American Studies, University of California, 1987 & 1990.

Emerson, Rupert. *From Empire to Nation: The Rise of Self-Assertion of Asian and African Peoples.* Cambridge, MA: Harvard University Press, 1960.

Eze, Emmanuel Chukwudi, ed. *Race and the Enlightenment: A Reader.* Cambridge, MA: Blackwell, 1997.

Fabio, Rojas. *From Black Power to Black Studies: How a Radical Social Movement Became an Academic Discipline.* Baltimore: Johns Hopkins University Press, 2007.

Falola, Toyin, and Christian Jennings, eds. *Africanizing Knowledge: African Studies across the Disciplines.* New Brunswick, NJ: Transaction Publishers, 2002.

Gates Jr., Henry Louis, and William L. Andrews, eds. *Pioneers of the Black Atlantic: Five Slave Narratives from the Enlightenment, 1772–1815.* Washington, DC: Civitas Counterpoint, 1998.

Geiss, Imanuel. *The Pan-African Movement: A History of Pan-Africanism in America, Europe and Africa.* Translated by Ann Keep. New York: Africana Publishing Co., 1974.

Gershenhorn, Jerry. *Melville J. Herskovits and the Racial Politics of Knowledge.* Lincoln: University of Nebraska Press, 2004.

Gilroy, Paul. *The Black Atlantic: Modernity and Double Consciousness.* Cambridge, MA: Harvard University Press, 1993.

Goggin, Jacqueline. *Carter G. Woodson: A Life in Black History.* Baton Rouge: Louisiana State University Press, 1993.

Guyer, Jane I. *African Studies in the United States: A Perspective.* Atlanta: African Studies Association Press, 1996.

Herskovits, Melville J. *The Myth of the Negro Past.* New York: Harper, 1941.

Huntington, Samuel P. *The Clash of Civilizations and the Making of World Order.* New York: Simon & Schuster, 1996.

Hunwick, John, and Eve Troutt Powell, *The African Diaspora in the Mediterranean Lands of Islam.* Princeton, NJ: Marcus Wiener Publishers, 2002.

Jalloh, Alusine, and Toyin Falola, eds. *The United States and West Africa: Interactions and Relations.* Rochester: University of Rochester Press, 2008.

James, C.L.R. *A History of Pan-African Revolt.* Chicago: Charles H. Kerr Publishing Company, 1995. Originally published in 1938.

James, Stanlie M., Frances Smith Foster, and Bervely Guy-Sheftall, eds. *Still Brave: The Evolution of Black Women's Studies.* New York: Feminist Press, 2009.

Jansen, G.H. *Afro-Asia and Non-Alignment.* London: Faber and Faber, 1966.

Jayasuriya, Shihan de Silva, and Richard Pankhurst, eds. *The African Diaspora in the Indian Ocean.* Trenton, NJ: Africa World Press, 2003.

Keaton, Trica Danielle, T. Denean Sharpley-Whiting, and Tyler Stovall, eds. *Black France/France Noire: The History and Politics of Blackness.* Durham: Duke University Press, 2012.

King James Bible.

Korang, Kwaku Larbi. *Writing Ghana, Imagining Africa*. Rochester: University of Rochester Press, 2009.

Lee, Christopher J., ed. *Making a World after Empire: The Bandung Moment and Its Political Afterlives*. Athens: Ohio University Press, 2010.

MacLeod, Erin. *Visions of Zion: Ethiopians and Rastafari in the Search for the Promised Land*. New York: New York University Press, 2014.

Magubane, Zine, ed. *Postmodernism, Postcoloniality and African Studies*. Trenton, NJ: Africa World Press, 2003.

Manning, Patrick. *Slavery and African Life: Occidental, Oriental, and African Slave Trades*. New York: Cambridge University Press, 1991.

Martin, William G., and Michael O. West, eds. *Out of One, Many Africas: Reconstructing the Study and Meaning of Africa*. Urbana: University of Illinois Press, 1999.

Meier, August, and Elliott Rudwick. *Black History and the Historical Profession, 1915–1980*. Urbana: University of Illinois Press, 1986.

Mishra, Pankaj. "Pakistan's Writers: Living in a Minefield." *New York Review of Books*, October 13, 2011.

Miyoshi, Masao, and Harry Harootunian, eds. *Learning Places: The Afterlives of Area Studies*. Durham: Duke University Press, 2002.

Moses, Wilson Jeremiah. *Alexander Crummell: A Study in Civilization and Discontent*. New York: Oxford University Press, 1989.

Moss, Jr., Alfred A. *The American Negro Academy: Voice of the Talented Tenth*. Baton Rouge: Louisiana State University Press, 1981.

Myrdal, Gunnar. *An American Dilemma: The Negro Problem and Modern Democracy*. 2 Vols. New York: Harper & Brothers, 1944.

Nkrumah, Kwame. *Ghana: The Autobiography of Kwame Nkrumah*. New York: Nelson, 1957.

Olaniyan, Tejumola, and James H. Sweet, eds. *The African Diaspora and the Disciplines*. Bloomington: Indiana University Press, 2010.

Post, Ken. "The Bible as Ideology: Ethiopianism in Jamaica, 1930–38." In *African Perspectives: Papers in the History, Politics and Economics of Africa Presented to Thomas Hodgkin*, edited by Christopher Allen and R.W. Johnson, 185–207. Cambridge: At the University Press, 1970.

Potkay, Adam, and Sandra Burr, eds. *Black Atlantic Writers of the Eighteenth Century: Living the New Exodus in England and the Americas*. New York: St. Martin's Press, 1995.

Quayson, Ato, and Girish Daswani, eds. *A Companion to Diaspora and Transnationalism*. Chichester, UK: Wiley Blackwell, 2013.

Reed Jr., Adolph, and Kenneth W. Warren, eds. *Renewing Black Intellectual History: The Ideological and Material Foundations of African American Thought*. Boulder: Paradigm Publishers, 2010.

*Report of the Gulbenkian Commission on the Restructuring of the Social Sciences*. Stanford: Stanford University Press, 1996.

Robinson, Armstead L., Craig C. Foster, and Donald H. Ogilvie, eds. *Black Studies in the University: A Symposium*. New Haven: Yale University Press, 1969.

Rodney, Walter. *The Groundings with My Brothers*. London: Bogle-L'Ouverture Publications Ltd, 1969.

Rogers, Ibram H. *The Black Campus Movement: Black Students and Racial Reconstruction in Higher Education, 1965–1972*. New York: Palgrave Macmillan, 2012.

Said, Edward W. *Orientalism*. New York: Vintage Books, 1994.

Szanton, David, ed. *The Politics of Knowledge: Area Studies and the Disciplines*. Berkeley: University of California Press, 2004.

Toure, Ahati N.N. *John Henrik Clarke and the Power of Africana History: Africalogical Quest for Decolonization and Sovereignty*. Trenton, NJ: Africa World Press, 2009.

Wang, Zuoyue. *In Sputnik's Shadow: The Presidents Science Advisory Committee and Cold War America*. New Brunswick: Rutgers University Press, 2008.

Waters, Neil L. ed. *Beyond the Area Studies Wars: Toward a New International Studies*. Middlebury, VT: Middlebury College Press, 2000.

Williams, Eric. *Capitalism & Slavery*. Chapel Hill: University of North Carolina Press, 1944.

Wright, Richard. *The Color Curtain: A Report on the Bandung Conference*. Jackson: University of Mississippi Press, 1994. First published 1956.

Zeleza, Tiyambe. *Manufacturing African Studies and Crises*. Dakar: CODESRIA, 1997.

# INDEX

Printed by Printforce, United Kingdom